Entertainment and Media Law in Ireland

ENTERTAINMENT AND MEDIA LAW IN IRELAND

By

SIMON SHIRE

CLARUS
PRESS

Published by
Clarus Press Ltd,
Griffith Campus,
South Circular Road,
Dublin 8.
www.claruspress.ie

Typeset by
Gough Typesetting Services,
Dublin

Printed by
CPI Anthony Rowe,
Chippenham,
Wiltshire

ISBN
Paperback edition: 978-1-911611-07-3
Hardback edition: 978-1-911611-91-2

A catalogue record for this book is available from the British Library

Preface

The timing of the within publication is providential in probing the sea of changes which the entertainment and media sector has undergone in recent years. These include enhanced artist/performer rights at EU level and by virtue of domestic legislation, more stringent data protection laws, the recent Supreme Court judgment in *Higgins* on defamation awards (together with a government report into proposed changes to the Defamation Act 2009), the move to self-assessment of the s 481 film/television tax credit, transposition into Irish law of the revised Audiovisual Media Services Directive, and establishment of the Media Commission to replace the Broadcasting Authority of Ireland. The breadth of recent UK and US case law informing certain parameters for successful prosecution of music copyright infringement civil litigation is also explored.

An exhaustive analysis of each discrete area of law (in this jurisdiction and internationally) is beyond the scope and purpose of *Entertainment and Media Law in Ireland*. A range of specialist legal textbooks is available dedicated to complex topics such as defamation and intellectual property, primarily targeted at legal practitioners and law students. The goal of this book, aimed at *all* persons providing entertainment and media services, be they company directors, event producers, radio personnel, journalists, filmmakers or musicians, is to navigate the fundamentals in a hands-on manner, and, for those already conversant with and engaged in the industry, to develop their knowledge against the backdrop of myriad legal principles at play. This book is therefore better viewed as a series of signposts in the form of best practice guidelines.

As circumstances may dictate, it is of paramount importance that film and music producers, media professionals and those engaged in the wider entertainment sector obtain independent legal advice from experienced entertainment and media law practitioners. Accounting and taxation advice will also be apposite. Each contract will be different, each set of facts unique. This book deliberately, for this reason, does not contain template agreements but does point to industry-wide minimum contractual requirements of broadcasters, stakeholders and other content financiers, as well as stressing the importance of adequate insurance cover, conducting due diligence, obtaining consents and mitigating risk. Creative prowess of content-creating practitioners aside, this structured legal and business affairs publication seeks then to equip readers with procedures to elude the common pitfalls, collate robust chain of title documentation where relevant and obviate any missing links in that chain.

Due to international rules on copyright, its infringement and enforcement, audiovisual producers when considering distribution avenues for their material, should ensure that the legal advice obtained relates to where their film or other output is being made and where it is to be commercially exploited. Certain legal principles discussed throughout this textbook will not apply outside Ireland. Defamation law for instance can differ radically between Ireland and the US. Contract law in common law territories will also differ to civil law systems. By way of further example, the equivalent of the 'fair dealing' defence to copyright infringement in Ireland and the UK is termed 'fair use' in the US where a range of disparate legal principles apply when seeking to invoke such exemption in that jurisdiction.

It is my intention that this textbook might serve producers and other practitioners well to better identify what is required of any given project, and hence how one might cost-effectively instruct legal and accounting professionals for specific advice on the project at hand. It should not, however, be relied upon exclusively and is not represented as a definitive interpretation or statement of the prevailing law. Moreover, while every effort was made to ensure accuracy, no liability is accepted by the author or Clarus Press for inadvertent errors or otherwise. Views expressed throughout represent those of the author.

I fervently hope that *Entertainment and Media Law in Ireland* will contribute to an augmented understanding and appreciation by its readers, multimedia creators, journalists and artists generally of what is involved in producing, and ultimately commercially disseminating, high quality, industry-standard content in an increasingly globalised market. To this end, it may serve some part in ensuring that this small island of storytellers, artists and performers continues to punch well above its weight in maintaining standards of excellence on the world stage.

I have endeavoured to state the law (and attendant developments in the entertainment and media fields) as of late April 2023. Since then, a notable change to which readers' attention is brought is the increase, announced in Budget 2024, in the eligible expenditure cap of the film/television tax credit (s 481) from €70 to €125 million, subject to EU state aid approval. Another is the reaction by key stakeholders to advancements in artificial intelligence, from actors' strike action to litigation by music publishers.

Simon Shire
19 October 2023

Table of Contents

PART II
AUDIOVISUAL, STAGE AND RADIO PRODUCTIONS

PART III
MUSIC PRODUCTION AND PERFORMANCES

PART IV
GENERAL ENTERTAINMENT

PART V
DIGITAL SAFETY, BROADCASTING REGULATION AND AUDIOVISUAL MEDIA SERVICES

PART VI
JOURNALISM LAW, REGULATION AND ETHICS

Table of Cases

Table of Legislation

IRELAND

Constitution

Pre-1922 Acts

Acts of the Oireachtas

Statutory Instruments

UK LEGISLATION

US LEGISLATION

EUROPE

EU Directives

INTERNATIONAL AGREEMENTS

Part I

Business Management, Regulation and Risk Mitigation

Chapter 1

Business Set-Up, Private Companies and Taxation/ Self-Assessment

INTRODUCTION

[1.1.01] A thorough exploration of company law is beyond the scope of this textbook.[1] Nonetheless, established practitioners in the media and entertainment sector will, as a matter of course, be operating squarely within the company law parameters outlined in this chapter. Furthermore, aspiring producers endeavouring to secure more substantial project funding are required by statute to incorporate for corporation tax credit financing. It is more likely too that a company will have professional supports in place relating to specialist legal and accounting advice on intellectual property ('IP') law, media insurance and raising funds from both public and private sources.

[1.1.02] Media practitioners must also be aware of the tax consequences of their operations, from the charging of value added tax ('VAT') on the supply of services,[2] engagement of personnel as employees, and hiring cast and crew as freelance contractors, to the treatment of loan-out agreements, calculating 'budgeted expenditure'[3] for s 481 (Taxes Consolidation Act 1997) purposes as discussed in Chapter 8 and the related matter of filing tax returns to include bi-monthly VAT returns which will greatly affect cashflow throughout the financial lifespan of a particular project.[4]

---

1 For a detailed analysis, readers are directed to specialised textbooks including Michael Forde and Hugh Kennedy, *Company Law* (5th ed, Round Hall, Dublin, 2017); G Brian Hutchinson, *Keane on Company Law* (3rd ed, Bloomsbury Professional, Dublin, 2016); Thomas B Courtney, *The Law of Companies* (4th ed, Bloomsbury Professional, Dublin, 2016), and Anthony Thuillier, *Company Law in Ireland* (2nd ed, Clarus Press, Dublin, 2015).

2 And goods where applicable, e.g. sale of special effects equipment.

3 This term refers to an amount expected to be expended on the production of a film or other production that qualifies for relief as either the 'total cost of production' or as 'eligible expenditure'.

4 Note that budgets are expressed net of VAT. For instance, a film director's fee may be €100,000 as inserted into the budget. However, at the current rate of VAT at 23 percent, €123,000 will need to be paid by the production company, most likely in tranches inclusive of VAT throughout the project. This extra €23,000 in total will thus need to be

The requirement for and benefits of incorporation

[1.1.03] With the exception of development loans[5] to individual applicants and the funding of certain short films, it is a prerequisite to Screen Ireland funding that the applicant Irish producer be an independent production company registered in Ireland with an office based in the State. The Arts Council also requires certain applicants such as venues or those in receipt of strategic funding awards to be registered companies, including community development and not-for-profit Revenue-approved charity organisations registered as companies limited by guarantee. This is also a requirement of the Media Commission (formerly the Broadcasting Authority of Ireland, 'the BAI')[6] which advances funds to either individuals or established legal entities incorporated in Ireland or within the EU.

[1.1.04] Additionally, in respect of s 481 of the Taxes Consolidation Act 1997 as amended ('TCA'), the cash tax credit is payable only to 'producer companies' as parent companies of 'qualifying companies' set up for each film or television project which incurs the costs of production. The subsidiary undertaking must be incorporated and resident in the State or be carrying on a trade in the State through a branch or agency and exist solely for the purposes of producing one qualifying project only. A producer company must, at the time of application to the relevant government department[7] for a culture certificate relating to a qualifying film,[8] be carrying on the trade of audiovisual productions. The requirement to have filed a corporation tax return with the Collector General following 21 months' trading as a producer company is a further condition which needs to be satisfied before making a claim for the credit.[9]

Duties arising under company law

[1.1.05] It is imperative that company owners,[10] directors, secretaries and other corporate officers or duly authorised persons are aware of their duties and obligations under company law. The implications for breaching the Companies Act 2014 as amended ('the Act') can be severe. The Supreme Court in a 2008

---

financed for cashflow purposes pending recoupment, periodically, of VAT refund sums from Revenue throughout and following completion of filming.

5 For example, screenplay development loans are available, at the time of writing, to writers/directors up to €16,000, either to individuals (€12,000) or teams of two or more individuals.

6 The Online Safety and Media Regulation Act 2022 (which commenced in late February 2023) established the Media Commission. The BAI was thus dissolved with its functions, powers, staff and property transferring to the Commission.

7 The relevant government department, at the time of writing, is the Department of Tourism, Culture, Arts, Gaeltacht, Sport and Media.

8 See Pt 3 of the Film Regulations 2019 (SI No 119 of 2019) – feature films, shorts of feature quality, television dramas (episodic or feature length), animation and eligible creative documentaries.

9 This requirement does not prohibit the producer company from making an application for a culture certificate before the 21-month period has elapsed.

10 Also termed members or shareholders.

judgment[11] described as "draconian" provisions under the Companies Act 1990, which have carried over to the Act, giving jurisdiction to restrict or disqualify an individual from acting as a company director or in related activities. Consequences of breaching the Act include conviction in the criminal courts that may result in the imposition of fines, a custodial sentence, or disentitlement to act as director or secretary for a specified number of years.

[1.1.06] Exposure to personal liability for company debts can also arise in a variety of circumstances notwithstanding the doctrine of separate legal personality[12] and the limited liability of company shareholders. A five-justice panelled Supreme Court in *WL Construction Ltd*[13] recently reaffirmed the position that, in certain circumstances, the 'corporate veil' can be lifted. In those proceedings a director of an insolvent company was held personally liable for legal costs of the litigation at bar.[14] In addition, banks or other creditors lending money to a company may require personal guarantees from directors/shareholders with the effect of rendering them personally liable in the event of repayment default.

[1.1.07] In relation to strict statutory duties governing bookkeeping and accounting, a company director cannot "act as a mere passive custodian of books and papers".[15] Proper accounts and records must be created in a particular form and maintained at all times:

> ...on a continuous and consistent basis and must be such that they will at any time enable the financial position of the company to be determined with reasonable accuracy.[16]

---

11 *Per* the late Mr Justice Adrian Hardiman in *Re Tralee Beef and Lamb Ltd (In Liquidation): Kavanagh v Delaney* [2008] IESC 1 referring *inter alia* to the possible constitutional injustice and fundamental unfairness of placing the "burden upon the respondent to prove, not only that he has acted responsibly and honestly in relation to the company but to prove the negative proposition '(there is no other reason'...)".

12 Emanating from the seminal company law decision by the former House of Lords (UK) in *Salomon v* A *Salomon & Co Ltd* [1897] AC 22.

13 *W.L. Construction Ltd v Chawke* [2019] IESC 74.

14 Mr Loughnane was the 99 percent shareholder and his litigation was dismissed for fraudulent amendment of invoices, the court refusing to accept unreliable evidence adduced by him at hearing. Loughnane mistakenly believed that in arranging for the insolvent company to bring the claim, and by not being a party to the litigation, he could avoid any personal liability for the legal costs of the defendants through the separate corporate personality of the company.

15 *Per* Shanley J in *Mantruck* (see fn 16).

16 *In the matter of Mantruck Services Ltd (In Liquidation) and in the matter of an application pursuant to section 150 and 204 of the Companies Act 1990* was a High Court judgment (*Mehigan v Duignan* [1997] 1 IR 340, commonly known as the *Mantruck Services* case) delivered by the late Mr Justice Peter Shanley. A County Roscommon company director and shareholder of Mantruck Services was declared personally liable to the company in the sum of €91,000 pursuant to s 204 of the Companies Act 1990 as a consequence of the contraventions of s 202 of that Act. In this landmark judgment, the first of its kind under the provisions of the Companies Act 1990, the judge also imposed a five-year restriction on the director.

Compliance and robust corporate governance

[1.1.08] Aside from general statutory and common law obligations, financial backers of projects including Screen Ireland, RTÉ, the Arts Council and the Media Commission will stipulate in the accounting and audit/inspection provisions of their development or production loan, distribution licence or funding award agreements specific requirements to include, where appropriate, Chartered Accountants Ireland M45 reporting accountants' audit certifications and the technical statement required for grant claims. Grant recipients must also comply with the responsibilities of a grantee set out by the Department of Public Expenditure and Reform in Circular 13/2014 in section five thereof.[17]

[1.1.09] While this chapter speaks to advisers and practitioners in the sector who are already company shareholders and officers, it also addresses, for those wishing to expand their practice to facilitate larger projects, the designated activity company ('DAC') which is typically incorporated as a special purpose vehicle ('SPV') by film production companies or other audiovisual project creators. A subsidiary SPV company is a legislative imperative in the case of s 481 tax credit funding. The chapter is likewise intended for the aspiring market entrant desirous to commence trading activities on a formal, structured and regulated footing in compliance with tax and company legislation.

[1.1.10] Thus, production companies, and content creators where relevant, should be armed with more than a passing familiarity with standard company law documentation. Conditions precedent in development and production loan applications with Screen Ireland by way of example will require copies of the subject company's constitution (both parent and subsidiary companies where appropriate) on each occasion, board resolutions, company director declarations, tax clearance certification and so forth. Company directors and shareholders must therefore be aware of their obligations in respect of board procedures and the statutorily-required keeping of minutes of meetings. This might apply as regards approving a loan for drawdown and registration with the Companies Registration Office ('CRO') of a financier's charge over a project's IP assets in the case of production and cashflow loans. They should also be conversant with such matters as the number of shares each company member owns, authorised and issued share capital levels, and the contents of the company's constitution, which contains the memorandum and articles of association in the case of subsidiary DACs.

Business types

[1.1.11] There are three main avenues for entrepreneurs relating to the manner

---

17 See Department of Public Expenditure and Reform, (Circular 13/2014) *Management of and Accountability for Grants from Exchequer Funds* (2014), circulars.gov.ie. Available at: www.circulars.gov.ie/pdf/circular/per/2014/13.pdf [Accessed 15 August 2020]. Further, the recipient must adhere to the statement of principles set out in Appendix 2 (and 1b) and of the circular's conditions and ensure that appropriate governance and oversight arrangements at board and employee level are in place.

in which they operate their trading activities as self-employed individuals or salaried company directors[18] and each will now be examined in brief.

SOLE TRADERS

[1.2.01] The first entity type is that operated by a sole trader. This unincorporated business form can be set up with minimal documentation and cost. One can commence immediately but in some cases will need to effect a business or 'trading as' name registration[19] with the CRO. Sole traders must also register with Revenue for income tax, and where appropriate, for employer taxes and VAT. The reason for business name registration is to allow the public to identify the persons behind each trading entity for litigation, service of formal notices and other purposes. Hence, when choosing a business name which differs in any way from the owner's true surname, that name, by statute, is to be duly registered with the CRO within one month of adoption of such name.[20]

Personal liability

[1.2.02] The downside to the sole trader model is exposure to personal liability if the business fails where outstanding debts remain which cannot be met from business assets. Accordingly, creditors can issue contract debt proceedings against the sole trader business, a prospect that might ultimately lead to bankruptcy or personal insolvency. The liabilities must, unless written off by a creditor,[21] be repaid from whatever assets remain in the business and/or otherwise be met from the debtor's personal property and assets. This is the primary reason why entrepreneurs are urged to take accounting advice on incorporating a company whereby company law can afford limited liability to the shareholders as owners. There are, however, exceptions to the limited liability of company members and officers. Such officers can be held personally liable if personal guarantees have been provided to creditors or, for instance, in the case of fraudulent trading or inadequate keeping of accounting records as further detailed below.

---

18 A company director can be employed by a company under a contract of employment. Individuals who are directors and owners of their own companies may also be on loan-out from such companies to third party production companies (including their subsidiary DACs) by way of loan-out or personal services agreement as discussed later in this chapter.

19 Name registration, using form RBN1 for individuals, can be effected using the companies' online registration environment (CORE) on the CRO website. Registration of business names ending in a domain name suffix such as '.ie', '.com' and '.net' or a prefix such as 'www' is considered undesirable for the purposes of s 14(1) of the Registration of Business Names Act 1963. Proof of domain name ownership is required to process such applications.

20 By way of illustration, Daniel Walsh might decide to trade as Edge Films. 'Edge Films' obviously does not reveal Mr Walsh's true identity. If his identity needs to be established (for instance where a creditor wishes to instigate debt recovery proceedings against Edge Films), the contact details, as public records, can be obtained from the CRO, some of which particulars will involve payment of a nominal fee. This sole trader business would therefore formally be styled "Daniel Walsh trading as Edge Films".

21 Note that, in the context of High Court bankruptcy proceedings, all unsecured debts are written off.

PARTNERSHIPS

[1.3.01] The second unincorporated business vehicle is that of a partnership[22] or 'firm' in statutory parlance. A partnership will have a minimum of two persons conducting business together with a view to making a profit. Two or more member partners share the investment and management of the business and thus the profits and responsibility for trading liabilities. If one does wish to enter into a partnership with another person or persons, it is advisable to consult a solicitor for specialist legal advice. This is to avoid default provisions of the Partnership Act 1890 – which may be wholly unintended – being applied to the business by a court when a dispute between partners leads to litigation.

[1.3.02] This can occur in respect of music band-member scenarios as outlined in Chapter 22 for which the above 19th century statute did not envisage, but it may nonetheless govern resolution of disputes. That eventuality could arise in the absence of a partnership agreement modifying application of the default statutory position.

[1.3.03] A further downside is personal exposure to partnership debts (though this can be mitigated to some degree in the case of members of incorporated[23] limited liability partnerships (LLPs), as opposed to general partnerships (by amendment of the 'joint-and-several' rule of partnership law)) in the same vein as that which applies to sole traders who can be rendered personally liable even after cessation of trade.

PRIVATE COMPANIES LIMITED BY SHARES

Introduction

[1.4.01] A private limited company denoted with the suffix 'Limited' or 'Ltd'[24] and incorporated under Pt 2 of the Act is the most common type of company in Ireland, generally the most recommended trading model and indeed, as discussed above, will be specifically required in some instances of raising production funds. The liability of members if the company is wound up is limited to the amount, if any, unpaid on the shares they hold.[25] Essentially, save for exceptions such as in the event of having traded recklessly or with intent to defraud creditors, the

---

22 Defined in s 1(2) of the Partnership Act 1890 as "the relationship which subsists between persons carrying on a business in common with a view to profit".

23 Registration must be effected in accordance with the Limited Partnerships Act 1907 as amended and accounts and returns must be submitted annually to the CRO. Solicitor firms operating as LLPs (since October 2019) need not however register with the CRO, partnerships of solicitors being governed instead by the 1890 Act.

24 The suffix CLG (company limited by guarantee – see Pt 18 of the Act) might otherwise apply to certain sectors including community charities and not-for-profit local arts centres funded by the Arts Council which will typically have a board of directors appointed on a voluntary (no remuneration) basis.

25 This means if they had subscribed for shares at a cost of €1,000 and have only paid €400 into the company's bank account thus far for these shares, their total exposure in the case of insolvent liquidation is merely the balance of €600.

owners of a limited company can walk away with impunity from company debts should the business fail to maintain solvency.

[1.4.02] A limited company may have only one director if it chooses. It can also be a single-member company and that member may also be a director. A separate company secretary must, however, be appointed who will perform important administrative functions. Under the Act, a limited company is not required to have stated objects in its constitution whereas an objects clause was a requirement in the memorandum of association under the former principal 1963 legislation. As a consequence, it can undertake any type of allowed business activity.

Raising finance and taxation benefits

[1.4.03] Another fundamental reason for incorporating a business is borne out of general credibility considerations: corporate status provides easier access to private equity finance, commercial loans and public funding. A company can raise money by issuing shares to new shareholders in return for a cash investment. This type of investor-backed financing is evidenced for instance on the television series *Dragons' Den*. Incorporation may also lead to taxation advantages in respect of income tax and strategic tax planning generally, and more specifically, for example, with respect to service companies which might apply to the manner in which music bands conduct business, and as regards 'loan-out' of company director services (see sections [1.6.14] to [1.6.17] below). Further, as already stated, having an incorporated company is a prerequisite to securing certain funding as is the case with most Screen Ireland lending and the s 481 film and television tax credit as detailed in Chapter 8.

[1.4.04] A charge[26] can also be created and registered in the CRO by a lender over company assets – for example, Screen Ireland will register a charge (the deed of charge will also include an assignment of rights)[27] over the film/television assets of a production company (and, where applicable, its subsidiary DAC) in respect of a specific project when advancing a production loan facility thereto.[28] In the case of the production account opened by the DAC, the relevant bank will need to consent, by acknowledgement of a notice of charge from the DAC chargor, to assignment of this security account to Screen Ireland as chargee and to the instructions from the DAC account-holder as set out in the notice. These matters should be discussed in advance with the company's bank manager before production funding is sought from Screen Ireland.

---

26 Similar to a mortgage or charge on a residential or commercial property as security for a mortgage loan, registered as an encumbrance or burden against the property in the Registry of Deeds or Land Registry respectively.

27 However, the borrower company will nonetheless be permitted to exploit the material by distribution or sales agency contract(s) as approved in advance by Screen Ireland.

28 This was previously the position too in respect of Screen Ireland development loans. Funding by Screen Ireland above certain levels for short films also necessitates registration of a charge.

Formation documents and company name considerations

[1.4.05] It is advisable to consult a solicitor, accountant or company formation office for the purposes of incorporating a company, drafting its one-document constitution which includes the articles of association,[29] and registering for taxes with Revenue.[30] The prescribed documents[31] can be completed expeditiously if no complex issues arise relating, for example, to share classes and governance procedures. The CRO may refuse to register a particular corporate name if it is identical or similar to a name already appearing on the register, is offensive or would suggest State sponsorship. A trading name should be registered[32] in the same manner as discussed for sole traders when it differs from the full company name.[33] A company promoter should also determine well in advance if the proposed business name has already been registered as a trademark.[34] Use of a trademarked name could render the company liable to trademark infringement proceedings. Prior registration of that name (or a very similar name by another business) with the Intellectual Property Office of Ireland ('the IPOI') will also preclude its registration by the company in the IPOI under primary and secondary trademark legislation (unless honest and concurrent use can be proven – see Chapter 12). From a practical business perspective, an internet domain name should also be procured as soon as possible to afford additional brand protection.

Single-member companies

[1.4.06] A single-member company is a company which is incorporated with one shareholder, or the membership of which is reduced to one person. However, the company must have at least one director and a separate company secretary. This secretary may also be a second director. Dual capacity of director/secretary for single-member companies is prohibited under ss 134 and 129(6) of the Act such that, for example, the statutory financial statements must be signed by the secretary and the director(s). Section 129(4) provides that the directors of a company shall have a duty to ensure that persons appointed as secretary have the skills or resources necessary to discharge their statutory and other duties.

---

29 Which in the case of limited companies replaces the memorandum of association and articles of association under the Companies Act 1963. Other company forms such as a DAC (see below) retain the memorandum of association and articles of association under the Act by way of a two-document constitution comprising these documents.

30 Using form TR2 which should also satisfy s 882 of the TCA which requires the company secretary of a new company to supply (form 11F) certain information to Revenue within 30 days of the company's commencing trading. Failure to comply can lead to the company's being struck off and/or penalties imposed both on the company and the company secretary.

31 Form A1 (whereon persons being over eighteen years of age will give their consent in writing to act as director(s) and another individual will give consent to act as company secretary). Signatures are also required from the shareholders in the subscribers' section and on the constitution document.

32 By submitting form RBN1B.

33 For instance, Murphy Hire Ltd trading as Murphy Hire or Low Cost Hire.

34 This search can be conducted online (ipoi.gov.ie) free of charge in the Intellectual Property Office of Ireland (formerly the Irish Patents Office) based in Kilkenny.

[1.4.07] The sole member can dispense with the holding of general meetings including annual general meetings ('AGMs'). The financial statements and reports that would normally be laid before the AGM of a company will nonetheless still need to be prepared.

DACs and entertainment law

[1.4.08] A new feature of the Act was the DAC, which is also limited by shares.[35] Unlike a limited company, DACs must have at least two directors and its constitution must include both a memorandum and articles of association. The relevance of the DAC to the entertainment sector is that, to avail of s 481,[36] production companies[37] must incorporate a 'qualifying company' (being a DAC) and enter into a contract with this subsidiary SPV in relation to the production of the qualifying film. Hence, there will be a production services agreement between the parent 'producer company' and its DAC subsidiary[38] as to covenants, conditions and obligations applying to production and delivery of the subject film/project. The DAC will also enter into legal agreements (e.g. a deed of charge and assignment as above) with stakeholders including Screen Ireland in the case, for example, of a production loan facility being advanced,[39] and with cast, crew and service providers (the parent company will also be party to finance agreements). Aside from s 481, a DAC might otherwise be utilised for a single project as a production company in its own right (that is, not being a subsidiary) so that it can be voluntarily wound up by its shareholders following project completion and finalisation of all accounting, tax and regulatory requirements.

Statutory obligations of directors and company secretaries

[1.4.09] *Registered office*: the company address must be a physical location, not merely a post office box number. The public (and the Office of the Director of Corporate Enforcement, 'the ODCE')[40] has the right to visit the company's registered office to inspect certain registers and documents and to deliver documents including formal service of notices and legal proceedings by hand and registered mail. A letter addressed to the company at its registered office

---

35 See Pt 16 of the Act. Like with a limited company (Ltd), the members' liability, if the company is wound up, is limited to the amount, if any, unpaid on the shares they hold.

36 Of the TCA.

37 Non-resident companies making a qualifying film or programme can also consider setting up an Irish company (or a branch/agency in the State carrying on trade as a production undertaking) to carry out production in order to benefit, if the spend is eligible, from the tax credit.

38 Note that, generally speaking, DACs may have their own subsidiary companies including subsidiary DACs which will apply in the case of large corporate structures but a complex group structure would rarely be required (nor would it be desirable for s 481 purposes) for the typical production company in the entertainment sphere.

39 Such agreements, security documents and conditions precedent to Screen Ireland production loans will be examined in Chapter 9.

40 Established pursuant to s 7 of the Company Law Enforcement Act 2001.

address must be capable of being delivered by An Post. It is mandatory to e-file any change of the registered office details.[41]

[1.4.10] *Nameplate outside registered office*: s 49(1)(a) of the Act provides that a company shall display its name in a conspicuous position in easily legible letters outside every office or place in which its business is carried on and at its registered office, even if that office is a director's private home. Failure to display the name as prescribed can result in criminal conviction and penalty (see category 4 offences at [1.4.28]).

[1.4.11] *Display of particulars on company documents and publications*: the following particulars are required by s 151 of the Act to be displayed by a company on its business letters, emails and order forms: the legal form of the company,[42] place of registration, registered number and registered office address. This includes on the company website, stationery, invoices, receipts and cheques. If a company contravenes this statutory requirement in s 49(1)(b) of the Act, the company and any officer who is in default shall be guilty of a category 4 offence.

[1.4.12] *Company seal*: pursuant to s 42 of the Act, a company shall have a common seal[43] that states the company's name, engraved in legible characters. This seal should be affixed, for example, to certain loan agreements, deeds of assignment of copyright, deeds of novation[44] from one company to another, share certificates (when persons become new shareholders) or on a lease entered into by the company for office space. Generally, affixation of the seal to a document will be effected in the presence of a director and a countersigning second director (or signed by a director and the secretary) but s 43 allows for this default position to be altered in the company's constitution to allow for one authorised person only to sign and seal.

[1.4.13] *Statutory registers and minute books*: every company is obliged to maintain (by making entries in bound books or in electronic form)[45] a combined company register which must be held at the registered office. This can be administered by the company secretary or company accountant and will include a register of directors and secretaries noting their contact details, and a register

---

41 Pursuant to s 50(3) of the Act using form B2. This mandatory e-filing, as with annual returns and changes in director and secretary details, is in accordance with SI No 458 of 2016 and s 897 of the Act.

42 There are a variety of company types, e.g. company limited by guarantee (CLG), public limited company (plc), unlimited company (uc) – the Companies (Accounting) Act 2017 contains a provision that unlimited companies, which are holding companies of undertakings whose members have limited liability, are deemed to be designated unlimited companies – and a DAC.

43 Certain retailers specialise in providing company seals with a cost typically of under fifty euro.

44 Of, for example, financial and other obligations such as delivery requirements for a film on completion of post-production, as made pursuant to an earlier development or other loan agreement.

45 See ss 213 and 214 of the Act.

of members.[46] Any change[47] to the register of directors and secretaries or their details must be notified online to the CRO within 14 days of its occurrence. It will also include a register of charges[48] – each instrument creating a charge over the company's assets (or certain specified assets relating to a particular audiovisual project in the case of a production company) must be recorded and filed with the CRO within 21 days of the charge being created;[49] a register of minutes of company meetings (that is, AGMs and extraordinary general meetings); and a register of minutes of directors' meetings, for example, documenting the passing of a resolution[50] to approve the drawing down of a loan from Screen Ireland (see Chapter 9 for further discussion).

[1.4.14] Failure to keep minutes of proceedings and meetings of directors can result in prosecution (s 166(6) of the Act). Minutes of proceedings of member meetings must be entered in the company books pursuant to s 199(1) of the Act and be produced under s 199(5) if required by the ODCE or facilities made available for inspecting and taking copies of the contents of the books as the ODCE may require. If a company fails to comply with subsection (1) or with a requirement made of it under subsection (5), the company and any of its officers in default shall be guilty of a category 4 offence.

[1.4.15] *Director (fiduciary) duties*: there is an obligation under s 228 of the Act on a director to act in good faith, to act honestly and responsibly, with all due care and skill, and to act according to the company's constitution. There is a further requirement to have regard to the interests of the company's employees as well as to the interests of the members. A director must avoid any conflict between the director's duties to the company and the director's other (including personal) interests, unless the director is released from his or her duty to the company in relation to the matter concerned, whether in accordance with provisions of the company's constitution or by a resolution of members in a general meeting. There is a duty on directors under s 231 of the Act to disclose any interest they have in contracts made by the company. The duties set out in the Act are not exhaustive and, where appropriate, directors should consider obtaining legal or accounting advice concerning compliance with such duties. The consequences for non-compliance, including disqualification and personal liability, can be far-reaching.

---

46 Required under ss 149 and 169 respectively of the Act.

47 By submitting form B10 electronically to the CRO.

48 The Registrar of Companies is required to maintain a register of charges pursuant to s 414 of the Act and s 418 provides that a company shall keep a copy of every instrument creating any charge in relation to it and requiring registration.

49 Form C1 is used to create a charge. Form C6 is filed by the chargeholder (chargee) after a charge has been fully satisfied (and the loan which the charge secured has been repaid) to remove the charge from the CRO's records for that company.

50 ss 191 to 198 of the Act set out the provisions in relation to special resolutions and ordinary resolutions – examples of resolutions include giving authority for a company to purchase its own shares, changing the company's name or its constitution, winding up the company voluntarily, and varying of class rights attaching to classes of shares. s 199 deals with the recording of minutes of proceedings of meetings of a company.

[1.4.16] *Filing annual returns*: an annual return is required to be delivered[51] by a company, whether trading or not, to the CRO at least once per year. Since the introduction of mandatory e-filing of certain documentation in June 2017, annual returns must be submitted online through CORE.[52] A new company is exempt from the obligation to annex financial statements to its first annual return, which is required to be made up to a date that is six months from its date of incorporation.[53]

[1.4.17] Although the company must lay full financial statements before an AGM, depending on the type and size of the company, it may be able to claim an exemption from filing full, or any, financial statements with the CRO.

Defaulting in the filing of annual returns

[1.4.18] Returns which are filed post-deadline with the CRO incur a late filing penalty.[54] A company will also lose eligibility for audit exemption if the annual return is not filed within the prescribed timescale. Pursuant to s 343 of the Act, applications for an extension of time to file an annual return may be made to either the High Court or to the District Court. These applications involve the incurrence of significant costs and should be avoided by filing returns diligently and in a timely fashion. The court may, if it is satisfied that it would be just to do so, make an order extending the time in which the annual return of the company, in relation to a particular year, may be delivered to the Registrar of Companies.

[1.4.19] In addition, an on-the-spot fine (and/or summary prosecution of the company and/or any officer in default) may be imposed by the CRO where the company has a record of persistent late filing. Fines of up to €5,000 can be imposed on conviction for breach of the annual return filing requirements – see category 3 offences below.

[1.4.20] A company may be struck off the register and dissolved for failure to file an annual return. Application for restoration can be made to the High Court under s 738 of the Act. If a company is struck off, its assets become vested in the Minister for Public Expenditure and Reform (this would prove highly problematic in the case of film assets, film finance and distribution licence

---

51 Using form B1.

52 See fn 41. The company secretary has 28 days from the annual return date to file the return online. Within a further 28 days, the signature page, financial statements and payment must be submitted.

53 It is, however, required to annex financial statements to its second annual return, which is required to be made up to a date not later than 18 months from its date of incorporation, and filed within 28 days.

54 A late filing penalty of €100 becomes due in respect of an annual return on the day after the expiry of the filing deadline, which is 28 days after the effective date of the return, with a daily penalty amount of €3 accruing thereafter, up to a maximum penalty of €1,200 per return. This penalty is in addition to the standard filing fee of €40 per return. Revenue has confirmed that late filing penalties are not tax deductible.

agreements),[55] and if the business continues to trade, the owners will no longer enjoy the benefit of limited liability and can be rendered personally responsible for any debts incurred so long as the company remains dissolved.[56] Any person who was a director of a company at the date of sending to that company a strike-off notice due to the non-filing of annual returns may be disqualified from acting as a company director by the High Court where the company is struck off leaving outstanding liabilities. Such order may be made by the court on the application of the ODCE disqualifying the company's director/s from acting as director or having any involvement in the management of any company, together with an order for the legal costs incurred in bringing such an application and the costs of investigating the matter.

[1.4.21] The CRO itself prosecutes companies and their directors for failure to file annual returns on time. Companies and directors may receive a conviction in respect of each year that annual returns are outstanding. A director with three such convictions may be disqualified from acting as a director or having any involvement in the management of any company.

Restriction and disqualification of company directors

[1.4.22] Sections 818 to 864 (together with s 683) of the Act provide for restriction and the more serious sanction of disqualification. Since its introduction (and subsequent secondary legislation setting out the statutory forms and notices),[57] it is possible for directors to submit to voluntary restriction and disqualification by accepting an undertaking not to act as a director, such undertakings to be registered by the ODCE with the CRO. This has resulted in many such voluntary arrangements and fewer court applications. The advantage for company directors is that they can avoid paying the legal costs involved were the matter to come before the courts. The tests applied by the courts when setting periods of disqualification and for granting restriction and disqualification orders were set out in the oft-cited case of *Re Clawhammer Ltd*,[58] the 2016 Court of Appeal ruling in *Walsh*,[59] and the judgments of Mr Justice David Keane in the *Leahy* cases (the first concerning an application for restriction under the Companies Act 1990 and the second under current legislation later that year),[60]

---

55 It is most unlikely this would occur in the case of well-established production companies whose film and television projects will be overseen by legal, accounting, tax and auditor practitioners whereby statutory compliance will be a prerequisite to obtaining private and public funding. Nonetheless it could occur in the case of inexperienced producers (as company directors/owners) with nascent companies whereby their equipment and other assets might potentially become vested in the State.

56 See also s 859 of the Act (persons acting while disqualified or restricted can be held liable for debts of the company) and s 836 (personal liability for debts of a company that is subject to restriction).

57 Companies Act 2014 (Disqualification and Restriction Undertakings) Regulations 2015 (SI No 222 of 2015).

58 [2005] IEHC 85.

59 *Director of Corporate Enforcement v Walsh* [2016] IECA 2 (otherwise cited as *Re Walfab Engineering Ltd*).

60 *Leahy v Doherty* [2016] IEHC 588; *Leahy v O'Keefe* [2016] IEHC 589.

as well as Haughton J's decision in *Wood Products*.[61] The ODCE's annual reports can also be consulted for further analysis in respect of the tests it applies and the rationale therefor.

[1.4.23] More recently, in the High Court case of *Re Winning Ways Ltd (In Liquidation)*,[62] there was a deficit as regards unsecured creditors which at liquidation exceeded one million euro. This led the court to the conclusion that the respondents had not demonstrated that they acted honestly and responsibly in relation to the affairs of the company. Accordingly, the learned judge, Quinn J, made a restriction declaration pursuant to s 819 of the Act that each respondent should not for a period of five years be appointed to act in any way directly or indirectly as a director or secretary of a company or be concerned in or take part in the formation or promotion of a company unless it could meet the requirements set out in s 819(3). As regards disqualification, the decision in *Kirby v Conlon*[63] illustrates that in cases where an applicant can establish serious misconduct on the part of a director, the court will make disqualification orders for a significant period, in that case 18 years.[64]

[1.4.24] The criteria historically applied in considering whether a party had acted honestly and responsibly are set out in High Court and Supreme Court jurisprudence since the late 1990s including the seminal decision of Shanley J in *Re La Moselle Clothing*,[65] the Supreme Court's ruling in *Re Squash (Ireland) Ltd*[66] (2001), the High Court's 2004 judgment in *Tralee Beef and Lamb*,[67] as successfully appealed by one restricted party (chartered accountant Simon Coyle) to the Supreme Court,[68] and the above-cited *Leahy* cases.[69]

---

61 *Wood Products (Longford) Ltd (In Liquidation) and in the matter of sections 819, 842 and 682 of the Companies Act 2014* [2017] IEHC 314.

62 [2020] IEHC 264.

63 *In the matter of the Companies Act 2014 and in the matter of Pembroke Dynamic Internet Services Ltd (In Liquidation)* [2021] IEHC 475.

64 Sanfey J stated that in deciding on a period of disqualification, "it is necessary to examine the company's history and the respondent's role in it, and the liquidator's investigation of its affairs". The court, in applying the principles set out in *Re Bovale Developments Ltd, Director of Corporate Enforcement v Bailey* [2013] IEHC 561, held that the period of disqualification should reflect the gravity of the conduct or wrongdoing of the director in question. It ruled that, in light of the serious fraud and diversion of charitable donations, a disqualification period of 18 years was appropriate. However, the court reduced this by two years based on mitigating factors including the respondent's age, the fact that he had previously been imprisoned and the fact that he entered into a settlement with the liquidator of the company.

65 [1998] 2 ILRM 345.

66 [2001] 3 IR 35.

67 *In the matter of Tralee Beef and Lamb Ltd (In Liquidation): Kavanagh v Delaney* (unreported, High Court, Finlay Geoghegan J, 20 July 2004).

68 Hardiman, Macken and Finnegan JJ [2008] IESC 1.

69 See also: *Re Swanpool Ltd; McLaughlin v Lannen* [2006] 2 ILRM 217; *Re James Murphy & Sons Sales (Dundalk) Ltd; Stafford v Murphy* [2010] IEHC 115; *Re Mitek Ltd; Grace v Kachkar* [2010] IESC 31, and *Re USIT World* [2015] IEHC 285.

Civil liability of disqualified or restricted persons for company debts

[1.4.25] Under s 859 of the Act, if, while restricted or disqualified, persons are acting in such prohibited manner or capacity when the company goes into insolvent liquidation, or if it goes into insolvent liquidation within 12 months of their so acting, the court may, on the application of the liquidator or any creditor of the company, declare them personally liable, without any limitation of liability, for all or any of the debts or other liabilities of the company incurred in the period during which they were acting in breach of restrictions or in breach of a disqualification order.

Criminal liability for officers, members and companies

[1.4.26] Offences are predominantly addressed in Pt 11 of the Act from ss 715 to 724 (covering *inter alia* companies in liquidation and fraudulent trading) and Pt 14 from ss 865 to 878, while s 785 deals with offences in respect of the requirement to produce books or documents. Criminal prosecutions are not limited to the Act however. For example, the DPP can prosecute pursuant to s 26 (using false instruments) of the Criminal Justice (Theft and Fraud Offences) Act 2001 and in respect of counts of theft under s 4 thereof. Prosecutions can be initiated by the ODCE having regard to its powers under the Company Law Enforcement Act 2001, the DPP, and, in some cases, by the Registrar of Companies as noted at [1.4.21], depending on the severity of the offence. Company directors and officers may be convicted of an offence as well as the company itself.

[1.4.27] Offences include material omissions as regards statements of company affairs; failing to make disclosures or to produce documents or accounts to a liquidator or otherwise; destroying, falsifying or concealing documents; completing a return, report, balance sheet or other document that is false in a material particular; and fraudulently parting with, altering or making an omission from a book or document. Section 722 (fraudulent trading) offences can arise at any time during a company's life (solvent or insolvent), thus imposing criminal liability on persons found guilty of fraudulent trading with intent to defraud creditors or for any fraudulent purposes. Fraudulent trading constitutes a category 1 offence.

[1.4.28] Under s 871 which prescribes the four categories of offence and the attendant penalties, a person guilty of an office on summary conviction (before a District Court judge) can be liable to a class A fine[70] or imprisonment for a term not exceeding 12 months or, on conviction on indictment (after trial before judge and jury in the Circuit Criminal Court), to a fine not exceeding €500,000 or imprisonment for a term not exceeding 10 years or both.[71]

---

70 A class A fine is that within the meaning of the Fines Act 2010 and is a fine not exceeding €5,000.

71 In respect of a category 1 offence, conviction on indictment can result in a term of imprisonment of up to 10 years and/or a €500,000 fine while a summary prosecution

The veil of incorporation

[1.4.29] It was firmly established by the House of Lords as a fundamental principle of British company law well over a hundred years ago in the case of *Salomon*[72] that a company is the agent of its members, even if all the shares are beneficially owned by one person. Accordingly, the acts of the company will not automatically be regarded as the acts of the members nor will the members be responsible as such for the debts and liabilities of the company. In other words, even if a shareholder owns 100 percent of a company, the company is a distinct legal entity, separate to its owner(s). The company is said to have a separate legal personality, recognised as such and separate from the members and directors of the company. However, case law and legislation has evolved over time to ensure that the corporate veil could be pierced or lifted and thereby render, in certain circumstances, company promoters, owners and directors personally liable in the civil courts for company debts.

Personal liability: lifting the veil in cases of fraudulent and reckless trading

[1.4.30] It is not intended to traverse the law on fraudulent and reckless trading and failure to keep proper books of account in any great detail. One would hope that expected astuteness, business acumen and competency aside, there are sufficient checks and balances in place to oversee the trading activities of production company directors and other practitioners in the entertainment and media field, whether that be compliance with conditions in a funding loan agreement, acting on legal advice, or adherence to internal and external accounting procedures. For the sake of completeness, however, some salient points must be made.

[1.4.31] If, in the course of winding up or examinership,[73] or if the court makes an order pursuant to s 610 (civil liability for fraudulent and reckless trading) of the Act, it appears that an officer was knowingly a party to the carrying on of the business of the company in a reckless manner or any person was knowingly a party to the carrying on of the business of the company with the intent to defraud its creditors or for any fraudulent purpose, then that officer or person may be held personally liable, without any limitation, for some or all of the debts of the company.

[1.4.32] Company officers will be regarded as being knowingly party to such

---

for a category 1 offence will result in a class A fine and/or a term of imprisonment of up to 12 months; conviction on indictment for a category 2 offence can result in a term of imprisonment of up to five years and/or a €50,000 fine, while a summary prosecution for a category 2 offence will result in a class A fine and/or a term of imprisonment of up to 12 months; category 3 relates to summary offences only, attracting a term on conviction of up to six months' imprisonment and/or a class A fine and, likewise, category 4 pertains to summary offences only, punishable by a class A fine.

72 *Salomon v A Salomon* & Co L*td* [1897] AC 22.

73 Examinership (ss 508 to 558 of the Act) is an option available to an insolvent company that enables it to explore all opportunities to provide for its survival.

conduct if, having regard to the general knowledge, skill and experience they might be expected to have, they ought to have known that their actions or the company's actions would cause loss to the creditors, or if they were party to the contracting of a debt and did not honestly believe on reasonable grounds that the company would be suitably placed to pay the debt when it fell due along with its other debts.

[1.4.33] The historical development of reckless trading can be traced from the seminal *Hefferon Kearns* case in 1993[74] and *Doherty Advertising*[75] in 2006 to the landmark decision on failure to keep proper accounts in *Mantruck Services*[76] some years later, to more recent decisions such as the Court of Appeal judgment in *Appleyard Motors*[77] *in* late 2016.

DIRECT AND INDIRECT BENEFICIAL OWNERSHIP OF COMPANIES

[1.5.01] The 4th[78] (4AMLD), 5th[79] and 6th[80] Money Laundering and Counter Terrorist Financing Directives mandated that EU Member States take action in this area in respect, *inter alia*, of records to identify ownership in companies.[81] The central Register of Beneficial Ownership of Companies and Industrial and Provident Societies ('the RBO') is a standalone register which has been established under anti-money laundering legislation and not pursuant to company law. However, the Registrar of Companies was appointed as its registrar with effect from 29 July 2019.

[1.5.02] Statutory Instrument No 560 of 2016, which required all corporate and legal entities to hold adequate, accurate and current information on their beneficial owner(s) in their internal register, was revoked and replaced by SI No 110 of 2019.[82] These latter regulations give effect to Art 30 of 4AMLD. The Criminal Justice (Money Laundering and Terrorist Financing) (Amendment) Act 2021 gives effect to the fifth Directive. Legislation is not required to transpose

74 *Re: Hefferon Kearns Ltd (No. 2)* [1993] 3 IR 191.

75 *In the matter of Doherty Advertising Ltd (In Official Liquidation) and in the matter of section 150 of the Companies Act 1990 and section 56 of the Companies Law Enforcement Act 2001* [2006] IEHC 88.

76 *supra* at fn 16.

77 *In Re Appleyard Motors Ltd & Cos Acts: Toomey Leasing Group Ltd v Sedgwick* [2016] IECA 280 overturning Binchy J in the High Court.

78 EU Directive 2015/849 [as amended by Art 1(15) of Directive 2018/843 of the European Parliament and of the Council of 30 May 2018] on the prevention of the use of the financial system for the purposes of money laundering or terrorist financing, amending Regulation (EU) No 648/2012 of the European Parliament and of the Council, and repealing Directive 2005/60/EC of the European Parliament and of the Council and Commission Directive 2006/70/EC.

79 Directive 2018/843.

80 Directive 2018/1673 (in effect for Member States on 3 December 2020 and requiring implementation by financial institutions by 3 June 2021).

81 With such details as PPSN, address and date of birth to be provided.

82 SI No 110 of 2019 – EU (Anti-Money Laundering: Beneficial Ownership of Corporate Entities) Regulations 2019. See also SI No 578 of 2019.

6AMLD into Irish law. Further, the EU (Anti-Money Laundering: Beneficial Ownership of Trusts) Regulations 2021 (SI No 194 of 2021) have revoked SI No 16 of 2019.

[1.5.03] All corporate and legal entities (other than companies listed on a regulated market) are required by 4AMLD to keep details of their beneficial ownerships on their own internal register.[83] Companies must thus identify their beneficial owners, keep their details on file and register these details with the RBO. This is in addition to meeting their existing statutory filing obligations with the CRO in relation to directors, shareholders and so forth. The filing of beneficial ownership data must be effected through the online portal on the RBO website and is therefore a process separate to the registration of information and forms under companies legislation. Restricted access to view beneficial ownership information/reports is only available to designated persons (including solicitors, accountants and financial institutions) while unrestricted access is granted to competent authorities such as An Garda Síochána, the Law Society of Ireland, the Department of Justice, and Revenue. In accordance with a November 2022 ruling[84] of the Court of Justice of the European Union, only the entity profile is available in terms of general public access, but will show the number of beneficial owners filed.

Beneficial owner defined

[1.5.04] A beneficial owner is defined in Art 3(6) 4AMLD as any natural person (and thus not a body corporate) who ultimately owns or controls a legal entity, either through direct or indirect ownership of a sufficient percentage of the shares or voting rights or ownership interest in the entity, or through control via other means. These include ownership (directly or indirectly) of more than 25 percent of the company shares; controlling (directly or indirectly) more than 25 percent of the company voting rights; and control via other means which is explained in Recital 13 of 4AMLD to include the criteria of control used for the purpose of preparing consolidated financial statements, such as through a shareholders' agreement, the exercise of dominant influence or the power to appoint senior management.

[1.5.05] If a relevant entity is a subsidiary owned by another corporate entity, any natural person who holds or controls a shareholding of 25 percent plus one share, or an ownership interest of more than 25 percent in the parent corporate entity, is a beneficial owner of the subsidiary. If a relevant entity is a subsidiary owned by multiple corporate entities, Art 3(6) states that a shareholding of 25

---

83 On 26 November 2018, the Criminal Justice (Money Laundering and Terrorist Financing) (Amendment) Act 2018 was commenced, transposing 4AMLD into Irish law. It should be noted that Art 30(1) of 4AMLD, dealing with the requirement of a body corporate or other legal entity to maintain its own register (local register) of beneficial owners, was already transposed into Irish law by the EU (Anti-Money Laundering: Beneficial Ownership of Corporate Entities) Regulations 2016.

84 *WM and Sovim SA v Luxembourg Business Registers,* joined cases C-37/20 and C-601/20.

percent plus one share or an ownership interest of more than 25 percent in a subsidiary held by multiple corporate entities which are under the control of the same natural person(s), shall be an indication of indirect beneficial ownership. Ultimately, it is a natural person who must be identified and entered on the RBO as the beneficial owner of the relevant entity, irrespective of how many layers of ownership there are in the company structure.[85]

[1.5.06] 25 percent plus one share does not mean 26 percent. In instances where companies have a large number of shares, a shareholder might have 25 percent of the overall available shares plus one extra share. For example, ABC Company Ltd has 1,000,000 shares at one euro each. If any person holds 250,000 (25 percent) or less shares, this person does not qualify under the requirement. However, if the shareholder owns or controls 250,001 shares, then that member qualifies as a beneficial owner and details of same must be duly registered.

Penalties

[1.5.07] If a relevant entity does not file with the RBO, it may be guilty of an offence and liable on summary conviction to a class A fine of up to €5,000 and on conviction on indictment to a fine of up to €500,000.

TAXATION/SELF-ASSESSMENT

Income tax, employer taxes and self-assessed contractors

[1.6.01] The taking of legal and accounting advice is always recommended in relation to matters of taxation as, for instance, the consequences for an individual worker, service provider or business can be severe if contracts are miscategorised for income tax purposes as being contracts of service or contracts for services. These matters are discussed in Chapter 17 in relation to crew contracts. Assistance, were confusion to arise relating to classification of a worker as a PAYE/Schedule E[86] employee or self-employed Schedule D contractor, can be obtained from the Department of Social Protection.[87]

[1.6.02] Within the entertainment and media sector, the treatment of income tax has been a source of controversy, contention and disquiet for several years and the position remains unresolved despite parliamentary debates in recent times probing the underlying issues. Legislation or guidance to put matters beyond

---

85 If, after having exhausted all possible means and provided there are no grounds for suspicion, no natural person is identified as a beneficial owner, or if there is any doubt that the person identified is the beneficial owner, the natural person who holds the position of senior managing official shall be recorded on the RBO as the beneficial owner (reg 5(4), SI No 110 of 2019). Relevant entities shall keep records of the actions taken to identify their beneficial owners (reg 5(5)).

86 Of the TCA.

87 The membership organisation Screen Producers Ireland can also be contacted as can unions and guilds, and seminars and training programmes are available from organisations such as Screen Skills Ireland.

doubt would be greatly welcomed. The burning issue is the prevalence (or not) of 'bogus' self-employment pertaining to workers who should be classified as employees being incorrectly classified as self-employed and vice versa, a matter that resulted in a €1.2 million settlement by RTÉ with Revenue in 2021 in respect of 81 such workers (see Chapter 17). The effect of being self-employed is a reduction in costs for the production company, meaning income tax is a matter for the self-employed contractor. Further, the contractor stands unentitled to employee benefits including annual leave, maternity leave and potential pension contributions and a wide array of statutory protections from unfair dismissal, redundancy and fixed-term work legislation.

[1.6.03] The uncertainty has not been aided by the withdrawal of guidance by Revenue issued in 2009 pertaining to taxation of individuals engaged in the Irish film industry. The difficulties were then compounded in the context of the definitions of eligible expenditure by the rather ill-conceived reference only to 'employees' in the Revenue guidance manual on s 481 issued in 2019 on foot of the current film regulations. The updated June 2022 guidelines do refer to self-employed persons however in respect of travel and subsistence expenses and it is still the case that heads of department are generally classed as self-employed persons (as are certain talent, crew and service providers).

[1.6.04] Revenue has issued guidance on the income provisions of the TCA and as updated in the Finance Act 2020.[88] Further, in July 2021, Revenue, the Department of Social Protection and the Workplace Relations Commission issued an updated (first prepared in 2001) *Code of Practice for Determining Employment or Self-Employment Status of Individuals*. Responsibility for decisions in relation to employment status in terms of PRSI rests with the Scope Section of the Department of Social Protection, charged with giving directions and information relating to the insurability of employment. Any person, business or its representatives may apply to have an employment investigated to ensure that the correct PRSI class is attributed.

Section 481 and income tax

[1.6.05] When applying to the relevant government department for a culture certificate in respect of a qualifying film as the first step in the s 481 tax credit application, the producer company must set out who will be hired for a film, whether they are employees (e.g. skills participants, line producer, production co-ordinator) or independent contractors (e.g. heads of department, writer, director, post-production service providers), the wages or fees payable, and the amount of 'person days' to be worked within and outside the State. In the case of contractors who are seeking to be paid expenses, it is essential that they submit invoices for such expenses (e.g. fuel, tolls and parking, subsistence costs

---

88 See, for example, Revenue, *Notes for Guidance – Taxes Consolidation Act 1997 Finance Act 2020 edition Schedules* (2021), revenue.ie. Available at: https://www.revenue.ie/ga/tax-professionals/documents/notes-for-guidance/tca/schedules.pdf [Accessed 20 March 2022].

and per diem payments). Any unvouched sums cannot count towards eligible expenditure.

[1.6.06] When preparing the budget as regards employee costs it is important, aside from deduction of PAYE income tax and other employee taxes, that account is also taken of employer taxes (employer PRSI, fringe benefit payments, holiday pay and so forth). Less experienced producers will be aware of the obligation to pay employee income tax as deducted from source but may omit to incorporate significant additional employer tax costs into the budget. It is therefore crucial in this connection to obtain detailed figures from the production accountant.

VAT and contractors

[1.6.07] A related matter is invoicing by independent contractors and whether they are VAT-registered (see thresholds below). If so, their fee invoice should be in the form of a VAT invoice submitted to the production company. Actors and crew working as waged or salaried employees under standard contracts of service are outside the scope of VAT given that, in these circumstances, there is no supply of services for VAT purposes.

Chargeable persons

[1.6.08] Under s 950 TCA, in general, a company director is a 'chargeable person' for income tax purposes. As a result, company directors are obliged to submit an Irish income tax return each year, even though all of their income may have been taxed at source under the PAYE system. There are, however, some exceptions. For example, non-proprietary directors are usually excluded from this obligation. A proprietary director is, in simple terms, a director who controls more than 15 percent of the company's shares.

Withholding tax

[1.6.09] Other considerations regularly confronting larger productions are the issues of loan-out companies generally (see below) and withholding tax on income earned (withholding tax on royalties might also arise). Simultaneously with the introduction of the new film tax credit, the government introduced a withholding tax on payments to non-EU/EEA artistes (principally meaning actors and voice-over artistes) for work rendered in Ireland. The withholding tax also applies to artistes using loan-out companies as will be discussed below. The rate of this tax is 20 percent but expenses incurred by the artiste (such as manager and agent fees, travel expenses and so forth) are deductible for this purpose. Revenue updated its film withholding tax ('FWT') guidelines in August 2021[89] and clarifies for instance that following the conclusion of the Brexit transition period (from 1 January 2021), UK artistes are also subject to the withholding tax; that where

---

89 See Revenue, *Film Withholding Tax* (2021), revenue.ie. Available at: https://www.revenue.ie/en/tax-professionals/tdm/income-tax-capital-gains-tax-corporation-tax/part-18/18-01a-01.pdf [Accessed 19 March 2022].

an individual is engaged in dual roles, for example, as both a director and as an actor, it will be necessary to apportion payments to the individual between the two roles; and that special considerations apply as regards US artistes.[90]

Corporation tax

[1.6.10] Taxation of profits from trading activities will depend on the business structures outlined earlier in this chapter. Partners in a band, for example, will be self-assessed and each will deal with their own individual tax affairs based on figures from the partnership accounts as referred to in Chapter 22. Sole traders will also be self-employed and submit self-assessment annual tax returns to Revenue. The position in respect of companies is more complicated. First, because returns must be filed both with the CRO and with Revenue and, secondly, there may be a number of tax types at play. There are advantages to trading as a company given that corporation tax is levied at a much lower rate than personal income tax. However, when director shareholders are employed by the company, they will be paying income tax on dividends and/or their salary as PAYE employees, and the company itself will be paying employer taxes and corporation tax.

[1.6.11] Accounting advice should be sought as how best to lawfully reduce one's taxation liabilities. Incorporation of a company at home or abroad[91] is an attractive option to which successful music artists, for instance, will commonly have recourse.[92]

---

90 Under the terms of Art 17 of the Double Taxation Treaty between Ireland and the USA (1997), where the amount of the payments, including expenses reimbursed or borne on behalf of the artiste, made by a qualifying company to a specified person in respect of artistic services does not exceed $20,000 or its equivalent in a tax year, then FWT is not to be applied to the payments. Where the amount of relevant payments and expenses exceeds $20,000 in a tax year, the full amount (excluding expenses) is subject to FWT. There are no equivalent provisions in double taxation treaties between Ireland and any other State.

91 U2, for instance, moved part of its business (publishing arm royalties and performance income) from Ireland to the Netherlands in 2006 after the government capped a previously unlimited tax break on artistic earnings at €250,000 a year. As a very high-grossing act through album sales, tour receipts and publishing/royalties income, the cap imposed in 2006 would have resulted in a multimillion euro tax bill. *The Irish Times* reported in 2018 that U2 and The Rolling Stones licensed their copyright to companies they established in the Netherlands, which in turn licensed it to companies in other countries. While the Netherlands companies received the bands' global royalties, tax would only be paid on what was earned in the Netherlands itself, allowing the groups to cut their tax bills (source: Barry O'Halloran, *U2 face closure of loophole they used to avoid paying their taxes* (2018), irishtimes.com. Available at: https://www.irishtimes.com/business/media-and-marketing/u2-face-closure-of-loophole-they-used-to-avoid-paying-their-taxes-1.3407927 [Accessed 3 January 2019].

92 Niall Horan (formerly of One Direction) by way of illustration incorporated two Irish companies Neon Haze Music Ltd and Jaredon Ltd in 2016 and 2017 respectively (source: Gordon Deegan, *Niall Horan pays himself €2.4m from two Irish companies* (2019), irishtimes.com. Available at: https://www.irishtimes.com/business/media-and-marketing/niall-horan-pays-himself-2-4m-from-two-irish-companies-1.3986201 [Accessed 18 August 2019]. Ed Sheeran Ltd is a UK entity which organises and negotiates Sheeran's touring arrangements.

[1.6.12] Another avenue is splitting artist revenues. For example, a writer might pen a novel. The income from book publishing might be dealt with under the writer's sole trader business as a novelist (and the author may additionally benefit from the artist exemption outlined below). However, the writer might also elect to form a company into which revenues from stage, radio productions and film rights (and associated gains such as spin-off production revenues, back-end income from producer net profit participation and sale of merchandising products) are channelled.

[1.6.13] Raising finance through s 481 Revenue cash funding is discussed in detail in Chapter 8 which involves the making of a self-assessment claim for film corporation tax credit relief by a producer company through Revenue's Online Service whereby the company amends its corporation tax return[93] for the relevant accounting period. A certificate issued on foot of a successful application entitles the producer company to a credit against its corporation tax liabilities. In the event that this credit exceeds the company's corporation tax for the qualifying period (and the company has no other outstanding taxes), the excess amount is paid by Revenue to the producer company.

Loan-out companies

[1.6.14] In the entertainment sector, a personal service company is a form of business entity whereby the company director's/owner's services are lent out by the 'lender' corporate body to a production company for a project (e.g. a film director). The service providers will typically be the sole shareholders and the company is used as a means to reduce their personal liability, protect their assets[94] and exploit taxation advantages. Loan-out companies are especially prominent in the entertainment and professional sports industries, as the subject services are typically performed on an individual contract basis and irregular sums of income will be received throughout the year.

[1.6.15] The loan-out company is engaged by external third parties to fulfil services, rather than the individual company officer directly. Consequently, it is the loan-out company that is referred to and liable in contracts to perform the services required. For example, a novelist writes a book but obtains accounting advice to incorporate a company such that the publishing agreement is between

---

Further, Cheryl Cole, Olly Murs and JLS all established Irish companies in 2012. The three acts had separate companies in the UK to handle their earnings there. Worldwide profits for British acts can be channelled through subsidiaries in Ireland, where corporation tax is 12.5 percent, compared with the 24 percent rate which formerly applied in the UK. One Direction's financial affairs were handled by Live Wire Business Management based in Limerick and London which also handled matters for Boyzone, Westlife and Girls Aloud (source: Colin Coyle, *Ireland is No 1 for tax haven stars* (2012), thetimes.co.uk. Available at: https://www.thetimes.co.uk/article/ireland-is-no-1-for-tax-haven-stars-vmjm07qzhr0 [Accessed 4 March 2018 and 20 March 2022].

93 Form CT1.

94 Through the doctrine of limited liability/separate legal personality of companies described earlier.

that company and the publisher. Similarly, a production company may lend its company director to perform individual producer services on a film it is producing (through its subsidiary DAC) and the contract will be between it as parent company and the DAC for the purposes of tax credit documentation. This arrangement will be effected for the tax advantages it may bestow due to expense deductions and the different treatment of corporation tax versus personal income an individual would pay, together with the lowering of profits on which tax will be paid by means of payment of a salary.[95]

[1.6.16] In the above examples, service providers will sign (in an appendix to the loan-out agreement) a letter of inducement for the benefit of the production company an undertaking in their personal capacity to *inter alia* perform the contractual obligations; authorise the lender company to make on their behalf the assignment of copyright and other IP rights in the product of the services being provided; repeat and make in a personal capacity as if set out in the letter of inducement all of the warranties and consents made and granted by the lender; confirm that payment of all fees due to the lender under the contract should be made to the lender; and undertake that if the lender should at any time cease trading, be struck off the Register of Companies or go into voluntary or involuntary liquidation, to perform all of the obligations and honour all of the liabilities of the lender pursuant to the contract as if the service provider were personally party to the agreement in lieu of the lender.

[1.6.17] Where a foreign loan-out company is hired by an Irish producer (such as when engaging the services of a director or head of department), there are other consequences to consider including tax residence rules, withholding tax and social security obligations of the Irish employer on which specialist accounting advice should be sought. If the foreign entity fails to operate the Irish income tax system correctly, the Irish authorities may seek the relevant amounts from the Irish host company.

VAT

[1.6.18] VAT (sales tax) treatment generally is a complex subject on which the services of accounting and book-keeping professionals should be consulted in

95 In a general corporate setting, the corporation pays tax on profits made from generating business revenues, and pays out a dividend to shareholders. Subsequently, these shareholders pay tax on the income received in the form of a dividend. However, in the loan-out corporation format, the creator of the corporation is typically the sole shareholder. To avoid paying tax twice, at the corporate and personal income tax levels, the loan-out corporation will pay out its profits to the sole shareholder as a salary or bonus. Since the payment is treated as a salary expense, it is tax deductible as it is a typical part of business operations, rather than the elective payment of a dividend, potentially minimising company profit to or near zero.

respect of VAT registration,[96] filing of VAT returns and VIES[97] returns where applicable, charging VAT on the supply of goods or services, recovering through VAT refund claims the VAT incurred on certain costs in making a production (note, as stated at the outset, that fees are stated net of VAT in production budgets), place of supply rules, and VAT arising on presale of distribution rights to a person established in Ireland (a presale of distribution rights to a business established in another EU Member State, or to any purchaser outside of the EU, is not within the scope of Irish VAT). Producers may also require accounting advice when supplying invoices to draw down loans from Screen Ireland and grant aid from local authorities and other public funding bodies or indeed when invoicing for their services and overheads by virtue of a production services agreement.

Completed films

[1.6.19] VAT is applicable on the supply of goods and services within the EU. Where an Irish-established company delivers a completed film to a company established in another EU Member State, Irish VAT should be chargeable at the zero-rate provided the recipient's foreign VAT number is stated on the Irish company's invoice, the film is physically dispatched to the other Member State within three months of the supply and evidence of the dispatch is retained by the Irish company. Film production may also avail of zero rating when the master negative is being exported to a company outside the EU but the supplier of the completed film would be able to recover VAT incurred in making the relevant film. Another consideration is that on larger projects the sale of peripheral goods connected to the distribution of a film such as books, magazines, children's clothing and the publication of sheet music might have one rate (e.g. zero-rated) while the sale of other merchandising such as DVDs, other clothing, posters, toys and e-books might be subject to VAT at the top rate.

[1.6.20] As regards supply of a completed film in Ireland, the supply of commissioned cinematographic and video film which records particular persons, objects or events supplied under an agreement to photograph those persons, objects or events is treated as a supply of goods liable to Irish VAT at the reduced rate of 13.5 percent. Other supplies of films or videos (e.g. films on DVD, Blu-ray or any other digitised media) are liable to Irish VAT at the standard rate which at the time of writing is set at 23 percent. Producers are advised to seek specialist accounting services when confronted with such taxation issues.

---

96 In general, once registered for VAT in Ireland (which is compulsory in the case of persons supplying services only after the turnover threshold of €37,500 in a calendar year has been reached; a threshold of €75,000 applies to persons supplying goods), Irish VAT incurred on costs directly relating to a person's vatable activities is recoverable subject to certain statutory restrictions on non-deductible items such as food and drink, accommodation (except accommodation in relation to qualifying conferences, and that which is eligible production spend in the case of s 481), entertainment, the purchase/hire of motor vehicles (except a partial VAT deduction on certain low-emission vehicles), petrol (VAT can be reclaimed on diesel) and other goods and services not purchased for business purposes.

97 European Commission VAT Information Exchange System.

Broadcaster commissions

[1.6.21] Specific rules apply in the case of commissioned material. Revenue has issued some guidelines (last reviewed September 2021)[98] on the VAT treatment of independent film and television productions, which should be read in conjunction with para 18 of Sch 3 to the VAT Consolidation Act 2010.

[1.6.22] Producers may avail of funding under the Broadcasting Funding Scheme,[99] established under the Broadcasting Act 2009, for production and development costs on high quality programmes on Irish culture, heritage and experience, programmes to improve adult literacy and programmes dealing with the themes of media literacy and global affairs. This scheme enables producers to share the revenues from their film, television or radio project with the funding body until such time as the funding body has recouped its investment. Funding provided under the scheme is outside the scope of VAT. Likewise, generally, in the case of production funding with a licence agreement and recoupable investment whereby there is granting of a licence only (being the right to broadcast the programme for a fixed period, together with other current and future exploitation rights)[100] this is the supply of a service chargeable at the standard rate of VAT in accordance with section 46(1)(a) of the above Act – however, the recoupable amount payable to the producer is deemed to be outside the scope of VAT.

EXEMPTIONS FOR CERTAIN EARNINGS OF WRITERS, COMPOSERS AND ARTISTS

[1.7.01] Section 195 TCA is designed to assist young artists on low incomes, the scheme originally being introduced in 1969 by then Finance Minister Charles Haughey to support local talent and attract artists to settle in Ireland. It exempts from income tax certain earnings of writers, music composers and artists which would otherwise be chargeable to tax under Case II of Schedule D[101] to include revenue arising from the publication, production or sale of books, screenplays, plays and musical compositions.[102] This applies whether they are living in Ireland

---

[98] See Revenue, *VAT Treatment of Independent Film and TV Productions* (2021), revenue.ie. Available at https://www.revenue.ie/en/tax-professionals/tdm/value-added-tax/part03-taxable-transactions-goods-ica-services/Goods/goods-independent-film-and-tv-productions.pdf [Accessed 18 March 2022].

[99] BAI (Sound and Vision), national broadcasters (RTÉ and TG4) and Screen Ireland.

[100] A characteristic of the supply of goods for VAT purposes is the transfer of ownership of the goods by agreement. For example, where a producer makes a programme and transfers ownership together with copyright of that programme, in its entirety, to another entity then there is a supply of goods for VAT purposes and that supply is liable to VAT at the reduced rate.

[101] Application for exemption can be made to the Income and Capital Taxes Division of Revenue at the Artist Exemption Unit, Dublin Castle by submitting the Artist 2 Claim and any supporting documentation.

[102] Other payments are exempt from tax when they are made to an artist who has received an artist's exemption, to include Arts Council bursaries and advance royalties from book publishing.

or in the EU/EEA.[103] The maximum amount of income which can be exempted in respect of an individual is €50,000 annually.

[1.7.02] Guidelines[104] (updated August 2021) were prepared under s 195(12) TCA by the Arts Council and the then Minister for Culture, Heritage and the Gaeltacht to which Revenue has recourse to determine (subject to an appeal mechanism)[105] whether a work is original and creative, and whether it is generally recognised as having cultural or artistic merit. The view has been expressed in this latter connection that the scheme has the potential to be undermined by the works of entertainers, singers and eligible ghost-written sports biographies. This tax scheme has also been criticised for casting too wide a net in terms of eligibility.[106]

[1.7.03] An original and creative work may fall within one of the following categories: a book or other writing, a play, a musical composition, a painting or other like picture, and a sculpture. As *per* Revenue guidelines,[107] books or other writings published primarily for students pursuing a course of study are ineligible as are adaptations, arrangements and versions of musical compositions by a person other than a bona fide composer who is also actively engaged in musical composition, and photographs or drawings that would not exist independently in their own right.

Cultural or artistic merit

[1.7.04] The relief applies to an individual who is determined by Revenue to have written, composed or executed either solely or jointly a work or works generally recognised as having cultural or artistic merit. In reaching a

---

103 For 2015 and subsequent years, eligibility for the relief was extended by s 5 of the Finance Act 2014 to an individual who is either resident or ordinarily resident and domiciled in one or more Member State of the EU, or in another EEA State, and not resident elsewhere.

104 See Revenue, *Exemption of Certain Earnings of Writers, Composers and Artists* (2021), revenue.ie. Available at: https://www.revenue.ie/en/tax-professionals/tdm/income-tax-capital-gains-tax-corporation-tax/part-07/07-01-10.pdf [Accessed 18 March 2022].

105 An appeal to the Appeal Commissioners is available to unsuccessful claimants. A determination of the Appeal Commissioners may be appealed on a point of law to the High Court.

106 *The Irish Independent* reported in August 2017 that 2,840 people availed of the scheme in 2015, with a cost to the taxpayer of €10.8 million – Mark O'Regan, *Artist tax exemption faces major shake-up over books loophole* (2017), independent.ie. Available at: https://www.independent.ie/irish-news/artist-tax-exemption-faces-major-shake-up-over-books-loophole-36072649.html [Accessed 20 September 2017 and 20 March 2022]. The article suggested, given high earner names such as Ryan Tubridy, Louis Walsh, Bertie Ahern, Ronan O'Gara, George Hook and Katherine Zappone who had availed of the exemption, one option being considered by then finance minister Paschal Donohoe was to reduce the tax-free allowance for those with proven financial resources. Under s 132 of the Finance Act 2012, s 195 TCA was amended to include a new subsection (16) such that Revenue may publish the name of an individual who is the subject of a determination. Publication may, as appropriate, include the title or category of the work of an individual.

107 Revenue, *Exemption of Certain Earnings of Writers, Composers and Artists* in Tax and Duty Manual (2017), Pt 7 Chapter 1.

determination, Revenue may consult any person or body of persons as might provide authoritative assistance in establishing whether a work is a qualifying work for the purposes of s 195.

[1.7.05] Where a claim is made in respect of an individual's general as opposed to a particular work, Revenue may request that individual to furnish such information or evidence as could be of assistance in reaching its determination such as a copy of a play or body of musical compositions. In the case of a painting or sculpture, it may require the individual to provide or arrange for viewing facilities and for accounts to be made available relating to the publication, production or sale of the work the income from which is the subject of the claim for exemption.

Chapter 2

Media, Event and Film Production Insurance

INTRODUCTION

[2.1.01] Errors and omissions ('E&O') insurance is a form of liability cover which is rather specific to the media sector[1] and to which audiovisual producers must, where applicable,[2] have regard in terms of subject content and cost. It is a critical issue too for radio content producers and broadcasters, online media and traditional print media in terms of exposure to damages for defamatory remarks made in content material. This chapter will also address production insurance policies including public liability and employer's liability cover taken out by film and television producers and a wide range of other entertainment practitioners.[3]

[2.1.02] E&O cover as a form of professional indemnity insurance should be embedded at the forefront of minds from the pre-production and distribution planning stages. Entertainment lawyers are frequently engaged by audiovisual producers to furnish an opinion to insurers and distributors/sales agents on legal clearances generally and the risks posed by a project and its commercial exploitation. Instructing such legal expert only at the rough cut or indeed final cut stage of output can prove problematic.

[2.1.03] At the most fundamental level is the copyright on which a subject film, television programme, radioplay, song, sound recording, theatrical or other production is centred. If the screenplay to a motion picture is adapted from a pre-existing play, the playwright's underlying rights must be cleared, which in most instances will involve payment of a substantial fee (and when based on a published book, a quitclaim letter should be sought from the publisher).

---

1 In other sectors such as in respect of legal, accounting, engineering and architectural services, the comparable insurance is styled 'professional indemnity' insurance.

2 It is invariably required on larger audiovisual projects for broadcast but may not necessarily be sought by financiers or broadcasters in the case for instance of short films or certain television programmes (and when the production lawyer can confirm that no legal issues arise or that the likelihood of claims or litigation is almost nil).

3 Including podcast producers, drone operators, music recording studios, circus operators, magic acts, dance companies and theatrical productions as well as, for instance, festival and other live music event organisers.

Screenwriters of original work and legacy writers of pre-existing material for adaptation, in addition to typically moderate option fees during the development phase, will receive compensation by way of an acquisition of film rights agreement providing for assignment of the required rights[4] and a writing/purchase fee. In certain cases, the original writer, for example, of a novel may potentially receive a percentage of back-end producer net profit participation money and a credit (e.g. associate producer credit if involved in some way with the production) in addition to an 'adapted from' credit.

[2.1.04] Authors of original screenplays and teleplays will be requested, as a standard term in writers' agreements, to offer a warranty to the commissioning producer that all material is (or where not already written, will be) original to them and does not infringe another's copyright-protected work or breach third party rights in terms of privacy, duty of confidence or defamation, and that it is not in contempt of court.[5]

Music clearance

[2.1.05] Music used in a project will require clearance from a production music library, under a broadcaster blanket licence with a collection society[6] or, where applicable (see Chapter 17), directly from the relevant music producer/record label[7] and the music publisher(s)/songwriter(s).[8] Sometimes the rights to music will be owned by one party only (e.g. a film score composer/sound designer who also records and performs the music and is thus the rightsholder of the sound recordings and the performances thereon). Film and television producers can become embroiled in litigation, firstly, where music is used that is not cleared with the copyright and related rights owners and, secondly, indirectly, if, for example, a composer writes a score but has plagiarised from legacy music. For this reason, as with screenwriters, composers will be required to warrant to the hiring production company that the music is original, free from claims and encumbrances and that they will indemnify the producer from damages and costs in the event of breach of such warranty. If the contract does not contain such warranty,[9] a production company may need to rely on its own E&O policy in the case of alleged music copyright infringement.

---

4 The screenwriter might retain certain other rights including novelisation, stage and radioplay rights.

5 Aside from E&O considerations, interference with an ongoing criminal investigation, prejudicing an extant criminal or civil trial and rules on court reporting and contempt of court are all additional matters to which serious thought must also be given by producers (particularly of investigative documentaries) given the potential exposure to prosecution.

6 With the Mechanical Copyright Protection Society/Irish Music Rights Organisation (MCPS/IMRO) as regards music publishing rights, and with Phonographic Performance Ireland (PPI) as regards sound recordings in the case of Irish productions shown by commercial or free-to-air public stations.

7 By master use licence agreement.

8 By synchronisation licence agreement.

9 Or the composer does not have professional indemnity insurance and is personally not a

[2.1.06] One must be cognisant when relying on a broadcaster's blanket music licence with MCPS/IMRO[10] and PPI[11] (see Chapters 17 and 23) that content originally destined say for RTÉ may well be released internationally on RTÉ Player (or indeed might ultimately be placed on a platform such as Netflix for broadcast in multiple territories. Another scenario might be that a co-funding broadcaster in another country such as England comes on board later on in a project which then likely rules out blanket licence possibilities for both broadcasters). If geo-blocked to Ireland, the blanket licence reliance should generally be in order and E&O cover for Ireland only may suffice. However, the E&O coverage may need in the future to be extended internationally and the policy amended accordingly. One would need to look at music clearance either at the outset for international use, or modify the music later by inserting, for instance, library music in place of commercial music (exploitation beyond Ireland may well necessitate highly expensive music clearance with collection societies and/or rightsholders directly for which there may be no budget funds remaining). However, national broadcasters are in recent times agreeing international usage terms with collection societies for their online catch-up players particularly in respect of the publishing side of music clearance, meaning the sound recording side would still require clearance directly with the rightsholders.

CASE LAW

[2.2.01] The worst case scenario is where a film itself plagiarises a pre-existing picture as occurred in the 1982 Australian case of *Zeccola v Universal City Studios Inc*,[12] discussed in Chapter 10 which concerned blatant infringement by the film *Great White* of copyright in a novel, screenplay and in the *Jaws* motion picture. The infringements allowed Universal to secure interlocutory injunctive relief and seizure of the intended release material to prevent exploitation of the offending film in the US. The two films were spectacularly similar on a multitude of grounds to include plotlines, characters, names and settings.

[2.2.02] In the Canadian Supreme Court decision in *Cinar Corporation v Robinson*[13] (2013), discussed at [10A.6.46] in the context of substantiality of copying, the seven-justice court confirmed that the concept for a children's television show *The Adventures of Robinson Curiosity* had been infringed. Claude Robinson had developed characters, drawn detailed sketches and storyboards, written scripts and synopses, and designed promotional materials for the *Curiosity* project. While the project failed to attract investment and was

---

'mark' for damages if simply unable to afford the payment of monetary damages to the aggrieved third party rightsholder.

10 *supra* at fn 6.

11 *ibid.*

12 [1982] FCA 271; 46 ALR 189; 67 FLR 225 (Federal Court, Victoria District, appeal from the Supreme Court of Victoria's judgment as trial court).

13 [2013] SCC 73; [2013] 3 SCR 1168.

shelved, the plaintiff subsequently discovered that directors and officers of Cinar Corporation who had been given access to his *Curiosity* project material were also involved in the production of a new children's television show, *Robinson Sucroë*. Robinson commenced an action for copyright infringement against the various coproducers and distributors of *Sucroë*. The court concluded that his copyright had in fact been infringed and ordered compensatory damages, disgorgement of profits and punitive damages.

[2.2.03] Plaintiffs Don Miller and Peter Hassinger were the co-authors of a screenplay entitled *The Dark Lady* about Shakespeare writing a new play and falling in love. They pitched the script to numerous studios including Miramax which ultimately produced the film *Shakespeare in Love*. The writers claimed the film infringed their work and filed an action for copyright breaches. While the court[14] agreed with the defendant Miramax that many of the similarities between the two works were scenes a faire (stock scenes) that were typical of and necessary for the shared subject matter such as locations and historical characters, it further held that there were sufficient similarities (such as Shakespeare suffering from writer's block, burning a manuscript and meeting a woman who knows his work by heart and inspires him to write and star in a new play) in protected expression to survive summary judgment. The case settled before full trial of the substantive issues.

[2.2.04] The producer of the classic 1939 film *Gone With The Wind* was unable to convince the underlying rights proprietor (novel author Margaret Mitchell) to authorise a sequel during her lifetime. After her death, MGM claimed that a subsequent agreement with her estate granted it the right to create such a sequel. In *Trust Co. Bank v MGM*,[15] the Eleventh Circuit appeals court affirmed that no such right had been granted.

[2.2.05] Turning then to infringement by a stageplay producer rather than a film studio, in 1979 an Atlanta theatre announced the opening of *Scarlett Fever*, an unauthorised musical play based on the film. MGM filed a copyright infringement action to enjoin the production. The court[16] found that the works were substantially similar in terms of characters, setting, plot and in many cases had identical dialogue. It rejected the defendant theatre's argument that the production was a protected parody, holding that although the play was presented in a humorous cabaret style and contained a few instances of arguable parody, it was predominantly not a critical commentary but a derivative homage to the original and hence unlawfully copied significant elements from the film.

[2.2.06] While from UK case law at least there appears to be no copyright in a

---

14 *Miller v Miramax Film Corp.*, 2001 US Dist LEXIS 25967 (CD Cal 2001).

15 772 F.2d 740 (11th Cir. 1985).

16 *MGM v Showcase Atlanta Coop. Prods., Inc* 479 F.Supp. 351 (N.D. Ga. 1979).

name, trademark infringement litigation (to include film merchandise,[17] as well as personal name misappropriation and publicity rights) has been a recurring issue through the decades in the US. For this reason, Irish producers are frequently required by US distributors (through the international sales agent's contract terms) to conduct and furnish a title clearance report.

[2.2.07] Kurt Unger wrote a screenplay entitled *Return from the River Kwai* similar to the story of the successful film *The Bridge on the River Kwai* produced by Tri-Star Pictures. When Tri-Star learned of the project, it filed suit for trademark infringement alleging that the title of the original film, though based on a geographical location, had acquired a secondary meaning. The court[18] in New York agreed and found that Unger had no legitimate reason to use the title *Return from the River Kwai* other than to confuse consumers into believing, incorrectly, that his script was an authorised sequel. Unger was thus permanently enjoined from using that title.

Due diligence

[2.3.01] Further examples of problematic content include uncleared archive material such as broadcasts or film clips, newspaper articles or photographs that appear on screen, published book covers, artwork, sculptures and improperly cleared music. In the latter regard, a song penned by two authors jointly might feature in a soundtrack but, through inadvertence, a synchronisation licence is signed with one writer only of the composition. Another instance might be use of a public domain Beethoven piece. While the composition itself is clearly outside of copyright protection, an orchestral sound recording from 1987 for instance would still be in copyright and require clearance from its owner by way of master use licence agreement.

[2.3.02] Accordingly, audiovisual producers must understand how copyright duration terms are computed (see [10A.8.01]) in relation to music, film, broadcasts, artistic works and so forth. A song may be public domain given the date of death of the author as might a sound recording, but performers thereon (or their estate) might nevertheless still be due performer royalties and this needs to be assessed when submitting music cue sheets to broadcasters/distributors, and in certain scenarios the performers' written consent may be required.[19] Further, differing copyright terms will apply, for example in the US, and, while an American song for inclusion in an Irish film may be public domain in Ireland or elsewhere in the EU so that its use is cleared in those territories, it

---

17 Merchandise arising out of *Gone With The Wind* for instance has been the subject of numerous trademark and copyright disputes.

18 *Tri-Star Pictures, Inc v Unger* 14 F.Supp.2d 339 (SDNY 1998).

19 If that performer did not assign performer rights to a label, music producer or film production company.

may still be in copyright in the US such that specific clearance will be necessary to commercially exploit the film in America.

[2.3.03] An experienced legal practitioner's input can be invaluable in reducing exposure to litigation and advising on, in the given circumstances, what can and cannot appear on screen, online, radio, print media or on stage. Furthermore, an opinion stating that the risk of claims is low can positively affect the cost of E&O cover or otherwise confirming that clearance procedures will be rigorously pursued pre-publication. Hence, advice should be sought at script stage for audiovisual content. Dropping an important scene, recourse to pixelation (full or partial) and costly post-production 'online' editing to prevent a trademark violation or defamation claim are highly unattractive options. So too is inserting a contractually guaranteed opening or end credit that has been inadvertently omitted after master negatives and DCPs (digital cinema packages) have been produced.

[2.3.04] Pre-production planning well in advance will inform producers of potential copyright infringement pitfalls, data protection and privacy issues, defamation and other potential legal claims to include breach of contract and breach of a duty of confidence. On the copyright front, a recent welcome development is the introduction pursuant to s 13 of the Copyright and Other Intellectual Property Law Provisions Act 2019[20] of an expansion of the fair dealing defences, namely, fair dealing with a work for the purposes of caricature, parody or pastiche shall not infringe the copyright in that work.

Defamatory content and jurisdictional considerations

[2.3.05] Legal advice will almost invariably be taken in respect of defamation law which might arise where, by way of illustration, a documentary film insinuates corruption, bribery or malpractice by an individual or corporation. A film destined for an American audience will have entirely different issues at play than a picture to be shown in Ireland where defamation laws are substantially more conservative and pro-plaintiff. In other words, content that might well give rise to a successful defamation claim in Ireland may not meet the test for defamatory content in another jurisdiction (especially in the case of documentaries, comedy or satirical productions) and consequently all content and intended target audiences should be borne in mind. The law of defamation is comprehensively addressed in Chapter 4.

[2.3.06] In Ireland, a malice element is only required as regards the tort of malicious falsehood (e.g. slander of goods) in s 42 of the Defamation Act 2009 but not as regards general defamation of an individual in ss 2 and 6 or a business (s 12) where a defamatory statement is actionable *per se* regardless of intent and

---

20 Amending s 52 of the Copyright and Related Rights Act 2000 by inserting a new subs (5).

irrespective of financial loss or proof of special damage. An exception arises however in the case of the s 19 defence of qualified privilege.[21]

THE BIRTH OF MODERN NEGLIGENCE LAW

[2.4.01] Having set up a business and commenced trading as described in the previous chapter, the next crucial consideration is the range of insurance covers required for production (e.g. street filming under permit from a local authority), screening, broadcast and other distribution channels. Insurance can shield business owners from liability to which they would otherwise be exposed if such cover was not in place. Most significantly, an insurance policy should serve to indemnify[22] a business against losses and damages caused to third party IP rightsholders, contractors, employees and others. Claims can arise on foot of a copyright or trademark infringement, contract breach, commission of a tort (civil wrong) in the case, for example, of a defamation,[23] breach of privacy action, or breach of duty of care giving rise to personal injuries and material damage to property caused by negligence.

[2.4.02] The need for general loss cover stems from the fact that a duty of care, under the law of negligence and the statutory duty of care which employers owe to their employees and third parties,[24] arises so as not to harm others and to duly compensate them for loss caused by the acts or omissions of tortfeasor businesses or their employees.[25] This historical and far-reaching 'neighbour' principle was espoused in the landmark 1932 'snail in a bottle'[26] case of *Donoghue v Stevenson*[27] wherein Lord Atkin, delivering the leading judgment in the former House of Lords,[28] held that:

---

21 The statutory defence of qualified privilege shall fail if, in relation to the publication of the statement in respect of which the action was brought, the plaintiff proves that the defendant acted with malice.

22 Namely, holding harmless an individual(s) or a business against legal responsibility for negligence (and breach of contract etc.) and to thereby compensate third parties for injuries caused by that negligence.

23 Defamation, copyright infringement or breach of contract would be covered under an E&O or professional indemnity insurance policy whereas personal injuries and property damage or loss claims would fall under a production's general insurance policy.

24 For instance, pursuant to s 8 of the Safety, Health and Welfare at Work Act 2005, s 12 (duties of employers to persons other than their employees such as suppliers or visitors coming on site) and under the wide-ranging Safety, Health and Welfare at Work (General Application) Regulations 2007 to 2016, some of which are discussed in the next chapter.

25 Generally, employers are vicariously liable for torts committed by their employees unless, for example, employees commit a criminal offence or act well outside the scope of their duties.

26 The plaintiff, a shop assistant, met a friend at a cafe in Paisley near Glasgow. Her friend ordered and paid for a pear and ice cream ginger beer for the plaintiff. When the ginger beer was poured into her glass, it was alleged the decomposing remains of a snail dropped out of the darkened, opaque bottle. Donoghue complained of stomach pains, and a doctor diagnosed gastroenteritis and shock.

27 [1932] AC 562.

28 The Supreme Court of the United Kingdom was established by Pt 3 of the Constitutional

> The rule that you are to love your neighbour becomes in law, you must not injure your neighbour; and the lawyer's question, Who is my neighbour? receives a restricted reply.[29] You must take reasonable care to avoid acts or omissions which you can reasonably foresee would be likely to injure your neighbour. Who, then, in law, is my neighbour? The answer seems to be – persons who are so closely and directly affected by my act that I ought reasonably to have them in contemplation as being so affected when I am directing my mind to the acts or omissions which are called in question.

[2.4.03] With those words, the modern law of negligence was born. Lord Atkin based his judgment on the Christian principle of loving thy neighbour and the parable of the good Samaritan. This term could now be applied to almost any relationship, in any circumstances. *Inter alia*, it covers personal injury, product liability and professional negligence. This noble but highly controversial principle was the inception of our existential compensation culture whereby injured parties are compensated for losses caused by the negligent acts of others including road traffic accidents, workplace injuries, and 'slip and fall' claims against, for example, supermarkets and local authorities owing to the presence of hazards.

THE NEED FOR PRODUCTION AND E&O INSURANCE COVER

[2.5.01] It is important to dispel two myths about insurance. The first is that public liability insurance covers injury to all persons and therefore includes employee injuries. It does not.[30] A separate policy should be effected to cover employees (hence the term 'employer's liability' insurance) as distinct from third parties such as contractors, suppliers, clients, visitors and the public at large. The second issue frequently misunderstood is that public liability insurance is not needed by a contractor if a premises or entity in or to which (e.g. a film production) the contractor will provide services is already covered by public liability. This is also not necessarily true.

[2.5.02] While that policy might indemnify the contractor's negligence, such insurance would generally be worded to cover only the negligence of the premises or production company policyholder and its employees (and not the negligence of third party contractors, such as engineers and film-set construction companies,

---

Reform Act 2005 and commenced work on 1 October 2009, assuming the judicial functions of the House of Lords.

29 In 1928, when the incident giving rise to the claim occurred, the common law only acknowledged that a duty of care was owed to people harmed by the negligent acts of others in specific and limited circumstances such as where a contract existed between the parties, or where a manufacturer was producing something dangerous, or was acting fraudulently. Thus, the plaintiff could not take legal action. As her friend had paid for the drink, it meant the plaintiff had not entered into a contract with the cafe owner. Clearly, neither Donoghue nor her friend had a contract with the manufacturer of the ginger beer. Further, the latter had not committed fraud, and ginger beer could hardly be described as dangerous so as to satisfy the limited test.

30 Unless it is a 'catch-all' policy covering a variety of loss/liability types under different sections.

who should have their own cover in place for public liability, employer liability and third party property damage). Nowadays, however, insurance for film, television, stageshow and music event producers will be catch-all or global in effect with a range of covers provided to potentially include liability for contractors for which, strictly speaking, the policyholder is not or at least should not be liable at law. In the case of location releases, however, and where producers hire a premises for shooting, the release will typically state that the location/venue insurance covers only its own negligent acts. The audiovisual producer will therefore be expected and required to have public liability, property damage and other relevant covers in place.

[2.5.03] Thus, a policy providing coverage to an entertainment venue will likely only cover negligence of that venue's owners, employees or agents. If, for example, a band causes injury to a patron during a gig due to the band's negligence (e.g. throwing a guitar into the crowd or crowd surfing), the band in all probability will not be indemnified by virtue of the venue's public liability policy if that venue is sued.[31] One could argue in this particular instance, however, that where the band was notorious for unruly behaviour, it was reasonably foreseeable by the venue that injury might occur to a patron and therefore the venue should have properly policed the band's antics to comply with its duty of care owed to the audience. In any event, the venue should confirm in advance with the act's manager that the band holds sufficient public liability insurance itself.

[2.5.04] While public liability and employer's liability insurance is not in fact specifically mandated by statute (nor of course is contents/property insurance)[32] in the manner in which, for example, motor insurance is obligatory, it has become a reality because of our modern-day claims culture. In the absence of insurance, a defendant, ordered to pay damages from its own resources in the case of significant injuries suffered by a third party and attendant Circuit Court or High Court legal costs on both sides, might well be forced out of business.

[2.5.05] Another instance of the need to obtain such policies is that landlords, when leasing commercial premises will include as standard a clause in the lease requiring that a policy of public liability insurance (and employer's liability, where staff will be employed at the premises) be produced either before the lease is signed or shortly thereafter (and in default, this would constitute a breach of the lease giving rise to its termination). The landlord will seek to ensure that it is not held responsible for any injuries or loss arising on its premises caused to invitees or patrons by its lessee production company or the lessee's agents or employees.

---

31 In which case the band can be sued directly, the venue and the band will be litigated against as co-defendants, or the venue will apply to join the band as a third party to the proceedings.

32 The statutory requirement for professional indemnity insurance, however, is regulated in the case, for instance, of solicitors.

[2.5.06] Insurance is a fact of life for all engaged in the entertainment and media business, be it a concert venue, theatre, magazine publisher, newspaper, public house, circus, horse-racing track, music recording studio, multimedia college, film production company or national public broadcaster. The hazard giving rise to injury could be a deficiency in manual handling training, bullying by colleagues, the inducement of stress, or, in respect of third parties, a local caterer might trip over a wire when delivering lunch on a film set.

Financier, broadcaster and local authority requirements

[2.5.07] Broadcasters which part-finance a production and public funders such as Screen Ireland will also require evidence of appropriate insurance cover in their distribution licence, grant funding and production loan agreements. As financial backers of a project during production and as also appearing in the credits, broadcasters and financiers need to insulate themselves from suit and therefore will require to be named as an additional insured on the relevant policies of public liability and E&O cover. Distributors and sales agents will likewise require confirmation of E&O cover and/or to be named as joint loss payees on the production company's policy. In certain scenarios, writers, directors, executive producers and individual producers will in addition request to be added to the E&O policy as a condition of their agreement with the production company.

[2.5.08] As will be seen in Chapter 14 when discussing film permits, public liability insurance (and employer's liability, where applicable) is a prerequisite when seeking filming permission from local authorities and state agencies. Most likely, evidence of cover may also be sought by owners of private property, particularly commercial property, to ensure they are indemnified by the producers for material damage to their property or any injuries occurring during filming. This applies to homeowners as much as it does to commercial spaces where production takes place. Standard and professionally drafted location agreements will cover this issue as a matter of course whereby the production will warrant that it holds the relevant insurance to thus afford solace to the proprietor before signing a location release.

[2.5.09] Financiers and distributors including broadcasters will at times require E&O cover to be in place even before the first day of principal photography occurs.[33] This deals not with physical injury but with the fallout for producers from failing in their duties as professionals, to include defaming a person in a television programme, invading a person's privacy, infringing the copyright of a songwriter or record company, breaching trademark law, or causing loss to a business, product or brand through negative association between the action on

---

33 This, for example, will cover promotional activities in the event that the producer provides early teaser material for online marketing purposes. Also, breaches of IP law can occur at pre-production stage where, for instance, material is used or copied for project development reasons that has not been cleared by the rightsholder(s).

screen and a real-life business or product which might suffer a diminution in sales or loss of reputation due to such adverse depiction, defamatory statements or negative connotations.

[2.5.10] Even if the producer organisation is innocent of wrongdoing, it will nonetheless have to discharge legal fees in mounting a defence. Indeed 'nuisance' or frivolous claims are frequently settled which could otherwise mushroom into a protracted distraction and costly course of litigation. The fees for drafting defence proceedings and settlement costs themselves can be substantial.

[2.5.11] Moreover, effective insurance cover can minimise the risks posed. It is helpful in the entertainment business to maintain a strong working relationship with an insurer or broker, grounded in trust,[34] transparency, co-operation and dependability. Insurers should be openly advised of all possible risks, updated if the need arises and their advice adopted on controls to be implemented to minimise or eliminate exposure to liability and damages.

Brokers and insurance companies

[2.5.12] Key players in the Irish and UK media insurance markets include AON (broker, policies underwritten by Hiscox); LHK Kelleher Insurance (broker)[35] and its London partner Entertainment Vision Sound (EVS) Insurers Brokers (policies underwritten, for example, by Tokio Marine HCC and Markel International Insurance); Chubb (insurance underwriter); MIB Insurance Services (broker, policies underwritten by Hiscox), and Joseph G Brady Insurance trading as EventInsure.

POLICY TYPES

[2.6.01] While every business to which the public and employees have physical access will require such insurance as public liability cover, employer's liability, fire and buildings cover[36] and contents insurance, we will concentrate for the most part in this chapter on film (to include commercials and music videos), radio and television production insurance. A production company may elect to take out a comprehensive, catch-all package to include public and employer's liability for the year together with equipment, vehicles and all productions to be filmed that year, or more likely a stand-alone, project-specific[37] E&O policy relating to

---

[34] Bearing in mind the overriding tenet of insurance law, being the common law doctrine of "utmost good faith" (*uberrimae fidei*) and disclosing all material facts and relevant information for consideration.

[35] The Dublin-based broker formerly known as The Insurance Shop has joined the LHK Group.

[36] If the business is renting the premises, the landlord will generally discharge the premium but will typically seek a full or partial refund. In the case of the premises forming part of a larger building, a proportionate contribution will be sought from the subject premises.

[37] E&O cover will be taken out for each specific project as the exploitation territories will

one film only (in tandem with general production insurance cover which will be required for shooting permits and locations agreements). Irrespective of policy type, regular engagement with the insurer is nonetheless required to advise of the specificities of the production underway and, for example, to add named parties to the policy such as financiers and local authorities issuing filming permits.

[2.6.02] In respect of production insurance, the following coverage would be considered for policy inclusion: negatives, travel, cast and talent,[38] wardrobe, props and motor insurance, as well as processing insurance to cover additional expenses in the event of physical loss or damage to rushes; physical loss or damage to a key location or facility; technical equipment insurance to cover physical loss/damage to equipment and mechanical breakdown of cameras, lighting, sound or grip equipment.

[2.6.03] Budget cover[39] (to include such matters as cast or talent insurance, faulty equipment and physical damage to footage/media processing) and travel insurance will also need to be considered on a case-by-case basis. Insuring the budget for defaults regarding funding (e.g. if a broadcaster fails to pay distribution licence fees on a presale) is a specialised area with a very limited availability, confined to very large productions, and requires financial background checks on the parties concerned and would be subject to a (performance) bond proposal form. Further, partially insuring a budget for finance-related default is not offered by insurers.

[2.6.04] Freelance media professionals' insurance can be purchased by contractors to include public/general liability, all-risks technical equipment, employer's liability and professional indemnity. Examples of persons for which this cover is available could be a special effects supplier, events planner, screenwriter,[40] journalist, director, editor, and practitioners supplying location sound, camera and lighting equipment. Electricians, carpenters and builders involved in stage and set construction/demolition will also require public liability insurance.

[2.6.05] Professional indemnity insurance offers protection for claims relating to services rendered which prove to be problematic in some respect. This policy

differ, as will the licence term with various sub-distributors and broadcasters, the content and attendant level of risk and so forth. Hence, an annual policy covering all projects would not necessarily be feasible or practical.

38 The age and health of the director, key cast and documentary contributors should always be carefully considered at pre-production stage as death or serious illness could derail a project.

39 The relevant sum is calculated net of producer fees.

40 Writer agreements will contain a clause whereby the writer will warrant to the producer that the content is original and not in breach of third party IP rights. Ideally, however, whether granted or not, the writer should at least seek an indemnity from the producer against all lawsuits such as defamation, product disparagement and breach of privacy (including for any matters arising during production) and to be named on the producer's E&O policy and production insurance policy as and where appropriate.

type might offer cover for compensation payable to remedy an error or cover any legal costs and damages due to negligence in the performance of one's duties or providing erroneous advice. This insurance is aimed at book and magazine publishers, multi-media providers, production companies, broadcasters and distributors. Professional indemnity insurance is also an important consideration and regulatory/professional practice requirement for legal/business affairs advisors (accountants, financial advisers, solicitors and barristers) and media accountants and ideally should cover errors and omissions of employees of these professionals also.

[2.6.06] Coverages include IP infringement (breaches of copyright, neighbouring rights and trademark legislation), defamation, emotional distress, plagiarism, breach of confidentiality, invasion of privacy, breach of contract, and the insured's failure to give credit or attribution of authorship having regard to moral rights discussed below.

E&O

[2.7.01] Before discussing this multimedia risk insurance, it is important to note a statutory exclusion that exists in relation to indemnification for defamation. Section 40 of the Defamation Act 2009 provides that an agreement to indemnify any person against civil liability for defamation in respect of the publication of any statement shall be lawful unless at the time of the publication that person knows that the statement is defamatory and does not reasonably believe that there is a defence to any action that might be brought. Neville Cox, co-author of *Defamation: Law and Practice* (2022) has stated that "whereas one can insure oneself against a defamation action, one cannot insure oneself in respect of a statement that one knows is indefensibly defamatory". [41]

[2.7.02] E&O cover will almost invariably be required by financiers, investors, distributors, sales agents and broadcasters. It is a requirement, generally, for distribution deals with theatrical, non-theatrical[42] and digital distributors, sales agents, television networks and online platforms – such distributors of media require the filmmaker to shield them from claims that may result when the production is released and aired for public consumption.

[2.7.03] Cover will need to be in place before release and some financiers require sight of an E&O insurance certificate to be in effect for the first day of principal photography before funds are advanced to the production company. Accordingly,

---

41 Neville Cox, *An Overview of the Defamation Act 2009* (2011) at p 5 in *Recent Developments in Defamation Law*, The Bar Council, Continuing Professional Development conference paper. For a detailed account of defamation law in Ireland see generally Neville Cox and Eoin McCullough, *Defamation: Law and Practice* (2nd ed, Clarus Press Dublin 2022).

42 Licensing of non-theatrical rights includes agreements with ships and airlines (and for educational uses).

one should always note the start date of the policy to ensure it extends to the required date to meet contractual requirements of distribution licences.[43] An application for cover from an insurance provider (or broker on its behalf) is submitted by way of proposal form which is then assessed by an underwriter. Ample time should be afforded to set other necessary arrangements in train. Distributors and broadcasters will outline the required licensing terms and limits in their agreements – for example, RTÉ and the BBC may mandate a specified minimum level of E&O cover per claim and in the aggregate[44] throughout the full licence period. The policy excess should also be carefully considered whereby the person seeking to rely on the insurance, the policy-holder, will be obliged to pay, for instance, the first €10,000 of a payout by the insurer in damages to a plaintiff who suffers loss.

[2.7.04] Expert legal advice on filming issues should be sought. A legal adviser will carry out due diligence and clearance checks to ensure that the chain of title is in order. Distributors and sales agents will typically request a formal opinion or chain of title report from the production lawyers to assess if the requisite written agreements have been signed with locations proprietors, writers, performers, documentary contributors and copyright owners and if all releases are in order such as those relating to data protection and privacy consents, music and trademarks. Otherwise, E&O providers will have standard detailed clearance procedures appended to their proposal forms to be followed by the producers in the first instance and ultimately to be verified by their legal adviser as having been implemented.

[2.7.05] The cost of E&O cover can be substantial, ranging from several hundred euro for a short film (if E&O is mandated as a condition to funding/broadcast) to several thousand euro and beyond for a live action, feature or documentary. Hence, it is useful to liaise with a range of insurers and brokers and to factor this essential cost into the project budget at the earliest possible juncture. Worldwide coverage should generally be sought and included to provide for borderless online release as well as international theatrical and television distribution. The policy should also provide for outside legal costs and fees in the event of a claim being brought by an aggrieved party.

Due diligence and risk mitigation

[2.7.06] Name-checking is a task to be routinely performed by a production's script and clearances expert. Take the example of a screenplay based on Mark Colbert, a fictional serial killer in Dublin 4 who works as a teacher. Checks should seek to confirm that there is no actual Mark Colbert working in Dublin 4 (or the local environs or Dublin generally) as a teacher. If there is, the character's name should be changed, preferably to something sufficiently unique that no-

43 If not, the policy can be modified or renewed upon payment of an additional fee.

44 E.g. one million euro/pound per claim and three million in aggregate.

one who is a local teacher bears that name. This will serve to obviate a person's being associated with a serial killer, albeit a fictional character, with the resultant time and legal costs expended on a trial grounded on breach of duty of care or potentially defamation.

Content

[2.7.07] Another problematic instance might manifest itself by way of a scene shot in a restaurant. Take the example of the use of clearly visible original paintings on the wall by a renowned artist, who has hired them to the restaurant at a fee or who may have them on sale there, has not been cleared under a prop licence agreement with the producer.[45] The rightsholder artist sues for copyright infringement, that is, reproduction of his work on screen which was not authorised. Ideally, a release agreement should have been executed and a payment made (if required) to the artist for depiction and reproduction of the paintings. E&O should cover this eventuality but it is more likely that in advance of that it would come under scrutiny at pre-broadcast clearance review by the production lawyer. This would then involve deleting or editing the scene, paying whatever after-the-fact sum the artist might demand if the art could not be removed from the scene, or pixelating the work which frequently, creatively, will not present a viable option.

[2.7.08] Documentaries frequently unearth contentious issues. It is essential that contributors sign (and parents or guardians in the case of contributors who are minors) a comprehensive release to cover capturing their input on camera for GDPR and privacy law issues, with a release from any defamation claims, a waiver of moral rights clause (to permit uninhibited editing – see [2.7.14]) and an agreement that no injunctive relief can be sought to prevent broadcast. In some cases, a life rights or collaboration agreement will also be required to be executed by the main subject to include access to archive and other personal materials such as photographs and home videos. In the case of the latter, while the subject may own the copyright to the photographs[46] and videos, it is important, for privacy law reasons, to ensure in so far as may be possible that all living persons appearing on screen are aware of the film and consent to its exploitation. This may not always be practicable and the production lawyer will advise accordingly on the potential risk level.

[2.7.09] Where the content discusses delicate topics such as sexual abuse, poverty

---

45 This is assuming the use is not 'incidental' as set out in case law discussed in Chapter 10 (incidental use is a statutory defence to alleged copyright infringement). One cannot claim incidental use if the artwork features, essentially as set dressing, for a prolonged duration in a scene(s), particularly where such scene may be pivotal.

46 For a discussion on copyright in photographs and the defence of fair dealing (as opposed to privacy law issues as may arise) see the discussion in Chapter 10 concerning 14 photographs of the Beckhams used in a BBC production entitled *Tabloid Tales* hosted by Piers Morgan which came before the English High Court in 2005.

or violence within the home, a thorough due diligence should be undertaken in respect of privacy, duty of confidence and defamation. Any allegations of violence, addiction and substance abuse must be capable of being corroborated by police records, hospital admittance notes, attendance at a family doctor, drug rehabilitation therapy and so forth. Furthermore, not naming individuals in an attempt to protect their anonymity is insufficient for defamatory statement purposes if the persons can readily be identified by context. Section 6(3) of the Defamation Act 2009 provides that a defamatory statement concerns a person if it could reasonably be understood as referring to that person.

[2.7.10] In a live action scenario, another example of high risk content is where drug use and a fight scene involving intoxicated characters wielding weapons or committing sexual acts is staged outside a clearly visible (real-life) business premises. Ideally, the owner's consent should have been obtained in a written location release or the name (and appearance) of the premises temporarily changed by the art department. The business owner may otherwise assert that reputational damage was caused where the impression has been created that the store and its environs are home to anti-social or violent criminal activity. Equally, if teenage characters are drinking from clearly visible branded alcohol bottles, a product disparagement claim might be taken by the manufacturer for alleged damage to its goodwill or indeed for corporate defamation. The film producer will seek to rely on E&O cover in this instance.

[2.7.11] The very title[47] of a production (if it leads to confusion as regards another film with the same name) could violate a third party trademark. Comprehensive E&O insurance should serve to indemnify producers and distributors from legal claims that may emerge in this scenario. To guard against registered trademark infringement, checks can be readily conducted in trademark databases in Ireland, the EU and elsewhere. In the case of unregistered trademarks, to avoid a passing off or other infringement action, thorough research will reveal if a business is trading under the name being considered for use in a production and hence if that business should be approached for consent and clearance purposes.

Clearance procedures to undertake

[2.7.12] One should begin clearance work at the inception of the film (or whatever media project it is) and continue during filming and throughout post-production. When employing the use of underlying works such as a book, scripts or screenplays, the chain of title of all works on which the production is based must be investigated and cleared back to the original copyright owners. This will determine if grants or assignments of rights (to the production company) in the chain of title permit the producers to license (or assign by outright sale)

[47] In the US, titles can be checked by title clearance companies in the US Copyright Office and the Library of Congress (and against all types of media including books and the internet) for similar uses.

the material used in the production to distributors, television stations and other media. Acquisition and distribution licence agreements will contain a warranty that the producer holds all necessary rights. If that transpires not to accord with reality, the producer will be in breach of such warranty for which it will have contractually agreed to indemnify the broadcaster or distributor if such licensee is litigated against by a third party claiming infringement.

[2.7.13] Signed agreements must be in place[48] between the production company and the individual producer(s), director, director of photography, creators, authors (including music copyright holders), writers, cast/performers, crew and any other persons providing material or services such as stills photographs by a camera operator for marketing purposes or a costume designer. Signed releases, to include data protection consents, must be obtained for faces, voices and likenesses of all actors, extras and contributors who are identifiable on screen.

[2.7.14] For moral rights reasons (see Chapters 10A and 10B), a release must authorise the producer to freely edit, modify, add to and/or delete material, alter the sequence of events or of any questions posed and/or answers provided (as in the context of a documentary film) and where relevant to fictionalise events or persons. In practice, all persons contributing to a production, whether it be an extra or the film director, will be required to sign an irrevocable waiver of moral rights in perpetuity to allow the producers full creative freedom and editorial control. An additional standard term will stipulate that damages in the case of breach of contract will be the only remedy such that an aggrieved cast or crew member cannot seek to injunct exploitation of the production.

[2.7.15] A documentary filmmaker will need to obtain permission (and likely pay a substantial archive licence fee) from the owner of in-copyright television and film footage, radio content, newspaper articles or of photographs (and if appropriate further procure consents from persons being depicted in or captured by the film footage and as visible from photographs to guard against breach of privacy or other lawsuits relating, for example, to celebrity personality rights or rights of publicity). When footage is being obtained from the major studios or agents on behalf of such studios, ample time (months rather than weeks) must be afforded to negotiation of rights and executing the necessary licence agreement due to the large volume of requests that these studios receive on a daily basis.

Royalty, (re)use payments and music clearance

[2.7.16] Regard must also be had to royalties and collection societies. Actors featured in archive footage may be entitled to residuals or reuse fees, and fees

---

48 Unless crew and other personnel are employees of the production company rather than independent contractors. If they are in fact employees, the employer will own the copyright in the product of their services unless an agreement has been reached to the contrary as will be discussed in Chapter 17, but in any event it is always prudent to have the matter clearly set out in writing.

may also be payable to director and screenwriter guilds internationally. When the major studios or archive libraries license content, they do so on the basis that it is the obligation of the licensee filmmaker to clear and pay for performance royalties and music clearance.[49]

[2.7.17] If not purchasing a licence for pre-cleared library or production music, commercial music rights will be procured from the composers and songwriters directly (in the event that MCPS/IMRO does not have a mandate to enter a synchronisation licence on their behalf) and from sound recording owners. This will bring film producers into contact with music publishers, music producers and/or record labels, and in some cases performers where the music producer or label has not been assigned performer rights in relation to the sound recording. This arises both with specially commissioned bespoke music for a project, and where clearing pre-existing commercial music (by way of synchronisation and mechanical use licences in the case of publishing, and master use licences in the case of sound recordings).

[2.7.18] Releases are further explored in Chapter 17 as are other pertinent issues throughout this book from trademark law, GDPR, defamation and privacy law to life rights.

PUBLIC LIABILITY INSURANCE

[2.8.01] Film production companies, and all other multimedia and entertainment businesses including television studios, theatres, stageshow and dance companies, owe a range of statutory obligations to persons coming onto their place of work which are under their control such as film sets. Examples of relevant statutes here are the Occupiers' Liability Act 1995; the Safety, Health and Welfare at Work Act 2005 (and Regulations made thereunder such as the Construction Regulations, Working at Height Regulations and Noise Regulations); the Civil Liability Act 1961, and the Road Traffic Acts. Chief among these is the responsibility not to endanger the safety of others by breaching a duty of care that will result in injury or harm being occasioned to them.

[2.8.02] In certain cases where a film permit is required, such as for public parks, open spaces and street filming, the local licensing authority will require the producer to provide evidence of a policy of public liability insurance (and for it to be included as a named insured or loss payee on the policy of insurance) to protect members of the public who may be injured by filming activities. This

[49] If archive footage is used which itself features music compositions, royalties are to be paid to the relevant collection society through the submission by audiovisual producers of music cue sheets to broadcasters (and distributors). Royalties would also arise in respect of the sound recordings comprising such compositions unless the rights to such recordings were assigned to the film or television producer by way of full buyout, work for hire arrangement when the archive production was being made.

is discussed in the next chapter as regards safety, health and welfare at work and Chapter 14 in relation to film permits.

[2.8.03] As already seen, another requirement for this type of cover will come in the form of a covenant in the production company's lease with its landlord (if it is a tenant of a commercial premises from where it operates its business).

EMPLOYER'S LIABILITY INSURANCE

[2.9.01] A company owes a duty of care not to injure its employees. With television and film productions, a policy should be in place to cover injury in the case of employees working at the (permanent) production company office or (temporary) base if on-set. This insurance will need to cover full-time employees of the production company as well as those working on a once-off film, music or advertising project or television production under a contract of employment with the production company. Independent contractors will be protected for injury caused by the producers' negligence under the production's public liability insurance and, ideally, such contractors will have effected their own policy of insurance for injury caused to others by their own negligent acts or omissions.

[2.9.02] Under vicarious liability principles of tort law, persons engaging independent contractors (e.g. camera operators) are not liable in law (as they would be for torts committed by employees) for civil wrongs committed by such contractors or the contractors' staff or agents. Therefore, independent contractors should be requested to provide evidence of their own public liability cover. Regardless of the legal principles at bar or the outcome of legal proceedings, if a claim is made in respect of a contractor's negligence on the production's insurance, it may adversely affect premia costs going forward. Contracts between contractors and producers should therefore contain an indemnity in favour of the producer for claims arising on foot of the contractor's negligent acts and omissions.

MUSIC INSURANCE

[2.10.01] Music insurance issues are covered in Chapter 25 to include those arising for touring bands and on music video productions.

SMALL UNMANNED AIRCRAFT (DRONE) INSURANCE

[2.11.01] For those providing aerial images to commercial clients and operators hired by film producers to record aerial shots, insurance is a mandatory condition required by the Irish Aviation Authority before issuance of pilot competency certificates, specific operating permissions and otherwise, pursuant to SI No 563 of 2015 being the Small Unmanned Aircraft (Drones) and Rockets Order 2015 and having further regard to EU Regulation 2019/947 (rules/procedures for operation of unmanned aircraft, effective from 30 December 2020). Such policies of insurance can include cover for injury to persons and property damage caused by flight operations and for professional indemnity in the case, for example, of unauthorised reproduction of copyrighted or trademarked items captured by the aerial footage. Examples of companies offering this specialist form of insurance include Starr Insurance in the UK and Coverdrone (Netherlands, with offices in the UK).

[2.11.02] Film and television producers should therefore contract with fully licensed drone operators who have in effect certain minimum levels of insurance cover such that they will be in a position to indemnify the hiring production company in the event of third party claims being initiated.

Chapter 3

Safety, Health and Welfare at Work

> *"The greatest failing of all on behalf of the company is a lack of communication, a lack because, if you have a risk assessment and you do not communicate it, what is the point of having one? That is the most serious breach here...If only they had included Mr Ford in all the discussions, he might have at least been alert to the dangers that he had to avoid".*[1]

INTRODUCTION

[3.1.01] These are remarks by Judge Francis Sheridan when sentencing at Aylesbury Crown Court, England in October 2016 arising out of a successful prosecution at Milton Keynes Magistrates' Court against a film production company which had failed to communicate effectively with Harrison Ford during production on the set of the Millennium Falcon spaceship in June 2014. Foodles Production (UK) Ltd, a company owned by Disney, was fined £1.6 million for health and safety breaches after Ford's left leg was crushed by a hydraulic door on the set of *Star Wars: The Force Awakens* while filming at Pinewood Studios. The prosecution informed the court that he was fortunate to escape with his life. Injuries the actor sustained were fractured tibia and fibula bones in his leg while a deep laceration to his left hand required plastic surgery.

[3.1.02] Safety on film sets hit news headlines globally in October 2021 in the most tragic and dramatic of circumstances when Alec Baldwin accidentally shot and fatally wounded cinematographer Halyna Hutchins. A prop gun he was holding was discharged during filming rehearsals in New Mexico of western movie *Rust*. Director Joel Souza also sustained a shoulder injury. The actor was handed the weapon during rehearsals by the assistant director who announced it was a "cold gun" indicating that it contained no live rounds and was safe to handle.

[3.1.03] Aside from criminal prosecution (Baldwin was charged by the Santa Fe District Attorney's office with two counts of involuntary manslaughter in

---

1 *R. v Foodles Production (UK) Ltd*, unreported, Aylesbury Crown Court, Sheridan J, 12 October 2016.

October 2021),[2] family of the deceased cinematographer filed a wrongful death lawsuit in February 2022 against crew members and producers, including Mr Baldwin, alleging that reckless conduct and cost-cutting measures endangered the crew. These proceedings were settled in October 2022 for an undisclosed sum. Baldwin himself has also filed suit.[3] The actor and producers face a separate civil lawsuit filed by the family of Ms Hutchins for alleged battery, intentional infliction of emotional distress, negligence and loss of consortium.

The rationale for safeguards

[3.1.04] In sum, failure to rigorously enforce safe work practices can lead to exposure to a claim for damages in a personal injuries action; a fatal injury action under Pt IV of the Civil Liability Act 1961 brought on behalf of the deceased's dependants; a potential claim for nervous shock where a duty of care is owed to secondary victims who come upon a seriously injured party on the basis of the principles set out by Keane J in the High Court decision in *Kelly v Hennessy*;[4] payment of the excess sum on an insurance policy; downtime and all attendant costs where a television or film production is suspended due to indisposition through injury of a key cast member, together with the time expended in statutorily reporting certain accidents and dangerous occurrences and cooperating with Health and Safety Authority ('HSA') investigations; low staff morale and absenteeism in the case of unsafe systems of work; loss of goodwill and reputational damage where health and safety breaches or prosecutions are reported in the press; and criminal trials leading to substantial penalties and potential imprisonment.

Halted productions

[3.1.05] Apart from obviating occurrences of serious injury and fatalities, the prevention of accidents can ensure that productions remain on time and on budget. While insurance is available, as mentioned in the previous chapter, to cover indisposition of key cast, that is of little solace when a production must be abandoned for several weeks when its star actor has sustained injuries. In August 2017, Tom Cruise fractured his ankle during a roof-jumping stunt in London for *Mission: Impossible – Fallout*. Production was halted for nine weeks, adding an estimated $80 million to the film's budget. Daniel Craig also fell victim to the demand for convincing stunts. In May 2019, shooting was suspended for two weeks on the 25th James Bond film, *No Time to Die*, after the actor injured

---

2 At the time of writing, a preliminary hearing date is yet to be set, but will determine whether the case will go to trial.

3 Against the film's armourer who was in charge of weapons on set and three other crew members, including assistant director Dave Halls, as a cross-complaint to a previous suit in which a different member of the crew had named Baldwin and others as defendants. His cross-complaint alleges negligence and seeks damages for the "immense grief" he endured as a result of Hutchins' death.

4 [1995] 3 IR 253.

his ankle. He slipped and fell while shooting a running scene in Jamaica and was flown thereafter to the US for minor surgery.

Civil liability

[3.1.06] Understanding the fundamentals of safety, health and welfare at work law, together with implementing procedures to minimise or eliminate exposure to risk and injury, is crucial to the effective management and success of any undertaking. Closely linked to this, for insurance purposes and otherwise, is understanding the statutory principles of occupiers' liability[5] as discussed later in this book in the context of fire safety and indoor events (see from [27.2.01]). Breaches of relevant statutory and common law obligations can and do give rise to both civil liability, in respect of claims for damages and losses arising from an injury at work, and criminal prosecution.

[3.1.07] A successful claim against a policy of public liability or employer's liability insurance could potentially render the cost of future insurance prohibitive for a company. Further, a portion of damages will generally be payable by the negligent employer or independent contractor on foot of the 'excess' provisions of the policy (e.g. where an employer might have to pay, for instance, the first €10,000 of the damages claim).

Injuries on set

[3.1.08] While many injuries in the film production sector relate to stunts whereby in the first instance stunt professionals are required to be formally qualified in a number of physical disciplines, including martial arts, horse riding and stunt driving, and secondly, these performers voluntarily assume risk and sign waivers to that effect in favour of the production company, that of course does not justify circumstances leading to a death or catastrophic injury occurring on set. There have been vast improvements in safety compared with previous decades but the volume of stunts and audiences' need for 'real' action has also increased dramatically. Accidents are not confined to action-packed adult content. In 2009, for instance, David Holmes, a stunt double for Daniel Radcliffe on the *Harry Potter* films, injured his spine and was rendered paralysed through a flying stunt.

[3.1.09] Recent years have seen an alarming number of fatalities occurring during filming. In July 2019 in Toronto, a special effects coordinator on the Warner Brothers television superhero series *Titans* lost his life after an accident at a special effects facility during preparation and testing for an upcoming shoot. Warren Appleby was reportedly struck by a piece of a car that became detached during the stunt test. In July 2017, the stunt performer John Bernecker died from head injuries on the set of *The Walking Dead* in Georgia after falling 20

---

5 Pursuant to the Occupiers' Liability Act 1995.

feet onto a concrete floor, missing a crash mat. A few months later, stunt rider Joi SJ Harris was fatally injured when she lost control of her motorcycle on the streets of Vancouver while filming *Deadpool 2*. A former professional road racer, Harris was a novice stunt rider. The stunt required her to not wear a helmet.[6]

[3.1.10] Closer to home, British professional stunt performer Joe Watts sustained a fractured skull and traumatic brain injury on the set of *Fast and Furious 9* whilst undertaking a stunt during which he was being thrown from a 25-foot balcony in July 2019 at Warner Brothers' Studios in Leavesden, Hertfordshire. Instead of remaining suspended by a wire mid-air, the stuntman hit the concrete floor and was taken to the Royal London Hospital by air ambulance where he was diagnosed with a fractured skull and placed in an induced coma for five days. Watts remains impaired by a number of physical and cognitive difficulties, for which as of September 2020, according to his personal injury legal advisors Irwin Mitchel, he was still undergoing physiotherapy, neuropsychology, speech and language therapy and occupational therapy. The matter prompted an investigation by the Health and Safety Executive as to the cause.

[3.1.11] Other high-profile examples of deaths caused and injuries suffered in the entertainment sector include the Hillsborough disaster,[7] the 1984 Pepsi commercial during which Michael Jackson's hair caught fire on stage,[8] the death of a teenage fan at a Smashing Pumpkins rock concert at the Point Theatre, Dublin in 1996[9] and the accidental on-set fatal shooting of Brandon Lee.[10] The public truly became aware of the dangers of movie-making only in 1982 when, during filming of *Twilight Zone: The Movie*, a helicopter flying just eight meters off the ground became engulfed in pyrotechnics and spun out of control, killing actor Vic Morrow and leading to the tragic loss of two child actors aged six and seven.

The courts' response to safety breaches

[3.1.12] There are already firm indications from criminal trial outcomes in Ireland that custodial sentences will be imposed for health and safety breaches

---

6 Steve Rose, *Film stunts under scrutiny after deaths and serious injuries* (2019), theguardian.com. Available at: https://www.theguardian.com/film/2019/jul/26/film-stunts-under-scrutiny-after-deaths-and-serious-injuries [Accessed 24 February 2021].

7 The Hillsborough disaster was a human crush at Hillsborough football stadium in Sheffield, England on 15 April 1989 resulting in almost 100 fatalities and hundreds of injuries.

8 Jackson appears at a short flight of steps at the back of the stage, and fireworks spark behind him as he dances down the steps. For the sixth take, however, Jackson was still at the top of the steps when the explosion took place. Pepsi paid him a $1.5 million settlement, money that he donated to a Californian medical centre which used it to fund a burns clinic named after him.

9 Concert-goers surged towards the stage and began trampling on one another despite a 110-strong security presence. The 17-year-old victim was crushed to such an extent that she suffered a heart attack.

10 An actor fired an improperly prepared prop gun that killed Lee (son of Bruce Lee) on the set of *The Crow* in 1993.

in the future (imprisonment has already been imposed as a sentence in some instances but all such sentences to date have been suspended in full). However, in the case of death or serious personal injury, the Circuit Criminal Court will very likely impose substantial fines (potentially up to three million euro). Because breach of safety legislation is a criminal offence (as well as potentially giving rise to a claim for civil damages for the tort of negligence, breach of duty of care and breach of statutory duties), the fines imposed by courts and paid into the exchequer by defendants are not covered by insurance and could in such scenarios have the effect of insolvency for an offending production company.

[3.1.13] Returning to financial and reputational fallout in terms of criminal sanctions for offending companies generally, a 2017 Court of Appeal judgment[11] delivered by Edwards J, considered an application by the Director of Public Prosecutions for resentencing of the defendant/respondent company, Kilsaran Concrete Ltd, on the grounds that a €125,000 fine imposed by Trim Circuit Court was unduly lenient in the case of a fatal industrial accident which resulted in the death of Barry Gargan on 6 September 2011 when he was crushed whilst working with a machine. In 2010, Kilsaran Concrete had purchased a fully automated piece of machinery for the manufacture of precast and standardised concrete products. A decision was taken to use the machine in an unorthodox manner to make bespoke products, and certain safety measures were overridden to render the machine more efficient and cost-effective.[12] The appellate court imposed a fine of the same magnitude imposed in the 2004 *Smurfit News Press* (see fn 36) decision in the sum of one million euro, the maximum fine payable by statute being three million euro. Edwards J stated:

> We consider that the gravity of this case, considered with reference to the range of punishments set by the Oireachtas, and having regard to the respondents' very significant culpability and the substantial harm done, merited a headline sentence involving a fine of €2,000,000. We will allow a 50% discount for the mitigating factors in the case. The final sentence therefore will be a fine of €1,000,000.[13]

[3.1.14] The DPP submitted that insufficient account was taken at trial of a number of aggravating factors pointing to the inherent and obvious danger presented by the system of work and the particular work practice adopted in this case, and contending that there is a clear distinction between a system which

---

11 *People (DPP) v Kilsaran Concrete Ltd* [2017] IECA 112 (Birmingham, Edwards, Hedigan JJ).

12 Further, Christy Bagnall, the most experienced operative at the plant, testified that he had previously expressed concerns over the safety of the procedure. Carl Griffin had instigated the unorthodox procedure. Bagnall indicated that despite his concerns, Griffin (who was a co-accused) insisted that this procedure should nonetheless be used. In the course of the proceedings, a student who had been working at the plant over the summer, gave evidence that he had earlier been involved in a "near miss" incident involving the same procedure in which he almost lost his life.

13 At para 96 of the judgment. The mitigating factors included a guilty plea, cooperation with the investigation, and prompt payment of compensation to the deceased's family.

presents inherent and obvious danger and an accident occurring due to an isolated instance of human error. A number of features here were indicative of an inherently dangerous system of work, involving the deliberate and conscious taking of an unjustified risk as opposed to an omission through negligence or inadvertence. Thus, in all the circumstances, the three-judge court was satisfied that the sentence was unduly lenient for an accident arising from a clear departure from the norm, and one caused by several errors of principle.

SAFE SYSTEM OF WORK

[3.2.01] A dangerous, unsafe, unplanned or uncomfortable workplace or system of work can also lead to low staff morale, tarnish a businesses goodwill, irreparably damage reputation (particularly if breaches are reported in the national press) and result in absenteeism and lack of productivity with an obvious knock-on effect for trading profits. There are myriad reasons, therefore, to pursue an ongoing commitment to attaining standards of excellence, and to achieve this, one must stay abreast of an ever-evolving working environment and the system/s of work at hand. At a minimum, the HSA's website[14] should be consulted sporadically by an organisation's safety officer and company directors for legal and practical updates.

[3.2.02] Health and safety issues apply as much to an administrative employee in a newspaper office or film/television production office[15] as they do to decibel levels in music recording studio live rooms and control rooms, an audio post-production studio, or to the erecting of scaffolding and construction of a building on a film set. Coupled with this are the employment law and human resource management issues of welfare law including maternity leave, welfare facilities (e.g. actor changing rooms and bathrooms on location) and parental leave.

CONTRACTS OF SERVICE[16] AND CONTRACTS FOR SERVICE[17]

[3.3.01] Safety has been afforded such elevated status by lawmakers that it should feature prominently in all contracts of employment and agreements with independent contractors. A clause which almost invariably features is the right to terminate the contract in the event that the hiring company's health and safety procedures are not rigorously adhered to so as to prevent injury or fatality. Ideally, employment contracts should specifically reference up-to-date legislation and any applicable codes of practice together with directing the signatory employee

---

14 www.hsa.ie.

15 A worker who, for example, is subjected to stress or repetitive strain injury while typing, screen glare or an unergonomic desk chair leading to back injury, or an employee who is a victim of bullying by a colleague or management arising out of the persistent imposition, for instance, of unreasonable targets and deadlines.

16 Relating to employees.

17 Relating to independent contractors.

to the company's safety policy, dignity at work policy, regulations and guidelines on matters ranging from bullying to sexual harassment, sick leave, disciplinary procedures, grievance procedures[18] and the company's approach to relieving and minimising stress. Contracts of employment, and agreements with contractors, should also set out the employees' own statutory requirements (to ensure their own safety and that of others) as specified in s 13 of the Safety, Health and Welfare At Work Act 2005 and provisions relating to persons in control of workplaces (s 15) and duties owing to persons who are not employees (s 12).

SAFETY, HEALTH AND WELFARE AT WORK ACT 2005

[3.4.01] Every employer should have more than a passing familiarity with the Safety, Health and Welfare at Work Act 2005 (as amended) ('the 2005 Act') which repealed the Safety, Health and Welfare at Work Act 1989 ('the 1989 Act'), the purpose of which was to give effect to EU (formerly EEC) legislation. More detailed and specific secondary legislation was also passed under and pursuant to the 2005 Act – thus, the Safety, Health and Welfare at Work (General Application) Regulations 2007[19] as amended regulate and inform such matters as personal protective equipment, working at height, protection of children and young persons, and pregnant, post-natal or breastfeeding employees.[20]

Safety statements

[3.4.02] Under s 20(8) of the 2005 Act, it shall be sufficient compliance with s 20 by an employer employing three or less employees to observe the terms of a code of practice,[21] if any, relating to safety statements which applies to the class of employment covering the type of work activity carried on by the employer. Self-employed persons must also commit to safeguarding their employees' health by preparing a safety statement. Where there are more than three employees, a full safety statement is required. A copy of a safety statement, or relevant extract thereof, shall be kept available for inspection at or near every place of work to which it relates while work is being carried out there.

[3.4.03] HSA inspectors regularly encounter generic safety statements that are prepared by an individual with no clear grasp of the activities undertaken by the employer.[22] A safety statement is a written document which specifies how health and safety will be managed within the business and it is the cornerstone

---

18 For example, if employees wish to voice safety and welfare concerns.

19 SI No 299 of 2007.

20 The Regulations also deal *inter alia* with use of work equipment, manual handling of loads, display screen equipment, electricity, control of noise at work, control of vibration at work, night and shift work, safety signs at places of work, first-aid, and explosive atmospheres.

21 See the HSA website for codes of practice available for download.

22 The HSA has therefore provided a simple video setting out the basics of what is required and expected of employers in this connection. In addition, besmart.ie is the HSA's free online tool that facilitates self-generation of workplace-specific risk assessments and a

of effective accident prevention and welfare management in any business. The safety statement will also cover risk assessments and the controls required to minimise the risks from the hazards in the workplace, as well as detailing the names of those responsible for putting them into practice. It must be reviewed and, if necessary, amended as required. This should be effected on an annual basis or more frequently if, for example, one's business changes and the employees are exposed to new hazards such as upon the introduction of revised work practices or new machinery/equipment, or when there is reason to believe that existing controls are no longer adequate, in the case, for instance, of a near-miss incident.

[3.4.04] The safety statement must be brought to the attention of the employees and to any other persons at the place of work who might be exposed to the specific risks outlined in the document. When bringing the safety statement to the attention of employees and other affected individuals such as clients, visitors and suppliers, it must be in a form, manner, and if necessary, a language that can be understood by all. On television and film productions,[23] ideally, all production staff and contractors should be made aware of the contents of the safety statement particularly where filming will occur over a period of weeks or months. In addition, the line producer as a matter of course will (alone if sufficiently experienced, or otherwise in tandem with the safety officer) conduct risk assessments for each filming location in advance of shooting taking place and duly report back to the individual producer/s.

Employer and employee duties under the 2005 Act

[3.4.05] Section 8 (employer duties) of the 2005 Act mandates that all work activities be managed and conducted so as to ensure, as far as reasonably practicable, the safety, health and welfare of persons at work. This involves designing, providing and maintaining a safe place of work that has safe means of access and exit; uses of plant and equipment that are safe and without risk to health; providing information, instruction, training and supervision regarding safety and health to employees; providing and maintaining welfare facilities (e.g. bathroom and breastfeeding facilities) for employees; preventing risks to other people at the place of work, and having plans in place in the case of emergency.

[3.4.06] Section 13 provides that employees, including those employed on a part-time or temporary basis, also have duties including complying with relevant laws and protecting their own safety and health, as well as the safety and health of anyone who may be affected by their acts or omissions at work; ensuring that they are not under the influence of any intoxicant to the extent that they could be a danger to themselves or others while at work; co-operating with their

safety statement. It covers hundreds of business types (including during construction) with clear guidelines of the risk assessment process.

23 Including filmic commercials (such as a Christmas campaign for a multinational corporation) and music video shoots that might span several days.

employer with regard to safety, health and welfare at work; using in the correct manner any equipment provided for safety protection; participating in safety and health training offered by their employer; reporting any dangerous situations, practices or defects that might endanger a person's safety, health or welfare, and not engaging in any improper conduct that could jeopardise their own safety or health or that of anyone else.

[3.4.07] In relation to s 19 (hazard identification and risk assessment) of the 2005 Act, the online HSA resource bank assists employers in carrying out mandatory written risk assessments in its three-step process of identifying unusual and other hazards, determining the level of risk and then implementing appropriate controls, and informing employees and others who might be affected.

[3.4.08] Sections 77 to 85 of the 2005 Act deal with offences, prosecution of offences and penalties. Section 80 imposes liability on company directors and officers. It provides that where an offence has been committed by the company and the act that constituted the offence has been authorised, or consented to by, or is attributable to connivance or neglect of a person, being a director, manager or similar officer of an undertaking or a person who purports to act in any such capacity, that person shall, as well as the undertaking,[24] be guilty of an offence and stand liable to prosecution. The penalties set out in s 78 are severe in order to serve as a clear deterrent. An accused who is convicted under s 77 on summary prosecution in the District Court can be ordered to pay a maximum fine of €5,000 per charge and/or serve a term of imprisonment of up to six months.

[24] In *People (DPP) v Technical Engineering and Tooling Services Ltd*, unreported, Circuit Criminal Court (Mullingar), Judge Kennedy, 12 May 2011, three company directors and the company itself were prosecuted in Mullingar Circuit Court (sitting in Tullamore) in 2011 arising from an incident in March 2006 whereby the drill bit from a milling machine struck an employee at speed. The employee died two days later from his injuries. The director defendants pleaded guilty to breaches of the 2005 Act and all received a one-year term of imprisonment suspended unconditionally. The accused company was fined €50,000 by Judge Anthony Kennedy and was ordered to pay the DPP's costs of €14,000 and the HSA's costs of €7,383. The judge noted there had been a "woeful failure" on behalf of the defendants to learn from a previous accident, that interlocks had been bypassed, handmade extension bars used, wrong data inputted, warnings on the machine ignored and that there was no inspection supervision. He said that the deceased was "killed by the accused, like being shot in the head with a bullet". Health and Safety Authority, *Prosecutions* (on indictment) (2011), hsa.ie. Case summary available at: http://www.hsa.ie/eng/Topics/Inspections/Prosecutions/Prosecutions_2011/#X-2013121311271618 [Accessed 2 February 2017].

On indictment,[25] an offender can be fined up to three million euro[26] per charge and/or be imprisoned for up to two years.[27]

[3.4.09] It is now an obligation under statute on persons charged to prove their innocence. This reverses the usual burden of proof in criminal trials and evidences the legislature's commitment to deterring breaches of statutory duties and the implementation of exacting standards of safety by employers to reduce the incidence of injuries and to save lives. Section 81 of the 2005 Act provides:

> In any proceedings for an offence...it shall be for the accused to prove that it was not practicable or not reasonably practicable to do more than was in fact done to satisfy the duty or requirement, or that there was no better practicable means than was in fact used to satisfy the duty or requirement.

CONSTRUCTION AND REMOVAL/DEMOLITION OF FILM SETS

[3.5.01] In larger organisations, it is necessary to engage the services of a full-time safety officer, or, in the case of construction of a substantial film set, the services of a qualified safety consultant such as an architect, engineer or other suitably qualified and experienced individual to fulfil the role of project supervisor for the design process ('PSDP') and construction stages ('PSCS') pursuant to the Construction Regulations referenced below.

[3.5.02] Employees on film and television productions, and producers themselves, most likely neither wish to assume onerous responsibilities of a PSDP/PSCS (as statutorily defined), nor indeed will they necessarily possess the requisite skill-set to effectively carry out these project supervisor roles to ensure safety. It is therefore advisable and desirable to engage an expert such as an experienced safety consultant, registered engineer or architect who themselves hold their own appropriate professional indemnity and public liability insurance cover.

[3.5.03] The purpose of the Safety, Health and Welfare at Work (Construction)

---

25 Trial by jury (though indictable cases can be run in the District Court in certain instances where the accused does not object to being tried summarily by a judge alone).

26 On 28 June 2018, for example, Tony Kirwan Civil Engineering Contractors Ltd pleaded guilty to three charges on indictment at Kilkenny Circuit Court. In April 2016, an employee had suffered personal injuries when the defendant company failed to ensure that a safe system of work was in place to protect persons working inside a trench box within an excavation from being struck by falling materials. The company pleaded guilty and was fined €200,000.

27 On 4 May 2018 at Letterkenny Circuit Court an accused employer pleaded guilty to one charge of failing in March 2012 to manage and conduct his undertaking in such a way that individuals at the place of work, who were not his employees, were not exposed to risks to their safety, health and welfare, in particular that he failed to take precautions in relation to a crane working near overhead power lines or to ensure that the said work was carried out safely and in accordance with ESB guidelines. He was sentenced to 12 months' imprisonment but the full term was suspended (see https://www.hsa.ie/eng/topics/inspections/prosecutions/prosecutions_2018/ [Accessed 19 January 2020]).

Regulations 2013[28] ('the 2013 Regulations') is to prescribe the main requirements for the protection of the safety, health and welfare of persons working on construction sites and to give further effect to Council Directive 92/57/EEC on the minimum safety and health requirements at temporary or mobile construction sites. Construction work is defined in reg 2(1) as meaning the carrying out of any building, civil engineering or engineering construction work including all those mentioned below and the assembly of prefabricated elements to form a structure and the regulations therefore capture the building and removal of film sets, concert and festival stages and so forth.

[3.5.04] The 2013 Regulations are designed to clarify and strengthen the general duties of all parties as regards securing occupational safety, health and welfare in construction work, including those of clients, project supervisors, designers, contractors and employees. They apply to all construction projects including the alteration, decoration, maintenance and repair of buildings and the installation, maintenance and removal of mechanical and other systems,[29] and the dismantling and demolition of structures. They place obligations on clients and designers to ensure that safety and health is taken into account before any construction work begins.

Safe Pass and audiovisual productions

[3.5.05] Safe Pass is a one-day safety awareness programme aimed at construction workers.[30] It can also be of benefit to riggers, stagehands, propmasters, painters, carpenters, electricians and anyone in film and television production who requires Safe Pass training. Safe Pass or an equivalent course is mandatory under the 2013 Regulations for general construction workers, apprentices and on-site students, on-site security workers and on-site drivers.[31] The aims of the programme generally are to raise the standard of safety awareness in the construction industry and ensure that all construction workers after completing the one-day programme can make a positive contribution to the prevention of accidents and ill-health while working on the site. The Safe Pass programme is operated and managed by Solas.

REPORTING OF ACCIDENTS AND DANGEROUS OCCURRENCES

[3.6.01] Certain accidents and dangerous occurrences must be reported to the HSA in line with the Safety, Health and Welfare at Work (Reporting of

---

28 SI No 291 of 2013. These regulations replaced and revoked the Safety, Health and Welfare at Work (Construction) Regulations 2006.

29 Electrical, gas, compressed air, hydraulic, telecommunication and computer systems for example fixed within or to structures.

30 Note that Safe Pass is a general awareness programme and does not negate the duty of the employer under the 2005 Act with regard to the provision of information, instruction and training to enable workers to carry out their duties safely.

31 See Sch 4 (Safety Awareness Scheme) of the Regulations (regs 4,19, 25 and 29).

Accidents and Dangerous Occurrences) Regulations 2016.[32] Failure to report constitutes an offence. Some key points in relation to reporting of accidents and dangerous occurrences are that only fatal and non-fatal injuries are reportable – diseases, occupational illnesses or any impairments of mental condition are not reportable. Fatal accidents must be reported immediately to the HSA or the Gardaí. Subsequently, the formal report should be submitted to the HSA within five working days of the death. Non-fatal accidents or dangerous occurrences should be reported to the HSA within ten working days of the event; and injuries to employees as a result of an accident while at work where the injury results in the employees' being unable to carry out their normal work duties for more than three consecutive days, excluding the day of the accident, must also be reported to the HSA.

NOTABLE PROSECUTIONS AND CASE LAW

[3.7.01] Adherence to safety law is a very real and ever-present obligation. Flagrant breaches give rise to multiple trials on indictment and summary prosecutions annually in the Circuit and District Criminal Courts. Pursuant to s 82 of the 2005 Act, the HSA has power to bring and prosecute summary proceedings in the District Court. The DPP prosecutes indictable offences. The most notable sentences (including suspended custodial sentences) handed down to date under the 1989 Act and its 2005 successor are Oran Pre-Cast Concrete Ltd[33] (reduced fine of €100,000 imposed by the Court of Criminal Appeal), Roseberry Construction Ltd[34] (Circuit Court fine of £200,000 imposed by

---

32 SI No 370 of 2016.

33 *People (DPP) v Oran Pre-Cast Concrete Ltd* [2003] JILL-CCA 121601 (Court of Criminal Appeal, *ex tempore*, 16 December 2003). The case involved an accident in which a 25-year-old employee fell to his death from a roof. A fine of €100,000 was imposed by the Court of Criminal Appeal overturning a €500,000 fine imposed by Castlebar Circuit Criminal Court, the highest ever fine handed down by the courts at that point for safety breaches. The appeal court set out the factors to be taken into account when assessing penalties, being degree of fault, the record of the company and how it has behaved since the events, and its ability to pay the fine. The circumstances were that two employees were tasked to fit a gutter while positioned on a mobile scaffolding tower but needed to step onto a roof due to the fault of a third party in failing to undertake adequate preparatory work. They were insufficiently harnessed and one man fell thirty feet to his death. It was specifically noted that there was no element of risk being taken specifically to save money.

34 *DPP v Roseberry Construction Ltd* [2003] 4 IR 338. A leading UK case, *R. v F. Howe & Son (Engineers) Ltd* [1999] 2 Cr App R 37, in the context of health and safety prosecutions, was adopted by the appellate court.

Groarke J upheld on appeal),[35] Smurfit News Press Ltd[36] (€1 million euro)[37] and Ellickson Engineering Ltd (€750,000).[38] A fine of €2 million euro was imposed in *Kilsaran Concrete*[39] discussed above but the sentence was reduced by half having regard to mitigating factors in the case.

THE COVID-19 PANDEMIC

[3.8.01] The Covid-19 pandemic had a profoundly detrimental effect on the entertainment sector chiefly for cinema theatres though it did spawn a major upsurge in the consumption of online content from home. While abated at the time of writing, incidences persist and an equally sinister threat may potentially arise in the future for which media professionals should be robustly prepared.

[3.8.02] Producers cannot obtain insurance cover against injury and death arising from a pandemic. Therefore, from a criminal law perspective (the 2005 Act is foremost a penal piece of legislation), one must assiduously enforce safety and health protocols on-set, in studios and in event spaces. From a civil law perspective and to guard against claims by parties (or by their estates in the

---

35 The trial judge commented that an accident at a construction site in Kildare which claimed the lives of two men would never have happened if there had not been "utter disregard" for health and safety on site. A trench, more than three meters in depth, was being excavated for sewage and the two workers were repairing pipes therein when one of the trench walls collapsed. When they were taken from the trench they were already deceased, having suffocated. The subcontractor who was in charge of the trench was also accused of reckless endangerment under the Non-Fatal Offences Against the Person Act 1997 and was sentenced to an 18-month prison term (suspended) and further fined £7,000. Groarke J described the failures as "carelessness of an extreme nature" leading to the loss of two lives in circumstances whereby actions were taken to save costs. He noted that concerns of employees of Roseberry Construction that supports be put in place went unheeded suggesting to the trial judge "recklessness of an extreme nature".

36 *People (DPP) v Smurfit News Press Ltd*, unreported, Circuit Criminal Court (Trim), Groarke J, 29 October 2004 (mentioned in: The Law Reform Commission, *Report on Corporate Killing* (LRC 77-2005).

37 The largest ever penalty at that juncture imposed for health and safety breaches in this jurisdiction. It followed investigations by the HSA into two serious accidents at the company plant in Kells, County Meath in April and May 2002. Groarke J said the company had displayed a "cavalier attitude" to safety and had placed the pursuit of profit over the safety of its workers. The court heard how both accidents had occurred within two weeks of each other and had arisen from almost identical circumstances. In the first incident, an employee was working at a printing press when his right leg became entrapped and he suffered a below-the-knee amputation. Two weeks later, another employee was seriously injured when his hand was trapped in a printing press. The man suffered a degloving injury to his left wrist. The cause of the accidents was attributed to inadequate guarding and a failure to prepare an adequate risk assessment as statutorily required in respect of the hazards involved in working on printing presses.

38 On 5 July 2017, proceedings on indictment were heard in Tralee Circuit Court against the accused company. In April 2004 at Killarney Plaza Hotel, a passenger lift was installed and the accused failed to ensure the machinery was erected or installed in a safe manner and without risk to health when in use.

39 *People (DPP) v Kilsaran Concrete Ltd* [2017] IECA 112.

case of death) that they have contracted the subject virus while on set, a waiver should be signed by all cast, talent and crew to the effect that they are voluntarily assuming risk and thereby indemnifying the production, crew, financiers and locations proprietors against injury or death. Further, in the case of a pandemic, social distancing should be observed, the amount of attendees on site minimised, and face-masks worn. During the Covid-19 crisis, regular testing by PCR and rapid-result antigen tests were conducted to protect those with underlying conditions, the elderly and those who might be vulnerable including pregnant employees and pregnant independent contractors.

Chapter 4

Defamation, Parody & Satire and *Norwich Pharmacal* Orders

The judgment of the Supreme Court on 7 March 2022[1] *in Higgins v Irish Aviation Authority concerns existing defamation law and does not take into account proposals by the Department of Justice for reform as published in its review report on 1 March 2022 including to potentially abolish juries in defamation cases. Nonetheless the justices' observations may well inform amendment in the future of the Defamation Act 2009.*

INTRODUCTION

[4.1.01] Defamation as a cause of action came hurtling very dramatically to the world's attention in the proceedings taken against each other by ex-spouses Amber Heard and Johnny Depp as decided by a Virginia jury in June 2022. While Depp's proceedings related to a press article in *The Washington Post* written by Heard in 2018[2] and though he was named in the article and he therefore claimed it cost him lucrative acting roles, this matter concerned domestic violence allegations in the context of a relationship. This chapter will focus on instances where a person's character and reputation are called into question by unrelated journalists via untrue news reports, false allegations in print media and online, and by means of audiovisual material such as in the case of a documentary programme or film.

[4.1.02] Defamation, whereby an individual's or entity's[3] reputation is injured in the eyes of reasonable members of society through publication of a defamatory

1 [2022] IESC 13.

2 In which she described herself as a "public figure representing domestic abuse". Heard countersued for defamation over statements Depp's attorney made about her abuse claims. The jury found that Heard defamed Depp in three separate statements in *The Washington Post* piece, and that Depp defamed Heard with one statement his attorney made. The jury awarded Depp $10 million in compensatory damages and $5 million in punitive damages. The jury awarded Heard $2 million in compensatory damages but nothing for punitive damages. Depp had sought $50 million in damages and Heard sought $100 million. Punitive damages in the state of Virginia are capped at $350,000 and the judge accordingly reduced the punitive damages award to that amount.

3 Corporate defamation is discussed in Chapter 5.

statement to one or more persons, is a highly specialised area of tort law to which whole textbooks, substantial in their own right, have been devoted. A table of key points with attendant sections of the Defamation Act 2009 ('the 2009 Act') noted (cases referred to therein being discussed throughout the chapter) at the outset may therefore be beneficial:

Limitation period	Action to be brought within one year (exceptionally extendable to two years).[4] A re-publication (e.g. a re-tweet or television broadcast of a defamatory newspaper article) is a new publication and the clock restarts from the date of such re-publication
Elements	Strict liability: intention irrelevant (with limited exceptions such as malice defeating the defence of qualified privilege); Actionable *per se*: no proof of actual/special/financial losses required
Jurisdiction	Circuit Court (judge sitting alone, damages cap of €75,000);[5] High Court (jury as trier of facts; judge or jury to assess quantum of damages); possible substitution of High Court's award by the Court of Appeal/Supreme Court
Defences	Innocent publication (s 27); consent to publish (s 25); truth; absolute privilege; qualified privilege; honest opinion; offer to make amends; apology; and fair and reasonable publication on a matter of public interest (s 26), reformulating in part the former *Reynolds* defence (House of Lords)

4 As clarified at para 47 of Phelan J's judgment in *Reidy v Pasek* [2022] IEHC 366 – see also *Oakes v Spar (Ireland) Ltd* [2019] IEHC 642 – application must be made prior to issuing proceedings within the two-year period; *Watson v Campos* [2016] IEHC 18 and *Rooney v Shell E&P Ltd* [2016] IEHC 63 (*obiter* comments that draft proceedings should be exhibited to an affidavit applying for extension); *Quinn v Reverse Defence Forces Representative Association* [2018] IEHC 684 (Barton J: extension of time only needs to be sought when a "statute barred plea" is raised in a defence, and *McKenna v Kerry County Council* [2020] IEHC 687 wherein Butler J adopted Barton J's reasoning but also said a plaintiff could still bring an application to obtain certainty).

5 See fn 68 (the previous cap as *per* s 41 of the Act was €50,000).

Notable cases	*Higgins* (2022): jury award of €387,000 in respect of three defamatory emails lowered by the Supreme Court to €202,500 (the Court of Appeal in 2020 upheld an appeal by the Irish Aviation Authority ('IAA'), reducing the award by 80 percent to €76,500 which included €6,500 in aggravated damages). MacMenamin J for the majority held the Court of Appeal erred in cutting general damages to €70,000 for what was "very serious defamation" and the appropriate figure for this was €175,000. Adding €50,000 for aggravated damages, and giving a 10 percent discount for the offer of amends by the IAA, this brought the amount to €202,500. In related proceedings, on 10 July 2018, the Supreme Court agreed with a 2016 decision of the Court of Appeal and held that damages fell, in the absence of agreement between the parties, to be determined by a jury and not by a judge in the ss 22 and 23 context of the amount of damages to be paid in a defamation action where an offer of amends has been made. *Higgins* is also seminal as it was the first occasion that jurors were provided guidelines (by the High Court trial judge) on quantum of damages by way of figures and ranges of awards in other cases with a view to guiding them on the amount of damages they should award for this defamation action. In the March 2022 ruling, the Supreme Court gave specific guidance (though not formal guidelines) suggesting four categories or brackets (see discussion below) of defamation awards *Kinsella* (2019): jury award of €10 million reduced by the Court of Appeal to €250,000 *Nolan* (2019): Court of Appeal upheld the award total of €310,000 for general, punitive and aggravated damages (€50,000 towards breach of the plaintiff's constitutional right to privacy, €30,000 for punitive damages, €30,000 for aggravated damages and €200,000 for general damages arising from the defamation) *Christie* (2017): High Court assessed the starting point for damages in this case at €200,000 but, applying a discount in the region of one third, reduced same to €140,000 in light of an offer of amends and apology. Court of Appeal used a €60,000 starting point and applied a 40 percent discount, thus reducing damages payable to €36,000

	Speedie (2017): Court of Appeal rejected the argument that an award of €85,000 was inadequate to compensate the plaintiff in respect of a defamatory article which had alleged that he assorted with known criminals *McDonagh* (2016): Jury award of €900,000 overturned by Court of Appeal. Upon further appeal to Supreme Court, had the case not settled, the court would have substituted the award for a figure as low as €75,000 *Leech* (2014): Jury award of €1,872,000 reduced by Supreme Court to €1.25 million. The defendant/ appellant publisher applied to the European Court of Human Rights claiming that this award of damages was still excessive and in breach of the guarantee of freedom of expression in Art 10 of the Convention. The court noted that the Supreme Court's judgment did not provide a comprehensive explanation for the final award, and failed to explain, apart from reference to principles which had been put to the jury in the High Court, how it arrived at the figure of €1.25 million.

Table 1: Summary of the statutory tort of defamation and damages awards

Reluctance of the courts to grant injunctions

[4.1.03] Though covered by the law of torts, in limited circumstances (outside of the injunctive relief provisions of s 33[6] of the 2009 Act in applications to prohibit, pending trial, the publication or further publication of a defamatory statement where a defamation action is already in being) the courts have discretion to otherwise grant the equity law remedy of an injunction where damages will be inappropriate.[7]

---

6 See *Lidl Ireland GmbH v Irish Farmers Association* [2021] IEHC 381 wherein the High Court *refused an* application by Lidl Ireland *for an injunction prohibiting the publication of two* advertisements by the IFA. Lidl claimed that the advertisements contained allegations that their own-brand milk was not Irish and that they had been misleading customers as to the provenance of their dairy products. Delivering judgment in the case, Allen J held that the defendants had a bona fide defence to the proceedings. The court held that the IFA could point to evidence that the Lidl milk was not Irish and that the labelling was designed to mislead customers about the source of the products. Accordingly, the court held that the factual disputes should be left to a jury to conclusively determine.

7 *Reynolds v Malocco* [1998] IEHC 175 (Kelly J) and as implied in the ruling of Clarke J in *Cogley* v RTÉ [2005] IEHC 180 discussed in Chapter 34. The plaintiff in *Reynolds* complained that extracts in a new magazine *Patrick* defamed him in two respects: the words in the natural and ordinary meaning or by innuendo alleged that he had been charged with permitting the sale of drugs in his nightclubs and/or that he permitted the sale of drugs on the premises and was benefiting therefrom. Alternatively, he was turning a blind eye to the sale of drugs on his premises and secondly, that he was a homosexual. The plaintiff alleged that the libel was so serious that it was one in which the court ought to intervene by the grant of an injunction. Without such injunction he would suffer loss

[4.1.04] In *Muwema v Facebook Ireland Ltd*,[8] the court held that the social network was not obliged to remove the defamatory posts of an anonymous third party. The court opted instead to exercise its discretion and made a *Norwich Pharmacal* order, forcing Facebook to reveal the identity of the user in question. Binchy J also found that the s 33 prohibitory order sought could only be available when the defendant had no defence which is reasonably likely to succeed and, in this instance, the defendant may well have been successful in availing of the innocent publication defence. On appeal, giving the decision of the three-judge Court of Appeal,[9] Peart J said he would not interfere with the High Court decision.

[4.1.05] In *Gilroy v O'Leary*,[10]Allen J came to the conclusion that the above threshold under s 33 is the same as that which applied at common law (see fn 63). Further, the application of the first plaintiff for an order for the removal of the subject video, having failed to satisfy the legal threshold for the granting of an order pursuant to s 33, was refused.

[4.1.06] In *Beaumont Hospital Board v O'Doherty*[11] however the High Court granted an interlocutory injunction against Gemma O'Doherty *for defamatory comments that she made about* Beaumont Hospital *and its director of nursing*. The court applied s 33 and held that O'Doherty had no defence that was reasonably likely to succeed.[12]

[4.1.07] Aside from the reasons expressed in *Reynolds v Malocco* (see fn 7) above, one of the underlying reasons, as explained by Clarke J in the *Cogley* decision discussed in Chapter 34, for the reluctance of the courts in this jurisdiction to grant injunctions at an interlocutory stage in relation to defamation stems from the fact that if the traditional basis for the grant of an interlocutory injunction (i.e. that the plaintiff had established a fair issue to be tried) was sufficient for the grant of an injunction in defamation proceedings, public debate on many issues would be largely stifled.

---

incapable of being compensated in monetary damages. The court stated that "damages are the normal remedy for defamation and injunctions are not. Nothing in this judgment should be taken to dilute that approach". In the present case, however, the question arose as to what damages the plaintiff would be likely to recover against the defendants at trial due to their particular financial circumstances. Kelly J thus concluded he was satisfied that his discretion must be exercised in favour of granting an injunction rather than refusing it. To refuse it would be to consign the plaintiff to a trial where damages would be an inadequate remedy because of the virtual impossibility of ever recovering any sum awarded.

8 [2016] IEHC 519.

9 [2018] IECA 104.

10 [2019] IEHC 52.

11 [2021] IEHC 469.

12 The defamatory comments related to three videos posted by Ms O'Doherty on her website which included allegations of serious criminal activity by the plaintiffs. It was claimed by O'Doherty that these statements were justified on the basis of truth. However, the court disagreed, noting that the defendant's comments were based largely on her own perceptions rather than facts.

[4.1.08] In publications or broadcasts which deal with important public issues, persons or bodies may necessarily be criticised from time to time. There will frequently be some basis for such persons or bodies to at least suggest that what is said of them is unfair to the point of being defamatory. If it were necessary only to establish the possibility of such an outcome in order that the publication or broadcast would be restrained, then a disproportionate effect on the conduct of public debate on issues of importance would result.

[4.1.09] In that regard it is important to note that the Constitution and the law generally both recognise the need for a vigorous and informed public debate on issues of importance. The Constitution accordingly confers absolute privilege on the debates of Dáil Éireann and Seanad Éireann. Any measures which would impose an excessive or unreasonable interference with the conditions necessary for such debate would require very substantial justification. Hence the reluctance of the courts in this jurisdiction (and also the European Court of Human Rights, 'the ECtHR') to justify prior restraint save in unusual circumstances and after "careful scrutiny".

Defamation examples

[4.1.10] Defamation can be obvious in the case, for example, of a magazine article that alleges a famous actor enjoyed an extra-marital affair which transpires to be untrue, founded only on unsubstantiated rumours from a dubious or unreliable source. Use of the caveat "alleged" will not shield a defendant from liability, nor will the words "innocent face?"[13] akin to an emoticon. A second instance, cited later in this chapter, the case of genuine and inadvertent mistake, is where a solicitor, rather than his client, is depicted as the defendant in criminal proceedings during a television news report. Defamatory statements can also include images, emoticons, sounds and gestures. Further, 'retail defamation' could occur for instance where a person is wrongly accused of shoplifting.

[4.1.11] However, a much more nuanced hypothetical example arises where exterior shots in a film show a readily identifiable house and the readily identifiable and idiosyncratic homeowner in a local community which are used in conjunction with interior shots (purporting, for the benefit of the audience, to be the same house) of a marijuana plant cultivation operation. The owner of such house, assuming of course his consent has not been obtained in advance to film his property's exterior, could certainly make a case for defamation if his home

[13] In *McAlpine v Bercow* [2013] EWHC 1342, Tugendhat J in the England and Wales High Court was asked to rule on the meaning of Bercow's tweet, particularly the phrase "innocent face" which the judge said was intended to be read "as a stage direction" with readers imagining that they can see Bercow's face as she asks the question in the tweet. The words direct the reader to imagine that the expression on her face is one of innocence, that is an expression which purports to indicate (sincerely, on the defendant's case, but insincerely or ironically on the claimant's case) that she does not know the answer to her question.

now (and forever more) becomes associated with illegal drugs or he is shunned by the community, even if such association stems from an entirely fictional narrative. Filmmakers, therefore, must be particularly vigilant that all potential avenues for litigation are meticulously explored through risk mitigation. This will be required in any event by the production's errors and omissions ('E&O') insurers – this topic has already been addressed in Chapter 2. Without E&O insurance, projects will not receive public funding or attract private financiers or distributors. All stakeholders need to insulate themselves from exposure to liability and hence defamation is an issue to which careful attention must invariably be paid.

[4.1.12] In recent years, the number of defamation cases taken in the courts has dramatically increased which is being linked to the growth in social media use.[14] The tort of defamation has the potential to witness the demise of a defendant's business (be it a regional radio station or independent film production company), particularly if there is no insurer to indemnify the action. Even when there is media insurance in place, a successful settlement or outcome at trial for the claimant may well mean, in the case of some insurers at least, that the prospects of obtaining future cover are cost-prohibitive or minimal. Ireland is a pro-plaintiff country in which to litigate a defamation action and jury awards can be staggering (although the Supreme Court and Court of Appeal have recently stemmed this tide as evident from case law throughout this chapter). A portion of damages may also have to be borne by the defendant business itself on foot of the 'excess' provisions of the policy (e.g. where it might have to discharge, for example, the first €10,000 of the damages claim).

[4.1.13] For these reasons, all practitioners in the entertainment and media sector engaged in content creation on a commercial basis should be armed with a firm grasp of defamation law principles and how they apply to their particular and unique business or project-specific circumstances, whether it be high-risk investigative journalism, the production of documentaries or the publication of a weekly newsletter.[15] In respect of investigative journalism, the case of Fr Reynolds will be discussed in Chapter 31. Damages estimated at between €750,000 and

---

14 In respect of UK law, see *McAlpine* (above, n 13), a landmark social media defamation case in 2013 between Conservative peer Lord McAlpine and Sally Bercow, spouse of the Speaker of the House of Commons. McAlpine alleged that he was defamed by comments implying that he was a paedophile published by the defendant on Twitter. This followed the broadcast on 2 November 2012 of a report by BBC Two's *Newsnight* which linked an unnamed "senior Conservative" politician to sex abuse claims. On 4 November 2012, Bercow tweeted "Why is Lord McAlpine trending? *innocent face*". When the allegations against McAlpine proved to be unfounded, the BBC subsequently apologised and paid him £185,000 in damages and the ITV television network paid him £125,000. McAlpine commenced legal actions against users of Twitter who had repeated the claims but users with fewer than 500 followers were allowed to settle the matter by making a donation of £25 to the BBC's Children in Need charity.

15 For deeper analysis of the law of defamation, see, for example, Neville Cox and Eoin McCullough, *Defamation: Law and Practice* (Clarus Press, Dublin, 2014).

€1 million[16] were paid to the plaintiff priest in a defamation action after a RTÉ journalist wrongly accused him of sexually assaulting a minor and fathering a child while working in Kenya. This was in addition to a financial sanction of €200,000 imposed on the national public broadcaster by the Broadcasting Authority of Ireland (BAI). RTÉ had the resources to foot such a bill. The same might not be the case of a cash-strapped independent production company especially in the absence of professional indemnity insurance.

THE CONSTITUTION AND THE EUROPEAN CONVENTION ON HUMAN RIGHTS

[4.2.01] Article 40.6.1°.i of the Constitution affirms that the State guarantees the right of citizens to express freely their convictions and opinions. This guarantee is qualified, however, and, accordingly, the right to freedom of expression in Ireland is not absolute. The article provides that, because of the importance of educating the public, the State will seek to ensure that the organs of public opinion such as the radio and the press maintain their right to liberty of expression, but this shall not be used to undermine public order, morality or the authority of the State.

[4.2.02] The right to freedom of expression is also guaranteed by Art 10(1) of the European Convention on Human Rights ('the ECHR') which provides that:

> Everyone has the right to freedom of expression. This right shall include freedom to hold opinions and to receive and impart information and ideas, without interference by public authority and regardless of frontiers.

Similar to our constitutional restraint, Art 10(2) subjects this freedom to such restrictions as:

> ...are necessary in a democratic society in the interests of national security, territorial integrity or public safety, for the prevention of disorder or crime, for the protection of health or morals, for the protection of the reputation or rights of others, for preventing the disclosure of information received in confidence or for maintaining the authority and impartiality of the judiciary.

[4.2.03] The third leg in this balancing act of competing rights is that the Constitution does not only guarantee freedom to the media. It also requires the State to respect, defend and vindicate the personal rights of citizens in Art 40.3.2° by stipulating that:

> The State shall, in particular, by its laws, protect as best it may from unjust attack (and, in the case of injustice done, vindicate) the life, person, good name and property rights of every citizen.

16 Dearbhail McDonald, *No winners as RTÉ settles libel case with ex-bishop* (2015), independent.ie. Available at: https://www.independent.ie/irish-news/courts/no-winners-as-rt-settles-libel-case-with-exbishop-31348610.html [Accessed 20 April 2018].

Thus, the Constitution guarantees both the right to a good name and the right to free speech, rights which come into conflict with one another in a satirical context for example. However, in defamation cases, the Irish courts are currently, according to the seminal textbook on the law of torts in Ireland,[17] reluctant to rely on these Constitutional protections, observing instead that rights are adequately protected by existing tort laws stemming from statute and common law precedent.

ECtHR ruling (2017) in Leech and subsequent Irish developments

[4.2.04] Before exploring the last leg of the long-running proceedings concerning Monica Leech, two salient points are necessary. Paul O'Higgins SC in his contribution to a Continuing Professional Development conference in 2011 on then recent developments in defamation law, commented that:

> While a range of cases both before and after the passing of the 2003 Act have stressed the similarities between the protection afforded to the right of freedom of expression under the Convention and the Constitution, it is suggested in this paper that the differences which exist at a textual level are being amplified by recent decisions of the European Court of Human Rights…and that the European Court is developing Article 10[18] and Article 8[19] jurisprudence which sits uncomfortably with the existing understanding of the equivalent Constitutional rights in this jurisdiction and which may conflict with the new defences provided for under the 2009 Act.[20]

[4.2.05] The combined effect of the passing into Irish law of the European Convention on Human Rights Act 2003 ('the 2003 Act') and the 2009 Act has been to create a complex intersection in defamation and media law between statutory provisions, constitutional protections, rules of common law and ECHR rights. Notwithstanding, in this arena, the Constitution reigns supreme, as affirmed by Fennelly J in the Supreme Court in *Mahon Tribunal v Keena* wherein he stated that:

> Although no issue arises in the present case of conflict between the Convention provisions and the Constitution, it is important to recall that, in the event of such conflict, it is the Constitution which must prevail.[21]

[4.2.06] The ECtHR delivered its landmark judgment on 15 June 2017 in the case of *Independent Newspapers (Ireland) Ltd v Ireland*[22] involving the long-

---

17 Bryan McMahon and William Binchy, *The Law of Torts* (4th ed, Butterworths, Dublin, 2013), para 34.05 at p 1241.

18 Concerning freedom of expression.

19 Right to respect for private and family life.

20 Paul O'Higgins SC, *The Phoney War* (2011) at p 2 in *Recent Developments in Defamation Law*. The Bar Council, Continuing Professional Development conference paper.

21 [2009] IESC 64 at para 44.

22 [2017] ECHR 567.

running Leech matter[23] which involved awarding of certain government contracts and rumours of an intimate relationship between the married consultant plaintiff and a government minister. The European Court's seven-judge Fifth Section unanimously held that a damages award made against an Irish newspaper for defamation violated the Art 10 right to freedom of expression. While the judgment concerned Irish defamation law prior to reforms brought about by the 2009 Act, it is still significant for signalling to Irish courts that:

> ...unpredictably high damages in libel cases are considered capable of having a chilling effect and they therefore require the most careful scrutiny and very strong justification.[24]

[4.2.07] Although the judgment had no impact on the €1.25 million figure payable to Leech, it was seen as an indication that the Irish legal system needed to control defamation damages being awarded in the State. This changing tide has in fact been reflected by recent Court of Appeal decisions cited in the table at the opening of this chapter. Indeed, the Supreme Court (March 2022) in *Higgins*[25] favoured trial judges giving specific guidance to juries by reference to a range of cases, suggesting four categories or brackets. The guidance is that very moderate defamation attracts awards between zero and €50,000; median cases between €50,000 and €120,000 and serious defamation between €125,000 and €199,000. MacMenamin J (as he then was) for the majority signalled that cases at the top of the scale would be more than €200,000 but noted that the courts had very seldom awarded more than €300,000.

[4.2.08] The ECtHR held that:

> ...further clarification was lacking regarding why, in particular, the highest ever award was required in a case which the Supreme Court did not categorise as one of the gravest and most serious libels.[26]

[4.2.09] This was particularly so given that the award had the capacity to act as a benchmark for future defamation awards and out-of-court settlements. Thus, the court found that the Supreme Court had failed to provide very strong justification for its award, and accordingly violated Art 10's guarantee of freedom of expression. It noted that the Supreme Court had found the High Court jury

---

23 *Leech v Independent Newspapers (Ireland) Ltd* [2014] IESC 79. One might ponder how an application to the ECtHR was capable of being brought by Independent Newspapers in terms of eligibility. The answer is that legal entities such as companies and associations, as well as individuals, can lodge an application to the Strasbourg court. Thus, the news and media company could bring an application for a judgment that the State had failed to protect its freedom of expression. The application could also be brought as it is a prerequisite for eligibility to bring a case to Strasbourg that all the national remedies have first been exhausted as was the case here given the Supreme Court ruling had substituted the jury award in the High Court.

24 At para 104 of the judgment, see also para 85.

25 [2022] IESC 13.

26 At para 100.

award of €1,872,000 disproportionate but failed to explain, apart from reference to generic principles which had been put to the jury in the High Court, how it arrived at the figure of €1.25 million.

DEFAMATION ACT 2009 KEY PROVISIONS; SOCIAL MEDIA CONTENT

[4.3.01] Any individual or business actively practising in the field of entertainment and media will, most likely, already be broadly familiar with the statutory framework for the tort of defamation and the defences available.

[4.3.02] A defamatory statement (concerning a living individual)[27] can be written or oral and the old distinction of slander and libel was abolished by the 2009 Act.[28] The statement need not necessarily name or identify anyone. It may suggest by implication or surrounding circumstances a person or persons by, for example, their profession, location or connections. Publication of a defamatory statement can take place in the traditional written media such as newspapers and magazines, but an increasing number of defamation actions are arising relating to posts made on microblogging and social media platforms such as Twitter (since the time of writing, Twitter has rebranded to X) and Facebook as discussed below.

[4.3.03] Section 8 of the 2009 Act obliges the parties to a defamation action to swear a verifying affidavit, similar to an affidavit of verification in a personal injuries action, attesting as to the truth[29] of pleadings and assertions or allegations

---

27 A deceased person cannot be defamed (McMahon and Binchy, *supra* at para 34.379; see also s 39 of the Act (causes of action for defamation vested in persons immediately before their death shall survive for the benefit of their estate. The Review Report recommended leaving s 39 as-is). Note, however, that ECtHR case law has accepted the possibility that courts may sometimes be required to protect the reputation of the deceased, within the scope of Art 8 of the ECHR. The same court's jurisprudence has also accepted that the reputation of a deceased member of a person's family might affect one's private life and identity, provided that there was a sufficiently close link between them. See also Chapter 18 on life rights. Further, note that US law (and potentially Indian common law too) provides for descendible publicity, personality and privacy rights (estates of deceased persons) and hence for productions to be broadcast in that territory, local legal advice should be sought in the case, for example, of documentaries where the subject and other parties depicted are deceased and where the material may be controversial. See discussion of US defamation (civil and criminal), descendible publicity and privacy rights in this connection in William H. Binder, *Publicity Rights and Defamation of the Deceased: Resurrection or R.I.P.?* (2002), DePaul University Journal of Art, Technology and Intellectual Property Law Vol 12, Issue 2, Article 3, pp 297-332; and Anushree Yewale, Riddhi Tulshian and Meghana Chandorkar, *Posthumous Survival of Privacy and Personality Rights: Part 1* (2021), TMT Law Practice (India). Available at: https://www.legal500.com/developments/thought-leadership/posthumous-survival-of-privacy-personality-rights-part-1/ [Accessed 5 April 2022].

28 Section 6(1). Note too that s 35 abolished the common law criminal offences of defamatory libel, seditious libel and obscene libel.

29 The making of a false or misleading (in any material respect) statement in an affidavit or knowingly making a statement that is false or misleading can give rise to criminal

of facts. In terms of the limitation of actions period, s 38 provides that a defamation action must be initiated in the courts within one year, although this can be extended to two years in exceptional circumstances (see the case law outlined in n 4 above). Previously, libel had a six-year limitation period and slander a three-year limitation period.

[4.3.04] For the specific tort of defamation itself, no proof of special damage or financial loss is required (but see s 42 of the 2009 Act in respect of malicious falsehood torts which, in fact, require special damage and intention or likelihood of causing financial loss).[30] All defamatory statements are actionable *per se*. This also applies as regards a body corporate (s 12) which can bring a defamation action (discussed in the Chapter 5). Accordingly, a body corporate may also bring a defamation action, again irrespective of whether it has sustained financial loss.[31]

[4.3.05] Section 6 of the 2009 Act provides that:

> The tort of defamation consists of the publication, by any means, of a defamatory statement concerning a person, to one or more than one person (other than the first-mentioned person).

A "defamatory statement" is defined in s 2 of the 2009 Act as "a statement that tends to injure a person's reputation in the eyes of reasonable members of society".[32] In other words, one must merely issue a statement that could injure a third party's reputation in the eyes of the community in order to be potentially liable for defamation. With a few exceptions,[33] the intent of the tortfeasor (be it

---

prosecution, with liability on summary conviction to a fine not exceeding €3,000, or imprisonment for a term not exceeding six months or to both; and on conviction on indictment, to a fine not exceeding €50,000, or imprisonment for a term not exceeding five years, or to both – s 8(7).

30 Section 6(5) of the 2009 Act.

31 The Review Report recommends a legislative provision (as applies in other common law jurisdictions) that a body corporate may not sue for defamation of its reputation unless it first shows that the statement has caused or is likely to cause serious harm: in the case of a body that trades for profit, this means serious financial loss, and to consider whether smaller entities such as SMEs should be exempted from this requirement.

32 The court will consider what is the "ordinary reasonable reader" of the statement, bearing in mind the medium through which it is published. The principles were recently re-stated by the Court of Appeal in *Gilchrist v Sunday Newspapers* [2017] IECA 191. Irvine J referred to the Supreme Court's *ex tempore* judgment of Hardiman J delivered on 12 October 2015 in *Travers v Sunday Newspapers Ltd* which upheld Hedigan J's ruling ([2012] IEHC 185). Hardiman J relied on *Lewis v Daily Telegraph Limited* [1964] AC 234 as support for the proposition that whether a particular publication is capable of bearing the meanings pleaded by a plaintiff is a question of impression and the court had to consider the whole of the publication, which included the "get up" – headlines, pictures and captions. All of this had to be taken into account. Further, it is permissible for a jury to look at a second article to see to whom an earlier article, which is alleged to be defamatory of a plaintiff, refers.

33 See s 19 (acting with malice defeats a plea of qualified privilege) and s 40 (knowing a statement is defamatory). Malice is also relevant as regards s 42 (malicious falsehood) of the 2009 Act as shall later be discussed.

satirical or, for example, coming or not with malice or ill-will)[34] is irrelevant and hence the strict liability nature of this civil wrong. As previously was the case in repealed legislation and in common law, defamatory statements are automatically deemed to be false. When invoking the s 16 "defence of truth" in defamation proceedings, it shall be for the defendant to prove that the statement in respect of which the action was brought is true in all material respects.[35]

Meaning and extent of publication

[4.3.06] As regards meaning and extent of publication of a statement published on Twitter, in the UK case *Monroe v Hopkins*,[36] the court noted that it would be wrong to engage in elaborate analysis of a 140 character tweet. Instead, an impressionistic approach is much more fitting and appropriate to that medium. This impressionistic approach must take account of the whole tweet and the context in which the ordinary reasonable reader would read it. That context includes matters of ordinary general knowledge and matters which were put before that reader via Twitter. Notwithstanding this, the court rejected the submission that normal principles should be set aside when considering the "wild west" of social media,[37] and that the statement should be taken less seriously simply because it was made on Twitter. It concluded that the ordinary reader of Twitter would hold the tweets to be defamatory.

[4.3.07] In relation to the meaning of a statement published on Facebook, in the UK Supreme Court case of *Stocker v Stocker*,[38] the court considered what would the words "he tried to strangle me" convey to the "ordinary reasonable reader" of a Facebook post. The High Court and Court of Appeal held that this meant Mr Stocker had tried to kill his wife, which was considered defamatory of him. The Supreme Court, however, was of the view that the trial judge, Mitting J, performed an overly analytical approach to arriving at the meaning of the statement, holding at para 47 that:

---

34 Malice is relevant however in two respects. Irvine J for the Court of Appeal in *Kinsella v Kenmare Resources plc* [2019] IECA 54 confirmed that, first, malice is relevant only in the event that publication occurred on an occasion of qualified privilege. Section 19(1) of the 2009 Act provides that in a defamation action, the defence of qualified privilege shall fail if, in relation to the publication of the statement in respect of which the action was brought, the plaintiff proves that the defendant acted with malice. Secondly, if there is evidence of malice or evidence to show that the defendant acted in a high-handed or malevolent manner with the result that the plaintiff's self-esteem was further damaged, then aggravated damages may be awarded – see para 115 and 130 of the judgment.

35 Section 16(2) adds a proviso however – in a defamation action in respect of a statement containing two or more distinct allegations against the plaintiff, the defence of truth shall not fail by reason only of the truth of every allegation not being proved, if the words not proved to be true do not materially injure the plaintiff's reputation having regard to the truth of the remaining allegations.

36 [2017] EWHC 433.

37 This term was used in *AB v Facebook* [2013] NIQB 14.

38 [2019] UKSC 17.

> ...he failed to conduct a realistic exploration of how the ordinary reader of the post would have understood it. Readers of Facebook posts do not subject them to close analysis.

[4.3.08] Given then that the statement was not capable of bearing the meaning suggested by Mrs Stocker, the court concluded:

> ...a reader does not splice the post into separate clauses, much less isolate individual words and contemplate their possible significance. Knowing that the author was alive, he or she would unquestionably have interpreted the post as meaning that Mr Stocker had grasped his wife by the throat and applied force to her neck rather than that he had tried deliberately to kill her.[39]

[4.3.09] Courts may consider the extent of initial publication, and difficulty in controlling its further dissemination. In *Cairns v Modi*[40] the plaintiff was awarded £90,000 for a tweet seen only by 65 people, as it was "impossible to track the scandal, to know what quarters the poison may reach". There has been inconsistency, however, as to whether defamation on social media will attract greater damages than in traditional media. Thus, in *AB v Facebook*[41] the plaintiff was awarded £35,000 whereby a Facebook page was equated with the main page of a leading newspaper or a popular television programme. While in *Monir v Wood*[42] a tweet which labelled the plaintiff a sex offender attracted £40,000, the court admitting it would have been £250,000 had it appeared in a national newspaper.[43]

[4.3.10] In relation to proof of publication online, evidence can be gathered through use of Google Analytics figures, number of followers or friends that the defendant has on Twitter (now X) and Facebook and the number of retweets, reposts and likes of a statement.

Defences

[4.3.11] The defences to defamation are truth (s 16) such that truth in all material respects must be proved,[44] absolute privilege (s 17),[45] qualified privilege (s 18), honest opinion as might apply, for example, to an impersonal (e.g. refraining from commenting on the personal appearance of a chef) restaurant review (the

---

39 At para 49 of the judgment.
40 [2012] EWHC 756.
41 [2013] NIQB 14.
42 [2018] EWHC 3525.
43 Referred to in Michael O'Doherty, *Defamation and Social Media* (2021) (paper for CPD Philanthropy lecture).
44 However, as already seen, if an allegation contains what might, simplistically, be termed major and minor allegations and defendants cannot prove the truth of the minor allegations, they can still avail of the defence if, by reason of the major allegations being proved, the remaining words do not materially injure the plaintiff – s 16(2).
45 Amended by Houses of the Oireachtas (Enquiries, Privileges and Procedures) Act 2013 and Parole Act 2019.

2009 Act introduced this defence but requires in s 20(2)(c) that the opinion relate to a matter of public interest,[46] consent to publish (s 25), fair and reasonable publication on a matter of public interest (s 26),[47] and innocent publication (s 27)).[48] Procedures are also in place for offers to make amends (where the person who or entity which published the defamatory statement offers to publish a correction and apology, and agrees to make a payment, whether accepted by the parties or assessed by a jury/appellate court,[49] to the plaintiff). If the maker of a defamatory statement publishes an apology with equal prominence, or offers to do so, it counts towards mitigation of any damages.

[4.3.12] The honest opinion (replacing the former 'fair comment') defence essentially seeks to protect the right to freedom of expression, by allowing for free expression and exchange of honestly held opinions on matters of public interest, subject to the conditions set out in s 20[50] and the mandatory but non-exhaustive list of factors in s 21 to which a court must have regard for the purposes of determining whether a statement was one of opinion or fact. It is relevant to critiques and reviews of matters of public interest and other matters held out for public scrutiny – for example, reviews of films, plays, books or restaurants, as well as the discussion of political, social and economic affairs. Section 20 *inter alia* provides that an opinion is honestly held if at the time of the publication of the statement, the defendant believed in the truth of the opinion or, where the defendant is not the author of the opinion, believed that the author believed it to be true.

---

46 Though matters that are deemed to be in the public interest are quite broad, and so the inclusion of this requirement does not unnecessarily restrict the scope of the defence.

47 This is a very complex and unwieldy defence. In determining whether the publication was fair and reasonable, the court must have regard to such matters as it considers relevant, including any or all of the ten criteria set out in s 26(2) of the 2009 Act. A defendant faces a considerable burden in seeking to raise it as seen in *Meegan v Times Newspapers Ltd* [2016] IECA 327. The Review Report recommends simplifying and clarifying the defence along the lines applied in the UK and Canada to provide a defence where a statement is on a matter of public interest, the publisher reasonably believed that its publication was in the public interest and the defendant acted responsibly in the circumstances relating to attempts at verifying the accuracy of the statement.

48 The Review Report calls for this defence to be applied to operators of websites in relation to user-generated comment subject to the obligation to take down content expeditiously and/or identify the poster if notified of defamatory content. It also suggests amending the defence to exempt a broadcaster from liability for a statement made by a contributor during a live broadcast, provided that it has taken reasonable precautions prior to the broadcast and exercises reasonable care during the broadcast.

49 It was believed from the passing of the 2009 Act onwards that "court" meant a judge sitting alone until the Supreme Court clarified in 2018 that "court" in the context of s 23 means a jury: *Higgins v Irish Aviation Authority* and *White v Sunday Newspapers Ltd* (the two cases were heard together) ([2018] IESC 29, [2018] 3 IR 374).

50 The 'honestly held' requirement for instance was not made out in *Cullen v Sheehy* [2017] IEHC 459 wherein the High Court held that a press release inaccurately presented some of the findings of a report of an independent review of the compulsory purchase of a piece of land by Wicklow County Council and made claims about a number of County Councillors when the report had not made any such findings.

[4.3.13] While the defences of truth and honest opinion are most likely the ones to be utilised by individuals or private entities, the defences of innocent publication or defences under the E-Commerce Regulations[51] are the likely defences to be relied on by social media platforms in respect of notice and takedown mechanisms. Fair and reasonable publication on a matter of public interest is the defence frequently advanced by newspapers.

[4.3.14] The Department of Justice in its March 2022 review report on the 2009 Act ('the Review Report') considered a number of changes to the honest opinion defence (such as removal of the requirement that the opinion must be on a matter of public interest) but recommended only the removal of the requirement on the defendant to prove that the opinion was believed to be true (the opinion however still having to be honestly held).

[4.3.15] Absolute privilege applies even if a statement has been made maliciously, for example, in either house of the Oireachtas by a senator or deputy, or in the European Parliament by a member of that parliament, or made by a judge or other person performing a judicial function, or by a party, witness, legal representative or juror in the course of proceedings presided over by a judge or other person performing a judicial function.[52] Here, the intention of the publisher is irrelevant. A fair, accurate and contemporaneous media report of Oireachtas or court proceedings is also absolutely privileged, even if the reporter is motivated by malice. Clearly this exception is aimed at allowing free speech for members of the judicial and legislative arms of government, and for accurate reports of their views.

[4.3.16] Qualified privilege (s 18 and Sch 1 of the 2009 Act) (privileged "without explanation or contradiction") attaches to communications where the informant has a legal, moral or social duty to communicate the information and the recipient has a similar duty to receive it (this defence was invoked by the Irish Aviation Authority in *Higgins* discussed below). For example, a person may write to an employer making allegations of dishonesty or incompetence against an employee. If the allegations are made in good faith, even if they are factually wrong, the communication is not actionable. This privilege is defeated

---

51 SI No 68 of 2003 – European Communities (Directive 2000/31/EC) Regulations 2003. A provider which hosts content (e.g. a social media platform) is not liable for information which it stores on its platform on condition that the provider does not have actual knowledge of illegal activity or information and, as regards claims for damages, is not aware of facts or circumstances from which the illegal activity or information is apparent; or the provider, upon obtaining such knowledge or awareness, acts expeditiously to remove or to disable access to the information. Further, social media platforms will rely on the defence of innocent publication whereby they are not the author, editor or publisher of the statement to which the action relates, they exercise reasonable care in relation to its publication, and did not know, and had no reason to believe, that what they did cause or contributed to the publication of a statement would give rise to a cause of action in defamation.

52 See s 17(2)(a) to (w) for the full list.

however by proof of malice (s 19). Qualified privilege is also granted *inter alia* for a determination of the Press Ombudsman or Press Council, and applies too to statements or reports of certain public meetings, organisations and bodies (such as local authorities and tribunals) "subject to explanation or contradiction". In these cases, publishers will lose the privilege if they fail to amend or clarify an erroneous statement.

Offer to make amends procedures

[4.3.17] Section 22 provides a statutory offer to make amends (which cannot be made after the delivery of the defence in the defamation action concerned, and if defendants in defamation actions plead the defence under this section, they shall not be entitled to plead any other defence in the action).[53] The effect of the offer is set out in s 23. The defence was designed to facilitate expeditious and more economic resolution of defamation actions.

[4.3.18] The procedures seek to soften, in the case of genuine error, the harshness of the strict liability nature of the tort whereby the intention of the tortfeasor is regarded as irrelevant. Where defendants have published an allegedly defamatory statement, they can offer to publish a suitable correction and apology and pay compensation and costs. In Britain, making such an offer leads to a discount in any damages that may be awarded at trial – as much as 50 percent.[54] This was echoed by the Supreme Court in *Higgins* in 2022 whereby in considering the discount to be applied following an offer of amends,[55] MacMenamin J suggested that courts take account of the "timing, content of the offer, and the conduct of the defendant", and operate on a scale of discount from zero to a "gold standard" of 50 percent. In the honourable justice's view, any inadequacy in the offer of amends should be dealt with via the discount percentage, not aggravated damages.

[4.3.19] If the offer is accepted and the parties cannot agree either the amount of damages or the terms of the apology then an application can be made to court (meaning a jury will decide on damages but has no function in approving the terms of the apology). The main advantage for the defendant in making such

53 However, a defendant who made an offer to make amends is not required to plead it as a defence in a defamation action.

54 Michael Kealey, *Defame and Fortune* (2010). *Law Society Gazette* (January/February issue), p 23.

55 Captain Higgins, a senior Aer Lingus pilot, also flew single-engine aircraft in his spare time. Emails were sent following an incident in which he had to make an emergency landing of a light aircraft in Wales. The emails, it was claimed, meant he had flown the aircraft unauthorised even though his papers were fully in order and in circumstances where the UK Civil Aviation Authority, following an investigation, considered the case closed. The IAA eventually offered an apology – which Captain Higgins said came six years too late after instituting legal proceedings – and an offer of amends was made. Ultimately, the matter of amends went before a High Court jury which awarded him €387,000, including €300,000 general damages. This award was substantially cut by the Supreme Court overturning an even lower figure that had been reached by the Court of Appeal.

an offer of amends is that it should be entitled to a discount of up to 50 percent on the amount of damages for doing so, together with significant costs savings if the case is resolved speedily. If plaintiffs reject the offer of amends, then they have to overcome the difficult hurdle of proving that the defendant knew or ought reasonably to have known at the time of the publication of the statement that it was false and defamatory of them. The benefit for plaintiffs is that the damage to their reputation is resolved quickly and effectively, without risk-laden, costly and protracted litigation.

[4.3.20] It is doubtful in light of a Court of Appeal decision in 2020 and its earlier ruling in 2016[56] as well as that of the Supreme Court's initial determination (10 July 2018)[57] in *Higgins* whether any party will deploy the offer of amends again,[58] at least under the current regime. The procedure would be of little appeal to a defendant if it resulted in the expense and risk associated with a jury trial. Another key reform of the 2009 Act has perhaps therefore become all but redundant. When providing that the "court" could decide the amount of damages if the parties did not agree, s 23(1)(c) failed to specify if "court" meant a judge or a jury.[59] Aer Lingus pilot Captain Padraig Higgins argued that the 2009 Act would have specified that it was intended a judge would rule on damages if that was its intention and that "court" must mean a jury. The Supreme Court agreed with the interpretation put forward by Captain Higgins' counsel.[60]

[4.3.21] The Department of Justice, after reviewing a range of submissions on possible reforms of the offer of amends procedure, has recommended to government, similar to the recommendation by a Joint Oireachtas Committee in 2016, that s 23 be amended to provide that the reference to the High Court (for the purposes of the assessment of damages under s 23(1)(c)) means a judge sitting without a jury. This recommendation will be moot, however, if the recommendation to abolish juries altogether is accepted. Another recommendation is for the 2009 Act to provide that the plaintiff must prove that the defendant acted recklessly as regards the defamatory publication to defeat the offer of amends as a defence.

---

56 [2020] IECA 157, [2016] IECA 322.

57 [2018] IESC 29.

58 The benefit for a defendant in submitting an offer to make amends in a situation whereby the damages cannot be agreed between the parties is that it empowers judges to apply a discount to the damages they believe should ordinarily be awarded. Discounts of up to 50 percent have been applied in the UK where a similar process obtains. However, the uncertainty as to what juries may award in damages will most likely deter defendants from availing of the procedure.

59 Though in s 31(8), for the purposes of s 31, "court" means, in relation to a defamation action brought in the High Court, the jury, if the High Court is sitting with a jury. The same holds true for s 26(4) and 32(3).

60 See paras 47 and 48 of the judgment of Dunne J.

Other key provisions

[4.3.22] Section 28 provides for a novel relief in the form of a declaratory order from the Circuit Court. This order will state that the statement was false and defamatory of the applicant.[61] Damages are of course also a remedy, as set out in s 31 and a correction order can be made by the courts, pursuant to s 30, and a prohibitory order pursuant to s 33 as mentioned below. Section 29 allows a defendant to pay a sum of money into court in satisfaction of the defamation action.

[4.3.23] Section 32 allows a court to order the defendant to pay aggravated and punitive damages where defendants have conducted their defence in a manner that aggravated the injury caused to the plaintiff's reputation by the defamatory statement, for instance, on account of the delay by the defendant in accepting responsibility for its conduct and in making an offer of amends. Binchy J for the Court of Appeal in *Higgins* considered that the sum of €15,000 properly reflected the conduct of the appellant between the publication of the defamatory statements and the making of the offer of amends. This overturned an award of €130,000 in respect of aggravated damages awarded by a jury after a seven-day High Court hearing in November 2019 (with Barton J presiding). In *Kinsella* (see fn 34 and [4.5.01]), the plaintiff had been awarded compensatory damages of €9 million and a further €1 million in aggravated damages in the High Court. The aggravated damages award was set aside in its entirety by the Court of Appeal in 2019. In *Higgins* (2022), the Supreme Court as noted above held that any inadequacy in the offer of amends should be dealt with via the discount percentage, not aggravated damages.

Injunctions to prohibit publication

[4.3.24] Courts are empowered to make an order prohibiting the publication of a defamatory statement[62] as seen in the High Court case of *Philpott v Irish Examiner Ltd* discussed from [33.4.03] in Chapter 33, the first written judgment considering the test for an injunction under the 2009 Act. Upon application of the plaintiff under s 33 of the 2009 Act,[63] the court may make an order prohibiting the publication or further publication of the statement in respect of which the application was made if in its opinion the statement is defamatory and the defendant has no defence to the action that is reasonably likely to succeed[64]

---

61 This is a swift device for persons who are not interested in compensation and who are solely concerned with remediation of their reputation. Plaintiffs who decide to pursue an application for a declaratory order will not be entitled to bring any other proceedings arising out of the offending statement.

62 Section 33 of the 2009 Act.

63 It was confirmed by Allen J in *Gilroy v O'Leary* [2019] IEHC 52 that the test in s 33 is the same test that is applicable to interim, interlocutory and permanent orders, concluding that it is the same as that which applied before the 2009 Act in relation to equitable injunctive relief generally.

64 As recently considered in *Lidl v Irish Farmers Association* [2021] IEHC 381. In *Muwema*

(this latter requirement may be reviewed by the legislature in the future to the effect that a plaintiff need not prove that there is no defence to the action).

Malicious falsehood

[4.3.25] In respect of the tort of slander of title, slander of goods or other malicious falsehood (collectively termed "malicious falsehood" in s 42 of the 2009 Act), plaintiffs must prove the statement was untrue, was published maliciously and referred to the plaintiffs, their property or their office, profession, calling, trade or business. In such actions, plaintiffs must further prove special damage (actual loss or material harm) or that the publication of the statement was calculated to cause and was likely to cause financial loss to the plaintiffs in respect of their property or their office, profession, calling, trade or business. Product disparagement (also termed product defamation, trade libel or slander of goods) is discussed in Chapter 5.

RECENT DEVELOPMENTS

[4.4.01] The 2009 Act defines defamatory statements to include statements "published on the internet"[65] but since then events have been overtaken at lightning speed by the explosive power, and the potential to cause irreparable damage to one's reputation, of social media – a subject which may well also involve the equitable jurisdiction of the courts to grant injunctions to compel the immediate removal of a tweet or post on Facebook for instance (where damages may not serve as an adequate remedy) or using the s 33 mechanisms.

Norwich Pharmacal Order

[4.4.02] Applications to court for a *Norwich Pharmacal* order ('NPO') are discussed at the end of this chapter. However, for present purposes, in *McKeogh v John Doe*,[66] the High Court ordered certain social networking and video hosting websites to disclose the identities of users who had defamed the plaintiff through their websites, claiming that he appeared in a YouTube video featuring an individual evading a taxi fare and posting disparaging comments about him.

---

v Facebook [2016] IEHC 519, the court held that a plaintiff would almost never be able to obtain injunctive relief against a social media platform. However, the Court of Justice of the EU in *Eva Glawischnig-Piesczek v Facebook Ireland* (C-18/18) held that it was not inconsistent with art 15 of the E-Commerce Directive (prohibition against monitoring) to compel Facebook to prevent the future uploading of not only identical material, but also "equivalent content", so long as the injunction was carefully particularised, and framed so as not to require an "independent assessment" of the material each time, which is taken to refer to manual supervision by staff.

65 Section 2 of the 2009 Act.

66 [2012] IEHC 95, discussed in Gráinne Murphy, *Norwich Pharmacal Orders in Ireland: Case Law So Far* (2016), lkshields.ie. Available at: https://www.lkshields.ie/news-insights/publication/norwich-pharmacal-orders-in-ireland-case-law-so-far [Accessed 27 April 2018].

The plaintiff, who had proven he was out of the country when the taxi incident occurred, had been misidentified in the video, and was granted a NPO to identify the online commenters. He was also granted orders that all material be removed from the internet. This injunction was appealed to the Supreme Court by a number of the defendants due to its far-reaching implications. This case was ultimately settled on undisclosed terms.

Actions against Facebook and Twitter (now X) users

[4.4.03] Social media defamation marks a new era for the tort of defamation. A common myth is that liability rests with the social media platform for allowing the publication of defamatory content on such platform. However, recent decisions in the Irish courts have ruled that liability can in fact rest with the user who published the content. Five cases in this connection are worthy of comment.

[4.4.04] First, a Donegal couple, Patricia Barnett and her husband Paddy Murphy, were awarded more than €30,000 in damages in January 2017 against a neighbour who posted a number of disparaging remarks against Mrs Barnett on her private and business Facebook pages (referring to her as being overweight and commenting that her exercise regime was not working). Barnett claimed the posts had occasioned harm personally and professionally (some clients had not revisited her podiatry business) because of the embarrassment the postings had caused. In addition, Mr Murphy had been falsely accused in these Facebook posts of having an affair with another woman. The couple initiated a defamation action which was decided at Letterkenny Circuit Court. The defendant admitted the action and apologised for the unjust attack on the couple's reputation.

[4.4.05] Judge James O'Donoghue described the posts as "scurrilous and reckless" and was satisfied that both plaintiffs were wronged and their names seriously sullied. He awarded Barnett €20,000 in damages and Murphy a further €12,500 in damages and ordered that one of them receive their costs in the case. The court also issued a general warning that the posting of Facebook comments was sometimes a "highly dangerous activity".[67]

[4.4.06] The second case is from June 2017 in which a defendant who posted a defamatory piece on Facebook about the national director of the country's game shooting body was ordered to pay €75,000 in damages (with costs also to the plaintiff) at Monaghan Circuit Court. In awarding the maximum allowable Circuit Court damages,[68] Judge John O'Hagan said his order should "teach

---

[67] Stephen Maguire, *Couple awarded €30,000 for Facebook defamation by neighbour* (2017), irishtimes.com. Available at: https://www.irishtimes.com/news/crime-and-law/courts/circuit-court/couple-awarded-30-000-for-facebook-defamation-by-neighbour-1.2940354 [Accessed 4 September 2017].

[68] The jurisdiction of the Circuit Court in civil proceedings (other than personal injury claims where the upper limit is €60,000) was increased by s 14 of the Court and Civil Law (Miscellaneous Provisions) Act 2013 to €75,000. The monetary jurisdiction for

people posting messages on the social media site to be very careful". The plaintiff took the action in relation to a Facebook comment posted which suggested that he, as its national director, had caused the National Regional Game Council to "go broke". This resulted in a confrontation that led to his being suspended on full pay. It transpired there was no truth in the claim posted by the defendant as the organisation was solvent at the time, with over €7 million in funding.[69]

[4.4.07] Thirdly, former secretary of Roscommon County Darts was awarded €65,000 (plus his costs) in damages at Carrick-on-Shannon Circuit Court in November 2017 after being defamed on Facebook, with an allegation, effectively, that he had stolen funds in the 1980s and 1990s. The plaintiff explained to the court that he was not involved in Roscommon County Darts in the 1980s, and only became involved in the late 1990s.[70]

[4.4.08] Fourthly, the HSE settled a case paying €40,000 to the mother of a child in foster care who claimed she was defamed when the foster carers posted on Facebook about the care of the boy by the mother.

[4.4.09] Lastly, in the Northern Ireland case of *Foster v Jessen*,[71] anonymous tweets were written in late 2019 alleging that then First Minister for Northern Ireland, Arlene Foster, had been discovered having an affair with one of her Close Protection Officers and that her marriage had broken down. On the evening of 23 December, the defendant, Christian Jessen, doctor and presenter of Channel 4's *Embarrassing Bodies* posted the following tweet:

> Rumours are bouncing around that the DUP's Arlene Foster has been busted having an affair. Isn't she the 'sanctity of marriage' preaching woman? It always comes to bite them in the arse in the end.

[4.4.10] The defendant had 311,000 followers on Twitter, and the post was retweeted 517 times and liked approximately 3,500 times. Solicitors for the plaintiff posted a message on Jessen's Twitter account the following day, demanding that the tweet be removed. Ultimately, it was not taken down until 7 January 2020. The court held that the duration of publication, the large numbers who became aware of the content of the defamatory statement and the significant number who republished it were important factors to take into account when determining the appropriate award.

---

defamation in the Circuit Court had previously been increased to €50,000 in 2009 by s 41 of the Act.

69 Patsy McArdle, *Man must pay €75k damages for Facebook 'defamation'* (2017), independent.ie. Available at: https://www.independent.ie/irish-news/man-must-pay-75k-damages-for-facebook-defamation-34808254.html [Accessed 4 September 2017].

70 Shane Phelan, *Hospital worker awarded €65k after being defamed on Facebook* (2017), independent.ie. Available at: https://www.independent.ie/irish-news/courts/hospital-worker-awarded-65k-after-being-defamed-on-facebook-36345960.html [Accessed 6 January 2018].

71 [2021] NIQB 56.

[4.4.11] In considering the proportionality of the award, the court compared it to the Northern Ireland equivalent of the Book of Quantum, which estimates the loss of an eye to be between £80,000 and £140,000, and amputation between £125,000 and £250,000. The court arrived at a sum of £125,000 plus costs.

Defamation tourism

[4.4.12] For a discussion on jurisdictional issues, the doctrine of *forum non conveniens* and the Brussels Recast Regulation, see para [10A.2.13], the Court of Justice of the EU decision in *eDate Advertising*[72] and the judgment of Heslin J in *Robbins v Buzzfeed UK Ltd.*[73] In late March 2023, acting Justice Minister Simon Harris signalled his intention to seek government approval to add provisions to new reform legislation to be published by year end to address defamation tourism where a plaintiff chooses to take the defamation case in a jurisdiction which awards the highest damages. There have been a number of these high-profile actions taken in Ireland in recent years where neither of the parties were resident in the state.

JURIES IN DEFAMATION ACTIONS

[4.5.01] Ireland is one of the sole remaining jurisdictions in which a jury determines defamation cases. One of the key recommendations of the Review Report is that juries be abolished such that a judge would both assess damages and rule on offer of amends hearings. The urgent need to address grossly disproportionate awards made by Irish juries[74] has already been addressed by the judiciary in recent years in overturning jury awards and substituting their own more reasonable sums (when compared to serious personal injury awards). It is noteworthy to ponder that if the ECtHR was signalling in *Leech* that unpredictably high damages have a "chilling effect," and require the most careful scrutiny and very strong justification, what might the same court's view have been on the *Kinsella* case where the award was €10 million (€9 million in compensatory damages and €1 million in aggravated damages)?[75] This (since

---

72 *eDate Advertising GmbH and Others v X and Société MGN Ltd* (joined cases C-509/09 and C-161/10, EU:C:2011:685).

73 [2021] IEHC 433. The court rejected arguments that jurisdiction based on the *eDate* decision requires that content must have been accessed, finding that the material must only be accessible within the territory of the member state.

74 In England and Wales, a cap has been placed on damages in defamation proceedings. If juries are not abolished in this jurisdiction, such a measure if introduced here would ensure that jury awards were within acceptable ranges.

75 This sum was awarded in November 2010 in *Kinsella v Kenmare Resources Plc* (unreported, High Court, de Valera J, 17 November 2010) involving a press release by a company that defamed a former vice-chairman and comments made that he had sleepwalked while on a business trip to Mozambique and during which trip he had woken a female secretary three times in one night, each time while wearing no clothes. The sum was reduced in 2019 by the Court of Appeal to €250,000 ([2019] IECA 54).

overturned) trial court award of €10 million was multiples of the previous record amount that was granted by the High Court jury in *Leech*.[76]

[4.5.02] Further, the Supreme Court signalled in its 2022 *Higgins* judgment that awards should generally not exceed €200,000. When taken with the possibility of juries being abolished from the defamation law system altogether, this would positively impact on heretofore high awards and trial costs. Where legal principles must be explained to jurors and directions or guidance provided by the trial judge by way of judge's charge, this inevitably leads to a longer trial than would arise in the case of an experienced judge hearing and determining the case alone.

[4.5.03] The *Higgins* High Court trial before Barton J was unique, being the first time that a jury was provided with details of damages awarded in other cases with a view to guiding the jury on the amount of damages it should award.[77] The jury was informed about landmark awards by the Court of Appeal and Supreme Court and the reasoning for them. Jurors were also instructed about the kind of damages awarded by judges in catastrophic personal injuries actions. Although rightly cautioned by the judge that no two defamation cases are the same, it was acknowledged that the jury could have regard to these other awards in deciding how much to award Captain Higgins. Despite its best efforts, the jury's award of €387,000 was in the mind of Binchy J delivering the Court of Appeal's judgment nonetheless "so unreasonable as to be disproportionate to the injury sustained" (the Supreme Court later increased his award of €76,500 to just over €200,000). The guidance the jury was provided with in relation to other awards, a reform intended by the 2009 Act to prevent such disproportionate awards, clearly did not succeed in its objective.

[4.5.04] It is worth restating Binchy J's summary of events which transpired in the High Court thus:

> The jury was provided with information about damages awarded in previous cases of defamation, as well as the maximum level of general damages in personal injury cases. This was the first case in which a jury was provided with such information… The jury was then informed as to the amount of the awards initially made in the cases of Leech (€1.87m) and Christie (€200,000) and the subsequent reduction of those awards on appeal (to €1.2m in Leech and €60,000 in Christie (before application of the discount)). The jury was also informed about the maximum amount payable for general damages in catastrophic injury cases (€500,000), although in his charge to the jury,

---

[76] Note however that the case was heard under the old defamation rules (and the current s 31 therefore did not apply) when the jury was only allowed general directions from the judge to quantify damages. As above, defamatory statements made after 1 January 2010 now come under the 2009 Act which provides for more detailed direction to the jury by the judge on the quantum of awards. It is likely that the absence of such guidance in this case contributed to the disproportionate award made at first instance.

[77] In spite of the provisions of the 2009 Act in s 31(2) which mandate that directions "shall" be given to the jury by a judge as to "the matter of damages" – such directions could have included comparisons with other awards/damages/injuries.

> the trial judge pointed out that this was increased to €700,000 in one case. Counsel for the appellant explained to the jury in some detail the facts of the Christie case and the reasons for the reduction of the award in that case. Counsel for the respondent explained to the jury the difficulties of comparing one case of defamation with another and in his charge to the jury, the trial judge did likewise. The trial judge also emphasised to the jury the need to be fair to both parties and to arrive at an award that was proportionate in all of the circumstances.[78]

RECENT CASE LAW ON DAMAGES

[4.6.01] In light of recent judicial decisions, the truly exceptional jury awards of the past can now be viewed as being of historical interest only. The cases of *Kinsella* (jury award of €10 million, reduced on appeal) and the 16-year *McDonagh* saga[79] (jury award of €900,000, reduced on appeal) remain important however given the vast reductions in the jury awards on appeal by the Court of Appeal and the Supreme Court.

[4.6.02] In *Christie,* the defamation consisted of a nine-second clip of television footage which mistakenly showed the solicitor for the defendant in a serious criminal trial rather than (as had been intended) the accused himself. In the High Court,[80] the trial judge (who for this purpose sat without a jury), O'Malley J, assessed the starting point of damages as €200,000. She nevertheless thought that it was appropriate to allow a discount in the region of one third in the light of the offer of amends and an apology. She accordingly awarded Mr Christie the sum of €140,000. TV3 appealed to the Court of Appeal arguing that the starting point of an award of €200,000 damages in a case of this kind was simply too high and that appropriate weight had not been given to the nature of the apology and the offer of amends. TV3 contended that the level of the discount should have been higher and suggested a figure of 50 percent. On the facts of the case, the appellate court agreed the appropriate starting point should have been €60,000.

[4.6.03] The Court of Appeal in *Kinsella* quoted[81] from its earlier decision in *Christie* and Hogan J's reasoning for holding that the €200,000 starting figure was too high where he had stated:

---

78 At para 89 of the judgment.

79 The *McDonagh* proceedings were settled just minutes before the Supreme Court was to deliver a majority judgment ([2017] IESC 46). This decision was to substitute the jury's €900,000 award for a figure as low as €75,000. The case concerned an action taken in the High Court in 2008 by Martin McDonagh, a member of the Traveller community, against a newspaper for branding him a "drug king". The unanimous decision of the Court of Appeal (*McDonagh v Sunday Newspapers Ltd* [2015] IECA 225) was to set aside the jury award. Hogan J said it was clear the jury verdict, so far as it concerned the drug dealing allegation, could not be allowed stand because, viewed objectively, the evidence overwhelmingly pointed to the conclusion that the respondent was indeed a drug dealer.

80 [2015] IEHC 694.

81 At para 256.

> ...None of this is to say that it was not a serious defamation, because it was. As I have already observed, the potential for confusion, distress and embarrassment was considerable and should not be minimised. It is rather to say that it was not a defamation of such a character as would merit a starting point in the region of €200,000 in terms of the assessment of damages. If that were indeed the starting point in a case of this kind, then, adapting the language of Henchy J. in *Barrett*,[82] the damages in respect of a deliberate, calculated accusation of serious wrongdoing by the plaintiff in which he had been mentioned by name would be 'astronomically high.'
>
> For my part, taking account all relevant factors–a once-off nine second broadcast, the fact that the plaintiff was not named, the very limited range of viewers who might think that the news item referred to Mr Christie, the absence of any animus towards the plaintiff, coupled with the fact that it was plainly a case of mistaken identity–I consider that these mitigate the otherwise very serious nature of the defamation. In the light of these factors, therefore, it is sufficient to state that this is not a defamation which would warrant a starting point in damages of €200,000 identified by the trial judge and that in these circumstances a starting point of €60,000 is appropriate and proportionate.

[4.6.04] The Court of Appeal in *Kinsella* signalled endorsement of the starting point figures used by Hogan J for the Court of Appeal in *Christie*.[83] In addition, in *Speedie*,[84] the Court of Appeal had rejected the argument that an award of €85,000 was inadequate to compensate the plaintiff in respect of a defamatory article which had alleged that he assorted with known criminals.

[4.6.05] Of course every case is different and must be determined on its own merits as evidenced in the *Diop*[85] *ruling* wherein Barr J awarded a black man a nominal €500 in damages and legal costs on appeal to the High Court over a "momentary" incident of defamation when a security guard on a Luas instructed him to leave the tram following incidents with 12 other black youths without tickets.

[4.6.06] Elsewhere, *The Sunday World* newspaper was ordered to pay compensatory, aggravated and punitive damages totalling €310,000 (which included €50,000 for breach of the plaintiff's constitutional right to privacy) to a former GAA footballer whom it "grossly defamed" (*per* O'Connor J sitting without a jury in the High Court).[86] The Court of Appeal (Peart J) upheld this level of damages in light of the "serious breach of his constitutional right of privacy" with €30,000 attributable to punitive damages, €30,000 for exemplary damages, and recalibrating the remainder of the High Court award to €200,000

---

82 Referring to *Barrett v Independent Newspapers* [1986] I.R. 13.
83 *Christie v TV3 Television Networks Ltd* [2017] IECA 128.
84 *Speedie v Sunday Newspapers Ltd* [2017] IECA 15.
85 *Diop v Transdev Dublin Light Rail* [2019] IEHC 849.
86 *Nolan v Sunday Newspapers Ltd* [2017] IEHC 367.

for general damages for defamation, and €50,000 for breach of the plaintiff's Constitutional right to privacy.[87]

[4.6.07] Meanwhile, solicitor Gerald Kean[88] was awarded €160,000 in damages and costs relating to an *Irish Daily Star* article concerning a visit by members of the Criminal Assets Bureau to his office.

Application of a discount for offer to make amends

[4.6.08] On 8 November 2016, the High Court gave a decision on two connected cases.[89] The plaintiffs had sued for defamation arising out of two articles in the *Donegal Times* newspaper. The defendants had made offers to make amends and ultimately the plaintiffs had refused the apologies and damages offered as part of the process.

[4.6.09] McDermott J, having regard to the High Court decision in *Christie* discounted the damages that he held were due to the plaintiffs by 20 percent and not (in the region of) the one third allowed in the *Christie* case.[90] The court reduced the discount on account of what it considered to be the lateness and insufficiency of the apology offered by the defendants. In addition, the court took a dim view of two articles published by the defendants after the offers to make amends had been made and which "rehashed" the earlier defamatory articles on foot of which the plaintiffs had sued.[91] As regards the subsequent articles, while the court rejected the plaintiffs' argument that these two articles could be a basis for seeking aggravated damages, given the manner in which the cases had been pleaded, it felt that it was more appropriate that the articles be taken into account in terms of the discount to be afforded to the defendants.

PARODY AND SATIRE

[4.7.01] Over the years, US courts at least have made it abundantly clear that parody and satire are not defamatory. That does not universally mean all satirists

---

87 *Nolan v Sunday Newspapers Ltd* [2019] IECA 141.

88 *Kean v Independent Star Ltd* [2018] IEHC 206.

89 *Ward v The Donegal Times Ltd* [2016] IEHC 711.

90 The *Christie* decision was subsequently overturned whereby the Court of Appeal reduced the starting figure of €200,000 to €60,000 and increased the level of discount from one third to 40 percent. Accordingly, it substituted a figure of €36,000 for the award of €140,000 made by the High Court as the sum to be paid to Mr Christie by way of damages for the inadvertent but defamatory news report.

91 As an aside, while the newspaper in question had a limited circulation of approximately 5,000 copies, the court noted that, in a small rural area, a newspaper can have a very large effect on local views and the regard neighbours will have for each other. While the breadth of publication, that is, circulation in this instance, was relevant to the amount of damages to be awarded, it seemed that the court equated the saturation effect of a local newspaper such as the *Donegal Times* in a small area with the impact that a national newspaper might have over a much broader area.

and comics emerge victorious from defamation lawsuits in America. It depends entirely on the facts but because parody and satire are seen as opinion, they are viewed in US jurisprudence as being non-defamatory. Irish and UK law is not as liberal (but see [10A.7.19] where in respect of a libel action by Sir Elton John the High Court essentially stated that irony and teasing do not amount to defamation). Before assessing the situation in this jurisdiction (with no corpus of authorities yet on the topic) whereby satire is not a ground of defence in a defamation claim, let us turn first to the seminal US Supreme Court ruling on the topic.

The Hustler magazine case

[4.7.02] The highly publicised 1988 US Supreme Court decision in *Hustler Magazine Inc v Falwell*[92] is perhaps best known for the portrayal thereof in the 1996 biographical drama film *The People vs. Larry Flynt* starring Woody Harrelson as physically disabled self-made millionaire and editor Larry Flynt,[93] alongside Courtney Love, with Edward Norton as Flynt's lawyer.

[4.7.03] This landmark ruling held, reversing the Fourth Circuit Court of Appeals, that parodies of public figures which could not reasonably be taken as true are protected against civil liability by the First (and Fourteenth) Amendment to the US Constitution (the right to free speech), even if intended to cause emotional distress. This would then prohibit public figures from recovering damages for the tort of intentional infliction of emotional distress if the emotional distress was caused by a caricature, parody or satire of the public figure which a reasonable person would not have interpreted as factual.

[4.7.04] The case bolstered the entertainment sector immensely and bestowed the strongest form of legal protection, in the form of a judgment from the highest court in the land, to those who depend on comedy, satire and parody for their livelihoods. Had the case been decided the other way, it would have stifled the outrageousness of comedy such as that contained in *South Park*, explosive stand-up comedy, comedic film and no-holds-barred talk shows. On this side of the Atlantic, however, while satire and parody have long been a feature of Irish entertainment from *Scrap Saturday*, *The Savage Eye* and *The Mario Rosenstock Show* to *Irish Pictorial Weekly* and *Callan's Kicks*, an article from the satire news website *Waterford Whispers News* involving media tycoon Denis O'Brien (discussed below) sounds an ominous warning bell as regards Irish defamation law. A second hurdle producers and broadcasters sometimes face is to ward off viewer complaints to the Media Commission as discussed in Chapter 31.

---

[92] 485 U.S. 46.

[93] Flynt had spent much of his life in a wheelchair after being shot by a white supremacist serial killer who allegedly disliked some of the inter-racial nature of the pornography that he published.

[4.7.05] The court's unanimous 8-0 decision[94] in *Hustler* ruled (Rehnquist CJ delivering judgment)[95] in favour of the defendant/appellant magazine, holding that a parody advertisement published in the magazine depicting televangelist and political commentator, Reverend Jerry Falwell, a nationally known minister and charismatic Christian televangelist, as an incestuous drunk, was protected speech since Falwell was a public figure and the parody could not have been reasonably considered believable.[96] Therefore, the court held that the emotional distress inflicted on the plaintiff by the advertisement was not a sufficient reason to deny the First Amendment protection to speech which was critical of public officials and public figures.

[4.7.06] Generally, a successful defamation case is notoriously difficult to achieve in the US because of the Constitutional protection of freedom of speech guaranteed by the First Amendment. If the defendant can show an absence of malice, the plaintiff's case will fail.[97] In the lower courts, arguments on behalf of Falwell convinced the judge and jury that, because of the nature of the satire used in *Hustler*, the publisher had taken a deliberate step to cause him both personal distress and harm – it showed malice in the publication of the satire. However, the Supreme Court stated that Falwell was a public figure and relied on his public characteristics, particularly his religious outlook, to further his business and, as such, was open to satire and ridicule, which should be protected by the Constitutional guarantee afforded to freedom of speech irrespective of intention

---

94 Justice Anthony Kennedy took no part in the consideration or decision.

95 With White J filing an opinion concurring in the judgment of the other seven justices.

96 The 1983 advertisement in *Hustler* was a parody of a Campari advertisement, featuring a mock interview with Falwell in which he admits that his "first time" was incest with his mother in an outhouse while intoxicated. The parody portrayed the respondent and his mother as drunk and immoral, and suggested that the respondent was a hypocrite who preached only when he was inebriated. In small print at the bottom of the page, the advertisement contained the disclaimer "ad parody — not to be taken seriously". The magazine's table of contents also listed the advertisement as "Fiction; Ad and Personality Parody". Falwell sued for $45 million, alleging invasion of privacy, libel and intentional infliction of emotional distress. A jury rejected the invasion of privacy and libel claims, holding that the parody could not have reasonably been taken to describe true events, but ruled in the plaintiff's favour on the emotional distress claim and awarded damages of $200,000, representing $100,000 in compensatory damages, as well as $50,000 each in punitive damages from Flynt personally and *Hustler* magazine. This was upheld in the appellate court. Flynt then appealed to the Supreme Court, which unanimously held that the First Amendment prevents public figures from recovering damages for emotional distress caused by parodies.

97 *New York Times Co. v Sullivan*, 376 U.S. 254 (1964) was a landmark US Supreme Court case that established the actual malice standard, which has to be met before press reports about public officials can be considered to be libellous; and hence allowed free reporting of the civil rights campaigns in southern United States. It is one of the key decisions supporting the freedom of the press. The actual malice standard requires that the plaintiff in a defamation case, if that person is a public official or public figure, prove that the publisher of the statement in question knew that the statement was false or acted in reckless disregard of its truth or falsity. Because of the extremely high burden of proof on the plaintiff, and the difficulty of proving the defendant's knowledge and intentions, such claims by public figures rarely prevail.

and malice. *Hustler* had a right to say whatever it pleased, however distasteful and unpleasant, provided it was clearly satirical and concerned a public figure.

[4.7.07] The film *Borat* is an example of the satirical form of humour in a cutting cultural exposition and commentary. Some of the numerous lawsuits instituted against the producers are discussed later in this book, but for other reasons (claims that releases from contributors were obtained by fraud and false pretence).

The South Park disclaimer

[4.7.08] Incidentally, the iconic and jocular disclaimer in the opening slates (before the title sequence) of *South Park* reads:

> ALL CHARACTERS AND EVENTS IN THIS SHOW—EVEN THOSE BASED ON REAL PEOPLE—ARE ENTIRELY FICTIONAL. ALL CELEBRITY VOICES ARE IMPERSONATED.....POORLY. THE FOLLOWING PROGRAM CONTAINS COARSE LANGUAGE AND DUE TO ITS CONTENT IT SHOULD NOT BE VIEWED BY ANYONE

which, in itself, of course is satirical and is thereby ridiculing disclaimers, censorship and American 'wholesomeness'. This is widely seen as a subversion and derision of all other disclaimers. One commentator, Stephen P. Pajović,[98] asserts the position as being, "Its prime intention coincides with the one the entire series has: parody. In this case, it is the legal disclaimer that is being lampooned". Interestingly, Hulu, the US subscription video-on-demand service, has placed its own disclaimer before *South Park's* disclaimer thus, "The following is intended only for mature audiences. Viewer discretion advised".

No distinction between satire and defamation in Ireland

[4.7.09] Thus, satire, such as the use of irony, sarcasm, ridicule and so forth, in exposing, denouncing or deriding vice and folly, for example, is a defence in the US for many actions of defamation. This is not so in Ireland. The 1991 Law Reform Commission report[99] noted there should not be a distinction between a satirical comment and any other defamatory comment solely on the basis that its object is to subject the target to derision or ridicule (rather than hatred or contempt). The Commission concluded by stating it accordingly recommended that there should be no special provision in relation to such material.

[4.7.10] The courts in the US draw a distinction between satire and defamation. There is also a legal defence of satire in New Zealand and Australia. In a Trinity

---

98 Stephen P. Pajović, *The (re)shaping of South Park's humor through literacy reference* (2014) in *Popular culture in 20th century Anglophone literature*, Faculty of Philosophy, University of Novi Sad, Serbia at pp 427-449.

99 *Report on The Civil Law of Defamation* (LRC CP 8-1991).

College Law Review article[100] on the issue, reference is made to one US lawyer's having described the difference as "defamation is a malicious lie passed off as truth; satire is a humorous skewering of a cultural or political event".[101] The latter author commences the piece as follows:

> With cases involving outrageous parody and satire, the path of least resistance has been to find the 'speech' non-defamatory as a matter of law. The rationale used to justify this conclusion is that no reasonable reader could understand the publication as an assertion of fact. The presumption is that satire so outrageous as to preclude belief is incapable of harming reputation.

Waterford Whispers News and Denis O'Brien

[4.7.11] In 2015, the Leinster-based satirical website, *Waterford Whispers News*, removed an article relating to businessman Denis O'Brien from its site, following a cease and desist letter and threat of legal action from solicitors representing him. Failure to comply, the letter warned, would lead them to "take all necessary steps to vindicate our client's good name and reputation".[102] The website newsroom wrote a piece set in a parallel universe in which the DPP prosecutes Denis O'Brien for bribing politicians. The article was then reposted by *Broadsheet.ie*. The story focused on the awarding of the state's second mobile phone licence to Mr O'Brien and the findings of the Moriarty Tribunal in relation to his dealings with the then Minister for Communications, Michael Lowry. The satirical article also featured an edited image of Mr O'Brien, portraying him as a convicted criminal. Ultimately, legal action was averted.

[4.7.12] Colm Williamston, editor of *Waterford Whispers News*, tweeted an image of a letter received from Meagher Solicitors, marked private and confidential, addressed to the website's publishers, Whispers Media Ltd. The letter called the "parallel universe" in which the article was set "a sham" and added the article was "a malicious and deliberate defamation of the most serious kind", and demanded it be removed from the website and all social media platforms within a tight timeframe.

[4.7.13] The net import, if one were to heed the potentially chilling upshot of this matter, is that there is no absolute right to freedom of speech in Ireland because citizens simultaneously enjoy a potent right to their good name under

---

100 Ross Malervy, *Satire in Irish law, and comparisons with other jurisdictions* (2018), *Trinity College Law Review* (Junior Editorial Board). Available at: http://trinitycollegelawreview.org/962-2/ [Accessed 2 March 2018].

101 Kelly/Warner Law, *Satire v. Defamation: A Legal Explanation* (2014), kellywarnerlaw.com. Available at: http://kellywarnerlaw.com/satire-v-defamation/ Kelly/Warner Law [Accessed 18 April 2018].

102 Colin Gleeson, *Waterford Whispers removes article after Denis O'Brien threat (2015), irishtimes.com*. Available at: https://www.irishtimes.com/news/ireland/irish-news/waterford-whispers-removes-article-after-denis-o-brien-threat-1.2309298 [Accessed 2 June 2019].

the Constitution. Sarah Kieran, solicitor of MediaLawyer Solicitors, spoke on RTÉ Radio One's *Morning Ireland*[103] in respect of the *Waterford Whispers* affair on 7 August 2015 outlining her belief that humour offers little defence in a defamation action:

> There is no such thing as an "only kidding" defence or that "I was messing". And the intention of the publisher, which is the person who publishes the piece, in this case, *Waterford Whispers*, it doesn't matter what their intention was, the law will automatically deem that they have to prove what they said was correct.

[4.7.14] As defamation is a tort of strict liability, the intention of the tortfeasor has traditionally been regarded as irrelevant. When asked by Rachael English, presenter, what sort of advice she might offer to a website, radio programme or newspaper columnist involved in satire, Ms Kieran replied, "Make sure that it's so surreal that it couldn't be true, be very incisive of what you say". This advice is echoed by RM/Warner Law where they suggest:

> The worst thing a satirist can do is not make their work outrageous enough. If a reasonable person could realistically construe a work as truthful, legal trouble will follow.[104]

[4.7.15] The above-cited Trinity College Law Review article submits in its conclusion that there should be a distinction drawn in law between satire and defamation arguing that there ought to be a more moderate approach than that taken in the US, wherein free speech has taken prevalence over the right of individuals to a good name and instead insisted on an approach where courts distinguish a person's "opinion" (protected under free speech) from "fantasy" designed to defame an individual.

NPOs AND DEFAMATION

[4.8.01] A NPO requires a respondent to disclose certain documents or information to the applicant, commonly used to identify the proper defendant to an action or to obtain information to plead a claim. *Norwich Pharmacal* relief is not generally available against a respondent who is likely to be a party to the potential proceedings. The respondent must, however, be either involved or "mixed up" in a wrongdoing, whether innocently or not. Being an injunction, a NPO is an equitable rather than common law remedy, and will be granted only where necessary in the interests of justice.

---

103 As reported in *No One is Beyond Satire* (2015), broadsheet.ie. Available at: https://www.broadsheet.ie/2015/08/07/no-one-is-beyond-satire/ [Accessed 20 April 2017].

104 RM Warner Law, *Satire v. Defamation: A Legal Explanation* (2014), kellywarnerlaw.com. Available at: https://kellywarnerlaw.com/satire-v-defamation [Accessed 15 August 2019].

[4.8.02] In *Norwich Pharmacal Co. v Commissioner of Customs and Excise*,[105] Lord Reid summarised the principle as follows:

> ...if through no fault of his own a person gets mixed up in the tortious acts of others so as to facilitate their wrong-doing he may incur no personal liability but he comes under a duty to assist the person who has been wronged by giving him full information and disclosing the identity of the wrong doers. I do not think that it matters whether he became so mixed up by voluntary action on his part or because it was his duty to do what he did. It may be that if this causes him expense the person seeking the information ought to reimburse him. But justice requires that he should cooperate in righting the wrong if he unwittingly facilitated its perpetration.

[4.8.03] The jurisdiction to grant NPOs was recognised by the Irish Supreme Court in *Megaleasing UK Ltd v Barrett*,[106] where the court cautioned that NPOs must be sparingly used as they are plainly open to abuse which the courts must be alert to prevent. At first instance, the High Court alone has jurisdiction to grant a NPO in this jurisdiction, thus precluding proceedings being litigated at more affordable cost in the District Court and Circuit Court.

Recent case law

[4.8.04] Social media routinely brings complications relating to identification. Individuals can post comments or content anonymously or under a pseudonym. However, for aggrieved parties to apply for relief in court, they must be able to identify the person making the impugned, offending or defamatory comment. The Irish courts have shown willingness in a number of cases to grant the necessary NPO against social media organisations requiring them to disclose details of the poster.[107] This type of application is therefore unusual in that the plaintiff may issue proceedings where the only relief sought is discovery of the identity of the wrongdoer, and there may be no cause of action against the defendant being asked to disclose this information.

[4.8.05] Matters took a further twist on 19 May 2021 when the High Court (Simons J) confirmed that it proposed to make a preliminary reference to the Court of Justice of the EU ('CJEU'), seeking clarity on the circumstances in which it can grant a NPO. This was in the context of proceedings issued by the Board of Management of Salesian Secondary College, Limerick against Facebook Ireland seeking a disclosure order to compel Facebook to identify the individual(s) behind an Instagram account, "Pallaskenrymemes". The account,

---

105 [1974] AC 133.

106 [1993] ILRM 497.

107 E.g. in *Petroceltic International plc v Aut O Mattic A8C Ireland Ltd* (unreported, High Court, Baker J, 20 August 2015, amended 8 September 2015). Petroceltic also secured an order requiring that the allegedly defamatory blog be removed in its entirety, including deletion of its URL, and that any data relating to the blogger and the blog be preserved for six months.

which was active between 14 and 24 October 2019, published a number of memes relating to individuals and events at the school, content which the court described as "coarse and vulgar". The disclosure order was sought by the school for the purpose of "dealing with" the individual(s) behind the account by way of "disciplinary or pastoral response". However, the school did not intend to bring any legal proceedings against those behind the account.

[4.8.06] The High Court proposed to refer a number of questions to the CJEU, including whether there is an implied right under the Charter of Fundamental Rights of the EU to post anonymously on the internet (subject to any countervailing objective of public interest); to determine what is the threshold to be met under the GDPR/the above charter before a social media platform can be compelled to disclose information about a user, and whether it is necessary for a third party seeking disclosure to establish a "strong prima facie case" of tortious wrongdoing and an intention to pursue legal proceedings; and further whether it is necessary for a national court to attempt to put the anonymous user on notice of an application for a disclosure order.

[4.8.07] Simons J noted that the application presented significant legal issues in respect of privacy, data protection and freedom of expression and indicated that there is a strong argument that persons using a social media platform anonymously have an expectation that their identity will not be disclosed without their consent (subject to any countervailing public interest in the disclosure of their identity, for example in the context of defamation proceedings). In addition, the judge noted that the school was inviting the court to depart from the longstanding requirement that an applicant seeking a disclosure order must have an intention to pursue legal proceedings for the alleged tortious wrongdoing. He said that the position advanced by the school would represent a significant departure from the existing case law of the Irish courts.

[4.8.08] In the 2015 case of *Walsh v Twitter International Company*,[108] the plaintiff, a whistleblower, took part in RTÉ's *Prime Time*, a leading current affairs television programme. He alleged that he was subsequently defamed by a tweet on social media and sought an order from the High Court directing that Twitter provide information which would assist in identifying the anonymous Twitter user and author of the allegedly defamatory tweet. Mac Eochaidh J granted the NPO sought following which the defendant provided the Twitter user's email address to the plaintiff.

[4.8.09] In February 2017, in the case of *Muwema v Facebook Ireland Ltd*,[109] the High Court refused (upheld on appeal)[110] to grant a NPO against Facebook requiring disclosure of the identity and location of an anonymous third party

---

[108] Unreported, High Court, Mac Eochaidh J, 2 October 2015.

[109] [2017] IEHC 69.

[110] [2018] IECA 104

('TVO') operating a Facebook page containing defamatory content. Binchy J found that if Facebook disclosed such information it would endanger the life of the third party (potential subjection to torture, cruel or inhumane treatment in Uganda). The court held that the right to a good name must give way to the right to life and bodily integrity in the event of a conflict. Further, Facebook had the means to communicate with TVO and to notify forthwith that unless the offending postings were removed within 14 days, the plaintiff would be entitled to renew his application for Norwich Pharmacal relief which would be granted.

Calls for reform

[4.8.10] The NPO application is a route not many would wish to traverse. William Fry Solicitors, in their submissions[111] to the Department of Justice[112] on possible reform of the Act, considered that having to seek this order in the age of social media was draconian in that it is prohibitively costly for an injured plaintiff, excessively slow and the damage will have been caused by the time the orders are obtained and enforced. Victims of defamation simply do not have the luxury of time if they wish to limit the number of persons who can view an offending post on social media. To adequately address this issue, the law firm suggested some form of amendment to the 2009 Act to facilitate a rapid take-down solution to protect the good name and reputation of social media users in Ireland rather than employing the only real equity law mechanism available, that of the injunction.

[4.8.11] Interestingly, in *EMI Records (Ireland) Ltd v UPC Communications Ireland Ltd*,[113] Charleton J commented that evidence shows that the process of obtaining a NPO is burdensome and ultimately futile (as a potential solution to the problem of internet piracy rather than defamation) and noted the time, trouble and expense involved in pursuit of this remedy. He suggested that NPOs could become simple and inexpensive if appropriate legislative intervention occurred, placing such an obligation (the obligation to address the problem of internet piracy) by law on the internet service providers by inexpensive application to the District Court.

[4.8.12] The Review Report calls for a statutory notice of complaint process to render it easier, quicker and cheaper to notify an online publisher (including intermediary platforms) of defamatory content and request its takedown, or request identification of the poster; and define a timeframe for the required expeditious removal of defamatory content. It further proposes the provision of a statutory power to the Circuit Court (as well as the High Court) to grant a

---

111 Fiona Barry and Mary Cooney, *Review of the Defamation Act 2009* (Submission of William Fry) (2016), justice.ie. Available at: http://www.justice.ie/en/JELR/William_Fry.pdf/Files/William_Fry.pdf [Accessed 26 April 2018].

112 Section 5 of the 2009 Act called for review of the Act within a five-year period of its commencement.

113 [2010] IEHC 377.

NPO directing an intermediary services provider to disclose the identity of an anonymous poster of defamatory material.

Chapter 5

Defamation of a Body Corporate and Product/Brand Disparagement

INTRODUCTION

[5.1.01] The statutory and common law torts of corporate defamation, commercial disparagement, trade libel, malicious falsehood or slander of goods relate to any statement, including via broadcasts, about a company, its services and products, or other trading entity, that is false and likely to adversely affect its reputation, profits, brand and business goodwill.

[5.1.02] Currently, the same legislative provisions for defamation apply to companies and other corporate entities as to individuals such that, with very limited exception, intention of the defendant is irrelevant.[1] As set out in the Defamation Act 2009 ('the 2009 Act'), the tort is actionable *per se* with no proof of actual financial loss required. However, in its defamation law review report published in March 2022 as discussed throughout the previous chapter, the Department of Justice has signalled that, to align with other common law jurisdictions, reform of s 12 of the 2009 Act might be considered such that a body corporate may not sue for defamation of its reputation unless (with possible exemptions from the requirement for smaller entities)[2] it first shows that the statement has caused or is likely to cause serious harm.[3] At present, a company may sue for defamation irrespective of whether it has sustained any financial loss.

[5.1.03] Atlanta, Georgia-based entertainment law attorney, Lee Morin[4] cites the

---

1 Except in the case of s 42 of the Defamation Act 2009 (an untrue statement published maliciously and calculated to cause and is likely to cause financial loss to the plaintiff or the plaintiff's property, office, profession, calling, trade or business), and otherwise, where a defendant has acted with malice, this conduct will defeat the s 19 defence of qualified privilege.

2 The rationale here is that in the case of a small entity (such as a SME), a financial loss may result in its going out of business before it is in a position to prove such loss in order to take a defamation action.

3 In the case of a body that trades for profit, this would mean serious, direct financial loss (e.g. a financial loss as a result of individuals or bodies deciding not to trade or associate themselves with it).

4 Lee Moran, *Got Consent? Legal Issues in Film, Pt. 2: The Script* (2015), morinentlaw.com.

decision in *Films of Distinction*[5] and proceedings[6] involving the movie *The Dark Knight Rises* as case law examples of commercial disparagement from television and film. In the former, the owner of *The Crime Channel* sued producers of *Relative Fear* on the basis that unauthorised use of its trademark led viewers to believe that those who watch its network become murderers. In the latter case, a computer software manufacturer of a product called Clean Slate brought suit against Warner Brothers for its portrayal in the Batman movie. In reality, the product protects public access to computers but the film depicted its usage by criminals to erase any trace of criminal activity.

[5.1.04] Product disparagement thus includes negative statements about a product or service, false comparisons of competing consumer products or services, and statements or depictions harming the reputation of a company. Danny Boyle's *Slumdog Millionaire*, for instance, was forced to cut scenes showing a Mercedes Benz filmed in a Mumbai slum because of the luxury car manufacturer's disquiet with such an image, according to the film's director. Boyle stated in an interview[7] that a scene wherein a Mercedes pulls up in a Mumbai ghetto, carrying a slumlord, and shots featuring Coca-Cola products had to be discarded as both corporations seemingly wished to disassociate their products from the urban Indian locations shown, fearing their brands would be tarnished. Where the Mercedes brand is used, the logo has been removed. Another example might be where a branded product features in a movie but is depicted as being defective or malfunctioning, such as in the case of a bus breaking down or a smartphone operating poorly.

[5.1.05] Film and television producers (as well as music video and commercials video makers) should carry out the necessary clearance procedures and ensure, if applicable, that a prop agreement is in place. This will, most likely, involve advance script clearance (and shooting script adjustment if required) by the company whose brand, business or premises is being filmed to ensure no defamation will occur, and more importantly, that the relevant release to be signed contains a waiver as to the bringing of claims in this connection. It is also an issue in which the project's legal advisors, financiers, insurers and distributors will take a keen interest.

[5.1.06] Moreover, filmmakers need to judiciously manage scenes involving violence, sex, anti-social behaviour and criminality to ensure that a shot or sequence does not defame any affected business. This is likely best achieved through script clearance. For example, the script might read "never drink in

---

Available at: http://morinentlaw.com/got-consent-legal-issues-film-pt-2-script/ [Accessed 22 April 2018].

5 *Films of Distinction Inc v Allegro Film Productions Inc*, 12 F. Supp. 2d 1068 (C.D. Cal. 1998).

6 *Fortres Grand Corp. v Warner Bros. Entertainment Inc*, 763 F.3d 696 (7th Cir. 2014).

7 Barbey Henderson, *Slumdog Millionaire censors out Merc in slum* (2008), hindustantimes.com. Available at: https://www.hindustantimes.com/india/slumdog-millionaire-censors-out-merc-in-slum/story-Cm4oxB96lvB6EuHqtY0jfM.html [Accessed 22 June 2017].

that bar – it's full of money launderers and crooks", with the relevant named (and real-life) business or private commercial property owner signing off on this scene and duly executing a location agreement or release, and/or requesting the art department to undertake the requisite set dressing (e.g. placing temporary fictional nameboard signs and logos to radically alter the look and feel of the premises and render it unidentifiable). As a last and least savoury resort, in the absence of a signed release, the premises can be altered in post-production using pixelation or image blurring techniques.

US CASE LAW – PRODUCT CRITIQUES

[5.2.01] Product and service disparagement also includes posting a comment on a website or making a statement via a blog, podcast or other publication (such as a radio advertisement) and therein associating a competitor's product with negative ideas or images; or an unfavourable (and untrue) review or critique of a product or service.

[5.2.02] *Bose Corp. v Consumers Union of United States Inc*[8] was a product disparagement case ultimately decided by the US Supreme Court. The court held, on a 6-3 vote, in favour of the defendant, the publisher of *Consumer Reports* magazine, ruling that proof of "actual malice" was necessary in product disparagement cases raising First Amendment issues as set out by the seminal 1963 case of *New York Times Co. v Sullivan* (see fn 97, Chapter 4). The court ruled that the First Circuit Court of Appeals had correctly concluded that Bose had not presented proof of actual malice. In Ireland, the malice element is only required as regards the tort of malicious falsehood (e.g. slander of goods) in s 42 of the 2009 Act but not as regards general defamation of a business in s 12 where a defamatory statement is actionable *per se* regardless of intent and irrespective of financial loss, and will further operate to defeat a s 19 qualified privilege defence. Producers therefore need to exercise caution if there is any potential exposure to a corporate defamation action.

[5.2.03] In 1970, *Consumer Reports* had published a review of an unusual loudspeaker system manufactured by Bose called the Bose 901. The review expressed scepticism of the system's quality and recommended that consumers delay purchase until they had investigated for themselves whether the loudspeaker system's unusual attributes would suit them. Bose objected to numerous statements in the article, including the sentences:

> Worse, individual instruments heard through the Bose system seemed to grow to gigantic proportions and tended to wander about the room. For instance, a violin appeared to be 10 feet (3.0 m) wide and a piano stretched from wall to wall.

---

[8] 466 U.S. 485 (1984).

[5.2.04] Bose demanded a retraction when it learned that *Consumer Reports* changed what the original reviewer wrote about the speakers in his pre-publication draft, which the magazine refused to do. Ultimately, however, the case was not decided in the petitioner's favour in the Supreme Court as malice was absent.

IRISH CASE LAW – PRODUCT DISPARAGEMENT GENERALLY

[5.3.01] In *Norbrook Laboratories Ltd*,[9] Kelly J set out the facts of the case stating that the first plaintiff developed and manufactured veterinary products, including one known as Life Aid Extra, while the second plaintiff marketed, distributed and sold veterinary products including Life Aid Extra. It was alleged that the defendant which was also engaged in the manufacture and sale of veterinary products, including one known as Lectade Plus, wrote to all members of the veterinary profession in Ireland in January 1994 in order to promote its product. The letter stated, *inter alia*, "Indeed a recently introduced competitor is seriously hypertonic thus running the risk of compounding the dehydration problem".

[5.3.02] The plaintiffs took umbrage to the letter in general but in particular the words referred to above, claiming that the reference was designed to and did in fact disparage the plaintiffs' product, Life Aid Extra. They further alleged that the words in question were false and were published maliciously or recklessly and that they were calculated to denigrate the plaintiffs' product and so to cause pecuniary damage to the plaintiffs. The plaintiffs went on to claim damages for slander of goods and defamation.

[5.3.03] The defendant maintained a bona fide belief and lack of malice on the part of the writer of the letter in suit and claimed qualified privilege. It specifically denied that the words complained of were understood to bear the meaning attributed to them by the plaintiffs, or any meaning defamatory of the plaintiffs. The defendant had been advised that it would be prudent to admit liability in respect of the allegation of slander of goods and in respect of certain of the allegations of defamation made by the plaintiffs, thus wishing to admit to certain of the innuendos and to make a lodgment in respect of them but to maintain its defence in respect of others.

[5.3.04] The court acceded to the defendant's application by directing that a payment into court by the defendant in respect of the plaintiffs' allegation of slander of goods, and in respect of some, but not all, of the plaintiffs' allegations of defamation, was a valid payment and in conformity with the provisions of Order 22 of the Rules of the Superior Courts,[10] provided that the notice of such

---

9 *Norbrook Laboratories Ltd and Norbrook Laboratories (Ireland) Ltd v Smithkline Beecham (Ireland) Ltd t/a Smithkline Beecham Animal Health* [1999] 2 IR 192.

10 SI No 15 of 1986 as amended *inter alia* by SI No 511 of 2009: Rules of the Superior Courts (Defamation) 2009.

lodgment specified the particular allegations in respect of which payment had been made and that the relevant admissions were made in the defence.

FILM EXAMPLES

[5.4.01] In respect of the film *Flight* starring Denzel Washington as a brave and skilful but alcoholic pilot, Budweiser brewer Anheuser-Busch was reportedly[11] unimpressed with the portrayal of its beer brand in the movie. *Deadline Hollywood*, an authoritative website source for breaking news in the entertainment industry, reported in November 2012 that the company had asked Paramount and the production company Image Movers to obscure all images of its flagship beer. In the drama, Denzel Washington plays an airline pilot accused of drinking before captaining a plane. It includes scenes showing Washington's character consuming alcoholic beverages, including Budweiser and assorted vodka brands. Budweiser vice president Robert McCarthy wrote a letter stating that Anheuser-Busch had no knowledge of the use or depiction of Budweiser before or during the film's production and was not contacted by the studio adding:

> We would never condone the misuse of our products, and have a long history of promoting responsible drinking and preventing drunk driving. It is disappointing that Image Movers, the production company, and Paramount chose to use one of our brands in this manner...We have asked the studio to obscure the Budweiser trademark in current digital copies of the movie and on all subsequent adaptations of the film, including DVD, On Demand, streaming and additional prints not yet distributed to theatres.

[5.4.02] KEO, a church-backed[12] beverage company from Cyprus, made the news in 2010 when it was reported that the drinks group was contemplating legal action after one of its beer products appeared in an American pornography film. KEO, the Greek abbreviation for Cyprus Wine Company, is the largest and most popular beverage company in Cyprus, with a history dating back to 1927.[13] The film's graphic scenes reveal a man and a woman in a tavern briefly discussing the beer and its 'Greek' origin before having intercourse. One scene shows the actress pouring the beer into her co-star's mouth from a bottle clasped in her cleavage. Talks were held with the church representatives to discuss taking legal action to remove the scenes from the film.

---

11 Nancy Tartaglione, *Budweiser Disappointed By Brand's Portrayal In 'Flight'* (2012), deadline.com. Available at: http://deadline.com/2012/11/budweiser-unhappy-obscure-brand-portrayal-drinking-flight-366738/ [Accessed 7 October 2017].

12 The Orthodox Church of Cyprus reportedly owns 20 percent of the company that produces the highly popular beer.

13 See *National Post* (Canada), *Church-backed company mulls lawsuit after beer used in porn movie* (2010), nationalpost.com. Available at: http://nationalpost.com/news/church-backed-company-mulls-lawsuit-after-beer-used-in-porn [Accessed 22 April 2018].

THE CURRENT[14] STATUTORY POSITION IN IRELAND

[5.5.01] Product disparagement can be a false statement about a product that causes harm to the manufacturer of such product by, for instance, comparing in a false or misleading manner one product or service to a competitor's in an advertisement. When that comparison is false or misleading, victims of product disparagement in the US can sue the perpetrators under both state product disparagement laws and the federal Lanham Act,[15] the law which has protected trademarks since 1947.

[5.5.02] In Ireland, plaintiffs have recourse to the malicious falsehood (including slander of goods) provisions of s 42 of 2009 Act and potentially too under s 14 (infringement of registered trademarks) of the Trade Marks Act 1996 as amended.[16] Trademark litigation is discussed in Chapter 12.

[5.5.03] In addition, as mentioned in the previous chapter, litigants in product or trade defamation proceedings can invoke s 12 of 2009 Act which provides that the provisions of the Act apply to a body corporate as they apply to a natural person, and a body corporate may bring a defamation action under the Act in respect of a statement concerning it that it claims is defamatory, whether or not it has incurred or is likely to incur financial loss as a result of the publication of that statement. The company or business need not prove financial loss arising out of and on foot of the defamatory statement. Note too that "statement" is defined in s 2 of the 2009 Act to include visual images, sounds, a broadcast on radio or television or published on the internet and hence a movie, advertisement or television programme which defames a company's product or service would be caught by s 12.

BREACH OF MORAL RIGHTS CLAIMS AS AN ALTERNATIVE TO DEFAMATION

[5.6.01] If a product is considered a work or artistic work under the wide definitions of same in s 2 of the Copyright and Related Rights Act 2000, the author/creator of that work (e.g. a vehicle, sculpture or building owner/designer) could potentially (and at a stretch) bring proceedings for breach of s 109 moral rights by a movie for instance. This section bestows a right on authors to object to any distortion, mutilation or other modification of, or other derogatory action in relation to, the work which would prejudice their reputation or the integrity

---

14 Subject to possible future legislative reforms as mentioned at the outset of this chapter.

15 The Lanham Act was enacted by Congress in 1946.

16 Section 14(3) as amended by the Patents (Amendment) Act 2006 and SI No 561 of 2018 (EU (Trade Marks) Regulations 2018) provides that a person shall infringe a registered trademark if that person uses in the course of trade a sign which is identical with or similar to the trademark where the trademark has a reputation in the state and the use of the sign, being without due cause, takes unfair advantage of, or is detrimental to, the distinctive character or the reputation of the trademark.

of the work. An example might be a product that is depicted in a film to not function properly or a documentary insinuating that a company manufactures defective products.

MALICIOUS FALSEHOOD

[5.7.01] As already seen in Chapter 4, in respect of the tort of slander of title or slander of goods, the plaintiff must prove the statement was untrue, was published maliciously and referred to the plaintiff's property, trade or business. In such actions, the plaintiff must prove special damage (actual loss or material harm) or that the publication of the statement was calculated to cause and was likely to cause financial loss to the plaintiff's property, trade or business.

Part II

Audiovisual, Stage and Radio Productions

Chapter 6

Film Distribution

This chapter will concentrate on film. While private entities like Netflix commission content from independent producers,[1] in the main, Irish television productions are produced with public broadcaster funding (and will often be co-funded by the Media Commission), or though private investment from Virgin Media for example. 'High-end' series can be solely financed by major studios or streamers, or entail a hybrid of private and public sources including Screen Ireland and EU moneys. Lower budgets can be funded exclusively by commission from RTÉ/TG4, or from both RTÉ and Media Commission funds. Otherwise, RTÉ might co-produce with say the BBC or another UK/EU broadcaster, or partner with a US streaming service via pre-sales to finance production. In the latter scenario, RTÉ will likely first enter a development agreement to fund the early scripts, a series pitch deck and bible.

The finance plan, creative team and co-financier parties can and do evolve from project development to distribution. Such details as set out in this chapter and Chapter 7 (as available at the relevant time from Screen Ireland, IMDb or otherwise) may differ somewhat from the eventual factual realities.

INTRODUCTION

[6.1.01] Distribution planning considerations in the practical sense fall outside the scope of this textbook in terms of audience reach and marketing strategies, as does comprehensive analysis of the typical (but sometimes negotiable) licensing terms one would expect to see in acquisition agreements between producers and distributors[2] or international sales agents. This chapter will focus instead on providing an overview of the critical elements that require detailed preparation, contingency planning and general foresight. Budgets, finance plans and cashflow funding/expenditure projections can and do change substantially throughout the lifetime of a project, with recourse then being had to astute lateral thinking when the circumstances dictate. In the first instance, a producer will do well to commence early talks with an experienced line producer or production manager in terms of costings and to engage regularly with specialist legal, accounting and tax consultancy practitioners from pre-production to film delivery and beyond.

1 Whether intended to be exhibited internationally on its platform or on a territory-specific basis (e.g. on Netflix Ireland or Netflix in Britain).

2 Distributors can be domestic or international. International distributors will sublicense to domestic/local distributors (e.g. those who have relationships with cinema chains) or buyers (e.g. television broadcasters or online platforms) in various territories.

[6.1.02] Distribution, in facilitating exhibition of a film in cinema and/or via home or mobile entertainment and in non-theatrical settings,[3] is a vital element in both the creative and financial processes. On the creative front, a producer will pitch a project to a broadcaster, public funder, private financier, online platform, sales agent or distributor based on demand and audience for the product with reference to demographics, style, genre and so forth. From the commercial realities perspective, a thorough knowledge of distribution will separate the novice from the experienced producer. Less seasoned producers might opt (often at their peril) to leave distribution strategy to when the film has been completed. However, as sales are inextricably linked to film financing, distribution planning should commence at inception stage and certainly by pre-production.

[6.1.03] Achieving sales for a film or other audiovisual output, whether by advance sale (pre-sale), pre-delivery or on/after completion, will demand a varied skillset from the people skills required to forge a team of business, legal, accounting and creative talent to drive a project to on-time and on-budget completion (and ideally financial success) to the multifaceted business nous that will be drawn upon pertaining to company law and taxation; IP rights;[4] budgets, finance plans, and the timing of cashflows; raising production moneys,[5] managing sales or other receipts to cover production costs and service repayments on and the discharge of loans and investments; production scheduling, cashflowing VAT payments,[6] reclaiming VAT on talent and cast and crew fees;[7] effecting insurance cover, and everything in between – be that an understanding of the disparate distribution models, the film tax credit, the mechanics of meeting technical and legal delivery requirements of the buyer(s), or cultivating industry contracts.

[6.1.04] For the sale of film or television material, all of the above, generally-speaking, will converge (though of course each project will have its own specificities as regards finance and otherwise). Documentary financing will likely

---

3 For instance, in-flight and cruise entertainment.

4 To include approvals and consents as may be required, for instance, from a documentary interviewee or person on whose story a drama film is based. Where a right of approval is not granted to such parties, they may otherwise seek meaningful consultation and final cut viewing rights.

5 Through state aid and/or private finance options.

6 Budget figures are expressed net of VAT. However, VAT will be payable on many contractor agreements such as a director loan-out agreement or on post-production editing, grading and technical deliverables fees. A production company (or its DAC in the case where a DAC is set up for a particular project or as necessitated by the tax credit requirements) will be VAT registered and can reclaim VAT on services (and on goods purchased where applicable). As the budget does not provide for this expenditure, pending a refund of VAT (which could be months from the time such outlay is expended), the film's cashflow plan needs to account for this and short-term financing may be required, e.g. through a loan, or holdback on payment of producer fees to finance VAT on payments to crew and the discharge of post house fees after delivery of the film.

7 In the case of VAT-registered contractors who will issue a fee for their services. Where persons are otherwise engaged as employees, the employer production company will be paying employer and employee taxes instead.

differ from distribution considerations attaching to selling action features, with the latter often more dependent on theatrical exhibition.

INTERNATIONAL SALES AGENTS AND DISTRIBUTORS

[6.2.01] The relationship between producers and sales agents/distributor licensees is now more collaborative in nature with the latter taking a more hands-on approach from script to screen. Sales agents will frequently also act as distributors. Equally, some will be involved in production financing, thus offering lines of credit, for example, for development funding[8] and P&A.[9] Such an agent may even co-finance an independent film or offer an advance to cashflow production pending sales receipts and public funding. Thus, in response to the diminishing pre-sales model, companies are diversifying and seeking new revenue streams, including utilising their own funds (or those of related companies that can offer equity or debt financing), raising finance from third parties, advising on development, casting, budget, production, co-production, post-production and global marketing strategies,[10] in some cases becoming *de facto* studios.

[6.2.02] The term 'sales agent' no longer aptly describes the more expansive services of London companies including WestEnd Films (sales agent for *The Breadwinner*), Protagonist Films (*The Lobster*), Abacus Media Rights (*Peter O'Toole: Along The Sky Road to Aqaba*),[11] Altitude Film Entertainment (*Black 47*),[12] Cornerstone Films (*Herself*),[13] Bankside Films (*An Cailín Ciúin*/*The Quiet Girl*) and HanWay Films (*Brooklyn*), some of which will take an executive producer position or otherwise part-finance a production.

---

8 Film Constellation, launched in 2016 by former WestEnd and HanWay executive Fabien Westerhoff, by way of example, is ostensibly a sales company. However, instead of the traditional sales agency model where films are filling a sales pipeline, the company reverse-engineers it by providing sales and production finance to producers. In addition to working with third-party lenders and equity players, Film Constellation is poised to draw on backing from parent company Playtime (the Paris-based sales group formerly known as Films Distribution). Constellation's investments manifest as sales advances, gap financing and financial co-productions structured from the Playtime Group's fund thus enabling fast-tracking of projects to market.

9 Prints and advertising.

10 The international rollout occurring via various distribution partners by providing marketing materials and artwork, and liaising with the talent to support the local publicity drives.

11 Abacus is an international UK distributor linked with sister company 101 Films in London/Dublin under the Amcomri Entertainment Inc umbrella.

12 Financiers for the project, reportedly, were Screen Ireland, Luxembourg Film Fund, BAI, TV3 (as it then was), Eurimages, Primemeridian Entertainment (an international production company based in Beverly Hills which develops, produces and finances film, television and other media) and Umedia (*The Artist*, Brussels and Paris-based vertically integrated international film group).

13 A Screen Ireland, BBC Films, BFI (British Film Institute) presentation of an Element Pictures and Merman Films production, with North American rights being acquired by Amazon Studios.

[6.2.03] While financing through pre-sales is seemingly steadily diminishing, the upshot is that UK sales agents are now offering a full service from early pre-production involvement right through to distribution. Such companies may engage from time to time with Screen Ireland and other state agencies including Northern Ireland Screen to mesh soft loans with private funding.[14] Some, while not necessarily offering lending services, might otherwise offer short-term cashflow solutions as secured against or fully recoupable from sales receipts in first position. For instance, to get filming up and running and while awaiting a contract signature payment[15] from a broadcaster buyer, the sales agent might advance the value of that contract signature sum to the producer.

[6.2.04] Particularly in higher budget productions where global sales receipts will need to meet a certain level to recoup the budget spend, an international sales agent is likely to be engaged on an exclusive basis to handle all sales.[16] That agent in turn will contract with distributors and sub-distributors throughout the world. As sales are generated and payments due from buyers are invoiced by the agent,[17] the sales agent's percentage fee will be deducted before releasing net funds to the production company. This will affect the budget, cashflow and the film tax credit[18] where applicable. Where a producer elects not to engage an agent, a deal can otherwise be concluded say with an Irish distributor for Irish and UK rights, and the producer might engage directly with distributors, broadcasters and buyers in other territories.

The financial drawbacks

[6.2.05] In spite of the fact that sales agents can prove invaluable for certain projects that may be difficult to finance absent soft money grants and state funding (or where such funding if secured is insufficient to complete the budget),

---

14 Treasure Entertainment's *Papi Chulo* was an Irish feature film to receive a distribution deal (and co-financing) with UK international sales agent (and finance provider/facilitator to market finance funds) Bankside Films arising out of such engagement.

15 On contract signing by Sky for example, an upfront payment of 25 percent of the overall licence fee payable by Sky might be due within 45 days as *per* the sublicence distribution contract. If the Sky sales figure is £160,000, the sales agent might advance £40,000 to the producer until that same sum is paid to the sales agent by Sky.

16 Some rights, however, might be reserved such as theatrical release rights in Ireland (in which case the producer might contract with an Irish distributor for this purpose) or perhaps television rights for the island of Ireland to allow sales to Irish broadcasters, for instance, to be eligible for substantial Media Commission grant funding. In the case where rights are sold by the agent to Sky UK, Sky, which also broadcasts simultaneously in Ireland, will treat Ireland and the UK essentially as one territory and cannot thus permit the producer to retain broadcast rights for Ireland. A further issue arising is that Sky broadcasts would not meet Media Commission requirements as Sky television is a subscription and not free-to-air service.

17 The sales agent will receive its fees on release of contract signature payments, any rough cut payments and on final/delivery payments by the pre-buyers.

18 Fees payable to a UK or US sales agent for example are not allowable for 'budgeted expenditure' purposes and are deemed non-qualifying pursuant to Pt 7 of the Film Regulations 2019 (SI No 119 of 2019) (reg 12).

their services are expensive (and indeed the percentage fee that applies to pre-sales will likely rise in the case of post-completion sales). Well-seasoned Irish producers may well have established working relationships with broadcasters in the UK such as the BBC and further afield. If certain commissions or cornerstone acquisition agreements can be negotiated directly, the savings on sales agent fees can be very significant and may pave the way for attracting equity investment to complete the finance plan, with investor recoupment coming from more elusive rest-of-world unsold territories to which the agent, with its network of buyers, is contracted to sell.

[6.2.06] In other words, a producer might pre-sell directly to a number of buyers in different territories: if the budget sum has still not been fully achieved, an equity investor could be approached to bridge that gap with possible repayment (whether at a profit or not) from further sales[19] after the film has been delivered to the principal financier(s). The catch to pre-selling in this manner however is that a film will receive a lower sales fee pre-delivery than it will realise on project completion due to the risks posed to any buyer entity which acquires[20] rights very early.

[6.2.07] The other downside to engaging a sales agent outside Ireland is that their fees will not be qualifying spend for tax credit purposes. This will reduce the figure on which the percentage-based tax credit sum is calculated and in turn may well result in the necessity for additional finance or a recalibration of budget sums and the overall finance plan. The fees accruing to foreign-based sales agents therefore dent the budget and the cash payment from Revenue.[21]

[6.2.08] Further, where Screen Ireland is advancing production moneys as co-funder, it will wield approval rights over the appointment of the sales agent and the terms of such appointment. This matter is taken up below.

DISTRIBUTION MODELS

[6.3.01] In order to sell the right to distribute a film,[22] a production company

---

19 Sales in certain territories or countries (e.g. Africa, Asia, South America, Israel, New Zealand or Portugal) may not necessarily realise much in the way of licence fees. However, when taken cumulatively (and when combined with fees from non-theatrical uses such as rights licensed to educational organisations and sale of hotel, ship and airline rights), these may rise to a level where an equity investor might recoup his or her unsecured loan/investment.

20 Likely by means of a licence rather than outright purchase by assignment.

21 Unless additional sales are achieved down the line which can be used to pay eligible production and post-production costs, to include any deferred fees.

22 The assets of a film are dissected into different markets and release 'windows' from cinema to domestic and foreign television distribution deals, subscription video-on-demand, transactional video-on-demand to electronic sell through (download to own). It is possible to sell theatrical and home entertainment rights together or separately. Television rights may also be separately sold. Either way, there will most likely be a theatrical window of

(either itself directly or via a distributor or agent) will enter into one or more acquisition/distribution agreements. The distributor may then enter agreements itself directly with sub-distributors in various world territories. There are a number of different forms such distribution licences may take including domestic and foreign pre-sales or territorial distribution agreements, television pre-sales[23], new media[24] and 'first look' deals[25] which refer to contracts, often with the major studios, granting a pre-emption right or right of first offer/refusal.

[6.3.02] As content is consumed online via streaming and downloads (such consumption rising very dramatically of course during the Covid-19 pandemic), save for the major tentpole blockbuster films that rely on cinema receipts to recoup production spend, the prevalence of or indeed need for theatrical windows has greatly diminished and material is often released to different media simultaneously (and where a theatrical window is required, it is a fraction, temporally, of what obtained in the past). This has simplified matters to some extent but timing and competing media/territories still call for consideration and an element of strategic planning. Issues concerning the premiere and the timing of festivals, television and online release as well as cinema release dates all need to be carefully juggled.

[6.3.03] International co-productions between countries will also influence distribution strategies for the producers given the wider pool of domestic markets made available.[26] Strong production partners of Irish producers to date include UK,[27] American and Canadian entities.

---

several weeks or months (much shorter perhaps for documentary feature films) to allow cinema exploitation to be optimised before home entertainment rights are then exploited.

23 In the US, syndication is also common, namely, the licence to broadcast television programmes by multiple television stations without recourse to a broadcast network. Broadcast programming is scheduled by television networks with local independent affiliates.

24 Via internet, mobile and smart devices, that is, video-on-demand or home entertainment distribution.

25 Such as that between Element Pictures and Fox Searchlight.

26 Co-production partnership collaborations can tap into the respective domestic funding and tax credit opportunities of each territory, European funding such as Eurimages, the network connections of each contributing partner, a wider net of writers, cinematographers, directors, editors, cast and crew, and of course the audiences of the home countries. An example in this regard was the 2020 animated film *Wolfwalkers* from Cartoon Saloon and Luxemburg's Melusine Productions. Financiers, reportedly, were Creative Europe MEDIA (EU slate development funding), Screen Ireland, BAI, RTÉ, Haut et Court, V & P Media (China), Luxembourg Film Fund, Novelle Aquitaine Fund, Canal+ and OCS (France). Cartoon Saloon also partnered with Dentsu Entertainment USA in 2019, having formed its ancillary rights division, to explore licensing and merchandising opportunities for its original IP (e.g. character toys, publishing and live-experiential events). Apple purchased the rights for *Wolfwalkers* in 2018.

27 *Wildfire* is one such example, being a Cowboy Films (UK), Samson Films (Ireland) and Tempesta Films (UK) production with development and production support from the British Film Institute (with use of national lottery receipts), Screen Ireland, Northern Ireland Screen, Wellcome Trust (UK) and with co-finance production support from Film4,

THE DYNAMICS OF FILM FINANCE, CASHFLOWING AND DISTRIBUTION

[6.4.01] A budget (essentially being an estimate of costs) is a living document that will change over time. Unplanned overspend will frequently result, and on occasion savings may prove possible to plug holes that unanticipated expenditure creates. Budgets, finance plans and cashflow documents will need to be updated and recalculated on a continuous basis. Intended stakeholders may decide not to proceed or additional project backers may come on board as a project develops over time. Contingency planning is therefore critical and the budget itself should contain a healthy contingency sum to cover unforeseen eventualities. The rule of thumb is a figure in the region of ten percent of the budget.

[6.4.02] It is imperative to appreciate the distinction between a project's being fully financed and production cashflow realities. Simply because there are fully executed finance agreements in place (as would be required for the tax credit) certainly does not mean that a product is green-lit so as to commence and/or complete principal photography.

[6.4.03] With pre-sales contracts being concluded in some cases before shooting even commences, film buyers are understandably not prepared to take the risk of advancing finance upfront (as they might be in the case of television productions where funds can be released in tranches to assist with cashflow). They may be amenable to advances being released at contract signing stage but such advance is likely to be only in the 20 to 30 percent range. Some buyers may in addition or in the alternative release funds at rough cut stage where the element of risk is very substantially reduced with principal photography out of the way. In all likelihood, the majority of the licence fee payable will not be available until delivery of the film and acceptance thereof by the purchasing party. Even then, non-negotiable and standard invoicing terms might dictate that payment is made weeks if not many months after delivery of the film and its attendant materials.

[6.4.04] The need to cashflow production spend then comes hurtling to the fore. This could be achieved in part, for example, by deferred or postponed producer, crew and post-production fees, a loan against the tax credit from a film fund,[28] a bridging loan (or overdraft) from a credit institution or boutique film finance house secured against contract signature payments and/or pre-sale delivery payments, an equity investor, or from producer and post-production house investment.[29] Producers may elect, to get the film over the line, to reinvest a

---

Sulcata Productions, Illium and Lexis Media (UK). International sales agents were Great Point Media (UK).

28 However there is a major limitation to this as later discussed in respect of the need to have at least 68 percent of the amount on which the tax credit is based available to spend without recourse to such moneys secured against the tax credit (the film tax credit is to be ringfenced to pay production costs and not debt). Such a loan would be of benefit only when substantial finance has already been received from other sources to repay debt.

29 Post houses (see fn 30) can assist with film financing when such business is part of or

portion of their fee back into the film (by deferral or loan) and a post-production company[30] might reduce its fee in return for a production credit that will serve its own general marketing strategy, or otherwise it might provide a cash investment secured against future sales which stand as collateral.

[6.4.05] Sequencing and timing is key. When availing of the tax credit, one must ensure the application for a qualifying film certificate to the Department of Tourism, Culture, Arts, Gaeltacht, Sport and Media is submitted at least 21 working days before shooting commences. In practice, given the voluminous supporting documentation that is required, the application should be furnished long before that to allow time to deal with departmental queries that may arise in respect of errors, incomplete or inconsistent documentation or where clarifications are sought. More broadly, to ultimately draw down the tax credit, signed financing agreements must be in place[31] and thus one source of finance affects the other and vice versa.

Competing interests/specific contractual provisions

[6.4.06] From a practical perspective, there may also be competing stakeholder interests at play. In return for their investment, buyers might well require corporate logo and executive producer credits. Specific credit wording (such as "in association with" or "presented by") could necessitate that the film be cut in different versions for different territories. Certain buyers might otherwise call for a film to be edited into two shorter versions.[32] Others may require dubbing into their native language and subtitling. Such requests will affect delivery timelines (and hence the timing of delivery sum payments) and will add to post costs if they are to be borne by the producer.[33] Teasers and trailers if required (including film poster and specific promotional material such as electronic press kits) will in many cases be further requested by the various buyers, again adding to overall costs.

[6.4.07] If there are conflicts between the rights and obligations of the producer, distributor(s) and buyers, completion guarantor (where one is required by one or more stakeholders) and financiers under the various contracts relating to the production and delivery of the film, those parties will usually enter into an inter-party agreement to resolve such inconsistencies. The inter-party or master agreement, if applicable, is usually prepared by the principal financier's legal

---

can partner with an entity that offers film finance, or by deferring fees to a later date (or reducing their fees that might otherwise be due at normal rates).

[30] Trigger Films (UK), for example, offers both film finance and post-production services.

[31] Producers can, however, apply to the department for the film certificate without signed finance agreements but ultimately these must be fully executed and certain minimum moneys (68 percent of the sum on which the tax credit is based) lodged to the production account before tax credit funds are released by Revenue.

[32] For television mini-series purposes for instance.

[33] While buyers will likely pay for dubbing, they may require the cost of subtitles to be borne by the production company.

counsel. The producer will be asked to furnish certain required documents and contracts to the completion guarantor for its review and approval.

SPECIALIST LEGAL SERVICES

[6.5.01] The production lawyer's role can be pivotal to film and television productions. Entertainment solicitors in Ireland and the UK can facilitate introductions between their third party connections (including distributors) and their clients, and indeed between their diverse client mix *inter se* from screenwriters and music composers to film directors and production companies. Their role is to assist on all legal/business affairs across IP rights clearance, writer option agreements, talent and crew contracts, pre-production, production, post-production, financing and distribution. They will also advise on chain of title and errors and omissions insurance, prepare chain of title reports for insurers, financiers and distributors, and provide expert guidance on risk minimisation as regards exposure flowing from (loan) security documents, possible copyright and trademark infringement and avoiding breaches of privacy and defamation law.

[6.5.02] As domestic and international co-productions become more commonplace because of the myriad benefits they can bestow, the lawyer's role becomes central in terms of reviewing all finance and co-production agreements[34] to include advising on distribution licensing or other acquisition agreements, soft loan funding, tax credit applications (in tandem with specialist accounting firms in this area), and commercial lending/security agreements.

SPECIALIST ACCOUNTING SERVICES

[6.6.01] In addition to legal fees, producers must be mindful of accounting and book-keeping fees. Aside from company formation and, where applicable eventual DAC wind-up costs and the fees for submitting accounts and annual returns to Revenue and the CRO, a film project may require the services of three or more sets of accountants – a tax consultant if relying on the film tax credit, an auditor who will produce a compliance report for s 481 purposes and the production accountant and/or book-keeper.[35] The latter will advise on VAT, payroll, employer taxes and so forth but will also be required to prepare cashflow income and expenditure figures as will be sought, for example, by a film fund lending against the tax credit, the tax consultant providing an opinion on eligibility for and amount of the credit, and Screen Ireland where Screen Ireland is co-financing production costs.

---

[34] For example, an official Eurimages co-production contract under the Council of Europe Convention on Cinematic Co-Production.

[35] A fourth accountant may be required to submit the s 481 corporation tax return amendment to Revenue if this is not submitted by the tax consultant or the production accountant.

[6.6.02] Significantly, like with sales agency fees, certain of these not insignificant spend items are non-qualifying fees under tax credit rules when they relate to financing of the film (e.g. costs of organising pre-sales moneys and professional fees associated with claiming 'tax shelters' or the film corporation tax credit including an opinion letter on the eligibility for a 'shelter' or the credit).

FILM FINANCING AND DISTRIBUTION

Pre-sales and minimum guarantees

[6.7.01] Before commencement of production, producers will oftentimes seek to enter into exclusive pre-sales contracts with distributors/broadcasters/buyers in various territories (e.g. North America, UK and Ireland, Nordic countries) based on the script and attached cast and director/producer team talent. Pre-sales agreements were very common if not indispensable in the past but are becoming less so. In former times, more than half of a film's budget could be financed before it went into production. With those contracts in hand, a financier (or bank which has a media arm) might cashflow production pending delivery payments from the buyers. That proposition generally no longer obtains but that is not to say that pre-sales, especially when combined with the tax credit, cannot be relied upon to substantially finance a film.

[6.7.02] Foreign pre-sales are licensing agreements between producers and national/ local distributors or broadcasters/online platforms directly, or much more likely, between the sales agent/distributor as exclusive licensee of global distribution rights and local sub-distributor as sublicensee, whereby the relevant distributor guarantees on completion of a film for cinema release to pay a fixed sum on the strength of expected revenues[36] in return for the right to theatrically distribute the film in a certain foreign territory (or, in the case of broadcasters, to pay an agreed licence fee for television broadcast and catch-up services).[37] The advance, called a minimum guarantee, is paid upon delivery and must therefore be discharged irrespective of how the film ultimately fares. It might be discharged by way of a cash advance upon signing of the agreement and then in one or more instalments over the course of production to be recouped from

---

36 It is an advance on (or paid in one or more tranches before) delivery with the expectation from the producers' perspective that net producer profits will ultimately be realised after payment of distribution fees and expenses, sales agent fees, production costs and loans. This advance, payable on delivery of the film may cover some of the film's production costs.

37 Television licensing abroad may also provide a production company with pre-sale financing. The production company could thus obtain a production loan using a syndication agreement as collateral. Moreover, the amount of the advance will depend on star attachments, genre, budget and whether in the case of a film it will be given a wide theatrical release. For higher television audience numbers, a theatrical release and the attendant advertising and promotional campaign are important in creating public awareness of the film (which in turn translates into potential television viewers).

film sales. In limited cases, the distributor of a film for theatrical release may otherwise pay a flat buy-out fee.

[6.7.03] While this model might apply to dramatic feature films (where, for instance, domestic market cinema receipts are the source of revenue) it is highly unlikely to arise in the case of documentaries. Sales agents prefer to rely on broadcaster commitments. In this manner, if the sales agent pitches a documentary to broadcasters in the UK, Germany and a network in the US for example for total broadcaster sublicensee fees of €575,000, this sum will be used to finance the film with other sources of finance including the tax credit. The sales agent will take its commission on delivery of the film[38] to these broadcasters and hence no real risk attaches. Sometimes, the licence fees that broadcasters or local territory subdistributors pay to acquire rights are also termed minimum guarantees.

[6.7.04] Pre-sales can count for anything from a small percentage to more than half of the budget of a film and may form the collateral for a production loan from a bank[39] or private cashflow lender (whether a company or high net worth individual). Application for a production loan can be submitted to a principal lender, backed by such pre-sales, together most likely with public funding grants and tax incentives in a structured financing approach to potentially include gap financing and an accompanying completion bond as will be discussed in more detail in the Chapter 7.

The future of pre-sales

[6.7.05] The pre-sales model has vastly diminished in value or dependability over the last number of years. It therefore becomes the role of the sales agent or exclusive distributor licensee to at least secure a sufficient number of pre-sales to give financiers sufficient confidence to support the project. Also, as already stated, several vertically integrated UK-based sales companies are now actively involved in financing. Moreover, the lack of pre-sales is exerting much more pressure on raising gap loans, soft money or equity financing. Even where pre-sales are achieved by sales agents, this comes at considerable cost.

---

38 If there are contract signature payments from one or more of the buyers, the sales agent will be due its proportionate fees at an early stage with the balance on delivery. In this regard, the producers need to be in a position to cashflow the payment of such fees (or reach agreement that the early payment be waived and not deducted at source, with full payment falling due on delivery in order to facilitate more moneys being available for production and post costs). Given, however, that it may take months to conclude a deal with a licensee (and all the while the sales agent is incurring staff fees on the project and overheads), the sales agent may be averse to waiting several further months for payment.

39 International Federation of Film Distributors' Associations, *Position Paper on the European Commission Proposal on Regulation on certain online transmissions of broadcasting organisations and retransmissions of television and radio programmes* (2017) (Revisited Sat/Cab) Brussels, p 6.

[6.7.06] If an agent organises a sale of a documentary feature to the BBC or Sky Arts, for example, in the sum of £450,000, this at 15 percent agency/distributor fees will cost the production nearly £70,000 (which further will not qualify as spend for the tax credit) and this additional cost will need to be covered by other sources to complete the finance plan such as from equity finance based on future revenues.[40] Equity financing however may likewise be difficult to arrange if key territories are already pre-sold (with receipts being used to finance production costs) and the rights are thus tied up for long periods, for example, five to seven years (the material may have little value beyond that and hence the equity investor may not recoup unless there are further sales in rest-of-world territories). However, it is the sales agent, with a proven track record and longstanding relationships with buyers that will have clout with key personnel in organisations throughout the world. Despite the high fees, without their input, the sale might not come to fruition.

[6.7.07] At lower budgets it is less common, according to Rodrigues Law, business and entertainment attorneys based in New York, to see finance plans consisting of pre-sales. The added fees and finance costs of a pre-sale deal make it impractical for such lower budget films. In most cases, in their experience, a producer should wholly disregard the prospect of pre-sales at budgets under $1 million. In addition to the finance costs, it is almost impossible to achieve star attachments with low-budget productions. Talent agents will also be desirous that their clients secure more lucrative work, the agent fee increasing of course in proportion to the actor fee.

The producer's position

[6.7.08] Obviously, producers will seek to negotiate as large a minimum guarantee as possible, since the money can be used to finance the production of the film, pay down production loans, discharge any sales agent's fees and expenses, repay or part-repay investors and pay any deferred fees to talent. In a typical distribution licence agreement between the producer and distributor, recoupable theatrical expenses are discharged off the top from gross receipts, and once paid, the net minimum guarantee sum is available from net proceeds. Ideally, the producer will receive this sum after delivery and, beyond that, a split in the revenues after the distributor has recouped its costs.

[6.7.09] While pre-sales serve to reduce the risk of loss for the producer, they equally reduce the potential for future income. Once a territory is sold (e.g. North America) it is sold for a number of years and therefore further licensing deals for America and Canada are precluded despite the vastness of such territory and wide-ranging sales potential. In addition, owing to very high distributor/agent fees and costs of financing cashflow pending delivery payments from the

---

[40] Such revenues may not materialise and hence the equity investor is exposed to risk, making such finance difficult to raise.

pre-sales, even with films that achieve breakout success, producers have found themselves short-changed. If the film is a hit, the production company would fare better if funding had been possible without pre-sales. Meanwhile, a national/regional distributor only receives its money back or generates a profit if the film destined for cinema release is successful at the box office.

[6.7.10] From the revenues of the film, the distributor (in a particular territory) recoups its payment of the minimum guarantee and deducts any theatrical print and advertising costs. The distributor also deducts its distribution fee. The size of the distribution fee generally increases with the amount of the minimum guarantee, having regard to the fact that the distributor's risk of not recouping the advance is greater. The distributor will usually recoup all these costs before the filmmaker can enjoy any overages. Thus, even if the film reports high grosses at the box office the producers may see little return.

Unlikelihood of distributor advances in the Irish market

[6.7.11] In Ireland it is worth stressing that domestic distributors (while they can invest to some extent in production costs to be recouped from sales) are unlikely to offer significant upfront advances.[41] Their role is to sell rights before or upon completion at a percentage of money received from cinema or television distribution and online sales. Pre-sales to reputable well-funded broadcasters (e.g. of documentary output and telefilms) or streaming platforms essentially guarantees that the film will be made and that the distributor will receive its fee. The strategy will generally be to embark on the international festival route and garner critics' interest. Awards bolster the marketing material which in turn drives audiences to cinemas at home and abroad, coupled with promotional interviews on chat shows by the principal cast. Theatrical success will then likely lead to television and streaming deals. At early stages of a project, it is impossible for an Irish distributor to predict how a film will fare on the home and international markets and hence the payment of an advance to acquire rights is not a viable or prudent option. In the case of *The Quiet Girl*, for example, which was the first Irish language film to be Oscar-nominated for best international feature, neither distributor Break Out Pictures nor director/writer Colm Bairéad had aspirations of an Oscar nomination especially for a film in the native language.

Gap financing

[6.7.12] After making a number of foreign pre-sale deals, the independent producer might have raised ample money to produce the film, while leaving open a number of unsold territories to which further sales can be made once the film is completed (usually at higher licensing fees). This strategy seeks to facilitate a profit being realised on the project for the production company. If

---

[41] If they do, it would be more along the lines of a secured cashflow loan rather than by way of the traditional minimum guarantee.

sufficient funds have not in fact been raised to complete the budget, recourse can be had to gap financing which will centre on sales estimates for such unsold remaining territories.

Production loans and completion bonds

[6.7.13] Because territorial distribution agreements do not always immediately result in upfront cash to the filmmaker to carry the costs of principal photography and post-production, as above, the production company may have to pledge the relevant local distribution agreement as collateral to borrow money from a traditional bank, film finance company, an investment fund or other media lender pending box office receipts. The distributor company may in turn execute a guarantee agreement which provides that it stands as guarantor of the loan. Since the lender is entitled to repayment regardless of the film's revenue or success, the distributor's guarantee of the loan places the lender in a position of much greater security than if the filmmaker is solely responsible for the loan. When the completed film is delivered to the distributor, the distributor will repay the loan directly to a lender who has provided production loan facilities.

[6.7.14] Likewise, in the case of the BBC/Sky example above, where a cashflow lender has provided a loan to a production secured against the delivery payments from these broadcasters, the exclusive distributor (which has facilitated the pre-sale), lender and production company will execute a notice of acceptance of assignment agreement. This agreement will assign the right to receive sales receipts (net of distributor/agency fees) to the lender instead of money flowing from the distributor to the production company and onto the lender. The direct payment therefore reduces risk for the lender. If the funds went directly to the production company, that production company could potentially default and neglect, fail or refuse to pay the lender.

[6.7.15] As a prerequisite for a loan, a financier/bank will often insist that the production company or distributor obtains a completion bond from a reputable bond company to ensure that the project is completed on-time and on-budget. In addition to the completion guarantee, the lender may require that the production company provide certificates of insurance coverage, including general liability and errors and omissions insurance, naming the financier as an additional insured given that, in the event of litigation, the lender may be named as a defendant.

SCREEN IRELAND PRODUCTION LOANS

[6.8.01] As the state's development agency for film, television and animation, Screen Ireland's function is to support the audiovisual sector in all respects. But donned with its lender hat, it will seek recoupment of the loans it advances to production companies (albeit perhaps in a 'limited recourse' manner). Producers must therefore commence distribution planning at the very inception of the project in order that Screen Ireland can ascertain if due consideration has been given to the avenues to market and making audience connection. Accordingly, funding applicants should detail geographic targeted audiences and audience demographics for the subject project, and preferably, look to how comparable titles have performed in the international and domestic marketplaces to investigate what successful paths to market have been employed for such similar works.

[6.8.02] Details are sought from Screen Ireland of the producer's Irish and international festival and PR strategy for the project generally, to possibly include release timings as well as a strategy for domestic distribution and international sales. If the project does not have a sales agent attached, the applicant producer must outline target sales agents, demonstrating a knowledge of their catalogue and track record. Knowledge of key distribution principles is therefore a prerequisite for producers to acquire funding at a level required for larger scale productions.

[6.8.03] Aside from setting out its own technical delivery requirements for the film to include a digital cinema package, Screen Ireland's entitlement to opening and closing credits and delivery of promotional material,[42] its conditions precedent in the loan agreement will mandate that executed copies of finance agreements be furnished, as well as (if Irish and foreign tax credits are being invoked) the tax credit opinion letter from a tax consultant and confirmation of the foreign tax credit amount in the case of a co-production; the borrower's suite of insurance documents,[43] and the complete application form for the cultural certificate in relation to the film as submitted to the Department of Arts and Culture for the purposes of securing s 481 funding from Revenue.

[6.8.04] Screen Ireland will advance production money in tranches throughout the film's production. Before the rough cut payment issues, a pre-release/pre-broadcast legal review will be required from an entertainment lawyer. This will seek to ensure that any potential IP rights infringements or other problematic issues relating to defamation, privacy or otherwise are remedied in time for final cut to minimise the risk of litigation against the producer and/or Screen Ireland as co-financier. Were litigation to arise such as based on breaches of pre-existing IP, it could tie up or indeed jeopardise release of the film and hence delay recoupment by Screen Ireland as lender.

Mandatory provisions in sales agency agreements

[6.8.05] Screen Ireland is contractually granted prior approval to any sales agent/distribution agreement between the borrower production and such party, as

---

42 E.g. approved publicity and behind the scenes stills photographs, an electronic press kit, film poster, promotional clips from the film/trailer and a press release.

43 These will require the interest of Screen Ireland to be noted thereon as an additional insured and joint loss payee as follows, "Fís Éireann/Screen Ireland and its officers, agents, directors, successors and assigns".

well as over the proposed commission fee and recoupable distribution expenses. In addition, it will require having approval of the 'broadcaster window'. The broadcaster window in the past at least meant the period of no less than twelve months commencing on the date of the first film festival screening of the film (within which it was agreed that the film would not be broadcast on television, on-demand or in any other format) to therefore allow for cinema release and box office receipts. Such film festival, being Irish or international, shall be subject to pre-approval by Screen Ireland. Television and theatrical window requirements or limitations can be flexible and cases can be made by producers for more latitude in this connection for the betterment of enhancing non-box office sales figures and accordingly leading to higher prospects of recoupment by Screen Ireland and other stakeholders.

[6.8.06] A dedicated schedule to the production agreement will set out provisions which are mandatory in the relevant sales agency agreement or other contract where an entity is appointed to market, sell, license or otherwise dispose of any rights in respect of the film to which Screen Ireland has lent money. Such mandatory terms will include warranties by the sales agent that it shall prepare sales estimates in respect of all intended commercial exploitation of the film to be approved in writing by Screen Ireland and will consult meaningfully with Screen Ireland with regard to the release dates, release patterns and marketing strategy for the film for the territory as defined in the distribution agreement and send to Screen Ireland statements of all sales derived by it from the exploitation of the picture.

[6.8.07] Additional warranties will include rights of inspection and audit by Screen Ireland or the producer in relation to the sales agent and all (sub) distributors. The agreement will further provide that gross receipts shall be distributed in accordance with and subject to the recoupment schedule (and/or collection agreement (if any)) of the production loan agreement between the borrower producer and Screen Ireland.

DISTRIBUTORS IN IRELAND

[6.9.01] Irish box office statistics for domestic films cogently underpin the view that securing a domestic distribution deal is more likely to lead to commercial success, theatrically at least, in Ireland. Leading Irish distributors are Volta Pictures (formerly Element Distribution, which works for instance with eOne) and Wildcard. Element Distribution in the past handled Studio Canal's[44] slate and direct acquisitions including, for instance, *Rosie* (sales agent Protagonist Pictures) penned by author and screenwriter Roddy Doyle. Notable Element

[44] The French-owned film and distribution company which holds one of the world's largest film libraries and is a subsidiary of media giant Vivendi.

releases in Ireland included *Song of the Sea* (for Studio Canal), *Room*, *The Lobster*, *The Guard*, *Frank* and *Garage*.

[6.9.02] Another key player in the Irish market is Wildcard Distribution (Garry Keane's *Gaza*,[45] *Amy*, detailing the life of music superstar Amy Whinehouse, *Patrick's Day*, *Life's A Breeze* starring Fionnula Flanagan and Pat Shortt, *The Young Offenders*, *Green Room* and *The Hole In The Ground*).[46] Established in early 2013, Wildcard acquires and releases films in Irish[47] and UK cinemas as well as internationally with broadcasters and platforms such as Amazon and Netflix.

[6.9.03] Eclipse Pictures also competes in the indigenous distribution market, as does Break Out Pictures (Damien Dempsey-based documentary *Love Yourself Today*, *Arracht*, Oscar short-listed *The Quiet Girl/An Cailín Ciúin*, *The Bright Side*, and *Phil Lynott: Songs For While I'm Away*). Eclipse-released films include Carmel Winters' Traveller community boxing drama *Float Like a Butterfly*,[48] *The Stag*, *Noble*, *Snap*, *Foxes*, *Stella Days* and *Dollhouse*. International companies which distribute Irish product in this territory include Lionsgate (e.g. *Sing Street*, *Maze*, *Brooklyn*), Paramount (*Shadow Dancer*, *Haywire*), Universal (*Notorious*, *The Queen of Ireland*, *Mrs. Brown's Boys D'Movie*) and eOne (*Jimmy's Hall*, *Calvary*, *The Last Right*, *Albert Nobbs*).

ERRORS AND OMISSIONS INSURANCE AND PRODUCER WARRANTIES

[6.10.01] Both the distribution licensing contract with a sales agent (or domestic and/or international distributor) and the production loan agreement with Screen Ireland (if Screen Ireland is co-financing) will detail express insurance requirements to include the level of cover required and the noting of additional parties on the suite of policy documents. They will also require the production company (or DAC in the case of a tax credit funded production) to provide a variety of warranties in respect of clearance of rights relating to data protection consents, music, performer and talent rights (including waiver of moral rights and a no-injunction clause), and in the case of documentaries, for the use of archival clips and photographs; and to offer indemnification in the case of

45 Donegal-based Real Films reportedly received a documentary production award of €100,000 in 2017 from Screen Ireland. The film was co-produced with Belfast-based Fine Point Films. The distributors/sales agents outside Ireland were Filmoption International and Indie Rights. It also received production funding from Northern Ireland Screen.

46 Additional successful releases include *Michael Inside*, *Black 47*, *Damo & Ivor: The Movie*, *Cardboard Gang*sters, *The Man Who Invented Christmas*, acclaimed space documentary *The Farthest* and *Bobby Sands: 66 Days*.

47 Working too with British distributors such as Altitude Films, Vertigo Releasing and Thunderbird on cinema releases in Ireland (e.g. *Diego Maradona*, *Amy*, *Child's Play*, *Lady Macbeth*).

48 A Samson Films production co-financed with BAI and RTÉ funding (with support also from the Creative Europe programme of the EU). The sales agent was WestEnd Films in London.

breach of such third party rights. These matters are comprehensively addressed throughout this book.

[6.10.02] Given that errors and omissions ('E&O') insurance for international distribution can be expensive especially when combined with production and travel insurance (including budget-related[49] insurances to cover for damage, equipment and data loss, cast and talent insurance and so forth), the producer may need to negotiate (via the sales agent) more restrictive terms with broadcasters and other buyers. For instance, a buyer may require E&O to be in place for the duration of the licence agreement (which may range from three to 15 years). The parties may therefore agree that three years' cover will be sufficient or that it can be renewed if deemed necessary.

[6.10.03] At times, extensive correspondence will become necessary between an insurance broker and the producer as a project develops and the production needs evolve. As financiers and broadcasters are added to a production, the schedules of insurance will require amendment to reflect additional insured/loss payees on the policies and to satisfy particular wording requirements.[50]

CURRENCY EXCHANGES RATES

[6.11.01] Currency fluctuations[51] that can arise concerning international sales with territories such as the UK, Canada or Australia may also prove problematic (in the case of satisfying pre-conditions to bridging or gap financing that any attendant reduction to receipts will be covered by the producer) and require early planning. If insurance cannot be obtained to hedge against this risk, the producer will need to forward-plan to plug a hole in the budget arising from less money being received from a licensee buyer by way of delivery payment due to adverse currency movements over time. This can come from the contingency sum in the budget or the producer may take the financial hit (at least until further sales, if any, materialise).

---

49 Note that collateral protection insurance to protect the budget itself (e.g. in the case of distributor/licensee default on payment of the agreed licence fee) suffers from a paucity of availability and would come more in the form of a performance bond which would require financial background checks on the parties concerned and as would be subject to a bond proposal form.

50 For instance, a broadcaster may require "ABC Limited, its parent, subsidiaries and related companies" while a sales agent or other stakeholder may require more extensive language along the lines of "Sales Agent Limited, its parent, subsidiary and affiliated companies, successors, sub-distributors, licensees, sub-licensees, advertisers, lenders and assigns and the respective officers, directors, shareholders, attorneys, employees, agents and any other representatives of any and all of the foregoing".

51 A sale fee for US/Canada distribution rights of US$100,000 (say €93,000) agreed in January 2023 for instance may transpire to be worth only €84,000 in March 2024 if 100 percent of the fee is paid on delivery in March 2024 at a much less favourable currency rate.

Chapter 7

Private Funding of Film

INTRODUCTION

[7.1.01] Over-reliance by producers on State[1] and European public funding can arguably stilt creativity.[2] Private funding, while more arduous in terms of production cashflow financing, can afford more latitude and potentially spawn more creative freedom, experimentation and artistic risk-taking, subject to any conditions imposed by the financial backers involved. In addition, raising finance from private sources should serve to cultivate a deeper appreciation of financial and international distribution planning and to augment producers' business acumen.

[7.1.02] A compromise (and often necessary) finance plan can be a blend of private and public sources with Screen Ireland, for example, routinely part-financing productions by virtue of development, production or strategic slate funding or otherwise. This chapter is not intended as a financial analysis but more as a cursory introductory discussion of funding types and to cultivate a general awareness amongst producers of opportunities for private investment and/or deals with distributors and international agents,[3] as might arise in the case of a co-production, or reliance by an Irish project on a production loan secured against pre-sales across multiple territories in domestic and foreign markets.

[7.1.03] In certain cases where budgets are tight, by seeking to fund a production from private sources, production companies may be compelled to adopt budgeting strategies that optimise production values but, where possible, at minimum cost. At the other end of the spectrum, to attract Netflix, Amazon

---

1 The reality, however, is that film financing without Screen Ireland and/or s 481 support would generally prove extremely difficult in practice in most instances.

2 In saying that, whenever possible, the tax credit, though coming with an array of strict conditions, compliance obligations and practical limitations, should of course always be considered as it comprises a cash payment from Revenue with no attendant costs apart from tax consultancy, auditing and legal fees.

3 Distributors can be domestic and deal with cinemas, streamers and television broadcasters in Ireland and the UK, or international and effect deals with national/regional/local distributors and buyers internationally. Sales agents likewise deal with distributors in each local territory on behalf of independent producers and enter into sublicensing arrangements.

Prime and other big player interest, bankable talent will need to be attached both on the creative and production fronts. Given the mass audiences for on-demand television output, projects are increasingly being pre-sold to streaming services such as Netflix and Apple TV. This drives the delivery of higher quality content and de-risks the many variables that could otherwise arise.

[7.1.04] Moreover, for medium and large scale productions, the norm nowadays is for producers, either solely or jointly with other Irish co-producers, to team with UK and international partners. Some may avail too of outside consultancy services to develop, package and finance feature films. As seen in the previous chapter, many sales agents by necessity are vertically integrated and offer production consultancy, film administration,[4] executive production,[5] financing and distribution services. Such companies can finance the production itself, post-production costs or concentrate on sales and marketing aspects. It is important when considering entering talks with a sales agent to understand which genre may whet its appetite for content. Altitude Films in London for example has a proven interest in biographical documentary content with notable names including *20 Feet From Stardom* and *Amy* but it also backs dramatic content.

[7.1.05] Thus, on the higher end of budget sums in an Irish context, *The Favourite* with a production budget well in excess of €10 million, was an Element Pictures and Scarlet Films (UK) production for co-financiers Fox Searchlight, publicly owned free-to-air British channel Film4 and Waypoint Entertainment (US) on the back of *The Lobster's* success.[6]

[7.1.06] With a more modest budget, aside from public funding in the two jurisdictions, Anglo-Irish co-production *Wildfire* by writer-director Cathy Brady, for instance, was part-financed by Great Point Media (UK) as sales agents[7] while Hugh O'Conor's comedy *Metal Heart* was part-funded by London-based Head Gear Films[8] and Bankside Films, the latter having acquired international sales rights.[9] WestEnd Films in London is another production, financing and international sales company which has partnered with Irish producers in the past (*The Breadwinner, Song Of The Sea* and *Albert Nobbs*).[10]

---

4 To ensure the best possible return for investors in the case of loan finance coming from a (hedge) fund, a close eye would be maintained on the progress of the production, the costs and the sales including analysis of costs reports and scheduling as well as watching dailies footage as forwarded by the production office.

5 Among others, Title Media (Belgium and LA, Catherine Dumonceaux and Giles Daoust), Epic Pictures (US, Patrick Ewald) and Creativity Capital (UK, Patrick Fischer) for instance co-executive produced horror thriller The Winter Lake shot in Leitrim and Sligo.

6 Also produced by Element and Scarlet with backers including Film4.

7 This British company established its US theatrical distribution arm in early 2018 with the aim of launching eight to 12 titles per year across the country.

8 Head Gear Films provides loans against the tax credit, loans secured by pre-sales, and gap funding.

9 Head Gear also invested in *Papi Chulo* with Bankside again handling film sales on that project.

10 All of which were nominated for Academy awards.

DISTRIBUTION AND FINANCE FEES – EFFECTS ON BUDGET (AND TAX CREDIT SUM)

[7.2.01] It is critical for producers to understand that if relying on an international distributor or sales agent to effect pre-sales to finance a film that the costs of this (in terms of the fees and promotional or other expenses)[11] are properly factored into the finance plan. In essence, the finance plan should include sales receipts licence fee figures net of distributor fees. Take a simple example of licensing of television and streaming rights to a British broadcaster and a North American online platform. The UK broadcaster invests £130,000 and the US platform invests $160,000, totalling say €300,000 gross. If the distributor fees are 20 percent of proceeds received, these €60,000 fees need to be accounted for in the budget, meaning the net receipts are €240,000 and not €300,000. Net receipts will further reduce when any distributor expenses and withholding taxes as say apply to German sales are taken into account.[12] A loan may be required to make up any budget shortfall to be plugged from further sales down the line (e.g. from further pre-sales or sales after the film has been completed).

[7.2.02] Hence, due consideration must be given to the timing of cashflow and expenditure. Irish film fund lenders advancing loans against the tax credit[13] will request evidence of all soft money sources (state funding)[14] and will also require details of signature and delivery payments by licensees, how sales agency fees will affect the budget, and the timing of receipts and disbursements. Very significantly, sales agency fees (in the case say of contracting with a UK sales agent) are not qualifying spend[15] for the purposes of the tax credit and therefore must be deducted from the figure on which the tax credit will be based leading to an ultimately lower tax credit sum. However, sales arising post-completion of the film will not present difficulties if the cost thereof (namely the sales agent or distributor fee) falls outside the budget, in other words where total receipts exceed the costs of production.

[7.2.03] Likewise, finance costs (legal, monthly fees on the principal borrowed sum, and lending arrangement fee) relating to loans will also be non-qualifying. In reducing the gross budget considerably, both sales agency fees and loan finance costs need to be assessed by the producer when ironing out cashflow requirements to determine the extent of the effect on the tax credit sum which will in turn impact the finance plan and overall budget.

---

11 Which will at least run into tens of thousands of euro.

12 It may take one to two years for the distributor to retrieve these taxes for onward payment of the net amount (net of distributor fees on that temporarily withheld sum) to the producer.

13 Funds for this purpose (e.g. the BCP or CFF schemes) might lend up to 90 percent of the tax credit sum secured against the first instalment of 90 percent of the tax credit received from Revenue.

14 For instance as awarded by the Media Commission and Screen Ireland.

15 See reg 12 of the Film Regulations 2019 (SI No 119 of 2019).

The 68 percent lodgement requirement (s 481 funding and borrowing restrictions)

[7.2.04] A critical consideration if relying on tax credit money to part-finance a production is the 68 percent lodgement requirement of the scheme. Before the first tranche drawdown of the film tax credit is effected by the producer company,[16] at least 68 percent of the sum on which the credit is based must be lodged to the qualifying DAC's bank account and a company director of the DAC will need to sign a certificate duly certifying to that effect. While Revenue of course permits producers to borrow from lenders to finance production pending release of the cash sum tax credit, such borrowed funds cannot be used to make up the amount to be lodged to the production bank account if they are to be repaid from the tax credit.[17] To be counted in the 68 percent lodgements total, the loan would have to be secured against other receipts such as pre-sales. The 68 percent then will comprise actual receipts to date (e.g. upfront advances and contract signature payments), loan money borrowed against delivery payments, equity investment, and soft money funding such as from Screen Ireland. Producer fees can be paid out from such funds and reinvested back into the production.[18] The transfer of money back to the production account in this manner can therefore form part of the 68 percent sum.

[7.2.05] Hence, to cashflow production early on (while awaiting delivery of payments from licensee pre-buyers such as national broadcasters in the EU) and to simultaneously meet this Revenue requirement, producers need to borrow[19]

---

16 The producer company applies for the tax credit, amends its own corporation tax return and moneys are paid by Revenue to the producer company. The producer company then lodges that sum to the production account held in the name of the qualifying subsidiary DAC to be expended on production and post-production costs.

17 Finance from a film fund that lends against the tax credit cannot be counted for the 68 percent lodgments floor sum (however, outside of this, funds can be borrowed from a film fund secured against the tax credit). Moreover, producers should not borrow against the tax credit to fund the 68 percent requirement then draw down the tax credit and repay the facility such that the production now does not have these funds available to it as needed to fund the film production – that is against the spirit of the early first instalment payment from Revenue.

18 The lodgment of funds back into the production account will count towards physical bank lodgements to make up the 68 percent floor amount. Producers might outright reinvest by unsecured loan (with the hope of recouping the reinvested fees when the film is completed and beyond the strictures of s 481 at that point, or temporarily reinvest by way of deferred fees). To count as eligible spend (and to thereby increase the tax credit sum), such deferred fees must be paid to producers within four months of acceptance of film delivery by one of the film buyers (e.g. a cornerstone broadcaster). Deferred fees, however, rank in second position in terms of recoupment after Screen Ireland (and distribution costs and commercial bank or other loans) if Screen Ireland has provided a production loan.

19 From a lender such as Head Gear in Britain or Principal Film Finance. Meanwhile, Finstock Capital, for instance, advances loan finance against tax credits in the UK which may be of benefit to Irish producers partnering, for example, with an English production company which has applied for the tax credit in that jurisdiction. Finstock offers loans based on the qualifying production expenditure and the post-production budget.

against other assets, such as pre-sales and not against the tax credit, or otherwise obtain more receipts at initial stages (e.g. negotiate higher contract signature payments or tranche payments throughout production). The rationale is that Revenue does not wish for tax credit funds to be used to pay down private lenders or finance fees. Tax credit money is to be used towards production costs to ensure the film is made[20] and that the Irish economy benefits in terms of eligible spend (crew and other service provider fees and the income tax generated thereon). Revenue guidelines (see Chapter 8) stipulate that finance must be made available to the producer company on terms whereby it will not be repaid until the film has been delivered and accepted.

Currency fluctuations and delivery payments

[7.2.06] If delivery of a film to its primary buyers/broadcasters is to be effected, for example in 12 months from contract signing, and pre-sales contracts for territories such as Britain, North America and Australia are drafted by reference to the pound and dollar, major downward currency fluctuations may radically affect delivery payments. Take the example of a pre-sale to a US buyer for $100,000. The buyer might agree to a 25 percent signature payment on signing of the contract. There is no issue with currency here as it will be known and should not vary much with the budget sum provision for this. However, the balance of 75 percent due on completion might equate to a considerably less euro equivalent in twelve or eighteen months if the dollar weakens against the euro.

[7.2.07] Accordingly, a cashflow lender providing funds with such delivery payment standing as collateral may require evidence of insurance for the budgetary variance[21] this will create or some form of hedging by the production such as producer fee holdbacks to cover any reduction in the delivery sum. A solution, to achieve certainty for the producer, is to have the contract in euro but the buyer is highly unlikely to accept such a term, asserting acceptance of its standard terms including invoicing and payment terms which will be expressed in the local currency to facilitate ease of bookkeeping.

SOURCES OF PRIVATE FINANCE

[7.3.01] Private financing comes in the form of producers' own finances[22]

---

20 Actual delivery of the film to Revenue, insertion of the government logo and funding acknowledgement wording in the end credits being further requirements of the scheme.

21 If the budget is dented by lower delivery payments, this may mean that a lender may not recoup all its fees and will want to be protected in this scenario to realise full return of the principal sum advanced, and payment of interest and fees. Such insurance is very difficult to obtain save in the case of large productions with major budgets.

22 Element Pictures, for example, contributed to *The Favourite's* budget, source: https://www.screendaily.com/features/20-years-in-the-making-the-story-behind-bafta-front-runner-the-favourite/5135627.article [Accessed 19 October 2019]. A producer investment need not necessarily mean actual cash injection by a producer though in reality it may ultimately

including those of co-production partners; equity funding from both individual and corporate investors;[23] commercial loans by way of debt financing from banks[24] secured by sales; investment from privately owned broadcasters or streaming platforms; advance project finance against tax incentive funding (tax credit lending);[25] debt financing from boutique market finance houses and managed hedge funds;[26] pre-sales (sometimes called minimum guarantees);[27] gap or mezzanine financing (also called senior debt) and bridge financing.

[7.3.02] Completion bonding is another source but coming more in the form of media insurance in the case of project abandonment or budget/shooting overruns. The latter is included in this chapter given that, where there is a mix of private finance and public funding by Screen Ireland, the latter will require a completion bond to be in place for projects with a global budget in excess of three million euro.

[7.3.03] Some film financing models such as those pertaining to pre-sales are experiencing a contraction stemming from the near[28] death of DVD and the growing popularity of on-demand consumption online. Accordingly, banks including Leumi, Coutts, Barclays and Cofiloisirs are wary about providing gap financing which is inextricably linked to pre-sales. Television projects on the other hand tend to already have solid backing and can often come fully financed.[29] A

---

equate to the same thing when a part of a producer's fee is paid out and then reinvested back into the budget (and then is not recouped).

23 Either by recoupable and secured cash loan and/or taking an equity percentage stake in the project with the hopes of realising a profit in addition to full repayment.

24 In France, Italy and Belgium a major player in the market is Cofiloisirs which is partially owned by BNP Paribas. Each of the critically acclaimed *La Dolce Vita* (Dir: Fellini, 1960), *Rome, Open City* (Dir: Rossellini, 1944), *Cinema Paradiso* (Dir: Tornatore, 1989) and *The Son's Room* (Dir: Moretti, 2001) received financing from this French lending institution. Its slate also includes *The Lobster*.

25 Goldfinch (with Bird Box Finance) offers loans secured against government creative industry tax credits, VAT reclaims, sales contracts, pre-sale contracts, minimum guarantees or regional soft money funds. Barclays Bank in the UK also discounts film tax credits against a fully funded film production by advancing funds until state moneys are received. Coutts Media Banking team in London provides extensive production finance capabilities against pre-sales and broadcaster commissions (contract discounting) and other acceptable collateral and provides advance project finance against appropriate tax incentives within the UK, and select tax incentives available overseas. See also BCP Asset Management's funding below.

26 E.g. Enterprise Investment Scheme in Britain. Lenders in this specialist media financing space include Creativity Capital, Soho Film Finance, The Fyzz Facility, Ingenious Media, Great Point Media, Head Gear, HH5 and Premiere Picture. 101 Films can also invest as a production partner.

27 These terms are not necessarily to be used interchangeably however as synonyms.

28 DVDs are still sold in certain areas such as rural and isolated parts of large American states where there are no internet services to facilitate streaming.

29 However, as bigger budget television financing tends to only be available on delivery (on smaller budgets, a broadcaster, for example, will generally pay its distribution licence fee in tranches throughout production), producers turn to private financiers to cashflow the project or to secure bridging loans.

typical project will have the cornerstone broadcaster, a co-production partner, a tax credit and, if there is a gap in the finance plan, depending on genre, script and attached talent, recourse can possibly be had to an advance from an international distributor or sales agent. Hence, television projects are perhaps easier to cashflow than their feature film brethren intended for cinematic release.

[7.3.04] Some British market financiers using EIS funds[30] aim to lure high net worth private investor individuals by, in some instances, offering end credits and opportunities to watch filming taking place, meet the cast or indeed to appear as an extra, attend premieres or private VIP screenings.[31] Investors may be afforded the chance to choose their preferred vehicle such as a company which focuses on financing the development, production and marketing of horror films or a SPV which invests in the development of animated feature films. EIS companies might undertake the film project as the production company, with a production services contract arrangement with the developer of the project, or as a provider of marketing services to the film's distribution company.

[7.3.05] Otherwise, in return for partial bankrolling of a project, production and distribution companies can hire film investment companies and hedge fund managers as executive producers. A company opening credit, individual credits, and corporate logo would be sought in such circumstances.

[7.3.06] The EIS market in the UK, however, appears to be suffering a decline and seems reserved for slates rather than single projects with investment being made based on long-term businesses. Slate finance is acknowledged to lower costs, reduce risk and raise returns for producers and investors alike.

[7.3.07] A sales agent company may also make an investment in a film with an advance, or, in order to secure the sales agency rights acquisition agreement from the producers in the first instance, take the place of a senior lender/gap financier. Hence, Protagonist Films which was sales agent for Blinder Films' *Love & Friendship* also co-financed the project.[32]

[7.3.08] Further, Irish distributors and post-production companies may co-finance as in the case of documentary *Katie* which was part-funded (with state backing)[33] by Wildcard Distribution,[34] *What Richard Did* and *Patrick's Day* by Screen Scene, and *Handsome Devil, Dublin Oldschool, Papi Chulo* and *The Stag* as

[30] Thus providing a range of tax benefits to the purchasers of shares in qualifying businesses.

[31] These benefits to investment are offered for example by Soho Film Finance.

[32] With the Irish Film Board (as it then was), Arte France Cinema, Netherlands Film Fund, French soficas Soficinema 11 and Cineimage 10 (a sofica entity is a television and film investor-led scheme whereby private individuals support the film sector in return for income tax benefits and potential returns on investment).

[33] Screen Ireland, BAI, RTÉ.

[34] The sales agent was WestEnd Films and the acquisition of international sales rights fell under its WeLove brand which focuses on a variety of formats for female audiences.

co-financed by post-production house Windmill Lane Pictures. Post houses, for instance, in lieu of making a cash injection, can reduce their post fees (outright or by deferred fees) which lowers the budget sum and can then be factored into the finance plan. Trigger Films in the UK, which do not invest pure gap money or equity, can otherwise offer production cashflow loans in the event they are engaged for post production services and sound/music editing.

[7.3.09] Four other types of financing are service fee deferrals (deferred fees for talent and postponed producer fees – this practice is largely discouraged having regard to the revenue waterfall considerations explored in section 11 below), crowdfunding, product placement or prop loans (all of which are discussed in brief at the end of the chapter) and invoice financing (termed discounting and factoring). In the case of the latter, an invoice financier may lend against pre-sales. The producer will adduce evidence of the pre-sales buyer having been invoiced for a payment (100 percent, or less if the buyer has part-paid the distribution licence fee on signing the licence agreement) due on delivery of the film and in the interim the sum advanced can be used to finance production and/or post-production costs.

EQUITY FUNDING

[7.4.01] Equity-based financing refers to the contribution of cash by investors to the production either in exchange for an ownership interest in the film, potential return of the investment[35] and potential net profits derived from the exploitation thereof, or by recoupable investment loan with no proprietary share. On the public funding side, Screen Ireland is likewise an equity investor by way of production loan facilities, and after distribution/sales agency fees are deducted 'off the top' from gross receipts, will require recoupment of such loan in first position in the manner set out in Chapter 9.

[7.4.02] Equity investors are essentially private individuals (equity funding is not provided by banks) who are interested in the film industry and wish to become involved. Otherwise, equity can be raised from media finance corporations[36] or media sector companies wishing to promote their brand and benefit from goodwill attaching to a drama film or feature documentary and the increased marketing exposure this offers. Their cash contribution is laden with risk, generally standing as an unsecured investment in return for intended repayment of the principal sum and a share of the profits, if any. All other sources of secured and unsecured funding including (in the case where Screen Ireland advances a

35 The investment is speculative and, laden with risk, depends on whether receipts are sufficient to return the investment after payment of distribution fees and expenses, secured lenders, production and post-production costs, certain deferred fees and so forth.

36 One such provider is Soho Film Finance which operates EIS funds for investors seeking a return on investment and tax relief. Lending involves the taking ownership of revenue rights.

production loan) any cash injection by the production company itself must first be recouped before an equity investment or loan is discharged and any profits accrue to the equity financier. Hence, equity investors rank last in the pecking order after 'hard money' commercial investors such as banks who will have a charge on film sales and, for example, repayment in first position recoupment of a 'soft' Screen Ireland loan on a pro rata *pari passu* basis.

[7.4.03] The picture must actually accrue net profits in order for these private investors to see any return. Relying on profits, equity investors will take a share with the film producers and any others who may have a contractual right to backend income from net profit distribution.[37] As a result, if a film performs poorly (if relying on theatrical sales to recoup production monies), equity investors in this connection will most likely recoup little or nothing of their funds. Accordingly, pure equity investors sit at the bottom of the revenue waterfall discussed below.

[7.4.04] It is noteworthy that even if a film grosses into the millions at the box office, investors may nonetheless see little or no return after all other parties who rank above them in priority including the distributors and sales agents, have taken substantial interest and fees and recouped their investment off the top from gross receipts. In saying that, if a movie performs well from theatrical release, equity investors might ultimately enjoy a return from television sales and exploitation of other rights (e.g. the soundtrack, sale of merchandise) over time as part of a long-term equity/profit-sharing agreement.

[7.4.05] While this source of funding may represent the dream scenario for a producer notwithstanding loss in certain cases of some IP ownership, it suffers from a paucity of availability as it stands unprotected with returns emanating only from potential net profits.

[7.4.06] Where the budget is very substantial and the expectation is that the picture will be a major success, it is imperative for such investor to require that a collection agent, a reputable intermediary financial institution, be appointed to the film to ensure the investor receives any profit share due after recoupment of the invested sum. Such independent agent will collect in all revenues from the film into a single account and distribute same pursuant to the recoupment schedule of the final production (inter-party) agreement to which others including banks and gap financiers, if any are in the mix, will also be party – lenders will incidentally in any event also insist on the appointment of a collection agent to protect their own loans.

---

[37] Such as writers or star actors who may have taken a modest fee upfront in return for the potential for more income after film distribution, and career advancement if the role aligns with their creative trajectory.

PRE-SALES TO DISTRIBUTORS, BROADCASTERS AND STREAMING PLATFORMS

[7.5.01] In a pre-sale agreement, as often negotiated by producers when attending the major film markets including Cannes, a distributor[38] or buyer agrees to acquire/purchase the distribution rights for a film before it has been produced, completed or released. The money is then paid into the production company's bank account and must be available to pay creditors when the film is completed or to finance production if an advance is made before completion. Accordingly, revenues are assured before a film is actually made. Such agreements equate to a percentage of the production budget. By way of illustration, a pre-sale to a major German national or regional public television/digital distribution broadcaster might be worth 10 to 20 percent of the budget (whereas a pre-sale to Spain, Nordic countries or Italy would likely yield a much lower percentage even if the film is dubbed into the relevant national language).

[7.5.02] Sales agents, based on past experiences of a similar film to that being sold, will have estimates for each territory worldwide – whether specific (e.g. Italy, Australia) or regional/continental (take the Benelux countries, Scandinavian countries, Middle East/Asia, South America or US/Canada). They will usually be divided into low, medium and high categories to assist them with their own financial projections and to discuss realistic receipts figures with a producer at early pre-production planning stage.

[7.5.03] As mentioned, the pre-sales market is contracting with banks and other lenders apprehensive about providing gap financing to plug any budget shortfall. Further, distributors are going to the safe havens of action thrillers and horror, genre-type material where there are well-defined audiences.

[7.5.04] Pre-sales are usually handled through a sales agent company which will contractually be granted the right to sell (by licence) the content produced by the production company, further selling this onto distributors in agreed territories. Often, such deals for Irish films are not made with an expectation of significant profit – as such, agents may accept sales that allow them to cover their expenses and make a modest return. Movies and animation projects might be a critical success rather than a box office hit and, accordingly, festival and other prestigious awards can boost a sales agent's profile significantly while in operations growth mode.

[7.5.05] It is worthy of note too that, traditionally, pre-sales are rare for an independent animation. Independent distributors are reluctant to pre-buy an animation, unless a film is led by a studio in the US. In saying that, given

---

38 A distributor for a particular territory such as the US (as opposed to an exclusive distributor company which acquires all world distribution rights from a producer for a film (being more akin to a sales agent) which will sell film rights to various national/local distributors and broadcasters around the world).

the major successes of Irish productions *Wolfwalkers*, *Song Of The Sea*, *The Breadwinner* and *Two By Two*, it is certainly an evolving space for the sector going forward. In the children's market, Irish animation studios frequently work with global broadcasters including Disney, Nickelodeon, Cartoon Network and the BBC.

[7.5.06] Gaining pre-sales is not readily accomplished by international distributors and sales agents. It follows that financing will be injected into development of films and content for specific audiences only where there is proven demand. The likelihood of pre-sales rests on the perceived strength of the project as assessed by each (sub)distributor/buyer after reviewing the script, the attached talent and the marketing strategy.

[7.5.07] In spite of the above, national distributors with well-worn distribution chains across theatre chain operators and television/online broadcasting seeking quality film product may be willing to engage with the independent production sector even from the development stage. This demand arises as the major studios are entering less output deals[39] and tend to distribute their product themselves directly. Hence the market for a constant supply of fresh, high-quality content from independent filmmakers. In particular, it is almost essential in the highly competitive current climate, whereby top-level production values and first-rate creative quality is the expected norm, that a 'star' actor forms part of the cast whose on-screen performance and off-screen promotional activities can drive the film in the relevant territory involved to achieve the target sales. Otherwise, the calibre of the director and producer team and their proven track record will drive sales forward. In the case of documentaries, there will need to be a clear demand and appetite for the subject. It may be a very contemporary and topical issue, or the documentary subject and contributors to the film may have a large following or otherwise pique audience interest as might arise in the fields of acting, business, politics, religion, art, sport and music.

Minimum guarantees

[7.5.08] Pre-sale contracts can provide for a minimum amount being paid upon future delivery of the picture. However, distributors may be willing to pay upfront around 20 percent (and beyond) on signing of the agreement to assist with production costs and the tax credit,[40] and the balance when the movie is delivered. Low-budget productions are perhaps more likely to attract a pre-sale during post-production with at least a rough edit of the film available, and a distributor may be willing to pay an advance upfront to cover completion costs.

[7.5.09] Thus, while advances can at times be payable by the distributor, most

---

[39] Whereby national distributors may, for example, have the exclusive right to distribute all of the films of a major studio in their territory.

[40] In terms of the 68 percent lodgement requirement discussed earlier.

of the value of the sale is payable on delivery. Accordingly, a producer requiring funds must finance the value of the sale until delivery. This is usually done with a loan from a specialist media lender (e.g. Head Gear in the UK) secured against the benefit of the underlying distribution contract(s). In other words, the balance pre-sale amount due from the distributor stands as collateral for a bank's production loan or other secured loan from a specialist media financier.

COMPLETION BONDS

[7.6.01] An important element of finalising the pre-sale process in certain instances will be a completion bond. Given that a lender bank depends on complete delivery of the film to trigger full repayment by the distributor, the producer is required to arrange for this special form of insurance which guarantees completion and delivery to principal distributors throughout the world.

[7.6.02] The inter-party production financing agreement is a master legal agreement which brings together and cites all legal agreements including by way of illustration distributor, gap financing, Eurimages (if applicable)[41] and Screen Ireland loan agreements. Each of the relevant parties contributing funding will be represented by their respective lawyers and it is this agreement that a completion bonder will analyse before signing the bond. On all productions with a global production budget in excess of €3 million, it is a strict requirement of Screen Ireland that an approved completion guarantor has been engaged in relation to the production where Screen Ireland's funding is to be made available during production.

[7.6.03] A bond by a guarantor (a major completion guarantor is European Film Bonds (UK, Denmark) which incidentally was party as co-claimant to proceedings (*European Film Bonds A/S v Lotus Holdings LLC*)[42] in relation to completion and delivery of the €19 million film *Starbright*) would cover additional costs where a film goes over-budget or beyond schedule (or in the case that the project is outright abandoned) such that these costs will not be a lender's responsibility. An example of a producer warranty in a completion contract would thus be that, prior to commencement of principal photography, all of the principal cast members shall have taken physical examinations to ensure they are in good health to see the production through to the end. Delayed filming due to talent or actor indisposition can lead to major costs overruns as discussed in Chapter 3. The completion guarantor will also require that the principal cast members be covered under the production insurance without any exclusions.

---

41 Note that Council of Europe (Eurimages) funding mentioned in Chapter 9 is recoupable from film receipts. Creative Europe (EU) moneys on the other hand are advanced by way of non-repayable grants.

42 [2019] EWHC 2116 (Ch), Deputy Master Henderson sitting in the High Court (business list).

[7.6.04] This insurance cover repays the outstanding loan to a lender bank in problematic scenarios outlined above. A bond provider will only issue a bond once satisfied that the independent producer will be poised to meet a set of other stringent conditions (e.g. not to materially modify the planned production without the guarantor's prior approval; the right to control all settlement negotiations in the event of disputes; the noting of its interest on production insurance policies; that errors and omissions insurance is in place; that the producer holds all rights; and prior approval of key personnel and locations in the film through review of the underlying legal agreements relating to the production of the film) and in some instances the completion guarantee provider will be granted the right or remedy to take over and finish the movie subject to the provisions of the completion guarantee and in accordance with the distribution and financing agreements.[43]

[7.6.05] While completion bonds are insurance that the film will be financed to completion if overruns occur, this does not necessarily mean that the guarantor will be out of pocket. After the film is finalised and released, the insurer will enforce its recoupment rights. The bond will contain a clause along the lines of:

> The Producer represents that if the Guarantor expends any Secured Sums (as defined in the Standard Terms hereto), and if such Secured Sums are not otherwise repaid to the Guarantor in full, the Guarantor shall have the right to recoup the unpaid balance of such Secured Sums from the Gross Receipts of the Film. Such right of recoupment shall be subject to the Prior Rights, which for the purposes of this Completion Agreement, consist of the rights and security interests of any financiers pursuant to the Financing Agreement.

[7.6.06] An example of an independent completion bond company is FFI Holdings plc (FFI) in the UK,[44] the parent of a group of companies, chief among them being its main operations subsidiary Film Finance, Inc (US), a world leader in completion contracts since the 1950s (e.g. *La La Land*, *12 Years A Slave*, *The Grand Budapest Hotel*). It has provided completion guarantees to all leading banks in the entertainment industry, major studios and distributors.

[7.6.07] An important milestone for the company was marked in 1982 when FFI provided a completion guarantee to Francis Ford Coppola for the 1983 films *Outsiders* and *Rumblefish*. After the troubled productions of *Apocalypse Now* (1979) and *One From The Heart* (1982), which had run disastrously over-budget, the studios were reluctant to work with Coppola. FFI's readiness to take the

---

[43] Monitoring processes will require the subject production company, in addition to copies of key production documents such as script, budget, cross-plot and schedules, to email in daily shooting progress reports and weekly cost sheets in order to properly evaluate the progress of the film. Bond companies may also make periodic visits to the shooting locations. In addition, monitoring may include the post-production of a film via schedules and updated cost reports until materials are finally delivered to the distributor(s).

[44] A boutique bond company example in the US is California-based UniFi (*The Shape of Water*).

risk enabled Coppola to make a successful comeback. The following full-page advert ran in *Variety*: "Film Finances Ltd congratulates Francis Ford Coppola on completing principal photography of *The Outsiders* on schedule and on budget". Given Coppola's then reputation in the industry, the message, 'on schedule and on budget', was a powerful calling-card which remains to this very day.

GAP FINANCING

[7.7.01] Gap financing is a short-term loan as traditionally secured against the film's unsold territories to cover a gap in the financing for the film.[45] After pre-sales have been agreed with buyers in national territories, loans can be advanced to producers against such further sales contracts. This form of high-interest lending covers any part of the budget not covered by equity, minimum guarantees from distributors and tax credits. The gap lender entity assumes very little risk and is well poised as a secured lender[46] in priority position to generate interest and fees from commercial exploitation of the subject project beyond return of the principal sum.

[7.7.02] Gap financiers such as independent film and television lender Goldfinch, Head Gear Films (which cashflows tax credits and pre-sales) are termed senior lenders and advance funds only when the relevant elements of production and production financing are in place (or are being put in place with another institution such as with a bridge loan facility). Being the last funding source in structured financing plans, some 70 to 80 percent of the budget would first need to be in place before actively exploring this form of financing.

[7.7.03] Further examples of gap financiers include Trigger Films and Creativity Capital in the UK. Creativity Capital part-financed[47] Phil Sheerin's horror thriller *The Winter Lake* for Tailored Films (Californian sales agent Epic Pictures also contributed funding) and Fantastic Films' *Sea Fever* (also distributed by Epic). Trigger Films in London is a tax credit-based, gap finance and film fund[48] financier.

---

45 Gap lending bridges the gap between the amount of money raised from all other sources in the finance plan and the sum needed to see film (or television) production through to completion. It thus finances any 'end money' or 'finishing funds' shortfall. It is a straight loan and there is no profit participation such as that potentially enjoyed by Screen Ireland, the production company itself or equity investors.

46 The loan is secured against receipts (including receivables such as potentially attaching to VAT refunds due from Revenue on VAT paid out from initial production moneys to crew and service providers) and the lender may also require personal and corporate guarantees from the producers and the production company.

47 With additional money from Screen Ireland, Creative Europe, WRAP Fund, BAI, Telefilm Canada, Title Media and FilmOption (Canadian distributor which also handled international sales and distribution on Andrew McConnell and Garry Keane's *Gaza*).

48 Applications being made to German public film funds.

BRIDGE FINANCING AND WORKING CAPITAL LOANS

[7.8.01] Bridge financing is a close relative of gap financing but arises early in the financing stream when a film producer needs to commence filming but does not have sufficient resources to hire the talent and crew while waiting for funding and loans to close. The producer will approach a short-term lender[49] to bridge the gap by way of working capital until the production loan is released or tax credit money is advanced. BCP Asset Management finance schemes in Ireland provide short-term finance to medium-sized film and television projects.

[7.8.02] *Wolfwalkers* animated fantasy adventure feature by renowned Kilkenny based Cartoon Saloon, directed by Oscar-nominated Tomm Moore and Ross Stewart was released to critical acclaim in October 2020.[50] *Wolfwalkers* had a limited theatrical release due to Covid-19 restrictions, but the project had already secured financial certainty through a pre-sale with Apple TV whereon it premiered in December 2020. BCP provided finance of €2 million during production. The scheme has also successfully funded other animated projects such as *Pete The Cat* (Amazon Prime, with BCP finance of €1 million) and *Dorg Van Dango* (RTÉ/Nickelodeon, €800,000 finance) as well as a range of live action features and television output,[51] some of which piqued the interest of Netflix.

ONLINE PRIVATE FUNDING SOURCES

[7.9.01] Film finance may also be facilitated by film and television funding and related services platforms. US-based site Slated, as well offering analytics software, matches projects with talent, financing and distribution. Another example is LA-based pitch2me.com.[52]

---

49 An example of a bridge financier in England is Principal Film Finance.

50 It is the third instalment of Moore's Irish folklore trilogy. *Wolfwalkers*, along with the first two instalments *The Secret of Kells* and *The Song of the Sea*, all received Oscar nominations for Best Animated Feature.

51 Outside of animation, other notable BCP financed projects include *I Am Not A Serial Killer, Black '47, Cardboard Gangsters, The Young Offenders, Can't Cope, Won't Cope, Hole in the Ground, Gaza* and *Darklands*.

52 This website may be of interest to aspiring producers needing assistance sourcing production financing. It is a membership-based platform open to investors, banks, studios, producers and distributors globally, founded in LA by Harold Lewis, a career entertainment banker in association with other finance, entertainment and technology professionals. Filmmakers upload the key elements of their project, and using the site's search engine, financiers can locate specific types of projects in which they have an interest in investing. At a moderate fee, producers may upload their projects with all the key elements including pitch videos to attract the type of debt and equity financing required from banks, equity providers, soft money sources and so forth. The attendant software offers a suite of analytical tools including a project viability or risk rating model, film ultimates (income and expense regressions and revenue waterfalls), net present value project valuators, ten-year annualised cashflow projections and territory by territory income stream calculators.

PRODUCT PLACEMENT, PROP LOANS, CROWDFUNDING AND NFTs

[7.10.01] Product placement refers to placement of a branded product in a scene for marketing purposes for which the producer will receive a fee. Aside from television series productions whereby brands might routinely feature in reality shows, this typically applies only to the blockbuster type undertaking rather than more modestly funded independent films, but that will not always be so, particularly where a star cast is attached to an independent picture. Advertising through product placement represents a growing share of funding whereby an advertiser pays to have its product visible on screen (a watch on the protagonist's wrist, a drink consumed by the hero, a van driven by the villain). The advertiser's participation can be financial or props/equipment-based, for example, lending of items for use on set in exchange for promoting the subject brand.

[7.10.02] Hence, budgeting does not always require a cash injection. Sourcing an expensive prop on loan from its owners is also a form of production funding given that such prop will, accordingly, not have to be purchased or hired. This is especially important in the case of vehicles and period or historical items. Securing royalty-free images and artwork can also benefit a production immensely. Availing of the services of a film and television clearance provider with important contacts in the industry can therefore serve a multitude of financially beneficial purposes.

[7.10.03] Crowdfunding, through dedicated platforms such as GoFundMe and Indiegogo, is generally employed for smaller budgets. *The Queen of Ireland*, which centred on the story of Panti Bliss, for example, surpassed its goal in 2014 of raising €50,000 on the Indiegogo website. In 2012, Mark O'Connor wrote and directed *Stalker*, a feature film project starring John Connors, Peter Coonan and Barry Keoghan and fully funded through a Kickstarter campaign. Meanwhile, Zach Braff's comedy *Wish I Were Here* raised in excess of $3 million via its campaign. Indeed, Kickstarter itself confirmed that 15 films funded through its platform screened at the 2017 Tribeca Film Festival, one of which, *Joe's Violin*, a short documentary, was nominated for an Oscar.

[7.10.04] VidAngel, a popular entertainment app released the multi-season series *The Chosen* about the life of Christ in 2019. The series was the number one crowdfunded media project in history, raising over $10 million from more than 16,000 investors. Elsewhere, with the help of a crowdfunding campaign in 2014, seven years after the television show was taken off air, *Veronica Mars* the movie reached its goal of $2 million in just twelve hours and raised almost $6 million in total.

[7.10.05] Crowdfunding can be donation-based cash or equity funding. It may in some cases bestow the title of co-producer, associate producer or executive producer on the investor. Otherwise, where the funding is donation-based, donors will often receive gifts in the way of an invite to an advance screening of the film, invitation to the set or inclusion in the closing credits/acknowledgements.

[7.10.06] Lastly, as regards non-fungible tokens ('NFTs'), everyday consumers can become film financiers by purchasing a profit share in a film through pre-sale NFTs. One film on the moviecoin.com platform that set a goal in 2022 of being 100 percent fully financed[53] through pre-sale NFTs and crypto crowd investment is *Oui Cannes* directed by Mark O'Connor.

PRIORITISATION OF RECOUPMENT, DEFERRED FEES AND PRODUCER RISK MITIGATION

[7.11.01] Producers must be mindful, from the very germination of a project's creation, of what is termed the 'revenue waterfall' – the manner and order in which return on investment is structured and prioritised. The 2017 Olsberg•SPI report into the audiovisual sector in Ireland defined it as a concept which shows how the revenues recouped from the exhibition of a piece of IP are distributed to the various organisations involved in its funding, production and distribution.[54]

[7.11.02] The waterfall metaphor details how money from foreign sales and domestic distribution deals might ultimately flow to the producers. The top of the waterfall is the money source and the bottom of the waterfall is the producer with obvious aspirations of backend returns from net profits in addition to the 'above the line' producer fee income.[55] Producers should be very reluctant to defer their fees in a picture, and if they elect to do so, should be assiduously cognisant of how this affects their position in the revenue waterfall and the associated risks, to the extent that if such fees are in fact deferred, the producers may be left with nothing after all funding parties have been repaid from sales proceeds. As the Olsberg reports puts it:

> Generating value through IP sales is, however, a significant challenge for production companies – financing mechanisms are intimately related to IP rights, and the generation of more funding for production will result in the producer being forced ever further down the recoupment 'waterfall' … Such a funding approach means that producers are often unlikely to see the benefit of successful productions, and therefore focus on making rather than selling, as this generates guaranteed revenues through fees and overhead.[56]

[7.11.03] Thus, in reality, producers' income is generated from their producer fees and not from net profits. As seen with equity financing above, with a limited

---

53 The target set was €250,000 and as of January 2023 only €30,000 had been raised.

54 Olsberg•SPI, *Economic Analysis of the Audiovisual Sector in the Republic of Ireland* (2017), p 3.

55 The producer, director and principal talent are above-the-line items in the budget with the costs of making the film and post-production being below-the-line items.

56 At p 40 of the report.

chance of generating back-end returns, companies across the value chain are not motivated to generate value from IP:

> ... even where a production has a significant box office return, the vast majority of the revenues are deducted before getting back to the production company involved in financing and producing the project. When we also consider the difficulty which Irish production companies have in holding onto IP, it becomes apparent why so many focus on producer fees and overheads as their source of revenues – it is a logical response to a market which acts to limit the benefits of success.[57]

[7.11.04] Aside from deferred fees, production companies should also be guarded as to injecting their own cash reserves into a project by way of equity investment. In recoupment priority, they would in such instance rank behind hard and soft money loans.

[7.11.05] The other major downside to deferred fees and producer investment is twofold in terms of the tax credit. Firstly, deferred fees must be paid within four months of acceptance of film delivery by a buyer and this may not always be possible.[58] If not discharged within this period, these fees will be counted as non-qualifying and will reduce the tax credit payable (or, if already accounted for at first instalment stage, it may result in clawback of relief and thus repayment to Revenue of a portion of the credit). Second, by injecting one's own fees to a disproportionate level, a (low budget) project may be ineligible for the tax credit. Producer investments need to be deducted as non-qualifying spend even if that money is being used for production. If producers have a fee in the budget and then also invest in the project, the view is that the investment made by the producers is effectively part-funding their fee so in effect the fee payment is deferred and as such would not be qualifying spend. Revenue will therefore require substantial sales contracts and other sources of funding.

[7.11.06] One upside to fees deferral is that if producers and any other talent and crew (including post-production service providers) agree to defer their fees, then that much less money needs to be raised to make the film, at least in the short run in terms of cashflow. The difficulty with this means of financing is that any affected persons are working for no remuneration[59] or in receipt of part-fees only, and are either vulnerable to certain variables (such as further sales being achieved in certain territories, and pre-sale delivery payments) or the film's ultimate success (e.g. following cinema release) in terms of eventual payment. It is an immense gamble given that deferred fees will be paid only after all loans and investors have fully recouped. Some producers may nevertheless compromise in

---

57 Appendix 2 (11.2, page v).

58 Due to invoicing terms of broadcasters (and the planned transmission date) whereby delivery payments might not be paid over for five or six months after completion.

59 If talent and crew are engaged as employees, the producer is obliged to pay wages, at least at national minimum wages levels. Deferred fees due to such persons are therefore reserved for cast and crew working as self-employed independent contractors.

this regard – even if no revenue is earned, it will catapult their careers, particularly if the movie achieves critical success. However, in light of the many years a film project will demand of a producer's time, the prospect of working for free is never attractive and should be considered only as a very last resort.

[7.11.07] A practical option to minimise risk might relate to reaching box office milestones. For instance, take a contract term whereby theatrical distribution expenses shall be recouped from 65 percent of gross receipts, after payment of a 35 percent commission to a national distributor; but for gross box office income, for instance, after €250,000, the 35 percent is instead split 25 percent distributor with the licensor producer retaining 10 percent. This 10 percent will form part of the recoupment pot for funders such as Screen Ireland meaning the producer will recoup any of its own cash investment sooner after loans are repaid and ultimately may realise a profit pursuant to the agreed profit-sharing arrangements.[60]

[60] In another scenario, agreement might be reached whereby a 'producer's corridor' or revenue corridor split can be employed. An example might be that a distributor company in France which has arranged theatrical distribution there affords the producer a 20 percent corridor and then uses 80 percent to recoup the minimum guarantee and/or marketing fees. The producer licensor is therefore sharing in each euro of sales while the distributor is simultaneously earning its off-the-top commission.

Chapter 8

Section 481

INTRODUCTION

[8.1.01] Both Revenue and the Department of Tourism, Culture, Arts, Gaeltacht, Sport and Media ('the Department') issued comprehensive guidelines in June 2022 and January 2021[1] respectively on the statutory s 481 (Taxes Consolidation Act 1997) ('s 481')[2] process, including in respect of the regional uplift, the culture test, industry development test, and the types of film (including certain shorts)[3] which are eligible for certification as set out in reg 5 of the Film Regulations 2019 ('the 2019 Regulations').[4] The intention of this chapter is not to restate the contents of those publications but to highlight some practical issues for early consideration. Specialist legal and accounting[5] advisers in any event are to hand to steer producers through the application, supporting documents, filing and compliance requirements.

[8.1.02] Before embarking on a whistlestop tour of the tax credit, one might ponder why such generous[6] tax relief is made available by Revenue in the first instance. The answer lies in the fact that the exchequer regains a multiple (some 3.5 times) of the cash it injects, arising from income tax, employer taxes and general spend in the economy resulting from the funded production.[7] The State

1 Updated in November 2022 to include guidance on application for digital games tax credit funding.

2 Section 481 of the Taxes Consolidation Act 1997 as amended.

3 Short films are now eligible for relief provided they are of feature film quality (reg 5(2) of the Film Regulations 2019). This was not the case under the 2015 Regulations. In addition, eligible television drama can be feature length or a multi-episodic series.

4 SI No 119 of 2019.

5 Examples of leading production accounting, film tax auditing and tax consulting practitioners in this field include Saffery Champness, Crowe, Brophy Gillespie, Mazars (Dublin and Galway), Clancy & Associates in Lucan, and Upton Ryan Chartered Accountants in Dundrum.

6 Leaving regional uplift provisions aside, the rate of tax credit is worth up to 32 percent of eligible Irish expenditure on a qualifying project which can amount to hundreds of thousands and, in some instances, millions of euro in the case of feature films and television series productions.

7 See PricewaterhouseCoopers spring 2020 and spring 2021 reports, *Section 481 & The Film/TV Industry Insights on the Sector's Contribution to the Irish Economy* (2020), and *The Film/TV Industry & Ireland's Economy: Insights report on the contribution of Section 481 Film Tax Credit supported production activity to the Irish economy.*

also benefits from tourists visiting locations where film and television productions were shot as well as from other cultural dividends detailed by Olsberg•SPI in its January 2023 report (*The Cultural Dividend Generated by Ireland's Section 481 Film and Television Incentive*) commissioned by Screen Ireland and as available on the latter's website.

[8.1.03] The second initial query might relate to the form of payment. A qualifying project certificate issued by the Department on foot of a successful application entitles the applicant company to a credit against its corporation tax liabilities, provided the conditions therein are fulfilled. In the event that this credit exceeds the company's corporation tax for the qualifying period (and the company has no other outstanding taxes), the excess amount is paid by Revenue to the applicant via electronic transfer lodgement. In other words, if the producer company's corporation tax liability is less than the credit, Revenue will pay the difference to the company. It is therefore effectively treated as an overpayment of corporation tax. The cash credit is then used towards production costs and is lodged by the applicant producer company to its qualifying subsidiary DAC as set up to produce the subject qualifying film or television project.

MINIMISING RISKS TO ELIGIBILITY

[8.2.01] As emphasised in Chapter 6, distribution considerations should be at the forefront of producers' minds from project inception. Even when certification is obtained from the Department certifying a project as eligible for the credit (and thus allowing onward application to be made to Revenue), circumstances may change throughout a project's life and early assumptions that were made as to ultimate sales and distribution may not materialise meaning, in effect, that a project does not in fact qualify and the claim will thus be abandoned. A primary concern in borderline cases is that the *de minimis* thresholds will not be met. A production cannot qualify if the value of the total cost of the production is less than €250,000 or if eligible expenditure is less than €125,000. Other factors may also derail a tax credit claim such as where injection by a production company of its own financial resources into a budget is disproportionately high and is not offset in time by sales down the line.

[8.2.02] It is therefore imperative, in keeping any producer own-funds investment levels within range so as to qualify for the credit (see [7.11.05]),[8] to consider securing funding from a number of sources, be that Screen Ireland,

---

[8] Injection by producers of their own funds is essentially treated by Revenue as deferred fees. If not paid back within four months of completion of the film (after formal acceptance of delivery by a buyer/licensee of distribution rights or first public screening), deferred fees cannot form part of the budget. Producer fees can, however, count towards the 68 percent lodgment requirement discussed in para [7.2.04] even in circumstances whereby the producer is paid fees from the production account but then partly or wholly reinvests them back into the bank account.

the Media Commission and commissioning/licensing agreements (including by way of development agreement funding, if any) with RTÉ, TG4, Virgin Media or BBC Northern Ireland, for example, or effecting international television and digital distribution pre-sales through a sales agent or international distributor.[9] Should the finance plan factor in an anticipated tax credit sum but it subsequently transpires that no Revenue payment will in fact arise, then the production company will be left exposed and may have to cover the amount of the hoped-for credit itself if production is to proceed to completion and commercial exploitation via cinema release or otherwise. Such resources may not be available leading to attempts at a late stage in the project to secure a loan or other financing through private investment.

[8.2.03] This could arise, for example, where the intention is that substantial deferred fees (e.g. to an individual producer, film director, executive producer or life rights documentary contributor-collaborator), which form part of the budget, will be discharged upon a sale of the film. If intended sales/investments ultimately do not occur in time or at all (even if a licence agreement had initially been countersigned by the parties),[10] Revenue's requirements in this regard cannot be fully satisfied.[11] This could lead to abandonment of the tax credit application altogether (where the thresholds cannot be met, or otherwise if executed finance agreements are not in place) or clawback by Revenue of sums already paid out in the initial instalment of the credit, or a reduction in the amount that was expected under the second instalment after film completion.

[8.2.04] The lesson here is that finance and distribution agreements must be considered at the earliest possible opportunity. Indeed Revenue, in keeping with its preconditions as mandated by the 2019 Regulations,[12] will not advance the credit unless fully executed agreements are in place. Further, section 4.3.2 of the above-mentioned Revenue guidelines state at p 27 that the funding must be made available to the producer company on terms whereby it will not be repaid until the film has been delivered and accepted. The funding must be made available by way of a cash contribution, for example by way of a loan.

---

9 In the case of film, anticipated receipts from theatrical distribution cannot be taken into account. Revenue requires evidence of actual sales by vouching countersigned agreements. In any event, the tax credit will be required to fund production long before the film is released in cinemas.

10 The buyer might since have become insolvent for instance or some other issue may arise, perhaps force majeure related, which gives rise to valid rescission of the contract.

11 Deferred fees do not form part of an acceptable budget for Revenue unless they are only deferred during production and paid within four months of completion of the film – see para [7.11] for practical considerations on recoupment position.

12 See reg 7(2)(a) and Tab H of Sch 2 which require the applicant to submit fully executed contracts for funding and evidence that any conditions that are required to be satisfied in those agreements for funding to commence have been fulfilled.

Legitimately raising the budget

[8.2.05] A related issue is budget. While budgets cannot be artificially inflated,[13] careful thought must nonetheless be given to meeting the statutory thresholds noted above when non-qualifying costs have been deducted (see [8.8.03]). Producers are perhaps then faced with a dilemma of always seeking to minimise costs while yet ensuring both high production values and that, in the case of lower budget projects, eligible expenditure exceeds €125,000 or that the total cost of the production is not less than €250,000.

[8.2.06] For documentaries where the production costs will generally be a fraction of those for dramatic feature films, to achieve domestic and international sales, the production and its marketing material[14] will need to entice audiences. Compelling music and sound design is often essential. Appropriate sums should thus be allocated to this element, ideally using an Irish composer or licensing commercial music from a major label with a branch in Ireland.[15] Moreover, budgets should include industry-level post-production and editing services, and provision for achieving the highest audio and pictorial quality attainable.[16] A budget will also inevitably increase if a decision were to be taken to extend the length of the film by inserting additional scenes. In addition, where applicable, spend can be justifiably increased by inclusion, for example, of broadcaster or print media archive footage and content.

THE STATUTORY PROVISIONS

[8.3.01] Tax relief provisions for film production have undergone a range of revisions since their first incarnation over 35 years ago in 1987, Ireland following Australia as one of the first film tax credit jurisdictions in the world. Film relief was originally an incentive scheme designed to promote investment in the sector by granting high-income investors (or corporates) tax relief on their invested sums. That personal tax credit scheme applying up to the end of 2015 was closed and replaced by the current model, film relief under corporation tax, which involves

---

[13] Hence, s 481 provides that Revenue may refuse to issue payment for a film if it has reason to believe that the budget, or any part thereof, has been artificially increased. It is also for this reason that only costs related to the qualifying film can be included (such that for instance the cost of IT equipment, lighting and a €50,000 camera to be used in the next five productions and not just in the qualifying film are excluded).

[14] Promotional material costs incidentally are not allowable but if they contain high-quality content this material, from a practical perspective, will lend itself well in any event to teasers, trailers and festival advertising.

[15] The fees can then count towards eligible Irish spend. Universal Ireland for instance can issue synchronisation licences (on the publishing side, the master side may require payment outside of Ireland) for US artists' music for example.

[16] Through use, by way of illustration of SFX, a professional drone operator, employment of props, renting of industry quality lighting and top-end sound and camera equipment.

a payable corporation tax credit to the producer company as introduced by the then Film Regulations 2015.[17]

[8.3.02] Further substantial changes to the tax incentive were introduced by s 26 of the Finance Act 2018 and the 2019 Regulations. Of most significance, the ministerial orders commencing s 26 (and later the remaining provisions of s 26)[18] had the effect of extending the sunset clause of s 481 to December 2024 and providing that claims for relief shall be made on a self-assessment basis, both of which recommendations were made in the below-mentioned Olsberg•SPI report from 2017. The intent was to accelerate the speed with which the application process will move.[19] Further, Budget 2023, as announced in late September 2022, confirmed an extension of the Irish film tax incentive to 2028 thus bringing reassurance to Irish film producers and those outside of Ireland wishing to shoot in Ireland and/or to co-produce with Irish partners.

[8.3.03] The Department is now at the administrative helm during the initial stage of the application, with payments to be released by Revenue as before.[20] Revenue is no longer directly involved in the application process itself. The regime change reinforces the need for accounting and legal advice generally, from pre-production to completion, in order that financial planning and commercial opportunities be optimised, and in relation to audits of 'budgeted expenditure' which refers to an amount expected to be expended on the production of the film that qualifies for relief as either the total cost of production or as eligible expenditure. Such advice should serve to avert the risks of tax penalties and indeed prosecution.[21]

[8.3.04] Another essential change was to balance the divergence between rural and urban activity so that production is not concentrated in urban (or production-rich) areas only of Dublin, Wicklow and Cork. This finally culminated in regional uplift provisions in 2019. Other investor-driven tax measures led, for instance, to investment in Troy Studios in Limerick which stood to benefit from some of the largest television projects Ireland has ever produced.

---

17 SI No 4 of 2015.

18 SI No 120 of 2019 and SI No 357 of 2019.

19 Backlog congestion was occurring for the small unit in Revenue assigned to s 481 applications arising in part from incorrect figures being claimed and the resultant need for heightened scrutiny of expense items included as eligible spend.

20 It is now a self-assessment model and compliance checks may be conducted by Revenue to ensure figures are not inflated to claim higher relief.

21 The new self-assessment regime means that interest, tax-geared penalties, prosecution (see producer liability and clawback of relief in section [8.14]) and attendant publication and are now firmly on the table in respect of suspect claims, be they artificially inflated or otherwise containing error when presented for certification to the Department and for onward payment by Revenue.

ESSENTIALS TO CONSIDER IN ADVANCE OF APPLICATION

[8.4.01] The first considerations will always be budget (bearing in mind the floor sums stated in para [8.2.01]), the finance plan and a synopsis of the project when obtaining preliminary advices from a specialist tax consultant in the area. The applicant producer company ('PC') will next need to be trading as a film production company for a certain period[22] before applying, and the tax adviser will generally require a letter from the company's auditor confirming the company's activities with up-to-date accounts to ensure the company does not have accumulated negative reserves, along with Revenue confirmation that the latest corporation tax return was filed on time. The adviser can then ascertain if the subject production company is the appropriate eligible entity to set up a subsidiary designated activity company ('DAC') for the production[23] and can meet certain basic requirements as a PC before effecting incorporation of the DAC qualifying company ('QC') in the CRO. The PC, QC and relevant shareholders[24] (personally) must further be tax compliant and in possession of an up-to-date tax clearance certificate.[25]

[8.4.02] Producers wishing to avail of the credit but have not yet incorporated a production company (e.g. they trade instead as a sole trader) in Ireland should do so as early as possible to ensure, first, that such company has been trading in the

22 Regulation 16(3) provides that the specified amount shall not be paid unless the PC has been carrying on the trade of film/television production for a period of 21 months prior to a claim being made under s 481(2G)(b). The PC must thus be trading for 21 months in advance of making a claim to the minister for a certificate as to qualifying film status. While it may submit an application for a cultural certificate before the 21-month period has elapsed, payment will not be made until 21 months have in fact elapsed, the 68 percent eligible expenditure lodgement requirement has been met and a corporation tax return is filed in line with legislative requirements.

23 The Irish work on the film must be carried out by a special purpose vehicle ('SPV'), a DAC, which is a company wholly owned by an Irish PC and is thus a 100 percent subsidiary thereof. Hence, QCs are SPVs incorporated for a specific purpose for which the shareholders wish the capacity of the company to be clearly defined (that is, for the production and exploitation of a film or television programme). SPVs last only for the duration of production and while records must be maintained for six years after production, the QC can be voluntarily wound up (dissolved) hence relieving directors beyond that of their statutory duties and the obligation to file annual returns with the CRO. Since the enactment of the Companies Act 2014, the vehicle type employed for s 481 is the DAC – see Pt 16 of that Act (ss 963 to 999). It is imperative, therefore, for producers to be cognisant of the legal and accounting requirements in terms of company law for which they will require specialist legal and accounting advice such that, for instance, a DAC must have at least two directors – see Chapter 1.

24 Each person who is either the beneficial owner of, or able directly or indirectly to control more than 15 percent of the ordinary share capital of the PC or the QC.

25 The s 481 tax consultant will, when relevant, and before providing a formal opinion that might be required by financiers, also require confirmation from the directors of the PC that the company is a film production trading company and that it will continue to trade for a period that is at least 12 months after the date of delivery of the subject production. The consultant will also need sight of a full copy of the s 481 qualifying film application to the Department, details of all queries raised and responses provided to the Department and copies of all financing contracts to meet the project's finance plan.

business of filmmaking for the requisite period and that, secondly, a corporation tax return has been filed within the temporal parameters outlined by Revenue.

Timing of applications

[8.4.03] It is vital to submit the application to the Department well in advance. The scheme mandates that the cultural certificate application should be sent at least 21 working days prior to the commencement of the main body of the Irish production. This, therefore, means at least a month in advance and producers might be found wanting if they delay. Filming activities might be scheduled only to find, on the advice of the production lawyer and tax accountant, that arrangements must be cancelled as there is not a sufficient window between the application submission date and the start of shooting. Further, it is highly recommended in any event that the application be sent in much sooner than four weeks before the commencement of principal photography.

[8.4.04] The practical reasons are threefold. First, the Department is quite likely to raise queries on the documents that have been submitted in support of the application and time needs to be devoted to resolving those queries and forwarding additional vouching paperwork. Secondly, the sooner the film certificate issues, the quicker it will be to hand to produce to financiers (e.g. a film fund) that may be lending against the tax credit pending its drawdown and film completion (see para [8.2.04] for the conditional element of such borrowing and repayment). Cashflow lenders, production loan providers (e.g. Screen Ireland), content licensees (e.g. broadcasters, streaming platforms) and the domestic or international distributor or foreign sales agent may also require sight of the tax credit certificate from the Department as it provides solace that the finance plan and the project generally has been subject to scrutiny and that substantial state money will be forthcoming which will part-fund production. Thirdly, for budgets exceeding €2 million, Screen Ireland will need to approve the proposed skills development plan (see section [8.11]). This approval process could potentially take several weeks and beyond.

Creative documentaries

[8.4.05] In terms of original content for documentary films, the nuances of this requirement might inadvertently be overlooked. Apart from specifically excluded projects, not every potentially eligible project will automatically qualify. The film must be produced on a commercial basis with a view to the realisation of profit and produced wholly or principally for exhibition to the public in festivals, cinemas, via broadcaster channels and so forth. Aside from having to meet the cultural and industry development tests, creative documentaries must, *inter alia*, be based on an original theme, preferably demonstrated by a script or treatment, the design and style of which bear the undeniable stamp of creative originality and personal perspective, and contain significant original filming and not merely report information.

[8.4.06] Thus, for example, a producer may run into difficulty in overcoming the first hurdle of obtaining a certification of the film as a qualifying film by the Department where the project is a biopic of a famous Irish poet but where this topic has been covered by other producers in the past and the intended film contains no fresh, unique and original insights or perspectives.

Tax credit amount

[8.4.07] In respect of a qualifying film, the maximum sum payable by Revenue will be an amount equal to 32 percent of: the lowest of the eligible expenditure amount (including the cost of international cast and crew, if any, working in the state), 80 percent of the total cost of production of the film[26] (including allowable overseas expenses), or €70 million. The maximum credit a PC can currently claim in respect of a film is therefore €22.4 million (being 32 percent of €70 million – Revenue rather confusingly in its "beneficiaries of tax relief" publications refers to an upper range of up to €30 million). In practice, the credit per project does not usually exceed €5 million and is most commonly less than €500,000. The Olsberg•SPI report[27] recommended an increase in the cap per project on eligible expenditure from €70 million to €100 million.[28] The aim here was to maximise the opportunities to attract higher budget productions to Ireland. This recommendation was not adopted by the government (however note since the time of writing, the cap was in fact increased in Budget 2024 even further than proposed to €125 million, subject to EU state approval).

The 68 percent lodgement requirement

[8.4.08] The first tax credit instalment (see [8.5.01]) can be claimed if either evidence is provided[29] that an amount equivalent to not less than 68 percent of eligible expenditure has been lodged to the production account held by the QC being a wholly owned subsidiary of the PC, or Screen Ireland/Media Commission[30] issue a certificate, having duly carried out rigorous due diligence in line with procedures approved by Revenue,[31] confirming that its requirements have been fulfilled to the extent it has agreed to release its production funding.

---

26 As previously noted, the total cost of production of the film must exceed €250,000 – s 481(2A)(iv).

27 Olsberg•SPI (with Nordicity), *Economic Analysis of the Audiovisual Sector in the Republic of Ireland* (2017). Available at: https://www.screenireland.ie/images/uploads/general/Olsberg_Report.pdf [Accessed 3 October 2021].

28 Note that s 17 of the Finance Act 2015 raised the cap from €50 million to €70 million subject to EU state aid approval which was obtained.

29 For instance, a company director of the QC will certify to that effect. Bank statements must also be available for inspection by Revenue.

30 This certificate can also now be issued by equivalent bodies established in an EEA state.

31 Regulation 7(2)(b)(ii) of the 2019 Regulations.

[8.4.09] The importance of this requirement cannot be overstated. Take the example where the eligible spend is computed (by estimation, pending final accounts) at €428,000 and 80 percent of the total cost of production (as reduced by non-qualifying spend) equates to €400,000. The lower amount is €400,000 is the figure on which the tax credit (at 32 percent of this) will be applied. There will accordingly need to be at least 68 percent of that sum (i.e. at least €272,000) sitting in the DAC bank account before application is made to draw down the first instalment of the tax credit.

[8.4.10] As mentioned at para [7.2.04], while Revenue permits producers to borrow from lenders to finance production pending release of the cash sum tax credit, such borrowed funds cannot be used to make up the amount to be lodged to the production bank account if they are to be repaid from the tax credit.

Skills development

[8.4.11] Training of existing and new practitioners in the industry is an important element of the scheme. It is crucial to plan well in advance for the employment of skills participants on the project. Details of such individuals are required when applying to the Department for a certificate. This is further addressed at section [8.11].

ADVANCE PAYMENT OF THE CREDIT

[8.5.01] The PC may, by submitting an amended corporation tax return[32] through Revenue's online service ('ROS') for the relevant accounting period, claim the tax credit in instalments of (up to)[33] 90 percent initially (during film production) and 10 percent within six months of completion, or in one single instalment of one hundred percent within six months of project completion. The reality is however that s 481 is a major source of film funding in Ireland and the cash is obviously required at production stage. Therefore, in practice, the credit will be payable in two instalments. The first instalment of up to 90 percent of the credit is payable before the film is produced (likely during the course of production),[34] based on the production budget. The final instalment

---

32 (Amended) Form CT1. This will, *inter alia*, set out the film certificate number, the date it issued from the Department, the total cost of production, eligible spend on individuals, goods and services and the total credit claimed. Relief can be claimed in respect of an accounting period for which a form CT1 has been completed and filed before the cultural certificate is received.

33 It may be prudent (for instance while awaiting further pre-sales/investment or where the level of costs is yet uncertain) to draw down a lower sum say of 80 or 85 percent to guard against the possibility of over-claiming which may give rise to a clawback or penalty by Revenue.

34 As seen in Chapter 7, 68 percent of the amount on which the tax credit is based must be lodged to the DAC bank account before Revenue will release the first tranche. This money will therefore have already been used to commence filming to achieve the delivery date for buyers and assist with obtaining more financing.

is due when the film has been completed, is based on the actual amounts spent, and is subject to audit and a compliance report from an independent auditor.

Cashflowing final spend items within statutory deadlines

[8.5.02] There may be a temptation to claim 90 percent to assist with cashflowing production, but in borderline cases drawing down between say 75 and 85 percent might be more prudent. Because substantial delays can and do occur in receiving pre-sale funds from buyers, and further (post final cut) sales can take time to complete, all costs might not be discharged in time for preparation of the compliance report (or indeed, as regards deferred fees, within four months of completion).

[8.5.03] To circumvent a possible clawback as referred to in para [8.14], the DAC could pay out individual producer fees fully or partially which can then be temporarily lent back to the production to cover cashflow needs such as VAT arising on fees (depending on the month of expenditure, the final VAT refund might not be released by Revenue for a number of months after the audit is concluded). This could be effected on the strength of a signed sales agreement where licence fees will arrive at some point in the near future from which the loan will be discharged. Examples of costs that may need to be covered in this fashion are auditor and tax consultant fees which can be repaid to the producers from the second tax credit payment and/or further sales. Other solutions in this connection could include loans from the film director or other talent (from their fees as paid out), a loan from a lender secured against a VAT refund or a loan secured against a sale. In sum, the PC can only claim the final tax credit payment after delivery of the film and a full audit has been completed. Auditors will only be in a position to conduct the audit once all of the final payments are made. Hence, timing is key and management of the tax claim applications require advance planning.

THE TWO-STEP CLAIM APPLICATION PROCESS

[8.6.01] Under the new self-assessment model, administration of the credit has been separated into two steps, the first being certification of the film as a qualifying film by the Department. The second step involves submitting a claim for film corporation tax credit relief by the PC through ROS whereby the PC amends form CT1 for the relevant accounting period. When the Department certificate issues, the information required to support a claim for credit as set out in Sch 2 to the 2019 Regulations (Tab A to Tab R) should be ready for consideration by Revenue if and when required at the time of making the claim, namely, that such documents will be made available to Revenue upon its request.

[8.6.02] The claim is made in full by the applicant PC through ROS within six months of completion of the film (reg 9) or, as will almost invariably be the case, by claiming up to 90 percent of the credit based on 'budgeted expenditure' during the course of production, with the balance being applied for within six months of completion. Completion is defined in reg 2 as the point at which any commissioning party confirms delivery and acceptance[35] of the qualifying film in accordance with written agreements, or, the date upon which the film has been screened or broadcast in a public viewing.[36] For the purposes of a series, completion relates to the entire series. Caution must be exercised in connection with this temporal deadline and the need to receive in (within six months of completion) sufficient sums that cover the cost of production and deferred fees given that delays may arise.

Delays

[8.6.03] Producers must be mindful that deferred fees must be paid within four months of completion, and indeed that submitting the compliance report ahead of the claim for the final instalment of the tax credit within six months following completion does not allow for as much time as one might consider to be the case. A common issue is the timing of release of payments from broadcasters and ultimately a sales agent or distributor in the event distribution rights have been assigned. Due to non-negotiable standard invoicing and payment terms, licence fees might not reach the DAC bank account for several months after completion and delivery of the film. Accordingly, recourse may need to be had to a cashflow loan or other source to discharge any outstanding production costs including deferred fees. The issue in turn is that, in the case of a cashflow loan, this can come at a substantial cost potentially meaning that (unless there are further receipts to cover such cost) less or insufficient funds will be available to pay creditors.

CONDITIONS TO BE SATISFIED

[8.7.01] Regulation 7(2) stipulates that prior to making a claim for Revenue to release the tax credit moneys, evidence, as above, by way of records in the form set out in Sch 2 must be available in respect of signed and fully executed finance agreements; bank statements demonstrating that an amount not less than 68 percent of the amount on which the tax credit is based has been lodged with a financial institution (namely into the QC production bank account), and details of any charges or liens over that amount; or a certificate from the

---

[35] Delivery of a film of broadcast quality is not dependent on the delivery of supplementary peripherals such as publicity material or alternative versions of the film for different formats such as online streaming. See the interpretation section (reg 2) definition of "delivery and acceptance".

[36] A limited test screening however (or even a festival screening) may be followed by additional reshoots or editing which can be evidenced in cost reporting. Accordingly, a full commercial release subsequently would constitute delivery and acceptance for the purposes of triggering completion. Generally, also, the screening of the (completed) film would trigger the commencement of the completion period.

Media Commission, Screen Ireland or equivalent bodies established in an EEA state, confirming that the body's requirements in relation to the financial and other arrangements for the film have been fulfilled;[37] the production budget broken down to show eligible expenditure, and where the eligible expenditure is greater than 50 percent of the total cost of production ('the TCP'), also the TCP; and signed production, financing, distribution, or film sale agreements, where relevant set out as *per* the tabs in Sch 2.

CALCULATING THE CREDIT: TCP V ELIGIBLE EXPENDITURE

[8.8.01] Section 26 of the Finance Act 2018 inserted a new definition for the TCP figure into s 481 as follows: qualifying expenditure that was wholly, exclusively and necessarily incurred to produce the film. This then begs the question of what is "qualifying expenditure", what constitutes non-qualifying and what is the meaning of "wholly, exclusively and necessarily incurred". Entertainment and publicity costs[38] for instance do not meet the latter requirement, neither do fees arising on company formation and CRO annual returns.[39] The purchase of crew transport vehicles for a period television drama may not meet the "wholly, exclusively and necessarily" test as they can be used in future productions whereas say 1920s motor cars and specific period costumes to make a period production will meet the test. *Per diem* subsistence or daily expenses including vouched travel expenses of employees involved in the production, which are subject to PAYE, should generally be accepted as should invoices from contractors relating to allowable *per diem* out-of-pocket expenses.

[8.8.02] Turning to qualifying expenditure as the constituent element in the TCP definition, *per* regs 11 and 12, qualifying expenditure on the production of a qualifying film shall include, subject to non-qualifying expenditure, all expenditure incurred on the production of the film in Ireland and elsewhere from the development phase up to and including post-production together with the cost of providing an archive print.

---

37 To the extent that such body has agreed to release its production funding to the PC, where the due diligence procedures performed by the body, prior to its issuing the certificate, have been approved by Revenue.

38 Examples include film posters, gifts, staff entertainment costs such as office parties and wrap parties, launch parties, web presence costs and social media campaigns.

39 See p 25 of the Revenue guidelines. Personal usage costs of the QC should also be removed as an expense. The cost of food and drink that does not serve an exclusive business purpose (in relation to the qualifying film) will not be deductible. Where a producer or actor elects to dine off-site during a shoot (where on-site catering is available) only a portion of this will be allowable. Similarly, an actor cannot submit a claim to the QC for evening meals consumed during private entertainment after the day's filming. Further, the full cost of, for example, several smartphones or laptops purchased for use by non-resident actors during a co-production shoot in Ireland will continue to have value and can be used when handed back on completion on other future productions. Hence, appropriate cost apportionment for these small capital items should be effected.

[8.8.03] Types of non-qualifying expenditure are set out in reg 12 and include finance fees (e.g. on a cashflow loan), costs of organising or providing pre-sales moneys, distribution fees and expenses, publicity costs (e.g. film website and posters), and capital expenditure on assets used in the production of the film which assets are not used up in that process. Deferred fees, as previously stated, are non-qualifying too unless the payment of such sums is made no later than four months after completion. Tax consultancy fees and legal fees arising on advices regarding s 481 are likewise not allowable.

[8.8.04] In summary, therefore, the PC must first review the total agreed budget and reduce it by any non-qualifying costs excluded under reg 12 to identify the qualifying expenditure. Next, it must again review the budget and, using the wholly, exclusively and necessarily test, identify any costs that need to be removed in order to calculate the TCP. Eligible expenditure in Ireland then needs to be computed in accordance with Pt 8 of the 2019 Regulations. This figure will be compared with the TCP to arrive at 'budgeted expenditure', being the sum to which the 32 percent will be applied. If TCP (as reduced down) is lower than the eligible spend figure, 32 percent will be applied to 80 percent of the TCP. If the lower figure of TCP and eligible expenditure is the eligible expenditure sum, then 32 percent will be applied to the latter.

[8.8.05] When stating the TCP in the CT1 claim form, this figure must exceed the eligible spend sum. 100 percent of the TCP amount will always be higher because certain ineligible spend can be qualifying spend while non-qualifying spend will never be eligible spend.[40] However 80 percent of TCP can be lower than total eligible spend and, if including this figure in the claim form calculations, it should be made clear that this is the reduced-down figure after deducting non-qualifying costs. Otherwise the claim will be queried or rejected.

Eligible expenditure

[8.8.06] Due to the territorial test (costs arising in Ireland), it will prove beneficial to use an Irish travel agent to book ferries, flights and accommodation overseas. While the direct booking by producers of hotels and international flights from production account money would be non-qualifying, when calculating eligible spend,[41] invoices discharged to a travel agent that made these travel arrangements are eligible.

Definitions

[8.8.07] Eligible expenditure is the portion of the TCP of a qualifying film

---

40 Foreign accommodation for crew (as not booked through an Irish travel agent) or use of a UK make-up artist for filming in Wales is ineligible spend as it is incurred for services outside of Ireland, but it counts as qualifying spend for TCP purposes.

41 As seen at para [8.8.04], both TCP (as reduced down) and eligible spend must be calculated and provided to Revenue to ascertain on which sum the credit will be claimed.

that is expended on the production of the film in the State. This expenditure must be incurred by the QC directly on the employment and hiring of eligible individuals on the production of the film or on the provision of certain goods, services and facilities (which may include an expense not directly incurred by the QC but charged to it).[42] Eligible individuals are individuals employed, or hired as contractors, by the QC for the purposes of producing a qualifying film. In order for goods, services and facilities to be categorised as qualifying expenditure they must be used or consumed within Ireland in the production of the qualifying film (reg 14); and be provided by persons (a 'relevant person') who are carrying out their business from a fixed place of business in Ireland.[43]

[8.8.08] Thus, where a French location sound operator provides services in Ireland but has a fixed place of business in France, the fees arising will not be eligible. Likewise, where a US cinematographer hired for an Irish/US co-production shoot carries out services for scenes shot in the US, the fees pertaining to the US leg of filming will be ineligible spend.

[8.8.09] Regulation 13 defines "provided within the State" as: in the case of goods which are dispatched or transported, that the dispatch or transportation to the person to whom they are provided begins in the State, and in the case of goods which are not dispatched or transported, that the goods are located in the State at the time they are provided; in the case of facilities, that the facilities are located in the State; in the case of transport, that the transportation takes place within the State, or, where transportation takes place across borders, that the journey begins or ends in the State; and in the case of a service, that the activities constituting such service are carried on in the State and that any goods, facilities or transport associated with such service satisfy any of the conditions above specified.[44] For instance, where the QC engages a Swedish special effects company or pays for a flight by the film director from London to Sweden (the journey must begin or end in Ireland), these cannot form part of eligible expenditure.

SCREEN IRELAND AND S 481

[8.9.01] When Screen Ireland and the tax credit are financing a production (along with other private investors or broadcasters as the case may be), Screen Ireland will conduct its own internal review of the applicant borrower production company's readiness to make a claim to Revenue. It will thus require, as well as sight of the culture certificate, a detailed letter of opinion from a tax consultant.

---

42 For instance, if the PC is a tenant and in turn rents or sublets some of its office or production set space to the QC, a portion of its rent payable to its commercial landlord may be an appropriate amount to charge the QC based firstly on the PC's own rent and secondly as duly and legitimately allocated, say on a floor space basis.

43 Regulations 15 and 13.

44 Regulation 14 classifies goods, services and facilities as qualifying expenditure where they are used or consumed in the state in the production of a qualifying film and are provided within the state by a relevant person directly or indirectly to a QC.

This will include a certification that company constitutional documents were reviewed, what assumptions were made in preparing the opinion, a statement that the PC and QC meet the criteria set out in s 481 and identifying the beneficial owners of the production company (both Screen Ireland and Revenue will wish to confirm that all relevant corporate entities and their owners are tax compliant).[45]

INTERNATIONAL CO-PRODUCTIONS

[8.10.01] Non-Irish persons (including non-EEA residents) are permitted to form a company in Ireland provided certain CRO conditions are met in respect of residency. Subject to one exception,[46] at least one of the directors for the time being of a company which is being incorporated is required to be resident in a Member State of the EEA. Foreign companies can also register a branch here.

[8.10.02] Foreign production companies, unless they have set up a production company in Ireland which has been trading in commercial film or television production for the requisite period, may partner with an Irish PC which will handle the Irish tax credit claim as part of the overall budget.[47]

SKILLS DEVELOPMENT PLAN AND UNDERTAKINGS BY COMPANY DIRECTORS[48]

[8.11.01] It is not proposed to recite the Department's guidance notes but some salient points are necessary in respect of the new training and skills development requirements.

[8.11.02] Films with eligible expenditure of under €2 million may provide a 'Tab F' skills development plan directly to the Department. Otherwise, the plan must first be submitted by the PC to Screen Ireland and Screen Skills Ireland. A minimum of two participants must be employed on the project for the purpose of developing their skills. A skills development participant must be engaged for every €177,500 of corporation tax credit claimed up to a maximum of eight participants.

---

45 The PC, QC, any company controlled by the PC, and each person who is either the beneficial owner of, or able directly or indirectly to control more than 15 percent of the ordinary share capital of the PC or the QC must be fully tax compliant.

46 The requirement to have at least one resident director from a Member State of the EEA does not apply to any company which for the time being holds a bond, in the prescribed form, in force to the value of €25,000 that will provide for certain eventualities in the event of a failure by the company to pay the whole or part of company law fines, or tax-related fines and penalties.

47 That is not to say that non-Irish producers cannot form a DAC in Ireland for a particular production that will not be reliant on the tax credit where they have sufficient funding without recourse to the tax credit. In cases where they wish to apply for a credit, however, the statutory requirements applying to both the PC and QC must be met.

48 To be signed by a company director of the PC and QC.

[8.11.03] The Department has provided a sample template to Screen Ireland for an agreed plan that applicants should complete and Screen Ireland's resultant template application forms A and B are available on its website. Part B can be submitted along with Part A or can be submitted after the first day of principal photography/first drawings on a date agreed in advance with Screen Ireland and Screen Skills Ireland. Once the application is approved, Screen Ireland will issue a letter of approval of the plan which will then be required to accompany the application for certification by the Department.

[8.11.04] A post-project skills development quality assurance compliance report will also be required from the PC. The PC will furnish this report in order to receive a final compliance certificate to accompany an application for the second tranche drawdown from Revenue.

COMPLETION BONDS

[8.12.01] Where relevant,[49] Revenue requires a completion bond contract (surety bond or guarantee) between guarantor and independent film financier to be executed. There is always the risk that film production will not be seen through to full completion. A completion bond, which is essentially an insurance policy covering liabilities in the event that a film must be abandoned, can help reduce this risk. It is not mandatory (see Tab I, Sch 2 and Tab I, Sch 3 of the 2019 Regulations) but where one is in place, evidence of this should be submitted with the application. This bond thus confirms that if for any reason the production is not completed Revenue will be fully reimbursed. In any event, where Screen Ireland funding comprises part of the finance plan, on all productions with a global production budget in excess of €3 million, it is a strict requirement of Screen Ireland that an approved completion guarantor has been engaged.

ADDITIONAL RECORD-KEEPING AND COMPLIANCE DOCUMENTS

[8.13.01] Section 481 provides that a company will not be regarded as a PC unless it provides, when requested by Revenue to do so, evidence to vouch each item of expenditure including records to be kept by virtue of s 886. Revenue may request sight of such records up to six years after delivery and acceptance of the qualifying film.

[8.13.02] Prior to making a claim for the final instalment, the PC must also prepare a compliance report. This includes the declaration set out in Sch 4 to the 2019 Regulations and the documents listed in Sch 5.

---

[49] Completion bonds may not be required where there is already evidence of the balance of funding having been lodged to the production account or in the instance of where, for example, the Media Commission has agreed to release production funding.

PRODUCER LIABILITY AND CLAWBACK OF RELIEF

[8.14.01] The cultural certificate from the Department will be based on the information submitted and on the understanding that the proposals will not contravene any of the conditions for relief. Any material change in the information supplied that may emerge as the project progresses must be notified to the Department. The question arises then, under the new self-assessment system, whether any matters or facts which transpire to be incorrect (or fraudulent) will render individual producers personally liable whereas, under the former system, Revenue was charged with the task of assessment. The answer is in the affirmative. The former scheme required upfront verification of claims and this meant that the normal tools to discourage incorrect claims – interest, penalties, publication and prosecution – were not available to Revenue. The self-assessment model changes this as claims under the self-assessment basis are subject to Revenue's *Code of Practice for Revenue Audit and Other Compliance Interventions* published in February 2017.[50]

[8.14.02] Revenue's role is now principally focused on the payment of the tax credit. In any event, imposition of liability, be it civil or criminal, merely highlights the advisability of seeking out experienced s 481 legal and accounting advisors from the very outset of any project.

[8.14.03] Revenue's guidance manual confirms that relief may be withdrawn for example where the PC fails to comply with any of the provisions of s 481 or the 2019 Regulations, fails to comply with any of the conditions specified in the culture certificate, is not fully tax compliant, or there is a reduction in the budgeted expenditure so that the amount claimed is in excess of 90 percent of the revised budgeted film corporation tax credit. Further, interest will accrue from the date on which the amount was paid by Revenue. Lastly, where a credit has been paid to a PC by Revenue and it is subsequently found that all or part of the amount is not in accordance with s 481, then the overpaid amount may be recovered from the company, any director of the company, or any person who is the beneficial owner or able to control more than 15 percent of the ordinary share capital of the PC or QC.

[8.14.04] In practice, where the first instalment drawn down was higher than what should have been claimed (when the tax credit is computed based on actual figures), this will likely mean a repayment of the excess to Revenue before the second instalment will be released (if the figures allow for such second payment).

---

50 See section 2 (investigation), section 3 (regularising tax affairs, self-correction without penalty, correcting innocent errors), section 4 (audit), section 5 (intervention, payment, settlement, interest/surcharges/penalties which may be in addition to a fine/imprisonment if also prosecuted for tax fraud), section 6 (publication of tax defaulters) and section 7 (prosecution, with a decision to prosecute or not being taken by the DPP). Available at: https://www.revenue.ie/en/self-assessment-and-self-employment/documents/code-of-practice-revenue-audit.pdf [Accessed 3 October 2021].

For instance, if the PC will be in funds from a further sale beyond the compliance report date (as can be vouched with a countersigned agreement) or in the case of deferred fees within four months of completion to be in a position to discharge same within that timeframe, it could lend funds to the DAC or borrow from a third party to pay outstanding payments (e.g. auditor fees) on the project and then recoup down the line.

LOW BUDGET PROJECTS

[8.15.01] When completing the state aid section of the Tab A application form for the Department, the PC will be requested to confirm whether or not the project is 'low budget' or 'difficult'. Low budget is defined as a production budget of less than €3 million. If the applicant wishes to apply for a derogation from the state aid funding limit for a difficult[51] project, the reasons that the project is considered to be difficult should be stated in Tab J. If difficult categorisation is sought for the project, documentation to this effect from Screen Ireland (and/or from the Media Commission) should be included outlining the reasons. Screen Ireland is authorised to certify a film to be made in Ireland as low budget or difficult for derogation purposes.

[51] Films the sole original version of which is in an official language of a member state with a limited territory, population or language area may be regarded as difficult audiovisual works in this context. Such works may include short films, films by first-time and second-time directors, documentaries, or low budget or otherwise commercially difficult works. A difficult film is a film of high quality that faces severely limited prospects of attracting commercial finance for its production and/or of achieving wide commercial distribution.

Chapter 9

Screen Ireland Funding

INTRODUCTION

[9.1.01] The Irish Film Board Act 1980 (as amended) provided for establishment of the Film Board. On 18 June 2018 the agency's name was changed by Ministerial Order to Fís Éireann/Screen Ireland to reflect the breadth of projects to which it lends support to include high-end television productions (e.g. *Normal People* in 2019). Screen Ireland in the present-day audiovisual sector performs the roles and functions of national development agency for the Irish film, television and animation industry. Its neighbouring equivalents are Northern Ireland Screen[1] and the British Film Institute ('the BFI'), a charitable organisation funded by the national lottery.[2]

[9.1.02] In tandem with its national training and development resource arm (Screen Skills Ireland), Screen Ireland supports and promotes development, production and distribution through repayable loan financing. Financing is available to cover the costs of Irish creative elements only. Development loans are repayable on the first day of principal photography,[3] whereas in the case of limited-recourse production and completion loan funding, Screen Ireland will expect to recoup in first position but on a pro rata and *pari passu* basis with any other equity investors (and ahead of any financial investment by the production company itself) and, where applicable, to receive an ongoing net profit share following loan recoupment.[4] Its involvement takes the form of investment in the production with a view to recoupment from sales.[5]

---

1 It is funded by the Department for the Economy and the Department for Communities and it is delegated by the Arts Council of Northern Ireland to administer lottery funding for film in that territory.

2 The BFI is the national agency with a remit to maximise and support the production of international feature films and television in the UK.

3 Screen Ireland does not receive a profit share in return for its development funding, nor does it require a charge to be registered in the CRO over the project's assets in the case of advancing development money to a production company. Some of the projects receiving development loans from Screen Ireland will not proceed into production and may eventually have to be written off.

4 For levels of recoupment on funded features and development loans, see Screen Ireland's annual reports available from the industry insights (reports and publications) section of its website.

5 From cinema receipts, sales to television and ancillary markets (cable, satellite, downloads

LEGAL REPRESENTATION

[9.2.01] Producers will be expected to engage the services of an entertainment law specialist[6] to assist with the loan drawdown and security documents process for production funding which will include advice on chain of title and IP generally, production services agreements where applicable,[7] company law matters, assignment and licensing of rights and so forth.[8] Other considerations relate to compliance with conditions precedent in production and development loan offers, drafting recoupment schedules for approval by Screen Ireland, and review of security documents which will lead to registration of first-ranking fixed and floating charges by Screen Ireland in the CRO against the project's assets. The latter will apply in the case of production loans generally and short films where (at the time of writing) the loan advanced exceeds €50,000. Development loans do not require registration of a charge, but as security until the loan is repaid from production funding, Screen Ireland takes an assignment of 50 percent of rights in the project.

[9.2.02] It is also worth noting that in the case of feature film completion funding applications, producers, particularly in the absence of legal representation, may not have necessarily achieved the exactitude required in respect of chain of title. An entertainment law practice therefore may be in a position to seek to cure, retrospectively, any defects in the chain of title[9] and to advise on the

---

and streaming), sale of film/television/character-related merchandise products and so forth, both in Ireland and worldwide.

6 Given Screen Ireland's very limited funding resources in relative terms (€33.06 million capital budget in 2023 including an administration budget of €4.68 million), loan applications thereto are fiercely competitive and the quality of the paperwork submitted must match the creative allure of the project. This culminates in the need to comprehensively understand the myriad of issues as presented throughout this book from company law and taxation; the tax credit; statutory skills participant training regimes under tax credit rules; production and professional indemnity insurance; safety, health and welfare at work legislation; animal welfare law where applicable; data protection consents; shooting permits; location clearances; clearance procedures during production and pre-broadcast; potential breach of third party rights (such as trademark infringement, defamation, breach of the duty of confidence and privacy); contempt of court; employment law issues including bullying, anti-harassment and equal opportunities considerations, as well as child protection and vulnerable persons legislation.

7 In the case of s 481 (Taxes Consolidation Act 1997) ('s 481') funding, Screen Ireland will issue a production loan agreement to the producer company and two deeds of charge and assignment, one in respect of the parent producer company and the other pertaining to the subsidiary DAC. A production services agreement will be entered into between the producer company and its subsidiary qualifying company.

8 Legal practitioners will advise on insurance, project financing, talent, cast and crew agreements and will further seek to ensure clearance of all material pre-broadcast, thus examining any potential defamation, data protection and privacy concerns, pre-existing footage, sound design services, music score, life rights, radio archive clips and performer rights as well as a review of trademarked and other IP-protected items or content appearing on screen.

9 This may involve re-issuing contracts to certain parties where deficiently drafted agreements did not include data protection consents and other minimum contractual terms required by Screen Ireland which serve to facilitate exploitation worldwide in perpetuity.

requisite elements (to include errors and omissions insurance ('E&O')) required for distribution. Legal expertise will, in addition, regularly be sought for the purpose of managing the contractual and financing elements of national and international co-productions as well as negotiating the terms of distribution licence agreements with television broadcasters, exclusive distributors and sales agents and/or ensuring that there is no conflict between the various agreements and the rights granted or restricted therein.

MINIMUM CONTRACTUAL REQUIREMENTS

[9.3.01] Producers must always be mindful of the minimum contractual requirements of Screen Ireland's development, production and completion loans which are clearly set out in its funding guidelines. Key provisions include data protection consents; warranties as to the originality of content (such that it does not comprise plagiarised material or otherwise infringe third party rights); the agreements entered must be freely assignable to Screen Ireland to allow it to enforce its security in the event of default on repayment or otherwise;[10] the borrower company must have secured in all its production agreements an assignment or licence of copyright[11] in perpetuity in all media worldwide; a grant of rental and lending rights; payment for reuse, repeat and similar rights; an irrevocable and unconditional waiver of all moral rights, and a waiver of injunctive relief.[12] Furthermore, in the case of development loans, no agreement can contain any provision which provides for a reversion of rights to the first holder of copyright (such as a writer) upon breach of the subject agreement or insolvency of the production company.[13]

[9.3.02] If the work is based on pre-existing literary content such as a short story or play, Screen Ireland will require a signed deed of quitclaim from the writer, publisher or theatrical producer as applicable. Further, any rights that are withheld by a screenwriter (e.g. radioplay, stageplay/musical and novelisation rights) must be subject to holdbacks approved by Screen Ireland so that the reserved rights are not exercised in a matter that might compete with or jeopardise full exploitation of the audiovisual project to which Screen Ireland is advancing loan moneys.

---

[10] This may be particularly important where Screen Ireland is the sole or primary funder of the project so that it can exercise control in respect of the exploitation of rights to manage and recoup its investment. The agency, for example, fully or substantially funded *Michael Inside*, *The Young Offenders*, *Dublin Oldschool*, *The Stag* and *Handsome Devil*.

[11] The grant of rights generally by non-exclusive licence will arise in the case of pre-existing commercial music.

[12] Such that any aggrieved contractual party cannot restrain the release of a film and in the case of contractual breach will be entitled to monetary damages only.

[13] Though rights can revert back to the rightsholder, for example, in a case whereby the project is inordinately delayed or production does not realise sufficient funding from various sources within perhaps three to five years to complete production.

[9.3.04] In cases such as production funding for feature film documentaries where Screen Ireland may be providing all the equity finance, it follows that it will have pre-approval rights to include prior consent to any material changes to line items in the budget and to any material re-allocations therein, and modification of any of the film specifications, agreements or documents referred to in the special terms of the loan agreement and as *per* its conditions precedent.

[9.3.05] It is therefore imperative at development and distribution planning stages that producers be mindful of the impact that negotiations with writers and other talent may have on the loan agreement with Screen Ireland in terms, for example, of reserved rights and holdback provisions, on-screen and paid ad credits and profit participation terms. Agreement reached should thus be couched first in terms of being conditional on obtaining development and/or production funding itself, and secondly as being subject to financier approval having regard to recoupment and distribution considerations.

[9.3.06] By way of illustration, a producer may wish to offer a director or screenwriter an executive producer credit in addition to the directing or writing services fee but such credit may well be subject to Screen Ireland (and other broadcaster/financier) approval. Likewise, the loan agreement will place conditions on sales agency matters to include prior approval of Screen Ireland on the borrower's appointment in the first instance of a sales agent for the project, the terms of the distribution agreement, appointment of a collection agent depending on budget levels, and may call for undertakings and warranties from the intended distributor (and matters governing agreement with sub-distributors and termination provisions in certain territories), as well as pre-approval rights in respect of the commission payable to the agent, receipts payable to the production company, matters relating to promotional expenses (such that they might need to be capped), recoupment of theatrical distribution expenses from gross receipts and so on.

PRODUCTION FUNDING

Loan conditions and recoupment of award moneys

[9.4.01] Conditions of funding are set out in the attendant guidelines. A fundamental principle of Screen Ireland funding for production is that the entire amount it invests in a project must be spent only on Irish personnel, goods and services. Other requirements include that on all productions with a global production budget in excess of €3 million an approved completion guarantor must be engaged.[14] The appointment of an approved collection agent is furthermore a usual requirement. All projects in receipt of funding must be eligible for E&O insurance and have an allowance for this within the submitted

[14] A completion bond (or other appropriate takeover arrangements) must likewise be in place in the case of Western Region Audiovisual Producers Fund ('WRAP') funding.

production budget. In addition, a provision must be made for a contingency sum of 10 percent of the production budget. Exceptions may be made in relation to documentaries on a case-by-case basis.

Share of producer and creatives in the recoupment corridor for future projects

[9.4.02] Under the new (internal) recoupment corridor system effective from October 2019, the Irish producer, Irish writer and Irish director of a feature film, television project, feature documentary or animated project in which Screen Ireland has provided production funding is now entitled to share in a recoupment corridor of up to 60 percent (previously 50 percent) of the amount recouped by Screen Ireland under the production loan agreement subject to certain terms and conditions. This enables Irish writers, directors and producers to share in the revenues generated by their productions by applying to draw moneys from the recoupment corridor (to be used for future creative endeavours).

[9.4.03] This corridor, as specified in a recoupment corridor agreement, is broken down as follows: 40 percent to the production company, 10 percent to the director, and 10 percent to the writer (in the case of documentaries the shares will be 45 percent to the production company, 10 percent to the director). To avail of any funds standing to the account of the recoupment corridor, each participant must complete and submit a recoupment corridor application form. The funds are to be used for further projects and do not therefore comprise income for the applicant corridor participants.

The application and loan drawdown process

[9.4.04] After completing an online application form wherein details of the script and project are particularised,[15] in the event of successful application whereby a provisional offer of commitment[16] or confirmation of a quantified award of production funding issues, a draft production loan contract will follow suit (together with a draft Screen Ireland recoupment corridor agreement as above). The production loan agreement will set out the proposed loan and manner of tranche payments (payable at different stages from counter-execution of the agreement through to delivery of the film and its technical materials),[17] finance plan details, loan recoupment provisions, matters as to distribution of net profits,

---

15 Together with information pertaining to its producers, creatives and principal contributors, heads of department, budget items, proposed financing and distribution plans as well as production bank account particulars, shooting details and information pertaining to deliverables.

16 The amount of the loan is not specified.

17 For instance, on the commencement of principal photography; receipt by Screen Ireland of an approved cost report; on completion of principal photography or receipt by Screen Ireland of an approved post-shoot cost report; on or after viewing and approval of a satisfactory rough cut and on receipt by Screen Ireland of acceptable proof of E&O insurance and attendant legal review; upon delivery of technical materials and receipt of approval of same from the IFI's Irish Film Archive.

chain of title requirements and conditions precedent as well as standard Screen Ireland general terms and conditions.

[9.4.05] General terms will include definitions, credits, warranties and indemnities, sale and distribution, s 481 requirements (if applicable), insurances, music clearance obligations, takeover rights in the event of default, repayment terms, and producer recoupment through Screen Ireland's corridor agreement. The appendices will seek a full budget for approval, breakdown of admissible Irish expenditure, a finance plan, cashflow funding and cashflow expenditure sums for approval, a loan recoupment schedule, film and archive delivery requirements, (if applicable) sales agent agreement mandatory provisions, a post-production facility house letter,[18] and a company director inducement letter setting out undertakings as to individual producer services for the borrower producer company.

Conditions precedent

[9.4.06] The conditions precedent provide that Screen Ireland shall not be under any obligation to advance the loan until the borrower has delivered complete, comprehensive and executed copies of a wide range of documents in a form satisfactory to and approved by Screen Ireland to include all chain of title documents, the production services agreement (where applicable between a producer company and its DAC in the case of reliance on s 481 funding), private equity investment agreements (including an investment agreement between the producer company and its DAC in s 481 eligible projects in the case of co-financing by the production company itself), and funding agreements with the Media Commission and broadcasters.

[9.4.07] The agency will also call for evidence of fees deferrals, a tax opinion letter where s 481 is part-financing the budget, the cultural certificate, security documents (see [9.4.14]), company director certificates, production and E&O insurance schedules, the health and safety policy for the film, animation or television production, principal contributor agreements (e.g. writer, director, cast, individual producers) and the production schedule.

[9.4.08] The conditions precedent will, in addition, mandate that company constitutional documents be furnished along with resolutions of the relevant board of directors authorising the acceptance and execution of the loan agreement and security documents, and all pertinent personal and corporate tax clearance certificates.

[9.4.09] The borrower company will undertake in this section of the loan

18 Undertaking to retain possession of the digital master (or any parts thereof) of the film and all other material including digital negatives, digital files, sound negatives and soundtracks from the time it reaches Screen Ireland's possession and to hold them to joint order.

agreement to ensure adequate budgetary provision for clearances, use fees, repeat fees and residuals to facilitate exploitation of the film throughout the world in all media. Lastly, where Screen Ireland elects at its discretion to advance any part of the loan prior to the borrower's satisfying all of the conditions precedent, the borrower will undertake to deliver any outstanding condition precedent requirements not met as soon as possible following any part of the loan being so advanced.

The recoupment schedule

[9.4.10] Funding is provided in the form of limited-recourse loans recoverable from a share of revenues arising on exploitation of the project and also entitling Screen Ireland to a share of net profits.

[9.4.11] The recoupment schedule is a key element in the loan agreement and will detail how total receipts will be applied in the specified priority and in payment of the specified amounts, being first to the approved sales agent(s) and/or distributor(s) in payment of the sales agent's and/or distributor's approved commission and approved expenses; and thereafter to Screen Ireland and the equity investors in the proportions of their cash investment until Screen Ireland has recouped its loan amount in first recoupment position. Thereafter, payment of deferred fees will rank in priority,[19] followed by the production company in the amount of the tax credit (where applicable). Finally, post-recoupment as above, the schedule will specify the manner in which net profits (if any) will be paid to Screen Ireland, the borrower applicant, other cash investors and any contributors who are contractually entitled to a share of net producer profits (e.g. writers and associate producers).

[9.4.12] The recoupment percentages (being proportions of cash invested relative to the total equity investment in the film) will be reflected in other financing agreements such as online distribution pre-sale agreements and equity investment agreements. Contracting with such parties will therefore require full disclosure by the production company of its arrangements with Screen Ireland and how the pre-agreed recoupment schedule will affect such investor.

[9.4.13] Depending on the specifics of the project and if Screen Ireland elects to apportion an amount equalling half of total net profits to the borrower production company as itself an investor and other equity investors, net profits will accordingly be divided half to Screen Ireland, the production company and equity investors as one pot, and the remaining half to the production company (and any other parties who are entitled to net profit participation, that is, a share in the producer's share of net profits).

---

[19] To satisfy s 481 requirements in this regard, deferred fees must be discharged within four months of completion of the film (see Chapter 8).

The security documents

[9.4.14] To protect its investment as funded by the taxpayer, Screen Ireland will, at the time of issuing a draft production loan agreement, also issue a deed of charge and assignment in respect (where there is an intended successful s 481 claim) of the producer company and its DAC. This makes provision for the worldwide exploitation rights being assigned (including ancillary publishing, spin-off and merchandising rights); covenants to pay and discharge the production loan; details of mortgage of and assignment by the chargor production company of its right, title and interest in and to the assigned rights by way of first-ranking mortgage to Screen Ireland as chargee; definitions of fixed and floating charges; enforcement terms, rights and powers of Screen Ireland as lender including appointment of a receiver; and release of the security upon discharge by the chargor of the secured obligations as defined.

[9.4.15] The deed of charge and assignment also contains a licensing provision such that, notwithstanding mortgage of the underlying IP and assignment of rights by the borrower production company to Screen Ireland, Screen Ireland grants to the chargor a licence to do all such things in respect of the collateral as may be necessary in connection with the development, pre-production, production and exploitation of the film in accordance with the production loan agreement. Such licence automatically terminates upon breach of the relevant loan agreements and security documents, default or the occurrence of any of the events specified such as inability to pay debts as they fall due leading to insolvency and wind-up, or it transpires that warranties and covenants given by the chargor company directors or any statements furnished by them prove to be incorrect or false.

[9.4.16] In the case of the deed of charge also being drafted in respect of a DAC, the schedule to that agreement will include a notice of charge from the DAC to the bank where the production account was opened authorising, where relevant, that bank to act in accordance with Screen Ireland instructions when enforcing its security (e.g. not to permit any further withdrawal of any funds) and instructing the bank to comply with the other requirements of the notice of charge by signing a form of acknowledgement of the notice of charge. This signed bank acknowledgement in turn, for example, acknowledges that on or after the receipt by the bank of a written notice from Screen Ireland (or its permitted assigns) or an appointed receiver notifying the bank that it is enforcing its rights pursuant to the deed of charge, the bank shall make all payments solely as Screen Ireland may direct and shall not otherwise permit payments or withdrawals from the moneys held in the account.

[9.4.17] In accordance with company law, Screen Ireland will file and register the deed of charge (or deeds if there is a DAC involved arising from s 481 funding) with the CRO against the company's film assets (and not against the company as a whole) within 21 days of its creation. The deed is sent to the borrower or its solicitor to arrange signing thereof through Revenue's online service. ROS is used for charge execution purposes in line with mandatory e-filing in the CRO of ROS-verified chargor and chargee signatures, even in cases where no s 481 money is being advanced.

[9.4.18] When the borrower applicant has fulfilled its obligations pursuant to the deed of charge and recoupment schedule in the production loan agreement, Screen Ireland will file and register satisfaction of the charge with the CRO so that the charge in respect of the production loan will no longer appear in the particulars of charge section of the borrower production company's official company printout.

PAVING THE WAY FOR FURTHER FUNDING

[9.5.01] The attachment of Screen Ireland to a project (even at development loan stage) will generally bolster endeavours to secure further funding from both private and public sources. Endorsement by the national agency instills confidence in backers of audiovisual content and, in the case of, for example, additional RTÉ or Virgin Media funding, this will have the knock-on effect of opening the gate to Media Commission money (the Commission providing funding at a late stage when other finance is securely in place). Secondly, a production loan from Screen Ireland will assist the finance plan and budget when applying for the tax credit.

EURIMAGES (COUNCIL OF EUROPE) AND EU FUNDING

[9.6.01] Aside from national funding from Screen Ireland, the Media Commission, national broadcasters, the Arts Council, the corporation tax credit and regional funding (e.g. from county councils; the WRAP fund), producers if teaming with international partners, can also seek to rely on European public funding.

[9.6.02] The European Convention on Cinematographic Co-Production 1992[20] as revised and renamed by subsequent October 2017 convention[21] relates to a cultural support fund (Eurimages) of the Council of Europe[22] (not to be confused with the EU Council). EU Regulation No 1295/2013 (as since repealed by

---

20 ETS No 147.

21 ETS No 220.

22 The Council of Europe is an international organisation, the stated aim of which is to uphold human rights, democracy and the rule of law in Europe. Founded in 1949, it has 47 member states and is distinct from the 27-nation EU and the EU Council in Brussels, Belgium. Unlike the EU, the Council of Europe cannot make binding laws but it does have the power to enforce select international agreements reached by contracting states on various topics. The best known body of the Council of Europe is the European Court of Human Rights which enforces the European Convention on Human Rights.

Regulation 2021/818)[23] on the other hand relates to the Creative Europe Media programme. It is possible for productions to be afforded financial assistance both from the EU and Council of Europe. *The Secret of Kells* benefitted from both funds for example as did *The Lobster*.

[9.6.03] An important difference between the EU funding and Eurimages is that the former is non-repayable grant funding. Eurimages soft loan money is repayable (with the exception of grants for less than €150,000) on the basis of revenues generated by the projects supported.[24]

FUTURE DEVELOPMENTS IN PUBLIC FUNDING

[9.7.01] Developments may be afoot in relation to a potential broadcasting levy and other possibilities (e.g. contribution to a national fund from Netflix) arising from the provisions of the revised Audiovisual Media Services Directive discussed in Chapter 32. For now, however, notwithstanding independent experts having testified to the sizeable contribution to the Irish economy brought about by filming production activity, the sector remains grossly underfunded. Both government and Revenue of course understand the positive impact the sector bestows on the exchequer and this is reflected to some extent in the s 481 tax credit which, aside from RTÉ-related productions, is the engine of the industry.

---

[23] Regulation (EU) No 1295/2013 of the European Parliament and of the Council of 11 December 2013 established the Creative Europe Programme (2014 to 2020). The 2021 Regulation established the programme for the period from 2021 to 2027.

[24] Eurimages support is therefore granted in the form of an advance on receipts repayable from the first euro of producer net receipts. Repayment is due up to 100 percent of the amount awarded. The support amount is repayable from producer net receipts at a rate equal to the percentage of the Eurimages share in the financing of the film, and after deduction of distribution guarantees and/or pre-sales necessary for the financing of the film upon which binding agreements have been concluded.

Chapter 10

Copyright, Moral Rights and Performer Rights

Part A: Chain of Title, Copyright and Moral Rights

INTRODUCTION TO CHAIN OF TITLE

[10A.1.01] Chain of title[1] in entertainment practice relates to contractual agreements pursuant to which a bundle of rights[2] are acquired to permit commercial exploitation of television programmes, films, concerts, radio show productions, theatrical performances and so on.[3] Fundamentally, it governs the copyrights, performer rights[4] and moral rights generated from and in such activities (and relating to pre-existing works where applicable)[5] but it can also, for example, encompass privacy law issues as governed, for instance, by a life rights or contributor/collaborator agreement, and the clearance of trademarked products

1 Chain of title is generally understood in the legal and banking fields to be a conveyancing term that describes how a current owner of a residential or commercial property has come to acquire good title to such property. Legal ownership is grounded upon and commences with a "good root of title". Title documents, however, refer not only to deeds of transfer, conveyances, leases, assignments, mortgages and probate documents but also to supporting documents including grants of planning permission, certificates of compliance with planning permission and building regulations, evidence of discharge of or exemption from taxes and so forth – essentially any documents that show good marketable title and which will facilitate sale, mortgage or other alienation of a property more readily. Similar concepts hold true in the entertainment sector. When we analyse title to land and buildings, we look to freehold (generally absolute ownership) and leasehold title (subject to covenants and conditions including rent, insurance, repair, restrictions on subletting etc.). In the same way, title to a film or a music album can be transmitted, bought and sold, licensed and passed on by succession such as under the provisions of a last will and testament. Copyrights in the form of proprietary rights, similar to their real and personal property brethren, can also come with restrictions, e.g. a licence granted by a production company to a distributor to theatrically or otherwise exploit a movie in France for three years, or the right granted by a songwriter's publisher to a film producer to use 25 seconds of a commercially released track in a movie for theatrical release worldwide.

2 Through assignment and/or licensing.

3 In the wider sense it relates also to record-keeping generally to comply with statutory and regulatory obligations, to meet insurance and funding requirements and for the purposes of deliverables.

4 For instance, of actors, singers, dancers and musicians.

5 Such as a short story or play.

and services. The chain should be unbroken, verifiable and documented. Any chinks such as a missing talent agreement, option agreement,[6] location release, prop release or music licence could prove fatal in terms of potentially exposing a production company, broadcaster or distributor to legal proceedings.

Funding requirements and regulatory compliance

[10A.1.02] Chain of title due diligence means an investigation by financiers, private and public service broadcasters, online streaming platforms, sales agents and distributors whose legal teams will trace back through a series or chain of rights to ensure that the production company has acquired all requisite legal authority and consents from every concerned party and contributor so as to commercially exploit a production. Thus, on formal delivery of a feature film, an entertainment lawyer will oftentimes be called upon to furnish a written opinion or chain of title report vouching that all IP matters are in order, to include, where applicable, reliance on exemptions to copyright infringement such as fair dealing and incidental inclusion of a third party's work.

[10A.1.03] More holistically, aside from talent, cast, crew and other production-related contracts, the producers must also document that proper procedures were followed in the case of regulatory obligations including in respect of permits and insurance, taxation, accounting, data protection and to fulfil funding requirements.[7] In the latter connection, for example, to avail of the s 481 (Taxes Consolidation Act 1997) ('s 481') film relief that may part-finance production, there are specific statutory requirements in respect of employment,[8] and training and skills development of participants on the production.

Avoiding litigation

[10A.1.04] Every stakeholder will have robust measures in place to resist writs being issued. Proceedings can be instituted against Irish productions by Irish and foreign plaintiffs – see international conventions at para [10A.2.11] below. To that end, evidence of errors and omissions ('E&O') cover will be sought from producers by distributors and financiers. As seen in the Canadian Supreme Court case of *Cinar* discussed later in this chapter (see 10A.6.46), both the co-production companies and the distributors of *Robinson Sucroë*, a children's television show, were named as defendants in circumstances whereby the creator

---

6 In respect of option agreements, proof of payments made to authors on foot of such agreement should be documented.

7 Evidencing, for example, adequate production insurance and errors and omission cover, and compliance with legislation and broadcasting codes such as in the case of safety laws, obtaining local authority permits for filming or road closures, employing child actors under ministerial licence, and where television show product placement or sponsorship rules are at issue.

8 For instance, gender equality, diversity and inclusion; safety, health and welfare legislation; adherence to minimum notice of employment terms.

of the original concept claimed the defendants had substantially copied his work. Separately, it is noteworthy too that defamation law (and parody/satire issues) will differ in Ireland and the US for instance and target markets must be judiciously considered by producers and/or their legal advisers when analysing script and content.

[10A.1.05] Further, in the *Zeccola* case (at para [10A.6.21]) we will see that a movie's exploitation in a particular territory (US) can be prohibited by injunction – here, blatant infringement of copyright in a novel, screenplay and in the *Jaws* motion picture by the film *Great White* allowed Universal to secure interlocutory relief and seizure of the offending copycat release. In addition, the 2016 *VMG Salsoul v Ciccone* 824 F.3d 871 (9th Cir. 2016) proceedings against Madonna in respect of the song *Vogue*[9] reinforce the mantra that one should always obtain permission where appropriate.

[10A.1.06] That case involved less than a half a second of music but landed the defendant pop icon (and song producer, label and publisher) in trial court and later in appellate court to ultimately vindicate that copyright had not been violated by virtue of the *de minimis* doctrine.[10] With hindsight, if Shep Pettibone, producer of *Vogue*, could rewind, he most likely would have sought clearance to use and modify the plaintiff's subject music segment. Though successful, the defendants were ordered to pay almost $1 million in defence legal costs.

Written assignments and waivers

[10A.1.07] In the entertainment sphere, oral agreements in the main[11] are wholly unsatisfactory given that various sections of the Copyright and Related Rights Act 2000 (as amended, and throughout this chapter referred to as 'the 2000 Act') provide, for example, that an assignment of the copyright in a work

---

9 Note separately that legal proceedings relating to *Madonna: Truth or Dare*, a docufiction chronicling the life of Madonna during her Blonde Ambition World Tour in 1990, were instituted in 1992 against the popstar and her production company wherein three dancers claimed that she had invaded their privacy during filming as well as alleging fraud and deceit, intentional misrepresentation, suppression of fact, and intentional infliction of emotional distress for displaying the men's private lives (and exposing homosexuality as regards two claimants) in the documentary. With a worldwide gross of $29 million, it was the highest-grossing documentary of all time, until *Bowling for Columbine* surpassed it in 2002.

10 For a discussion on this in an Irish context see the classic statement on where this principle should be applied contained in the judgment of Henchy J in the Supreme Court's decision in *Monaghan UDC v Alf-a-Bet Publications Ltd* [1980] ILRM 64, at p 69, referred to in the Labour Court case *Patrick Hall v Irish Water* [TED161] in which it set out the approach to be adopted where a technical breach of legislation had no practical consequence for the plaintiff. This principle is encapsulated in the Latin maxim *de minimis non curat lex* (the law does not concern itself with trifles).

11 There can be exceptions relating to other matters in the employer/employee sphere such as arose in the *Robin Ray* decision mentioned below at [10A.6.14] and in *Mei Fields* below where the courts can entertain oral agreements.

(whether in whole or in part) is not effective unless it is in writing and signed by or on behalf of the assignor. The same holds true for waivers of moral rights and assignments of performer rights.[12]

Valid assignment

[10A.1.08] In the 2018 *Mei Fields* case, the UK court was faced with interpreting if the following handwritten document gave rise to a valid assignment of copyright:

> I, Mei Fields, as owner of the copyright of my designs, allow my works to be used by MEI FIELDS DESIGNS LTD, and transfer ownership of copyright. My designs may be licensed with my permission. These include all works dating from 1st January 2000 and future works until further notice or termination.[13]

[10A.1.09] The plaintiff company relied on this document as being an effective assignment at law, or, in the alternative, as an effective exclusive licence. The defendants averred that the document was not an assignment, and was no more than a bare non-exclusive licence which was terminable at the will of Mrs Fields. Mr David Stone (sitting as an IPEC[14] judge) commented that the law on construction of contracts had recently been the subject of several judgments helpfully summarised by Popplewell J in *Lukoil Asia Pacific Pte Ltd v Ocean Tankers (Pte) Ltd*[15] as follows (at para 8):

> There is an abundance of recent high authority[16] on the principles applicable to the construction of commercial documents… The court's task is to ascertain the objective meaning of the language which the parties have chosen in which to express their agreement. The court must consider the language used and ascertain what a reasonable person…would have understood the parties to have meant. The court must consider the contract as a whole and, depending on the nature, formality and quality of drafting of the contract, give more or less weight to elements of the wider context in reaching its view as to the objective meaning of the language used. If there are two possible constructions, the court is entitled to prefer the construction which is consistent with business common sense and to reject the other.

[10A.1.10] The court applied Popplewell J's summary to the facts before it. The

---

12 See s 120(3) of the 2000 Act – assignment and licensing of copyright works; s 116(2) – waiver of author moral rights shall be in writing and signed by the person waiving the right concerned; s 293(3) – assignment and licensing of a performer's rights are ineffective unless in writing and signed by or on behalf of the assignor; and s 316(2) – waiver of moral rights in performances shall be in writing and signed by the person waiving the right.

13 [2018] EWHC 1332 (IPEC) at para 80.

14 Intellectual Property Enterprise Court (a specialist division of the High Court of England and Wales).

15 [2018] EWHC 163 (Comm).

16 Referring to *Investors Compensation Scheme Ltd v West Bromwich Building Society* [1998] 1 WLR 896; *Chartbrook Ltd v Persimmon Homes Ltd* [2009] 1 AC 1101; *Re Sigma Finance Corp* [2010] 1 All ER 571; Rainy *Sky SA v Kookmin Bank* [2011] 1 WLR 2900; *Arnold v Britton* [2015] AC 1619; and *Wood v Capita Insurance Services Ltd* [2017] AC 1173.

handwritten document was clearly unsatisfactory in legal terms, being internally inconsistent. If an assignment, it should not also make reference to licensing or termination. If a licence, then the word "assignment" is misplaced. The judge therefore looked at the commercial context to determine which interpretation was consistent with business common sense. In doing so, the court reached the conclusion that the document was an assignment.[17]

Contract clauses to assign copyright and related rights

[10A.1.11] Persons who are hired as independent contractors[18] will own the copyright in their own creations. Thus, their agreements, as standard, will need to assign the products of their services to the production company. If this was not the case, the production simply could not proceed as all rights must ultimately vest in the company (except in the case for example of certain music licences which grant specific rights only). Such contracts will invariably also provide for a waiver of moral rights as discussed from para [10A.9.01] to ensure that the production cannot be injuncted and exploitation prevented in the case of a dispute.

Work for hire

[10A.1.12] The US Supreme Court case of *Reid*[19] in the late 1980s exemplifies the employee versus contractor position in terms of copyright ownership in an area of US law referred to as "work for hire". The ownership of works for hire belong to a third party (e.g. production company or record label) rather than the creator.[20] Generally, employers automatically own the copyright of their employees, and are therefore considered the legal author, but not of hired contractors.[21] A work for hire in US copyright law is therefore a work that is

---

17 This interpretation was more consistent with the commercial consequences. The plaintiff company had proceeded to license Fields' card designs to third parties. These licences were not expressed to be sublicences. Whilst some of the words of the document were inconsistent with that interpretation, interpreting it as an assignment did less violence in the judge's view to the main claim "I ... transfer ownership of copyright" than interpreting the document as a licence. Hence, the document was effective to assign any copyright owned by Fields to the company.

18 Which will be the norm for heads of department and crew in film, stage and other short-term productions where cast too might also be contractors.

19 *Community for Creative Non-Violence v Reid*, 490 US 730 (1989).

20 *Fifty-Six Hope Road Music Ltd v UMG Recordings* 08 CIV. 6143 (DLC) (S.D.N.Y. 10 September 2010) was a case brought by the heirs of Bob Marley who claimed ownership of the renewal copyrights in some of Marley's famous sound recordings. The US District Court for the Southern District of New York in 2010 granted UMG's motion for partial summary judgment, dismissing the plaintiffs' claim to the copyrights in question. The court held that, through its predecessor-in-interest, UMG is the statutory "author" of the recordings, which were "works for hire" for purposes of the Copyright Act of 1909. As such, UMG is the owner of the initial and renewal term copyrights in the recordings.

21 Unless the work is custom-ordered or commissioned from the contractor and both parties agree in writing that the services are performed on a work for hire basis. The position in the UK was laid out by the Court of Appeal in *R Griggs Group v Evans* [2005] EWCA Civ 11 (the mere fact that the contractor has been commissioned is insufficient to entitle

subject to copyright and is created by employees as part of their job or some limited types of works for which the parties agree in writing to the work for hire designation.

[10A.1.13] Justice Thurgood Marshall, delivering the court's opinion, held that Reid was an independent contractor, not an employee and accordingly the work was not "made for hire" and therefore belonged to Reid.[22]

[10A.1.14] Present-day contracts with both contractors and employees will almost invariably provide that the subject work is in fact a work for hire so that the production company is the equivalent of an employer (for US law purposes) and in any case will be the contractual owner by virtue of an assignment therein from relevant contractors of their copyright in the work/services in question.

Reassignment in the case of dissolution of assignee company

[10A.1.15] It is important in any contract purporting or intending to assign copyright to an assignee company[23] that any rights transferred thereto will revert to the assignor if the assignee company is dissolved by liquidation or otherwise in the future. The same holds true in the case of insolvency or bankruptcy if the assignee is a sole trader individual.

[10A.1.16] In the case of Screen Ireland development loans whereby it takes a share of copyright as security for the production loan funding advanced, one of its minimum contract terms requirements is that no agreement (e.g. with a screenplay writer) can contain any provision which provides for a reversion of rights to that writer arising on breach of contract, bankruptcy or insolvency of the production company (though rights might otherwise revert).[24] This certainty of rights ownership protects the production company and its assignees. Because of financial investment in the project, its assets need to be guarded and ultimately commercially exploited by the financiers.

COPYRIGHT: AN OVERVIEW

[10A.2.01] The first disrupter to IP rights was perhaps Gutenberg's printing press

---

the client to the copyright. The contractor is entitled to retain the copyright in default of some express or implied term to the contrary effect).

22 The court determined that the defendant's commission was not "specially ordered or commissioned" under the work for hire statutory definition. Reid supplied his own tools, was without any extensive supervision and was free in the way he met his deadlines. The plaintiff could not assign more projects to him and paid him in the normal manner independent contractors are remunerated.

23 For instance where a producer sells concept or television format rights to a third party entity.

24 For example, if the project cannot obtain production financing and is not developed within a period of five years.

in the 15th century, later followed by the modern photocopier. The Statute of Anne,[25] the world's first copyright statute which recognised that authors should be the primary beneficiaries of copyright protection and not the all-powerful printing companies and stationers of the time, followed in Britain in 1710 and set the maximum[26] term of 28 years for copyright protection. This milestone statute was a catalyst for enactment of copyright legislation internationally such as in the US in 1790 and France a few years later.[27] Aside from international conventions through the years such as the Berne (1886), Rome (1961) and WIPO (1996) treaties, EU law has shaped copyright evolution in this jurisdiction including, for instance, enactment of the Copyright and Other Intellectual Property Law Provisions Act 2019 ('the 2019 Act') which affects such matters as parody as a fair dealing defence to copyright infringement,[28] and the EU (Copyright and Related Rights in the Digital Single Market) Regulations 2021[29] as discussed in Chapter 11 which transposed the hotly debated 2019 Directive on Copyright in the Digital Single Market into Irish law.

[10A.2.02] Copyright or authors' rights are IP rights granted by statute[30] (both in Ireland and in domestic laws around the world) and under international conventions[31] to authors as creators of works. Section 17 of the 2000 Act provides *inter alia* that copyright subsists in original literary, dramatic, artistic or musical works, sound recordings, films, broadcasts or cable programmes.[32] The basis of copyright protection is that, *per* Lord Wilberforce, "one man must not be able to appropriate the result of another's labour".[33] Creators (termed "authors" in statutory parlance) of a work such as a song, book or play hold the copyright in that work. This means that they have the exclusive right to display,

---

25 Long title: An Act for the Encouragement of Learning, by Vesting the Copies of Printed Books in the Authors or Purchasers of such Copies, during the Times therein mentioned.

26 14 years extendable by a further 14-year period.

27 Dr Mark Hyland, *European Copyright Law, from the Printing Press to the Digital Age – A Journey of Constant Change* (2020). IMRO and Law Society Annual Copyright Lecture. Law Society of Ireland, at p 6.

28 This, however, does not affect defamation law.

29 SI No 567 of 2021.

30 EU Directives, as transposed into national law, have also exerted great influence on this area of legal practice and recent developments in this regard will be discussed in Chapter 11.

31 The Berne Convention 1886 (discussed at [10A.2.11] and [10A.7.01]) was applied, for example, by Buxton LJ in *Norowzian v Arks Ltd (No 2)* [1999] EWCA Civ 3014.

32 Copyright may also subsist in design arrangements, either as a graphic work or as a work of artistic craftsmanship. See *Response Clothing Ltd v The Edinburgh Woollen Mill Ltd* [2020] EWHC 148 (IPEC), Directive 98/71/EC of the European Parliament and of the Council of 13 October 1998 on the legal protection of designs, the Industrial Designs Act 2001 (repealing the Acts of 1927 and 1929) and ss 78 and 79 of the 2000 Act.

33 *LB (Plastics) Ltd v Swish Products Ltd* [1979] RPC 551 (House of Lords). This case is a leading authority for the proposition that it is for the plaintiff to establish and prove as a matter of fact that copying has taken place. Proof of copying will usually begin with the establishment of similarity combined with proof of access to the plaintiff's works. Once access and similarity are established, the burden will move to the defendant to establish independent creation.

perform, create or authorise reproductions or copies of their works. In the case of audiovisual works, the original copyright creators such as screenplay writers will assign their rights to the production company. In the case of commercial music, labels and publishers will license rights to the production.

Related rights

[10A.2.03] Performers, music producers/labels and broadcasters who make works available to the public also enjoy statutorily-protected related rights.[34] RTÉ, for instance, which produces a programme in-house will own the copyright in that programme as broadcast and can generate revenue in archive fees over time if segments of that broadcast are reused by third parties in subsequent documentaries for example. Musicians and actors hold performer rights and will assign rights to film and television producers. Musician performers on a master sound recording used in a film, as well as a release fee if the music is specially commissioned, are entitled to royalties from music collection societies each time the film is shown in public. Actors, in certain territories (e.g. UK and US), are entitled to reuse and repeat fees. This is not the position in Ireland but lobbying by actor representatives and unions continues so as to reach parity with our British counterparts.

Economic rights and succession law

[10A.2.04] Economic rights enable rightsholders to control the use of their works and other protected material and ensure payment and income for their use. They normally take the form of exclusive rights, notably to authorise or prohibit the making and distribution of copies as well as communication to the public. An example is the right given by a playwright to a theatre to perform a play written by that playwright or the right granted by a novelist to a filmmaker to adapt the story to a screenplay. These rights[35] and the terms of their protection are harmonised at EU level.

[10A.2.05] Hence, as copyright and any related or neighbouring right is a form of property, the right may be transferred to another party or entity, such as to film producer, theatrical production, music publisher, distributor or to Screen Ireland[36] and can also be transmitted by will or intestacy[37] under the rules of succession law.[38] During one's lifetime, this can be effected via sale or partial sale

---

[34] Sometimes referred to as "neighbouring" rights.

[35] Another is the right of the owner of the copyright in a literary, dramatic, musical or artistic work, sound recording or a film to grant or refuse authorisation for cable retransmission of a broadcast or cable programme from another EU member state in which the work is included. See s 174 of the 2000 Act and Directives 93/83/EEC and (EU) 2019/789.

[36] In certain cases, Screen Ireland will require a share of copyright in the project.

[37] See s 120 of the 2000 Act.

[38] For this reason, claims of IP infringement or in respect of other IP-related matters can be taken by estates of deceased rightsholders. See, for example, the Martin Gaye proceedings in relation to Ed Sheeran and separately as regards the *Blurred Lines* track discussed at

by assignment or by licence (whereby permission for use is granted). Licences to use copyrighted material, such as a pop song in a television commercial, can be granted on an exclusive or non-exclusive basis as detailed in Chapter 23.

International enforcement

[10A.2.06] One might question how, where a producer uses a Columbian or Swedish song in a film shown in Irish cinemas that has not been cleared for such use, the copyright holders may file suit here against such producer. If it is broadcast on US television, for example, they will most likely bring proceedings against the US distributors in the US for ease of access to the courts and for cost implications. In respect of Irish dissemination, the rightsholders can likewise issue legal proceedings in this jurisdiction for damages or to injunct further public showings. This stems from our obligations under international copyright law and the principle of national treatment as below.

[10A.2.07] A global system of copyright enforcement exists, established by six conventions. At the heart of the system is the principle of national treatment, meaning that copyright and related rights owners will be treated as if they are nationals of the territory in which the infringement is taking place and can claim the protection of copyright laws there and bring proceedings for copyright violation. Copyright owners desirous of using this international system must be prepared, however, to sue in a foreign jurisdiction with the added difficulties and costs that may be involved.

[10A.2.08] The relevant conventions *inter alia* require contracting states to protect trademarks, copyright and related rights and provide specific remedies for infringement as well as enforcement and dispute resolution procedures. Protection and enforcement of all IP rights is a balancing exercise between producers and users in a manner conducive to social and economic welfare, cognisant of the respective rights and obligations.

[10A.2.09] In September 2022, for example, it was ruled by US District Judge Louis Stanton in Manhattan that English singer-songwriter Ed Sheeran must face trial in one of three lawsuits alleging that he copied his 2014 smash hit *Thinking Out Loud* from Marvin Gaye's 1973 classic *Let's Get It On*. Likewise, *F.B.T. Productions, LLC v Let Them Eat Vinyl Distribution Ltd*,[39] concerned Marshall Mathers' (Eminem's) lesser known and less successful first album entitled *Infinite* recorded in 1996 and (partially unsuccessful) proceedings instituted in England by this US company.

[24.6.25] and [24.6.02] respectively. And in early 2022, Jimi Hendrix's estate sued the bandmates' heirs after an alleged royalties and copyright threat.

39 [2019] EWHC 829 (IPEC).

[10A.2.10] Further, in *Lucasfilm Ltd v Ainsworth,*[40] the British Supreme Court held that a US copyright infringement action was justiciable in the English courts. Although the infringing acts were taking place in the US, the defendant was a UK national and domiciled there, which gave the English courts personal jurisdiction over him. Meanwhile, in *Editions Musicales v Universal Music Publishing Ltd*[41] the claimant, EMA, a French music publishing company, brought an action in England in September 2011 against the first two defendants (Universal and Sony/ATV) seeking a declaration that EMA owned the copyright to *Alright Alright, Alright* released in 1973 by the band Mungo Jerry which it was alleged was a copy of the French hit song *Et Moi, Et Moi, Et Moi.*[42]

The international conventions

[10A.2.11] The six principal copyright conventions are: the Berne Convention 1886; the 1952 Universal Copyright Convention (UCC);[43] the Rome Convention 1961;[44] the Agreement on Trade-Related Aspects of Intellectual Property Rights (TRIPS) signed in 1995 between all the member nations of the World Trade Organisation; followed by the World Intellectual Property Organisation (WIPO) Copyright Treaty 1996 and the WIPO Performances and Phonograms Treaty (effective from 2002). The Copyright Directive 2001[45] also known as the Information Society Directive or the InfoSoc Directive (as amended by the Directive on Copyright in the Digital Single Market 2019) implemented the 1996 WIPO Copyright Treaty. Lastly, the Beijing Treaty on Audiovisual Performances (adopted in 2012 and ratified in 2020) *inter alia* grants relevant performers moral rights and four kinds of economic rights for their performances as fixed in audiovisual fixations for instance as used in films, being the rights of reproduction, distribution, rental and the right of making available.[46]

---

40 [2011] UKSC 39.

41 [2017] EWHC 1058 (IPEC).

42 In *Performing Right Society Ltd v Qatar Airways* [2020] EWHC 1872 (Ch), the English High Court ruled in favour of the Performing Right Society ('PRS') in a question over whether a landmark copyright infringement case against the defendant airline should be heard by the English courts. PRS was seeking damages from Qatar Airways ('QA') for using its members' repertoire without a music licence being in place. The airline, which operates over 200,000 flights per year, and offers music as part of its in-flight service had never remunerated PRS members, songwriters, composers or music publishers for the use of their IP. PRS contended that infringement was taking place in the UK, Qatar and/or any other signatory country to the Berne Convention, WIPO Copyright Treaty or TRIPS Agreement whenever a relevant QA aircraft was present in a country, either on the ground or in the territorial airspace of a country.

43 To include Latin America and the US which had issues with elements of Berne.

44 Which added protection for performers, sound recordings and broadcast organisations.

45 Directive 2001/29/EC of the European Parliament and of the Council of 22 May 2001 on the harmonisation of certain aspects of copyright and related rights in the information society.

46 The treaty also covers unfixed (live) performances. It is the first international treaty aimed at protecting audiovisual performances. A right to equitable remuneration for any broadcasting and communication to the public – as art 8(2) of the Rental and Lending Directive 2006/115 grants to phonograms – does not exist for audiovisual recordings.

[10A.2.12] Signatory countries to the above IP treaties cannot require copyright owners to follow particular formalities (such as registering their copyright in that country) before being allowed to take advantage of national treatment there. However, the UCC provides that, if formalities are required in any particular country, that country must regard them as satisfied where the copyright owners mark their work with a copyright notice comprising the copyright symbol (©) together with the author's name and year of publication. TRIPS provides that copyright must be granted automatically, and not based upon any formality such as registration (as was previously specified in the Berne Convention).[47]

The Recast Brussels Regulation 2012[48]

[10A.2.13] The Recast Brussels Regulation 2012 ('the Recast Regulation') which repealed and replaced the 2001 Brussels Regulation[49] has EU-wide effect and governs jurisdiction and the recognition and enforcement of judgments (given after 10 January 2015) in civil and commercial matters across the union. Jurisdiction or 'choice of court' agreements are commonly used in commercial agreements. Under the 2001 Brussels Regulation, Member State courts were obliged to recognise such agreements, provided at least one of the parties was domiciled in the EU. The Recast Regulation removes that requirement. Now, where parties to a contract, regardless of their domicile, agree that the courts of a particular Member State will have jurisdiction to settle any disputes which arise in connection with the contract, the jurisdiction clause must be recognised by all EU Member State courts.[50]

The Enforcement Directive

[10A.2.14] Directive 2004/48/EC[51] as mentioned in (pre-Brexit) IPEC decisions such as that of Hacon J in *Tumber v ITN*[52] when applying the provisions thereof, bolstered the rights of creators by harmonising civil remedies and measures available for the enforcement of IP rights across the EU.[53] Article 3(1) provides

---

47 When the US joined the convention on 1 March 1989 it continued to make statutory damages and attorneys' fees only available for registered works.

48 Regulation (EU) No 1215/2012 of the European Parliament and of the Council of 12 December 2012 on jurisdiction and the recognition and enforcement of judgments in civil and commercial matters (Recast Brussels Regulation) (effective from January 2015).

49 Council Regulation (EC) No 44/2001 of 22 December 2000 on jurisdiction and the recognition and enforcement of judgments in civil and commercial matters, which came into force on 1 March 2002.

50 For further discussion see Keith Smith, David Strahan, Florence Loric and Nicholas Cole, *The Recast Brussels Regulation: What It Means For Commercial Parties* (2015). Available at: http://www.arthurcox.com/wp-content/uploads/2015/02/Arthur-Cox-The-Recast-Brussels-Regulation-What-It-Means-For-Commercial-Parties-Feb-2015.pdf [Accessed 9 May 2018].

51 Of the European Parliament and of the Council of 29 April 2004 on the enforcement of intellectual property rights.

52 [2017] EWHC 3093 (IPEC).

53 Articles 13, 14 and 15 of the Directive deal with damages, legal costs and publicity

that Member States shall provide for the measures, procedures and remedies necessary to ensure the enforcement of the IP rights covered by the Directive. Those measures, procedures and remedies shall be fair and equitable and not be unnecessarily complicated or costly, or entail unreasonable time-limits or unwarranted delays. The European Communities (Enforcement of Intellectual Property Rights) Regulations 2006[54] transposed into Irish law those aspects of the Directive which were at that point not available under Irish law.

Access to the courts in Ireland

[10A.2.15] The Copyright and Other Intellectual Property Law Provisions Act 2019[55] (throughout this chapter referred to as 'the 2019 Act') which amends the principal 2000 Act also made consequential amendments to other jurisdictional legislation to facilitate improved access to the courts system for IP infringement claims. There was a strong imperative to improve access to the courts and aid the enforcement by individuals and companies of their IP rights in a timely, efficient and inexpensive manner. The 2019 Act thus permits the admission of IP disputes to the District Court and Circuit Court and for the amounts up to the monetary jurisdictions of those courts, namely up to €15,000, and between €15,001 and €75,000 respectively.[56]

[10A.2.16] In the longer term, this should lead to the development of a greater wealth of case law and precedent to benefit all parties.[57] It is also likely that, due

---

measures, that is, publication of judicial decisions. Matters to be taken into account by the competent judicial authorities of member states when ordering damages payable by culpable defendant infringers to the rightsholders, as appropriate to the actual prejudice suffered, include the negative economic consequences, to also encompass lost profits which the injured party has suffered, any unfair profits made by the infringer and, in appropriate cases, elements other than economic factors, such as the moral prejudice caused to the rightsholder by the infringements. As an alternative, courts may, in applicable cases, set the damages as a lump sum on the basis of elements such as at least the amount of royalties or fees which would have been due if the infringer had requested authorisation to use the IP right in question. Article 14 provides that member states shall ensure that reasonable and proportionate legal costs and other expenses incurred by the successful party, as a general rule, be borne by the unsuccessful party, unless equity does not allow this. In respect of advertising and publishing court decisions, Art 15 mandates that member states shall ensure that, in legal proceedings instituted for infringement of an IP right, the judicial authorities may order, at the request of the applicant and at the expense of the infringer, appropriate measures for the dissemination of the information concerning the decision, including displaying the decision and publishing it in full or in part. Member states may provide for other additional publicity measures which are appropriate to the particular circumstances, including prominent advertising.

54 SI No 360 of 2006.

55 Commenced by SI No 586 of 2019 (signed by the Minister for Business, Enterprise and Innovation on 26 November 2019 with an effective date of 2 December 2019).

56 The new statutory provisions therefore promote easier access, particularly for lower value cases of IP infringements which can be taken in the District Court with attendant savings in terms both of time and substantial legal costs. In higher value cases, it was not always economically feasible to prosecute same before the High Court (commercial list).

57 In addition, in the longer term, the increased enforcement activity by rightsholders may

to the reduced cost burden of taking enforcement actions, there may be higher numbers of cases taken and an increase in the numbers of legal practitioners specialising in IP matters, potentially leading to an overall reduction in legal costs for such expertise. This also helps to maintain Ireland's reputation as a high-performing country with regard to IP enforcement at all levels.[58]

NO COPYRIGHT IN NAMES

[10A.3.01] In *Dick v Yates*[59] (1881) it was held that a title is not long enough to constitute a literary work so as to attract copyright protection. The Court of Appeal's decision in the *Elvisly Yours* case[60] is discussed in Chapter 12 (trademarks), wherein the court confirmed the decision of Laddie J in the High Court disallowing registration in the UK of various name-related marks. Laddie J made it clear that (trademarks aside) the appellant could not own the words Elvis and Elvis Presley stating "there is nothing akin to copyright in a name" and continuing:

> Even if Elvis Presley was still alive, he would not be entitled to stop a fan from naming his son, his dog or goldfish, his car or his house "Elvis" or "Elvis Presley" simply by reason of the fact that it was the name given to him at birth by his parents. To stop the use of the whole or part of his name by another he would need to show that as a result of such use, the other person is invading some legally recognised right.

[10A.3.02] *Exxon Corporation v Exxon Insurance Consultants International Ltd*[61] is a leading authority in English law on the existence of copyright in a name alone and the infringement of a trademark. The Court of Appeal found that typically there is no copyright in a name, invented or otherwise[62] (and that a trademark can only be infringed when the infringing party shares part of the market segment).

---

lead to a change in the behaviour of competitors, users and consumers, as the increased likelihood of court action against infringements results in reduced levels of infringement overall.

58 A departmental Regulatory Impact Analysis (Department of Business, Enterprise and Innovation, *Regulatory Impact Analysis, Copyright and Other Intellectual Property Law Provisions Bill 2018*) of the Bill before it became the 2019 Act in evaluating the Copyright Review Committee's *Modernising Copyright* report of 2013 identified this as being important to attract research and development and other innovation sectors to develop and retain their IP in Ireland and its conclusions were also in keeping with other government policies such as the Innovation 2020 strategy and the Knowledge Development Box. This is a factor that has been discussed in many academic papers, with a WIPO Journal article expressing it clearly: "Countries that are perceived as having a clear, simple, effective and expeditious judicial system could display higher levels of investment. Firms may also conduct more R&D in these countries, for example, as this factor may facilitate their ability to appropriate benefits of their innovative activity".

59 (1881) 18 Ch D 76.

60 *Elvis Presley Enterprises Inc v Sid Shaw Elvisly Yours* [1999] RPC 567.

61 [1982] Ch 119; [1982] RPC 69.

62 Single letter commands used within a computer program, and those with longer names, even if clearly recorded in the source code, are unlikely to be entitled to a copyright.

[10A.3.03] However, television/film and animation character names, brand names, iconic building names and so forth can be registered as trademarks as can personal names although Chapter 12 sets out the practical difficulties sometimes faced in registering celebrity names as trademarks. In addition, use of a name (in a case where no trademark has been registered by the plaintiff) can give rise to a claim for passing off in tort law. The 2018 High Court of England and Wales decision in *Martinez T/A Prick v Prick Me Baby One More Time Ltd T/A Prick*[63] is a case in point.[64]

[10A.3.04] Notwithstanding the seemingly very clear copyright law position, due to possible passing off actions,[65] claims in respect of statutorily-registered trademarks, and the frequent requirement of distributors for a name/title check to be conducted (particularly in the US), it is advisable to conduct due diligence on a project's name to satisfy E&O insurers. In *Warner Bros Entertainment, Inc v The Global Asylum, Inc* No. 13-55352 (9th Cir. 2013), the law firm Jenner & Block successfully prevented a low-budget movie originally called *Age of the Hobbits* from being distributed under that name, arguing that the title unlawfully sought to ride the wave of Warner Brothers' blockbuster *The Hobbit: An Unexpected Journey*. The court issued a preliminary injunction barring Asylum from advertising, selling or distributing any film titled *Age of the Hobbits* or using any mark that is similar to *The Hobbit* or *The Hobbit: An Unexpected Journey*. The Ninth Circuit affirmed the injunction in October 2013.

[10A.3.05] In *Universal City Studios LLC v Global Asylum Inc*, Universal Studios prosecuted a trademark, unfair competition and copyright claim against a film studio that produced and distributed in the US and internationally a "mockbuster" DVD that copied the title, title design and key art for Universal's 2012 motion picture *Battleship*. Following litigation in the UK and in California, the defendant settled and agreed to change the title, title design and artwork to a non-infringing format for all distribution of the DVD worldwide.

[10A.3.06] By way of final example, the surname of the Rabbitte family in Roddy Doyle's book *The Snapper* seemingly had to be changed in his screenplay

---

63 [2018] EWHC 776 (IPEC).

64 Though the claimant's action for passing off ultimately failed on the grounds that the judge was satisfied that the use of the word 'PRICK' by the defendants did not amount to a material misrepresentation that the goods and services offered by the defendants were those of the claimants or were somehow authorised by or connected with the claimants. This was a dispute between a tattoo artist (and his company) and a retailer of cacti about the use of the trading name PRICK. Prick Tattoos was well known as Martinez had created and applied tattoos to Amy Winehouse. In 2016, Leon (the second defendant) opened a cactus and succulent plant shop called Prick through a company of which she is the sole director and shareholder called Prick Me Baby One More Time Ltd. The plaintiffs claimed that the defendants' use of the word PRICK in the context of the first defendant's business selling cacti and succulents amounted to passing off.

65 Arising with unregistered trademarks where there is a likelihood of customer confusion.

for a film of the same name to Curley due to *The Commitments* movie in 1991 which featured the same characters.

COPYRIGHT IN INTERVIEWS

[10A.4.01] Interviews should always be covered by a release agreement signed by the contributor to cover both the assignment of performer rights[66] and for data protection consent and privacy/duty of confidentiality purposes. In the case of a documentary film, a contributor agreement will need to be signed and the issue of life rights agreements may also arise (see Chapter 18).

[10A.4.02] When a freelance journalist conducts a recorded interview with a public figure, and then types it up in a verbatim report, the journalist, not the interviewee, would own copyright in the report. In *Hager v ECW Press Ltd*[67] the Federal Court of Canada (*per* Reed J) stated:

> [U]nder Anglo-Canadian law, insofar as private interviews are concerned, it is the person who reduces the oral statements to a fixed form that acquires copyright therein. That individual is considered to be the originator of the work.

[10A.4.03] This proposition was affirmed in *Neugebauer v Labieniec*[68] (reversed on other grounds on appeal) by Simpson J (Federal Court) who further remarked that "people do not have copyright in a work simply because they are its subjects or respond to questions in interviews", at para 39. Both *Hager* and *Neugebauer* relied significantly on prior findings of the Ontario Court of Appeal in the below-mentioned *Gould decision.*

[10A.4.04] However, some words of caution are apposite. If the freelance journalist was in fact employed in a contract for service (e.g. for a newspaper) and the report was generated in the course of employment, the employer may be the presumptive owner. If a third-party recorded the interview, that party could have a claim to copyright in the sound recording and/or cinematographic work (which a verbatim transcription might infringe) depending on the nature of the recording and whether it was made under the journalist's direction.

[10A.4.05] Furthermore, if the interviewee had prior access to the questions, and particularly if answers were fixed (e.g. written out) before the interview, a court might find that the journalist's report (and recording) actually infringed the interviewee's copyright, at least insofar as the "work" containing the prepared answers is concerned. The court in *Gould* (see fn 101) seemed focused on the casual and informal nature of the conversations between interviewee Gould

---

[66] And payment of equitable consideration even if only nominal in amount or to reflect the fact that some form of money's worth has been paid.

[67] [1999] 2 FC 287, 1998 CanLII 9115 (FC).

[68] 2009 FC 666.

and bookwriter Carroll, and the spontaneous and offhanded nature of Gould's remarks. Thus, if Gould had provided something that amounted to more than "oral utterances", a different analysis may well have applied.

JOINT AUTHORSHIP

[10A.5.01] This area of IP law as it applies to music creation is comprehensively discussed with references to case law in Chapter 22. This chapter will instead discuss the legal principles as they apply in other artistic contexts such as in plays or in film.

[10A.5.02] As will be seen from the statutory definition in the following section, a work of joint authorship means a work produced by the collaboration of two or more authors in which the contribution of each author is not distinct from that of the other author or authors. For example, adding a scene to an existing play would not render the author of the additional scene a joint author of the full play unless there had been some collaboration and common design at the time the copyright work was created.

[10A.5.03] A film is treated in Ireland as a work of joint authorship unless the producer and the principal director are the same person. This in practice necessitates that directors assign their copyright in the film to the production company in a director's agreement.

[10A.5.04] The most significant recent case concerning the law of joint authorship (see Chapter 22) is the *Martin v Kogan* judgment[69] of the High Court of England in January 2021 (Meade J) which arose from a full retrial ordered by the Court of Appeal in October 2019,[70] reversing Hacon J's decision in November 2017[71] in the same court, IPEC.[72] The proceedings concerned rights to the screenplay for *Florence Foster Jenkins* starring Meryl Streep and Hugh Grant. The court ultimately found Kogan's authorship contribution to amount to 20 percent. Mr Justice Meade also delivered a follow-up decision in May 2021[73] in relation to the very net issue in these proceedings of IMDb credits.

[10A.5.05] Hacon J had originally held that the weight of the evidence supported Martin's claim to have been the sole writer of the drafts of the screenplay with only limited input from Kogan, which consisted of musical expressions of a technical nature, along with helpful criticism and some minor plot suggestions. This input was insufficient to qualify Kogan as a joint author. Martin was thus entitled to a declaration that he was the sole author of the screenplay. Upon

---

69 [2021] EWHC 24 (Ch).
70 [2019] EWCA Civ 164.
71 [2017] EWHC 2927 (IPEC).
72 The IP Enterprise Court (High Court, Chancery Division).
73 [2021] EWHC 1242 (IPEC).

retrial, however, following Kogan's successful appeal in the Court of Appeal, Meade J found that the screenplay work was in fact jointly authored. The Court of Appeal in considering extensive citations of authority summarised (at para 53 of its judgment) eleven legal principles applicable to addressing joint authorship as set out in Chapter 22.[74]

THE 2000 ACT AS AMENDED

[10A.6.01] IP law in Ireland, as it applies to entertainment, media and the arts, is governed in the main by the 2000 Act. The term IP generally, to include trademarks, designs and patents, refers to intangible creations of the mind such as inventions; literary and artistic works; designs; symbols; names and logos used in commerce. The 2000 Act also governs the "related" (neighbouring) rights afforded to performers, producers and broadcasters which are the rights of a creative work not connected with the work's actual author such as dance performances, music performances and sound recordings. Rights related to copyright will in addition include moral rights.

[10A.6.02] The treatment of copyright-protected material in audiovisual content is the most crucial legal consideration for producers. A frequently occurring example of this are issues relating to clothing, branded products or services, paintings, posters or artwork on walls, copyrighted wallpaper, published books as visible on shelves or dressers, and indeed iconic buildings and vehicles. For detailed exploration of these matters including music licensing, see Chapters 12, 14, 17 and 23.

Definitions

[10A.6.03] The 2000 Act defines "artistic works" in s 2(1)[75] as photographs, paintings, drawings, diagrams, maps, charts, plans, engravings, etchings, lithographs, woodcuts, prints or similar works, collages or sculptures. Therefore, subject to any statutory defence, beer company logos, for example, may potentially be caught by this provision such that filming of a line of taps of Budweiser, Guinness and Carlsberg in a bar scene might well infringe the copyrights (but more likely the trademarks) of these breweries if their consent was not obtained in advance.[76] Artistic works also include works of architecture, being either buildings or models for buildings, and works of artistic craftsmanship, e.g. a costume used for a period film.

---

[74] See also the judgment in *Mei Fields Designs* cited at para [10A.1.08] above.

[75] Note certain definitions in s 2(1) were amended by s 4 of the 2019 Act.

[76] However, such infringement is unlikely as the capturing of these trademarks on camera might well constitute an incidental use only (a statutory exception to copyright infringement) if it would not unreasonably prejudice the rights of its registered owner. In saying that, one must always be mindful of context and the issues discussed in Chapter 5 (defamation and product disparagement) and Chapter 12 (trademark infringement) should be assessed by the production's entertainment lawyer.

[10A.6.04] Artistic work is protected in s 17 to include buildings and structures. Accordingly, by recording/filming a building or structure, one is in fact copying or reproducing that building on screen and technically, therefore, permission should be sought from the owner and hence the use of location and prop agreements. However, incidental use is permitted as discussed below. There is also a statutory exemption available in s 93 of the 2000 Act in relation to representation (e.g. filming) of certain artistic works on public display such as buildings and works of artistic craftsmanship where permanently situated in a public place or in premises open to the public.

[10A.6.05] "Film" means a fixation on any medium from which a moving image may, by any means, be produced, perceived or communicated through a device and therefore includes shorts, music videos, documentaries for television/ cinema release and so forth.

[10A.6.06] "Work" means a literary, dramatic, musical or artistic work, sound recording, film, broadcast, cable programme, typographical arrangement of a published edition or an original database and includes a computer program.[77] Dramatic works include choreographic works or works of mime.

[10A.6.07] "A work of joint authorship" (s 22(1)) means a work produced by the collaboration of two or more authors in which the contribution of each author is not distinct from that of the other author or authors. Joint authorship is explored above with reference to recent case law developments in the UK. It is also affected by the 2019 Directive and transposing legislation.

Music copyright and related rights

[10A.6.08] In respect of IP attaching to music, a recorded song has potentially six elements in terms of rights: first, lyrics, being a "literary work" owned by the songwriter(s) or controlled by a music publisher; secondly, melody or music composition, being a "musical work" owned by the songwriter(s) or controlled by a music publisher; thirdly, the sound recording copyright owned by the music producer of that recording or a record label; fourthly, performer rights owned by the songwriter as vocalist/musician (if performing on the subject track) and by band members, singers, backing vocalists, arrangers and session/studio musicians; fifthly, moral rights of the songwriter; and lastly, moral rights of the performers/contributors.

Meaning of 'producer'

[10A.6.09] The s 2(1)[78] definition in the 2000 Act of "producer", in relation to a

---

77 Except in Pt II, Chapter 7 of the 2000 Act (moral rights) where "work" only means "literary, dramatic, musical or artistic work or film".

78 Section 2 was amended by Ministerial Order (European Communities (Copyright and

film or sound recording, means the person by whom the arrangements necessary for the making of the film or sound recording, as the case may be, are undertaken.

[10A.6.10] Confusion can often arise as to who is the music producer for the purposes of a sound recording particularly where there is no label and perhaps a lead band member takes charge. While the producer will either self-produce performances or book a studio session, pay the recording and mastering fees, organise session musicians, arrange a band's compositions for enhanced production values and so forth so that such person is clearly the "producer", it is best to immediately register the subject tracks with a collection society such as with Phonographic Performance Ireland or other collection society (e.g. PPL in the UK) or private company (e.g. Kobalt Music) to essentially put the matter beyond doubt. Such registration and copyright papers (including keeping signed musician releases on file) will greatly assist should ownership of the masters fall for dispute resolution, aside of course from ensuring the producer obtains public performance royalties and has the requisite legal authority to enter into master use licences for the purposes of film, advertising and other commercial exploitations of the material.

Producer case law

[10A.6.11] The 2015 IPEC case of *Henry Hadaway Organisation v Pickwick Group Ltd*[79] very usefully summarises a number of authorities relating to how the term producer is perceived by the courts. To Ms Melissa Clarke sitting as a deputy judge of the High Court, these decisions made it clear that the statutory test of "the person by whom the arrangements necessary for the making of the film are undertaken" is a "question of fact in each case" and provided some guidance on how that determination was to be approached.[80] The judgment of Sir Mervyn Davies in *Century Communications v Mayfair Entertainment*[81] involving the shooting of a film in China by a Hong Kong company is also illustrative.

Copyright in a film under EU law

[10A.6.12] Turning to the critically important default legal position that the producer and director of a film project are joint owners in Ireland, it is noteworthy that the rental and lending right Directive in 2006[82] which replaced

Related Rights) Regulations 2004 (SI No 16 of 2004)) which completed the transposition into Irish law of Directive 2001/29/EC on the Harmonisation of Certain Aspects of Copyright and Related Rights in the Information Society; the Broadcasting Act 2009, and of the Copyright and Other Intellectual Property Law Provisions Act 2019 (s 4).

79 [2015] EWHC 3407 (IPEC).

80 At para 49.

81 [1993] EMLR 335. See also *Beggars Banquet v Carlton Television* [1993] EMLR 349; *A&M Records Ltd v Video Collection International Ltd* [1995] EMLR 25, and *Slater v Wimmer* [2012] EWPCC 7. *Century Communications*, *Beggars Banquet* and *Slater* relate to the production of films while *A&M Records* relates to a sound recording.

82 Directive 2006/115/EC of the European Parliament and of the Council of

and repealed a 1992 Directive[83] provides in Art 2(2) that the principal director of a cinematographic or audiovisual work shall be considered as its author or one of its authors. Member States may provide for others to be considered as its co-authors (including screenplay writers). Ireland considers directors and producers in the 2000 Act to be joint authors and the practice is for directors to assign their copyright to the producer[84] (or production company more likely) in the directing services agreement. Bearing in mind the Directive and differing national copyright statutes across the EU, when an Irish film is being shot outside Ireland on continental Europe, it is important (where a country might deem a number of parties to be the joint owners of a film) to first ensure that all relevant rights are assigned to the production company and secondly that Ireland will be the relevant jurisdiction in the case of any legal disputes such that the production company will in fact be the owner to which rights have been assigned by the director.

Course of employment case law

[10A.6.13] *Per* s 21 of the 2000 Act, the owner of copyright is the author, meaning the person who creates the work (including contractors such as directors of cinematography and actors, and for this reason the products of their services must be assigned to the production company for audiovisual exploitation). For example, a photographer is the owner in the case of a photograph, a songwriter in the case of lyrics and melody, the music producer in the case of a sound recording, and the producer and principal director (as joint authors) in the case of a film and, as now expressly provided for in s 7 of the 2019 Act,[85] its soundtrack too.[86] Where an employee in the course of employment creates the work, the employer, pursuant to s 23, is the owner of the copyright in the work, unless an agreement to the contrary exists.

[10A.6.14] There is no requirement for an agreement to the contrary to be in writing: it can be oral or implied.[87] In *Robin Ray v Classic FM PLC*[88] it was argued that the consultancy agreement which governed the relationship between Mr Ray and Classic FM was a contract for services and not of employment. Lightman J rejected this and instead found that there was a contract of employment. Hence the statutory position prevailed (employer being the default owner of

---

12 December 2006 on rental right and lending right and on certain rights related to copyright in the field of intellectual property.

83 Council Directive 92/100/EEC.

84 If the producer is a sole trader or to a firm of producers if two or more producers are in partnership together.

85 Amending s 21 of the 2000 Act.

86 This default legal position will be altered in all commercial scenarios in a directing services agreement such that directors will assign their joint authorship in order that ownership, instead, is held solely by the film production company.

87 *Copinger and Skone James on Copyright* (17th ed, Sweet & Maxwell), paragraph 5-26.

88 [1988] FSR 622.

employee creations unless there was an agreement modifying this). As there was no agreement to the contrary, the employer owned the copyright.

[10A.6.15] For a full and extensive discussion of undertaking a task that may attract copyright in the course or scope of employment, see the aforementioned *Mei Fields* decision[89] wherein David Stone (sitting as an IPEC judge) held[90] that whether or not given acts were carried out in the course of employment for the purposes of the relevant legislation is a multifactorial assessment[91] and no single factor is likely to be determinative.

Future copyright

[10A.6.16] Future copyright, that is, prospective ownership of copyright, such as with screenplays or scripts not yet written or which require further drafting and polishing, is governed by s 121 of the 2000 Act. Where, by an agreement made in relation to future copyright and signed by or on behalf of the prospective owner of the copyright, that owner purports to assign the future copyright to another person or entity, then, where on the copyright coming into existence the assignee[92] would be entitled as against all other persons to require the copyright to be vested in such assignee, the copyright shall vest in the assignee.[93] In respect of prospective ownership of performers' property rights, see s 294.

[10A.6.17] An example of this is when a writer of a story featuring a character for use in a film is required[94] to sign away future rights to use of that character in sequel movies, television spinoffs or for merchandise products purposes. An agent for such writer will rigorously seek to retain that copyright. A compromise might be, as well as in consideration of a considerable fee for the film rights to the first movie, that the same writer is offered a right of first refusal to write further scripts for future productions in good faith on customary industry terms.

[10A.6.18] In a general sense, production agreements will contain a clause assigning "present and future copyright" to put the matter beyond doubt. This ensures at an early development stage or during production when contracts are being signed that material not yet written or recorded (or in respect of future services to be rendered) will form part of the assigned rights.

89 [2018] EWHC 1332 (IPEC).

90 At para 42.

91 Relevant factors may include the terms of the contract of employment; where the work was created; whether the work was created during normal office hours; who provided the materials for the work to be created; the level of direction provided to the author; whether the author can refuse to create the work(s); and whether the work is "integral" to the business.

92 Or successor in title.

93 Or successor in title or any other person claiming rights under an estate.

94 In an option and purchase/assignment agreement.

No protection for mere ideas

[10A.6.19] Copyright does not subsist in ideas. Section 17(3) of the 2000 Act provides that copyright protection shall not extend to the ideas and principles which underlie any element of a work. It relates instead to the form of expression, the physical form such as a book, MP4 file or WAV file. In terms of show format rights, the formats to internationally televised audition and entertainment shows from *X Factor* to *First Dates* are protected by copyright. In 1993, Chief Justice Mason[95] for the Australian High Court in *Autodesk Inc v Dyason* (No 2)[96] concerning copyright in a computer program, referred to this idea-expression divide as the "dominant principle in copyright law".

[10A.6.20] Accordingly, if a writer is discussing a film idea with a potential investor or producer, it is prudent to insist on execution of a non-disclosure or shopping agreement to protect the idea given that ideas themselves are not protected by copyright law while just existing in the creator's mind. A non-disclosure agreement is an enforceable contract and it will also evidence how the concept originated in the event of a later dispute. It is important too to give mere ideas written form such as in a treatment which will attract the courts' protection. The 2013 Canadian Supreme Court case of *Cinar* (see para [10A.6.46]) provides case law authority for the proposition that copyright resides in proposals, treatments and formats.

[10A.6.21] In an earlier Australian case too in 1982 of *Zeccola v Universal City Studios Inc*,[97] concerning blatant violation of copyright to the film *Jaws*, it was confirmed there is no copyright in the idea of a theme or a story but the matter did not rest there. Counsel for the appellants submitted that both films, *Jaws* and *Great White* are genre films based upon the idea of a savage monster menacing a community. Each is a film about a killer shark terrorising human beings and it was said that neither film was entitled to protection as there is no copyright in that general idea. The appellants also sought to dissect the films and to exclude from consideration stock scenes and banal events.

[10A.6.22] The appellate court was not swayed by such arguments holding *Great White* did not simply exploit a general idea, and that there may be a time where a combination of events and characters reaches sufficient complexity as to give rise to dramatic work copyright. Lockhart and Fitzgerald JJ thus noted that copyright subsists in the combination of situations, events and scenes which constitute the particular working out or expression of the idea or theme. If a literary or dramatic work is not wholly original there is no copyright in the unoriginal part so as to prevent its use. Here the trial judge at first instance had closely

---

95 The High Court of Australia, as the last court of appeal, is the equivalent of the Supreme Court in Ireland and in the UK.

96 (1993) 111 ALR 385.

97 [1982] FCA 271; 46 ALR 189; 67 FLR 225 (Federal Court, Victoria District, appeal from the Supreme Court of Victoria's judgment as trial court).

analysed the two films. Notwithstanding that the subject matter of the film *Jaws* was not particularly striking, the trial court held the view, in essence, that the combination of the principal situations, singular events and basic characters was sufficient to constitute an original work that was susceptible of protection under the law of copyright.[98]

[10A.6.23] *Reyher v Children's Television Workshop*[99] was a US case where the author and illustrator of a children's book sued a company that had published a television skit and a magazine story with a similar title and plot, claiming copyright infringement. The story was based on an old Russian folk tale. The court found that the plot or theme was not subject to copyright, and there had been no infringement since the book and the story or skit were quite different in all other respects. The court used the "total concept and feel" standard in reaching its decision and held that the essence of infringement lies in taking not a general theme but its particular expression through similarities of treatment, details, scenes, events and characterisation.

Tangible medium and fixation; registering copyright

[10A.6.24] Section 18 of the 2000 Act provides that copyright shall not subsist in a literary, dramatic or musical work or an original database until that work is recorded in writing or otherwise by or with the consent of the author (e.g. upon first fixation of a sound recording – that is not to say of course that performer rights do not arise in the case of live performances such as with live broadcasts).[100] Ergo, copyright takes effect as soon as the work is put on paper, film or other fixed medium such as Blu-ray disc, internet upload and so forth.[101] It is therefore automatic and no formalities are required. However, it is always best (see, for example, the Universal Copyright Convention above) to use the © and ℗ (phonographic copyright for sound recordings) symbols for the purposes of remedies in infringement proceedings. Software is also available nowadays to time-stamp works and thus keep a valuable evidentiary record.

---

[98] Moreover, this case did not centre on the main idea of a dangerous shark. The two films were spectacularly similar on a multitude of grounds each of which was explored in some detail by the trial judge to include plotlines, characters, names and settings.

[99] 533 F.2d 87 (Court of Appeals, 2nd Cir. 1976).

[100] See s 203(1)(b) of the 2000 Act.

[101] In the Canadian case of *Gould Estate v Stoddart Publishing Co Ltd* 39 OR (3d) 545; [1998] OJ No 1894, the Ontario Court of Appeal held that the oral statements (taken from audio recordings of interviews in 1956) of renowned classical pianist Glenn Gould could not be protected by copyright because there was no fixation. Gould was not reading from a speech, nor had he pre-prepared anything that was said. Jock Carroll as the author of the text and captions in a 1995 book (which contained 70 photographs from the 1956 interviews, as well a narrative that was largely based on the old notes and recordings, including many quotations by Gould) was the owner of the copyright in the written material the appellants were attempting to suppress. Mr Justice Finlayson stated that in protecting Carroll's artistic creation, the law permitted the public to benefit from an insight into Gould's early years to which it would otherwise be denied.

[10A.6.25] In the US, copyright (e.g. to music/lyrics and sound recordings) can be registered in the Library of Congress in Washington DC and registration, though not required, is helpful in terms of proofs and evidence in the case of a dispute or litigation.[102] Registration renders one's ownership part of the public record and allows rightsholders to sue for monetary damages in the event of proceedings regarding ownership. Registered works may be eligible for statutory damages and legal fees in successful litigation.

[10A.6.26] There is no registration procedure for copyright works under Irish copyright law, copyright protection is automatic and arises upon the creation of an original work[103] (however, music compositions, sound recordings and musical performances should of course be registered with collection societies for the purposes of ensuring royalties flow to the respective rightsholders). It is noteworthy too that s 139 of the 2000 Act reverses the usual onus of proof that applies in civil actions. Copyright shall be presumed to subsist in a work until the contrary is proved by the defendant.

Remedies for infringement

[10A.6.27] Before discussing how creators can control and restrict their works and enforce their rights, it is opportune to mention, what may well be obvious, that copyright shall not subsist in a work which infringes, or to the extent that it infringes, the copyright in another work – s 17(5) of the 2000 Act.

[10A.6.28] It is also noteworthy to mention in passing two decisions which are outside the scope of this textbook relating to online copyright infringement and the granting of Norwich Pharmacal Orders[104] as previously referred to in Chapter 4 in the context of defamation. The High Court cases of *EMI Records v Eircom Ltd*[105] and *Sony Music Entertainment (Ireland) Ltd v UPC Communications Ireland Ltd*[106] can be consulted in this connection.

---

[102] If registration is effected, owners will have *prima facie* evidence that they were the first to create the work meaning that the other side bears the burden of proof to prove that the work is not that of the registered owner.

[103] However, it is beneficial to note that WIPO has expanded its services targeting innovators and creators active in the digital economy by becoming a trusted Time Stamping Authority (TSA). On 27 May 2020, WIPO launched a new tool called 'WIPO PROOF' to deliver this service.

[104] Norwich Pharmacal relief is an equitable remedy given by the court which compels the respondent to disclose certain information or documents to the applicant only where it is deemed necessary and where the interests of justice require it. This form of order is primarily sought as a means of identifying the appropriate defendant to an action or obtaining information which is required to plead a claim. It is commonly sought against an innocent intermediary who, although not directly involved in the offending activity, holds information or documentation required for the issuing of proceedings.

[105] [2005] IEHC 233.

[106] [2015] IEHC 317, [2015] IEHC 386.

Acts restricted by statute

[10A.6.29] Section 37 of the 2000 Act as amended by s 11 of the 2019 Act provides that (subject to the exceptions such as education, library and private use and of course authorised licensing) the owner of the copyright in a work has the exclusive right to undertake, prohibit or authorise others to undertake all or any of the following acts, namely to copy the work;[107] to make available to the public the work such as via broadcasting, on-demand lending services, video, DVD rentals and so forth; and to make an adaptation of the work (such as from novel to screenplay or arranging a cover song differently to the original music). The copyright in a work is infringed by a person who without the licence of the copyright owner undertakes, or authorises another to undertake, any of these acts restricted by copyright.

Case law

[10A.6.30] In March 2013, singer-songwriter Johnny Duhan settled a long running legal dispute with RTÉ and a Dutch television production company over the alleged unlicensed reproduction of a performance of his song *The Voyage* by The Three Tenors. In an action launched in 2002, the plaintiff sued production companies Radius Television Production Ltd and TV Matters BV (Amsterdam) as well as RTÉ Commercial Enterprises Ltd over what he claimed was unlicensed reproduction, in the form of CDs, video recordings and other media, of the song as performed by the trio group. It was alleged the recordings took place during a date in 1999 at the RDS in Dublin and at different venues in the US. Duhan contended that those recordings of *The Voyage* amounted to an infringement of his copyright and moral rights in the song as made famous by singer Christy Moore.

[10A.6.31] The case had come before the courts in 2007 when Mr Justice Dan Herbert ordered that the claimant was entitled to limited legal disclosure (discovery) of documents, files, notes, records and correspondence in the defendants' possession relating to any performance of *The Voyage* produced by them within the EU during the period 1 January 1999 to 21 December 2002.

[10A.6.32] The defendants denied the claims, and had argued they were strangers to the precise authorship and copyright entitlement alleged by Duhan in the song. At the High Court in 2013, the plaintiff, representing himself, informed Laffoy J that the action had been resolved.[108]

---

[107] Under EU law too, rightholders (e.g. performers, authors and phonogram producers) have an exclusive right (the right of reproduction) which allows them to prohibit anyone from making a copy of their performance, work or recording, unless they obtain prior permission.

[108] As part of the settlement, it was also agreed that some €34,000 that had previously been lodged into court by the defendants was to be paid to the plaintiff. Two of the defendant companies (the third company had been struck off the register of companies) consented to the settlement and the court struck out the action. Source: Aodhan O'Faolain, *Songwriter settles long-running RTE dispute over 'The Voyage' song* (2013), independent.ie. Available at:

Civil and criminal liability

[10A.6.33] If a copyright owner's (including performer's) rights are infringed (lawful exceptions to infringement are discussed later), there are statutory remedies available under ss 127, 131 to 134, 303, 304 and 308 of the 2000 Act such that all relief by way of damages, account of profits, injunction or otherwise is available to the plaintiff as it is available in respect of the infringement of any other property rights. The 2000 Act allows also for application to be made to court for orders in respect of seizure and delivery up of infringing material. Further, the legislation provides for criminal offences and, consequently, infringers could face both civil liability and criminal conviction for piracy, unlawful copying/recording of a work, illegal downloading of music, films and software.[109]

[10A.6.34] Furthermore, ss 128 and 304 provide for the possibility of aggravated or exemplary damages or both in addition to or as an alternative to compensating the plaintiff just in the way of general damages (e.g. for financial loss). In the Canadian *Cinar* decision below at para [10A.6.46], punitive damages were awarded in addition to compensatory damages (as were non-pecuniary damages for psychological suffering).[110]

[10A.6.35] In July 2017, the High Court ruled that singer Tommy Fleming suffered "a serious setback"[111] following unauthorised broadcasts of his *Voice of Hope* DVD on an Irish television station, Irish TV, and was thus entitled to damages. The singer, his wife and manager Tina Mitchell Fleming, and their company TF Productions, were awarded a total of €150,000 damages against the broadcaster Irish TV. The station broadcast a promotional DVD sent out by the singer in relation to his 2004 recording *Voice of Hope* but under the title *The Tommy Fleming Musical Extravaganza*. The infringing broadcasts occurred in December 2014.

---

https://www.independent.ie/irish-news/courts/songwriter-settles-longrunning-rte-dispute-over-the-voyage-song-29128899.html [Accessed 12 April 2017].

109 In Japan, Isamu Kaneko, the developer of P2P file-sharing program Winny was indicted for aiding in copyright infringement. This was the first case in which a computer program developer faced a criminal charge for assisting in the copyright infringement by the program's users. In 2006, the Kyoto District Court found Kaneko guilty and fined him ¥1.5 million (in excess of €10,000). On appeal in 2009, the Osaka High Court overturned the lower court's decision. Finally, in 2011, the Supreme Court upheld the acquittal, holding that Kaneko did not intentionally induce infringement and was therefore not responsible for the users' unlawful actions. The prosecution could not prove that he had any intention to promote the software for illegal use.

110 This head of damage would arise in Ireland only in respect of cases such as "nervous shock", road workplace and other personal injury claims arising out of the defendant's negligence or for example in the case of a teacher who is subjected to bullying, harassment and infliction of emotional suffering.

111 Mr Fleming contended he would never have used the term "extravaganza" in relation to his work which to him meant "circus". He claimed he had been adversely affected because the *Voice of Hope* had been broadcast on a small channel with low ratings. This had compromised his ability to be featured on major broadcasters.

[10A.6.36] Gilligan J held the Flemings were entitled to €100,000 by way of damages for IP infringement, and TF Productions was awarded €50,000 in damages as a contribution to the money it expended on minimising its losses. The plaintiffs had incurred sums on hiring extra staff, marketing and advertising to redress the drop in ticket sales caused by the defendant's breach. The judge also awarded the three plaintiffs their legal costs against the defendants.

Prior access to pre-existing work

[10A.6.37] When determining whether unlawful copying of a prior or legacy work has occurred, courts will look to whether a defendant had access to that work.[112] The Court of Appeal decision in the British case of *Baigent v Random House Group Ltd*[113] (in which the allegation against American author Dan Brown was for infringement by *The Da Vinci Code* in taking the central themes of the claimants' book *The Holy Blood and The Holy Grail*[114] rather than of direct textual copying), which although decided before *Infopaq*,[115] is nonetheless helpful. Mummery LJ enumerated a number of issues likely to arise for decision in a case of alleged infringement of literary copyright, and in respect of access, relied on the following question:

> What access, direct or indirect, did the author of the alleged infringing work have to the original copyright work? Unless there was some evidence from which access can be directly proved or properly inferred, it will not be possible to establish a causal connection between the two works, which is essential if the claimants are to prove that the defendant's work is a copy.[116]

---

112 In *Ogunkoya v Harding* [2017] EWHC 470 (IPEC) Miss Recorder Amanda Michaels (Recorder in the UK means a part-time Circuit or High Court judge), while ultimately denying the plaintiff author's claim, accepted, in respect of alleged copyright infringement pertaining to three chapters of a book written by the claimant, that the defendant author clearly had access to that book. It had previously been purchased from the plaintiff by the defendant's mother.

113 [2007] EWCA Civ 247.

114 Brown admitted that he had referred to the earlier work in the course of research but denied copyright infringement. The claimants alleged that the defendant had copied the central theme of the work. At first instance Mr Justice Peter Smith found that six chapters of DVC were largely derived from HBHG but rejected the claim of copying – the claimants had not created a central theme as alleged and therefore no such theme could have been copied. The claimants appealed. The appeal was dismissed. The judge had been correct to consider whether the central theme was the central theme of HBHG (as opposed to one of several), and was entitled to come to the finding of fact which he did. Since there had been no central theme to copy and accordingly no substantial part copied, the issue of possible misdirection was irrelevant. The intention of the copier is irrelevant as a matter of law and animus furandi "should not be invoked in the future" (*per* Lloyd LJ).

115 Discussed below from para [10A.6.44]. The Court of Justice of the EU held that it is possible for relatively short parts of a longer work to be protected from copying where those parts of themselves form an expression of the author's intellectual creation.

116 At para 124(2) of the judgment.

Copying or reproducing a "substantial part" of the original

[10A.6.38] Copyright will be infringed if, without the permission of the copyright owner, any of the restricted acts are carried out in relation to the whole or a substantial part of the work (directly or indirectly). A substantial part of a work is a part of the work that represents a substantial portion of the author's skill and judgment expressed therein.[117] The burden of proof is on the claimant.[118] If copying is denied, but the defendant had access to the work and there is a sufficient degree of objective similarity between the copyright work and the alleged infringement, there is a rebuttable presumption that copying took place.

[10A.6.39] In the British case *Ashley Wilde Group Ltd v BCPL Ltd*,[119] Clarke J dismissed a claim for infringement of copyright in a prototype fabric for use in a celebrity-branded duvet cover, the *Kylie Minogue At Home* brand. The court held that it did not find the similarities between the Evangeline Design and the Amore products were sufficiently close, numerous or extensive to be more likely the result of copying than coincidence. The court was satisfied that the Amore products were independently designed and not copied. The court relied on dicta at p 2425 from Lord Millet in *Designers Guild v Russell Williams Textiles*[120] thus:

> It is at this stage that similarities may be disregarded because they are commonplace, unoriginal or consist of general ideas. If the plaintiff demonstrates sufficient similarity, not in the works as a whole but in the features which he alleges have been copied, and establishes that the defendant had prior access to the copyright work, the burden passes to the defendant to satisfy the judge that, despite the similarities, they did not result from copying.

[10A.6.40] The Guinness advert decision in the 1999 UK Court of Appeal case of *Norowzian v Arks Ltd (No. 2)*[121] produced what many might consider to be a rather surprising result. The case involved the hugely successful *Anticipation* advert which featured the actor, Joe McKinney, dancing around a large pint of Guinness while waiting for it to settle. In the course of the production of the film the editor had used a similar jump cutting technique to that used by renowned British director Mehdi Norowzian in a short piece entitled *Joy* with no dialogue, which was shot using a static camera on a London rooftop and

---

[117] In *Temple Island Collections Ltd v New English Teas* [2012] EWPCC 1 Judge Birss QC in the England and Wales Patents County Court held at para 63 that the defendants' work did reproduce a substantial part of the claimant's artistic work. In the end the issue turns on a qualitative assessment of the reproduced elements. The elements which had been reproduced were a substantial part of the claimant's work because, despite the absence of some important compositional elements, they still included the key combination of what the judge called the visual contrast features with the basic composition of the scene itself. Further in the earlier House of Lords case *Ladbroke (Football) Ltd v William Hill (Football) Ltd* [1964] 1 All E.R. 465 Lord Pearce at p 481 stated that, "Whether a part is substantial must be decided by its quality rather than its quantity".

[118] See House of Lords ruling in *LB (Plastics) Ltd v Swish Products Ltd* [1979] RPC 551.

[119] [2019] EWHC 3166 (IPEC).

[120] [2000] 1 WLR 2416, [2000] UKHL 58.

[121] [1999] EWCA Civ 3014.

comprised a jump cut sequence[122] of a man performing an extended dance of exuberance against a plain canvas background.

[10A.6.41] While the Court of Appeal unanimously held that the content of *Joy* as a film (including the use of film and editing techniques) could enjoy copyright protection (but not the artistic techniques demonstrated in it) as a dramatic work, it ruled that *Anticipation* did not significantly copy any portion of *Joy* and dismissed the proceedings. Ultimately, Norowzian was ordered to pay £200,000 in legal costs. The law lords stated in their very succinct judgment they had found it impossible to decide whether *Anticipation* was or included a copy of a substantial part of Norowzian's film:

> As the judge recognised, the highest it can be put in favour of the claimant is that there is a striking similarity between the filming and editing styles and techniques used by the respective directors of the two films. But no copyright subsists in mere style or technique...So here, the subject matter of the two films being, as the judge said, very different one from the other, the similarities of style and technique are insufficient to give the claimant a cause of action against the defendants.

[10A.6.42] Compared with US jurisprudence on, for example, music copyright law, as analysed in some detail in Chapter 24, the reasoning employed is far from sophisticated or comprehensive. However, simplicity (as opposed to over-analysis) can avoid the conflicting and unfair judgments that have been delivered across the Atlantic in such cases as *Gaye v Williams* (the *Blurred Lines* track – see para [24.6.02]) in which, unlike the within action, the majority of the three-judge appeals court in the view of dissenting judge, Judge Nguyen, had accomplished what no one had before – copyrighting a musical style.

[10A.6.43] As to comparing the films in their entirety Buxton LJ noted as follows:

> What therefore was original about *Joy* was indeed what was said to be the subject of the copyright: the film *as a whole*. The theme and originality of *Joy* was, as Mr Norowzian›s evidence stressed, a representation in stylised form of a young man hesitating with tension when coming amongst a group of unknown people but gradually gaining self-confidence. That essence and originality of *Joy* is however not reproduced at all in *Anticipation*. The drinker is not hesitant, but impatient. The only tension from which he suffers is not that of introspection, but of separation from his drink: as the advertiser of the drink no doubt wished to convey. For that reason, I am doubtful whether there

[122] Described at pp 70-71 by the trial judge, Mr Justice Rattee, thus: "This is a film editing process whereby the editor excises pieces of the original film within a sequence of movements by the actor, with the result that on the edited version of the film he appears to have performed successively, without an interval, two movements that in reality could not have immediately succeeded each other. . . The result of this technique being used in editing is, of course, a film apparently containing sudden changes in position by the actor or dancer which could never have been performed as successive movements in reality. This gives the finished film what was referred to in the course of the trial before me as a surreal effect".

has been any copying at all of *Joy* in its status as a copyright work. And even if that is not so, the nature of *Joy*, and of what gives it its copyright protection as a work, must affect the question of whether *Joy* has been substantially copied.

Further case law on 'substantial part'

[10A.6.44] To assess whether there has been copying of a substantial part, courts must look at the part of the copyright work which has been copied (not the copy) and assess substantiality on a qualitative not a quantitative basis [*Designers Guild Ltd v Russell Williams (Textiles) Ltd.*[123] However, (pre-Brexit) English[124] and European case law (*Infopaq International A/S v Danske Dagblades Forening*)[125] indicates that the test for whether a substantial part is taken has been replaced (or at least supplemented) by the question of whether or not part of the author's own intellectual creation has been taken, at least in relation to those rights that have been harmonised within the EU under the copyright Directives. EU law takes supremacy over national laws on treaty matters.

[10A.6.45] Section 37(3) of the 2000 Act (as substituted by the 2019 Act) is to be construed in conformity with Directive 2001/29/EC[126] ('the InfoSoc Directive'). In the landmark ruling in *Infopaq*, the CJEU held in 2009 that it is possible for relatively short parts of a longer work to be protected from copying where those parts of themselves form an expression of the author's intellectual creation. In *SAS Institute Inc v World Programming Ltd*[127] Lewison LJ held (at para 38) that, following *Infopaq*, the test for determining whether a restricted act has been done in relation to a substantial part of the work is whether that part contains elements which are the expression of the intellectual creation of the author of the work.[128]

[10A.6.46] *Cinar Corporation v Robinson*,[129] an immensely important iteration

---

123 [2001] 1 WLR 2416.

124 *Newspaper Licensing Agency Ltd and Others v Meltwater Holdings BV and Others* [2011] EWCA Civ 890.

125 C-5/08.

126 Directive 2001/29/EC of the European Parliament and of the Council of 22 May 2001 on the harmonisation of certain aspects of copyright and related rights in the information society.

127 [2013] EWCA Civ 1482, [2014] RPC 8.

128 The CJEU developed the *Infopaq* concept two years later in *Painer* by stating that an intellectual creation is an author's own "if it reflects the author's personality". That will be the case "if the author was able to express his creative abilities in the production of the work by making free and creative choices", "stamp[ing] the work created with his 'personal touch'" ("his personality"), *Painer v Standard VerlagsGmbH*, (C145/10), (§ 88-89, 92 and 94). And in *ATB Sales Ltd v Rich Energey Ltd* [2019] EWHC 1207 (IPEC) Clarke J (sitting as a judge of the High Court) put the matter very plainly when she stated, in considering whether a substantial part of a copyrighted work has been taken, that what matters is the extent to which that part contains elements which express the intellectual creation of the author, "If it contains elements which express the intellectual creation of the author, then it is a substantial part. If it does not, it is not".

129 [2013] SCC 73; [2013] 3 SCR 1168.

on the law of substantiality in copyright infringement concerned the concept for a television show for children. On 8 September 1995, the plaintiff/respondent watched on television the first episode of a new children's television show, *Robinson Sucroë* ('*Sucroë*'). As he perceived it, *Sucroë* was a blatant copy of *The Adventures of Robinson Curiosity* which he had spent years developing. The plaintiff subsequently discovered that the several parties who had been given access to his *Curiosity* project were also involved in the production of *Sucroë*. The Supreme Court of Canada unanimously *per* (former) Chief Justice, McLachlin J (all six other justices concurring) dismissed the appeal on liability and concluded that copyright was infringed and ordered compensatory damages, disgorgement of profits, and punitive damages, thus part-allowing Robinson (and co-plaintiff Nilem's) appeal.

[10A.6.47] The court agreed with the trial court that the cumulative effect of the features copied from the work must be considered to determine whether those features amount to a substantial part of the creator's skill and judgment expressed in his work as a whole (not dissecting the subject work into its component parts).[130] The Supreme Court noted that the question of whether there had been substantial copying focuses on whether the copied features constitute a substantial part of the plaintiff's work, not whether they amount to a substantial part of the defendant's work and held that the alteration of copied features or their integration into a work that is notably different from the plaintiff's work does not necessarily preclude a claim that a substantial part of a work has been copied.[131]

Substantiality and access tests in music copyright claims

[10A.6.48] Chapter 24 examines recent landmark rulings in music copyright law

---

[130] To determine what elements of *Curiosity* were original; to exclude nonprotectable features of the author's work (such as ideas, elements drawn from the public domain, and generic elements commonplace in children's television shows); and thirdly to compare what remained of *Curiosity* after this "weedingout" process to *Sucroë*, and determine whether a substantial part of *Curiosity* was reproduced.

[131] The appellants further argued that the trial judge based the bulk of his findings pertaining to the issue of substantial copying on inadmissible and unnecessary expert evidence claiming the expert evidence was not necessary to assist the court because the question of whether a substantial part has been copied must be assessed from the perspective of the layperson in the intended audience for the works at issue. The court considered that the perspective of the layperson in the intended audience for the works at issue is a useful one. It has the merit of keeping the analysis of similarities concrete and grounded in the works themselves, rather than in esoteric theories about the works. However, the question always remains whether a substantial part of the plaintiff's work was copied. This question should be answered from the perspective of a person whose senses and knowledge allow such person to fully assess and appreciate all relevant aspects, patent and latent, of the works at issue. In some cases, it may be necessary to go beyond the perspective of a layperson in the intended audience for the work, and to call upon an expert to place the trial judge in the shoes of someone reasonably versed in the relevant art or technology. In the present case, the necessary criterion of the test for the admissibility of expert evidence was satisfied.

including the claimant's unsuccessful suit in *Skidmore v Led Zeppelin* concerning the iconic introduction to *Stairway to Heaven*, the highly controversial decision relating to *Blurred Lines* in *Gaye v Williams* and High Court proceedings in the UK case against Ed Sheeran unsuccessfully taken by songwriters Sami Chokri and Ross O'Donoghue in respect of Sheeran's hit *Shape Of You.*

EXEMPTIONS FROM COPYRIGHT RESTRICTIONS

[10A.7.01] Exceptions to copyright infringement are constrained by the Berne three-step test which defines the freedom of signatory countries to create exceptions and limitations to copyrights. In essence, it is a way to restrict the kinds of permitted fair uses in national laws. The three-step test was first enacted in the 1967 revision of the Berne Convention. It provides:

> It shall be a matter for legislation in the countries of the Union[132] to permit the reproduction of such works [a] in certain special cases, provided that [b] such reproduction does not conflict with a normal exploitation of the work and [c] does not unreasonably prejudice the legitimate interests of the author.

[10A.7.02] The three-step test has already established an effective means of preventing the excessive application of limitations and exceptions. Most international copyright agreements since then have incorporated aspects of this test. Versions of the test may be found in the TRIPS Agreement (Art 13), the WIPO Copyright Treaty (Art 10), several EU copyright Directives, and numerous bilateral agreements. Even when national legislation does not explicitly incorporate the test, judges oftentimes rely upon it when construing and applying their national copyright laws.

[10A.7.03] The coverage of the different versions of the test varies somewhat. By way of example, whereas the third step of the Berne Convention test requires that an exception or limitation "not unreasonably prejudice the legitimate interests of the author," the third step of the TRIPS test requires that an exception or limitation "not unreasonably prejudice the legitimate interests of the right holder". This is a change that shifts attention away from the interests of creators toward the economic interests of the companies that acquire copyrights from the original creators.

Fair dealing in statute and case law

[10A.7.04] Fair dealing is a defence in Ireland and the UK but it is more restrictive than the wide range of exceptions found in the US equivalent defence of fair use. Sections 49 to 52 of the 2000 Act (amended by the 2019 Act) cover

[132] The countries to which the convention applies constitute a "union" for the protection of the rights of authors in their literary and artistic works – Art 1.

fair dealing[133] in relation to research or private study (s 50); fair dealing as regards criticism or review of a work (s 51); and incidental inclusion (e.g. fleeting/transient/minimal inclusion; or for caricature, parody or pastiche purposes) of copyright material (s 52; see also Art 17(7) of the 2019 Directive on Copyright in the Digital Single Market regarding excepted uses of protected content by online content-sharing service providers) that is accordingly protected under that section and by the legal principle of *de minimis* non curat lex (the law does not concern itself with insignificant, trifling matters). Fair dealing is defined in s 50[134] as meaning the making use of a literary, dramatic, musical or artistic work, film, sound recording, broadcast, and so forth which has already been lawfully made available to the public for a purpose and to an extent which will not unreasonably prejudice the interests of the owner of the copyright.

[10A.7.05] Section 51 of the 2000 Act (as amended by s 12 of the 2019 Act) provides that fair dealing with a work for the purposes of criticism or review of "that" work or "another work" or of a performance of a work (e.g. a critic's review of a play) shall not infringe any copyright in the work where the criticism or review is accompanied by a sufficient acknowledgement. Sufficient acknowledgement means identifying the work concerned by its title or other description and naming the author.[135] The definitional inclusion of "another work" is important. A documentary on celebrated UK street artist Banksy might therefore include photographs of a third party rightsholder that have not been properly cleared for use in the film. The producers may then seek, depending on the circumstances, to rely on fair dealing with the photographs for the purpose of review of "another work" being the works of Banksy.

[10A.7.06] The landmark 2005 case of *Fraser-Woodward Ltd v BBC*[136] permitted a liberal interpretation and application of the defence (though producers should continue to exercise caution and always seek a licence from relevant rightsholders when practicable and deemed necessary). The case arose out of the BBC programme *Tabloid Tales* hosted by former *Daily Mirror* editor, Piers Morgan. In one episode of the series, 14 photographs of the Beckhams were featured. None of these appearances had been licensed by the plaintiff company owner of the copyright in those photographs. The plaintiff thus argued fair dealing did not apply as there was no critique or review of the quality or content of the photographs themselves. However, the High Court court *per* Mann J held that it was sufficient that there be a criticism or review of the idea or philosophy

---

133 Described as "fair use" in the US – however, the fair use doctrine in the US is much more expansive than the limited statutorily-defined fair dealing exceptions in the UK and Ireland.

134 For the purposes of Pt 2 (copyright provisions) of the 2000 Act – it is further defined in s 221 in respect of performances.

135 Unless in the case of a work which has been lawfully made available to the public it was so made available anonymously, or in the case of a work which has not been made available to the public, it is not possible for a person without previous knowledge of the facts to ascertain the identity of the author of the work by reasonable enquiry.

136 [2005] EWHC 472 (Ch).

underlying a certain style of journalism as manifested in the copyright works. The decision is also worthy of examination for its review of what is 'fair' generally in terms of lengths of television clips featuring a copyright work and so forth.

[10A.7.07] In the *Harper* case,[137] US President Ford had licensed his publication rights to Harper & Row, which had contracted for excerpts of the memoirs to be printed in *Time* magazine. Instead, *The Nation* magazine published 300 to 400 words of verbatim quotes from the 500-page book without the permission of Ford, Harper & Row, or *Time*. Based on this prior publication, *Time* withdrew from the contract (as it was permitted to do by a clause therein), and Harper & Row filed suit against *The Nation* for copyright infringement.

[10A.7.08] Here, the Supreme Court ultimately held that *The Nation's* actions in quoting the memoirs were not protected by fair use privilege. The public interest in learning about a historical figure's impressions of a historic event was held not to be sufficient to show fair use of material otherwise protected by copyright.

[10A.7.09] In the landmark *South Park* judgment[138] in 2012 the three-judge Court of Appeals for the Seventh Circuit (per Cudahy J) affirmed the District Court's decision that the impugned *South Park* parody of a song squarely fell within fair use. Importantly, the appeals court also agreed that it was proper (but very unusual in a copyright lawsuit) to dispose of the case early, on a motion to dismiss, without lengthy discovery.

[10A.7.10] The court proceeded to consider the four, non-exhaustive factors contained in the (US) Copyright Act of 1976 that a court must consider in determining whether a particular use of a copyrighted work is a fair use: the purpose and character of the use; the nature of the copyrighted work; the amount and substantiality of the portion used in relation to the copyrighted work as a whole; and lastly, the effect of the use upon the potential market for or value of the copyrighted work. Moreover, the case is precedent for ending a lawsuit before trial which can help content creators avoid the costs of litigation brought about by frivolous claims, and is one of the most cited precedents in recent history in the realm of important legal decisions in entertainment law jurisprudence. Here a large portion was copied, and for commercial gain, and it was not radically transformative – but yet the court held its use to be fair use.

Sufficient acknowledgement

[10A.7.11] In *Tumber v Independent Television News Ltd*[139] (2017) Hacon J for the English High Court had no issue in finding a sufficient acknowledgement

---

[137] *Harper & Row v Nation Enterprises* 471 US 539 (1985).

[138] *Brownmark Films, LLC v Comedy Partners,* 682 F.3d 687 (7th Cir. 2012).

[139] [2017] EWHC 3093 (IPEC) during the preliminary trial/case management conference to hear certain applications and strike out certain defences.

had occurred in circumstances whereby Tumber wrote a love poem, said to be the longest love poem ever written, which gained some publicity and came to the notice of ITN and was uploaded on its website. The piece clearly credited and "sufficiently acknowledged" Tumber as the author thereof.

[10A.7.12] In terms of fair dealing generally, the court referred (at para 21) to a judgment of Arnold J in *England and Wales Cricket Board Ltd v Tixdaq Ltd*[140] in which he had in turn quoted with approval three criteria laid out in Laddie, Prescott and Vitoria's copyright law textbook, namely, first, said to be the most important, whether the alleged fair dealing is in fact commercially competing with the proprietor's exploitation of the copyright work. The second most important factor is said to be whether the work has already been published or otherwise exposed to the public. The third most important factor is said to be the amount and importance of the work that has been taken.

Incidental inclusion

[10A.7.13] Section 52(1) of the 2000 Act provides that the copyright in a work is not infringed by its inclusion in an incidental manner in another work. Section 52(3) provides that a work shall not be regarded as included in an incidental manner in another work in circumstances whereby the interests of the owner of the copyright are unreasonably prejudiced. Prejudice would arise, for instance, where the owner should receive payment in the form of a licence or usage fee but no such payment has been made. Section 52(4) states that the copyright in a work which has been lawfully made available to the public is not infringed by the use of quotations or extracts from the work, where such use does not prejudice the interests of the owner of the copyright in that work and such use is accompanied by a sufficient acknowledgement.

[10A.7.14] If a documentary on planning law corruption features an interview with a politician but in doing so captures a painting by a well-known artist hanging on the wall, the use of the artwork in those circumstances would likely be regarded as incidental. It is not part of the story and the interests of the copyright owner artist are not being (unreasonably) prejudiced.

[10A.7.15] In *Fraser* above, the incidental use defence was rejected by Mann J as regards all the photographs bar one. The odd one out was a small photo of the Beckhams appearing within a newspaper headline. The focus of the relevant sequence in the programme was on the headline throughout the four seconds in which it appeared. It was also shown together with two other headlines and all were being depicted as examples of sensational headlines. The judge considered that the appearance of this particular photograph was purely incidental and therefore copyright was not infringed. In all other cases, there was

---

[140] [2016] EWHC 575 (Ch).

a "further purpose" to the appearance of the photograph. This was "to provide or demonstrate the context of the image" and hence the use was not incidental.

[10A.7.16] Further examples of incidental use are iconic buildings, structures and identifiable business premises in wide establishing shots at the start of a movie where there is no close-up of any single identifiable building. Incidental use would also arise in a crowd scene where branded clothes are being worn or a shot of congested traffic with visible vehicle brand names. It would be impractical and cost prohibitive for producers to obtain copyright[141] and trademark clearance for each and every use. Courts and rightsowners alike are aware of this.

[10A.7.17] Difficulties will arise, however, in the case of close-ups where props are integral or central to a scene such as where they are prominently used for set dressing or relate to the action and dialogue.[142] Here, it is essential that clearance procedures be followed and releases or licences obtained from the copyright (and trademark, if applicable) owners. Otherwise, in default of having been paid for licensing and authorising such use, the owners' interests, and potentially their reputation and goodwill depending on the sequence or shots, may have been prejudiced. If the scene compromises the rightsholders' integrity in any manner, a claim for damages or proceedings for injunctive relief pre-release of the film might arise (for example, a commercial pop song has been edited without authorisation from the copyright holders and sound recording owners in a scene where a body is being severed with a hacksaw). Such proceedings could claim for breach of copyright (and potentially performer rights depending on the facts) as well as for moral rights infringement.

Fair dealing for caricature, parody or pastiche

[10A.7.18] Section 52(5) of the 2000 Act was inserted by s 13 of the 2019 Act and provides that fair dealing with a work for the purposes of caricature, parody or pastiche shall not infringe the copyright in that work.[143] This new subsection takes account of certain exceptions to copyright permitted by the above-cited InfoSoc Directive and places the defence in Irish law on a firm statutory footing.

[10A.7.19] The new exception does not affect moral rights (discussed from [10A.9.01]), however, which the author of the parodied work enjoys, meaning that if a parody is disparaging of the original work, the author may be able to

[141] In the sense here of a logo or image being a drawing or print of copyright-protected artistic work.

[142] In the UK case of *Football Association Premier League v Panini UK Ltd* [2004] FSR 1, the Court of Appeal considered whether the use of logos in photographs on stickers and sticker albums could be regarded as incidental use. The court was of the view that it was necessary to consider the reasons why the work had been included in another. Ultimately, the inclusion of the work cannot be considered incidental where its inclusion is essential to the object for which the image was created.

[143] s 221 of the 2000 Act was amended by s 30 of the 2019 Act in relation to fair dealing with a recording of a performance for the purposes of caricature, parody or pastiche.

litigate about the derogatory treatment of his or her creation. Neither does it affect the law of defamation. It is worth noting that, over the years, US courts have made it abundantly clear that parody and satire are not defamatory. That does not universally mean all satirists and biting comics emerge victorious from defamation lawsuits in America. It depends entirely on the facts but because parody and satire are seen as opinion, they are viewed in US jurisprudence as being non-defamatory. Irish and UK law is not as liberal (however, in the *Elton John* decision by the High Court in 2008[144] it was held that the tort of defamation had not been made out against a *Guardian* columnist. Tugendhat J was of the view that irony and teasing do not amount to defamation.[145] The ruling thus offers protection to writers of satirical articles clearly not meant to be taken seriously. The Court of Appeal later refused the singer leave to appeal).

The Irish, UK and EU positions

[10A.7.20] Article 5 (exceptions and limitations) of the InfoSoc Directive lists the copyright exceptions which Member States may apply to copyright and related rights. The Directive gave EU Member States significant freedom in certain aspects of transposition. Only parts of the Directive were implemented by Ireland[146] as many of the rights and exceptions were already contained in the pre-existing 2000 Act. Article 5(3)(k) permits use of copyrighted material for the purpose of caricature, parody or pastiche.

[10A.7.21] Pastiche is a musical or other artistic composition made up of selections from various sources or one that imitates the style of another artist or period. Thus, the YouTube music and other 'mash-ups' like those referred to below would fall under this classification and, provided their use is deemed fair dealing, they might not offend against copyright law. How much copying from a work is fair or unfair is an issue ultimately decided by a court, taking into account the interests and rights of the copyright owner as well as the freedom of expression of the person relying upon the parody exception. In making this decision, a court will typically take a number of different factors into account, such as the amount of the work that has been copied. It is often necessary to take a substantial part of the original work in order to parody it (so that the audience can recognise it as a parody).

[10A.7.22] Campaigners for the introduction of the exception in UK law argued parodists such as Cassetteboy, who is famous for online mash-up comedy sketches of shows including *The Apprentice* and *Dragons' Den* and for disguising

---

[144] *John v Guardian News & Media Ltd* [2008] EWHC 3066.

[145] The singer claimed that the impugned article suggested that his commitment to his aids foundation charity is so insincere that he hosts the annual White Tie and Tiara ball knowing that only a small proportion of the money raised will go to the charity, and that he uses the event as an occasion for meeting celebrities and/or self-promotion.

[146] See EU (Copyright and Related Rights) Regulations 2012 (SI No 59 of 2012) and European Communities (Copyright and Related Rights) Regulations 2004 (SI No 16 of 2004).

his identity with a giant cassette tape on his head, should be celebrated, not censored.[147] In one instance, as a result of action from the owners of copyright in the parodied works, YouTube was obliged to take down videos in Britain such as *Newport State of Mind* (a parody of Jay Z and Alicia Keys' *Empire State of Mind*) which seemed to flag a failure of the UK to keep up with other territories, like the USA, which has long recognised the right to parody under the doctrine of fair use.[148] The lack of an exception for parody had obvious implications for freedom of expression.[149]

Prince, the Dancing Baby case, fair use and takedown notices

US case law

[10A.7.23] In 2007, Universal, which administered Prince's music publishing, targeted a YouTube clip of a baby dancing as *Let's Go Crazy* played in the background claiming it violated copyright according to the Digital Millennium Copyright Act ('DMCA').

[10A.7.24] The infant's mother Stephanie Lenz took legal action (with assistance from the Electronic Frontier Foundation (EFF)) citing lawful fair use. In July 2007, Lenz sued Universal for misrepresentation under the DMCA, and sought a declaration from the court that her use of the copyrighted song was non-infringing. According to the DMCA, copyright-holders must consider whether use of the material was permissible (e.g. fair use) and issue a statement to the service provider that they have a good faith belief that use of the material in the manner complained of is not authorised by them as copyright owners, their agents, or the law.

[10A.7.25] The legal dispute[150] which followed lasted more than a decade and

---

[147] Dan Smith, *A New Law State of Mind – UK Parody Exception to Copyright Infringement Comes into Force – 1 October* (2014). Available at: https://gowlingwlg.com/en/insights-resources/articles/2014/a-new-law-state-of-mind-uk-parody-exception-to-c [Accessed 23 April 2018].

[148] A parody of *Empire State of Mind* by Alicia Keys and Jay Z, used to promote the charms of south east Wales, was famously removed after a copyright claim by EMI.

[149] Thus, in May 2011, Professor Ian Hargreaves, Professor of Digital Economy at Cardiff University, former BBC Director of News and Current Affairs, and newspaper editor, as chair of the specialist review group, delivered a review recommending that the UK's failure to implement all of the copyright exceptions available under EU law was also harmful to innovation and economic growth. The *Hargreaves Review of Intellectual Property and Growth*, or *Digital Opportunity–A review of Intellectual Property and Growth*, was an independent review of the UK's IP system, focusing on UK copyright law. Professor Ian Hargreaves was commissioned to chair a review of how the IP framework supports economic growth and innovation in November 2010 by Prime Minister David Cameron.

[150] *Lenz v Universal Music Corp.*, 801 F3d 1126 (9th Cir 2015) is a decision by the US Court of Appeals for the Ninth Circuit affirming the ruling in 2008 of the US District Court for the Northern District of California, holding that copyright holders must consider fair use in good faith before issuing a takedown notice for content posted on the internet. The Digital Millennium Copyright Act is a 1998 US copyright law that implements

even outlasted Prince himself. The matter ultimately came before the US Supreme Court in June 2017 which upheld the decision of the Ninth Circuit Court of Appeals. The US District Court for the Northern District of California had initially held that copyright-holders, as above, must consider fair use in good faith before issuing a takedown notice for content posted on the internet.

[10A.7.26] Section 512 of the DMCA created the so-called "notice and takedown" system which gives service providers immunity from copyright liability for content posted by users if the providers take it down when they are notified that it is infringing. However, s 512 notices can often target lawful material too. To discourage such abuse, Congress ensured that the DMCA included a series of checks and balances, including s 512(f), which affords users the ability to hold copyright-owners accountable if they send a DMCA notice in bad faith.

[10A.7.27] Lenz claimed that Universal's takedown notice was a misrepresentation in violation of s 512(f). In response, Universal argued that copyright-owners should not have to consider fair use before sending DMCA takedown notices. The Ninth Circuit rejected this argument, holding that the DMCA requires copyright-owners to consider whether works are lawful fair uses *before* sending takedown notices targeting them. The appeals court made clear that fair use is not an "infringement to be excused" but instead is not copyright infringement at all.[151]

[10A.7.28] Elsewhere, the 1964 case of *Berlin v EC Publications, Inc*[152] was decided by the US Court of Appeals for the Second Circuit and involved the right by the defendants to parody in satirical fashion the lyrics to several of the plaintiffs' well-known melodies. Again in 1986, it was held, this time by the Ninth Circuit in *Fisher v Dees*,[153] that parody of a song performance was fair use. In *Campbell v Acuff-Rose Music, Inc*,[154] the US Supreme Court established in 1994 that a commercial parody can qualify as fair use. The fact that revenue is generated by a work does not render it impossible for fair use to apply; it is merely one of the components of a fair use analysis.

---

two 1996 treaties of WIPO. Section 512 of the DMCA created the so-called "notice and takedown" system which gives service providers immunity from copyright liability for content posted by users if the providers take it down when they are notified that it is infringing.

[151] The Ninth Circuit also ruled that, when considering claims under s 512(f), copyright holders should be held to a subjective standard. In other words, senders of false infringement notices could be excused so long as they subjectively believed that the material they targeted was infringing. EFF was disappointed with this aspect of the ruling as it entailed that a subjective belief in infringement can excuse a wrongful takedown notice no matter how unreasonable that belief. Source: *Electronic Frontier Foundation, Lenz v Universal* (2018), https://www.eff.org/cases/lenz-v-universal. After the Ninth Circuit's ruling, both Lenz and Universal petitioned the Supreme Court for review. The Supreme Court denied both parties' petitions and the parties later agreed to a settlement in 2018.

[152] 329 F.2d 541 (2nd Cir. 1964).

[153] 794 F.2d 432 (9th Cir. 1886).

[154] 510 US 569 (1994).

[10A.7.29] In permitting unauthorised parody, the *Suntrust v Houghton Mifflin Co.,*[155] decision followed the previous decision in *Campbell* and extended the *Campbell* principle (a parody's commercial character is only one element that should be weighed up in a fair use inquiry) from songs to novels. The US Court of Appeals for the Eleventh Circuit found against Margaret Mitchell's *Gone with the Wind* and vacated an injunction prohibiting the publisher of Alice Randall's *The Wind Done Gone* from distributing the book. The creation and publication of a carefully written parody novel in the US thus counted as fair use. Despite stating that substantial portions of Mitchell's work were used, the Court of Appeals found that the likely outcome of a full adjudication of the rights involved was a finding of fair use.

New EU law

[10A.7.30] The Digital Services Act (a late 2022 EU Regulation, see Chapter 30), the provisions of which are to be policed in Ireland by the Media Commission, will have a bearing on take-down notices going forward. Intermediary service providers must implement a notice and action mechanism for content that users consider illegal. Content deemed illegal must be removed expeditiously. Providers must also provide users with a statement of reasons whenever they delete or block access to their content for content moderation purposes.

DURATION OF COPYRIGHT

[10A.8.01] Regulations introduced in 2013[156] transposed Directive 2011/77/EU[157] into Irish law. In line with the Directive, the Regulations extended the term of protection for performers and for (music) producers of sound recordings from 50 to 70 years as outlined in Table 1 below.[158]

---

[155] 268 F.3d 1257 (11th Cir. 2001).

[156] The EU (Term of Protection of Copyright and Certain Related Rights) (Directive 2011/77/EU) Regulations 2013 (SI No 411 of 2013) ('the Regulations').

[157] Directive of the European Parliament and of the Council of 27 September 2011 (amending Directive 2006/116/EC on the term of protection of copyright and certain related rights).

[158] The Regulations also introduced new measures to benefit performers in sound recordings in the later stages of their career such as a 20 percent fund for session musicians to obtain additional payments during the extended 20-year term; a provision whereby performers can reclaim their rights from producers if, in the extended period, a record company does not market a recording, and a 'clean slate' provision whereby producers will not be entitled to make deductions from the contractual royalties due to featured performers during the extended term of protection.

Literary, dramatic, musical and artistic works	Copyright protection expires 70 years after the death of the author/creator (s 24 of the 2000 Act as amended by reg 3 and as amended further by s 8 of the 2019 Act – see below)
Films	Copyright protection expires 70 years after the last of the following dies: the director, the author of the screenplay, the author of the dialogue of the film, or the author of the music composed for use in the film (s 25)
Sound recordings	Copyright protection expires 50 years after the sound recording is made or if it is made available to the public then 70 years from the date it was made available to the public (s 26 as amended by reg 3) where the sound recording is created on or after 1 November 2013 or where the rights of the performer and the producer would still have been protected on 1 November 2013 had the Regulations not come into operation on that date
Broadcasts	Copyright protection expires 50 years after the broadcast is first transmitted
The typographical arrangement of a published edition	Copyright protection expires 50 years after the date it is first made available to the public.

Table 1: duration of copyright

[10A.8.02] It must be noted that copyright periods in other territories such as the US differ considerably. When seeking to rely on the public domain exemption, producers need to ensure that the relevant period has in fact elapsed. While the time period after which a work enters the public domain may be shorter in some cases in Ireland, if distribution and exploitation is planned for the US where periods are longer, due consideration must be had to computing the periods correctly. That might mean that while a work is cleared for use in Ireland that is not necessarily so in another country and the clearance mechanisms for this will involve additional cost.

Extended rights period

[10A.8.03] Music performers' main sources of income from recordings on which they have performed are royalties from public performance and broadcast of those recordings, sales royalties, and (only if/where applicable) master use income (relating to synchronisation of music with audiovisual material) for featured performers via their record contract. Prior to the Regulations the above income ceased 50 years after the first release or communication to the public of the recording. Once the legislation was introduced this provided an additional 20 years of sales, licensing and public performance income for performers, including session musicians, from each of the recordings on which they performed.

[10A.8.04] The scope of the extended term Directive is regrettably limited to the musical field only. In other words, the duration of performers' rights in recordings of performances other than in sound recordings, such as in films or television programmes, remains at only 50 years.

MORAL RIGHTS

[10A.9.01] Moral rights are non-economic in nature. A value cannot necessarily be placed thereon. They relate to the integrity of a work and a creator's reputation. For example, *Ice Ice Baby* is associated (due to melodic similarities/sampling) with the original Queen/Bowie work *Under Pressure* and this was not a consequence authorised or envisaged by the latter artists, neither was it welcomed by all accounts!

[10A.9.02] Moral rights include the right to claim authorship of a work (s 107 of the 2000 Act) and the right *per* s 109 to object to any derogatory action taken in respect of that work. An instance of the latter is the words and/or melody of an original song being changed (in bad or dubious taste, or otherwise) by a cover version artist without prior authorisation from the rightsholder. A dispute arose[159] for instance when celebrated folk singer Mary Black had recorded songwriter Jimmy MacCarthy's *No Frontiers* but omitted the last four lines which the lyricist considered to represent the kernel of the song. Following a legal battle, removal of those lines going forward was prohibited. In terms of music television shows, an arranger might be hired to write new arrangements to pre-existing commercial 'chart' song works that are in copyright. If an arrangement does not stay true to the original melody as written (or if there are lyrical changes), this would require consent from the legacy rightsholder(s) directly in terms of copyright (adaptation) and moral rights (integrity) as, strictly speaking, it would not be covered in Ireland by national broadcaster blanket licences with the relevant music publishers' collection societies.

[10A.9.03] Hence, moral rights protect authors' personal or intellectual relation to their work. They are not harmonised at EU level. Scope and duration of moral rights varies within the union. Member states protect the right to be named as an author (paternity right) and the right to integrity of the work but the scope

---

[159] *Magic, music and me …* (2000), independent.ie. Available at: https://www.independent.ie/entertainment/books/magic-music-and-me—26257422.html [Accessed 4 November 2021].

of the integrity right is not the same throughout the EU territory. In many member states, authors cannot waive their moral rights. This is not the case in Ireland however where legislation (in s 116 and 316 of the 2000 Act) allows for such waiver of moral rights.[160]

[10A.9.04] To ensure that recorded footage can be used, edited and reused at the absolute sole discretion of production companies, it is of paramount importance that writer, director, contributor, performer, cast and crew and all other production contracts invariably contain a waiver of moral rights provision. As seen in the previous chapter, waiver of moral rights is a minimum contractual requirement for development and production loans upon which Screen Ireland insists that producer borrowers obtain. In respect of co-writers or other joint authors, it is important that all rightsholders waive their moral rights as s 117 of the 2000 Act provides that a waiver made under s 116 of the paternity right or the integrity right by one joint author shall not affect the rights of the other joint authors.

[10A.9.05] As regards succession law issues, s 119 states that on the death of a person entitled to the paternity and integrity rights, the right passes by testamentary disposition to such person as the person entitled to the right may direct and where there is no direction as to whom the right passes but the copyright in the work concerned forms part of an estate, the right passes to the person to whom the copyright passes. On intestacy, it is exercisable by the personal representatives of the person entitled to the right.

[10A.9.06] Therefore, for instance, a deceased's estate can prevent a singer/producer, who wants to change the lyrics or arrangement of the deceased's song, from making any such changes which might prejudice or adversely affect the original work/author. The same holds true as regards adapting a book to a screenplay and making significant changes thereto. The legal personal representatives/administrators of the deceased should be approached for their consent and to agree terms.

Case law

[10A.9.07] In *Gilliam v American Broadcasting Companies, Inc*[161] (1976) the British comedy group Monty Python claimed in the US Court of Appeals (Second Circuit) that the ABC had violated its copyright and caused damage to its artistic reputation by broadcasting drastically edited versions of several

---

160 Although moral rights, unlike copyright and related rights, cannot be assigned or alienated in any manner in this jurisdiction (but can be passed on under succession law).

161 538 F.2d 14 (2nd Cir.1976).

of its shows.[162] The court agreed and directed the District Court to issue the preliminary injunction sought.[163]

[10A.9.08] In *Snow v The Eaton Centre Ltd*[164] the plaintiff was commissioned to create a sculpture called *Flight Stop* consisting of a number of geese in flight in the atrium of the Toronto Eaton Centre. During the Christmas season of 1981, the defendant centre placed red ribbons around the necks of the geese. Mr Snow brought an action for injunctive relief to have the bows removed arguing that the ribbons offended the integrity of and distorted his work and hence violated his moral rights. The Ontario High Court *per* O'Brien J held that the sculpture's integrity was "distorted, mutilated or otherwise modified" which was "to the prejudice of the honour or reputation of the author" contrary to the relevant section of Canadian copyright legislation. The court heard testimony from the plaintiff as well as from experts in the art community[165] in relation to the prejudicial effect of the defendant's action to Snow's honour and reputation.

Infringement

[10A.9.09] Section 137 of the 2000 Act provides that infringement of the integrity, paternity and other rights in ss 107, 109, 113 and 114 is actionable as a breach of statutory duty owed to the person entitled to the right concerned. A person may apply to the appropriate court for damages or other relief in respect of an infringement of a right conferred by those sections. In proceedings for infringement of the right conferred by s 109 (integrity right), the court may grant an injunction prohibiting any act unless a sufficient disclaimer is made, on such terms and in such a manner as is approved of by the court, dissociating the person entitled to the right from the treatment of the work. Similarly, s 319, in the context of performer rights, sets out the remedies in the same manner as above as regards violation of performer moral rights in s 309 (paternity right), s 311 (integrity right) and s 314 (false attribution).

Duration of moral rights

[10A.9.10] Section s 115(1) of the 2000 Act provides that the paternity right and

---

[162] Some of the editing had been carried out in order to make time for commercials; other material had been edited, according to ABC, because the original programmes contained offensive or obscene matter.

[163] It was held that the appellants demonstrated that the excising done for ABC impaired the integrity of the original work and that the comedy group's contract with the BBC had been violated. The permission granted to the BBC (which could license the transmission of recordings of the television programmes in any overseas territory) to broadcast the shows did not confer the right to edit the work and no such authorisation had been given by the copyright holders of the scripts.

[164] 70 CPR (2d) 105 (1982), [1982] OJ No 3645.

[165] Copyright legislation in Canada has since been amended such that any modification to a painting, sculpture or engraving is deemed to prejudice the author. For those types of works, no evidence of actual prejudice is required.

the integrity right shall subsist for the same period of time as the copyright in the work subsists (e.g. 70 years from date of death of the author in the case of a book, 50 years after broadcast in the case of a broadcast). In respect of moral rights in performances, s 315 (as substituted by the EU (Term of Protection of Copyright and Certain Related Rights) (Directive 2011/77/EU) Regulations 2013) applies thus: moral rights in a performance shall expire 50 years after the date of the performance, subject to the 50 year term being extended to 70 years (from the date the recording is first so made available) in the case of a sound recording.[166]

[166] In regard to which the rights of the performer and the producer would still have been protected on 1 November 2013, had the Regulations not come into operation on that date; or that is created on or after 1 November 2013.

Part B: Copyright and Related Rights: Performer Rights

INTRODUCTION

[10B.1.01] The international,[1] EU and national legal frameworks underpinning performer rights can unfortunately be summarised as nothing short of a complex, undesirable and inequitable mess. This is borne out in two seminal recent studies, the UK parliament's investigation during the Covid-19 pandemic into the economics of music streaming and the comprehensive AEPO[2]-ARTIS report on performers' rights as updated in November 2022. Even decisions of the Court of Justice of the European Union ('CJEU'), when interpreting disparate union law, have been conflicting and potentially give rise to confusion,[3] while the international treaties have differing definitions, inclusions and exclusions. Further, the 2019 EU Directive on Copyright in the Digital Single Market ('the 2019 Directive') was a compromise on competing interests and stopped short of conferring performers (and authors) with unwaivable remuneration rights that would have ensured when such performers transfer their exclusive rights, that fair remuneration could still be guaranteed.

[10B.1.02] A rather bizarre fact perhaps not known by the general public is that US and international songwriters who also self-produce their music and own the masters (or who are otherwise signed to a record label) do not receive public performance royalties for radioplay and terrestrial television broadcasts in America. The US does not recognise traditional neighbouring rights (however, while the US does not have a traditional collection society[4] for neighbouring rights royalties, there is a designated collection society agency (Sound Exchange) as established by the US government that collects digital radio royalties for broadcast on non-terrestrial radio, namely satellite radio like SiriusXM, and internet radio like Pandora, iHeartRadio and other webcasters). This leads to an absurdity whereby even superstars such as Adele or U2 do not receive income (on the master side[5] of song income) from say traditional radioplay in the US. As regards actors as performers, however, the US does compensate these performers for the use of their audiovisual works when they are retransmitted on cable channels or broadcast publicly. This means that Irish actors who register

---

1 Treaties and conventions concerning IP rights.

2 Association of European Performers Organisations (Belgium) which represents 37 performers' collective management organisations in 26 countries.

3 See for example *OSA v Léčebné lázně Mariánské Lázně* (C-351/12); *Società Consortile Fonografici v Marco Del Corso* (C-135/10); and *Reha v GEMA* (Case C-117/15).

4 Equivalent to Phonographic Performance Ireland ('PPI') or Phonographic Performance Ltd ('PPL') in the UK.

5 The songwriters however of course receive publishing income from collection societies such as ASCAP and BMI arising from public performance of their music on traditional radio and television (and via the Harry Fox Agency which provides physical product and permanent download licensing and royalty services to US publishers and labels in terms of mechanical reproductions).

their subject performances with Recorded Artists Actors Performers (RAAP) can derive income from such use.

[10B.1.03] US broadcasters are exempt from paying music performers and labels when sound recordings are performed on terrestrial radio or television because the broadcast industry has successfully lobbied and argued that their playing artists' music promotes artists as artists. The US is one of only four countries in the world that does not pay a royalty to the sound recording owner in this manner. The other three are North Korea, Iran and China.

[10B.1.04] Given the untenable situation going forward whereby, following the CJEU's ruling in *RAAP v PPI* discussed at para [10B.7.04] whereby US performers are entitled to receive royalties from the public performance of sound recordings in the EEA,[6] it is only a matter of time before the US reciprocates so that Irish and other non-US performers properly receive performance royalties from radio airplay and television broadcasts in the US. These matters, together with a discussion of performer rights collection societies, mechanical reproduction income for performers from streaming or otherwise, producer 'points' and other income that does in fact accrue to master sound recording owners through synchronisation/master use licensing are discussed in Chapter 23.

Unequal treatment of music performers

[10B.1.05] Disparity exists between performers in the music industry versus actor and dancer performers in the audiovisual field[7] (even in the musical field, discrimination is perpetrated between audio and audiovisual recordings leading to absurd situations – for instance, an opera recorded on an audiovisual fixation will be protected only for 50 years whereas the same opera, regarding its musical part on the sound recording, will be protected for 70 years). The Beijing Treaty on audiovisual performers which entered into force in 2020 sought to rectify this in part at least and expand performer rights but it remains to be ratified by the EU. Further, inequity clearly persists in the music sector between composer rights and performer rights. Moreover, legislation within the EU is unwieldy, complex and piecemeal and, in certain cases where choices are left to Member States in the manner in which they enforce rights, this has led to unharmonious approaches across the union.

---

6 To obtain these, independent artists will need to engage a rights management company or manager to register their clients' performances in various territories. In the case of signed acts, Universal for example has a branch in Ireland and can register its US artists' performances with PPI and RAAP (Recorded Artists Actors Performers).

7 The term of protection of audiovisual performances is twenty years shorter than that of musical performances. That limits the period in which actors may benefit from existing remuneration mechanisms that currently exist under EU law. There are also fewer remuneration mechanisms available to audiovisual performers (as compared to performers in the music sector), which in turn limits the possibilities available to collection management organisations to collect on their behalf.

[10B.1.06] In June 2022, the European Commission confirmed that the introduction of an unwaivable right to equitable remuneration collected from users and subject to collective management, would be a valid way of transposing the 2019 Directive and would therefore achieve the goal of ensuring performers receive appropriate and proportionate remuneration. It is the responsibility of the European Commission to monitor how Member States have implemented the 2019 Directive and for now at least it is a wholly unsatisfactory case of 'wait and see'.

[10B.1.07] Moreover, the choice made in the 1990s to structure performers' rights on the basis of exclusive rights has proven to be ineffective in the 21st century. Where performers are granted a remuneration right subject to compulsory collective management (see [10B.6.10]), they are guaranteed to receive a reasonable financial benefit. Conversely, where they have been granted an exclusive right (decision-making power to authorise or to prohibit the use of their work), such an outcome is highly uncertain.

Inequity between music performers and music producers/labels

[10B.1.08] The imbalanced commercial negotiating power between performers and producers has led to contractual practices that are one-sided, unfair and outdated. In the music sector, the lack of a remuneration right for online exploitation makes it impossible for many musicians to make a living from their profession as the market shifts towards a digital music market. In the audiovisual sector, the continuing practice of rights 'buyouts' prevents performers from sharing in the success of the works to which they make a vital contribution. The exclusive making available right, as the only tool provided to performers to assist them in obtaining fair remuneration from new technological uses, has utterly failed and the situation must change in order to comply with the 2019 Directive. Introducing soft law such as the mere principle of "fair contracts" between producers and performers does not work in practice. The most reliable way in which this can be done is to introduce a right to equitable remuneration for online exploitation. This presents no legal or practical difficulties, as the approach taken in countries such as Spain has shown.[8]

[10B.1.09] With effect from June 2022, performers in the EU are entitled to receive transparent information from producers regarding the exploitation of their performances.[9] It is still too early to see what impact this has had. Major record labels in particular have concluded multimillion euro agreements with platforms such as TikTok and Facebook. The terms of these agreements are confidential.

---

8 At p 73 of the AEPO-AERTIS 2022 report. Available at: https://www.aepo-artis.org/wp-content/uploads/2022/11/AEPO-ARTIS_Performers_Rights_Study_2022_digital.pdf [Accessed 13 February 2023].

9 The recognition by the EU legislature that performers are entitled to receive transparent information from producers is to be commended. However, historically performers have been unwilling to confront producers for fear of being 'blacklisted'.

In the audiovisual sector, buyout practices continue to limit the possibility for actors to receive information on the revenues generated from their work. If that remains the case, it will be impossible for performers to determine whether they are receiving a fair share of the value of their work.

MUSIC STREAMING

[10B.2.01] The current revenue share from streaming gives the record label the majority of a track's revenue. This comes from a model which applied to physical sales, where labels had overheads such as manufacturing, storing and transporting CDs. Songwriters and publishers are left with the smallest share of revenue, despite being integral to the creative process. Music creators and music publishers argue that this model is outdated and unfair as these overheads simply do not apply to digital music production.

[10B.2.02] The money that a subscriber pays (or revenue generated from advertising on freemium services) is paid into a "pot". From that pot (approximately) 30 percent is retained by the platform, 15 percent is paid to the songwriters and the remaining 55 percent is paid to the record label. No money is paid directly to the performers. The record label may or may not pass on a share of its revenue to performers, but this will depend on the contract the performers have been able to negotiate with the record label. Non-featured artists will always receive zero. Their contracts grant them no royalties whatsoever from streaming.[10] As a result, regardless of their contribution to the recording, they do not share in its success.

[10B.2.03] It remains to be seen whether the legislative intervention of the contract adjustment provisions contained in Art 20 of the 2019 Directive (discussed in Chapter 11) will enable performers to override these contractual provisions, but for practical reasons this is unlikely. Making a claim against a producer or record label will inevitably adversely affect the prospect of obtaining further work.

CONTRACTS WITH PERFORMERS (THE MUSIC PRODUCER/ RECORD LABEL PERSPECTIVE)

[10B.3.01] Before exploring performer rights and equitable remuneration payable to performers generally, it is important to flag at the outset the advisability of requiring, when contracting with music performers, that they warrant in the agreement being executed that they in fact have the legal authority to sign. For

[10] Elsewhere, for traditional music consumption by public performance (e.g. retail shops, cinemas, radio and linear television broadcasts) equitable remuneration will arise, that is, a performer right whereby performers (including non-featured performers such as backup singers) have a statutory right to share in recording revenues of a song, regardless of their royalty rates (and their outstanding debts with a label through advances, if applicable).

example, a singer, session musician or band member might be under ongoing obligations with a manager by way of management agreement, or otherwise on foot of contractual commitments with a record label, and therefore the manager/record label may at times need to authorise and/or sign the contract as well as the artist.

[10B.3.02] In the case of exclusive recording or performance services, the performer contract in favour of an audiovisual production company may contain a clause exempting the subject performance from the general exclusivity provision and the record label will sign this agreement in addition to the performer. In this way, a performing artist (signed to a label as an album recording artist and for touring services only) requested by a third party to perform in a particular television programme, multi-artist concert event or a corporate advertisement for instance will be free to render those services.

[10B.3.03] As with copyright generally, on foot of exclusive statutory rights they hold, performers can authorise or restrict the use, recording, broadcast, copying, lending and rental of their work. Mindful of such exclusive rights afforded in ss 203 to 207 of the Copyright and Related Rights Act 2000 as amended ('the 2000 Act') as well as new data protection controls, in an audiovisual context, to permit producers to use, record and commercially exploit a performance, a performer will grant consent to the producer in relation to an array of uses and media as well as authorising biographical material concerning and images of the performer to be potentially used in connection with advertising, publicising and exploiting the relevant content,[11] and in respect of assigning rental and lending rights discussed below.

[10B.3.04] Contracts with performers will invariably require performers to waive their moral rights (to allow the production company use and edit the performance as it sees fit), to agree that, in the event of dispute, damages will be the sole remedy, and that injunctive or other equitable relief such as rescission of the release agreement cannot be sought.

DURATION OF PERFORMER RIGHTS

[10B.4.01] Section 291 of the 2000 Act as substituted by the EU (Term of Protection of Copyright and Certain Related Rights) (Directive 2011/77/EU) Regulations 2013 ('the 2013 Regulations')[12] provides that performer rights, in

---

[11] In respect of a film, rights might also extend to merchandising of any product, commodity, service or series, if any, based on the performer's role/character in the picture.

[12] SI No 411 of 2013, EU (Term of Protection of Copyright and Certain Related Rights) (Directive 2011/77/EU) Regulations 2013. Article 1(2) of the term extension Directive extended the term of protection for sound recordings in the EU from 50 to 70 years from the date that the recording was first published or communicated to the public. Consequently, the term of protection for performers whose performance is fixed in a sound recording is also extended from 50 to 70 years.

respect of sound recordings, shall expire 50 years after the date of the performance (calculated from the first day of January of the year following the event). However, if a recording of the performance is lawfully made available to the public the rights shall expire 70 years from the date the recording is first so made available.

[10B.4.02] The term of protection of audiovisual performances (by actors) is 20 years shorter than musical performances. Accordingly, this limits the period during which actors may benefit from remuneration mechanisms that currently exist under EU law. It can be seen that, without any justification, EU law grants audiovisual performers fewer rights than their colleagues working in the music sector. Performers' rights in recordings of performances other than in sound recordings, such as in films, remains at only 50 years.

[10B.4.03] The 2011/77/EU 'term extension' Directive as transposed in Ireland by the 2013 Regulations (see fn 12) ensures that performers receiving non-recurring remuneration (that is, they obtain a one-off payment only) also benefit in practice from the term extension. This means that non-featured performers not benefiting from royalties on the exploitation of the recordings are granted an unwaivable right to obtain annual supplementary remuneration from the record producer from the 50th year of the term of protection up to the 70th year.[13] For these non-featured performers in the audio sector, there is evidence that they are beginning to benefit from this right and this remuneration has started to be collected and distributed in the majority of EU Member States.[14]

[10B.4.04] A second additional measure introduced by the term extension Directive is the so-called "use it or lose it" clause. This clause can be invoked by all performers, regardless of whether they benefit from recurring remuneration (royalties) or not. If record producers fail to use a record for exploitation,

---

13 The record producer must, at least once a year, allocate 20 percent of revenue (before deduction of any costs) derived from the reproduction, distribution and making available of the sound recording to performers that received a lump-sum buy-out at the time of the recording. The collection and distribution of this annual supplementary remuneration is to be administered by collection management organisations. In the calculation of the overall amount to be allocated to performers, no account should be taken of revenue that the producer has derived from the rental of recordings, of revenue from broadcasting and communication to the public or of compensation for private copying (on the ground that in most EU countries and on the basis of the acquis communautaire, these uses are subject to remuneration already shared between performers and producers).

14 A common problem however is that it has proved difficult to adequately obtain information from phonogram producers that would enable performers' collection societies to trace the performers who are entitled to receive this remuneration since this information is held or ought to be held by the producers. Unfortunately, for a number of phonograms, information regarding non-featured artists who should benefit from this remuneration is not always easily available (despite common principles on performers' moral rights and their right to be identified as a performer in the performance). With the dematerialisation of phonograms (i.e. the change from physical formats such as vinyl and CDs to digital files), this problem may increase in the future if non-featured artists are not included in the metadata accompanying the file.

performers have the unwaivable right to terminate the contract with the record producer.[15] From anecdotal evidence, however, there have been no reports to collection societies of performers having exercised the right to terminate the contract with the record producer under these provisions.[16]

[10B.4.05] The "clean slate" provision is the third and last additional measure introduced by the term extension Directive which only concerns performers who have transferred their rights in return for a recurring remuneration. According to this provision, a royalty or remuneration rate should be paid to performers during the extended period, writing off any 'unrecouped' advances. Similar to use it or lost it, most collection societies are not aware of any performer benefiting from this provision. In practice, it is highly unlikely that, if a recording has not been very commercially successful during the initial period of 50 years, there will be any significant use of the work in the following 20 years. Therefore, the amount of remuneration generated by this provision is minimal. In practice, in any event, this provision has been superseded to some extent by a welcome initiative on the part of major record labels to write off unrecouped amounts after a 20-year period.

EXEMPTED ACTS

Fair dealing and incidental use

[10B.5.01] Similar to copyright, certain acts are exempted from what otherwise might constitute infringements of performer rights (ss 220 to 241 of the 2000 Act, amended as and where applicable by ss 30 to 33 of the Copyright and Other Intellectual Property Law Provisions Act 2019) such as fair dealing criticism or review (with caricature, parody and pastiche also now permitted by s 221(2)), incidental use, copying of a performance for the purpose of instruction, playing a sound recording at an educational establishment or anything done for the purposes of parliamentary or judicial proceedings. Article 17(7) of the 2019 Directive regarding excepted uses of protected content by online content-sharing service providers also references the existing permitted uses of quotation, review and parody.

Private copying

[10B.5.02] EU law recognises that the private copying (e.g. blank media) exception can cause copyright owners to lose money. The corrective principle is that the purchase price of a storage device (e.g. USB drive, smartphone, tablet

---

15 This right may be exercised if the producer fails to carry out both of the acts of exploitation within a year of having been notified by a performer of their intention to terminate the contract. Performers may terminate their contracts in accordance with the applicable national law. The aim of this provision is to guarantee a real exploitation of the recording for which the rights were transferred to the producer, often with the benefit of exclusivity.

16 p 72 of the (2022) AEPO-ARTIS report.

or external hard drive) includes a share payable by the consumer to remunerate creators, authors, performers, publishers and producers, hence the private copying "levy". The ruling in the *Austro-Mechana v Strato AG*[17] case was very important in confirming that private copying remuneration is payable in respect of reproductions made on any medium including cloud storage.

[10B.5.03] Most Member States of the EU realised quite early that in view of technical developments and the resulting widespread use of reproductions made by individuals, a ban on private copying simply could not be enforced and have introduced in their national legislation an exception for private use, linked to an entitlement to remuneration for the rightsholders paid by collecting societies. While Ireland did not implement the private copying exemption under Art 5(2)(b) of the InfoSoc Directive (2001/29/EC) or put in place a corresponding remuneration scheme, rightsholders can nevertheless benefit from remuneration for private copying from those countries which do provide for private copying remuneration (all of the EU, but not the UK).[18] Incidentally, AEPO-ARTIS notes in its report that Ireland's actions were not in compliance with Art 5.[19]

[10B.5.04] The amount collected from private copying accounts for an essential part of the revenues received by performers from collection societies.[20] In 2013, remuneration for acts of private copying accounted for approximately 22 percent of the total revenue collected by the European performers' organisations. This percentage increased to almost 30 percent in 2014 and has remained stable until

---

17 C-433/20.

18 The only Member State that did not have a private copying exception and, consequently, a payment of the corresponding remuneration to rightsholders. In the UK, when a consumer makes a private copy of a recording, it is in fact an infringement of the exclusive right of reproduction. The High Court ruled in *British Academy of Songwriters, Composers and Authors v Secretary for Business Innovation and Skills* [2015] EWHC 1723 (Admin) that the statutory private copying exception as regards not paying attendant performer remuneration was unlawful (in practice, however, no action can be taken against these consumers). Currently in the UK, there is an ongoing call for a system of private copying remuneration system (or "Smart Fund") to be introduced, which would address this situation: https://thesmartfund.co.uk. The Smart Fund is a proposal by culture industry organisations to ensure creators and performers are remunerated fairly. Essentially, it would mirror "traditional" EU private copying systems, with the revenue collected from manufacturers of devices and carriers being administered by collective management organisations and paid out to creators and local community projects with a focus on digital creativity and skills.

19 Given that any proposed exception in Ireland would have been almost identical to the failed UK exception, and the Regulatory Impact Analysis' expectation of the Department of Business, Enterprise and Innovation that it would almost certainly be legally challenged and struck down, it was decided not to progress the Copyright Review Committee's recommendation in this area as a provision in the 2019 Act.

20 As well as the disparity in amounts collected, there is also disparity across the EU in the manner in which the private copying remuneration collected is shared in the music and audiovisual sectors between authors, performers and producers. Commonly, the amount collected is shared equally, with each of these categories of rightholders receiving one third of the amount collected. The percentages vary in Poland, Portugal and Lithuania.

2021.[21] Equitable remuneration for broadcasting and communication to the public remains the highest source of collection for performers' collecting societies, representing 46 percent of their overall collection[22] though in Ireland the income when shared between all relevant performers is very low.[23]

EU LAW AND EXCLUSIVE PERFORMER RIGHTS

[10B.6.01] European legislation on performer rights consists of the recognition of exclusive rights: attributing to rightsholders the decision-making power to authorise or to prohibit the use of their work. Exclusive rights concern the fixation, reproduction, sale, publishing, distribution, rental, lending, broadcasting, communication to the public, and the making available on demand of performances (see Arts 3 to 9 of the rental and lending rights Directive 2006/115/EC, ss 202 to 208[24] of the 2000 Act[25] as amended)[26] and the fair remuneration rights set out in Pt 6 of the EU (Copyright and Related Rights in the Digital Single Market) Regulations 2021 which transpose the relevant provisions of the 2019 Directive.

[10B.6.02] In practice, however, musicians and actors will assign their rental and lending rights in an audiovisual release contract that provides that the one-off contractual fee for the subject performance includes equitable remuneration for this additional grant of rights (from a financial point of view, in 2023 the rental right is of very little significance in any event).[27] In other words, agreements with performers will provide for a global transfer of all their exclusive rights, for the whole protection period, and, moreover, for a fixed and final fee. The difficulty is that the release fee itself may not be substantial to begin with although

21 p 58 of the AEPO-ARTIS report.

22 *ibid* at p 44. Collection for broadcasting and communication to the public over the period 2011 to 2017 amounted to on average 67 percent of overall collection.

23 According to AEPO, the average total annual figure collected by PPI (as distributed by RAAP) for the relevant performers in the years 2011 to 2017 was just shy of €1.2 million in respect of equitable remuneration for broadcasting and €1.64 million generated in the way of equitable remuneration for communication to the public. When split annually between the amount of performers involved, the figures are almost negligible in terms of artist performer income.

24 Note s 10 of the Copyright and Related Rights (Amendment) Act 2007 amended s 205(5)(g) of the 2000 Act. Section 205 (new subsection inserted after subs (9)) was also amended by the EU (Copyright and Related Rights) Regulations 2012 (SI No 59 of 2012).

25 The 2000 Act *inter alia* gave effect to 92/100/EEC of 19 November 1992 on the rental and lending right as later codified, repealed and replaced by Directive 2006/115/EC.

26 By the 2007 Act (see fn 24), SI No 20 of 2009, SI No 59 of 2012 and SI No 411 of 2013. Performer rights, actions for infringement and so forth have also been amended by the 2019 Act.

27 In any case, it has always been limited to the audiovisual sector. The phonographic industry did not allow the rental of phonograms. Its relevance is likely to continue to decrease, at least for the period it is applied only to physical media and not streaming, as is currently the case.

obviously in-demand top performers will attract sums commensurate with their skills and reputation.

[10B.6.03] To compound matters, the vast majority of countries in the EU have not collected any remuneration whatsoever for performers for the making available on demand of their performances. Essentially the argument from performer advocates is that 21st century streaming platforms acting as radio stations or video rental shops should pay remuneration like any other radio station or video rental shop. The stated aim of the Belgian government during its presidency of the EU in 2023 is to introduce an EU-wide right to unwaivable equitable remuneration for music and audiovisual streaming. If this can be achieved, it would be the biggest step forward in performers' rights in decades.

[10B.6.04] The 2019 Directive sought to correct this but contracts since then are providing by way of "full buyout" clauses that performers waive their rights to the contract adjustment provisions of the Directive (see Chapter 11) and the above domestic Regulations such that a claim will not be made by performers against the production company for further payments (or to revoke the rights granted). While this appears manifestly unfair and against the spirit of the new legislation, it has at least ignited informed discussion in the industry. Producers are now duly considering the adequacy of the intended full buyout fee much more judiciously, and perhaps from the perspective of ultimately whether a judge would likewise consider the remuneration paid to in fact be equitable. The trend going forward will be somewhat more significant fees.

Exclusive rights versus remuneration rights

[10B.6.05] Exclusive rights are transferable by nature. In practice, the consequence is that producers (usually a music record company or television/film producer or independent film production company) will insist that performers transfer all of their exclusive rights to them when contracting with the performer for a particular performance.[28] As addressed below, in the case of film production agreement between a producer and performers, the latter shall be presumed (unless the agreement provides to the contrary) to have transferred their rental rights (though this is without prejudice to the right of performers to receive equitable remuneration in respect of the rental right).

[10B.6.06] Accordingly, at the time performers make a recording or give a performance, they are entirely reliant on and bound by the terms of the contract that they have signed with the producer. Such contracts usually make provision for the payment to the performer of an overall lump sum, which can often be

[28] If this occurs, performers can no longer control future uses whereas writers of a song for example, because they retain control of reproduction rights, this allows them to authorise the synchronisation of their work on many more occasions and in many more areas (e.g. films or television commercials).

quite low.[29] Due to these commercial realities, very few performers' collective management organisations ('CMOs') in the EU are thus able to exercise and manage exclusive rights on behalf of performers and the possibility to administer such rights is limited and has remained, until now at least (recent legislative changes might engender improvements), the exception rather than practice.[30]

[10B.6.07] As distinct from an exclusive right, a remuneration right is merely a right to receive a payment when a work is used. It does not give rightsholders the possibility to authorise or prohibit use of the work and the remuneration directly collected by their CMO from the users thereof is not dependent upon any authorisation from the performers. Hence, remuneration rights alone do not give rightsholders the possibility to authorise or to prohibit the exploitation of their work (as do exclusive rights) but at least ensure them an income. They are generally considered as non-transferable, which means that they remain in the hands of the performers concerned, regardless of signed contract provisions. This is also the case for the equitable remuneration guaranteed for broadcasting and communication to the public of fixed performances (mostly for phonograms). Accordingly, most performers across the EU are depending much more on remuneration rights say from radioplay of music and the remuneration from private copying than on the exclusive rights to receive an income from the exploitation of their rights.

The weaker position of performers

[10B.6.08] This situation is very different to the position of authors and the manner in which authors' exclusive rights are exercised. First of all, authors' rights were created centuries prior to performers' rights. The latter came into being following on from the Rome Convention in 1961. Authors' rights are traditionally more accepted and respected than performers' rights.[31] Moreover, authors may create a work independently and then grant a mandate to a CMO to exercise the exclusive rights on their behalf such as a songwriter granting authority to the Mechanical Copyright Protection Society to negotiate terms with a movie producer of a synchronisation licence and the fee payable for use of a song in a film.

[10B.6.09] CMOs, which are in a far stronger bargaining position than

---

29 This will not always be the case. In-demand session and orchestral players will command respectable hourly studio rates, but aside from future radio and other public performance royalties if they register the performance with RAAP (see fn 6), the payment will be a one-off and they will sign away future exclusive rights.

30 And even where CMOs do in fact administer rights it will represent only a small fraction of performers' exclusive rights.

31 For example, while Art 3(1) of InfoSoc Directive 2001/29/EC grants authors an exclusive right for "any communication to the public", including making available, under Art 3(2), performers are only granted an exclusive right with respect to the type of communication to the public that constitutes making available on demand of fixations of their performances.

individual authors or performers, can negotiate favourable and equitable contractual arrangements with producers. It can be seen therefore that in the case of authors, the exclusive right is indeed a powerful tool. For performers, however, that same exclusive right is in practice of far less benefit. Consequently, collection made by performers' CMOs is mostly in respect of remuneration rights only, while collection by authors' CMOs is predominantly based on the collective exercise of exclusive rights.

Equitable remuneration

[10B.6.10] In parallel to the exclusive performer rights above, performers in the EU enjoy three main sources of remuneration: a right to equitable remuneration for broadcasting and communication to the public of their performances, a right to equitable remuneration for rental, based on an exclusive right when transferred, and a remuneration for private copying as a counterpart for the use of the corresponding exception to the reproduction right (which as seen does not apply in Ireland).

[10B.6.11] In terms of broadcasting and communication to the public of fixations, the audiovisual sector does not benefit from the remuneration guaranteed to the music sector. A right to equitable remuneration for any broadcasting and communication to the public, as Art 8(2) of EU Directive 2006/115 grants to phonograms, does not exist for audiovisual recordings and hence, at the international level, the Beijing Treaty is the first treaty aimed at protecting audiovisual performances. Incidentally, the CJEU held in *Atresmedia Corporación de Medios de Comunicación S.A. v Asociación de Gestión de Derechos Intelectuales* (Case-147/19) that the rental and lending right provisions must be interpreted as meaning that the single equitable remuneration need not be paid by the user (in this case a television broadcaster) where it makes a communication to the public of an audiovisual recording containing the fixation of an audiovisual work in which a phonogram or a reproduction of that phonogram has been incorporated. However the court stressed that remuneration could otherwise be paid under contract between the holders of the rights in phonograms (music producers/performers) and the audiovisual works producers seeking to incorporate the prior music sound recordings into such works.

RAAP

Registering a performance with RAAP

[10B.7.01] While music performers may (or may not, at their own volition) register their performance with Recorded Artists Actors Performers ('RAAP') in Ireland (British musicians, actors, dancers and other performers should register with Phonographic Performance Ltd (see fn 4) and BECS, the British Equity Collecting Society for performers' audiovisual rights), the royalty income received will be lower than that of authors such as songwriters as collected by the Irish Music Rights Organisation (IMRO) and/or the Mechanical Copyright Protection Society (MCPS). Oftentimes they will neglect or fail to register and hence receive no royalty income at all (even if their performance features in films or on television).

[10B.7.02] Music producers can also register with RAAP *qua* performer. If producers (and say sound/mixing engineers) contribute to a sound recording (e.g. by playing a guitar riff), they can register with RAAP to obtain performer royalties as well as obtaining PPI royalties in relation to ownership of the master itself.[32]

The RAAP v PPI rulings (CJEU and Irish High Court)

[10B.7.03] Regarding performances fixed in a phonogram, the Rome Convention introduced the principle that if such sound recording is used directly for broadcasting or any communication to the public, then a single equitable remuneration must be paid by the user. It was clear from the wording that this single remuneration was to be shared between both performers and the phonogram producers (record labels in the main). In 1996, this principle was upheld with approval in the WIPO Treaty. In the vast majority of EU Member States the amount of equitable remuneration is shared on a 50:50 basis between performers and producers.[33]

[10B.7.04] The long-running legal battle in *RAAP v PPI*[34] concerned royalties collected by the Irish neighbouring rights' collecting society, PPI (which collects equitable remuneration, that is, public performance, broadcast and webcast royalties on behalf of record labels) and whether such moneys are and, if not, should be, distributed back to all performers, including performers who are nationals in, or residents of, countries located outside the EU. Simons J in the High Court had made a reference under art 267 of the Lisbon Treaty to the CJEU for the reasons set out in detail in a judgment he delivered in January 2019.[35] The reference concerned the interpretation of the rental and lending

---

[32] That is if the producer has not assigned default statutory ownership of the sound recording to the band, artist/s or audiovisual producer by way of work for hire agreement. In *Bamgboye* discussed in Chapter 22, the defendant as music producer claimed he carried out all the performing of the subject dance track. However, the court held that the claimant who added electronic drum and other parts while acting as sound engineering assistant was entitled to performer rights as well as a share in the compositional rights.

[33] This method has been established in national legislation in some cases, but in others it is merely a matter of established practice. Similarly, some national legislation specifies that it is compulsory for collection of the equitable remuneration to be administered by a single CMO, whereas in some countries collective management is applied as a matter of practice rather than law.

[34] *Recorded Artists Actors Performers Ltd v Phonographic Performance (Ireland) Ltd* [2021] IEHC 22.

[35] [2019] IEHC 2.

rights Directive (Directive 2006/115/EC). The CJEU delivered its judgment (*RAAP v PPI*) in September 2020.[36]

[10B.7.05] The CJEU held in a ground-breaking decision that all performers, regardless of nationality, are entitled to equitable remuneration, without exception, provided that the use of the relevant commercial phonogram occurs within the EEA. In Ireland, as in many other European countries, the law did not permit the sharing of equitable remuneration with nationals of a country where the same right is not recognised for Irish performers. This has historically had significant relevance for the US which does not operate a system of paying public performance or broadcast royalties to artist performers. In practice, this has meant that US artists have been left out of other international systems for sharing in equitable remuneration payments (or similar local equivalents) not only in Europe, but also in Australia, Japan and elsewhere. The ruling signals a significant shift in the system for US performers and will have considerable practical implications for EU labels.

[10B.7.06] The High Court proceedings were then relisted before Simons J on 29 January 2021 who held, *inter alia*, that the right to remuneration accorded to owners of sound recordings in respect of the broadcasting and of any communication to the public in the state of the said sound recordings be equally accorded to all performers whose performances are incorporated on the said sound recordings. Prior to this and unlike in other EU countries, this sharing of remuneration was not done on the basis of a 50:50 split at source. PPI unilaterally calculated the share to which performers were entitled and obliged RAAP to request the payment for each performer separately.

SATELLITE BROADCASTING AND CABLE RETRANSMISSIONS

[10B.8.01] Council Directive 93/83/EEC (as amended) on the co-ordination of certain rules concerning copyright and rights related to copyright applicable to satellite broadcasting and cable retransmissions, while giving for the first time a single European definition of broadcasting and communication to the public by satellite, relates directly to the pre-existing right of communication to the public and broadcasting as introduced in Directive 92/100/EEC (now 2006/115/EC). The 2018 AEPO report states that eight percent of the total collection moneys captured in the study came from cable retransmission rights.

[10B.8.02] Directive 93/83/EEC applied only to satellite broadcasting or cable retransmission. In particular, it did not apply to online transmissions and therefore did not take into account the technological developments of the digital age. Hence, Directive (EU) 2019/789[37] (the Online Broadcasting

[36] Case C-265/19 *Recorded Artists Actors Performers Ltd v Phonographic Performance (Ireland) Ltd, Minister for Jobs, Enterprise and Innovation, Ireland, Attorney General.*

[37] Of the European Parliament and of the Council of 17 April 2019 laying down rules on

and Retransmission Directive) was introduced. The Council adopted both the Digital Single Market Directive and the Online Broadcasting and Retransmission Directive on 15 April 2019. The latter aims to promote the cross-border provision of online services ancillary to broadcasts and to alleviate heavy rights-clearing burdens by establishing the country of origin principle, on the one hand, and by extending the system of mandatory collective management to all types of radio and television retransmissions, on the other hand. It also lays down rules on television and radio broadcasts via the technique of direct injection.[38] The Directive was transposed into Irish law in July 2022 by statutory instrument.[39]

[10B.8.03] The introduction of the Directive to take account of changing technologies is welcome as Belgium, Finland, France, Greece, Ireland, Italy, Norway and Serbia were not collecting remuneration for performers under this right. This is for varying reasons such as the must-carry exemption[40] or ongoing litigation.

EQUITABLE REMUNERATION FOR BROADCASTING AND COMMUNICATION TO THE PUBLIC OF COMMERCIAL PHONOGRAMS

[10B.9.01] As above, in both the audio and audiovisual sectors, performers almost always transfer their "making available right" to the producer, at best for a single all-inclusive fee which in many cases can be woefully insignificant. Only a few performers of great repute manage to negotiate directly the payment of royalties for the exploitation of their performances. In respect of collection for making available, in 2017 collection occurred in only eight of the 26 countries covered in AEPO's 2018 study (excluding those countries where a negligible amount was obtained).

[10B.9.02] As regards the right to equitable remuneration for broadcasting and communication to the public of commercial phonograms set out in Art 8(2) of the rental and lending Directive 2006/115/EC, as a large percentage of streams on platforms such as Spotify and Deezer are non-interactive or "passive" streams, these fall under the provisions of Art 8(2), and accordingly remuneration ought to be paid to performers. Currently, this is not happening and performers are therefore being denied a remuneration to which they are entitled under existing legislation. In the same Directive, performers are granted a right to

the exercise of copyright and related rights applicable to certain online transmissions of broadcasting organisations and retransmissions of television and radio programmes, and amending Council Directive 93/83/EEC.

38 For a detailed analysis see Alexander De Bleeckere and Olivier Vrins, *In the shadow of the DSM Directive: the new Online Broadcasting and Retransmission Directive* (2019), altius.com. (Altius Blog, 20 June 2019, Altius Lawyers, Belgium).

39 EU (Copyright and Related Rights Applicable to Certain Online Transmissions and Retransmissions) Regulations 2022 (SI No 357 of 2022).

40 See Chapter 32.

remuneration (upon the transfer of the exclusive right) for rental. This provided a source of revenue when films in which their performances are incorporated were rented from high street video-rental shops. Today, these shops have almost all disappeared. However, digital streaming platforms such as Amazon Prime and Apple TV now offer subscribers the same opportunity to "rent" films, albeit online. Despite sharing all properties of a high street shop, these platforms pay no remuneration as a result of an antiquated legal anomaly.[41]

RENTAL AND LENDING RIGHTS

[10B.10.01] The above-cited rental and lending Directive introduced an unwaivable remuneration right aimed at guaranteeing that these incomes would be shared. The principle behind this is positive for performers. However, because the right is not subject to compulsory collective management and there is no legal obligation on the users to pay performers, in practice the amounts that performers on audiovisual productions receive is very low.[42]

[10B.10.02] Article 4 imposed on Member States the principle that where performers have transferred or assigned their rental right concerning a phonogram or an original or copy of a film to a phonogram or film producer, those performers shall retain the right to obtain an equitable remuneration for the rental. However, these provisions are considerably weakened given the fact that the Directive introduces a presumption of transfer of rental right in the event of a film production. Pursuant to Art 3(4), Member States are obliged to implement in their national legislation a rebuttable presumption that performers have transferred their rental right to the film producer when a contract concerning the production of a film is concluded (s 207 of the 2000 Act so provides in Ireland).

[10B.10.03] In practice, the performers' exclusive right here is often transferred to the phonogram or audiovisual producer in individual contracts without a specific equitable remuneration. This practice is extended by the presumption of transfer as above if a contract concerning the production of a film is concluded. This often means no remuneration accrues for the transfer of this right. It appears at least from the 2018 AEPO report that rental right remuneration in Ireland was nil for all years examined.

41 These 21st century types of use are deemed not to be covered by the rental right but are instead deemed to be covered by a completely different right: the making available right. This is because the rental right is considered to apply only to tangible/physical copies. In other words, if a film is fixed on a DVD and a consumer pays to access and use it for 48 hours it is "rental". If it is fixed in a computer file and accessed via Amazon Prime for 48 hours it is "making available".

42 Rental is limited to the audiovisual sector, as the phonographic industry has chosen to prohibit the rental of phonograms.

Chapter 11

New Rights for Content Authors and Performers: Directive on Copyright and Related Rights in the Digital Single Market

INTRODUCTION

[11.1.01] The EU Directive on Copyright in the Digital Single Market (2019/790) ('the 2019 Directive') was transposed by Statutory Instrument in November 2021 into domestic Irish legislation.[1] It affects a range of industry practitioners from authors/content creators including screenplay writers, music composers, film directors, journalists and photographers in the context of copyright through to performers including actors, musicians, singers, dancers and other performing artists in terms of related rights. It therefore has a bearing for contract law purposes on audiovisual and other media content production companies as well as for music publishers and producers/record labels entering agreements with such authors and neighbouring rights holders. The 2019 Directive also impacts users of content and distributors of such content. The purpose of this chapter is to set out in practical terms the benefits this long-debated EU legislation bestows on creators and performers. The legislation did not go far enough, but advancing rights a number of steps in the right direction, it can be built upon in the future.

[11.1.02] The 2019 Directive is not retrospective in effect. It applies in respect of all works and other subject matter that are protected by national law in the field of copyright on or after the implementation date of 7 June 2021. It, therefore, applies without prejudice to any acts concluded and rights acquired before that date. Article 27 provides that agreements for the licence or transfer of rights of authors and performers shall be subject to the transparency obligation set out in Art 19 as from the later date of 7 June 2022.

[11.1.03] In short, the 2019 Directive contains a number of provisions that will

---

1 EU (Copyright and Related Rights in the Digital Single Market) Regulations 2021 (SI No 567 of 2021). By its actual implementation deadline of 7 June 2021, only the Netherlands, Hungary and Germany appeared to have had fully implemented the 2019 Directive.

further harmonise copyright exceptions in the areas of research, education and cultural preservation, provide protection for press publishers for the online use of their content[2] and measures to address the 'value gap' whereby rightsholders can, it is hoped at least, derive greater economic value for the use of their content online. The latter will be achieved by affording creators rights to greater access to information on the use of their works, as well as the ability in exceptional circumstances to renegotiate agreements into which they entered with their contractual counterparts.

[11.1.04] From a wide standpoint in terms of the need for the 2019 Directive at all, it was considered[3] that intervention in a national context would not be robustly efficient to address the identified problems (notably because such measures would lack scale) and could create new obstacles and market fragmentation. Accordingly, action at EU level was deemed necessary in order to ensure legal certainty for creators, performers, those investing in content, and for distributors and users.[4] Moreover the 2019 Directive aspires to allow rightsholders to better exercise their rights in the online environment and guarantee a level playing field in the digital single market.

[11.1.05] From a practical perspective, the 2019 Directive will inevitably lead (and already has led) to change in the standard type contracts which have been employed in the industry over many years. Even though this EU legislation did not fall for transposition by EU Member States until 7 June 2021, it had prompted Netflix prior to that to take account of its fair remuneration provisions in Germany. In addition, it will be interesting to observe how it will sit with existing case law. As regards provision of transparent information, Art 19(4)[5] introduces the 'significance of contribution' clause and provides that:

> Member States may decide that the obligation set out in paragraph 1 of this Article does not apply when the contribution of the author or performer is not significant having regard to the overall work or performance, unless the author or performer demonstrates that he or she requires the information for the

---

2 Art 15 is intended to ensure greater protection for press publishers by creating a neighbouring press publishers' right. This should allow press publishers to receive remuneration for the online exploitation of their works by news aggregators without preventing users from making lawful use of those works and thus help in ensuring the sustainability of the publishing industry.

3 EU Commission Staff Working Document, *Executive Summary of the Impact Assessment on the modernisation of EU copyright rules accompanying the document proposal for a Directive of the European Parliament and of the Council on copyright in the Digital Single Market* (2016), Brussels, 14 September 2016, SWD/2016/0302.

4 By facilitating provision of greater choice of content.

5 Art 19(1) provides that Member States shall ensure that authors and performers receive on a regular basis, at least once a year, and taking into account the specificities of each sector, up to date, relevant and comprehensive information on the exploitation of their works and performances from the parties to whom they have licensed or transferred their rights, or their successors in title, in particular as regards modes of exploitation, all revenues generated and remuneration due.

exercise of his or her rights under Article 20(1)[6] and requests the information for that purpose.

[11.1.06] UK case law has proven repeatedly that the weight of a contribution is difficult to assess from the outset (e.g. *Beckingham v Hodgens* (2003) and *Fisher v Brooker* (2009)).[7] Contributions by session musicians, for instance, can become the hook of a song or leave an imprint that was not foreseen at the time of release of a track. Considering that most creators have very little bargaining power, this assessment is left to the producer party, and it was initially believed that the large majority of creators were likely not to witness any real benefit in this connection.[8] The then Department of Business, Enterprise and Innovation queried in its *Consultation Paper No. 4*, inviting input from industry stakeholders on how best to transpose the 2019 Directive,[9] what criteria should be used to determine that the "contribution of the author or performer is not significant" if Ireland opted to transpose the voluntary provision of art 19(4).

[11.1.07] Regulation 27 of the transposing EU (Copyright and Related Rights in the Digital Single Market) Regulations 2021 (SI No 567 of 2021, 'the 2021 Regulations') makes no reference to this contribution and hence Ireland did not adopt the voluntary position of the Art 19(4). Thus, in the case of this jurisdiction at least, the position of authors and performers whose input might not be significant has not been diluted as regards the transparency obligations. However, reg 28 (contract adjustment mechanism) does provide that the assessment of a claim by an author or performer as to whether remuneration originally agreed[10]

---

6 Member states shall ensure that, in the absence of an applicable collective bargaining agreement providing for a mechanism comparable to that set out in Art 20, authors and performers or their representatives are entitled to claim additional, appropriate and fair remuneration from the party with whom they entered into a contract for the exploitation of their rights, or from the successors in title of such party, when the remuneration originally agreed turns out to be disproportionately low compared to all the subsequent relevant revenues derived from the exploitation of the works or performances.

7 As discussed in *Appendix 1* to Chapter 22.

8 Ananay Aguilar, *The New Copyright Directive: Fair remuneration in exploitation contracts of authors and performers – Part 1, Articles 18 and 19* (2019), University of Cambridge. Available at: https://copyrightblog.kluweriplaw.com/2019/07/15/the-new-copyright-directive-fair-remuneration-in-exploitation-contracts-of-authors-and-performers-part-1-articles-18-and-19/ [Accessed 3 September 2021].

9 Art 29 provides that Member States shall bring into force the laws, regulations and administrative provisions necessary to comply with the 2019 Directive by 7 June 2021 (this proved aspirational as practically all Member States missed this deadline). The Irish government in late 2019 welcomed submissions from all stakeholders as to suggestions on the transposition into Irish law of the Directive's wide and sweeping provisions which leave discretion to Member States as to implementation of certain aspects thereof. The Department (Copyright Section, Intellectual Property Unit) opted to conduct a series of public consultations, four in total, regarding transposition. Each consultation was allotted four weeks to allow for submissions from interested parties including Screen Producers Ireland, film producers and leading entertainment law practitioners in Ireland.

10 Between authors/performers and the parties with whom they entered into a contract for the exploitation of their rights in a work or performance, or from the successors in title of such party.

transpires to be disproportionately low compared to all the subsequent relevant revenues[11] derived from the exploitation of the work or performance shall *inter alia* take into account the specific circumstances of each case, including the contribution of the author or performer.

[11.1.08] Likewise, while Art 22(1) provides that Member States shall ensure that where authors or performers have licensed or transferred their rights in a work or other protected subject matter on an exclusive basis, they may revoke in whole or in part the licence or the transfer of rights where there is a lack of exploitation of that work, Art 22(2)(b) counters this somewhat by providing that where a work or other subject matter contains the contribution of more than one author or performer, national law may take into account the relative importance of the individual contributions, and the legitimate interests of all authors and performers affected by the application of the revocation mechanism by an individual author or performer. However, again, the Irish legislature has chosen not to adopt this voluntary provision and reg 29 omits any reference from the 2019 Directive of the relative importance of the individual contributions of authors or performers in cases where there are more than one author or performer. In spite of this, contracts with contributors/performers as drafted by audiovisual (or audio) producers will typically require a waiver of the right of revocation (and therefore render what the 2019 Directive is trying to achieve redundant).[12]

[11.1.09] Moreover, as regards fees payable, the operation of 'full buyout' clauses might henceforth dwindle to some degree although it is crucial to note that the 2019 Directive envisages the continuing use of lump sums payments as constituting Art 18 appropriate and proportionate remuneration but that "it should not be the rule".[13] Where they are included in author or performer agreements, the payment of a merely nominal consideration as has sometimes been the case thus far (such as with documentary participants, certain music composers/performers and extras actors) may well be a hazardous practice for producers going forward in light of the enhanced rights the 2019 Directive contemplates, notwithstanding that nominal consideration is fully permissible in common law as being 'sufficient'.

[11.1.10] In the aftermath of the 2021 Regulations coming into force in Ireland, specific reference is typically being made thereto in contracts and to the 2019 Directive. Where no reference is expressly made, the subject contract

---

[11] Including, where applicable, merchandising revenues.

[12] A typical clause might read, "Contributor acknowledges that the production of the Programme requires the contributions of a plurality of authors and performers and accordingly Contributor irrevocably waives any rights of revocation or similar right to which Contributor may (in the absence of this paragraph) be entitled at any time pursuant to Article 22 of the EU Directive on Copyright in the Digital Single Market (2019/790) and pursuant to any enactments of Ireland and any other jurisdiction whose purpose is to transpose in national law such directive in whole or in part".

[13] See preamble to the 2019 Directive at Recital 73.

should nonetheless take cognisance of the EU/national law governing the now augmented author and performer rights. Indeed, provisions seeking to contract out of rights granted and obligations imposed by the new legislation would be deemed unenforceable. Article 23(1) thus expressly prevents parties from overriding Arts 19 to 21. Regulation 31 of the transposing regulations in Ireland provides that any contractual provision that prevents compliance with regs 27 (transparency obligations) or 28 (contract adjustment mechanism) shall be unenforceable in relation to authors and performers. That is not to say, however, that lawyers do not seek to lawfully circumvent the legislation by recourse to waivers being signed by rightsholders. It thus remains to be seen how the courts will view the effect and enforceability of such waivers.

Circumventing the new enhanced rights in contracts

[11.1.11] As seen in the preceding chapter, the 2019 Directive stopped short of conferring performers and authors with unwaivable remuneration rights that would have ensured when they transfer their exclusive rights, fair remuneration could still be guaranteed. Contracts since then are providing by way of 'full buyout' clauses that authors/performers waive their rights to the contract adjustment provisions of the 2019 Directive and the 2021 Regulations with the effect that they sign away the right to claim against the production company for further payments (or to revoke the rights granted).

[11.1.12] Specifically, they are being called upon to acknowledge the proposed fee as adequate for the purposes of 'full buyout' equitable payment (and that it is fair, appropriate and proportionate) such that a claim will not be made against the producer (or other party seeking buyout) for further payments whether pursuant to reg 28 of the 2021 Regulations and/or Art 20 of the 2019 Directive, and that any right of revocation to which they may otherwise be entitled pursuant to reg 29 and/or Art 22 of the 2019 Directive is thereby waived. It will prove interesting as to whether these express waivers will be challenged in the courts. For now, it seems that unless further unwaivable rights are guaranteed in law for authors and performers that producers might be immune from suit when the provisions of the 2019 Directive and the 2021 Regulations are viewed holistically. As regards the revocation provisions, Member States may provide that any contractual provision derogating from the revocation mechanism provided for in Art 22 is enforceable only if it is based on a collective bargaining agreement. That might well suggest that the type of waivers being adopted in this connection would be enforceable. The 2021 Regulations do not specifically deal with this point relating to enforceability. Again, it will take litigation to test the lawfulness of such contractual clauses.

Brexit

[11.1.13] A final introductory point to note is the impact of Brexit on

Irish creatives who might be contracting with British counterparts such as music publishers, record labels or film producers. The UK left the EU in 2020 before the implementation deadline for the 2019 Directive, and in any event, it had earlier confirmed that it would not implement the (spirit of the) 2019 Directive in its own laws. Therefore, once fully implemented by each Member State (as of 15 February 2023, the European Commission decided to refer Bulgaria, Denmark, Finland, Latvia, Portugal and Poland to the Court of Justice of the EU ('the CJEU') following their failure to notify complete transposition measures in respect of the 2019 Directive's implementation), the copyright position in the EU will be different to that applying in Britain. At a stretch, an Irish music composer, for instance, with a strong track record and who is in high demand for film scoring might circumvent this issue (to avail of the protections offered by the 2019 Directive) by insisting that the governing law of the contract is Ireland (and thus Irish/EU rules apply) and not England. The other alternative is to negotiate express inclusion into the contract of the same enhanced rights that the 2019 Directive affords across the EU. One would expect however in time that Britain, to keep apace as a major creative hub, will enact legislation that aligns somewhat closely to the core provisions of the 2019 Directive.

THE VALUE GAP

[11.2.01] The 2019 Directive, designed to stem the transfer of value and hence close the 'value gap' (such that rightsholders would receive a fair share of the value that is generated by the use of their works), unearthed a storm of controversy from the days when it was initially proposed in 2016 and weathered a raft of intense lobbying of EU politicians by the music sector[14] to be met with robust resistance and counter-lobbying from the technology giants such as Google and Amazon as well as from internet freedom campaigners. Netflix, Facebook, YouTube, Instagram and TikTok must now observe legal obligations in respect of film, music and other protected content. Aside from freedom of expression arguments,[15] the extent of lobbying witnessed can be explained by market size

14 In July 2018, Sir Paul McCartney wrote in an open letter to the European Parliament that "the value gap jeopardises the music ecosystem. We need an internet that is fair and sustainable for all. But today some User Upload Content platforms refuse to compensate artists and all music creators fairly for their work, while they exploit it for their own profit. The value gap is that gulf between the value these platforms derive from music and the value they pay creators". Source: Rhian Daly, *Paul McCartney calls on MEPs to back music copyright law change* (2018). Available at: https://www.nme.com/news/music/paul-mccartney-calls-meps-back-music-copyright-law-change-2349934 [Accessed 26 July 2019].

15 Free speech advocates impugned the 2019 Directive in its draft stages as amounting to a meme ban. However, the protection of legitimate uses (the parody exception, caricature, parody, quotation, criticism and review) in art 17(7) allow GIFs and other memes to continue to be shared freely. This was confirmed by EU Commission FAQs issued on 4 June 2021: "Does the Copyright Directive prevent users from expressing themselves in the same way as now? Are memes and GIFs banned?" The reply given was, "No. Uploading memes and other content generated by users for purposes of quotation, criticism, review,

and the fact that the EU's creative industry is estimated to be valued at over half a trillion euro.[16]

[11.2.02] The lobbyists on behalf of music composers ultimately proved triumphant such that the position of rightsholders in their negotiations with online platforms has been strengthened, information must now be imparted in relation to how publishers, labels and music producers exploit works, and having regard to the 2019 Directive's 'better-seller' article and revocation mechanism[17] discussed below. Nevertheless, it remains to be seen how the broad framework of the Directive will be interpreted in practice and how its provisions will be implemented throughout the EU's Member States. As is oftentimes the case with Directives, Member States were afforded wide discretion as to the manner in which this Directive was to be transposed into domestic law.

SCOPE AND AFFECTED PARTIES

[11.3.01] The objective was to make EU copyright rules fit for the digital age. The market, with a substantial number of sectors in the wider economy being copyright intensive, is highly significant given the numbers employed in the entertainment industry. The ramifications, therefore, are far-reaching.

[11.3.02] The 2019 Directive was agreed between the Council, the European Parliament and the Commission on 13 February 2019 and then approved by Parliament on 26 March 2019 and endorsed by the Council on 15 April 2019. It amends the InfoSoc Directive from 2001[18] which largely predates what we now know as social media and its purview extends to the above-mentioned market players including Google/YouTube which may and will have to sign licensing agreements with songwriters, musicians and performers (or their representatives) in relation to use of their creative IP output.

[11.3.03] It is hoped, with strengthened bargaining powers, that screenwriters, songwriters, musicians, composers and actors should now find it somewhat less difficult to negotiate with their contractual partners (to include audiovisual

---

caricature, parody and pastiche (like GIFs or similar) is specifically allowed. Users are able to continue to upload such content online, but the new rules bring clarity in this respect and apply in all EU Member States. Until now, copyright exceptions allowing these uses were only optional and Member States were free not to implement them. Under the Copyright Directive, this is no longer the case: Member States are obliged to allow these uses. This is a particularly important step for the freedom of expression online".

16 According to the European Commission in 2018, the cultural and creative industries (including the fashion industry) generate around €509 billion per year and employ 12 million in full-time jobs, which constitutes some 7.5 percent of the EU's total employment.

17 Affecting licensing agreements between creators and music publishers or producers for instance.

18 The Copyright Directive (Directive 2001/29/EC) of the European Parliament and of the Council of 22 May 2001 on the harmonisation of certain aspects of copyright and related rights in the information society.

producers, record labels and music publishers) in order to receive enhanced remuneration for the use of their works and performances. In addition, creators in the audiovisual and music sectors should henceforth be poised to exert more control over the use of their songs and performances or otherwise in films and other formats uploaded on online platforms and, the intended outcome is, will be better compensated therefor.

ENHANCED AUTHOR AND PERFORMER RIGHTS

[11.4.01] Perhaps of most potency, beyond the new online platform licensing and remuneration issues which shall shortly be discussed, is the contract adjustment mechanism and right of revocation provisions of Arts 20 and 22 respectively. With all things contract law, the devil is in the detail however and the Directive is scant on the minutia. This is hardly surprising however considering the mammoth difficulties in striking some semblance of a balance between competing interests to push this piece of legislation ultimately across the line. What is certain is that all measures to tighten artist protection, even if incremental and unclear in practical terms for now at least as to extent and being subject to ongoing policy review over the medium term, comprise a movement in the right direction and must be welcomed.

Contract adjustment mechanism ('better-seller' clause) (Art 20/reg 28)

[11.4.02] Certain contracts for the exploitation of rights can be of a lengthy duration. The Art 20 provisions will allow rightsholders, without prejudice to the law applicable to contracts in Member States, to review and adjust existing contracts. The article equips authors and performers (or their representatives) with the right to claim additional, appropriate and fair remuneration from the party with whom they entered into a contract for the exploitation of their rights, or from the successors in title of such party, where the remuneration originally agreed transpires to be disproportionately low compared with all subsequent revenues (including, where applicable, merchandising income) derived from exploitation of their works or performances. This mechanism does not apply to collective bargaining agreements that contain a comparable contract adjustment mechanism, or agreements concluded by collective management organisations or independent management entities or other entities subject to national rules implementing the Collective Rights Management Directive.[19]

[11.4.03] The better-seller clause will therefore allow a creator, for example a screenwriter or a musician whose work or performance has achieved unanticipated success, to assert a claim to this (additional and unforeseen) success if the originally agreed remuneration with the film/television production company

[19] Which concerns collective management of copyright and related rights and multi-territorial licensing of rights in musical works for online use in the internal market.

or record label is clearly disproportionate to the actual generated revenues. This mechanism has existed in several Member States for quite some time but it has now been extended to the entire EU.

Contractual freedom of the parties

[11.4.04] Freedom to contract should not be affected by the 2019 Directive's provisions. Rightsholders cannot be obliged to give an authorisation or to conclude licensing agreements say with YouTube for use of their music. On the flip side, contractual freedom means too that authors are free to accept or reject the types of waivers that are being commonly used to obviate the Arts 20 (contract adjustment) and 22 (right of revocation) effects of the 2019 Directive. If authors and performers are unwilling to sign away their rights, producers will likely always have alternatives in terms of authors/performers and content providers who will be amenable to signing a waiver not to institute claims for further fees or seeking revocation of rights they had previously granted to a producer or platform. Meanwhile, the point is made by Baden-Powell and Heeley[20] that the secondary impact of these new rights is that investors desirous to fund content may be deterred by the idea that a carefully negotiated and legally binding contract can potentially be adjusted or even revoked under the 2019 Directive. The full effect of the Directive therefore remains to be seen.

[11.4.05] (In the absence of a waiver of rights provision in a contract) reg 28(4) of the 2021 Regulations provides that where an author or performer makes such a claim by electronic or other means, the party with whom that author or performer has entered into a contract shall provide a written response addressing the substance of the claim within one month of receiving that written claim. Regulation 28(5) further provides that without prejudice to judicial remedies, disputes under the 2021 Regulations may be submitted to a mediator in accordance with the Mediation Act 2017 or, where appropriate, to an arbitrator in accordance with the Arbitration Act 2010.

Right of revocation (Art 22/reg 29)

[11.4.06] When authors or performers transfer their rights, such as where a screenwriter assigns the film rights in a script or where a composer transfers stage rights to a theatre production company in respect of a musical, or they license their rights on an exclusive basis, there is an expectation that their work or performance will be exploited. In the event that this does not occur, Art 22 of the 2019 Directive stipulates that the author or performer may revoke in whole or in part the licence or the transfer of rights where there is a lack of exploitation of that work.

---

20 Baden-Powell and Heeley, "Copyright in the Digital Single Market–long-debated Directive approved" (2019) *Entertainment Law Review* 30(5), 143-147.

[11.4.07] The rationale here is that copyrighted works are created to be used and shared with an audience. Any work that is not exploited is a loss for European culture. However, works are frequently locked up in long-term contracts and creators until this point, absent a contract clause permitting re-assignment of rights by way of reversion, generally had no way to renegotiate even if there was active commercial exploitation of the subject material from which they were not receiving revenues (or if there were little or no attempts at commercial exploitation at all). This type of scenario has also arisen for certain American singer-songwriters as discussed in Chapter 22.[21]

[11.4.08] The revocation mechanism will potentially allow creators to regain their rights in cases where their works are not being exploited at all. A number of procedural guarantees, which Member States will be able to complement on a sector specific basis, however, will ensure that the legitimate interests of producers, publishers and investors are likewise considered in the balancing act. For example, the revocation mechanism will only be capable of invocation within a reasonable time after the licensing agreement has been concluded (as implemented by reg 29(2) of the the 2021 Regulations). Creators will also be obliged to notify producers or publishers of their intention to revoke the rights within a reasonable timeframe. This is to ensure that the producers or publishers have the opportunity to start exploiting the work if they so desire.

[11.4.09] The Art 22 right will not apply where exploitation is predominantly due to circumstances which the artist could reasonably be expected to remedy. Furthermore, as above, the revocation mechanism can only be exercised after a reasonable time following the conclusion of the relevant contract, and artists must provide notice of an appropriate deadline for exploitation. Once the deadline has expired, the artist can choose either to revoke the contract or to terminate its exclusivity rather than revoking it outright (Art 22(2) and reg 29(3)(b)). Member States may provide that contractual provisions aimed at avoiding the revocation mechanism are enforceable only if based on a collective bargaining agreement, a point to which we shall later return. This is not the case *per* reg 29.

[11.4.10] Member States have a margin of discretion over how they implement the right of revocation, taking into account the specificities of the different sectors and the different types of works and performances; and where a work/ performance contains the contribution of more than one author or performer, the relative importance of the individual contributions, and the legitimate interests of all artists affected by the application of the revocation mechanism by an individual author or performer. As afore-mentioned, Ireland has not chosen to adopt this route and reg 29 does not implement these voluntary provisions.

---

21 See recording contract litigation section.

Transparency obligation (Art 19/reg 27)

[11.4.11] While Art 19 on first inspection appears to make great waves, on closer examination (as regards opt-outs for Member States),[22] some may argue that the transparency obligation has been watered down to the point of rendering it nearly ineffective. Fortunately for Irish creatives however the implementing Regulations clearly side with authors and performers in not adopting the voluntary provisions of the article (see the following paragraph). Nonetheless few could argue that a fair balance must be struck as to allowing authors and creators by law access to information that may affect their income and, on the other hand, not imposing an unworkable burden on producers and others in terms of administration especially where it may be disproportionate in some cases to small gains for the creators (or indeed no gain accruing to them at all) after the information is duly made available to them.

[11.4.12] For this reason, the 2019 Directive afforded full latitude to Member States in this regard to legislate how they saw fit. In Ireland, reg 27 of the transposing legislation make no reference to this disproportionate administrative burden to temper the transparency obligations and accordingly record labels for instance cannot argue that an information request is disproportionate and creates too high an administrative burden in an effort to restrict or limit the information they furnish to the artist seeking such documentation. Neither does reg 27 include reference to the transparency obligation not applying when, using the wording of Art 19(4), the contribution of authors or performers is not significant having regard to the overall work or performance unless the authors or performers demonstrate that they require the information for the exercise of their contract adjustment rights under Art 20(1) and request the information for that purpose.

[11.4.13] Recital 75 to the 2019 Directive's preamble explains that as songwriters and performers tend to be in the weaker contractual position when they grant licences or transfer their rights, they require information to assess the continued economic value thereof compared to the actual remuneration initially received for such licence or transfer, but they frequently face a lack of transparency. Therefore, the sharing of adequate and accurate information by their contractual counterparts is important for openness and balance in the system.

[11.4.14] While contracts do, as a matter of course, contain accounting and audit provisions where there is a fee-splitting arrangement or otherwise and for

[22] Member States may limit the types and level of information reasonably expected in duly justified cases where the administrative burden would become disproportionate in the light of the revenues generated by the exploitation or performance of a work; introduce an exception where a contribution of the author or performer is not significant having regard to the overall work or performance, unless the artists demonstrate that they require the information, and request it, in order to exercise the right to claim additional remuneration provided under Art 20(1); and exempt collective bargaining agreements that are subject to transparency rules, provided that they meet the criteria at Art 19(1) to (4).

a collection agent to be appointed to administer receipts from the exploitation of a film for example, the 2019 Directive might help standardise the position where the author is in fact entitled to a share in the exploitation revenue or indeed if placed in a position where remuneration should be adjusted. Article 19 will ensure that authors and performers have access to an increased level of information about the exploitation of their works and performances to allow them assess their economic value.

[11.4.15] For example, screenwriters (who are contractually due backend producer net profit participation income) who seek it[23] are entitled to receive regular information from the film producer on the exploitation of the film to which they have contributed, including on the generated revenues. If the film achieves unexpected success and accrues much higher revenues than initially expected, the information obtained this way (either by contract and/or relying on the 2019 Directive/2021 Regulations) can be the basis for a review of the remuneration for the screenwriter through a contract adjustment mechanism. In another scenario where accounting and auditing entitlements are absent from the contract, the 2019 Directive provides for such entitlements.

[11.4.16] The information that the 2019 Directive prescribes as being mandatory in relevant circumstances should be up-to-date to allow access to recent data, relevant to the exploitation of the work or performance, and comprehensive in a way that it covers all sources of relevant revenues including merchandising revenues where applicable. As long as exploitation is ongoing, contractual counterparts of authors and performers should provide information available to them on all modes of exploitation and on all relevant revenues worldwide with a regularity that is appropriate for the sector at hand, but at least annually.

[11.4.17] The information should be provided in a manner that is comprehensible to the author or performer and it should allow the effective assessment of the economic value of the rights in question. The transparency obligation should nevertheless apply only where copyright-relevant rights are concerned. Moreover, the information must be proportionate and effective in ensuring a high level of transparency in every sector.

[11.4.18] Hence, reg 27 obliges the contractual counterpart, at least once annually, to provide the author of performer with a clear, detailed description

---

[23] While compliance with reg 27 (producers and others to whom rights have been licensed or transferred "shall" provide information on exploitation and revenues) is mandatory, in practice this is very unlikely, due to time and cost, to be actioned unless the licensor or assigner of rights in fact requests the information. It is noteworthy however that reg 31 provides that any contractual provision that prevents compliance with regs 27 (and 28) is unenforceable, and therefore this transparency right cannot be denied to rightsholders (though, as seen, a waiver can be requested from a rightsholder in respect of the contract adjustment mechanism which in effect negates the Art 20 right). Further, authors and performers are entitled to be notified of their rights under this regulation.

of how any work or performance the subject of the licence or transfer has been exploited worldwide during the relevant period; an itemised list of the euro value of all copyright revenues generated worldwide during the relevant period, including, where applicable, merchandising revenues, and notification of the author or performer's rights under this regulation.

[11.4.19] Moreover, the Art 19 provisions may serve to overcome the age-old concern that assignees or exclusive licensees can oftentimes neglect older content without actively re-releasing or promoting it on a continuing basis. Further, the creators will be better informed on the exploitation of their works and hence better poised firstly to determine if the exploitation efforts in respect thereof are adequate and, second, to assess their economic value so as potentially to obtain a fairer remuneration therefrom. Accordingly, Art 20 is designed to operate in conjunction with Art 19.

[11.4.20] Member states shall also ensure that, where the rights have subsequently been licensed, authors and performers or their representatives shall, at their request, receive from sublicensees additional information, in the event that their first contractual counterpart does not hold all the necessary information. Where that additional information is requested, the first contractual counterpart of authors and performers shall provide information on the identity of those sublicensees. Regulation 29(3) provides that a sublicensee who receives a request from an author or performer for additional details that are required to be provided under para (1) shall, as soon as practicable after receipt of the request, provide those additional details by electronic or other means.

[11.4.21] The transparency obligation does not apply to agreements concluded by collective management organisations or independent management entities[24] or other entities subject to the national rules implementing the Collective Rights Management Directive.[25] Therefore, if the Mechanical Copyright Protection Society Ireland, under mandate from its member, negotiates a synchronisation licence for use from its repertoire of that member's song in a film, the above rules will not apply. The fee and terms agreed at the time of signing the licence will thus not be subject to future scrutiny regardless of how the film performs and how it is exploited.

---

24 Defined in the EU (Collective Rights Management) (Directive 2014/26/EU) Regulations 2016 (SI No 156 of 2016), as any organisation which is authorised by law or by way of assignment, licence or any other contractual arrangement to manage copyright or rights related to copyright on behalf of more than one rightsholder, for the collective benefit of the rightsholders, as its sole or main purpose, and which is neither owned nor controlled, directly or indirectly, wholly or in part, by rightsholders, and organised on a for-profit basis.

25 Directive 2014/26/EU of the European Parliament and of the Council of 26 February 2014 on collective management of copyright and related rights and multi-territorial licensing of rights in musical works for online use in the internal market.

Alternative dispute resolution procedure (Art 21/reg 24)

[11.4.22] Disputes over transparency and contract adjustments must be capable pursuant to Art 21 of being submitted to a voluntary, alternative dispute resolution ('ADR') procedure and representative organisations must be empowered to initiate such procedures at the specific request of artists. This measure is welcomed as it will facilitate expedience and save on court costs.

[11.4.23] Incidentally, however, a recent legislative change[26] in Ireland as seen in Chapter 10A fosters improved access to the courts system in any event by permitting the admission of IP disputes to the District Court and Circuit Court, particularly for lower value cases of infringements which can be taken in the District Court up to a value of €15,000.[27] In terms of ADR, the reg 28(5) contract adjustment mechanism thus provides that, without prejudice to judicial remedies, disputes under that Regulation may be submitted to a mediator in accordance with the Mediation Act 2017 or, where appropriate, to an arbitrator in accordance with the Arbitration Act 2010. The same holds true *per* reg 27(9) for disputes under the transparency obligation above.

[11.4.24] The rationale[28] for Art 21 was that authors and performers are often reluctant to enforce their rights against their contractual partners before a court or tribunal. Member States must therefore provide for an ADR procedure that addresses claims by authors and performers related to obligations of transparency and the contract adjustment mechanism. For that purpose, Member States can either establish a new body or mechanism, or rely on an existing one that fulfils the conditions established by the 2019 Directive, irrespective of whether those bodies or mechanisms are industry-led or public, including when part of the national judicial system.

Appropriate and proportionate remuneration (Art 18/reg 26)

[11.4.25] In terms of the impact of Art 18 on making available on demand, the 2019 Directive stops short of explicitly introducing an unwaivable right to remuneration for streaming subject to compulsory collective management. Belgium however of its own accord introduced a new right to remuneration specifically for online content sharing. This right to remuneration arises where performers have transferred their exclusive right to authorise or prohibit the communication to the public of their performances. It is non-transferable, cannot be waived and can only be managed by a performers' CMO.

[11.4.26] A much welcomed development in the 2019 Directive is the Art 18

---

26 ss 40 and 41 of the Copyright and Other Intellectual Property Law Provisions Act 2019.

27 Therefore, rightsholders are now free to file certain claims in lower courts where they may be heard in a timelier manner and will incur lower legal costs than if such proceedings were brought in the Commercial Court which is the dedicated IP court of the High Court.

28 See Recital 79 of the preamble to the 2019 Directive.

principle whereby Member States shall ensure that where authors and performers license or transfer their exclusive rights for the exploitation of their works or other subject matter, they are entitled to receive appropriate and proportionate remuneration. This remuneration is not waivable. Prior to the enhanced remuneration which the 2019 Directive and transposing regulations may bestow, performers had and still have an exclusive right that was and is commonly signed-off in standard 'full buyout' contracts as regards future revenues, including from streaming (though the performers can nonetheless receive modest statutorily-protected income through public performance royalties from their contribution to sound recordings). The new laws may therefore also buttress the position of non-featured performers and session musicians on studio recordings. Featured performers (e.g. band singers or backing vocalists) obviously fare better and depending on say their record contract deal may be entitled to a share of record sales on an ongoing basis.

[11.4.27] When a track that includes contributions from one or more non-featured artists is streamed, downloaded or purchased physically, those artists are not paid (other than public performance royalties from collection societies at low amounts). Instead, as noted in Chapter 10B, session musicians are only entitled, by way of reversionary rights, to an equal share of 20 percent of gross revenues from physical and online sales, which is referred to as the non-featured performers fund or session fund, after 50 years since the publication of the recording.

[11.4.28] The preamble[29] to the 2019 Directive explains that the remuneration of authors and performers should be appropriate and proportionate to the actual or potential economic value of the licensed or transferred rights, taking into account the author's or performer's contribution to the overall work and all other circumstances, such as market practices or the actual exploitation of the work. A lump sum payment can also constitute proportionate remuneration but it should not be the rule. Member states are thus given the freedom to define specific cases for the application of lump sums, taking into account the specificities of each sector. Member States can implement Art 18 through different existing or newly introduced mechanisms, which could include collective bargaining and other mechanisms, provided that such mechanisms are in conformity with applicable EU law.

[11.4.29] In the implementation in national law of this principle, Member States shall be free to use different mechanisms and take into account the principle of contractual freedom and a fair balance of rights and interests. Historically, new artists frequently held a weak bargaining position when negotiating their contracts. This new provision bolsters their lot considerably and it is good fortune that the word "appropriate" accompanies the notoriously-hard-to-determine word "proportionate".

---

[29] See Recital 73.

[11.4.30] Unlike contract law principles of common law where consideration can be deemed 'sufficient' if it is say one euro, pound or dollar or indeed where zero monetary consideration has been paid but some other form of ('money's worth') consideration is forthcoming,[30] it is unlikely that less established artists will henceforth accept paltry sums when exclusively licensing or indeed selling their material[31] if they are armed with the knowledge that EU and Irish law dictates that the sums payable must be appropriate and that they do not have to accept ten euro for instance as being 'equitable remuneration' for the grant of certain rights. On the other hand, assignees or licensees may argue that the 2019 Directive's requirement for appropriate and proportionate remuneration could place too onerous a burden on them in specific circumstances.

[11.4.31] Further, in the absence of any guidance, it is impossible to quantify what remuneration (if indeed any has been paid) might be deemed "disproportionately low". Clearly, this could lead to disputes, an issue which is covered in Art 21 as above. However, if a performer becomes involved in a dispute with a producer, this greatly damages the relationship between performer and producer which can have a highly detrimental effect on the prospect of working again with that producer.

[11.4.32] In Irish law, reg 26 has regrettably not sufficiently fleshed out the scant detail of the 2019 Directive as to the meanings of "appropriate" and "proportionate". It simply borrows much of the wording of Recital 73 of the said preamble in providing that:

> Remuneration under Paragraph (1) shall be considered appropriate and proportionate where it is proportionate to the actual or potential economic value of the licensed or transferred rights, taking into account the author's or performer's contribution to the overall work or other subject matter and all other circumstances of the case, such as market practices or the actual exploitation of the work or other subject matter, including, where applicable, merchandising revenues.

[11.4.33] Perhaps quite unhelpfully for practitioners, it does not include the preamble wording that, "A lump sum payment can also constitute proportionate remuneration but it should not be the rule". Regardless, aggrieved authors and performers can rely on the spirit of the 2019 Directive in this connection. Moreover, the Directive imposes a mandatory obligation of ensuring that where authors and performers license or transfer their exclusive rights for the exploitation of their works, they are entitled to receive appropriate and proportionate remuneration. This, like the implementing 2021 Regulations,

---

30 Although this clearly may not be adequate consideration, the courts will generally not intervene in the absence of undue influence or unconscionable bargain.

31 Whereby they would obtain an upfront fee as well as potential future public performance royalties depending on the terms of sale.

puts the matter beyond any doubt at least in a general sense and enhances in law, to some extent, the remuneration position of creatives for the very first time.

Interplay with other legislation

[11.4.34] Recital 77 of the preamble explains that it should not be necessary to apply the Art 19 transparency obligations to Collective Management Organisations ('CMOs'), independent management entities or other entities as they are already subject to transparency obligations set out under Art 18 of the Collective Rights Management ('CRM') Directive. Those organisations are required to comply with the provisions set out in the EU (Collective Rights Management) (Directive 2014/26/EU) Regulations 2016 ('the 2016 Regulations'),[32] which transposed the CRM Directive in Ireland. Equally, as per Recital 78, the Art 20 mechanism should not apply to contracts concluded by CMOs, independent management entities or other entities (that are likewise subject to said Regulations) on the basis that the CRM Directive regulating them already has such provisions.

[11.4.35] For example, reg 14 of the 2016 Regulations provides that a CMO (e.g. the Mechanical Copyright Protection Society) shall ensure that rightsholders receive appropriate remuneration for the use of their rights; that tariffs for exclusive rights and rights to remuneration are reasonable in relation to, among other things, the economic value of the use of the rights in trade, taking into account the nature and scope of the use of the work and other subject matter, and the economic value of the service provided by the CMO; and that CMOs shall inform the users concerned of the criteria used for the setting of those tariffs.

[11.4.36] In the case where rightsholders have mandated their CMO to negotiate licences on their behalf, and the CMO does not have a contract adjustment mechanism in place for its contracts with licensee users, the effects of the above derogation can be undone by members. The rightsholders are free to withdraw from their assignment of public performance rights with a particular CMO (and register with another instead or a publisher in the case of composition rights) or request that the mandate they might have granted when registering for membership be nullified such that only they can negotiate directly with the party seeking use of their work. It will be interesting to ascertain how MCPS and other collection societies might voluntarily amend their rules in light of the 2019 Directive and its implementing legislation in Ireland to deal with such matters as contract adjustment and licence revocation.

Conclusion

[11.4.37] The rival interests have resulted in more nuanced provisions of the 2019 Directive being adopted to accommodate both sides of the debate. Numerous

[32] SI No 156 of 2016.

uncertainties about how the principles will work in practice have been left to Member States to determine in implementing the Directive. Baden-Powell and Heeley[33] opine that entertainment companies may contend that existing policies are more flexible and fluid than the imposition of a potentially over-rigid framework for re-negotiations, and it therefore seems quite likely that intense lobbying will continue well into the future to secure workable outcomes.

[11.4.38] Moreover, the new measures are set to have a wide-ranging impact on how copyright-protected content is produced and exploited within the EU. This will in turn have a significant effect on how executives and legal practitioners alike negotiate and draft entertainment-related contracts and there is some way to go before the full extent of the impact can be assessed and critiqued based on empirical evidence. Article 30 provides that the Commission will carry out a review of the 2019 Directive and present a report of the findings to the European Parliament.

ARTICLE 17 LICENSING AGREEMENTS WITH ONLINE CONTENT-SHARING SERVICE PROVIDERS

[11.5.01] In summary, Art 17 is a provision intended to address the value gap whereby rightsholders are receiving less remuneration despite the increased usage of their works. The objective is that it will place creators in a better position to receive remuneration for the online exploitation of their works without preventing users from making lawful usage thereof, while being minimally burdensome on sharing platforms.[34] It aims to encourage the conclusion of agreements for the use of content and to generate additional revenues for rightsholders and to afford them facilities to better exploit and control the distribution of their content online. The Commission hopes, in a balancing exercise, that holding sharing platforms liable for user-generated content will encourage them to conclude fair licensing agreements with creators, who as a result will be able to achieve remuneration that has often eluded them in the past.

[11.5.02] The platforms covered by the new rules are considered to be carrying out acts covered by copyright (i.e. performing acts of communication or making available to the public) for which they need to obtain an authorisation from the rightsholders concerned. In situations where there are no licensing agreements concluded with rightsholders, the platforms need to take certain actions if they

---

33 *supra* at fn 20.

34 A sharing platform is an information society service provider whose main purpose (or one of its main purposes) is to store and offer the public access to a large amount of copyright-protected works uploaded by its users, which it organises and promotes for profit-making purposes. Article 2(6) of the Directive lists certain entity types that are not considered sharing platforms under the Directive. For example, not-for-profit encyclopaedias, such as Wikipedia, will be specifically excluded from the definition of online content-sharing service providers. Thus, internet users will continue uploading content on Wikipedia and other similar platforms as they have done to date.

want to avoid liability. In particular, they need to make best efforts to obtain an authorisation, and, secondly make best efforts to ensure the unavailability of unauthorised content regarding which rightsholders have provided necessary and relevant information, and thirdly, act expeditiously to remove any unauthorised content uploaded by users following a notice received and also make their best efforts to prevent future uploads.

[11.5.03] Accordingly, Art 17 aims to render online content-sharing service providers (YouTube, Vimeo, Instagram and Facebook for instance as opposed to host-licensed content such as on Netflix and Spotify) liable for infringing content and obliges them to negotiate fair licensing agreements with rightsholders and actively prevent infringing content from appearing on their platforms. Going forward, it will be key for online platforms to establish whether their activities are even caught by Art 17. A platform is only subject to Art 17 if it hosts (author unauthorised, copyright-infringing) content uploaded by third party users that is thus made available to the public.

[11.5.04] The old rules stemmed from the e-Commerce Directive.[35] Under this legislation, proceedings could not necessarily be instituted against content-sharing platforms for the unauthorised display of copyrighted content that had been uploaded by their users. A content-sharing platform was defined as a mere conduit that simply received information from its users and provided access thereto. Hence, a platform's users were responsible for ensuring that the content they uploaded was not copyrighted, and the users could be litigated against by rightsholders. To escape liability, a content-sharing platform needed simply to act expeditiously and remove the offending content *after* receiving notice from the rightsholder.

[11.5.05] There are certain types of content[36] that are exempted from the Art 17 rules, namely quotation, criticism, review (Art 17(7)(a) such as movie reviews and certain educational content) and use for the purposes of caricature, parody or pastiche (Art 17(7)(b) such as memes and satire).[37] However, some still argue that the new rules will cause content-sharing platforms to be so vigilant in screening

---

[35] Directive 2000/31/EC of the European Parliament and of the Council of 8 June 2000 on certain legal aspects of information society services, in particular electronic commerce, in the Internal Market.

[36] Art 2(6) provides that providers of services, such as not-for-profit online encyclopedias, not-for-profit educational and scientific repositories, open source software-developing and sharing platforms, providers of electronic communications services as defined in Directive (EU) 2018/1972, online marketplaces, business-to-business cloud services and cloud services that allow users to upload content for their own use, are not "online content-sharing service providers" within the meaning of the Directive. Hence, for example, Wikipedia, GitHub, eBay, Three and DropBox activities are specifically excluded where relevant.

[37] These provisions are mirrored in s 13 of the Copyright and Other Intellectual Property Law Provisions Act 2019 which amends s 52 of the Copyright and Related Rights Act 2000 by inserting thereto: "Fair dealing with a work for the purposes of caricature, parody or pastiche shall not infringe the copyright in that work".

user-uploaded content that memes could potentially disappear. This is despite the fact that Art 17(8) clearly provides that the application of Art 17 "shall not lead to any general monitoring obligation" being imposed by Member State legislation. This was reinforced by the Commission in June 2021 when it stated, "The Directive does not impose upload filters nor does it require user-uploaded platforms to apply any specific technology to recognise illegal content".[38]

[11.5.06] Article 17 is transposed by regs 18 to 21 which govern the use of protected content by online content-sharing service providers; liability of those service providers where no authorisation is obtained; and removal of certain content and protection of freedom of expression.[39]

Sharing platform obligations and EU case law

[11.5.07] If a licence is not concluded (for example because rightsholders do not wish to do so), the online platforms will, pursuant to Art 17(4), have to employ their "best efforts" to ensure that content which is not authorised by the rightsholders and for which they have provided the platforms with relevant and necessary information, is rendered unavailable.[40] Moreover, upon receiving a notification from rightsholders, they will have to remove specific unauthorised content from their websites. However, not to place excessive burden on small and young platforms,[41] the 2019 Directive provides a specific regime for start-ups and smaller companies which will be subject to less burdensome rules.

[11.5.08] On request, rightsholders must be provided with adequate information on the functioning of a sharing platform's practices in relation to the cooperation required under Art 17(4) and information on the use of content covered by licence agreements. Sharing platforms are obliged to make an effective and

---

38 See also Communication from the Commission to the European Parliament and the Council, *Guidance on Article 17 of Directive 2019/790 on Copyright in the Digital Single Market* (2020). COM(2021) 288. Available at: https://eur-lex.europa.eu/legal-content/EN/TXT/?uri=COM%3A2021%3A288%3AFIN&qid=1622805308826 [Accessed 14 October 2021].

39 A user of online content-sharing service providers in Ireland may rely on the existing exceptions or limitations provided for, by or under Pts II and III of the Copyright and Related Rights Act 2000 when uploading and making available content on such services.

40 This is certainly not a novel concept. Some platforms like YouTube had long since invested in systems to try to identify the provenance of content and to reconcile conflicts between rightsholders, and the Directive will in many ways provide a statutory underpinning for those efforts, but without being unduly prescriptive about the technological means to achieve the desired result.

41 Companies that are less than three years old, with turnover of under €10 million and less than five million monthly unique users. Those start-ups only need to comply with Art 17(4)(a) and (c), but excluding the requirement to make best efforts to prevent future uploads. When determining whether sharing platforms have complied with Art 17(4), and in light of the principle of proportionality, account will be taken of the type, audience and size of the service and the type of works uploaded by users; and the availability of suitable and effective means and their cost to service providers.

expeditious complaint and redress mechanism available in the event of disputes concerning the disabling of access to or the removal of works uploaded by users. Where rightsholders request that access to their works be disabled or removed, they must justify their reasoning via a "sufficiently substantiated notice". Any complaints must be processed without undue delay, and decisions to disable access to or remove content should be subject to human review (Art 17(9)). This is an unwieldy requirement to monitor. Access and removal requests are, in reality, unlikely to be reviewed by a human in every instance given the sheer volumes involved.

[11.5.09] Although sharing platforms are provided with a defence where they are unable to obtain a licence, it remains uncertain how Art 17(4) will ultimately work in practice or what will satisfy the best efforts requirement as the Commission's guidance on this issue is somewhat nebulous.[42] The case of *Republic of Poland v European Parliament and Council of the European Union* (C-401/19) in which the Polish government asked the Court of Justice of the EU (CJEU) to annul parts of Art 17 (in particular Art 17(4)(b) and (c)) on the basis that they violate the right to freedom of expression and information granted under Arts 11 and 13 of the EU Charter of Fundamental Rights (seeing these provisions as a form of censorship) sheds some light. In April 2022, the court dismissed the action holding that the obligation, on online content-sharing service providers, to review, prior to its dissemination to the public, the content that users wish to upload to their platforms, is accompanied by the necessary safeguards to ensure that such obligation is compatible with freedom of expression and information.

[11.5.10] For further analysis, readers are directed to the CJEU's June 2021 judgment in joined cases *Frank Peterson v Google LLC* and *Elsevier Inc v Cyando AG (C-682/18 (YouTube) and C-683/18 (Cyando))* concerning platform liability for copyright-infringing user uploads under Art 3(1) InfoSoc Directive and Art 14(1) of the E-Commerce Directive. Here the court ruled that internet platforms are not liable in principle for the unauthorised uploads of users, unless the platforms fail to take action to remove or block access to the content. The judgment also made clear that the interpretations provided in this ruling applied solely to the law as it was prior to the entry into force of the 2019 Directive and Art 17. The court, in a departure from the opinion of Advocate General Saugmandsgaard Øe, did not engage with Art 17 in any form.

---

[42] The notion of 'best efforts' is not defined and no reference is made to national law, hence it is an autonomous notion of EU law and it should be transposed by Member States in accordance with the guidance and interpreted in light of the aim and the objectives of Art 17. The guidance reiterates that the application of Art 17(4) should not lead to any general monitoring and must not affect legitimate uses (e.g. uses covered by copyright exceptions). As to filtering and automated tools, the guidance does stress that such technology cannot tell if a work is legitimate or not. Such technological tools could therefore be over-zealous in their blocking of legitimate uploads which leads to conflict with Art 17(7).

EU Digital Services Act

[11.5.11] The EU Digital Services Act[43] ('the DSA') was formally signed into law on 19 October 2022 and, being a Regulation, has been directly applicable in the EU from 16 November 2022[44] with two compliance dates in particular being relevant, 17 February 2023 and 17 February 2024 depending on the intermediary service provider (offering its services in the European single market, whether established in the EU or outside). Organisations for which the DSA applies are *inter alia* required to adopt procedures for swiftly handling take-down notices, informing users in certain circumstances and addressing complaints. Each Member State shall designate a competent authority as its Digital Services Coordinator ('DSC'). All Member States are required to have designated their DSC by 17 February 2024. For Ireland, the DSC is the Media Commission. The provisions of the DSA (and the Digital Market Act)[45] are outlined further in Chapter 30.

---

43 Regulation EU 2022/2065.

44 New legislation, however, will need to be passed in Ireland to provide for the implementation of the DSA, including to designate competent authorities and to provide necessary powers in relation to the enforcement of the DSA.

45 Regulation EU 2022/1925.

Chapter 12

Trademarks, Trademark Infringement and Passing Off

INTRODUCTION

[12.1.01] Trademark law affects disparate facets of the entertainment and media sector from motion marks and multimedia marks for websites,[1] online content and commercials,[2] to the clearance processes involved in musicals, plays, music videos,[3] television content, webcasts and films. It can also have a bearing on the raising of finance and generation of revenue for filmmakers and radioshow producers arising from product placement advertising and brand sponsorship. Trademarking of goods and IP such as characters, clothing, stationery, toys and posters for merchandising and licensing also arises, as does registration of celebrity names. This area of law can play an important role in protecting IP assets through registering a brand name, enhancing freedom to operate, and creating income-earning potential whether that be a band, music recording

---

1 In Europe, the EU updated its legislation only quite recently by way of the 2015 Trade Marks Directive (Directive (EU) 2015/2436) to permit easier registration of non-traditional marks. EU Member States are now all expected to have harmonised their laws with the Directive. Today, a mark needs only to be represented in a manner "which enables the competent authorities and the public to determine the clear and precise subject matter of the protection". The representation must be "self-contained, easily accessible, intelligible, durable and objective". A motion mark must be represented by either a video file or a series of still sequential images showing the movements or position changes. 2019 was marked by the grant of the first ever moving multimedia mark in the UK. The Japanese company Toshiba was granted protection for the company's logo featuring origami-style folding coloured triangles. Whilst it had been possible to register motion marks before this, submissions were required to be illustrated graphically. Under the new system, applicants can now submit their moving, hologram or sound trade mark using a multimedia file.

2 The EU (Trade Marks) Regulations 2018 (SI No 561 of 2018) for example explicitly provide at reg 11 (amending s 14 of the Trade Marks Act 1996) that the use of a trademark in comparative advertising in a manner that is contrary to the EC (Misleading and Comparative Marketing Communications) Regulations 2007 (SI No 774 of 2007) (e.g. denigrating or taking unfair advantage of a trademark) constitutes an act of infringement.

3 In *Mattel, Inc v MCA Records, Inc* 296 F.3d 894 (9th Cir. 2002), Mattel claimed that its Barbie trademark was tarnished by the song *Barbie Girl* because the song supported "promiscuity, lewdness, and the stereotyping and denigration of young". Note however that trademark parody might be afforded a defence (in the US at least, the theory being there is no likelihood of confusion because a parody will not be taken seriously). See discussion too of the short film *Logorama* below.

studio, stageshow, dance company, franchise television format, film, game, book or ezine for example.

[12.1.02] Registration of a mark at national, EU or international level should serve to put others on notice of the prior owner's rights and thereby reduce the likelihood of infringement.[4] Another benefit is that it reduces operational risks for investors and manufacturers. Local partners in another territory (take a T-shirt, toy or game production factory in Asia for instance) may require trademark registration as a condition to the commercial agreement reached.[5]

[12.1.03] Mark registration including for a word, product, service name,[6] logo, artistic illustration, phrase, slogan, sound design[7] and packaging[8] will also have the effect of elevating the value of a business due to the statutory protections it affords and given the element of prestige that attaches to trademark proprietary rights. It will facilitate marketing efforts too as some social media platforms require evidence of trademark ownership and, more widely, trademark registration will assist in preventing commercial misuse as platforms will have reporting policies in place. Further, the ® registered trademark symbol[9] increases consumer trust in that the brand owner is indicating to customers that its product/service, its provenance and the commercial origin thereof is worthy of protection. In addition to trademark registration, marks should also be registered promptly as

---

4 See the decision of then Controller of Patents, Designs and Trade Marks issued on 24 October 2018 whereby Simco Ltd and Freemantle Media Ltd (owners of EU mark "Got Talent" and proprietors of international marks including Britain's Got Talent and America's Got Talent) succeeded in preventing registration of a mark "Ireland's Got Talent Blanchardstown's Got Talent Irellywood" by Rebecca Omakaro on the grounds that her application offended against s 10(2)(b) of the Trade Marks Act 1996 – a likelihood of confusion on the part of the public, and the likelihood of association with the opponent's earlier Got Talent marks; and s 10(3) – use of the mark applied for would take unfair advantage of, or be detrimental to, the distinctive character or reputation of the opponents' marks. *Written Grounds – Trade Marks Act, 1996 (2018-Current)* (2018), ipoi.ie. Available at: https://www.ipoi.gov.ie/en/law-practice/written-grounds/trade-marks-act-1996-from-year-2018-current/irelands-got-talent.pdf [Accessed 1 July 2021].

5 They may be investing money, resources and their reputation in making products available in their countries to their own customers and clients. They are also vulnerable for local knock-offs if the product has not been trademarked.

6 In the US for instance trademarks (goods) are distinguished from service marks (SM) (services) but throughout the world the word 'trademark' is generally used to denote both.

7 For instance, the MGM lion's roar or the opening sounds to the Netflix application.

8 Other trademark types are combined marks (standard characters and a figurative element), shape marks (e.g three-dimensional shape, including containers, packaging, the product itself or its appearance, position mark (e.g. labels on the pockets of jeans or on shoes), colours, sounds or a combination of sounds, motion marks, multimedia marks (image and sound) and hologram marks – all as recognised by r 5 of the Trade Marks (Amendment) Rules 2018 (SI No 562 of 2018) which inserted r 12(A) into the principal Trade Mark Rules 2006, and reg 4 of the EU (Trade Marks) Regulations 2018 (SI No 561 of 2018) giving effect to Directive (EU) 2015/2436).

9 The TM symbol on the other hand can be used to assert proprietary rights over unregistered marks and where applications for registration are pending.

usernames and account names on the main platforms, which names are assigned on a first come, first serve basis.[10]

[12.1.04] Confusion and misapprehension concerning titles, names and what can and cannot be shown on film or other medium often arises. This area of law is technical in nature and uncertainty can exist among practitioners in the entertainment industry about what precisely constitutes infringement. This chapter will seek to illuminate certain of its nuances through references to case law.

[12.1.05] Examples of familiar Irish trademarks or marks registered in this jurisdiction include Slane,[11] U2, Heineken, Sky, Star Trek, Levi Strauss, Ferrari, Rolling Stones, Aviva Stadium and Zara. This short list gives an inkling as to the breadth of products and services which are afforded statutory protection upon successful trademark registration. Registered trademarks offer an exclusive right of use for commercial purposes, comprise a highly valuable asset and are rigorously protected by their owners as highlighted during the production of *Slumdog Millionaire* discussed at [12.16.01].

CLEARANCE

[12.2.01] A key question for consideration is whether each and every use should be cleared by licence or prop release agreement signed by the registered owner (or the rightsholder of an unregistered trademark where the subject mark has not been statutorily registered). If not, a film or television production may in certain cases potentially fall foul of defamation law as explored in Chapter 5 (product disparagement) and/or trademark law. The rule of thumb is that provided the use depicted (which might primarily be limited to background use) shows the product or service in the intended usual manner of use or mode of operation, such use should not infringe the owner's rights. At EU trademark level, Regulation 2017/1001 may also provide some guidance on the matter.[12]

---

[10] To constitute a trademark infringement, social media platforms can require that the username or account name be actually used in a commercial context that infringes the trademark rights. A username or account name on its own will most likely not constitute infringement.

[11] The US multinational that produces Jack Daniel's whiskey registered the name "Slane" as a trademark. The registration of the trademark throughout the EU (by the EU Intellectual Property Office based in Spain) by a subsidiary of the Kentucky-based Brown Forman emerged after a business in the County Meath village, wishing to use "Slane" in its title, found it was blocked from doing so. The trademark prohibits companies from using "Slane" in any alcoholic drink brands, or merchandise such as sports bags, mugs, hats, golf balls, umbrellas, key rings or sweatshirts. The trademark right to the word Slane was granted in 2016 to Slane Castle Irish Whiskey Ltd, a company incorporated by Lord Henry Mountcharles and his son Alexander in 2009 and sold to Brown Forman in 2015.

[12] See para [12.5.03]. Recital 21 provides that use of a trademark by third parties for the purpose of artistic expression should be considered as being fair as long as it is at the same time in accordance with honest practices in industrial and commercial matters.

[12.2.02] Otherwise the production of movies and other entertainment media would be rendered virtually out of reach (for example, if all apparel in a movie had to be custom-designed by the wardrobe department so that no well-known trademarks appeared). However, this industry rule of thumb is certainly not absolute and great caution must be exercised in the particular circumstances and context at hand. The default legal position must be: if in doubt, seek permission. Moreover, careful consideration must be given to any prop or other content, the use or depiction of which could infringe the IP rights of its proprietors. One instance is a movie title itself that transpires to be the same as an existing book title, product or business as was the case with rapper 50 Cent's film *All Things Fall Apart* discussed below.

Litigation examples

[12.2.03] RTÉ was served with High Court proceedings 2013 in respect of its *Damo and Ivor* comedy show when the rightsholder of the name "Damo", which had been registered several years prior in relation to entertainment services, music and lyrics, claimed trademark infringement.

[12.2.04] A major legal battle in relation to the smash hit *Glee* television series will be outlined in this chapter pitting a chain of UK comedy clubs (owned by Comedy Enterprises Ltd which in turn owns the trademark "the glee CLUB") against Twentieth Century Fox, the makers of *Glee*. The plaintiff company was successful in its trademark infringement claim at trial and again on appeal in the Court of Appeal. One remaining net issue was then listed for final hearing in the UK Supreme Court in November 2017. However, by agreement on confidential terms between the parties, the appeal by Fox was withdrawn in advance of the hearing date.[13] While initially there were major fears by the defendant corporation on foot of the trial court decision mandating a name change for the television show, the settlement concerned matters of financial compensation only.

[12.2.05] Another instance might be the unauthorised use of an image. Celebrity driver Damon Hill was granted trademarks of his own portrait[14] – use of such image in a documentary drama about amateur racing car drivers for example without authorisation or payment of an agreed licence fee could well infringe the owner's property rights[15] (even if, on the separate law of copyright front, the use might potentially be exempted under fair dealing provisions).

Furthermore, this Regulation should be applied in a way that ensures full respect for fundamental rights and freedoms, and in particular the freedom of expression.

13 See The Supreme Court (UK), News, *Appeal Withdrawn* (2017). Available at: https://www.supremecourt.uk/news/appeal-withdrawn-twentieth-century-fox-film-corporation-v-comic-enterprises-limited.html [Accessed 24 July 2019].

14 Image of his eyes staring from his crash helmet.

15 Likewise, Eric Cantona registered his likeness as a trademark while Rayne Rooney registered his name and signature in 2002, before he became a recognised household name.

[12.2.06] Corporate rightsholders will diligently manage and protect their IP rights. When various public interest groups began referring to the Reagan administration's strategic defence initiative as the "star wars" program, Lucasfilm sued for trademark infringement.[16] Other well-policed brands are Marvel Comics, the characters of Disney or Pixar, and products emanating from the works of Tolkien. The JRR Tolkien estate holds numerous trademarks based on the writer's material including the word/name "shire"[17] and the Tolkien name itself.

[12.2.07] Before analysing the complexities of trademark law and further instances of trademark reproduction and depiction on camera or otherwise, it may be helpful to summarise standard due diligence clearance procedures which, as a matter of practice, might be undertaken in accordance with specific legal advices for the subject production at hand:

1. Audiovisual and stage productions must avoid implying an association with or endorsement by a product/service/business without prior approval. Obtaining approval after the event could prove prohibitively costly (for instance reshooting a scene/sequence) if not impossible. Footage of certain iconic buildings for example should not be used in the marketing or promotions for a film.

16 The US District Court for the District of Columbia ruled however that Lucasfilm could not control the use of the phrase in a non-commercial context and could not prevent it from entering into the common parlance (*Lucasfilm Ltd v High Frontier*, 622 F Supp 931 (DDC 1985)).

17 s 15(2) (as amended) of the Trade Marks Act 1996, however, provides that a registered trademark shall not be infringed by the use by a person of his own name or address and hence a David Shire for instance could legally use the name Shire in Ireland for commercial purposes. This was tempered with more expanded infringement provisions in the amending EU (Trade Marks) Regulations 2018 (SI No 561 of 2018) such that the "own name" defence is no longer available to corporate entities; the Regulations limit it to natural persons, meaning that only individuals can use their own name without infringing an identical or confusingly similar name that is a registered trademark (e.g. Smyths or McDonald's). Another related change is that using a trademark as part of a trade or company name can now constitute an act of infringement – see reg 11 amending s 14(4) of the Trade Marks Act 1996.

2. Instructing a film clearance practitioner or entertainment lawyer to analyse the script (and its title)[18] well in advance of production to allow time, if deemed necessary, for agreement to be reached and a licence or prop/depiction release executed is always advisable. Where issues may arise in a particular distribution territory, local legal advice may prove necessary. Issues might arise, for example, as to day or night shooting of the Eiffel Tower. Recording of iconic buildings such as the Empire State Building, the Hollywood sign and the Spire in Dublin are classic examples of where approval and case-by-case licensing fee payments are or may be required (e.g. if the Spire is to appear in a commercial).

   The rough and final cuts of a film or television programme should also be viewed by an experienced legal practitioner to ascertain if any issues have been missed as might arise where unplanned changes occurred during shooting, new props were introduced or there were pick-up shots which resulted in script/locational changes.

3. Where applicable, a clearance company can be retained to vet the script and to run name,[19] signature, and title checks[20] against individuals, businesses, products and services as well as conducting due diligence on slogans, phrases and catchphrases.[21] Claims can arise in the most unexpected of scenarios as in the case of the *Titanic*[22] and hence pending applications for trademark registration should also be searched.

---

18 See *Tri-Star Pictures, Inc v Unger* discussed at [2.2.07].

19 Trademarks can be searched free of charge too in the IPOI.

20 The late Nigerian novelist Chinua Achebe found himself at the centre of an unlikely dispute with 50 Cent (Curtis Jackson) in 2011. Lawyers for Achebe took issue with the rapper's shooting of a film with the same name of his influential 1958 novel *Things Fall Apart*. Despite an alleged offer to pay one million dollars to retain the title, Jackson's production eventually conceded defeat and changed the film's name to *All Things Fall Apart*. Interestingly, Achebe himself did not coin the phrase, nor was it trademarked to him. It first appeared in a poem written by William Butler Yeats in 1919, a line that Achebe used in his work. This case shows the merits of conducting name checks well in advance. One's bargaining powers are all but dissipated after the event when a movie has been completed and moneys expended on marketing and promotion.

21 The phrase Hakuna Matata translated means "no problems" or "no worries" and is a common expression throughout east Africa. To the rest of the world, it is best known as a song from the *Lion King*. Walt Disney registered a trademark for the phrase for their merchandise and certain newspapers accused the company of stealing from Kenyan culture by claiming ownership of the phrase. However, the trademark itself is not new, US records showing it was first filed back in 1994 coinciding with the movie's original release. See: BBC News, *Hakuna Matata' and other unlikely trademarked phrases* (2018). Available at: https://www.bbc.com/news/world-46384204 [Accessed 1 August 2021]. Further, Paris Hilton's signature catchphrase on *The Simple Life* reality television show is also brought to mind and her long legal battle with Hallmark whereby the company had portrayed her as a waitress using the catchphrase on a spoof greetings card. Hilton had registered the trademark in 2004. Hallmark cited free speech as its defence and the two parties settled out of court for an unknown sum.

22 A panel of three US administrative trademark judges on The Trademark Trial and Appeal Board (US) ruled in *R.M.S. Titanic, Inc v R.M.S. Ltd N.Y.C.* (30 November 1999, file no 91099005) that the owner (James Korn) of a retail store near Times Square does not

4. The art department can be consulted if items such as mock book covers, newspapers and bottle labels are needed for the production or if set dressing can be employed to conceal a trademark in a scene. Continuity personnel should also be highly vigilant as to use of trademarked items during shooting. Otherwise, where trademarked products must be used, one can ascertain with the film editor how blurring can be tastefully effectuated or the product disguised. With technology, it is possible to remove some trademark infringements from already-shot material but it is best to plan for this troublesome eventuality in advance of filming. Alternatively, discussion can be had pertaining to camera angles/focus with the director of photography and camera operators. Simply turning a Sprite bottle around so that its label is not visible is not sufficient[23] if the use may tarnish the brand (e.g. a paedophile documentary subject who frequently sips from a bottle of Sprite).
5. For routine city scenes in Dublin for example, it is helpful to establish relationships with bus, tram and rail operators, private property owners, the city council and local businesses (e.g. a bar or restaurant where scenes could habitually be shot without fear of trademark infringement claims). If the production involves post office or bank robberies, the press office of An Post or management of a particular bank should be consulted. If there is use associated with crime or a scene/sequence brings a negative connotation, the product/service owner will need to assess the context, approve the script or request edits or indeed removal. In questionable cases, it may be more prudent to remove the trademarked brand altogether such as a well-known hotel clearly and closely appearing in the background of a violent scene or one depicting antisocial conduct.

---

have the right to trademark the names Titanic and R.M.S. Titanic on his clothing. By letter he had informed Twentieth Century Fox, the maker of James Cameron's blockbuster movie *Titanic*, that it owed him royalties for any clothing it had sold bearing the name, as well as Dodger Endemol Theatrical Productions, the producers of the musical *Titanic*. The applicant was known as a respected expert on military furnishings and had supplied Broadway and Hollywood with original clothing for major shows and movies. Fox filed applications, relative to the film, that covered posters, stationery, videos, Christmas tree decorations and, like Mr Korn, clothing. After he learned of the movie, he wrote to Fox and director James Cameron offering his services, noting he held the trademark registrations related to the Titanic and that he was willing to negotiate licensing agreements. The studio responded pointing out the applicant did not in fact yet own all the trademarks and confirming that no licensing agreement would be concluded. Oppositions by Fox and R.M.S. Titanic, Inc (the New York company that had been raising artefacts from the ship since 1987) to Korn's petition were sustained on the ground that the applied-for marks, as used by the applicant, failed to function as trademarks for the applicant's goods and were merely ornamental uses. Although the issue ultimately had no significant adverse consequence for Fox, the matter serves to epitomise how unlikely complications can emerge from the woodwork and that one can never be too careful when naming a project, particularly where the budget is not insubstantial.

23 The owners trademarked the distinctive shape and colours of their container as a recognisable link back to their product.

6.	With television productions, one must be mindful of product placement and sponsorship rules discussed later in this textbook (such as prohibitions in relation to the advertising of cigarettes).
7.	As well as trademark law issues, producers should be aware of exposure to related copyright, passing off and corporate defamation actions.

Table 1: Customary trademark and E&O clearance procedures

PRODUCER REVENUES FROM USE AND OWNERSHIP OF TRADEMARKS

[12.3.01] To shift emphasis now away from infringement, the benefits that third party marks or ownership of one's own IP can bestow will be mooted in terms, firstly, of paid product placement, and secondly, through exploitation of character merchandising, *Peppa Pig* and *Frozen* being well-known examples.

[12.3.02] Product placement (and sponsorship)[24] can in certain circumstances be explored as a means of production financing. While of course largely reserved for blockbuster scale movies and major television productions, if the script in lower budget independent films is compelling and/or the producers have attracted well-known 'bankable' talent, a rightsholder brand may see advertising potential and invest. The investment need not be monetary but could instead constitute prop placement rather than paid product placement and nonetheless thereby add production value, the supply of a sports car or luxury item on loan being two instances.

[12.3.03] Product placement, such as frequently occurs with alcoholic drinks and vehicles, is used as a source of funding in return for brand exposure. In olden days of the industry, manufacturers approached a likely prospect of product placement as a way of surreptitiously marketing their products in a positive light without being heavy-handed as blatant advertising can often become. Product placement may nonetheless come with a downside too as overt marketing can dilute the creative and artistic mettle of filmmakers who may be reluctant to have their work used by producers as a platform for the promotion of products. Frequently, subtle product placement where the item is just distinguishable in the background alone is of value to the trademark holder. It associates the brand in a way that seems natural as in the case of a leading actor eating a bowl of cereal. Excessive or aggressive advertising on the other hand can feel forced with astute audiences being attuned to manipulation efforts by marketeers.

Character merchandising

[12.3.04] Popeye the Sailor, the Teenage Mutant Hero Turtles and Tarzan

[24] Where applicable such as with music artists, sports personalities, radio and television shows.

exemplify the possibility of use by the owners of these fictional characters[25] not only for their primary purpose in books, comics, movies, broadcasts and so forth but also for the secondary exploitation of the characters' gained reputation, by granting licences for manufacturing and mass market distribution of posters, T-shirts, toys and badges.

[12.3.05] It may thus be lucrative for producers, writers, illustrators, animators and playwrights to trademark characters, phrases, logos or otherwise from works, singularly or as a series.[26] The earlier the trademark is registered, the more power and control a producer holds in negotiating royalties and other rights. James Bond and 007 come to mind as film titles and characters that gained global appeal, originating from books written by Ian Fleming. Other examples include Bart Simpson, Harry Potter, Batman, Winnie the Pooh and Thomas The Tank Engine. Often, the main characters can be worth even more than the film title or television series itself (take Mickey Mouse, Donald Duck, Peppa Pig) in terms of merchandise products.

REGISTERING A TRADEMARK AND JURISDICTIONAL SCOPE

[12.4.01] An applicant for registration[27] most likely will choose to engage the services of a registered trademark agent attorney.[28] An application may be made either before the mark is put in use or afterwards. An application should be made to register a mark as soon as possible to ensure priority over any other applicant who applies to register the same or similar mark. Trademark renewal should be effected every ten years.[29]

[12.4.02] Applications in Ireland may be refused pursuant to s 10 of the Trade Marks Act 1996 ('the 1996 Act') when the trademark conflicts with prior trademark rights. Having two identical (or very similar) trademarks for the same type of product could cause confusion among consumers. If the trademark is

---

25 Personality merchandising and image rights relating to real persons are discussed in Chapter 18.

26 s 46 of the Trade Marks Act 1996 (as amended by SI No 346 of 2001 and SI No 561 of 2018) makes provision *inter alia* for the registration of a series of trademarks in one registration. A series of trademarks means a number of trademarks which resemble each other as to their material particulars and differ only in respect of the matter of a non-distinctive character which does not substantially affect the identity of the trademark.

27 At relatively modest fees (€70 initial application fee per class and, if successful, a registration fee of €177 being payable) given the power and control a trademark can wield for its owner.

28 While oftentimes considered an American term, 'attorney' is used in other common law jurisdictions as in the case of 'powers of attorney'. In Ireland, trademark law practitioners are also styled 'attorneys'.

29 The full schedule of fees relating to trademarks is contained in the Patents, Trademarks and Designs (Fees) Rules 2001 (SI No 482 of 2001); Patents, Trademarks and Designs (Fees) (Amendment) Rules 2012 (SI No 30 of 2012); and the Patents, Trade Marks and Designs (Fees) (Amendment) Rules 2018 (SI No 564 of 2018).

considered to be identical or confusingly similar to an existing one for identical or similar products, the application will be rejected.[30]

Concurrent/prior use and opposition proceedings

[12.4.03] If wishing to register a brand name, service or production title, it is advisable to commence that registration at the earliest possible opportunity. Notwithstanding, applying to register a trademark (that has previously been registered, is similar to an earlier mark, or in respect of which an earlier right exists) will not always prove an impossible feat. The 1996 Act provides a legal mechanism whereby even if an earlier mark has been registered in Ireland or in the EU already, it may be possible for another party to apply, grounded on statutory declaration by the applicant, for that same or similar mark if there is no likelihood of confusion on the part of the public, which includes the likelihood of association of the later trademark with the earlier trademark.

[12.4.04] Pursuant to s 12 of the 1996 Act (raising of relative grounds in case of honest concurrent use), notwithstanding an earlier mark, an applicant can apply to demonstrate to the satisfaction of the Controller of Intellectual Property (previously the Controller of Patents Designs and Trade Marks),[31] in defence to a notice of opposition to registration having been filed[32] by the earlier proprietor or rightsholder, that there has been honest concurrent use of the trademark for which registration is sought. Also, of course, consent of the earlier rightsholder will permit registration to proceed by virtue of s 10(6) of the 1996 Act.

---

30 In *Allergan Inc v Ocean Healthcare Ltd* [2008] IEHC 189, McGovern J in the Commercial Court considered the defendant's products could likely cause confusion in the minds of the plaintiff's customers or the public. The judge was satisfied both products were marketed at the same consumers and found visual, aural and conceptual similarities between the products' marks including the product name (Botoina versus Botox). And in *British Amateur Gymnastics Association v UK Gymnastics Ltd* [2020] EWHC 1678 (IPEC), the Enterprise Court found that UK registered trademarks for "British Gymnastics, More than a sport" and "British Gymnastics" were infringed by the defendants' use of "UK Gymnastics" in logos and as a word mark. The court also upheld the claimant's claim for passing off. See further *Natural Instinct Ltd v Natures Menu Ltd* [2020] EWHC 617 (IPEC). The defendant launched its True Instinct brand of pet food. Given the similarity of the marks, the identity of the goods, the enhanced distinctiveness of the earlier mark and the average degree of attention of the average consumer, the judge had no problem in finding that there was a likelihood of confusion, and consequently found infringement of the claimant's earlier mark. Mr David Stone sitting as Enterprise Court judge held that the defendant was likely to receive a "leg up" as a result of the mental link formed in consumers' minds, which constituted an unfair advantage gained from the earlier mark. The claimant's passing off claim action also succeeded. The court found that the evidence overwhelmingly proved that the claimant had goodwill in Natural Instinct and in the earlier mark. The judge used the findings of a likelihood of confusion to hold that there would be a misrepresentation to consumers and damage flowing from this misrepresentation.

31 s 4 of the Copyright and Other Intellectual Property Law Provisions Act 2019 amended s 2 of the 1996 Act.

32 Within three months of publication of the successful application for the later trademark.

[12.4.05] The Controller issued procedures[33] to trademark practitioners in 2011 wherein discretion is afforded to the Controller (previously refusal was mandatory in certain instances). The Controller will now take various factors into account when assessing whether a case of honest concurrent use exists that justifies the registration of a mark pursuant to s 12 of the 1996 Act. The main factors are the extent of use in duration, area and volume; the degree of confusion likely between the trademarks in question; whether any instances of confusion have in fact occurred; the honesty or otherwise of the concurrent use;[34] and the relative inconvenience that would be caused to the respective parties if the applicant's trademark were registered.[35]

Worldwide protection

[12.4.06] If trademark protection is required beyond Irish shores, application can be made to the EU Intellectual Property Office in Alicante, Spain for a trademark which will provide registration in all Member States of the EU or under the Madrid Protocol. This protocol is an international system of registration administered by the World Intellectual Property Organisation (WIPO), which maintains the International Register of Marks.[36]

Paris Convention for the Protection of Industrial Property

[12.4.07] The Paris Convention, adopted in 1883, applies to industrial property in the widest sense, including patents, trademarks, industrial designs, service marks, trade names, geographical indications and the repression of unfair competition. This international agreement was the first major step taken to help creators ensure, through national treatment[37] and priority of filing mechanisms, that their intellectual works were protected in other countries of the union

33 See IPOI, *New Trade Mark Procedures Regarding Claims of Honest Concurrent Use* (2011), ipoi.gov.ie. Available at: https://www.ipoi.gov.ie/en/law-practice/legislation/trade-marks/trade-marks-practice-and-procedures/honest-concurrent-use-procedure.pdf [Accessed 15 July 2021].

34 Factors to be considered here are whether the applicant copied the cited mark or adopted its mark with the knowledge that the mark was identical or very similar to the cited mark, or used its mark surreptitiously.

35 In terms of inconvenience to the applicant, in the exercise of the discretion granted to the Controller, the Controller will consider such matters as exposure to infringement proceedings, loss of goodwill and the necessity to adopt a new trademark. Factors which the Controller will take into account in terms of inconvenience to the earlier rightsholder are diversion of trade due to confusion in the marketplace, the need to re-label products to minimise confusion, and dilution of its rights in the trademark and any other factors which may be deemed relevant to the opposition proceedings.

36 See https://www.ipoi.gov.ie/en/types-of-ip/trade-marks/understanding-trade-marks/protection-abroad/international-madrid-protocol/international-madrid-protocol.html [Accessed 1 August 2021]._Ireland ratified the Madrid Protocol in 2001. Consequently, the Madrid Protocol governs international trademark applications received in the IPOI.

37 Natural (and legal persons) who are either national of or domiciled in a state party to the convention shall, as regards the protection of industrial property, enjoy in all the other countries of the union, the advantages that their respective laws grant to nationals.

that was created. The central concept is that each Member State shall afford to nationals of other member countries the same protection it affords to its own nationals.

Trade Related Aspects of International Property Rights (TRIPS) (1994)

[12.4.08] TRIPS relates to the protection of certain IP rights, including trademark protection, under the auspices of the World Trade Organisation ('WTO'). It ensures a minimum threshold of IP rights applies in all Member States which are members of the WTO.

REGULATION OF TRADEMARK USAGE IN IRISH AND EU AUDIOVISUAL PRODUCTIONS

[12.5.01] In Ireland, the legal basis for the principles discussed in this chapter stems from s 14(3) of the 1996 Act (as substituted by the provisions of s 39 of the Patents (Amendment) Act 2006 and as further amended by reg 11 of the EU (Trade Marks) Regulations 2018)[38] which provides that a person shall infringe a registered trademark if that person uses in the course of trade in relation to goods or services a sign which is identical with, or similar to, the trademark irrespective of whether it is used in relation to goods or services which are identical with, similar to, or not similar to, those for which the trademark is registered where the trademark has a reputation in the state and the use of the sign, being without due cause, takes unfair advantage of, or is detrimental to, the distinctive character or the reputation of the trademark.

[12.5.02] Section 14(6) stipulates that nothing in the preceding provisions of s 14 shall be construed as preventing the use of a registered trademark by any person for the purpose of identifying goods or services as those of the proprietor or licensee of the registered trademark; but any such use, otherwise than in accordance with honest practices in industrial or commercial matters, shall be treated as infringing the registered trademark if the use without due cause takes unfair advantage of, or is detrimental to, the distinctive character or reputation of the trademark.

[12.5.03] Recital 21 of Regulation 2017/1001[39] on the EU trademark states:

> ... Furthermore, the proprietor should not be entitled to prevent the fair and honest use of the EU trademark for the purpose of identifying or referring to

---

38 SI No 561 of 2018.

39 Repealing *inter alia* certain of EU Regulation 2015/2424 of the European Parliament and of the Council of December 16, 2015. Directive (EU) 2015/2436 of the European Parliament and of the Council to approximate the laws of Member States relating to trademarks (Recast) has also been transposed into Irish law by SI No 561 of 2018. See further SI Nos 562, 563 and 564 of 2018 relating to trademark legislation amendments and introduction of new rules.

> the goods or services as those of the proprietor... Use of a trademark by third parties for the purpose of artistic expression should be considered as being fair as long as it is at the same time in accordance with honest practices in industrial and commercial matters. Furthermore, this Regulation should be applied in a way that ensures full respect for fundamental rights and freedoms and in particular the freedom of expression.

[12.5.04] While the final sentence does not afford a specific defence to trademark infringement, it at least opens the debate as to possible acceptable exceptions to unauthorised use and might suggest that further reform of the law at EU level is in the offing.

ACCESS TO THE COURTS

[12.6.01] It is worth mentioning in passing that s 2 of the 1996 Act which defined "court" as the High Court, and other provisions thereof, were amended by the Copyright and Other Intellectual Property Law Provisions Act 2019 ('the 2019 Act'), ss 84 to 107 of which relate to courts and fines. The 2019 Act thus recognised the high if not prohibitive costs associated with IP litigation, and therefore permits the taking of smaller claims before the District and Circuit Courts. The former is now empowered to hear actions related to small IP (including trademark) infringement claims and the Circuit Court will hear claims in excess of €75,000.

[12.6.02] It is also noteworthy that the 2019 Act (s 88) amended s 24 of the 1996 Act which deals with remedies for groundless threats of infringement proceedings such that where a person threatens another with proceedings for infringement of a registered trademark other than in certain enumerated circumstances, any person aggrieved may apply to court for relief seeking a declaration that the threats are unjustifiable, an injunction against the continuance of the threats, or damages in respect of any loss sustained by the threats. The District, Circuit or High Court can now hear any such claims.[40]

DEPICTION OF TRADEMARKS IN AUDIOVISUAL WORKS

[12.7.01] Trademarks may be protected by statute when they are registered, and even when they are not, by the law of passing off under common law principles. The relationship between trademarks and the film industry has long been close. One famous example is the Aston Martin cars used in the James Bond movies. Such is the pervasiveness of trademarks that in any given scene filmmakers

---

40 For a full discussion, see the Law Commission (UK) Consultation Paper No 212 *Patents, Trade Marks and Design Rights: Groundless Threats* (2013) which comprehensively analyses the equivalent s 21 of the Trade Marks Act 1994 (as amended by the Intellectual Property (Unjustified Threats) Act 2017 and SI No 771 of 2017 (UK)) with reference to comparisons in a number of jurisdictions.

or performers may have inadvertently used a number of different trademarks without even realising they have done so.

[12.7.02] As stated above, a trademark will not (necessarily) be infringed if products or services are being shown for their intended purpose. One may be able to film a car logo when an actor is driving because such actor is merely demonstrating the intended purpose of the vehicle.[41] An important proviso is that use of the trademark must conform to honest commercial practices. The impression of a commercial relationship between the proprietor of the product and the film or performance cannot be implied where none exists, or in circumstances whereby the depicted action unfairly tarnishes a trademark. For example, if a plotline features a villain committing illegal acts using a trademarked item, that very likely may not be a honest commercial portrayal. Thus, it may not serve the Adidas brand well to have a murderer or rapist character depicted in a scene wearing an Adidas tracksuit.

Flight

[12.7.03] A useful illustration of honest commercial use is provided by the motion picture *Flight* starring Denzel Washington. The lead character is an alcoholic and his addiction is central to the story. Depicting some of the specific brands he was consuming to excess did not bode well with the brandholders Anheuser-Busch and the distributor of Stolichnaya vodka. However, because of the artistic merit likely to be found in the film, there was little legal recourse available for the trademark proprietors.

Logorama

[12.7.04] A much more audacious example of unauthorised trademark usage comes in the form of the 2009 short film *Logorama* which won high accolades at Cannes and an Academy Award. The French animated film by H5 used thousands of logos and trademarks of worldwide corporations in a fanciful depiction of an alternative world. Those marks most clearly were not being depicted through their use in the film in the manner for which they were intended. Fast food icon Ronald McDonald is the film's antagonist, who sprays machine-gun fire, curses, and takes hostages. However, no legal proceedings seemed to have ensued. While the film may be provocative, it was perhaps unlikely to provoke lawsuits from trademark holders, especially after securing its position as an Academy Award recipient and in light of the fact that it was satirical[42] in nature, a chaotic critique of corporate rule.

---

[41] If a trademark is accidentally filmed in the background, it is important to satisfy oneself the intended purpose of a product or service is merely being indicated. The inclusion should not give rise to any adverse impression in relation to that trademark.

[42] See trademark parody below.

Caterpillar Inc v Walt Disney

[12.7.05] *Caterpillar Inc v Walt Disney*[43] is a decision from 2003 in respect of *George of the Jungle 2* involved particulars of scenes wherein the villain in a children's comedy is set to destroy a forest with a line of bulldozers until George heroically swoops in. The plaintiff company sued on foot of the use of its equipment as the chosen instruments of evil claiming infringement – unauthorised use or misuse of its trademark; tarnishment – the denigrating of the product marked by its trademark within the marketplace thus lowering its established reputation; and dilution – the confusion between its trademarked goods and others in the mind of the consumer.

[12.7.06] The US District Court for the Central District of Illinois found that the bulldozers were used as one would expect bulldozers to be used, that is, to move earth, fell trees and so forth. The fact that the filmmakers showed the well-marked devices performing the function for which they were intended did nothing to affect the reputation of the equipment regardless of who was supposedly operating them. In addition, since the only bulldozers used in the film were those produced by Caterpillar there was little basis for audience confusion as to other bulldozer brands. Furthermore, in terms of dilution or tarnishment, there was nothing in the film to even remotely suggest that Caterpillar products were defective or of low quality. Moreover, the court was swayed by the fantastical nature of the movie. In terms of the crux of the issue, use, chief judge McDade J stated:[44]

> Caterpillar points out that the narrator at various stages describes its products as "deleterious dozers," and "maniacal machines." In a sense, Caterpillar is arguing that the narrator is giving anthropomorphic attributes to the bulldozers, thereby somehow implying that the machines are directly responsible for the attempted destruction of Ape Mountain. However, it is clear to even the most credulous viewer or child that the bulldozers in the movie are operated by humans and are merely inanimate implements of Lyle's environmentally unfriendly schemes. Accordingly, the Court does not find that Caterpillar is likely to succeed on its claims of trademark dilution.

[12.7.07] Although the challenged trademark depictions here were ultimately protected, the studio likely incurred significant legal costs to prevail. In hindsight, no doubt it would have been prudent to furnish Caterpillar the script in advance and seek its approval. Moreover, whenever filmmakers can reduce or eliminate a potential risk, it seems logical and commercially prudent to do so.

LANDMARKS AND ICONIC BUILDINGS

[12.8.01] Many well-known landmarks including the Hollywood sign and Empire State Building are protected as trademarks (brand and image rights as well

---

43 287 F. Supp. 2d 913.

44 At para 29 of the court's judgment.

as architect or design copyrights may also attach as in the case of night filming of the Eiffel Tower where rights, separate to the public domain building, relate to the design of the lighting creation). Permission may be required to show or reproduce any trademarks that are visible on the building (whether interior or exterior). For example, the London Eye bears branding and, accordingly, consent to include these trademarks in a film may need to be obtained if the trademarks are prominently visible in the film. There may also be copyright, as separate IP, in any logos, designs or artworks visible on or in the building.

[12.8.02] A building may also be considered to represent an individual or institution, even if no logos are visible. For example, Anfield Stadium could be said to represent or be synonymous with Liverpool FC. It is arguable that including certain buildings in a movie could amount to a representation to the public that the film is associated with or endorsed by a certain individual, institution or entity. This might amount to passing off. Footage of any such buildings should, in particular, not be used in the marketing or promotions for a film and consideration should be given as to whether a disclaimer needs to be included clarifying that the picture is not endorsed or licensed by the relevant association. In addition, if the plot suggested that a famous (albeit fictional) football club was involved in a match-fixing scandal and used footage of Anfield to represent the grounds of such football club, this might be considered defamatory of the Liverpool team and its management.

[12.8.03] Most or all of Donald Trump's buildings appear to be trademarked such that if producers and directors wish to use such structures in movies or advertisements, they must seek permission and/or discharge a fee for the shooting rights. The facade of Biltmore House, the 'largest private residence' in the US is also trademarked. Its trademark holder routinely receives royalties and fees for its appearances in films and other media. In New York, trademarked buildings and landmarks include the Chrysler building, Yankee Stadium and 30 Rockefeller Plaza.

[12.8.04] In relation to iconic landmarks in Ireland (particularly in the capital), the payment of permit fees may likewise arise. Filming of the Spire and on Ha'penny Bridge will potentially set producers of commercials (television and other brand advertising filming) back some two thousand euro. For non-commercials, film and television producers will instead pay flat fee public shooting permit sums.[45] Notwithstanding s 93 of the Copyright and Related Rights Act 2000 (representation of certain artistic works on public display do not give rise to infringement), the rationale here is presumably that the city council will recoup some of its capital costs, the Samuel Beckett Bridge for instance costing some €60 million. The substantial photocall and commercial advertising fees above are likewise imposed to raise revenue to promote events and festivals.

[45] In the region of €300 to €500 per production for medium and large production budgets, as defined.

GENERAL PROPS

[12.9.01] Featuring an article from a newspaper or magazine can also introduce exposure risks. Aside from publication/journalist issues as to copyright, the newspaper title may be trademarked. The same holds true for book covers, CDs, posters, artworks and so forth.

[12.9.02] The question often arises as to logos appearing on T-shirts. Further, can one depict a crowd scene where different vehicle models are discernible, as are well-known restaurants (e.g. Burger King) or clothing/footwear brands such as Nike? While a legal defence may apply in terms of copyrights (fair dealing or incidental use), the same might not hold true having regard to trademark law. The question is a legal one and the advisability of obtaining (and paying for, as appropriate) licences/releases should be carefully considered on a case by case basis having regard to the script, context and camera shot types.

TRADEMARK PARODY

[12.10.01] There is, at the time of writing, no legislative exemptions for trademark parody in Ireland and the EU as apply with copyright law. There is some indication as above however, in the existing EU legislation (albeit in recital form only) that a defence may be enacted in the future gleaned from the reference to the fair use of a trademark by third parties "for the purpose of artistic expression" and to the "freedom of expression".

[12.10.02] One thesis[46] considers that an explicit inclusion of the parody exception in EU trademark law might be recommended for cases of non-commercial expression and mixed expression but not for cases of merely commercial expression. Commercial speech includes commercial advertising, promises and solicitations while non-commercial speech includes political speech or a biographical movie for example. The latter has secured the highest degree of freedom of expression protection under the US Constitution.

[12.10.03] Meanwhile, since 2001, the EU has had parody legislation in effect in connection with copyright law. The InfoSoc Directive (as amended)[47] provides that Member States may allow exceptions or limitations to the exclusive rights of a copyright holder "for the purpose of caricature, parody or pastiche; and Art 17(7) of the 2019 Directive on Copyright in the Digital Single Market (Directive (EU) 2019/790) provides that Member States shall ensure that users in each Member State may rely on any of the following existing exceptions or

---

46 Marta Carmona López, *Should European Trademark Law Include an Explicit Parody Exception as a Limitation to Trademark Rights?* (2019) (Thesis: Master Programme in Intellectual Property Law, Uppsala University, Sweden). Available at: https://www.diva-portal.org/smash/get/diva2:1324852/FULLTEXT01.pdf [Accessed 20 February 2022].

47 2001/29/EC of the European Parliament and of the Council of 22 May 2001, art 5(3)(k).

limitations when uploading and making available content generated by users on online content-sharing services: quotation, criticism, review, and use for the purpose of caricature, parody or pastiche. The latter exceptions were introduced into Irish copyright law by the Copyright and Other Intellectual Property Law Provisions Act 2019.

[12.10.04] In the 2014 copyright case of *Deckmyn*,[48] the Court of Justice of the EU ('CJEU') observed that there is no definition in EU law of the meaning and scope of a parody. Thus, such meaning should be determined based on everyday language. In light of this, the essential characteristics of a parody were found "first, to evoke an existing work while being noticeably different from it, and, secondly, to constitute an expression of humour or mockery". Nonetheless, the court stated that, when determining the applicability of the parody exception, it is for the Member States' courts to strike a fair balance between the rightsholders' interests and the rights of those who seek to make use of copyrighted works, by taking into account all the circumstances of the case, including for instance, the fact that the parody conveys a discriminatory message which has the effect of associating the protected work with such a message.

[12.10.05] It is reasonable to assume that the above copyright law principles might also apply to parody in the context of trademark law. However, the issue is not straightforward: while in the US the courts are more inclined to apply a parody fair use defence, Europe is still quite reluctant to uphold such protection for would-be defendants, especially against the commercial non-authorised use of a well-known trademark.

[12.10.06] The CJEU has signaled that it is not likely to entertain parody defenses in future trademark infringement and opposition cases. In *The Polo/Lauren Company, LP v OHIM*[49] it held that the graphic representation of a boy on a bicycle holding a polo mallet was a parody of the well-known polo player device and that its use, without due cause, infringed the trademark rights of the famous fashion house, because it took unfair advantage of, or was detrimental to, the distinctive character or the repute of a trademark.

[12.10.07] In accordance with European case law, Italian courts have traditionally considered the ironic use of well-known trademarks for commercial purposes as a trademark infringement. In two cases in Milan it was held that the use of a third party's trademark would be justified where it is implemented as an artistic work (the best known example is Andy Warhol's Campbell's Soup Cans) but the parody defence would not apply in cases where a well-known trademark is used in someone else's goods as a decorative element. The cases concerned the ironic use of certain fashion iconic trademarks of Chanel and Louis Vuitton on

48 *Deckmyn v Vandersteen* C-201/13 (3 September 2014).

49 Case T-265/13 (18 September 2014).

T-shirts produced and marketed by an infringing company under the trademark "Happiness is a $10 tee".[50]

[12.10.08] Even where a defence is in fact afforded (as in the case of the US), parodists must walk a fine line.[51] On the one hand, if their parody does not call to mind the original, then the public will not get the joke[52] and the parody fails. On the other hand, if the parody does not simultaneously (and somewhat paradoxically) communicate to the public that it is not the original, then parodists may find themselves without a defence.

PASSING OFF AND CASE LAW

[12.11.01] The 1996 Act provides in s 7(2) that no proceedings may be instituted thereunder to prevent infringement of or recover damages for an unregistered trademark. However, infringement of such unregistered property rights is nonetheless protected under the common law principles of passing off.

[12.11.02] Passing off is a tort that is similar to a form of misleading and deceptive conduct. In the *Glee* decision at first instance,[53] the High Court judge

---

50 Elena Varese, *A new provision for trademark parody – is it a joke?* (2016) DLA Piper, dlapiper.com. Available at: https://www.dlapiper.com/en/us/insights/publications/2016/05/law-a-la-mode-inta-special/a-new-provision-for-trademark-parody/ [Accessed 11 March 2019].

51 The Second Circuit in *Dallas Cowboys Cheerleaders, Inc v Pussycat Cinema Ltd*, 604 F.2d 200 (2nd Cir. 1979) found a likelihood of confusion in the use of the Dallas Cowboy cheerleading uniforms in the sexually explicit film *Debbie Does Dallas*. The last several minutes of the film depicted a cheerleader engaged in various sexual escapades. The defendant argued that the film was merely a parody protected by the US Constitution. The court disagreed, stating that the defendant's movie may convey a barely discernible message but that does not entitle it to appropriate the plaintiff's trademark in the process of conveying that message stating that there are numerous ways in which defendants may comment on sexuality in athletics without infringing the plaintiff's trademark. And in *Coca-Cola Co v Alma-Leo U.S.A., Inc*, 719 F. Supp. 725 (1989), 728–29 (ND Ill 1989) the District Court for the Eastern District of New York failed to find the humour (the sale of bubble gum in the form of a white powder with a texture similar to cocaine in a bottle closely resembling a Coca-Cola bottle both injured the reputation and diluted the source-identifying distinctiveness of the Coca-Cola mark) and determined that Coca Cola's cultural status as an international icon would be damaged by the poster parody linking this symbol to the enjoyment of drugs.

52 Parodies do not always arise from a sense of humour. In *Smith v Wal-Mart Stores, Inc* 537 F. Supp. 2d 1302, 1309 (2008), the successful plaintiff held the fervent view that the defendant retail corporation which operates a chain of hypermarkets, discount department stores and grocery stores had a destructive effect on communities, and on the US generally.

53 The case of *Comic Enterprises Ltd v Twentieth Century Fox Film Corp* [2014] EWHC 185 (ChD) typifies in the most dramatic fashion how a production can potentially be derailed or exposed to protracted legal proceedings (though ultimately the plaintiff was not requesting a name change for the television programme, compensatory damages were the remedy being sought). The claimant company, trading as The Glee Club, operated a number of live entertainment venues in the UK used primarily for stand-up comedy. It owned a UK-registered trademark relating to a series of two device marks which included the words "The Glee Club" as registered in respect of a variety of entertainment services

ruled that the plaintiff's trademark had been infringed by the US television show but rejected the claim that passing off had occurred, ruling that in law there had been no misrepresentation. The tort is made out when advertisers for example utilise some form of expression or imagery that is commonly associated with a well-known brand or celebrity in their advertising, and do so in a way that implies that the brand or celebrity has endorsed the usage, and at the same time leverages the reputation of the brand or celebrity to promote themselves.[54] This being the case, even if actors are not the owner of the underlying copyright material (film production companies being the 'authors'), they could still be the victim of passing off if a brand takes issues with some aspect of a character or role they perform. In this instance however it is likely that their actor agreement will contain an indemnity by the producers for copyright infringements by the production.

[12.11.03] Passing off is commonly confused with copyright infringement. However, copyright infringement occurs simply when a substantial[55] portion of a copyright-protected work is reproduced without permission. Passing off goes one step further, whereby a passing off uses the relevant work in a manner that suggests there is an endorsement or connection between the subject and the advertiser or other user. Thus, in *Thomas*,[56] the plaintiff claimed passing off by

---

since 1999. The Glee musical comedy television series (as also released in the UK from 2009) with associated concert tours and merchandise used the sign "glee" in similar lettering to the plaintiff's mark. In a preliminary ruling on the case two years prior, a judge in the patents county court had made a reference to potentially "catastrophic consequences" for Twentieth Century Fox. The High Court held that the defendant/appellant's activities infringed the respondent's registered trademark but the claim in passing off failed. The appellant appealed and the respondent cross-appealed but the Court of Appeal [2016] EWCA Civ 41 dismissed both. Fox lodged appeal papers with the Supreme Court on three grounds. The Supreme Court hearing was scheduled for November 2017. However, by agreement reached in and around October 2017 on confidential terms between the parties, the appeal by Fox was withdrawn. Moreover, the High Court held that Fox infringed a trademark and had potentially "put off" comedy club customers, and had no objective justification for trademark infringements likely to cause confusion. The deputy High Court judge ruled there was a likelihood of confusion and Fox's use caused dilution and tarnishing. In trademark infringement cases, there is no requirement for actual confusion (see Millett LJ in *Harrods v Harrodian School* [1996] EWCA Civ 1315). The legal test as set out by the Court of Appeal (paras 26 to 34 of the judgment [2012] EWCA Civ 24) is the likelihood of confusion. This test was applied again in *George v Bond* [2020] EWHC 3863 (IPEC) and involves a global assessment: taking everything into account, including the visual, aural and conceptual similarity between the marks, and the similarity of the respective services.

54 *Rogers v Grimaldi* 875 F.2d 994 though not a parody or passing off case was an unsuccessful action decided by the US Court of Appeals for the Second Circuit whereby actress Ginger Rogers alleged in her proceedings that the use of "Ginger and Fred" as the title of a fictional movie violated her common law right of publicity by falsely implying that the film was about her and that she had endorsed it. The film depicted two struggling dancers in Italy in the 1940s. The dancers were known to their audience as Ginger and Fred and sometimes imitated Ginger Rogers and Fred Astaire.

55 Substantiality being a legal construct for interpretation and it does not always mean substantial in the normal everyday meaning of the word.

56 *Thomas v Luv One Luv All Promotions Ltd* [2020] EWHC 1565 (IPEC).

the defendants (who were using the performance name Luv Injection Sound) through use of names and signs relating to a music group known as Love Injection or less frequently Luv Injection, and that use by the defendants (of certain musical records of performances of the original group as part of the defendants' performances) passed its group off as the claimant's group. The claimant therefore sought an injunction against further passing off by the defendants, transfer of the records, transfer or cancellation of a registered trademark and damages or an account of profits at his election.[57]

[12.11.04] Even where a prudent filmmaker or theatre production is careful not to feature any registered trademarks, they may nonetheless be liable for passing off. This is because unregistered (and registered) trademarks attract protection under the common law to prevent copycat products. Passing off serves to protect the goodwill, namely, the reputation attached to existing goods or services. Where a party uses a mark, get-up or trade dress similar to an existing product resulting in confusion as to origin amongst consumers, then that party may be liable to a claim of passing off where this is likely to cause damage to the rightsholder in terms of loss of sales or adverse reputational fallout.

[12.11.05] If it were too costly to pay a fee for certain brands to appear in the production and as a result mock-ups of brands, logos or slogans are carefully made and devised which are very similar to an existing product, liability may nonetheless still result if it causes confusion and actual or potential damage to the rightsholder. For example, if a performance features a laptop with a mock-up of the Apple logo that was very similar but clearly not the same, this could amount to passing off (and registered trademark infringement). When making adaptations from someone else's play, musical or film, this can also amount to a passing off. Similar caution must also be made in choosing film/performance titles, and using

---

57 In relation to the fashion industry, see *Freddy SPA v Hugz Clothing Ltd* [2020] EWHC 3032 (IPEC). The judge (Mr David Stone sitting as deputy judge) held that Hugz had passed off the Freddy jeans in the conventional sense (i.e. attempting to create an association in the minds of consumers between the two brands). More interesting was the court's consideration of passing off in relation to post-sale confusion. This is the situation where a consumer knows that Hugz are unconnected to Freddy when buying the Hugz jeans, but buys them anyway, wanting other consumers to believe that their Hugz jeans are associated with Freddy and its jeans. The judge bore in mind that it was well-established in case law that such confusion is actionable as a matter of trademark law, but in relation to passing office the question had rarely been considered. He found that the owner of goodwill in a product is entitled to have this goodwill protected throughout the life of the product, not just at the point of sale and concluded that there had been passing off on the basis of post-sale, as well as point-of-sale, misrepresentation. This is a unique finding, whereby confusing post-sale use of similar aesthetic design elements on an article of clothing (as opposed to trademarks, such as brand names or logos) can be used as a basis for passing off. If post-sale confusion can now be relied on in passing off claims, fashion designers will have an additional tool in the fight against copycats. Extending passing off to include post-sale confusion would close the gap between trademark law and passing off, and ensure that the purpose of the tort cannot be subverted by the mere use of a disclaimer, or other circumstances, to remove confusion.

celebrity-likeness or giving the impression of a celebrity endorsement when no such endorsement in fact exists.

[12.11.06] In the 1970s there were a number of cases in which merchandising rights were not found to exist by the English courts. These included *Tavener Rutledge Ltd v Trexapalm Ltd* (Kojak lollipops, an 'unauthorised' local lollipop retailer succeeded against the plaintiff makers of the television programme),[58] *Lyngstad v Anabas* (T-shirts bearing photograph images of the pop group Abba, injunction refused)[59] and *Wombles v Womble Skip Hire* (skips for collecting waste branded Womble).[60] These cases highlighted difficulties with the 'common field of activity' hurdle as the plaintiff and defendant business activities were dissimilar.

The Teenage Mutant Ninja Turtles

[12.11.07] However, in *Mirage Studios v Counter Feat Clothing Co Ltd*,[61] Sir Nicholas Browne-Wilkinson accepted that the claimant had proved the public did expect goods bearing the image of a famous cartoon character to be licensed. As other jurisdictions such as Australia (see *Crocodile Dundee* below) started to realise the true potential of character merchandising and the accompanying commercial gain, the UK courts caught up. True recognition of the utility of passing off in such claims came through this decision which involved the production of clothing bearing images of the iconic turtles. Mirage Studios made significant profit from the sale of merchandise. Accordingly it was unsurprising that the court held that they also held goodwill in the clothing trade. The pleadings clearly satisfied the requirements of passing off: the claimant had goodwill, there was a misrepresentation through unauthorised sales, which in turn could damage Mirage Studios' trade.

[12.11.08] Australian courts have developed the law of passing off to something akin to a right of image and personality through a number of high-profile decisions. In the 1969 case of *Henderson v Radio Corp.*[62] the defendant used a photograph of the claimants, well-known professional ballroom dancers, while dancing, as an album cover. The Australian High Court[63] considered that customers of the defendants could be misled as to whether the claimants had approved or recommended the album and this was sufficient for an action of passing off.

---

[58] [1977] RPC 275 (High Court, Walton J).

[59] [1977] FSR 62. Oliver J expressed the view that the public would not believe that a music group was responsible for all memorabilia bearing its name or image. This is especially so if the music group itself is not in the business of selling memorabilia (T-shirts, mugs and the like).

[60] [1975] FSR 488.

[61] [1991] FSR 145.

[62] [1969] RPC 218.

[63] The final court of appeal and thus the highest court in that jurisdiction.

Crocodile Dundee

[12.11.09] The leading Australian case is *Pacific Dunlop Ltd v Hogan*[64] which involved proceedings brought by Paul Hogan, famously known for the role of Mick 'Crocodile' Dundee. Pacific Dunlop, a shoe manufacturer, used a character dressed in a costume similar to that worn by Hogan in the films in its television advertisement campaign and one advert contained a spoof scene based on a famous scene from the film involving a mugging, substituting the knife reference with leather shoes.

[12.11.10] Hogan's claim for passing off was upheld and an appeal was dismissed on the basis that the public would assume that he had licensed or endorsed Pacific Dunlop to use the image of Crocodile Dundee.[65] Despite not actually damaging Hogan's career, the court believed the advert that mimicked his film character could damage his own potential marketing opportunities. This demonstrates the requirement for a common field of activity had become no more than an indicator for the likelihood of confusion. In terms of registered trademarks (as opposed to unregistered marks for which the tort of passing off can provide a legal remedy), we also saw in para [12.5.01] that a registered trademark can be infringed irrespective of whether it is used (say in a film or commercial) in relation to goods or services which are not similar to those for which the trademark is registered.

[12.11.11] In a previous case involving Hogan and the character Crocodile Dundee (*Hogan v Koala Dundee Pty Ltd*)[66] in 1988, the actor brought an action against the proprietors of Koala Dundee stores. These stores sold T-shirts and other items recognised from the films to be typical of those coming from the Australian outback. The stores' logo was a koala bear in Crocodile Dundee "get-up". Hogan sought an injunction and damages. The court held that it was now the law of Australia that the creator of a sufficiently famous character having certain visual or other traits may prevent others using his character to sell their goods and may assign the right to so use the character; furthermore, the inventor's rights accrue even where he has never carried on any business at all, other than the writing or making of the work in which the character appears.[67]

[12.11.12] Hogan also took legal action in 2017 against burger chain Grill'd in response to its continued use of the expression "That's not a knife. This is a knife" on packaging used for dining in its restaurants. The company credited the expression it used on the packaging to Paul Hogan's character in the film. Hogan filed a lawsuit accusing Grill'd of misleading or deceptive conduct by

---

64 23 FCR 553 (1989).

65 *Per* Beaumont and Burchett JJ, dissent by Sheppard J.

66 83 ALR 187 (1988).

67 Ben Challis, *The Right Image?* (2007), Music Law Updates. Available at: http://www.musiclawupdates.com/?p=171 [Accessed 29 July 2019].

associating itself with the Hogan brand without consent. Reuters reported[68] in early February 2018 that Grill'd had paid Aus$20,000 to the actor and a charity to settle the dispute. An interesting point of note again was that it was the actor, Paul Hogan, taking action for the misuse of the phrase (though of course he co-wrote the screenplay also).

Eddie Irvine and the tort of false endorsement

[12.11.13] It is a well-established fact that one of the benefits of the common law system is the ease of change. Laddie J commented on this in the *Irvine* judgment, noting that change enabled the law to evolve with the constant state of flux of the commercial market. This malleability was demonstrated through the development of passing off to the point of creating a new tort: false endorsement. The *Irvine* case was the first time the courts had accepted that passing off can protect image rights. Until *Irvine v Talksport Ltd*[69] where the Formula One racing driver Eddie Irvine successfully brought a passing off action against UK radio station Talksport, celebrities were generally unable to prevent the use of their image using the tort of passing off, as the claimant and defendant rarely fell within a common field of activity. *Irvine* expanded passing off to include false endorsement claims, rejecting the need for a common field of activity.

[12.11.14] In the past, the courts had struggled with the need for a common field of activity, causing many passing off claims to fail. As a common law tort, the case law has developed over time on a case by case basis, becoming increasingly strict as the judiciary appears to accept the possibility of commercial success. In light of *Mirage*, it is doubtful that the common field requirement remains relevant when discussing character merchandising and image rights.

[12.11.15] The development of the law on character merchandising and image rights appears to have spun 180 degrees. In the 19th century the judiciary did not believe that there should be a monopoly over a particular character. Now the courts seem more willing to accept that inferior or unofficial merchandise can be damaging to a reputation. They also appear to realise that character merchandising is now an accepted activity that accompanies fame. Singers and bands will want to release merchandise, films likewise. Those who have built up a reputation and therefore goodwill now appear to have the right to protect same from being imitated.

USE OF NAMES AND IMAGES/LIKENESSES

[12.12.01] Interestingly, from a legal standpoint, there is no copyright inherent

---

68 See https://www.reuters.com/article/us-australia-lawsuit-crocodile/australian-burger-chain-settles-dispute-with-crocodile-dundee-actor-idUSKBN1FS0F5 [Accessed 29 July 2019].

69 [2002] 2 All ER 414.

in a name.[70] The primary means to protect a name is by trademark registration.[71] Trademarks may even extend to personal names[72] and nicknames. This mode of registration is very different from business name registration and is much more powerful in result given that the latter does not convey any significant rights or protection and is simply a statutory obligation in Ireland under the Registration of Business Names Act 1963 to identify the persons behind a business.

[12.12.02] In the *Elvisly Yours* judgment, Laddie J referred to the *Tarzan*

---

70 In *Elvis Presley Enterprises Inc v Sid Shaw Elvisly Yours* [1999] EWCA Civ 964 the plaintiff, a London trader, carried on the business of a souvenir shop under the name "Elvisly Yours" for which he owned a registered trademark in the UK. Elvis Presley Enterprises, Inc ('EPEI'), the marketing arm and legal successor of Presley's estate had applied to register three trademarks. The Court of Appeal confirmed the decision of Laddie J in the High Court overturning a Trademarks Registry decision to allow EPEI to register the various marks. In the High Court judgment, Mr Justice Laddie began by making it clear that EPEI could not (trademarks aside) own the words Elvis and Elvis Presley stating "there is nothing akin to copyright in a name". On appeal by EPEI, Lord Justice Brown stated that there should be no assumption that only celebrities or their successors may ever market their own character, adding that monopolies should not be so readily created. This was positive news for traders and for the freedom of artistic expression or otherwise, although this decision does not give carte-blanche to unofficial merchandisers to exploit celebrities' names. Moreover, the crux of the issue was that Elvis as a trademark had very low inherent distinctiveness. Members of the public would purchase Elvis merchandise because it bore the name and likeness of Elvis Presley and not because it came from a particular source. Further, in trademark registration proceedings involving the face/likeness of Diana Princess of Wales by her estate and the trustees of her memorial, in reaching the decision [2001] ETMR 254, Mr Allan James, acting on behalf of the Registrar of the UK Trademarks Registry, had to consider whether people would think, on seeing merchandise with a picture of Diana's face, that it was a badge of origin or mere decoration. He also considered whether the image of Diana had been used for trading before the application. The decision against the estate illustrates in dramatic terms again the paradox of trademark law: sometimes a name and image can become too well-known and too widely used to serve as a trademark. Note however there were subsequent trademark applications by the Memorial Fund which in fact proved successful but a commentary thereon is outside the scope of this chapter.

71 See for instance *APT Training & Consultancy Ltd v Birmingham & Solihull Mental Health NHS Trust* [2019] EWHC 19 (IPEC). The court ruled that a NHS trust infringed a consultancy's trademark in its promotion of mental health services. APT had trademarked the word RAID (Reinforce Appropriate, Implode Destructive) in respect of services relating to psychology, behavioural problems, business and commerce. The trust had provided services using the RAID name but to stand for 'Rapid Assessment Interface and Discharge'. It accepted it had used the claimant's sign but denied this amounted to an infringement of registered trademarks or passing off as the service was different. Clarke J ruled that she was "satisfied on the balance of probabilities that there is a likelihood of confusion". She said the trust's use of the earlier trademark and name in relation to its service "would cause the average consumer to believe that they come from the claimants or that they are economically linked to the claimants" and found there was infringement.

72 Justin Bieber's attorneys registered his name to protect it and all associated merchandise to include toys, stationery, clothes and cosmetics. Five-year-old Harper Beckham's name was also registered in late 2016 and reserved for exclusive use in the entertainment industry, should a career in music, television or film await this son of widely-famed David and Victoria Beckham.

trademark decision of the Court of Appeal.[73] In that case, Tarzan, which had once been a distinctive word, had, by the time it was applied for as a trademark, become a household name following the success of the Tarzan books and films.[74] It was held, dismissing the appeal, that as the word Tarzan had passed into the language and was well-known by every adult and by most children, it failed to qualify for registration as an invented word. If the mark had been applied for at the time of its creation, no doubt registration could have been achieved. In fact, a registration for Tarzan in respect of films has since been achieved under UK legislation.

[12.12.03] *Tarzan* and *Elvis Presley* thus suggested that the more well-known the character is, the less protection there is, in the sense that once a fictional character has achieved fame, the creator probably can no longer apply to protect its name by means of a trademark.[75] This was also the issue in Linkin Park LLC's trademark application whereby it was held[76] that at the application date, the mark Linkin Park had already acquired a well-established meaning of denoting the respective music group (similar to the situation in the *Tarzan* case) and Mr Richard Arnold QC accepted that this led to the paradox that the group was worse off than it would have been had it applied before the band became well known.[77]

CHOOSING FILM TITLES AND CONDUCTING SEARCHES

[12.13.01] In Ireland and Britain, there is no rule which prohibits the registration of a title as a national or EU trademark, provided it can meet the basic requirements imposed on all trademarks. A lack of the requisite distinctiveness can be overcome through careful management of the manner in which a trademark is exploited, to educate the public about its function as an identifier of commercial (as opposed to merely artistic) origin; and indeed many film titles are protected as registered trademarks. The main value of film title trademarks is the licensing of related ancillary merchandise and the ability to police unauthorised products.

[12.13.02] Using a title which is identical to a registered trademark in respect of

---

73 [1970] RPC 450.

74 The applicant, an American company which was exclusively entitled to produce films, records and merchandise centred on the character Tarzan, applied to register the word TARZAN in respect of films and magnetic tape recordings and in respect of games, toys, playthings, and gymnastics and sporting articles. The Registrar refused to register the mark on the grounds that TARZAN was not an invented word, that it had a direct reference to the character and quality of goods and that it was not distinctive. An appeal to the High Court was dismissed and the applicant appealed further to the Court of Appeal which decided against granting the trademark.

75 BM Nyman, "Passing off–sale of 'unofficial' merchandise" (1997) *Entertainment Law Review* 8(5) pp E94-95.

76 [2006] ETMR 74.

77 A Wood, "Linkin Park fails to hit a sweet note" (2005) *Entertainment Law Review* 16(5) pp 134-6 at p 135.

goods or services which are identical to those for which it is registered without permission will, on the face of it, amount to trademark infringement. Using a name which is similar may also infringe if there is a likelihood of confusion. As above, even if a title or name is not registered as a trademark, it may nevertheless be protected as an unregistered trademark under the law of passing off.[78] If appropriate trademark clearance searches reveal an existing trademark, or if a producer has already started using a name and then becomes aware of a potentially conflicting earlier trademark, the implications of this need to be considered very carefully.

[12.13.03] Depending on the stage of production, one may be able to adopt a different title, attempt to negotiate a licence to use the title from the trademark owner, and in some cases it may be possible to avoid the issue entirely. For example, as argued by counsel in *Arsenal Football Club plc v Reed*,[79] it may be feasible to contend, for some jurisdictions at least, that the name one proposes to use does not constitute 'trademark use' (in the legal sense) at all, or that it is merely descriptive of the subject matter or other characteristics of the film,

---

78 Thus the High Court in *Asian Business Publications Ltd v British Asian Achievers Awards Ltd* [2019] EWHC 1094 (IPEC) held that passing off had occurred where the claimant ran the Asian Achievers Awards and the first defendant adopted the name British Asian Achievers Awards for a similar event. The judge was satisfied that simply by adding the word 'British' to the claimant's name, the defendants had not sufficiently distinguished their event from the claimant's event or done enough to stop confusion arising. Hence there was a risk that a substantial number of potential attendees at or sponsors of the claimant's event would be confused into thinking that the defendants' event was that of the claimant or was connected with it.

79 [2003] EWCA Civ 696. Reed was a street vendor of Arsenal-branded goods such as scarves, hats and shirts. Arsenal commenced High Court proceedings claiming he was passing himself off as being connected with the club and of violating its trademark in the club logo – a shield and a cannon contrary to the trademark legislation. The court determined that Reed was not guilty of passing off by deliberately misleading purchasers, because there was no evidence of purchasers being confused as to the origin of the goods (e.g. consumers would expect to find the official merchandise to be sold in shops, not on the street). It then considered the question of trademark infringement, and decided that the use of the logos on Reed's goods was merely a badge of allegiance to the football club and did not amount to trademark infringement. The Court of Justice of the EU ('CJEU') (giving an art 234, now art 267 TFEU, preliminary ruling) disagreed with Laddie J and confirmed that the use of the logos did amount to trademark infringement. However, the trial judge was of the view that the CJEU had overstepped its remit and made a decision on the facts and not the law. Arsenal appealed and the Court of Appeal took the view that Laddie J should have followed the view of the CJEU, namely, the sale of unofficial branded merchandise did amount to trademark infringement. The fact that the logo was being used as a badge of allegiance was irrelevant. According to the Court of Appeal, the crucial factor was whether the selling of unofficial merchandise was likely to damage the trademark, or jeopardise the guarantee of ownership that stemmed from the trademark. The ruling appears to introduce the principle of dilution into UK trademark law. Under this principle the rights of the trademark proprietor go beyond preventing use by others of the trademark to mislead consumers and enable the proprietor to prevent use by others simply to protect the exclusivity of the trademark and the goodwill associated with it. The position regarding sports clubs is now clear. Other trademark proprietors will not be slow to assert the same expanded merchandising rights as those afforded to Arsenal.

which could constitute a defence. Equally, producers may be able to make certain changes to the way the title, and the film generally, are presented; for instance, to ensure they do not mislead the public into believing they have been licensed or authorised by the owner of the earlier trademark, so as to render a passing off action less likely to succeed.

[12.13.04] The *Damo and Ivor* action[80] highlights the need to conduct name checks against registered trademarks (and indeed pending applications). The Intellectual Property Office can conduct a search of the national trademark database and the EU database for pending applications in consideration of a fee. The same holds true for the US Patent and Trademark Office whereby that office itself, clearance practitioners and trademark attorneys can conduct the relevant searches. In the UK, the services of the Intellectual Property Office can likewise be employed.

HISTORIC WORDS/NAMES

[12.14.01] History does not appear to represent an issue in trademark law. Although the Olympics are thousands of years old, the US Supreme Court upheld the right of the US Olympic Committee to trademark the name in 1987.

PRODUCT PLACEMENT

[12.15.01] As previously stated, some companies will actively encourage the use of their products in film. From the 1990s, in action movies like *Mission Impossible* to television shows including *House of Cards* and *Modern Family*, Apple products occasionally find their way into the central plot. Apple's marketing chief Phil Schiller once explained[81] that the company works closely with Hollywood to secure as much screen time as possible for its computers and iPhones, and, while it is common to see Apple products casually being used, there have also been instances where an Apple product has enjoyed a primary plot point or is conspicuously referenced or depicted during a pivotal scene.[82]

---

80 In 2013, singer/songwriter Damien O'Regan issued High Court proceedings against national broadcaster RTÉ and comedian Andrew Quirke for alleged trademark infringement over their use of the name "Damo" in the *Damo and Ivor* television comedy just days before it was set to air. Had the action not been struck out for lacking in merit, it would have presented the first character mark case before the Irish courts. According to the then Irish Patents Office, the plaintiff registered the name Damo in relation to entertainment services, music and lyrics many years prior. McGovern J was informed that the use of the name Damo was a clear breach of the claimant's trademark and evidence was adduced that he had not given his consent for its use by Quirke. Ken Fogarty SC for O'Regan contended the infringement would damage the goodwill his client had spent years building and hence an injunction was being sought.

81 Yoni Heisler, *Apple's most obvious product placement in movies and TV* (2015), networkworld.com. Available at: https://www.networkworld.com/article/2887929/ios/apples-most-obvious-product-placement-in-movies-and-tv.html [Accessed 12 September 2017].

82 If one wishes to feature an Apple product in a film, for example, an email request for

[12.15.02] The advantages for film producers of product placement are numerous. *Castaway*, by way of example, features several brands including Snickers and Fedex. Total time exposure in the movie for the Fedex brand was reportedly more than 15 minutes and instead of cash the company provided airplanes, uniforms, trucks and packages to the producers. It also helped of course that CEO Fred Smith was an investor in the film production company. Another notable example from the television world is the sponsorship by Australian supermarket giant Coles of the series *My Kitchen Rules* which features contestants shopping for foodstuffs in a local Coles supermarket in each episode and use of its branded carrier bag. It also regularly features close-up images of car brand logos and sequences where a particular vehicle is used to drive participants and chef judges.

REMEDYING OR OBVIATING INFRINGEMENT

[12.16.01] Perhaps the most high-profile example of a contentious trademark issue in recent film history relates to Mercedes-Benz and Coca-Cola, both of which insisted on their logos and markings being removed from scenes in *Slumdog Millionaire* because they sought to avoid being associated with a non-flattering Mumbai slum,[83] a move director Danny Boyle referred to as "product displacement".

[12.16.02] Both the soft drinks corporation (wanting to remain anonymous but readily emerging in any event publicly as Coca-Cola) and Mercedes demanded that key scenes featuring their brands be excised based on the contention that their drinks products and cars would suffer from association with the poverty depicted in the movie. Thus, for scenes shot in Mumbai slums (or depicting gangsters driving and/or owning a Mercedes), the Mercedes markings were removed. Mercedes was willing, however, to provide cars for scenes evidencing opulence and wealth (where the gangster's car was parked outside his mansion and in respect of a vehicle hired by wealthy American tourists) as this would tally with the company's branding as producer of top-end, luxury products.

[12.16.03] In somewhat of a peculiar about-turn on the matter, however, it was noteworthy that the car manufacturer did not appear to have issue with use of a Mercedes to mass murderous effect in 2017's hit television thriller series *Mr.*

---

permission (outlining how the product fits into the project) can be sent to Apple using the link below. Apple will want to ensure that its product is not brought into disrepute (e.g. an actor stating on screen that the battery life on an iPhone is too short or a fraudster using an iMac to commit a cybercrime): https://www.apple.com/legal/intellectual-property/rightsandpermissions.html. See also *Guidelines for Using Apple Trademarks and Copyrights*. Available at: https://www.apple.com/legal/intellectual-property/guidelinesfor3rdparties.html [Accessed 1 August 2021].

[83] Claude Brodesser-Akner, *Coke, Mercedes Avoid Gritty Film Cameos* (2008), adage.com. Available at: http://adage.com/article/madisonvine-news/coke-mercedes-avoid-gritty-film-cameos-slumdog/132301/ [Accessed 13 September 2017].

Mercedes based on Stephen King's novel and starring Brendan Gleeson as retired Ohio detective Bill Hodges investigating the criminal actions of psychopath serial killer Brady Hartsfield.

[12.16.04] Returning to *Slumdog*, producers of the film were also asked to remove the Coca-Cola branding from a scene where a beggar offers a bottle of Coke to the protagonists. Boyle explained in a post-screening interview for *The Times* that there is a scene where children are on a rubbish dump and are offered bottles of the popular fizzy drink. There were calls for the name Coca-Cola to be removed and the labels painted over for fear that the product would be sullied. This situation, which greatly vexed the renowned movie director, was resolved at very considerable post- production cost, reportedly into the tens of thousands of pounds.

Product 'displacement'

[12.16.05] Product displacement is usually achieved via digital pixelation or removal of a logo physically (e.g. a brandname from the grill or rear of a car). This occurs in order to avoid the payment of licensing fees, if the trademark owner objects, or if a broadcaster would rather not publicise a product for free (if the owners have not paid for it to be included in a programme).

[12.16.06] Fictionalised product displacement uses a completely fictional brand and/or product which closely resembles and mimics a real product or brand. The idea here is that viewers can make close correlation with an already existing non-fictional brand that they may use on a daily basis. The protagonists in *Scrubs* were often seen mingling at a coffee shop known as Coffee Bucks which closely resembles the logo, colour and theme of Starbucks. *My Name is Earl* also used a similar technique with the fictional candy bar by the name of TitTat Candy which closely resembles the Kit Kat chocolate bar. For reasons explained earlier in this chapter, however, embarking on such course of action could be fraught with danger.

[12.16.07] The practice of product displacement is also frequently seen on reality television shows which do not have clearance to display the logos or products of non-sponsor companies. This accounts for the frequent appearance of pixel mosaics and blurring of logo T-shirts and other instances on productions such as *Survivor* and *America's Next Top Model.*

THE CONSEQUENCES OF INFRINGEMENT

[12.17.01] In both breach of a registered trademark and passing off cases, the court is likely to order the infringer to remove from the subject work trademarks used without permission and account to the owner for any damage suffered or for any unfair benefit gained from use thereof. There are also potential criminal law sanctions for the unauthorised use of a trademark.[84] However, the most likely consequence would be that the film or performance in question is prevented from being released to the public and the infringer ordered to pay damages. Such eventuality would spell disaster to the filmmakers or performance organisers in the case of a live stageshow.

CONCLUSION

[12.18.01] Given the sheer volume of case law on the topic of trademark infringement and the conflicting judicial decisions over time (although the law seems well settled in certain areas such as passing off), it would be an imprudent producer who fails to seek clearance from trademark owners where appropriate. In saying that, a deep understanding of the underlying legal principles and a comprehensive knowledge of the line of authorities could equip a producer with sufficient armoury to make a judgment call and to successfully persuade a court. The downside to defending legal proceedings however is time lost and substantial cost.

[84] ss 92-95 of the 1996 Act as amended by the Copyright and Other Intellectual Property Law Provisions Act 2019.

Chapter 13

GDPR and the Data Protection Act 2018

INTRODUCTION

[13.1.01] While the enactment of the EU General Data Protection Regulation[1] ('GDPR') has brought data protection to the fore for every business, Member States have been subject to data protection rules since EC Directive 95/46/EC on the protection of individuals with regard to the processing of personal data and on the free movement of such data (although the UK already had domestic legislation in place since 1984, and Ireland since 1988). A subsequent British statute, the (then) Data Protection Act 1998 ('the 1998 UK Act') had not been the subject of judicial interpretation except for a passing reference by Brooke LJ in the Court of Appeal judgment in *Douglas v Hello! Ltd*[2] whereby mention was made to s 13 thereof at p 983 concerning the granting to an individual of the statutory right to compensation for damage (including distress, in certain specified circumstances) against a "data controller" who contravened any of the requirements of the 1998 UK Act, the entitlement being subject to any of the defences the Act may provide.

[13.1.02] Data protection legislation in the context of media law came up for discussion shortly afterwards again in *Campbell v Mirror Group Newspapers Ltd*[3] whereby Naomi Campbell was awarded a modest total sum of £3,500 in damages by the High Court for breach of confidentiality and for compensation under s 13 (compensation for failure to comply with certain requirements) of the 1998 UK Act. Mr Justice Morland also awarded aggravated damages assessed in the amount of £1,000. These proceedings, ultimately coming for decision by the House of Lords in 2004, arising out of publication by the *Mirror* of an article detailing supermodel Campbell's attendance at Narcotics Anonymous meetings, and printing photographs of her leaving such a meeting, are further discussed below.

---

1 EU Regulation 2016/679 of the European Parliament and of the Council dated 27 April 2016.

2 [2001] QB 967.

3 [2002] EWHC 499 (QB) (see fn 24 for House of Lords ruling).

[13.1.03] Data protection is a fundamental right set out in art 8 of the EU Charter of Fundamental Rights ratified in December 2000, which states that individuals have the right to the protection of personal data concerning them; such data must be processed fairly for specified purposes and on the basis of the consent of the person concerned, or some other legitimate basis laid down by law, and that individuals have the right of access to data which has been collected concerning them, and the right to have it rectified.

[13.1.04] Individuals are therefore entitled to have their personal data protected, used only in a fair and lawful way, and made available to them when they require a copy. If persons feel that their personal data is incorrect, rectification can be duly requested and effected. The GDPR which came into effect in May 2018 protects a number of basic rights such as right of access and the right to be informed. However, data protection is not an absolute right. It must always be balanced against other fundamental rights and there may be circumstances under which an organisation could have grounds to refuse to grant individuals' requests to exercise their data protection rights. There are also certain limitations contained within the data protection rights as set out in the Regulation.

[13.1.05] Moreover, the main objective of the GDPR is to allow data subjects to exercise more control over their personal data, as well as bestowing a more comprehensive understanding of how that personal data is used. The GDPR only applies to personal data, which effectively means any information that can be used, directly or indirectly, to identify a living individual.

[13.1.06] This chapter will focus on data protection as it applies to entertainment and media law. It is not concerned with general company or business-wide matters of data protection by data controllers as apply to security, processing and administration of personal data held in respect of clients, suppliers, staff and so forth. These matters will be governed by the organisation's privacy and data protection policies.

Consent as a requirement for production funding

[13.1.07] Given the potentially very serious practical and cost ramifications for data protection breaches as later discussed, financiers of audiovisual productions including Screen Ireland and RTÉ will ensure in their production loan/rights acquisition agreements that the matter of data protection is assiduously contemplated by film and television producers (and any other parties providing audiovisual content). Producers will be required to warrant in such agreements that their activities throughout production will be in compliance with the GDPR and the Data Protection Acts 1988 to 2018. This will include the signing by talent, crew, actors, interview contributors, music composers and performers of a release agreement that contains a data protection consent. The importance of this cannot be overstated. Obtaining consent is an express legal requirement.

[13.1.08] If the data subject's consent is given in the context of a written declaration which also concerns other matters, the request for consent shall be presented in a manner which is clearly distinguishable from the other matters, in an intelligible and easily accessible form, using clear and plain language. Therefore, in contracts with contributors to an audiovisual project such as cast, crew and interviewees, there should be a conspicuous separate clause (with its own heading) governing data protection. Producers ideally will also make their data protection, privacy and social media policies freely available to data subjects who may wish to consult them (see paras [13.4.09], and [13.5.02] in respect of special categories of personal data).

'Sharenting'

[13.1.09] Lastly a word on consents given on behalf of minors by their parents or their guardians. Releases for child actors and performers will be signed by their parents (see the European Court of Human Rights decision in *IVT v Romania* discussed in Chapter 35 in respect of broadcast of a television interview by an 11-year old which had been conducted without obtaining parental consent). It is recommended that these agreements be signed by the minors themselves too for the reasons outlined at the end of Chapter 15.

[13.1.10] This issue has come to the fore in recent times as regards actions potentially being taken by children against their parents and/or film and television producers arising from the use and exploitation of material posted online by parents of their children but without the express consent of the child (see Chapter 35 on privacy law). At EU level, at least one such case has come before the courts whereby a Dutch District Court judge (Gelderland District Court, 13 May 2020, case number C/05/368427) ordered a woman to remove photographs of her grandchildren from Facebook after she posted the images without permission from the children's mother in breach of the GDPR and privacy law.

GDPR

[13.2.01] The GDPR repealed and replaced the existing data protection framework under the above-cited 1995 Data Protection Directive. Regulations generally being 'directly applicable', do not require transposition into national law of Member States. Irish legislation was therefore necessary only to implement certain article provisions such as national handling by the Data Protection Commission ('DPC') or the courts relating to the issue of fines and compensation.[4] Thus, organisations involved in data processing of any sort need to be acutely aware that the GDPR itself affects and addresses them directly in terms of the obligations it imposes. It emphasises transparency, security

4 Note that the Data Protection Act 2018 largely repeals and revokes the Data Protection Acts 1988 to 2003 but some provisions thereof have been retained such as in relation to law enforcement and matters of state security.

and accountability by data controllers and processors, while at the same time standardising and strengthening the right of EU citizens to data privacy.

[13.2.02] The GDPR sets out more extensive obligations on data controllers and processors, and provides strengthened protections for data subjects. Rights of data subjects are set out at Arts 12 to 23 and include the right to be forgotten,[5] a right of access and in respect of erasure, rectification and restriction of processing.

Standard contractual clauses (transfer of personal data to third countries)

[13.2.03] It is worthy of mention in passing, the finer details lying outside the scope of this textbook, that in June 2021 on foot of the EU Court of Justice's ('CJEU') decision in *Schrems II*[6] in July 2020 which arose following a referral of a number of questions to the CJEU by Costello J in the High Court, the European Commission took a further step to reinforce legal certainty under the GDPR by adopting two new sets of standard contractual clauses (SCCs), intended to allow safe and free cross-border data transfers (e.g. from Ireland to the US). The SCCs come in the form of implementing decisions under the GDPR and provide tools for data transfers between controllers and processors, and transfers of personal data to non-EU third countries being countries outside the EEA.

---

5 In *Savage v Data Protection Commissioner* [2018] IEHC 122, the High Court delivered its first judgment on the "right to be forgotten" in Ireland. The case concerned a complaint made to the Data Protection Commission about Google's refusal to delist an URL link to a webpage for a discussion forum. The DPC decided that there had been no contravention of the Data Protection Act 1988 Act as the relevant link was accurate, in that it represented an opinion about the claimant that was expressed by a user of the discussion forum, rather than a verified fact. The Circuit Court allowed the claimant's appeal on the basis that it was not clear from the URL title that the original poster was expressing his/her opinion, and the URL title was therefore inaccurate. The court said that if the expression was an opinion, it should have been presented within quotation marks or parenthesis. The High Court overturned the Circuit Court's decision, finding that it had erred in not considering the underlying article to which the URL link related. If the Circuit Court had done so, it could not have come to the conclusion that the URL title was inaccurate data, factually incorrect or had the appearance of fact. The High Court also noted that Google does not carry out an editing function, and to oblige Google to place quotation marks around a URL link would involve an editing process.

6 *Data Protection Commissioner v Facebook Ireland Ltd* (Case C-311/18): in this landmark decision, the court upheld the validity of standard contractual clauses ("SCCs") in principle as a means for companies to transfer data to non-EU third countries, subject to important caveats on their use in practice. However, the EU-US Privacy Shield which facilitates the transfer of data between Europe and the US, has been deemed invalid. This case stemmed from a complaint made by Facebook user Maximilian Schrems to the Irish Data Protection Commissioner in June 2013 in relation to the processing of his personal data by Facebook. The CJEU invalidated the Safe Harbour Decision in October 2015, which was replaced by the Privacy Shield in July 2016. Mr Schrems went on to reformulate his complaint to the DPC in December 2015 to focus on the validity of SCCs, contending that US domestic legislation does not afford the same protections over personal data as exist under EU law. On 12 April 2018, the Irish High Court had referred a number of questions to the EU court.

[13.2.04] Following the judgment in *Schrems II*, the DPC decided to commence an "own volition" inquiry under s 110 of the Data Protection Act 2018 ('the 2018 Act') to consider whether the actions of Facebook Ireland in making transfers of personal data relating to individuals in the EU/EEA are lawful and whether any corrective power should be exercised by the DPC in that regard. Both Facebook and Mr Schrems brought judicial review proceedings as decided by Barniville J in May 2021.[7] The court dismissed Facebook's challenge to the DPC investigation into Facebook's international transfers of personal data.

GDPR definitions

[13.2.05] "Personal data" is defined in art 4 as meaning any information relating to an identified or identifiable natural person ("data subject"); an identifiable natural person is one who can be identified, directly or indirectly,[8] in particular by reference to an identifier such as a name, address, date of birth, email address, phone number, or location data or to one or more factors specific to the physical, physiological, genetic, mental, economic, cultural or social identity of that natural person – examples include identification through a photograph, video or audio (once it is clear to whom that information relates, or it is reasonably possible to find out). In *Nowak v Data Protection Commissioner*,[9] the CJEU adopted a broad interpretation of the concept of personal data holding that the written answers submitted by a candidate at an exam, and any comments made by an examiner constitute personal data as it is information that relates to the candidate. The meaning of personal data and its scope within the context of data access requests were considered in a series of cases by the High Court in 2018 and subsequently by the Court of Appeal.[10]

[13.2.06] Personal data does not have to be in written form, it can also be information about what a data subject looks or sounds like, for example photographs, audio or video recordings, but data protection law only applies where that information is processed by 'automated means' (such as electronically) or as part of some other sort of filing system. This is nothing new however – such

---

7 See *Facebook Ireland Ltd v Data Protection Commission and Schrems* [2020] 617 JR, [2021] IEHC 336.

8 Personal data can be information where the data subject is identified – "John's favourite colour is blue" – or where the subject is 'identifiable' – "John's sister's favourite colour is blue" (where his sister's identity is unknown, but could be ascertained using context and/or additional information). Even where personal information is partially anonymised or pseudonymised (but this could be reversed and the data subject could possibly be identified using additional information), it should still be considered personal data. However, if information is truly anonymised, irreversibly, and could not be traced back to an identified person, it is not considered personal data.

9 C-434/16, 20 December 2017.

10 *Nowak v DPC* [2018] IEHC 117; see also *Nowak v DPC* [2018] IEHC 118; *Nowak v DPC* [2018] IEHC 443; *Nowak v DPC* [2020] IECA 174 and [2020] IECA 175; *Nowak v DPC* [2018] IESCDET 196 and *Nowak v DPC* [2020] IESCDET 144. For recent case law on data protection, see the Data Protection Commission: https://www.dataprotection.ie/en/dpc-guidance/law/judgments.

video footage would also fall within the definition of "personal data" under the older legislative framework (the 1995 Directive and the Data Protection Act 1988[11] in Ireland).

[13.2.07] Data protection rights do not concern corporate entities such that written consent from a company to enter a particular contract is not required. If for instance a corporate service provider to a film production is entering a production contract, it is the company directors and employees as individuals who benefit from data protection legislation. Information about companies or public authorities is not personal data. However, information about individuals acting as sole traders, employees, partners and company directors where they are individually identifiable and the information relates to them as an individual may constitute personal data.

Living individuals

[13.2.08] Recital 27 of the GDPR clarifies that the GDPR does not apply to the personal data of deceased persons and indicates that Member States may provide for rules regarding the processing of personal data of deceased persons. Section 1 of the Data Protection Act 1988 defines "personal data" as meaning data relating to a living individual who can be identified either from the data or from the data in conjunction with other information in the possession of the data controller. Hence, data relating to deceased persons is ruled out if their estates were to seek to obtain access, post-mortem, to social media files and so forth.

Processing and control

[13.2.09] The term "processing" (Art 4(2) GDPR and as now governed by the Data Protection Act 2018) refers to any operation or set of operations performed on personal data. Processing includes storing, collecting, retrieving, using, combining, erasing and destroying personal data, and can involve automated or manual operations. A "data controller" (Art 4(7)) refers to a person, company or other body which alone or jointly with others decides the purposes and methods of processing personal data. A "data processor" refers to a person, company or other body which processes personal data on behalf of a data controller (Art 4(8)). Processors do not decide how or why processing takes place, but instead carry out processing on the orders of a controller.

Notable fines

[13.2.10] Compliance with GDPR for filmmakers, content producers, print

11 s 1 of that Act defines "personal data" as meaning data relating to a living individual who can be identified either from the data or from the data in conjunction with other information in the possession of the data controller. See ss 7 and 8 of the 2018 Act in respect of repeals and revocation of the 1988 Act and the provisions thereof which have survived the enactment of the 2018 Act.

media, online publishers and indeed social media platforms is much more onerous, although similar to what formerly obtained, than previous domestic data protection law with provision for substantial fines and compensation arising out of data breaches by data controllers and processors.

[13.2.11] By way of illustration generally, Amazon fell victim to the GDPR enforcement mechanisms when fined a record €746 million by Luxembourg's privacy regulator in July 2021 for failing to process personal data in compliance with the GDPR's consent rules, Amazon in the immediate aftermath however signalling its intent to appeal the ruling. The Luxembourg Administrative Tribunal will hear the appeal in January 2024.

[13.2.12] The highest GDPR fine of 2022 (€405 million) was levied against Meta-owned social networking platform Instagram by the Irish Data Protection Commission. It related to Instagram's violation of children's privacy through the publication of email addresses and phone numbers. Children aged between 13 and 17 using the platform were permitted to use business accounts where both the email addresses and phone numbers could be accessed. In addition, the accounts were not set to private by default and could be viewed by the public in some instances.

Damages for data protection actions

[13.2.13] If the 2018 Act is breached, a data subject may initiate court proceedings as termed a "data protection action" in s 117. The Circuit Court concurrently with the High Court has jurisdiction to hear and determine data protection actions. The compensation recoverable in a data protection action in the Circuit Court shall not exceed the amount standing prescribed as the limit of that court's jurisdiction in tort actions (€75,000). The court hearing a data protection action shall have the power to grant to the plaintiff an injunction or declaration, or compensation for damage suffered by the plaintiff as a result of the infringement of a relevant enactment. Irish data protection actions can now include claims for compensation for stress and emotional suffering, whereas prior to the GDPR, only compensation for financial and other material loss could be recovered in Ireland.[12]

[13.2.14] "Damage" is now clearly defined as including physical damage (Recital 75 GDPR, among others) and "material and non-material damage" (see Art 82 GDPR and ss 128(9) and 117(10) of the 2018 Act). Material damage

---

12 Thus in *Collins v FBD Insurance Plc* [2013] IEHC 137 Feeney J overturned the Circuit Court which had awarded general damages in the sum of €15,000 for distress caused to the plaintiff for various data protection breaches by the defendant in the course of handling the plaintiff's insurance claim for the theft of his van. The High Court found that individuals must prove that they have in fact suffered damage arising from a breach of their data protection rights before they can be entitled to compensation, and furthermore that non-financial loss was not recoverable.

involves actual damage that is quantifiable, and non-material damage covers any non-financial damage, such as pain and suffering, shame, affronts to dignity, trauma and anxiety. It remains to be seen how the Irish courts[13] will approach compensating a person for non-material damage, including in terms of defining the concept and in assessing the quantum of damages to be awarded.[14] Where the GDPR has been infringed, there is liability (whether or not distress is caused) unless a controller or processor can prove it is not the source of non-compliance (Art 82). Significantly, a litigant does not have to prove fault or negligence to initiate proceedings.

The landmark ruling in Österreichische Post

[13.2.15] Even more significantly still, the CJEU ruled in early May 2023 (C-300/21)[15] that there is no threshold that non-material damage needs to pass before data subjects can make a claim. Mere upset might suffice. The Austrian Supreme Court had proposed the ECJ would introduce a threshold for such claims. The decision explains that:

> making compensation for non-pecuniary damage subject to a certain threshold of seriousness would risk undermining the consistency of the regime established by the GDPR, since the graduation of such a threshold, on which the possibility or otherwise of obtaining that compensation would depend, would be liable to fluctuate according to the assessment of the judges.

[13] However, some guidance has now come from the CJEU on non-material damage claims. Both Germany (see fn 14) and Austria had requested separate preliminary rulings from the CJEU on a number of issues in relation to compensation and claims for non-material damage. The Austrian matter (*Österreichische Post), post-CJEU ruling,* has been sent back to the domestic court for assessment of damages.

[14] Germany's Federal Constitutional Court ruled that the CJEU must be asked to clarify when a claim for damages is recognised under Art 82 and when damage is to be assumed. The court overturned a ruling of the Goslar local court from 2019 in respect of the unlawful sending of an advertising email. The recipient had filed a lawsuit because his email address had been used without his consent in breach of Art 6. In addition to injunctive relief and information about his stored data, he also claimed damages under Art 82. The local court ruled that the recipient of the advertisement was not entitled to non-material damages due to the lack of materiality. It had only been a single advertising email which had not been sent at an inopportune time, which had clearly shown that it was advertising due to its appearance and which had not made it necessary to deal with it at length, the court said. However, since the GDPR is EU law and there was (at that point) no CJEU case law on this issue, the federal court concluded that the question of when non-material damage gives rise to a claim for financial compensation must be referred to the EU court.

[15] *UI v Österreichische Post AG.* The plaintiff involved, an Austrian attorney, sought €1,000 in damages from a postal service provider after an algorithm processed his personal data – in a manner which the courts found to be illegal – and extrapolated that he likely supported mega libertarian right-wing populist types in the country's far-right Freedom Party (FPÖ). UI was angered and offended after he learned about the affinity specifically attributed to him by Österreichische Post when he performed a subject access request. In the original filing, he said that he had not consented to the processing of his personal data, and additionally had found the assignation insulting and shameful, as well as extremely damaging to his reputation. In addition, Österreichische Post's conduct caused him great upset and a loss of confidence, and also a feeling of public exposure.

The court also offered some clarity around assessment of damages more generally, saying it was for the legal system of each Member State to decide.

Case law

[13.2.16] In a seminal UK judgment in November 2021 that is set to alter the landscape of non-material damage claims in Britain and beyond, the Supreme Court in *Lloyd v Google LLC*[16] rejected the idea that non-material breaches of the Data Protection Act 1998 entitle claimants to compensation for "loss of control" of their personal data. The court held that, on the proper interpretation of s 13 of the above legislation, the term "damage" refers to material damage or mental distress distinct from, and caused by, unlawful processing of personal data in contravention of the Act, and does not refer to the act of unlawful processing itself. The court thus held that claims under UK law (post-Brexit) must reach a threshold of seriousness to be eligible for compensation.

[13.2.17] The Dublin Circuit Court in the case of *Cunniam v Parcel Connect Ltd* [2023] IECC 1 granted a stay in January 2023 on proceedings brought by a data subject where non-material damages were alleged, pending six decisions awaited from the CJEU relating to non-material damage claims. The court held that not granting the stay would substantially prejudice the defendants' case, and would lead to the risk of an irreconcilable judgment being produced by the court. A decision is also awaited in the Dublin Circuit Court case (record number 2019/04546) of *Kaminski v Ballymaguire Foods Ltd*.

[13.2.18] Elsewhere, *obiter* comments by Whelan J for the Court of Appeal in *Shawl Property Investments v A&B* [2021] IECA 53 state that nothing in the 2018 Act "suggests that a data protection action is a tort of strict liability" and regard should be had to the principle of proportionality in evaluating claims for breaches of the GDPR. There has been no consideration of Art 82 in any written decision of the Irish superior courts to date. Meanwhile, the Advocate General delivered an opinion in the *Österreichische Post AG* case above which was welcomed by parties facing data breach claims as it required a *de minimis* threshold

---

[16] [2021] UKSC 50. As regards British class action type lawsuits, Google won its appeal after the Supreme Court was not persuaded to allow privacy damage to be compensated for collectively, killing off that claim and damaging the prospect of similarly representative privacy litigations. However, an action in respect of possible GDPR/privacy law breaches has been instituted against TikTok by a (then) 12-year-old girl who was granted anonymity by the court to bring the claim that the social networking site is processing children's data unlawfully. In March 2022, the High Court allowed the matter to proceed and to serve TikTok's overseas entities, including in China, the Cayman Islands and the US. In 2023, the UK Information Commissioner's Office issued TikTok with a fine of £12.7 million for breaching UK data protection law, including rules intended to protect children (whereby TikTok would have needed to obtain parental consent to lawfully process data relating to minors). Meanwhile, the Dutch Data Protection Authority imposed a fine of €750,000 in 2021 on TikTok for violating the privacy of young children.

of damage to be met in a claim for non-material damages arising from a GDPR breach.[17] However, as seen, the CJEU did not follow this opinion.

CONSENT TO RECORD AND PUBLISH

[13.3.01] Audiovisual producers henceforth need to review their release forms used with interviewees and other contributors who appear in documentaries and to include data protection clauses in actor, performer (including music performer) and crew agreements.[18] The same holds true for dance, theatre and stage productions. Individuals by law withdraw their consent to appear in a film, even if consent was originally given. However, producers may have a legitimate interest in using sound and audiovisual recordings of individuals even if consent as initially provided were to subsequently be withdrawn. It is nonetheless important to be able to demonstrate that due consideration has been given to the impact of persons appearing in a film and that a data protection policy is made available to the data subjects concerned when requested.

Journalistic and freedom of expression exemption

[13.3.02] There are certain exemptions contained within s 43 of the 2018 Act[19] which section gives effect to Art 85 of the GDPR, which provides that it is for national law to reconcile the right to the protection of personal data with the right to freedom of expression and information.[20] This exemption which replaced the freedom of expression exemption for public interest journalism formerly set out in s 22 of the Data Protection Acts 1988 to 2003 is of broader application. Section 43 contains a challenging test to apply in practice and provides little guidance to those wishing to avail of the exemption (however it provides that in order to take account of the importance of the right to freedom of expression

---

17 Davinia Brennan and Thomas Condon, *Irish Circuit Court Stays Compensation Claim For Non-Material Damages* (2023). Matheson (solicitors). Available at: https://www.matheson.com/insights/detail/irish-circuit-court-stays-compensation-claim-for-non-material-damages [Accessed 11 April 2023].

18 And relating to performers such as dancers in music videos.

19 The processing of personal data for the purpose of exercising the right to freedom of expression and information, including processing for journalistic purposes or for the purposes of academic, artistic or literary expression, shall be exempt from compliance with a provision specified in s 43(2) where, having regard to the importance of the right of freedom of expression and information in a democratic society, compliance with the provision would be incompatible with such purposes. The DPC may, on its own initiative, refer any question of law which involves consideration of whether processing of personal data is exempt in accordance with s 43(1) to the High Court for its determination. An appeal shall by leave of the High Court lie from a determination of that court on a question of law pursuant to s 43(3) to the Court of Appeal. In order to take account of the importance of the right to freedom of expression and information in a democratic society that right shall be interpreted in a broad manner [as *per* s 43(5)].

20 Both the right to protection of personal data and the right to freedom of expression and information are enshrined in Arts 8 and 11 of the EU Charter of Fundamental Rights respectively.

and information in a democratic society the right shall be interpreted in a broad manner). Moreover, the section makes clear that in the event of a conflict between the GDPR and the right to freedom of expression and information, the right to freedom of expression and information takes precedence.

[13.3.03] Cases before the Data Protection Commission and the courts are likely to play a significant role in the formulation of more detailed guidelines on the operation of this exemption in Irish law. The exemption in using personal data with a view to publishing journalistic material might primarily relate to e-creation of journalistic material for use on-air or online where there is no commercial gain for the station.[21]

[13.3.04] In early 2020, the Commission has this to say on the matter of personal data being used for the purpose of exercising the right to freedom of expression, including for journalistic, academic, artistic or literary purposes:

> In practice this means that data protection law may not assist someone who is upset at an opinion being expressed about them in a newspaper article or other media – as the publisher may be able to rely on a 'journalistic exemption' which allows for publication of the personal data in question. The idea behind this is that a free press plays an important role in society and that society would not benefit from restricting the ability of news outlets to publish opinions about identifiable individuals when reporting matters in the public interest...It is worth noting that there may be other legal avenues, aside from data protection, available to individuals who are aggrieved at an expression of opinion about them appearing in the news.[22]

The Campbell proceedings

[13.3.05] In *Campbell*,[23] the court considered whether the subject personal data released by the newspaper of the supermodel was sensitive personal data defined *inter alia* in the 1998 UK Act (since then replaced by the UK's own post-Brexit GDPR) as concerning the racial or ethnic origin of the data subject and her physical or mental health or condition. The judge stated at paras 85 to 87:

> In my judgment the contention, that the published photographs of the claimant are sensitive personal data because they consist of information as to her racial or ethnic origin, has no materiality or relevance to the circumstances of this case. The claimant is proud to be a leading black fashion model and it is part of her life style and profession to be photographed as a black woman. She has suffered no damage or distress because the photographs disclose that she is black.

---

21 Such as where it is not for the purposes of advertising or sponsorship sales or competitions.

22 Data Protection Commission, *Opinions–Everyone's got one, but does data protection law apply to them?* (2020). Available at: https://www.dataprotection.ie/en/dpc-guidance/blogs/opinions-everyones-got-one-does-data-protection-law-apply-them#:~:text=One%20example%20of%20the%20interaction,%2C%20including%20for%20journalistic%2C%20academic%2C [Accessed 11 April 2023].

23 *supra* at fn 3.

> However, it should not be understood that I am ruling that images whether photographic or otherwise that disclose whether from physical characteristic or dress racial or ethnic origins cannot amount to sensitive personal data.
>
> In my judgment the information as to the nature of and details of the therapy that the claimant was receiving at Narcotics Anonymous including the photographs with captions was clearly information as to her physical or mental health or condition, that is her drug addiction and therefore "sensitive personal data".

[13.3.06] It was argued on behalf of the defendant newspaper that it had a statutory defence (under s 32 of the 1998 UK Act as to a possible journalistic defence)[24] or exemption (aimed at limiting a disproportionate restraint on freedom of expression by publication such as the granting of injunctions to stop publication) being that the processing was undertaken with a view to the publication of journalistic material; the data controller reasonably believed that having regard in particular to the special importance of the public interest in freedom of expression, publication would be in the public interest, and the data controller reasonably believed that, in all the circumstances, compliance with that provision was incompatible with the special purposes of journalism as provided for in s 3 of the 1998 UK Act.

[13.3.07] However, Morland J held the defendant was not entitled to exemption from liability under s 32. That section had no application to the claimant's entitlement to compensation under s 13 of the Act for distress caused by the publication. Moreover he was of the view that disclosure of details of the claimant's therapy was not in the substantial public interest. It was not in connection with the commission of drug offences but the claimant's efforts to avoid committing drug offences.

[13.3.08] In relation to a s 13(3) defence (proof that in this case the publisher had taken such care as in all the circumstances was reasonably required to comply with the requirement concerned) the judge has this to say at para 121:

> In my judgment the defendant has utterly failed to establish a Section 13(3) defence. Indeed in his evidence Mr Piers Morgan made it clear that in his opinion the claimant had lost all right to privacy.

[13.3.09] The court concluded (at paras 163 to 164) in addition to holding that the total sum for damages for breach of confidentiality and for compensation under s 13 of the 1998 UK Act was £3,500:

---

24 Where under that section the processing is undertaken with a view to the publication by any person of any journalistic, literary or artistic material, the data controller reasonably believes that, having regard in particular to the special importance of the public interest in freedom of expression, publication would be in the public interest, and the data controller reasonably believes that, in all the circumstances, compliance with that provision is incompatible with the "special purpose" of journalism.

> Yet I am not satisfied that Miss Campbell suffered any significantly increased distress or injury to feelings from the manner in which the defendants conducted the trial.
>
> However, I am satisfied that Miss Carroll's article sounds in aggravated damages. That article did not only criticise the merits of her claim in strong and colourful language but also to use Mr Caldecott's phrase "Trashed her as a person" in a highly offensive and hurtful manner. That trashing entitles her to aggravated damages. I assess aggravated damages in the sum of £1000.

[13.3.10] By a three-to-two majority, the House of Lords in its judgment[25] reinstated the damages awarded in the High Court, and reversed the Court of Appeal's award of costs in favour of the *Mirror* against Campbell, the Court of Appeal decision having relied heavily on the fact that Campbell had denied having a drugs problem.

Public interest

[13.3.11] Where the GDPR and Irish domestic law are not observed, there may be a public interest reason or defence. Necessary and proportionate restrictions (s 60 of the 2018 Act) on obligations of controllers and rights of data subjects under the GDPR may arise for important objectives of general public interest such as for the prevention, detection, investigation and prosecution of criminal offences. Domestic legislation may be made in the future restricting GDPR rights and obligations where such restrictions are necessary for the purposes of safeguarding important objectives of general public interest including preventing threats to public security and public safety; preventing, detecting, investigating and prosecuting breaches of discipline by, or the unfitness or incompetence of, persons who are or were authorised by law to carry on a profession or any other regulated activity; and preventing, detecting, investigating or prosecuting breaches of ethics for regulated professions. Other important objectives of public interest include safeguarding public health, social security, social protection and humanitarian activities, protecting the health, safety, dignity and wellbeing of individuals at work against risks arising out of or in connection with their employment, and protecting members of the public against dishonesty or other improper conduct of persons in the provision of banking, insurance, investment or other financial services.

CONTRIBUTOR RELEASES: GROUNDS FOR USE OF PERSONAL DATA

[13.4.01] Personal data can only be used (i.e. controlled or processed) if a business has lawful grounds to do so. Under the GDPR, it is arguably more difficult for those grounds to be lawfully engaged. Perhaps the most significant change is

---

[25] *Campbell v Mirror Group Newspapers Ltd* [2004] UKHL 22.

to the most often-cited ground for processing, namely, consent. If businesses process personal data on this ground, they do so on the basis that the individual to whom the personal data relates has agreed for the data to be processed and used in a specific way. In the context of video content, producers should typically have individuals sign releases or consent forms which are intended to allow an individual's personal data to be controlled and processed. Contributors should be made aware for what purposes their data will be used and, in the case of minors, this needs to be carefully explained to and understood by their parents or legal guardians before they (and the relevant child where applicable) sign such release.

[13.4.02] Consent must be freely given, specific, informed and unambiguous. Such consent must also be given by individuals providing "clear affirmative action" that they consent to processing. In other words, businesses can no longer imply consent from an individual. For example, it may be that some filmmakers have traditionally been of the view that, by the fact that contributors have agreed to be sound-recorded as part of a documentary, television production, radio podcast or interview, they have likewise consented to their image being used in conjunction with (for instance in advertising and promoting) that project or for their name to be released. However, attempting to demonstrate that valid consent has been obtained in this way is highly unlikely to comply with the requirements of the GDPR. Instead, it is in practice required that production companies would need to expressly obtain active consent from an individual that the footage/recording is to be used for each specific purpose. It would not be sufficient to state that, because individuals agreed to be filmed, that they also by extension agreed for that footage to be used as part of a marketing campaign.

[13.4.03] Further, at the time of obtaining consent, individuals should be specifically made aware (*per* Art 13(2)(c) GDPR) that they are free to withdraw consent at any time but also that this would not (necessarily) render processing on the basis of consent being given prior to withdrawal unlawful. If consent is withdrawn, processing must cease, although exemptions can arise as is the case with possible s 43 (2018 Act) artistic/freedom of expression exceptions cited above and in light of the matters set out in the next section below.

Legitimate interest in using personal data

[13.4.04] Audiovisual producers (and media organisations generally) may incur very substantial expenditure in creating content which they intend to use as part of their marketing and branding for years to come or indeed much larger sums again for production and exploitation of a film/television programme. If that video content is created on the basis of individuals having consented to use of their imagery, but that consent can be withdrawn at any time, is there a risk that the producer will be required to stop using that footage if consent is withdrawn? Not necessarily. Consent is not the only ground for processing data under the GDPR.

[13.4.05] It may well be the case that a second lawful ground for processing by a business having a "legitimate interest" will be relied upon much more by producers. For most activities, a company may well be permitted to continue to use and process personal data even if individuals have withdrawn their consent for the business to do so, on the basis of the producer's having such "legitimate interest", the most flexible of the six lawful bases for data processing (though of course it should not be the default basis for all processing). One needs to be transparent when relying on legitimate interests, clearly explaining in the relevant privacy policy what are the legitimate interests of the processing.

[13.4.06] The term "legitimate interest" is not well defined under the GDPR and its scope is open to interpretation. This is arguably a positive for producers. In brief, a business is likely to have a legitimate interest in continuing to process personal data where there is a real commercial interest being pursued through such continuation of data processing; the processing is absolutely necessary in order for the business to pursue that interest (i.e. the interest cannot be pursued in another way which is proportionate); and the processing is balanced against the impact such processing will have on the fundamental rights and freedoms of data subjects.

[13.4.07] As such, whether or not legitimate interest will be relied upon is a matter of degree and individual circumstance. For example, in considering whether or not it is proportionate and legitimate for a business to continue using video footage which contains imagery of identifiable individuals who have withdrawn consent to its use, will depend on various factors such as where the footage will be used, if the individuals are a main element of the footage or whether, for instance, the footage indicates that the individuals have links or associations with people or a particular ideology which they no longer have. Other factors are the likely impact for those individuals of continuing to use the footage and the impact on the business so processing. In particular, controllers should pay special attention and afford extra protection to the interests or fundamental rights and freedoms of the data subject where the data subject is a child.

[13.4.08] In relation to whether legitimate interests pursued by the controller or by a third party are to be overridden by the interests or fundamental rights and freedoms of the data subject, the DPC commented in its December 2019 guidance note, *Legal Bases for Processing Personal Data* that:

> A large part of the balancing test undertaken by controllers should also be based on common sense and the expectations of the data subject: If a data subject would not reasonably expect this type of processing of their personal data, or if it would cause unjustified harm to their interests, rights, or freedoms, their interests are likely to override the legitimate interests upon which the controller is seeking to rely. Similarly, the greater the intrusion a certain processing operation has on the data protection rights of an individual, the greater the justification needed to ground that processing. A balancing test is needed as a controller's interests will not always align with the interests of the

data subject(s). However, where there is a conflict or tension between these interests it is not the case that processing can never take place, but rather the controller can only process the personal data where their interests provide a clear and proportionate justification for the impact on the individual.

Privacy policies (including data protection and social media policies)

[13.4.09] One of the key requirements under the GDPR is that businesses demonstrate that they have considered the impact their control or processing will have on individuals, and that they have, through risk assessment, put preventative measures in place to limit such impact. It is also recommended that businesses ensure that they are able to evidence that they have considered the grounds on which data will be processed. If organisations can illustrate that they have done this, the negative impact upon them in the event of a data breach is likely to be reduced. A robust manner in which this can be proven is by setting this information out in an up-to-date privacy policy, clearly outlining all the basic information a controller and processor must provide at the time of collecting and processing personal data under the GDPR. This information includes when, how and why data is processed, and the grounds for doing so. Having individuals agree that this information has been provided to them at the time of collecting data will assist in proving compliance with the Regulation.

SPECIAL CATEGORIES OF PERSONAL DATA (ART 9 GDPR)

[13.5.01] Certain special categories of personal data should not be processed except in limited circumstances. Processing of personal data revealing racial or ethnic origin, political opinions, religious or philosophical beliefs, or trade union membership, and the processing of genetic data, biometric data for the purpose of uniquely identifying a natural person, data concerning health or data concerning a natural person's sex life or sexual orientation is prohibited except as below.

[13.5.02] Such processing requires both a legal basis under Art 6 (lawfulness of processing) as well as meeting one of the exceptions in Art 9 (such as explicit consent or protection of vital interests) which allow such data to be processed. It is the responsibility of controllers to identify on which legal basis they are relying for each type of processing of personal data in which they engage. This information should be provided to data subjects, as part of the principle of transparency, and controllers should be poised to identify the legal basis on which they are relying for processing if asked by a data subject or the DPC.

DATA PROTECTION COMMISSION

[13.6.01] The DPC which replaced the Data Protection Commissioner is the national independent data protection authority responsible for upholding the fundamental right of individuals in the EU to have their personal data protected.

Hence, the DPC is the Irish supervisory authority for the GDPR and also has functions and powers related to other important regulatory frameworks including the Law Enforcement Directive[26] and the Irish e-Privacy Regulations (2011).[27] The DPC was established in May 2018 pursuant to s 10 of the 2018 Act. Part 2 (ss 9-27) of the Act sets out its powers, functions, self-regulation procedures as well as provisions in relation, for example, to Commission membership (s 15 allows for up to three Commissioners for Data Protection – at present there is one commissioner only, Helen Dixon, and six deputy commissioners/department heads), and accountability of the commissioner(s) to Oireachtas committees.

Administrative fines

[13.6.02] Section 136 of the 2018 Act sets out the powers of the DPC to decide to impose administrative fines.[28] Section 137 concerns appeals against the imposition of administrative fines – a controller or processor that is the subject of a decision to impose an administrative fine may, within 28 days from the date on which notice of the decision concerned was given to it, appeal to the court against the decision. The court may confirm the decision the subject of the appeal; replace the decision with such other decision as it considers just and appropriate, including a decision to impose a different fine or no fine; or annul the decision (s 142(3)). The court shall act in accordance with art 83 GDPR. "Court" means the Circuit Court where the amount of the administrative fine the subject of the appeal does not exceed €75,000, or in any other case, the High Court (s 142 (6)).

[13.6.03] Where a controller or processor does not appeal in accordance with the provisions of s 142 against a decision by the DPC to impose an administrative fine on the controller or processor, the DPC shall, as soon as is practicable after the expiration of the period referred to in s 142(1) (within 28 days from the date on which notice of the fine decision was given to the controller/processor) and on notice to the controller or processor concerned, make an application in a summary manner to the Circuit Court for confirmation of the decision. The Circuit Court shall on the hearing of an application confirm the decision the subject of the application unless it sees good reason not to do so (s 143(2)).

Offences

[13.6.04] Aside from offences as found throughout the 2018 Act (such as failure

---

26 Directive EU 2016/680.

27 SI No 336 of 2011 giving effect to two EU Directives.

28 For example, in *Data Protection Commission v Tusla* (unreported, Dublin Circuit Court, 4 November 2020, record number 2020/02845), on the application of the DPC, an order was made by the Circuit Court pursuant to s 143(2) of the 2018 Act confirming an administrative fine levied by the DPC on Tusla (in the sum of €75,000) pursuant to a decision of the DPC dated 7 April 2020 following an inquiry taken under the Act. Costs were also awarded to the DPC.

to comply with an information notice or enforcement notice, or obstructing or impeding authorised officers appointed by the DPC under s 129 in the performance of their functions) and aside too from the administrative fines provisions below, s 144 relates to unauthorised disclosure by a data processor[29] who will be liable on summary conviction, to a class A fine (maximum fine on summary conviction €5,000) or imprisonment for a term not exceeding 12 months or both; or, on conviction on indictment, to a fine not exceeding €50,000 or imprisonment for a term not exceeding five years, or both. The offence contains a *mens rea* requirement of "knowingly" or "recklessly" contravening the section.

[13.6.05] Section 145 (disclosure by a person of personal data obtained without prior authority from the controller or processor) will give rise, *inter alia*, to liability on summary conviction, to a class A fine or imprisonment for a term not exceeding 12 months or both; or, on conviction on indictment, to a fine not exceeding €50,000 or imprisonment for a term not exceeding five years, or both.

[13.6.06] Section 146 governs offences by directors and officers of bodies corporate. Where an offence under the 2018 Act is committed by a body corporate and is proved to have been committed with the consent or connivance of, or to be attributable to any neglect on the part of, a person being a director, manager, secretary or other officer of the body corporate or a person who was purporting to act in any such capacity, that person, as well as the body corporate, shall be guilty of that offence and shall be liable to be proceeded against and punished as if guilty of the first-mentioned offence.

[13.6.07] Section 147 deals with the issue of prosecution of summary offences by the DPC. Notwithstanding s 10(4) of the Petty Sessions (Ireland) Act 1851 (the usual time period for charges to be brought as regards minor offences is within six months), summary proceedings for an offence under the Act may be brought at any time within three years from the date on which the offence was alleged to have been committed, or if, at the expiry of that period, persons against whom the proceedings are to be brought are outside the state, within six months of the date on which they next enter the state, whichever is the later, provided that no such proceedings shall be commenced later than five years from the date on which the offence concerned was alleged to have been committed.

Fines and enforcement; civil law damages

[13.6.08] The GDPR itself (Art 83(4) and (5)) significantly increases the scope and nature of administrative fines for non-compliance, with the effect that failure to address data protection compliance obligations could prove very costly, in financial terms, for businesses. Organisations will be potentially subject to fines of up to ten million euro or two percent of total worldwide annual turnover (whichever is greater) for serious breaches; and €20 million or four percent of

29 Without the prior authority of the controller on behalf of whom the data are processed.

total worldwide annual turnover (whichever is greater) for very serious breaches. In addition, and for the first time under Irish law, as above-mentioned, data subjects will have a right to sue for non-material damage in addition to material damage arising from data privacy breaches.

Chapter 14

Filming Permits and Drone Operation

INTRODUCTION

[14.1.01] The practical and legal considerations for obtaining filming permits and attendant insurance cover should be fully explored by producers at pre-production stage. Statutory time periods may need to be factored in such as in the case of road closures or application notice periods to be observed under local authority bye-laws.

[14.1.02] A film director must have the capacity to exercise full control of a shoot and this, when shooting in public, can only be assured when all necessary permits and insurances are in place. In the case of production insurance, it is a condition set by public financiers (e.g. Screen Ireland) and broadcasters which will require to be named as joint loss payees on such policy. Failing to possess the requisite permit, permission or licence in the case of public and private locations, use of props and depiction of copyrighted or trademarked items results in corners being cut and filming in a heightened state of unease, which in turn almost invariably engenders legal and other complications which cannot necessarily be remedied in the editing suite. The rule is therefore simple – obtain a permit for exterior locations where one is required.[1] In the case of interior shooting, consent will also be required from the owner or occupier with a location release agreement being signed to ward off litigation claims.

[14.1.03] Not least because of its generous tax incentives, Ireland is a film friendly nation and a wealth of systems are in place to assist, not deter, creative productions. The services of Coillte, Waterways Ireland, county film commissions and each of the twenty-six county councils, city councils (Dublin, Cork, Galway), city and county councils (Limerick and Waterford) or town councils across Ireland are readily available to filmmakers.[2]

---

1 Special dispensations on permit fees may apply to low-budget or micro-budget films and projects where any revenues are intended for charity or comprise student productions.

2 In addition, Screen Ireland operates a database of over 1,000 regional film locations as well as comprehensive online databases of production companies, crew and service companies outside Dublin. It provides contact details for the Network of Regional Film Offices throughout Ireland. The Irish Film and Television Network also provides an online database

[14.1.04] On all medium to large productions, producers will likely retain the services of a locations scout and/or a unit production manager to arrange all permits, payment of fees and to effect submission of attendant application documentation. Such crew should be armed too with location agreements/ licences or releases in the case of private residential premises and commercial or public properties including any sets involving hotels, retail outlets, bars, restaurants and state-owned buildings.

[14.1.05] This chapter summarises the wider issues surrounding audiovisual productions from crowd release notices, data protection laws and drone operations to erecting temporary structures, obtaining permits for certain filming equipment and machinery, road closures, nudity, use of replica firearms and explosions, the procedures for dressing cast in fake Garda uniforms and advising local residents of an upcoming shoot. It will also address risk assessments to be conducted by the production's health and safety consultant required as part of a producer's statutory safety obligations and as pre-requisites to the issuance of a filming permit in Ireland and in fulfilment of public financier requirements as to safety procedures.[3]

[14.1.06] The same factors apply if shooting in the UK, mainland Europe or elsewhere – a producer's first port of call could be the national equivalent of Screen Ireland or Screen Producers Ireland which can assist with local crew knowledge and resources and with key information pertaining to local authority procedures. Moreover, producers are highly recommended to engage the services of an experienced locations manager who has worked on a multitude of diverse projects.[4]

CONSEQUENCES FOR FAILURE TO PROCURE PERMITS AND PRODUCTION INSURANCE

[14.2.01] Failure to procure a permit when required may lead to criminal prosecution under the local bye-laws of the various city and county councils throughout Ireland. Aside from non-compliance with insurance requirements as specified by public funders, if a policy of public liability insurance is not in

---

of location resources from architectural to urban, rural, historical, coastal and specialist (such as golf courses, stables, cemeteries, zoos and swimming pools). Local knowledge and information on what documentation is required in terms of permit applications can be requested from each local authority throughout Ireland.

3 In the case of a film production loan for example, Screen Ireland will require, as a condition precedent, a copy of the producer borrower company's health and safety policy relating to the film.

4 Such locations manager or unit production manager would advise for example that the Office of Public Works is to be approached for a permit rather than Dublin City Council in relation to buildings and offices of central government departments and agencies, and that filming in St Stephen's Green or the Iveagh Gardens likewise requires the green light from the OPW/Heritage Ireland rather than from the city council.

place, particularly for filming in urban areas, together with the necessary permit, a production company runs the risk of losing professional credibility: cast and crew will expect matters to be meticulously organised in advance. On-the-fly guerrilla shooting is never advisable. Ireland is a small island nation and filmmakers can quickly alienate themselves from the authorities in the case of repeated breaches of legislation and local regulation. In the event of not possessing a permit, a production may well be shut down with resultant time and cost sequelae and, of course, reputational damage.

[14.2.02] Additionally, in the absence of insurance, in the circumstances of a material damage or personal injuries claim against a production company, litigation proceedings could, if money is not available to meet a settlement pay-out or court award of damages, result in the winding up of a production company under the Companies Act 2014 and sale of its assets and equipment to satisfy such claim. Worse still, if operating as a sole trader, the owner is personally liable for business debts.

[14.2.03] If operating absent a permit, as alluded to in the introduction, short-cuts will inevitably be taken in haste. This may well result in a realisation by the film editor that certain rushes are unusable (in the case, for example, of distinguishable but uncleared passers-by[5] appearing in the background or an insurmountable IP law issue presenting). Frenzied filming will mean that control over the production set is lost. A director will ideally require ample time in a fully managed setting to allow for multiple scene takes. Only by holding a permit and public liability insurance can peace of mind be secured and a professional, safe and well-planned system of work guaranteed.

[14.2.04] Lastly, cast and their agents and production crew (and of course investors, funding bodies and insurers) will expect all pertinent paperwork to be in place and will offer their services on the basis that the producers will observe local authority bye-laws and safety legislation. Failure to apply for permits or insurance may mean that a film is doomed before it even begins. It may also constitute breach of funder and crew contracts in certain instances.

PRIVATE PROPERTY

[14.3.01] A permit from a private land or buildings owner is not required. Instead, the owner's consent to film there by way of licence will be necessitated through execution of a location agreement or release form by the occupier or the owner's duly authorised agent or representative.[6] To guard against injury to any party during filming, owners of private property, being reluctant to claim

---

5 Clearance in this connection is achieved through placement at the filming location(s) of crowd release notices as discussed from [14.12.02].

6 For instance, a tenant of commercial property, or a restaurant or music venue manager on behalf of the proprietor/tenant occupier.

against their home, business or public liability insurance, will typically seek an indemnity from the film producer or film production company to hold the property owner harmless against all claims that may arise due to the filming operations, including for any damage occasioned to the property. The producer, therefore, will need to effect appropriate personal injury and material damage insurance cover. From the producer's perspective, the agreement will require the owner to waive any claims for defamation, privacy and breaches of IP rights, as well as indemnifying the production for accidents or loss to third parties arising from the owner's negligence.

PRIVATE AND PUBLIC PROPERTY (EXTERIOR FILMING)

[14.4.01] Simply because one holds public liability insurance and a filming permit does not mean that directors are thereby given free rein to film whatever they choose with impunity. One seemingly innocuous example is where a row of cars is filmed and some car registration plates are clearly visible (in which case data protection and privacy considerations arise as discussed below). Another instance is that filming is not permitted outside Department of Justice properties, Department of Defence properties, national embassies, consulate offices or airports (except where express consent might be granted in a particular case).

[14.4.02] Further still, a third party business's reputation, trade or goodwill may be damaged if, for example, a sex, crime, fight or drug-use scene were to be filmed outside one of its supermarket properties. This may well land a production in the High Court defending a claim for defamation (s 12 of the Defamation Act 2009 states the provisions of that Act apply to a body corporate in the same manner as they apply to a natural person).[7] Defamatory statements as defined in s 2 of the statute include visual images and sounds and, consequently, this would include film clips which are "published" when aired.

[14.4.03] A business will be keen to ensure its trade or premises does not become associated with antisocial or criminal behaviour, which adverse association may ensue when the film is released. The owner's[8] consent (such owner having most likely perused the script in the case of questionable material) should therefore be obtained and a release signed. Otherwise, the name of the business should not be visible on screen. Alternatively, set dressing could be employed to disguise the premises.

---

7 A company may accordingly bring a defamation action under the Act in respect of a statement concerning it which that body corporate claims is defamatory whether or not it has incurred or is likely to incur financial loss as a result of the publication of that statement. There may be legislative reforms in the future however to provide for a financial loss requirement.

8 Ideally, a company director or the company secretary should give consent on behalf of the company in the case of a company. In the case of a sole trader business, the person who owns the business will give the requisite consent.

[14.4.04] Protection for certain property owners is bolstered as further outlined below by the Copyright and Related Rights Act 2000 ('the 2000 Act'), s 52(3) of which provides that the copyright in a "work" (including a building with copyright-protected elements such as architectural design or artwork) shall not be regarded as included in an incidental manner[9] in another work where it is included in a manner where the interests of the owner of the copyright are unreasonably prejudiced. Prejudice may result where a licence/location fee should have been paid but was not, or the work was reproduced without the owner's consent (which, depending on the script and action on-screen, may also have a bearing on attendant moral rights in the event of derogatory or other adverse treatment of the work). Again, a location agreement will put these matters beyond doubt.

Artistic works on public display

[14.4.05] There is a statutory exemption in relation to copyright pertaining to public buildings and representation of certain artistic works on public display. Section 93 of the 2000 Act provides that copyright in buildings, sculptures, models for buildings and works of artistic craftsmanship, where permanently situated in a public place or in premises open to the public, is not infringed by for instance making a photograph or film of it, or broadcasting or including in a cable programme service, an image of it, or by the making available to the public of copies thereof. However, there are separate bye-laws in place by city and county councils which nonetheless may require a fee as part of the permit process for shooting an iconic city image or structure for example (see para [14.8.01]).

Other considerations

[14.4.06] Another issue relates to product placement. Broadcasters in particular do not wish to offer organisations free advertising by having their business (or product/service) shown for a considerable period on screen. They may seek to limit or restrict this practice in their distribution agreements with the licensor production company. This eventuality is also restricted by BAI/Media Commission product placement rules discussed later in Chapter 31.

[14.4.07] Finally, the issue of copyright arises. Section 1 of the 2000 Act defines artistic works (irrespective of their artistic quality) so as to include works of architecture (e.g. buildings) and works of artistic craftsmanship (say a wooden or metal advertising sign or shopfront name-board). Pursuant to s 17 of the 2000 Act, copyright subsists in artistic works and it follows that they cannot be unlawfully copied or reproduced (in this case, on film). This is tempered with an exception contained in s 52(1) which is termed "incidental use" thus – the copyright in a work is not infringed by its inclusion in an incidental manner in

---

9 Incidental inclusion can act as a defence to copyright infringement in certain specified circumstances as set out in Chapter 10A.

another work (namely a film for present purposes). Therefore, a fleeting, transient shot of a business premises which does not prejudice the interests of the owner will not be regarded as copyright infringement. If it does in fact prejudice the owner's interest (such as where a licence fee should have been paid for depiction usage in a pivotal scene), it will not be regarded as incidental use and the producer may thus be liable in the event of a claim for damages.

[14.4.08] All that being said, as a general rule, one may shoot a street scene where all businesses and shops are filmed collectively in a sweeping sense by means of a wide establishing shot or otherwise. If this were not the case, films with urban landscapes would never get made. It is only where close-ups are taken or prolonged sequences of (a readily identifiable) business premises are filmed (or indeed where they form part of the plot/narrative) that the above considerations arise. However, because there may be defamation (as above) and trademark law concerns (e.g. depiction of a business name/logo) as well as copyright issues, where there is any doubt, a property owner should be contacted about signing a release.

AN GARDA SÍOCHÁNA: SERVICES AND POTENTIAL OFFENCES

[14.5.01] Film producers may engage the services of Garda members to perform duties to which they would not normally be assigned. This work is oftentimes undertaken by members of the force who would otherwise be off duty. It is generally the practice to charge organisations for the costs of duties performed by Garda members inside the event (such as at concerts and football matches) but the costs of policing duties performed outside the event such as traffic and beat controls additional to those normally performed at the location are not paid by the organisation hosting the event but fall to be paid from the Garda Vote (Garda budget). However, the promoters may be requested to make a contribution towards those public policing costs.

[14.5.02] Hence, producers wishing to retain the services of non-public duty Garda members should contact the Finance Directorate at Garda Headquarters in the Phoenix Park, Dublin to inquire as to the level of such costs when preparing their film production budget. For city centre filming in the capital, producers must also supply to Dublin City Council the name of the relevant Garda station and the number of Gardaí required as part of the street permit application process analysed below.

Impersonating the Gardaí

[14.5.03] It is an offence under ss 60 and 61 of the Garda Síochána Act 2005 to impersonate a member of the Gardaí or to have in one's possession any article, equipment or vehicle containing or having on it any distinctive badge or crest so closely resembling the badge or crest of An Garda Síochána as to be likely to deceive. However, s 61(2) permits the wearing by cast and crew of any (Garda) uniform or dress in a performance in a theatre, on film or on television or other media, or, with the prior approval of the Garda Commissioner, in a public place in the course of making a film, television or other media production.

[14.5.04] In addition, police supervision (as well as local authority permission) is recommended (or at least that contact be duly made with the Gardaí) if intending to use mock-up vehicles (use of fake registration plates would ordinarily constitute an offence under the Road Traffic Act 1961 as amended), replica Garda vehicles or where stunts (including those involving pretend emergency services personnel) are taking place or the management of traffic flow is needed.

Use of firearms, fire and pyrotechnics (fireworks, smoke effects)

[14.5.05] If such props are being deployed on set, additional permissions will be required. The use of firearms by a suitably qualified armourer requires a permit from the Department of Justice and Equality. The Garda Commissioner's Film Office must also be advised of all scenes involving the use of firearms (to include prop/replica firearms in interior or exterior locations). If a scene contemplates dangerous stunts such as the burning of a vehicle, the local fire brigade must be notified and the blaze safely extinguished immediately after the shoot has been completed. The safety issues outlined in Chapter 3 are also of paramount importance.

Nudity, exposure and sexual content

[14.5.06] Section 5 of the Criminal Justice (Public Order) Act 1994 as amended provides for offensive conduct in public to be dealt with on a summary basis (by a District Court judge), with fines reaching up to a maximum of €1,000.[10] Offensive conduct means any unreasonable behaviour which, having regard to all the circumstances, is likely to cause serious offence or serious annoyance to any person who is, or might reasonably be expected to be, aware of such behaviour. Thus, it is prudent to notify the Gardaí and local residents (if practicable) in advance of the filming of feigned public disorder activities by actors and extras.

[14.5.07] Section 45 of the Criminal Law (Sexual Offences) Act 2017 deals with exposure and offensive conduct of a sexual nature. Examples are exposure of genitalia, engaging in sexual intercourse, an act of buggery or an act of masturbation in a public place. To ensure, therefore, that a production featuring scenes of sexual conduct does not fall foul of the above provisions, it is essential to contact the Gardaí if featuring nudity, sexual scenes or perceived nudity. Ireland's first nudist-friendly beach was opened in April 2018 in Dalkey, County Dublin. This might, therefore, exclude nudist activity on that beach from the

---

[10] The maximum fine of £500 was increased by s 22 of the Intoxicating Liquor Act 2008 to €1,000.

above permissions. Notwithstanding, a beach permit would be required (see [14.11.02]).

ROAD CLOSURES

[14.6.01] Film producers (or their agents on set) are prohibited by statute from closing a public road, however rural, small or remote, without lawful authority. To do so constitutes a criminal offence. Section 75 of the Roads Act 1993 governs the temporary closure of roads by a roads authority (for example, a city or county council) as do the Roads Regulations 1994 ('the 1994 Regulations')[11] made under this legislation.

[14.6.02] If application for a road closure is required, it is essential to submit the requisite documentation as early as possible (at least two months in advance). The rationale for this is that the 1994 Regulations mandate that a roads authority publish its intention to close a road at least 14 days in advance in a minimum of one newspaper circulating in the area where the road is situated and furthermore to write to the superintendent of An Garda Síochána for the district in which the road is situated. The public is then statutorily entitled to voice objection to this road closure.

[14.6.03] Here is where a locations manager, from a practical perspective, can wield experience in advance discussions (depending on the size of the locality concerned) with the local residents and garner support and goodwill for the intended film shoot. Where the roads authority decides to close the road in accordance with s 75 of the Roads Act 1993, it must again give notice (at least seven days) in the newspaper(s) where the notice of intention was published of its decision to close the road. The Garda superintendent must also be further notified.

[14.6.04] Road closure applications to the relevant local authority are summarised in *Appendix 1* together with an attendant discussion on removal of road markings and the temporary suspension of parking bays.

ERECTING TEMPORARY STRUCTURES IN PUBLIC PLACES

[14.7.01] A production company may need to erect a temporary structure in a public place (to which the public may or will have access) to include platforms, raised seating, arches, tents, marquees, stage sets, lighting rigs, sound towers, camera platforms, film sets, green screens, elevated screens, floodlights, barriers, fencing, bridges and so forth. At least one month's notice should be afforded to the relevant council when submitting an application for such proposed structures. A schedule of temporary structures to include sizes, locations, drawings,

---

[11] SI No 119 of 1994, Pt VIII, art 12.

specifications and structure types should be included as part of the application together with the name and contact details for the structural engineer who will oversee the design, erection and dismantling of temporary structures. These particulars will assist in assessing whether the strict requirements of the Building Control Section of the council will be met. For more on the role of project supervisors for the design process and construction stages as *per* construction regulations made under the Safety, Health and Welfare at Work Act 2005, see Chapter 3. The structural engineer's certificate, in relation to the erection of temporary structures, must be submitted by email[12] prior to the event or filming concerned being commenced.

FILMING ICONIC CITY IMAGES

[14.8.01] In Dublin, the city council levies charges for commercial filming for television advertising, commercial shoots for brands and photo-calls. One might be requested to pay up to €2,000 to film iconic images in Dublin such as the Samuel Beckett Bridge or the Spire but this cost only arises with commercials: the flat rates otherwise levied for filming generally are set out in local authority permit guidelines.[13] Hence the need for advance budgeting and comprehensive pre-production meetings when planning an advertising shoot or photo-call.

LETTERS TO LOCAL RESIDENTS

[14.9.01] All neighbouring residents and businesses affected by any filming should be notified well in advance (ideally two to four weeks) of filming arrangements in their area. A copy of the proposed letter must be supplied to the relevant city or county council's film liaison officer for approval prior to circulation. Any correspondence sent to residents and businesses should fully outline the intended filming and include such particulars as production company details, locations manager contact details, dates, times and locations of filming, planned stunts and use of special effects, lighting plans, parking proposals and information pertaining to any road closures/traffic control (dates, times and areas affected).

CREDITING THE LOCAL AUTHORITY IN END CREDITS

[14.10.01] Local government should be credited in the production titles for its assistance in the making of the programme/film/series and its logo included. For outside the capital city, producers should make contact with the relevant local authority to ascertain whether crediting is in fact mandatory. Even if not

---

12 In the case of Dublin city centre to buildingcontrol@dublincity.ie.

13 For example, in relation to Dublin city centre, forms and guidance notes are available at https://www.dublincity.ie/filming. See also *Dublin City Council, Parks & Open Spaces Bye-laws 2002.*

specifically required, it is a matter of courtesy to acknowledge all assistance received in the making of a production. Most likely, further productions will be made in the future and it is best to keep all state bodies and local governments firmly on side.

DUBLIN CITY COUNCIL:[14] PERMIT APPLICATION PROCESS

[14.11.01] The multi-staged permit application process is set out at *Appendix 2.*

Filming in parks, open spaces and beaches

[14.11.02] In accordance with Dublin City Council Parks and Open Spaces Bye-Laws 2002, written permission is required from the council to engage in any commercial activity in any park or open space managed by the council. An application for a permit must be made by any individual or group wishing to use any park or open space for any event, filming, photography, photo-calls, fashion shoots and product launches of any type. A person or group who contravenes a provision of the Parks Bye-Laws is liable to a fine.

[14.11.03] This permit application form should be forwarded to Parks and Landscapes Services by email[15] at least 10 working days in advance.[16] The applicant must submit evidence of public liability insurance cover with the level of indemnity generally to be not less than €6.5 million in respect of any one incident. Employer's liability cover of some €13 million is also required where individuals or companies are hiring crew under contracts of employment (rather than engaging them as independent contractors). Dublin City Council must be specifically indemnified and named on the policy.

DATA PROTECTION ACTS AND GDPR

[14.12.01] Data protection issues have been discussed in the previous chapter in respect of talent, actors, crew and other contributors. When filming in areas to which the public have access, a crowd release is also required.

---

14 Given the size/population of the capital city and the vast range of locations and resources open to filmmakers there, the above permit application process is intended as a case study. Similar procedures apply outside of Dublin and the relevant local authorities should be contacted for details.

15 Parks@dublincity.ie.

16 As regards filming on Bull Island (to include Dollymount Beach), a site map showing the exact location of the proposed filming/activity should be submitted to the National Parks and Wildlife Service (District Conservation Officer) by the production company. If filming on Bull Island, a vehicle permit is required to access the beach. In respect of filming on Ringsend Beach, to gain access through the barrier to the beach, permission is required from Electric Ireland.

Crowd release/notice

[14.12.02] A clearly conspicuous public notice should be placed in situ outside of set entry and on the perimeter of a filming area. Further, a record (by film-recording/photographs) of this notice should be stored with the chain of title documents. The notice will ideally state the date and producer contact details, provide a summary of the production and intended uses (e.g. for national television broadcast) and make clear that filming is in process. Aside from GDPR considerations, local authorities, as part of a permit application process, will also require the placement of such signage.

[14.12.03] The notice will outline that entry into the filming area will give rise to consent being expressly given for GDPR purposes (to use of one's appearance and voice in any and all media and formats worldwide in perpetuity) and, while such consent may be later withdrawn, data processing may nonetheless be permitted having regard to the legitimate interests of the producer and the processing of personal data for the purpose of exercising the right to freedom of expression including processing for journalistic purposes or for the purposes of artistic or literary expression. The notice should also advise that if a member of the public does not agree to the conditions of the notice they should not enter, and to contact a member of crew for specific information relating to the production and the intended uses of recorded material.

FORESTRY, WATERWAYS AND SHOOTING AT NATIONAL MONUMENTS

[14.13.01] Coillte, Waterways Ireland, The Office of Public Works and Heritage Ireland permit application procedures are set out in *Appendix 3*.

DRONE OPERATIONS LICENSING AND REGULATION

[14.14.01] From 1 December 2015, certain drones based on their weight must be registered with the Irish Aviation Authority ('IAA') in Dublin as *per* two[17] sets of Regulations made in 2015: the Small Unmanned Aircraft (Drones) and Rockets Order 2015 ('SUA Order') and the Irish Aviation Authority (Nationality and Registration of Aircraft) Order 2015 which governs the use of larger drones, and having further regard to EU Regulation 2019/947 (rules and procedures for operation of unmanned aircraft, effective from 30/12/20). Flight and drone operation approval is to be sought in advance from the IAA.

[14.14.02] The SUA Order contains a number of limitations for the operation of drones including a prohibition on presenting a hazard to another aircraft in flight, if operated over an assembly of people, over urban areas, in civil or

[17] SI No 563 of 2015 and SI No 107 of 2015.

military controlled airspace and in restricted areas such as military installations and prisons – unless the person operating the drone has permission from the landowner for take-off and landing.[18] In addition, drone users cannot operate their equipment in public parks, at sporting events or public beaches (although a specific exemption could be requested, for instance, in the case of beaches).

[14.14.03] Pilot competency certificates are issued by the IAA annually. When certified, flights may be conducted in accordance with the conditions contained in the pilot's operations manual (as approved by the IAA), including a documented risk assessment for each operation. The drone may generally be operated within 300 meters from the point of operation. However, operators may be specifically authorised by the IAA in writing to conduct extended visual line of sight SUA operations to 500 meters (maximum range from drone pilot). Obtaining insurance cover for operation of the relevant SUA is required by the IAA as a precondition to issuance of a specific operating permission.

Application for a drone permit from local authorities

[14.14.04] In Dublin city centre (and similarly for the Dublin county councils), a permit application must be submitted to Dublin City Council[19] at least seven days in advance of proposed drone filming together with the requisite flat fee.[20] As above, flight and usage approval must be sought from the IAA. The terms and conditions of filming are the same as those which pertain to other permit types including submission of evidence of public liability insurance and indemnifying Dublin City Council to the required minimum sum level. Proof of employer's liability may also be requested where relevant.

[14.14.05] The production company will be expected to indemnify any third party property owners, whose property is intended for use as a film location (and for take-off or landing), against any claims or proceedings arising directly from any injury to persons or damage to property as a result of the activities of the production company or its agents. Producers must not cause a disturbance or safety hazard or impede the mobility of pedestrians, goods or services without adequate prior consultation. If required, all road closures must be applied for and agreed in advance of filming. Drone operations shall not interfere with vehicular or pedestrian traffic unless specific application is made therefor, with a traffic management plan being received and approved by An Garda Síochána and Dublin City Council.

---

18 Other statutory restrictions include that use must be further than 300m from the person operating the drone; not within 120m of any person or over 400 feet (120 metres) above ground level, not closer than 5km from an aerodrome, or operated in a negligent or reckless manner so as to endanger life or property of others.

19 Or to the other councils such as Fingal or South Dublin County Council.

20 In the order of €75.

Use of drones not permitted at national monument sites

[14.14.06] The use of drones is not permitted at national monument sites (such as at Kilkenny Castle) which are under the charge of Heritage Ireland/The Office of Public Works. Notwithstanding, the IAA may exempt persons or operations from the provisions of the SUA Order or specifically grant permission for use of a drone in a particular scenario – for example, consent was obtained to film footage for the final scenes of *Star Wars: The Force Awakens* on Sceilig Mhichíl off the coast of Portmagee in south west County Kerry.

Data protection and drone usage

[14.14.07] Having regard to data minimisation principles of art 5 of the GDPR, processing of personal data must be adequate, relevant and limited to what is necessary in relation to the purposes for which they are processed. Personal data should be processed only if the purpose of the processing could not reasonably be fulfilled by other means.[21] This means that the data from such processing should be limited to what is strictly necessary to achieve a specific purpose. Thus, drones equipped with different technologies[22] for data collection should only collect information that is necessary for achieving the purpose pursued by this collection. For example, a camera on a drone which serves to take aerial photographs of landscapes should not be used for recording faces or other personal information.

[14.14.08] Mechanisms should be considered that automatically blur faces when they are inadvertently filmed during a data collection to ensure that unintended capture of personal data is avoided or removed. In 2015, the Data Protection Commissioner advised that there are several practical steps one can take to ensure that compliance with data protection legislation is achieved when using drones, to include, ensuring consent of the individuals whose personal data will be captured is obtained; by making timely use of notifications, signage, media, or publicity; having robust security and access controls in place to ensure only authorised persons have access to the images; and using a software programme that automatically deletes the remaining personal data collected once the task is completed. In May 2022, the Data Protection Commission ('the DPC') established under the 2018 legislation provided specific guidance on the use of drones capable of recording video.[23]

---

21 This requires, in particular, ensuring that the period for which the personal data are stored is limited to a strict maximum.

22 E.g. camera, thermal imaging, GPS, altimeter, motion, radio frequency equipment and other sensors.

23 Data Protection Commission, *Guidance on the Use of Drones* (2022). Available at: https://www.dataprotection.ie/sites/default/files/uploads/2022-05/Guidance%20on%20the%20use%20of%20drones%20-%20May%202022%20Final.pdf [Accessed 11 April 2023]. See also *Video Recording/CCTV, Dash Cams, Action Cams, Drones and Other Video Recording Equipment* (2019). Available at: https://www.dataprotection.ie/en/dpc-guidance/video-recording [Accessed 4 August 2021].

Privacy impact assessment

[14.14.09] Those using drones for commercial purposes should also ensure that a privacy impact assessment is completed prior to the use of same. This is effectively an audit of the proposed use of drone technology and takes account of the people and organisations involved, the purpose of the operation, the type of drone and the combination of sensing technology used, identifying the risks to personal data protection, the necessary safeguards to address those risks, and the measurement and adjustment of those safeguards when in use.

[14.14.10] If required, appropriate contracts should be executed with the professional licensed operator exhibiting its drone usage policy for record-keeping purposes. These documents will protect a production company if a claim is made or a complaint is submitted to the DPC. It is crucial, therefore, when retaining the services of a drone operator, that the operator produces vouching paperwork as to registration and drone usage experience in a commercial context. As outlined above, such experience encompasses more than a passing familiarity with data protection laws. The consequences for a production company for breaches of GDPR law and national legislation can be severe having in mind the administrative sanctions discussed in Chapter 13.

DPC enforcement examples

[14.14.11] While an October 2020 decision[24] of the DPC in respect of Waterford City and County Council concerned law enforcement, it is nonetheless indicative of the DPC's very strict enforcement of the Data Protection Act 2018 Act ('the 2018 Act'). It could also inform producers who are engaged in surreptitious investigative filming for television reporting purposes. This decision considered the processing of personal data through a broad range of technologies including CCTV systems, drones, dash cams and covert cameras the purposes of which included preventing, detecting and prosecuting littering offences, public safety, crime prevention and investigation, and preventing anti-social behaviour. All of these devices capture visual images of individuals. It is possible to identify individuals from such images. Thus, the data processed by the devices includes 'personal data'.

[14.14.12] The council had used drones since the summer 2017 to monitor compliance on permitted waste sites and to prevent dumping on illegal waste sites. The drones were used to take aerial photos and videos of the sites. The images

---

24 *Decision of the Data Protection Commission under Sections 111 and 124 of the Data Protection Act 2018 in the Case of 04/SIU/2018 relating to: Waterford City and County Council Own-Volition Inquiry under Sections 110 and 123 Data Protection Act, 2018 on foot of Data Protection Audit Conducted under Section 136 of the Data Protection Act regarding The Surveillance of citizens by the State for Law Enforcement Purposes* (2020), dataprotection.ie. Available at: https://www.dataprotection.ie/sites/default/files/uploads/2021-02/21.10.2020_Decision_IN-04-SIU-2018_WaterfordCity%26CountyCouncil.pdf [Accessed 28 March 2022].

allow the scale and type of waste to be clearly demonstrated in prosecutions. The council relied on the Waste Management Act 1996 and the Water Pollution Act 1977 as a lawful basis for this processing. While the council's processing of personal data by means of drones may be validly based on the Waste Management Act 1996, the Commissioner (Helen Dixon) found that the council's processing of personal data by means of dash cams and covert cameras infringed ss 71(1)(a) and 71(2) of the 2018 Act because there is no lawful basis for such processing of personal data in EU law or the law of the state.

[14.14.13] As regards the council's functions of preventing, investigating, detecting and prosecuting waste-related criminal offences, this requires a balancing of the personal data being processed against the aims that the processing seeks to achieve. If there is a less intrusive means to achieve those aims, the processing will fail the test. The Commissioner therefore found that the council failed to demonstrate that the use of drones was capable of achieving its aims and that no less intrusive means existed between 25 May 2018 and the date on which the impact assessment was finalised in September 2019.

[14.14.14] Further, the Commissioner *inter alia* found (and thus issued a reprimand) that the council infringed s 75 of the 2018 Act by failing to communicate the statutory prerequisites of the Waste Management Act 1996 in its final policy on the use of drones. This omission constituted a failure to implement appropriate organisational measures to protect against unauthorised and unlawful processing prior to implementing data protection policies for their use. The council was also ordered to bring its processing of personal data by means of CCTV and drones into compliance with s 90 of the 2018 Act by ensuring that data subjects are provided with all of the information required by the section as achieved by updating the council's website.

Wexford County Council

[14.14.15] The DPC also ruled (*per* Eunice Delaney, Deputy Commissioner) in October 2020 that Wexford County Council failed to adhere to the legislation by using drones to monitor public movement during the Covid-19 lockdown. The council had been redeploying its UAV drones from monitoring of illegal dumping to surveillance of caravan parks and holiday homes, designed to ensure compliance with the Covid-19 travel limits of two kilometres that were in place at the time. However, no data protection impact assessment, a prerequisite for any project likely to have privacy implications under the GDPR, had been carried out prior to the project's start, and a complaint was lodged with the DPC.

[14.14.16] The local authority submitted that it had no case to answer as any people or vehicles filmed were unidentifiable. Images captured it said were distant and of low image quality and thus did not contain any personal identifiable information. As there was no personal data captured in the drone deployment, it was the council's view that no data processing took place.

[14.14.17] While the Deputy Commissioner, having examined the drone footage available, agreed that the captured film by design did not contain any personal or vehicle registration data, it said that an assessment should still have been carried out given that the drones deployed constituted a system carrying out surveillance which had the potential to collect personal data.

[14.14.18] However, she said that, given the council had moved to amend its drone policy so that an impact assessment would be carried out before the future purchase or use of drones, and given that no identifiable footage had been recorded, no further action would be taken.

Airspace – trespass and nuisance by drone operation

[14.14.19] In principle, any unauthorised intrusion into airspace is capable of being an actionable trespass so that any owner of land whose airspace rights are infringed can seek damages and/or an injunction to restrain the trespass. However, section 55 of the Air Navigation and Transport Act 1936 (as amended by s 47 of the Air Navigation and Transport Act 1988) provides that no action for trespass or nuisance shall lie by reason of the flight of aircraft over property at a height which is reasonable taking into consideration wind, weather and all reasonable circumstances. Further, the concept of a trespasser (as opposed to visitors and recreational users) in the Occupiers' Liability Act 1995 may muddy the waters somewhat.

[14.14.20] In *Keating & Co Ltd v Jervis Shopping Centre Ltd*[25] the High Court *per* Keane J court treated an airspace intrusion (use of a tower crane by the defendant builders over the plaintiff's public house) as trespass and awarded the plaintiff damages. The decision established the principles that an invasion of lower stratum airspace is prima facie actionable in trespass and often in nuisance.

[14.14.21] In the English case of *Bernstein of Leigh v Skyviews & General Ltd* the plaintiff sued the defendant for trespass where the defendant had taken an aerial photo of the plaintiff's property which he then attempted to sell to the plaintiff. The case was influential in clarifying that landowners do not own all airspace above their property and that there was "a need to balance the rights of an owner to enjoy the use of his land against the right of the general public to take advantage with all that science has to offer in the use of air space".[26]

[14.14.22] It appears that the borders between the lower and upper strata of airspace have never been quantified due to the hesitancy of the courts to define

---

25 [1997] 1 IR 512.

26 [1978] QB 479 at 485.

the scope of airspace within a landowner's domain.[27] In most cases judges have held that the lower stratum is unlikely to reach an altitude of more than 200 metres above roof level as otherwise satellites and aircrafts could be accused of trespass. Legal immunity has been granted to overflying aircraft engaged in "innocent passage" in the upper stratum of airspace. However, courts have refused to treat industrial surveillance and invasive photographs of celebrities' homes as "innocent passage". The UK Independent Press Standards Organisation upheld a breach of privacy complaint from the Duke of York after a certain tabloid sent a helicopter over the grounds of his property on 19 June 2015 to capture photographs of Princess Eugenie's 25th birthday preparations.

[14.14.23] To overcome the above challenges, it is important for evidentiary reasons for commercial drones to maintain altitude and co-ordinate tracking logs.

---

27 Dr Kathryn O'Sullivan, *Low-flying drones and ownership of airspace in Ireland* (2016). Available at: https://hdl.handle.net/10344/5127 [Accessed 13 May 2021].

Appendix 1

Road closures, road markings removal and parking suspension

[A1.1.01] The application to the roads authority will contain a number of particulars including details of the length of the road to be affected, details of any alternative route or routes which will be available while the road is temporarily closed, provision for pedestrians and local access, the location and details of signage, and, the applicant must also provide a sketch of the site showing the compound, location of materials, plant, equipment and so forth. The public road cannot be used for the location of site huts without the prior written permission of the relevant Roadworks Control Unit. The roads authority needs to assess the application thereby necessitating, for example, Dublin City Council, to require six weeks' advance notice, a traffic management plan and an advertising/administration fee.[28] The applicant must also discharge road space charges based on traffic impact and importance of the route in question (daily charge per linear metre per lane per number of days for use of a public road with a given designation).[29]

[A1.1.02] The applicant must indemnify the council against all claims arising in connection with the road closure for the period and times during which the road closure is in place and therefore must undertake to maintain a public liability insurance policy with the local authority being named thereon.

[A1.1.03] When the proposed works result in the removal of statutory road signs, the signs will be removed at the commencement of the proposed works and replaced at the completion of the works by the Roadworks Control Unit at the applicant's expense. Any other signage associated with the road closure and the maintenance of same is at the applicant's expense. In addition, the applicant shall pay, where appropriate, any other expenses incurred by the council such as the suspension of parking bays (thus compensating for loss of revenue to the local authority during the period of road closure) whereby a daily charge is levied for these suspensions based on the relevant tariff zone, the temporary removal and temporary disguising or removal/replacement/reinstatement of road markings and pay-and-display parking machines.[30]

---

28 At the time of writing in the order of €2,375.

29 All roads within the council's area have been given a traffic impact number based on the road's traffic importance with fees for Traffic Impact 5 costing substantially more than for Impact 1.

30 A list of charges is available on request from the council, but these charges do not usually apply in most cases.

Appendix 2

Permit application process for Dublin City Council[31]

[A2.1.01] The first matter concerns into which category the filming falls and therefore which application form applies – television commercials and advertisements; micro, small, medium and large filming applications; applications for filming in parks/open spaces and beaches; or the take-off and landing zones for unmanned aircraft (drones) permission form. One should provide as much notice as possible to the council (typically ten days to five weeks but eight weeks may often be required depending on the project).

[A2.1.02] The following details are to be furnished: information relating to cast, names of the health and safety officer and armourer in the case of replica gunfire use, whether animals and children will be on set, specifics in respect of equipment, street dressing, production budget, crowd management, crowd control barriers, scaffolding, generators, welfare facilities (e.g. portaloos), crew, scene descriptions including any stunts, car chases and driving sequences, proposals to remove street furniture or turn off street lights, effecting fake snow or wetting down streets, production schedules, start and finish times, whether non-public duty Gardaí and security are required,[32] traffic and pedestrian management, waste management, a risk assessment and copy public liability and employer's liability insurance policies with an indemnity in favour of Dublin City Council for the minimum required sums.

[A2.1.03] Application should additionally be made for other auxiliary council services to service the production such as road closures, public parking suspensions and temporary positioning of plant and equipment, all of which require a health and safety statement, public liability cover to the requisite level and the placing on duty of banksmen/pointsmen. A permit is required together with payment of a fee when the positioning of a mobile crane/hoist/cherry picker/vehicle[33] on a public road or footpath results in obstruction to a lane of traffic or interferes with pedestrian traffic flow. If heavy goods vehicles are being used, a HGV permit is also required. Traffic management arrangements are to comply with Traffic Signs Manual (Chapter 8), *Temporary Traffic Measures and Signs for Roadworks* published by the Department of Transport in August 2019.

31 See https://www.dublincity.ie/filming for the various application forms.

32 Together with the name of the DMR (Dublin Metropolitan Region) division station.

33 See https://www.dublincity.ie/residential/transportation/apply-licence-or-permit/cranes-hoists-and-vehicles-permits.

Provision must be made too for the safe passage of vehicular/pedestrian traffic around the mobile crane or other plant in use.

[A2.1.04] All application forms with any vouching attachments (such as insurance particulars, traffic/pedestrian management plans and risk assessments) are to be emailed to the Events and Tourism Promotion Unit.[34] In respect of emergency plans and procedures mandated by s 11 of the Safety, Health and Welfare at Work Act 2005 or otherwise, it is the responsibility of producers to ensure that all emergency medical technicians, paramedics and advanced paramedics who may be required to be on site for a shoot are registered with the Pre-Hospital Emergency Care Council and that the person responsible for drawing up and implementing the production's health and safety statement and risk assessment plan is competent to do so.

[A2.1.05] The application will be reviewed by the film liaison officer who will contact the production team if any clarification or further information is required. The application will be circulated to the relevant statutory partners and council departments who review and coordinate services for film productions. Occasionally, larger productions may necessitate meetings with the film liaison officer and nominated officials to discuss the production and how best to plan the filming and coordinate with the city partners to keep the impact on the city to a minimum. If no additional information or action is entailed, the film liaison officer will raise an invoice for the production. If other costs are incurred, such as parking fees for the film production office/base or for road closures, the individual departments in Dublin City Council will make direct contact with the production company or its locations manager.

[A2.1.06] Finally, once the production and other fees, if applicable, are paid, the permit to film in Dublin is issued to the production company. There is no refund if filming is cancelled after a permit has been granted. All late applications (if accepted) will result in double the relevant application fee for all productions that do not meet the required lead-in time.

TERMS AND CONDITIONS

[A2.2.01] Any applications for filming that do not have any impact on the flow of traffic (or a significant pedestrian impact) must be submitted to Dublin City Council ten working days before the intended date of filming. Applications (including photoshoots) that require road closures and/or a traffic management plan require a six-week lead-in time prior to the date of proposed filming. Applications relating to medium and large-scale productions must be submitted at least 21 days in advance of the date for which permission is sought (but a much longer period would be advised).

---

34 Events@dublincity.ie.

[A2.2.02] The site plan should contain full details of all infrastructures to be used as part of the activity such as dolly tracks, cranes, low loaders, scissor lifts, lights, pedestrian access, toilets, signage, security, electrical cables, power outlets, and litter minimisation. In addition, a reinstatement plan may apply if street furniture and so forth will be affected during filming. Furthermore, a risk management plan must be submitted to include identification of any risks, measurement of the risks and the proposed management of those risks. A related matter is submission of medical personnel and first aid information. The numbers involved in the production will determine if the shoot requires security personnel. The applicant's health and safety officer, carrying out the site-specific risk assessment, will determine the number of security personnel required.

[A2.2.03] In relation to rules to which the production company must adhere, the following apply: there must be no obstruction of access to or egress from retail or other premises and noise levels should not cause a nuisance, with due consideration being afforded to any noise-sensitive premises in the area. Generators should be baffled or integrated within the mobile generator vehicle. As regards litter management, the applicant must ensure that the area is left in and restored to the condition in which it was found. Sufficiently sized 'filming in progress' signs should be used with the signs clearly posted in public view.

Appendix 3

Coillte, Waterways Ireland, The Office of Public Works and Heritage Ireland permit application procedures

COILLTE

[A3.1.01] Coillte, offering specially discounted rates for smaller low-budget productions, has amassed a proven track record in providing filming locations. In 2014 alone, it hosted productions including *The Lobster, Love/Hate* and *Vikings*. All filming, photography or other events are subject to a financial charge depending on the size and structure of the production or event.[35]

[A3.1.02] A formal request for a filming licence should be submitted online at least three weeks in advance using an online application. This form requests basic details regarding contact information for the locations manager, estimated number of people and vehicles on site (including proof of motor vehicle insurance), proposed scene content/nature of production, photographic shoot or event and proposed locations. Coillte requires to be specifically indemnified against any potential damages arising from the proposed production/event and for evidence of insurance to the required levels to be submitted.

[A3.1.03] Applications for a location agreement will be considered on a case-by-case basis, taking into account the production's risk assessment, possible impacts on day-to-day forest operations, other forest users and the forest environment. Larger projects or projects potentially impacting on the Coillte estate may be subject to a formal debriefing/site audit to ensure that all agreed conditions, including restitution of the site, have been met.

[A3.1.04] A production company may film at night, subject to consultation with Coillte's neighbouring private landowners, minimal local disturbance and notification to the local Gardaí.

WATERWAYS IRELAND

[A3.2.01] Waterways Ireland[36] can assist filmmakers wishing to film scenes at

---

35 See http://www.coillte.ie/media/2020/01/Recreational-Licences_2020.pdf.

36 Based in County Fermanagh, Northern Ireland and Carrick-on-Shannon, County Leitrim; waterwaysireland.org.

or on rivers, lakes and canals across Ireland. All filmmakers and photographers are asked to complete a detailed filming approval application form supplied by its press office, with proof of public liability insurance and a risk assessment. For large-scale or more complex productions, a site meeting will be required to discuss the details and logistics of the request.

[A3.2.02] The press office will advise of any potential fees to be incurred in relation to the filming request. If fees are to be levied, the production must acknowledge in writing that it wishes to continue with the proposed filming and agree to discharge the fees payable. If permission is granted, an indemnification will be issued for signature and witnessing. It must be returned to Waterways Ireland for the affixing of its corporate seal.

THE OFFICE OF PUBLIC WORKS (OPW) AND HERITAGE IRELAND

[A3.3.01] The OPW with headquarters in Trim, County Meath is responsible for managing, maintaining and preserving approximately 750 national monuments under state ownership and care. The OPW and Heritage Ireland are also responsible for managing a wide range of historic properties such as Emo Court in County Laois and a multitude of lands and properties including Iveagh Gardens, Rathfarnham Castle, the National Botanic Gardens, Phoenix Park, St Stephen's Green, Dublin Castle, the Royal Hospital in Kilmainham, the National Museum and National Library in Dublin, Adare Castle in Limerick, the Hill of Tara in Meath and Castletown House in County Kildare.

[A3.3.02] In addition, the OPW manages the state's property portfolio including buildings and offices of central government departments and agencies. Where permission is granted for filming, the OPW requires the production company to provide it with evidence of public liability insurance cover. In order to afford OPW staff at its sites sufficient notice that film shooting is to take place, the OPW requires 48 hours' advance notice from production companies.

Chapter 15

Employment of Children and Young Persons

INTRODUCTION

[15.1.01] The Protection of Young Persons (Employment) Act 1996 as amended ('the 1996 Act') was enacted to give effect to a European Communities Council Directive passed in 1994.[1] This statute prescribes criminal sanctions for failure to comply with its provisions.[2]

[15.1.02] The 1996 Act applies generally to young employees under 18 years of age. Under s 1 (as amended by s 31 of the Education Welfare Act 2000), a "child" means a person who has not reached the age of 16 years. A "young person" means a person who has reached 16 years but has not reached the age of 18 years, that is, 16 and 17-year-olds.

[15.1.03] It is important to point out that the legislation only applies between employers and employees, an employee being defined in the interpretation section of the 1996 Act as "a child or a young person who has entered into or works under (or, where the employment has ceased, entered into or worked under) a contract of employment". Therefore, using a child as an extra in an amateur short film, for a few days' voluntary work experience or training in a radio station, concert venue or local newspaper for instance would not be caught by the provisions of the statute.

[15.1.04] Since 1 January 2023,[3] the national minimum wage[4] is €11.30 per hour for persons of the age of 20 or older. Young persons, however, are only guaranteed up to 70 percent of the national minimum wage which amounts to €7.91 per hour.[5] Employers are of course at liberty to pay in excess of the minimum wage if they wish, but they are not required to do so by law.

---

1 Council Directive 94/33/EC of 22 June 1994.

2 With fines up to €1,904.61 and continuing contraventions potentially attracting a fine of up to €317.43 per day (s 25).

3 National Minimum Wage Order 2022 (SI No 500 of 2022).

4 Minimum wage rates were introduced in Ireland by the National Minimum Wage Act 2000.

5 The rate, at 80 percent for persons aged 18 years, is €9.04 and at 90 percent is €10.17 for those aged 19.

Garda vetting where applicable

[15.1.05] Audiovisual producers employing children should also be aware of the provisions of the National Vetting Bureau (Children and Vulnerable Persons) Acts 2012 to 2016 and the vetting procedures for persons working with children (who are already required to be vetted in any event under Children First legislation/guidelines referred to at the end of this chapter). The primary purpose of this legislation is to put the procedures that had been developed by the Garda Vetting Unit to vet these applications into law (as previously conducted on the basis of a voluntary code – vetting is now mandatory whereupon a vetting disclosure in respect of the relevant person intended to work with children is to issue from the bureau).

[15.1.06] Garda vetting is conducted on behalf of registered organisations only and is not conducted for individual persons on a personal basis. Section 3 of the 1996 Act provides that the Act shall not apply to certain work or activities such as in the case of family relationships, work activities in the course of a personal relationship for no fee, and the giving of assistance by an individual on an occasional basis for no commercial consideration (at no fee).

EMPLOYMENT IN CULTURAL, ARTISTIC, SPORTS OR ADVERTISING ACTIVITIES

[15.2.01] In general, the Act prohibits the employment of children under 16 years of age. Employers may, nonetheless, recruit 14 and 15-year-olds on light work during the school holidays, part-time during the school term (over 15s only, and for a maximum of eight hours in the week) and as part of an approved work experience or education programme where the work is not harmful to their safety, health or development. Children can also be employed in cultural, artistic, sports or advertising work which does not interfere with their attendance at school, vocational guidance or training programmes.

[15.2.02] Section 3 of the 1996 Act permits the relevant minister[6] to authorise in individual cases, by way of licence, employment of a child in cultural, artistic, sports or advertising activities. The three age categories are: children under seven, children between seven and 13, and children/young persons between 13 and 17 years of age. Applications for such licence are to be submitted before employment commences to the Licensing Section of the Workplace Relations Commission ('the WRC') in County Carlow which may issue the licence on behalf of the minister with certain conditions attaching. The WRC has provided notes on employing a child by licence for film/television and theatre which can be downloaded from its website.[7]

6 The Minister for Enterprise and Employment (at the time of writing, the relevant department is at present styled the Department of Enterprise, Trade and Employment).

7 Workplace Relations Commission, *Protection of Young Persons (Employment) Act 1996 Note on employing a child by licence under Section 3(2) Film/TV Licence,* workplacerelations.ie. Available at: https://www.workplacerelations.ie/en/publications_forms/notes_on_

Licence conditions

[15.2.03] The type of activities for which licence applications are made would typically be television commercials, series or films that require the presence of a child for more protracted contract periods. The licence sets out the conditions under which the child may be employed, such as general conditions concerning parental consent permitting the work; supervision and education arrangements; availing of the services of a chaperon for up to 12 children where their parents or guardians are not present; parental consent for total or partial nudity; meals, nightwork beyond 7pm (permitted only if essential),[8] arrangements for getting home and the maximum working times and minimum breaks appropriate to each group.

[15.2.04] The employer should apply in writing for a licence at least 21 days before the employment commences. The application form may be downloaded from the WRC website as can the requisite form to be completed by the principal of the school where the child is a student, agreeing to the child's absence from school.

[15.2.05] Section 9 of the 1996 Act allows for an exception to the legislation to apply in the case of employment of close relatives (such as a grandchild, child, sister or brother), for example, in a bar, recording studio, cinema, theatre, live music venue or film production business which is a family undertaking, provided the health, welfare and safety of the employees affected will not be endangered.

[15.2.06] It is mandatory in all cases for employers to comply with the obligations imposed in the Safety, Health and Welfare at Work Act 2005 (and Regulations made thereunder including those governing manual handling, provision of personal protective equipment, working at heights and relating to the control of noise).

[15.2.07] Section 5 of the 1996 Act provides that before a young person or child is employed, an employer shall require the production of a copy birth certificate or other satisfactory evidence of age and, in the case of a child, obtain written permission from the parent or guardian. A register or other satisfactory record must also be maintained detailing the date of birth, the time the young person or child commences and finishes work each day, the rate of wages or salary paid and the total amount paid by way of wages or salary.

Statutory display of abstract by way of poster

[15.2.08] Section 12 requires that all employers shall display at the principal

---

employing_young_persons_in_film_tv.pdf; theatre: https://www.workplacerelations.ie/en/publications_forms/notes_on_employing_young_persons_in_theatre.pdf [Accessed 13 April 2023].

8 This applies to children over 13. For younger children, the cut-off time is either 4.30pm (under seven years of age) or 5pm (between seven and 13) unless there are exceptional circumstances.

entrances to the premises where any of their employees work, and in such other places as an inspector[9] may require, in such a position that it may be easily read by employees so employed, the prescribed abstract of the 1996 Act (a summary of the Act should also be provided by leaflet or otherwise). The wording of such abstract was set out by the then minister by way of secondary legislation regulations[10] passed by the Oireachtas in 2007 which summarises the principal rules on employing persons under 18. The WRC has helpfully designed an information poster which employers should duly display.[11] In light of the fines potentially payable for commission of offences under the 1996 Act, it is vital therefore that employers do in fact display an abstract of the Act.

EMPLOYMENT IN A LICENSED PREMISES (PUBLIC HOUSES)

[15.3.01] The Protection of Young Persons Act 1996 (Employment in Licensed Premises) Regulations 2001[12] permit young people employed on general duties in a licensed premises (including bars, restaurants and hotels) to be required to work up to 11pm on a day that does not immediately precede a school day during a school term where the young person is attending school.

[15.3.02] Employers who employ young persons to carry out general duties in a licensed premises must have regard to the Code of Practice Concerning the Employment of Young Persons in Licensed Premises published by the WRC (previously by the Department of Enterprise, Trade and Employment in 2001).[13] This covers such issues as equality, discrimination, parental consent, the provision of written terms and conditions, induction training, continuing education and training, study time,[14] bullying and sexual harassment.

VIEWER COMPLAINTS TO THE BAI REGARDING CHILD ACTORS

[15.4.01] In November 2014, the Broadcasting Authority of Ireland ('BAI') rejected[15] three complaints by three different complainants against four episodes of RTÉ 2's *The Savage Eye* aired in May and June 2014 which took offence to

---

9 "Inspector" means a person appointed by the relevant minister by virtue of s 22 to be an inspector for the purposes of the 1996 Act.

10 Protection of Young Persons (Employment) (Prescribed Abstract) Regulations 1997 (SI No 3 of 1997).

11 Available at: https://www.workplacerelations.ie/en/publications_forms/under_18_a3_poster.pdf [Accessed 16 March 2022].

12 SI No 350 of 2001.

13 Available at: https://www.workplacerelations.ie/en/publications_forms/code_of_practice_-_employment_of_young_persons_in_licensed_premises.pdf [Accessed 31 May 2020].

14 Provision is to be made for students with impending examinations. These should allow for study leave and leave to sit the exams, without having to work excessive hours in the period approaching the exams. Employers shall ensure that students' jobs are protected in the event of their returning to work following study/exam leave.

15 Broadcasting Authority of Ireland, *Broadcasting Complaints Decisions* (November 2014),

the use of "foul mouthed language" by children featured in the programme, and claimed that all child sketches should have been deleted from the programme. Each was critical of children being included, stating that they were involved in "sexualised dancing" and, in another scene, a young person was discussing cutting off a man's genitals and stuffing them in his mouth. Additionally, all complaints cited the use of an anti-Protestant sketch, while another made reference to an anti-Catholic element in one episode.

[15.4.02] The BAI rejected the complaints stating that a pre-airing warning was broadcast on RTÉ 2 (the programmes were also shown after the watershed of 9pm) and noting that the content was satirical. The complaints committee also observed that the programme chose to lampoon those who hold prejudicial views against other members of society stating that, as regards the impugned content, the character in the sketch was playing a Catholic priest who was inculcating children in his classroom with sectarian beliefs in respect of members of the Protestant faith. The committee also stated that the parents of the children who were in the show had consented to their inclusion in the programme (and were aware in advance of content, suitably explaining it to their children when necessary) and that RTÉ had in place a range of measures to protect the interests and welfare of the children during production. While the committee acknowledged that satirical content can often "walk a tight rope", it stated that "facets of society are open to scrutiny and are regularly challenged through the medium of comedy, which can be hard-hitting" and was of the view that a significant majority of the audience would have understood the sketches in this context.

CHILD PERFORMER RIGHTS; GDPR

[15.5.01] While an employer is the author of a work created by its employees (unless the parties agree to the contrary) pursuant to s 23(1)(a) of the Copyright and Related Rights Act 2000, Pts II (copyright) and III (performers' rights) of the 2000 Act stand separate to each other. In the case of performances given by child employees therefore, as with any adult performers, employers should have such child employees sign (through their parents/guardians) a release for IP reasons and for data protection law purposes. Section 29 of the Data Protection Act 2018 provides that for the purposes of the application of the General Data Protection Regulation (Regulation (EU) 2016/679, 'GDPR') in Ireland, a reference to "child" in GDPR shall be taken to be a reference to a person under the age of 18 years (in relation to information society services, the age for the purposes of GDPR is 16).

[15.5.02] In all cases of contributors to media productions, consent must be given to processing of personal data (Art 6, GDPR) such as the use by a production

---

pp 12, 17 and 23. Available at: https://www.rte.ie/documents/news/bai-decisions-november2014.pdf [Accessed 5 August 2017].

company of the products of a child actor's services in a film or commercial. Two points are salient: first, that written consent be provided on behalf of an employee under the age of 18 by that child's parents or guardians. Second, when signing a release setting out the fee payable, IP matters as above, intended uses (e.g. in any and all media and formats throughout the universe in perpetuity, including for promotional purposes) and so forth, the request for/written declaration of consent in the section of the contract dealing with GDPR must be presented in a manner which is clearly distinguishable from the other matters, in an intelligible and easily accessible form, using clear and plain language.

[15.5.03] This will necessitate recourse by the producer employer to a more detailed release as may apply to adult employees on the production. The contract will refer to precautions to be taken in respect of child actors, welfare procedures, the need for the child and parent/guardian to fully understand the context, character/role and effect on the child (as regards privacy/fame in the context say of peers and school), the contractual inclusion of the parent/guardian, and it should explicitly deal with the provision of information in relation to the production, its content and potential impact (ideally a child psychologist may be involved in certain instances). It is further noteworthy that child data subjects, like any other data subject, may withdraw their consent at any time (Art 7, GDPR) though permitted exceptions (see Chapter 13) may arise which producers can seek to invoke if the eventuality occurs. This, by law, should be set out in the agreement.

[15.5.04] It is best practice to have the minor sign the release too whether in the case of acting contracts or say in the case of a child of a documentary adult contributor where the film deals with intimate family issues, violence, abuse, pornography, drug use, crime and so forth. This may assist in warding off claims (against the producer and/or parents) when the child comes of age alleging that the child's privacy or confidentiality rights were infringed. This matter was alluded to in the introduction to Chapter 13 under 'sharenting' (see also the discussion in Chapter 35 of the European Court of Human Rights' judgment in *IVT v Romania*: broadcast of a television interview by a child conducted without parental consent).

[15.5.05] It may be particularly relevant where a parent posts embarrassing or compromising photographs of a child (or which images may conjure up intensely sensitive issues) that might adversely affect that child in later life (or on a practical level during teenage years if subjected to ridicule or bullying). In more serious matters, the production should advise the parent to obtain independent legal advice. The legal adviser may recommend that the child speak with a psychologist or other professional to explain the ramifications of entering the contract and to ensure the minor fully understands the nature of the documentary or other filmed material.

Other legislation and guidelines

[15.6.01] The Children First Act 2015 ('the 2015 Act') also applies to the employment[16] of children for those engaged in providing "relevant services" which are set out in Sch 1 thereof to include any work or activity which consists *inter alia* of the provision of cultural and other activities to children whether or not for commercial or any other consideration. This might include for example participation by children in theatrical productions to be attended by children. Section 11 of the 2015 Act relates to risk assessments such that service providers must undertake an assessment of any potential for harm to a child while availing of the service; prepare a written statement (a "child safeguarding statement") specifying the service being provided and the principles and procedures to be observed to ensure as far as practicable that a child, while availing of the service, is safe from harm; and appoint a relevant person for the purposes of Pt 2 of the statute.

[15.6.02] Further, the Department of Children and Youth Affairs' *Children First: National Guidelines for the Protection and Welfare of Children*, first published in 1999 and revised in 2017, comprises the national guidance for social workers, professionals, organisations and individuals to help keep children safe and protected from harm. The guidance seeks to assist people to recognise where a child is being abused or neglected, and to report reasonable concerns about abuse or neglect to Tusla, the Child and Family Agency. The guidance also assists organisations working with children with information about best practice in child safeguarding. In January 2019, the guidance was amended by way of an addendum to ensure that online safety is specifically accounted for in child safeguarding statements.

[15.6.03] The above legislation and guidance is of relevance when funding moneys are being made available by the Arts Council, state departments or county councils. It will be a condition of the funding that the recipient (e.g. arts centre or theatre) comply with the Act and best practice in this regard and to have in place a child safeguarding statement.

---

16 Children may otherwise offer services on a voluntary basis.

Chapter 16

Animal Actors and Circus Animals

"No animals were harmed in the making of..."

INTRODUCTION

[16.1.01] Another important layer to entertainment regulation, on this occasion more in the realm of ethics, with which filmmakers and others in the industry need to be familiar when applicable, are the requisite welfare standards for animal actors. It is an offence to harm an animal (ss 11 and 12 of the Animal Health and Welfare Act 2013 as amended). The use of animals is not limited to the classical circus. Stage productions, including opera, magic shows and theatre can occasionally incorporate ponies, rabbits, birds or dogs into performances and films can feature a wide variety of animals. Animals should at all times be kept under the supervision of an experienced animal handler or 'wrangler' to ensure the highest level of care and protection. Where necessary, a veterinary surgeon should also be retained by the production company.

Use of animals in *The Hobbit* trilogy

[16.2.01] A high-profile example of alleged animal mistreatment is that pertaining to *The Hobbit*. Peter Jackson and the producers of *The Hobbit* trilogy outright rejected allegations made by animal wranglers involved in making the films that the production was responsible for the deaths of as many as 27 animals on set in New Zealand. *The Hollywood Reporter* stated in a 2012 article[1] that The Associated Press had reported that some 150 animals were housed at a farm near Wellington and that unsafe conditions led to the deaths of horses, goats, chickens and sheep. In a statement given to the magazine by the filmmakers it was contended:

> The producers of The Hobbit take the welfare of all animals very seriously and have always pursued the highest standard of care for animals in their charge. Any incidents that occurred that were brought to their attention as regards to this care were immediately investigated and appropriate action taken. This

1 Erin Carlson, *Peter Jackson Denies 'Hobbit' Animal Claims* (2012), hollwoodreporter.com. Available at: https://www.hollywoodreporter.com/heat-vision/peter-jackson-denies-hobbit-animal-392242 [Accessed 14 May 2018].

> includes hundreds of thousands of dollars that were spent on upgrading housing and stable facilities in early 2011.
>
> The producers completely reject the accusations that 27 animals died due to mistreatment during the making of the films. Extraordinary measures were taken to make sure that animals were not used during action sequences or any other sequence that might create undue stress for the animals involved. Over 55 percent of all shots using animals in The Hobbit are in fact computer generated; this includes horses, ponies, rabbits, hedgehogs, birds, deer, elk, mice, wild boars and wolves.
>
> The American Humane Association (AHA) was on hand to monitor all use of animals by the production. No animals died or were harmed on set during filming.
>
> We regret that some of these accusations by wranglers who were dismissed from the film over a year ago are only now being brought to our attention. We are currently investigating these new allegations and are attempting to speak with all parties involved to establish the truth.

ARTS COUNCIL FUNDING

[16.3.01] The Arts Council stance on animal welfare in Ireland is indicative in this discussion albeit applying only to arts projects concerning the council. Arts activities that feature one or more animals in any performance or exhibit one or more animals to the public in association with a performance shall be awarded and provided funding subject to compliance with all general conditions of funding by the council as well as the requirements enumerated in its *Framework for the Welfare of Animals Presented in the Arts* document which was published in January 2009.[2] The Arts Council in its Animal Welfare Policy Statement refers to the World Animal Health Organisation's adoption of the internationally recognised "Five Freedoms"[3] as part of its Guiding Principles of Animal Welfare.

[16.3.02] The Irish Society for the Prevention of Cruelty to Animals ('ISPCA'), however, was critical in its 2016 report *Wild Animals in Travelling Circuses* of the Art Council's stance on the matter stating:

> Notwithstanding the apparent inability of circuses to comply with the Animal Welfare Framework, the policy document explicitly states that the "Council has neither regulatory authority nor the technical expertise to assess animal

---

2 Available at: http://www.artscouncil.ie/uploadedFiles/AC_Animal_Framework_ENG_Web.pdf [Accessed 31 May 2021].

3 Freedom from hunger and thirst by ready access to fresh water and a diet to maintain full health and vigour; freedom from discomfort by providing an appropriate environment including shelter and a comfortable resting area; freedom from pain, injury and disease by prevention or rapid diagnosis and treatment of disease and injury; freedom to express normal patterns of behaviour by providing sufficient space, proper facilities and company of the animal's own kind; and freedom from fear and distress by ensuring conditions and treatment that avoid mental suffering.

welfare" (Framework for the Welfare of Animals Presented in the Arts, 2008, p 3). This position was confirmed in a meeting in 2014 between the ISPCA and the Arts Council and raises serious concerns over the validity and potential efficacy of the policy. If there is no way of the Art Council assessing organisations for compliance with animal welfare standards, the policy arguably becomes meaningless.[4]

AMERICAN HUMANE AND THE "NO ANIMALS WERE HARMED" DISCLAIMER

[16.4.01] Founded in 1877, American Humane is charged with ensuring the safety, welfare and wellbeing of animals. It works in association with the US film and television industry to protect the wellbeing of animal actors and promote the human-animal bond. Its staff attends on set to protect animal actors.

[16.4.02] The organisation monitors animals in filmed media and holds the exclusive right in the US to award its "No Animals Were Harmed" end credit certification to productions that meet its standard of care for animal actors. American Humane works with production personnel and trainers in the pre-production planning stage, monitors the animals on set during production, and enforces American Humane's *Guidelines for the Safe Use of Animals in Filmed Media*. It also investigates allegations of mistreatment and cruelty and sanctions productions that do not meet its standards of humane animal treatment. American Humane currently monitors 70 percent of known animal action in film and television productions in the US. This amounts to approximately 2,000 productions annually.[5]

LOVE/HATE EPISODE DEPICTING ANIMAL CRUELTY

[16.5.01] Ireland has also adopted this form of disclaimer in programme end credits when applicable. The highly successful television crime drama series *Love/Hate* managed, however, to spark major controversy in 2013 when the machine-gunning of a cat in the opening episode of the new series that year incited more complaints than a double murder depicted in the previous season. Seven disgruntled viewers called RTÉ and ten more emailed complaints to the station after the episode opened with a cat being machine-gunned to death.[6] By comparison, an episode in the previous series, featuring the fatal shooting of

---

4 Elizabeth Tyson, *Wild Animals in Travelling Circuses* (2016), p 7. Available at: https://www.ispca.ie/images/pages/ISPCACircusCampaignReportFeb_2016.pdf [Accessed 3 May 2019].

5 See https://www.americanhumane.org/initiative/no-animals-were-harmed/ [Accessed 14 May 2018].

6 Laura Butler and Louise Hogan, *Fur flies after cat 'shot' in opener of new Love/Hate series* (2013), independent.ie. Available at: https://www.independent.ie/entertainment/tv-radio/fur-flies-after-cat-shot-in-opener-of-new-lovehate-series-29641568.html [Accessed 15 May 2018].

a man and a woman, sparked five complaints. Numerous complaints were also lodged in an earlier series when a character is depicted killing a swan.

[16.5.02] According to *The Irish Independent*, the ISPCA labelled the scene "sick and horrendous". The broadcaster issued a statement that no animal was harmed during the making of *Love/Hate* series four. A RTÉ spokeswoman explained that the cat was at all times under the supervision of an experienced animal handler. She confirmed the blood was computer generated and no fake blood was used near the cat. The cat was anaesthetised by a vet to ensure it played dead.

WILD ANIMALS PROHIBITED FOR CIRCUSES

[16.6.01] Ireland, like many other EU Member States, legislates against use of wild animals. Since January 2018, wild animals have been banned in Irish circuses. The then Minister for Agriculture Michael Creed signed secondary legislation[7] in November 2017, made under the above-cited 2013 Act, which prohibits the use of wild animals in circuses, wild animals being defined in reg 2 of the Circuses (Prohibition on Use of Wild Animals) Regulations 2017 as "an animal of a kind not commonly domesticated in the State".

7 Circuses (Prohibition on Use of Wild Animals) Regulations 2017 (SI No 482 of 2017).

Chapter 17

Crew Agreements, Production Releases and Music Clearance

CREW AGREEMENTS

[17.1.01] For a contract (oral or written)[1] to be legally binding and thus enforceable by courts, tribunals or arbitrators, it must have the following components: intention to create legal relations,[2] the parties must have legal capacity,[3] and there will be evidence of an offer, acceptance and consideration. Consideration in contract law refers to money or money's worth.[4] An example of money's worth might be where an independent contractor actor (as opposed to an employee who will be guaranteed a wage by law) performs services gratis[5] in return or exchange for permission from the producer to use the subject film (or more likely clips therefrom after its release date) in a showreel as a springboard to assist in procuring future roles. Alternatively, in the case of extras for instance on location, a nominal fee combined with catering facilities provided by the

---

1 All entertainment and media contracts should be in writing for chain of title purposes generally and due to the requirement in the Copyright and Related Rights Act 2000 that assignments must be in writing to be valid as explained in Chapter 10A.

2 See UK Supreme Court judgment in *RTS Flexible Systems Ltd v Molerei Alois Muller GmbH* [2010] UKSC 14, Irish Supreme Court case in *McCabe Builders (Dublin) Ltd v Sagamu Developments* [2009] IESC 31 (*per* Fennelly J overturning Charleton J in the High Court that there was no binding contract and holding that the courts should seek to give effect to the apparent intentions of parties to enter into binding contracts) and *Edwards v Skyways Ltd* [1964] All ER 494 at 499-500 cited with approval for instance in *O'Rourke v Talbot Ireland Ltd* [1984] ILRM 587.

3 The parties must be of sound mind and generally, subject to exceptions, minors cannot enter a contract – their parent or guardian must do so on their behalf. In the case of companies, the status of the entity should be 'normal' in the CRO and not dissolved.

4 Clark states that the best definition of consideration is that of Sir Frederick Pollock who argued that consideration is the price a promisee pays in return for a promise when he said, "An act of forbearance of the one party, or the promise thereof, is the price for which the promise of the other is bought, and the promise thus given for value is enforceable", Robert Clark, *Contract Law in Ireland* (8th ed, Round Hall, Dublin, 2016), p 67.

5 The contract should nonetheless, for legal certainty, contain a nominal consideration say of €1 or €10. The 2019 EU Directive on Copyright in the Digital Single Market (and 2021 transposing legislation in Ireland) as discussed elsewhere in this book, which *inter alia* seeks to ensure fair (appropriate and proportionate) remuneration, may however see the demise of nominal fees.

production office and travel or other *per diem* expenses should suffice in terms of the requisite consideration needed for the agreement to have force.

[17.1.02] Absent undue influence or duress, unconscionable bargain and improvident transactions,[6] the courts are not concerned with adequacy of amount (but see the discussions on fair remuneration in Chapters 10 and 11; and in respect of employees, under statute law, they must of course receive the prevailing minimum wage). Heretofore at least, judges needed merely to be satisfied that the consideration was sufficient rather than adequate.[7] Thus, one would regularly encounter consideration of €1 or €10 in a contract.[8] An example might be €10 (as additional consideration in a contract with a substantial fee providing for acquiring television broadcast rights), payable from a broadcaster to a licensor producer, for a first refusal right to some aspect of a future project; or say €200 as an initial option fee to a writer for film rights to underlying IP such as a novel. In light of the Directive on Copyright in the Digital Single Market (*Directive (EU) 2019/790*) discussed in Chapter 11 ('the 2019 Directive'), however, it is likely that a movement away from nominal consideration sums will be witnessed particularly in music composer and sound recording agreements as well as in performer contracts generally.

[17.1.03] Equally, actor, extras or performer day releases will routinely feature a modest consideration of perhaps fifty to one hundred euro in return for assignment of all performer rights by the actor to the production company (this will be more if an actor is requesting industry norm union/Irish Equity rates[9] and, again, given the 2019 Directive, it is highly likely that payments to performers will no longer be nominal). If the actor is volunteering services free of charge, a consideration of some sort should ideally still apply so that same can be vouched as part of the chain of title. If a performer is providing services as an employee (rather than voluntarily or as a contractor), payment of at least

---

6 See the Court of Appeal decision *Allied Irish Bank Plc v DX* [2020] IECA 308. Further, the law of equity supplements (or indeed compliments) and runs parallel to the common law. Contract law is a subset of the common law which was built up through centuries of decisions in the courts of Britain, USA and so forth and hence the terms 'case' law or judge-made law. Equity is concerned with fairness and justice and the courts can invoke their equitable jurisdiction to set aside for example a transaction on the grounds of its improvidence – see *Carroll v Carroll* [1998] IEHC 42 and the Supreme Court judgment in [1999] IESC 11.

7 Ellis J remarked in *Kennedy v Kennedy* (Unreported, High Court, 12 January 1984) that once there is consideration its adequacy is irrelevant to its validity and enforceability.

8 Even where real property is being transferred as might be the case where ownership in common areas is being transferred by the developer of a housing estate to the owners' management company.

9 See below sections on developments in collective agreements for discussion of possible reform (Irish Equity and Screen Producers Ireland) of the impugned repeat fees and residuals customary buyout provisions to come into line with UK and international practice.

the per hour minimum wage[10] will arise. An insufficient flat fee which would fall foul of employment legislation in terms of hours worked.

[17.1.04] Whatever the consideration sum, it is important that it is in fact paid to the payee. This is because the contract's remuneration clause will provide for receipt of the consideration to have been acknowledged by the payee for chain of title purposes.

Developments in collective agreements

[17.1.05] More generally as regards sector working conditions and contract terms, the Workplace Relations Commission holds the view[11] that strong consideration should be given to the establishment of a formal structure for the resolution of industrial relations issues and has confirmed a willingness to offer its services in this process. A helpful development in this connection was the new Irish Film Agreement between the actors' representative body Irish Equity and Screen Producers Ireland ('SPI'), effective from 1 February 2021. This agreement, which regrettably unravelled shortly thereafter,[12] was to augment the existing television drama and docudrama agreements between Irish Equity and SPI. In addition to providing a standardisation of terms and conditions for film, it sought to formalise the then existing film rate card which was timely in light of the 2019 Directive and coming in tandem too with the updated and modernised SIPTU/SPI Shooting Crew Agreement (effective from January 2021) and the reaffirmed commitment to maintaining good work practices within the industry for artists and crew, thus positioning Ireland as a more attractive location to shoot feature films and high-end television drama.

Buyout clauses in actor agreements

[17.1.06] Since then, members of Irish Equity and Equity UK have partnered together to call for equal treatment and enhanced working conditions for Ireland-based performers working on international co-productions in the country. Both unions have claimed international production companies are applying lesser terms and conditions to Ireland-based actors and that equal rights are being

---

10 €11.30 from 1 January 2023 (there are age-related exceptions).

11 Advisory Service, Workplace Relations Commission, *Audit of the Independent Film and Television Drama Production Sector in the Republic of Ireland* (2020). Available at: https://www.workplacerelations.ie/en/news-media/workplace_relations_notices/wrc-audit-of-the-independent-film-and-television-drama-production-sector-in-the-republic-of-ireland.pdf [Accessed 3 October 2020].

12 Actors started a campaign against the terms of the agreement and focused on its failings when compared with agreements in, for example, the UK and the US. The discontent led to a seven-hour Equity AGM in late March 2021, at which a new executive was elected and resolved to renegotiate the agreement with SPI. Any renegotiation with SPI is to primarily focus on the share-out with performers of so-called residuals payments that are made to producers on foot of programme sales and repeat screenings, which are an industry standard in other jurisdictions. Also on the agenda are working time arrangements.

denied to local performers on production sets despite generous subsidies from the s 481 of the Taxes Consolidation Act 1997 ('s 481') tax credit. Equity UK has pointed out that when working on the same film or television production, UK performers do so on standard Equity union contracts that entitle them to receive payments for royalties, residuals and repeats while Irish colleagues are on non-union contracts that do not.

[17.1.07] For both television series and films, the minimum terms and conditions of performers can thus favour non-resident performers over local hire. The assignment of performer rights which rights are protected in legislation fall far below the international norm in terms of payment. It is these rights which could potentially produce residual payments for performers. In actor and crew contracts, however, rights are typically assigned by way of full 'buyout' as discussed in Chapter 10B. This is not an issue where the acting fees are substantial for leading cast (or the agents of such cast may in some cases push for a percentage too of net producer profits) but where support actor fees are not as significant as they should be, gaining rights to residual or passive income for repeats and reuses both in Ireland and abroad would be a welcome development in the future for such performers.

Miscategorisation of employees for income tax

[17.1.08] Throughout this book emphasis is laid on risk mitigation. Continuing in that vein is to guard against incorrect tax treatment of film cast and crew for financial gain, and indeed in relation to protection of artists in the wider entertainment and media sector as a whole. An increasingly problematic reality, as likewise obtains in the construction field in particular, is the miscategorisation of employees in certain instances as freelance independent contractors ('ICs') in the film and television industry, termed 'false self-employment' by Revenue, with resultant substantial losses to the exchequer and a denial to workers of a suite of statutory rights enshrined under domestic and EU law alike.

[17.1.09] It is therefore no surprise that both Revenue and the Oireachtas are actively examining this area for potential pathways to reform in an effort to prevent or target abuse of the tax system and employment protection rights. It is perhaps only a matter of time before the legislature introduces a new criminal offence of wilfully and knowingly misclassifying an employee as being self-employed.[13] The Workplace Relations Commission is also set to be granted wider powers in order to tackle the issue of unfair treatment or penalisation of persons

---

[13] While the Employment (Miscellaneous Provisions) Bill 2017 originally included a provision whereby an employer who incorrectly designated an employee as a self-employed contractor could face a fine of up to €5,000 and/or imprisonment, or both, this did not survive enactment of the Act in 2018. The foremost concern was that if issues related to bogus self-employment were included, it would delay the passage of the legislation as a whole.

who request that their tax and work status be duly reviewed.[14] For now, where a determination is made that a worker has been incorrectly classified as being self-employed, the employer will be required to pay the relevant PRSI contributions for the employee for the full period in question and may be subject to a range of penalties under the Social Welfare Consolidation Act 2005.

[17.1.10] In July 2021, Revenue, the Department of Social Protection and the Workplace Relations Commission issued an updated (first prepared in 2001) *Code of Practice for Determining Employment or Self-Employment Status of Individuals.*[15] This code provides significantly more detail around the factors considered in case law[16] determining contracts for service (contractors) as distinct from a contract of service (employment) including mutuality of obligation, substitution, the enterprise test, integration and control which are considered below.

[17.1.11] In January 2018, the Department of Employment Affairs and Social Protection and the Department of Finance published a joint report entitled *The Use of Intermediary-Type Structures and Self-Employed Arrangements: Implications for Social Insurance and Tax Revenues*. Revenue was also involved in the preparation of the report. The report examined the potential loss to the exchequer arising from the misclassification of workers as being self-employed, stating therein:

> Although illustrative, the data does indicate the potential loss to the exchequer for a person engaged in work at a rate equivalent to the average industrial wage (€37,500) amounts to €5,000 per annum. This rises to €8,000 per annum at a payment level of €60,000 and €15,000 per annum at a payment level of €100,000 per annum.[17]

[17.1.12] Accordingly, it is imperative, first, that employers do not misclassify

---

14 s 11 of the Employment (Miscellaneous Provisions) Act 2018 already provides for protection against penalisation in certain circumstances but this could be extended in time to cover the issue under discussion.

15 See https://www.revenue.ie/en/self-assessment-and-self-employment/documents/code-of-practice-on-employment-status.pdf [Accessed 10 September 2021].

16 Appendix 4 to the code lists a number of relevant cases to include *Karshan (Midlands) Ltd t/a Dominos Pizza* [2019] IEHC 894; *National Museum of Ireland v Minister for Social Protection* [2016] IEHC 135; *Monnie McKayed v Forbidden City Ltd t/a Translations.ie* [2016] IEHC 722, and the recent UK Supreme Court decision in *Uber BV v Aslam* [2021] UKSC 5.

17 At p 19 thereof. Also, the annual report of the Comptroller and Auditor General published in September 2018 examined the issue of self-employment, with a specific emphasis on PRSI contributions by the self-employed in the aftermath of work conducted by the special investigations unit of the Department of Employment Affairs and Social Protection. In 2017 the unit initiated a campaign specifically focused on the construction sector. As a result of this activity, €60.2 million was recovered by Revenue and nearly 500 subcontractors were reclassified as employees. The Comptroller and Auditor General concluded that because there is no employer PRSI contribution for workers who are classified as self-employed, this creates an economic incentive for certain individuals to be improperly treated as self-employed.

employees and, secondly, that they conversely ensure, by requiring vouching Revenue documentation or otherwise, that ICs who present or hold themselves out as ICs are in fact ICs.[18] The advices of the production company's HR consultants, solicitors, bookkeepers and accountants should be sought in this connection and, as mentioned in Chapter 1, the Scope Section in the Department of Social Protection can, on application, determine employment status with a view to deciding the appropriate class of PRSI for an individual.

Consequences for misclassification

[17.1.13] The import for production companies could be that if they engage an IC over a significant period but it is subsequently determined by Revenue that the appropriate tax treatment for the individual was PAYE/PRSI rather than self-assessment, they could be rendered liable for very significant arrears of employer taxes.[19] Where Revenue finds that a worker's status has incorrectly been classified, it demands that backdated employer PRSI at a minimum be paid by the employer. Indeed, accountants TaxAssist have confirmed that fines of €50,000 are now commonplace for cases where bogus self-employment is identified.[20] Revenue will often then turn its attention to the 'contractors' themselves and pursue them too to ensure their taxes were correctly filed.

[17.1.14] The issue is further complicated by the fact that worker compensation is paid by a special purpose vehicle DAC set up for each separate film production or television series in the case of s 481 recipient producers. This might entail ICs working for multiple DACs over many projects by the same producers when they should have been treated as employees with all concomitant employee and/or social welfare benefits. If the practice is a means of evasion, in light of the major tax credit benefits accruing to the producer company, this lends further urgency to reform of the sector and to defining in law for the first time the meaning of 'employee'.

---

[18] A suitable indemnification clause will require contractors (who should warrant that they own and operate a business on their own account, are registered for self-assessment with Revenue and shall adduce vouching documentation) to agree that they shall be liable to the exclusion of the hiring production company for all taxes, levies, charges and payments to Revenue and/or the Department of Social Welfare and indemnifying the production company against any such liabilities including penalties or interest. Contractors may also be requested to agree to reimburse to the producer any arrears of employer/employee taxes that Revenue may seek from the producer on the basis of its determination that the contractor was erroneously self-employed.

[19] PRSI (from 1 January 2023) amounts to 11.05 percent paid on total or gross weekly earnings over €441. It is 8.8 percent for weekly earnings below that figure.

[20] Charlie Weston, *Employers warned over bogus self-employment* (2019), independent.ie. Available at: https://www.independent.ie/business/jobs/employers-warned-over-bogus-self-employment-38073151.html [Accessed 14 August 2021].

RTÉ settlement of €1.2 million with Revenue

[17.1.15] It was announced in March 2021 that RTÉ had offered staff contracts to 81 freelancers or self-employed contractors after Revenue raised concerns over their trading relationship with the national public broadcaster and arising out of Public Accounts Committee hearings on the matter. This followed a Revenue analysis of 157 RTÉ self-employment contracts, and a consultancy report commissioned by RTÉ in 2018 from law firm Eversheds Sutherland on a list of 433 freelancers or contractors providing services across the organisation. The report recommended that RTÉ should review and update its policy on the engagement of freelancers, and develop clear guidelines as to when and how to engage a contractor or employee.

[17.1.16] Renewed focus was cast on the Department of Social Protection's investigation of the treatment of the said 81 RTÉ workers after the broadcaster acknowledged it had made a settlement of €1.2 million with Revenue due to those workers having been improperly engaged as individual contractors rather than full-time employees.

Employees and ICs

[17.1.17] The audiovisual and music industry engages a large proportion of cast and crew personnel on an IC basis to include actors, directors, producers, location sound engineers, directors of photography and audio/editing post-production services. The reason for this, apart from contract term length which in most cases may be short compared with an employment situation, is that the production company or hiring party is thereby under no obligation as regards statutory requirements or entitlements such as pertaining to maternity leave that apply to PAYE/Schedule D employees (an exception is safety legislation as the production must protect the safety and welfare of all persons hired).[21] Neither will it be liable for employer taxes.

[17.1.18] The term 'employee' is generally defined as a person who has entered into or works under a contract of employment – but, as clearly evidenced from case law, the distinction is often clouded. The terms 'worker' and 'employee' are not defined in Irish law. This results in ambiguity on how to determine whether to engage workers on a contract for service or directly as employees, hence increasing the risk of misclassification.

[17.1.19] An employee works under a contract of service[22] whereas an IC is

---

[21] s 15(1)(a) of the Safety, Health and Welfare at Work Act 2005 provides that s 15 (duties owed to non-employees) applies to a person who has control to any extent of a non-domestic place of work that has been made available as a place of work to persons other than employees. See also s 12.

[22] The Terms of Employment (Information) Act 1994 (s 1) defines a contract of employment *inter alia* as a contract of service.

retained pursuant to a contract for service. The essential distinction is that employers must have regard to employment law statutes and attendant employee entitlements such as hours of work, holidays (including public holiday pay or time off in lieu), unfair dismissal law (depending on length of continuous employment), redundancy procedures[23] and maternity leave. There may in addition be pension considerations particularly if in respect of public sector workers (such as for RTÉ or TG4). An employer must also pay an employee's PAYE, PRSI and USC. Further, while some form of sick pay is included in employment contracts, ICs would not be entitled to same. If they do not work, they receive no pay. Lastly, fixed-term workers legislation (which can bestow job security)[24] does not apply to ICs.

[17.1.20] An IC is hired on an as-needed, specified purpose or project basis such as where a director is employed over a three-month period to direct a series of television programme episodes or where a designer is hired by a media company to create a website. The IC receives a fee having issued a number of invoices or one invoice upon completion. The hiring company does not have responsibility to pay any taxes on behalf of contractors who must manage their own tax affairs through self-assessment.

[17.1.21] Therefore, it is clearly more cumbersome for production companies to hire employees and to file regular employer and employee taxes/returns as well as maintaining statutory records in respect of annual leave and working time, and complying with the Minimum Terms and Notice of Employment Acts 1973-2005.[25] However, it may in fact make sense for larger long-running productions (take *Fair City*, *Vikings* or *Peaky Blinders*) to hire cast, extras and crew on an employee basis particularly where workers require a level of job certainty and employee benefits and are less inclined to file their own self-assessment tax returns. The same might hold true for national public radio broadcasters and private operators such as Today fm who may hire researchers and presenters on an employee rather than IC basis for radio shows spanning several months or long-running shows over many years.

The tests employed: IC v employee

[17.1.22] If an individual is to be hired on an IC basis, this should in fact

23 It should be noted that being classified as an 'employee' does not necessarily afford automatic access to statutory rights. An important further threshold that must be crossed in many cases is that of continuity of employment. Hence, to acquire rights under unfair dismissals or redundancy legislation, for example, employees must also demonstrate that they have been in continuous employment on a full-time basis by the employer for a specified period (52 weeks under s 2(1)(a) of the Unfair Dismissals Act 1977, as amended, and 104 weeks under s 4(1) of the Redundancy Payments Act 1967).

24 Protection of Employees (Fixed-Term Work) Act 2003 as amended.

25 And the Employment (Miscellaneous Provisions) Act 2018 which *inter alia* relates to casual work and permissible zero-hours contracts in limited circumstances.

represent the reality. There are a range of tests adopted by Revenue and the courts. Revenue published guidelines in this regard in 2009 entitled *Guidance Note: Taxation of Individuals Engaged in the Irish Film Industry* and an updated version thereof was awaited. However, it seems the afore-mentioned July 2021 code comprises the relevant updates.

[17.1.23] Over the years, various approaches have been used by courts and tribunals to determine the employment status of individuals. These include the control test, the 'in enterprise on one's own account' test, the mutuality of obligation test, the integration test (albeit to a lesser extent recently), and the right of substitution[26] test.

[17.1.24] When looking at the criteria, one must consider the working conditions and the employment as a whole. The main question will always be whether the relevant individuals work as persons in business on their own account. This will help decide if they are free agents with economic independence from the hiring party. It is clear from case law that the courts and employment law fora will look past the label the parties themselves have given the contract and will consider all factors relating to the working relationship to ascertain its true nature.

[17.1.25] Criteria on how to determine if individuals are self-employed include whether they have a fixed place of business, own their own business and are exposed to financial risk (for example, they may have to bear the cost of redoing faulty or substandard work carried out under the contract); assume responsibility for investment and management in the business and can profit from the management, scheduling or performance of the work; if they cost, quote and agree a fee for the services, have control over what, how, when and where the work is performed and whether they do it personally or are free to hire other people; can provide the same services to more than one person or business at the same time and thus on a non-exclusive basis; provide the materials, equipment and machinery, and provide their own insurance cover.

[17.1.26] The Supreme Court decision in *Henry Denny & Sons (Ireland) Ltd v The Minister for Social Welfare*[27] examined the issue of whether or not a shop demonstrator was an employee. Despite the contract's stipulating that she was not an employee and the fact that she was responsible for her own tax affairs, Keane J, with whom Murphy J and Hamilton CJ agreed, held that she was an employee, applying a combination of tests. He noted that the inference that a person is engaged in business on his own account can be more readily drawn

---

26 The Code of Practice states that the ability to hire subcontractors or other people to do the work is one of the factors which would be indicative of contractor status. However, the Supreme Court, in *Castleisland Breeding Society v Minister for Social and Family Affairs* [2004] IESC 40 looked at this factor and found that a prohibition on the use of substitutes without prior approval was not fatal to a finding of self-employed contractor status.

27 [1998] 1 IR 34.

where he employs others to assist in the business. Keane J stated that in general a person will be regarded as providing his services under a contract of service and not as an independent contractor where he is performing those services for another person and not for himself.

[17.1.27] In making this assessment, cognisance had to be taken of the degree of control, the contract of employment and its express and implied terms, the level of integration[28] of individuals into the workplace, whether they provide equipment, premises, investment or employment for others, and whether they work on their own account. Other factors include whether persons engaged receive holiday pay, sick pay or are part of the pension scheme. Requirements to be at work during specified hours and to wear a certain uniform provided by the hiring party were also relevant to the court's assessment.

The enterprise test

[17.1.28] This entrepreneurial (or economic reality) test examines whether persons are performing services in a business on their own account and have an opportunity to make a profit. If so, then they will almost certainly be regarded as an independent contractor. The test originated in the UK decision of *Market Investigations v Minister for Social Welfare*.[29] It looks at a range of factors (e.g. whether workers have helpers, whether they take a financial risk) and asks whether or not the worker is actually running a separate business. According to Cooke J:

> The fundamental test to be applied is this: 'Is the person who has engaged himself to perform these services performing them as a person in business on his own account?' If the answer to that question is 'yes' then the contract is a contract for services. If the answer is 'no' then the contract is a contract of service.[30]

[17.1.29] Co-authors Daly and Doherty[31] observe that this test was noted with approval by Blayney J in the High Court decision in *O'Coindealbhain v Mooney*[32]

---

28 Integration test – this involves an examination as to the extent to which an individual has been integrated into a workforce. The general position set down in the UK in *Stevenson Jordan and Harrison Ltd v MacDonald and Evans* [1952] 1 TLR 101 is that under a contract of service an individual is employed as part of the business whereas under a contract for service the individual is only an accessory to it. In the *Sunday Tribune* case, *In Re Sunday Tribune* [1984] IR 505, a freelance journalist who received commission in advance but was under no obligation to the newspaper to publish her work was held to be hired under a contract for services. By contrast a 'staff' journalist working 50 weeks per year for the newspaper was an integral part of the newspaper and therefore had a contract of service. This case illustrates that the nature of the work itself is not always significant, as both journalists did the same substantive work (writing columns for the newspaper) but each had a different employment status – B Daly and M Doherty, *Principles of Irish Employment Law* (Clarus Press, Dublin, 2010), chapter 3.

29 [1969] 2 QB 173.

30 [1969] 2 QB 173 at 184.

31 *supra* at fn 28.

32 [1990] 1 IR 422.

and comment that although it has the attraction of clarity, in reality it is less of a conceptual categorisation and more of an approach, which encourages the courts to examine a range of features of the work relationship and come to a conclusion, on balance, as to how it should be classified. The authors also refer to the comments of Edwards J in *Minister of Agriculture and Food v Barry*[33] where he pointed out that this test could not be treated as being of universal application where the issue for determination involves the broader question as to what is the nature of a particular work relationship between two parties.[34]

[17.1.30] This is because in certain cases a work relationship is not capable of being defined in terms of a simple choice as to whether it is governed by a contract of service or a contract for services (for example in the case of a statutory office holder). On appeal (which overruled Hedigan J in related proceedings), the Supreme Court[35] confirmed *per* Charleton J (using Edward J's wording) that there is no one-size-fits-all universal test. Setting aside the High Court's decision, the justices found that the Employment Appeals Tribunal ('EAT') (as it then was) should be allowed determine, based on the facts, whether an employment relationship between the parties existed. The court did not comment at length on the mutuality of obligations aspect of the trial judge's ruling but did deem it a critical component.

Mutuality of obligation

[17.1.31] This test examines whether the employer is obliged to provide work for the employee and whether the employee is obliged to perform that work. It was considered in *Barry* above. Temporary veterinary inspectors had lost their jobs at a Galtee plant in 2004. They sought notice and redundancy payments which the minister resisted based on an argument that they were self-employed contractors rather than employees. The matter came before the EAT three times, twice in the High Court and ultimately before the Supreme Court which sent the matter back to the EAT for a rehearing. This further decision by the EAT that they were self-employed contractors as there was not sufficient mutuality of obligation was appealed (for the third time) to the High Court.

[17.1.32] If this mutuality is not present, then there is no contract of employment. Edwards J referred to a UK case which called it the irreducible minimum of mutual obligation necessary to create a contract of service.[36] In particular, he pointed to the fact that if there is no mutuality of obligation:

> ...it is not necessary to go any further. Whatever the relationship is, it cannot amount to a contract of service. However, if mutuality of obligation is found

---

[33] [2008] IEHC 216.

[34] [2009] 1 IR 215 and [2008] IEHC 216; see also [2011] IEHC 43 (Hedigan J).

[35] [2015] IESC 63 at para 9.

[36] *Carmichael v National Power plc* (1999) ICR 1226.

to exist, the mere fact of its existence is not, of itself, determinative of the nature of the relationship and it is necessary to examine the relationship further.

[17.1.33] This test was the first of several that were considered in determining whether the vets were employees or contractors: if the mutuality of obligation hurdle was not passed then the other tests, such as control, enterprise, integration and right of substitution are essentially immaterial. The majority of the Supreme Court was not satisfied that the claimants had established that there was mutuality of obligation between them and the minister. Passing this test is deemed to be essential for the claim they were employees to proceed, and it is only then necessary to consider other factors.

[17.1.34] The test was addressed again by Lavan J in *Ahktar Mansoor v Minister for Justice*[37] and further considered by the High Court (Ní Raifeartaigh J) in *McKayed v Forbidden City Ltd*[38] which referred extensively to the judgment in *Barry*. This latter case involved a translator who was engaged by the defendant and claimed to be an employee. The High Court found that the fact that he had been given work on a regular basis for a particular period did not create an obligation to provide work. Also of note was that the fact of being on-call did not convince the court that he was an employee – it was found that the translator was free to refuse work when called by the defendant (whether he did so or not).

The essentials for entertainment contracts

[17.1.35] Aside from fees, deferred fees as sometimes arise in the case of tight budgets, profit sharing in talent contracts (if applicable), credits, warranties, engagement term, post-release availability for publicity, insurance provisions, and other standard terms, the first essential clause in all contracts is assignment (or licence)[39] of rights such as performer rights of actors and assignment to the production company of copyrights of default IP owners under statute (e.g. film directors and music composers) and others who may be deemed to have created IP during a project including costume and set designers, SFX companies and animators.

[17.1.36] The second contractual imperative, being waiver of moral rights, was examined in Chapter 10A. Moral rights under Irish law cannot be assigned and are consequently waived by rightsholders instead in favour of the hiring party. An example of a moral rights infringement action is a cast member suing for a change made in the editing suite that compromises what the actor believes is the artistic integrity of a key scene. However, the production lawyer might determine that the scene as shot infringes the copyright of a number of artists whereby their paintings prominently appear (in the background) on screen but

---

37 [2010] IEHC 389.

38 [2016] IEHC 722.

39 Licences are frequently used for example in distribution contracts and in music use contracts.

have not been cleared by such authors or their agents, and the scene must be modified accordingly. Therefore, it will be asserted that the production company firstly has full and final editorial control contractually and secondly that the actor freely signed an agreement which contains a clause providing for waiver of all moral rights in and to the film unconditionally and irrevocably.

[17.1.37] Thirdly, a 'no injunction' clause ensures that an aggrieved party to an agreement (e.g. where an independent contractor claims he has not been paid, in circumstances whereby the producer company contends that the services provided were substandard) can only take action for a monetary sum and not apply to court for equitable relief to delay or prevent exploitation and broadcast of the subject picture.[40]

[17.1.38] As well as these three core clauses which will feature as standard minimums in every contract (including for example short-form releases signed by extras or session musicians on a sound recording), whether for the benefit or not of Screen Ireland which expressly requires certain minimum contractual terms, funders including broadcasters will, as seen in Chapter 13, require production contracts to also include a data protection consent declaration as standard for chain of title, insurance and regulatory purposes. A fifth clause of relevance is a boilerplate clause in respect of contracts for service confirming that no relationship of employment exists between the parties.

Torts of ICs

[17.1.39] An employer, and thus its insurer, is vicariously liable for the torts or civil wrongs (e.g. negligence causing injury to the cast or public on set) committed by employees under its employer's liability insurance policy. This is not so in the case of ICs who should be requested to adduce evidence of their own public liability or production insurance so that in the case of their own negligent acts or omissions, the hiring production company will be indemnified, as a contract term, against personal injury, material loss and property damage claims by injured parties.

[17.1.40] A statutory example is contained in s 7 of the Occupiers' Liability Act 1995 which provides that an occupier (which can include a production company)[41] of premises shall not be liable to an entrant for injury or damage

---

40 Injunctions will, in any event, in the main, only be granted where damages are not an appropriate remedy (and hence proceedings for non-payment of a director's fee for example would not necessarily pass the test – irreparable injury to his reputation however might successfully ground such an application for equitable relief). The refined test for preliminary injunctions was stated by the Supreme Court in *Merck Sharp & Dohme Corp v Clonmel Healthcare Ltd* [2019] IESC 65.

41 "Occupier" is defined in s 1 of this Act in relation to any premises as meaning a person exercising such control over the state of the premises that it is reasonable to impose upon that person a duty towards an entrant in respect of a particular danger thereon and, where there is more than one occupier of the same premises, the extent of the duty of each

caused to the entrant or property of the entrant by reason of a danger existing on the premises due to the negligence of an IC hired by the occupier if the occupier has taken all reasonable care in the circumstances (including such steps as occupiers ought reasonably to have taken to satisfy themselves that the IC was competent to do the work concerned) unless the occupier has or ought to have had knowledge of the fact that the work was not properly done.

PRODUCTION RELEASES

[17.2.01] The need for releases has been identified at length already in Pts I and II of this book flowing from the various stakeholder requirements. The requisite agreements are also summarised in Chapter 25 in respect of shooting music videos whereby the same gamut of issues arises as for films, television and commercials. Contracts needed for stageshow and radio productions are discussed in Chapters 19 and 20 respectively.

[17.2.02] Each project will have its own specificities and each legal agreement may or will have bespoke and project-specific clauses. Fledgling producers relying on a generic 'template from the web' do so at their peril. Furthermore, it is essential that every contract satisfies the minimum requirements set out above to include a data protection consent.

[17.2.03] It may be opportune at this juncture to table the most frequently encountered contracts and other legal documentation that should comprise or otherwise supplement the chain of title and compliance papers to allow for full and unimpeded commercial exploitation of the project at hand [note that distribution and financing agreements including broadcasting rights acquisition licences, loan and investment agreements are excluded from the below table as is company law documentation (e.g. director certificates approving the drawdown of a production loan; deeds of charge) and other chain of title documents (e.g. deeds of novation assigning rights to a party who takes over rights or a full production from another person or entity)]:

---

occupier towards an entrant depends on the degree of control each of them has over the state of the premises and the particular danger thereon and whether, as respects each of them, the entrant concerned is a visitor, recreational user or trespasser.

Document	**Reason therefor**
General filming-in-public permit, drone use permit, vehicles and plant/heavy equipment permit and road closure licence Garda Síochána clearance	To ensure a breach of local bye-laws or an offence under road traffic legislation is not committed and to indemnify the local authority against injuries/property damage claims To ensure an offence is not committed when employing or deploying fires, imitation firearms, Garda vehicles, uniforms, badges etc. and when depicting nudity, indecent exposure or what would otherwise constitute criminal activity
Iconic images/street sculpture release (e.g. Eiffel Tower, Samuel Beckett Bridge)	To ensure there is no breach of copyrights, trademarks or moral rights of creator, and no breach of local filming production bye-laws
Location agreement	To ensure there is no breach of copyright (buildings and designs can also be 'works') and to minimise or remove risk of a claim for defamation of a business, breach of privacy in the case of owners/occupiers of private premises, or breach of trademark law if a logo/name is captured on film; to indemnify the owner against claims; to agree a no-injunction/damages only clause
Props release (e.g. use of a copyrighted poster or magazine cover; use of trademarked equipment or vehicle) Archive licence agreement	To ensure trademark law is not infringed or copyright law breached and to protect against product disparagement claims; to agree a no-injunction/damages only clause To obtain rights to use archive photographs, recordings, broadcasts, newspapers etc.

Document	**Reason therefor**
Where applicable, broadcaster approval of product placement in television content (films and certain other productions are exempt from PP rules)[42]	Having regard to advertising, sponsorship and product placement statutory broadcasting rules
Talent (e.g. directors, producers), actor, crew and extras agreements, crowd release notices, contributor agreements for documentaries with specific clauses required for minor (child) contributors; contributor agreements for stageplay and dance productions, voice-over performer contracts for animation projects	To ensure copyright/performer rights are assigned to the production company (parents or guardians to sign in the case of child actors); to provide for waiver of moral rights and no injunction in the case of breach of agreement; and to comply with employment law (employees) and tax legislation (employees and independent contractors)
Data protection law consent and crowd release notice; drone usage policy where applicable	To set out the legal basis for filming for the purposes of the GDPR and national data protection law and so not to offend against one's right to privacy
Life rights/collaboration agreement	To ensure access to a range of personal material and to guard against breach of privacy, breach of duty of confidence and defamation claims; to agree a no-injunction/damages only clause
Master use licence agreement (sound recordings)	To obtain permission from a record producer or label to use a sound recording so that copyright and performer rights are not infringed or moral rights breached; to agree a no-injunction/damages only clause

42 Paid product placement is only permitted in cinematographic works, television films, sport, dramas including one-off dramas, drama series and serials (excluding docu-dramas) and light entertainment programmes (excluding talk/chat shows that regularly include 20 percent or more of news and current affairs content) – see section 10.2 of BAI's 2017 General Commercial Communications Code. Note that despite establishment of the Media Commission, unless revoked or amended, the BAI codes remain effective in respect of broadcasts – see para [31.4.01].

Document	**Reason therefor**
Synch licence agreement / mechanical rights licence	To obtain clearance or licence from a writer, publisher, collection society or label to use a song/track in a production so that copyrights or moral rights are not infringed; to agree a no-injunction/damages only clause
Assignment (sale, subject to minimum 'writer share' royalties where applicable) or licence (permitting defined usage) by music composers; artist, musician and performer releases (e.g. lead vocalists, band members, session musicians, backing singers, dancers, music video cast; and data protection consent forms	To purchase copyright in a song from a composer (and to obtain the waiver of moral rights) or to license the use of a song; and to obtain the right to exploit performer rights (and a grant of lending/rental/reuse rights); to agree a no-injunction/damages only clause; to obtain data protection consents for GDPR purposes for capturing one's image or performance on film
Letters of waiver from record labels and music publishers	To exempt a writer, performer or recording artist bound to an exclusive agreement from performing services for a third party (such as a one-off live performance or writing for/ performing on the soundtrack for a television programme)
Writer or co-writer agreement (including for theatre and stageshows), option agreement and supplemental agreements; publisher release/ quitclaim (where writer has licensed publishing rights including film rights to a book publisher); certificates of authorship	Primarily (aside from matters of fees, warranties and other customary terms) to obtain copyright clearance and waiver of moral rights to permit full exploitation of a project and to extend or modify pre-existing rights granted by the copyright holders; to agree a no-injunction/damages only clause
Screenplay/teleplay agreement	To obtain copyright clearance and waiver of moral rights to permit full exploitation of a project; to agree a no-injunction/damages only clause
Image rights release	Permission to use a personality's image for a commercial to prevent a claim for passing off or breach of privacy; to agree a no-injunction/damages only clause

Document	**Reason therefor**
Licence from minister/WRC	When employing a child on a production to ensure no offence is committed by failing to obtain a licence
(Online) public performance and music streaming licence (e.g. music streaming services, dance company streaming performances online which contain music)	Contact to be made with IMRO/PPI on the applicable licence that may be required for the specificities of the production/business
Policies of insurance	For permit, production and errors and omissions purposes
Production services agreement	Primarily (aside from matters of fees, warranties and other customary terms) to assign copyright in a production to the commissioning party together with the benefit of other grants and waivers of rights (e.g. between a producer company and its qualifying company subsidiary for the purposes of the film tax credit; engagement of an Irish production company to produce a commercial for a Belgian beer company)

Table 1: Releases and chain of title documentation

MUSIC CLEARANCE

[17.3.01] What follows for present purposes is a cursory tour of the considerations needed for clearing music for a film, dissemination of content online, use of music in radio and television commercials and so forth. Music clearance for stageshows and radio programming is discussed in Chapters 19 and 20. This section will also discuss production or library music as a more cost effective alternative to using commercial music.[43] Aside from new entrant or relatively recently established operators such as Artlist, Pond5 or West One and veteran international music licensing companies including BMG, the Mechanical Copyright Protection Society ('MCPS') in Ireland and Britain also offers production music to music users including film producers and advertising agencies. MCPS production/library music licensing covers both the publishing (compositional) and sound recording (master) sides of music clearance.

[43] When the intended content is for worldwide use (and not limited to Ireland under blanket music licensing schemes as explored later in this section).

The wider backdrop of music rights

[17.3.02] Music publishing, licensing of sound recording rights, works registration and royalties income are explored in Chapter 23. So too is the meaning of 'purchase' of songs, sound recordings and performer rights, and the concept of 'full buyout' in one of multiple contractual forms that can take.[44] Chapter 23 also looks to the wider music law issues, more in the vein of the economics of rights control and asset management, for consideration beyond the summary of music clearance in this chapter. This includes income streams for audiovisual producers who acquire music copyrights both in terms of publishing and sound recordings.

Contracts required

[17.3.03] At the most fundamental level, independent legal advice should be taken by audiovisual producers in respect of composer agreements for specially commissioned music (this may involve further performer releases and data protection consents if third party performers and session musicians perform on the soundtrack recordings), and drafting or review of synchronisation licences (from songwriters/publishers) and master use licences (relevant to the separate record label or music producer owned sound recordings) in the case of including commercial music in the subject project. Specialist music licensing experts and music supervisors can also be retained to liaise with music collection societies and, where applicable, to negotiate terms with record label and publisher rightsholders directly.

Contract terms

[17.3.04] It is imperative that music licensing/assignment contracts serve their purpose as comprehensively as possible in terms of the three core elements set out in paras [17.1.35] to [17.1.37] above[45] but also as to territory definition (e.g. worldwide) and medium/device/format (e.g. online, cinema, in-flight, festival, television and financier websites/social media channels). For audiovisual productions, a further consideration is the matter of rental and lending rights and equitable consideration for performances on sound recordings for inclusion in film content as outlined in Chapter 10B.

[17.3.05] The release agreement must cite a consideration payable, however

---

44 An informal survey of music licensing trends by Music Creators North America indicates that there are at least four basic categories of copyright transactions being offered internationally to songwriters and composers all being described simply as 'buyouts' as used to describe certain copyright assignments and licensing transactions, executed with third parties such as film/video production companies, distributors and administrators of musical works. Available at: https://thescl.com/wp-content/uploads/2020/05/Defining-Buyouts-and-Other-Copyright-Transactions.pdf [Accessed 9 September 2021].

45 Licence to use (or full buyout by assignment subject to future royalties or not), waiver of moral rights, and a 'no injunction/no equitable relief' clause.

nominal the amount might be in certain scenarios, to constitute a valid, enforceable agreement. If the monetary consideration is nil (it is best however that at least a nominal consideration be inserted), the money's worth should be stated as might arise with advancement of the artist's career by the promotion of his music in a film and the attendant publicity generated. Nil or nominal consideration is highly unlikely going forward however save for exceptional cases in light of the 2019 Directive and its fair remuneration and other requirements.

[17.3.06] In terms of performer rights, it is not necessary to obtain consents when using a commercial track (say featuring a 20-member choir) from each individual performer and musician. It should be sufficient to obtain the consent of the owner of the sound recording which features all such performances as the music producer or label, to which the various performers will have been required to assign their performer rights by means of a release before or after rendering the performance, is the default statutory 'author' of the recording.

[17.3.07] If however, a documentary film producer wishes to use archive music video footage (e.g. from a *Top of the Pops* episode in the 1970s), first while paying an archive fee to the broadcaster as legal owner of that broadcast, ideally, releases should also be obtained from performers in that video permitting the inclusion of their image in the production at hand. For example, if the documentary centres on politicised bands but the band shown in the archived footage had no political or activist associations, they could file a defamation action if their reputation is sullied in some manner. A release from such performers will contain an indemnity against legal actions in favour of the documentary producer.

Most favoured nations; step deals

[17.3.08] A convention in the music industry pertaining to synchronisation and masters use licensing is that rightsholders might be willing to offer their music to a film producer on a most-favoured nations basis. For example, if the Rolling Stones music publishers agree to license a segment of one of their compositions for €10,000, the sound recording owners may equally be willing to offer a licence at a rate not exceeding €10,000. With internationally successful acts, their publishers will likely be the publishing arm of a major record label (Sony, Warner or Universal) and on the sound recording side, the label will also be a major (indeed publishing and master rights may be held by just one label).

[17.3.09] Music licensing can be prohibitively expensive. However, independent filmmakers planning to show their films at film festivals can often negotiate a reduced fee for a festival use licence. These reduced rates are based on limited screenings of the film. Once the film has been sold for theatrical release, the fees will increase based on the significant increase in viewership and potential increased revenues (it is best to negotiate this increased fee in advance).

Negotiating in advance for possible future performances in different types of media (theatrical, television, cable, internet) is often referred to as a step deal.

End credits

[17.3.10] To protect artist/performer and music producer moral rights, where a commercial song or specially commissioned piece features in a movie, the end credits should acknowledge the writers and recording rightsholders and state from whom consent was obtained by licence. Even if moral rights are waived generally, it is most likely the paternity rights will be excepted. Readers will be readily familiar with film credits to include 'written by', 'performed by' and 'licensed courtesy of…' terminology that appears towards the latter part of the end credits relating to music used in film productions.

Clearance requirements of financiers and distributors

[17.3.11] Screen Ireland contractually requires that all rights relating to a project be cleared worldwide and in perpetuity across all media. This includes rights in all underlying materials, actor performances, documentary participation and musical performances, music compositions and recordings, archive footage and so forth. Further, all projects in receipt of funding must be eligible for E&O cover and the relevant insurer will likewise require confirmation that all rights to the commercial or production music used, sound design and/or score for the soundtrack have been cleared. Further still, acquisition rights/distribution agreements with broadcasters including RTÉ, Virgin Media and the BBC will contain warranties that the production company holds all necessary rights and is not in violation of any composer, performer and sound recording IP and that it will, in reliance on its E&O cover, indemnify the licensee broadcaster from all claims of copyright infringement.

[17.3.12] For material to be broadcast in Ireland (whereby, in applicable cases, music licensing is governed by the Irish Music Rights Organisation ('IMRO')/ Mechanical Copyright Protection Society ('MCPS')/Phonographic Performance Ireland ('PPI') blanket licences), this warranty will be to the effect that the producer holds all the rights in the subject programme/film with the exception of such performing rights in any music which are controlled by performing rights societies and which are available to the broadcaster, it being agreed that the broadcaster shall be responsible for collection society licence fees, with the licensor production company being otherwise responsible for all other synchronisation and non-society performance payments.[46]

[46] For instance, there may be a number of songs used in the production and music might be used from an artist who is not registered as a member with IMRO/MCPS or other collection society, or the music may not yet have been registered by works registration form. This artist will need to be paid directly by the audiovisual producer (in lieu of collection society royalties).

Public domain

[17.3.13] In the case of reproductions of out-of-copyright public domain works (e.g. Beethoven works, sufficiently old traditional Irish compositions, and sound recordings produced or first made available to the public more than 50 years prior to 1 November 2013 (note: for post-1 November 2013 recordings, the term is 70 years for recordings of music performances which were lawfully made available to public)),[47] there must be a master use licence for any sound recording whereby the composition is out of copyright but the relevant sound recording thereof is still under copyright protection. Producers might assume that a Mozart composition is public domain and royalty free. It is – but only on the compositional side. If there is an in-copyright sound recording produced say in 1981 containing the musical works which a film producer sources on YouTube or elsewhere, permission, as with any other commercial track, must be obtained from the sound recording proprietor.

Mandate by publishers/songwriters to MCPS

[17.3.14] Synchronisation licensing refers to using music in film, adverts, video games, internet television advertising, viral advertising, music streamed in the background of a website or other audiovisual productions where the music is synchronised with other media. MCPS (where it holds the mandate[48] by virtue of its standard membership application to license specific musical works for use in productions on behalf of its music publisher, songwriter and composer members) provides a track clearing service.

[17.3.15] The service is for those wishing to use a specific musical work (which has been commercially released for retail sale) in a production for international use[49] (or where, in the context of domestic broadcast, an exclusion applies to

---

47 s 26 of the Copyright and Related Rights Act 2000 specified this 50-year period. This was amended by SI No 411 of 2013 (EU (Term of Protection of Copyright and Certain Related Rights) (Directive 2011/77/EU) Regulations 2013) to extend the term to 70 years.

48 Within the parameters of blanket licensing for general entertainment television programmes broadcast in Ireland, this mandate is automatically included in the MCPS membership agreement. Exclusions are not available. For the use of non-production music in audio (e.g. karaoke) and audiovisual productions (e.g. films for theatrical release, radio and television advertising, and television programming), members have the option to exclude these licences from MCPS control. The options are as follows: MCPS only whereby MCPS has the exclusive right to issue the licence for the relevant use after having gained prior approval for the use from the member; member only whereby MCPS has no right to license or negotiate on the member's behalf for the relevant mandate; and MCPS on first call whereby either the member or MCPS has the right to issue the licence, depending upon whom the user of the music contacted first. If MCPS is contacted first, MCPS must nonetheless obtain prior approval for the use from its member creator (or publisher).

49 And thus not covered by blanket licensing arrangements unless the production is fully funded by say RTÉ whereby RTÉ may require to upload the content on its Player for Ireland's worldwide diaspora (e.g. a live music event to mark a special occasion). This, on the publishing side, can be covered by IMRO/MCPS blanket performing and reproduction/mechanical licensing (excluding North America) but producers need to ascertain the

blanket licensing such as a song needed for the opening credits sequence) and for which MCPS must therefore first attain approval from its member rightsholders and agree a fee. For music of international artists, MCPS (where it has a mandate to do so) will liaise with the relevant rightsholders or entities. This expedites the process and obviates the need for music users to make cross-border enquiries. International publishers will have joined MCPS as overseas members or may have subpublishers based in Ireland.

[17.3.16] Part of the application includes a statement about the intended track and to what use it will be put. The rightsholder songwriter/publisher member will either approve or reject such use in the subject production. If the request has been successful, MCPS will confirm the licence fee payable. All rates are negotiated on a case-by-case basis.

[17.3.17] Where MCPS does not in fact hold the mandate to license music on behalf of a particular rightsowner member, it can nonetheless facilitate contact being made with the parties who will be in a position to license it directly to the applicant music user.

[17.3.18] MCPS has no involvement in sound recordings and master use rights (unless in the case of MCPS production music). For content not covered by the PPI blanket licences with national broadcasters for Irish uses (for instance, where not fully funded by RTÉ or at least 50 percent funded by RTÉ with say Media Commission support, or not geoblocked to Ireland for linear transmissions and catch-up on RTÉ Player such that a programme cannot be accessed in Northern Ireland), PPI can be contacted in the case of difficulty tracing sound recording proprietorship. PPI represents record labels and music producers and holds their contact details.[50] Through PPI (and if otherwise unable to identify ownership and contact details), audiovisual producers can thus ascertain the rightsholders of masters (and music videos) and negotiate a master use licence and payment of a use fee with them directly. Other than that, PPI's role is limited to ensuring

---

position of worldwide use with the broadcaster and PPI, and may well need to clear sound recordings with rightsholders directly. Further, even when covered by blanket licence, artist publishers/agents and record labels may require RTÉ to geo-block particular territories (e.g. Australia). Outside of using a pre-existing commercial song, however, it is important to note that PPI blanket licensing may be moot. If a broadcaster commissions a music event for example with live performances for a subsequent edited television programme, it will require to own all resulting IP in the independent producer's live sound recordings (save in the case of artists signed to major record labels – see below). It will not be using the legacy sound recordings. In this instance, only cue sheets will be required to be submitted to the broadcaster in order that any performers who register their performances with RAAP (see fn 56) will receive royalties for public performance broadcasts (from RAAP through PPI). If major label artists perform on the show, their label (as exclusive rightsholder to its artists performances) will require ownership of the sound recording for its own commercial purposes later and will license the use thereof for the subject production and its broadcast (to include for international uses if applicable).

50 PPI is affiliated with sister organisations throughout the world and hence will have the requisite details pertaining to sound recording rights at home and abroad.

that labels and performers are paid[51] via royalties for Irish and overseas public performances of their work.

The web of rights in music clearance

[17.3.19] To fully exploit film and television output internationally, a deep understanding of music law requires *inter alia* a knowledge of copyright and multiple rightsowner possibilities (as in the case of co-writers and their respective publishers as may be applicable and which may operate in different jurisdictions), moral rights,[52] performance rights, duration of copyright/moral rights and performer rights, public domain material, and defences to copyright infringement.[53] On the sound recording side, ownership may also be shared between different record labels such that for example a certain label may control North American rights while interests may be vested in one or more additional record companies in respect of rest of world rights. The duration of copyright attaching to sound recordings will further need to be taken into account when producers are seeking to use what they believe is in the public domain.

[17.3.20] A specific consideration for record labels is that their artists' music will be used strictly for the subject production and not in any manner that would state or imply endorsement by the artists of any service or product other than the event or production at hand.

[17.3.21] Creators and users of music need to be further mindful of licence restrictions and prohibitions imposed by production music libraries, such that, for instance, music assets licensed from Artlist unsurprisingly cannot be used in the context of pornography.[54] Rightsholders may otherwise wish to limit acceptable usage so that, by way of illustration, the licensed music shall not be used in the opening title sequences or in promotional material and that its inclusion is thus confined to the subject production itself. If this applies, the producer must ensure that broadcasters are aware of these restrictions when advertising the film or programme in advance of broadcast.

Reuse fees/royalties to legacy music composers (use of archives)

[17.3.22] Lastly is the issue of reuse fees for music embedded in archive film clips. Audiovisual clips will be licensed to documentary producers from the major studios on the basis that where applicable the producers will clear any music therein (acting performer reuse fees to actor guilds may also arise as may

51 In addition to any master use fee agreed between the film producer and the sound recording owner (when the subject use is not covered by broadcaster blanket licence).

52 The song cannot be adapted/changed/edited, treated in a derogatory manner and so forth.

53 Such as parody, fair dealing exemptions and incidental inclusion uses.

54 Neither can they be used to encourage violence, racism, hate, threats and discrimination against any person based on race, religion, sexual orientation, community or nationality; violating privacy, or in a defamatory manner.

royalties to be paid to screenwriter and director guilds) in terms, for example, of score composer rights and submission of a cue sheet for royalty payment purposes. Ultimately it depends on what deal was reached between the studio and composer when the archive film was made and whether compositions were assigned to the film studio. The major composers typically retain and register their copyright ownership of scores which would then need to be cleared separately to the audiovisual elements of the archive clips being licensed (and music cue sheets for the film would also list such composer's music for the purposes of public performance royalties).

Broadcaster blanket licences for music in Irish television

[17.3.23] Commercial music (e.g. a John Denver track) in Irish general entertainment television programmes broadcast by Irish broadcasters can generally (there are exceptions) be covered under blanket licence (take *First Dates* or *Don't Tell The Bride*). The broadcaster simply pays an annual or/and one-time fee to IMRO and MCPS[55] and, in respect of broadcast of sound recordings in television programmes, a further broadcaster licence is required from PPI in order that sound recording owners and performers thereon will receive public performance royalties from PPI and Recorded Artists Actors Performers[56] respectively.

[17.3.24] However, there are important restrictions, most notably that usage will (generally) be confined to Irish distribution, the music cannot be altered (e.g. resequenced), used in opening credits or for advertising purposes in commercials or promotional material. In the case of such excluded uses, these must be individually negotiated with the the publishing rightsholders directly (or MCPS on their behalf) and the labels directly in regard to sound recording rights, outside of blanket licensing arrangements, which likely will add very considerable time and cost – and while if broadcaster blanket licensing does not prove possible MCPS can nonetheless issue a blanket licence to independent producers as well as to licensed broadcasters, unfortunately the same does not hold true with PPI which does not at present offer such clearance. Use of music in a deliberately derogatory, obscene or demeaning way to its composer, author or the performing artist also falls outside the blanket licensing scheme and would require prior approval from the IP owners.

[17.3.25] PPI licenses television and radio broadcasters to play copyrighted recorded music as part of their programming. It is important that the audiovisual

---

[55] A performing licence from IMRO allows Media Commission-licensed broadcasters to broadcast content featuring musical works, while the mechanical licence from MCPS allows them to reproduce or synchronise musical works into their original programming (whether produced in-house or commissioned from independent production companies) for broadcast in Ireland (and potentially worldwide through permitted broadcaster licensees and/or on RTÉ Player – see fn 49).

[56] Recorded Artists Actors Performers is commonly known as RAAP.

producer's commissioning contract with the broadcaster (note certain rights acquisitions such as by way of pre-sale, where broadcaster investment does not meet a certain threshold as set against say Media Commission funding, may not be eligible under blanket licence rules if not a 'full commission') contains a provision that the broadcaster will obtain and pay for the necessary licence required from PPI as well as IMRO/MCPS so that music can be used in the subject programme or telefilm. Some broadcaster funding contracts will refer only to IMRO (MCPS should also be negotiated for inclusion) but, where a blanket licence is possible, it is essential (where a hit song is planned for placement) that PPI is also included as otherwise the producer would need to clear master rights individually which will disproportionately affect the programme budget. In all cases, the producer will be obliged to submit music cue sheets to the broadcaster which in turn will provide same to the collection societies to ensure all relevant rightsholders receive public performance royalties from the relevant broadcast(s) and on-demand uses.

MCPS secondary exploitation licence agreement

[17.3.26] Broadcasters' on-demand players are oftentimes geo-blocked as this would otherwise present licensing difficulties or lead to breach of distribution contracts with various stakeholders. However in certain cases where uses for 'qualifying programmes' are intended beyond Ireland (material for cinematic exploitation being excluded)[57] and the audiovisual content contains MCPS members' music, audiovisual producers can contact MCPS to discuss music licensing options where the subject programme has already been broadcast in Ireland or is scheduled for broadcast within Ireland. Examples of uses are in-flight entertainment on aircraft and viewing at non-fee paying television programme festivals (such as MIPCOM in Cannes) and free to air analogue or digital transmissions by broadcasters internationally. The important proviso here is that sound recordings are not covered and masters owners' prior approval is required (which likely will lead to payment of a master use fee).

Broadcaster on-demand services (e.g. RTÉ Player) and geoblocking

[17.3.27] Some but not all of TG4's content has rights restrictions such that the broadcaster might make such content available on the island of Ireland only. RTÉ will likewise geoblock programmes to honour distribution contracts independent producers have in place with other programme (co)financiers, and arising from music licensing considerations. For example, a production co-financed by RTÉ and BBC NI will mean that RTÉ has broadcast rights in Ireland (including the television premiere) for a particular term, typically five years (and non-exclusive

[57] This restricted secondary exploitation licence also only covers musical works. It does not cover sound recordings (other than production music controlled by MCPS). As PPI does not offer a track clearing service, the masters owners will need to be contacted directly for uses outside of Ireland that do not fall within the PPI blanket licence system.

rights in Northern Ireland) while BBC will have the premiere rights in Northern Ireland (and because BBC is broadcast in Ireland too, BBC will be afforded broadcast rights in the republic after the RTÉ premiere). In other words, RTÉ will not make the relevant programme episode available on the RTÉ Player in Northern Ireland until after the BBC transmission of that episode when RTÉ will then be able to continue to exercise its on-demand rights in Northern Ireland on a non-exclusive basis.

[17.3.28] This is not an issue for the majority of programmes but it will add complications if the programme contains commercial music. The blanket licences RTÉ will have in place with IMRO, MCPS and PPI would confine the broadcast of the subject programme to Ireland only where a co-financier such as the BBC will be broadcasting in the UK and hence the licensing scheme will not apply at all. Likewise, if the BBC is contributing an insubstantial sum by way of pre-sale rather than a full commission, it likewise cannot rely on PRS/PPL (the UK equivalents of IMRO/PPI) blanket licensing. Broadcasts outside of the state in this fashion would mean negotiating licence fees directly with the various musical rights and sound recording rightsholders. For most programmes intended for RTÉ, these costs might render the budget unworkable. However, for programmes funded by RTÉ/the Media Commission that will be broadcast in Ireland only, RTÉ does have an agreement in place with MCPS in relation to international uses on its Player (see fn 49).

[17.3.29] Specially commissioned music in any event will very likely be cleared for all media worldwide[58] as will production music (and hence Northern Ireland or elsewhere will not present an issue) but the use of commercial music (e.g. an Adele track) would be enormously expensive if recourse could not be had to the broadcaster blanket licence systems. However, if say Netflix were to later acquire the programme for dissemination worldwide (and not merely on Netflix Ireland), commercial music could then be more extensively considered (and the soundtrack reworked) as the licence/acquisition fee payable by Netflix would allow the producers rethink the music licensing arrangements (or indeed Netflix has its own blanket licensing arrangements in place with collection societies).

[17.3.30] In respect of music programmes (featuring live or pre-recorded artist performances) the independent producer commissioned by RTÉ may have cleared uses worldwide as a matter of course. However, artists attached to major labels like Universal might well come with strict contractual restrictions. Therefore, while RTÉ could be in a position, in terms of technologies and rights clearance, to transmit the programme worldwide on its Player, certain territories may need to be blocked due to specific record label requirements relating to their artists. Further, North America is excluded from the RTÉ/MCPS blanket licensing scheme on the publishing side. Another issue is that membership of collection

---

58 For instance, if Screen Ireland is co-funding a project with RTÉ and the Media Commission, it will require music to be cleared for all uses worldwide.

societies (such as IMRO) is not necessarily permanent. As an alternative, some rightsholders nowadays are registering with the likes of Kobalt (publishing) and Peermusic (masters/neighbouring rights) for their royalties management and de-registering with the non-for-profit societies. Thus, while a production may have cleared music at one point in time under the broadcaster blanket licensing arrangements, this may not be the case in the future which would require the matter to be revisited, likely leading to future costs.

Online transmission and retransmission of certain television and radio programmes

[17.3.31] The situation at the time of writing is in a state of flux given the 2019 'SatCab' Directive on online transmission and retransmission of television and radio programmes[59] which was transposed into national law by the government in July 2022 by SI No 357 of 2022. It remains to be seen in practice how this Directive may or will affect blanket music licensing. The stated purpose of the SatCab Directive is to lay down rules to enhance cross-border access to a greater number of television and radio programmes by facilitating the clearance of rights for the provision of online services that are ancillary to the broadcast of certain types of television and radio programmes and for their retransmission.

[17.3.32] The SatCab Directive also lays down rules for the transmission of television and radio programmes through "direct injection" which is a process increasingly used by broadcasters to exhibit their programmes to the public. Instead of transmitting their programmes directly to the public over the air or by wire, broadcasters send their programmes to distributors which in turn transmit them to the public.

[17.3.33] To address the difficulties associated with copyright clearance, the country-of-origin principle provides that rights required to make certain programmes available on broadcasters' online services (for instance their catch-up services) are to be cleared only for the broadcaster's country of principal establishment (instead of all EU member states in which the broadcaster wishes to make its programmes available). The Directive applies to all radio programmes, but only to television programmes that are news and current affairs programmes, or fully financed own productions of the broadcasting organisation.

---

59 'SatCab' Directive (EU) 2019/789 of 17 April 2019 amending Directive 93/83/EEC. The country of origin principle contained therein applies to all online radio programmes and to certain online television programmes being news and current affairs programmes and programmes that are fully-financed own productions of the broadcasting organisations. It does not apply to television productions acquired from third parties or commissioned by the broadcasters from independent producers. Television broadcasts of sport events are also excluded. Broadcasters are not obliged to make such programmes available online across borders and the country of origin principle is therefore an enabling mechanism for broadcasters who may wish to offer programmes on their online services across EU member state territories.

[17.3.34] Moreover, the SatCab Directive extends the system of mandatory collective management (currently applicable to cable retransmissions only) to retransmission services provided through other means such as satellite, digital terrestrial or online technologies. This system allows retransmission operators to clear the necessary rights in a simpler manner. They need to clear the relevant rights with broadcasters whose channels they retransmit and with collective management organisations (e.g. IMRO) and not with several individual rightsholders on a one-to-one basis (SI No 357 of 2022 therefore amends ss 103 and 174 of the Copyright and Related Rights Act 2000). The charges to be paid for the relevant rights may be calculated on the basis of the revenues of the broadcasting organisation.

Alternatives to using commercial music

[17.3.35] Sometimes a music supervisor, with a sizeable budget, for a film or television series may specifically require commercial music such as a Stevie Wonder, Metallica or Dolly Parton song to add enhanced production value or because the mood or lyrics thematically align with a particular sequence in the film to great dramatic effect (take Journey's *Don't Stop Believin'* used in the final scenes of *The Sopranos*). However, for smaller independent productions, obtaining the necessary rights and legally clearing the use of such music can be a painstaking and cost-prohibitive process (unless the project is for television broadcast and is covered under national blanket licence rules). Some songs may be co-owned by multiple artists and controlled by a number of publishers (with sound recordings also to be cleared by record labels) and registered with a variety of collection societies worldwide. Clearance will most likely require the paid services of an expert music clearance practitioner. Therefore, it is prudent to consider three more economical alternatives.

Production (library) music

[17.3.36] The first is broadcast quality production or library music (e.g. Artlist, IMRO/MCPS production music,[60] PRS production music (to which its MCPS UK arm has outsourced its licensing administration), Universal production music and JW[61] Media Music to name but a few) which is music specifically written for inclusion in audio (e.g. radio drama or documentaries, podcasts, or for advertising jingles) and audiovisual productions. This has the added advantage of the sound recordings also having been cleared. Often the composer will write, perform and record music (and will hence hold the publishing, performer and master rights) that is licensed or sold to film production music libraries.

---

60 Anyone wishing to use IMRO production music must first sign up to the MCPS code of conduct, an agreement between MCPS and music users which defines the terms of how production music may be used and the procedure for making licence applications.

61 Josef Weinberger (London) – see also Chapter 19 on stageshow licensing by Josef Weinberger.

[17.3.37] Another distinct advantage to library music is that content is generally available for advertising and promotional uses as well as in the production itself. This is not always the case with commercial music whereby use of the music in teasers and trailers might oftentimes be expressly prohibited.

[17.3.38] One slight drawback to using services such as those offered by Artist is that the licence is non-exclusive. Therefore, one might hear the same music in several productions which impacts on its uniqueness. Second, the licence does not cover payment of royalties to performance rights organisations. Hence, the producer or broadcaster will need to submit music cue sheets to IMRO and PPI in respect of assets licensed from Artlist, Pond5 and so forth in order that the creators thereof are further remunerated in royalties distributions arising out of public performances of the material. The submission of music cue sheets arises across the board however whether covered by blanket licence, collection society production music or as sourced from operators such as Artlist.

Commissioning music for a film

[17.3.39] The second option is specially commissioning a songwriter or composer at an agreed fee to write a song, score music or sound designs for a project and to assign,[62] part-assign (sale subject to usage conditions and/or future royalty splits) or license rights by synchronisation licence agreement to the film/television show producer.

[17.3.40] As regards assignment, 'sale' or intended 'full buy-out' of rights may still leave the matter of royalties to be addressed. While sound recordings can be sold (but with performers, which may include the composer as music performer thereon, typically remaining entitled to royalties from exploitation of the sound recording in different media),[63] seasoned industry-savvy writers of music will generally retain at least their full writer share which comprises half of the publishing income for performance income and mechanical royalties.[64] The composer agreement will reflect how that half (or more if the composer

62 Outright buyout of writer share and publisher share so that the artist will not generate future royalties – such a deal would be reflected most likely in a substantial consideration sum payable. IMRO may query a work registration where the usually sacrosanct writer share is not being registered for a composer/songwriter (see fn 64).

63 Here, there is statutory intervention for such a performer. An artist-songwriter who also sings and/or plays on the track has the right to equitable remuneration from the owner of the copyright in a sound recording which, after assignment, will be the film or television producer. This right can only be assigned to a collection society (*per* s 208 of the Copyright and Related Rights Act 2000 as amended, 'the 2000 Act'). Thus, unless there is a full buyout of performer rights to preclude royalties in the future (royalties instead passing to the new owner if it registers with RAAP as proprietary rightsholder), performers will directly receive royalties for registered performances in the usual fashion.

64 Legal ownership will not necessarily affect royalties. Despite assigning rights, writers of a song will generally be entitled to at least 50 percent of the public performance royalties. Collection societies operate on this basis and would need sight of a legal agreement to register a work otherwise.

negotiates a better deal) will be paid – for example, that the film producer will register the track(s) as publisher (if a member of IMRO/MCPS) or will itself assign rights to a music publisher which will register the works to ensure both the film producer and the writer receive whatever royalty splits have been agreed.

[17.3.41] Nowadays, composers will also in effect be producers as they will have home studio and digital music capabilities allowing them to record as well as write. They are then in a position to deal with both sound recording rights and song rights in a combined composer/music producer agreement. In the case of their hiring session musicians to play instruments live in studio or elsewhere (or indeed to render performances of digital instruments), the contract will usually require that composers pay for such performers from their own fee and secure all performance releases from any persons performing on the recording and to produce such signed releases when delivering the recording to the commissioning film producer.

[17.3.42] In situations whereby the film producer records live performances as in the case of a documentary or action picture featuring a traditional[65] Irish music session in a public house, the producer will be default legal owner of the sound recording but will need to obtain releases from the music performers who contributed to the film or programme by musical performance (or other appearance on camera to include interviews).

Dealings with music producers

[17.3.43] If the composer uses the services of a music producer to record the subject music, the music producer will assign the master rights to the recording if that is what the contract provides in a work for hire type arrangement with the film production company,[66] or more likely, he will assign the rights to the composer and the composer in turn will assign those rights to the film producer. However, should the music producer instead wish to outright own the masters (depending perhaps on level of creative input) notwithstanding engineering/ music producer fees paid, and not assign any and all rights he may have by statutory default in the recording, the sound recording will instead be licensed to the film producer by way of master use licence from the music producer.

[17.3.44] The other scenario of course is that dealings between the composer and

---

[65] If the music compositions are out of copyright or have long been in the public domain, no need arises to obtain writer clearance.

[66] In Chapter 10A it was seen that the default owner of a recording is the producer thereof. 'Producer' is defined in s 2 of the 2000 Act in relation to a film or sound recording as the person by whom the arrangements necessary for the making of the film or sound recording, as the case may be, are undertaken. Thus, for the avoidance of doubt, the composer here will require the music producer to assign any and all rights he may have in the master (and an assignment in respect of performer rights if the music producer also performs on the track).

music producer will be on the basis that it is the composer who is the statutory 'producer' and thus author of the sound recording as the person arranging and paying for the recording and the music producer's services – it is best however in any cases where there may be ambiguity in this regard to put the matter beyond doubt so that, if the music producer is deemed for whatever reason to be the 'producer' for statutory definition purposes, he assigns any and all rights to the composer.

[17.3.45] This sort of agreement would need to be discussed well in advance. The film producer hiring a composer to compose and arrange the recording will generally require the composer to assign rights to the music and to the recording if he self- produces or hires a music producer. If (which the contract will typically require) the composer hires in third parties to perform on, engineer, produce and provide mastering services for a sound recording, the composer will give a warranty that all such persons will sign a release assigning their copyright and related rights[67] and waiving their moral rights.

Using an emerging band's music

[17.3.46] The third eventuality is to use music of a less well-known artist or band rather than an internationally successful pop song (that would attract very substantial synchronisation licence and master use fees perhaps into the thousands if not tens of thousands of euro). Those artists or bands, if fledgling, may well be willing to license the use of their music to an audiovisual producer for a very moderate fee. If the film or television programme performs well, there are obvious advantages to the artist or band concerned in terms of revenue from public performance royalties (received each time the film/programme is broadcast or repeated) or if their legacy songs on the soundtrack receive renewed radio airplay or are streamed online – take the 25-year old song *After All* by Cork band The Frank and Walters which enjoyed a major resurgence in Ireland and the UK after featuring in *The Young Offenders* television series. The knock-on effect for the artists, if they control the masters, is most likely a rise in sales and income through downloads and streaming. More importantly, they will also have more opportunities for live performance and touring income on the back of a surge in popularity.

[17.3.47] The artist giving consent must not be precluded by prior contract or otherwise from doing so (such as a performer or songwriter who is exclusively tied into a record label deal (see ss 215 and 302 of the 2000 Act) or publishing contract (see s 122) and therefore the clearance of such label or publisher may/would also be required by way of letter of waiver or consent),[68] and must otherwise

67 This will not affect public performance royalties due to the performers. A vocalist for example will be entitled to equitable remuneration by way of royalties from RAAP for the vocal performances on the music sound recording used in a film.

68 Or the label/publisher can join as a party to the release/music licensing contract.

have full legal authority to give consent and to license or assign the rights being sought. In the case of three songwriters, one co-author signature is insufficient. All co-writers will need to execute the subject synchronisation licence or release.

[17.3.48] Care must be exercised where releases are being signed 'on behalf of' a band. That is fully in order if the band (a 'firm' in partnership law parlance as will be seen in Chapter 22) is a partnership[69] as is most likely the case. However, if a band is a company, the person signing the release must be a director or other duly authorised officer of the company so as to lawfully bind the company.

Commissioning the recording of a cover song for a production

[17.3.49] When a gig is played in a public house or other venue by a cover band, the cover band will not require permission from the original songwriters to perform the tracks. It would render local live music virtually unworkable. However, the original writers should nonetheless receive payment through public performance royalties. The band is thus expected to list any cover songs performed in its gig-list submission to IMRO.[70]

[17.3.50] In the film, television and streaming sector, pre-existing material can likewise be covered by subsequent artists but in this case more likely for the purposes of evading the need to pay expensive master use royalties to a record label. The original recording would not be used and permission in respect thereof does not arise. Clearance would nonetheless be required from the songwriters to synchronise their work (lyrics and melody) in the subject project.

[17.3.51] There is no requirement, unlike with a song composition, for a sound recording to be original so as to attract copyright protection. Section 17(2) of the Copyright and Related Rights Act 2000 Act specifies that copyright subsists in original literary, dramatic, musical or artistic works whereas it likewise subsists in sound recordings, films, broadcasts or cable programmes but the latter grouping is not prefaced with the word 'original'. Ergo, by re-recording a song, film producers (or music producers if they retain master ownership) will own fresh copyright in this new recording for inclusion in a television production, advertisement, film, stageshow or radio release.

[17.3.52] It can oftentimes be wrongly assumed that provided that the original creator ultimately receives royalties that a song can be covered and used at will.[71]

---

69 s 5 of the Partnership Act 1890 provides that every partner is an agent of the firm and his other partners for the purpose of the business of the partnership; and the acts of every partner who does any act for carrying on in the usual way business of the kind carried on by the firm of which he is a member bind the firm and his partners.

70 Sound recording royalties will not arise unless the band is using backing tracks of the original material. It will be playing the music live.

71 In the US the position for covering other creators' music is governed by a compulsory licence system allowing artists to legally sell their rendition of another song based on a

As a matter of law[72] and courtesy, for a radio release, permission should be obtained from MCPS. For inclusion of a cover song in a film, a synchronisation licence will be required (unless covered by broadcaster blanket licence in the case of a general entertainment television programme) from the legacy writer to place the original composition in timed relation to the action in the film. The cover artist will receive no royalties from IMRO or MCPS (not being a writer/publisher of the piece – cover songs are not registered with IMRO)[73] and it is the original creator who will stand to receive public performance royalties.

Moral rights and covers

[17.3.53] Failing to obtain permission from the original rightsholder wholly neglects the issue of moral rights and possible intended changes to the melody/arrangement and lyrics of the piece as written. Songwriters can object to a cover (which is an adaptation of a work outlawed by statute in the absence of prior authority) if, for example, the song is used in bad taste, is taken out of context, the musical arrangement is changed, the lyrics are altered or they come to the conclusion that the project does not match or fit the track which could thus potentially injure their reputation (e.g. if used in pornography, in a sordid or crime-related depiction, or for political or religious purposes).

[17.3.54] In summary, to cover a song especially where the arrangement might be altered, it is necessary to contact the writers (or publishers) so that they can consider their moral rights and grant permission for the intended use. Otherwise, without compromising the integrity of the original composition, a person may release a cover version of a song once the appropriate licence has been obtained from MCPS. Any permission for changes to lyrics or arrangements must be sought directly from the copyright holder. This also applies on large productions including *American Idol* where the contestant wishes to use a new arrangement (to be played live by the show's houseband or where a backing track has to be specially produced for that arrangement).

---

set royalty payment scale. It is obtainable for any song that has already been previously recorded and sold with the consent of the original musical copyright holder. Unlike a traditional music copyright licence, the terms for a compulsory cover licence are established by the US Copyright Office rather than the artist or record label. Also, a compulsory cover licence does not require negotiations with the original rightsholder provided a notice of intent to obtain a licence is sent to the copyright owner a month before sale of the cover song. In saying that, depending on use, say change of an arrangement for an *America's Got Talent* performance by a contestant, clearance would be required.

72 s 37 (rights restricted by copyright in a work) of the 2000 Act.

73 In the case of covers for radio and online release, cover artists will receive public performances royalties from RAAP as performers on sound recordings, and separately, will receive record royalties (at whatever percentage is agreed in the contract) from their label for single sales and downloads (if signed to a label).

Chapter 18

Life Rights; Right of Publicity; Commercials, Image Rights & False Endorsement; Passing Off

INTRODUCTION TO LIFE RIGHTS

[18.1.01] *Catch Me If You Can*, *My Left Foot*, *In the Name of the Father*, *Rocketman*, *The Iron Lady*, *Argo*, *The Disaster Artist*, *Spotlight*, *Steve Jobs*, *The Social Network*, *Bohemian Rhapsody* and *The Big Short* are just a handful of examples from a long list of successful film titles based on life stories. True stories can also be adapted for live stageshow exploitation in musicals or plays, Andrew Lloyd Webber and Tim Rice's *Evita* being an example. The advantage to creating content inspired by true life events is simple – the story in each case is already written, which in itself results in considerable cost benefits.[1] Biopics will require a writer, however, to pen a screenplay centred on the already well-known underlying events.

[18.1.02] It may be opportune and highly advisable, but not always necessary, for a filmmaker or stage musical producer to purchase the rights to a person's life story by way of depiction release or other such contract.[2] Take the example of a documentary chronicling the life of an Irish soccer or other sports personality who achieves a level of success, descends into a life of crime and drugtaking, emerges stoically at the other end and sets up a charitable foundation to help illiterate adults obtain a third level education. This inspiring tale might attract the attention of bookwriters and film producers. A non-disclosure agreement could be considered as a first port of call and a producer may subsequently persuade such sports personality not to enter into discussions with competitor producers, and ultimately talks could culminate in the purchase of story rights.

---

1 Melissa Fish, "The 'Real Life': Life Story Rights in the United Kingdom" (2013), *Entertainment Law Review*, (24) 6, pp 196-198.

2 In relation to stage rights, producer Lin-Manuel Miranda obtained consents that were not necessarily required for the *Hamilton* stageshow. This course of action did nothing but catapult him to the ultimate success the production enjoyed with endorsement from a variety of artists whose work was sampled.

The need for a life rights agreement

[18.1.03] Notwithstanding courts' liberal attitude to freedom of expression, the above documentary can be achieved without the consent of and legal agreement with the former soccer personality but there is always the threat of a breach of privacy or data protection claim[3] or a defamation action if the documentary veers into fiction and dramatises untrue facts which injure the subject's reputation in the eyes of the public. Moreover, failing to seek permission from a living individual subject could also affect eligibility for errors and omissions ('E&O') cover discussed below which may or will render funding and distribution options impossible. Further, financiers such as Screen Ireland might require a contractual agreement to be in place as a prerequisite to funding. Accordingly, the more sensible route is to obtain the subject's blessing and strike an agreement.[4] This will buttress the documentary or feature drama by allowing the filmmaker access, which would not otherwise be available, to personal and private historical information, diaries, photographs, documents, amateur film clips and so forth but will also assist in interviewing family and friends who are made aware that the sports star has agreed to participate in, support and endorse the project. The subject may even be willing to co-write, script-consult, serve as executive or associate producer or assist with funding.

[18.1.04] Astute producers will thus enter into an option/acquisition agreement with the subjects to be portrayed with a right to acquire (either outright or by non-exclusive licence) the rights to their story. Typically, producers may take an option over the life rights for a certain period of time rather than acquiring them outright in order to lower their initial development expenses and cushion the blow if the project fails to be financed. Essentially, the contract is a form of cooperation agreement whereby individuals allow the producer to fictionalise or document their life events in return for a fee. They can sometimes also agree to assist in promotional efforts and may be offered rights of consultation during production.

Documentaries

[18.1.05] A documentary subject's rights are dictated by two interrelated factors, namely the rights granted by contract with the filmmakers and the rights granted by law. A well-drafted contract will set out a documentary subject's rights and obligations, including what avenues are open if production is halted or does not come to completed fruition for whatever reason. It will also outline whether such participant will have production and creative input, or will simply act as a conduit for storytelling. In the case of the first factor, the contract will govern

---

[3] Having regard for example to art 8 of the European Convention on Human Rights.

[4] Spielberg's production company DreamWorks SKG (founded by Steven Spielberg, Jeffrey Katzenberg and David Geffen) adopted a no-risk strategy when it purchased the rights to Merhan Karimi Nasseri's life story for the romantic comedy *The Terminal* starring Tom Hanks whose character is based on Nasseri.

whether the subject will have an ownership stake in the film and potentially even take control of the production by means of rights reversion, buying up all the footage and/or hiring a new production team to complete the film if it runs into difficulty. With the second factor, the question of withdrawal of consent under the GDPR (or if there is no contract, privacy law and defamation issues may arise) for use of portrayed subjects' likenesses and stories is a pivotal consideration as is the level of oversight they will be granted, if any, to control how they will be depicted and presented on camera.

[18.1.06] Absent a written contributor/collaboration agreement or similar life rights contract, the law requires filmmakers to obtain their subjects' permission (by signed release) in any event to screen the finished product for an audience when the subject is actually actively participating in the project by way of interviews. Failure to do this means they could be in violation of their subjects' rights, exposing them then to claims including breach of performer rights,[5] defamation, breach of the duty of confidence, invasion of privacy, breach of data protection, or breach of one's right to publicity as recognised in the US and as somewhat inappropriately termed 'image rights' in Ireland and the UK.[6]

[18.1.07] Moreover, life rights will be acquired in writing by a seasoned producer, not only to ensure the subject's cooperation with the production, but also to appease the concerns of insurance companies, financiers and studios/distributors. Insurance companies will not provide the necessary errors and omissions coverage if there is a strong likelihood the production would be left open to liability by failing to secure these rights. Financiers will likewise refrain from backing a film where the main subject's story is not secured, and studios, online platforms and distributors will most likely not purchase a film if there is a potential threat of a defamation and/or invasion of privacy claim.

[18.1.08] That is not to say that biographical documentaries or films cannot be produced where the subject is not participating in the production (see para [18.1.16]), and the US First Amendment constitutional freedom of expression can allow producers to use an American person's name or likeness without prior approval as discussed in the *Appendix* with reference to such cases as *Sarver v Chartier* 813 F.3d 891 (9th Cir. 2016) concerning the Oscar-winning film *The Hurt Locker*). The subject may be deceased and, if living, productions can be made that are not defamatory and are thus based on facts or verifiable truths or

---

5 Within the meaning of s 202 of the Copyright Act 2000 (a performance is given by an actor in a film or by other performances in literary, dramatic, musical or artistic works).

6 Broadly speaking, publicity rights in the US are subjects' ability to control the commercial use of their name, image, likeness, story, or any other specific aspect of identity. The rights and remedies vary state by state, but they are often considered part of an overarching right of privacy which is recognised in all 50 states. Seventeen states (most notably New York and California) have statutes preventing the unauthorised use of a person's identity. The remaining states protect it through common law.

on non-defamatory[7] information already in the public domain, and which do not invade the privacy of the subject. Where living however, as above, it is the preferred route that the subject be engaged and a contract signed.

The perils of relying on the truth[8] defence in defamation actions

[18.1.09] The UK's Entertainment Law Review neatly summarised the defamation suit risks facing producers in a 2016 article[9] thus:

> A producer will often rely on the assumption that they are safe from a defamation claim on the basis that the depiction of an individual is true. However, there are inherent risks in this approach given that the portrayal of any individual is a subjective exercise in itself. Indeed, truth is a fluid concept. In the creative exercises of writing and directing, a scriptwriter or director may not necessarily have the risk of defamation at the forefront of their minds but rather, and quite rightly given their roles, how to create a compelling story. The truth may inevitably become more 'colourful' during this process. Whilst the 'justification' or 'truth' defence certainly exists under English law, what is important to note here is that the defence in itself does not prevent an aggrieved individual bringing the claim in the first place and applying for injunctive relief on these grounds. Although the claim may be successfully defended, the consequences of litigation and, potentially, the delays in releasing the film or television programme due to an injunction could be significant. The other issue with relying on the idea that 'if it's true it cannot be defamatory' is that not all sources are reliable. Given that most evidence is anecdotal by nature, it is difficult to ensure the 'real' truth and verify the information or accounts that form the basis for a script and content of a film or television programme.

Detainment: The James Bolger murder

[18.1.10] *Detainment* by director Vincent Lambe is an Irish film addressing the real-life abduction, torture and murder of two-year-old James Bolger in England in 1993 by Liverpool 10-year-olds Jon Venables and Robert Thompson. While the consent of the long since deceased toddler was obviously not in issue, the moral and ethical issues surrounding the production's failure to liaise with his parents in this immensely sensitive case came hurtling to the fore. It was shortlisted in the 2019 Live Action Short Film category of the Oscar nominations. Lambe based his work on police transcripts and from surveillance recordings. The victim's mother, Denise Fergus, appeared on UK and Irish television revealing in no uncertain terms that neither she nor her ex-husband had been informed of the film in advance and appealing for a boycott and a retraction of the Academy award nomination and/or a withdrawal of the film from the ceremony by the

---

7 Note that re-publishing of defamatory content can give rise to a claim in defamation.

8 See s 16 of the Defamation Act 2009.

9 Melissa Fish, "Life Story Rights in the UK: Ten Top Tips For Producers" (2016). Available at: https://www.fieldfisher.com/publications/2016/12/life-story-rights-in-the-uk-10-top-tips-for-producers (republished from an *Entertainment Law Review* article) [Accessed 15 January 2019].

director. Lambe apologised for not informing the family before production and denied making the film for financial gain.

[18.1.11] *Detainment*, which became embroiled in unsavoury and arguably avoidable controversy, demonstrates how a movie project could otherwise have benefitted from a blessing of the subject (or in this case the deceased subject's parents). The director's contention was that emotional involvement of the family might have disproportionately influenced how the facts were depicted. In the final analysis, it is perhaps true to say that in all of the circumstances the better course of action would have been to procure the parents' consent to produce a documentary involving a story so intimately and painfully connected to them with resultant gains for authenticity.

Data protection legislation

[18.1.12] Another key but frequently missed issue is data protection and GDPR requirements. A written consent, coupled with a release, is advised notwithstanding the latitude potentially granted by s 43 (data processing and freedom of expression and information, including processing for journalistic purposes or for the purposes of academic, artistic or literary expression) of the Data Protection Act 2018. The relevant legal issues in this connection were covered in Chapter 13.

Deceased subjects

[18.1.13] The freedom which productions of this type allow has prompted a deluge of films and television programmes in recent years, including the cinematic Oscar-winning portrayal of Abraham Lincoln by Fox and ITV's television series *Mr Selfridge*. If the subject is deceased, the threat of an action from heirs will not arise as an action for defamation only applies to living persons (or where the action for defamation in the case of pecuniary damages, rather than general damages for pain and suffering, was instituted before the subject's death).[10] It is important to recognise though that some jurisdictions such as France and the US are not so forgiving and do have post-mortem rights of publicity and thus where international release is intended local counsel should ideally be consulted in certain territories.[11]

---

[10] See s 39 (survival of cause of action on death) of the Defamation Act 2009 and Chapter 4 (Survival of the Defamation Action) of the Law Reform Commission's *Consultation Paper on the Civil Law of Defamation*, LRC CP 3-1991.

[11] Melissa Fish, *supra* at fn 9. See also the discussion of US defamation (civil and criminal), descendible publicity and privacy rights in this connection in William H. Binder, "Publicity Rights and Defamation of the Deceased: Resurrection or R.I.P.?" (2002) 12(2) *DePaul University Journal of Art, Technology and Intellectual Property Law* 297-332; and Anushree Yewale, Riddhi Tulshian and Meghana Chandorkar, "Posthumous Survival of Privacy and Personality Rights: Part 1" (2021) *TMT Law Practice* (India). Available at: https://www.legal500.com/developments/thought-leadership/posthumous-survival-of-privacy-personality-rights-part-1/ [Accessed 5 April 2022].

[18.1.14] European Court of Human Rights case law has accepted the possibility that courts may sometimes be required to protect the reputation of the deceased, within the scope of Art 8 of the European Convention on Human Rights ('the ECHR'). The same court's jurisprudence has also accepted that the reputation of a deceased member of a person's family might affect one's private life and identity, provided that there was a sufficiently close link between them.

Legal status of life rights

[18.1.15] The first myth to debunk is the one which professes that we own the rights to our own life stories. Aside from judicially recognised personality rights discussed later but through the medium of the tort of passing off rather than image rights *per se*, it appears there is no legal basis in law for asserting this in copyright, trademark or any part of IP law. Provided that information has been obtained lawfully, there is technically nothing to prevent a producer making a film or a programme based on one's life events. It is this fact which has allowed celebrity-based programmes such as *E! True Hollywood Story* or indeed the unauthorised biography to exist. It is not the potential infringement of an IP right which producers should be concerned about but the associated risks that arise with the public portrayal of an individual such as the constitutionally protected right to one's good name.

[18.1.16] Life rights are not a commodity that warrant copyright protection. As above, our life rights are not necessarily rights we own and therefore exclusivity in the true sense cannot be granted in respect thereof.[12] In the IP arena, a bundle of protective rights does not accompany one's personal life journey (unless of course in the case of a book written by the subject, works by an artist or compositions in respect of musicians for instance). This means that a number of television programmes or films may be based on the same story as occurred with Steve Jobs. However, while entering into a non-exclusive contract with an individual by way of option or other agreement will not impede the creation of other productions forever, it generally at least offers first dibbs and prevents competition from other producers for the term of the option or other relevant legal agreement.

Clearing additional sources

[18.1.17] Rather than embarking on a life rights (or life story) agreement route, the subject to be portrayed on screen may have written an autobiography. This would then entail executing an option and purchase agreement with the author and/or publisher to adapt the book into a screenplay, clear the film rights in the work and negate any copyright infringement claims. In 2011 in the case of

12 Life rights agreements with subjects will of course seek to ensure exclusivity to prevent rival producers from undertaking a project about the same subject.

Hodgson v Isaac[13] a county court in the UK, the (misnamed) Patents County Court for England and Wales, ruled, *per* Judge Birss that the defendant's film script which told the story of the claimant's life had infringed the copyright in the claimant's autobiography. The judge found that elements reproduced in the script were not simply a generic story about a disabled football fan but constituted a substantial part of the story told in the book and were not based purely on conversations the defendant had with the claimant.

[18.1.18] As well as obtaining material from the subject, information may need to be gleaned from newspaper articles, magazines and books, audiovisual, online media or radio archives, or an existing documentary. The consent of journalists, newspapers, photographers and authors will in some cases need to be obtained for copyright clearance purposes. In relation to feature film or television remakes of a pre-existing documentary based on real events, where the story is being told largely in the same fashion as the documentary, the consent of the documentary's producers will ideally be required to ward off copyright claims. This course of action would bring the added advantage of piggy-backing the success and promotion of that prior documentary.

Breach of privacy

[18.1.19] This area of law, underpinned by the ECHR (and by implied constitutional rights), is discussed in Chapter 35. Article 8 of the Convention, to which, pursuant to human rights legislation in Ireland[14] and the UK[15] the courts must have regard, provides that persons enjoy the right to respect for their private and family life and their home correspondence. In *Campbell v MGN Ltd*,[16] the House of Lords held that the *Daily Mirror* had breached Naomi Campbell's rights by publishing reports and pictures of her attendance at Narcotics Anonymous meetings. For present purposes, however, at least in terms of well-known public figures, successfully arguing a breach of privacy claim may prove difficult. Elizabeth Taylor for instance was unable to enjoin the release of NBC's docudrama based on an unauthorised television biography of her life.

Breach of confidence and new privacy torts

[18.1.20] Another possible claim arising in the case of productions based on real events is an equitable remedy for breach of confidence (a duty of confidence

13 [2010] EWPCC 37. Paul Hodgson was disabled as a result of childhood meningitis. In 2000 he self-published his autobiography. He wrote the book to challenge the stereotype of the wheelchair-bound victim. It tells the story of his life as a fan of Darlington Football Club, his relationship with his family and his experiences in school, employment and community care.

14 s 4 (interpretation of convention provisions) of the European Convention on Human Rights Act 2003.

15 Human Rights Act 1988 (UK).

16 *Campbell v MGN Ltd* [2004] UKHL 22; [2004] 2 AC 457.

arises when confidential information comes to the knowledge of a person in circumstances in which it would be unfair if it were disclosed to others) stemming from a judgment of the Lord Chancellor, Lord Cottenham, in which he restrained the defendant from publishing a catalogue of private etchings made by Queen Victoria and Prince Albert.[17] Breach of confidence was recognised in 2016 in Canada as a new tort by the Ontario Supreme Court of Justice together with a new privacy tort of "publication of embarrassing private facts".

[18.1.21] In *Doe 464533*,[18] a plaintiff brought an action for damages against her ex-boyfriend after he posted a sexually explicit video of her on an internet pornography website.[19] The court held the plaintiff had proven this cause of action by demonstrating that the defendant had posted the intimate video online without her authorisation which a reasonable person would find to be highly offensive and because there was no legitimate public interest in the footage. The court awarded the plaintiff $100,000 in damages. In Ireland, such conduct now constitutes a criminal offence under Coco's Law.[20]

[18.1.22] The court thus defined the new privacy tort as publicising a matter concerning the private life of another, if the matter publicised or the act of publication is highly offensive to a reasonable person, and the matter is not of legitimate public concern. Private matters protected by the tort could include sexual relationships, family quarrels, or humiliating illnesses. The disclosure of the private facts must be a public disclosure meaning the disclosure must be to the public at large, as opposed to a private disclosure to a small group. The facts disclosed must be private facts meaning not facts that are generally known. The court noted that although private facts on the internet in a social media age are increasingly rare, they remain worthy of protection.

[18.1.23] Breach of confidence is also discussed in the 2016 UK Supreme Court decision in *PJS v News Group Newspapers Ltd*[21] (see Chapter 34 on media injunctions) wherein the court endorsed and vindicated the approach of lower courts in other cases in ruling that the tort of misuse of private information protects different values to breach of confidence and an injunction can still

---

17 *Prince Albert v Strange* (1849) 18 LJ Ch.

18 In *Doe 464533 v ND* (2016 ONSC 541).

19 The new Ontario law requires three elements to be proven in such claims: the information must have the necessary quality of confidence (meaning, the information is private and personal and not otherwise publicly available); the information must have been disclosed in circumstances where there is an obligation of confidence (meaning, there was a direct promise to keep the information private, or the circumstances that make it clear that the information was intended to be confidential and not meant to be circulated widely without express consent); and there must have been an unauthorised use of that information to the detriment of the party communicating it (detriment can be in the form of economic losses or psychological and emotional harm).

20 See s 2 of the Harassment, Harmful Communications and Related Offences Act 2020. This legislation was commenced by the Minister for Justice on 10 February 2021.

21 [2016] UKSC 26.

have value even if the information it protects is known to some. The tort and its development from its earlier equity origins was also considered by the House of Lords in *Campbell* as discussed in Chapter 35.

Douglas v Hello!

[18.1.24] The law of confidential information can protect commercial aspects of image rights, following the House of Lords' 2007 ruling in *Douglas v Hello!*[22] However, the information must have the requisite degree of confidence – in *Douglas*, steps had been taken to preclude publication of wedding photos by anyone besides the magazine which had by contract been given the exclusive right to do so.

[18.1.25] The attempt by the celebrity couple and *OK!* to prevent publication of the unauthorised images initially failed when the Court of Appeal overturned an interim injunction on 23 November 2000 with the result that both *OK!* and *Hello!* rushed to print. Editions of both magazines containing photographs of the wedding hit the newsstands on 24 November 2000. Following *Hello!'s* publication of the unauthorised photographs, the couple and *OK!* commenced an action against *Hello!* for damages. Both claimants were successful at first instance but in the Court of Appeal the decision in favour of *OK!* was reversed. Thus, the position of the parties after the Court of Appeal's decision was that *Hello!* was liable to the couple for breach of their privacy, with damages assessed at £14,600, while *OK!'s* claim on breach of confidence was refused. *OK!* appealed to the House of Lords. With majority support, the award of £1,033,156 in favour of *OK!* made by Lindsay J at first instance was reinstated.

[18.1.26] *OK!'s* appeal regarding the photographs was based on two separate claims, namely interference by unlawful means with its contractual or business relations or a breach of its equitable right to confidentiality in photographic images of the wedding. We shall concentrate on the former but it must be said that the judgment as a whole is conflicting, confusing and problematic on a number of fronts, not least because the question of whether or not the information was worthy of protection as "confidential" became somewhat redundant on a practical level because "once the approved pictures were published, albeit simultaneously,

22 [2003] EWHC 786 (Ch) (Lindsay J); [2005] EWCA Civ 595 (Court of Appeal); [2007] 4 All ER 545 (House of Lords). Michael Douglas and Catherine Zeta-Jones were a celebrity couple who sold exclusive photography rights of their wedding to *OK!* magazine. An unauthorised freelance photographer gained access to the wedding and sold pictures to the rival *Hello!* magazine. Reversing the judgment of the Court of Appeal, the final court of appeal held that *OK!* had paid one million pounds for the benefit of the obligation of confidence imposed upon all those present at the wedding in respect of any photographs of the wedding and was entitled to enforce that obligation. Note the Douglas couple's only connection at House of Lords stage was as the first-named party in the case report. They were not involved in the litigation at bar.

publication of the unapproved pictures was not a breach of confidence" (Lord Nicholls, dissenting).

[18.1.27] In other words, if *OK!* itself published the pictures, how could it then claim breach of confidence by *Hello!*? Yet while Lord Nicholls held that this publication by *OK!* destroyed its claim to confidentiality, the majority decided that *Hello!*'s actions still constituted a breach of confidence. Moreover, the decision, rather poorly reasoned, leaves a number of unanswered questions on which we will not dwell at this juncture.[23] It is uncertain whether the decision is of strong (or indeed any) persuasive authority for a similar case which might come before the Irish courts.

[18.1.28] The judgment would appear to mean that, where individuals control information regarding themselves (whether details of their personal lives or photographic images of a particular event), then they can protect it by way of privacy, and can also exploit it commercially by passing rights to the information to other parties – rights which can be enforced through the doctrine of breach of confidence. In the words of Lord Hoffmann:

> Some may view with distaste a world in which information about the events of a wedding… should be sold in the market in the same way as information about how to make a better mousetrap. But being a celebrity or publishing a celebrity magazine are lawful trades and I see no reason why they should be outlawed from such protection as the law of confidence may offer.[24]

Criminal law sanctions

[18.1.29] Mention was made above of posting an intimate video online without authorisation which a reasonable person might find to be highly offensive. While the Harassment, Harmful Communications and Related Offences Act 2020 (see Chapter 30) stops short of imposing civil liability on defendants, it does of course prescribe criminal liability which in effect (conviction and sentencing) is much more serious in nature, reputationally at least, than the potential exposure to civil law damages. Offences relate to distributing, publishing or threatening to distribute or publish intimate images without consent with intent to cause harm or being reckless as to whether harm is caused; recording, distributing or publishing intimate images without consent; and distributing, publishing or sending threatening or grossly offensive communication.

[18.1.30] Though of course seasoned film producers acting on legal advice will not engage in conduct of this sort, it is important nonetheless to bear the statute in mind in the case of inadvertent breach (say in the case of s 3: recording, distributing or publishing intimate images of another person without

---

23 See discussion and analysis in: Gillian Black, "OK! for Some: Douglas v Hello! in the House of Lords" (2007) *Edinburgh Law Review*, (11)3, pp 402-07.

24 Para 124 of the judgment.

consent – while ss 2 and 4 have a *mens rea* requirement of intent or recklessness, a s 3 offence is made out if the recording, distribution or publication seriously interferes with that other person's peace and privacy or causes alarm, distress or harm to that other person).

Errors and omissions insurance

[18.1.31] One of the most important considerations for financiers looking to invest in content is confirmation of E&O cover, which most likely will be a condition precedent to financing (and will be required too by any distribution/sales agency contract). Without evidence of consent from the portrayed individual(s), underwriters are highly unlikely to grant cover. In the alternative, they may well levy a higher premium in light of the risk of claims that may follow. Producers requiring investment for their projects should therefore bear this in mind during the development process and when being asked to provide clean chain of title documents. Indeed, Screen Ireland will require life rights agreements in appropriate circumstances as a condition to funding. Particular attention should be paid to adaptation, life rights or any necessary archival materials that are essential to the project ensuring also the rights are available worldwide in perpetuity in all forms of media.

Collaboration

[18.1.32] As alluded to above, aside from the astuteness of executing a legal agreement, myriad practical benefits flow from willing and active participation by the subject, as succinctly described in the UK *Entertainment Law Review* thus:[25]

> Whilst the legal benefits of involving the portrayed individual are important to consider, it is also worth noting the practical, commercial benefits to a collaborative approach. Engaging an individual gives the production team access to additional personal information, historical records and interviews, all of which could provide valuable insight on a creative level. There may be information which is not in the public domain or accessible through any medium other than from an individual themselves. Reducing reliance on third parties and getting the primary account directly from its source can help to avoid gaps in a story or information out of context. Having an individual backing a project can also help with marketing and promotion of the content. Any endorsement from an individual should lend credibility to the story and increase the effectiveness of the narrative.

Ideally, life story agreements or general contributor releases should also be concluded with family and friends featured in the film, ensuring first that such third party sources are not already under obligation in any confidentiality agreements with the subject or other third party producers.

---

25 *supra* at fn 9.

Private versus public figures

[18.1.33] Whether the film's subject is a private individual, public official or public figure will have a significant bearing. Public officials and figures have opened more of their lives to public scrutiny, and consequently more of their lives can be portrayed without invading their privacy. Indeed, a celebrity's decision to be in the public arena, and to profit therefrom, may preclude a successful lawsuit advancing a breach of privacy argument.

[18.1.34] In the US, public officials and figures must meet a much higher burden of proof in order to establish defamation or invasion of privacy. They must prove that a defamer intentionally spread a falsehood or acted with reckless disregard of the truth.[26] In Ireland, the much criticised and unnecessarily complex s 26 of the Defamation Act 2009 (with which juries[27] must grapple rather than an experienced judge when a case is taken in the High Court), concerning fair and reasonable publication on a matter of public interest, deals in part with the issue.[28]

[18.1.35] It states that it shall be a defence to defamation proceedings for the defendant to prove that the statement in respect of which the action was brought was published in good faith, and in the course of, or for the purpose of, the discussion of a subject of public interest, the discussion of which was for the public benefit; in all of the circumstances of the case, the manner and extent of publication of the statement did not exceed that which was reasonably sufficient; and in all of the circumstances of the case, it was fair and reasonable to publish the statement. Even for the trained lawyer, that is a mouthful! This section may be overhauled (through simplification, along the lines of the equivalent UK provision) in time however given the Department of Justice's review of defamation law report (2022) as discussed in Chapter 4.

[18.1.36] In the US, the only causes of action celebrities or public figures have against the use of their name, likeness or life story in non-commercial speech is for false light or libel.[29] In the below-cited *Seale* judgment, while certain events were fictionalised in the film *Panther*, the court held that the film did not either portray Seale in a false light or constitute libel although Seale tried to argue both points.[30]

---

26 Mark Litwak, *Dealmaking in the Film & TV Industry: From Negotiations to Final Contracts* (4th ed, Silman-James Press, Hollywood CA, 2017) (Chapter 3 Permission to Portray People and Places, Depiction and Location Releases).

27 Juries for defamation cases are an exception to the rule in civil law courtrooms in Ireland. The other exceptions are false imprisonment and assault cases (and prior to 1988, juries sat in personal injuries actions). There are calls for juries to be abolished for defamation trials – see Chapter 4.

28 See Chapter 4 for an analysis of the section.

29 In Irish law, there is no longer a distinction between the torts of libel and slander. Both come under the umbrella of defamation in the Defamation Act 2009.

30 The court nonetheless ruled that Seale's name and likeness on a CD related to the film constituted a commercial use of his name and likeness and was thus prohibited without a release.

Fictionalising

[18.1.37] The possibility of fictionalising a true story could also be considered to obviate the necessity for a depiction release. Names of the individuals involved can be changed as can locations in order that the real-life people are not recognisable to the public. The obvious downside is that the story's very appeal may be predicated on the fact that it is a true story which is the very attraction for viewers. Hence the need perhaps to explore the possibility of a life rights agreement instead.

Terms of a life rights agreement

[18.1.38] The purchase or assignment of life story rights can be structured as either an option/purchase deal or as an assignment without a prior option, both often coming with a reversion clause. A reversion clause provides that in the event the rights are not exploited within a certain number of years such as in the case where production cannot be financed, then all rights would revert to the subject. This provision protects subjects if they have sold life story rights to a producer who never exploits them, and another producer is subsequently interested in making such a film.

Extent of rights

[18.1.39] The parties must determine at the outset the extent of the rights granted. The filmmaker will require worldwide exploitation rights. Lawyers for the assignor of life rights on the other hand will oftentimes insist on retaining rights such as stageshow rights, novelisation and radio rights, and negotiation for the grant of remake, sequel, prequel and merchandising rights may also be key. It is important for the producer to acquire rights as extensive as possible as early as practicable so as to avoid seeking, renegotiating or securing them at a later date when the subject may well call for much more substantial remuneration particularly if the project has secured funding at that point or, if already distributed in its initial carnation (e.g. as a documentary), has performed well and the producers then envisage a spin-off production(s).

[18.1.40] The agreement should include a very broad release of all rights to the producer and a "hold harmless" indemnity provision for defamation, breach of privacy, breach of confidence claims and so forth. The production company should also specifically be granted the right to fictionalise and to change names in its sole discretion. Moreover, the prospect of litigation should be limited to monetary damages for breach of contract arising out of the failure to honour certain aspects of the contract, such that injunctive proceedings cannot be initiated to halt the production. The producer will seek to insist on provisions granting exclusive rights to the story, as well as to any photographs, documents, or other media related to the life story. This helps to ensure that subjects of the life story do not grant others the right to produce adaptations of their story.

Additional provisions could require the subject to make public appearances and participate in marketing efforts for the project.

Restrictions, rights to literary material

[18.1.41] It is advantageous to place a restriction on subjects' right to authorise any other biographical work based upon their life story and the freedom to provide personal documents or information to third parties. Usually, however, an exclusion is negotiated which grants the subject the right to appear on news interviews and sometimes to appear in documentary films that would not interfere with the producer's dramatised film.

[18.1.42] The film producer might want to also consider obtaining options for film rights in any previously published biography of the subject to the extent that this is possible within budgetary constraints. This could allow the producer to use certain facts and events that may appear only in this biography as protected under copyright and it would also prevent third parties from obtaining rights from the author of the biography.

Obtaining family consent: third party agreements

[18.1.43] Where practicable, the agreement may contain a clause that obliges the subject to obtain (or at least undertake or make best endeavours to obtain) written releases from family members, colleagues and friends who will contribute to the filmmaking pursuits by way of portrayal in the film or providing unfettered access to quotes, documents or information that may not otherwise be available from other sources.[31] This approach engages the individual involved and provides the production team additional personal information, historical records and interview opportunities, all of which could provide valuable insight on a creative level. In the case of teams, associations or groups, if the producer is planning to document the life of a sporting legend, for instance, it is opportune to gather all team members together and purchase or otherwise obtain all rights simultaneously.

[18.1.44] In addition, as stated, the filmmaker should be afforded the right to fictionalise or change names of characters (if the relevant persons do not agree to participate) thus allowing flexibility and an insurance policy against issues which may carry the potential to derail the entire project.

Publicity

[18.1.45] As previously noted, other matters to contemplate in life story rights

---

[31] If signed releases cannot be obtained from family and friends from the outset, the subject should at least be contractually obligated to cooperate with the producer in seeking to obtain these releases.

agreements are voluntary or obligatory participation by the subject in the marketing and publicity efforts for the film and, if needed, to act as a consultant to the screenwriter in the case of a dramatic film or the production team in the case of a documentary.

Assignment of rights

[18.1.46] The agreement will contain an assignment of rights provision in favour of the producer for financing and distribution agreement purposes so that it can be assigned or novated to a third party. The producer may need to assign or license rights to potential stakeholders such as Screen Ireland, a broadcaster, a distributor company, Netflix or a film studio. It may otherwise seek to sell on a project at a profit after development, or may require (or be obliged to source) another producer to take over the project in the case of financial difficulties.

Consideration

[18.1.47] The agreement should recite the consideration (money or anything of value) exchanged, even if only nominal such as €10 (courts generally in contract law disputes do not concern themselves with the adequacy of payment made)[32] as a contract can only be binding and enforceable with consideration. Otherwise, without money passing, a producer's efforts to develop a project could be deemed sufficient consideration for an option/purchase agreement. In addition, there are other means to compensate the subject of a life story besides a flat fixed fee if a fee is in fact to be paid. A percentage of producer net profits could be offered (this is not a wise option however for either party due to revenue waterfall considerations discussed in Chapter 7), an executive or associate producer credit, or consulting fees and/or bonuses to be paid when the film is eventually exploited in ancillary markets.

Warranties

[18.1.48] In terms of warranties, the producer will require the life rights subject to contractually refrain from ever suing for an invasion of privacy (and for breach of rights of publicity in the US), breach of confidence or for defamation, even if the producer takes some creative liberties in the means in which the story is presented. Likewise, the producer will seek a provision granting, in the producer's absolute discretion, a right to embellish, fictionalise, dramatise and adapt the story in any manner desirable. To obviate the life story subject's concerns of a prejudicial and negative portrayal in the film, a possible option is the right (in lieu of prior approval rights) to meaningful consultation in relation to the

---

32 However, in certain areas of copyright and related rights law such as performer rights, remuneration must be "equitable" as *per* national and EU legislation (see Chapters 10B and 11). If subjects appear in the film, they will accrue statutory protection (as regards rental rights and exploitation of their performance on sound recordings) and hence the consideration should in fact be equitable.

screenplay, treatment or rough cut of the film, with final and absolute editorial control being reserved to the producer's prerogative.

Approval and consultation

[18.1.49] An issue that can engender the most contentious negotiation in life story rights agreements and militate against the conclusion of a deal is script and/or final cut approval or some manner of control over how the subject is portrayed, outcomes any producer should avoid at all costs as no financier will accept this.[33] Compromises include the subject's exercising approval over the treatment, selection of a reputable and trustworthy writer, or dangling the offer of a creative or story consultant credit. A further potential concession could be to limit the subject matter and period portrayed, for example, to not include details of domestic violence that the subject had perpetrated, an acrimonious divorce or a period when the subject was incarcerated, in rehabilitation, or suffering from substance abuse.

RIGHT OF PUBLICITY IN THE US

[18.2.01] The right of publicity across the Atlantic is discussed in the *Appendix* for three purposes. First, US case law fleshes out the requirements for a successful case in that jurisdiction and thus illuminates the general legal principles (which may be in some way relevant or broadly similar should such a case with similar facts come before the Irish courts). Secondly, in the absence of directly relevant precedent in this jurisdiction, such decisions could be cited by counsel in Irish proceedings as non-binding, persuasive authority from another common law country – it must be noted however that entertainment law differs substantially in the two jurisdictions in many respects – Irish judges would tend to follow UK courts rather than their American brethren. Thirdly, Irish producers may be contracting with US-based life rights subjects or undertaking an unauthorised biographical film (namely where the subject, or the subject's family if the subject is deceased, has not signed a release and agreed to participate) to be distributed in North America.

COMMERCIALS, IMAGE RIGHTS AND FALSE ENDORSEMENT

[18.3.01] Production companies are frequently commissioned to shoot advertising videos or other promotional content. One cannot blindly follow a client brief and must be cognisant of the underlying legal issues to guard against legal action by the client, third parties or both. This is less so perhaps if

---

33 If granted, an approval right would afford the subject the power to control development of the production and conceivably to shut it down. Even if an approval right is not in fact granted, any language in the contract that agrees to portray the subject in a truthful or in a non-derogatory manner is fraught with danger and should be sidestepped.

the commissioning brand takes ownership of the video by assignment of rights from the producer (in a services agreement) and indemnifies the production company against all actions, but such assignment and full indemnification may not always take place meaning that the production company will be a mark for damages in the event of a successful suit.

[18.3.02] The umbrella term 'personality right' is commonly used in the US. A personality right in effect encompasses both a right of privacy and a right of publicity. In Ireland, a right of privacy is already protected as an implied constitutional right. It is therefore unlikely to be considered by the Irish courts to fall within the realm of what most legal practitioners would consider an 'image right'. Instead, an image right in this jurisdiction is more likely to be considered akin to the US right of publicity, which is intended to not only protect personalities' image, but also their name, mannerisms, voice and gestures. The term image right is therefore a misnomer and does not fully capture all aspects of a personality's distinctive attributes. Hence, the more accurate and better encompassing term is a right of publicity.[34]

Eddie Irvine

[18.3.03] The facts of the 2003 Court of Appeal (UK) decision in *Irvine v Talksport*[35] concerning false endorsements and passing off were that the defendant used a distorted image of the claimant, a famous Formula One racing driver, to endorse its product. The defendant operated a radio station called Talksport, which had formerly been known as Talk Radio. Its marketing company sent out promotional material to a number of people responsible for the placement of advertisements. The material included a brochure featuring on its cover a picture of the claimant. The right to use the picture had been legally obtained, but the marketing company had doctored the picture, removing the mobile phone that the claimant was holding and replacing it with a radio with the words "Talk Radio". Mr Irvine was dressed in the racing gear of the Ferrari team and apparently holding up to his left ear a small radio on which the station's logo clearly appeared. Irvine was depicted with his right hand raised to his right ear, as if to block out background noise from revving racing car engines, thus creating the impression that he is listening intently to the radio, and hence (given the logo) to Talk Radio.

[18.3.04] The claimant brought an action for passing off on the basis that it was understood by the market that he had endorsed the radio station. The court stated it could take judicial notice of the fact that it was common for famous people to exploit their names and images by way of endorsement. It was held that the

---

34 Tierney IP, *Rights of Publicity and Personal Portrayal in Ireland* (2018), tierneyip.com. Available at: http://www.tierneyip.com/wp-content/uploads/2018/08/Rights-of-Publicity-and-Personal-Portrayal-in-Ireland.pdf [Accessed 30 July 2019].

35 [2003] 2 All ER 881.

claimant did have a substantial reputation or goodwill, that the defendant had created a false message and accordingly was liable.

[18.3.05] The court, *per* Parker LJ, found that Irvine had a property right in his goodwill which he could protect from unlicensed appropriation consisting of a false claim or suggestion of endorsement of a third party's goods or business. Nothing prevented an action for passing off succeeding in a false endorsement case. The claimant had to show significant reputation and goodwill, and that a false message had been delivered which would have been understood by sufficient people to indicate his desire to associate himself with the defendant. His fame and personality were being exploited and a misrepresentation had been made to the relevant public that he endorsed the defendant's radio station.

[18.3.06] The court also held[36] that the unchallenged evidence led ineluctably to the conclusion that the defendant would in all probability have had to pay at least £25,000 in order to enable it to do lawfully that which it did unlawfully (that is to say, represent by means of the image appearing on the front of the leaflet, that Irvine had endorsed Talk Radio) and thus varied the High Court's award of damages in an order made by Laddie J in the sum of £2,000 and substituted a figure of £25,000 instead.

[18.3.07] Thus, to succeed in a false endorsement case, a claimant must demonstrate that, at the time of the acts complained of, he had a significant reputation or goodwill and that the actions of the defendant gave rise to a false message which would be understood by a not insignificant section of his market that his goods have been endorsed, recommended or approved of by the claimant.

[18.3.08] The *Irvine* case brings English passing off law up to date with modern commercial reality.[37] It does not provide any ammunition however for the proponents of more extensive personality rights for celebrities in the UK. Laddie LJ (the same judge who rejected a trademark claim in respect of unofficial Elvis Presley merchandise and stating that "there is nothing akin to a copyright in a name") made it clear in his judgment that the possible development of merchandising rights was an entirely separate issue.

[18.3.09] The *Irvine* proceedings involved a false suggestion of positive endorsement of an advertiser's product. It leaves open the question whether there can be liability for passing off in the more usual situation where an advertisement merely implies that celebrities have agreed to the use of their name or likeness in an advertisement, without going on to imply actual endorsement of the advertised product. In practice, lawyers advising in this field will continue to

---

36 See paras 114 and 116 of the judgment.

37 Charles Swan (Swan Turton Solicitors), *Eddie Irvine v Talksport: False endorsements and passing off* (2002). Available at: https://swanturton.com/eddie-irvine-v-talksport-false-endorsements-and-passing-off/ [Accessed 30 July 2019].

assume that false suggestions of authorisation are equally vulnerable to passing off claims as they are to false suggestions of endorsement.

Roy Keane

[18.3.10] In this High Court action A&L Goodbody, solicitors for Roy Keane, Ireland's former soccer squad assistant manager, instituted proceedings on its client's behalf against bookmaker Paddy Power in 2016. The defendant had parked a large truck near the Aviva Stadium where Ireland was playing Scotland in a European Championship soccer qualifier with a mocked-up billboard image of the star as William Braveheart Wallace. The advertisement referenced Scottish voters' rejection of independence. The action was later settled on undisclosed terms and Mr Justice Brian McGovern[38] was advised the dispute had been resolved to the satisfaction of both parties and could be struck out from the Commercial Court list. In his action, Keane claimed damages, including aggravated damages, alleging his image had been used without his prior knowledge or consent. He also argued his constitutional rights had been breached and further took offence to the advertisement's being couched in crude and vulgar terms towards Scottish people and its making a derisory reference to the outcome of the 2014 Scottish independence referendum when the electorate decided to remain within the UK.

[18.3.11] The world-renowned former soccer player contended the tone and content of the advertisement did not represent his views or amount to anything he would say even in a humorous context. The disparaging message on the billboard posters had the effect of endangering and harming his connection with Scotland. In the pleadings Keane claimed his image was very deliberately used by Paddy Power, which company he alleged is well known for its controversial approach to marketing, for its commercial benefit as part of the bookmaker's advertising campaign centred on the Ireland-Scotland game. It was claimed the soccer legend's image was central to the poster campaign given his high profile.

Douglas v Hello!

[18.3.12] The law of confidential information can also protect commercial aspects of image rights, following *Douglas v Hello!* discussed from para [18.1.24]. However, the information must have the requisite degree of confidence.

PASSING OFF

[18.4.01] The tort of passing off, often used to enforce unregistered trademark rights, is being increasingly used by celebrities to protect their images based on three principles: that the defendants are passing off on the goodwill generated by the public image of the claimants, in other words that goodwill or

---

38 Later appointed to the Court of Appeal, retiring from the bench in 2020.

reputation attaches to the goods or services of the claimants; that the use of the celebrity image suggests an endorsement of the product or service; and that the unauthorised use of the image denies the plaintiffs their earning power.

[18.4.02] In recent years, personal endorsements by celebrities and sports stars have highlighted the value which can be attributed to a person's image. For some individuals, their image is their brand which, if in danger of being devalued or damaged, must be protected.

[18.4.03] Without a free-standing image right, an alternative right of action must be argued in order to seek legal protection from the courts. The common law tort of passing off has traditionally been relied on by famous persons to prevent the unauthorised use of their image. However, certain grounds as above must be established in order to be granted protection by judges in such circumstances.

[18.4.04] Passing off protects against any misrepresentation in respect of a good's origin where the representation made is likely to mislead or confuse the public. The test for passing off was established in the House of Lords judgment in *Reckitt v Borden Inc.*[39] This Jif-Lemon case established the classic trinity of passing off, namely the three elements central to any case. A claimant in passing off must establish that goodwill or reputation attaches to the goods or services of the claimant; that a misrepresentation by a third party (whether intentional or not) leads the public to believe that the goods or services offered by that party are the goods or services of the claimant; and that the misrepresentation causes damage to the claimant. The Irish High Court adopted this test in *DSG Retail Ireland Ltd v PC World Ltd.*[40]

[18.4.05] Passing off is a flexible legal remedy which can be invoked in a variety of circumstances. It is for this reason that it has been utilised by individuals, such as celebrities and sports stars, who wish to prevent the use of their image by third parties.

[18.4.06] Confusion caused by misrepresentation is at the heart of any action for passing off. In *Irvine*, the court held that a misrepresentation could occur where a third party's product or service appeared to be endorsed by the individual whose image was being used and in such circumstances an action in passing off could arise. It was recognised that a substantial part of Irvine's income was through endorsement and misuse of his image could dilute his reputation thereby causing him damage.

Rihanna

[18.4.07] In July 2013, the High Court for England and Wales granted an

---

39 [1990] 1 All ER 873.

40 [1998] IEHC 3.

injunction to Rihanna which prevented Topshop from selling a T-shirt which displayed her image.[41] It was held that the sale of the T-shirt amounted to passing off as it encouraged customers to buy the shirt believing it was endorsed by the superstar and that she had consented to the use of her image. Topshop appealed the High Court's decision.

[18.4.08] In January 2015, the Court of Appeal[42] upheld the trial court decision whereby Birss J was entitled to find that the sale by Topshop of the T-shirt amounted to passing off. The appellate court *per* Kitchin LJ agreed that the use of Rihanna's image on the garment amounted to a misrepresentation and passing off by Topshop resulting in damage to the goodwill she held as a fashion icon. It is worth noting however that a solitary event may not be sufficient to establish misrepresentation and each case will be assessed on its own particular merits.

[18.4.09] The court made reference to two particular facts. Rihanna had a previous association with Topshop through a personal shopping competition for fans and her involvement had been promoted by Topshop through its Twitter account. The court considered this to evidence the shop's desire to link itself to the singer's celebrity profile. Secondly, the image used on the T-shirt which although licensed from a third party photographer was similar to the promotional images used by Rihanna for her Talk, Talk, Talk album (same clothes and hair) and so could be considered by the public as being an authorised publicity shot. It was held that these two points in combination amounted to a misrepresentation.

[18.4.10] The fact that there was no indication of artist authorisation on the swing tag or neck label pointed firmly against authorisation but was not strong enough to negate the impression that the garment was authorised. Although a good number of purchasers would buy the T-shirt without giving the question of authorisation any thought at all, a substantial portion of those considering the product would be induced to think it was a garment authorised by the artist and thus motivate them to purchase the product (or because of the value of the perceived authorisation itself). In both cases, they would have been deceived.

[18.4.11] If, as Birss J had found in the High Court, a substantial number of purchasers were likely to be deceived into buying the T-shirt because of a false belief that it had been authorised by Rihanna, then that would obviously be damaging to her goodwill. It would amount to sales lost to her merchandising business and represent a loss of control of reputation in the fashion sphere.

[18.4.12] This decision, whilst acknowledging that no express image right exists,[43] reaffirms that celebrities may seek to control the use of their image

---

41 *Rihanna Fenty v Arcadia Group Brands Ltd (t/a Topshop)* [2013] EWHC 2310 (ChD).

42 [2015] EWCA Civ 3.

43 Maria Edgeworth (Leman Solicitors), *Your Face or Mine – The Protection of 'Image Rights' in the UK and Ireland* (2015). Available at: https://leman.ie/your-face-or-mine-the-protection-of-image-rights-in-the-uk-and-ireland/ [Accessed 17 March 2019].

through an action in passing off. The courts have become more willing to recognise the value in a famous person's image and that unauthorised use by a trader in promoting its product can suggest endorsement and result in the dilution of a celebrity's brand.

Appendix

US right of publicity case law

RECOGNITION OF THE RIGHT OF PUBLICITY

[A1.1.01] The right of publicity secures the inherent right of all human beings to control the commercial use of their identity.[44] In California, the right of publicity is defined in statute as the right to control the commercial use of one's name or likeness (and any other recognisable aspects of one's life) against unauthorised exploitation. This then might conflict with First Amendment constitutionally-enshrined rights concerning freedom of speech and freedom of the press. Pursuant to the First Amendment, the entitlement exists to write about and creatively interpret the facts of a person's life in a film. However, as always where the balance of competing rights is at play, that protection is limited. Thus, it is best practice when promoting a film using a subject's name and likeness to secure the individual's life rights in order to avoid legal action.

[A1.1.02] Every state in the US recognises the right of publicity, that is, that persons have the right to prevent unauthorised commercial use of their name and likeness (non-commercial use is permissible as later discussed). Some states protect this under the right of publicity while others recognise this as a right of privacy. In New York, the right of publicity only applies to living persons while in other states permission may need to be obtained from the subject's estate. California recognises a continued right of publicity for deceased persons up to 70 years after death.

[A1.1.03] The Californian right of publicity also protects celebrities from appropriation of their performance or persona, in a variety of contexts where the defendant appropriates the economic value that the plaintiff has built in an identity or performance. In *No Doubt v Activision Publishing Inc*,[45] rock band No Doubt was permitted to sue a game company that used computer-generated images of the band in its video game. In *Hilton v Hallmark Cards*, the US Court of Appeals for the Ninth Circuit held that Paris Hilton could pursue a right of publicity claim for Hallmark's use of her image and catch phrase ("that's hot") from her television show in one of its greeting cards.[46] Here, merchandising a celebrity's image without that person's consent, the prevention of which is the core of the right of publicity, was not protected by the First Amendment so as to afford a defence to Hallmark. Moreover, in *White v Samsung Electronics*

---

[44] J. Thomas McCarthy, *The Rights of Publicity and Privacy* (2nd ed, Thomson/West, New York, 2016).

[45] 192 Cal App 4th 1018, 1023 (2011).

[46] 599 F.3d 894 at 899 (9th Cir. 2009).

America Inc,[47] the court stated that California's interest was in preventing "the exploitation of celebrity to sell products, and an attempt to take a free ride on a celebrity's celebrity value".[48]

[A1.1.04] Rapper Riff Raff (born Jody Christian) also confirmed in 2013 that he would bring proceedings (claiming up to ten million dollars in damages) alleging that one of the main characters in the movie *Spring Breakers*, Alien, who is played by James Franco misappropriated his likeness claiming there was a strong resemblance between him and Alien's character. The proceedings do not seem to have been filed and matters ultimately came full circle as Franco subsequently starred in Riff Raff's music video *Only in America*, a track from the rapper's Peach Panther album.

PERMISSIBLE USES BY FILMMAKERS

The Hurt Locker

[A1.2.01] This 2009 Oscar-winning motion picture tells the story of fictional Army Sergeant First Class William James, portrayed by Jeremy Renner, as he leads a team of specialists disarming explosive devices during the Iraq War. The critically acclaimed film won six Academy Awards including Best Picture, Best Director[49] and Best Original Screenplay for Mark Boal. Boal based the screenplay on his personal coverage of the Iraq War where he observed Sergeant Jeffrey Sarver and later interviewed him on home soil.[50] Sarver, a non-celebrity, asserted that Boal, without authorisation, published a factual account about him in *Playboy* magazine, then later fictionalised and appropriated his life story in the film.

[A1.2.02] In 2016, the Ninth Circuit ruled[51] that Sarver's right to publicity was trumped by the First Amendment rights of the filmmakers. The plaintiff had claimed that in basing the main character on his life story, the movie violated his right of publicity, in addition to defaming him and portraying him in a false light. The court held, *per* O'Scannlain J, in the oft-quoted passage that:

In sum, *The Hurt Locker* is speech that is fully protected by the First Amendment, which safeguards the storytellers and artists who take the raw materials of life – including the stories of real individuals, ordinary and extraordinary – and transform them into art, be it articles, books, movies, or plays.[52]

---

47 971 F.2d 1395, 1397-99, 1401 n.3 (9th Cir. 1992).

48 *ibid* at 1401 n.3.8.

49 Kathryn Bigelow, the first female director to win this award. There have been two others since.

50 Edwin Komen, *First Amendment SLAPPs Publicity Right Plaintiff in "Hurt Locker" Case* (2016), intellectualpropertylawblog. Available at: https://www.intellectualpropertylawblog.com/archives/first-amendment-slapps-publicity-right-plaintiff-in-hurt-locker [Accessed 23 June 2021].

51 *Sarver v Chartier* 813 F.3d 891 (9th Cir. 2016).

52 At p 26 of the judgment (813 F.3d 891, 905).

[A1.2.03] The Strategic Lawsuit Against Public Policy statute was enacted to allow early dismissal of meritless actions which might otherwise inhibit the exercise of First Amendment rights through costly and time-consuming litigation. The statute authorises dismissal where the defendant demonstrates the impugned actions are in furtherance of protected First Amendment activity, thus shifting the burden to the plaintiff to demonstrate a probability of success on the merits.

[A1.2.04] The appellate court had no difficulty in finding that the motion picture was an expressive work about a matter of public interest entitled to the highest level of constitutional protection. The court stated that the film was not speech proposing a commercial transaction, in contrast to commercial speech where an individual's publicity rights may more readily prevail (such that speech which either appropriates the economic value of a performance or persona or seeks to capitalise on a celebrity's image in commercial advertisements stands unprotected by the First Amendment against a Californian right of publicity claim). Therefore, a line of the court's own precedents in earlier cases relying on the lesser protection afforded to commercial speech by defendants is apposite when set against the non-commercial speech uses in the instant case.

[A1.2.05] The court, as examples of commercial speech which is less protected by a First Amendment defence, as well as *Hilton* cited[53] *Keller v Electronic Arts, Inc*, wherein it upheld an action by a college football player who sought to prevent the use of his likeness in the defendant's video game[54] (and *Davis v Electronic Arts, Inc*[55] upholding a right of publicity action challenging the defendant's use of professional football player likenesses in a video game). The court noted that the video game "literally recreates [the football player] in the very setting in which he has achieved renown"[56] and interfered with his ability to capitalise on his athletic success which took "talent and years of hard work on the football field"[57] to build.

[A1.2.06] Likewise, the court had previously upheld actions involving celebrities challenging the use of their images in commercial advertising (*Newcombe v Adolf Coors Co*,[58] wherein California's right of publicity law applied to the use of Dodgers' pitcher Don Newcombe's image in a printed beer advertisement, and the above-cited *White* decision – use of the plaintiff's likeness as a robot in an advertisement for VCRs). The court in *Sarver* thus stated:

> In sum, our precedents have held that speech which either appropriates the economic value of a performance or persona or seeks to capitalize off a celebrity's image in commercial advertisements is unprotected by the First

---

[53] At pp 23-25 of the judgment.
[54] 724 F.3d 1268 (9th Cir. 2013).
[55] 775 F.3d 1172 (9th Cir. 2015).
[56] 724 F.3d.1268 at 1271.
[57] *ibid* at 1277 n.9, 1281.
[58] 157 F.3d 686, 691–94 (9th Cir. 1998).

Amendment against a California right-of-publicity claim. Such lines of cases are not applicable here.

[A1.2.07] In relation to the defamation element of the claim, Sarver's allegations did not stand up in light of the film as a whole. The court agreed with the District Court that a reasonable viewer of the film would be left with the conclusion that the character Will James was a heroic figure, albeit one struggling with certain internal conflicts. Directly contrary to Sarver's allegations, Sergeant James exhibits compassion for various Iraqi citizens, including a young boy and a man trapped in a suicide vest, appears to care for and miss his son, and occasionally departs from military protocol in an effort to save human lives. Even if the claimant was correct that certain aspects of James' character were unflattering, it did not support the conclusion that the film's overall depiction of Will James could reasonably be seen to defame Sarver.

[A1.2.08] While (in the US at least) the decision should provide substantial comfort to filmmakers telling stories based upon or inspired by real-life events, whether such films portray the real persons by name or fictionalise the story for dramatic purposes, the best practice is nonetheless to duly obtain consent. Indeed, the *Sarver* decision in the view of one commentator[59] exposes the dangers of failing to understand the origins, development and justifications of the right of publicity. Ignoring earlier right of publicity cases and the works of important scholars,[60] the *Sarver* court seemed in that writer's view blinded by the recent influx of celebrity right of publicity claims, and suggests that only celebrities are worthy of protection from right of publicity violations, at least in cases where the defendants' speech is expressive in nature. By overlooking some of the right of publicity's justifications, and misapplying others, *Sarver* may lead future courts to strip non-celebrities of a right meant for "every human being".[61] Now, more than ever, as average persons' social media presence provides easy access to their photographs, videos, and more, it is worthwhile to explore non-celebrities' ability to control the uses of their identities.

Ginger & Fred

[A1.2.09] Another earlier landmark decision in the US emanating from a film based on real lives concerned the Fellini movie *Ginger and Fred.* Non-commercial speech (and a biographical film constitutes non-commercial speech) has First Amendment protection and therefore signed releases are not necessary to depict public figures. *Rogers v Grimaldi*[62] was not a case involving a biography, but the use of the names of dancers Ginger (Rogers) and Fred (Astaire) in the title of a film directed by famed Italian filmmaker Federico Fellini. The US District Court

---

59 Noa Dreymann, "John Doe's Right of Publicity" (2018) 32 *Berkeley Tech. L.J.* 673.

60 Citing for example Melville B. Nimmer, "The Right of Publicity", (1954) *Law and Contemporary Problems,* (19)2, pp. 203-223.

61 J. Thomas McCarthy, *supra* at fn 44.

62 695 F Supp 112 (S.D.N.Y. 1988).

for the Southern District of New York in 1988 held (as affirmed on appeal) that, even though the film was not a biography of Fred Astaire and Ginger Rogers, the contents of the film were reasonably related to the use of their names. The court stated that:

> ...having determined that the speech in question is artistic expression, ... the speech at issue here is not primarily intended to serve as a commercial purpose, the prohibitions of the Lanham Act do not apply and the film is entitled to the full scope of protection under the First Amendment.

[A1.2.10] This rule applies even to films that use a public figure's name or likeness for non-biographical material so long as the use is reasonably related to the content – and it is especially true for material that is biographical. Over the years, there have been several attempts to derail biographical films and live stage productions by the subjects of the productions. These attempts have been unsuccessful. A number of cases have allowed the use of fictional events in biographical films, even though no permission was obtained from the subjects or their estates.[63] Thus, in the US, not all events depicted must be true and based on real events. Such cases involved the silent film star Rudolph Valentino,[64] the mystery writer Agatha Christie[65] and the former Black Panther party member Bobby Seale.[66]

Feud: Bette and Joan

[A1.2.11] In January 2019, the US Supreme Court rejected 102-year-old actress Olivia de Havilland's petition to review the dismissal of her lawsuit brought against the makers of FX's docudrama miniseries arising from the portrayal of her therein. The actress, best known for her role in *Gone With The Wind,* claimed that Catherine Zeta-Jones' depiction of her in the series violated her right of publicity, represented her in a false light and damaged her professional reputation for integrity, honesty, generosity, self-sacrifice and dignity. Her contention was that she had been unfairly depicted as a vulgar hypocrite and gossip who casually disparaged friends and family, claiming the series cast unsavoury aspersions as regards crude language she had used in the past. The actress also sought compensation for the use of her name and likeness in the show.

[A1.2.12] The proceedings were previously dismissed by the California Court of Appeal (Second Appellate District)[67] on First Amendment grounds in light

---

63 Stephen Rodner, *Life story rights: What's possible and what's not* (2008), hollywoodreporter.com. Available at: https://www.hollywoodreporter.com/news/life-story-rights-whats-whats-103334 [Accessed 18 April 2019].

64 *Gugliemi v Spelling-Goldberg Productions*, 25 Cal 3d 860 (1979).

65 *Hicks v Casablanca Records*, 464 F.Supp 426 SDNY (1978).

66 *Seale v Gramercy Pictures* 964 F.Supp 918, ED Pa (1997).

67 *De Havilland v FX Networks, LLC* 21 Cal App 5th 845 (2018).

of the fact that the series depiction of the plaintiff was transformative work[68] of artistic expression in nature (taking the raw materials of life and transforming them into art), holding that if the case were to be successfully made out it would negatively impact the rights of screenwriters and producers to develop creative works that dramatise historical events or public figures. Finding that the plaintiff would not be in a position to demonstrate a probability of prevailing on the merits of her claims, de Havilland's complaint was stricken under California's anti-SLAPP statute, a law, as we have seen, designed to curtail frivolous legal actions impinging First Amendment activity.

[A1.2.13] The appellate court, citing the precedent of three earlier authorities concluded that:

> Publishing a fictitious work about a real person cannot mean the author, by virtue of writing fiction, has acted with actual malice…Recognizing this, in cases where the claimed highly offensive or defamatory aspect of the portrayal is implied, courts have required plaintiffs to show that the defendant "intended to convey the defamatory impression." De Havilland must demonstrate that FX either deliberately cast her statements in an equivocal fashion in the hope of insinuating a defamatory import to the reader, or that it knew or acted in reckless disregard of whether its words would be interpreted by the average reader as defamatory statements of fact.[69]

The court was of the view that the plaintiff would not be capable of so demonstrating as the portrayal of her was not highly offensive to a reasonable person as a matter of law.

MAGAZINE USES

Dustin Hoffman

[A1.3.01] In the case of *Hoffman v Capital Cities/ABC Inc*,[70] Dustin Hoffman filed a complaint against Los Angeles Magazine's ('LAM') parent company, Capital Cities/ABC, Inc. LAM had digitally edited an image of Hoffman's character from the film *Tootsie* to impose his head on the body of a male model who was wearing a woman's dress and shoes, along with the caption, "Dustin Hoffman isn't a drag in a butter-colored silk gown by Richard Tyler and Ralph Lauren heels". The complaint alleged that LAM's publication of the image misappropriated the actor's name and likeness, thereby violating California's common law and his statutory publicity right since LAM had not obtained permission from Hoffman to publish this image. While in this instance the court ruled against the claimant on First Amendment grounds by holding that the magazine's appropriation of identity was "communicative" rather than

---

68 An affirmative defence formulated by the California Supreme Court in *Comedy III Productions v Saderup* 25 Cal 4th 387 (2001).

69 pp 35-36 of the judgment.

70 *Hoffman v Capital Cities/ABC Inc*, 255 F.3d 1180 (9th Cir. 2001).

"commercial" and that the article published was not commercial speech, what is interesting to note is that the complaint was based on the argument that Hoffman's name and likeness is an extremely valuable commodity and that he does not permit commercial use of his identity.

Chapter 19

Stage Productions

INTRODUCTION

[19.1.01] Many of the considerations that apply to film and television production can apply likewise to stage productions. Accordingly, many of the chapters contained in this textbook including those related to insurance, safety legislation, cast and crew contracts, data protection, releases, defamation and trademarks pertain too to theatrical productions. The treatment of copyright, however, will generally differ to screenwriting in terms of more expansive rights typically afforded to playwrights.

[19.1.02] Authors of theatrical plays and musicals can enjoy significantly broader rights than their screenwriting counterparts. Historically, playwrights and composers and lyricists of musicals were afforded the utmost deference in creative matters relating to their work. Notwithstanding, the turning of the tide in today's world is alluded to later.

[19.1.03] This chapter will analyse typical production contracts and briefly consider, for the benefit of emerging theatre practitioners and trainees, some common myths associated with amateur productions, followed by an examination of 'grand' performance rights licences (as required to use another's musical composition in a stage show),[1] 'small' rights music licensing,[2] and

---

1 Grand rights or dramatic performing rights cover the right to present a dramatico-musical show (i.e. with words and music) in its entirety on stage, or, when enough of the piece is performed to convey a section of the story such as an act, a scene or significant excerpt in a staged, semi-staged or concert performance. Grand rights thus refer to the right to perform musical compositions within the context of a dramatic work, a term typically referring to stage performances such as musical theatre. This, according to the UK Music Publishers Association, might involve the creation of an entire dramatico-musical work (such as *My Fair Lady*, *West Side Story* or *Hairspray*), or the use of popular compositions in compilation/jukebox musicals (such as *Petticoats and Dreamboats* which uses a number of popular songs from the rock and roll era of the late 50s and early 60s interpolated into a new storyline).

2 Small rights relate to non-dramatic works, that is, music not specially written for a dramatic presentation, e.g. a song from a musical may be performed on the radio or in a live concert with no visual reference to the original stage show. This is an instance of the possibility of having a small rights performance of a work from a grand right presentation. The more usual example however of small rights might be the use of a CD to play pre-show or post-show music.

the royalties which flow to copyright-holders whose melodies and lyrics and sound recordings are used in stage productions. In addition, the type of fair use sampling and music rights clearance employed in the smash hit show *Hamilton* will be discussed, together with pay and conditions of theatre cast and crew, stage show controversies and mention of the major international theatrical licensing companies.

OWNERSHIP OF RIGHTS

[19.2.01] Under copyright legislation, the author of a play or musical is its owner and enjoys, *inter alia*, the exclusive right to authorise (or not) the creation of derivative works including third party stage productions or audiovisual productions adapted from the underlying work.[3] Any change to the text of a play, book, lyric or score of a musical is such a derivative use and would require the express consent of the copyright owner. The staging of a production of a play or musical also involves another exclusive right held by the author, namely, the right to perform the work publicly and thus the right to authorise others to present it in theatres. A written contract between author and stage producer will specify the conditions under which the production may be presented, some of which terms will be outlined below.

[19.2.02] Screenwriters on the other hand will assign film/television/streaming rights to audiovisual producers by means of a writer's agreement (with certain rights often being reserved by the author such as book publishing, radioplay productions and stage rights, subject to holdback provisions – see [19.6.04]. Their relevant film rights are therefore sold and the writers cede ownership and control but possibly, depending on the writers' track records, they may be in a position to negotiate certain consultation rights, additional main and billing credits, and a percentage of producer net profits on the back end. They will invariably also be required to waive their moral rights allowing the producer to ultimately[4] make changes and edits to suit production and post-production demands. Meanwhile, authors of pre-existing musicals (commissions to write new works would likely call for a full assignment of rights if the fee is substantial) can retain, assign or license rights as they might please. Even where rights are assigned to a production company, the writer might nonetheless successfully negotiate broad approval rights.

[19.2.03] Before Andrew Lloyd Webber had written a single hit song, he had observed 'grand rights' in publishing contracts, the ongoing financial control over theatrical productions, an issue to which not sufficient attention was paid in the 1960s. He evidently managed to retain rights to an impressive eighty

3 See ss 17 and 37 of the Copyright and Related Rights Act 2000 relating to subsistence of copyright and for actions by third parties that can be restricted by copyright owners.

4 And beyond the lengthy and involved writer and producer rewrite/redrafts/polishes process contained in the contract.

percent of his productions.[5] The international theatre rights licensing agency and music publisher, The Musical Company, handles his slate.[6] A guide fee for staging of a Lloyd Webber musical might be in the region of 15 percent of the total gross box office receipts from all performances[7] as well as the hire costs of any cast and music materials required for the licensed show.

DISPELLING AMATEUR PRODUCTION MYTHS

[19.3.01] Unless the underlying work is in the public domain (e.g. Shakespeare plays), local drama societies do not have free reign to stage plays and musicals even if presented without an admittance fee in private settings. Amateur[8] dramatic productions[9] must be duly licensed by way of non-professional performance rights licence application (or professional rights licence application in the case of professional productions) and the attendant fee paid.[10] The Drama League of Ireland ('DLI') office is regarded as the primary point of contact for acquiring amateur rights for plays. Hence, contact should be made with DLI prior to commencing rehearsals to ensure that the amateur performance rights are in fact available. Not all plays are available for amateur production and some frequently have temporary geographical or other restrictions due for instance to existing exclusive licences granted to theatres. Restrictions regularly apply to the works, for example, of playwrights Samuel Beckett and Brian Friel.[11]

[19.3.02] A new play will likely not be released for amateur performance until its professional stage life has been fully exploited commercially. Similarly, when an existing play is revived professionally, amateur rights are often restricted or wholly withdrawn for a period to protect the professional production's box office income.

[19.3.03] DLI can advise on the availability of plays on behalf of the agencies which it represents but might also assist with contact details in respect of

---

5 Adam Gopnik, *Did Andrew Lloyd Webber Ruin the Musical or Rescue It?* (2018), The New Yorker. Available at: https://www.newyorker.com/magazine/2018/03/12/did-andrew-lloyd-webber-ruin-the-musical-or-rescue-it [Accessed 10 August 2021].

6 The company also manages the musical theatre songs of songwriters Tim Rice and Marvin Hamlisch if one were to seek mechanical and synchronisation licences for uses outside of theatre such as in a film score or commercial advertisements on television or online.

7 See https://themusicalcompany.com/faq/.

8 *Per* the Drama League of Ireland, actors in a professional production must either be members of Equity (see Chapter 21) or trained and/or recognised professional actors who work in the business. Amateur actors, on the other hand, perform as a leisure activity and earn their living by other means.

9 It is a requirement of some of the agents which DLI represents that the maximum theatre capacity for an amateur production should not exceed 300.

10 In general, full length amateur plays cost in the region of €100 per performance and one-act plays cost about half that per performance.

11 See https://www.dli.ie/drama/performing-rights.

playwrights whom it does not represent.[12] DLI, significantly, is the authorised agent for, amongst others, Dramatists Play Services, Inc (see below), The Society of Authors (UK), and Josef Weinberger Ltd which is the UK and other European territories' representative of the prestigious Broadway show catalogues of Music Theatre International.

[19.3.04] An amateur licence will contain strict conditions that the unaltered play title and the name of the author must appear clearly on posters and all other promotional material. The publicity material must also indicate that it is an amateur production. No changes of any kind may be made without the permission of the author. This includes changing the sex of characters, inserting 'bad' language or making modifications to the time and place/setting of the play.

Monitoring royalties (licensing performance rights of plays)

[19.3.05] Another myth to debunk is that certain performances are private and hence the issue of payment relating to performance rights does not arise. Performances given in clubs, halls or any public places are public performances, including church halls and function rooms of public houses. A production must be licensed if it is witnessed by the general public regardless of whether there is an admittance charge,[13] although the fee payable to DLI (or to the author where DLI is not the author's agent) will reduce for use of an excerpt only from a play. The rationale for licensing is that performances before audiences lower the earning potential of a play for which the author must accordingly be compensated in the form of royalty fees.

[19.3.06] Where certain music features, as well as a tariff payable to the Irish Music Rights Organisation ('IMRO') under standard Tariff VT which applies to performances of copyrighted music within the repertoire controlled by IMRO in theatrical presentations, stage plays or variety shows to which admittance is gained by purchase of a ticket or by subscription, amateur dramatic societies must also pay a modest annual charge under Phonographic Performance Ireland ('PPI') licence (Tariff 44)[14] as part of the IMRO/PPI dual licence system detailed in Chapter 23 for the public performance of sound recordings in terms of royalties

---

12 For example, DLI licenses rights to amateur productions of John B Keane plays but for professional productions of *The Field* for example, stage producers should contact Mercier Press in Cork rather than DLI. A producer wishing to stage a Martin McDonagh play would be directed to contact the Samuel French theatrical company in London in the case of *Hangmen* or *The Pillowman*, the Dramatists Play Services, Inc in New York if applying to stage *The Pillowman* in the US or Canada (subject to special clearance for New York and Los Angeles), or Nordiska, the international performing rights agency for plays and musicals staged in Iceland, Norway, Sweden and Denmark if seeking to host a performance of *The Pillowman, Hangman, A Skull in Connemara, The Cripple of Inismaan* or other McDonagh works in those Nordic territories.

13 However, as regards commercial music used in the show, IMRO Tariff VT does not apply in respect of small rights discussed below where there is no admission charge.

14 See https://imro.ie/wp-content/uploads/2023/01/Tariff-44-2023.pdf.

distributable to record producers (and singers/performers on a track paid by Recorded Artists Actors Performers ('RAAP') via PPI if they have registered their performances with RAAP) which is used solely as background music during the entry and exit of audiences and during the intervals.

[19.3.07] If a play is performed by members of a school before an audience of staff and students, it is classified as an educational exercise and no licence is required either for use of sound recordings or in relation to a dramatic or musical work.[15] However, if any persons from outside the school are admitted (families and friends), the production becomes public, licences are required and royalties accrue to the copyright holders by way of intermittent distribution payments.

[19.3.08] DLI, through a team of volunteers throughout the country, regularly monitors local newspapers, roadside signs and other publications with a view to identifying all dramatic performances, both licensed and unlicensed. In cases where plays are identified, for which fees have not been paid, a set of procedures, which have been agreed with the agents which it represents, are initiated. A planned show could therefore suffer the fate of cancellation.

[19.3.09] Finally, as regards recording an amateur play, the issuing of a performing licence does not include recording rights. Recording rights may be available for some plays, for others DLI will need to refer the show director/producer to the author's agents and in other cases such grant of recording rights may be not available at all.

FILMING PROFESSIONAL STAGE SHOWS

[19.4.01] As seen, copyright law bestows on authors the exclusive right to control the reproduction of their work. When Music Theatre International, one of the world's leading theatrical licensing agencies discussed at end of this chapter, for example, grants a licence for a live stage production of a show that it represents, that licence does not include the right to record it as well since the authors retain the exclusive right to decide when or if their work is recorded in any way.

[19.4.02] For most titles licensed by Theatrical Rights Worldwide (also discussed below), this licensing company can offer permission to create a video of the subject production. A video licence agreement, outlining special conditions and usage limitations, must be completed and returned with the requisite fees.

[19.4.03] In respect of Lloyd Webber works, The Musical Company which handles his repertoire can consider requests from producers in the UK and Ireland to film their productions of *Joseph and the Amazing Technicolour Dreamcoat* and *The Likes of Us* (both musicals with lyrics by Tim Rice and music by Andrew

[15] s 55 (performing, playing or showing work in the course of activities of educational establishments) of the Copyright and Related Rights Act 2000.

Lloyd Webber). However, filming requests in respect of the authors' other works are not currently entertained.[16]

COPYRIGHT IN STAGE RIGHTS

[19.5.01] A live stage show is a "work" as defined in s 2 of the Copyright and Related Rights Act 2000 ('the 2000 Act') including, *inter alia*, a literary, dramatic, musical or artistic work. A dramatic work includes a choreographic work or a work of mime. Pursuant to s 17 of the 2000 Act, the owner of the copyright in any work may undertake or authorise other persons in relation to that work to undertake certain acts in the state, being acts which are designated by the Act as acts restricted by copyright in a work of that description. Unauthorised or unlicensed reproductions and performances of a work or illicit recordings[17] of a show are subject to both criminal prosecution and civil law proceedings.[18]

[19.5.02] Copyright subsists in a playwright or the creator/author of a stage show who will therefore own and control its productions. However, in the case of a specially commissioned show (written as a 'work for hire'), the commissioning party would generally pay for the rights by way of full buyout. Otherwise, if not a contract for service, the commissioning party might be an employer of a playwright (e.g. a theatre) and such employer would be the first owner of any copyright in the work pursuant to s 23(1)(a) of the 2000 Act, being a work made by an employee in the course of employment, unless there is a written agreement to the contrary whereby the employee might retain some or all ownership rights. Where playwrights contractually retain all copyright they will grant a licence to a relevant theatre(s) to stage the play.

Duration and public domain

[19.5.03] In Ireland (and throughout the EU),[19] copyright protection expires 70 years after the death of the author.[20] Therefore, certain plays and musicals will be freely in the public domain and their use will not be subject to copyright restrictions. The obvious example is the work of William Shakespeare or the comic opera output of Victorian era theatrical dramatic/composer partnership

---

16 See https://themusicalcompany.com/faq/.

17 As defined in s 210 of the Copyright and Related Rights Act 2000.

18 See ss 11-13, 140 and 258 of the 2000 Act as amended by the Copyright and Other Intellectual Property Law Provisions Act 2019.

19 Directive 2006/116/EC of the European Parliament and of the Council of 12 December 2016 on the term of protection of copyright and certain related rights – the duration of the rights of an author of a literary or artistic work was lengthened from 50 years to 70 years post-death.

20 For works made for hire and anonymous and pseudonymous US works, the duration of copyright is 95 years from first publication or 120 years from creation, whichever is shorter (unless the author's identity is later revealed in the US Copyright Office (part of the Library of Congress) records, in which case the term becomes the author's life plus 70 years). Source: US Copyright Office, see https://www.copyright.gov/circs/circ15a.pdf.

Gilbert and Sullivan (e.g. *The Pirates of Penzance*). Likewise, the fairytales of French author, Charles Perrault, as derived from folk stories (*Little Red Riding Hood*, *Cinderella* and *Puss in Boots*) are all copyright free and can be adapted to theatre, film, opera and ballet as was the case with Tchaikovsky's ballet *The Sleeping Beauty* which premiered at the Mariinsky Theatre in Saint Petersburg on 15 January 1890, becoming one of the classical repertoire's most famous ballets. Shakespeare work can not only freely be used in monetary terms but it can also be extensively changed and adulterated, thus offering the production director total creative freedom without any concern of author moral rights infringement.[21]

[19.5.04] The plays of George Bernard Shaw who died in 1950 allowed his heirs to generate income from his work for a period after his death until 31 December 2021 when they fell into the public domain.[22]

[19.5.05] Translation or adaptations of out-of-copyright works may still be subject to copyright law. In some countries (e.g. Denmark and in the UK pursuant to the UK Theatre Minimum Terms Contract),[23] the person who adapts a play or the translator of a foreign play, for instance, is also protected as an originator.

Neighbouring rights

[19.5.06] Rights not connected with the work's actual author also fall for consideration. A play will have actors. A musical will have actors, singers and musicians. These participants in a live stage show are bestowed a bundle of performer rights by the 2000 Act. They also enjoy statutorily recognised rights when their performance is recorded and is reproduced for a television special for example. These performers will be required in their contract to assign their rights to the show producer lest the producer's freedom to commercially exploit the show to its fullest potential will be restrained.

[19.5.07] However, performers must, under the 2019 EU Copyright Directive and transposing legislation in Ireland in November 2021 (see Chapter 11) receive fair ("appropriate and proportionate") remuneration. Statute also provides, as regards equitable remuneration to performers (e.g. singers in a musical that is

---

21 Unless based on a modern adaptation/production of the relevant play (with newly added elements) which is still in copyright.

22 Pursuant to s 35 of the 2000 Act, the 70-year term shall be calculated from the first day of January of the year following the event that gives rise to that term, thus 70 years from January 1951. The minimum term of protection laid down by the Berne Convention for the Protection of Literary and Artistic Works 1886, namely the life of the author and 50 years after his death, was intended to provide protection for the author and the first two generations of his descendants. The average lifespan in the European Community grew longer, to the point where this term was no longer sufficient to cover two generations and hence the term was changed to 70 years by art 1 of Directive 2006/116/EC above.

23 Agreement between the UK Theatre Association and Writers' Guild of Great Britain and the Scottish Society of Playwrights of 29 April 2014, amended in 2017.

broadcast on television) for exploitation of sound recordings featuring their performances, that performer rights cannot be assigned other than to a collection society.[24] In the case of certain audiovisual uses, remuneration paid should also include for the grant of rental and lending rights as discussed in Chapter 10B.

Filmed recordings of stage productions

[19.5.08] It is important to note too that film directors/producers commissioned to record a live musical or play will be the first copyright owner of that film given that a film is a work of joint authorship by a producer and principal director (unless the producer and the principal director are the same person) pursuant to s 21(b) of the 2000 Act. The contract governing such recording will accordingly most likely assign these rights to the show author or to the relevant theatre to alter the default statutory position.

GRANT OF STAGE RIGHTS

[19.6.01] When playwrights pen a play for exhibition in theatres, they will grant production rights (by way of exclusive or non-exclusive licences) to the show's producer or to a theatre to stage the play by presenting paid public performances of same.[25] Subject to any such performance licences, and unless otherwise agreed, the author as statutory IP owner of the play itself, will retain legal and beneficial ownership in the show in perpetuity. Minimum terms of the production contract will often be based in each territory on union or collective agreement between theatre associations and writers' guilds. The Writers Guild of Ireland[26] in Temple Bar, Dublin is the representative body for writers in Ireland for the stage, radio and screen. It is a member of the International Affiliation of Writers Guilds and the Federation of Scriptwriters in Europe. It has a joint membership agreement with the Writers' Guild of Great Britain and an agreement with the Authors Licensing and Collecting Society.[27]

[19.6.02] The production period is the period from signing the agreement to the end of the run of a specified number of performances of the play or show

---

24 To RAAP if the performance works are registered in Ireland or to other collection societies if the works are registered in another jurisdiction(s) [which collection society will forward moneys back to an Irish performer through PPI/RAAP if that performer and the relevant performance(s) is registered with RAAP]. PPI which represents owners of sound recordings (music producers and record labels) will first receive royalty payments for sound recording uses and then distribute them via RAAP to performers.

25 In respect of dramatico-musical works (e.g. ballets, operas, musicals), the creator will grant a grand rights performing licence to the theatre regarding the entire composition. This is to be distinguished from another grand rights licence which creators/theatres themselves would need to obtain from the relevant copyright holders if a commercial song was used in the show.

26 See script.ie.

27 See http://irishtheatre.ie/resources/theatre_support_organisations/168/writers_guild_of_ireland.

at the theatre's facilities and the theatre may be granted the right to extend its option of the play for a period of months (or years) thereafter upon payment of a further advance as described below at [19.6.18] to [19.6.20]. The first series of performances will be the world premiere professional stage production over a number of weeks or months. If the theatre fails to present the play or show within the agreed production period, the theatre's rights to produce the play (and to the ancillary consultative services of the author if that has been agreed) shall then automatically terminate and all rights revert to the author.

[19.6.03] It is likely (in agreements with writers of renown) that the contract will provide that the theatre may not assign rights in the play/show to any third party but may sub-license rights acquired where the sub-licensee is presenting substantially the theatre's original production. The writer may be afforded the right to approve such sublicence but with a probable proviso that such approval is not to be unreasonably withheld or delayed.

Holdback of rights by the author

[19.6.04] To protect the theatre's investment (let us call it 'Theatre X'), the agreement might also provide that the author shall not grant other theatres the right to exhibit or perform the play or show within a certain radius of Theatre X or by means of radio, television, film and so forth. This restriction, to prevent any other production from competing or adversely affecting full commercial exploitation of the show by Theatre X, would serve to safeguard Theatre X's costs in hiring cast and stage crew, and as expended on rehearsals, production, marketing and stage design. This restriction would not necessarily prevent the author, however, from entering into other contractual agreements for presentation of the play/show with other persons during the production period provided the date of such presentations occurs after the date the exclusive rights to Theatre X of the play/show contractually expire.

[19.6.05] Theatre X would of course seek too to agree that it could invoke the right at any time during the term of the licence or option in the designated area (or in any of the territories covered by the agreement) to authorise the televising or sound broadcasting of excerpts from performances of the play, and/or use those excerpts for the purpose of publicity or promotion of the production.

Reservation and holdback of stage rights by brethren screenplay writers

[19.6.06] When a film producer options and later purchases an already written screenplay (or simply commissions a new and original screenplay by writer's agreement), the writer when dealing with film rights will wish to retain publishing rights to any future book based on the screenplay, dramatic radio rights and lucrative stage rights. As well as obtaining a fee from the screenplay and possibly backend sums, additional income will then potentially be generated outside of the subject movie through disparate media and creative forms.

[19.6.07] However, in light of production costs of a film or television content, a production company will require its full and unhindered exploitation of the film to be protected by requesting that authors refrain from exercising such reserved rights for a period (usually three to five years) to allow the film enjoy freedom from competition and to optimise its revenues from cinema, online and television sales. The author will therefore need to agree such holdback provision. If *Once*, for instance, had been in theatres as a musical before the film was released or during its exhibition window, it certainly may have diminished the poignancy of the film and reduced audience numbers.

Reservation of film rights by play and musicals writers

[19.6.08] Similarly, reservations and holdback provisions can apply to theatre. Writers/composers of a play or musical will want to exhaust their theatre opportunities before it is adapted for the screen. A classic example here is *Hamilton* which would have enjoyed a six and a half year run (with attendant album releases) from its creation and off-Broadway debut in February 2015 at The Public Theatre until its planned cinematic debut in October 2021. However, due to the impact of the Covid-19 pandemic on the film industry, *Hamilton* was instead released worldwide to stream on Disney+ in July 2020 and became one of the most-streamed films of that year. This release by Disney with the original cast as directed by Tommy Kail is a recording of a live stage performance which occurred in 2015. The Pulitzer Prize-winning writer Lin-Manuel Miranda always expected to release *Hamilton* to the wider world once "a decided-upon majority of audiences" had availed of the opportunity to "see the show live on stage as intended".[28]

[19.6.09] Another example in terms of adapting a play to a film occurred with *Disco Pigs* (2001) starring Elaine Cassidy and Cillian Murphy based on the 1996 play of the same name. In this instance, the screenplay writer and the original playwright were the same person (Enda Walsh), but where a film is based on a play, the same grant of rights by the author would occur as that which applies to purchasing the film rights to a book. Other notable examples are the plays *A Streetcar Named Desire* and *Cat on a Hot Tin Roof* by US playwright Tennessee Williams which were adapted into Academy Award-winning and nominated pictures respectively. In Ireland, John B Keane's play was adapted for *The Field* directed by Jim Sheridan and starring Richard Harris. The reverse can also happen where films are adapted. Multi-Oscar-nominated *The Shawshank Redemption* for instance was recently recreated for the stage.

---

28 Christopher Rosen, *The Hamilton* Movie Is Real, and Disney Will Release It Next Year (2020), Vanity Fair. Available at: https://www.vanityfair.com/hollywood/2020/02/hamilton-movie-release-date [Accessed 10 August 2021].

No waiver of moral rights

[19.6.10] Unlike in the case of films or television productions where the screenplay author will be required under contract to waive statutory moral rights,[29] a playwright or musical author will aim to retain IP rights and thus wield full artistic approval and control. A theatre or production house may not always therefore necessarily insist on such waiver. Consequently, any additions, omissions or alterations in the manuscript of the show, including dialogue and stage directions, will not occur without the written consent of the author arising on foot of the underlying licence agreement.[30] Any material uncured violation of such provision would be cause for the author to declare the entire production contract null and void. This prior artistic approval can be likened to licensing a commercial song for use in a film or television production – no changes thereto can be made unless authorised by the relevant songwriter (and master sound recording proprietor in the case where the original sound recording is also used and modified rather than recording a new version with fresh master copyright).

Provisions in respect of rehearsals and creative approvals

[19.6.11] Furthermore, show authors who retain moral rights and copyright, whether in residence (if perhaps living local to the theatre) or not will typically make themselves available for all necessary casting sessions and would be entitled to recoup out-of-pocket expenses for travel, accommodation and so forth.[31] The writer would accordingly have the right to attend readings, workshops, rehearsals and previews. The theatre (or its representatives) and the author will, in general, mutually select and approve the cast for the production, such approval not to be unreasonably withheld by either party. It is likely though in the case where the theatre is expending large sums on the production (as may be funded by central/local government) that the theatre will negotiate final editorial control and will require operational and oversight control in all key aspects.

[19.6.12] Theatres are normally expected to agree that the play shall be presented with a cast, director, music director if applicable, scenic, lighting, costume and sound design, and where applicable, a stage combat/fight director, choreographer/dance director and music conductor as shall be mutually approved by the parties and that the author shall have the right to confer with the theatre to approve production elements. This should be on the proviso that the writer pay due

---

[29] As discussed in Chapter 10A, moral rights of authors pursuant to ss 107-119 of the 2000 Act refer to non-economic rights including the paternity right, integrity right and the right not to have a work falsely attributed to them as authors.

[30] Any agreed changes that are so made in the manuscript, alterations or incidental dialogue and stage directions as accepted by the author would thereupon become the property of the author.

[31] A fee may also arise for attendance at script meetings, production and design meetings, production-related articles, publicity interviews and other promotional activities as well as for contributions to or compilation of the show's programme which will be available to the audience at an additional fee.

regard to the theatre's artistic and financial resources and taking into account the production budget.

A changing tide?

[19.6.13] In a July 2013 article by *The Guardian*, a question was posed thus, "Should a playwright have the final say over a production?". This was in response to an incident on the opening night of a play, *Alienation*, by disgruntled Australian playwright Lachlan Philpott. Due to creative differences, the writer removed his name from the production and placed a note on every seat in the auditorium declaring, "This production does not reflect my original scripted or communicated intentions as the playwright". The Perth Theatre Company later refuted the assertion by issuing a statement iterating that it strongly disagreed and was disappointed with these statements, considering them to be inaccurate and unwarranted.[32]

[19.6.14] The incident spurred theatre practitioners to re-examine the power and authority of the playwright and to probe whether changes are needed (if indeed they are possible at all). It also raised interesting issues about how much theatre is a collaborative enterprise and whether the writer as creator should have supremacy. Los Angeles based entertainment law attorney, Gordon Firemark, makes mention of Polish theorist Grotowski and others who have argued that a text simply suggests rather than determines a performance,[33] asking why it seems perfectly acceptable to modify Shakespeare but not permissible to cut lines from Philpott. The obvious answer is that Shakespeare's work is in the public domain.

[19.6.15] However, copyright aside, if the artistic output of the world's most talented playwright is not sacrosanct, it begs the question as to why theatres might be at the whim of contemporary writers. Ultimately, it is a matter for contractual negotiation between the parties but perhaps the industry will, in time, dictate that the rights of playwrights align with those which pertain to their screenwriting brethren who are afforded much less eminence.

Warranties given by the author

[19.6.16] The most fundamental of authors' warranties in a production contract is that (and again in respect of a playwright or musical show composer of renown as opposed to a less eminent writer providing services on a work for hire basis) they are the sole author of the play/musical and the sole owner of all copyright in all languages throughout the world, are in full control of the rights granted in the agreement and that (to the best of the writers' belief) the play contains

32 Lyn Garden, *Should a playwright have the final say over a production?* (2013). The Guardian. Available at: https://www.theguardian.com/stage/theatreblog/2013/jul/25/playwright-final-say-theatre-production [Accessed 10 August 2021].

33 See https://firemark.com/2013/08/03/why-theatre-authors-are-more-powerful-than-screenwriters/.

no defamatory material or other content that might give rise to a third party claim relating to music copyright, trademark infringement, passing off, breach of contract, breach of confidentiality, privacy or data protection, or violation of any other IP rights including moral rights.

[19.6.17] The contract will therefore further provide that the author shall fully and effectually hold harmless and indemnify the theatre against any losses, costs, expenses (including reasonable attorney's fees) and damages caused by or arising out of any breach of the representations or warranties therein made. Resulting from this clause, a policy of insurance might also be required from the author by the theatre (or film producer if the play is to be adapted to film) in this regard to ensure that the plaintiff has access to the deep pocket resources of an insurance company rather than the personal financial resources of authors (or their trading company or business) and that the defendant theatre, if sued, will be indemnified against a damages settlement or compensatory award by a court. In some cases however, depending on track record and bargaining position, writers may require the theatre or producer to note their name on the theatre/producer's own errors and omissions policy.

Advances and royalties

[19.6.18] In consideration of the right to produce and present the play publicly, the theatre most likely will pay an advance to the author upon signing the production contract. Depending on whether the production is commissioned or non-commissioned, there may be a number of payments by the licensee to the licensor (due upon signing of the contract, upon first and further deliveries of the property being licensed to allow for alterations and revisions) or by way of lump sum. In the case of a non-commissioned work, there should be contractual provision for at least some revisions required from the producer by the author in respect of the already written work.

[19.6.19] These advance payments are expressed as being non-returnable, but recoupable or offset from royalties earned in the future under the agreement. In other words, an advance sum is to constitute a non-returnable downpayment against royalties and is therefore a guaranteed minimum royalty payment. For example, if a playwright licenses the subject work to a theatre in return for five percent royalties on ticket sales and a €5,000 advance against those royalties, in this case, the author would immediately receive the €5,000 and further royalty payments would be withheld until the theatre's takings from box office ticket sales reached €100,000 (thus allowing for costs recoupment); after that point, the five percent royalty would be paid on any additional sales.

[19.6.20] Otherwise, or in addition to the initial advance, a royalty will often be payable by the theatre on a percentage of the gross weekly box office receipts[34] or a stated amount for each paid public performance, whichever is greater. This payment may increase if the play/show is extended beyond its announced limited run or a number of specified performances. Furthermore, should the theatre recoup its investment during the limited designated run of the production, or during the extension, the author might be paid yet another higher percentage of the gross weekly box office receipts or a fixed sum for each paid public performance, whichever amount is the greater. Moreover, there will in all probability be a split of gross box office receipts between the writer and theatre (e.g. 20/80) for the first production run and a royalty pool will be created for future performances and exploitation of subsidiary rights based on a points system (e.g. 15 points to the composer(s) and 5 to the theatre of a total of 20 points).

Exploitation of the sound recording of a musical

[19.6.21] If the theatre sound-records a musical and then exploits that sound recording of the show, notwithstanding that the composer will own first copyright in the compositions, the theatre might expect (given the production costs and payment of sound engineers and performers) to own the masters of that sound recording and not to assign its default statutory authorship rights as the music/show producer. Otherwise, the theatre and composer may decide to split any net income from exploitation of any sound recording(s) of the musical. To ensure receipt of public performance royalties (aside from any master use licence fees that might be negotiated by the master's owner and a third party licensee), the recording(s) should be registered with Phonographic Performance Ireland.

Proceeds to theatres from authors' subsidiary rights

[19.6.22] Although the relationship between the parties may be limited to the production of the play or show as above, there may well be a recognition by the author that, through a successful production, the theatre has made a contribution to the value thereof. Hence, if the theatre, as the originating theatre to which an exclusive licence has been granted for the initial run of shows, has produced a minimum number of performances since the official opening, the author may agree that the theatre shall be entitled to receive a percentage of the author's net proceeds derived from the disposition of subsidiary rights (see below) occurring within a certain period (say two years) following the final performance of the play/show at the theatre (excluding perhaps proceeds from performances of the play/show in other territories).

[19.6.23] Subsidiary rights could include major regional theatres; touring productions; worldwide motion pictures; free, pay, or cable television; DVD

[34] All sums received by the theatre from ticket sales less, for example, any admission taxes, customary commissions, group discounts for group sales and fees paid to credit card companies from ticket sales.

and Blu-ray, and all other kinds of visual and audiovisual productions; radio and sound recordings. If the author sells audiovisual rights in respect of film, television and so forth during a certain period (for example, five years) following the final performance of the play at the originating theatre, the latter might also be entitled to receive a small percentage of the author's net proceeds derived from exploiting such subsidiary rights.

Actor agreements

[19.6.24] Minimum actor remuneration (the contract can provide for more favourable terms) in the UK and Ireland is dictated by union rules as set out by the respective Equity UK[35] and Irish Equity (with royalties, in certain cases, to be discharged by RAAP) which is part of the Services Industrial Professional and Technical Union (SIPTU) which are discussed in Chapter 21. The executive of Irish Equity negotiates minimum terms and conditions agreements with producers and their representatives. It also liaises with its international partners on the standards for these agreements through affiliation with the International Federation of Actors (Federation Internationale des Acteurs, FAI) and its counterpart societies in the UK, USA, Canada and so forth.

Stage show income for music composers

[19.6.25] With the prevalence nowadays of streaming and downloads, the high revenues from music are reserved for the superstar acts who can gain back lost radio and CD sales income from international touring and merchandise sales. In the film music sector, while not every songwriter or composer gets to soar the heights of John Williams or Ennio Morricone, business-savvy songwriters in recent times might, if their creative ethos permits, seek song placement via synchronisation licensing in a videogame, advert, television programme or motion picture in order to generate viable alternative income streams.

[19.6.26] However, composers should keep in mind that perhaps the most lucrative of all copyrights attaches to musicals and other live stage performances, that of grand rights. The shows *West Side Story*, *The Sound of Music*, *Once*, *Jesus Christ Superstar*, *Phantom of the Opera*, *Cats*, *Shrek*, *Alice in Wonderland*, *Beauty and the Beast*, *Aladdin* and *Les Misérables* readily spring to mind. The upside to a successful stage show or operetta, be it Broadway, off Broadway, the West End or elsewhere, is its sheer longevity. An astute move, to future-proof one's creative career, might be to align oneself with a theatre or musicals producer such as the

---

[35] As regards film and television productions of stage shows, the British Equity Collection Society (BECS) pays royalties to its members when their work is copied for private use, rented in video shops, retransmitted on cable channels or publicly broadcast. BECS negotiates a share of the revenue generated in this way for British-made productions that are exploited in the countries where performers' rights are enshrined in law. BECS has agreements in place with international collecting societies.

Riverdance collaboration between composer Bill Whelan, (executive) producer Moya Doherty and her spouse, show director John McColgan.

[19.6.27] Aside from royalties from IMRO emanating from use of one's songs or music as curtain or incidental music, significant revenues are earned from grand rights whereby a fee, pursuant to a licence agreement or assignment, is paid from a theatrical production to the songwriter for interpolated music which forms part of the actual action of the show as in the case, for example, of Glen Hansard's music in *Once*, a musical based on the 2007 film of the same name by John Carney. Like in the film, music and lyrics were by Glen Hansard and Markéta Irglová including the Oscar-scooping *Falling Slowly*. The script for the musical was written by Enda Walsh. The stage show premiered at the New York Theatre Workshop in 2011 before transferring to Broadway in 2012. It has since spawned international tours of the show.

FAIR USE AS AN EXCEPTION TO COPYRIGHT INFRINGEMENT AND PAYMENT OF MUSIC LICENSING FEES/ROYALTIES

[19.7.01] Larry Iser, managing partner at Santa Monica law firm, Kinsella Weitzman Iser & Aldisert LLP, and lecturer on IP law at the University of Southern California frequently litigates IP disputes and has represented music artists including The Beatles, Michael Jackson and Jackson Browne.[36] He explains in a series of online articles that writer/composer Lin-Manuel Miranda licensed or otherwise obtained permission for what became the theatre sensation *Hamilton* to use the many references in his score and libretto to iconic music and lyrics of the past, from operetta of the 1800s to modern day hip-hop and R&B, notwithstanding that having recourse to the doctrine of fair use[37] in the US, he did not necessarily need to clear all those uses.[38]

[19.7.02] In Ireland, depending entirely on context, fair dealing (the fair use equivalent) may allow what would otherwise constitute unauthorised use provided it does not prejudice the interests of the rightsholder (such as where a licence fee should have been paid for the use but was not; or in the statutorily-permitted case of parody).[39]

---

36 See https://kwikalaw.com/our-attorneys/lawrence-iser/.

37 Fair use is a legal principle that promotes freedom of expression by permitting the unlicensed use of copyright-protected works in certain circumstances. Traditionally, in the US, courts adjudicated fair use by considering four factors, the first of which is whether the accused work is "transformative" of the original. Over time, the courts (particularly in the Second Circuit, which ultimately would decide copyright disputes concerning Broadway shows) have focused on this factor as the defining issue in the fair use analysis, to the point where it now overshadows the other factors.

38 Note that application of, and principles governing, fair use in the US differ considerably from the statutory fair dealing provisions in Ireland and the UK.

39 Fair dealing is governed by s 52 of the 2000 Act as amended. Section 52(4) provides that the copyright in a work which has been lawfully made available to the public is not infringed by the use of quotations or extracts from the work, where such use does not prejudice the

[19.7.03] *Hamilton* is a hip-hop history lesson that incorporates musical works from the past with an entirely different aesthetic, purpose and audience than the original works and is peppered throughout with modern-day music references. Larry Iser explains that after his first 2016 post in *Forbes*[40] he received a call from Deborah Mannis-Gardner, President of DMG Clearances, Inc and music clearance expert who was responsible for clearing all (grand rights) of Lin-Manuel Miranda's references to musical theatre and popular music. DMG is known for representing the stars of the industry and clearing difficult copyrights from artists such as Led Zeppelin, The Beatles, Prince and AC/DC, as well as intricate multi-song mash-ups. Mannis-Gardner agreed with the assertion that *Hamilton* was protected by fair use. It was Mannis-Gardner's understanding, however, that Miranda specifically wished to license all of his references to and samples from prior music out of respect and to garner added appreciation worldwide for the rap genre.

[19.7.04] By taking a form of entertainment (hip-hop) not typically associated with musical theatre and by combining the genres of pop, R&B, hip-hop and musical theatre into a rather accurate show, historically, about one of America's lesser-known founding fathers, all of whom are portrayed by non-white talent, Miranda created the poster child for transformative works. By way of illustration, Eminem's famous hip-hop (*8 Mile*) battles were transformed into cabinet debates over international neutrality and the assumption of state debts in the creation of the national monetary system. The third song from Act 1 *My Shot* is reminiscent of Eminem's *Lose Yourself.* Notorious B.I.G.'s *Ten Crack Commandments* were transformed into Hamilton's "Ten Duel Commandments" that governed the fatal duel between Hamilton and Burr. Gilbert and Sullivan's introduction of their *I am the very model of a modern major-general* song was humorously transformed into the patter of General George Washington.

[19.7.05] Moreover, Miranda's admiration for hip-hop and R&B is evidenced by means of a homage type tribute and sampling from a large number of artists including Jay Z (*Izzo (H.O.V.A.)*), DMX (*Party Up (Up in Here)*), Beyoncé (*Countdown*), Prodigy and Mary J. Blige. Although fair use was permissible and the show creator thereby clearly acknowledged in some cases the source of his

---

interests of the owner of the copyright in that work and such use is accompanied by a sufficient acknowledgement. Section 13 of the Copyright and Other Intellectual Property Law Provisions Act 2019 (inserting a new s 52(5) into the 2000 Act) also provides that fair dealing with a work for the purposes of caricature, parody or pastiche shall not infringe the copyright in that work. For the purposes of the present discussion of theatrical shows for commercial gain, fair dealing is highly unlikely to afford any would-be defendant (e.g. who breaches music, or other copyright laws that might apply for instance to the use of IP-protected props on stage) a defence.

[40] Larry Iser, *'Hamilton' And Copyright: Lin-Manuel Miranda Had His Eyes On Music History* (2016), forbes.com. Available at: https://www.forbes.com/sites/legalentertainment/2016/06/16/hamilton-and-copyright-lin-manuel-miranda-had-his-eyes-on-music-history/?sh=4e92139650f8 [Accessed 10 August 2021].

inspiration and referenced the relevant artists or music, he also sought consent where relevant and cleared the intended uses.

SMALL PERFORMING RIGHTS AND THIRD PARTY MUSIC RIGHTSHOLDERS

[19.8.01] While it is true that most venues pay IMRO for blanket music licences which allow for the performance of music in a public setting, the rights granted by IMRO (and PPI, through IMRO, which accounts for royalties for sound recordings by dual licence) cover only the so-called 'small' performing rights. Typically, in the general sense, this includes royalties to songwriters from radio airplay, live performances in a restaurant or bar, background music in a workplace, retail outlet and so forth. In a theatrical setting, the use of a CD to play pre-show or post-show music, or a revue type performance or concert will give rise to public performance royalties.

[19.8.02] However, where the music in question is important to the arc of the show, the issue of 'grand' performing rights arises. Small rights (relating to non-dramatic works) refer to music not specially written for a dramatic presentation (e.g. using an Otis Redding song as curtain/interval music). It is possible to have a small rights performance of a work from a grand right presentation, for instance, a song from a musical may be performed on the radio or in a live concert with no visual reference to the original show. This would constitute a small rights performance and hence be controlled by performing rights societies.

[19.8.03] Small rights is therefore a term employed to cover performances of individual songs in a concert or cabaret-type setting. Most schools, heritage/cultural centres, local community halls, churches,[41] restaurants and clubs pay an annual fee to obtain a blanket licence from IMRO that covers the small rights use of all music in its catalogue for the year. The annual blanket licence does not permit dramatic performances of songs. The songs can be performed only in cabaret style. While it is sometimes difficult to draw a distinction between dramatic and non-dramatic performances, a dramatic performance usually involves using a song to tell a story or as part of a story or plot. A blanket licence does not permit the use of dialogue from the show nor of course sets, costumes and/or choreography that invoke the original show.

[19.8.04] Theatrical licensing agencies will occasionally be approached by groups seeking either to create a revue based on a composer's body of work or centred around a theme (e.g. love songs), or take existing songs from shows and incorporate them into a new dramatic context. Neither of these examples would be covered under a small rights licence since their thematic nature or

41 See para 3.13, IMRO Standard Tariff GP.

imposed storyline would create what is considered a dramatico-musical work under copyright law.

Interpolated music and incidental music

[19.8.05] PRS for Music in the UK and IMRO in Ireland control small rights in the British and Irish territories whereby two categories of use are recognised – interpolated music and incidental music. The former describes music that is either performed by, or audible to, a character in a drama. This kind of music is not authorised by PRS in Britain or IMRO licences held by venues and so a specific licence application must be made in advance of performances, even if a standard PRS licence or IMRO annual blanket licence is already held by the relevant theatre. Royalties resulting from interpolated music performances are charged directly to the applicant, usually the producing/performing party. Songwriter members of IMRO may opt to license show producers directly for the use of their works as interpolated music and applications can be referred by IMRO to the publishers or writers concerned for this option to be considered.

[19.8.06] Incidental or 'curtain' music is that which is not audible to a character in a drama, such as music used for transitions, intervals, pre- and post-show, scene changes and so forth.[42] IMRO defines this small right category of incidental music in Tariff VT,[43] rates effective from 1 January 2023, as music heard by the theatre audience as an accompaniment to a theatrical production or variety show, but which is not performed by or intended to be audible to any of the characters in the theatrical production or variety show.[44] This type of music use is automatically covered by venues' blanket licence pursuant to the terms of IMRO Tariff VT and PPI Tariff 36[45] (current rates effective from 1 January 2023). Note that the dual IMRO/PPI annual licence contract (administered by IMRO) does not apply to Tariff VT and reference must thus be made to the above two individual tariffs of these performing rights societies.

Obligation to obtain a copyright music licence

[19.8.07] Where a theatre is using commercial music (not written by the stage show author/composer) for its production (e.g. by way of exit, curtain or

---

42 Music usage during the opening, interval and exiting of an event is described by IMRO in Tariff VT as curtain, overture, entr'acte and exit music.

43 This tariff applies to performances of copyright music within the repertoire controlled by IMRO in theatrical presentations, stage plays or variety shows, admittance to which is gained by purchase of a ticket or by subscription. It does not apply to performances at premises to which there is no admission charge.

44 Variety shows, as also defined in the tariff, mean stage entertainments, however designated, in the nature of variety revues, pantomime or theatrical productions as distinct from musical entertainments consisting entirely or almost entirely of controlled light or popular music and from concerts or recitals of such music.

45 See https://imro.ie/wp-content/uploads/2023/01/VT-Tariff-0123-1223.pdf and https://imro.ie/wp-content/uploads/2023/01/Tariff-36-2023.pdf.

incidental music), the primary obligation rests on the proprietor of the premises hosting the theatrical production which features musical works[46] to obtain the necessary licences from IMRO and PPI respectively in advance of the planned staged event to permit the public performance of musical works in the repertoires controlled by the societies and to pay all royalties due thereon in accordance with the tariffs. In the event that the proprietor of the premises proves to IMRO's satisfaction in advance of the event that the event promoter holds a licence from IMRO for the event, IMRO will not require an additional licence to be obtained by the proprietor of the premises for the event.

[19.8.08] If the proprietor or event promoter omits to apply for and obtain a licence in advance of the event and the live event proceeds, royalties will be payable at the unlicensed rate in para 5 of Tariff VT. Any performances not declared are unauthorised and constitute an infringement of copyright and will be charged as unlicensed performances.

Obligation to submit returns to IMRO

[19.8.09] In the case of all events licensed under Tariff VT, the proprietor of the premises or event promoter must send IMRO in the format specified, along with the details required in para 5.2.3 of the tariff, particulars of all musical works performed at each event in the way of programme details and a setlist.[47]

Royalties payable

[19.8.10] IMRO distinguishes between performances of its members' music at stage plays versus performances at variety shows or other theatrical presentations. The former commands an annual/weekly fee based on a capacity of under or over 1,000 seats. The latter type shows generate income for songwriters/publishers as calculated by applying a percentage rate to the net revenue receipts from each show.

Music rights clearances and moral rights

[19.8.11] The matter does not end there. A production contract will seek the

---

46 Including live, recorded, instrumental, electronic, digital or by any other means.

47 No later than one month after an event has taken place, or if a number of events are held by the proprietor of the premises or event promoter, within 30 days of the end of the month in which the event or series of events takes place, the proprietor of the premises or event promoter must submit to IMRO a statement(s) for each event(s) in accordance with a format outlined by IMRO, detailing for each individual event such particulars as details of the capacity of the event, ticket prices paid by purchasers, actual number of tickets sold at each ticket price, selling agent and credit card commissions included in the ticket price paid by purchasers, total gross receipts from ticket sales, number of complimentary tickets allocated, setlist in respect of all performers, duration of performing time and duration of each musical work performed during the total performing time and details of any sponsorship and advertising revenue other than revenue generated from ticket sales.

grant of unencumbered rights from the writer to the theatre as regards third parties. Accordingly, the rights to use incidental music (as above) or interpolated music (see below in relation to grand rights) must be cleared by the writer (or theatre for example in respect of curtain music) by way of licence from IMRO (if IMRO's repertoire contains that music and IMRO is mandated to license its use) as must rights from the record producer in terms of sound recording master use. This is the monetary element which will be handled by IMPO/PPI through royalty tariffs or directly with the songwriter/composer/publisher pursuant to contract whereby a fee will be agreed.

[19.8.12] However, if changes are to be made to music in a show, the rightsholders will also need to give their consent directly (outside of blanket licensing) for moral rights (integrity) purposes or waive their moral rights. Moral rights provisions in the 2000 Act dictate that no derogatory treatment can occur, nor any amendment, mutilation or distortion be made which might prejudice the integrity of a piece, and the reputation of its creator, without the consent of the party seeking to effectuate such modifications.

Royalties for use of sound recordings

[19.8.13] With current rates effective from 1 January 2023 theatrical production companies must pay, on an annual basis, a specified sum per week for daily performances pursuant to PPI Tariff 36 or a sum per performance for performances for the public use of sound recordings solely as background music during the entry and exit of audiences and during the intervals and during the action of shows when required.

GRAND RIGHTS

[19.9.01] As outlined at the outset, grand rights or dramatic performing rights arise in respect of performances of a composition in a dramatic setting, such as within a stage play, musical, opera or ballet where the composition becomes part of the story, plot or theme of the performance. A dramatico-musical work is defined in IMRO's Articles of Association as an opera, an operetta, musical play, revue or pantomime, insofar as it consists of words and music written expressly therefor. Licensing is undertaken and managed by the appropriate rightsholder. A classic example of a grand rights use is where a character in the show sings a popular song, or recites the lyrics to a pop song. Grand rights are not administered by IMRO or other performing rights societies such as BMI or ASCAP in the USA. Exceptions exist in relation to excerpts of certain durations and as outlined below.[48]

[19.9.02] In respect of pantomime, although this theatrical format contains a

---

[48] See https://imro.ie/faq/do-imro-administer-grand-rights/ [Accessed 10 August 2021].

dramatic story, in Britain, it is an exception to the general rule. Pantomime is automatically licensed by PPS for Music and application for an interpolated music licence does not therefore need to be submitted directly to the rightsholders/publishers.[49]

[19.9.03] The performing right in dramatico-musical works and ballets is administered by IMRO when these works are performed by means of films which were made primarily for the purpose of exhibition in cinemas (and this control extends also to television broadcasting of such films). IMRO also controls performances of these works when given in public by means of radio or television sets (for example in a hotel lounge or a public house). In addition, all ballet music – complete or in excerpt – is controlled by IMRO when not accompanied by a visual representation of ballet. Unlike dramatico-musical works, ballet music is therefore considered to have a grand right whether or not the music was written specially. Third, if a dramatico-musical work (of specially written music) begins its performance life as a film, broadcast, record, tape or CD and is later adapted to the stage, IMRO does not control the stage performance of such an adaptation. However, pre-existing musical works used in films which are later adapted to the stage are normally controlled by IMRO in the first instance.

[19.9.04] Aside then from the limited exceptions above, grand rights are controlled by the composers themselves and/or their music publishers. In order, therefore, to secure the necessary rights and permissions, the producer of the show must identify each song's composer or publisher and negotiate the terms of a licence. In some instances, the playwright may have pre-negotiated a royalty rate to be paid for uses of songs contained within the show, in others, the producer may have to offer a royalty based on a percentage of gross box office receipts. In many cases, the publisher of the song will require a guaranteed minimum fee. When multiple songs are included in a show, it is often possible to negotiate a favoured-nations deal, or a pooled royalty for music, in which each song receives a pro-rata share of the pool.

[19.9.05] Another point of concern is the scope and duration of the licence granted. It can certainly occur that songs have to be withdrawn from a musical because of licence expirations, or holdback provisions imposed by publishers. Show directors, producers and playwrights would do well to anticipate these problematic music licensing issues when selecting music to incorporate into a show. One's bargaining position is all but removed if negotiating the royalty rate just hours before the show is scheduled to open.

49 See https://www.prsformusic.com/royalties/theatre-royalties-and-grand-rights.

THE DRAMA OF LAWSUITS

Anastasia

[19.10.01] In April 2018, a federal judge ruling on a US copyright suit rejected arguments by lawyers for prolific playwright Terrence McNally (second-named defendant) that his work, a Broadway musical *Anastasia,* and a 1940s play were not substantially similar.[50] In late 2016, Jean-Etienne de Becdelievre, heir of playwright Marcelle Maurette (and Tams-Witmark Music Library, Inc) initiated legal proceedings against the writer and Anastasia Musical LLC ('AML'). The plaintiffs contended the show infringed on Maurette's tale of a young woman who claims to be Grand Duchess Anastasia Romanov, the daughter of Russian Tsar Nicholas II who was killed by revolutionaries along with his wife and other children. While some of the play is loosely based on history, de Becdelievre argued much of the dialogue, characters and plot are fictional and therefore fall under copyright protection.

[19.10.02] The heir claimed the play was licensed to Twentieth Century Fox for a 1956 film and a 1997 animated feature, but that he retained all rights in live stage performances. According to his pleadings, Fox unlawfully transferred rights it did not possess to AML to produce the musical, which opened at the Broadhurst Theatre in April 2017. McNally, who wrote the show's book, moved for summary judgment arguing the play and the musical were not substantially similar.

[19.10.03] US District Judge Alvin Hellerstein (southern district of New York) disagreed and denied the motion. Hellerstein J found that McNally was aware of the licensing history and obtained a licence from Fox which imposed on producers an obligation to use all reasonable efforts to secure live stage rights:

> [E]ven in the realm of historical work, and especially in cases involving historical fiction, the right to build on a prior author's work is not absolute...Put differently, to the extent that plaintiffs seek to assert copyright protection over the historical underpinnings of the Play, their claim must fail. But the fictionalized elements that are built on top of the historical skeleton are subject to copyright protection, and these fictionalized elements form the basis of plaintiffs' claim.[51]

After parsing through the works and excluding from consideration any non-copyrightable historical facts, the court held the works share "significant commonalities not traced to any documented historical record".

---

[50] Ashley Cullins, *'Anastasia' Musical Lawsuit Steps Towards Trial as Judge Evaluates Similarities in Hollywood Fiction* (2018), hollywoodreporter.com. Available at: https://www.hollywoodreporter.com/business/business-news/anastasia-musical-lawsuit-steps-trial-as-judge-evaluates-similarities-historical-fiction-1099289/ [Accessed 10 August 2021].

[51] *De Becdelievre v Anastasia Musical LLC* 16 Civ 9471 (AKH) (2018), pp 14-15.

Riverdance

[19.10.04] Shortly after hitting the spotlight at the April 1994 Eurovision as the lead male in *Riverdance*, Michael Flatley was released from his contract in 1995. Flatley issued a writ against the production company Abhann Productions Ltd after disputes arose over pay, artistic control and profit-sharing. At the time of the split, British publications reported that Flatley had overplayed his hand when he threatened to quit if his request for a higher salary and for royalties on dance routines he had created was refused.[52] He left the show and subsequently developed *Lord of the Dance*.

[19.10.05] A legal adviser to Flatley told *The Irish Times* in 1995 that his client was suing the Riverdance producers on contractual grounds, claiming he was entitled to two percent of the gross earnings of the *Riverdance* shows.[53] An estimate of the show's turnover at the time of the news article in 1999 was £400 million. In August 1999, it was announced via joint statement from the parties in dispute that the proceedings had been settled. The statement acknowledged Flatley's contribution to the original development of *Riverdance*.

The Phantom of the Opera

[19.10.06] The song *The Music of the Night* from *The Phantom of the Opera* was the subject of controversy after the estate of Giacomo Puccini filed proceedings against Lloyd Webber. Puccini's estate had argued that the melody in the lyrics "silently the senses abandon their defences" was plagiarised from an excerpt of the opera *La Fanciulla del West*. The matter was settled out of court. Lloyd Webber had originally planned to use the melody for *The Music of the Night* under different lyrics for his show *Aspects of Love*, but that song, titled *Married Man*, was cut from the final version of *Aspects*. It is widely reported that an undisclosed sum was paid to the Puccini estate to resolve embarrassing claims of music plagiarism.

INTERNATIONAL LICENSING AGENCIES

Music Theatre International

[19.11.01] Founded in 1952, Music Theatre International ('MTI') is one of the world's leading theatrical licensing agencies, granting theatres from around the world the rights to perform the greatest selection of musicals from Broadway and beyond (e.g. *West Side Story*, *The Lion King JR.*, *Wizard of Oz*, *Mamma Mia*,

---

[52] Valerie Gladstone, *The Man Behind The Duel Between Irish Blockbusters* (1997). The New York Times. Available at: https://www.nytimes.com/1997/03/02/theater/the-man-behind-the-duel-between-irish-blockbusters.html [Accessed 10 August 2021].

[53] Jim Dunne, *Flatley's 'Riverdance' court action is settled* (1999). The Irish Times. Available at: https://www.irishtimes.com/news/flatley-s-riverdance-court-action-is-settled-1.219662. [Accessed 10 August 2021].

Matilda, *Frozen JR.*, *Aladdin*, *Beauty and the Beast*, *Annie*, *Mary Poppins*, *Billy Elliot*). MTI works directly with the composers, lyricists and book writers of these musicals to provide official scripts, musical materials and theatrical resources for professional and amateur theatre productions in the US and worldwide.[54] The rights which MTI is authorised to grant under its contracts with its author clients are limited to grand rights covering the right to present the show, in its entirety, on stage. These rights do not include performance of a single song or medleys (small rights), videotaping, use of a logo or merchandising (although the granting of additional rights may prove possible on a case by case basis).

[19.11.02] When a theatre or producer is granted a performance licence by MTI, by law, the duly licensed show must be performed as-is. During rehearsals, directors or producers may believe that some changes are required to make the show work in their theatres. They may thus hold the mistaken belief that 'minor' adjustments to a show (such as changing the gender of a character, changing the name of a town to give it local significance, adding songs that appeared in the movie version of the musical, etc.) is inconsequential to its integrity, or they otherwise opine they have the right to experiment with the author's intentions as an expression of their own artistic vision. Occasionally, new versions of shows are created when the authors (or persons whom the authors have approved) reconceive the piece. However, only the authors have the right to make these revisions, and they rarely grant third parties permission to do so.

[19.11.03] Any unauthorised changes of American works will violate the authors' rights under US federal law (where the show is presented in the US) and international copyright law (where the show is presented outside the US). Without prior permission from MTI, unauthorised revisions to the show would not only expose theatres (and indeed the entire production staff, cast and crew) to liability in infringement claims by authors but also to a claim by MTI for breaching the terms of the licence agreement.

[19.11.04] Turning now to use of logos in a theatre show, like other elements of a production, logos are covered by both copyright and trademark law. Using the original logo without obtaining permission from the rightsholder is prohibited. MTI has obtained rights to license certain logos. Logos can legally be used in conjunction with the promotion of a show – on posters, programs and flyers – but organisations must ensure that such logos are original and do not violate the rights of third parties. If an organisation is seeking to create merchandise, such as T-shirts, mugs and keychains which will be sold to the public, a separate licensing agreement must be obtained.

Josef Weinberger (London)

[19.11.05] Josef Weinberger founded his publishing business in Vienna in 1885.

---

54 See https://www.mtishows.com/about.

Through an association with Johann Strauss II, he began licensing performances of Strauss' operettas. The principal Viennese operetta composers are represented in this catalogue and the company has expanded into several other musical genres over the years including British musicals of the 1990s. Its associated production music library, JW Media Music Ltd, is a leader in the field of production music for broadcast. Josef Weinberger is also a representative for the UK and other European territories of the Broadway show catalogues of MTI.[55]

The Musical Company

[19.11.06] As well as licensing the work of Lord Andrew Lloyd Webber,[56] the Musical Company provides support to creators and producers of musicals with the aim of bringing the subject theatre show to a wide audience. Operating from headquarters in New York, with offices in London and Los Angeles, the Musical Company is owned by two industry-leading companies, Andrew Lloyd Webber's The Really Useful Group and Concord Music.

Theatrical Rights Worldwide

[19.11.07] With headquarters in London and New York, Theatrical Rights Worldwide (TRW) represents Broadway shows, West End shows, and a wide variety of off-Broadway, off-West End and regional shows. Notable names include *Flashdance*, *Grease*, *Saturday Night Fever*, *Ghost*, *The Bodyguard* and *Priscilla Queen of the Dessert*.[57]

---

55 See https://www.josef-weinberger.com/musicals.html and http://www.mtishows.co.uk/.
56 See https://alwshowlicensing.com/theatrical-licensing/.
57 See https://www.theatricalrights.co.uk/shows/.

Chapter 20

Radio Documentaries

INTRODUCTION

[20.1.01] Radio content creation for documentary and dramatic productions can offer aspiring independent audiovisual producers the opportunity to hone their creative, scriptwriting, business and production skills. When compared with audiovisual content intended for the competitive television market, high quality radio material for commercial, community and national public service radio stations will likely, for market entrants at least, result more readily in broadcast. Indeed, if producers wish to avail of state funding, the Media Commission[1] will only advance production funding for radio programmes that will be broadcast by an eligible broadcaster.[2] Achieving successful distribution and content exploitation in turn buttresses one's track record in the entertainment industry generally. Radio can thus present career opportunities not just in its own lane but in the wider fields of film and television production to which production skills are readily transferable.

[20.1.02] In addition, radio rights in content can offer further income stream opportunities for screenwriters, playwrights and novelists. Writers will frequently seek to retain or reserve radio (and stageshow) rights when optioning and assigning film or television rights to an audiovisual producer based on their literary works. This will allow them, often subject to holdback for a certain period of time to permit full exploitation of a film or television programme or series, to ultimately enter into contracts with radioshow producers and theatre production companies based on the novel, play or screenplay and any adaptations thereof.

[20.1.03] The production of radio programming entails similar elements as those which obtain in film, television, stageshows, dance productions and theatre. However, the crew will plainly be smaller in number (often two or three), the budget a fraction of what would be required for brethren television and film productions. In the absence of visual content, legal issues surrounding trademarks, data protection and copyrighted elements as might be recorded by camera and reproduced on screen do not arise in many instances. Nonetheless,

---

1 Formerly the BAI – see Chapter 31.

2 At application stage, the Media Commission requires applicants to provide a letter of commitment from such broadcaster.

the contractual documents and funding agreements are broadly similar. Producers meanwhile must be no less mindful for instance of chain of title matters, defamation and privacy law, insurance, health and safety during production, production scheduling and funding compliance than would apply to larger audiovisual projects.

UNDERLYING RIGHTS AND FUNDING CONTRACTS

[20.2.01] Chain of title applies too to radio productions and hence the same IP and rights clearance processes require consideration as with all other forms of entertainment for commercial exploitation and public dissemination. Content may be based on pre-existing copyrighted material for which agreements will be signed with rightsholders and publishers, or it may involve an original treatment and script for which a writer's agreement will be in place. Other legal documentation will include funding and distribution licensing or acquisition agreements with commissioning entities or otherwise.

[20.2.02] The suite of production contracts may involve cast and crew agreements to include (voice) actor, researcher, presenter, narration and voiceover agreements, permits,[3] a life rights agreement, an errors and omissions ('E&O') insurance policy, production insurance,[4] individual producer contracts, a director agreement,[5] location agreements (where sound recording equipment and crew enter upon a premises to record a scene, carry out interviews or conduct research),[6] music licensing agreements[7] and contributor agreements. There may also be sponsorship of a radio programme subject to the terms of an agreement between the production company/broadcaster and the sponsor company advertising its product or services.[8]

[20.2.03] A programme licensing and investment agreement (such as with

---

3 If recording audio or filming in public places.

4 E.g. for conducting on-street interviews, capturing live footage or recording interviews in private and public settings, and for conducting out-of-office research.

5 If, on a larger production, a director's services are retained in addition to the radio content producers.

6 Usually for one-to-one street interviews a hand-held sound recording device will be employed and the need for a permit from the local authority will not arise – where boom polls are required to capture sound, the need for a shooting permit may arise (and in some cases crowd release forms should be sought, particularly where a person's voice will distinctly appear in the documentary).

7 Using a library of pre-cleared music or a MCPS licence for use of its members' production music repertoire, sound design agreements, contracts with composers for specially commissioned music or with songwriters/publishers, and songwriter/sound recording rightsholders in the case of commercial music (reproduction/dubbing and master use licences). Otherwise, if the radio programme will be confined to Ireland (and thus where radio programmes are uploaded online, the website will be geoblocked), producers and broadcasters can seek to rely on blanket licence mechanisms.

8 See rules governing sponsorship laid out in the Media Commission/BAI's *General Commercial Communications Code* (June 2017) as discussed in Chapter 31.

RTÉ for the premiere broadcast and any subsequent repeats on-air or made available online) or other distribution agreement will also be required, as well as a production agreement assigning ownership of the documentary (and its full underlying sound recordings) or dramatic radioplay from the individual producers to the production company.[9] In the case of commissioned content, a production services agreement or acquisition agreement will be in place between the production company and the commissioning broadcaster or online content provider to govern the specifications, budget, deliverables, rights granted and so forth.

[20.2.04] It will be necessary at times for producers to conduct research from biographies (which may necessitate acknowledgements for moral rights reasons, and consent or payment for copyright purposes if quoting therefrom),[10] to fact-check a range of informational sources, to include sound recordings in the programme as imported from video footage or audio recordings, and to obtain archive recordings of radio and television clips and other pertinent background material.

[20.2.05] Clearing the rights to use archives generally requires payment of significant fees particularly if from a national broadcaster such as RTÉ or the BBC. This would arise say for content to be broadcast on Today fm that will include RTÉ archive material. If providing radio content to RTÉ that will include RTÉ's own archive material however these fees will or may be waived or heavily discounted in the case of commissioned programming.

[20.2.06] In Ireland, a broadcaster is considered an author by s 21 of the Copyright and Related Rights Act 2000 ('the 2000 Act') as "the person[11] making the broadcast" and hence is the organisation from which a release or licence is to be sought in the case of using archive broadcast material.[12] Additionally, releases may be necessary from other rightsholders such as content authors and performers within the meaning of the Act who contributed to that material depending on what terms were agreed between them and the broadcaster at the time in relation

---

9 Under s 21 of the Copyright and Related Rights Act 2000, producers are the default owners of the copyright in a radio documentary (radio content is audio only and hence, being a sound recording, unlike a film, the director/producer are not joint owners). Therefore for funding arrangements and so forth, individual producers will assign same to the production company in order that the latter can freely contract with licensee distributors.

10 Some copying of material will be covered by fair dealing exceptions such as news reporting, criticism or review but the subject material title/description, and the author, must be duly acknowledged. Note however the Media Commission does not fund primarily news and current affairs content.

11 Note s 18(c) of the later Interpretation Act 2005 defines "person" *inter alia* as "person shall be read as importing a body corporate (whether a corporation aggregate or a corporation sole)" and hence in the context above "person" as regards broadcasts would be the networks/broadcasters (who would own the output of individual producers/presenters working as employees or contracted under a 'work for hire' contract for service agreement).

12 Any music featured in the documentary may however need to be cleared separately.

to formats and media, reuse and so forth. Although it is likely that the broadcaster (which self-produces content in-house)[13] will have obtained all rights for all uses in perpetuity, privacy rights and data protection consents for example may need to be considered for including performances and interviews from archive material in new material, as might the law of defamation (or contempt of court and court reporting rules) depending on the context.

Copyright exception

[20.2.07] Caricature, parody or pastiche is now governed by statute[14] and provides a defence to infringement of copyright claims in the form of a fair dealing exception (radio producers may also be in a position to rely on fair dealing rules generally as discussed in Chapter 10A). Therefore, a radio documentary maker can parody a work such as a commercial song, play, television clip, radio interview or film segment without fear of an action for copyright breach by the author of that work. This will not absolve a defendant in the case of a defamation claim however and, in the case of use of commercial music, it will have implications for blanket music licensing discussed below.

PUBLIC FUNDING

[20.3.01] In terms of finance agreements, funding will generally be sought from national and regional broadcasters directly by way of commissions and/or through the Media Commission/BAI's Sound and Vision scheme.[15] Individuals and established legal entities[16] are eligible to apply. At application stage, the Media Commission requires applicants to provide a letter of commitment from a broadcaster[17] which confirms agreement to broadcast the programme in line with the scheme's requirements. Further, the eligible broadcaster attached to the project must commit to broadcasting the proposed programme(s) at peak times.[18] Completed programming funded by the Commission can also be distributed (in whole or in part) online before being broadcast on radio, namely having regard to 'digital first' principles.[19] It may well also be a condition of funding that the

---

13 For productions that are licensed from independent producers the broadcaster may negotiate archive rights in perpetuity (as distinct from broadcast rights for linear and on-demand exploitation of full programmes, which rights might oftentimes be for a period of five years) in order that it can include clips in later (in-house) productions or to monetise the content by way of future licensing to producers seeking archive material.

14 s 13 of the Copyright and Other Intellectual Property Law Provisions Act 2019 which amended s 52 of the 2000 Act.

15 At the time of writing, the current scheme is S&V4.

16 Individuals must be Irish or EU nationals/residents. Legal entities must be incorporated in Ireland or the EU.

17 A broadcaster licensed by the BAI/Media Commission or a RTÉ service.

18 For radio programming, this is from 7am to 9pm with exceptions, for instance, for children's programming.

19 The requirement for the 'digital first' release is that the audio programme(s) must be made digitally available within 12 months of the delivery of the content to the broadcaster. The

broadcaster or the Commission obtains rights to archive the programme(s) for its own future uses and exploitation, or in the public interest generally.

[20.3.02] Under EU regulations concerning state aid, the maximum grant aid intensity permissible is limited to 50 percent. However, programmes specified under the Broadcasting Act 2009 (the Act is to be amended and reformed as discussed in Chapter 31), generally fall within the three exclusions to the upper limit. These exclusions relate to programmes which are difficult to make, low-budget or which counteract the limited geographic extension of certain languages and cultures. Accordingly, the scheme can potentially fund a maximum of 95 percent of the costs in the eligible budget.

[20.3.03] Applications to the Media Commission for standalone development or completion funding are not eligible. Eligible costs are the costs associated with the production and delivery of the programme(s) and, in addition to general production expenditure, may include financial, legal and banking costs. Development costs may be eligible provided they are directly related to the production of the programme and have been supported by budget notes.

CASE EXAMPLE OF RADIO PROGRAMME PRODUCTION

[20.4.01] To illustrate by case study what legal and business considerations might attach to producing a radio programme documentary, journalist Steve Cummins'[20] IMRO-award winning production for RTÉ Radio One, *Sin-é: Jeff Buckley's Irish Odyssey*,[21] (2016) is explored in the *Appendix*.

BLANKET LICENCES

[20.5.01] If commercial music (pre-cleared production music is discussed below at [20.6.01]) is used in a radio production by an independent producer for a public or private broadcaster it might be presumed that such reproduction of that music will be covered under the station's blanket radio licence for Irish Music Rights Organisation/Mechanical Copyright Protection Society/Phonographic Performance Ireland (IMRO/MCPS/PPI) purposes. This will not necessarily be the case as it will depend on context and there are considerations other

---

Media Commission will permit a digital first release only where the application has met certain requirements such as all or part of the programme being made available digitally first e.g. a pre-transmission distribution via a radio station's website, such as a podcast, before appearing as a broadcast; using 'digital first' to promote the programme; and making additional material available such as content intended for the production but not used in the final cut, e.g. extended interviews.

20 Steve Cummins is a journalist with *The Irish Times*, *The Sunday Times* and *NME*. His work has also appeared in *Hot Press*, *Nylon*, the *Irish Independent* and the *Irish Examiner*, among numerous other publications worldwide.

21 Available to download at https://www.rte.ie/radio1/podcast/podcast_documentaryonone.xml.

than copyright such as moral rights and blanket licence limitations (e.g. online radioshow playback if available beyond Ireland) to include no derogatory uses and editing. If the music is adapted or edited in some manner, this could well constitute a breach of s 43 of the 2000 Act (infringement by adaptation) or might otherwise constitute reproduction without due clearance. Adaptation in relation to a musical work includes arrangement or other alteration of the work (e.g change of lyrics, music, resequencing of chorus/verses or the language of the lyrics).

[20.5.02] Thus, while the playing of the music itself (in whole or in part) may be captured by the blanket licence and the copyright owners will thereby receive public performance royalties (the radio producer supplying to the broadcaster a cue sheet in relation to the track or tracks used for onward forwarding to IMRO/ PPI),[22] a release or licence should be obtained to ensure that where there are any changes to the work such changes are cleared, and second, to ensure that the owners have waived their moral rights in respect of use of the material in the radio production at hand.

[20.5.03] In circumstances whereby RTÉ licenses a programme having commissioned and funded same from an independent producer or produces it in-house itself, this should be covered under its IMRO radio broadcaster blanket agreement[23]in conjunction with the MCPS radio blanket licence in respect of music publishing (and the PPI blanket agreement in relation to sound recordings). IMRO royalty rates to broadcasters are calculated as the higher of a fixed annual fee and a percentage of revenue, subject to the level of music broadcast by the station.

[20.5.04] For rights excluded under the blanket licence, these must be individually negotiated and cleared with the rightsholders (writer/publisher and sound recording owners). Prior consent of the copyright owners in such instances is required unless the music is (pre-cleared) production music. Many songwriters/composers will in any event have mandated MCPS to license their works on their behalf. Some however will have elected when registering with MCPS to license production companies directly themselves for synchronisation uses and other purposes. Therefore, if MCPS is not in a position to arrange a licence because it is not mandated to do so or the music is not covered by blanket licence, it will direct licensees to the relevant copyright owner.

PPI licence (sound recordings)

[20.5.05] PPI, which represents owners of sound recordings (record labels

---

[22] Broadcasters are required to submit on a monthly basis to IMRO information on all musical works broadcast on the service.

[23] Such IMRO licence also covers the use of MCPS production music/sound recordings of MCPS-registered creators/publishers for use within Ireland. For international uses (and thus not covered by the blanket licence, see the IMRO rate card cited below).

and music producers), is mandated to license the copying of recorded music in certain restricted circumstances including to independent radio producers making programmes for a PPI-licensed broadcaster such as RTÉ.

[20.5.06] If the radio programme has been commissioned by a PPI-licensed broadcaster in Ireland, then the dubbing or embedding of commercial music therein should be covered by blanket agreement between PPI and the broadcaster. Contact can be made with PPI providing the name of the broadcaster for which the production is being made and the details of the tracks required for use to ensure the broadcaster/tracks are covered. If a radio programme is being made 'on spec' for sale by licence to a broadcaster, PPI cannot license the dubbing of recorded music. Accordingly, permission must be sought directly from the owners of the copyright in the recordings.

Licence limitations

[20.5.07] The downside to the above blanket licensing schemes is that there are restrictive limitations at play in respect of which E&O insurers will require full knowledge, particularly in terms of broadcast territory[24] or territories if commercial music used in the radio programme is not covered by blanket licence. Adaptation, alteration, sampling or arrangement of MCPS members' commercial music requires prior approval from the copyright owner. Use of music in a deliberately derogatory manner is also excluded as is certain editing. Independent producers, if they obtain their own blanket licence, will only be covered for uses within Ireland. If the production is intended for international distribution, rights will need to be individually negotiated (note that MCPS's secondary exploitation/programme sales licence as applies say to in-flight entertainment relates only to audiovisual productions).

PRODUCTION MUSIC

[20.6.01] To overcome the above challenges and if (often instrumental) production music were to suit a particular radio production, the producer may therefore elect to use say MCPS production music instead of commercial music, the advantage being pre-clearance for all usage types worldwide in perpetuity (for the lifetime of the production). There are no copyright owner permissions to obtain. Clearance covers sound recordings as well as song rights (the music is both written and recorded by professional songwriters, composers and musicians who also own the master rights). IMRO's 2022 rate card setting out fees payable by music users in this regard is available online.[25] For further discussion, see [17.3.36] and *Appendix 1* in Chapter 23.

---

24 If the exploitation of the radio programme is online such that it could be accessed internationally, there may well be geoblocking issues to consider so as to limit broadcaster website features (podcasts, catch-up shows etc.) to a particular territory or territories.

25 IMRO MCPS *Rate Card 2022 Production Music,* imro.ie. Available at: https://imro.ie/

Appendix

The making of "Sin-é: Jeff Buckley's Irish Odyssey"

[A1.1.01] Through his definitive cover version of Leonard Cohen's *Hallelujah*, haunting vocal talents and classic debut album, Jeff Buckley became a music icon. The young American west coast singer-songwriter was on the cusp of prolific international success before his tragic accidental death in 1997 in Tennessee and Northern Mississippi's Wolf River at the age of only 30.[26] Emerging from New York's East Village in lower Manhattan in the early 1990s, Buckley honed his unique talent during his formative,[27] experimental years at Sin-é, a bustling Irish café on St Mark's Place years before the limousines started to line up there with record executives. The small coffee house attracted East Village artists, writers and musicians of the time and was founded by Irishman Shane Doyle and his business partner Karl Geary. It was famed for its late-night celebrity music sessions before it closed its doors in 1995. Sin-é became Jeff's de facto workshop and a mecca for a new breed of Irish emigrants and celebrities alike, drawing in acts from the Hothouse Flowers, Carole King, Bono, the Edge, to Iggy Pop, Paul Simon, Sinéad O'Connor and Shane MacGowan.[28]

[A1.1.02] On the eve of what would have been Buckley's 50th birthday, journalist Steve Cummins' documentary as broadcast on RTÉ Radio 1 explored the Californian singer's untold connections with Ireland,[29] unearthing a previously undiscovered recording of Buckley's first-ever Irish performance at the Trinity Ball in 1992 as an unsigned artist. His brief role with The Commitments, his friendship with musicians Glen Hansard and Mark Geary and his legendary Irish performances at Whelan's[30] are also touched upon. Cummins (co-producer) researched, produced, recorded and edited.

[A1.1.03] The documentary was recorded in Dublin, Kildare, Westmeath,

---

wp-content/uploads/2022/01/IMRO-MCPS-Ireland-2022-Rate-Card.pdf [Accessed 29 March 2022].

26 He impulsively decided to take a swim in the river fully clothed and wearing boots when caught in a current caused by a passing boat. His body was found three days later and the death was ruled an accidental drowning.

27 At Sin-é, the young singer washed dishes and waited on tables while otherwise using his Monday night residency to test his new material and shape his creative vision, sometimes to a crowd of only five listeners.

28 RTÉ Doc On One, *Sin-é: Jeff Buckley's Irish Odyssey* (2006), rte.ie. Available at: https://www.rte.ie/radio1/doconone/2016/1104/829140-sin-e-jeff-buckleys-irish-odyssey/ [Accessed 17 July 2021].

29 Buckley having ancestral roots in Cork.

30 Wexford Street, Dublin.

Galway and New York.[31] It was co-produced by Tim Desmond, long-standing producer with RTÉ's 'Doc On One' team since 2013 producing both his own documentaries and supervising the production of documentaries with independent documentary-makers.

[A1.1.04] To thoroughly explore Buckley's Irish connections, the owners of Sin-é,[32] Irish promoters who staged his shows in Ireland[33] and Buckley's mother, Mary Guibert were interviewed by Cummins. He also spoke to regular fellow performer at Sin-é Katell Keineg and band member/friend Hansard.[34] Equally, fellow musician and friend through Sin-é, Mark Geary, brother of co-owner Karl Geary, also makes contributions to the programme.

[A1.1.05] Contracts would therefore have been signed with all such contributors for the copyright, duty of confidence, privacy and data protection reasons outlined below as would have been the case too for the following additional contributors: American songwriter Tom Clarke who played at Sin-é, former record-company scout Dubliner Michael Murphy[35] who speaks about Buckley's visits to Ireland, and Murphy's parents, with whom the singer stayed in Foxrock on Buckley's very first outing to Dublin in May 1992. There is also a brief voice recording of the present occupier of the former Sin-é space[36] and quotes from Steve Berkowitz, A&R (artists and repertoire) executive and producer at Columbia Records (Cummins may in this connection have spoken to him directly or made use of archive footage). Finally, archive footage from a US radio interview with a young Jeff Buckley is used in the programme for which clearance would have been required from the broadcaster station (or reliance may have been replaced on fair dealing in terms of critique of Buckley's musical works).

INTERVIEW CHALLENGES AND THIRD-PARTY COLLABORATION

[A1.2.01] The approval and consultation issues discussed in Chapter 18 come

---

31 See Steve Cummins, *Jeff Buckley Radio Documentary*. Available on: https://www.stevecummins.com/radiovideo [Accessed 18 July 2021].

32 Above-named Dubliners Shane Doyle and Karl Geary who set up the café in 1989.

33 Dave Allen who booked him to play Whelan's as a major recording artist in 1994 (then venue manager at Whelan's) and Michael Murphy who arranged Buckley's set at the Trinity Ball.

34 Living in LA, and eager to relocate to New York, Buckley spotted an opportunity. The *Commitments* film was about to open in the US, and the producers were seeking musicians to play at premiere parties in LA, Chicago and New York. In the summer of 1991 Buckley was hired as a guitar player and technician to Glen Hansard of The Frames. Source: Steve Cummins, *Jeff Buckley – The Irish Connection* (2014) as originally published in *The Irish Independent* (2007). Available on: http://www.stevecummins.com/features/jeff-buckley-the-irish-connection [Accessed 18 July 2021].

35 Murphy was A&R with label Imago and wished to sign Buckley who ultimately contracted with Columbia Records. Some years prior, Murphy had organised the singer's set at the Trinity Ball as an unknown.

36 An Israeli delicatessen called Holyland.

to the fore too in respect of radio documentaries exploring the life and times of celebrities. Cummins reflects that Buckley's tragic death, some 20 years prior at that point, was still raw in the memory of some who expressed reluctance to speak on record. Others were difficult to locate. Those who did not wish to feature instead spoke with him at length off the record and provided crucial information to help ensure the accuracy of the backstory.

[A1.2.02] In delving into events more than two decades ago, some recollections would, understandably, prove hazy. Cummins explains that dates, times, places and sequences of events could differ from one person to the next. Accordingly, to ensure the factual context was robust, the secondary research conducted was extensive from biographies to other works and archive audio. These in themselves unearthed some conflicting accounts and reinforced Cummins' belief that in the absence of Buckley himself he needed to attend at the epicentre of the story and made arrangements to visit New York.

[A1.2.03] Cummins describes the information and fact-checking process thus:

> At the time, there wasn't much to feed this fascination. These were pre-internet days and Buckley wasn't a big star. There wasn't a ream of interviews to read or other fans to communicate with. There was no access to video footage or much other audio content to listen to. You couldn't simply type his name into a computer and be inundated with suggestions. Any information about him that I did glean was piecemeal, but in its strange way, this helped to hold my interest.[37]

Cummins for example confirmed Buckley's presence in Ireland in the early 1990s from first hand witness accounts, photographs of Buckley staying at the host Murphy family in Foxrock, video shots of his walking the streets of Dublin, a recording of his performance at the Trinity Ball, material evidencing his two appearances at Whelan's and his last Irish performance at the Tivoli Theatre in 1995 before his subsequent untimely death.

THE MAKING OF

[A1.3.01] The primary legal issue in radio, and indeed any documentary, as and where applicable, is obtaining consents and releases from the participants (this may at times involve executing a life rights agreement). The 2000 Act defines a performance and sets out performer rights and remedies in the case of performer right infringement. Participating in an interview involves recording of that live interview. That then forms part of a sound recording to which the performer can assert further rights. Performer rights have already been examined in Chapter 10B.

---

[37] RTÉ Culture, *Jeff Buckley's story through Irish eyes – Documentary on One* (2016), rte.ie. Available on: https://www.rte.ie/culture/2016/1111/830958-jeff-buckleys-story-through-irish-eyes-documentary-on-one/ [Accessed 18 July 2021].

[A1.3.02] Within Ireland (similar provisions will exist in other jurisdictions), s 202 of the 2000 Act defines "performance" as the performance of any actors, singers, musicians, dancers or other persons who act, sing, deliver, declaim, play in, interpret or otherwise perform literary, dramatic, musical or artistic works or expressions of works of folklore, which is a live performance given by one or more individuals, and shall include a performance of a variety act or any similar presentation. Subsection 202(4) defines recording in relation to a performance as meaning any fixation made directly or indirectly from the live performance, made from a broadcast of, or cable programme including, the performance, or made directly or indirectly from the live performance.

[A1.3.03] Section 203 bestows on performers the exclusive right to authorise or prohibit the making of a recording of the whole or any substantial part of a qualifying performance directly from the live performance; the broadcasting live, or including live in a cable programme service, of the whole or any substantial part of a qualifying performance, or the making of a recording of the whole or any substantial part of a qualifying performance directly from a broadcast of, or cable programme including, the live performance.

[A1.3.04] The above rights as conferred on performers are infringed by a person who, without the consent of the performer, undertakes or authorises another to undertake any of the aforementioned acts. The rights of a performer are not infringed however by the making of a recording by persons for their private and domestic use and hence reference is made for present purposes to documentaries intended for release to the general public, with commercial gain accruing to the producers and broadcasters through advertising, sponsorship, onward licensing of the programme or otherwise.

[A1.3.05] Flowing from the above statutorily-protected rights, performers hold rights pursuant to ss 204 to 208 relating to reproduction, making available to the public copies of recordings of performances, a distribution right, a rental and lending right, and a right to equitable remuneration for exploitation of the sound recording containing their performance. Consents and releases address these rights. Firstly, consent is required to include personal data, names and so forth in the production. Second, performer rights must be assigned to the production company to permit lawful reproduction and broadcasting of the subject performance.

[A1.3.06] The third consideration is a matter of insurance and indemnity. By having a contributor sign a release, it should serve to protect the production company against defamation actions and breaches of privacy, copyright, moral rights and the duty of confidence. Releases must also contain an express data protection consent from interview and contributor subjects having regard to GDPR and the Data Protection Acts. Releases aside, one could potentially argue however that the terms of the contract itself were breached by the production entity in some fashion if it fails in its duties, obligations and warranties to the contributor under the agreement. A comprehensive E&O policy should indemnify producers in respect of the latter breach of contract eventuality.

[A1.3.07] The production company must ensure above all else that an injunction cannot be brought by contributors (if ultimately there is discontent with some aspect of the end product such as where it makes them appear in a negative light) and accordingly that the only remedy in the event of a dispute will be monetary damages rather than enjoining the release and broadcast of the documentary. Some contributors may understandably be wary in this regard and the diplomacy tactics discussed in Chapter 18 should be carefully contemplated by documentary-makers. For example, a contributor may wish to read a script or interview questions in advance or to be consulted for approval before the programme airs (this should be avoided where possible as it may scupper funding opportunities – producers/broadcasters should always assert the right to edit at their absolute discretion by way of final editorial control).

[A1.3.08] Consideration, where applicable (e.g. where music is specially composed for a radio programme), must be given to fair remuneration. This is particularly so if the documentary soars heights commercially as would not necessarily be the case with the Jeff Buckley programme at bar. This documentary pre-dated the 2019 Copyright Directive but henceforth producers must bear it in mind when paying the contract's consideration fee. It is likely here that the contributors were paid a nominal sum only (e.g. one dollar) (to ensure that the prerequisite of consideration for a valid and binding contract was met) as the documentary is a cultural and music history exposé of a shy artist who died prematurely more than a commercial product for mass release.[38] While contributors need not be paid (*per diem* expenses will suffice), music as licensed or specially composed will require fees to be paid to composers, commercial music rightsholders (unless covered by broadcaster blanket licence) or a production music library.

Legal agreements

[A1.3.09] Aside from financing agreements, policies of E&O and production insurance,[39] producer Steve Cummins would have signed a writer agreement with his production company or sole trader business in order that such production entity, by virtue of assignment, would hold all attendant copyrights and related rights to the project in order to contract with RTÉ. The story is narrated by

[38] Though of course it is a product that could be played on radio stations internationally given the renown of Buckley provided the music releases are in order beyond any blanket licences for domestic use – however given the Irish connections, its appeal is primarily in Ireland and the US.

[39] To cover for public liability for on-location public, street and interior premises recordings of interviews in Ireland and the US.

Lillian Smith[40] and sound supervision is by Ciaran Cullen. Accordingly, talent/crew agreements would have been executed for copyright and performer rights reasons and to govern standard issues such as production schedule, consideration (fee payable), credits, warranties and indemnities, confidentiality and publicity requirements (if any). Crew agreements also contain waiver of moral rights provisions as standard to afford full discretion to the production company in terms of editing of the recorded material.

[A1.3.10] The documentary commences with an extract from *The Commitments* film featuring the voice of Colm Meaney, thus requiring clearance from the production company of that movie (as would potentially[41] an extract from the US television show on which Sinéad O'Connor appeared as used in the radio programme). Michael Murphy too as rightsholder most likely granted a licence for his sound recording of the 1992 Trinity Ball, at which Buckley played to his first large audience of some 1,000 patrons, to be used in the documentary.

[A1.3.11] In terms of the rough, improvised Buckley recordings (from Sin-é Monday night sessions and recordings from gigs at Whelan's) featured in the documentary, the location proprietors or other relevant persons own the copyright to same having captured these sessions on a sound recording device, thus necessitating a licence or release form to be executed permitting the reproduction thereof. In respect of the commercial recordings (the official Sin-é recording by Columbia Records and studio recording of *Hallelujah* or any other songs from Buckley's back catalogue for example) and any further background or commercial songs used, as above, there are three potential avenues that would have been open to the co-producers of this radio programme – their own blanket licence if held one, the broadcaster's blanket licence (depending on territorial exploitation), or procuring consents from the copyright owners directly.

[A1.3.12] As noted, adaptation, alteration, sampling or arrangement of commercial music is prohibited without prior approval from the individual rightsholders. Therefore, in this Sin-é production, if any edits were to be made to the featured sound recordings (or if the radio programme were to be licensed for international use on say German or US radio and hence falling outside the scope of an Irish blanket licence), the consent of the record label (Columbia) would be required and a dubbing licence (permitting use of the compositions in the documentary) and master use licence (permitting reproduction of the sound recordings) obtained. These licences can typically be prohibitively expensive but in the case of *Sin-é: Jeff Buckley's Irish Odyssey* the segments of the songs used are insubstantial which would greatly reduce the price payable if the producer elected to obtain international rights or otherwise required direct consent from the IP rightsholders due to blanket licence limitations.

---

40 For celebrity voiceover engagements, agents will typically be involved in negotiating the terms of the contract and the remuneration payable.

41 Unless caught by the fair dealing defence in this jurisdiction and fair use under US law.

Chapter 21

Royalties and Residuals for Actors, Writers, Directors and Producers

INTRODUCTION

[21.1.01] Imagine an actor is hired by a production company to perform in a marketing video for a client's website and she is paid €300. No contract is signed between the two parties. The video proves so successful that the very same video is placed in a national television advertising campaign but without obtaining advance clearance from the actor. The actor then approaches the company demanding a significant payment for this subsequent television commercial. What are the respective parties' rights?

[21.1.02] In the instance of a dispute, the law will protect the actor as her performance rights, as *per* Pt III (rights in performances) of the Copyright and Related Rights Act 2000 ('the 2000 Act') have been breached. She did not consent to broadcast of the website video on television. The actor can therefore seek to enforce payment by threatening to sue for damages (including for breach of data protection law) or to enjoin the advertising campaign by way of injunction.[1] In this scenario there was no contract in place. For substantially funded audiovisual productions, a contract will be in place for chain of title, funding and insurance reasons and, further, there will almost invariably be a clause stating that damages are the sole remedy and an injunctive remedy is precluded. This guarantees that the broadcast and exploitation of costly productions is not jeopardised with mammoth legal and financial fall-out.

[21.1.03] One avenue might be to agree a figure for use of the actor's performance for just the television commercial, or, if it is intended to further use the video for a variety of marketing purposes, the best approach would be to purchase the right to use her performance in any and all media throughout the universe in perpetuity. The latter should have been achieved at the very outset by way of a contract provision when negotiating an all-in fee with the actress. Alternatively,

---

1 It is doubtful however injunctive relief would be granted as it is a prerequisite for an injunction that damages will not be an adequate remedy. Here, damages may well compensate the actor – but that might not be the case and the court has discretionary powers in deciding whether or not to grant the relief sought.

an additional fee could have been agreed at contract signing stage for reuse/reproductions of her performance. When the actor's consent is required for subsequent future uses, she can exact a premium sum as the other party is in a weak position due to having clearly infringed copyright law to that point. Hence, it is imperative to have in place provisions relating to productions of derivative material, sequels, prequels, remakes, reuses, repeats and spin-offs so that certainty is enshrined and, on the artist side, to ensure that actors do not naively sign away important revenue streams, and conversely, that actors do not hold production companies to ransom.

[21.1.04] Sections 202 to 308 in Pt III and ss 309 to 319 in Pt IV (performers' moral rights) of the 2000 Act place performers' rights on a firm, statutorily-protected footing. Thus, actors, extras, voice-over performers, documentary contributors and persons performing stunts own and accrue copyright and other rights in their performances. These include recording and broadcast rights, the making of copies of a recording (reproduction right), the making available right (the making available to the public of copies of recordings), distribution rights, rental and lending rights and the right to equitable remuneration for exploitation on a sound recording which includes the relevant performance. This lasts for 50 years from the date of the performance or 70 years (previously 50 years) from when a recording of such performance is first lawfully made available to the public (s 291 as amended).[2]

QUALIFYING PERSONS

[21.2.01] Because Irish law cannot of course legislate for the whole world, the 2000 Act limits its protection to qualified persons, qualified performances and qualifying countries as defined in ss 287 to 289. In s 287, a qualifying country means Ireland, another Member State of the EEA or to the extent that an order made by the government under s 289 so provides, a country designated under that section. A qualifying individual means a citizen or subject of, or an individual domiciled or ordinarily resident in, a qualifying country; and qualifying person means an Irish citizen, or an individual domiciled or ordinarily resident in the state.

[21.2.02] It is for this reason that actor, musician and other performer (e.g. dancer, stuntsperson) contracts will generally have provisions akin to "the Artist warrants and undertakes that the Artist is a 'qualifying person' within the meaning of the Copyright and Related Rights Act 2000" and is currently entitled to work in Ireland as the case may be.

---

2 SI No 411 of 2013 EU (Term of Protection of Copyright and Certain Related Rights) (Directive 2011/77/EU) Regulations 2013 transposed Directive 2011/77/EU (amending Directive 2006/116/EC on the term of protection of copyright and certain related rights) into Irish law and substituted a new s 291 into the 2000 Act.

RESIDUALS AND BACKEND PAYMENTS

[21.3.01] Actor contracts (typically based on collective bargaining agreements stipulating minimum fees/salaries and so forth between actor unions and producer company member bodies and organisations as will be discussed below) should ideally guarantee that actors are compensated for the distribution or exhibition of their work beyond its initial use.[3] This is particularly true having regard to the provisions and spirit of the 2019 Copyright Directive ('the 2019 Directive') discussed in Chapter 11.

[21.3.02] Nonetheless, the 2019 Directive does not rule out the 'full buyout' of rights by one-off lump sum payment (the fee need only be fair and proportionate, though as seen in that chapter, there is a contract adjustment mechanism in more exceptional cases). For decades, the Irish acting sector, unlike as obtains in the UK, has not provided for residuals. It is only a matter of time however before this long-established and comparatively highly unfair practice ends, whether arising from strict application of the Directive and its implementing Regulations (as enacted by the Oireachtas in November 2021) or simply to achieve parity with jurisdictions both within and outside the EU where actors can earn generous royalties long into the future (particularly as occurs in the case of US actors).

[21.3.03] These royalty payments are called residuals (also termed ongoing payments or passive income) and include income from film and television re-runs, home video/DVD/Blu-ray releases,[4] and exhibition on pay television and subscription video-on-demand services.

[21.3.04] Obligation, where it exists, to account for and discharge residuals payments does not necessarily depend on profitability, but can be triggered by the project's exhibition alone as is the case with directors' residuals for example in the US Directors Guild of America system. If a production company sells a programme for a repeat broadcast, it will receive a fee. From that fee the company will pay the actor the agreed repeat percentage owed to the actor. Hence, profitability is not an issue in this context and should not be used as an argument by production companies in resisting inclusion of such ongoing payment provisions. These additional payments come from further income from exploitation and they do not add to the cost of production as some producers may argue.

[21.3.05] Different formulas apply worldwide depending on the nature of

---

3 It is not just actors or musicians who can receive residuals. Screenwriters, production companies and directors can also benefit from backend and residual payments which will be negotiated into the contracts by their agents, legal representatives, unions or trade organisations.

4 BECS (see below) does not collect revenue for video and DVD/Blu-ray programme sales because there is no performers' remuneration right covering this use of performers' work. What moneys are paid for DVDs is determined by the terms of one's original contract which will normally be governed by a collective agreement between Equity and the producer.

the project and where it is used. Residuals can be based, for instance, on gross receipts or the period of time a project is exhibited. In Ireland, it is more likely that residuals for 'star' actors in film, if agreed at all (more likely the upfront actor fee will be sufficiently large to include a buy-out of all rights so that residuals will never arise) might be calculated based on an agreed calculation method for producer net profits. This will not preclude actors however from obtaining royalties for which they are statutorily entitled (e.g. right to equitable remuneration where a performer transfers his rental rights to the producer). This is further discussed in the context of EU and Irish legislation in the directors' royalties section below. Properly drafted contracts in this regard however will invariably state that the actor's fee includes equitable remuneration for lending and rental rights.

[21.3.06] For simplicity, let us imagine a broad rule of thumb as follows: the television production company retains 80 percent of the fees earned from re-runs. The other 20 percent is paid to the various performers and off-camera crew who have negotiated residual payments or where such payments are part of their union contract. This guideline is not in fact too far off the mark – in the UK, if a television series (for example *Downton Abbey*) is sold to another market, some 17 percent of the sales are divided up among the actors.[5]

COLLECTION OF ACTOR ROYALTIES

[21.4.01] From a sound recording perspective, the situation in Ireland differs to that which pertains in the UK. Music performers in Ireland receive royalties as distributed from Recorded Artists Actors Performers ('RAAP') (as collected by PPI, that is, Phonographic Performance Ireland) and the equivalent in the UK is PPL, Phonographic Performance Limited, which collects royalties for sound recording owners and performers on sound recordings. However, PPL only deals with music licensing and does not concern itself with rights attaching to audiovisual productions unless there is a music element that impacts its members. RAAP on the other hand has actors as members along with its music performer members and has recently begun collecting royalties for actors in respect of audiovisual rights (incidentally 'sound recordings' in the 2000 Act are not limited to phonograms and encompass audiovisual recordings). RAAP thus administers remuneration for actors for their work in film and television from rental, retransmission and certain other exploitation of these works. UK actors receive royalties from another collection society called BECS (see 21.6.02 below), part of actors' union Equity UK. Each year, Equity UK distributes payments for use of members' work in television and film re-runs, sales of DVDs, videos and audio recordings such as cast albums.

5 Ronan McGreevy, *Irish producers and actors at loggerheads over future copyright payments* (2013), irishtimes.com. Available at: https://www.irishtimes.com/culture/irish-producers-and-actors-at-loggerheads-over-future-copyright-payments-1.1440289 [Accessed 10 August 2017].

[21.4.02] Unlike its UK counterpart, the Irish Equity union has not founded a collective management organisation as yet but nonetheless campaigns for actor rights in matters ranging from working time and working conditions to minimum rates of pay. It is recommending that compliance with copyright legislation (in essence adherence by producers to the letter and spirit of the 2019 Directive so that full buyout practices end) be a listed and mandatory requirement when applying for direct funding and for the s 481 tax credit. At present, the tax credit only mandates compliance with employment (and safety) legislation.

[21.4.03] In this jurisdiction, if the performance of an actor on the audio recordings for a film or other project (i.e. the sound recordings of dialogue) have been registered with RAAP and have been played in public or broadcast on television or radio, performers are entitled to equitable remuneration royalties. The performance given on that recording must be a qualifying performance as above. Thus, RAAP also represents actors and claims royalties on their behalf in respect of their audiovisual rights.

BUYOUTS OF ACTOR RIGHTS (AND FUTURE ENTITLEMENT TO RESIDUALS)

[21.5.01] For some 30 years Irish actors have been signing buyout contracts that cut performers out of the residual income pot. According to Irish Equity, Irish actors are financially discriminated against particularly pertaining to co-productions and hence the union is seeking something close to the existing UK Equity agreement that covers both television and film productions and whereby ongoing residual and usage payments feature in the standard BBC and ITV agreements. An agreement was reached in late 2020 for new standard terms, to include royalties and (re)usage fees, between Irish Equity and Screen Producers Ireland effective from 1 February 2021 but as outlined below Equity members subsequently rejected the pact and developments are awaited in this connection at the time of writing.

[21.5.02] Meanwhile the effects of implementation of the 2019 Directive are also awaited. In particular, full buy-out clauses might henceforth dwindle in use although it is crucial to note that the 2019 Directive envisages the continuing use of lump sums payments as constituting art 18 appropriate and proportionate remuneration but that "it should not be the rule".[6]

[21.5.03] It is worthy of note too that provision is made in Screen Ireland production loan agreement wording which mandates that the borrower production company undertakes to ensure adequate budgetary provision for clearances, use fees, repeat fees[7] and residuals to facilitate the exploitation of the

---

6 See preamble to the 2019 Directive at Recital 73.

7 As there is no legislative or other requirement at present for payment of residuals to Irish actors, the Screen Ireland loan agreement clause is referring in the main to use of archives

subject film throughout the world in all media. Failure to do so will result in the borrower being prohibited from applying for further funding from Screen Ireland. Thus, while reuse and repeat fees for Irish actors are not the custom and practice in this country, they could and should be paid.

INTERNATIONAL AND IRISH ACTOR UNIONS

[21.6.01] Irish Equity,[8] Equity UK as set up in 1930, and Actors' Equity USA as founded in 1913[9] represent actors, dancers, theatre directors, stage and set designers, stage managers and other creative practitioners. There is also an Equity association in Canada, Australia, New Zealand and other similar unions throughout the world. Aside from actor-specific unions, actors might also be members of trade unions such as SIPTU in Ireland which unions advocate on their behalf in terms of employment rights and so forth. Like Equity, Bectu (Broadcasting, Entertainment, Cinematograph and Theatre Union) in the UK is another sector-specific union.

[21.6.02] As mentioned, Irish Equity has not founded a collective management organisation as yet to collect royalties for its members. Equity UK established the British Equity Collecting Society ('BECS') in 1998 in order to enforce its members' rights in Britain and collect revenue from the compulsory collective administration of rights in other EU Member States. Performers in many European countries are compensated for the use of their audiovisual work and their legal rights entitle them to remuneration when their work is copied for private use, rented in video shops, retransmitted on cable channels or publicly broadcast. BECS negotiates a share of the revenue generated in this way for British-made productions that are exploited in such territories and has agreements in place with collecting societies throughout the EU.[10]

---

for documentary feature films where reuse fees may arise for non-Irish actors appearing in archive films and television programmes included in such documentaries. Indeed, when obtaining audiovisual archives from the major studios such as Warner, archive libraries such as Producers Library in Hollywood or independent producers/IP management organisations, their standard contract will provide that stock and other footage is fully cleared for worldwide use in all media but with the strict proviso that it is a matter for the licensee producer to obtain and pay for, where applicable, all guild fees (e.g. pertaining to writers, directors and music composer collection societies). The licensee will need to indemnify and hold harmless the archive provider in this connection.

8 Part of SIPTU, Services Industrial Professional and Technical Union.

9 Note that Actors' Equity (USA) represents live theatrical performances rather than television and film actors who are represented by SAG-AFTRA.

10 In respect of graded productions, if performers' rights revenue from European sources is not already split between performers by the originating collecting society, BECS apportions performer shares according to time spent on screen and programme duration. This entails classifying productions as either "film character" or "ensemble" and grading performances according to the importance of the character played. Performers' rights dues are only paid to credited cast members. Film character productions are split into four grades: principal performers being leading characters in a production around whom the story revolves, featured performers being major characters who are integral to the storyline but secondary

THE IRISH POSITION

[21.7.01] In March 2016, as regards indigenous Irish television drama, Screen Producers Ireland and Irish Equity concluded negotiations on a collective agreement in relation to residual payments with the objective of aligning certain aspects of the Irish television drama sector with international standards. Negotiations were ongoing as regards film and other aspects of television productions in Ireland for another three year agreement. The SPI/Irish Equity Irish Film Agreement came into force on 1 February 2021 but shortly thereafter things began to unravel. Actors started a campaign against the terms of the agreement and focused on its failings when compared with current agreements in, for example, the UK and the US. The discontent led to a seven-hour Equity AGM in late March, at which a new executive was elected and resolved to renegotiate the agreement with SPI.

[21.7.02] The above developments were set in part against the backdrop of a dispute in relation to *Vikings*, the Canadian-Irish co-production distributed by MGM. In 2012, Irish Equity was in ongoing negotiations with Morgan O'Sullivan's World 2000 Entertainment for a local agreement on *Vikings*. Performers on the series were offered full buyout agreements which was unacceptable to Irish Equity as it sought to ensure a share in residuals for its members.

THE COST OF RESIDUALS FOR BROADCASTERS AND STREAMERS

[21.8.01] BBC bosses believed in 2011 that screening episodes of expensive dramas such as period-piece *South Riding* four times in a week would be an easy means to reduce costs. However, it quickly emerged that actors' royalty fees would cost more than new programming. According to trade magazine *Broadcast*, the BBC-made show cost £900,000 an episode, with its stars, including Anna Maxwell Martin as Sarah Burton, collecting £165,000 for a first repeat of the show in peak-time on BBC2. With US-made international smash hits *Friends*, *Dallas* and *The Big Bang Theory* the stakes are much higher again. However, in the case of streaming services such as Netflix and Amazon, it is widely understood that all but negligible residuals sums are paid to actors and writers when their work is re-aired. It is in all likelihood only a matter of time before this reality will end if powerful unions in the US in particular advocate strike action on matters of pay.

SCREENWRITER ROYALTIES AND PROFIT SHARING

[21.9.01] Royalties to writers and playwrights from publication of novels, books

to the principals, secondary performers being secondary characters who, whilst part of the storyline, do not have a focal role, and cast members being all remaining characters on the cast list.

and plays is straightforward and the position will be clearly set out in the author publishing agreement. The situation in respect of screenplay royalties however is not yet highly advanced in Ireland as there is no statutorily recognised collection society. Writers, apart from their fee for writing a script, will seek directly or more likely through an agent to garner additional income, for example, arising from script consultation services throughout film production or an executive or associate producer credit and an accompanying fee. Additional revenue streams might consist of a small percentage share in net producer profits and attendant accounting and audit provisions (which contract provisions have now been bolstered by the transparency obligations and better seller clause of the 2019 Directive).

[21.9.02] A further income stream can be generated from television broadcasts. The reality of the levels at stake were noted in the English High Court by Mr Justice Meade in *Martin v Kogan*[11] discussed in the next chapter in respect of royalties due to the screenplay writer of *Florence Foster Jenkins* when he stated at para 382 of his judgment:

> I was also told on behalf of Mr Martin that he has received a little over £12,000 collected by the ALCS in respect of overseas television transmissions.

[21.9.03] The Writers Guild of Ireland,[12] formerly the Irish Playwrights and Screenwriters Guild, is the representative body for writers in Ireland for the stage and screen. Unlike in Britain, it has not established a collecting society for copying and other royalties. In 1977, the Writers' Guild of Great Britain ('WGGB') trade union representing professional authors formed the Authors' Licensing and Collecting Society ('ALCS') which Irish writers can also join. WGGB has a reciprocal membership and services arrangement with The Writers Guild of Ireland. UK WGGB members who achieve television or film writing contracts in the US can join the Writers Guild of America.

[21.9.04] ALCS members sign a mandate that authorises the society to license and collect royalties on their behalf at home and abroad with the subject rights ranging from photocopying, scanning and cable retransmission in the UK and internationally, to reproduction in journals.

[21.9.05] The Irish writers' guild is endeavouring to make strides in terms of collective bargaining for its members and routinely advises writers on standard contract terms. The position in the UK is streamlined by reference to rate cards which include reuse royalties in the case of feature films for example. WGGB agreements for television, theatre, radio and film cover minimum fees as well as working practices, repeat fees, credits and so forth.

---

11 [2021] EWHC 24 (Ch).

12 See script.ie

Primary and secondary rights

[21.9.06] ALCS distributes royalties only in respect of secondary or subsidiary rights. Primary rights stem from publication of a book and are paid to writers through their publisher directly. Secondary uses involve situations where a third party uses a work that has already been distributed to the public such as when schools photocopy books they own, or libraries lend books, or overseas television companies retransmit UK television signals. Royalties from secondary rights are paid to writers through ALCS – unless the royalties come from UK library lending by way of the public lending right[13] which scheme also provides registration for the Irish PLR scheme on behalf of Public Lending Remuneration Ireland.

DIRECTOR ROYALTIES

[21.10.01] The Screen Directors Guild of Ireland ('SDGI') is the representative body for over 220 director members involved in the Irish and international audiovisual industry. These include directors of feature films, fiction, documentary, television drama, short films, commercials and animation. It is a member of the European Federation of Directors Organisations and is affiliated to the International Affiliation of English-Speaking Directors Organisations. It receives funding from Screen Ireland and The Arts Council. SDGI operates an audiovisual collecting society (Screen Directors Guild Collecting Society, 'SDCS') which collects remuneration for secondary usage of directors' work and has 14 bilateral agreements with foreign collecting societies. It is registered as a licensing body with the Intellectual Property Office of Ireland. Payments from the secondary exploitation of qualifying works vary from country to country and are regulated by criteria such as transmission type and programme type.

SDGI member contracts

[21.10.02] It is mentioned in passing that SDGI members will negotiate contracts with producers in accordance with SDGI minimum terms such as that rental and lending rights payments and secondary rights and other payments discussed below collected by the guild and/or any other collecting societies be payable to the director and not become the entitlement of the production company or any other entities; that in respect of any entitlement to a share in producer net profits calculation, definition and payment must be favoured nations with all other participants in profits, including financiers, actors and the production company, and that if director fees are to be deferred this must be a first position deferment before any other deferments, or if this is impossible, pro-rata with other deferments.

---

13 In the UK, the public lending right is a legal right to payment from the Department of Digital, Culture, Media and Sport funding for eligible book contributors when their books are borrowed from public libraries.

Royalties and the rental and lending rights Directive

[21.10.03] SDGI was established to collect on directors' entitlement to payments from the exploitation of their work nationally and internationally. Throughout the EU and in several other countries, film and television directors are legally recognised as being authors of their work. This right of authorship may give directors an entitlement to receive payment for certain uses of their work – such as cable retransmission, private copying, video rentals. These payments are administered through the international network of authors' collecting societies. In Ireland, as previously noted in Chapter 10A, the principal director and the producer are the joint authors of a film (and its soundtrack) or television programme. However, as mandated by financing agreements, the directing services agreement will invariably assign copyright from the director to the production company so that the production company is free at its sole discretion to exploit the content.

[21.10.04] However, the matter does not end there. Directive 2006/115/EC (replacing a 1992 Directive) ('the 2006 Directive') on rental, lending and on certain rights related to copyright in the field of IP sought to harmonise these rights EU-wide. Owners of copyright have a right to authorise or prohibit rental or lending of original and copies of copyright works. Rental means making available for a limited period for direct or indirect economic or commercial value. Lending involves making available for use for a limited period not for direct or indirect economic or commercial advantage when made through establishments accessible to the public.

[21.10.05] The author holds the rental and lending right. This includes directors, performing artists and phonograph producers. Where authors or performing artists have transferred their rental right concerning the phonogram or copy of the film, they retain the right to obtain equitable remuneration from the rental. This, pursuant to Art 5 of the 2006 Directive and (in respect of the lending right) s 125 of the 2000 Act cannot be waived but its administration may be entrusted to collecting societies.

[21.10.06] In cases where a director is also a producer who has established a company say for producing documentaries, it is of note as mentioned in Chapter 32 that s 103 of the 2000 Act (the cable copyright exemption) has been repealed by s 75 of the Online Safety and Media Regulation Act 2022. Section 103 permitted cable operators based in Ireland to retransmit works (including audiovisual works) protected by copyright that are broadcast in the state and the "must-carry" channels without obtaining permission from the copyright holders or paying retransmission fees.

[21.10.07] This means that Irish production companies were not fairly paid for their works, unlike many of their European counterparts. Continuing that exemption would have resulted in a loss of revenue to both broadcasters and rightsholders including producers. Repeal of the exemption may therefore provide a pathway to appropriate payment being made to these rightsholders.

[21.10.08] The same holds true in respect of the 2019 Directive on (re) transmission of certain online television and radio programmes as transposed into national law by SI No 357 of 2022. This legislation will help to ensure that rightsholders are adequately compensated when their works are used in programmes transmitted through direct injection, namely that when broadcasters transmit their programme-carrying signals exclusively to distributors, and the latter transmit these to the public, there is an act of communication to the public, in which both the broadcaster and the distributors participate, and for which authorisation from rightsholders must be sought.

UK collections

[21.10.09] British directors receive an annual payment for the secondary use of their work under the terms of the Directors' Rights Agreement agreed with broadcasters and independent producers in 2006. Directors UK is charged with the responsibility of devising, implementing and administering a scheme for the distribution of payments to individual directors. This takes account of the type of programme, the length and the form of the secondary use. The scheme is based on information supplied by broadcasters. Here, SDCS has no national agreement with Irish broadcasters and independent producers relating to payments for freelance directors for the secondary use of their work but is advocating to establish a national agreement for all directors.

PRODUCERS' REPRESENTATIVE BODY AND PRODUCER ROYALTIES

[21.11.01] Screen Producers Ireland is a representative group which advocates for the interests of independent producers in Ireland as well as seeking to raise the sector's profile for the purposes of achieving increased investment in the industry. It liaises on policy matters with government, unions, industry bodies, broadcasters and negotiates terms of trade. Its counterpart in the UK is PACT.

AGICOA

[21.11.02] Established in 1981 and based in Geneva, the Association of International Collective Management of Audiovisual Works is the largest collective management organisation of audiovisual producers globally. It is a non-profit that negotiates, collects and distributes royalties from the use of audiovisual works, whether via cable, satellite, mobile or any other similar means. It operates under the terms of audiovisual copyright law set by the

Berne Convention, the CABSAT 1 Directive[14] and CABSAT 2.[15] AGICOA pays royalties on independently produced works such as feature films, telefilms, short films, animation, series and game shows. The royalties are typically paid during the year following the end of the broadcasting year.

[21.11.03] Secondary rights are the rights that operators must acquire to distribute to the public television content that includes producers' audiovisual work. AGICOA concludes licences with such operators and collects the royalties on behalf of producers. It then distributes such moneys to its members including Irish producers. Any individual or legal entity holding distribution rights of audiovisual works can register with the association. Registration is free (management fees are deducted from royalties due). Royalty claims can be backdated as producers are entitled to claim royalties within three years following the broadcast of the relevant works.

---

14 The satellite broadcasting and cable retransmission directive (93/83/EEC).

15 Online broadcast and retransmission directive (EU 2019/789).

Part III

Music Production and Performances

Chapter 22

Joint Authorship, Band Partnership Agreements and Recording Contract/Artist Management Litigation

JOINT AUTHORSHIP: INTRODUCTION

[22.1.01] The most significant recent development concerning the law of joint authorship is the *Martin v Kogan* judgment[1] of the High Court of England in January 2021 (Meade J). This decision arose from a full retrial ordered by the Court of Appeal in October 2019,[2] reversing Hacon J's judgment of 22 November 2017[3] in the same court, IPEC.[4] The proceedings concerned an application by Nicholas Martin for a declaration of sole authorship of a film screenplay relating to the picture *Florence Foster Jenkins* released in 2016. The court found Kogan's authorship contribution to amount to 20 percent. Meade J also delivered a follow-up decision in May 2021[5] in relation to the very net issue of credits whereby the judge allowed the IMDb credits stand, namely "Nicholas Martin (written by); Julia Kogan (written by) (originally uncredited)".

[22.1.02] Hacon J had held that the weight of the evidence supported Martin's claim to have been the sole writer of the drafts of the screenplay with only limited input from Kogan, which consisted of musical expressions of a technical nature, along with helpful criticism and some minor plot suggestions. This input was insufficient to qualify Kogan as a joint author. Martin was thus entitled to a declaration that he was the sole author of the screenplay. Upon retrial however following Kogan's successful appeal in the Court of Appeal, Meade J found that the screenplay work was in fact jointly authored. His ruling is discussed below.

[22.1.03] Creative endeavours are often collaborative by their very nature given the sheer scale of music, stage, film or other productions. Songwriting is

---

1 [2021] EWHC 24 (Ch).
2 [2019] EWCA Civ 164.
3 [2017] EWHC 2927 (IPEC).
4 The IP Enterprise Court (High Court, Chancery Division).
5 [2021] EWHC 1242 (IPEC).

no exception as exemplified by the joint output of Lennon/McCartney, Jagger/Richards and Elton John/Bernie Taupin. The matter becomes more complicated where musicians and band members can become co-authors with the lead writer of a song through their performance in that song, as demonstrated from the case law. Artists and their management teams are now more acutely aware than ever of songwriting credits. Performers will strive whenever possible to secure some piece of the writing and publishing share of royalties distribution by contributing in some manner or means to compositional elements of music and/or lyrics in a track.

Legal structure of bands

[22.1.04] It is always worth probing, in respect of compositions and music creation through collaborative effort by a band, what is the business structure of the group and whether there is any contractual or other relationship between the members. Are they in a partnership (or a partnership at will)[6] with a view to realising profits or has a service company been formed which employs the band members? If the former, the Partnership Act 1890, in the absence of a formal written agreement modifying the default statutory provisions, will apply, most likely with unintended consequences not envisaged by the band when they co-write a song together.[7] If band leaders are of the view that they are entitled, as the driving force behind lyrics and music, to half or more of the songwriters' share of copyright, they may well be surprised to ascertain an unforeseen reality if the band is deemed in fact to comprise a partnership.

[22.1.05] In the absence of a partnership deed setting out percentage shares, the partnership's profits, by default, will be split between the member partners equally. This in effect would mean that revenues from any mechanical reproductions royalties and synchronisation licensing deals and arising through public performance royalties would be split in equal proportions, again, not a result that might not be intended by the group members. Other important practical consequences of a band's being deemed a partnership are set out later in this chapter as addressed by the 1998 decision of the Court of Appeal in the case of *Morrissey* (The Smiths).

Contract provisions to circumvent or evidence joint authorship

[22.1.06] Given the differing approaches judges have taken to the issue of

---

6 A partnership at will is understood as being an informal arrangement whereby there is no fixed or formal arrangement with regard to the activities of the partnership. This concept was discussed in some detail by Clarke J in *Thomas v Luv One Luv All Promotions Ltd* [2020] EWHC 1565 (IPEC) in relation to two British musical groups where the members of one earlier band split and continued their music careers separately.

7 In the US, this calls for a discussion of partnership law and the law of joint work. In respect of partnership law generally in Ireland, all the partners are entitled to share equally in the capital and profits of the business, and must contribute equally towards the losses.

composition and performance of a composition, there is possibly no area of music law which requires more attention to IP considerations than the complexities and peculiarities of joint authorship. It was certainly unhelpful when a leading case (*Hadley*) on the matter relating to the band Spandau Ballet as will later be analysed, despite the court's best efforts to grapple with the underlying concepts, was laced with an illogical thought process. That decision, however, in view of the line of authorities since then, must be viewed with caution and as being of very dubious precedent for reasons later canvassed. The current position in respect of the law of joint authorship as it applies to copyright, in Britain at least, is now set out in Meade J's judgment having regard to 11 principles laid out for him by the Court of Appeal.

[22.1.07] The simplest and only robust means to ward off potential disputes and litigation alleging copyright infringement, unjust enrichment or otherwise seeking injunctive relief is for both parties to each independently instruct an experienced entertainment lawyer to draft and agree contract terms setting out the position in very clear terms. For example, if two songwriters co-write a song and a dispute arises, it is likely (because of substantial collaboration and significant contributions from both) that ownership will be deemed 50:50.[8] However, this may not be the songwriters' intention who reach consensus that one contributed 20 percent and the other 80.[9]

[22.1.08] If this is in fact the intention, the respective percentages (e.g. proportions of 30, 25 and 45 percent in the case of three songwriters who agree on those writing credit contributions) should be registered by Irish artists with IMRO and MCPS rather than agreeing loosely, orally, on the matter. This will be supplementally vouched by a works registration form and by a legal instrument signed by all songwriters, such as a publishing contract or co-writers' agreement, which verifies the position. In the event of legal proceedings, recourse can then readily be had to the song registration papers. The best example of simplicity and clarity is perhaps offered by the fact that the four U2 band members have an equal share in all songwriting credits and the resultant royalties and publishing income.

[22.1.09] In the case of a strings arranger/composer, for example, who is contracted by a songwriter/producer to write the orchestral parts in a pop track to an existing underlying melody structure, the songwriter/producer should request that a release be signed assigning rights in that arrangement/strings composition.[10] The songwriter is then free to license (or sell by assignment, but subject to the guaranteed minimum writer share of half of total publishing

---

8 Case law (*Martin, Fisher, Bamgboye* – see discussions at [22.1.15] and *Appendix 1*) reveals however that that there is no requirement that joint authorship necessarily involves equality on a 50:50 basis. It is possible to conceive of a joint ownership in unequal shares in principle and in practice.

9 This may even be the case notwithstanding that a publisher has erroneously registered the respective songwriting shares with a performance rights organisation.

10 As seen in Chapter 10A, to meet the requirements of copyright legislation, such assignment

royalties) the track in a neat fashion, with a clean and readily demonstrable chain of title, to a publisher, record label, advertising company, music library, television/film producer, theatre company and so forth.

[22.1.10] The reason for such assignment is that copyright can also exist in an arrangement or orchestration of a musical work or a part thereof quite separately from the copyright in the original musical work.[11] If A writes an original composition and B then helps him arrange it, A will remain owner of the copyright in the original version, while A and B can be joint owners of copyright in the new arrangement. Since an arrangement or transcription of a musical work is an adaptation of original compositional work by A, B will require the consent of A (or if the work has been assigned to a publisher, the consent of that publisher) to make an arrangement of it.[12] An agreement can then be made between A and B that some share of copyright in the arrangement (but not in the original work) will be attributed to B. Often permission to make a new arrangement is only granted however on the basis that 100 percent of the new arrangement is assigned to the original composer (or the publisher as applicable) as the person commissioning the arrangement upon payment of a fee for such arrangement services.

Music industry conventions at odds with the law

[22.1.11] There appears to be a hierarchy within popular music, with vocalists and guitarists at the top, followed by bass players and, at the bottom layer of the

---

must be in writing (and unassignable moral rights should ideally be waived in writing by the composer/arranger).

11 In *Godfrey v Lees* [1995] EMLR 307 the claimant had acted as an orchestral arranger and piano/organ accompanist for the group Barclay James Harvest which enjoyed success in the late 1960s and early 1970s. He contributed arrangements and accompaniment to various works on the group's two albums. Godfrey was not a member of the group and the group members had never considered that he was entitled to any share in the music copyrights in the songs to which he contributed. In 1971 he ceased to work with the group. In 1985 he issued the first of two sets of proceedings in which he claimed a share in the music copyrights and a share of the income therefrom. In coming to his decision, Blackburne J made it clear that it was unnecessary for each joint author of a musical work to establish that "his contribution to the work is equal in terms of either quantity, quality or originality to that of his collaborators". He also emphasised that the qualifying threshold was not high. Referring to *Redwood Music v Chappell* [1982] RPC 109 the judge commented that this case was not concerned with joint authorship but it well demonstrates how little originality is required of a person's contribution to a piece of music in order to attract copyright in the altered work which results. Blackburne J went on to find that Godfrey was a joint author of the various works on which he played. The claim to a share of the earnings from the music copyrights nevertheless failed on the basis that Godfrey was estopped by his conduct in allowing the band members to proceed for fourteen years under the assumption that he did not claim any interest in the music copyrights. The estoppel issue came before the courts again in later cases and the *Godfrey* decision in this regard has effectively been reversed by the Court of Appeal.

12 Adaptation of a work is an act restricted by copyright in a work – see s 37(1)(c) of the Copyright and Related Rights Act 2000 as amended. See also s 43 (infringement by adaptation of works).

pyramid, the drummer. The convention is that the songwriters who compose the chords of a song and its main vocal melody are to be considered its authors and entitled to the entire music copyright. The group members who contribute the other musical parts are not considered to have earned a share of the music copyright and, still less, any adept session musician brought in to add a musical part on an instrument which no group member can play.[13]

[22.1.12] This convention is squarely at odds however with the legal reality as extrapolated from the outcomes of a number of senior court decisions on the issue, most notably the House of Lords in *Fisher* discussed in *Appendix 1* (see also the comments of Mummery LJ in *Sawkins* below as to specific elements of a musical creation). *Godfrey v Lees*[14] is significant as it clarified once more that a contribution can be minor and nonetheless attach joint author rights and that it need not be a contribution to the composition of the song itself – arrangements are also clearly covered. It is time, therefore, that attitudes and practices move with judicial developments. Case law clearly makes manifest that custom and practice, which can have a bearing on contract law cases generally, is not (or is no longer) heeded by the judiciary in the instant field which instead must interpret statutory IP law provisions to the particular facts of each dispute.

Collaborative band compositions: Stuart v Barrett[15]

[22.1.13] Where a group composes a song together in a jam session, it is generally accepted by the courts that the group members are joint authors and thus joint owners of the music copyright. Even in this creatively collaborative setting, a session musician on the other hand is unlikely to be considered for a share of the music copyright (this will not always be the case however depending on the facts, see *Beckingham* below) but a band member may well. In *Stuart*, the High Court of England and Wales awarded the drummer a share in the copyright to the songs in question as, in the court's view, a drummer can significantly influence the whole composition such that the drums contribution was part of the composition as performed, not of the performance only. The court was called upon to determine authorship of a piece of music which had evolved from a jamming session. In his judgment, Sir Thomas Morison QC (sitting as judge) described the scene as:

> Someone started to play and the rest joined in and improvised and improved the original idea. The final piece was indeed the product of the joint compositional skills of all the members of the group present at the time.[16]

---

[13] Dominic Free, *Beckingham v. Hodgens: The Session Musician's Claim to Music Copyright*, (2002) 1(3) *The Entertainment and Sports Law Journal* 93–97. In *Hodgens* the court held that a session musician had a valid claim for joint authorship to the extent of 50 percent.

[14] *supra* at fn 11.

[15] [1994] EMLR 448.

[16] *ibid*, p 455 of the law reports.

[22.1.14] He did further comment nonetheless that one member of a pop group may have an idea which is so nearly perfected that compositional input of any of the other members of the group would be regarded as insignificant.

Joint authorship legislation and the ruling in Martin v Kogan

[22.1.15] Before assessing the authorities, it is useful to set out the statutory provision which underpins these decisions. The law in Ireland on joint authorship is set out in the provisions of s 22 of the Copyright and Related Rights Act 2000. The same provision in the UK has guided and informed the decisions made in that jurisdiction. Section 22 provides that a work of joint authorship means a work produced by the collaboration of two or more authors in which the contribution of each author is not distinct from that of the other author or author.[17] Case law fleshes out the interpretation of this section as seen from pronouncements on the identical UK equivalent in s 10 of the Copyright, Designs and Patents Act 1988. The respective shares of joint authors are not required to be equal, but can reflect, pro rata, the relative amounts of their contributions. Joint authors are only entitled to such share in the copyright as their contribution merits.

[22.1.16] In *Martin*, the Court of Appeal considered whether it was open to Martin to treat this case as one that had to be analysed by reference to Kogan's contribution to the final draft of the screenplay for the film or whether Kogan's contribution should be determined by all of the drafts produced. The court thus held that Hacon J at the initial trial erred in looking only at the final version screenplay and not taking account of contributions to earlier drafts (and the documents that preceded them to include five draft treatments).[18] The court considered extensive citations of authority, and summarised (at para 53) the legal principles applicable to addressing joint authorship thus:

1. A work of joint authorship is a work produced by the collaboration of all the people who created it.
2. There will be a collaboration where those people undertake jointly to create the work with a common design as to its general outline, and where they share the labour of working it out. The first task for the court in such a

---

[17] In *Hodgens* discussed in *Appendix 1* the court ruled in respect of the subject violin parts, "I do not believe that a contribution to the arrangement of a song of the kind I am concerned with in this case is 'separate' in the sense in which that word is used in the section. The added part is heavily dependent on what is there already. Stripped of the voices and other instruments, the violin part would sound odd, and lose meaning. The final musical expression—what the audience will hear—is a joint one". That contributions must not be separate can also be summarised by saying that they are merged into a unitary whole.

[18] The Court of Appeal also considered the extent to which it was able to review the findings of fact made. It reviewed and commented on the documentary evidence that had been taken into account but also identified documentary and witness evidence that had not been considered. The court therefore found that Hacon J had failed to make essential primary findings of fact on the main issues in the case. As a result, the court felt it had no choice but to order a retrial.

case is to determine the nature of the co-operation between the putative joint authors which resulted in the creation of the work.

3. Derivative works do not qualify. Works where one of the putative authors only provides editorial corrections or critique, but where there is no wider collaboration, do not qualify. Ad hoc suggestions of phrases or ideas where there is no wider collaboration do not qualify.
4. In determining whether there is a collaboration to create a literary or artistic work it is never enough to ask "who did the writing?". Authors can collaborate to create a work in many different ways. For example there may be joint authorship if one person creates the plot and the other writes the words, or if either or both of these types of labour is shared.
5. Joint authors must be authors, in the sense that they must have contributed a significant amount of the skill which went into the creation of the work. Again, it is not correct to focus exclusively on who fixed the work in writing. The statutory concept of an author includes all those who created, selected or gathered together the detailed concepts or emotions which the words have fixed in writing.
6. Contributions which are not "authorial" in the above sense do not count. What counts as an authorial contribution is acutely sensitive to the nature of the copyright work in question.
7. The question of what is enough of a contribution is to be judged by the Infopaq test, i.e. whether the putative joint author has contributed elements which expressed that person's own intellectual creation. The essence of that term is that the person in question must have exercised free and expressive choices. The more restrictive the choices the less likely it will be that they satisfy the test.
8. The contribution of a putative joint author must not be distinct.
9. There is no further requirement that the authors must have subjectively intended to create a work of joint authorship.
10. The fact that one of the authors has the final say on what goes into the work may have some relevance to whether there is a collaboration, but is not conclusive. The author with the final say must be given credit in deciding on the relative proportions of ownership, for the extra work involved in making those choices.
11. It follows that the respective shares of joint authors are not required to be equal, but can reflect, pro rata, the relative amounts of their contributions.

[22.1.17] The Court of Appeal also rejected Hacon J's identification of development of plot and character as secondary skills, the primary skill (the said trial judge had said) being choice of words. In doing so, the court explained that a screenplay is a dramatic work. The Lord Justices criticised Hacon J's description of a screenplay as a literary work, like a novel, and the primary skill being the selection and arrangement of words in the course of setting them down, and viewed it as a wrongful approach to describe inventing plot and character as a secondary skill.

Ruling of Meade J upon full retrial

[22.1.18] The retrial judge found as a matter of fact that Kogan had the original idea of a screenplay about Florence Foster Jenkins, the American socialite and amateur soprano. This is almost the only thing he said that she had contributed alone (there were also a few words of dialogue in the nature of technical musical terms). He furthermore found that creative discussions went far beyond the mere sounding board relationship on which Martin and Kogan had started out. They maintained a pattern of behaviour in contributing possibilities for characters, feeling, main events and musical content. This amounted to a common design as to general outline and a sharing of labour. The judge doubted if they would have agreed at the time that their intention was to create a work of joint authorship as such, not least given Martin's attitude to what he thought of as "writing", but the Court of Appeal made clear in point nine of its statement of principles above that that is not a separate requirement.

[22.1.19] During the period when the screenplay itself was being written on Final Draft software by Martin, Kogan provided comments and input, often at Martin's request, that went well beyond mere editing. During the period when the film was in early production and Stephen Frears was involved as director, Kogan's input was in relation to musical feeling and content, similar to the ideas she contributed initially, but of much more limited scope, and she provided this input in response to specific requests by or through Martin in relation to certain individual aspects of the intended musical content and context.[19]

[22.1.20] It was accepted by Martin that Kogan's contribution was authorial but in the absence of this acceptance Meade J would certainly, he stated, in any event have held that the contribution was authorial because it resided in the "creation, selection and gathering together of detailed concepts and emotions which the words have fixed in writing", quoting the Court of Appeal. The mere idea to make a screenplay about Jenkins would not have been authorial on its own. Instead, her "highly creative and imaginative" contribution was an expression of her own intellectual creation as required by the *Infopaq* test.[20] The fact that Martin had the final decision did not mean that Kogan's contribution was not an expression of her own intellectual creation.

[22.1.21] As to distinct or separate contributions (lack of distinctiveness is a requirement for joint authorship to arise in the first place), the characterisation

[19] Meade J thus noted at para 317 of his judgment that Kogan had a feeling for the musicality of the screenplay and its interaction with the characters and their development. She had an understanding of musical tuition and the feel of the world of opera and 1940s New York. She made plot and character suggestions based on this and furthermore made some suggestions for dialogue which were worked up with Martin into important scenes.

[20] In the landmark ruling in *Infopaq* discussed in Chapter 10A (Case C-5/08, [2010] FSR 20), the Court of Justice of the EU held in July 2009 that it is possible for relatively short parts of a longer work to be protected from copying where those parts of themselves form an expression of the author's intellectual creation.

and musicality run right through the whole film. In relation to certain scenes it was impossible for Meade J to say who contributed what (apart from the odd technical word that came from Kogan).

[22.1.22] In relation to relative amounts of contributions, the Court of Appeal stated in point 11 above that, "It follows that respective shares of joint authors are not required to be equal, but can reflect, pro rata, the relative amounts of their contributions". The conclusions the retrial judge reached were that there is a presumption in favour of equal shares as between joint authors; joint authors may provide otherwise by agreement (not relevant in this case); there may be circumstances where the court is not able to reach any different conclusion than equal shares; but if circumstances justify a different result than equal shares the court may so decide, assigning shares pro rata to their individual contributions; and the decision is a highly subjective one and may be approached on a broad-brush basis.

[22.1.23] He considered the circumstances clearly justified an allocation different to 50:50; indeed a 50:50 decision would in his view be an obvious injustice given how much greater was the work of Martin. Kogan's contribution was less than half of the early (treatment) stage and Martin did virtually all the work in the actual screenplay writing on Final Draft taking into account the work and effort, both qualitative and quantitative, that went into this second period was considerably greater than the first stage, and was undertaken much more by Martin. The first period represented about one third of the overall creation, with Kogan contributing about one third of it. The second period represented about two thirds of the overall creation, with Kogan contributing only about one tenth. This culminated in a little under 20 percent contributed by Kogan.

Estoppel

[22.1.24] As regards the estoppel/acquiescence and lack of consent issues in the case, Meade J considered the three basic elements of a proprietary estoppel had been made out, the parties agreeing that the existence of an estoppel would require Kogan to know that the 'Film Companies' (who optioned the screenplay and then financed and produced the film)[21] believed they were free to commercialise the screenplay without interference from Kogan; for the Film Companies to rely on their belief; and for the Film Companies to incur a detriment as a result. It was then also necessary to consider unconscionability, but it could not alone be a basis for finding an estoppel.

[22.1.25] Having all this in mind, the retrial court concluded that Kogan was estopped from seeking an injunction against the Film Companies or any restriction on the form in which they distribute the film, or any financial relief

[21] Second to fifth-named claimants Big Hat Stories Ltd, Florence Film Ltd, Pathe Productions Ltd and Qwerty Films Ltd.

against them, so long as they pay to her 20 percent of anything owing by them to Martin in the future. She was also estopped from withdrawing her consent to their commercialisation of the film.

[22.1.26] The court allowed Kogan to seek damages for moral rights (exploiting the screenplay without her consent and without her being afforded a credit). The claimants (who were seeking a declaration of full ownership by Martin) were entitled to rely on consent by Kogan down to the point when it became clear as between them that she would obtain no writer's credit and the relationship of trust between the parties had irretrievably broken down (by March 2015) when Kogan withdrew her consent in relation to the claimants. On this basis, Kogan was held entitled to an inquiry as to damages or an account of profits against Martin (and Big Hat Stores Ltd as second claimant) for the period after she withdrew her consent. Martin's (and the second claimant's) acts of dealing with the screenplay thereafter (making copies in the course of improving the screenplay for shooting and the like) on the findings of Meade J constituted infringements.

Further case law

[22.1.27] For readers requiring an involved discussion of further case law, a number of key decisions are detailed in *Appendix 1* to include *Fisher* (dispute in respect of the stand out organ solos in a *Whiter Shade of Pale* – whereby the court, as upheld in the Court of Appeal and House of Lords[22] ruled that Procul Harum band member organist Fisher was entitled to a 40 percent share in the musical copyright of the song despite only asserting his arrangement copyright claim some 38 years later), *Hadley* (litigation between Spandau Ballet members in which it was held, in respect of the most significant claim of band member Steve Norman to be joint author of the song *True* arising from his saxophone solo, that Gary Kemp alone who had always been credited as the composer and lyricist of all the group's songs except one was the sole author – it is now considered this judgment was wrongly decided), and *Hodgens.*

[22.1.28] The latter case concerned a dispute over the introductory violin parts to the Bluebells' *Young at Heart* by a session musician whereby it was held, as affirmed in the Court of Appeal, to be a valid claim for joint authorship (50 percent) and thus royalties, entitling the claimant to damages in respect of, or an account of profits arising from, any infringement of his copyright over the relevant years and into the future.

[22.1.29] *Appendix 1* also analyses the judgment in *Bamgboye* which is interesting not just in the context of joint authorship but also in terms of a share to performer royalties from exploitation of a sound recording. The defendant as music producer

---

22 On the net issue of delay, the House of Lords overturned the Court of Appeal and held there were no time limits under English law in copyright claims.

claimed he carried out all the performing of the subject dance track. However, the court held that the claimant who added electronic drum and other parts while acting as sound engineering assistant was entitled to performer rights as well as a share in the compositional rights.

BAND PARTNERSHIP AGREEMENTS

[22.2.01] It is somewhat interesting with the exception perhaps (in terms of outcome as opposed to application of relevant law) of the above-cited *Stuart* decision[23] that partnership law did not form discussion in all of the aforementioned cases (although the plaintiff in the *Godfrey* as outlined later made a claim that there had been an oral agreement or a common understanding that the income from the group's activities would be shared equally between the four members of the group and himself). The reason for this perhaps is that the proceedings did not involve band members other than in the cases of *Morrissey* and *Hadley*. In the latter an oral agreement was apparently in place as to songwriting credits (which may alter the default partnership law position). For a discussion on partnerships at will as might apply with group members or former band members, see *Thomas v Luv One Luv All Promotions Ltd*.[24]

[22.2.02] With agreements as to assignment of rights in consideration of a fee in respect of session musicians and hired-in arrangers and composers, the issue of partnership does not arise. Ideally then, for the sake of absolute clarity, the contract should contain the standard boilerplate provision stating that no relationship of partnership or joint venture is deemed to exist.

Insurance and liability

[22.2.03] The nucleus of the band may be in partnership and employ or contract other players as and when necessary, for instance, to play live. These contractual arrangements need to be unambiguous, if such other players are not to claim that they are also partners. If outside musicians are hired (e.g. for six months to record an album) as employees, the partnership becomes vicariously liable for their negligent actions and should therefore certainly consider employer's liability insurance in addition to public liability insurance. Independent contractor performers on the other hand should adduce proof of their own public liability insurance to indemnify the partnership for negligence committed by such contractors (for example while on tour or during large-scale live performances on stage) for which the partnership is not and should not, at law, be held liable.

---

23 And the *Fisher* decision but in that case Fisher was a band member for only a couple of years and his leaving would automatically have dissolved the partnership had there been a partnership in place and this would certainly have muddied the waters in terms of the complexity of his copyright case as a whole and the timespan of pre- and post-partnership royalties (if there was in fact a partnership).

24 [2020] EWHC 1565 (IPEC).

Partnership legislation

[22.2.04] For the purposes of simplicity, brevity and direct relevance to the music sector, the below summary of the law excludes certain legislation relating to limiting partnership members' liability. Most likely a successful group will incorporate a company for tax benefit and other financial reasons rather than form a limited partnership.

[22.2.05] If a band does agree to form a general partnership, it is highly advisable that a solicitor drafts the deed of partnership. Otherwise, default legislative provisions will apply as alluded to at the outset of this chapter and will supply a partnership agreement often with very unintended and potentially harsh results. Waller LJ put the matter in *Morrissey* (see [22.2.08]) thus:

> I think it is important to stress it is perhaps easier for those who have the law of partnership in mind to appreciate that there is a presumption of equality and no presumption of inequality created by a greater contribution being made by one or two partners. It is understandable if a non-lawyer starts from a different position. It may also have been unpalatable to contemplate that partners even factually dominant partners, who wish to vary the terms from equality to some different proportion must face up to making absolutely clear that the only basis on which they will continue is on a different and unequal basis thus putting at risk the joint venture itself, but that is what has to be done if a variation is to be achieved.

[22.2.06] Section 19 of the Partnership Act 1890 ('the 1890 Act') provides that the mutual rights and duties of partners, whether ascertained by agreement or defined by the 1890 Act, may be varied by the consent of all the partners, and such consent may be either express or inferred from a course of dealing. The partnership agreement will thus ensure certainty and clarity and assist in avoiding disputes in the event that the group disbands, a band member leaves or is requested by the other members to part ways due to incompetence, skill deficiencies or otherwise (possibly in less dramatic circumstances than Pete Best's replacement by Ringo Starr!). Section 25 stipulates that no majority of the partners can expel any partner unless a power to do so has been conferred by express agreement between the partners. This statutory provision alone should be sufficient reason for band members to draft a partnership agreement if that is the business vehicle they choose to adopt for the band.

Default provisions in the absence of a partnership agreement

[22.2.07] Without an agreement, the default provisions of s 24 would apply such that, for instance, all the partners are entitled to share equally in the capital and profits of the business, and must contribute equally towards the losses whether of capital or otherwise sustained by such business; and the partnership must indemnify all partners in respect of payments made and personal liabilities incurred by them in the ordinary and proper conduct of the business of the partnership; or in or about anything necessarily done for the preservation of the business or property of the partnership. In addition, if a partner, without the consent of the other partners, carries on any business of the same nature as and competing with that of the partnership, that partner must account for and pay over to the partnership all profits made in that business (s 30). A final example of unintended consequence is that (again subject to any agreement that might exist between the partners), every partnership is dissolved as regards all the partners by the death or bankruptcy of any partner.

Joyce v Morrissey

[22.2.08] Section 24 (the same 1890 Act applies in England and Ireland) was considered by the Court of Appeal in *Morrissey*[25] in relation to the presumption that all partners share equally in the capital and profits of the business. The Smiths band was a partnership comprising four members: the plaintiff (Joyce), the first defendant (Morrissey), the second defendant (Marr) and Andy Rourke. Rourke was initially a party to the litigation but settled his claim very shortly after the writ was issued.[26] The group disbanded in 1987.

[22.2.09] Joyce was the drummer and in March 1989 he issued proceedings claiming a declaration that he was a partner in the band entitled to a 25 percent share of all net profits arising out of the activities (other than songwriting or publishing in respect of which an agreement existed that Joyce would have no share) of The Smiths. By the time the issues came to be tried before Judge Weeks QC (sitting as a judge of the High Court) it was not in dispute that Joyce was a partner.[27] The only bone of contention remaining was whether he was an equal partner entitled to one quarter of the profits arising out of the activities (other than songwriting or publishing) of the band. The High Court found in favour of the plaintiff (ordering that he receive approximately one million pounds in back payments and 25 percent henceforth). Morrissey, alone, then pursued an appeal which proceedings were unanimously dismissed by the three-panel Court of Appeal.[28] Application for leave to appeal to the House of Lords was also refused.

[22.2.10] It was Joyce's case that, apart from the agreement that he should not be entitled to share in the profits resulting from songwriting and publishing, there was no other agreement which disentitled him from sharing equally in the capital and profits of the business such as recording income streams. It was the defendants' case that it was a term of the partnership that profits would be shared in the proportions Morrissey and Marr 40 percent each, Joyce and Rourke 10 percent each. They did not assert or seek to establish an express agreement to

---

25 [1998] EWCA Civ 1711; [1999] EMLR 233.

26 Rourke, who reportedly was in financial difficulty, settled almost immediately after the summons was served for a lump sum of £83,000, renouncing all further claims, and in return for ten percent of future royalties.

27 It was also accepted that the partnership was dissolved as from 31 May 1987 and that the affairs of the partnership should be wound up.

28 Thorpe and Gibson LJJ concurring with Waller LJ.

that effect but alleged that the same was to be inferred from conduct, relying on various matters including certain alleged discussions between the parties together with references to accounts, meetings and correspondence with solicitors and accountants.

[22.2.11] To the trial judge, the evidence was overwhelming that there was no agreement formal or oral rebutting the presumption of equality contained in s 24. As regards the allegation that Joyce and Rourke throughout received sums equivalent to ten percent of the profits from the activities of the band, Weeks J had found that this was factually incorrect. He held that in one year the drawings of Messrs Rourke and Joyce amounted to one quarter of those of Marr, but that no clear pattern emerged. Further, in 1984, Mr Bowen, solicitor for Messrs Morrissey and Marr stated that "in principle they will be equally entitled to the net profits of the business". In another letter a number of days letter he stated:

> I was also concerned that there was no agreement between the individual members of the band. I took the view that as a matter of law the members of The Smiths were all equal partners although I was of course aware that this kind of arrangement was not acceptable to Morrissey or Johnny Marr.

[22.2.12] Of the extra work and responsibilities undertaken by Messrs Morrissey and Marr (such as taking risks as signatories to contracts and being defendants to proceedings of which Messrs Rourke and Joyce were not), Waller LJ delivering the lead speech held:

> … it is clear as a matter of partnership law that the fact that one or more partners makes a greater contribution than others in no way displaces the presumption of equality: see *Lindley & Banks* (17th Edition) para 19-22:
>
>> "Whether, therefore, partners have contributed money equally or unequally, whether or not they are on a par as regards skill, connection or character, whether they have or have not laboured equally for the benefit of the firm, their shares will be considered equal, unless some agreement to the contrary can be shown to have been entered into."

The Lord Justice continued stating:

> …once it is established as it was in this case that the partnership was from its commencement on the basis of equality, for Mr Morrissey to establish that there was a variation from equality, he must show that Mr Joyce accepted in a contractual sense that that was the basis on which the Group were to continue, and for there to be a contractual acceptance the terms must be certain, and there must be consideration. If there is to be a variation of this type of partnership where there is no express partnership deed providing powers to make variations, the consideration will normally be provided by the agreement not to terminate the partnership if the new terms are agreed…

[22.2.13] From a review of the evidence presented and testimony adduced at trial, the Court of Appeal dismissed Morrissey's appeal proceedings and upheld the verdict of Weeks J holding the trial judge was correct to conclude that the basis on which The Smiths commenced their partnership both as a fact and as presumed by law was never varied. All band members were thus equal partners for the purposes of net profit distribution on all activities other than songwriting and publishing. The long-running matter from 1989 is said to have cost Morrissey over £1.5 million in recovered royalties and legal fees to late 2005 (and Joyce was to receive all the recording royalties from Smiths' albums until the amount, plus interest, he was owed was fully discharged).[29] The case highlights the extreme perils of partnership law for the unwary band member.

Definitions

[22.2.14] The 1890 Act defines a partnership as two or more individuals "carrying on a business in common with a view of profit". Persons who have entered into partnership with one another are for the purposes of the Act collectively called a "firm" (s 4) and the name under which their business is carried on is called the firm name. Provided that the members of the band are sharing income and debts, then the broad view is that they are in partnership. A songwriting team, string quartet, acoustic duo, ensemble, brass band and so on may equally be a partnership (as might a dancing, comedic or other performance troupe). This is of significance as, where there is no written agreement (and sometimes even where there is but poorly drafted), the Act which is certainly not a statute framed with bands in mind, provides that each member of the band is individually liable for all group debts incurred while a partner, and not just for that partner's share of the group debts, and that all equipment will belong to the partnership and not to any one member (s 20). Members, in the absence of an agreement to the contrary, may therefore find their own equipment becomes a band asset when they join and that same cannot necessarily be taken away when they leave.

Further default provisions

[22.2.15] Section 5 of the 1890 Act provides that every partner is an agent of the firm and his other partners for the purpose of the business of the partnership; and the acts of every partner who does any act for carrying on in the usual way business of the kind carried on by the firm of which he is a member bind the firm and his partners, unless the partner so acting has in fact no authority to act for the firm in the particular matter, and the person with whom he is dealing either knows that he has no authority, or does not know or believe him to be a partner. Thus, any member of the band has the authority to bind the rest of his partners and to incur debts in the name of the partnership. Accordingly, it is in every band member's interest to keep abreast of what actions other members

[29] As a result of his subsequent absence from the jurisdiction while Morrissey was in the US, Joyce secured a default judgment against him for final backpayment moneys owed. *The Irish Times* reported in 2006 that, "Morrissey has gone on the record alleging that Joyce took out third party orders against Morrissey's personal bank account in the UK" – Brian Boyd, *These Charmless Men* (2006), irishtimes.com. Available at: https://www.irishtimes.com/culture/these-charmless-men-1.1289123 [Accessed 24 July 2019].

are taking in the band name and to agree in advance what they are permitted to do without informing the others in advance.

[22.2.16] Section 6 provides that any act or instrument relating to the business of the firm done or executed in the firm's name, or in any other manner showing an intention to bind the firm, by any duly authorised person, whether a partner or not, is binding on the firm and all the partners.

[22.2.17] In terms of liability, ss 9-12 provide *inter alia* that every partner in a firm is liable jointly and severally with the other co-partners for all debts and obligations of the firm incurred while he is a partner; and where, by any wrongful act or omission of any partner acting in the ordinary course of the business of the firm, or with the authority of his co-partners, loss or injury is caused to any person not being a partner in the firm, or any penalty is incurred, the firm is liable therefor to the same extent as the partner so acting or omitting to act; and where one partner acting within the scope of his apparent authority receives the money or property of a third person and misapplies it, the firm is liable to make good the loss.

[22.2.18] Section 17 deals with the issue of liabilities of incoming and outgoing partners thus: a person who is admitted as a partner into an existing firm does not thereby become liable to the creditors of the firm for anything done before he became a partner. A partner who retires from a firm does not thereby cease to be liable for partnership debts or obligations incurred before his retirement. A retiring partner may be discharged from any existing liabilities however by an agreement to that effect between himself and the members of the firm as newly constituted and the creditors, and this agreement may be either express or inferred as a fact from the course of dealings between the creditors and the firm as newly constituted.

[22.2.19] In the absence of agreement, the leaving of a member (upon giving notice as is required by the statute) will automatically dissolve the partnership and the leaving member is entitled to apply to court to wind up the partnership's affairs to force a distribution of the assets. This may prove problematic if a band is about to play a tour.

[22.2.20] On dissolution, the partners' authority, rights and obligations continue, so far as may be necessary, to wind up the partnership and complete outstanding partnership contracts. This could mean the leaving member's having to, or having the right to, play any booked gigs.

[22.2.21] The band name will be treated as one of the assets of the partnership and (unless there is an agreement to the contrary) it is owned by all of the members of the firm equally. Consequently, where one member (perhaps the founding member) conceived the name, but is expelled by a majority of partners by prior express agreement conferring such right of expulsion, he could lose that name to the continuing partners. Where the band breaks up and all the former members seek to each use the name for their own new bands, this will inevitably lead to confusion and dispute (see *Thomas* at [22.2.01] above). Legally, no single former partner has the right to use it without the majority's express permission, and accordingly, if the band splits, equally no-one can use the name unless agreement is reached.

[22.2.22] Band members may be content that one or more of the above default statutory provisions should apply but, for the sake of certainty, it is always prudent and advisable to have a written partnership agreement varying the default position and, if certain aspects of the Partnership Act are to be avoided, it is essential.

[22.2.23] In respect of taxation, since the advent of the self-assessment system for income tax, partnerships are no longer taxed separately but each partner's share of partnership profits should be declared in that partner's own self-assessment tax return and hence partnership accounts will nonetheless still have to be prepared for Revenue purposes.

Limited companies

[22.2.24] Many professional bands form a limited company through which to trade and provide their musical services. This type of arrangement is often called a service company. The band members will then often be the shareholders, directors and employees of their own company.

[22.2.25] The limited personal liability a company affords is often considered to outweigh the extra formalities of forming and administering a company, and the fact that a company's income is effectively taxed twice, once as company income in the form of corporation tax and again as income of the band member (as a shareholder or employee). In contrast, a partner's personal liability for partnership debts or claims is unlimited, which could mean bankruptcy if the band is exposed to a substantial claim for damages for which it stands uninsured. On the upside, partnership accounts do not have to be publicly made available whereas upon payment of a fee all company accounts are available to any member of the public from the Companies Registration Office.

RECORDING CONTRACT/ARTIST MANAGEMENT LITIGATION

Introduction

[22.3.01] In the music industry, recording contracts with the majors and larger independent labels are valuable and highly sought after by voracious artists who dream of one day garnering worldwide recognition, though this route is becoming somewhat less desirable or indeed necessary with digital distribution, social media and given that artists wish to control more of their income streams.[30] Distracted by the promise of fame and fortune, many musicians if unrepresented can hastily overlook the restrictive or potentially exploitative nature of recording agreements. Such restrictions can have detrimental consequences as epitomised in the examples set out hereunder. Prince faced a 40-year tumultuous battle for control over his music, comparing a record contract with Warner[31] to slavery[32] and challenging certain music streaming practices.[33] While oftentimes alienating his fans and the public at large with his ongoing feud with the label, he did however raise awareness for the plight of artists and was triumphant in his fight to control his music and all aspects of his creativity.

[22.3.02] On the one hand, legal disputes between musicians and their recording companies shed light on the necessity perhaps of governments to legislate in protecting artists from the damaging consequences of unfair contracts. This has occurred to some extent within the EU with the advent of the Directive on Copyright and Related Rights in the Digital Single Market (2019) (see Chapter 11 on contract adjustment mechanisms and licence revocation, but it remains to be seen how the Directive itself (and Irish legislation transposing same) will be implemented by practitioners in the industry and interpreted by the courts at national and EU level). On the other hand, recording contracts are legally binding agreements freely entered into with, one would expect, the benefit of specialist legal advice.

[22.3.03] As such, the courts may be unlikely to undo an enforceable contract which meets the ingredients in contract law of a valid agreement unless there is justifiable reason to do so or if the law of equity is invoked as would be the case (where monetary damages will not provide a suitable remedy) in an injunction

30 Artists can avail of direct-to-market online distribution channels and thus self-manage, self-release and self-publish (or through a digital aggregator such as TuneCore). Alternatively, they can license material to music publishers and music libraries.

31 This is against the backdrop of Prince's success with Diamonds And Pearls which spurred Warner Brothers to double their efforts to extend Prince's contract which was about to expire, and in August 1992 they signed a six-album extension worth $100m – the largest recording contract up to that time for a solo artist. Does this constitute slavery?!

32 His argument was that he was signed to Warner and it, as a result, owned and controlled his name as well as any music released under that name. He changed his name to that of a symbol and was referred to, variously, as "Symbol", "Squiggle" or "the Artist Formerly Known as Prince". This coincided with George Michael's ill-fated attempt to resile from his contract with Sony. Prince appeared with the word "slave" written on his cheek repeatedly in music videos and public appearances, including on *Today* in 1996 and at the 1995 Brit Awards. His acceptance speech was "Prince. In concert: perfectly free. On record: slave".

33 He pulled his songs from all streaming services except for Tidal, which exclusively released his last two albums in 2015. Previous to that, Prince had engaged in releasing albums himself online via a subscription service on NPG Music Club, which was then replaced by Lotusflow3r.com in 2009, which sold his music as well as tickets to his shows. Prince's early attempts to sell directly to fans online was clearly an influence on Radiohead, then out of contract with EMI, when the band released *In Rainbows* in 2007 as a 'pay what you like' download. Nine Inch Nails has also released directly to its fans thereby defying traditional distribution routes.

compelling a defendant to take a particular action or desist from certain business practices, or an order for specific performance mandating the performance of a contract or aspects thereof where, for instance, there has been inaction to the detriment of the artist's career. Equity law such as an order for rescission to end a contract operates alongside or concurrently with the common law, with discretionary powers afforded to judges, to accord fairness and bring flexibility and good conscience to bear.

[22.3.04] In the Pink Floyd proceedings discussed in the next section, Lord Neuberger MR for the Court of Appeal cited House of Lords (*per* Lord Hoffman) precedent in this regard thus:

> ...the court does "not readily accept that people have made mistakes in formal documents" – *Chartbrook* [2009] 1 AC 1101, para 23. He also pointed out in paragraph 20, that, as the court, and therefore the notional reasonable person, cannot take into account the antecedent negotiations, the fact that the natural meaning of the words appears to produce "a bad bargain" for one of the parties or an "unduly favourable" result for another, is not enough to justify the conclusion that something has gone wrong. One is normally looking for an outcome which is "arbitrary" or "irrational", before a mistake argument will run.[34]

Contractual provisions

Term

[22.3.05] Primarily, legal regimes regarding the term (period of time an individual is bound to a contract and affected thereafter by sunset clauses post-termination as to income splits) of management or record contracts could be re-evaluated to allow artists to legally dissolve their agreements after periods of inactivity, especially when it is through no fault of their own. This has already occurred in principle at least with the passing of the above-cited Directive. In the US, under Californian law, no personal services contract can bind an employee for more than seven years.[35] The one exception to this are recording artists, thus raising the issue of repealing California's Labor Code 2855(b) (a Bill was drafted by one parliamentarian to that effect in early 2021).

---

34 *Pink Floyd Music Ltd v EMI Records Ltd* [2010] EWCA Civ 1429, para 20.

35 Some twenty years ago, led by Don Henley, a number of recording artists and artist advocates negotiated for months in the California State Senate for the passage of a state bill that called for a repeal of 2855(b), the section of the code that exempts recording artists and which would have allowed musical acts to be held to the same contract terms as employees. The artists faced a powerful foe on the other side in The Recording Industry Association of America, which represents the interests of the major labels. The RIAA was responsible for amendment (b) to Statute 2855 in the first place in 1987. Though the RIAA offered up some compromises, such as limiting the number of albums for which a label could sue artists should the artists leave after seven years with records still remaining on their contract, the original subsection (b) allows labels to sue for damages for all undelivered albums. The two sides could never come to anything near a workable compromise and matters ended there.

[22.3.06] Actors routinely use the seven-year rule as a negotiating tactic – the *Modern Family* cast for example brought proceedings against 20th Century Fox Television under the statute as they renegotiated their contract. In 1944 actress Olivia De Haviland successfully invoked the relevant provision of the former Civil Code in her seminal action against Warner Brothers Pictures. Artists including Metallica, Courtney Love and Don Henley also sought to be released from their contracts citing the statute but settlements were reached before a ruling on the legislation could be reached.[36]

[22.3.07] Most record labels call for two albums with an option to sign the artist for at least one or two more. The reasoning behind the long-term option is because a major studio can often invest very substantial sums in an artist's career, and it may be years before the label recoups its investment and begins to realise a profit. On the artist side, a multi-album deal could tie up an act for several years if not decades which will prove problematic especially if there are creative differences between the artist and label executives. Additionally, if the label is sold (such as when Universal acquired EMI in 2012 or Warner Music Group purchased EMI assets including Parlophone), artists' contracts will be assigned to a new company with which they may never have envisaged signing and differing opinions could thus emerge as to ethos, vision and creativity. Lastly, with many labels now demanding 360 deals with the record company also potentially receiving a share of touring, merchandising, endorsements and other ancillary income above and beyond record sales, the financial stakes are even higher.

Assignment of contracts to another label (or manager)

[22.3.08] While independent labels have grown in stature, the three majors (Universal, Sony and Warner) still have a firm grip on the music industry. Even when signing with perhaps a more benign indie label, lawyers and artists should be cognisant of assignment provisions. A once amicable relationship between artist and label more akin to a partnership can develop tentacles if the contract is sold on by assignment or novation to a major studio. Moreover, if top acts including Prince, George Michael, Dixie Chicks, Bruce Springsteen and the like can become entangled in contractual and legal disputes (albeit arising from agreements entered at an early stage of their careers), the fate of aspiring artists

---

36 Melinda Newman, *Following Kesha's Court Decision, Is It Time To Reexamine The Seven-Year Contract Statute* (2016), forbes.com. Available at: https://www.forbes.com/sites/melindanewman/2016/02/22/following-keshas-court-decision-is-it-time-to-reexamine-the-7-year-contract-statute/#41a68cc7175c [Accessed 3 April 2019]. Section 2855(b) provides that persons rendering services for "the production of phonorecords may not invoke the [Seven Year Rule] without first giving written notice to the employer" and further, the company (label) "shall have the right to recover damages for a breach of the contract occurring during its term in an action commenced during or after its term". While record companies cannot force artists to work beyond seven years, they can recover damages for material required under the contract that was not delivered.

can be on very shaky ground if it is not underpinned by robust and pragmatic legal advice and an equitable contract.

Accounting provisions

[22.3.09] Highly adept music lawyers and accountants will at times be called upon to scrutinise in particular the oftentimes complex accounting and auditing provisions relating to net revenues and record royalties owing to their artist clients as highlighted in the Dixie Chicks dispute outlined below. Indeed, even the Court of Appeal Lord Justices differed in interpreting certain provisions of a licence agreement between Pink Floyd and EMI. Further, notwithstanding that artists may be successful in their disputes, the lapsed time often causes considerable harm to their career such as occurred in the George Michael and Bruce Springsteen cases.

[22.3.10] In saying all that, with global success comes leverage for artists and a bargaining power to renegotiate the terms of their contracts. The Beatles and The Rolling Stones were in a position to achieve this in the mid-1960s.

Pink Floyd royalties claim

[22.3.11] The appeal (for summary judgment) to the Court of Appeal in *Pink Floyd Music Ltd v EMI Records Ltd*[37] was brought by EMI against a decision of the Chancellor of the High Court, Sir Andrew Morritt,[38] in favour of the rock band as regards the group's royalties claim. The case raised issues of interpretation relating to two agreements which EMI entered into with the band's service companies in 1999. The agreement governed the overseas and UK sales of five named albums (and two single tracks) and incorporated the provisions of a master (sound recordings) licence agreement. The two agreements terminated all earlier agreements and their effect was to confer licences on EMI to exploit those albums on specific terms.

[22.3.12] In March 2007, the plaintiff-respondent company notified EMI that, in accordance with its rights under clause 7 of the master licence agreement, it had appointed accountants Prager & Fenton to carry out an audit of the royalty statements provided by EMI for the period from July 2002 to September 2007. In July 2008, Prager & Fenton produced a report indicating that, in its view, there were fifteen areas of under-accounting amounting to a total value of more than £10 million. In March 2009, the group issued proceedings based on that expert assessment. EMI's defence was served and in October 2009 the claimant service company furnished a reply and applied for summary judgment in the High Court.

---

37 [2010] EWCA Civ 1429.

38 *Pink Floyd Music Ltd v EMI Records Ltd* [2010] EWHC 533 (ChD).

[22.3.13] All but four of the fifteen claims were settled before the appeal application reached the Court of Appeal. The four claims remaining for consideration by the three Lord Justices sitting were based on allegations that EMI used an incorrect base price for digital sales; wrongly exploited the works in the albums in the form of single track downloads; wrongly exploited those works in the form of ringtones and streaming; and did not include digital income from single track downloads – in sum, the case being essentially that there were owing to the band substantial underpayments of royalties over many years. The Chancellor at first instance made an order in Pink Floyd's favour.

[22.3.14] The EMI appeal, which concerned contract law issues of construction of individually negotiated written agreements, was dismissed by the majority (Carnwath LJ dissenting in part). Before the court could be satisfied that something had "gone wrong", it had to be satisfied both that there has been "a clear mistake" and that it is clear "what correction ought to be made".[39] Moreover, the Master of the Rolls was of the view, as regards the clauses under review (whether the master licence extended to digital recordings as well as physical products – clause 4.13 referred to "Records" and "Albums"), that the licence did extend to digital recordings – the Chancellor, agreeing with Pink Floyd, had also held in the High Court that the agreement did in fact include digital recordings:

> In all these circumstances, I have reached the conclusion that clause 4.13, unlike clause 9(d)(i), is not by any means a clearly drafted provision, whose effect is unambiguous as a matter of language, and that it is therefore quite permissible, indeed positively appropriate, to invoke commercial common sense to assist on the issue of clarifying a rather opaque provision.[40]

[22.3.15] Lord Neuberger MR thus upheld the Chancellor's order and dismissed the appeal. Lord Justice Laws concurred stating:

> I therefore see the case as one where the purpose of the provision is clear but the language is equivocal. In those circumstances, on established principles we should construe the contract so as to give effect to its demonstrated purpose. That is what the Chancellor and the Master of the Rolls have done, and so would I.[41]

George Michael

[22.3.16] The case taken by George Michael (Georgios Panayiotou) against Sony in 1992 best illustrates the potential perils for artists of entering into contracts with their label or indeed with their manager. Despite the havoc it wreaked for

---

39 At para 21 of Lord Neuberger MR's judgment citing Lord Hoffmann in *Chartbrook Ltd v Persimmon Homes Ltd* [2009] 1 AC 1101, paras 22-24, approving the analysis of Brightman LJ in *East v Pantiles (Plant Hire) Ltd* (1981) 263 EG 61, as refined by Carnwath LJ in *KPMG LLP v Network Rail Infrastructure Ltd* [2007] Bus LR 1336.

40 At para 60.

41 At para 75.

the artist's career (recording only two albums of new material in two decades following the litigation and denting his armoury for major success in America), it serves as an eternal reminder to all aspiring artists to firstly approach multi-album deals with extreme caution and, secondly, to avail of the advices of a seasoned entertainment lawyer (although in this matter the popstar in fact had the benefit of independent legal advice).[42]

[22.3.17] On the other side of the coin, Robbie Williams' signing of a record-breaking £80 million contract with EMI in 2002 comprised the biggest music deal in British history, the contract including a number of provisos, including the label's ceding greater creative control to him and a commitment to breaking the British popstar into the US market. The deal was brokered by Ingenious Media, a UK corporate finance advisory business (also mentioned in Chapter 7 in terms of film finance).

[22.3.18] In *Panayiotou v Sony Music Entertainment (UK) Ltd,*[43]the plaintiff entertainer argued that his recording contract constituted an unreasonable restraint of trade or was rendered void by art 85(2) of the EEC Treaty directed at maintaining freedom of competition within the common market, and that it manifested in inequality of earnings and bargaining power. Michael alleged that the defendant had failed to promote his album Listen Without Prejudice Vol 1 with due vigour as a form of victimisation when the artist decided to downplay his status as a sex symbol in an effort to disassociate himself from his past with pop duo Wham!. Michael described his situation as "professional slavery" because his contract required that he produce music and cede copyright to Sony for many years, leaving him no control over how the music would be marketed, nor placing a reciprocal requirement that the label invest in promotion.[44] This comparison with slavery was echoed a year after the George Michael proceedings were initiated when Prince commenced in-public legal wrangling with Warner in 1993.

[22.3.19] In the plaintiff's view, there was a clear imbalance of power resulting in a long-term lack of control over his career. Had the case succeeded, it might have curtailed the practice of signing artists to multi-album contracts. The court however wholly rejected the claims. A summary of the proceedings and the

---

42 Parker J was of the view that the subject agreement was genuine and bona fide and freely entered into. Mr Michael had the benefit of one of the most experienced advisers and toughest negotiators in the business.

43 [1994] ChD 142.

44 There was no question of slavery in terms of remuneration. According to the *Independent* (UK), the popstar received advances and royalties of more than £11 million pounds during 1988 alone under the 1988 agreement: Ying Hui Tan, *Law Report: Recording agreement enforceable: Panayiotou and others v Sony Music Entertainment (UK) Ltd–Chancery Division (Mr Justice Jonathan Parker), 1 June 1994* (2011). Available at: https://www.independent.co.uk/news/uk/law-report-recording-agreement-enforceable-panayiotou-and-others-v-sony-music-entertainment-uk-ltd-1424669.html [Accessed 28 March 2019].

judgment is set out in *Appendix 2* together with further litigation examples in respect of The Dixie Chicks, Courtney Love and teen idol JoJo.

Bruce Springsteen: artist-manager proceedings

[22.3.20] On 27 July 1976, Springsteen filed a lawsuit against his manager and publisher Mike Appel who had co-produced the Born to Run album with Springsteen's future manager Jon Landau.[45] Two days later, Appel countersued, seeking to prevent Springsteen from working on his next album with Landau. An injunction was granted pending full hearing but the matter was ultimately settled between the parties on undisclosed confidential terms. The dispute arose after Springsteen had been made aware that the contracts he had signed with Appel in 1972 meant he would never reap the full benefits of his work. When New York Supreme Court Judge Arnold Fein granted Appel his injunction, Springsteen in effect found himself banned from entering the studio with his preferred collaborator. The legal battle that followed placed his recording career on hold for 12 months, at the very point he should have been capitalising on Born to Run.

[22.3.21] The rockstar disclosed details to a courtroom in an unrelated case[46] concerning his early career, to include his having to rely on handouts from his first professional management team, Messrs Jim Cretecos and Mike Appel of Laurel Canyon Productions. Despite releasing several successful albums in the early 1970s, he failed to realise monetary gain. Springsteen explained from the witness box in these proceedings that despite the success, he was impecunious.[47]

[22.3.22] After ten months of litigation and nearly two years after Born to Run had catapulted him to national celebrity, Springsteen and Appel settled and parted ways forever. The move finally enabled Springsteen to record a follow-up to Born to Run with Landau, the producer of his choice. The case serves as a reminder to artists that the business and legal affairs element of content creation and its exploitation is, or at least should be, as important as the creative process itself.

[22.3.23] Details of the settlement with former manager/publisher Mike Appel

---

45 Keith Cameron, *Bruce Springsteen: 'People thought we were gone. Finished'* (2010), guardian.com. Available at: https://www.theguardian.com/music/2010/sep/23/bruce-springsteen-darkness-edge-town [Accessed 28 March 2019].

46 To prevent defendant Masquerade selling a CD of 19 songs called Before the Fame, which had never been released or were out-takes from his first albums: Irishtimes.com, *Springsteen tells court of living in near poverty* (1998). Available at: https://www.irishtimes.com/news/springsteen-tells-court-of-living-in-near-poverty-1.201760 [Accessed 28 March 2019].

47 He revealed that before his first album, the successful Greetings from Asbury Park, his home was a sleeping bag on the floor of a friend's apartment in New York. Sometimes Appel would give him a "few bucks" or Cretecos "might help you with $10 if you were in a bind or something". Appel reportedly had given him only one financial statement in their entire legal relationship and Springsteen remained impoverished during the first three albums.

are scant.[48] Counsel for manager Appel stated that the settlement provided his former client with "substantial economic benefits, including a share of the profits from the first three albums". Also included was a five-year deal between Laurel Canyon Productions, Appel's company, and CBS Records, a third party to the litigation. "Substantial" reportedly means Appel was to receive several hundred thousand dollars from Springsteen and CBS for relinquishing his interest in Springsteen. The three contracts (publishing, recording and management) which bound Springsteen to Appel's Laurel Canyon Productions were rescinded. His recording agreement with Columbia Records was renegotiated and Springsteen would, going forward, self-administer all of his publishing. Appel was to continue receiving some proceeds from the records and publishing from Springsteen's first three albums but held no administration rights thereto.

[22.3.24] The crucial allegations in Springsteen's complaint against Appel were fraud (representing himself as a knowledgeable and experienced businessman), undue influence and breach of trust. Appel, as an artist manager, had a fiduciary duty – a continuing obligation, by the trust Springsteen placed in him, to act honourably in the best interests of his client. The Laurel Canyon management, according to particulars of claim filed in the proceedings, suffered from a conflict of interest that ran directly counter to that fiduciary obligation. The agreement provided that Appel's managerial responsibility was suspended in any of Springsteen's dealings with Laurel Canyon companies; it also denied Springsteen the right to retain any advisers other than Appel.

48 David McGee, *Bruce Springsteen Reclaims the Future* (1977), rollingstone.com. Available at: https://www.rollingstone.com/music/music-news/bruce-springsteen-reclaims-the-future-179300/ [Accessed 13 July 2021].

Appendix 1

Further case law on joint authorship

Fisher v Brooker

[A1.1.01] In *Fisher v Brooker*[49] the claimant was the organist in the original line-up of Procul Harum from 1967 to 1969. The first defendant Gary Brooker was the band's singer and pianist.[50] In early 1967, Brooker wrote the music and Keith Reid wrote the lyrics for the original version of *A Whiter Shade of Pale* (referred to in the judgment of Blackburne J as "the Song"),[51] and Brooker made a demo tape of himself singing the Song to his own piano accompaniment. Subsequently, Matthew Fisher was recruited as the band's organist. After rehearsals, the band recorded the version of the Song (referred to in the judgment as "the Work") performed by Brooker, Fisher, Ray Royer (guitar), David Knights (bass) and Bill Eyden (a session drummer) which was commercially released in May 1967. No credit was accorded to Fisher as composer of the organ parts, nor was he acknowledged as joint author in the publicity and product material.

[A1.1.02] In terms of extraordinary delay (the proceedings only being instituted in 2005) to which we shall later return, the trial court held on this point that, for so long as the claimant chose not to make and establish his claim, the defendants had no reason to think that they were not entitled to the payments they received. Moreover, for so long as Fisher allowed the collection societies to account to the defendants, notwithstanding his long held belief that as co-writer of the music he was entitled to share in the musical copyright or at the least to be recognised as having co-written the Work, he must be taken to have gratuitously (at no monetary consideration) licensed the exploitation of his copyright. Two of three judges in the Court of Appeal disagreed with the trial judge, Blackburne J, on this issue of delay[52] which would have resulted in the otherwise successful

---

49 [2006] EWHC 3239 (ChD).

50 The second defendant claimed to be the assignee of the rights of Essex Music Ltd under the group's publishing and recording contracts.

51 The track ultimately became one of the most successful popular songs of the late 1960s selling (at the time of the judgment) over six million copies worldwide with, according to the judgment, over 770 versions of the song since having been performed by other groups.

52 [2008] EWCA Civ 287 at para 115: Murmery LJ delivering the Court of Appeal majority judgment (as reversed on appeal) was of the firm view that the claimant was guilty of excessive and inexcusable delay in asserting his claim to title to a joint interest in the Work stating he had silently stood by and acquiesced in the defendants' commercial exploitation of the Work for 38 years. His acquiescence led the defendants to act for a very long period on the basis that the entire copyright in the Work was theirs. They controlled the commercial exploitation of the Work without any reference or reward to him. His

claim to copyright being dismissed. However, the House of Lords unanimously overturned the majority decision in the Court of Appeal, leaving the trial judge's orders stand that the delay in bringing the case had not caused any harm to the other writers who had, in fact, benefited financially from it and adding that there were no time limits under English law in copyright claims.

[A1.1.03] In respect of the mechanics of the joint authorship claim itself, the repeated eight-bar introduction features the famous solo on the Hammond organ by Fisher. On the question of who created the organ solo, there was ultimately little dispute between Fisher and Brooker that Fisher had created it to fit the musical context provided by the Song. Blackburne J thus held as follows:

> Reviewing the evidence as a whole, it is abundantly clear to me that Mr Fisher's instrumental introduction (i.e. the organ solo as heard in the first eight bars of the Work and as repeated) is sufficiently different from what Mr Brooker had composed on the piano to qualify in law, and by a wide margin, as an original contribution to the Work. The result in law is that Mr Fisher qualifies to be regarded as a joint author of the Work and, subject to the points to which I shall next turn, to share in the ownership of the musical copyright in it.[53]

[A1.1.04] On the issue then of percentage ownership in the musical copyright, the learned judge could see no reason in principle why the claimant's share in the Work should not be something less than an equal undivided share if the circumstances justified that result, in other words that a finding of a smaller than equal share to the claimant was permissible under the law. In an earlier judgment of *Bamgboye v Reed*[54] the court there had declared the claimant to be entitled to a 33 percent share in the musical copyright and two thirds to the defendant. The claimant had sought 50 percent.[55]

---

acquiescence thus made it unconscionable and inequitable for him to seek to exercise control over the commercial exploitation of the copyright in the Work. The combination of a declaration of a joint interest and a declaration of revocation of the implied consent would enable him to control future commercial exploitation by means of a final injunction against the defendants.

53 At para 42.

54 [2004] EMLR 5.

55 Miss Hazel Williamson QC (sitting as a judge of the High Court) summarised the matter neatly thus, "However, I do not find that this creative input is as great as the 50%, which he claims. He has more musical and original creative talent in this regard than he has been given credit for, but Mr Reed certainly has considerably more experience, many more ideas and more flare, I find, as to the possibilities of effects, embellishments and general arrangement of the piece. … Mr Reed, for example, put in the "wobble base" and it was Mr Reed's ideas to put in the chops which are very distinctive. Indeed, Mr Bamgboye acknowledged that they were Mr Reed's idea. I find that they all were. Mr Bamgboye also acknowledged that ideas only stayed in if Mr Reed liked them and not if he did not. It follows that the ultimate selection of the ideas on the track was Mr Reed's and not Mr Bamgboye's, either because they were Mr Reed's in the first place, or because if they were Mr Bamgboye's they were selected, in effect, by Mr Reed. Mr Reed's contribution was, therefore, greater. In the end, I have come to the conclusion on the evidence that their respective contributions are fairly represented as one third on the part of Mr Bamgboye and two-thirds on the part of Mr Reed (at para 77 of her judgment).

[A1.1.05] Returning to *Fisher*, the plaintiff's pleaded claim was likewise for a 50 percent share. The question ultimately, in the court's view, is a highly subjective one and Blackbourne J concluded that Fisher's interest in the Work should be reflected by according him a 40 percent share in the musical copyright. His contribution to the overall work was on any view substantial but not, in the court's judgment, as substantial as that of Brooker. The trial court findings as to Fisher's contribution (in respect of the stand-out organ solo) to the Work were subsequently upheld by the Court of Appeal.[56] Furthermore, although the defendants did not pursue that issue in the House of Lords, the final court endorsed the Court of Appeal's conclusion ([2009] UKHL 41 at para 41).

Delay as a defence

[A1.1.06] As did Christopher Floyd QC sitting as a deputy High Court judge in *Beckingham* below, Blackburne J went on to hold in his ruling that the claimant was not estopped from revoking the gratuitous licence he had impliedly granted nor was he otherwise barred (that is, statute-barred) by reason of his delay of 38 years in asserting his claim. A majority of the Court of Appeal[57] held that Fisher was disentitled, due to delay, to declarations that he jointly owned the copyright, and that he had revoked the implied licence by reason of his delay in making the claim, but that conclusion was unanimously reversed by the House of Lords in July 2009.

[A1.1.07] One of the striking features of the claim is that it was made decades after the Work was first released. The plaintiff did not suggest he or anyone on his behalf ever formally raised his claim until the matter was mentioned in a letter dated 19 March 2004 from the solicitors then acting for him to Brooker's manager wherein it was represented that their client should have been entitled to a writer's share of royalties from the outset and that he had "clearly been the victim of a lot of bad advice right from the beginning".[58] Accepting that any monetary claim could not go back decades, the concern as expressed in that letter was to address the position for the future, not the past. The court ultimately concurred and held that royalties were due to the claimant only after initiating his claim.

[A1.1.08] Blackburne J conceded that of all the issues in the dispute, this is the one that troubled him most. In appropriate circumstances, the court has power to dismiss a claim where, with the passage of time, it is no longer possible to have a fair trial of the issues.[59] Absence of key witnesses or documents, memory

---

56 [2008] EWCA Civ 287 at para 44.

57 David Richards J in his dissenting view to that of Mummery LJ and Sir Paul Kennedy on the issue of dismissing the claimant's otherwise successful claim to copyright on the grounds of long delay stated at para 139 that, "Where the defendants retain all past earnings and have suffered no detriment from Mr Fisher's delay, there is in my view no injustice if his interest in the copyright is now established for the future".

58 See para 15 of the judgment.

59 (Separate from the question whether, even if Fisher established his claim, he should be

loss or uncertainty as to facts or events are all considerations in a trial concerning inordinate delay which is potentially prejudicial and grossly unfair to a defendant.

[A1.1.09] The key issue affected by the delay is who composed the distinctive eight-bar melody of the organ solo. There were only two contenders, Fisher and Brooker. Although there were inevitably many matters which neither could remember, both seemed, in the court's view, well able to recall the broad course of events and, in particular, the roles each had played in the process of composition. The judge also opined that a matter as fundamental to the Work as knowing who it was that devised the distinctive and famous organ solo was scarcely likely to escape the memory of those who claim authorship.

Timespan of royalty claim

[A1.1.10] The court was not persuaded that Fisher had established any restitutionary right against the defendants in circumstances whereby he had "sat back and permitted the two societies to account to the defendants for royalties in respect of the musical copyright in the Work for nearly 40 years".[60] Furthermore, for so long as the claimant chose not to make and establish his claim, the defendants had no reason to think that they were not entitled to the payments they received from collection societies and Fisher must then be taken to have gratuitously licensed the exploitation of his copyright. Accordingly, on this issue, Blackburne J concluded:

> Given those circumstances there is, in my judgment, no injustice to Mr Fisher in the fact that the defendants have received all of the royalties prior to receiving the letters before action. The claim was issued on 31 May 2005. In my judgment, any right by Mr Fisher to share in the royalties only arose from that time.

[A1.1.11] Moreover, it follows from this case that it will oftentimes be the case that a recorded piece of music created through performance is sufficiently original over any antecedent musical work to attract copyright and, secondly, that piece of music will frequently be a work of joint authorship between some or all of the musicians.[61] The law on joint authorship has now been summarised in any event in *Martin v Kogan*.

---

denied any particular relief by reason of his excessive delay in bringing his claim, for example by reference to the defence of laches).

60 At para 94.

61 (Mr Justice) Richard Arnold, *Reflections on The Triumph of Music: Copyrights and Performers' Rights in Music* (2009), Oxford Intellectual Property Invited Speaker Seminar, p 12. Arnold also refers to scholarly analyses which reach similar conclusions: Lionel Bently, "Authorship of Popular Music in UK Copyright Law", (2009) 12(2) *Information, Communication & Society* 179 and Prof. Andreas Rahmatian, "The Concepts of 'Musical Work' and 'Originality' in UK Copyright Law – Sawkins v Hyperion as a Test Case", (2009) 40(5) *International Review of Intellectual Property and Competition Law* 560-591.

Hadley v Kemp[62]

[A1.2.01] In *Hadley* the claimants were the lead vocalist Tony Hadley, drummer John Keeble and guitarist/saxophonist/percussionist Steve Norman in the band Spandau Ballet. The first defendant Gary Kemp was the group's guitarist, keyboard player and backing singer. The other defendant was Gary Kemp's publishing company.[63] Gary Kemp had always been credited as the composer and lyricist of all the group's songs bar one. The principal dispute in the case centred on a purported oral agreement between Gary Kemp and the other members of the group to share publishing income from the songs. In the alternative to their contract claim, the plaintiffs claimed that they were the joint authors of the music for the songs on the band's first four albums.

[A1.2.02] For present purposes, the most significant claim was that of Steve Norman to be joint author of the song *True*. Norman's saxophone solo in *True* is 16 bars long, and it lasts 35 seconds, just under nine percent of the whole track. Park J said this was the most famous of Norman's saxophone solos, and described it "particularly attractive" and "particularly felicitous".[64] It was conceded to be memorable by the defendants' expert musicologist. The judge found as a fact that, in common with Norman's other saxophone solos, the notes which Norman played were not devised by Gary Kemp, but were improvised by Norman. Despite this, he held that Gary Kemp was the sole author of *True*.

[A1.2.03] The decision is problematic for a number of reasons and has been heavily criticised by a number of expert commentators. First, it fails to distinguish between the original songs created by Gary Kemp accompanying himself on the guitar or piano and the arrangements of the songs which were recorded by Spandau Ballet for commercial release. Indeed, the learned judge did not even use the word "arrangement" in the parts of his decision dealing with the plaintiffs' claims.[65]

[A1.2.04] Secondly, in determining the issue as to joint authorship, Mr Justice Park required that the putative joint author should have made a contribution which possessed "significant creative originality".[66] This, in the view of IP law specialist, Sir Richard David Arnold (former UK High Court justice and Court of Appeal lord justice since July 2019) in one of his papers cited in this chapter, conflates two distinct questions: first, whether the work the subject of the claim is original over any antecedent work so as to attract a fresh copyright; and secondly, who made a sufficient contribution to the work to rank as one of its authors.

---

62 [1998] EMLR 588.

63 The fifth member of the group, the bass guitarist Martin Kemp, was not a party to the litigation.

64 At p 650 of the law reports.

65 In assessing claims to co-authorship of musical works, the vital first step is for the court correctly to identify the work the subject of the claim to copyright and to distinguish it from any antecedent work.

66 At p 644.

[A1.2.05] Thirdly, in applying his criterion of "significant creative originality", Park J expressly discounted what he termed "significant performing originality", holding that this was the wrong kind of skill and labour to be protected by the copyright in a musical work. In this regard, the judge placed considerable weight on evidence given by the defendants' expert musicologist Guy Protheroe stating:

> I should perhaps make clear that, as I understand him, he does not dispute that the existence of a space for a saxophone improvisation may be an element in the work. His point, with which I concur, is that the particular improvisation which Mr Norman played and which featured on the master recording was not in itself a significant part of the musical work.

[A1.2.06] This led Park J to suggest *obiter* that another potential obstacle to Norman's claim was the requirement that the contribution of each joint author not be separate from that of the other or others:[67]

> … there is an obvious argument that a wholly improvised passage which Mr Norman supplied at a point where Mr Kemp left a space for him to supply it was separate from Mr Kemp's contribution to the song.

[A1.2.07] The judgment also contains a suggestion that an improvising soloist unconsciously reflects the basic melody of a song which appears to be an attempt to downgrade the soloist's skill and labour. It is not an accurate description of the art of improvisation, since it is conventional for a soloist consciously to improvise more or less closely upon the theme. Whether it is conscious or unconscious does not matter, however. What matters is the end result.

[A1.2.08] The upshot of Park J's analysis (and it is clear from his reasoning that the learned judge had no experience of the mechanics of music) is either that the sixteen bars of notes comprising the saxophone solo have no author at all or that their author was Gary Kemp. Both conclusions are irreconcilable with the judge's finding that the notes were improvised by Norman.

Beckingham v Hodgens

[A1.3.01] In *Beckingham v Hodgens*[68] the claimant (professionally known as Bobby Valentino) was a violinist and a session musician. The first defendant (Robert Hodgens) was the guitarist and leader of the band The Bluebells. The dispute concerned the authorship of the song *Young at Heart* and the issue of liability for infringement of copyright in the music of a version of the song by The Bluebells. In the action he claimed that he not merely performed but wrote the violin part which features in the introduction to the record, consisting of four bars (repeated three times during the song), without any significant input from anyone else; and that his contribution in writing the violin part was such

---

[67] At p 650.

[68] [2002] EWHC 2143 (ChD), [2002] EMLR 45.

as to render him a joint author of the music (referred to as "the Work" in the judgment) and hence a joint owner of the copyright therein. That assertion was denied by Hodgens, who claimed to have written all the music (including the violin part) himself. Hodgens alleged that at the recording session Valentino merely followed instructions in relation to the violin part given by him. The court (Mr Christopher Floyd QC sitting as a deputy High Court judge) found in favour of Valentino on this issue and upheld his copyright claim.

[A1.3.02] The proceedings also included a claim grounded on estoppel (previously summarised in the words of Lord Justice Oliver as whether it would be unconscionable for a party to be permitted to deny that which, knowingly, or unknowingly, he has allowed or encouraged another to assume to his detriment).[69] Following its release in mid-1984, The Bluebells' version of the song (incorporating the disputed violin part), achieved a degree of commercial success, reaching number eight in the charts. At that time, Valentino made no claim to be a joint author of the music. Indeed, his own evidence was that he had informed Hodgens in around 1984 that he had taken advice as to whether he should make such a claim but had decided not to do so. In the first period of the song's success, from 1984, Valentino certainly knowingly permitted The Bluebells to assume that he would make no claim to a share in the royalty income they were receiving from exploitation of the Work.[70]

[A1.3.03] However in 1986 the Bluebells disbanded and in 1993 The Bluebells' version of the song was (adventitiously so far as the parties were concerned) used as backing in a Volkswagen commercial. This caused a substantial resurgence in its popularity, as a result of which it reappeared in the charts and was at number one for a number of weeks. Its success was such that the group reformed for the purpose of performing it on a number of occasions on *Top of the Pops*. Following this resurgence of popularity, Valentino, for the first time, claimed a share of future royalties on the basis that he was a joint author of the music. His evidence was that he made this claim in March 1993; Hodgens' evidence was that he did not do so until November 1997 at the earliest and that in any event Valentino was estopped on grounds of unconscionability from revoking the licence.

[A1.3.04] Returning to the copyright issues, the song was initially written by Robert Hodgens with his then girlfriend Siobhan Fahey for the group Bananarama and recorded by them. Hodgens wrote the music, and he and Fahey co-wrote the lyrics. It was originally performed in a northern soul style.

---

69 *Taylor's Fashions Ltd v Liverpool Victoria Trustees* [1982] 1 QB 133 at 151H-152A.

70 This caused the deputy High Court judge to comment:

> "If matters had rested there, and if it were necessary to do so, I would have no hesitation in holding that any attempt by Mr Valentino to change his position in relation to those royalties, brought after the passage of so many years, would be unconscionable. However the Claimant recognises that he has no such claim, having impliedly licensed all such use. Any claim to such royalty income would in any event now be statute barred" (at para 64 of his judgment).

Subsequently it was covered by The Bluebells in a country style. Valentino was hired to play violin on the recording. The deputy High Court judge found that Hodgens gave Valentino an idea of the sort of thing he wanted by indicating the country style, the underlying chords and the rhythm, but held, "That does not, however, mean that Mr Hodgens was the author of the violin part".[71]

[A1.3.05] Instead, the judge found that Valentino had created the violin part by reversing a country lick used elsewhere in the song and drawing on the introduction to a song he had composed previously. It was common ground in that case that The Bluebells' version of *Young at Heart* was an original music work compared to the Bananarama version. In considering whether Bobby Valentino was a joint author of The Bluebells' version, the court held that there were three requirements which had to be met under s 11(3) of the 1956 Act (the relevant copyright Act applying at the time of composition), namely, there must be collaboration in the creation of the work, there must be a contribution from each joint author, and the contribution must not be 'separate'. He went on to find that each of these requirements was satisfied. So far as the second requirement was concerned, he found that the violin part made a significant and original contribution of the right kind of skill and labour to The Bluebells' version. As to the third, he said:

> I do not believe that a contribution to the arrangement of a song of the kind I am concerned with in this case is 'separate' in the sense in which that word is used in the section. The added part is heavily dependent on what is there already. Stripped of the voices and other instruments, the violin part would sound odd, and lose meaning. The final musical expression—what the audience will hear—is a joint one.

Temporal extent of royalties claim

[A1.3.06] The court order thus declared that Valentino is a joint author of the Work and joint owner (to the extent of 50 percent) of the copyright therein; that in 1984 he had gratuitously licensed Hodgens to exploit the copyright in the Work but that he was entitled to, and did, revoke that licence in March 1993; and that he was entitled to claim damages in respect of, or an account of profits arising from, any infringement of his copyright in the Work on or after 18 October 1993.

Estoppel

[A1.3.07] Thus, by contrast with *Godfrey* (and the ruling by Park J on delay in *Hadley*), Mr Floyd QC sitting as deputy judge held that Valentino was not estopped from revoking the gratuitous licence he had impliedly granted to exploit the work. The Court of Appeal subsequently refused Hodgens permission

---

[71] At para 38.

to appeal against the judge's findings of fact with regard to joint authorship.[72] Permission was granted however to challenge the lower court's conclusion with regard to estoppel, but the appeal was dismissed. The court, *per* Lord Justice Parker, turning to the seven specific factors[73] on which counsel sought to rely as raising an estoppel against Valentino, stated[74] it had no hesitation in upholding the High Court's decision on the estoppel issue and would therefore dismiss the appeal.

Intention as to joint authorship irrelevant

[A1.3.08] The Court of Appeal then addressed a submission made by counsel for Hodgens to the effect that the subsection imposed a further requirement, the requirement of an intention as to joint authorship, as the deputy judge put it (in para 47 of the judgment), "a joint intention to create a joint work". The judge rejected this contention and counsel therefore sought permission to appeal against that holding.

[A1.3.09] In support, counsel relied principally on a decision of Mr Justice Cohen in the Supreme Court of British Columbia in *Darryl Neudorf v Network Expressions*[75] concerning the well-known singer Sarah McLachlan. After an extensive review of authorities in Canada, the US and England, Cohen J said at pp 962-3:

> In the result I find that the test for joint authorship that should be applied to the facts in the instant case is as follows:
> i) Did the plaintiff contribute significant original expression to the songs? If yes,
> ii) Did each of the plaintiff and Ms McLachlan intend that their contributions be merged into a unitary whole? If yes,
> iii) Did each of the plaintiff and Ms McLachlan intend the other to be a joint author of the song?

[A1.3.10] The deputy judge failed to see any basis in the English cases, or in the statutory definition which he was bound to apply, for the importation of this extra requirement of common intention as to joint authorship. Plainly, for there

---

72 *Beckingham v Hodgens* [2002] EWCA Civ 1901 and *Hodgens v Beckingham* [2003] EWCA Civ 143.

73 Such as the delay in making the claim (around nine years if the claim was first made in March 1993; almost fourteen years if it was first made in November 1997), the terms of the representations made by Valentino in around 1984 to the effect that he would not make such a claim, the effect of the claim on Hodgens' professional reputation, the opportunity for excising the violin part from the recording had Valentino asserted a claim to joint authorship prior to the release of the recording in mid-1984, and the trial judge's refusal to allow Hodgens to lead evidence to the effect that he had spent the royalties which he had received pre-1993 in reliance on Valentino's representations that he would not be making any claim to them.

74 [2003] EWCA Civ 143, para 48.

75 [1999] RPC 935.

to be a collaboration at all, the parties must have a common design to produce the work. Those authors who reach the threshold of a significant and original contribution in furtherance of that common design should then, in the view of Mr Floyd QC, be entitled to call themselves a co-author. Any other test, he said, introduces undesirable problems of proof for which he could see no basis in the relevant copyright Act.

[A1.3.11] The Court of Appeal agreed there was nothing in the express wording of s 11(3) of the relevant statute which warranted the imposition of such a requirement (this was also borne out in *Martin*). The only requirements for a work of joint authorship expressed in s 11(3) were that the authors should have collaborated and that their contributions should not be separate. The court went on to cite Keating J in the 1871 case *Levy v Rutley* (dealing with a play rather than a song)[76] in support for reaching this conclusion:

> I fail to discover any evidence that there was any co-operation of the two in the design of this piece [a play], or in its execution, or in any improvements either in the plot or the general structure…If the plaintiff and the author had agreed together to rearrange the plot, and so to produce a more attractive piece out of the original materials, possibly that might have made them joint authors of the whole. So, if two persons undertake jointly to write a play, agreeing in the general outline and design, and sharing the labour of working it out, each would be contributing to the whole production, and they might be said to be joint authors of it. But, to constitute joint authorship, there must be a common design. Nothing of the sort appears here. The plaintiff made mere additions to a complete piece, which did not in themselves amount to a dramatic piece, but were intended only to make the play more attractive to the audience.

[A1.3.12] In *Levy*, perhaps the earliest recorded case on joint authorship, Byles J found joint authorship could exist (it was not held to exist in the case before him)[77] even if one person had contributed only a very small amount of work to the execution as long as there was prosecution of a preconcerted joint design. Keating J concurred with this view that although it may not be necessary that each should contribute the same amount of labour, there must be a joint labouring in furtherance of a common design.

[A1.3.13] Moreover, reverting to the instant *Beckingham v Hodgens* judgment, the trial court (as affirmed on appeal) held that The Bluebells' version was created by a collaboration between Hodgens and Valentino in furtherance of a common design. Whilst accepting that it was ultimately a question of fact and degree for the court, both sides called expert evidence on the question of whether the violin part made a significant and original contribution to The Bluebells' version of *Young at Heart*. Both experts considered the violin riff memorable and catchy.

---

[76] (1871) LR 6 CP 523.

[77] As the defendant wrote the play and the plaintiff subsequently added a scene and made some minor alterations and additions – and hence the whole play was not originally co-authored by them jointly in different portions.

Mr Chandler, a musicologist and copyright consultant called by the claimant, viewed the violin part as more memorable than anything else in the song. Mr Protheroe, the expert called by the defence, was inclined to accord the chorus rather more importance, yet nevertheless described the violin part as a reasonably striking feature of the work. In the end the dispute between them came down to whether the violin part made its contribution largely or wholly because of its prominence at the beginning of the work.

Sawkins v Hyperion[78] *and the import for electronic music*

[A1.4.01] It can now be seen from the subsequent decision of the Court of Appeal in *Sawkins v Hyperion* that, if anything, Blackburne J in *Godfrey* understated how little is required by way of changes to an antecedent musical work in order for the altered work to be original so as to attract a fresh copyright.

[A1.4.02] Here the Court of Appeal was directly confronted with the question of what is music in the context of an issue as to whether performing editions of 17th century French baroque music were original musical works and thus protected by copyright. In determining whether the editions were original, an important issue was whether aspects such as the figuring of the bass, ornamentation and performance directions were part of the musical work, since most of the plaintiff's editorial interventions concerned those aspects. Mummery LJ answered this question in the affirmative:

> But the fixation in the written score or on a record is not in itself the music in which copyright subsists. There is no reason why, for example, a recording of a person's spontaneous singing, whistling or humming or of improvisations of sounds by a group of people with or without musical instruments should not be regarded as 'music' for copyright purposes.
>
> …
>
> In principle, there is no reason for regarding the actual notes of music as the only matter covered by musical copyright, any more than, in the case of a dramatic work, only the words to be spoken by the actors are covered by dramatic copyright...It is wrong in principle to single out the notes as uniquely significant for copyright purposes and to proceed to deny copyright to the other elements that make some contribution to the sound of the music when performed, such as performing indications, tempo and performance practice indicators, if they are the product of a person's effort, skill and time…

[A1.4.03] Although *Sawkins* concerned written scores for musical performance, Mummery LJ's reasoning makes it clear that the position is the same with regard to electronically recorded music. It follows that all aspects of the music which affect the recorded sounds form part of the musical work contained in the recording.

---

[78] [2005] EWCA Civ 565, [2005] 1 WLR 3281.

***Bamgboye v Reed*[79]**

[A1.5.01] In *Brighton v Jones*,[80] Park J noted that a finding of joint authorship did not mean (contrary to his earlier view) that the joint author was bound to be an equal owner of the copyright. A joint author needed to have made a significant contribution to the creation of the work though his contribution did not need to be equal in magnitude to the contribution of the other joint author(s).[81] Hazel Williamson QC sitting as a deputy High Court judge in *Bamgboye* held that the nature and extent of the claimant's contribution as a joint author entitled him to a one third share in the copyright.[82]

[A1.5.02] Bamgboye in his proceedings laid claim to a share in the copyright in respect of the original musical work dance track *Bouncing Flow*, the copyright in respect of a sound recording and to his performer rights. Reed claimed he produced the music for the song and contended that as far as Bamgboye had any input, this was entirely at his direction, assisting him only as a sound engineer – in other words, merely helping him to record his own ideas. He also denied that the plaintiff had any rights in the sound recording of the output that was eventually made and that he had any performer's rights in that regard. The defendant was thus alleging that he himself carried out all the performing.

[A1.5.03] The plaintiff gave evidence that his input commenced when Reed had a partial drum pattern already laid on an eight-bar loop. From this point he helped by adding further drums and crash cymbal effects, such that, in his view, he was creator of half the drum element in the piece, although he accepted that Reed added snare patterns and had created what was already on the tape. Bamgboye also claimed it was he who, in effect, composed the eight measures which provided the bassline, a subsidiary bassline, and which bars were further recorded with string parts and became, with a slight variation, the melody of the piece. Moreover, he asserted having performed approximately 50 percent contribution to the creation of the drum part; the creation of the leading bassline on the synthesizer and the whole of the synthesized string section which constitutes the melody.

[A1.5.04] Referring to the defendant's keyboard abilities, the judge stated in rejecting his arguments on the issue, that he did not have the musical training to effect certain parts of the composition.[83] The court was therefore wholly satisfied

---

79 [2002] EWHC 2922 (QB), [2004] EMLR 5.

80 [2004] EWHC 1157(ChD).

81 The claimant director was found not to have been a joint author of a play with the playwright. Aside from five reasons enumerated by the judge, a contract was in existence in any event which provided that the defendant writer owned the copyright to the play.

82 Subsequently, as noted earlier, Blackburne J held in *Fisher* that the claimant was entitled to a 40 percent share in the musical copyright of *A Whiter Shade of Pale*, an assessment which went unchallenged on appeal. It may therefore be taken to be settled that joint authors are only entitled to such share in the copyright as their contribution merits.

83 She noted, "I am not at all convinced that he could ever have got to the rather more

that the subsidiary melodic bass lines, whether in the bass or in the string part were, in fact, played in by the claimant. The court also accepted his evidence that this musical idea is an idea that came from him, that he played it and volunteered it, and that the defendant approved of same and it therefore remained on the mix as an enhancement. The court rejected the defence argument which suggested Reed was humming a basic tune to Bamgboye who was therefore acting as no more than an engineering scribe in recording it. Instead, the judge favoured evidence that the defendant found the claimant useful and helpful because of his ideas, and these ideas were not confined merely to engineering because Bamgboye was at times, in his enthusiasm, volunteering original ideas which Reed was then able to creatively incorporate into the composition. Consequently, the judge was satisfied "they were indeed, on occasions, working together".

[A1.5.05] Accordingly, the court held that Bamgboye did contribute the melody, added significantly to the drum pattern and crashes, contributed effects and had significant creative input into the making of the musical piece that was recorded as *Bouncing Flow*. However, the learned judge did not quantify this creative input as great as the 50 percent which was claimed in the proceedings.

[A1.5.06] In connection with the plaintiff's claim to rights in the sound recording, the judge was of the view that no such right existed. The defendant was clearly the producer and thus legal owner (or 'author' in statutory parlance) of the sound recording, being the person by whom the arrangements necessary for the making of the sound recording (or film, as applicable) are undertaken.

[A1.5.07] Finally, in relation to the plaintiff's claims to assert performer's rights in respect of the sound recording, the court was satisfied that Bamgboye played the bass melody and the "busy bass" and the "octave parts on the keyboard into the computer" and this, in the view of the court, consisted of a performance which bestowed on the claimant the attendant statutory rights (in respect of which public performance royalties would accrue).

---

complicated — I think it is called the "busy base" — part of the composition. I do not find it credible either, that he would have taken the time to doggedly amend notes on the computer to produce the subtly different versions of the notes, i.e. the lengths of the notes, that one sees on the printout of recording produced by the Logic Audio files. To amend their length to such a minute degree as is evidenced from what is actually recorded on the tape would have been extraordinarily pedantic and tedious. I also rather doubt if he could have achieved the arpeggio line on his own, as it involves a very quick movement of intervals through various notes. I find that this evidence suggests clearly that these items were played in by human hand, and by somebody with at least a degree of formal musical training to enable them to do so. That can only have been Mr Bamgboye".

Appendix 2

Further case law on artist/ label disputes

George Michael

[A2.1.01] Innervision and its 1982 contract with Wham! were acquired by Sony Music Entertainment in 1987. Following Wham!'s success and subsequent break-up, Michael renegotiated a new eight-album deal with Sony as a solo artist in 1988. This deal was further renegotiated in 1990 to reflect Michael's superstar status, achieving terms comparable to similarly high-grossing artists. *Listen Without Prejudice* represented a new direction for the artist, downplaying the sex symbol status he had cultivated with Wham! in favour of a more reserved identity as a serious-minded musician. He decided not to place his image on the album cover and declined to appear in promotional videos.

[A2.1.02] Michael alleged that Sony under-promoted his new album in response to these decisions, he further alleged that the contract restricted him from negotiating with a new label and prevented him from managing his professional image as he saw fit. Moreover, the singer-songwriter, even though he had renegotiated his deal in 1990, felt increasingly despondent with his temporally long-reaching and onerous contract which he deemed exploitative and sought to have declared invalid. Michael strongly objected to the terms by which Sony possessed ultimate power of approval, being contractually poised to reject any material of which it did not approve and restrain him from recording for any other label.

[A2.1.03] It was common practice in the recording industry to sign many artists on the rise like Wham!, banking that long-term profits from the few commercial successes would absorb the losses from promoting the remainder. A decision holding Michael's contract unenforceable could have dramatically reduced the expected return on investment for signing and promoting an emerging artist, leading to label fears that the practice would end. Michael argued that the structure of the industry concentrated power in too few hands, and that these companies competed by selling music, but not in the terms offered to new artists. This he contended led to an imbalance of power, whereby the artist was contractually obligated to produce a set number of albums of acceptable quality and cede copyright to the label, but the label did not bear a reciprocal obligation to market and promote the product, in accordance with the artist's wishes or otherwise.

[A2.1.04] The artist was advanced a sum of one million pounds in February

1992 under the terms of the 1990 contract; this amount was returned to Sony in August of the same year in preparation for filing suit in October. The star issued proceedings in 1992, and Justice Jonathan Parker ruled on the matter on 1 June 1994. The plaintiff's claims were wholly rejected. Parker J held that Michael's contracts were reasonable and fair, especially in consideration of his access to expert legal advice, several renegotiations, and terms comparable to the industry standard for an artist of his commercial success.

[A2.1.05] Leaving aside the origin of the new eight-album deal with Sony as a solo artist in the 1988 agreement, its provisions were justifiable: the label had a legitimate and enforceable recoupment interest in an exclusive contract of some duration. Restraint of trade under Art 85 of the Treaty of Rome which concerned trade between Member States accordingly was held not to apply. Further, the agreement did not have the requisite effect on trade in the context of the market for pop records and the requisite anti-competitive effect was not established. Lastly, by activating its terms in requesting an advance in 1992, the singer affirmed the 1988 agreement.

[A2.1.06] As regards determining whether the contract satisfied the test in *Nordenfelt v Maxim Nordenfelt Guns and Ammunition Co Ltd,*[84] which involved reasonableness as between the parties and reasonableness in the public interest, the court was of the view that there was a clear public interest in upholding genuine and proper compromises and Mr Michael was seeking to have a central part of the compromise declared unenforceable. In relation to Sony's acquiescence agreement which was accepted, Parker J was of the belief it would be unfair to Sony and unconscionable to allow Michael several years later to assert that the 1988 agreement was unenforceable.

[A2.1.07] George Michael parted with the company in 1995, signing with DreamWorks for North America and with Virgin for elsewhere. Sources close to the negotiations at the time said Sony was to receive a cash sum of $30-40 million as a payment to release the star. This was to be paid by DreamWorks and Virgin against their earnings from the release of subsequent albums.[85] To end with a bizarre turn, the artist ultimately re-signed with Sony in 2003, albeit in circumstances whereby the case continued to trouble him.

The Dixie Chicks

[A2.2.01] The Dixie Chicks' dispute with Sony escalated in July 2001 after the trio sent a letter notifying the Japanese corporation that the country act would no longer record for it. Sony responded with a lawsuit alleging it was owed

---

84 (1894) AC 535.

85 Billboard.com, *George Michael has signed a new worldwide recording deal with the U.K. arm of Sony Music, the company he left in the '90s after a drawn-out court battle* (2003). Available at: https://www.billboard.com/articles/news/68127/george-michael-re-signs-with-sony [Accessed 13 July 2021].

damages for five undelivered albums, the value of which the company estimated at more than $100 million.

[A2.2.02] The band, having reportedly sold nearly 20 million albums, generating more than $175 million in revenue for the label in four years, filed a $4.1 million countersuit against Sony Music Entertainment in August 2001 in response to its breach of contract complaint.[86] The proceedings alleged breach of the group's exclusive recording agreement, fraud, breach of fiduciary duty and violation of the federal Racketeer Influenced and Corrupt Organization Act, claiming to the tune of four million dollars that the label had withheld such sums by *inter alia* underreporting sales figures/royalties and overcharging for company services. Sony officials dismissed the Dixie Chicks' contentions as a "sham" attempt to resile from the group's recording contract.

[A2.2.03] At its core, the performers' suit called into question the "unconscionable" terms that young artists are required to accept when signing a standard industry recording agreement. Like most entry-level artists, the band had no bargaining power when its first contract was drafted, the suit claimed, allowing Sony to treat its standard offer as non-negotiable. Within months, the singers had joined the burgeoning artists' rights movement,[87] lobbying legislators in Sacramento to evaluate recording contracts and curb industry accounting practices designed to prejudice the rights of fledgling artists. The group also appeared at a concert benefit to raise funds for the Recording Artists Coalition, a nascent trade group comprising 100 top-selling acts seeking reforms in the music business. Behind the scenes, representatives for the Dixie Chicks met with rival EMI Group and Bertelsmann Music Group to shop for a new deal based on a new model involving smaller advances, larger backend royalties, fewer deductions and more transparent accounting provisions. Unable to reach agreement with any of Sony's competitors, less than ten months after accusing Sony of "systematic thievery", the Dixie Chicks signed a lucrative new pact with the company.[88]

Courtney Love and Vivendi Universal

[A2.3.01] The judge in a breach of contract case in 2001, involving rock star Courtney Love's alternative rock band (Hole) and Vivendi Universal, requested

---

86 Andrew Dansby, *Dixie Chicks Sue Sony–Band says label owes them millions in royalties* (2001), rollingstone.com. Available at: https://www.rollingstone.com/music/music-news/dixie-chicks-sue-sony-236628/ [Accessed 8 August 2020].

87 Among those who threatened legal action against their lables were Don Henley, Luther Vandross and Beck: Chuck Philips, *Dixie Chicks, Sony End Feud With a New Deal* (2002), latimes.com. Available at: https://www.latimes.com/archives/la-xpm-2002-jun-17-fi-dixie17-story.html [Accessed 8 August 2020].

88 *supra* at fn 86. The Dixie Chicks' management team, the Firm, forged a new deal with an estimated $20 million signing advance. The pact required that the musicians reimburse Sony for about $15 million from record sales before collecting royalties. Sony reportedly agreed to significantly boost the Nashville trio's royalty rate to some twenty percent.

that the parties resolve the matter[89] out of court. After the rockstar filed her complaint to rescind the band's contract, the claimant publicly condemned what she described as the "unconscionable and unlawful" business and accounting practices of the major record labels. The suit gave impetus to a movement by other stars to demand fairer contracts, health benefits and other reforms.

[A2.3.02] Settlement was reached that released Love from her recording contract and affirmed her ownership of several unreleased recordings by Hole. As part of the compromise agreement, the artist reportedly granted permission to Universal to release additional records by Nirvana, the seminal grunge rock band led by her late husband Kurt Cobain, including a previously unreleased song. Universal was also to pay an estimated $12-million advance to be split among Love and the two surviving members of Nirvana.[90]

JoJo and Blackground Records

[A2.4.01] In 2014 popstar JoJo was freed from the shackles of her record deal after a claim she instituted in the New York State Supreme Court[91] in July 2013 relating to a contract she signed when only a minor at the age of 12 to which she was unwillingly bound for almost seven years. The decade-long battle centred on her restrictive contract with Blackground Records. Though she prepared extensively to release her new album, producing multiple recordings of many songs and participating in countless promotional photo shoots, the artist was ultimately unable to release new music to the general public. After Blackground Records lost its distribution at Interscope, the record company was unable to distribute any of her music; however, the contract's exclusivity clause held her hostage. Years of litigation later, the court ruled in JoJo's favour allowing her to be released from the agreement.[92] In spite of her victory, considerable damage was occasioned to her career as her name had slowly waned from the popular music scene.

---

89 Love's dispute with Universal erupted in December 1999 when she notified it that she would no longer record for the company because it had improperly acquired her contract from another label. Universal sued Love in January 2000, demanding compensation for five undelivered albums. Love countersued in February 2001, claiming that the record industry's long-term contracts violate California's so-called seven-year statute whereby entertainers cannot be tied to any company for more than seven years.

90 Jeff Leeds (with contribution from Geoff Boucher), *Courtney Love Settles Suit Against Vivendi Universal* (2002), latimes.com. Available at: https://www.latimes.com/archives/la-xpm-2002-oct-01-fi-courtney1-story.html [Accessed 9 August 2020].

91 Unusually, despite its misleading name, this is a trial court and not the highest court in the state.

92 By the label's claiming that the recording contract remained in full force and effect, the artist argued that she suffered irreparable damage to her professional career, forfeiting other business opportunities so long as she remained contracted to Blackbird and its imprint Da Family. These might include touring, merchandise, endorsements, the ability to make connections in the industry and to generate favourable publicity.

Chapter 23

Music Publishing, Master Recordings, Royalties, Collection Societies & Music Streaming

INTRODUCTION: THE INNATE COMPLEXITY OF MUSIC RIGHTS

[23.1.01] Music publishing and music rights management is complex simply because there are myriad moving parts. A creator might be a self-producing, self-releasing artist and thus entitled to all income from publishing[1] and master recording (or 'phonogram') uses but may on the other hand be signed to both a record label and a music publisher (or to a label which also has a publishing arm).[2] Otherwise, recording artists may be signed only to a publisher and not a label, or signed to a label but not a publisher. Even the simplest scenario of a self-producing writer can quickly become complicated in terms of rights ownership and works administration if that writer enters into legal agreements with film producers, music libraries, or media companies in search of synchronisation licence music material for their clients for product or service branding purposes.

[23.1.02] The accounting for, distribution and receipt of writer share, publisher share and sound recording income[3] and the timing of such income receipts will depend on an array of factors (transparency around exploitation of works, as helped to some extent by the 2019 Copyright Directive, is discussed in Chapter 11 as is potential contract adjustment and recapturing of rights).[4] There is copyright ownership in the songs (lyrics and melody, there may also be an arrangement component to such ownership) versus the sound recording and the manner in which income generated from each will be divided between all relevant parties. Performers, in addition, wield IP rights in the way of performer

---

1 Unless, say, in contract with a music library by way of exclusive licence and/or non-exclusive licences with other libraries, music distributors or publishers.

2 A recent survey of Association of Independent Music (UK) members found that 89 percent of independent record labels reported having business interests beyond just recordings, with 81 percent declaring interests in publishing (as well as 46 percent being involved in artist management and 35 percent being creators themselves).

3 From sale/download/streaming and sound recording public performance royalties.

4 The Directive did not mandate that contract adjustment and licence revocation be unwaivable and hence artists likely will be requested in many cases to waive these rights, thus undermining the spirit of the Directive.

neighbouring rights. Performer income from public performance royalties is affected by whether a singer/performer is a featured or non-featured artist or musician on a relevant track (and, due to the current legislative regime, session musicians receive nothing from music streaming platforms).

[23.1.03] Performance income from public performance royalties is affected by whether a singer/performer is a featured or non-featured artist or musician on a relevant track. Record royalties from CD sales or downloads will be governed by a contract.[5] If there is a band, income received will further be affected by the band's agreement *inter se*. Extent of publishing income will depend on whether the material has been licensed to a publisher to handle the administration of rights.

[23.1.04] Master use licences (for uses of sound recordings say in a film or stage musical)[6] and synchronisation licenses (for uses of compositions) add further layers of complexity as do agreements with music libraries or collection management organisations ('CMOs') for production and commercial music. If there are co-writers to a song, all such writers must clear the rights for the given use for synchronisation licence purposes. The administration of rights is further affected by what rights have been granted (if any) in relation to a CMO's contractual entitlement to enter such deals on behalf of members. Mechanical royalties and the payment thereof, for instance, by record labels to publishers adds more convolution.

[23.1.05] And these are just some issues in the rights management and income discussion. Others include merchandising, live, live-stream and tour performance income (usually matters for a band/artist manager and record label rather than a publisher), and licensing of rights for stageshows and theatrical productions. "Covering" a well-known music artist's material brings additional considerations to the fore.[7] Mechanical royalties will need to be paid to the original writers who will be in receipt too of public performance income from performances by the cover artist. The cover artists will receive only performer royalties from the cover version sound recording[8] and a share of CD or online sales (record royalties) if signed with a label.

---

5 Income from music streaming, payable by platforms, will be discussed in the end section.

6 As well as the record label or producer that owns the master, the performers on the recording may potentially share in the master use fee too depending on the terms of their contract and will in any event receive public performance royalties from exploitation of the sound recording to which they have contributed.

7 Conversely, a well-known artist may cover a less well-known writer's material.

8 If covering original music, a music producer or label will record a new sound recording version to which the cover artist will perform. Copyright in that version will vest wholly in that producer or label. There is no copyright infringement as a sound recording, unlike a song, need not be an original work – see s 17(2) of the Copyright and Related Rights Act 2000 whereby copyright can vest in (new) sound recordings, and sound recordings unlike musical works are not prefaced with the word "original". The rationale is that the sound recording is simply a recording of an original composition written by a songwriter. While sound recordings are of course protected by copyright, re-recording a pre-existing

COPYRIGHT AS A FORM OF PROPERTY

[23.2.01] In relation to dealing with copyright as a form of property in Ireland, the Copyright and Related Rights Act 2000 ('the 2000 Act') first provides[9] that the copyright in a work is transmissible by assignment, by testamentary disposition or by operation of law, as personal or moveable property. Accordingly, it can be bought and sold. Secondly, where writers, performers and individual sound recording owners[10] are deceased, their estates will instead receive the royalties or other income due such as deriving from synchronisation and master use licence agreements. Thirdly, a transmission of the copyright in a work by assignment may be partial, so as to apply to one or more but not all of the acts the copyright owner has the right to undertake or authorise, and to part but not the whole of the period for which the copyright in the work is to subsist (s 120(s) of the 2000 Act).[11]

[23.2.02] Hence, assignment can be partial with restrictions attaching in the subject agreement. This is frequently the position in respect of composer contracts for music usage in an audiovisual production and particularly where the music creators are renowned, well-seasoned practitioners with a working knowledge of rights administration who wish to bolster their contractual position.

[23.2.03] Moreover, there are wider music law issues, more in the vein of the economics of rights control and asset management, for consideration beyond the summary of music publishing in this chapter. Whether aware or not, audiovisual production companies, if through a custom and practice of securing full assignment of rights where possible, can trigger far-reaching consequences for artists, composers, performers and their own balance sheet. From a commercial perspective, successful film and television production companies will manage and exploit their assets effectively. A broad understanding of the music industry as a whole can serve to achieve this objective when contracting for soundtrack and score content and planning holistically for the production company's future. This is especially true when large sums are being expended on commissioning and recording new music.

[23.2.04] Another more global issue film producers now face is the related matter of contract adjustment and licence revocation provisions in the 2019 EU Directive on Copyright in the Digital Single Market discussed in Chapter 11 as well as accounting and transparency obligations which can be onerous and in some cases disproportionately time-consuming.

---

recording of a song (in other words recording a new version sound recording) does not constitute copyright infringement.

9 s 120.

10 Being 'natural persons' as distinct from a corporate entity.

11 s 293 of the 2000 Act refers to partial assignment (or by testamentary disposition) of performers' property rights.

MUSIC PUBLISHING

[23.3.01] The broad bundle of rights that are associated with a musical copyright are known as publishing rights. These rights are not defined by statute but rather are terms recognised in the music industry. Music publishing relates to varying streams of income derived by songwriters, composers and publishers from music compositions (described in legislation and court decisions as "musical works").

[23.3.02] Royalties in the main will be collected on behalf of artists by a CMO such as the Irish Music Rights Organisation ('IMRO'), MCPS,[12] PRS for Music in the UK,[13] or BMI or ASCAP in the US.[14] They can also be collected by digital music aggregators[15] such as Tunecore which upload artist material to download and streaming platforms such as iTunes, Amazon, Spotify or market leader YouTube.[16] Other players in the collections market include Kobalt Music Group which is an independent rights management and music publishing company.[17]

Income streams

[23.3.03] Royalties result in payments to rightsholders for radio airplay, use of music in retail outlets, webcasting, radio advertisements and radio productions, as well as music videos broadcast on television or other media. More substantial

---

12 The Mechanical Copyright Protection Society in Ireland. MCPS represents thousands of (domestic and international) composers and publishers of music. Through its reciprocal agreements with other collecting organisations around the world, it also represents the interests of music copyright owners in other countries. MCPS licenses companies and individuals who record musical works and collects and distributes the royalties payable under those licences. MCPS Ireland is a branch office that only administers mechanical activities in Ireland and does not deal with international collections. All international royalties will flow from MCPS head office in London and are paid directly to members. Thus, for member writers and publishers wishing to avail of international collection of mechanical royalties, they need (through MCPS Ireland) to register with MCPS in the UK (though they can register with IMRO for international collection of public performance royalties – they need not register with PRS in the UK unless they elect to do so).

13 PRS (Performing Right Society) is made up of two separate collecting societies, PRS and MCPS, which operate together. PRS collects and distributes royalties for musical works that have been performed or played, while MCPS collects and distributes royalties for musical works that have been reproduced or copied.

14 In the US, mechanical royalties are collected by the Mechanical Licensing Collective (MLC) as founded in 2018 and the Harry Fox Agency (HFA). Sound recording royalties for online uses are collected by SoundExchange.

15 The artist retains copyright and the aggregators charge a set-up fee and a percentage, say around 15 percent, by way of commission from royalties collected for the artist and a percentage of synchronisation fees if artists have mandated the aggregator to negotiate licences on their behalf.

16 Data from the Recording Industry Association of America shows that YouTube commands at least a 51 percent global market share in terms of streams, more than Spotify, Apple, Tidal, Deezer and Napster combined.

17 On the sound recording end, as distinct from the music publishing/compositional side of music rights, Peermusic is a global independent leader in neighbouring rights offering worldwide collections for both recording rights owners and artist performers (featured and non-featured).

public performance royalties and income will also accrue for use of music through television broadcasting, video gaming, and "grand" rights[18] relating to use of music in theatrical settings (see Chapter 19). Other forms of income are generated from sheet music and printed lyrics,[19] use of music for ringtone purposes, jukeboxes and website background music. It is noteworthy that per-stream or play rates by YouTube and Spotify are a small fraction of one cent and this negligible streaming income discussion is taken up at the end of the chapter.

[23.3.04] Fees for synchronisation licences whereby music is used in a film, television shows, online adverts, television and radio commercials, videogames, fashion show productions and major sporting events (if synchronised with visuals) can also be negotiated between music users and rightsholders by CMOs where the CMO has been mandated to so negotiate. Otherwise, songwriters themselves (if self-published/self-releasing) or their publisher will contract directly with the party seeking to use the subject music material as in the case where the user requires for example to change the arrangement or lyrics (as this affects moral rights, CMOs are not mandated by rightsholders in this connection).

[23.3.05] Music publishing stands entirely aside from sound recordings (though some record labels will also of course have a publishing division). Public performance royalties to sound recording owners from the public playing of those 'masters' flow to labels or music producers[20] through a collection system administered by CMOs (e.g. PPL in the UK, PPI in Ireland) which stand wholly separate to the publishing rights CMOs (e.g. IMRO in Ireland, BMI in the US).

---

18 Grand or dramatic rights refer to the use of a song in a dramatic context (whether or not the song is originally written for a dramatic musical production). This expression is generally understood to refer to performances of dramatico-musical works (an opera, an operetta, musical play, revue or pantomime, insofar as it consists of words and music written expressly therefor) and ballets. Grand rights are often withheld from grants of rights to the music publisher and are controlled directly by authors or their representatives. The royalties derived from the exploitation of grand rights are typically in the form of a percentage of gross weekly box-office receipts or a flat per performance fee.

19 See para [23.3.06].

20 Though legislatively-guaranteed 'equitable remuneration' also accrues to performers, see Chapter 10B, where performances are exploited in sound recordings. PPI collects equitable remuneration for performers when their recorded music is broadcast on radio or played in public spaces. This is a statutory right, and is not determined by a recording agreement, nor can it be bought or sold (assignment to PPI excepted). PPI was established in 1968 to administer record company rights (Irish recordings by music producers and those owned by Irish and multinational record companies) in the public performance, broadcasting and reproduction of their recordings. PPI formerly issued licences to businesses and organisations from all sectors across Ireland playing recorded music and music videos in public. Under the new dual system, IMRO is now charged with this task. These can range from cinemas, bars, nightclubs, shops and hotels to offices, factories, gyms, universities and local authorities. It also licenses music suppliers to copy recorded music for services such as in-store music systems, jukeboxes, compilations for exercise classes and in-flight entertainment systems. PPI additionally licenses television and radio broadcasters to play copyrighted recorded music as part of their programming.

If songwriters self-produce,[21] they will be the legal 'authors' of the sound recording and hence can derive income from masters in addition to songwriting publishing income. Where music producers are contracted on a work for hire full buyout basis (e.g. by a label, band or audiovisual producer) they might nonetheless be in a position to negotiate points.[22]

[23.3.06] Other income to songwriters/publishers accrues from print rights, namely, the rights to issue licences for printed versions of the compositions, including single-song sheet music. Print rights may be included in a general grant of rights to a third-party music publisher or may be licensed separately to a company whose primary business is the printing and sale of music. The fees payable to the songwriters for the exercise of print rights can typically be based on a percentage of the retail list price.

[23.3.07] Additional income to rightholders on both the publishing and masters side (aside from synchronisation and master uses as above) arise from the sale, streaming and download of tracks either physically or online. If artists, performers and producers have a record deal, these sales receipts will be determined by the agreed splits in their recording contract (and so fall outside the public performance royalties systems administered by CMOs).

[23.3.08] Thus, music publishing refers to compositions only. However, two income sources may be of simultaneous relevance. A film producer requiring to use a commercial song in a movie will require a master use licence for the sound recording from the rightsholder and a synchronisation licence from the writer(s)/publisher(s). Often a fee is agreed on a most favoured nations basis such that the fee to both the master owners and publishing rightsholders will be the same. This is more likely to arise where the fees are high and a number of tracks are being sought for use by the film producer.[23]

Writer and publisher shares of total publishing income

[23.3.09] There are two shares of royalties when a song (composition of lyrics and melody) is exploited, a writer's share and a publisher's share. This is based in practice, not law. Where songwriters self-publish, the matter is moot. They will receive the full share of song/composition/publishing income. It is critical

---

21 Or are assigned rights from a music producer they hire to produce a track or album.

22 Producer points are also commonly referred to as album points, producer percentage, or producer royalties based on the revenue earned by the recording.

23 In the case of Irish television productions for transmission by national broadcasters and films commissioned by such broadcasters from the independent sector, the use of songs (as opposed to sound recordings which must be individually negotiated with owners, or it may potentially be covered under broadcaster licence with PPI) might, depending on use and context and financing arrangements for the project, be covered by blanket licences of the broadcaster with MCPS and IMRO. This leads to very substantial savings in music clearance costs.

to understand that total publishing income from a song includes the writer share as well as the publisher share.

[23.3.10] Traditionally, 50 percent of the income derived from the exploitation of a composition is deemed to constitute the publisher share and 50 percent the writer share. So, by extension, if there are two published co-writers on a song, there are four shares assigned to that song: two writer shares and two publisher shares. The manner in which those shares are divided depends on the contracts, if any, entered into by the writer(s).

[23.3.11] Thus, total publishing income from a song is divided into two equal parts, a writer share (50 percent) and a publisher share (50 percent). If writers do not sign with a publisher, namely they self-publish, they will obtain 100 percent of the total publishing pie, in other words all public performance and all mechanical[24] royalties (including income from any synchronisation deals). If writers sign a publishing deal, they will always[25] at least retain the full writer share (being half of the total income). The publisher does not share in this income nor can it be used to recoup advances. Writers receive their writer share directly from their CMO even if their publishers have not yet fully recouped their costs and advance payments made to the writers.

[23.3.12] If a writer is signed to an exclusive publishing agreement with a publisher and the deal is a 50/50 co-publishing arrangement in terms of the publisher share, for every song written, the songwriter receives half of the publisher share (together with the full writer share). The publisher obtains the other half of the publishing share (being one quarter of total song income). Many new writers will enter "straight" publishing deals[26] whereby the publisher is in receipt of all of the publishing share (being half of total song income, referred to by some CMOs as 6/12ths) and the risk for the publisher is therefore reduced in terms of its outlay such as promotional material and any advance paid to the songwriters.

[23.3.13] If a writer signs on a 75/25 publisher share basis, the publisher will obtain only 25 percent of the publisher share of publishing income and therefore one eight or 12.5 percent of total publishing income. The writer will retain the full writer share (four eights) and 75 percent of the remaining half (75 percent of 50 equals 37.5 percent equating to 3/8 of total income). The total percentage to the writer is therefore 87.5 percent or 7/8 of total song/publishing income.

---

24 Stemming from reproductions of music material (a track used in an online advert; music streaming) (see also fn 28).

25 An exception is the case of a full buyout such as in the case of sale of a back catalogue by a major artist (Dylan, Springsteen) whereby in consideration of a large fee the writer may sell the music and thus forego future public performance royalties and synchronisation fees.

26 On a 100 percent writer share, 100 percent publisher share basis.

Total publishing % (WS & PS)	Writer/publisher splits of PS %	Writer % of total	Publisher % of total
100	0/100	50	50
100	50/50	75	25
100	75/25	87.5	12.5

Table 1: Examples of publisher share splits

[23.3.14] Some find it helpful to think of total publishing as 200 percent,[27] with 100 percent writer share (as guaranteed by CMOs) and 100 percent publisher share. If there is a 50/50 split as to publisher share, the writer obtains 100 percent writer share and half of the 100 percent publisher share and therefore 150/200, being 75 percent or three quarters of total income. If there is a 75/25 split, the writer gets 100 percent writer share and 75 percent of the publisher share, 175/200 being 7/8 or 87.5 percent. When there is a "straight" deal (commercial music), the songwriter does not participate in the publisher share at all and the total songwriting income is split half to the writer and half to the publisher. When music libraries (production music) speak of a 50/50 split however this will relate to the publisher share. The songwriter would thus be entitled to half of the publisher share (and hence 75 percent of total song income).

[23.3.15] It is important when registering works with IMRO/MCPS that the registration is effected correctly as to splits in performance royalties and mechanical royalties,[28] to which we shall later return. While the mechanical royalty can be inserted at 100 percent in favour of the publisher,[29] the percentage figure in the performance royalty due to and filed for the publisher cannot

---

27 BMI in the US considers payments to songwriters, composers and publishers as a single unit equal to 200 percent. Where there is the usual division of performance royalties between songwriters and publishers, the total writer share will be 100 percent (half of the available 200 percent), and the total publisher shares will be the remaining 100 percent. The following rules apply with respect to the division of the 200 percent royalty: the total publisher shares may not exceed 100 percent; if the agreement between the publisher and songwriter provides for the songwriter or composer to receive more than 100 percent, the work should be registered with BMI indicating the percentages allocable; and where no performing rights (or only partial performing rights) have been assigned to a publisher, the songwriters or composers will receive the entire 200 percent (or the balance of the entire 200 percent) in the same ratio as their respective writer shares.

28 Mechanical rights refer, *inter alia*, to rights to include a composition in a sound recording including for digital download and ringtones. In the US, once a song has been published, anyone can record it as long as the statutory mechanical licence is obtained and the statutory fee paid. Many US copyright owners authorise the Harry Fox Agency to issue mechanical rights licences on their behalf. In Ireland, MCPS may have the authority to license its members' music for cover songs, inclusion in film and so forth. If not, it can assist in making contact directly with the rightsholder. The right (or not) for example to issue a synchronisation licence is granted to MCPS by a songwriter when registering a particular track.

29 Which entity or individual will then pay out 50 percent of whatever share has been agreed – or instead of the publisher receiving all and paying out, the writer can receive directly if say 50 and 50 are entered between publisher and writer(s) – however it is usual for the

exceed 50 percent (in order that the writer obtains the full writer share). CMOs will not accept agreements that entitle the publisher to more than a 50 percent performance share.

[23.3.16] One must remember too that each contract will have its own specificities. It may not for example be an across-the-board 50/50 or 60/40 split of the publisher share. Instead, the writer could for instance be on 60/40 for performance income, 75/25 for mechanical income (deriving from reproductions – see below) and 50/50 for synchronisation income.

[23.3.17] Let us take the straightforward example of a publishing contract between publisher Chappell and U2 in the mid 1980s. The contract was a three-album deal for five million dollars. Chappell published all songs in return for 50 cents per album. Within eight months, The Joshua Tree had sold 14 million copies. Chappell received back seven million from its investment of five million and thus profited to the tune of some two million dollars.

Exclusive and non-exclusive licences; benefits of publishing deals

[23.3.18] For a discussion on exclusive and non-exclusive licences (including single song assignments) and the advantages of signing with a publisher/music library, see *Appendix 1.*

Cover songs (and new arrangements): royalties and moral rights

[23.3.19] While cover artists and bands do not earn as much as the original writer(s) who rightly obtain the lion's share of royalties,[30] the cover artists will receive public performance royalties (from say streaming and radio airplay) from their performance on the new sound recording created for the new rendition of the song. They will further receive income from live performances (as split on an agreed percentage with their manager from ticket sales) and a split of sales through downloads or otherwise, in accordance with the terms of their recording contract. Additionally, if the cover version is used in say a television commercial or film, while the original writer(s) will obtain synchronisation fees in respect of the composition, the artist (if self-producing) or the artist label will receive master use licence fees from use of the cover sound recording as split between the artist and label according to the contract terms. In respect of new arrangements of public domain works (e.g. a traditional Irish piece), the composer will create fresh copyright, solely owned by that arranger. If, however, a songwriter/composer wishes to write a new arrangement of an existing song and to change the melody as originally written (and/or change the lyrics), consent will be required from

---

publisher to receive in 100 percent of the mechanical royalties as these will be used to cover any advances that might have been be paid to the writer upfront on signing.

[30] In the form of public performance royalties paid out by CMOs and mechanical royalties payable to CMOs by cover artists' labels for reproducing the original work on cover singles, EPs and albums.

the rightsholder for this adaptation. The rightsholder may require a split in publishing and to be registered as co-writer with collection societies, or may be willing (if the changes made are very substantial) to allow the arranger to fully own the adapted work. However, the former is much more likely to be the case in order that the legacy writer will benefit from new income streams.

[23.3.20] It is not merely economic rights that must be considered. There are also non-economic rights at play such as paternity and crediting rights, and other moral rights (which may not be waived, or not, by contract), which affect how music can and cannot be used and adapted. If an artist wishes to cover a legacy work but requires to adapt the lyrics and/or melody/arrangement, the original writer's consent must be sought. If not, even though the song rightsholders will receive mechanical royalties for the reproduction and public performance royalties from say airplay of the cover version, they could otherwise issue legal proceedings for moral rights infringement in a scenario whereby the cover version is not to their taste, does not align with their creative ethos, morals or ethics, or the rightsholders feel that their reputation or the song's integrity has been compromised, mutilated or subjected to derogatory treatment.

Blanket licence restrictions

[23.3.21] It is for the above reasons that restrictions apply to blanket licensing by broadcasters for use of music in their transmissions. It is worth noting too that aside from exclusions for editing, adaptation, integrity and bad taste moral rights considerations as above, a CMO may not be in a position to authorise use of its members' music where a track is to be used in the opening credits[31] of a television or film production or where the programme is intended for international use by a range of buyers (the MCPS/IMRO blanket licence will generally cover Ireland only, and where international use by a broadcaster's licensees in other territories or via an Irish broadcaster's catch-up services is covered under blanket licence, the sound recording rights will still need to be cleared through the rightsholders if not covered by PPI blanket licensing – see Chapter 17). In these scenarios (where the CMO does not wield the requisite authority from the rightsholder), the music user will need to negotiate with the rightsholder[32] directly for consent and/or a licence and not through MCPS. IMRO's and MCPS' role will then be confined to administering royalty payments in the usual manner from use and exploitation in public of the subject material by a cover artist or audiovisual producer.

WORKS REGISTRATIONS: SONGS AND MASTERS

[23.4.01] Co-writing/joint authorship of compositions, registration of one's

[31] Where MCPS has been granted a mandate by its (Irish or international) member to do so, it will be in a position to negotiate a fee and issue a licence to an audiovisual producer.

[32] Songwriter, composer or music publisher.

works with IMRO, MCPS, PPI and RAAP whether as songwriter, composer, publisher, music producer, record label or music performer is critical to unlocking royalty income. *Appendix 2* outlines the registration process and discusses ISRC codes relating to masters, the importance of metadata, and the "black box".

FILM PRODUCERS: MUSIC PUBLISHING AND MASTER RIGHTS

[23.5.01] Film and television producers, having invested considerably by way of composer/music producer fees,[33] may wish to exploit the master for other uses in the future such as a derivative spin-off production. It will therefore require full or partial assignment of the sound recordings and a share in the compositional IP. In these instances, the film producer itself will not need further master use or synchronisation licences from the composer/producer down the line given that the subject agreement will grant the composer's consent in this regard in relation to the composition and will likewise waive moral rights pertaining to any other work incorporating in whole or in part the products of the composer's services produced and or exploited by the audiovisual producer in any manner.[34]

[23.5.02] Accordingly, to maximise revenues from an investment perspective when a composition is acquired by a film production company from a composer, or indeed to recoup music budget costs, it is opportune for the producer to either appoint an outside publisher to administer the rights or register as a publisher itself with IMRO and MCPS. The IMRO requirements in this connection are having at least ten works in one's publishing catalogue, at least five of which having received some form of commercial exploitation (release of a film containing such music will suffice). Post-registration as a music publisher, the film production company can register music tracks to which it has been assigned rights in its film slate over time and thus perform publishing services. This may be commercially prudent if the audiovisual producer frequently commissions writers to pen material for inclusion in films and other projects.

[23.5.03] Bearing in mind that writers are entitled to their full writer share, total publishing income will therefore be split between the parties, sometimes on a 50/50 basis with the writers obtaining their full writer share and the film producer standing entitled to the full publisher's share of one half of total song income. The parties might otherwise agree a lesser share to accrue to the audiovisual producer. Indeed the songwriter/composer might give up no publishing rights at all and simply license the use of the music for the relevant audiovisual project (and for its attendant promotional activities).

---

33 If not relying on broadcaster blanket licences for Irish audience commissioned content.

34 If the film producer which owns the master is approached by a third party producer however for the right to use the master in a wholly unrelated production, that third party producer will however require a synchronisation licence from the composer who has retained song rights. The film producer will receive master use fees and the composer will obtain synchronisation licence fees.

[23.5.04] On the masters side, if the composer self-produces the music and agrees to an assignment of IP therein, the film producer can also register the recorded material with PPI (and with RAAP)[35] so as to benefit from public performance royalties.

[23.5.05] For more on income streams for audiovisual producers who acquire music rights and can thus seek to recoup some of their music clearance budget or further derive income from other exploitation of the subject music by way of master use licence agreements or otherwise, see *Appendix 3*.

Soundtrack albums

[23.5.06] In respect of full film soundtracks, while the production company will own same[36] (inclusion of a song on the album will however of course require prior approval from the owners) and can generate income from sale through download and streaming, the music writers will obtain mechanical royalty income from physical and online reproductions (and may obtain public performance[37] royalties) while the performers will obtain public performance royalties.[38] The sound recording owners of the masters on the soundtrack will also receive public performance royalties if/where applicable. It is important to note that inclusion of a track/master in a soundtrack album would first need to be negotiated with the rightsholders who, if consent for use is granted, likely will require a reasonable share of the audiovisual producer's receipts (from streaming, downloads and physical sales).

ADDITIONAL CONSIDERATIONS FOR MUSIC USAGE

[23.6.01] In sum, the above sections highlight merely some examples of the plethora of moving parts. Additionally, there is sampling of music (which brings with it the composition and sound recording aspects of those samples) and

---

35 In the case of performances by the composer on the track if the composer-performer likewise assigns all performer rights by full buyout to the film producer. RAAP, though intended for performers, also permits membership by any proprietor of rights in performances.

36 A director and producer jointly own a film and its soundtrack pursuant to s 21 of the 2000 Act as amended by s 7 of the Copyright and Other Intellectual Property Law Provisions Act 2019. A directing services agreement will assign the director's share in the film and soundtrack rights to the production company as a standard term. The production company will then exclusively own and control the film and its soundtrack (subject to underlying rightsholder prior consents/agreements –commercial music will be only licensed and not assigned) and can generate income from the soundtrack via sales through downloads and streaming.

37 For instance, if a song or musical piece specially written for a film and taken from a soundtrack album is played on radio.

38 If the music is streamed online, say on YouTube, as opposed to the soundtrack album's being purchased by download and listened to privately on personal devices.

remixing. Hip-hop records typically have a long list of co-publishers as there may be multiple samples and thus multiple owners of copyright.

[23.6.02] The use of songs and recordings as covered by blanket licences (e.g. as held by RTÉ, Virgin Media or the BBC for instance with CMOs)[39] is covered in Chapter 17 from paras [17.3.23] to [17.3.30] wherein geoblocking of catch-up broadcaster services is also addressed.

[23.6.03] The sale or part-assignment of back catalogues and matters concerning reversion of rights are outlined in *Appendix 4* to this chapter.[40]

[23.6.04] And we have not yet even mentioned the gamechanger – streaming giants Spotify, Deezer, Google, YouTube, Apple and so forth and their relationships with artists, labels and publishers and the split of income arising from such relationships. There will also be pre-existing relationships between the artist, label and publishers themselves. Contractual relations in this regard are now governed too by the 2019 Copyright Directive as transposed into Irish law (see Chapter 11).

ROYALTY TYPES AND USE FEES

Record/sales royalties

[23.7.01] There are a number of royalty payments (or licence fees in the case of master use and synchronisation licence agreements) relating to music, some of which will be administered by CMOs, some of which will not as in the case of record royalties. These are paid directly by the record company to the singer/band and are based on the number of albums or singles sold. The rates are determined by the recording contract. Superstars may achieve up to about 25 percent (Michael Jackson is believed to have negotiated a 50 percent deal with his label) while new acts with no proven track record and thus no bargaining strength might fetch in the region of 10 to 20 percent of the wholesale price of a CD, namely the published price to dealer record stores. This may equate (after producer fees, packaging costs etc) to something in the order of €1 to €2.50 of income per album to a pop band or artist. Nowadays, however, the income to artists in this manner accrues from a percentage of single or album downloads.

---

39 PPI for example licenses television stations to include recorded music and music videos in their transmissions (rightholders receive payment through the submission of cue sheets by broadcasters to the CMOs as provided by film and television producers).

40 If one compares it to owning a property, it can be rented out say for 10 years and then sold. With songs, one can earn royalties say for ten years before deciding to sell on the catalogue outright. By fully assigning ownership rights, a songwriter loses control and revenue making opportunities.

Mechanical royalties

[23.7.02] Songwriters receive royalties from the record company (through MCPS) for recording of their songs on CD and other formats. These are approximately 8.5 percent of the wholesale price of a record, the price at which it is sold to record stores.[41] The publisher of the song will take a share of this 8.5 percent depending on the agreed split of royalties between songwriter and publisher. If songwriters own their own publishing (as in the case of U2), they receive the full mechanical royalty as well as the record royalties discussed above. In Ireland and the UK, mechanical royalties are paid by record companies to MCPS which then distributes moneys to songwriters and publishers. Once the publisher registers the song with the MCPS, it can then collect mechanical income from sales. Thus, a record label which releases an album does not pay the publisher directly, as they would in the US.

Mechanical royalties, synchronisation licence fees and most favoured nations

[23.7.03] Mechanical royalties for songwriters also arise in the case of movies, trailers, television programmes, videogames, ringtones, adverts and so forth in which their song, or a part thereof, whether musically, lyrically or both, appears. A synchronisation fee, negotiated as between the publisher/songwriter[42] (or CMO if mandated to so negotiate) and music user, is paid pursuant to a contract and the public performance royalties discussed below also follow on from public broadcast of the song.

[23.7.04] A practice known as "most favoured nations" has developed over time whereby film producers, for instance, wishing to include part of a song in their movie, will negotiate a rate with the record company for the sound recording and the publisher (on behalf of the songwriter) must match this fee as regards the composition, or vice versa. This can be a helpful tool when there are a number of labels and publishers involved because if a competitive price is secured as a synchronisation or master use fee from one publisher or label, the others should follow suit. For further discussion and an outline of 'step' deals that might commence with a reduced rate initially say for film festival use, see paras [17.3.08] and [17.3.09].

---

[41] MCPS issues Audio-Only Product (AP2) licences to companies and individuals that manufacture or distribute audio-only products for retail sale in Ireland. The product formats covered include CD, vinyl and DVD audio and this licence enables the licence-holder to manufacture audio-only products and distribute audio-only products for retail sale. The AP2 licence covers the payment of mechanical royalties only, which are paid to music publishers (or songwriters directly if there is no publishing deal in place) for the use of musical works. Sound recording rights must be licensed directly from record companies where applicable.

[42] And record company which holds the sound recording rights but in this case in the form of a master use fee.

Public performance royalties

[23.7.05] These fall into two camps, the first being royalties for songwriters collected by IMRO based on IMRO's tariff system relating to compositions,[43] and the second being royalties payable to the record company and performers on a track in respect of the sound recording. These are paid by businesses and music users to PPI based on PPI tariffs through the dual licensing system administered by IMRO. Record company income is paid by PPI itself but royalties to performers (singers and musicians) are paid by PPI to RAAP which then pays its performer members. Public performance royalties also accrue to rightsholders under the broadcaster blanket licensing system. PPI engages PPL in the UK as its agent to assist with the licensing of television uses in Ireland of its members' music.

Digital performance royalties (USA)

[23.7.06] Sound recording performance rights are sometimes referred to as neighbouring rights. With a significant slice of worldwide royalties, the US is the main market for neighbouring rights, even though the collection of such rights is limited to the public performance of sound recordings on digital medium only.[44] Unlike most of the world, the US does not apply sound recordings performance rights to broadcast radio, terrestrial radio and performance of sound recordings in bars, restaurants or other public places. This practice most likely will change however in the not too distant future.[45] This issue is further discussed in *Appendix 5*.

Streaming royalties

[23.7.07] Music streaming is considered at the end of this chapter.

COLLECTION SOCIETIES

[23.8.01] The relevant public performance collection societies in Ireland are IMRO, MCPS, PPI and RAAP.[46] The UK counterparts for copyright and

---

[43] As used in retail outlets, public houses, hotels, cinemas, broadcasts, online, radio and television airplay and so forth.

[44] Such as online radio like Pandora, satellite broadcasting like Sirius/XM and also online streaming of terrestrial radio transmission like iHeartRadio.

[45] Given, for one reason at least, the *RAAP v PPI* EU Court of Justice ruling (see [10B.7.04]). CMOs must pay US performers and labels for public performance of sounds recordings. The US at some stage will have to reciprocate and most likely US performers will lobby for legislative changes in this regard in any event for domestic exploitation of their performances. If and when that system is in place it will pave the way for EU and other performers worldwide to be paid for US radioplay and other forms of traditional dissemination.

[46] Recorded Artists Actors Performers.

performance royalties collections are PRS and PPL.[47] Royalties for public performances of music accrue to rightsholders when that music is used anywhere outside of the domestic environment for which payment[48] is to be made to the songwriter, record producer/label and performers.

[23.8.02] While membership of IMRO is free, it distributes royalties to both its members and the international overseas societies that are affiliated to it less a deduction for its operating costs. However, IMRO does not apply any additional administration charges on overseas public performance royalty earnings.[49]

[23.8.03] Likewise, PPI deducts its operations costs from member royalty payments before the net distribution amount is paid out to the member.

[23.8.04] MCPS generates revenue in part from the fees it levies on the synchronisation licences it issues (e.g. for a worldwide synchronisation licence in perpetuity for a song used in the film's opening credits sequence selected from the MCPS member repertoire of commercial music). It also generates income from content creators using its production music library services, and from publisher registration fees.

Cross border royalty issues – international conventions

[23.8.05] How can performers, labels and music producers collect sound recording performance royalties in territories where they are not nationals and may not have direct agreements with the relevant societies? The answer derives from the application of the provisions set out in the Rome Convention and the WPPT (WIPO[50] Performances and Phonograms Treaty). The same holds true for worldwide publishing royalties. These matters are discussed further in *Appendix 6*.

The statutory basis for tariffs set by collection societies

[23.8.06] Royalties are not specifically defined in Irish legislation. However, the legal basis for royalties stems from a variety of sections in the 2000 Act including s 177 (notification of charges by a licensing body to the Controller of Intellectual Property),[51] s 38 (incorporating a sound recording in a broadcast, or the right for example of a retail store to play a sound recording in public), and

---

47 PRS means PRS for Music Limited. This society deals with mechanical and performing rights; PPL means Phonographic Performance Limited.

48 Exceptions arise, however, for example, in the case of fair dealings and performances of works in an educational context (Chapter 6 of the 2000 Act) as discussed in Chapter 10A.

49 Most other performing right organisations apply additional administration charges on overseas public performance royalties before passing royalties onto their members. The rationale for no charge in this respect by IMRO is that the CMOs overseas will have deducted their fees before transmitting payments to IMRO and imposition of a further fee by IMRO would result in double-charging of members.

50 World Intellectual Property Organisation.

51 Formerly the Controller of Patents, Designs and Trade Marks. Section 2 of the 2000 Act

s 208 (performers' rights to equitable remuneration for exploitation of sound recordings on which they performed).

[23.8.07] The overriding protection afforded to copyright holders is contained in s 37 (acts restricted by copyright) of the 2000 Act which provides that the owner of the copyright in a work has the exclusive right to undertake or authorise others to undertake copying of the work, the making available of the work to the public, and adapting the work. Similar provisions in the Act relate to rights stemming from performances (e.g. s 203). Under s 149, a licensing body,[52] is one that negotiates copyright licences and whose objects include the granting of licences relating to works of more than one copyright owner.

[23.8.08] A licensing scheme, *per* s 149(1), means a scheme (whether described as a tariff or by any other name) specifying the classes of case in which the operator of the scheme or the person on whose behalf that operator acts is willing to grant copyright licences and the terms on which licences would be granted in those classes of case. Hence, this section allows for the tariffs currently set by IMRO and PPI and is the backdrop against which artists and record companies grant/assign rights to IMRO and PPI to act as agents on their behalf in respect of royalty payment collections.

[23.8.09] Irish and EU CMOs are also regulated by EU legislation on collective management arrangements as discussed elsewhere throughout this book.

The dual licensing system (IMRO and PPI)

[23.8.10] Businesses in Ireland that play recorded music in public were formerly obliged by statute to obtain two licences covering two separate copyrights, one covering the public performance of the musical work on behalf of songwriters, composers and music publishers (administered by IMRO), and the other covering the public performance of the sound recording on behalf of record producers and performers[53] (administered by PPI). However, since 1 January 2016, PPI has

---

was amended by s 4 of the Copyright and Other Intellectual Property Law Provisions Act 2019.

52 Art 3 of the Copyright and Related Rights (Register of Copyright Licensing Bodies) Regulations 2002 (SI No 463 of 2002) provides that the Controller of Patents, Designs and Trade Marks (now the Controller of Intellectual Property) shall establish and maintain a register of Copyright Licensing Bodies.

53 Artists/singers, featured and non-featured artists, session musicians, orchestral players and so forth (for performers to receive royalties they must actually register their particular performance with RAAP which will receive funds from PPI). Irish and UK law provides performers with a right to equitable remuneration, such as when recorded music is played in public or broadcast via radio. Because this right legally cannot be transferred or waived, in these instances non-featured artists receive a payment alongside (albeit at a lesser rate than) featured artists from the performers' overall share. Where a recording is incorporated in a music video or is used as a backing track for performers to mime or sing live to within a broadcast, session musicians on the recording have also been entitled to payments though at a low amount.

outsourced this responsibility to IMRO under the new dual licensing system for all public performances administered by IMRO such that two separate licences are not required from the two separate organisations.

[23.8.11] PPI (with backend administration of both (label) member royalty and (RAAP-registered) performer royalty distributions outsourced to PPL in the UK such that PPI members have a PPL account/login) collects record company and performer income. However, in respect of the performers' share, this is paid by PPI to RAAP which then distributes the moneys due to its performer members.[54] Airplay and public performance royalties for recordings (e.g. television broadcast, use of music in retail outlets, nightclubs, cinemas, aircraft or at a sports stadium) are split fifty/fifty between the record company and the performers. Note that IMRO tariffs alone are payable if a business uses live performances only at music venues.[55] PPI tariffs apply in respect of sound recordings. For a discussion on licences applicable to stage productions, see Chapter 19.

How royalties and music usage are assessed

[23.8.12] Royalties are calculated via differing methods (e.g. census box office figures for cinema, set-lists collected from music promoters for live events).[56] National radio stations will submit daily playlists to the CMOs[57]while small community and regional stations might be sampled by the CMOs as to their music usage. CMOs will charge commercial radio stations a fixed percentage of each station's net broadcasting revenue by way of an annual blanket licence fee covering all the station's performing, mechanical and sound recording usage. The CMOs also collect royalties for their members through television blanket licensing and other means. IMRO obtains programme details (logs of music works) from broadcasters and selected other music users licensed by IMRO. Generally speaking, broadcasters (and film distributors) are required to submit complete returns of all music used.

---

54 RAAP also collects royalties due to actors on foot of broadcast of their performance as mentioned in Chapter 21.

55 This is because the performers are playing live as opposed to using a copyrighted sound recording as a backing track.

56 Generally these are larger invoiced events where the majority of net revenue is paid to the headline act and the remainder to the support act(s). Where an event (say more than eight acts play) is classed as a festival, the royalties might be split evenly between all acts.

57 All the largest radio stations (and indeed, all BBC stations) are census stations. This means every single track which is played is reported to PRS and therefore the songwriters will receive royalties for the broadcast (hundreds of thousands of streams on Spotify might generate the same amount of income from a single spot play on BBC Radio 2). Every week the BBC publishes its new playlists for the week which are split into A-list, B List and C List. If on the A-list the airplay might average around 25 plays per week, which for a four-minute track could generate in the region of £1,000 weekly in gross performance royalties. A sampled station is a smaller station with a much lower audience share than a census station. Thus, a local station might be sampled say ninety days of the year. That means, if a track gets played on one of those ninety days then the writer will receive royalties, if not, then no income accrues.

Multiple songwriters/contributors

[23.8.13] For present-day Top 40 type music, there are often likely to be several creators contributing to a song's writing process. This means that revenues allocated to song rightsholders are often divided between more parties than on the recording side. It is not unusual for songwriters to share revenues for writing credits with at least three to four other songwriters, if not more. *Havana* by Camila Cabello, *Uptown Funk* by Mark Ronson featuring Bruno Mars and *Strip That Down* by Liam Payne featuring Quavo credit ten, twelve and fifteen writers respectively. Sometimes the recording artist may also contribute to the writing of songs or otherwise negotiate a credit, points or writing fee.

[23.8.14] Sampling is also prevalent. When writers sample a song they give up a share of the copyright, immediately having the songwriters of that sampled song involved in the rights mix.

[23.8.15] A producer, who is a producer-writer, may also augment a track and add creative elements and therefore gain from a share in song IP. There can be a number of further people in the studio control room who may be afforded a percentage. Often, major artists will also require a percentage of the song rights irrespective of whether or not they contributed to it. Indeed, the latter practice, whereby songwriting revenues have become fair game, have become an industry norm to the extent that they are summarised by the maxim 'add/change a word, take a third'.

Changing CMO / termination of membership

[23.8.16] EU Directive 2014/26 governs the rights of CMO members in respect of membership termination (for example if an Irish songwriter enters into a contract with Kobalt (publisher/collecting society in the UK and wishes to terminate with IMRO/MCPS and register instead with Kobalt).[58] Rightholders have the right to terminate the authorisation to manage rights, categories of rights or types of works and other subject matter granted by them to a CMO or to withdraw from a CMO any of the rights, categories of rights or types of works and other subject matter of their choice for the territories of their choice, upon serving reasonable notice not exceeding six months (to terminate with RAAP for instance three months' notice is required). The CMO may decide that such termination or withdrawal is to take effect only at the end of the financial year.

[58] Performing rights for PRS member songwriters published by Kobalt are covered by the ICE licensing deals. However, the mechanical rights are licensed directly with the digital service providers (e.g. Netflix, YouTube, Spotify, Deezer, GooglePlay, Apple Music, Soundcloud, iTunes. TikTok and Amazon) via arrangements made by Kobalt and are not included in the ICE licence deals. ICE was created by UK, Swedish and German CMOs PRS, STIM and GEMA. In addition the ICE Core includes repertoires of IMRO and the independent publishers Peermusic, Downtown/Songtrust and Concord. ICE offers a suite of services for publishers, CMOs and rightsholders with services including copyright administration, multi-territorial online licensing and processing solutions.

Timing of royalty distributions by CMOs

[23.8.17] Place of writing, sound recording and performance registration will affect the timing of payment. An American singer-songwriter in an Irish band will most likely receive writer public performance (e.g. radioplay) income later than her Irish bandmate for Irish and EU uses as she will likely be registered with say BMI in the US rather than IMRO and due to the timelag in royalties reaching BMI and thereafter being distributed to her. If registered with RAAP here, however, she will receive royalties from any performances (on sound recordings) she has registered that are performed publicly as collected by PPI (otherwise, she may for instance use a neighbouring rights administration service in the US[59] or elsewhere which has international label partners which collect royalties in each relevant territory throughout the world). Since a landmark EU Court of Justice judgment in September 2020, US performers are entitled to royalties from PPI (and through other CMOs throughout the EU) for sound recordings played pursuant to the rental and lending rights Directive (Directive 2006/115/EC) (and under international treaties – the Rome Convention and WPPT as discussed in Chapter 10A).

[23.8.18] Otherwise, a composer/producer/performer might be contracted by a label on an independent contractor basis to create content and that label likely will register the track in its own jurisdiction (say in the UK or US) rather than the writer registering the works in Ireland, and stating on the works registration form the CMOs of the Irish writer/producer. It will take longer for income to reach IMRO (and RAAP)[60] in this case. Territory affects royalty income. For US airplay, RAAP-registered members in Ireland will not receive television broadcast or radio public performance royalties from the sound recording. They will however receive income from online uses (including online radio and streaming) through SoundExchange which will forward moneys to PPI for distribution through RAAP.

[23.8.19] In terms of sound recordings, the record label (as a producer of phonograms) plays the central role in the supply chain for performers in the music industry both in the online and offline environment. In most cases, featured artists and session musicians transfer virtually all their rights to phonogram producers when signing a record agreement, with the exception of the right to equitable remuneration for the broadcasting and the communication to the

---

59 Note that ASCAP, SESAC and BMI collect only in relation to song royalties and not for sound recordings. The collection of such neighbouring rights is limited to the public performance of sound recordings on digital medium only (such as online radio or online streaming of terrestrial radio transmission like iHeartRadio). Unlike most of the world, the USA does not apply sound recordings performance rights to broadcast radio, terrestrial radio and performance of sound recordings in bars, restaurants or other public places. Digital royalties are collected by SoundExchange, the sole collective rights management organisation designated by the US Congress to collect and distribute digital performance royalties for sound recordings.

60 No PPI royalties will accrue if the writer/producer assigns rights in the master to the label.

public of commercial sound recordings, pursuant to Art 8 of the EU Rental and Lending Rights Directive (2006/115) (and s 208 of the 2000 Act). The contracts signed by featured artists and session musicians with phonogram producers may include either a buy-out of rights with a one-off payment, an entitlement to royalties or a combination of both. The role of the CROs is thus restricted, mainly to the collection of moneys for the communication to the public and broadcasting rights with no input as to music streaming income.

MUSIC STREAMING

[23.9.01] Streaming is now plainly the dominant mode of music consumption globally. As a consequence, it has been the subject in recent years of a UK parliamentary committee report[61] as compiled after hearings with a range of veteran stakeholders from artist writers, musicians and producers to publishers, labels, platforms, music lawyers, royalties accountants, academics and CMO personnel. The report is important given the output of music from the UK where streaming reportedly now makes up more than 70 percent of UK recorded music revenues. Further, according to NME, one in every ten tracks streamed globally is by a British artist.

[23.9.02] When one explores the negligible income figures[62] the stark picture becomes clear and explains why, if change is not effected, the income model for artists is simply not sustainable when streaming is now the dominant force. This has led many performers to treat streaming services as a promotional tool rather than a sustainable form of income. Several musicians in the parliamentary probe noted that a presence on streaming services is necessary to be discovered and 'heard', meaning that withdrawing works from these services is not practical and could stymie future success. Venues and promoters have come to expect a Spotify presence and use this to evaluate whether to book an act.

[23.9.03] Because streaming is exploited by the 'making available' right under copyright law, performers who are signed to a record deal are paid according

61 House of Commons Digital, Culture, Media and Sport Committee, *Economics of Music Streaming* (2021). Second Report, published 15 July 2021.

62 Singer/songwriter Fiona Bevan disclosed to the UK partialmentary committee that one track that she co-wrote, of which her share was 48 percent, earned her approximately £100 on an album that was the fastest-selling solo artist album of the year at the time of release and reached number one in the UK album charts. Successful songwriters and composers also provided written testimony, both publicly and confidentially, about low rates of remuneration for successful songs. One songwriter and composer, who co-wrote a NME and Rolling Stone award-winning song that was streamed 137 million times on Spotify, received a royalty of merely £3,013.47. Another prominent songwriter and producer received approximately €352 in Spotify payments over three years from a one-third writing share for a song that was streamed over 14 million times. Yet another composer and artist, who has created music for some of the biggest films in the world, wrote confidentially that more money accrues from a track being played on television than out of millions of record streams.

to the terms of their contract with their record label from streaming revenue. This differs from other forms of music consumption, such as a rental, licence, or broadcast. The major music companies and independent record labels have consistently asserted that music streaming is straightforwardly 'making available', and therefore performers should be remunerated as though it was a sale.[63] Advocates for change are calling on the UK government to reclassify streaming as communication to the public both on the basis of streaming's substantial functional distinction from downloading and similarity to radio, and for greater consistency between the song and recording sides.[64]

[23.9.04] Solid precedent for this exists in the EU. Under the Spanish system, by way of illustration, performers are presumed to have transferred the exclusive right under the terms of their contract, which the producer (i.e. the record label) retains, whilst the unwaivable and non-transferrable remuneration right allows performers to be paid when music is streamed. In that territory, equitable remuneration is paid by the user of the sound recording (in this instance, the streaming services) to the rightsholders via the Spanish collecting society AIE. The Spanish system has been in place since 2006, when Spanish law that transposed the 2001 EU 'InfoSoc' Directive came into force.

[23.9.05] In terms of non-featured artists,[65] these performers transfer their rights to music producers/labels and audiovisual producers in exchange for a one-off session fee[66] rather than an ongoing royalty payment from revenues earned. They are thus effectively bought out of their rights to future revenues, including from streaming. This means that, when a track that includes contributions from one or more non-featured artists is streamed, downloaded or purchased physically, those artists are not paid.[67]

[23.9.06] In essence, the report recommended that the British government

63 The argument is that music consumers can play what they want when they want it (and for however long they wish) and skip tracks as they please. That is not like broadcast where such consumer choice does not feature.

64 A solution is to apply the right to equitable remuneration to the making available right in a similar way to the rental right. As such, an additive 'digital music remuneration' payment would be made to performers through their collecting societies when their music is streamed or downloaded. Greater pay to the performers (and less to the labels) would also appropriately reflect the diminished costs of production and distribution associated with digital consumption (as opposed to the costs that apply to labels for physical products, or more correctly, that used to apply in the past).

65 Professional artists such as backing vocalists, orchestral players or specialist musicians who are hired to perform on a recording or tour on a work for hire basis.

66 In the UK the minimum rate for this payment is negotiated through periodic collective bargaining agreements between the BPI, representing record labels, and the Musicians' Union, representing session musicians. The current agreement, negotiated in 2019, is set at £130 for a standard three-hour session.

67 Instead, session musicians are only entitled to an equal share of 20 percent of gross revenues from physical and online sales, which is referred to as the non-featured performers fund or session fund, after 50 years from publication of the recording.

introduce a right to equitable digital music remuneration. In terms of the royalty pot of moneys payable to the industry, the master rightsholders were found to receive the majority of the revenues that accrue to the music industry rightsholders. The phonogram rightsholders receive approximately 55 percent of the gross revenue pot. Song rightsholders therefore receive approximately 15 percent. The remaining 30 percent represents platform administration fees. Put another way, the master rightsholders receive approximately 78.5 percent (55/70) of revenues distributed to the industry while song rightsholders receive approximately 21.5 percent (15/70).

[23.9.07] The right to equitable remuneration bestows an unwaivable, non-transferrable statutory right to payment when certain copyright controls are exploited. This is paid according to industry standard rates (which have no statutory basis though, as seen, case law has confirmed the position) which currently stands at 50:50 between the label and performers.[68]

[23.9.08] In Britain, in terms of platform licensing, PRS and ICE (International Copyright Enterprise) have licensing agreements with a range of digital service providers, such as Netflix, YouTube, Spotify, Deezer, GooglePlay, Apple Music, Soundcloud, Tidal, iTunes and Amazon.

---

68 Two advantages to this proposal are that, first, equitable remuneration is not subject to recoupment, meaning that performers would be paid when their tracks are streamed regardless of whether their recordings have earned out on the initial label investment and expenditure. Second, equitable remuneration could help redress some of the disparity faced by legacy performers who are paid according to the terms of pre-digital contracts at much lower royalty rates, despite the fact that these artists often generate significant revenues for the industry.

Appendix 1

Exclusive and non-exclusive licences; benefits of publishing deals

PRODUCTION MUSIC

[A1.1.01] Of fundamental importance in music licensing is the type of licence on offer from or with the rightsholder writer or publisher. Music libraries or contracts with music distribution companies will seek to obtain rights from writers for uses of their material (usually this will be instrumental production music but it may also be full tracks with sung lyrics) in various media such as television productions and advertising. Music libraries such as Audio Network, West One Music, Universal Production Music or Artlist allow users such as audiovisual producers (or more particularly music supervisors on films and television series) and advertising agencies to source material that is pre-cleared as to use (both in terms of composition rights and the sound recordings). CMOs including the IMRO/MCPS and PRS repertoire also offer this service to music users and have extensive repertoires of production music.

EXCLUSIVE AND NON-EXCLUSIVE LICENCES

[A1.2.01] If a licence is offered by a songwriter to a library/distributor on an exclusive basis, only that music library or distributor can exploit the track (even to the exclusion of the writer[69] who cannot enter into separate deals with third parties or release the music on different media). This type of licence typically requires a more substantial fee to be paid upfront as there is incentive for the licensee to generate more revenue by actively exploiting the material through diverse avenues. A non-exclusive licence means that the writer can contract with a number of different libraries or distributors. This will fetch a lower fee as the music loses its uniqueness if it could potentially appear in multiple adverts or television productions for example, and accordingly may be less attractive to music supervisors.

69 See for example s 122 of the 2000 Act which provides that an "exclusive licence" means a licence in writing which is signed by or on behalf of an owner or prospective owner of the copyright which authorises the licensee, to the exclusion of all other persons, including the person granting the licence, to exercise a right which would otherwise be exercisable exclusively by the copyright owner and references to an exclusive licensee shall be construed accordingly.

SIGNING WITH A PUBLISHER OR LIBRARY

[A1.3.01] One of the biggest revenue streams for music artists is through publishing, be it self-publishing or contracting with a publishing house. This is particularly true given the sharp decline in record sales and the need to generate income from other means of music exploitation such as advertising. Artists must now look to alternative, regular and recurrent sources of (passive) income. A publisher deals with the writers of music and lyrics and is not necessarily concerned with musicians and vocalists. They may be one and the same within a band of course but the process of composing music derives income from its own sources. A publisher promotes use of the compositions it represents, and is responsible for ensuring that the money earned therefrom is collected and paid to the writers. An example of an Irish music publisher is Elevate Music which among others represents the music of Cathy Davey, Aslan and Westlife.

[A1.3.02] Artists, in the same vein as book writers, will generally assign all works created during a certain time[70] (publisher as opposed to writer share, the latter will not be assigned) or grant administrative control of their songs to the publisher for a set period of time. The latter can administer the songs on behalf of the songwriters, thus ensuring prompt registration with CMOs at home and internationally and deriving further royalties income for the public performance or mechanical reproduction of music (such as with song placements in film or adverts and where a third party established artist wishes to cover a track, record and release same).

[A1.3.03] Publishers can also assist with obtaining record deals, distribution and encouraging collaborations with other writers. Moreover, a publisher is in charge of promoting and circulating a songwriter's music in order that it can be creatively and commercially exploited for use. Successful publishers will therefore have cultivated an extensive network of contacts over time to ensure their artists' music is heard by a wide audience to be used for diverse purposes in multiple media forms.

[A1.3.04] Writers (particularly a well-established artist) may license all their works to a music publisher or library with an income split agreed[71] between the

---

70 In exchange for a share of generated income and monthly or termly payments that are treated as recoupable advances whereby publisher costs and outlay are recoupable from future revenues due to the artist. Other typical types of arrangements between authors and music publishers include co-publishing agreements, under which the copyright ownership is shared by the author or heir/estate and publisher and the songwriter also takes a share of the publisher's income; administration agreements, under which the author retains the copyright ownership and the publisher administers the rights under licence for a period of time for an administration fee; and co-administration or participation agreements under which the author retains the copyright ownership and co-administers the rights with the publisher.

71 With music libraries, splits of 50/50 total publishing (writer obtains full writer share, publisher obtains full publisher share) and 75/25 are common (in the latter case, the writer obtains the full writer share and half of the publisher share).

parties depending on respective bargaining positions. The advantage is that the publisher will administer all rights, effect works registrations and ensure that the writer receives income due from various sources (excluding sound recording/ performer income and touring income which will be a matter in most instances for a record label and artist manager or agent). A publisher (or more likely a manager or agent) may also deal with branding rights, sponsorship deals (e.g. clothing, footwear, drinks, sports) and so forth.

[A1.3.05] Another advantage of signing with a publisher company is that where its artists co-write, it will administer the rights as regards co-registration with other publishers to which the co-writer(s) might be contracted. This paperwork can be somewhat cumbersome (especially if there are CMOs involved in different jurisdictions to which the co-writers or publishers are affiliated). To ensure correct submissions are made, signing with a reputable publisher should achieve this. Publishers will also be vigilant in respect of film and television uses that cue sheets are submitted to the relevant broadcasters by film/television producers to ensure in turn CMOs will distribute moneys based on the subject usages.

Individual song agreements

[A1.3.06] While an exclusive songwriter agreement covers all the writer's music, writers starting out in their career are more likely to test the market when building up their repertoire and reputation by assigning rights in specific works on a case by case basis by way of single song assignment in exchange for a portion of revenue. Though songs or instrumentals can of course be assigned outright,[72] the reality is that the writers will be entitled to retain their paternity right (a moral right, being the right to be credited as songwriter) and their writer share in terms of public performance royalties for radio airplay, television uses, and other public performances.

POTENTIAL PITFALL TO PUBLISHING DEALS

[A1.4.01] The publisher or distributor will often obtain the full publisher share which will (or may, terms depending) also include synchronisation licence fees. Thus, if a song appears in a film, the writer, very significantly, will not share in the fee for this but will only obtain public performance and mechanical royalties. It is essential firstly that either the licensee publisher or the writer registers the track(s) with a CMO so that the writer receives the writer share royalties. Further, in deals where a writer may be signing away synchronisation licence fees, it is recommended that legal advice be taken to ensure the contract is otherwise of

[72] Most usually however by sale of back catalogues by major artists at high level figures who may then, depending on the sale terms, forfeit their right to obtain future royalties and the purchaser will then step into their shoes in terms of all entitlements to publishing income.

benefit to the writer and to ensure the writer clearly understands the practical realities at play.

Appendix 2

Co-writing/joint authorship of compositions, works registration, ISRCs[73] (sound recordings) and metadata

CO-WRITING

[A2.1.01] Music copyright ownership might be shared between a number of co-writers or band members equally or in differing percentages. In law, a band might be a partnership and the partnership agreement may provide for a range of income splits depending on creative contributions. Louis Tomlinson as lead songwriter in the globally successful teen band One Direction wrote (solely or in collaboration with professional songwriters or other band members) many of their hits and presumably his vastly additional income was reflected in his share of writer and potentially publisher share royalties. In the case of other famous collaborations such as Elton John (music) and Bernie Taupin (lyrics) this dynamic duo would have shared songwriting royalties in agreed splits as *per* publishing contracts.

[A2.1.02] A sole writer might self-produce and will thus receive all record royalties and performance royalties from the sound recording, and all publishing royalties from the song itself in the form of public performance royalties (together with mechanical royalties) and possibly synchronisation licence fees. If that writer is signed with a publisher, this income will be distributed in defined splits and depending on whether an advance was paid to the artist or if other costs must be recouped from the artist share of total publishing income.

[A2.1.03] If there is more than one songwriter and/or publisher, the mathematics (and indeed contractual documentation and works registration paperwork) can become somewhat unwieldy. Take the example of *Arthur's Theme* (*The Best That You Can Do*) co-written by Christopher Cross, Burt Bacharach and others. BMI controls half of total publishing (being 25 percent on the writer side on behalf of its members, and 25 on the publishing side). ASCAP controls half of the other half. There are five co-publishing companies all of which are affiliated with BMI and ASCAP.

73 Songs and recordings are all each given unique identifiers called an International Standard Musical Works Code (ISWC) and International Standard Recording Code (ISRC) respectively to help authenticate them, distinguish them from other works and catalogue the relevant rightsholders.

[A2.1.04] Taking another example, *Ain't Going Down Till the Sun Comes Up* written by Garth Brooks, Edwin Williams and Kent Blazy, total publishing is split 66.7 percent ASCAP (33.35 of each of the writer and publisher shares) and BMI 33.3 percent (16.67 percent of each of the writer and publisher shares). There are four co-publishers including Sony (ASCAP) and Universal Music (BMI).

[A2.1.05] International registrations will arise where publishing companies and writers are in different territories. *Bad Habits* by Ed Sheeran for instance is 66.67 percent controlled by BMI in the US (to which CMO co-writer Johnny McDaid is affiliated) with the remainder in the management of PRS in the UK to which Ed Sheeran as co-writer and Sony/ATV Music Publishing (UK) Ltd as co-publisher are affiliated.

WORKS REGISTRATION

[A2.2.01] With IMRO/MCPS[74] the writer(s), or their heirs and administrators when deceased, by default will be credited with no less than 50 percent of the overall royalty (reflecting all the writer share and perhaps some or all of the publisher share). Copies of all writer assignments must be enclosed. If division of royalties is not specified upon works registration, half will default to the writer and half to the publisher. As regards mechanical royalties, MCPS in Ireland and the UK in respect of published music pays all of the royalties to the publisher which in turn will account to the writer(s) in accordance with agreed contract terms. With unpublished music (as self-published by a creator), 100 percent of the royalties will be paid to the writer(s) with MCPS membership.

REGISTRATION OF PERFORMANCES

[A2.3.01] What is certain is that all creators should register their works (on each and every occasion after creation) in terms of public performance royalties. This is not an issue generally with songwriters who will typically be cognisant of the imperative to income generation of registering with IMRO and MCPS. It is often overlooked however by performers in a band and by session musicians who may be entitled to a share in public performance income from sound recordings depending on whether they are featured or non-featured artists. However it is imperative that performers actually register their performance on a sound recording with RAAP (registration of the recording by the owner with PPI will not suffice). Creators and performers can greatly benefit from obtaining independent legal advice to best safeguard their rights and optimise their income-generating power.

[A2.3.02] As regards PPI and RAAP works registration, once registered, a performer and a record label can backdate royalties up to six years as this is the

---

[74] And as applies with PRS in Britain.

length of time that PPI will hold unclaimed money (RAAP can backdate Irish airplay royalties three years). Foreign airplay varies from country to country but the standard term is also three years. A performance generally includes all audible contributions to the recording (such as guitar or vocals). In addition, certain inaudible contributions (such as the contribution made by a conductor or studio producer) may also be treated as a performance, where the conductor/studio producer conducts or provides a similar musical direction to another performer's live performance as it is being recorded. Performers are requested to select a role to identify their contribution (e.g. role "BVC" for backing vocals).

ISRCs

[A2.4.01] International Standard Recording Codes (ISRCs) should be embedded within recorded audio by record labels, before a track is released. These ISRCs are internationally recognised and are the tracking codes which monitor where and when recorded audio has been broadcast around the world. Broadcasters report on ISRC activity and regularly send this information to the relevant CMOs so that royalties can be calculated.

THE BLACK BOX

[A2.5.01] Because the recording and song rights are licensed separately and often held by different music creators and companies, many labels do not supply the relevant ISRC/ISWC when licensing music to streaming services, meaning that songwriters often lose out altogether when music is streamed.

METADATA

[A2.6.01] Mismatched, incomplete or missing metadata[75] can result in delays to creator royalties for months or even years. At worst, this can result in payments being misallocated or otherwise consigned as unclaimed or non-attributable royalties to black boxes. The UK parliamentary hearings and report on music streaming undertaken during Covid-19 noted that black boxes consisted of $2.5 billion in unallocated income in 2019 alone. After a period of time, black boxes are then assigned pro-rata to streams that have been correctly identified, which is established in standard publishing agreements. This means that those creators (and publishers/labels) particularly who are most listened to, are effectively paid twice: first for their own streams, and then for streams that cannot be allocated.

---

[75] First, there is the descriptive metadata, which details the contents of a track, such as the title, album, track number, genre, and so on. Secondly, there is the ownership metadata, which details the creators, their corporate partners, the contractual terms agreed by them, and so on. Thirdly, there is the recommendation metadata, which are tags applied and constantly refined by the service using signals such as observed and quantified user behaviour that enable its recommendation systems to function in the most effective manner.

More recently, PPL has changed how it allocates black box income: performers' share of reallocated revenues are now allocated to causes such as the Momentum Fund, which tries to identify and support up-and-coming artists (it should be noted, however, that labels do not contribute to the Momentum Fund).

Appendix 3

Income streams for audiovisual producers who acquire music rights

PUBLISHING

[A3.1.01] Rights may be assigned (or assigned with restrictions so that in essence it is a partial assignment) in certain cases instead of being licensed, such as might apply with full buyouts. Otherwise, for example, a composer of a commissioned piece for a film who also produces it through self-recording or hiring a studio and performers[76] will seek to retain all publishing rights, subject only to a synchronisation licence agreement allowing use of the music in the film in perpetuity in all territories (but likely subject to non-compete holdback provisions).[77] The composer may nonetheless be willing in that scenario to assign the master rights to the film producer.

[A3.1.02] If a film composer writes specially commissioned music for a television programme or film and retains all song rights, the film/television producer will receive no public performance royalties from the music and will simply be licensing its use for the audiovisual project. If however the audiovisual producer is assigned all song rights (assignment involves matters of administration and control but may not necessarily affect royalties) this producer will receive all the publisher's share of the total publishing income but the composer will nevertheless receive the full writer share.

[A3.1.03] This then in effect is a partial buyout only whereby the fees paid are not sufficiently large to justify a full legal buyout.[78] The commissioning producer will be assigned (up to) half of the total publishing rights in the song or music track[79] (a half being the full publisher share) and the hired writer will retain the full writer share which represents the remaining half of total publishing income from public performance royalties and mechanical royalties. Splits in relation to synchronisation income might be negotiated separately to the agreed split in relation to public performance royalties. Or, there may be no contractual

---

76 And will thereby hold both publishing and master rights as first copyright author.

77 To allow first exploitation of the film containing this new commissioned music for a reasonable period before the composer puts it to further uses.

78 If the film producer is to obtain all rights in perpetuity and forego royalties forever, IMRO/MCPS will need to be satisfied by vouching legal documentation that the customary (if not sacrosanct) position of the writer's being entitled by default to at least the full writer share can be altered.

79 Being the full publisher share, with the producer registering with IMRO and MCPS the works and agreed splits and with the right to control and administer the works going forward.

entitlement by the writer to synchronisation fees, the film producer being the registered owner of the song.

[A3.1.04] In this instance, as publisher, the film or television producer (or it may sign with an outside publisher to administer the rights on its behalf) will be paid the total sum of any mechanical royalties that result from exploitation of the composition as received from MCPS[80] and in turn will pay fifty percent thereof to the composer, whereas the composer will be paid the writer share directly from IMRO. In the case where the composition is used in an unrelated third party production (such as a television commercial or new television series) the audiovisual producer as owner will receive all synchronisation licence fees (unless otherwise agreed). Both the audiovisual producer and the music composer will share, however, 50/50 in respect of public performance royalties (if that has been contractually agreed).

SOUND RECORDING ROYALTIES

[A3.1.05] Other than ensuring that all music performances have been cleared by release contract,[81] income from sound recording royalties are not of concern to audiovisual producers who have not been assigned master rights from a composer/producer who has also recorded the material or arranged and paid performers to so record and thus owns the masters (if that is what the contract provides). The film/television producer will receive no royalties in this regard, and it is the sound recording owner who will be ultimately paid after the producer submits cue sheets to the relevant broadcaster or distributor. In this instance (where there is no assignment of sound recording ownership) the contract between masters owner and audiovisual producer will simply contain a master use licence permitting the latter to use the sound recordings (in the film/television programme) ideally (from the audiovisual producer's perspective) in perpetuity worldwide.[82]

[A3.1.06] If however an Irish film producer is assigned master rights to a specially commissioned recording, such producer (or a label on its behalf) will itself receive any PPI moneys due from public performance of the recording on radio, in cinema or on television if it registers as a label with PPI and in turn

80 For instance from cinema exhibition of the subject film (cinemas pay an annual fee to IMRO/MCPS for their blanket licences) in Ireland and abroad (sister collection societies will forward moneys to IMRO), or from television broadcast in Ireland (whether under the blanket licensing system or not).

81 With commissioned music, the composers or songwriters will warrant in their contract that all hired musicians and performers have signed a release. With commercial music obtained from a record label, the performers on the sound recording should already have signed a release by virtue of their label/artist contract or otherwise.

82 In the case of a composer who is also engaged to arrange studio time, recording, mixing, mastering and delivery of the sound recordings but who might also perform on the recording, for example, the piano track, and will therein grant performer rights and consents required under the Act.

registers the subject sound recordings. It will also receive master use fees if the sound recording is incorporated into any future third party productions (e.g. a television commercial or short film).

[A3.1.07] For the sake of completeness, it is worth restating a point mentioned in Chapter 10B. The Court of Justice of the EU held in late 2020 in the case of *Atresmedia Corporación de Medios de Comunicación S.A.* (see [10B.6.11]) that the rental and lending right provisions must be interpreted as meaning that the single equitable remuneration does not need to be paid by the user (in this case a television broadcaster) where it makes a communication to the public of an audiovisual recording containing the fixation of an audiovisual work in which a phonogram or a reproduction of that phonogram has been incorporated. The court found that an audiovisual recording containing the fixation of an audiovisual work cannot be classified as a "phonogram". Further, given that an audiovisual recording containing the fixation of an audiovisual work cannot be classified as a "phonogram", then such a recording also cannot constitute a reproduction of a phonogram and therefore, the communication to the public of an audiovisual recording containing the fixation of an audiovisual work does not give rise to the right to the single equitable remuneration.

[A3.1.08] This is a landmark case as it has a significant impact in the audiovisual broadcasting market (including television channels, streaming platforms and video-on-demand services) throughout Europe. It confirmed that each time a film or television show where a pre-existing phonogram has been synchronised is broadcasted, television stations and platforms in Europe will not have to pay music producers nor music artists for the public communication of that film or series.

[A3.1.09] However the CJEU said this conclusion did not mean that performers and phonogram producers cannot claim for remuneration in relation to the broadcast of a phonogram. Appropriate remuneration for the related rights in a phonogram should be paid as a result of contractual arrangements between the holders of the music producer/label and performer rights in phonograms and the producers of audiovisual works. Also of course, equitable remuneration must be paid to performing artists and phonogram producers for the broadcasting of phonograms by radio and television (as opposed to those incorporated into audiovisual productions) as was discussed in the Dutch Association for the Exploitation of Related Rights case of *SENA v Nederlandse Omroep Stichting* (Case C-245/00) in terms of the criteria used by Member States in calculating what constitutes equitable remuneration that operates by reference to variable and fixed factors, such as the number of hours of phonograms broadcast, the viewing and listening densities achieved by the radio and television broadcasters represented by the broadcast organisation and so forth.

Appendix 4

Reversion of rights and sale of music rights

REVERSION OF RIGHTS

[A4.1.01] In the EU there are now two reversion mechanisms, firstly the right of revocation as provided for in Art 22 of the 2019 Copyright Directive (Directive (EU) 2019/790) whereby the author or performer may revoke in whole or in part the licence or the transfer of rights where there is a lack of exploitation of that work or other protected subject matter as outlined in Chapter 11.

[A4.1.02] Second, reversionary rights arise in the long term (after 50 years) for performers as to sound recordings (the 'use it or lose it' principle) as provided for in Directive 2011/77 amending Directive 2006/116/EC on the term of protection of copyright and certain related rights.[83] Even though non-featured artists' rights are generally bought out by a once-off fee (and subject only to receipt of the right to equitable remuneration from CMOs as regards royalties such as when recorded music is played in public or broadcast via radio) and therefore do not obtain streaming, download or physical sales income, session musicians are nonetheless entitled to an equal share of 20 percent of gross revenues from physical and online sales, which is referred to as the non-featured performers fund or session fund after 50 years from the publication of the recording. The legislation states that a musician cannot waive the right to this income.

[A4.1.03] In the US, as regards song rights, there is a statutory entitlement to regain one's back catalogue 35 years after its sale by assignment, a move undertaken by Bob Dylan in late 2020 to bolster value before he proceeded to sell his entire publishing catalogue of 600 songs to Universal for the reported sum of $300 million.

[A4.1.04] Legal proceedings filed in 2017 against Sony/ATV Music Publishing

---

83 Performers will usually assign their performers' rights in a sound recording to the producer in return for a single or recurring payment. After 50 years from publication, if the producer is not commercially exploiting a sound recording the performer can give notice to the producer of his intention to claim back the rights that he assigned to the producer. If after one year, the producer has failed to commercially exploit the recording, the copyright in the recording will expire and the performer's rights in the recording revert back to the performer. The transposing Regulations allow performers to only reclaim their own rights in the sound recording. If they chose to exploit the recording for their own commercial benefit (such as sales at gigs or performances) they would still need the permission of the other performers on the sound recording and the owners of any copyright in the music and lyrics.

relating to songwriter Paul McCartney's reversionary interests in music previously sold to Michael Jackson were settled the following year. Jackson had outbid him in 1985 to buy the Associated Television Corporation's back catalogue which included The Beatles' tracks.[84] Duran Duran however were unsuccessful in their pursuit to reclaim their copyright, Mr Justice Richard Arnold in the English High Court holding for the publisher.[85]

[A4.1.05] John Waite and David Johansen instituted suits claiming Sony and Universal had infringed their rights by refusing to accept termination notices that would allow them to reclaim their master rights in old recordings, in the US at least.[86] In 2012 Victor Willis, the Village People lyricist and performer succeeded in reclaiming the rights to 33 songs he wrote. In May 2012, a judge granted Willis' motion to dismiss publishers' claims against his proceedings, allowing the termination to go forward. The Eagles, Billy Joel, Paul McCartney, Prince and Bruce Springsteen also each exercised their statutory right under the Copyright Act 1976.

SALE OF MUSIC RIGHTS

[A4.2.01] In the very unlikely event of full legal buyout by a film producer where the writer share too will pass to the film producer or (more likely) some other purchaser of song rights (e.g. a publishing company acquiring a song or catalogue for a specified term), IMRO will need to see contractual evidence of the full assignment of rights where no future public performance publishing royalties will accrue to the writer (or during the retention period, see below, if the buyer has been assigned rights for a specified number of years). If the writer holds the master rights too, however, the writer can otherwise obtain master use licence fees and sound recording public performance royalties into the future.[87]

---

84 In the 1990s, Jackson sold half of his share to Sony and in 2016 Sony bought out Jackson's estate for its half, giving Sony all of the 4,000 song catalogue of ATV Music, which included 250 of Lennon/McCartney songs.

85 *Gloucester Place Music Ltd v Le Bon & Ors* [2016] EWHC 3091 (Ch). This test case against Sony/ASTV sought clarity on whether or not British songwriters who assigned copyrights in their songs to a British publisher under English contract law could reclaim those rights in the US by employing the reversion right contained within American copyright law.

86 In *Waite v UMG Recordings, Inc* 450 F. Supp. 3d 430 (S.D.N.Y. 2020) a federal District Court ruled *per* Caplin J on 31 March 2020 that the applicants could proceed with their class action lawsuit alleging copyright termination and infringement claims against Universal Music. In a separate judgment (*Johansen v Sony Music Entertainment*), the court ruled in the same vein allowing the claimants to proceed with their class action against seeking actual and/or statutory damages for sound recordings that Sony had continued to exploit after the effective date of the termination notices.

87 In the case of music specially commissioned for film, it is probable master rights will be transferred to the film production company which will have paid for the recordings and ideally will have registered essentially as a label with PPI to ensure receipt of any public performances royalties – but while record royalties will accrue to the film producer for public performance of the masters in this instance, the writer if a performer on the sound

Sale of catalogues between publishing companies

[A4.2.02] It is important to stress first that sales of catalogues are subject to underlying writer rights to income and second that there is a temporal element. Let us take a catalogue of 800 songs comprising the works of 50 artists. The net publisher share ('NPS') is the percentage that will equate to a value determined by the contract splits agreed between the publisher and the writer when the songs were assigned to the publishing company by the respective writers. Let us assume the average NPS is 40 percent, namely the contract royalty splits were on average 60/40 with the writers. The writers must be paid their share of income irrespective of which entity owns the catalogue. Hence its value can only be based on the publisher's share.

[A4.2.03] As to the time component, if overall there are still 15 years left on the retention period[88] this means that for the next 15 years after the end of the term the publisher will still receive the NPS but after that time the copyrights will revert to the composers or original copyright owners.

recording, can still obtain performer royalties from RAAP by way of equitable remuneration entitlements.

88 If there is a five-year term the contract may also state that the copyrights are retained for five years after the term. The overall length of time the copyrights will be assigned or licensed to the publisher will be ten years but the writer can exit the agreement after five years if the terms have not been met or the writer wishes to contract with another publisher. However, even if signed with a replacement publisher (for new material), the material written to date will remain with the previous publisher until the retention period has expired (the artist may have received advances throughout the contract. It takes the publisher time to receive income from around the world, to activate cover songs and other uses of the material and to make a profit and financial return). At the end of the retention period the copyrights will return to the writer.

Appendix 5

SoundExchange (US sound recording/digital performance royalties CMO)

[A5.1.01] The revenue generated from airplay on satellite and internet radio is collected in the US by SoundExchange which splits royalties between the artist and the label. SoundExchange is a non-profit CMO. It is the sole organisation designated by the US Library of Congress to collect and distribute digital royalties for sound recordings. The US is not a signatory to the Rome Convention because in 1961 it did not recognise sound recordings as copyrightable subject matter. Only in 1995 were sound recordings granted a limited digital public performance right.

[A5.1.02] While royalties for songwriting, publishing and composition in the US are covered by organisations such as ASCAP, BMI and SESAC, SoundExchange administers the statutory licence which allows services to stream artistic content while paying a fixed rate for each play. More than 3,000 digital radio services rely on the statutory licence to access any commercially available sound recording. Non-interactive digital streaming services such as internet radio, satellite radio, and cable TV music services are also eligible to use the statutory licence.

[A5.1.03] The US Copyright Act specifies how SoundExchange divides and distributes the royalties: 50 percent go to the sound recording copyright owner; 45 percent is distributed to the featured recording artist; and 5 percent is sent to an independent administrator which further distributes those royalties to non-featured musicians and vocalists.

[A5.1.04] SoundExchange has collection agreements with counterpart organisations in countries around the world including PPI and RAAP in Ireland and PPL in the UK. These agreements allow it to collect and pay US artists and rightsholders royalties when their music is played in those countries. Likewise, while PPI covers only Ireland it has bilateral arrangements with other CMOs including PPL (UK), SoundExchange (US) and Re:Sound (Canada) such that Irish performers and producers/labels can obtain royalties from streaming of their music in other jurisdictions.

[A5.1.05] In Ireland, legislation gives performers on sound recordings a right of equitable remuneration for a share of the proceeds for uses of the sound recordings. Therefore, when a sound recording is broadcasted in Ireland, the performers on those sound recordings have a right against the producer or the record label as to a share of their revenue from that usage. From a legal standpoint, it is very different from the US statutory licence regime where the featured artist's share is as against the user of the sound recording, not the record company.

[A5.1.06] In terms of music publishing and streaming in the US, streaming platforms pay mechanical royalties to the publisher through the local CMO. On-demand downloads and physical sales on the other hand are paid by the master's owner to the publishers. In both scenarios, the middleman between the streaming platforms/record labels and the copyright holders is Harry Fox Agency which collects all mechanicals and distributes them according to the rates set by the Copyright Royalty Board.

Appendix 6

International collections; cross border royalty issues – international conventions

INTERNATIONAL COLLECTIONS

[A6.1.01] For Irish performers registered with RAAP, overseas performers' societies (such as PPL UK, or SoundExchange in the US as regards digital performance royalties) have entered into reciprocal agreements with RAAP. This means that when sound recordings containing Irish performers' work are used in other territories, the fees are repatriated and distributed to those performers in Ireland.

[A6.1.02] IMRO distributes royalties collected from a range of local music service providers ('MSPs'). IMRO has partnered with a number of affiliated societies such as with PRS in the UK and SACEM in France to offer licences to multi-territorial MSPs. Therefore, for pan-European services, IMRO members will receive the majority of their digital royalties as overseas income.

[A6.1.03] During 2016, new licensing agreements were negotiated by IMRO with RTÉ, Netflix and cable operators. It has deployed audio recognition technologies in overseas territories to track its repertoire on international broadcast networks.

International treaties

[A6.2.01] Article 2 of the Rome Convention details the level of protection that it grants nationals of contracting states in each other's territories. Contracting states owe nationals of other territories the same level of protection they recognise for their own nationals. Articles 4 and 5 specify that sound recordings made by nationals of contracting states, first recorded in contracting states, or first published in contracting states, are eligible for national treatment. Similarly, a performer's performance will be granted national treatment if it was rendered in a contracting state, incorporated in a protected sound recording, or if not recorded, broadcast from a contracting state. Article 12 sets out the equitable remuneration for performers, producers or both for secondary uses of their sound recordings (e.g. broadcasting, communication to the public).

[A6.2.02] Article 4 of the The WIPO Performances and Phonograms Treaty (effective from 2002) sets out the treaty's national treatment requirements.

Contracting parties must grant nationals of other contracting parties the same level of protection they grant to their own nationals. Article 3 imports the qualification criteria for performers and producers from the Rome Convention (Arts 4 and 5). Thus, performers and producers who would be entitled to national treatment under Arts 4 and 5 of the Rome Convention are entitled to national treatment under Art 3 of the WPPT, as if all members of the WPPT were Rome Convention members. This ensures that US performers' and producers' eligibility is analysed in the same way even though the US is not a Rome Convention signatory.

[A6.2.03] Article 15 of the WPPT details the equitable remuneration right of performers and producers and largely follows the provisions of Art 12 of the Rome Convention. Article 4 of the WPPT requires contracting parties to provide full national treatment to each other's nationals. This concept of "like-for-like" treatment is often referred to as "reciprocity" and is distinct from national treatment.

Chapter 24

Music Copyright Infringement Litigation

INTRODUCTION

[24.1.01] The last five years have been a turbulent period for a wide array of international pop superstars who have found themselves defending music copyright infringement cases. However, the landmark ruling[1] in early 2020 by the Ninth Circuit federal appeal court headquartered in San Francisco in the long-running Led Zeppelin battle, from which Jimmy Page and Robert Plant ultimately emerged victorious, seems to have stemmed the tide. Most recently, in early May 2023, Ed Sheeran and his legal team successfully proved to a federal Manhattan jury that he independently created *Thinking Out Loud* in defence of a claim that he violated the copyright in Marvin Gaye's classic hit *Let's Get It On*.[2]

[24.1.02] On this side of the Atlantic, two recent cases are of particular importance. While US law can be invoked in Ireland and England as persuasive authority and decisions of American courts can be cited here, it is much more likely that case law from our neighbours in the UK will be followed or distinguished in any Irish music copyright cases (and in matters of EU law of course Irish courts are bound to follow the EU Court of Justice's decisions). Indeed in *Sheeran v Chokri*[3] (a case against Ed Sheeran and others) and *Smith v Dryden*[4] (proceedings brought against the band Rudimental) no mention whatsoever was made by High Court trial judge Zacaroli J of the recent body of seminal US jurisprudence in this area, the judge solely applying precedent from the UK superior courts and the relevant statutory provisions.

POTENTIAL DEFENDANTS

[24.2.01] In Ireland, reading s 37(2) of the Copyright and Related Rights Act

1 952 F 3d 1051 (9th Cir. 2020).
2 At the time of writing, it is possible that an appeal may be taken by the claimant against the jury verdict (but given the line of authority finding in favour of defendants in recent years that might be unlikely).
3 [2022] EWHC 827. Sheeran counterclaimed for a declaration of non-infringement (and hence appears as the plaintiff).
4 [2021] EWHC 2277 (IPEC).

2000 ('the 2000 Act'), a record company, recording artist, music publisher, movie production company (where a song features in a film's soundtrack) and a film distributor or broadcaster may all have participated in copyright infringement given that copyright in a work is infringed by a person who without the licence of the copyright owner undertakes, or authorises another to undertake, any of the acts restricted by copyright. Restricted rights are copying, adapting and making works available to the public.[5]

[24.2.02] This is significant given not just a claim being instituted against a defendant artist by the original creator of the work but also providing access to the 'deep pockets' of the defendant's record label, music publishers, film producers and film distributors where applicable.[6]

PROOFS FOR COURT

Originality

[24.3.01] As to originality requirements in Ireland, the UK and across EU member states, following the EU Court of Justice decision in *Infopaq* as discussed in Chapter 10A, it is possible for relatively short parts of a longer work to be protected from copying where those parts of themselves form "an expression of the author's intellectual creation". For present purposes, originality (as confirmed by the English Court of Appeal in *Martin v Kogan* [2021] EWHC 24 (Ch) discussed in Chapter 22, see section [22.1.16]), thus refers to whether one has contributed elements (in a prior or later work) which expressed that person's own intellectual creation (personal intellectual creation bearing the stamp of the author or reflecting the author's personality or personal touch).[7] Prior to this,

---

5 See also s 45 of the 2000 Act (secondary infringement: dealing with an infringing copy, e.g. selling, renting or lending an infringing copy of a work).

6 The motion picture *Me Before You* contains in its soundtrack the track *Photograph* by Ed Sheeran. Lawyers in a copyright suit against Sheeran, his touring company, publishers and record labels claimed in their 2016 complaint filed in a Californian District Court that the song's presence was heavily promoted by the movie, with a portion of the very chorus which they alleged was copied by the defendants being included in two trailers promoting the film. Incidentally, no allegations were made against the film producers or distributors in this action (the suit was instituted against labels and publishers who licensed the song's use and gained revenues from the exploitation of the movie). Similarly, in the *You Raise Me Up* proceedings discussed later at [24.6.21] (*Johannsongs-Publishing Ltd v Løvland*), aside from the writers, music publishers including Peermusic, Universal Music Publishing and Warner, as well as streaming and download platforms Apple and Spotify, were all named as co-defendants. In The Weeknd proceedings (*Clover v Tesfaye* discussed at [24.6.17]), a long list of defendants other than the songwriters were also party to the claim to include an artist management company, Universal (both as label and publisher), Kobalt Music Publishing and Warner Chappell.

7 For example, through the choice, sequence and combination of words or music that the author may express his creativity in an original manner and achieve a result that is an intellectual creation. However, the European Court did not rule out that certain isolated sentences or parts of sentences may be suitable for conveying the originality of a newspaper article, so that they are able to be the expression of an intellectual creation themselves.

the test to be applied in determining whether a work was original for copyright purposes was to ascertain if it was the result of its author's own skill and labour.[8]

[24.3.02] Jury instruction number 16 in the trial court in the *Skidmore* (Led Zeppelin) proceedings stated that copyright "does not protect ideas, themes or common musical elements, such as descending chromatic scales, arpeggios or short sequences of three notes."[9] This is mirrored in Ireland in s 17 of the 2000 Act which provides that copyright protection shall not extend to the ideas and principles which underlie any element of a work. Therefore, copying of unprotected ideas is permitted and there must be actual copying of constituent elements of the work that are original and accordingly are protected.

[24.3.03] Thus, copyright does not extend to common or trite musical elements that are firmly rooted in the genre's tradition. These building blocks belong in the public domain and cannot be exclusively appropriated by any particular author. Authors borrow from predecessors' works to create new ones. Giving exclusive rights to the first author who incorporated an idea, concept, or common element would frustrate the purpose of copyright law and curtail the creation of new music.

Copying

[24.3.04] Copying may be established by proving that the infringer had access to[10] the plaintiff's copyrighted work (and actually heard it)[11] and that the works at issue are sufficiently similar in their protected elements. After examining

---

See also *Football Dataco Ltd v Yahoo! UK Ltd* (Case C-604/10); *Bezpečnostní softwarová asociace v Ministerstvo kultury* [2011] FSR 18, (Case C-393/09); and *Painer v Standard Verlags GmbH* [2012] ECDR 6, (C-145/10).

8 See for instance *University of London Press v University Tutorial Press* [1916] 2 Ch 601, at 609-610, *per* Peterson J; *Ladbroke (Football) v William Hill (Football)* [1964] 1 WLR 273; *Independent Television Publications Ltd v Time Out Ltd* [1984] FSR 64. See also *Newspaper Licensing Agency Ltd v Meltwater Holding BV* [2010] EWHC 3099 (Ch), and before the Court of Appeal [2011] EWCA 890 Civ, [2012] RPC 1. The High Court in the latter case, affirmed by the Court of Appeal, held that the defendant's copying of titles and short extracts of newspaper articles as part of its business as a commercial media monitoring service could infringe copyright. When assessing the relevance of the *Infopaq* decision, the High Court found that the CJEU in *Infopaq* only restated the originality test but did not alter it. If the text extract taken amounts to an expression of the intellectual creation of the author (test of quality instead of test of substantiality, i.e. the taking of a substantial part), copyright subsistence and infringement is possible. The Court of Appeal held that "intellectual creation", as referred to by the CJEU, relates to the question of origin, not novelty or merit; therefore, *Infopaq* did not qualify the long-standing originality test of the classical English cases such as the above-cited *University of London Press* and *Ladbroke*.

9 At p 34 of the opinion (952 F.3d 1051, 9th Cir. 2020), also *Swirsky v Carey* – descending chromatic scales and arpeggios cannot be copyrighted by any particular composer, 376 F.3d 841 (9th Cir. 2004) at 851.

10 *Designers Guild* (below at fn 13), *per* Lord Millett at p 2425E; *Baigent v Random House* [2007] EWCA Civ 247 at [4].

11 See para 26 of Zacaroli J's judgment in *Sheeran v Chokri* (discussed at [24.5.02]).

similarities and the differences (in music cases, it is the sounds of melody that are more important than the notes – this depends to a large degree on the aural perception of the judge),[12] a court must judge whether the particular similarities relied on are sufficiently close, numerous or extensive to be more likely to be the result of copying than of coincidence. It is at this stage that similarities may be disregarded because they are commonplace, unoriginal, or consist of general ideas.[13]

Substantiality

[24.3.05] To amount to an infringement, the copying must be of either the original work or a "substantial part" of it: s 37 of the 2000 Act (see [24.3.12]). The test is not about quantity but rather whether the part in question contains elements which are the expression of the intellectual creation of the author of the work.[14] The essential consideration is to ask whether a defendant has taken that which conferred originality on the claimant's copyright work (or a substantial part of it).[15]

Valid copyright

[24.3.06] Second, claimants must be in a position to establish that they hold valid copyright to a song. While copyright protection is automatic under Irish legislation (in the case of music when it is written and/or recorded) and does not need to be registered, the plaintiff should be capable of proving when the song was written, recorded and released to the public (e.g. when uploaded to a website). There is a statutory presumption in s 139(2) of the 2000 Act, however, that copyright shall be presumed to subsist in a work until the contrary is proved. In the US, however, registration of a work is necessary before litigating and to ensure legal costs can be recovered.

[24.3.07] Section 127 further provides that where in an action for infringement of the copyright in a work the defendant does not admit that the plaintiff is the owner of the copyright the court may direct that evidence in relation to ownership of the copyright be given on affidavit and the court may decide the issue having considered any affidavit presented to it unless it is satisfied that any conflict of evidence between the affidavits may not be resolved other than by hearing oral testimony in which case the court may order that oral evidence may be adduced. Hearsay evidence may be accepted for the purposes of any hearing under s 129(3).

---

12 *Francis Day & Hunter v Bron* [1963] 1 Ch 587, *per* Upjohn LJ at p 618.

13 As observed by Lord Millett in *Designers Guild v Russell Williams* [2000] 1 WLR 2416 at p 2425E-F.

14 *Newspaper Licensing Agency Ltd v Meltwater Holding BV* [2011] EWCA Civ 890, at [24]-[28], applying *Infopaq*.

15 *Mitchell v BBC* [2011] EWPCC 42, *per* Birss J at [28]-[29].

[24.3.08] Section 139(4) provides that where a name purporting to be that of the author of a work or of the owner or exclusive licensee[16] of the copyright, as the case may be, appears on copies of the work, or a copy of a work bears or incorporates a statement, label or other mark indicating that a person is the author of the work or the owner or exclusive licensee of the copyright, as the case may be, that name, statement, label or mark shall be admissible as evidence of the fact stated or indicated which shall be presumed to be correct, unless the contrary is proved. In addition, the presumptions set out in s 139 shall apply to the same extent in any actions relating to an infringement which occurred before the date on which copies of a work were first lawfully made available to the public.

Access to prior work

[24.3.09] Thirdly, the issue arises as to how defendants in music copyright infringement cases became aware of the prior work, how they had access thereto and how familiar they were therewith.[17]

[24.3.10] As previously observed, the burden of proof for demonstrating copying is on the claimant (see the House of Lords ruling in *LB (Plastics) Ltd v Swish Products Ltd*, fn 33, Chapter 10A). While counsel for the claimant in *Smith v Dryden* (see [24.5.21]) urged the trial judge Zacaroli J to draw clear inferences from the high degree of similarities between the two songs, and from the possibility of access given the overlapping professional and personal circles involving Ms Smith and the defendants, he nevertheless did not suggest that this gave rise to any shift in the legal burden of proof.

[24.3.11] If copying is denied, and the defendant had access to the work and there is a sufficient degree of objective similarity between the copyright work and the alleged infringement, there is a rebuttable presumption that copying took place. Hence, once access and similarity are established, the burden will move to the defendant to establish independent creation.[18]

[24.3.12] In this jurisdiction, pursuant to s 37(3) of the 2000 Act as amended by s 11 of the Copyright and Other Property Law Provisions Act 2019, references

---

16 See s 122 of the 2000 Act.

17 This issue was fatal to a claim in *Loomis v Cornish* (836 F.3d 991 (9th Cir. 2016) at p 995) against Jessie J and her record label (Universal) which was upheld in their favour on appeal in the Ninth Circuit appellate court. So too was it fatal in The Weeknd proceedings as outlined below.

18 In the US, where no proof of access to the copyrighted work exists, a copyright plaintiff can still make out a case of infringement by showing that the songs were strikingly similar – *Three Boys Music Corp. v Bolton* 212 F.3d 477, 485 (9th Cir. 2000). Otherwise, the more compelling the similarities supporting an inference of copying, the less compelling the evidence of access need be – *Rentmeester v Nike, Inc* 883 F.3d 1111 (9th Cir. 2018) at 1124 quoted in *Skidmore v Led Zeppelin* 952 F.3d 1051 (9th Cir. 2020) at p 30 of the opinion.

to the undertaking of an act restricted by the copyright in a work shall relate to the work as a whole or (as above) to any substantial part of the work and to whether the act is undertaken directly or indirectly. In relation to adducing corroborating evidence in court, a report, if required, would be sought from an expert musicologist comparing the original track with the allegedly unlawful piece. Much case law hinges on the concept of substantiality where borrowing, copying or theft from another work occurs, whether by sampling or taking merely a measure/bar or two from a piece or incorporating/adapting some element of its 'hook'. Hence this is a qualitative, not quantitative, question.

Independent creation

[24.3.13] Fourth, because independent creation is a complete defence to copyright infringement (no matter how similar the plaintiff's and the defendant's works are, if the defendant created his independently, without knowledge of or exposure to the plaintiff's work, the defendant is not liable for infringement), a plaintiff must prove that a defendant copied the work ("actual copying", even if subconsciously done).[19] Copyright law does not forbid all copying (copying of generic unprotected ideas for example is permitted), only the unauthorised copying of protected works.

[24.3.14] Therefore, in order to establish infringement, it is not enough to show that lyrics/melody of the respective notes/passages of the legacy piece and the allegedly infringing copy are materially similar or even the same. It is necessary to demonstrate, by showing a causal nexus, actual copying of the copyrighted work. As Birss J (as he then was) put it, in *Mitchell v BBC*[20] at [33]:

> [t]he defendant's work must be causally connected to the work of the original author. If it is an independent work, then, though identical in every way, there is no infringement.

[24.3.15] As to the test to be applied in considering the question of copying generally, the directions of Wilberforce J (on the requisite "composite elements") in *Francis Day & Hunter Ltd v Bron*[21] remain a valuable guide:

> The final question to be resolved is whether the plaintiffs' work has been copied or reproduced, and it seems to me that the answer can only be reached by a judgment of fact upon a number of composite elements: The degree of familiarity (if proved at all, or properly inferred) with the plaintiffs' work, the character of the work, particularly its qualities of impressing the mind and memory, the objective similarity of the defendants' work, the inherent probability that such similarity as is found could be due to coincidence, the existence of other influences upon the defendant composer, and not least the

---

19 Inadvertent or subconscious copying is sufficient (in which case the state of mind of the defendant is not in issue).

20 [2011] EWPCC 42.

21 [1963] 1 Ch 587 (cited with approval by Wilmer LJ in the Court of Appeal at p 614-615).

quality of the defendant composer's own evidence on the presence or otherwise in his mind of the plaintiffs' work.

POSSIBLE RECOVERY OPTIONS FOR PLAINTIFF ARTISTS[22]

[24.4.01] In Ireland, an aggrieved claimant can first submit a complaint to IMRO/the Mechanical Copyright Protection Society and may also issue legal proceedings for one or more of the following: an injunction preventing further copyright infringement of the work by the defendant (and/or its withdrawal from the market); damages for breach of copyright, that is, in respect of economic rights (commercial exploitation of the impugned track to date) and moral rights (right to be identified as the author, i.e. paternity right; and integrity right, namely the right to object to modification, adaptation or otherwise of the work); a credit on the track the subject of the proceedings; and, lastly, a share in future royalties. MCPS could also be requested to suspend royalty payments pending the outcome of litigation.

[24.4.02] Plaintiff Sami Chokri filed High Court papers in England against Ed Sheeran (with the latter countersuing) and pending final determination at trial, he scored an initial victory when he submitted a copyright infringement complaint to PRS (IMRO's sister collection society in the UK) which decided against Sheeran and suspended royalties due on *Shape of You,* the chorus of which was alleged by Chokri to have copied his work *Oh Why*. In line with PRS' dispute and duplicate claims policy, it is the responsibility of claimants to resolve the dispute between them and the allegedly infringing party or via an external legal process. PRS meanwhile may pause royalty distributions until the matter is resolved, owing a duty to its members to ensure that fair remuneration is paid to the rightful creators of that work.

[24.4.03] It is important to note too that aggravated or exemplary damages or both can be awarded pursuant to s 128 of the 2000 Act – this threat of action could prove useful in persuading the defence to engage in settlement talks at an early stage in the dispute.

RECENT UK CASE LAW

[24.5.01] The Irish courts do not appear to have ruled on the salient issues here. Therefore, in the absence of relevant domestic case law, the judiciary in Ireland may well consider precedent from other common law countries to have persuasive authoritative value, particularly those of the highest courts such as the Supreme Court of the UK, US or Canada and the High Court of Australia (the highest court in that territory)[23] and appellate or 'senior' courts such as the High Court

---

[22] Or their estate if deceased.

[23] In *Cogley v RTÉ* [2005] IEHC 180, for example, Clarke J cited with approval a decision

of England and Wales (and much less likely, given differences in the law, from rulings say of the Ninth Circuit federal court in the US).

High Court: Ed Sheeran (2022)

[24.5.02] As above, the royalties for *Shape of You* ('*Shape*') remained frozen by PRS since 10 May 2018. Singer-songwriter Chokri argued that the impugned track plagiarised a substantial part of his song, using a musicologist report which suggested that the lyrics "oh why, oh why, oh why" were similar to those of "Oh I, Oh I, Oh I" in *Shape*. Other similarities claimed included structure of the lyrics between the choruses, tone, harmonic progression, texture, melodic fills and rhythmic clicking. Chokri also accused Sheeran of unauthorised use (or otherwise) of material from others including TLC and Shaggy in his songs whereby Sheeran was forced to include Shaggy in the credits of Liam Payne's *Strip That Down* which Sheeran co-wrote with Payne and two others, after using part of the melody from the hit *It Wasn't Me*.

[24.5.03] As a result, Sheeran, together with Steven McCutcheon (songwriter, second claimant), Johnny McDaid[24] of Snow Patrol fame (songwriter, third claimant), Sony Music, Kobalt Music and others brought a counterclaim within days of hearing of the freezing of royalties against Chokri and others seeking a declaration that the song did not infringe the defendants' song. Sheeran also alleged that Chokri has damaged his reputation and blocked his revenue streams, royalties having been suspended by PRS[25] pending final judicial determination on the legal issues at hand (the full hearing occurred in March 2022 with judgment delivered the following month).

[24.5.04] Sheeran's arguments were that there are significant differences between the songs such as lyrical content, keys, musical content of fills and rhythm of clicking sounds. Further, since "I" and "why" are different words, it is only the "oh" that is similar which does not amount to a substantial part of the song, nor

---

of the New Zealand Court of Appeal in *TV3 Network Services Ltd v Fahey* (1999) 2 NZLR 129 and applied same to the facts before him.

24 The High Court noted in April 2022 after full hearing that it was not until after they had been cross-examined that it was made clear that Messrs McCutcheon and McDaid were not accused of deliberate (or subconscious) copying. The allegation of deliberate and conscious copying (of music and not lyrics) was made, therefore, only against Sheeran (albeit that if this allegation was made out, the consequences would impact on each of the claimants as owners of the copyright in *Shape of You*). Alternatively, the defendants contended that he did so subconsciously. The leading English case on subconscious copying is *Francis Day & Hunter v Bron* [1963] 1 Ch 587 in which the Court of Appeal established that, although it was possible to demonstrate that a person had infringed copyright without intending to do so, it was nevertheless necessary to establish "proof of familiarity" with the allegedly copied work, as a prerequisite to establishing infringement, and that there was a causal link between the alleged infringing work and the original work.

25 Zacaroli J noted in his (April 2022) judgment that the claimants were justified in thinking that by the defendants' putting *Shape of You* into suspense at the PRS this was a tactic designed to extract a settlement.

is it protected by copyright since it is an unoriginal element. Additionally, his lawyers contended that the tone and composition techniques, such as clicking, are merely ideas and are too general to be the expression of ideas.

Similar fact evidence

[24.5.05] Significantly, Chokri sought to rely on similar fact evidence to support the argument that the first to third claimants were, consciously or subconsciously, in the habit of appropriating the compositional skill and labour of other songwriters during a songwriting session on 12 October 2016 from a US hotel room while Sheeran was on tour with McDaid's band, Snow Patrol. This included that the (cross-)claimants also created the song *Strip That Down* (later recorded by Liam Payne formerly of One Direction) which itself became the subject of a copyright dispute and now includes the creators of the song *It Wasn't Me* who receive 25 percent[26] of PRS royalties. The same occurred in relation to the subject track *Shape of You* itself as it was alleged that it was copied in part from TLC's *No Scrubs* since the writers thereof also now appear as co-authors and receive a 15 percent share[27] of the PRS royalties. A further dispute arose in respect of alleged copying by Sheeran's song *Photograph* (also written by Sheeran and McDaid) from a prior song *Amazing*[28] following which there was a (no admission of liability) settlement agreement and 35 percent[29] of the PRS royalties now go to the writers of the latter together with a lump sum payment of $5.4 million.

[24.5.06] Deputy Master Jefferis at first instance (in early application/pleadings stage in June 2019) declined to strike out the allegations against Sheeran based on similar evidence (of copying). Citing two House of Lords decisions,[30] Sheeran appealed and the matter was heard by Mr Justice Christopher Nugee (as he was then)[31] who denied the appeal[32] and therefore left the reference to the other songs (as potential evidence of widespread copying by Sheeran) on the pleadings as they stood. The matter would then be taken up at full trial of the action with the benefit of oral evidence.

---

[26] Being half (50 percent) of the writer share (25 percent being the total writer/publisher share). Song royalties are generally (it depends on the contract between publisher and artist) split 50 percent songwriters/50 percent publishers. PRS in the UK for example operates a 50/50 default – if division of royalties is not specified, 50 percent will default to the writer and 50 percent to the publisher.

[27] 30 percent of the writer share.

[28] Songwriters Martin Harrington and Thomas Leonard suggested *Photograph* has a similar structure and composition to their song *Amazing* which was released by former *X Factor* winner Matt Cardle in 2012.

[29] Being 70 percent of the writer share.

[30] See the two-step test of Lord Bingham in *O'Brien v Chief Constable of South Wales Police* [1973] AC 729 at 756 who in turn had cited Lord Simon in *DPP v Kilbourne* [1973] AC 729 at 756.

[31] Nugee J has since been appointed to the Court of Appeal and is now styled Lord Justice Nugee.

[32] [2019] EWHC 3584 (ChD).

[24.5.07] The Deputy Master held (in light of the above publishing splits reached after settlement) that these royalty splits showed that there was some real acceptance by the claimants that there had been copying and seemed to be logically probative of the possibility of the same thing happening in the case before him regarding *Shape.*[33] This decision was upheld by Nugee J on appeal whereby similar fact evidence would be allowed at the substantive hearing.[34] In dismissing the application for a strike-out, he noted that if costs had to be borne by third parties (such as Liam Payne) and the claimants, so be it. They would not be disproportionate. Nonetheless, it was noted by the court that there was nothing to prevent the pleadings being struck out at a later stage for lack of particularisation.

The outcome of the full High Court trial

[24.5.08] Before analysing the decision of Zacaroli J itself on the substantive issues, it is opportune to conclude examination of the similar fact evidence element. In analysing the *Amazing* track first as against *Shape*, the judge noted the shape of the melody in each case follows a very similar pattern. Similarity alone, however, is not enough to establish copying, "let alone deliberate copying (which is the only point to which the allegation of similar fact evidence is said to go)".[35] Moreover, they are each set to the same repeated four-chord sequence which is itself so commonplace in pop music that, in the judge's view, it could not be suggested that *Shape* is copied from any other particular song.

[24.5.09] Secondly, it was submitted by counsel that songwriting speed was indicative of copying. The court rejected such submission. The fact that Sheeran works surprisingly quickly when penning music was corroborated by those who have worked with him many times. The clear picture gained from all those that collaborate with him in writing songs is that "he has a rare ability to come up with lyrical and melodic ideas, and connect them together to create catchy songs, at great speed".[36]

---

33 In relation to *Strip That Down*, there was a clearance for 25 percent of the full writer/publisher total (or half the writer share) making it more probable that the claimants could see a risk of copying being established. In relation to *Photograph*, the settlement was 35 percent of the total, which would equate mathematically at least to 70 percent of the writer share, and as such there was a real chance that copying might be established.

34 Nugee J referred to *Mattel Inc v Woolbro* [2003] EWHC 2412 in noting that the risk of including this evidence is to create, to quote Laddie J, an assumption that "once a thief, always a thief". However, where there has been an instance of similarity between songs that might have been a coincidence, it is less likely to be a coincidence where there are three instances citing *Rex v Sims* [1946] KB 531 (at 540), Lord Denning at p 127 in the Court of Appeal decision in *Music Publishing v De Woolfe* [1976] 1 Ch 119 which case established the admissibility of evidence of other instances of copying (as later referred to in the judgment of Zacaroli J after full trial of the Sheeran action), and the late Henry Carr J in the more recent (trademark) case of *Trump International Ltd v DTTM Operations LLC* [2019] EWHC 769 (Ch).

35 At para 156 of the judgment [2022] EWHC 827 (Ch).

36 At para 67.

[24.5.10] Staying with *Amazing*, the defendants contended that the sheer size of the above-cited settlement was indicative of an admission of conscious copying. To the court however this only indicated an appreciation that there was a substantial risk of losing a case of copyright infringement, which would have come before a jury in the US, and that it was therefore in Sheeran's and McDaid's commercial interests to reach a settlement instead of expending an ordinate amount of time and costs going to trial. It was important for the judge to note that a finding of even subconscious copying was sufficient to mean they would lose the case.[37] In view of the objective similarities between the songs there was a clear risk of that.[38]

[24.5.11] For these reasons, Zacaroli J rejected the contention that Sheeran deliberately copied *Amazing* when co-writing *Photograph* with McDaid, and that it therefore provided any reason to suppose that they deliberately copied the lyrics "oh why" when co-writing *Shape*.

[24.5.12] In relation to *No Scrubs/Shape*, in an early version of *Shape*, Sheeran deliberately referenced the US R&B band TLC by using the line "TLC on the jukebox", and in that context intended to use a part of the melody from its song *No Scrubs* and to clear this through Sony Music Publishing. However, Sheeran then changed the melody of the pre-chorus and believed clearance was no longer required. Clearance was then sought and obtained, and credit was given to the writers of *No Scrubs*. The claimants did so on the advice of their US lawyer. Zacaroli J concluded that the circumstances in which the pre-chorus of *Shape* initially copied from *No Scrubs*, but was changed so that it no longer did so, did not provide any support for the contention of copying and concealing levelled at Sheeran. In any event, having compared the relevant passage in *Shape* with *No Scrubs*, from an English law perspective, he found there are insufficient similarities between them to demonstrate that *Shape* continued to include a substantial part of *No Scrubs*.[39]

[24.5.13] *Strip That Down* (written by Sheeran and McCutcheon in October 2016) was alleged to have been copied from a *It Wasn't Me* as recorded and released by Orville Burrell under the stage name Shaggy in 2000. However, in the view of the court, the circumstances in which *Strip That Down* was written provided no evidence of a propensity to copy and conceal. The claimants'

---

37 At para 165.

38 It was unnecessary for the trial judge to reach a conclusion on subconscious copying, and he would have had difficulty doing so in any event without exploring the extent to which Sheeran or McDaid had access to *Amazing* and what other possible sources existed for the melody in *Photograph*.

39 All this is in the context of both songs using only notes from the minor pentatonic scale. There are limited ways to set a two-bar phrase predominantly using (in the case of *No Scrubs*) only three tones or (in the case of *Shape*) five tones. Given the vast number of songs written to the minor pentatonic scale it is inherently likely that on a close examination superficial similarities can be identified between selected parts of a great many songs.

evidence was that the similarity between *Strip That Down* and *It Wasn't Me* was noticed after it had been written (and thus was an instance of subconscious copying) but long before the song was released in May 2017.

[24.5.14] Once the similarity had been noticed, the matter was passed to a musicologist, Peter Oxendale, for review. His opinion was that the similarities were such that clearance would be required or the track would need to be changed. Clearance was duly sought and obtained in January 2017. The immediate suggestion of seeking clearance reinforced the conclusion that Sheeran "was being open and honest".[40] The defendants also contended that the speed at which *Strip That Down* was written was itself "indicative of copying". The court had already dealt with this earlier in its judgement and again rejected that general proposition.

[24.5.15] In relation to alleged copying from Bob Dillon's *Lay Lady Lay* in a song *Lift Me Up* (which did not make the relevant album at the time), merely because the relevant phrases[41] use the words "lay", "lady" and "a while/awhile" was not enough in Zacaroli J's judgment to render Sheeran and McDaid's words a copy of a substantial part of the song *Lay Lady Lay*. Accordingly, he rejected the suggestion that this was an example of deliberate copying or otherwise provided any support for the claim in relation to *Shape*.

[24.5.16] Finally, the defendants relied on the lyrics Sheeran wrote to a rap,[42] entitled *Take It Back* in 2013. This was not invoked as similar fact evidence because there was no suggestion that the words were copied from anywhere else. Instead, it was relied on as an apparent admission by Sheeran that he was in the habit of plagiarising others. This was rejected by the judge who accepted Sheeran's evidence that the line "I never want to get bitten because plagiarism is hidden" simply meant that he did not want to find that someone plagiarised his work by "taking his flow". Moreover, in relation to Sheeran's evidence generally, the court was of the view that Sheeran presented his evidence straightforwardly and honestly in an attempt to assist the court.

Ruling on alleged copying

[24.5.17] In terms of shorthand definitions used by the judge, he referred to the post-chorus eight-bar passage in issue, neutrally, as the 'OI Phrase'. The defendants had contended that the OI Phrase is copied from the eight-bar chorus of *Oh Why*, in which the phrase "oh why" is repeated to the tune of the first four notes of the rising minor pentatonic scale (commencing on F#). The

---

40 At para 180.

41 "Little lady lay with me a while" versus "Lay lady lay, lay across my big brass bed; Stay lady stay, stay with your man awhile".

42 "I'm not a rapper, I'm a singer with a flow, I've got a habit of spitting quicker lyrics you know, You found me ripping the writtens out of pages they sit in, I never want to get bitten because plagiarism is hidden".

judge referred to this catchy and memorable phrase, clearly central to the song *Oh Why* as the 'OW Hook'.

[24.5.18] It was the court's finding that the use of the said first four notes for the melody is so short, simple, commonplace and obvious in the context of the rest of the song that it was not credible Sheeran sought out inspiration from other songs to devise it. As to the combination of elements upon which the defendants relied, even if Sheeran had gone looking for inspiration, then, the court stated, *Oh Why* is far from an obvious source, given the stark contrast between the dark mood created by the OW Hook in *Oh Why* and the upbeat, dance feel that Sheeran was endeavouring to create with *Shape*.

[24.5.19] In totality,[43] the court concluded that while there are similarities between the OW Hook and the OI Phrase, there are also significant differences. As to the elements that are similar, Zacaroli J's analysis of the musical elements of *Shape* more broadly, of the writing process and the evolution of the OI Phrase is that these provided compelling evidence that the OI Phrase originated from sources other than *Oh Why*. All the evidence relating to access by Sheeran to *Oh Why* (whether by its being shared with him by others or by his finding it himself) provided no more than a speculative foundation for Sheeran's having heard *Oh Why*. The court concluded that Sheeran had not heard *Oh Why* and in any event that he did not deliberately copy the OI Phrase from the OW Hook. Finally, the court was equally satisfied that Sheeran did not subconsciously copy *Oh Why* in creating *Shape*.

Takeaway for songwriters

[24.5.20] Despite the litigation victory here, the experience for Ed Sheeran in exonerating his name and expending time in court has resulted in his stated intention to record the songwriting process going forward. The recordings will serve as evidentiary proofs in the event of future copyright infringement claims.

Smith v Dryden (Rudimental case)[44]

[24.5.21] Smith is the composer and lyricist of a song *Can You Tell Me* which was never released commercially, but in October 2007 Smith performed an acoustic version of the song that was recorded for the purposes of a short promotional video, containing an interview with her interspersed with performances of some of her songs. The first to fifth defendants (but predominantly the fourth

---

[43] In relation to determining where the burden of proof lay, the court stated *obiter* that the evidence of similarities and access was insufficient to shift the evidential burden so far as deliberate copying is concerned to the claimants; the defendants failed to satisfy the burden of establishing that Sheeran copied the OI Phrase from the OW Hook; and even if the evidential burden had shifted to the claimants, they had established Sheeran did not deliberately copy the OI Phrase from the OW Hook.

[44] [2021] EWHC 2277 (IPEC).

defendant, James Newman and fifth defendant, Edward Jonathan Harris) are the composers and lyricists of a song *Waiting All Night*. The track was released as a single in April 2013 by the band Rudimental of which the first three defendants are members.

[24.5.22] Smith claimed that the lyrics and melody of the chorus of *Waiting All Night* were copied from *Can You Tell Me*, and constituted an infringement of her copyright. Although the claim was brought against all the Rudimental defendants (as they all had co-writing credits on *Waiting All Night*), by the end of the trial the allegation of copying was pursued against Newman alone. It was accepted that the contributions to the song by the other Rudimental defendants related to other aspects that were not copied from *Can You Tell Me*.

[24.5.23] Having regard to each of the composite elements referred to by Wilberforce J (at para [24.3.15] above), the court *per* Zacaroli J concluded that Newman did not copy any part of *Can You Tell Me* in creating *Waiting All Night* and thus dismissed Smith's claim. In assessing the likelihood that Newman copied *Can You Tell Me*, the composite elements of particular relevance in this case were the similarities between *Can You Tell Me* and the final version of *Waiting All Night*; the availability of *Can You Tell Me*, generally, by the time *Waiting All Night* was written; the likelihood that Newman had access to *Can You Tell* Me by reference to the "overlapping circles" relied on by the claimant; and the process of creating *Waiting All Night* as evidenced by a voice memo recorded during songwriting by Newman. This last element was of particular importance in the case because it provided a contemporaneous insight into the composition and evolution of *Waiting All Night*.

[24.5.24] While there are objective similarities between the choruses of both songs, there are differences which, in the context of a simple melody which spans only three different tones, are not insignificant, and it was plausible in the judge's view that two persons trying to write a hit song in the genre of *Waiting All Night* would come up with the lyric "tell me that you need me" and would set it to music in a way that is similar to *Can You Tell Me*.

[24.5.25] On the basis of all the evidence seen and heard by the trial judge it was unlikely in his view that Newman had access to *Can You Tell Me*. It was never produced commercially, and it was thus impossible that Newman would have heard it in passing, for example, being played in the background on a radio. Although the Smith promotional video was posted to two social media sites, and made available in 2007 to some people in the music industry, the claimant's case that Newman would have accessed the video was, in the court's view, extremely weak and involved too many tenuous links.

[24.5.26] The best evidence as to what actually occurred in relation to the evolution of the impugned song was the voice memo. The judgment refers to two recordings that demonstrate the creative process for *Waiting All Night*. The first is a voice memo made by Newman on his iPhone in June 2012, recording his informal first writing session for *Waiting All Night*. This was of critical importance because it was the claimant's case that Newman copied *Can You Tell Me* in writing the relevant parts of *Waiting All Night* that appear in the voice memo.

[24.5.27] It was Smith's assertion on copying by Newman that it was clear, upon hearing the voice memo in court that Newman had, before he started playing, two aspects of the song very clearly in mind. First, the opening phrase: "I've been waiting all night for you to bring me back around" and, second, the phrase "tell me that you want me, tell me that you need me", which first appears at one minute 27 seconds into the voice memo. However in Zacaroli J's view, a close analysis of the voice memo indicates that while both the words, melody and chord progression for the opening line to the song were in Newman's head before he started recording the voice memo, the remainder of the song, including, crucially, the passage alleged to have been copied from *Can You Tell Me*, emerges through trial and error as he experiments with various ideas.

[24.5.28] The fact that the opening phrase was in Newman's head before he started is evident from the way the words, tune and chord progression flow almost seamlessly from the start of the recording. None of these elements, however, were in the opinion of the court similar to *Can You Tell Me*, "the words are self-evidently different and the tune bears no resemblance to either the verse or chorus of *Can You Tell Me*.[45]

[24.5.29] A close analysis of the voice memo thus provided strong support for the conclusion that Newman came up spontaneously and independently with the allegedly offending lyrics and melody in the course of trying out various ideas.

SUMMARY OF RECENT US CASE LAW

[24.6.01] The outcomes of a number of recent US decisions are now outlined given their importance in that jurisdiction more so than for comparability with the body of law on music copyright from the UK. Further, while there are substantial differences in the analysis of copyright infringement in US and UK law, a pro-defendant trend seems to be emerging strongly and a firm indication that baseless claims will not pass the test of judicial scrutiny in light of all the evidence as will be presented at trial.

Blurred Lines (Williams v Gaye)

[24.6.02] This appeal court decision[46] from early 2018 wherein Pharrell Williams

---

45 At para 72 of the judgment.

46 895 F.3d 1106 as amended 11 July 2018 (9th Cir. 2018). The majority of the court initially defended use of the inverse ratio rule (see below) against the dissent's criticism because

and Robin Thicke ('the Thicke parties') filed suit for a declaratory judgment of non-infringement,[47] is one of the most important (or at least was until largely overtaken by the ruling in *Skidmore* discussed next) and heavily criticised case in music copyright history. The Thicke parties were ordered to pay $5.3 million. Additionally, the Gaye estate will henceforth receive half of any future songwriter and publishing revenues generated[48] by the 2013 hit *Blurred Lines* for infringement of Marvin Gaye's 1977 number one hit song *Got to Give It Up* after it was held to be substantially similar to Gaye's song. This 2-1 majority ruling sent shockwaves throughout the industry.

[24.6.03] If one were to side with the arguments of scathingly dissenting judge Nguyen J in *Gaye* (who was also a member of the majority of the bench in *Skidmore*) – and it is difficult not to having regard to her compellingly reasoned points, based squarely on precedent including that of the US Supreme Court and legal, musical and factual dissections – it would appear that *Gaye* was wrongly decided by the majority of the other two judges on the three-judge appellate panel in improperly expanding the scope of copyright protection to the feel or groove of a song. The Ninth Circuit unfortunately denied an application by the Thicke parties for an en banc rehearing and hence that decision, though heavily criticised by commentators, still stands.

Stairway to Heaven (*Skidmore v Led Zeppelin*)

[24.6.04] The norm in the Ninth Circuit is for a panel of three judges to hear an appeal. An en banc hearing is a session in which a case is heard by the limited full bench of 11 judges to maintain uniformity of decisions within the circuit. The entire bench in the Ninth Circuit consists of 29 active judges which may hear cases in truly exceptional circumstances or an appellant may advance directly to the Supreme Court.

[24.6.05] In spring 2020, by 9-2 majority[49] the en banc 11-judge court restored a jury verdict which found Led Zeppelin's *Stairway to Heaven* did not infringe rights in an instrumental entitled *Taurus* by the band Spirit. This decision suggests that any precedent legal practitioners believed might have been set by the earlier highly controversial *Blurred Lines* case above is not in fact impacting on similar litigation. Moreover, judges appear to be taking a more restrained view of music copyright lawsuits and seem keen to narrow the reach of the *Gaye* judgment.

---

the rule was "binding precedent" that the panel was "bound to apply." 885 F.3d 1150, 1163 n.6 (9th Cir. 2018) but in an amended opinion, the court deleted all references to the rule.

47 The Gaye estate made an infringement demand on Williams and Thicke after hearing *Blurred Lines*. Negotiations failed, prompting Williams and Thicke to file suit for a declaratory judgment of non-infringement on 15 August 2013. Hence, Williams and Thicke were plaintiffs rather than defendants in these proceedings.

48 This was in lieu of lessening the original jury verdict of $7.3m by $2m.

49 *Skidmore v Led Zeppelin* 952 F.3d 1051 (9th Cir. 2020).

[24.6.06] *Skidmore* overturned the Ninth Circuit's own long-standing precedent on the inverse ratio rule[50] which rule made it easier for plaintiffs to sue and (although decided on rather narrow technical and procedural grounds) proceeded to uphold a jury finding of non-infringement by writers Page and Plant. Under the common law doctrine of *stare decisis*, as applied in the federal court system, only a court sitting en banc or the US Supreme Court can overrule a prior decision in the same circuit; in other words, one panel (say of three judges) cannot overrule another. This is what occurred in *Skidmore* and the en banc court joined the majority of other circuits in America and reversed its inverse ratio rule which it had been inconsistently and confusingly applied for decades.[51]

[24.6.07] In October 2020, the US Supreme Court, without giving reasons (it is not so obliged) denied the plaintiff's petition for *certiorari*[52] and hence matters rested with the Circuit Court's en banc judgment.[53]

[24.6.08] This trial and appeal litigation, perhaps the most famous in music copyright history, related to a song written by guitarist Randy Wolfe and performed by his LA-based progressive rock group Spirit. His song called *Taurus* was written in 1968. Led Zeppelin released *Stairway to Heaven* in 1971. Wolfe's estate claimed that Led Zeppelin and its guitarist Jimmy Page and vocalist Robert Plant copied portions of *Taurus*.

[24.6.09] Proceedings were instituted in 2014, 43 years from the release of *Stairway to Heaven* (the Supreme Court having ruled in 2014 that laches[54] would not bar a copyright infringement lawsuit),[55] and the matter was ultimately

---

50 At p 26 of the ruling – "We have stated that substantial similarity is inextricably linked to the issue of access and have adhered to what is known as the 'inverse ratio rule,' which requires a lower standard of proof of substantial similarity when a high degree of access is shown" citing *Three Boys Music Corp. v Bolton* 212 F.3d 477 (9th Cir. 2000) at 485 quoting *Smith v Jackson* 84 F.3d 1213, 1218 (9th Cir. 1996). That is, the stronger the evidence of access, the less compelling the similarities between the two works need be in order to give rise to an inference of copying, *Rentmeester* 883 F.3d 1111 (9th Cir. 2018) at 1124. This would have the obvious effect of making a copyright infringement claim more readily provable.

51 Moreover, in sum, the en banc court stated that the inverse ratio rule improperly dictated how the jury should reach its decision. The burden of proof in a civil case is preponderance of the evidence. Yet this judge-made rule could fittingly be called the "inverse burden rule".

52 *Certiorari*, in common-law jurisdictions, is a writ issued by a superior court for the reexamination of an action of a lower court.

53 On 6 August 2000, Skidmore filed a petition for a writ of *certiorari* asking the Supreme Court to "resolve two issues of first impression, first, whether a deposit lead sheet defines a copyright under the relevant 1909 Copyright Act, and second, whether the Ninth Circuit's evisceration of the substantial similarity extrinsic test should be reversed. On 5 October 2020, the Supreme Court denied the petition. The justices did not offer any explanation as to why the case was not to be reviewed.

54 Unreasonable delay, referring to a lack of diligence and activity in making a legal claim.

55 See *Petrella v Metro-Goldwyn-Mayer, Inc* 572 US 663, 668 (2014).

decided in March 2020 by the en banc Ninth Circuit court.[56] The court affirmed the District Court judgment and the jury's verdict that *Stairway to Heaven* did not infringe *Taurus* given that while Plant and Page may have heard *Taurus* before they created *Stairway to Heaven* the songs were not "extrinsically" similar.[57]

[24.6.10] The first part, the extrinsic test (for the court to apply), compares the objective similarities of specific expressive elements in the two works. Crucially, because only substantial similarity in protectable expression may constitute actionable copying that results in infringement liability, it is essential to distinguish between the protected and unprotected material in a plaintiff's work. The second part, the intrinsic test (for the jury), tests for similarity of expression from the standpoint of the ordinary reasonable observer, with no expert assistance. Both tests must be satisfied for the works to be deemed substantially similar.

[24.6.11] The majority opinion in *Skidmore* referred to the US Supreme Court's opinion in *Feist*[58] wherein it was stated that copyright only protects the author's original expression in a work. The court also confirmed, as regards requirements for originality, that the work be created independently by the work's author (without knowledge of or exposure to the plaintiff's work) and contain "at least some minimal creativity." Thus, in California, the fact of a work's being original as long as it was independently created is not sufficient on its own – originality requires at least minimal creativity, a modicum of creative spark in addition to independent creation.

Katy Perry

[24.6.12] Christian hip-hop rapper Marcus Gray first sued Katy Perry (Katherine Hudson) in 2014 alleging she had plagiarised an eight-note riff from his track *Joyful Noise*. A jury agreed and awarded him $2.78 million. District Judge Christina Snyder (California) vacated the jury award post-trial however (after a post-trial motion for dismissal, which motions ask the court to find that no reasonable jury could have come to its conclusion on a legally sufficient evidentiary basis) and held that the melody was not "particularly unique or rare".

[24.6.13] The decision was made within ten days of the *Skidmore* judgment which was cited. The elements comprising the ostinato (repeating instrumental

---

56 Subject to a potential appeal to the Supreme Court or the full bench of the Ninth Circuit appeals court. As stated, however, the former refused to hear the matter.

57 The jury found that both Page and Plant had access to the musical composition *Taurus* before *Stairway to Heaven* was created. Once the jury made that finding, the remaining questions on the jury verdict form related to substantial similarity of the works. In answer to the question of whether "original elements of the musical composition *Taurus* are extrinsically similar to *Stairway to Heaven*", the jury said no. Because the extrinsic test was not satisfied, the jury did not reach the intrinsic test. These findings ended the jury's copyright analysis.

58 *Feist Publications, Inc v Rural Telephone Service Co.*, 499 US 340 (1991).

figure) in *Joyful Noise* were not, either individually or as a combination, copyrightable original expression. Hence, a repeated eight note melodic phrase was not substantial[59] enough to enjoy copyright protection, essentially being too basic for any one artist to monopolise.[60] *Skidmore* had held that common musical elements employed in multiple songs cannot be protected by copyright. Expressions that are standard, stock or common to a particular subject matter or medium are not protectable under copyright law.[61]

[24.6.14] The plaintiffs appealed Snyder J's ruling. Upholding her decision in *Gray v Hudson*,[62] the Ninth Circuit in March 2022 declared that the original verdict could have suffocated musical creativity. *Dark Horse* did not infringe *Joyful Noise* because the musical components at issue were not protectable under copyright law. The appeal court thus held that the common musical notes in *Joyful Noise* lacked the originality required for copyright protection. Reiterating longstanding principles of copyright law, the court noted the "famously low bar for originality" (but this low threshold for copyrightability still "*does* require at least a modicum of creativity").

[24.6.15] Copyright protection does not extend to "common or trite musical elements, or commonplace elements that are firmly rooted in the genre's tradition."[63] The Ninth Circuit concluded that the *Joyful Noise* ostinato was a "conventional arrangement of musical building blocks" amounting to nothing more than an unoriginal "two-note snippet of a descending minor scale". Further, given the limited number of expressive choices available to an eight note sequence, the court found that allowing such a copyright would amount to an:

> ... improper monopoly over two-note pitch sequences or even the minor scale

59 'Substantial' need not be literally construed such that a number of seconds or a couple of borrowed words or beats have been held in some US cases (in other circuits) to suffice. On the other hand, McKeown J delivering the majority opinion in *Skidmore* noted that, "We have never extended copyright protection to just a few notes. Instead we have held that "a four-note sequence common in the music field" is not the copyrightable expression in a song, *Granite Music Corp. v United Artists Corp.* 532 F.2d 718, 721 (9th Cir. (1976). In the context of a sound recording copyright, we have also concluded that taking six seconds of the plaintiff's four-and-a-half-minute sound recording – spanning three notes – is de minimis, inactionable copying".

60 Accordingly, the claimant was "trying to own the basic building blocks of music".

61 *Satava v Lowry*, 323 F.3d 805, 810 (9th Cir. 2003) citing *See v Durang*, 711 F.2d 141, 143 (9th Cir. 1983).

62 28 F 4th 87 (9th Cir. 2022).

63 Similarly, the court noted, the two songs' timbre (sound quality) from the use of synthesizers has long been commonplace in popular music. Their melodic shape (or the way the melody moves through musical space) simply reflect rules of consonance common in popular music and that use standard tools to build and resolve dramatic tension. The two songs' pitch sequence are merely basic musical building blocks of a melody – and while a melody may be copyrightable, the abstract pitch sequence that is only a component of that melody is not. Further, the songs' textures (the way different musical elements are mixed together, such as parts played by different instruments) are too abstract of a similarity to be legally cognisable.

> itself, especially in light of the limited number of expressive choices available when it comes to an eight-note repeated musical figure".[64]

But the court reiterated how a protectable combination can arise from an original "selection and arrangement" of unprotectable elements).[65]

[24.6.16] The case also raises important practical considerations including in respect of originality which, in the view of Fenwick & West LLP attorneys, can serve as both a sword and shield in copyright infringement arguments.[66] While Katy Perry comes out victorious as non-infringing in this case, the opinion simultaneously signals the weaknesses in the *Dark Horse* song's copyright itself. If the ostinato in *Joyful Noise* is unprotectable, then the similar elements in the ostinato in *Dark Horse* could be unprotectable, too, thus opening the door to more songs using similar-sounding elements without running the risk of infringement.

The Weeknd (Abel Tesfaye)

[24.6.17] In 2019 the Weeknd was sued in the federal District Court for the Central District of California for copyright infringement, accused by a trio of British songwriters of copying their song *I Need to Love* in The Weeknd's track *A Lonely Night* which appeared on his Grammy Award-winning 2016 album Starboy. In July 2020 the court dismissed the lawsuit on the grounds that there was insufficient evidence that the song copied substantial elements from the plaintiffs' song and in October 2021, the Court of Appeals for the Ninth Circuit affirmed this dismissal.[67]

[24.6.18] Because the plaintiffs lacked direct evidence of copying, they needed to demonstrate copying circumstantially by showing that first the defendants had access to the plaintiffs' work[68] and second that the two works share similarities

---

64 At pp 28-29 of the opinion of Smith J for the court.

65 Here, the court concluded that the ostinatos at issue consist entirely of commonplace musical elements, and that the similarities between them do not arise out of an original combination of these elements. In *Skidmore*, as regards a collection of otherwise unprotected elements, the court said these may be found eligible for copyright protection under the extrinsic test but only if those elements are numerous enough and their "selection and arrangement" original enough that their combination constitutes an original work of authorship. For a plaintiff who seeks to apply this theory of protection to work where there is a narrow range of available creative choices, the defendants' work, the court held, would necessarily have to be "virtually identical to the plaintiff's work in order to be substantially similar".

66 Eric Ball and Ryan Kwock, *Katy Perry's "Dark Horse" Comes Out in Front: Ninth Circuit Affairs No Infringement in Copyright lawsuit.* Available at: https://www.fenwick.com/insights/publications/katy-perrys-dark-horse-comes-out-in-front-ninth-circuit-affirms-no-infringement-in-copyright-lawsuit [Accessed 30 April 2023].

67 *Clover v Tesfaye* (9th Cir. 2021) Case No. 20-55861.

68 In *Loomis v Cornish* 836 F.3d 991 (9th Cir. 2016), the proceedings were an unsuccessful claim relating to alleged copying by Jessica Cornish's (Jessie J) *Domino* of a two-measure vocal melody from another songwriter, Will Loomis. The three-judge appeals panel affirmed

probative of copying, in other words, a "striking similarity." The court held the plaintiffs failed to establish a genuine dispute as to either.

[24.6.19] The claimants alleged that one of The Weeknd's producers had access to *I Need to Love* because Universal Music, The Weeknd's record label, once owned the rights to their song.[69] For access, the allegation that the defendants may have heard *I Need to Love* through a large song catalogue amounted, in the court's view, to no more than "bare corporate receipt and their admission that *I Need to Love* was never released to the public or generated any royalties indicated there was no reasonable possibility of access through widespread dissemination.

[24.6.20] For striking similarity, the plaintiffs failed to prove the two works are so similar that their resemblance can be explained only by "copying rather than…coincidence, independent creation, or prior common source". The plaintiffs also failed to timely or adequately address evidence of a prior common source: Blondie's 1979 song *Heart of Glass* and thus the plaintiffs failed to raise a genuine dispute as to copying.[70]

You Raise Me Up

[24.6.21] Johannsongs-Publishing Ltd, owner of a 1977 song written by Icelandic singer-songwriter Johann Helgason, initiated proceedings against Rolf Løvland (the Norwegian songwriter who wrote *You Raise Me Up* in 2001 as popularised by Josh Groban), Universal Music Group Recordings and Warner Records, among others in 2018. In April 2022 the claimant failed to convince the US Supreme Court to review the Ninth Circuit's copyright standard. Johannsongs petitioned the court to invalidate the two-part test for substantial similarity applied by the Court of Appeals for the Ninth Circuit. It argued a separate test used by the Second Circuit would be enough to revive its claims that *You Raise Me Up* infringed the song *Söknuður*.

[24.6.22] The Ninth Circuit has regard to shared, protectable elements between works in an objective "extrinsic" test. If it finds enough, it then considers the overall feel of the works in the subjective "intrinsic" test. The Second Circuit applies an "ordinary observer test". Johannsongs argued the Ninth Circuit's test is logically flawed as a robotic analysis cannot capture the soul of music or art.

---

the District Court's summary judgment in favour of the defendants holding that Loomis did not put forth any potentially admissible evidence to establish that the *Domino* songwriters had access to his *Bright Red Chords*, either on a chain-of-events theory or a widespread-dissemination theory. Accordingly, he failed to establish copyright infringement.

69 The claimants contended The Weeknd may have heard *I Need to Love* through a large song catalogue offered by Universal Music. They further admitted that *I Need to Love* was never released to the public or generated any royalties.

70 The songs were not sufficiently similar to prove their resemblance could have only come from copying. The court stated the songwriters' argument was undercut by evidence that both songs were influenced by *Heart of Glass*.

[24.6.23] The District Court for the Central District of California awarded the defendants summary judgment (but denied them attorney's fees) in early April 2020 (just weeks on the heels of *Skidmore*) finding that the impugned song was not substantially similar to the Icelandic song *Soknudur* as a matter of law, and excluding the plaintiff's expert musicologist reports as unreliable, unhelpful and inadmissible. Moreover the defendant expert's report established that *Soknudur* and *You Raise Me Up* lack substantial structural, harmonic, rhythmic and melodic similarities.

[24.6.24] The Ninth Circuit later affirmed in November 2021 (Case No. 20-55552, 9th Cir. 2021), holding that Johannsongs failed to provide enough evidence showing that the two songs are substantially similar. The court held that Johannsongs' expert in her "fatally flawed" report did not effectively filter out similarities between the songs that can be attributed to prior works.[71] A panel of three judges considered that most of the similarities between the compositions are attributable to prior art. That prior art includes the Irish folk song *Londonderry Air* best known for being incorporated into *Danny Boy* both of which are in the public domain.

Griffin v Sheeran (2023)

[24.6.25] Ed Sheeran faced a $100 million lawsuit in *Griffin v Sheeran*[72] accusing him of copying Marvin Gaye's *Let's Get It On* in his 2014 Grammy-winning song *Thinking Out Loud* by taking major harmonic progressions and rhythmic elements therefrom. Manhattan federal District Court Judge Louis Stanton, in rejecting Sheeran's request to dismiss the proceedings without a jury trial, held there were substantial similarities between several of the two works' musical elements. This included their bass lines and percussion.

[24.6.26] This case involved specificities regarding the legacy Gaye copyright technically covering only simple sheet music (the court ruling that such copyrights for Gaye music are strictly limited to the bare bones version). Judge Stanton cited *Skidmore* stating he would likely disallow the plaintiffs' legal team from playing jurors the famous recorded version at trial.[73] That, taken with the complexities of US music copyright law and the substantial differences in approach with the

---

71 The expert admitted that she did not conduct a prior art investigation or filter out any unprotectable elements that derive from prior art as required by the extrinsic test. These failures rendered the report legally deficient and irrelevant.

72 The plaintiffs were Kathryn Townsend Griffin and other heirs to the estate of Edward Townsend, the co-author (with Gaye) of Marvin Gaye's *Let's Get It On*.

73 A quirk of the relevant copyright law governed how the jury could hear the two songs. The case involved only the compositions underlying both tracks, namely the lyrics, melodies and chords that can be notated on paper, and not their recordings. For older songs like *Let's Get It On* copyright is limited to the sheet music, or "deposit copy," that was originally submitted to the US Copyright Office. On *Let's Get It On*, that notation was skeletal. That meant that the jury never heard Gaye's original recording during trial. Instead, the defendants supplied a computer-generated recreation of what appears on the deposit copy,

UK position (which Ireland invariably tends to follow or distinguish in terms of precedent), means that the decision is of more general than legal interest to Irish practitioners. The trial commenced in late April 2023 taken by the heirs of co-writer Ed Townsend, Katherine Townsend Griffin.

[24.6.27] The claimants alleged that the British star's 2014 number one has "striking similarities" to *Let's Get It On* and "overt common elements" that infringed their copyright. In early May 2023, a New York federal jury reached the conclusion in under three hours' deliberation that Sheeran did not infringe copyright of *Let's Get It On,* thus deciding he independently created *Thinking Out Loud.* When asked by his lawyer to explain how he came up with the track, the performer/songwriter gave a mini-performance to the jury.[74] He explained that writing a song was second nature to him, adding he uses his own version of phonetics to create songs quickly, claiming he could write up to nine in a day.

[24.6.28] The two tracks share a similar syncopated chord pattern, the "heart" of *Let's Get It On.* Sheeran never denied that the chords in the two songs are similar, but described them as commonplace musical building blocks that have turned up in dozens of other songs. He further stated, "These chords are common building blocks which were used to create music long before *Let's Get It On* was written and will be used to make music long after we are all gone".

---

complete with a robotic voice rendering the lyrics in question. On the other hand, the studio recording of Sheeran's song was heard multiple times.

74 Sheeran sang the words, "I'm singing out loud", just enough to be heard, before stating, "and then the words fall in" as he attempted to convince the jury about how he wrote the music.

Chapter 25

Music Insurance; Shooting Music Videos

MUSIC INSURANCE

[25.1.01] Insurance cover can be obtained by a range of music practitioners from performing artists to songwriters and orchestras.[1] It will also be sought by festival and indoor event organisers as well as record labels, producers and recording studios. Where applicable, in the case of international tours, quotes should be sought for cover on a worldwide basis.

[25.1.02] Standard coverage extends to matters including public liability for death or injury to a member of the public or the artist/band; instruments (repair, replacement and theft); equipment whether owned or hired on tour (faults, accidental damage and theft) and whether on stage, in transit or in storage; merchandise and vehicles. In cases where staff are employed, employers will obtain cover under an employer's liability policy for injuries sustained at work. Insurance can shield employers from financial exposure in the event that employees issue legal proceedings for damages arising from employer negligence or breaches of statutory duty.

[25.1.03] Due to decline in the traditional means of income generation through CD/record sales, artists and bands must now take to the road to ensure a constant revenue stream. Thus, another important facet of music insurance cover is for cancellation and non-appearance. Examples include illness, accidents, other events preventing appearance (such as family bereavement) or adverse weather preventing an outdoor show. This type of policy can protect a substantial financial investment in terms of tour costs or artist performance fees in the event that a show cannot proceed. Festival organisers likewise will insure against public

---

1 An example of a music insurance broker is MIB (Media Insurance Broker) with offices in Herbert Lane, Dublin 2. MIB provides insurance to bands, artists, DJs, producers, composers, festivals, recording studios, management companies, record labels and freelancers. Cover options include for travel, E&O (professional indemnity), employer liability, public liability, equipment (owned or hired), personal accident and cancellation/non-appearance. Other providers include AON, Chubb Ireland and Musician Insurance in Swords, County Dublin. MIS Underwriting in Dundalk, County Louth provides cover for musical instruments as does Lark Music (Aston Lark Ireland) in Dublin 22.

liability, employer liability, hired plant and equipment, cancellation due to inclement weather and non-appearance of key acts.

[25.1.04] Aside from equipment cover, policies can also be written for artists and bands such that attendant performers including tour musicians and backing vocalists or choirs will be covered for injury. Accordingly, the policy may and should cover all band members, musicians, vocalists, dancers and crew. In addition, public liability covering loss and injury to third parties should ideally provide coverage for all shows throughout the year, irrespective of location and capacity.

[25.1.05] Record labels, producers, recording studios and music/film colleges can arrange appropriate cover for equipment loss or damage, public and employer liability, buildings (e.g. fire damage), business interruption, business equipment and stock such as DVDs and CDs as well as professional indemnity insurance.

[25.1.06] Production insurance (including employer and public liability, cast, equipment and rushes) is required for the filming of music videos in the same vein as any feature film, television production, short film or documentary to cover for personal injuries, property damage, trademark and copyright infringement, defamation, breach of privacy, product or brand disparagement and so forth. Releases, consents and clearance procedures for music videos are discussed below. Errors and omissions ('E&O') insurance may also be required depending on the nature and content of the video and its intended distribution channels.

[25.1.07] Lastly, professional songwriters may require to effect a policy of media insurance providing for E&O or professional indemnity insurance. All contracts with music libraries, film producers and record labels will require the songwriter to warrant in the composer/label agreement that the material to be delivered will be original and not in breach of third party rights or subject to any claims, prior agreements or encumbrance, and further to indemnify the commissioning party from breach by the songwriter of such warranty and the contract itself. If the composer is also the producer, similar warranties will be required to clear all rights and performances featured in the sound recording.

[25.1.08] Should it transpire that a song used by a television producer infringed an earlier work from which the songwriter substantially copied lyrics and/ or melody (and the original writer institutes legal proceedings for copyright infringement against the television production), the audiovisual producer would seek to be indemnified under the songwriter's insurance cover and issue breach of contract proceedings in the case of a dispute. More likely, however, the songwriter will not have effected such insurance and the production company would have recourse to its own E&O policy in the event of a compensation payout.

SHOOTING MUSIC VIDEOS

[25.2.01] A fitting way to commence this section on the legal and business issues pertaining to music video production is by anecdotal reference to the portfolio of Dublin-born, London-based Steve Barron. The writer had the privilege of attending *In Conversation: Steve Barron* held at Windmill Lane Recording Studios[2] in late 2017 as hosted by the Irish Film and Television Academy. Barron — feature film, television and music video director — was a catalyst in catapulting MTV to soaring heights with such pioneering and iconic[3] directorial work on videos for Michael Jackson's *Billy Jean*, *Take on Me* by Norwegian synthpop band A-ha, The Jam, David Bowie, Madonna, Dire Straits, Bryan Adams and a host of 1980s international acts.

[25.2.02] An aspect of the talk which resonated with this writer at least related to the IP rights of a director and how those rights, generally, will be sold (by assignment of one's authorship rights to the video), leading to future pecuniary disadvantage for such filmmaker. In deciding whether to accept a one-off director's fee in return for assignment of ownership (remember a producer and director by statutory default jointly own a film and a music video is a film) rather than retaining a stake and having entitlement to a fee plus a share in future income from public performance royalties (e.g. television usage), synchronisation licensing or otherwise, much will depend on the reputation, status and bargaining power of the director. It is noteworthy too that, unlike a music performer on a sound recording who is entitled to equitable remuneration royalties from broadcasts of music videos, a director who has assigned any authorship rights to the music video film would not be so entitled to lifetime royalties. The real payoff to directors who accept buy-out deals would be career progression after each successful video, hence paving the way for negotiating more favourable contract terms in the future on lucrative, well-funded projects.

[25.2.03] The days of one-off lump sum contract payments may however be somewhat drawing to a close having regard to the Directive on Copyright in the Digital Single Market explored in Chapter 11 (and national transposing legislation in November 2021). The Directive seeks to ensure fair, appropriate and proportionate remuneration for authors and lays down a contract adjustment provision (in the event that the subject work performs better than expected, leading to a potential right to additional fees if the originally agreed moneys are disproportionately low compared to all subsequent revenues derived from the work) and the right of revocation if copyright is assigned or licensed to a third party but is not duly exploited. The issue with this is that the Directive did not bestow unwaivable rights and contracts now sidestep the Directive's provision

---

2 On 19 November 2017.

3 He employed three-dimensional animation, rotoscoping animation (a technique from 1914 onwards to trace over motion picture footage, frame by frame when realistic action is required as used in A-ha's *Take On Me*) and the technique of a film within a film such as in Human League's *Don't You Want Me*.

by requiring authors to waive their rights to future income beyond the one-off contractor fee.

MUSIC VIDEO AS A FILM

[25.3.01] A music video is a short film and ought to be treated as such by its director (and producer if there is one) with all concomitant artistic, legal and business considerations from writing a treatment, storyboard and/or shooting script through to financing, production, marketing, distribution and promotion. An example of a filmic production with a major budget film crew would be Justin Timberlake's six-minute plus *Say Something* featuring Chris Stapleton directed by Arturo Perez Jr and produced by La Blogothèque. The video was filmed in one continuous shot in Los Angeles' ornate and epic set Bradbury Building (which appeared in the 1982 cult science fiction film *Blade Runner*) and features intricate filming through elevators, stairways and culminating to an atrium filled with a 60-person choir.

[25.3.02] Akin to producing feature or short drama films, carefully planned pre-production and storyboarding is advised with detailed assessment of the IP (copyright and related rights; third party trademarks; design rights[4]), filming permit, insurance, risk assessment and safety issues arising. Legal agreements and releases will be drafted in respect of locations and props as well as to assign participant cast and crew rights to the moviemaker (that is, if the director/producer is to retain copyright in the music video – a band/label may well require the director to assign authorship rights in a work for hire arrangement). From a creative standpoint, matters of set and production design, mise en scène, graphic design, wardrobe and make-up need to be thoroughly planned in advance as do preparing for the post-production editing process to include CGI, special effects, sound optimisation and colour correction.[5] Moreover, as part of the pre-production process, a budget must be formulated and due analysis undertaken to achieve strong production values.

[25.3.03] While filmic videos with unlimited budgets are reserved for the superstars such as Justin Timberlake or Miley Cyrus costing into the hundreds of thousands and indeed millions, this is the exception nowadays due to the manner in which music is consumed via downloading and streaming, often without an accompanying video such as with Spotify or with a video employing only lyrics transitions or animation.[6] However, less grandiose independent productions

---

4 Design rights in two and three-dimensional products are a form of IP as can be registered in the Intellectual Property Office of Ireland and thereby become protected. In the EU, a Registered Community Design is a design right that is enforceable in the Member States of the EU. At international level, application can be made for protection in the World Intellectual Property Organisation.

5 To remedy, for instance, tone, lighting and skin blemish issues.

6 Where animation is employed, an independent contractor agreement will be signed by

but with aspirations nonetheless of high production values can also come with a pricetag into the tens of thousands (when local authority permit, private/public location fees, legal fees and insurance costs are added to the shooting, pre-production and post-production spend). The entire project might span several months despite the fact that shooting will often require one or two full production days only with some additional pick-up shooting time where required.

INDEPENDENT LABEL VIDEO

[25.4.01] The question arises as to whether the band itself is commissioning a director to shoot the video or if a record company is at the helm. Independent labels through their recording contracts may allow their artists full control and freedom in relation to executing the desired vision – indeed they may wholeheartedly encourage the band to produce and fund the video where the record label is itself of limited resources. Therefore, the agreement (or at least creative consultations) would be bi-party instead or tripartite and accordingly involve a much greater degree of collaboration between the director and the band members, at least until the final output is to be reviewed by the record label if one exists. If a major or mini-major label is involved, it most likely will exert control over the entire creative process principally stemming from the fact that it is funding the budget.

PRIOR CONTRACTUAL COMMITMENTS OF PERFORMERS AND FREEDOM TO CONTRACT

[25.5.01] If the music video producer/director requires to retain ownership of the IP in the video for future income purposes, it is always imperative to ascertain if hired-in backing singers, stunt artists, dancers, choreographers or freelance musicians have the authority to enter into production contracts. For example, their publishing, recording, management or agency/artist representation contract may stipulate that future performer rights have been assigned (or exclusively licensed) to that publishing company, label, manager or agency. Thus, in this scenario, it is not the artists or performers concerned that must consent by way of release to their performance in a music video by the video producer/director but the relevant performance rightsholder.[7] In saying that, for data protection and privacy reasons, consents will also be obtained from the performers personally.

[25.5.02] In the case of a director commissioned as a work for hire, assignment of video ownership will be effected from that filmmaker to the band (if unsigned and self-publishing) or label (sometimes music publishers too will commission

---

the animator to assign all rights to the producer/director of the music video (or record label/commissioning music publisher as the case may be).

7 The rightsholder (e.g. artist agent or manager) can either join in as a party to the contract between the video producer and performer or execute a letter of waiver of the exclusive performance rights for the purposes of shooting the third party subject video.

videos for their artists), and the band/label will therefore need to ensure that the filmmaker has ascertained that session musicians, actors or a hired choir for example are not precluded from prior contracts from assigning their performer rights and that they are free to sign the subject release form. The release can be for the benefit of the band/label directly or the director. If between director and performer, the director's own work for hire contract will assign the benefit of any contracts entered directly by the director to the band/label.

PRODUCTION BUDGETS AND FUNDING

[25.6.01] For independent productions where an artist or band will not have access to the deep pockets of a major record label and accordingly the independent outfit may not have sufficient resources to finance a professional video, crowd-funding could be a viable option. Donor rewards might include on-site access by fans to the filming set(s) and meeting their music heroes in the flesh. Another is a bank term loan on foot of a business plan outlining the expected sales receipts from the track or ultimate touring revenues.

[25.6.02] Otherwise, if a band has incorporated a service company as described in Chapter 1 it may be able to raise loan finance/equity investment by allowing a charge to be created on (current/future) company assets or by issuing company shares in return for investment. There may also be local schemes available to support regional talent as in the case, for instance, of Limerick Enterprise Development Partnership (LEDP) which contributed by way of loan agreement to studio recording and music video costs of a project on which the writer of this textbook acted as producer.[8]

[25.6.03] In recent times, as arises with blockbuster movies, commercial branding or sponsorship has emerged as a potential source of funding for music videos, including for emerging artists. However, the artist or band would obviously need to enjoy a solid fanbase so that the product being advertised within the music video can reach a wide audience. From a creative angle, product placement invariably should be used sparingly and with careful restraint but there may be subtle ways to incorporate products. This might involve teaming with an advertising agency that has an overarching campaign in mind for a brand and the music video is thereby a strategic and valuable asset to that marketing scheme.

[25.6.04] A most efficient use of resources is to attract talent to offer their services at nominal cost. The payoff is, first, the glamour of participating in a music video

8 *Santa Claus is Rockin'* performed by New Yorker Bradley Gillis, written by Limerick's Glen Shire and produced by Simon Shire at Windmill Lane Recording Studios, Dublin involving over 60 contributors (2012). Available at: https://www.youtube.com/watch?v=Tm7dutTZu40); music video directed by Maurice Linnane. LEDP was founded as a charitable trust in 1999 with a founding objective of economic, social and educational development of the Limerick region and the city.

and, second, résumé enhancement especially if the video succeeds commercially. A classic example in this connection is the video to accompany Hozier's *Take Me To Church* which was shot in Cork on a budget of €1,500[9] as directed by Brendan Canty and Conal Thomson of the then emerging production house Feel Good Lost. The music video was released in 2013. It went viral (at the time of writing with some 0.72 billion views on YouTube alone) and Hozier, as an Irish act, ultimately achieved almost unparalleled breakthrough success in the US, particularly in 2019 when his new album *Wasteland, Baby!* debuted at number one on the Billboard 200 albums chart. Feel Good Lost has since progressed to producing television adverts for Gas Networks Ireland and promotional material for Sky Sports, Budweiser and videos for Irish singer-songwriter Gavin James.

[25.6.05] If music videos are thus considered an art form rather than a commercial (fee-making) opportunity by cast and crew who offer their services at modest rates,[10] the budget can otherwise be channeled into attaining high production values. Directors and producers of music videos may well return the favour to them on future commercial opportunities such as brand advertising supported projects by rehiring those same actors and crew members.

[25.6.06] Another popular method of music video production is in a controlled setting such as a music studio while the artists are live-recording or in an empty concert hall or music venue. In addition, animation is an option which many consider as a budget-maximising alternative to a high-scale video with actors and exterior shooting on-location which will require permits, additional hired equipment and insurance.

[25.6.07] In terms of remuneration, music video directors generally charge a minimum fee or a percentage of the production budget (perhaps up to ten percent) for their services. For smaller productions, a flat fee is therefore more lucrative from the director's standpoint. Some will require to retain at least some share of ownership of copyright in the film and an entitlement to ongoing passive income from public performance royalties or other income streams.

COPYRIGHT, RELATED RIGHTS AND ISRCs

[25.7.01] The artist, band or the relevant music publisher/label would typically

---

9 Eoin Edwards, *How a €1,500 video made in Cork made Hozier the biggest name in music* (2015), irishexaminer.com. Available at: https://www.irishexaminer.com/lifestyle/artsfilmtv/take-me-to-fame-hoziers-cork-made-video-310955.html [Accessed 20 March 2019].

10 Note that for performer (and crew) release contract purposes whereby actors assign (other than their rights to equitable consideration which can only be assigned to RAAP) their performer rights to the music video producer (or band/publisher/label as appropriate) and waive their moral rights, they should, having regard to contract law principles, be given some form of consideration at least (e.g. €10) and for fair remuneration reasons as set out in Chapters 11 and 23.

require the director (and the producer if applicable) of the video to assign ownership rights in that video in consideration of the fee paid to such director. This will facilitate unimpeded control and monetisation of the work in the future. By default, under s 21 of the Copyright and Related Rights Act 2000, the producer and principal director *per* joint authorship provisions are the authors of a film.

[25.7.02] To then ensure public performance royalties are paid to the artist, band or the relevant music publisher/label (as assigned copyright holder of the video and first owner of the song composition and master sound recording) from Phonographic Performance Ireland ('PPI') or other collection society for television plays and online exploitation (e.g. YouTube) of the video, an International Standard Recording Code ('ISRC') should be obtained from PPI or other collection society to which the copyright holder is affiliated. This is free of charge. The ISRC system is the international system for the identification of recorded music and music videos. Each ISRC is a unique identifier that can be permanently encoded into a recording or music video. Encoded ISRCs automatically identify recordings for PPI in this jurisdiction or PPL (Phonographic Performance Ltd, 'PPL') payments in the UK. The Irish Music Rights Organisation and the Mechanical Copyright Protection Society on the other hand will pay the songwriter/publisher royalties due on the composition from public performance of the music video.

[25.7.03] Conversely, the music video director should seek to retain ownership rights unless a handsome fee is on offer for an assignment of those rights. Steve Barron explained that he forfeited decades of public performance royalties (for instance from television broadcasting of the works) on some of the most successful music videos of all time by taking a one-off fee from record companies (although he did manage to secure a negligible percentage of sales from singles in a few cases). While the songwriter(s) and sound recording owner will benefit from public performance royalties, music video directors should certainly endeavour for instance to agree a split in any income obtained from streaming and download of the video, particularly in respect of YouTube monetisation.

Licensing fees from secondary uses of music videos

[25.7.04] While successful music videos will not always spawn a career for directors in film or television projects as they did in Barron's case (he was offered feature films after his triumphant output on *Billy Jean*), it is nonetheless important to consider the lifetime of a music video and the revenue it could potentially generate in public performance royalties and synchronisation licensing fees[11]

[11] While the songwriter(s) will obtain synchronisation fees (and public performance royalties including mechanical royalties) relating to the underlying composition in the video (unless such future synch fees have been waived in the music video director/producer contract in favour of the filmmaker, or shared between the parties), the use of the music video (e.g.

(e.g. when the video is used in a commercial or as archive footage in a television production) decades down the line from its launch. Master use fees and royalties will likewise arise for the sound recording owner relating to the subject music track of the video.[12]

CLEARING SOUND RECORDING USES FOR MUSIC VIDEOS AND COMMERCIALS; MORAL RIGHTS

[25.8.01] For a sound recording to be included in a music video or television advertising campaign for a product or service (which features music), its use must first be cleared by the appropriate master use copyright holder, be that an unsigned band or artist, record label or music producer, and a synchronisation licence obtained from the songwriter(s)/publisher. This would not ordinarily present any problematic issues given that it is quite obvious a track will be required to accompany the related music video. However, individual music producers own or control master rights (as the first default copyright owners under legislation), as opposed to a record label, they may have artistic reservations about the style of the video such that it might injure their professional reputation if not the right fit. The task then is to convince music producers (as legal 'authors' of a master) in that eventuality to waive their moral rights in that video or re-conceptualise the narrative so that it accords more with the integrity of the sound recording. U2 for example have famously turned down offers to use their music in major advertising campaigns.

[25.8.02] By way of illustration, the sound recording producer may have been at pains to achieve a classic analogue sound. An ultra-modern contemporary music video (or commercial) might therefore fly in the face of such tonal warmth and texture. A 'retro' video may be more in keeping with the recording. This is mentioned as a potential issue only. Moral rights would more frequently arise as regards use of the melody and lyrics. Signed songwriters will have waived their moral rights in favour of an independent label or major label which thus ensures that they cannot object to aspects of music video production in the event of a dispute as to creative aspects thereof.

COVER VIDEOS AND THE UNDERLYING SONG COMPOSITION

[25.9.01] In order, in strict adherence to copyright laws, to post a cover video (with a new/cover sound recording of the track) online in Ireland, a licence needs to be obtained from MCPS or the songwriting rightsholders directly if they have not mandated MCPS to issue licences on their behalf. However, YouTube has

---

as an archive piece in a film or later third party music video) which has its own copyright as a film, will attract synchronisation/archive use fees for the video owner.

12 Master use fees in relation to the sound recording of the track which is embedded in the video will go to the owner (e.g. unsigned band that self-produces/label/music producer).

developed its own system for cover artists. YouTube's technologies recognise a video as a cover and will duly notify the original rightsholder/song publisher. This publisher will either take monetisation or demand that the poster take down the unauthorised video. Monetisation splits the payment between YouTube and the publisher. Each of these are weighed against the possibility of worldwide views (and streaming royalties, albeit at a very low rate) for the original artist if the cover were to perform exceptionally.

PERFORMER RELEASES, CROWD RELEASES, LOCATION AGREEMENTS AND CREW CONTRACTS

[25.10.01] Release agreements are as necessary for music videos as they are for motion pictures and other audiovisual productions discussed in Chapter 17. They ensure that releasors (including musicians, actors, extras, stunt performers and dancers) acknowledge that they (or, if applicable, their publisher/label/agent if performer rights have been assigned by contract) have consented to their appearance in the video. In the case of third party individuals and businesses featured, a contributor, location or prop agreement will cover depiction of persons, premises, property/business names and product/service/prop usage in terms of ensuring no passing off, breach of privacy, defamation, trademark, publicity rights or design right law will ensue. As previously stated, regardless of the contractual situation as to performer rights, performers should also be asked to sign releases to further guard against data protection and privacy breach claims.

[25.10.02] To ward off court proceedings, record label lawyers will mandate for their own productions that participants such as actors, extras, stunt personnel and dancers featured in a video must sign a personal release, including the artist[13] and musicians if there is footage of these artists. Here, the persons signing the release grant the label[14] all rights to use their performance in the video in all media in perpetuity. Performing artists retain their right to equitable remuneration however for exploitation of the sound recording embedded in the video if they register their performance with RAAP which represents actors and musicians. Royalties can then accrue from public performance of the video.

[25.10.03] If filming in a public place, anyone recognisable in the video should be requested to sign a release to cover IP, privacy law issues and data protection consent. If shooting an audience or crowd such as in a concert venue for a live performance, a large sign (crowd release) should be conspicuously displayed notifying persons who enter that they have consented to potentially appearing

---

13 More likely however the record label agreement between the artist and label will already cover assignment of rights including music video performances.

14 If the video director is not hired on a contractor/work for hire basis and will therefore retain video ownership under the default authorship provisions of copyright legislation in Ireland, the participant/artist/band will grant performer rights to this director in terms of performances in the video.

in a music video. However, if the video features a person from the audience (e.g. close-up frame), that person should ideally in addition sign a personal release. Location releases will also be required indemnifying the filmmaker against future claims by the location owner. For filming in public areas, a permit from the local authority must be obtained having first evidenced that public liability/ production insurance is in place.

[25.10.04] Crew contracts will further be required to detail the relationship between them as independent contractors and the music video director/producer (or publisher/label if such entity if producing the video). For example, costume designer self-employed contractors will be required to waive moral rights to ensure that equitable proceedings for an injunction cannot be instituted to prevent release of the music video in the event that the designers are not satisfied with the final edit and claim that it is damaging to their professional reputation. Otherwise, contracts with electricians, camera operators, location sound crew, make-up artists and so forth will be signed to govern terms such as fee, locations/ travel, warranties, insurance, indemnification,[15] termination of agreement and provision for a replacement contractor in the face of incompetent output or breach of contract and so forth.

DATA PROTECTION

[25.11.01] Capturing one's face on camera triggers data protection (and privacy law) considerations. This was the case formerly under older data protection legislation which has (largely) been overtaken by the GDPR and the Data Protection Act 2018 ('the 2018 Act'). These issues are considered in Chapter 13. The withdrawal provisions of the legislation are tempered by legitimate business interests. Given the time, effort and money to be expended in music video production, when taken together with a signed data protection consent form and a signed release (which places contractual obligations on the performer/ participant), it is likely that a court might rule, in the event of dispute, that such consent cannot in fact be withdrawn. Each case is taken on its own merits of course and as set against the backdrop of the artistic/freedom of expression exception in s 43 of the 2018 Act.

[25.11.02] To be in a position to vouch that fully informed consent was freely and willingly obtained, the consent form and prior discussion with the participant should outline the concept for the music video, what is being filmed, what is expected of the performers/contributors, how they will be depicted or represented in the finished edit, and how and where the music video will be exploited (e.g. a television music channel or online).

---

15 Contractors should hold their own public liability insurance so that the video director is not liable (and is thus 'held harmless') for torts/negligence committed by such contractors or their agents/employees.

TRADEMARKS

[25.12.01] The issues discussed in Chapter 12 also apply to filming music videos and commercials featuring music. When a trademark is prominently featured, it is reasonable to assume the brand is sponsoring the video and hence confusion is caused, to the potential detriment of the rightsholder, thus potentially giving rise to registered trademark infringement or a passing off action in the case of unregistered marks. This is averted by obtaining permission and clearing the use by depiction release or prop agreement. However, for well-known artists, brands can in fact sponsor the video by paying for product placement. Nowadays, as above, many independent artists use branding to help fund their videos.

PRODUCT DISPARAGEMENT

[25.13.01] Depicting a brand's name, logo or business premises negatively in a music video could prompt a cease and desist letter requiring removal of a music video from a website, withdrawal from television broadcasting, or indeed it could result in defamation proceedings after the event. An example might be filming of a beach party, at which Heineken cans are clearly visible, that descends into horseplay, violence or drunken sexual activity. Like with motion picture, television and documentary production, there are steps to be taken to overcome such obstacles including mock products designed by the art department, set dressing to conceal a business name, obtaining prior consent and signing a release contract (by providing the script in advance if required), blurring, editing the script/narrative to ensure defamatory material is removed or that trademarks are not visible and, moreover, consulting with an entertainment lawyer.

ARTWORK, PROPS AND ARCHIVES

[25.14.01] Using material protected by copyright, trademark, design right legislation and the law of passing off in respect of unregistered trademarks should be avoided unless consent is obtained from the rightsholder. This includes, in respect of copyright, artwork on walls, vehicles, computers, book covers, magazines, posters, clothing and background radio/broadcast clips.

[25.14.02] Music videos on occasion will include historic archive film or audio clips (e.g. political, wartime, civil unrest, or sport oriented). Take Michael Jackson's *Man In The Mirror* which is peppered with real-world images. This will require clearance as would apply for a documentary film [the filmmaker might otherwise seek to rely on permitted exceptions to copyright infringement such as parody and other fair dealing (but that leaves the matter of defamation open)].

[25.14.03] If including clips from broadcasters for example, the cost of this needs to be factored in early as archive clearance, depending on the content, can be disproportionately expensive, so much so that alternatives may need to be considered such as fully cleared stock footage from a reputable library.

PERMITS

[25.15.01] A range of statute law or local bye-law issues can arise in relation to music video shooting to include road closures, use of fireworks, firearms, blank bullets, hiring licensed gun wranglers on set, fake police uniforms and emergency service vehicles as well as public nudity and obscenity concerns, all matters as discussed in Chapter 14.

SAFETY AND WELFARE; OCCUPIERS' LIABILITY

[25.16.01] The oft-cited example of the life-altering injuries sustained by Michael Jackson during the infamous Pepsi commercial immediately springs to mind as a stark reminder of the perils of filmmaking. By their very nature, music videos can contain frenetic action, feigned protests, fighting, crowd scenes, stunts which include extreme sports, fire, pyrotechnic displays, firearms, explosions, demolition, exotic animals, car chases, planes, helicopters and boats but they can also be filmed on difficult or inherently risk-laden terrain such as mountaintops, beaches, poolsides, forests, on or near water, rooftops, derelict buildings and so forth.

[25.16.02] The provisions of the Occupiers' Liability Act 1995 (where applicable when producing and controlling a set/location) and the Safety, Health and Welfare at Work Act 2005 ('the 2005 Act') (and the Regulations made thereunder such as those involving construction of film-sets, working at heights and noise regulations) must be closely observed as detailed in Chapter 3. It is advisable to discuss options with one's public liability insurer or legal representative in advance and to conduct thorough risk assessments of the chosen locations but also, where necessary, to have safety consultants and paramedics on site. In the case of construction or demolition, it may be necessary to retain an engineer or architect to project-supervise in line with onerous and detailed construction regulations or otherwise in compliance with law.

[25.16.03] In the case where the director or production company requires employees or temporary employees/agency workers to assist with filming, the 2005 Act imposes obligations in s 8 in respect of providing welfare facilities such that a three-day video shoot in a remote forest or mountain landscape for instance should come equipped with suitable temporary accommodation, food provisions, access to water, sanitation facilities and whatever else may be essential to life, safety, hygiene, privacy and dignity. Such matters of course all come at a substantial cost to be provided for at budgeting stage. As regards use of crew contractors, s 12 imposes duties on employers/hiring parties to persons who are not their employees.

Part IV

General Entertainment

Chapter 26

Occasional Licences for Marquees; Licensing of Concerts, Festivals, Public Events; Theatre Licences

OCCASIONAL LICENCES FOR MARQUEES

[26.1.01] In order to raise finance, sporting and other unincorporated associations, which in some cases may also be registered charities, need not depend exclusively on subscription moneys, raffles and their club lottery. Events and festivals, annual or otherwise, can be held on the grounds of the club to coincide perhaps with sporting fixtures and entertainment such as a dinner-dance function. The advantage of erecting a weather-proof marquee, tent or other such structure is substantially increased capacity beyond the four walls of the clubhouse and onto the grounds, with significant fundraising potential. However, whereas the clubhouse may be licensed to sell alcohol which can be consumed on-site, the large exterior tent outside is not. The means to overcome the otherwise unlawful sale and consumption of alcohol in the marquee is to apply to court for an Occasional Licence for the proposed event.

[26.1.02] These licence applications are made in the District Court. In relative terms, attendant outlay to include legal costs, excise duty and court stamp duty is rather insubstantial when set against potential revenue streams from ticket sales and income from meals and the sale of liquor.

Legislation

[26.1.03] Section 11 of the Intoxicating Liquor Act 1962 ('the 1962 Act') governs the application process for Occasional Licences. This provision was amended, *inter alia*, by s 1 of the Intoxicating Liquor Act 1977, and ss 10 and 4 of the Intoxicating Liquor Acts 2000 and 2018 respectively. Order 76 of the District Court Rules 1997[1] sets out the rules pertaining to Occasional Licence applications and Form 76.1 of Sch C to the Rules provides that where the

1 SI No 93 of 1997. Order 76 was amended by the District Court (Intoxicating Liquor) Rules 2018 (SI No 566 of 2018).

application is granted, the licence shall be in accordance with the prescribed court order wording of Form 76(1).

Steps in the court application process

[26.1.04] A notice of application is drafted setting out the licensee's name and place of residence, the premises to which the on-licence attaches, the unlicensed premises (marquee) for which the Occasional Licence is sought and the special event to which the application relates, together with the times and days during which intoxicating liquor is to be sold. This notice of application is then furnished to the local District Court Clerk and to the officer in charge of An Garda Síochána of the relevant district not later than 48 hours before the intended event (longer notice should be afforded in practice in the event that the Gardaí may raise issues of concern and to ensure the notice is in fact received and processed on time). Although not required under legislation, it is nonetheless advisable and prudent to also serve a copy of such notice of application on the local Fire Officer as a matter of courtesy.

[26.1.05] Statutory declarations of service should then be drafted confirming that the notices of application were duly served on the parties mentioned above and lodged with the District Court Clerk. Finally, a hearing will take place in the District Court during which application the judge will either grant or deny the application.

[26.1.06] An Occasional Licence shall operate to exempt the persons to whom they are granted (if and so long as they comply with the conditions subject to which it is granted, and the special event for which the licence is granted is held in compliance with the relevant provisions of subsection (2) and (10) of s 11 of the 1962 Act) from the provisions of the Licensing Acts 1833 to 2018 relating to the sale and supply of intoxicating liquor at the place and during the time for which the licence is granted.

[26.1.07] The special event can last for up to six days (an extension from three days to six days was provided for in s 1 of the Intoxicating Liquor Act 1977). It can be held on a Sunday[2] but not on Christmas Day. The Good Friday exclusion was removed by the Intoxicating Liquor (Amendment) Act 2018.[3] The licence may be granted from 8am to 10pm (and later if there is a substantial meal served or a dance is the subject entertainment). There is no limit on the amount of occasional licences for which the same applicant may apply in a year.

[26.1.08] In the case of licensed premises, members of An Garda Síochána may,[4]

2 s 11 of the 1962 Act was amended by s 10 of the Intoxicating Liquor Act 2000.

3 s 4(a) thereof amended s 11(5) of the Intoxicating Liquor Act 1962.

4 Under s 23 of the Licensing (Ireland) Act 1874 as amended by s 22(4) of the Intoxicating Liquor Act 1927.

for the purpose of preventing or detecting the violation of any of the provisions of the Intoxicating Liquor Acts which it is their duty to enforce, at all times enter on any licensed premises and on any premises in respect of which an Occasional Licence is in force.

Possible legislative reform

[26.1.09] The Commission on Liquor Licensing, in its Second Interim Report (July 2002) recommended[5] reforms in relation to two aspects of the current arrangements. As regards eligibility criteria, at present, only the holder of an on-licence is eligible to apply for an Occasional Licence. This has two particular consequences in the view of the commission members. First, the operation of temporary bars in connection with local festivals, celebrations and so forth is reserved to existing licensees and, secondly, the capacity of catering and special event companies to serve intoxicating liquor in the course of their commercial activities is restricted.

[26.1.10] This latter type of business has expanded significantly in the recent past. The reasons for limiting the granting of Occasional Licences to existing licensees may be related to a recognition that expertise and legal knowledge is required for the sale of intoxicating liquor, even on a temporary basis. On the other hand, the commission members opined, the fact that an applicant for an on-licence who has no direct experience of the bar trade can cite the employment of an experienced bar manager as evidence of suitability of character for the purposes of obtaining an on-licence is indicative of a certain level of flexibility in this area.

[26.1.11] There would seem to be no obstacle in principle, therefore, to allowing organisers of festivals, agricultural shows and other events, as well as companies in the catering or special events sector, to obtain an Occasional Licence where they can demonstrate the availability of the required expertise. Accordingly, the commission recommended that provision be made for granting Occasional Licences to non-licence holders who can demonstrate, to the satisfaction of the District Court, their suitability to hold such licences and the availability of the necessary expertise.

[26.1.12] One area of uncertainty in relation to the operation of Occasional Licences, in the view of the commission, relates to offences committed at the event in respect of which the licence was granted. The commission considered it desirable to remove this uncertainty. Moreover, since it may not be possible to enforce certain penalties, e.g. temporary closure orders, in respect of Occasional Licences, the lodgement of a substantial security or bond with the court as a form of guarantee that the event will operate in accordance with licensing laws

---

5 See section 4.4, Pt 3 (Hours of Trading) at p 23 thereof. Available at: http://www.justice.ie/en/JELR/Liquor%20Licensing%202nd%20Report.pdf/Files/Liquor%20Licensing%202nd%20Report.pdf [Accessed 22 November 2017].

was a move recommended by the commission at this interim report stage for consideration by the Oireachtas.[6]

[26.1.13] Thus, in its final report (April 2003),[7] the commission set out Recommendations 15 to 17 as follows:

> 15. Provision should be made for granting occasional licences to non-licence holders who can demonstrate their suitability to hold such licences and the availability of the necessary expertise (reason: to enable organisers of local festivals etc who can avail of persons with the relevant experience and qualifications to obtain a licence for such events);
>
> 16. The appropriate licensing laws should apply in any place licensed for the sale of intoxicating liquor under an occasional licence (reason: to clarify the law in relation to occasional licences and to ensure that if they are abused the proper remedies will apply);
>
> 17. Holders of special restaurant licences should be permitted to apply for occasional licences on the same basis as other on-licence holders (reason: to eliminate disparities between the holders of special restaurant licences and other on-licence holders in connection with applications for occasional licences).

LICENSING OF CONCERTS, FESTIVALS AND OTHER PUBLIC EVENTS

[26.2.01] Licences are required for the major music festivals in Ireland including Slane, Marley Park and Electric Picnic. The term "subject to licence" is frequently used when marketing the staging of certain events and festivals. The purpose of this section is to examine the meaning of such term and the issue is best illustrated by reference to the internationally publicised Garth Brooks Croke Park debacle in 2014 which led to legislative changes in this area by way of the introduction of new Regulations.

The cancelled Garth Brooks concerts at Croke Park (2014)

[26.2.02] In early 2014, Aiken Promotions announced that American performer Brooks would play two dates in Croke Park in July 2014. One Direction were also scheduled to play three dates in May. The country star had already played there in 1997 to some 130,000 fans while the stadium was under construction and extension. A third date was added to the July fixtures as was a fourth. On 6 February, a fifth and final date was added and, at this juncture, almost one in ten people in Ireland had purchased a ticket with an overall spend in excess of €28 million. However, by mid February, the local residents had begun to publicly air

---

6 *ibid* at pp 23-24 thereof.

7 See Appendix 5 (Recommendations from Previous Commission Reports) of Commission on Liquor Licensing *Final Report* at p 123, justice.ie. Available at: http://www.justice.ie/en/JELR/FinalReport.pdf/Files/FinalReport.pdf [Accessed 22 November 2017].

their fervent concerns at the disruption to their lives during the concert period in terms of noise, litter, traffic management and potential anti-social behaviour. They then set about vehemently resisting the setting of a five-consecutive-concert precedent (incidentally, Garth Brooks was approved to play five Croke Park concerts from 9-17 September 2022 as matters came full circle, again amidst vehement local opposition).

[26.2.03] They vowed to file injunctive relief proceedings to prevent the concerts proceeding, alleging that this issue did not centre on the Garth Brooks concerts alone. Concert issues had been raging for 20 years as explained by solicitor for the objecting residents, Anthony Fay.[8]

[26.2.04] It then transpired that Dublin City Council had sanctioned only three of the five would-be concerts. The council refused to grant a licence for the remaining two concerts as three concerts had already been played at Croke Park earlier that year. Artist Garth Brooks insisted that it would be five concerts or none at all and, ultimately, he cancelled the three permitted performances.

[26.2.05] The local residents group was also critical that tickets had gone on sale for the concerts in April, when the application for a concert licence was only filed with Dublin City Council that month. They claimed this was in breach of the Pt 16 of the Planning and Development Act 2000 which states that an application must be filed ten weeks prior, with a five-week period for objections.

Legislation

[26.2.06] Sections 229 to 241, Pt XVI (events and funfairs) of the Planning and Development Act 2000 ('the 2000 Act') regulate the holding of music festivals and other events. An event is defined in s 229 as, *inter alia*, a public performance which takes place wholly or mainly in the open air or in a structure with no roof or a partial, temporary or retractable roof, a tent or similar temporary structure and which is comprised of music, dancing, displays of public entertainment or any activity of a like kind. Article 183, Pt 16 (Licensing of Outdoor Events) of the Planning and Development Regulations 2001 discussed below states that an event at which the audience comprises 5,000 or more people shall be an event prescribed for the purposes of s 230 of the 2000 Act.

[26.2.07] Section 240 of the 2000 Act provides that the holding of such event and works directly or solely relating to the holding of such an event shall not be construed as "development" within the meaning of the 2000 Act and hence planning permission is not required. Section 230 obliges the organiser, promoter or holder of an event to obtain a licence. It is accordingly an offence to organise

8 Sinéad O'Carroll, *Permission granted for just THREE of the scheduled five Garth Brooks concerts* (2014), thejournal.ie. Available at: http://www.thejournal.ie/garth-brooks-permission-1551169-Jul2014/ [Accessed 2 January 2018].

and hold an event without having first procured such licence. A licence is defined in s 229 as a licence granted by a local authority under s 231. Local authorities themselves are exempted from the obligation in s 230 to obtain a licence when they hold an event (s 230(4)).

Section 231–grant of licence

[26.2.08] Section 231(3)(a) provides that, where an application for a licence is made in accordance with regulations under this section (see the Regulations passed in 2015 as discussed at para [26.2.13] below), the local authority may decide to grant the licence, grant the licence subject to such conditions as it considers appropriate or refuse the licence.

[26.2.09] In considering such application, the local authority shall have regard to any information relating to the application furnished to it by the applicant; any consultations with persons and bodies which must be consulted in relation to a licence; any submissions or observations by the public or otherwise; whether events have previously been held on the land concerned; the matters referred to in subsection (4) below; and any guidelines or codes of practice issued by the Minister for Housing, Local Government and Heritage or by any other minister of the government.

[26.2.10] Subsection (4) provides that the conditions subject to which a licence is granted may relate to all or any of the following: compliance with any guidelines or codes of practice issued by the minister; securing the safety of persons at the event; the provision of adequate facilities for the health and welfare of persons at the event including the provision of sanitary facilities; protection of the environment including the control of litter; maintenance of public order; avoidance or minimisation of disruption to the neighbourhood; ensuring the provision of adequate means of transport to and from the event; the number of events which are permitted at a venue within a specified period not exceeding one year; the payment of a financial contribution to the authority of a specified amount or an amount calculated on a specified basis towards the estimated cost to the local authority of measures taken by the authority in connection with the event (where the event is held wholly or mainly for profit); the payment of a financial contribution to a person or body consulted in accordance with subsection 2(e); maintaining public liability insurance; and the display of notices for persons attending the event as to their obligations and conduct at the event.

Conditions attaching to a licence

[26.2.11] By way of illustration, the August 2012 MCD concert events featuring Van Morrison, David Guetta and Kasabian at Marlay Park in Dublin were granted, according to *The Irish Times*, by Dún Laoghaire-Rathdown County Council subject to 53 conditions (relating to issues of concern raised by the

Gardaí, South Dublin County Council, the HSE and Dublin Fire Brigade) including in respect of traffic management plans, car parking, alcohol sale, security, stewarding and the numbers of non-public duty Gardaí. In relation to the provision of non-public duty Gardaí to police the concerts, one of the conditions attached to the licence noted that "the numbers employed on non-public duty will vary depending on the audience size, profile, risk assessment and the artist performing". It further stated that "all associated costs" were to be covered by the promoter.

[26.2.12] In a letter sent to the Dún Laoghaire-Rathdown County Council planning department on March 22 regarding the application, Chief Superintendent Michael O'Sullivan referred to the fact that no artist details had been supplied with the application stating that An Garda Síochána wished to reserve the right to review its requirements of the concert promoter and to make stipulations in relation to the sale of spirits at the bar concessions when the artist for each event was confirmed and the associated audience age profile and demographic was known. He explained this was necessary as the demographic of the audience, social strata, gender mix, average age and other such factors would vary greatly depending on the artists with concomitant implications for provision of police services.[9]

Outdoor event licensing and ticket sales: the new planning regulations

[26.2.13] As stated above, the Garth Brooks affair led to change in secondary legislation and hence the Planning and Development Regulations 2001[10] ('the 2001 Regulations') were amended by the Planning and Development (Amendment) Regulations 2015[11] which came into effect on 1 October 2015. Some of the key changes to Pt 16 (arts 182 to 199) of the 2001 Regulations are that it is now mandatory for events promoters to have a pre-application consultation meeting with the relevant local authority prior to submitting an event licence application. They further require the submission of the prescribed Form 9 of Sch 3 (see substituted art 184) preliminary risk assessment of the proposed event by the proposed applicant to the local authority prior to the pre-application consultation meeting. In addition, they mandate further pre-application consultation meetings and a revised preliminary risk assessment to be submitted by the proposed applicant if additional events are proposed to those outlined in the original preliminary risk assessment.

[26.2.14] The new regulations call for a statement of compliance from the applicant that there have been no substantial or repeated breaches of a licence,

---

9 Jim Carroll, *Licence for Marlay Park concerts granted subject to 53 conditions* (2012), irishtimes.com. Available at: https://www.irishtimes.com/blogs/ontherecord/2012/07/25/licence-for-marlay-park-concerts-subject-to-53-conditions/ [Accessed 29 December 2017].

10 SI No 600 of 2001.

11 SI No 264 of 2015.

or conditions of a licence issued to the applicant by any local authority in the previous 24 months. Very significantly, event promoters are not be entitled to advertise or sell tickets for events prior to the holding of a pre-application consultation meeting with the relevant local authority and, where tickets for events have been advertised and sold prior to the holding of a pre-application consultation meeting, an application for an event licence will not be accepted by the relevant local authority.

[26.2.15] Event licensing applications must be lodged with the relevant local authority at least 13 weeks in advance of the proposed event (formerly ten weeks) and local authorities must make their decision on an event licence application no later than four weeks in advance of the proposed event. Where it is proposed to add performances to a schedule already announced (as was the case with the Garth Brooks proposed concerts in 2014 which increased from two to five), a further pre-application consultation meeting will be required to take place before the announcement of any additional dates; and finally, the public consultation period in relation to event licence applications was reduced to three weeks (formerly five weeks).

[26.2.16] The new regulations follow on from the establishment of a Review Group in October 2014 by then Minister Alan Kelly to examine the event licensing regulations and to make recommendations on possible changes to the legislation following issues which arose in relation to the licensing of certain proposed outdoor events in the summer of 2014. The Review Group, which was chaired by the Department of the Environment, Community and Local Government,[12] and comprised representation from other government departments, state agencies and local authorities, met six times during the period October 2014 to March 2015. The Review Group also met with the four main promoters of outdoor events in Ireland (MCD, Aiken Promotions, Festival Republic and POD) who were invited to make presentations of their experience with the existing legislative provisions and to suggest potential changes that might be required.

[26.2.17] In addition, the Review Group initiated a month-long public consultation in November 2014 during which some 50 submissions were received from venue owners, residents' associations, local authorities, statutory bodies, industry operators and members of the public. All submissions received during the public consultation were published on the department's website.

Conclusion: outdoor event licensing

[26.2.18] The changes announced to the event licensing regime were intended to ensure more certainty, to balance the views of all stakeholders involved and

12 At the time of writing, this department is styled the Department of Housing, Local Government and Heritage.

implement more fit-for-purpose and streamlined procedures in relation to the granting of such licences. In particular, the notion of promoters advertising and selling tickets for events before having any pre-application consultation meeting with the relevant local authority in relation to a proposed event is a practice consigned to history.

Funfairs

[26.2.19] The control of funfairs is regulated by s 239 of the 2000 Act which defines fairground equipment, obliges the organisers of a funfair to hold a valid certificate of safety in respect of such equipment and outlines such matters as applications for and the grant of certificates of safety for fairground equipment; payment of prescribed fees; the notice period to be given to a local authority for holding of a funfair; offences for breach of the legislation; the immediate cessation of the use of any fairground equipment without a valid certificate of safety and for other breaches; the removal, within a specified time, of any fairground equipment, temporary buildings or structures, plant, machinery or similar equipment which the local authority believes is intended to be used in relation to the funfair; and the restoration of the land to its prior condition within a specified time.

[26.2.20] Section 239(5) made provision that the relevant minister shall by regulations provide for such matters of procedure, administration and control as appear to the minister to be necessary or expedient in relation to applications for and the grant of certificates of safety for fairground equipment. Hence, the Planning and Development Act 2000 (Certification of Fairground Equipment) Regulations 2003[13] and the Planning and Development Act 2000 (Certification of Fairground Equipment) (Amendment) Regulations 2007[14] were signed into law.

Crowd control by the Gardaí

[26.2.21] The purpose of crowd control at public events is to maintain public peace and order and ensure the safety of all who are gathered there. Part III of the Criminal Justice (Public Order) Act 1994 is based on the recommendations of the Hamilton Committee on Public Safety and Crowd Control chaired by then High Court judge Mr Justice Liam Hamilton.[15] That committee was established in the wake of the Hillsborough disaster in the UK in 1989.

[26.2.22] Section 21 of that Act empowers the Gardaí to place barriers on roads up to one mile (1.6 km) from where a particular event is taking place. The decision on the placing of barriers must be made by a Garda who is of

---

13 SI No 449 of 2003.
14 SI No 590 of 2007.
15 The late Hamilton J served as Chief Justice of the Supreme Court from 1994 to 2000.

superintendent rank or higher. When the barriers are in place, the Gardaí are allowed to prohibit people from crossing or passing the barrier if the person does not have a ticket for the event. The Garda may also seize any alcohol or disposable drinks containers or any offensive article at the barrier before allowing a person to proceed to the event.

THEATRE LICENCES

The history of Theatre Licences: The Point Depot and Tivoli Theatre cases

[26.3.01] Under the misapprehension that Theatre Licences had to be granted under Royal Patent or a special Act of Parliament, no Theatre Licences existed between 1930 and 1981 according to James Woods, Commissioner for Oaths, author, barrister and former Limerick District Court Clerk.[16] In conducting research for the 1981 edition of his liquor licensing guide, he discovered that a Music and Singing Licence would entitle the holder to apply for a Theatre Licence. The first Theatre Licence to be granted under a Music and Singing Licence was to the former Theatre Royal in Limerick in 1981.

[26.3.02] A late licence could be obtained on foot of a Music and Singing Licence (regulated by the Public Health Acts Amendment Act 1890) if venues could satisfy Revenue that they were operating a bona fide theatre. Theatre licences were believed to be confined to theatres but Woods argued successfully that, provided entertainment was offered and the venue held a Music and Singing Licence, "even though you were a pub you could also be granted this licence." Costello's Tavern in Baker Place, Limerick was one of the first public houses to benefit from Woods' advice in having both a Publican's Licence and a Theatre Licence attached, obviating the need for expensive special exemption orders for late night sale of alcohol.

[26.3.03] In 1991, solicitor Bill Holohan took a case to the High Court for one of Ireland's premier entertainment venues (The Point Depot, now the 3Arena) arguing that a public entertainment venue is entitled to a licence to serve intoxicating liquor. It had been accepted for one hundred years that it could not. Mr Holohan's legal argument was accepted by the court, culminating in the creation of what became known as the modern day Theatre Licence.

[26.3.04] The 1998 Supreme Court case stated appeal in *DPP v Tivoli Cinema Ltd*[17] by the prosecution against a dismissal in the District Court related to the defendant proprietor (represented again by Holohan Law) of premises at Francis Street, Dublin known as the Tivoli Theatre, a custom-built premises developed

---

16 Drinks Industry Ireland, *James Woods–Liquor Licensing guru* (2012), drinksindustryireland.ie. Available at: http://www.drinksindustryireland.ie/james-woods-liquor-licensing-guru/ [Accessed 3 May 2018].

17 [1999] 2 IR 260; [1998] IESC 54.

over the years 1986 to 1993 (which until recently operated as a music venue). On the first storey, there was a modern theatre. On the ground floor, there was also a modern theatre. It had a stage but there was no fixed seating. The floor was concrete and, depending upon the entertainment being provided, it may or may not have had seating laid out for its audience. The premises had all necessary planning permissions and local authority approvals.

[26.3.05] The proceedings related solely to the use of the ground floor theatre for late night music concerts when the seating was not in use. The defendant was at all material times the holder in respect of its premises of a music, singing and public entertainment licence issued under the provisions of the Public Health (Ireland) Act 1890 and a licence under s 7 of the Excise Act 1835 and such premises were accordingly a "theatre" for the purposes of the Intoxicating Liquor Act 1927 ('the 1927 Act'). The essential element so far as it related to the case was that s 7 provides for a licence to issue to "other places of public entertainment". There is no specific definition of such other places of public entertainment.

[26.3.06] The downstairs theatre was visited on three occasions in 1994 by Garda officers on nights when late night concerts were taking place on the premises. Prosecutions were brought against the defendant on the basis, *inter alia*, that as there were no seats, it was a breach of s 20 of the 1927 Act to allow persons to enter after 9.30pm. The proceedings having been dismissed, the prosecutor appealed by way of case stated. One question which arose for determination was whether the District Court judge was correct in law in interpreting the word "seat" as including a place for standing, it being the undisputed evidence that there were no seats available for patrons at the premises of the accused on the occasions in question.

[26.3.07] The court held, *per* Barron J, the word "seat" should be interpreted as including a place for standing. Sections 20 and 21 of the 1927 Act should be interpreted on the basis that the court was dealing not only with theatres but also with other places of public entertainment which might be organised on a slightly different basis — the result being that people do not have to be seated, and thus, standing concerts are allowed in law.

Current law governing Theatre Licences

[26.3.08] Previously, Theatre Licences were issued by Revenue without any court certificate following presentation by the applicant of a public Music and Singing Licence (obtained from the District Court). Trading hours depended on the duration of performances in the theatre but there was no definition of performance or theatre in the legislation with the result that certain premises remained open until 3am or 5am. The sale of alcohol in premises with Theatre Licences is now permitted only during normal licensing hours, or during extended opening hours under a Special Exemption Order granted by the District Court. The law was amended to provide that the issue of a Theatre Licence is subject to production of a District Court certificate.

[26.3.09] A Music and Singing Licence is first required from the District Court before applying for a Theatre Licence from Revenue. Application is made to the Annual District Licensing Court and, upon receipt of the court certificate, same is submitted to the National Excise Licence Office. A new Music and Singing Licence is required each year to renew one's Publican's Licence (Ordinary) Theatre Licence.

The legislation on extended opening hours

[26.3.10] A new s 5 (Special Exemption Orders) of the 1927 Act was inserted by s 11 of the Intoxicating Liquor Act 2003. Section 5 was then amended by s 10 of the Intoxicating Liquor Act 2008. The conditions under which Special Exemption Orders can be made require the operation of a CCTV system and compliance with fire safety standards. Objections may be made by the Gardaí under public order grounds.

Chapter 27

Fire Safety, Occupiers' Liability, Event Security and Licensing Indoor Events

FIRE SAFETY

[27.1.01] The Stardust nightclub disaster[1] on Valentine's Day 1981 claimed the lives of 48 patrons and injured 214 others at an Artane venue in Dublin attended by more than 800 persons. Due to an electrical fault, a fire started in a non-planning compliant first-floor storeroom which contained dangerously flammable materials including large gallon drums of cooking oil. The fire apparently ignited after flames on the roof from the storeroom came through the roof tiles and fell onto the backrest and the top of a seating bench covered in PVC-coated polyester fabric. It then spread to plywood tables and upholstered seats and patrons began to notice smoke as carpet tiled walls and the ceiling caught flame. The ceiling collapsed, the lights failed and thick black smoke engulfed the ballroom.

[27.1.02] A tribunal of inquiry under then High Court judge, Keane J[2] concluded in November 1981 that the fire was probably caused by arson. This finding, which has been disputed ever since, legally exonerated the owners from responsibility.[3] However, the inquiry was damning in its criticism of the safety standards. Keane J also criticised the owners and management of the Stardust for recklessly dangerous practices when it was discovered that some emergency exit doors had been locked and impeded on the night of the fire. Not surprisingly, the aftermath led to a range of recommendations being made and implemented in relation to fire safety.

---

1 The Greenvale Hotel teenage crushing tragedy in 2019 (County Tyrone) is also discussed at the end of this chapter.

2 Keane J was subsequently appointed to the Supreme Court in 1996 and served as Chief Justice in the early 2000s.

3 There have been a number of enquiries since. After a senior counsel report to the Dáil in 2009, the public record was corrected and the original arson conclusion removed as the cause due to there being no evidence to suggest that the fire was started maliciously. In 2019 the Attorney General confirmed that fresh inquests would be held because there was an insufficiency of inquiry as to how the deaths occurred.

[27.1.03] According to the *Irish Examiner*, awards totalling £10.4 million were made.[4] Those with the most severe injuries received the largest amounts, but none received more than £200,000, a rather modest sum perhaps in the case of a lifelong disability. Five victims received £100,000 or more, 24 received in excess of £50,000, and the majority of claimants received somewhere between £5,000 and £10,000. Parents who lost children were among the largest group, their payment in respect of each death set at a maximum of £7,500.

[27.1.04] The Stardust fire disaster has often been cited as a case study in fire-safety neglect. Few involved in construction, planning, event-staging or the fire service have escaped a lesson on the catastrophic mixture of low-level standards, light-touch regulation and negligence that led to the inferno. Inquest proceedings before Dublin district coroner Dr Myra Cullinane will commence on 25 April 2023 and at the time of writing a jury has been empanelled. The fresh inquests into the tragedy, which will re-examine the circumstances related to the death of 48 young people, were first ordered by the Attorney General in September 2019.[5]

Legislation

[27.1.05] The current Irish building control system was introduced as a direct response to the Stardust tragedy; consequently, the legislation is now weighted heavily on a rigorous process of fire safety design certification by local authorities. In one generation this brought about a culture change as the principles of fire safety became widely understood and the construction industry responded. The backbone of the system has been resources and training for dedicated staff in the local authorities. The success of this policy is demonstrated in the fact that in the four-year period 2010 to 2013 there was only one fire fatality in non-residential buildings in Ireland.[6]

[27.1.06] The Fire Services Act 1981 ('the 1981 Act'), applicable to both outdoor and enclosed venues, introduced in the wake of the disaster was amended, *inter alia*, by Pt 3 (ss 24 to 34) of the Licensing of Indoor Events Act 2003 ('the 2003

---

4 Caroline O'Doherty, *How fire that destroyed the Stardust in 1981 devastated lives for decades* (2018), irishexaminer.ie. Available at: https://www.irishexaminer.com/breakingnews/views/how-fire-that-destroyed-the-stardust-in-1981-devastated-lives-for-decades-827585.html. [Accessed 2 March 2018].

5 In 2022, the former manager of the Stardust brought a High Court challenge related to the inquests. Lawyers for Eamon Butterly sought the judicial review to prevent the coroner from conducting the inquest in a way in which he believed would make him "a target for a verdict of unlawful killing". Butterly failed in this application and Mr Justice Charles Meenan said "it is for the coroner, having heard all the evidence…and considered the submissions of the parties, to direct the jury as to the permissible verdicts".

6 Source: Department of the Environment, Community & Local Government statistics referred to in Orla Hegarty, *Stardust Remembered | Building Control is about protecting life, not property (Part 1)* (2015), bregsforum.com. Available at: http://www.bregsforum.com/2015/02/13/stardust-remembered-building-control-is-about-protecting-life-not-property-part-1/ [Accessed 2 March 18].

Act').[7] Serious offences, such as contravening fire safety regulations in relation to the size, design and use of buildings, the provision of adequate fire escape facilities and the maximum number of occupants allowed under the regulations, may be punished on conviction on indictment with a fine of up to €130,000 or a prison sentence of up to two years or both.[8]

[27.1.07] Section 18 (as amended by s 29 of the 2003 Act) of the 1981 Act provides that it shall be the duty of every person having control over premises to which the section applies to take all reasonable measures to guard against the outbreak of fire on such premises, provide reasonable fire safety measures for the premises and prepare and provide appropriate fire safety procedures, to be applied at all times, for ensuring the safety of persons on such premises.

[27.1.08] It is worth noting that the definition of buildings in s 2 of the 1981 Act (as amended by s 24 of the 2003 Act) includes temporary buildings, structures and erections. This would encompass the types of buildings at music festivals and other social events.

The Building Control Regulations 1997 to 2020[9]

[27.1.09] The Building Control Regulations as made under the Building Control Act 1990 as amended provide, *inter alia*, for a system of fire safety certificates to vouch that building designs comply with fire safety requirements. Developers of every new building, with the exception of certain domestic buildings, are required to obtain a fire safety certificate.[10] Although there are different certificates for different kinds of development, it is necessary for developers in all cases to send their plans and designs to their local fire authority. Developers' plans are inspected by senior fire services staff who ensure that adequate escape facilities are present and that the building is designed in a manner that prevents and limits the spread of a fire. If they are satisfied, a certificate is then issued by the building control authority.

[27.1.10] Under the provisions of the Fire Services Acts 1981 and 2003, authorised inspectors from the fire services can visit and inspect any building within their jurisdiction. They may ask for such details as the number of employees or occupants in the building, the purpose of any room or area in the building and the materials used in the building's construction. The inspectors can also examine the water supply and are permitted to bring any necessary

---

7 See Licensing of Indoor Events Act 2003 (Commencement) Order 2003 (SI No 291 of 2003). Note that Pt 2 (ss 5 to 23) of the 2003 Act has yet to be commenced. Sections 1-4 have also yet to be commenced.

8 s 25 of the 2003 Act, which substituted a new s 5 of the 1981 Act.

9 See for example SI No 496 of 1997, SI No 9 of 2014 and SI No 113 of 2020.

10 This does not exempt houses and apartments however from compliance with building regulations generally in relation to fire safety. Apartment blocks do require fire safety certification.

equipment with them onto a site and examine or test any heating, lighting or ventilation systems and any substances used or stored within a premises.

[27.1.11] Owners of property may be requested by a fire services inspector to provide drawings or plans of buildings under their ownership. The owner is legally obliged to provide a satisfactory response to the inspector. If inspectors are not satisfied with what they discover, application can be made to the High Court for an order requiring the removal, alteration or making safe of any structure, service, fitting or piece of equipment, or an order restricting construction work at the site or prohibiting the use of a building until the required changes have been effected. If the High Court grants such an order, its terms are legally binding on the owner of the building or site. Offenders can face a fine of up to €3,000 and/or up to six months' imprisonment.

[27.1.12] If fire services inspectors are refused entry, obstructed or impeded in their duties, such offence is punishable by a fine of up to €3,000 and/or six months imprisonment.[11] A fire services inspector can apply to the District Court for a warrant if refused entry to a building or site.

OCCUPIERS' LIABILITY

[27.2.01] Breach of occupiers' liability can give rise to civil claims and may be pleaded in the form of breach of statutory duty in legal proceedings. In the entertainment sector, an occupier[12] might be the proprietor of a concert venue, a production company on a film set or the tenant of offices operating a radio station.

[27.2.02] Under s 3 of the Occupiers' Liability Act 1995 ('the Act'), an occupier of premises owes a duty of care ("the common duty of care") towards a visitor onto such premises except in so far as the occupier extends, restricts, modifies or excludes that duty in accordance with s 5. The common duty of care means a duty to take such care as is reasonable in all the circumstances to ensure that a visitor to the premises does not suffer injury or damage by reason of any danger

11 Art 5 of the 2014 Building Control (Amendment) Regulations (SI No 9 of 2014) which inserted a new Art 6A into the principal 1997 regulations.

12 "Occupier" in relation to any premises means a person exercising such control over the state of the premises that it is reasonable to impose upon that person a duty towards an entrant in respect of a particular danger thereon and, where there is more than one occupier of the same premises, the extent of the duty of each occupier towards an entrant depends on the degree of control each of them has over the state of the premises and the particular danger thereon and whether, as respects each of them, the entrant concerned is a visitor, recreational user or trespasser – s 1, Occupiers' Liability Act 1995.

existing thereon.[13] The Court of Appeal in *Byrne v Ardenheath*[14] (2017) assessing a visitor's regard to her own safety and welfare held that a defendant was entitled to assume that an adult exercising reasonable care would avoid a wet grassy slope, particularly when considering the presence of a 6-inch kerbstone, the fact that she was wearing shoes that provided little grip, and that she needed to go no further than some ten feet to leave the subject car park through an entrance using a tarmacadam surface.[15]

[27.2.03] As regards recreational users[16] and trespassers, in respect of a danger existing on a premises, an occupier owes towards a recreator user of the premises or a trespasser thereon ("the person") a duty not to injure the person or damage the property of the person intentionally, and not to act with reckless disregard for the person or the property of the person except in so far as the occupier modifies or excludes the duty in accordance with s 5.

[27.2.04] In determining whether or not an occupier has so acted with reckless disregard, reference shall be had (s 4(2) of the Act) to all the circumstances of the case, including whether the occupier knew or had reasonable grounds for believing that a danger existed on the premises; whether the occupier knew or had reasonable grounds for believing that the person and, in the case of damage, property of the person, was or was likely to be on the premises; whether the danger was one against which, in all the circumstances, the occupier might reasonably be expected to provide protection for the person and property of the person; the burden on the occupier of eliminating the danger or of protecting the person and property of the person from the danger, taking into account the difficulty, expense or impracticability, having regard to the character of the premises and the degree of the danger, of so doing; the conduct of persons (and the care shown for their own safety); the nature of any warning given by the occupier or another person of the danger; and whether or not the person

---

13 Having regard to the care which visitors may reasonably be expected to take for their own safety and, if the visitor is on the premises in the company of another person, the extent of the supervision and control the latter person may reasonably be expected to exercise over the visitor's activities.

14 [2017] 1 IECA 293.

15 In May 2018, the High Court *per* Twomey J in *O'Connor v Wexford County Council* [2018] IEHC 232 applied the reasoning of the Court of Appeal in *Ardenheath* when it dismissed a personal injuries claim arising from a slip and fall at work, on grounds that the plaintiff, who was a water inspector, did not exercise common sense, and failed to take reasonable care for his own safety by using the steep incline to access a manhole when there was a flat route a modest distance away. The law on personal injuries as laid down by the Court of Appeal was again applied by Mr Justice Twomey in *Comerford v Carlow County Council* [2017] 1 IEHC 720. Proceedings were also dismissed by the High Court in *Van Dalsen v Davy Hickey Properties Ltd* [2016] IEHC 717 and in *Chambers v Powerscourt Estates Ltd* [2016] IEHC 717.

16 Defined in s 1 of the Act as an entrant who, with or without the occupier's permission or at the occupier's implied invitation, is present on premises without a charge (other than a reasonable charge in respect of the cost of providing vehicle parking facilities) being imposed for the purpose of engaging in a recreational activity.

was on the premises in the company of another person and, if so, the extent of the supervision and control the latter person might reasonably be expected to exercise over the other's activities.

[27.2.05] Section 4(3) provides that where a person enters onto premises for the purpose of committing an offence (and this includes attempted offences) or, while present thereon, commits an offence, the occupier shall not be liable for a breach of the duty imposed by subsection (1)(b) unless a court determines otherwise in the interests of justice.

Disclaimer notices

[27.2.06] Section 5 of the Act provides that occupiers may by express agreement or notice restrict, modify or exclude their duty towards visitors. This often manifests itself in the form of a prominent warning/disclaimer notice or sign outside the normal access point to a premises warning not to trespass on private property, and that if one does so, entry is at one's own risk. Such a restriction, modification or exclusion shall not bind a visitor unless it is reasonable in all the circumstances, and in the case where an occupier purports by notice to so restrict, modify or exclude that duty, the occupier must have taken reasonable steps to bring the notice to the attention of the visitor.

[27.2.07] In determining for the purposes of s 5(3)[17] whether or not an occupier has acted with reckless disregard, consideration shall be had to all the circumstances of the case including, where appropriate, the matters specified in s 4(2) above. Finally, where injury or damage is caused to a visitor or property of a visitor by a danger of which the visitor had been warned by the occupier or another person, the warning is not, without more, to be treated as absolving the occupier from liability unless, in all the circumstances, it was enough to enable the visitor, by having regard to the warning, to avoid the injury or damage so caused (s 5(5)).

No liability (generally) for independent contractors

[27.2.08] Section 7 states that an occupier of premises shall not be liable to an entrant for injury or damage caused to the entrant or property of the entrant by reason of a danger existing on the premises due to the negligence of an independent contractor hired by the occupier if the occupier has taken all reasonable care in the circumstances (including such steps as occupiers ought reasonably to have taken to satisfy themselves that the independent contractor was competent to do the work concerned) unless the occupier has or ought to

---

17 s 5(3) provides that in respect of a danger existing on premises, a restriction, modification or exclusion shall not be taken as allowing an occupier to injure a visitor or damage the property of a visitor intentionally or to act with reckless disregard for a visitor or the property of a visitor.

have had knowledge of the fact that the work was not properly carried out by the contractor.

EVENT SECURITY AND THE PRIVATE SECURITY AUTHORITY

[27.3.01] To comply with their common law duty of care and any relevant statutory duties in relation to safety, planning legislation, event licensing or otherwise, businesses providing entertainment and managing social venues, including bars and music festivals, must employ security personnel (door supervisors and security guards) to safeguard patrons. Pursuant to s 38 of the Private Security Services Act 2004 ('the 2004 Act') there is a prohibition on employment of an unlicensed person.

[27.3.02] Applicants for a licence to engage in security provision must be made under s 21 of the 2004 Act to the Private Security Authority ('PSA'). This aspect of the entertainment industry is also regulated by the Private Security (Licensing and Standards) Regulations 2012[18] ('the 2012 Regulations') which revoked prior regulations and which were amended by the Private Security (Licensing and Standards) (Locksmith) Regulations 2016[19] together with the Private Security (Licensing and Standards) (Event Security) Regulations 2014.[20] This latter secondary legislation prescribes the standards with which security contractors will need to comply when providing security at events such as concerts, sporting occasions and other gatherings.

[27.3.03] The Authority is empowered in s 51 of the 2004 Act thus: it may, with the consent of the Minister for Justice, make regulations to provide for any matter referred to in the 2004 Act. An example of such regulations includes the above-mentioned 2014 regulations.

[27.3.04] Pursuant to PSA 39:2014 (event security licensing requirements and standards), the security organisation hired for the subject event shall have and make available to a client a statement signed and dated by a principal of the organisation of its compliance with all relevant legislation and shall state specifically its compliance, where relevant, with the following: Planning and Development Act 2000; Licensing of Indoor Events Act 2003; Code of Practice For Safety At Indoor Concerts (Department of the Environment and Local Government: 1998); Code of Practice For Safety At Outdoor Pop Concerts and Other Outdoor Musical Events (Department of Education: 1996); Safety, Health and Welfare at Work Act 2005, and the 2004 Act itself.

---

18 SI No 144 of 2012. See also SI No 147 of 2012.

19 SI No 343 of 2016.

20 SI No 302 of 2014 – reg 7 of these Regulations amends/substitutes reg 4 of the 2012 Regulations and *inter alia* prescribes the following categories of licence which may be granted by the Authority to a private security employer or an independent contractor – door supervisor (event security) licence; and door supervisor (licensed premises) licence.

[27.3.05] These standards outline the security requirements in terms of staffing, uniforms, threats and violence by patrons, general and venue-specific training, special training (e.g. command and control system operations, communication systems, pit crews, searches, removal of persons), the event security management plan and handling emergencies, risk assessment, hazard identification (and the attendant control measures to eliminate, isolate, reduce or manage those risks), incident reporting; and consulting with An Garda Síochána, government bodies, local authorities, emergency services and risk assessment consultants on likely security hazards as well as conducting assessments of crowd dynamics, environmental factors (e.g. outdoor, terrain, weather, lighting, traffic and pedestrian flow, intoxication, etc.).

[27.3.06] Clients of event security contractors under the 2004 Act such as public houses, nightclubs or premises where a dance or music event is taking place have obligations under s 15 thereof in respect of the power and entry provisions relating to PSA inspectors. Such clients shall allow inspectors from the PSA access to any venue where a security service is being provided. Clients shall also produce any records, books or other documents or information which it is necessary for PSA inspectors to see in the exercise of their functions. Such documents would include, but are not limited to, risk assessments and risk assessment surveys, risk control plans, event security management plans, assignment instructions, the site plan, attendance registers for event security staff and incident reports. Security service clients shall afford to a PSA inspector such facilities and assistance within their control or responsibility to enable inspectors to exercise their powers.

THE LICENSING OF INDOOR EVENTS ACT 2003

[27.4.01] A ministerial commencement order[21] in 2003 commenced Pt 3 (amendments to the Fire Services Act 1981) only of the 2003 Act. The remainder of the Act (ss 1-23) was not commenced. The purpose of this 2003 legislation is to make provision for the licensing of certain indoor events by fire authorities, to make some miscellaneous amendments to the 1981 Act and make better provision for enforcement. The enactment of the statute arose from the need to implement the recommendations of the Hamilton Committee on Crowd Control[22] at indoor concerts and the development of the Code of Practice for Safety at Indoor Concerts when it became apparent that existing licensing systems governing such events did not adequately cater for matters such as public safety and crowd management. While the code applied to outdoor events, it stated

---

21 Licensing of Indoor Events Act 2003 (Commencement) Order 2003 (SI No 291 of 2003).

22 In 1989 the government of the day tasked then High Court judge Hamilton J to chair a committee on public safety and crowd control the terms of reference of which included, "To examine and report to the government on the adequacy of all existing provisions, including legislative provisions, relating to public safety and crowd control at major events and music festivals and concerts and to make such recommendations as seem to them appropriate".

clearly that the parameters for good organisation of an indoor pop concert were basically similar. This issue was topical around the time of coroner inquests into crowd trampling which led to the death of a teenager at a Smashing Pumpkins concert at The Point Depot in Dublin in May 1996.

[27.4.02] There are currently no regulations requiring a local authority to license or approve an event of less than 5,000-person capacity (however, there are certain codes of practice which may be considered). An application can be made to the courts for a licence for certain activities that may be present at indoor events (e.g. liquor licence, dance licence, music and singing licence). The local fire authority (along with other notice parties) is to be notified of these applications to the court. When a notification of a licensing application has been received, the fire authority may carry out an inspection, request information, and, if satisfied, provide to the court a letter of no objection with certain conditions attached. The letter of no objection or objection from the fire authority is considered by the court during its review of the application and will inform the court's subsequent decision to grant or deny the licensing application.

[27.4.03] In all cases, all organisers of indoor events are required to cater for the health and safety, including fire safety, of persons on the premises under the provisions of the following legislation: Safety Health and Welfare at Work Act 2005; Safety, Health and Welfare at Work (General Application) Regulations 2007 to 2021; Fire Services Acts 1981 and 2003; Places of Assembly (Ease of Escape) Regulations 1985[23]; Code of Practice for the Management of Fire Safety in Places of Assembly; and the Code of Practice for Fire Safety of Furnishings and Fittings in Places of Assembly (1989).

[27.4.04] In addition, as seen above, there is in place a code of practice covering safety at indoor and outdoor concerts: Code of Practice for Fire Safety at Indoor Concerts 1998 ('the 1998 Code') (Department of Environment and Local Government) and the Code of Practice for Safety at Outdoor Pop Concerts and Other Musical Events (Department of Education, 1996).

[27.4.05] The 1998 Code points to the dangers inherent in particularly vigorous forms of audience participation, such as crowd surfing, crowd diving and moshing (members of a standing audience crashing violently into each other). The code also warns against performances containing:

> ...any material or activity which could overexcite the audience or endanger safety. Performers should remain within the stage area throughout the performance and should not incite or encourage any dangerous or unacceptable behaviour on the part of the audience.[24]

---

23 SI No 249 of 1985.

24 Para 3.9 at p 13 of the 1998 Code.

The code also identifies the tendency of people at such concerts to crowd towards the stage as a matter for serious concern:

> In the interests of comfort and safety, seating represents the preferred way of accommodating people at a concert, avoiding many of the risks associated with standing concerts.[25]

[27.4.06] The 1998 Code provides practical advice too and guidance for concert promoters on other matters such as event planning and management, the use of barriers, stewarding and the provision of emergency medical facilities. Furthermore, it deals of course with fire precautions and fire safety and structural matters.

Safety legislation

[27.4.07] In addition to security requirements as outlined above, licensed and other event premises must be mindful of all times of the provisions of the Safety, Health and Welfare at Work Act 2005 discussed in Chapter 3. As well as s 8 provisions relating to duties owed to employees, s 12 thereof provides that all employers shall manage and conduct their undertaking in such a way as to ensure, so far as is reasonably practicable, that in the course of the work being carried on, individuals at the place of work (not being employees) are not exposed to risks to their safety, health or welfare. Section 15 sets out duties of persons in control of places of work.

[27.4.08] Section 11 mandates that every employer shall, in preparing and revising as necessary adequate plans and procedures to be followed and measures to be taken in the case of an emergency or serious and imminent danger, provide the necessary measures to be taken as appropriate to the place of work for first aid fire-fighting and the evacuation of employees and any other individual present in the place of work; arrange any necessary contacts with the appropriate emergency services, in particular with regard to first aid, emergency medical care, rescue work and fire-fighting; designate employees who are required to implement plans, procedures and measures, and ensure that the number of those employees, their training and the equipment available to them are adequate, taking into account either or both the size of and specific hazards relating to the place of work.

The Greenvale Hotel crushing fatalities

[27.4.09] Tragedy struck on St Patrick's Day in March 2019 at a Tyrone hotel in Northern Ireland, venue to a 500-capacity teenage disco. Some 600 young people were seeking to gain access to Greenvale Hotel in Cookstown, County Tyrone after being dropped off by buses shortly before 9.30pm on a Sunday evening. Due to patrons arriving in large numbers in close succession, a crush

---

25 Para 3.3 at p 12.

towards the front door of the hotel ensued and three teenagers lost their lives having been trodden underfoot. Following the tragedy, hotel proprietor Michael McElhatton and a 40-year-old man, understood to be a member of the hotel's door staff, were arrested on suspicion of manslaughter.

[27.4.10] The three gross negligence manslaughter charges (one for each fatality) against the proprietor and a self-employed person working at the hotel (and separate offences concerning contravening the Health and Safety at Work (Northern Ireland) Order 1978) came before Dungannon Magistrates' Court in December 2022 and the matter was adjourned to early 2023 due to the substantial volume of documentation.

Chapter 28

Permits for Busking and Street Performances

INTRODUCTION

[28.1.01] Dublin's Grafton Street and Galway city centre naturally spring to mind when referring to busking in Ireland. A review of the attendant regulation of street performances for each city/county/town council nationwide is obviously not practicable and to take matters out of the capital city, we will concentrate on the relevant bye-laws that apply in Galway where Ed Sheeran, for one, began to hone his craft as a 12-year-old musical prodigy on its city streets. Similar rules apply around the country and the applicable local authority website or arts office can be consulted for specifics. A summary of the Dublin city bye-laws is set out at the end of this chapter.

Legislation

[28.1.02] Section 199 of the Local Government Act 2001 ('the 2001 Act') grants power to local authorities to make bye-laws for or in relation to the use, operation, protection, regulation or management of any land, services, or any other matter provided by or under the control or management of the local authority. The provisions relating to bye-laws are contained in ss 198 to 211 of Pt 19 of the 2001 Act as amended by the Local Government Reform Act 2014.

[28.1.03] The Galway City Council Street Performance and Busking Bye-Laws 2019, effective from 1 January 2020, repealed the Street Performance (Prohibited Periods) Bye-Laws 2011. They are policed by community wardens and members of An Garda Síochána.

Restrictions and derogations

[28.1.04] The majority of councillors who voted for the new laws which regulate the pedestrianised city centre[1] spoke of the need to take account of city centre

1 The new bye-laws cover the "protected streetscape" running from the top of Williamsgate

businesses, pointing to access issues caused by crowds watching performances. The rules, which were deemed by the outraged artist community to curb freedom of expression and creativity in the city, ban the use of amplification or backing tracks by buskers before 6pm and also restrict so-called 'circle acts' that attract large crowds of bystanders congregating around them during business hours. Amplification using an electronic device to create or increase the volume of a musical instrument or vocal performance is no longer permitted. The use of drum kits is also banned at all times.

[28.1.05] Buskers may however seek derogations to the bye-laws such as those which might be granted to permit use of drums and circle acts before 6pm during major events and festival periods, subject to application to the Chief Executive Officer who is authorised, in consultation with members of Galway City Council, to issue an Executive Order in respect of any such derogations.

Definitions

[28.1.06] "Circle acts" mean street performers who have a structured performance or routine that requires the reservation of a specific space and necessitates the audience to stop, watch and/or to participate. Such performances may incorporate elements of street theatre, puppetry, dance, comedy, fire manipulation, juggling and acrobatics and may involve the use of dangerous properties (such as flammable substances and sharp objects) as part of the act and thus public liability insurance (of approximately €6.5 million in cover) may be required by the council depending on the act. "Perform" means to engage in any type of public performance or exhibition with the reasonable expectation or opportunity of receiving donations, and includes the playing of musical instruments, singing, reciting, dancing, acting, juggling, magical tricks, street theatre, pavement art, sand sculpture, modeling and carving.

Performance times

[28.1.07] To ensure street performances do not generate noise nuisance to the public and nearby businesses, a street performer shall not perform in a public place[2] either before 10am or after 11pm during the months of April to October and may not perform in a public place either before 10am or after 10pm during the months of November to March, save and except silent acts such as human statues, pavement artists, balloon modelers, which body of performers shall be excluded from the time limits and proximity rules.

[28.1.08] A street performer is only permitted to perform for a maximum of two hours in a public place and shall not be entitled to charge a fee to members

---

Street to the end of Quay Street.

2 "Public place" includes any footpath, footway or road, open space, beach, public park or green space being in the charge or ownership of Galway City Council.

of the public, other than gifts or donations by the public to acknowledge that performance. Once the period of two hours has lapsed, the street performer must relocate to a different place not within 35 meters of the previous place. A street performer shall not act, say, do or sing anything that is likely to cause alarm, distress or offence to any member of the public, any business owner or occupier, the city council and/or any member of An Garda Síochána.

[28.1.09] A street performer shall not reserve a location/area while not performing, thereby preventing its use by another street performer. In addition, a street performer shall not obstruct the public's access to and egress from any premises and must immediately cease a performance in circumstances where a crowd has gathered thereby preventing the movement of pedestrians. Grafton Street in Dublin was closed in 2016 thus scuppering Glen Hansard's famous Christmas busking in aid of homeless charities due to crowd control and crowd safety concerns given that such a large audience had gathered, thereby impeding or preventing free flow and passage of people in the street.

Offences

[28.1.10] Where a bye-law is contravened, a community warden or Garda may serve a fixed charge notice (€75 with an increase to €150 if not paid within four weeks) in respect of the contravention.[3] Any person who contravenes any provision of the bye-laws or who prevents, attempts to prevent or encourages any other person to prevent, or attempt to prevent the exercise by a community warden (or other duly authorised person) and/or a member of An Garda Síochána from exercising a power conferred by the bye-laws shall be guilty of an offence and shall be liable on summary conviction to fine not exceeding €1,500.

[28.1.11] Finally, pursuant to s 204(3)(d) of the 2001 Act, where a member of An Garda Síochána forms the opinion that an offence is being or has been committed under the bye-laws, that member may arrest the person without warrant.

DUBLIN CITY COUNCIL: STREET PERFORMANCE BYE-LAWS

[28.2.01] Updated Street Performers Bye-Laws come into effect in August 2016 resulting in important changes to the 2015 bye-laws including backing tracks no longer being permitted; performers can now only remain on Grafton Street for one hour before moving; performances must start and end on the hour mark; a two-week visitor permit has been introduced; new permits[4] are subject to a six-week probation period, and acoustic performance is now possible in

---

3 Summary proceedings may be instituted if the €150 late penalty is not paid within 56 days.

4 Permit applications (annual fee of €30, a fee of €60 applies to annual amplification permits) are made to: Licensing Section, Culture, Recreation and Economic Services, Block 4,

the Temple Bar prohibited place (map of prohibited locations may be viewed online) but the area where amplified busking is banned has been extended. Street performance permit applications, amplification permit applications and visitor street performance permit application forms can be downloaded from city council website.[5]

[28.2.02] A performer must display a performance permit and have it clearly visible at all times during a performance in a public place; hold and display a permit to use amplification if using amplifiers; ensure a performance does not cause offence; comply with a lawful request of an authorised officer of the city council or a member of An Garda Síochána; and hold public liability insurance if using props or the act involves danger to the public.

[28.2.03] A performer must not perform before 9am (11am on pedestrianised streets where delivery vehicles operate), not perform after 11pm, not perform in a prohibited area and not perform twice in the same location on the same day. In addition, performers must not offer CDs or other merchandise for sale, outstay the maximum performance time of two hours (or one hour on Grafton Street), block entrances or cause obstruction on a street, exceed a volume level of 80db (75db in the Temple Bar area), use backing tracks or other recorded music, charge members of the public a fee for a performance or solicit, coerce or otherwise encourage members of the public into making a donation. The use of lewd, offensive or derogatory language or conduct is strictly prohibited and such behaviour will most likely result in withdrawal of a permit and imposition of a sanction for breach of the bye-laws.

Ground Floor, Civic Offices, Wood Quay, Dublin 8 or by email to: streetperformers@dublincity.ie.

5 See https://www.dublincity.ie/business/business-licences/street-performance#:~:text=Performers%20can%20only%20stay%20on,a%20six%2Dweek%20probation%20period. [Accessed 5 April 2023].

Chapter 29

Regulation of Gambling and Lotteries; Premium Rate Services; Commission for Communications Regulation

GAMBLING AND LOTTERIES

[29.1.01] According to *The Irish Post*,[1] more than 6,000 people work in betting shops, and another 1,000 are employed by online operators. Casinos are open 24/7, horse racing is a national pastime, and fixed odds betting terminals are commonplace on the shop floor of bookmaker outlets. However, Irish gambling is in a place of transition, with gaming laws thought by many in this service industry to be outdated and in need of tighter control and regulation to, *inter alia*, tackle organised crime and money laundering as well as compulsive or excessive gambling gambling. To this end, Chapter 4 of the Gambling Regulation Bill 2022 proposes the application of a percentage of gambling retailers' annual turnover to the establishment of a social impact fund to promote socially responsible playing (see s 52(3)). In a similar vein, in relation to lotteries, legislation passed in 2019 provides that in respect of lotteries with a total prize value of up to €30,000 per week, 25 percent of proceeds must be allocated to charitable or philanthropic purposes.[2]

[29.1.02] The 2022 Bill, when passed, seeks to comprehensively reform the regulation of gambling activities and to provide for an independent Gambling Regulatory Authority (the Media Commission which replaced the BAI shall also have regard, pursuant to the Online Safety and Media Regulation Act 2022, to the regulation of gambling). The Department of Justice's Statement of Strategy 2021-2023 set out the commitment to establish a gambling regulator focused on public safety and wellbeing, covering gambling online and in person, and the powers to regulate advertising, gambling websites and apps.

---

1 Lewis Webb, *Is This The Year Ireland's Gambling Control Bill Finally Comes Into Play?* (2019), irishpost.com. Available at: https://www.irishpost.com/business/2019-year-irelands-gambling-control-bill-finally-comes-play-164801 [Accessed 3 March 2019].

2 s 12 of the Gaming and Lotteries (Amendment) Act 2019 substituting a new s 28 in the principal Gaming and Lotteries Act 1956 (s 28(10)(e)).

[29.1.03] An interesting starting point for assessing the rather shambolic state of the law in this area of the entertainment sector is a High Court decision in June 2015 and a Circuit Court ruling in March 2017. Irish law clearly states, based on public policy grounds in particular, that gambling debts cannot be enforced (note, however, that different rules apply to lotteries, prize bonds, horse-racing and dog-racing for example).[3] The rule applies not just to gamblers seeking payment, but also to casinos, bookmakers and online gambling services seeking to collect debts. In respect of the latter, however, regulation has been introduced as will be discussed later in the chapter to take due account of modern realities (since the time of legislation passed as far back as 1956) and new technologies. It appears that the rationale is not merely a moral objection to gambling, but also reflects a concern that a series of disputed bets might end up in the courts, adding to an already brimming caseload.

[29.1.04] Section 36 of the Gaming and Lotteries Act 1956 ('the 1956 Act') whereby every contract by way of gaming or wagering is void, was neither repealed nor amended by the Gaming and Lotteries (Amendment) Act 2019 discussed at the end of this section. However, the 2022 Bill when enacted will repeal the 1956 Act. Section 9 specifically refers to abolishment of the s 36 rule.

Court decisions (under the soon to be repealed 1956 Act)

[29.1.05] The defendant in *Sporting Index Ltd v O'Shea*[4] appealed an order of the Master of the High Court deeming two judgments, obtained in the County Court in London against the defendant, enforceable (pre-Brexit) in this jurisdiction. The first judgment related to the indebtedness of the defendant arising from regulated contracts in the form of spread bets on the outcome of specified sporting events. The second judgment obtained in 2013 related to the plaintiff's costs of an application by the defendant to set aside the first judgment.

[29.1.06] The defendant opened an online spread betting account with the plaintiff, a UK based company specialising in sports spread betting. The defendant placed a bet on a Heineken Cup rugby match and lost. The plaintiff permitted the betting account to become overdrawn, resulting in the liability for gambling debts which were at issue in the UK proceedings. The defendant submitted a limited defence to the plaintiff's claim in the County Court outlining the reckless nature of the plaintiff's conduct by permitting his account to go overdrawn in circumstances whereby he did not request such facility. The defendant further contended that such proceedings should have been initiated in Ireland as he was domiciled in Ireland during the UK proceedings.

---

3 For instance, the Irish Horseracing Industry Act 1994 and the Horse and Greyhound Racing Act 2001 in relation to gambling under the auspices of Horse Racing Ireland; the Greyhound Industry Act 1958 in relation to gambling under the auspices of Bord na gCon (Irish Greyhound Board), and the National Lottery Act 2013 in relation to the National Lottery.

4 [2015] IEHC 407.

[29.1.07] The plaintiff subsequently obtained judgment in London in the sum of €118,058.99 together with costs of the action summarily assessed in the sum of £17,500. On 20 May 2014, pursuant to an ex parte application on the part of the plaintiff, the Master of the High Court made orders deeming both UK judgments enforceable in this state, together with the costs of the application. These orders were subsequently served on the defendant. By notice of motion dated 26 August 2014, the defendant appealed those orders.

[29.1.08] Therefore, the question for the High Court (Mac Eochaidh J)[5] in Ireland to consider was whether enforcement within this jurisdiction of the first and second judgments might be denied on the basis that such enforcement would be manifestly contrary to public policy in Ireland. It was the contention of the plaintiff that this was not an obstacle to recognition and enforcement of the English court orders because the court would be enforcing the court orders and not the gambling debts themselves.

[29.1.09] European Council Regulation 44/2001 (since repealed by the 2012 EU 'Recast' Regulation), which replaced the earlier 1968 Brussels Convention, had as its aim, *inter alia*, the harmonious administration of justice within the EU. It was incorporated into Irish law under the Jurisdiction of Courts and Enforcement of Judgments (Amendment) Act 2012. The defendant relied on Art 34(1) thereof as the basis for his assertion that the judgments should not be recognised in this jurisdiction. Article 34(1) stated that a judgment shall not be recognised if such recognition is manifestly contrary to public policy in the member state in which recognition is sought.

[29.1.10] The defendant also submitted, in respect of the public policy exception, that the Oireachtas clearly prohibited the enforcement of any betting contracts and same are deemed null and void pursuant to s 36 of the 1956 Act which states:

> 36 (1) Every contract by way of gaming or wagering is void.
> (2) No action shall lie for the recovery of any money or thing which is alleged to be won or to have been paid upon a wager or which has been deposited to abide the event on which a wager is made.
> (3) A promise, express or implied, to pay any person any money paid by him under or in respect of a contract to which this section applies or to pay any money by way of commission, fee, reward or otherwise in respect of the contract or of any services connected with the contract is void and no action shall lie for the recovery of any such money.

[29.1.11] The court rejected the argument that the public policy exception did not apply in the instant case. In its view, the intention of the legislature in relation to the relevant provisions of the Act was perfectly clear. The enforcement of any betting contracts is prohibited (as above, this will shortly change) and Mac Eochaidh J was satisfied that the statute constitutes a rule of law regarded

---

[5] Who proceeded to become a judge of the General Court of the EU.

as essential in the legal order of this state. There was a manifest conflict between the foreign court order arising from a gambling debt and Irish public policy as expressed in the 1956 statute on the control of gambling.

[29.1.12] While the Council Regulation contained an absolute prohibition of any review of the substance of the foreign court order (Arts 26 and 45(2)), the court was nevertheless not prohibited from knowing what was the substance of the proceedings. An affidavit on behalf of the plaintiff and the affidavit sworn by the defendant confirmed that the foreign court order was for the defendant's gambling debts. Thus, the court stated at para 24:

> Enforcing the court order would have the effect of enforcing a gambling debt in the State. The debt and the order are as inseparable as "the dancer from the dance". The law prohibits any enforcement of such in this State. Further, the Regulation directs that a foreign court order "shall not be recognised" if recognition is manifestly contrary to public policy in Ireland and as I so find I am prohibited from recognising the order of the London Court.

[29.1.13] Mac Eochaidh J took a different view, however, of the order referable to the costs of the proceedings incurred by the plaintiff in seeking to enforce the gambling debt. He did not regard this order as constituting enforcement of a gambling debt. The moneys were not owed from a betting transaction. They related to litigation expenses only and the order was therefore enforceable in the ordinary way under the Regulation. In light of the foregoing, the defendant's appeal was upheld with respect to the order for €118,058.99 but refused with respect to the order for £17,500.00.[6]

Circuit Court

[29.1.14] There is no legal guarantee in Irish law that gamblers will be paid their winnings, a judge in the Circuit Court held in March 2017 in the case of *Mirwais v Automatic Amusements Ltd.*[7] Judge Francis Comerford made the ruling in an action brought by Sayed Mirwais against Automatic Amusements Ltd, which trades as D1 Casino, and also against casino director Michael Donnelly for a debt of almost €12,000 won while playing on an electronic, automated roulette machine.

[29.1.15] Judge Comerford referred to the 1956 Act which states (s 36(2)) that no action shall lie for the recovery of any money or thing which is alleged to be won or to have been paid upon a wager and warned that:

> If you happen to be too lucky while placing a bet or gambling, the person can simply say 'no you're not entitled to the money'. That is simply the law in Ireland.

---

6 At para 27 of the judgment.

7 Unreported, Circuit Court, Comerford J, 20 March 2017.

[29.1.16] In a country with reportedly the third highest rate of *per capita* gambling losses in the world, about €470 per adult per year, this ruling seemed to stack the odds against punters in a most unfavourable way.[8] Yet, one obvious advantage, according to *The Irish Times*, of the (soon to be repealed) prohibition is that people who 'bet the house' on a particular outcome while in the pub on a Saturday night, would not subsequently find themselves up before the courts defending a failure to pay.[9]

Reform and historical development of the law

[29.1.17] There have been a number of official government-commissioned reports published on the issue of legalising casinos since the passing of the 1956 Act. As the law stands, casinos are prohibited in Ireland, yet every city and large town in the country has at least one 'private members club'. Some are open 24 hours a day, sell alcohol throughout those hours, and allegedly admit people without membership even if this is required under anti-money laundering laws.[10] The (scheme of the) then Gambling Control Bill 2013, published by former Minister Alan Shatter, ruled out the possibility of introducing 'Las Vegas-style' super-casinos such as that backed by independent TD, Michael Lowry, which had been proposed for Tipperary.

[29.1.18] The report of the Casino Committee in 2008[11] referred[12] to the Financial Action Task Force Report published in February 2006 and stated that casinos were included as a designated body for the purposes of s 32 of the Criminal Justice Act 1994 under reg 8 of the Criminal Justice Act (Section 32) Regulations 2003.[13] Casinos were therefore subject to anti-money laundering legislation. There are no licensed casinos in Ireland and no entities operate under the title of a casino. However, the evaluation team noted that there were private clubs operating in Ireland that offer casino-like facilities – poker, blackjack and roulette albeit they are not titled as casinos.[14] The report outlined the potentially

---

8 Irish Examiner Editorial, *When a gambling win is not a win: Casino wins row over winnings* (2017), irishexaminer.com. Available at: https://www.irishexaminer.com/viewpoints/ourview/when-a-gambling-win-is-not-a-win-casino-wins-row-over-winnings-445712.html [Accessed 5 May 2018].

9 Colm Keena, *Is any bet a sure thing under Irish gambling law?* (2017), irishtimes.com. Available at: https://www.irishtimes.com/news/crime-and-law/is-any-bet-a-sure-thing-under-irish-gambling-law-1.3017596 [Accessed 24 April 2017].

10 Stephen Rogers and Jimmy Woulfe, *Gambling law rules out 'super' casinos* (2013), irishexaminer.com. Available at: https://www.irishexaminer.com/ireland/gambling-law-rules-out-super-casinos-236956.html [Accessed 5 May 2018].

11 Department of Justice, Equality and Law Reform, *Regulating Gaming in Ireland* (2008). Available at: https://www.justice.ie/en/JELR/Casino%20(Eng)%20for%20Web.pdf/Files/Casino%20(Eng)%20for%20Web.pdf [Accessed 24 March 2022].

12 At para 1.2.6, p 3.

13 SI No 242 of 2003.

14 Financial Action Task Force, *Third Mutual Evaluation / Detailed Assessment Report, Anti-Money Laundering and Combating the Financing of Terrorism: Ireland* (2006), paras 35 and 36, p 21.

illicit operation of private gaming clubs in Ireland (see para 577 thereof) and stated that this system did create the potential for real risks as regards anti-money laundering and combating the financing of terrorism.[15]

Restricted gaming permissible

[29.1.19] It is worth noting, however, that gaming was and is permissible in restricted circumstances. Amusement hall machines were adapted on foot of a Supreme Court decision in 1969[16] which held that operation of machines of this kind was not in fact permissible having regard to s 10 of the 1956 Act which prohibited the operation of any slot machine that was designed to deliver, when successfully operated, a money prize or a token or other article. Legislation was thus passed in 1970 to legalise the operation of appropriately adapted slot machines which do not pay out directly to the player but require the intervention of an attendant to enable players to collect their prize. The operation of these machines in amusement halls, particularly at seaside resorts, was seen by the government as an attraction for holidaymakers and benefitted the tourist trade. Accordingly, s 1 of the Gaming and Lotteries Act 1970 repealed s 10 of the principal 1956 Act.

The Betting (Amendment) Act 2015

[29.1.20] The Betting (Amendment) Act 2015 ('the 2015 Act') amends the Betting Act 1931 and provides for the licensing of remote (online) bookmakers and betting intermediaries for the first time. With betting practices and offerings having changed significantly, particularly in the past decade, the 2015 Act extends the regulatory regime beyond the traditional notion of bookmaking. The Act's most significant aim is to create a regulatory system for remote bookmakers (such as by internet or telephone) and betting intermediaries (otherwise known as "betting exchanges") which may not necessarily have a physical presence in the state but offer betting services to Irish customers.

[29.1.21] The 2015 Act thus introduces two new types of licence – a remote bookmaker's licence for operators offering remote betting to customers based in Ireland (i.e. internet and mobile betting providers) and a remote betting

---

15 At Table 2, section 4, pp 164-165.

16 Mentioned in Report of the Interdepartmental Group (Department of Justice, Equality and Law Reform), *Review of the Gaming and Lotteries Acts 1956-86* (2000). Available at: http://www.justice.ie/en/JELR/GamingLotteriesActs.pdf/Files/GamingLotteriesActs.pdf [Accessed 3 November 2017]. The Supreme Court upheld the view of a District Justice that the operation of particular gaming machines (which had been in wide usage throughout the country) was in fact contrary to the principal Act. The machines had been adapted in order to circumvent the blanket prohibition in the Act of a machine delivering, when successfully operated, a money prize. Winnings were delivered to the player by an indirect route, usually by channelling the coins through a chute at the rear, to an operator who would then hand the money to the player. The Act was subsequently amended in 1970 in order to remove the original prohibition (under s 10).

intermediary's licence for operators who facilitate Irish customers making bets (i.e. betting exchanges). Remote betting operators are required to obtain their relevant licence regardless of whether or not they have a physical presence in Ireland. They also have to pay tax on betting transactions with Irish customers.

[29.1.22] Separately, current holders of retail bookmakers' licences are required, on the expiry of those licences, to apply for a new licence in accordance with the new licensing application process set out in the 2015 Act. An interesting feature of the Act is that a bookmaker operating under a bookmaker's licence can now also accept bets placed remotely, provided the value of those bets in any one year does not exceed the lower of €250,000 or ten percent of the bookmaker's turnover in that year.

[29.1.23] The new licence application process involves a two-stage process. First, the applicant (which can now be a corporate entity as well as an individual) must apply for a Certificate of Personal Fitness ('COPF') from either the Gardaí or the Minister for Justice depending on the type of licence being applied for and whether the applicant is resident in Ireland or elsewhere (ss 7 and 8). Secondly, an application must be submitted to Revenue together with the COPF and the relevant excise duty to obtain the actual licence. Revenue will ensure that the applicant has a valid tax clearance certificate before issuing a licence.

[29.1.24] The excise duty on the initial grant and renewal of a bookmaker's licence is €500. The excise duty on the initial grant of a remote bookmaker's licence and a remote betting intermediary's licence is €10,000.[17] On the renewal of these latter two licences, the excise duty is also €10,000 together with an additional amount linked to the level of annual turnover/level of annual commission earnings in the previous year. The legislation also extended the one percent turnover-based "betting duty" which applies to bookmakers, to remote bookmakers. The betting duty for remote bookmakers is one percent of every bet entered into with persons in the state. A betting intermediary duty applies to remote betting intermediaries at a rate of 15 percent of commission charges.

[29.1.25] A licence is valid for two years and a bookmaker's licence will expire on 30 November[18] of every second year following the enactment of the legislation. A remote betting licence or remote betting intermediary's licence will expire on 30 June of the second year following the enactment of the legislation.

[29.1.26] It is an offence to operate as a bookmaker, a remote bookmaker or as a remote betting intermediary without a licence. The penalty for operating without a licence is a fine of up to €5,000 on summary conviction or a fine of up to €150,000 for a first offence (€300,000 for repeat offenders) or imprisonment

---

17 s 33, which amends s 64 of the Finance Act 2002.

18 s 13, which substituted a new s 7 for s 7 of the Betting Act 1931.

for up to five years, or both, on conviction on indictment (s 4, which amends the Betting Act 1931 by substituting a new s 2).

Lotteries

[29.1.27] In May 2017, *The Irish Independent* ran an article[19] on foot of an interview with then junior justice minister David Stanton during which he stated that he feared certain lotteries, including some raising funds for GAA clubs, were operating without approval or in breach of restrictions on the size of prizes. He believed many sporting club lottos and locally-run raffles are operating illegally and albeit flouting the law do so, most likely, due to lack of awareness. Notwithstanding, it appears that no prosecutions have arisen.

[29.1.28] The law currently limits the size of weekly prize pots in such lotteries to €5,000, where a permit is issued by a Garda Superintendent and €30,000 where a lottery licence is granted by a District Court. Garda-issued permits last for six months, but difficulties can emerge when the size of the lottery prize grows larger than anticipated if the jackpot rolls over.

Gaming and Lotteries (Amendment) Act 2019

[29.1.29] As under the 1956 Act (to be repealed), a gaming licence is required from Revenue for gaming machines but Revenue is now required to create and maintain a register of gaming licences pursuant to the Gaming and Lotteries (Amendment) Act 2019 ('the 2019 Act'). Prize draws which operate for marketing purposes do not need a licence or permit under the Act, provided that the total value of the prizes does not exceed €2,500 and that those taking part are not charged for entry or redeeming the prize. Lotteries that are held for charitable or philanthropic purposes do not require a permit or a licence, provided certain conditions are met.

[29.1.30] This statute sets a new limit of €500 on the maximum payout from gaming machines and lifts the maximum stake per game in a licensed venue to €5 per player.[20] The minimum age to gamble has increased from 16 to 18 years.[21]

[29.1.31] The 2019 Act also seeks to improve permit and licensing application processes, setting out more clearly the conditions required for promoters of gaming and lottery activity, whether applying to a Garda superintendent for a

---

19 Shane Phelan, *Minister to crack down on 'wild west' illegal raffles and lotteries at sports clubs* (2017), independent.ie. Available at: https://www.independent.ie/irish-news/minister-to-crack-down-on-wild-west-illegal-raffles-and-lotteries-at-sports-clubs-35690035.html [Accessed 5 May 2018].

20 s 5 which substituted a new s 14 into the 1956 Act.

21 The 2019 Act thus standardises the legal age for all gambling activities at 18 years (a new s 9A(9) of the 1956 Act was inserted by s 4; s 14(4) of the 1956 Act is substituted by s 5 of the 2019 Act, and s 25 inserts s 4A into the Totalisator Act 1929).

permit, to Revenue, or the District Court for a licence. These changes include the following: a valid permit or licence is required to promote gaming and it is an offence to do so without a permit or licence;[22] there is a new application process for a permit for gaming to be issued by a Garda superintendent for charitable or philanthropic purposes or for private benefit, with a maximum stake of €10 and a maximum prize limit per game of €3,000;[23] and the District Court may attach to its certificate conditions limiting the hours during which gaming may be carried on, restricting the kinds of gaming, and the extent to which particular kinds of gaming may be carried on.[24]

[29.1.32] Revenue is required to establish and maintain a register of gaming licences accessible online;[25] certain lotteries promoted for the benefit of a charitable or philanthropic purpose and not for the promoter's benefit will not require a permit or licence – in such circumstances, the prize will be limited to €1,000 and no more than 1,500 tickets at a maximum price of €5 can be sold;[26] and the current maximum prize amount of €30,000 remains in place for a lottery licensed by the District Court – however, provision is made for a prize fund limit of €360,000 where a once-off annual lottery is promoted under a District Court licence (s 12 which substituted a new s 28 in the principal Act).

PREMIUM RATE SERVICES

[29.2.01] Premium rate services ('PRS') are defined in s 3 of the Communications Regulation (Premium Rate Services and Electronic Communications Infrastructure) Act 2010 as amended[27] ('the 2010 Act'), having all of the following characteristics: the provision of the content of communications other than a broadcasting service, through an e-communications network or by using an e-communications service; and where there is a charge for the provision of the service which exceeds the cost attributable to communications carriage alone; and such charge is paid by the end user of the service directly or indirectly to the provider of the e-communications network or e-communications service used in connection with the provision of the service by means of a billing or other agreed payment mechanism. PRS providers are individuals, organisations or companies that provide PRS over one of the telephone/mobile networks in Ireland.

[29.2.02] Hence, PRS are goods and services which one can purchase using a landline, mobile phone, the internet, interactive digital television or facsimile device.[28] The range of PRS has grown considerably in recent years, allowing access

---

22 s 3 which substitutes a new s 4 into the principal 1956 Act.
23 s 4 which inserts subsection (9A) into the principal Act.
24 s 6 which amends s 15 of the principal Act.
25 s 7 which inserts s 19A into the principal Act.
26 s 9 which inserts s 26A into the principal Act.
27 Most recently by the Online Safety and Media Regulation Act 2022.
28 Premium rate voice services have a 15 prefix (e.g. 1515 or 1530) and premium rate text services are five-digit short codes beginning with the number 5. Calls and texts to PRS

to information, advice and entertainment services as well as facilitating audience participation in television and radio shows. Examples include television voting (for example, *The X Factor*), television show competitions (e.g. Phonovation text service in respect of *The Late Late Show* home audience competitions), chatline and dating services, donations to charities (e.g. to Christmas FM to assist with diverse charities annually), and psychics or other entertainment services. Entertainment services include, but are not limited to, sexual entertainment services, chatline services, and any PRS involving any tarot, horoscope, 'hoax' or 'windup' services.

Licensing

[29.2.03] The Communications (Licensing of Premium Rate Services) Regulations 2012[29] ('the PRS Regulations') govern the issuing of licences to PRS providers. ComReg published a Code of Practice on 15 May 2014 with effective date 3 June 2014.[30] Compliance with the code is a condition of a PRS licence in accordance with ss 7(3) and 15(6) of the 2010 Act and reg 7 of the PRS Regulations. ComReg, pursuant to s 7(1)(a) of the 2010 Act, has set out in regs 3 and 4 of the PRS Regulations the class or type of PRS which is required to be licensed under s 6 of the Act, referred to as "specified PRS". All PRS providers in Ireland must comply with the strictures of the code. This seeks to ensure consumer protection when using national PRS and to set in place procedures to deal with consumer complaints that arise from using these services.

[29.2.04] The code contains restrictions and imposes requirements with regard to the promotion of PRS and other forms of commercial practices that may be engaged in by PRS providers. These aspects of the code are to be interpreted and understood in light of the provisions of the Unfair Commercial Practices Directive (2005/29/EC) and the Consumer Protection Act 2007 as amended which implements this Directive in Ireland. In particular, practices that are identified in the code will be assessed by reference to their fairness within the meaning of the Directive and by reference to whether they are likely to influence a consumer's decision regarding purchasing or paying for PRS.

Enforcement

[29.2.05] In 2017, ComReg (see below) commenced an investigation into the provision of the (once-off) AppMob PRS by Zamano Solutions Ltd following compliance monitoring and on foot of consumer complaints in respect of alleged

---

typically cost more than ordinary telephone calls/texts depending on the prefix number or shortcode.

[29] SI No 111 of 2012.

[30] This code of practice was made by ComReg pursuant to s 15 of the Communications Regulation (Premium Rate Services and Electronic Communications Infrastructure) Act 2010 and ss 10(1)(d)(ii) and 12(d) of the Communications Regulation Act 2002 (as amended).

breaches of the code of practice. The AppMob, a content PRS, provided end users with access to premium content for a single charge. End users who engaged with the PRS would receive a link to retrieve content such as games, ringtones and wallpapers to their mobile phones. The total cost of the service was €15 and was charged by way of six reverse-billed messages charged at €2.50 per message.

[29.2.06] Following the investigation, ComReg found that the AppMob PRS was not compliant with certain requirements of the code (including provisions relating to the information that must be provided to end users before they incurred any charges) and, therefore, was in breach of a condition of its PRS licence. ComReg also considered that end users who engaged with a particular promotion for Zamano's AppMob were entered into the PRS without their prior knowledge or consent.

[29.2.07] As the promotion failed to provide pricing information and any material details relating to the PRS, which would allow end users to make an informed transactional decision, consumers who responded to the promotion were misled into entering the service and subsequently incurred charges. Zamano was required to remedy the finding of non-compliance in respect of the breaches of the code and to refund affected end users by 22 June 2017 pursuant to s 9 of the 2010 Act.[31]

[29.2.08] In December 2020 the text service company was fined €5,000 after pleading guilty at Kilkenny District Court to two charges relating to s 13 of the Act after a case was brought by ComReg. The court heard that two people had been charged for receiving text messages with links to adult content to which they had not subscribed or consented.

THE COMMISSION FOR COMMUNICATIONS REGULATION

[29.3.01] The Commission for Communications Regulation ('ComReg') is the statutory body, established under s 6 of the Communications Regulation Act 2002,[32] responsible for the regulation and enforcement[33] of the electronic communications sector (telecommunications, roaming, broadband, radio communications, broadcasting transmission and premium rate services) as well as the postal sector.

[29.3.02] It succeeded the Office of the Director of Telecommunications

---

31 Commission for Communications Regulation, *A Finding of Non-Compliance with the Premium Rate Service ("PRS") Licence Conditions Zamano Solutions Ltd* (2017), comreg.ie. Available at: https://www.comreg.ie/finding-non-compliance-premium-rate-service-prs-licence-conditions-zamano-solutions-ltd/ [Accessed 2 July 2017].

32 As amended by the Communications Regulation (Amendment) Act 2007.

33 The commission has prosecutorial powers to bring District Court summary criminal proceedings pursuant to s 43 of the 2002 Act (as substituted by new s 43 provisions, see s 11 of the 2007 Act).

Regulation and its remit also includes the issuing of wireless telegraphy licences and operating a system of consumer complaints handling, from disability and access issues to terms and conditions, billing and disputed charges, contract duration, termination fees and unsolicited contact being made to would-be customers by service providers and direct marketing companies. It operates as a collegiate body, with decisions taken collectively by the commissioners. As of April 2023, there are two commissioners. Part of the rationale for the establishment of a new regulator was political pressure from the licensed radio community which felt that pirate operators were compromising their listenership figures. A spate of Garda and ESB-assisted raids by ComReg ensued (see spectrum compliance below).

Enforcement

[29.3.03] The might and muscle of ComReg was evidenced in 2016 when Eir (previously Eircom) was fined €3 million by ComReg for breaching a number of performance targets in connection with the reparation of phone services in rural areas due to stormy weather and flooding in 2015. As a universal service provider for fixed-line telephone services, Eir has responsibilities to maintain connectivity. Eircom submitted a *force majeure* claim in June 2016 and sought relief in respect of fault repair time performance. The submission set out the basis for Eircom's *force majeure* claim as being the "exceptional weather events in January, November and December 2015". In addition, Eircom submitted an expert report on the weather conditions in support of its claim. ComReg found that the *force majeure* conditions applied in the month of December 2015 but that the January and November 2015 weather events did not constitute *force majeure* events. Eircom paid ComReg a penalty of €3,094,000 in December 2016 for the breaches.[34]

Licensing of wireless telegraphy equipment

[29.3.04] The possession and use of radio equipment in Ireland is governed by the Wireless Telegraphy Act 1926 as amended which stipulates that an appropriate wireless telegraphy licence must be held, unless licence exempted. ComReg is the authority charged with the authorisation of wireless telegraphy equipment in Ireland, with the exception of ships radio licensing.[35] An authorisation may take the form of either a licence, which will be issued subject to compliance with specific conditions, or a licence exemption. A licence may be issued under

[34] Eoin Burke-Kennedy, *Eir fined €3m for breaching rural service obligations* (2017), irishtimes.com. Available at: https://www.irishtimes.com/business/technology/eir-fined-3m-for-breaching-rural-service-obligations-1.3046575 [Accessed 15 September 2017].

[35] Since 15 May 2007, the responsibility for the licensing of radio communications equipment on Irish ships and associated certificates of competency has transferred to the Maritime Radio Affairs Unit of the Department of Transport.

the Wireless Telegraphy Act 1926 as amended by s 182[36] of the Broadcasting Act 2009.

[29.3.05] As will be discussed in Chapter 31, the Broadcasting Authority of Ireland (to be replaced by the Media Commission which has already been established in law, see the next chapter) is responsible for the licensing of radio and television services additional to those provided by RTÉ, TG4 and the Houses of the Oireachtas Channel, Oireachtas TV.

[29.3.06] In managing the radio spectrum, ComReg has set down specific rules and regulations for the possession and use of many forms of radio equipment. These regulations specify the licensing regime or exempt the radio equipment from licensing. Unlicensed or non-compliant possession or use of radio equipment is illegal, rendering offenders liable to prosecution. Annual licences granted must be renewed.

Spectrum compliance – pirate radio stations

[29.3.07] ComReg's Spectrum Compliance Unit offers protection to the radio services of licensed operators by tracing and eliminating unwanted interference. It is also responsible for ensuring that all radio equipment is operated in accordance with current legislation and takes appropriate action where breaches are uncovered. This includes the Wireless Telegraphy Acts 1926 to 2009[37] and the Broadcasting and Wireless Telegraphy Act 1988 as amended.

[29.3.08] Possession of an apparatus for wireless telegraphy without a valid licence is an offence under s 3 of the Wireless Telegraphy Acts 1926 to 2009, liable on summary conviction to a class A fine not exceeding €5,000[38] and on conviction on indictment to a fine not exceeding €250,000.

[29.3.09] The Spectrum Compliance Unit regularly executes search warrants, issued pursuant to s 8 of the Wireless Telegraphy Acts 1926 to 2009. Such enforcement operations typically target unlicensed broadcasters (pirate radio stations), sellers of non-compliant radio equipment such as mobile phone repeaters and those who refuse to cease the operation of equipment causing harmful interference.

[29.3.10] In February, 2003 ComReg claimed[39] that airplanes using Dublin Airport were placed in grave danger after their radio frequencies were scrambled

---

36 Which substituted for ss 5-9 of the 1926 Act the new ss 5-9 as set out in Sch 2 to the 2009 Act.

37 s 180, the collective citations provision of the Broadcasting Act 2009 Act provides that the Wireless Telegraphy Acts 1926 to 1988 and ss 181(1) to (7) and (9), and s 182 of the 2009 Act may be cited together as the Wireless Telegraphy Acts 1926 to 2009.

38 Defined in s 3 of the Fines Act 2010 as a fine not exceeding €5,000.

39 Helen Bruce, *Pirate radio stations endangered aircraft* (2003), independent.ie.

by a local pirate radio station. The station had interfered with the frequency used to guide airplanes from Dublin to Manchester Airport, where UK air traffic control had sounded the alarm. The station's antenna in Donnycarney were forcibly shut down by ComReg thus opening presenters, engineers and financial backers liable to imprisonment and substantial fines.

[29.3.11] Elsewhere, former Radio Limerick One (RLO) was warned by ComReg that it posed a serious danger to public safety and was taken off the air in January 2003[40] after a no-advance-warning raid by ComReg. Its frequency clashed with that of airplanes landing at Cork. A spokeswoman for ComReg said the Irish Aviation Authority ('IAA') had never dealt with a more serious level of interference than that produced by RLO, reported to it by the IAA in late December 2002. She added that Ireland's estimated 70 pirate radio stations not only clashed with frequencies reserved for aviation, but also with mobile phones, legitimate radio broadcasts and the emergency services. She denied RLO's claim that €50,000 worth of equipment at its communications tower in Cratloe, County Clare was destroyed by ComReg, insisting that the main antenna and cables had to be removed under a court warrant to stop transmission.

[29.3.12] A major crackdown on Dublin pirate stations at mountainside transmitter sites at Three Rock and Killinarden[41] was undertaken by ComReg in May 2003, with the new regulator armed with more resources than its predecessor. A series of raids was conducted over two days involving assistance from the Gardaí and ESB staff and resulting in more pirate stations being disbanded.

Premium rate services

[29.3.13] As afore-mentioned, ComReg also regulates the provision of premium rate services including chatline and dating services, television voting and competitions, and donations to charities.

Available at: http://www.independent.ie/irish-news/pirate-radio-stations-endangered-aircraft-26228843.html [Accessed 16 September 2017].

40 Two other pirate stations in the county suffered a similar fate in 2002, being closed down by ComReg after complaints by Aer Rianta in Shannon that their signals were interfering with air traffic control.

41 Irishtimes.com, *Why are the pirates being rounded up now?* (2003). Available at: https://www.irishtimes.com/news/why-are-the-pirates-being-rounded-up-now-1.360155 [Accessed 15 September 2017].

Part V

Digital Safety, Broadcasting Regulation and Audiovisual Media Services

Chapter 30

Harmful Content Regulation; Establishment of the Media Commission; and the EU Digital Services Act Package

INTRODUCTION

[30.1.01] The government published the Online Safety and Media Regulation Bill[1] on 12 January 2022. The Online Safety and Media Regulation Act 2022 ('the 2022 Act') was signed into law by the President in December 2022 and was commenced in large part in March 2023. This statute has established the Media Commission to replace the Broadcasting Authority of Ireland ('BAI') and provide for the appointment of an Online Safety Commissioner, substantially amend the Broadcasting Act 2009 ('the Principal Act') and implement the revised Audiovisual Media Services Directive by regulating *inter alia* video-sharing platforms such as YouTube, other online media and traditional media broadcasters. The Principal Act, and the Online Safety and Media Regulation Act 2022 in so far as it amends the Principal Act, may be collectively cited as the Broadcasting and Other Media Regulation Acts 2009 and 2022.

[30.1.02] The government has confirmed that the new Media Commission regulator will also take on the role of Digital Services Coordinator for Ireland under the Digital Services Act ('DSA').[2] The DSA, being an EU Regulation which is directly applicable in all member states, entered into force in November 2022 though the majority of its provisions do not take effect until February 2024.

[30.1.03] The 2022 Act, in transposing the revised Audiovisual Media Services Directive into Irish law, places the regulation of video on-demand services on a direct statutory footing and aligns the regulation of such services with television broadcasting services. For instance, there will be an obligation for professional video on-demand services which provide news and current affairs content to meet the same standards as required by television broadcasters (see the provision

1 Which integrated the Broadcasting (Amendment) Bill 2019.

2 Regulation EU 2022/2065 of the European Parliament and of the Council of 19 October 2022 on a Single Market For Digital Services and amending Directive 2000/31/EC.

for the making of media service codes and media service rules in ss 46N-46R, and the obligations set out in ss 46J to 46M). A provider of an audiovisual on-demand media service shall not broadcast harmful and unduly offensive material. Further, it shall ensure that the privacy of individuals is not unreasonably encroached upon, and that news and current affairs programming is presented in a fair, objective and impartial manner. Audiovisual on-demand media service providers also have an obligation to observe advertising restrictions and controls.

[30.1.04] In addition, the 2022 Act augments[3] the protections afforded by the Harassment, Harmful Communications and Related Offences Act 2020 (Coco's law, 'the 2020 Act')[4] which legislation amended the law relating to harassment and provides for offences pertaining to the recording, distribution or publication of intimate images without consent with intent to cause harm[5] and seeks to protect the anonymity of victims of those offences, as well as prescribing offences involving the distribution, publication or sending of threatening or grossly offensive communication.

[30.1.05] Online safety codes to be made by the Commission in furtherance of s 139K and to be applied to designated online services will deal with a wide range of issues, including measures to be taken by online services to tackle the availability of harmful online content, for example cyberbullying material, on their services.

[30.1.06] Moreover, digital literacy and safety has come to the fore in recent years as it is an area inherently fraught with danger. This is set against the backdrop too of the GDPR, Art 6 of which states that personal data may not be processed unless there is at least one legal basis to do so. One of the six stated lawful purposes in the Regulation are the legitimate interests of a data controller or a third party. However, these interests can be overridden by interests of data subjects or their rights according to the Charter of Fundamental Rights of the EU[6] especially in the case of children. The government is thus set to end the era of self-regulation in the social media industry.

---

3 See Sch 3 of the Principal Act (as inserted after Sch 2 by s 46 of the 2022 Act) which sets out harmful online content offence-specific categories.

4 The legislation was named after 21-year-old Nicole ('Coco') Fox who took her own life in 2018 after being bullied on social media.

5 Or being reckless as to whether harm is caused (s 2 of the 2020 Act).

6 The charter was ratified in December 2000 but did not have full legal effect until the entry into force of the Treaty of Lisbon on 1 December 2009. Under the charter, the EU must act and legislate consistently with the charter and the EU courts may and will strike down legislation adopted by the EU's institutions that contravenes it. The charter applies to the institutions of the EU and its member states when implementing EU law.

PROVISIONS OF THE 2022 ACT

[30.2.01] In early January 2020, then communications minister Richard Bruton commented in respect of the proposed Bill that:

> This new law is one of the first of its kind in the world, and is breaking new ground in terms of how online services will be required to deal with harmful content.[7]

[30.2.02] The Principal Act provides in new s 11(7) (under s 8 of the 2022 Act, Pt 2 of the Principal Act was substituted by a new part) for the appointment of an Online Safety Commissioner(s) as part of a wider Media Commission to oversee the new regulatory framework for online safety. The Commissioner will govern this new framework through binding online safety codes and far-reaching statutory powers.

[30.2.03] Harmful online content is defined in new s 139A of the Principal Act as being such if it falls with the offence-specific categories enemerated (e.g. online content by which a person publishes or broadcasts matter likely to lead members of the public to identify a person as the person charged with a rape offence), falls within one of the other categories of online content defined in subsection (3) (e.g. online content by which a person bullies or humiliates another person), or if it gives to any risk to a person's life or risk of significant harm to a person's physical or mental health, where the harm is reasonably foreseeable.

Administrative financial sanctions and court-imposed fines

[30.2.04] In terms of administrative financial sanctions, the Law Reform Commission in its October 2018 *Report on Regulatory Powers and Corporate Offences*[8] described the power to impose such financial sanctions as "one of the most effective" in the regulatory toolkit and that:

> ...the power to impose administrative financial sanctions is both valuable and necessary in ensuring that financial and economic regulators have the requisite powers to achieve their regulatory objectives.[9]

[30.2.05] Traditionally, regulatory bodies have only been permitted to avail of such powers in limited legal contexts, such as to give effect to EU legislation. This is the case, for example, with the Data Protection Commission. However, recent case law (*Purcell v Central Bank*)[10] and the recommendations of the said

---

7 Gazette Desk, Law Society of Ireland, *Online safety could be pinned on digital leaders* (2020). Available at: https://www.lawsociety.ie/gazette/top-stories/digital-leaders-could-be-held-personally-responsible-for-online-safety-breaches—minister/ [Accessed 3 June 2021].

8 Available at: https://www.lawreform.ie/_fileupload/Completed%20Projects/LRC%20119-2018%20Regulatory%20Powers%20and%20Corporate%20Offences%20Volume%201.pdf [Accessed 20 June 2021].

9 *ibid* at p 105 of the report.

10 [2016] IEHC 514.

report have highlighted that financial sanctions are permissible where they do not constitute the administration of justice by a non-court entity. Certain safeguards must be built into such a system whereby sanctions will be subject to confirmation by a court.

[30.2.06] The procedure for administrative fines arises by virtue of s 47 of the 2022 Act which inserted a new Pt 8B (investigations and sanctions, including prosecution of offences) into the Principal Act (Pt 8, Chapters 1 to 8, ss 139ZG to 139ZZI). Administrative financial sanctions may be imposed where a regulated entity has failed to comply with a decision issued by the Commission (if satisfied on the balance of probabilities that the provider has committed the contravention to which the investigation relates).[11]

[30.2.07] The Commission will not have the power to make a final determination in this regard (save where a regulated entity expressly elects for the Commission to do so) and decisions to impose such sanctions will require court confirmation. A regulated entity may also appeal the decision to the "appropriate court".[12] The upper amount of the administrative financial sanction that the Commission may seek to impose on an online service (including an individual) under the Act is €20 million or, in the case of an undertaking, ten percent of relevant turnover of the financial year preceding the date of the decision, whichever is higher.

[30.2.08] Failure to comply with a notice to end contravention or a content limitation notice (where online content is harmful, requiring the provider to remove or disable access to it or to limit its availability) gives rise to category 1 and 3 offences respectively as set out in ss 139ZZH(1) and 139ZZH(3).

Balancing of rights

[30.2.09] The key thematic issue here (see new s 7 in newly substituted Pt 2 of the Principal Act, powers and functions of Commission)[13] centres on how the development of legislation will take into account the need to balance the right of safety with other rights, such as freedom or liberty of expression,[14] the interests of children, ensuring broadcasting services and audiovisual on-demand

11 The procedures governing oral hearings arise by virtue of s 48 of the 2022 Act which inserted a new Sch 4 into the Principal Act (ss 139ZK(3), 139ZR(3) and (4) or 139ZU(2)(a)).

12 Meaning, where no administrative financial sanction is imposed or where the amount of any administrative financial sanction imposed does not exceed €75,000, or such other sum as stands specified in law as that court's jurisdiction in tort, the Circuit Court, or in any other case, the High Court.

13 A new Pt 2 of the Principal Act was substituted by s 8 of the 2022 Act.

14 The right to freedom of expression does not only apply to expression which is considered positive by a majority but also to expression which is provocative, challenging, and even potentially distressing. In addition, safeguards must be adopted to ensure that blanket monitoring of communications would not be ethically or legally permissible in pursuing the regulation of harmful online content.

media services available in the state are open and pluralistic, freedom of religion, freedom of the press, the right to privacy, and the right to conduct a business and to innovate.

[30.2.10] Directions given and sanctions pursued by the regulator must be proportionate such that legal sanctions and their consequences on persons, legal or natural, must be proportionate to the nature of the undesirable behaviour in question.

Compliance and Media Commission powers

[30.2.11] The 2022 Act provides for extensive powers of the Commission including investigation into contractor affairs and termination or suspension of contracts. Section 50 of the Principal Act is amended by s 14 of the 2022 Act and s 51 is amended by s 15 of the 2022 Act. The former s 53 which dealt with investigations into broadcaster affairs has been repealed as have ss 52, 54, 55 and 56, namely Chapter 2 (financial sanctions) of Pt 5 of the Principal Act has been repealed in full. As stated above, new Pt 8B (ss 139ZG to 139ZZI) now prescribes the rules and procedures for investigations and sanctions, including administrative financial sanctions. Administrative financial sanctions are governed by ss 139ZU to 139ZZA.

[30.2.12] For the purposes of an investigation, authorised officers will also now be empowered to enter any place where they have reasonable grounds for believing that an activity connected with a broadcasting service, audiovisual on-demand media service or designated online service is taking place (s 139ZK, new Pt 8B of the Principal Act). Search warrant applications to the District Court as would apply for instance where consent to enter a dwelling has not been given to an officer are dealt with in s 139ZL.

[30.2.13] As well as the notices mentioned above that it can issue, the Commission may also apply to the High Court for an order requiring an internet service provider or a provider of an application store service to block access in the state to a relevant online service or an audiovisual on-demand media service.

Complaints

[30.2.14] Sections 11-13 of the 2022 Act amend ss 47-49 of the Principal Act in relation to the statutory viewer complaints procedures and the right of reply as will be further discussed in the next chapter.

THE EU DIGITAL SERVICES ACT PACKAGE

[30.3.01] The Digital Services Act ('DSA')[15] and the Digital Market Act ('DMA')[16] together constitute the DSA Package and introduce rules in the DMA for designated platforms that act as "gatekeepers" in the digital sector.[17] These companies need to be designated as gatekeeper for at least one of the so-called "core platform services" enumerated in the DMA (such as online search engines, online social networking services and video-sharing platform services, Art 2). The same company can be designated as gatekeeper for several core platform services.

[30.3.02] Examples of changes that gatekeepers will have to implement include ensuring end users can easily unsubscribe from core platform services or uninstall pre-installed core platform services, providing business users with access to the data generated by their activities on the gatekeeper's platform, and banning the tracking of end users outside of the gatekeepers' core platform service for the purpose of targeted advertising without effective consent having been granted.

[30.3.03] The DSA moreover aims to provide clearer and more standardised rules for digital content. It applies to intermediary services offered to recipients of the service that have their place of establishment or are located in the EU, irrespective of where the providers of those intermediary services have their place of establishment.

[30.3.04] Platform governance has been at the forefront of the technology and media spaces recently given the rise in cyberbullying, hate speech and other harms online. There is a requirement in Art 18 DSA for providers of hosting services to notify law enforcement of any suspicion that a criminal offence involving a threat to the life or safety of a person or persons has or is likely to take place. In particular, the DSA will regulate how platforms moderate content, advertise, and use algorithms for recommendation systems.

[30.3.05] The DSA will not replace the e-Commerce Directive, which remains the cornerstone legal framework for all digital services. However, in order to provide greater harmonisation, it incorporates the existing rules exempting online intermediaries from liability of the content they host under certain conditions to ensure innovative services can continue to emerge and scale up in the single

---

15 *supra* at fn 2.

16 Regulation EU 2022/1925 of the European Parliament and of the Council of 14 September 2022 on contestable and fair markets in the digital sector and amending Directives (EU) 2019/1937 and (EU) 2020/1828.

17 The DMA establishes a set of narrowly defined objective criteria for qualifying a large online platform as a so-called "gatekeeper". These criteria will be met if a company has a strong economic position, significant impact on the internal market and is active in multiple EU countries, has a strong intermediation position, meaning that it links a large user base to a large number of businesses, has or is about to have an entrenched and durable position in the market, meaning that it is stable over time if the company met the two criteria above in each of the last three financial years.

market. Further, the DSA is without prejudice to EU copyright and related rights law and its transposition in the member states.

Content removal

[30.3.06] The DSA harmonises the process by which platforms are notified and must take subsequent action on illegal content. More concretely, once notified by trusted flaggers (Art 22 status of 'trusted flagger' is awarded by the Digital Services Coordinator, in Ireland's case, by the Media Commission). Platforms will have to remove illegal content expeditiously. The DSA also stipulates that users be informed about, and can contest removal of content by platforms, having access to dispute resolution mechanisms in their own country. In the event platforms are not currently providing explanations to users about their removal decisions, this process must be instituted. Specific pieces of information are required in this explanation such as the legal ground for illegal content, whether the action involves removal or demonetisation, whether the action was in response to a notice submitted or based on voluntary own-initiative investigations, or whether automation was used in the decision.

Proactive approach

[30.3.07] Platforms and other intermediaries are not liable for users' unlawful behaviour unless they are aware of illegal acts and fail to remove them. This shielding of legal liability aims to encourage companies to be more proactive when moderating the content on their platform. Only if the flagged content is evidently manifestly illegal (see Art 23) can such notices give rise to 'actual knowledge' (see Recital 22). Information should be considered to be manifestly illegal content and notices or complaints should be considered manifestly unfounded where it is evident to a layperson, without any substantive analysis, that the content is illegal or, respectively, that the notices or complaints are unfounded (Recital 63). This assists in solving the potential disincentives around voluntary measures taken by small platforms. The DSA reinforces that diligent platforms are not liable for illegal content they detect themselves. Small platforms can now use this as a means to further invest in robust content moderation practices.

Notice/action mechanisms

[30.3.08] Notices flagging purportedly illegal content must be sufficiently precise (Recitals 22 and 53, Art 16), namely that providers should be able to determine illegality without needing a substantive analysis or legal review. When actioning these notices, platforms must ensure that responses are targeted so that fundamental rights, including free expression, and others outlined in the EU Charter of Fundamental Rights, are upheld. The DSA also foresees measures against misuse which allows online platforms to potentially suspend individuals who misuse the notice and action mechanism and/or complaint handling systems, as long as the decision to suspend is assessed on a case-by-case basis.[18]

Enforcement

[30.3.09] In terms of the DSA, if a provider/platform does not comply with the Regulation, the European Commission can, *inter alia*, impose fines of up to 6 percent of the company's total worldwide annual turnover (Art 74) or periodic penalty payments (maximum amount shall be 5 percent of the average daily worldwide turnover, Art 76). Fines potentially levied on a gatekeeper pursuant to the DMA are set out in Art 30 (for instance, not exceeding 10 percent of its total worldwide turnover in the preceding financial year; up to 20 percent of its total worldwide turnover in the preceding financial year where the Commission finds that a gatekeeper has committed the same or a similar infringement).

Damages in civil cases

[30.3.10] The DMA and DSA are Regulations containing precise obligations and prohibitions for gatekeepers and platforms which can be enforced directly in national courts. This will facilitate direct actions for damages by those harmed by the conduct of non-complying organisations.

---

18 World Economic Forum, *Here's how the Digital Services Act changes content moderation* (2022). Available at: https://www.weforum.org/agenda/2022/12/how-companies-prepare-digital-services-act/ [Accessed 1 May 2023].

Chapter 31

The Media Commission: Compliance, Enforcement, Codes & Standards

INTRODUCTION

[31.1.01] As noted in the previous chapter, the BAI and its statutory committees have been dissolved and replaced by the Media Commission with its functions, powers, staff and property transferred thereto. The Online Safety and Media Regulation Act 2022 ('the 2022 Act') amended, updated and modernised the Broadcasting Act 2009 ('the Principal Act').[1] In doing so however in this manner, the amended Principal Act is quite difficult indeed to navigate in terms of sections numbering and the layout of the new parts and schedules. It would perhaps have been preferable to start afresh, repeal the Principal Act in its entirety and bring all the new legislative reforms neatly under one broadcasting and online safety statute. Notwithstanding this, it is hoped the Law Reform Commission will publish a consolidated version of the legislation in due course.

[31.1.02] The objectives of the new legislation is in part related to the state's obligation to transpose the revised Audiovisual Media Services Directive[2] ('AVMSD') discussed in Chapter 32 and to ensure online safety for audiences and content consumers.

MEDIA COMMISSION

[31.2.01] The new Commission will (at the time of writing, four appointments are to be confirmed[3] by the arts, culture and media minister) be headed by an

1 The Principal Act almost immediately upon enactment thereof came to be seen as an analogue piece of legislation in an online world. In the midst of how content is now consumed through online sources, traditional public free to air broadcasting on RTÉ or subscription-based services such as Sky or Virgin Media are competing for audiences with the major streaming services thus rendering the very concept of broadcasting quite outdated in a digital world. Both domestic and EU legislation accordingly has had to adjust both to remain relevant and fit for purpose and to take account of changing consumption habits globally.

2 Directive (EU) 2018/1808.

3 Jeremy Godfrey as Executive Chairperson; Niamh Hodnett as Online Safety Commissioner;

executive chairperson who will have overall responsibility for the management of the organisation. In addition to the executive chairperson, a number of commissioners are to be appointed. One of the appointees to the Commission will serve as the Online Safety Commissioner.

[31.2.02] The Commission has been assigned a range of functions including promoting and protecting the interests of the public in relation to online, audiovisual and audio content; devising and implementing codes and rules (termed "media service codes" and "media service rules") to be observed by both broadcasters (including sound broadcasters) and entities operating designated online services and audiovisual on-demand media services and to take enforcement action where breaches are identified; preparing and submitting proposals to government for a scheme or schemes for the granting of funds to support the production of audiovisual content and sound broadcasting content; and imposing a levy on regulated media services and designated online services in order to ensure the commission is sufficiently resourced to properly execute its statutory functions.

[31.2.03] Section 8 the 2022 Act (in substituting a new Pt 2 in the Principal Act) provides for the Commission to make (new s 21) "levy orders" (the legal basis for this provision is Art 13 of the revised AVMSD) pertaining to the imposition of a content production levy on media services providers established in the state or which target audiences in the state sufficient to meet the Commission's expenses and its working capital requirements in the relevant "levy period", in so far as those expenses and requirements are not met in any other way. This applies to providers of both linear and on-demand services. A levy order shall not impose a levy on a provider providing only a community broadcasting service. The new s 22 of the Principal Act deals with enforcement of levy orders and related offences.

[31.2.04] In making provision by levy order for the method of calculation of a levy and for any exemption or deferral, the Commission shall consider the relevance of factors to include the financing of a provider (including any public funding), the desirability of promoting new or innovative services, and the nature and scale of services provided by a provider.

Levies to fund schemes to support the production of European works

[31.2.05] Section 159E of new Pt 10A (as inserted into the Principal Act by s 54 of the 2022 Act) contains provisions in respect of the European works levy to be paid by media service providers under the jurisdiction of the state or which target audiences in the state and are established in another EU Member State (or third country).[4] The method of calculation of a levy in the latter case shall

---

Rónán Ó Domhnaill as Media Development Commissioner; and Celene Craig as Broadcasting Commissioner.

4 European works include works originating in third countries that are European states

be based on the revenue earned by the provider in the state from any audiovisual media service which it provides here. Such a levy shall not apply for instance to a media service provider with a low audience or a low turnover or in respect of a service exempted under any rules made by the Commission (where it would be impracticable or unjustified by reason of the nature of the service, or the general theme of audiovisual programmes provided by the service, to impose those obligations).

[31.2.06] The Commission may prepare a scheme for approval from the Minister for Tourism, Culture, Arts, Gaeltacht, Sport and Media for funds to be granted, out of the proceeds of any levy, to media service providers which are under the jurisdiction of the state, or target audiences in the state and are established in another Member State to provide support for the production of European works included, or to be included, in the schedule of an audiovisual broadcasting service, or in the catalogue of an audiovisual on-demand media service, provided by the provider.

[31.2.07] The kinds of support for which funds may be granted under a scheme shall be support of such of the following: new audiovisual programmes relating to Irish culture, language, history, heritage, society and sport; the experiences of the people of the island of Ireland, including the experiences of people of Irish ancestry living abroad; environmental sustainability and climate change; human rights including equality, diversity and inclusion; news, current affairs and international affairs; science or education; and new audiovisual programmes to improve adult literacy or improve media literacy.

COMPLIANCE AND ENFORCEMENT

[31.3.01] While the outcome of the BAI's broadcasting complaints decisions in the past was that they were published periodically on its website and distributed to the media,[5] they did not lead to punitive sanctions against broadcasters. However, in sufficiently serious cases, these decisions (henceforth to be made by the Commission) relating to providers of broadcasting services (and audiovisual ondemand media services and designated online services) can pave the way for what were formerly statutory investigations under s 53[6] which in turn can potentially lead to the imposition of very substantial financial penalties (termed "administrative financial sanctions" in the 2022 Act; under the now repealed s

party to the European Convention on Transfrontier Television of the Council of Europe done at Strasbourg on 5 May 1989.

5 Going forward, s 139ZT(5) of the revised Principal Act relates to notice and publication of decisions of the Commission on its website.

6 s 53 was repealed by s 73 of the 2022 Act as was the entirety of Chapter 2 of Pt 5 of the Principal Act.

54, the upper limit for financial sanctions was €250,000 – this has been vastly increased).[7]

[31.3.02] It is worth noting that the 2022 Act stops short of imposing civil liability in favour of listeners/viewers for breaches of the amended Principal Act by broadcasters in claims that might otherwise be taken, for instance, grounded on duty of care, breach of statutory duty or negligent infliction of emotional distress.

[31.3.03] Further, the amount of sanctions shall not in the case of an individual provider be such as would be likely to cause the individual to be adjudicated bankrupt and in the case of a provider that is not an individual such as would be likely to cause the provider to cease trading (as might happen, given already limited resources, if substantial sanctions under the new range were applied to national public broadcaster).

[31.3.04] Under the updated legislation, matters to be considered in determining the amount of financial sanctions (see s 139ZW(3), new Pt 8B of the Principal Act) include the nature, gravity and duration of the contravention; the degree of harm to particular people or to the public caused as a result of the contravention; the extent of any failure by the provider to co-operate with an investigation; any gain (financial or otherwise) made or any loss avoided by the provider or by any person in which that provider has a pecuniary interest or beneficial interest as a consequence of the contravention; the nature and timeliness of any steps taken by the provider to bring the contravention to an end, and any steps taken by the provider to remedy the consequences of the contravention.[8]

The (former) s 53 statutory investigation

[31.3.05] Aside from core functions such as licensing radio and television services and its role in media mergers which was assigned to the BAI under Pt 4 (Media Mergers)[9] of the Competition and Consumer Protection Act 2014, one of the

---

7 In the case of an individual up to €20,000,000, or in the case of a provider that is not an individual, €20,000,000 or, if greater, ten percent of the relevant turnover of the provider in the financial year preceding the date of the decision under s 139ZK to impose the sanction.

8 Other relevant factors include the absence or ineffectiveness of internal mechanisms or procedures intended to prevent such a contravention; the extent to which the contravention was contributed to by the act or omission of a third party, and the extent to which the provider took steps to identify, and mitigate the effect of, that act or omission; the extent to which the contravention was contributed to by circumstances beyond the control of the provider; the extent to which the management of the provider knew, or ought to have known, that the contravention was occurring or would occur; and the turnover of the provider in the financial years during which the contravention occurred and the ability of the provider to pay a sanction.

9 s 74 of the Consumer Protection Act 2014 which inserted Pt 3A into the Competition Act 2002. The Competition and Consumer Protection Commission reviews media mergers on their narrow economic impact, while the BAI (now Media Commission) examines proposed mergers on a cross-media ownership basis and whether it damages

Commission's key statutory functions (apart from also encouraging compliance with the provisions of the Broadcasting and Other Media Regulation Acts 2009 and 2022 and any relevant codes and rules made thereunder, including by the publication of guidance as to how those provisions may be complied with) is the independent regulation of traditional broadcasting standards and procedures and those now relating to audiovisual ondemand media services providers and others.

[31.3.06] Investigators are charged with investigative, enforcement, compliance and reporting powers and functions. Section 50 of the Principal Act as amended provides for investigators to initiate statutory investigations where there is apparent non-compliance by a broadcaster, broadcasting contractor or other service provider.

[31.3.07] Section 50 which relates to contractors or content providers was never previously invoked by the BAI. However, an investigation pursuant to the now repealed s 53 which applied to broadcasters was undertaken to examine the making and broadcast of *Mission to Prey* by RTÉ in 2011. A second statutory investigation in respect of RTÉ's *The Frontline Presidential Debate* was narrowly averted later that same year as will shortly be discussed given the BAI's conclusion that a s 53 investigation would not have added sufficiently to what had been learned since the breaches so as to justify its instigation.

[31.3.08] Thus, the *Mission to Prey* documentary is the solitary example of practical application of enforcement, with financial sanctions, of the former BAI's regulatory powers in respect of breaches of the then s 39 (duties of broadcasters)[10] under the Principal Act and in relation to the then s 55 sanctions. This programme was described by Noel Curran, the former Director General of RTÉ as "one of the gravest editorial mistakes ever made" in the history of RTÉ broadcasting. On 5 April 2012, the BAI issued a notification pursuant to the then s 54(4) in which it set out an indicative financial sanction of €200,000 as being appropriate. After submissions by RTÉ, and having regard to the matters

media plurality. *The Irish Times* (article dated 18 April 2018) confirmed that the BAI was requested in January 2017 by the then Minister for Communications, Climate Action and Environment, Denis Naughten, to conduct a full media merger examination of the planned takeover by Irish News and Media (INM) of Celtic Media Group (which owns the *Anglo-Celt* in Cavan, the *Meath Chronicle* and the *Connaught Telegraph*) having regard to the level of ownership of media companies, broadcast and print, by Denis O'Brien, INM's biggest shareholder. However, the intended merger was aborted. In 2018, following certain revelations concerning, *inter alia,* potential inside information [reported to have been passed between INM then chairman and Mr O'Brien, in possible breach of stock market rules (chairman sharing information with the major shareholder)], the transaction details became politically controversial for the minister. The BAI had been given 80 days to examine if the takeover would be damaging media plurality in Ireland because it would have increased INM's ownership of regional newspapers from 13 to 20. Ultimately, INM and Celtic Media decided to resile from the proposed deal by mutual consent in June 2017 shortly before the minister was due to consider the BAI's report on the acquisition.

10 Duties of broadcasters are now set out in new Pt 3B of the Principal Act (see ss 46I to 46M).

set out in the provisions of s 56 (now repealed), the BAI subsequently determined in May 2012 that such level of sanction was in fact appropriate.

[31.3.09] There is no absolute, universally shared sense of what standards are, or should be, observed. Legitimate concerns may arise that a litany of prohibitions could ultimately constrain effective broadcasting. The Investigating Officer, Anna Carragher[11] in the *Mission to Prey* s 53 investigation discussed below prefaced her report with a summary of the delicate balancing act required:

> I approach this task as someone who has a deep appreciation of the role that broadcasting and investigative journalism plays in a free, fair and well informed society and the role it also plays in holding government and institutions to account. But broadcasting's powerful place in our society also brings heavy responsibilities and it is right and proper that those who hold others to account are themselves held accountable.

[31.3.10] Carragher was most likely mindful of the statutory objectives and functions of the BAI as previously out in ss 25 and 26 of the Principal Act such as providing a regulatory environment that would sustain independent and impartial journalism and endeavouring to ensure that the democratic values enshrined in the Constitution, especially those relating to rightful liberty of expression, are upheld, whilst yet monitoring that expression, regulating content and ensuring that measures taken are proportionate having regard to the statutory objectives.

Mission to Prey

[31.3.11] A spin-off series of *Prime Time*, namely *Prime Time Investigates* (now *RTÉ Investigates*) previously aired on Monday nights featuring investigative journalism and undercover reporting. The series was officially cancelled in April 2012 after RTÉ's Aoife Kavanagh, who promptly resigned, defamed Fr Kevin Reynolds in an episode broadcast on RTÉ One in May 2011 with the title *Mission to Prey* during which Kavanagh falsely accused Fr Reynolds of sexually assaulting a woman and fathering a child in Kenya. The BAI report found that:

> Second-hand repetition of gossip appears to have been treated as corroboration, as Ms Kavanagh did not appear to have met or questioned colleagues who, according to the primary source, were aware of the allegations.

[31.3.12] Ms Carragher stated that it was highly desirable that the legal affairs team have earlier input into programmes that are likely to be high-risk or contentious. Her report found that RTÉ had made serious errors in the production and its transmission. She was of the view that, of the former s 39 (broadcaster duties) breaches, ss 39(1)(b) and 39(1)(e) in particular had been

[11] Former Controller of BBC Northern Ireland where she was editorially responsible for all BBC Northern Ireland output.

contravened.[12] The former stipulated that every broadcaster shall ensure that the broadcast treatment of current affairs, including matters which are either of public controversy or the subject of current public debate, is fair to all interests concerned and that the broadcast matter is presented in an objective and impartial manner and without any expression of the broadcaster's own views. The latter subsection stipulated that every broadcaster shall ensure that in programmes broadcast, and in the means employed to make such programmes, the privacy of individuals is not unreasonably encroached upon.

The Frontline presidential debate

[31.3.13] During this televised debate in 2011, the presenter, Pat Kenny, read out a tweet that caused insurmountable hurdles for the then frontrunner presidential candidate Seán Gallagher. The tweet, which transpired to be bogus, and purporting to be from the presidential campaign of Martin McGuinness involved brown-envelope-type allegations concerning fundraising by Mr Gallagher for Fianna Fáil and collecting a cheque for €5,000 from a dubious source. It became apparent during the course of the programme that such tweet was in fact false. However, its falsity was not revealed to the live audience or the public audience viewers. Mr Gallagher subsequently lost the election.

[31.3.14] At its meeting on 20 November 2011, the BAI compliance committee considered a report and other related material provided to it by RTÉ which dealt with the broadcaster's editorial review of the programme. It issued a statement on 22 November. From its review of the report already made public by RTÉ and a review of a working document upon which the report was based, and taking into account complaints upheld by the BAI in respect of the use during this programme of an unverified tweet, it was evident to the committee that the production of this programme fell significantly short of the standards expected by the public of Irish broadcasters.

[31.3.15] The report, the working document and the earlier findings of the committee highlighted the serious and significant editorial failings that took place during a television debate of utmost public importance and interest. It was the view of the committee that those failings related to the fundamentals of journalistic practice and could, in its opinion, have been avoided had the broadcaster applied established good practice in the conduct of a news and current affairs debate to the standard required for a presidential election.

[31.3.16] The committee considered the necessity and desirability of instigating a statutory investigation into the televised debate. The committee ultimately decided, however, that such an investigation was not warranted in respect of this

12 Pt 3 (ss 39-46) of the Principal Act was repealed. The 2022 Act inserted a new Pt 3B (ss 46I-46R) into the Principal Act in relation to codes and rules applying to broadcasters and service providers.

programme. In reaching this decision, the committee had regard to a number of factors including that the debate programme had already been the subject of an examination by the committee further to the statutory complaints process. Six complaints in relation to the use of an unverified tweet were upheld and the broadcaster had announced on-air the findings of the committee. The decisions of the committee had also been published and, arising from this, RTÉ had initiated and completed a review of the programme.

[31.3.17] The programme resulted in defamation proceedings being instituted against RTÉ. Irish Legal News reported[13] subsequent to a settlement reached on 19 December 2017 that damages reported to be in the region of €130,000 had been agreed. A trial had been due to commence at the High Court early in 2018. Mr Gallagher had sought a declaration that the programme was unfairly edited, presented and directed by RTÉ in a fashion injurious to his electoral prospects.

The aftermath of the 2011 breaches

[31.3.18] On foot of the deficiencies outlined above and the Fr Reynolds scandal earlier that year, RTÉ reviewed and revised its approach to the management and production of news and current affairs programming. This included changes in key staff, management processes and journalism guidelines including policies in respect of the use of social media during programming. A number of recommendations were also made in respect of the production of future election debates to be scheduled on RTÉ, including the introduction of greater editorial oversight and measures to ensure that the selection and use of audiences in such debates is fair, objective and impartial.

[31.3.19] Arising by virtue of RTÉ's many failings, interim revised internal guidelines for journalists and editors were published in April 2012. It was announced that a new Editorial Standards Board was to be established to maintain and monitor the standards of content produced by the broadcaster. RTÉ's December 2013 (revised) *Programme Content Standards* (a general guide to standards and practices for staff and independent programme-makers) replaced the 2008 guidelines, s 4 thereof confirming the establishment of the new board. These specifically address issues of concern for those involved in editorial coverage of news and current affairs content. However, any programme or part thereof which deals with current affairs topics should be treated as current affairs content even if produced by other departments, for example factual, lifestyle or entertainment/music. The guidelines are subject to regular review. The RTÉ Journalism & Content Guidelines 2020, being the third iteration since 2012, were formulated by the RTÉ Editorial Standards Board.

---

13 Irish Legal News, *Paul Tweed secured damages from RTE for ex-presidential candidate* (2017), irishlegal.com. Available at: http://www.irishlegal.com/9936/paul-tweed-secures-damages-rte-ex-presidential-candidate/ [Accessed 27 April 2018].

[31.3.20] Examples of changes introduced include that any proposal to proceed with a programme despite legal advice concerning a significant or serious risk must be referred to the Director of News and Current Affairs or the Director of Content. The Director of News and Current Affairs or the Director of Content must assess any proposal to use secret recording in any content intended for use by RTÉ.[14] Programme legal advice must always be obtained in advance of any proposed report that may identify a child involved, in any capacity, in criminal court proceedings, or a child involved in illegal or anti-social activity. News pieces and other items involving exceptional circumstances will be dealt with on the day of transmission, but must be flagged at the earliest possible opportunity as requiring legal advice.

[31.3.21] The guidelines stress that editorial staff must exercise great caution when relying on information from individuals gleaned from social media sites, be alert as to reporting second-hand information and astute as to possible hidden agenda. They are urged to corroborate wherever possible and to perform due diligence on the identity of any contributor intended to be used as well as verifying content that appears on other sites before running the story, and to attribute the source clearly so that the audience can access the information and its source.

[31.3.22] The guidelines further provide that doorstepping,[15] that is, an interview with a person who was not expected to be interviewed for broadcast, should normally be a last resort and not used simply for dramatic effect. Any proposal to doorstep an individual must be approved in advance by the relevant managing or senior editor.

[31.3.23] Moreover, the purpose of the Editorial Standards Board, as convened by the Head of Editorial Standards and Compliance, is to maintain and monitor content standards. The board is independent of existing editorial lines within output divisions. Where a significant investigative programme is planned, the board will function as a separate and additional resource which can be used to further scrutinise the content pre-broadcast. In such cases, production teams shall present a detailed report to the board at least five working days in advance of scheduled transmission to enable it to assess the quality of the report, the reliability of the evidence assembled which supports the claims being made and to determine if the public interest is best served by the report's being broadcast.

---

14 Note (but in the context of law enforcement) the decision of the Data Protection Commissioner in 2020 against Waterford County Council in respect of covert filming targeted at illegal dumping and other illegal activity by the public discussed at the end of Chapter 14 in the context of drone and other footage. The potential s 43 (Data Protection Act 2018) defence (freedom of expression) may also be relevant and/or arguments in respect of the public interest.

15 s 13 of the guidelines.

DUTIES, CODES AND RULES APPLYING TO MEDIA SERVICE PROVIDERS AND SOUND BROADCASTERS; CONTINUING APPLICATION OF BAI CODES

[31.4.01] Section 49N(11) as inserted into the Principal Act provides that, unless otherwise amended or revoked by the Commission, the broadcasting codes referred to below shall continue to apply to broadcasters only. Pursuant to s 46N and O, the Commission may make new "media service codes" and "media service rules" in respect of other media service providers.

[31.4.02] Broadcasting codes, rules and standards (see new Pt 3B, ss 46I-46R of the amended Principal Act) support Irish audiences in holding broadcasters, both television and radio, and other relevant service providers to account while informing broadcasters, viewers and listeners of the standards expected in disseminating content. The codes are of relevance to independent producers as much as they are to commissioning broadcasters. The rights acquisition contract between for instance an outside producer and a broadcaster will vest final editorial control in the broadcaster as commissioning entity or distribution licensee. This will allow the broadcaster, pre-broadcast, to ensure that the content does not infringe the relevant code and upholds the requisitive standards. For in-house productions by broadcasters themselves, staff and independent contractors from directors and producers to researchers and presenters will likewise need to adhere to the codes.

[31.4.03] The *Code of Fairness, Objectivity and Impartiality* (2013) relates to news and current affairs content while the *General Commercial Communications Code* (2017) sets out rules pertaining to advertising, sponsorship, product placement and other forms of commercial promotion. The *Children's Commercial Communications Code* (2013) governs advertising, sponsorship, product placement and other forms of commercial promotion aimed at children or broadcast in or around children's programming.[16] The main aim of the *Code of Programme Standards* (2015) is to promote responsible broadcasting.

Complaints

[31.4.04] Complaints can be made to the Commission under s 48 as amended of the Principal Act in relation to broadcasts or programme material. A person may make a complaint that there has been a failure to comply with ss 46J, 46K, 46L, 46M(2) or (3), a media service code, a media service rule, s 46P(1) or (2), s 106(3) or s 127(6). A complaint shall be made in writing to the Commission not more than 30 days after where the complaint relates to one broadcast, the date of the broadcast; where the complaint relates to two or more unrelated broadcasts, the date of the earlier or earliest, as the case may be, of those broadcasts; where

---

16 It includes, for instance, rules on the promotion to children of food that is high in fat, salt or sugar.

the complaint relates to two or more related broadcasts, of which at least two are made on different dates, the later or latest of those dates; or where the complaint relates to programme material made available on an audiovisual on-demand media service, the date the programme material ceased to be available on that service. The s 48 procedures are discussed further below.

Right of reply

[31.4.05] The right of reply scheme (s 49 as amended by s 13 of the 2022 Act) provides for a right of reply statement that facilitates the correction of false information which has been broadcast and has resulted in a person's honour or reputation being impugned. Each broadcaster must include a copy of the scheme on its website and information on the station's staff member who deals with such requests. A request for a right of reply should be submitted to the broadcaster in the first instance. If complainants are not satisfied with the response from the broadcaster, their request can be referred to the Commission. When making a complaint to the Commission directly rather than first canvassing the matter with the broadcaster concerned, statutory time limits as set out in s 49 apply.

Code of Fairness, Objectivity and Impartiality

[31.4.06] This code requires broadcasters to deal fairly with persons referred to in news and current affairs content and to present views and facts in a manner which does not misrepresent those views or facts or render them misleading. Steps taken must be sufficient to provide interviewees with information to allow ample preparation for the interview. Further, interviewees must be afforded enough time to offer their opinions and respond to challenges during the programme to ensure that proportionality and fairness is achieved by the presenter.

[31.4.07] An instance of breach of the code occurred when a RTÉ *Six-One News* episode on 23 January 2018 referred to a report of court proceedings at Ennis District Court in which the complainant appeared as the defendant. The report presented information about the court proceedings, including details of the arrest and subsequent charges, but failed to mention details from the defence case or the fact that the defendant was acquitted of certain charges. The court proceedings had concluded prior to the broadcast but the broadcast nevertheless did not include all available facts. The exclusion of the acquittal, in particular, rendered the report misleading and unfair. The BAI complaints committee was mindful that the update on the story was not received by the broadcaster until six minutes prior to broadcast, however, the code states that:

> Accuracy is a fundamental principle associated with the broadcast of news and current affairs content and should always take priority over the speed with which content can be delivered.

[31.4.08] The committee noted that the broadcaster did not include the updated information, nor did the report include reference to the fact that the trial was ongoing at the time of preparation.

Code of Programme Standards

[31.4.09] This code requires broadcasters to take into account general community standards when making programmes. It acknowledges that harm or (undue) offence (see ss 46J and 46N(6)(a) of the revised Principal Act) may be caused by the programme or by the context in which it is heard because the material does not align with audience expectations. Broadcasters are, as a result, obliged to have due regard for audience expectations and, in live programming, to take timely corrective action where unplanned content is likely to have caused offence. Broadcasters are also required to exercise due care when broadcasting content with which audiences may identify and which can cause distress, particularly in relation to content such as sexual violence. Breach of the code can lead in practice to severe consequences for presenters as occurred in respect of the suspension of George Hook for inappropriate comments made about the sexual assault of a woman in the UK and issues of personal and parental responsibility during his Newstalk radio show which led to submission of a listener complaint to the BAI.

[31.4.10] The code seeks to promote responsible broadcasting in which access to information, entertainment and education, and a range of views, are enhanced while undue offence and harm are reduced. Programming as a force for public good and to enrich people's lives through entertainment can be provocative and deal with sensitive issues. The code therefore acknowledges the diversity of tastes and interests that exist in contemporary Irish society and aims to encourage and facilitate broadcasting that caters for this diversity.

[31.4.11] One of the functions of comedy for example is to push the boundaries of acceptable speech. The misuse of religious views, images, practices and beliefs in certain programme material has the potential to cause offence and this is recognised as part of the code. At the same time, the code recognises that content can be aired which may cause offence but which is justified for creative, editorial or other reasons.

[31.4.12] Broadcasters are required to comply with all seven guiding principles underpinning this code which are respect for community standards; importance of context; protection from harm; protection of children; respect for persons and groups in society; protection of the public interest, and respect for privacy. These principles are indivisible, meaning that all programme material must conform to all of the principles.

The s 48[17] statutory complaints process

[31.4.13] Under the Principal Act, viewers and listeners to Irish radio and television services can invoke the mechanisms of the s 48 complaints process.[18] Non-compliance with broadcaster and media service provider duties might include that the privacy of an individual was unreasonably encroached upon or that programme content can reasonably be regarded as causing harm or undue offence.

[31.4.14] The Commission shall either refer a complaint to the broadcaster or provider of an audiovisual on-demand media service concerned (for its consideration in accordance with a code of practice) or dismiss it within 60 working days from the date on which the complaint is received and shall publish notice of the fact of the reference or dismissal on its website.

[31.4.15] In assessing complaints, the Commission will have regard to the relevant codes and rules, the written material submitted by the relevant parties, together with the subject content/broadcast material.

General Commercial Communications Code

[31.4.16] This 2017 code sets out the rules with which Irish radio and television stations must comply relating to the airing of advertising, sponsorship, product placement and other forms of commercial communications. It was developed by the BAI following a statutory review, in pursuance of s 45(3) of the Principal Act,[19] of the 2010 code[20] and a public consultation on a revised draft.

[31.4.17] Updates made in this revision include the provision of greater clarity on the distinction between sponsorship and product placement. The stated objective of the revised code is to give the public audience the confidence that commercial communications on television and radio are legal, decent, honest, truthful and protect its interests.[21] The code is also intended to provide greater clarity and certainty for Irish broadcasters on the standards that they should apply. Additionally, the code seeks to ensure that commercial communications

---

17 ss 11-13 of the 2022 Act amend ss 47-49 of the Principal Act in relation to the statutory complaints procedures and the right of reply.

18 Grounded on the alleged breach by broadcasters of statutory duties, broadcasting codes or rules.

19 s 45(3) of the Principal Act required the BAI to review the effect of a broadcasting code every four years (see new s 46R(3)).

20 The *General Commercial Communications Code* was introduced in 2010 under s 42 of the Principal Act to regulate advertising, sponsorship, product placement and other forms of commercial communication on Irish broadcasting services, having regard, *inter alia*, to the Audiovisual Media Services Directive introduced in 2010 (2010/13/EU), a simplified and codified version of three earlier Council/European Parliament Directives and the EC (Audiovisual Media Services) Regulations 2010 (SI No 258 of 2010).

21 Audiences are afforded the statutory right to submit complaints where they believe the code has been breached.

do not impinge on the editorial integrity of broadcasts and the independence of broadcasters from influence by brands as regards programme scheduling for instance.

Product placement

[31.4.18] The advent of paid product placement on television since 2011 came with a relaxation of European law. Product placement and advertiser-funded programming have grown to become an important source of revenue for Irish broadcasters.

[31.4.19] While prop placement and paid product placement are permitted in cinematographic works (and television films), certain rules also apply to these forms of audience content.[22]

[31.4.20] Whether or not outside producers will be in receipt of a share of revenues from sponsorship and product placement, they will need in any event to consult with the broadcaster's relevant department head on any deals made by the latter as editing may be required (such as in respect of product placement announcements in the programme and closing credits) to comply with the appropriate rules and Commission monitoring.

[31.4.21] In January 2018[23] Virgin Media Solutions entered a brand exposure contract with Chilean wine Casillero del Diablo as the new sponsor of the then TV3 *Red Rock* series. In 2017, Virgin Media Solutions launched Mirriad In-Video technology in Ireland in a number of episodes of *Red Rock*, which incorporated real-time Virgin Media outdoor campaigns in multiple episodes. Virgin Media Solutions extended this digital product placement opportunity to incorporate Casillero Del Diablo products into the show in the post-production phase.

[31.4.22] Product placement is defined in the *General Commercial Communications Code* as "any form of commercial communication on television consisting of the inclusion of or reference to a product, a service or the trademark thereof so that it is featured within a programme".[24] The decisive criterion distinguishing product placement from sponsorship is the fact that in respect of product placement the reference to a product or service is built into the action of a programme. In contrast, sponsor announcements or references may be shown

---

22 Split-screen advertising, for instance, is not permitted in cinematographic works or television films – r 7.4 of the *General Commercial Communications Code*. Rule 10.9(a) also forbids product placement of tobacco products or cigarettes or product placement from undertakings the principal activity of which is the manufacture or sale of cigarettes or other tobacco products.

23 Adworld.ie, *Casillero del Diablo to Sponsor TV3's New Series of Red Rock* (2018). Available at: https://www.adworld.ie/2018/01/19/casillero-del-diablo-sponsor-tv3s-new-series-red-rock/ [Accessed 25 April 2018].

24 s 2 (general definitions and exclusions), p 8 of the code.

during a programme but are not part of the plot or narrative of the programme. The display of logos or branding in programme content is considered product placement.

[31.4.23] For the purposes of the code, there is a distinction between two types of product placement as provided for in AVSMD. Paid product placement occurs where a third party provides products and services for inclusion within a television programme for payment or similar consideration to the broadcaster. Prop placement occurs where a third party provides products and services for inclusion within a television programme free of charge and the total value of all the products and services featured in a single scheduled episode of a programme is of significant value (see below).

[31.4.24] The placement of products in programme content shall be editorially justified and shall not give undue prominence to the products or services in question. Product integration, where programme content, including storylines, is tailored around a product, service or facility provided through a product placement arrangement, is not permissible. Thematic placement, where programme content, including storylines, is tailored around a specific theme, e.g. the beliefs, policies, aims and objectives of the product or service provider, is also not permitted. Product placement is permissible only in circumstances whereby the reference to a product or service is simply built into, in some fashion, the action of a programme.

[31.4.25] Audiences shall be clearly informed of the existence of product placement. Programmes containing product placement shall be appropriately identified by an announcement at the start and the end of the programme, and when a programme resumes after an advertising break, in order to avoid any confusion on the part of the audience. The Commission may prescribe the form of a product placement announcement from time to time including its text, logo, size, colour, font type and audio message, and broadcasters shall ensure product placement announcements comply with the form and any related guidance prescribed by the Commission. This rule does not apply when broadcasting television programmes that have neither been produced nor commissioned by the broadcaster or a company affiliated to the broadcaster.

Paid product placement

[31.4.26] Paid product placement is permitted only in cinematographic works, television films, sport, dramas, including one-off dramas, drama series and serials (excluding docu-dramas) and light entertainment programmes (excluding talk/chat shows that regularly include 20 percent or more of news and current affairs content).[25]

---

[25] r 10.2 of the code.

[31.4.27] Prop placement is permitted in all programmes but shall not affect the integrity of such programmes, in particular, news and current affairs programmes. Prop placement in children's programmes is not permitted in the case of products/services that may not feature in children's programmes (e.g. alcohol and HFSS foods) and in the case of other relevant restrictions.

[31.4.28] The closing credits of a programme containing product placement shall include the name of the providers and the products and services provided. Broadcasters shall keep a record of the programmes in which product placement occurs, the placement in each programme, the value of each individual placement and whether it is paid product placement or prop placement. This information must be available to the media regulator upon request in the context of compliance monitoring or in instances where a complaint is investigated. This information must also be available in respect of any independent programmes commissioned by the broadcaster.

Prop placement

[31.4.29] Products and services featured within a television programme free of charge, and where the total value of all those products and services featured within a single scheduled episode of a programme is not of significant value, does not constitute product placement. However, where the featuring of such products and services is unduly prominent, is not editorially justified and/or could be construed as a commercial communication, the Commission may rely on the provisions of the code prohibiting surreptitious commercial communications.

[31.4.30] Products and services are deemed of significant value where the total value of all products and services featured in a single episode of a programme exceeds €1,000. The Commission reserves the right to amend this interpretation of significant value from time to time as it sees fit and such amendments will be published on its website.

Sponsorship

[31.4.31] Sponsorship and advertising around programmes concerns revenues for broadcasters[26] rather than producers although there may be instances where income will accrue in this connection to the producer.[27] It is also relevant to the

---

[26] In licensing agreements between independent producers and RTÉ, the latter will insist on having the sole right to arrange for sponsorship in respect of RTÉ's exploitation of the programme. Any such arrangement will be the subject of a contract entered into and negotiated between RTÉ and the sponsor(s) and RTÉ would be entitled to retain all proceeds of such sponsorship. Any other sponsorship (including any product placement) related to the programme would require the prior written agreement of RTÉ.

[27] In the case of revenues from competitions for instance (or from audience voting) then such revenues might be split between the producer and the broadcaster in predetermined contractual splits.

extent that it may assist with licensing deals for series productions. If the content performs well in series one, it is likely that a broadcaster will back further series given the opportunities that may be presented to the broadcaster for sponsorship deals grounded on the show's popularity. Certain content however, despite its success, will not lend itself to a sponsorship deal. *Love/Hate* for example was unable to attract a sponsor given its criminal underworld themes.

[31.4.32] Sponsorship might partially fund the making of the programme. In a limited number of cases, a specific contract can be negotiated whereby some or all of the sponsorship funding can go directly to the production's budget to enhance the programme. In exceptional circumstances, sponsorship income can be used to directly fund the production. This applies to a situation whereby, without sponsorship funding, the programme could not be made. The arrangement can only be entered into with the approval of the relevant television or radio boards. The same guidelines apply to independent producers as in-house producers.

[31.4.33] Sponsorship of television and radio programmes has enjoyed a long history. The term 'soap opera' stems from the fact that the sponsors and producers of many early American television and radio dramas were soap manufacturers. Indeed, RTÉ derives approximately half of its income from commercial sources.[28] Sponsorship can range from a simple on-air association with a single programme to a long-term, fully-integrated exclusive partnership including branded content, product placement, branded events, promotions, competitions and licensing. In addition to payment to RTÉ, Virgin Media or other broadcaster in return for sponsorship recognition, companies can offer sponsorship in kind by providing services or goods to a programme. The same guidelines apply in these instances as when the sponsorship involves cash payments.

[31.4.34] Public service broadcasting requires editorial independence of commercial or financial interests. Hence the existence of clear guidelines on advertising, audiences, product placement and sponsorship. In addition, there is a prohibition in the *General Commercial Communications Code* on the sponsoring of news and current affairs programmes. Neither can there be sponsorship in children's and religious programming. This rule however does not prohibit the sponsorship of weather, entertainment and traffic items.[29]

---

[28] RTÉ in April 2018 for example advertised a sponsorship offer in respect of *Can't Cope Won't Cope* and *Say Yes To The Dress* with the cost of the package for sponsoring both shows coming in at €130,000 with 104 sponsorship stings and pre-rolls on RTÉ Player's 21-day catch up. Elsewhere, *The Irish Times* reported in December 1999 that the most recent RTÉ signing was a one-year £500,000 deal with Irish Life and Permanent to sponsor the new series of the popular medical drama *ER*. Another visible television sponsorship on Irish television at that time was Eircom's link with *Weatherline*. At an annual cost of £600,000, the sheer frequency and high viewing figures for the weather forecast were particularly important for the company that year during its name change from Telecom Éireann to Eircom.

[29] r 8.8.

[31.4.35] Sponsorship is defined[30] in the *General Commercial Communications Code* as:

> any contribution made by a public or private undertaking or natural person not engaged in providing radio or television services or in the production of sound broadcasting or audiovisual works, to the financing of television and/or radio services or programmes with a view to promoting its name, its trade mark, its image, its activities, its products or its services.

[31.4.36] The contribution may be in the form of direct funding, provision of facilities or services, or the supply of goods/prizes. Advertising is a message from a commercial or other body contained in a recognisable and separate commercial break. Sponsorship credits stand apart from commercial breaks and the minutage allowed for them.

[31.4.37] Sponsorship is similarly defined in AVMSD as meaning:

> any contribution made by a public or private undertaking or natural person not engaged in providing media services or in the production of content, to the financing of media services or content with a view to promoting its name, its trademark, its image, its activities or its products.

[31.4.38] Sponsor announcements or references may be shown during a programme but shall not form part of the plot or narrative, namely, they are limited to announcements declaring the sponsorship arrangement (such as "sponsored by" and "brought to you by") and announcements for sponsored competitions.[31]Rules governing sponsorship on television (including competitions) and sponsorship on radio (including competitions) are set out in rr 8 and 9 of the code respectively.[32] Rule 8.3 stipulates that there shall be a clear distinction between sponsorship and product placement.

[31.4.39] There must be a clear separation between sponsorship and advertising for the audience.[33] There is no prohibition, however, on the inclusion of advertisements for a programme sponsor during advertisement breaks. Furthermore a sponsor must not have any editorial input or involvement in programming or scheduling, nor should there be reasonable grounds on the part of the viewer to believe that input or influence does exist. Rule 8.4 mandates that audiences shall be clearly informed of the existence of a sponsorship agreement. Sponsored programmes shall be clearly identified as such by the name, logo

---

30 At p 9 thereof.

31 r 8.3.

32 At pp 21-24.

33 Sponsorship must not constitute advertising as defined in the code, and sponsored programmes shall not directly encourage the purchase or rental of goods or services. A sponsorship announcement or reference shall not make special promotional references to a product or service (e.g. sales and discounts); include advertising copy, prices, endorsements or calls to purchase; or afford undue prominence to a product or service of the sponsor, though reference to more than one product or service is permitted.

and/or any other symbol of the sponsor such as a reference to its product(s) or service(s) or a distinctive sign thereof in an appropriate way for programmes at the beginning, during and/or at the end of the programmes.

Chapter 32

Audiovisual Media Services Directive; Directive on Certain Online Transmissions and Retransmissions of Television and Radio Programmes

INTRODUCTION

[32.1.01] The revised Audiovisual Media Services Directive (the 'AVMSD') was adopted in early November 2018 and introduced a number of key changes to the original 2010 version thereof.[1] Missing its implementation deadline in September 2020, it was transposed into Irish law by the Online Safety and Media Regulation Act 2022 ('the 2022 Act'), discussed in Chapter 30. It governs EU-wide coordination of national legislation on all audiovisual media, both traditional television broadcasts and on-demand services.

[32.1.02] The AVMSD overhauls the existing Directive to account for the ongoing convergence of television and internet services. Certain audiovisual rules which extend now to video-sharing platforms such as YouTube, as well as audiovisual content shared on social media services including Facebook, are covered by the Directive as outlined below including a new approach for video-sharing platforms to protect minors, to fight hate speech and ensure adherence to basic advertising standards.[2] The AVMSD also seeks to guarantee the independence of national media regulators.

[32.1.03] As discussed in Chapter 30, the legislation requires media services providers to protect minors from harmful content, such as scheduling restrictions, technical measures and visual indicators. In addition, the AVMSD mandates

---

1 Directive 2010/13/EU of the European Parliament and of the Council of 10 March 2010 on the coordination of certain provisions laid down by law, regulation or administrative action in Member States concerning the provision of audiovisual media services. The revised legislation is Directive (EU) 2018/1808.

2 The Directive will therefore work in tandem with the objectives of the EU Digital Services Act.

that Member States must ensure that audiovisual content does not contain any incitement to hatred based on race, sex, religion or nationality.

[32.1.04] The AVMSD[3] also assures across Member States that events of major importance are available on a free-to-air basis for their population. This aims to avoid a situation whereby, for example, a major sports event like the Olympic Games or a landmark national ceremony would only be available on pay-per-view basis or a subscription-based television channel.

[32.1.05] Further, the AVMSD provides that professional video-on-demand services which provide news and current affairs content shall meet the same journalistic standards as required by television broadcasters (see para [30.1.03]).

[32.1.06] The country-of-origin principle is a cornerstone of the AVMSD. According to this principle, each Member State is legally responsible for all audiovisual media services originating from its own country. This means media services providers come under the jurisdiction of only one EU country rather than being regulated by authorities from multiple territories.

IMPLEMENTATION IN IRELAND

[32.2.01] The government was obliged to transpose the AVMSD into Irish law by 19 September 2020, delays no doubt being exacerbated by the Covid-19 pandemic. The 2022 Act which finally transposed the AVMSD was signed by the President in December 2022. The statute in very large part was commenced on 15 March 2023 by ministerial order (SI No 71 of 2023).

Opportunity for content creators

[32.2.02] At the heart of the AVMSD lies quotas for European works meaning video-on-demand platforms must make at least 30 percent of their catalogues European. This obligation does not, however, apply to on-demand services with low turnover[4] or a low audience.[5] The quota thus opens up a much larger market

---

3 Further, see Art 14 of the 2010 Directive. SI No 465 of 2017 was enacted pursuant to Art 14. The events specified in the schedule thereto (e.g. the All-Ireland senior inter-county football and hurling finals) such as Six Nations rugby games are designated as events of major importance to society for which the right of a qualifying broadcaster to provide coverage on a live basis and in whole on free television services should be provided in the public interest.

4 Micro enterprises (with annual turnover of less than two million euro) should *a priori* be excluded from the European works obligation, unless it would be proportionate to include them (for example in small Member States where even micro enterprises may have a significant market presence).

5 For linear services, cross-border channels with an audience share below two percent in a targeted Member State should be considered to have a low audience. For on-demand services, EU Commission guidance from July 2020 recommends determining audience numbers by reference to the number of users/viewers of a particular service, for example,

for Irish audiovisual producers and all related practitioners and service providers from cast and crew to music composers and SFX companies given the potential for a greater pool of work.

[32.2.03] On the downside in practical terms, the Media Commission/BAI Sound and Vision scheme[6] is tied to commissions from linear free-to-air broadcasters RTÉ and TG4 and to private commercially-owned Virgin Media, the channels of which are available on Saorview. At present, therefore, only producers with commissions from free-to-air broadcasters can avail of Media Commission funds. Companies that wish to pitch solely to say Sky[7] or streaming platforms such as Netflix cannot benefit from Media Commission moneys.

New industry (content funding) levies to assist the sector

[32.2.04] Under the existing regime, Member States may require media service providers to make financial contributions to the production of European works and in 2018 Netflix was unsuccessful in a case challenging its obligation to contribute to Germany's aid scheme for the funding of film production and distribution.[8] Article 13 of the AVMSD provides that Member States may additionally require financial contribution from providers who are not under their jurisdiction but who target audiences in their territory:

> 1. Member States shall ensure that media service providers of on-demand audiovisual media services under their jurisdiction secure at least a

---

the number of paying subscribers for a subscription service such as Netflix. Providers with an audience share of less than one percent within a given Member State should be deemed to have a low audience.

6 Which distributes some €14 million annually from licence fee receipts to television and radio producers.

7 While Sky of course broadcasts in Ireland, it is a subscription model and therefore not free to air.

8 Case T-818/16 *Netflix International BV v European Commission.* The CJEU found inadmissible Netflix's application for the annulment of the European Commission's 2016 decision on Germany's aid scheme for the funding of film production, distribution and exhibition being financed by a special levy imposed on undertakings in the cinema and video industry and the broadcasting sector. In March 2014, Germany informed the Commission of an amendment to the existing aid scheme, which extended liability for the levy to providers of video-on-demand services established outside Germany receiving revenue from customers in Germany through a German-language internet presence. The amendment was to apply from the date of its approval by the Commission until 31 December 2016, and if the Commission approved the scheme, the levy would be recovered retroactively as from the date of the entry into force of the amendment, namely 1 January 2014. On 1 September 2016, the Commission issued its decision, and found that the measures were compatible with the Treaty on the Functioning of the European Union (TFEU), and did not infringe the AVMSD (2010/13/EU). Following the decision, Netflix International, an online video-streaming service established in the Netherlands that launched its service in Germany in 2014 and became subject to the levy, applied to the EU court to have the decision annulled. Netflix International, together with its parent Netflix Inc, argued that the Commission's decision had been based on an incorrect interpretation of the AVMSD and infringed the TFEU. However, without addressing the substance of Netflix's application, the court declared the application inadmissible.

30 percent share of European works in their catalogues and ensure prominence of those works.

2. Where Member States require media service providers under their jurisdiction to contribute financially to the production of European works, including via direct investment in content and contribution to national funds, they may also require media service providers targeting audiences in their territories, but established in other Member States to make such financial contributions, which shall be proportionate and non-discriminatory.
3. In the case referred to in para 2, the financial contribution shall be based only on the revenues earned in the targeted Member States. If the Member State where the provider is established imposes such a financial contribution, it shall take into account any financial contributions imposed by targeted Member States. Any financial contribution shall comply with Union law, in particular with State aid rules.

[32.2.05] The AVMSD therefore paves the way for imposing a long sought-after levy on overseas broadcasters which target Irish viewers. Currently, channels such as Channel 4 and Sky stream services here known as opt-outs, with advertisements targeting Irish audiences. These generate significant revenues in Ireland. While Brexit means that UK broadcasters targeting Irish audiences are no longer part of media service providers "established in other Member States", the 2022 Act provides for the Media Commission to impose levies on audiovisual media services and providers of designated online services generally.

[32.2.06] Across the EU, a substantial percentage (up to some 40 percent) of national funding for indigenous film is sourced through industry levies. In Ireland, funding is exclusively from the taxpayer in the form of the television licence fee or annual exchequer allocations for instance to the Screen Ireland budget. Screen Ireland estimates that Irish audiences and advertisers pay more than €2 billion annually to providers of audiovisual entertainment that are based overseas. Against the backdrop of a global television boom, the Irish television sector is battling to remain afloat. Despite Screen Ireland's keen interest in supporting high-end television projects to include *Darklands* and *Normal People*, it currently has resources in the order of merely two million euro to attribute to such purposes which needless to say is woefully inadequate in the case where a high-quality series might cost say up to three million euro per episode to produce.

[32.2.07] Accordingly, the opening up in time of existing funding to other projects could be effected, in tandem with a parallel move to oblige say YouTube Premium, Apple, Netflix, HBO, Disney Plus or Amazon Prime to make a formal contribution to the Irish media industry. The new Directive affords the state the opportunity to usher in levies (based on revenues earned in Ireland) on audiovisual services that are established in this jurisdiction (Apple and Google both have European headquarters here) or are regulated in another EU state (for instance Spanish headquartered Rakuten TV; Netflix and Amazon have European headquarters in Amsterdam and Luxembourg respectively) but target Irish audiences and to then apply those funds to support Irish creative talent.

These levies are discussed at paras [31.2.03] to [31.2.07]. Among the Member States that have chosen to introduce financial obligations, most have opted to introduce direct investment obligations (production and/or rights acquisition) as opposed to paying a levy to a support fund.[9]

[32.2.08] In relation to non-EU companies (e.g. US providers) and the establishment in the EU requirement, certain key providers will have either a parent undertaking or a subsidiary undertaking which is established in a EU Member State. Furthermore, Art 2 of the AVSMD set out establishment of media service provider[10] rules in this connection in terms of head offices, workforce, economic links and so forth so as to bring them under the AVSMD umbrella (and hence the levy imposition options of Member States). Moreover, and more generally, to bolster protection of the Union's security (e.g. in terms of child safety online), non-EU third countries such as China fall under EU regulation if they wish to trade with the EU. TikTok is one such company (but has a base in Dublin in any event).

[32.2.09] A levy on streaming services such as Netflix and Amazon Prime will therefore be considered by the Media Commission. In late 2021, the Oireachtas Media Committee not only recommended a new content levy on online media services but also clearly stated that it should only be accessed by the Irish independent production sector. This levy, at no extra cost to the exchequer, has been identified by economic consultants Indecon as having a potential to raise a minimum of €23 million in additional funding for the creation of original Irish content.[11] Any sum of this magnitude (and beyond) is extremely significant given that, for comparison sake, it roughly equates to Screen Ireland's total annual net budget for production funding purposes. The committee also recommended that the measure not be introduced until its viability can be researched and reviewed

---

9 See European Audiovisual Observatory, *Investing in European works: the obligations on VOD providers* (2022) at p 25. Available at: https://rm.coe.int/iris-plus-2022en2-financial-obligations-for-vod-services/1680a6889c [Accessed 30 April 2023].

10 If a media service provider has its head office in one Member State but editorial decisions on the audiovisual media service are taken in another Member State, the media service provider shall be deemed to be established in the Member State where a significant part of the workforce involved in the pursuit of the programme-related audiovisual media service activity operates. If a significant part of the workforce involved in the pursuit of the programme-related audiovisual media service activity operates in each of those Member States, the media service provider shall be deemed to be established in the Member State where it has its head office. If a significant part of the workforce involved in the pursuit of the programme-related audiovisual media service activity operates in neither of those Member States, the media service provider shall be deemed to be established in the Member State where it first began its activity in accordance with the law of that Member State, provided that it maintains a stable and effective link with the economy of that Member State.

11 James Ward, *Dail committee calls for levy on streaming platforms to fund Irish content* (2021), independent.ie. Available at: https://www.independent.ie/breaking-news/irish-news/dail-committee-calls-for-levy-on-streaming-platforms-to-fund-irish-content-41009019.html [Accessed 28 April 2022].

by the Media Commission. How exactly developments in this connection evolve will be closely monitored by all relevant stakeholders.

REGULATION OF VIDEO-SHARING PLATFORM SERVICES

[32.3.01] The AVMSD regulates video-sharing platform services ('VSPS') for the first time. This is a highly significant development towards the regulation of these platforms which have thus far fallen outside of the remit of the 2010 Directive altogether. A VSPS is a platform or part of a platform the principal purpose of which is the provision of programmes, user-generated videos or both to the general public, for which the platform does not have editorial responsibility,[12] in order to "inform, entertain or educate, by means of electronic communications network".[13] This includes YouTube, Vimeo and online newspapers which post video content to their sites.

[32.3.02] Under the AVMSD, VSPS are subject to a number of different restrictions and obligations, including relating to sponsorship and product placements, hidden advertising and so forth. In addition, Member States are required to ensure that VSPS under their jurisdiction take appropriate measures to protect minors from harmful content and to protect the general public from content containing incitement to violence or hatred, as well as content involving public provocation to commit a terrorist offence.

[32.3.03] The AVMSD retains the country of origin principle which provides that once a television or on-demand service provider has obtained a broadcasting licence from one Member State, and complies with the regulatory rules of that Member State, it can broadcast its service into all other Member States across the EU without having to meet any further regulatory hurdles. The AVMSD introduces some changes to the criteria by which a service can establish itself in a Member State and these may prove to be of particular interest, in the wake of Brexit, to UK-based services.

[32.3.04] The derogations from the country of origin principle under the AVMSD are more streamlined and now extend to all media services, not just television broadcasters, where a service manifestly, seriously and gravely infringes the prohibition on content involving incitement to violence or hatred, or public provocation to commit a terrorist offence or which prejudices or presents a serious and grave risk of prejudice to public health or public security.[14]

---

[12] Editorial responsibility as defined in s 2 of the Broadcasting Act 2009 (as amended by s 3 of the 2022 Act) means the exercise of effective control both over the selection of the programmes and over their organisation in a programme schedule or in a catalogue. Editorial responsibility does not necessarily imply any legal liability for the content or the services provided (adapted from the definition of editorial responsibility in the AVSMD).

[13] Article 1(aa).

[14] These derogations are subject to certain conditions, which now include a requirement that

[32.3.05] The AVMSD requires Member States to encourage the use of co-regulation and fostering of self-regulation through national codes of conduct, as well as through EU codes of conduct, which may be drawn up by media service providers, video- sharing platform providers or organisations representing them. The AVMSD recognises that Member States are free to require media service providers under their jurisdiction to comply with more detailed or stricter rules.

RETRANSMISSION FEES

[32.4.01] It is noteworthy in passing that it is open to the government to permit RTÉ to charge retransmission fees to Sky and other similar media providers which hitherto have escaped any such levy due to the wording of the Broadcasting Act 2009[15] which does not refer to any such payment and thus precludes negotiation on this point. Imposing such a fee would enhance RTÉ's coffers. In addition, under the same "must-offer" legislation, should Facebook, Google, Amazon or Apple wish to launch a television proposition in Ireland, they can simply request RTÉ's linear television channels. RTÉ is obliged in law, as it currently stands, to offer its channels to them free of any fees, an eventuality which to some may appear absurd. In terms of platforms however the situation has been altered by (new) s 128B of the 2009 Act (must-carry and must-offer obligations for platforms).[16]

[32.4.02] Retransmission fees are fees paid by pay-tv platforms which in Ireland include eir, Sky, Virgin Media and Vodafone to broadcasters for the right to distribute (or retransmit) the broadcasters' channels. In Ireland, the free-to-air RTÉ, TG4 and Virgin Media channels are distributed over a variety of pay-tv platforms. Currently these platforms do not pay retransmission fees to broadcasters for carrying their channels and broadcasters do not pay for transmission of their channels by the platforms. In its March 2018 report,[17] the Oireachtas Joint Committee on Communications, Climate Action and Environment recommended that public service broadcasters should be permitted to charge retransmission fees to service providers (the charge would be paid to the now Media Commission). If implemented, the imposition of such a fee could help the amelioration of RTÉ's straitened financial circumstances with positive knock-on consequences for the independent producers commissioned to supply content to the public service broadcaster.

---

the Member State has respected the right of defence of the service provider and given it an opportunity to express its views on the alleged infringement.

15 s 77 thereof.

16 "Platform" means a service, transmitted by means of an electronic communications network and accessed by the use of an interactive guide, which re-transmits or makes available more than one audiovisual media service, including at least one audiovisual on-demand media service.

17 Joint Committee on Communications, Climate Action and Environment, *Report of the Joint Committee on the Pre-Legislative Scrutiny of the General Scheme of a Broadcasting (Amendment) Bill 2017 and Retransmission Fees* (2018), p 4.

[32.4.03] The 2022 Act did not introduce any changes to the relevant statutory provision however[18] but this may well be revisited in the future. In this jurisdiction, proponents of retransmission fees were seeking amendment of s 77 of the 2009 Act to allow broadcasters the right to negotiate commercial terms without necessarily seeking to impose mandatory payments on the pay-tv platforms, but rather to ensure that the question of payment could at least be negotiated by the parties.

Repeal of the cable copyright exemption

[32.4.04] Section 10 of the Broadcasting (Amendment) Bill 2019 sought to repeal the cable copyright exemption as provided for in s 103 of the Copyright and Related Rights Act 2000. That section permitted cable operators based in Ireland[19] to retransmit works (including audiovisual works) protected by copyright that were broadcast in the state and the "must-carry" channels without obtaining permission from the copyright holders or paying retransmission fees. This meant that Irish production companies were not fairly paid for their works, unlike many of their European counterparts. Continuing that exemption would have resulted in a loss of revenue to RTÉ, TG4 and Virgin and, in particular, to rightsholders including actors, producers and musicians.

[32.4.05] Section 75 of the 2022 Act has thus repealed both the s 103 (Irish broadcasters) exemption as regards reception and retransmission of broadcasts in cable programmes services as applying to copyright under the Copyright and Related Rights Act 2000 ('the 2000 Act'), and s 251 of the same Act as applying to performers' rights. By repealing this provision, the rightsholders for the content have the flexibility to negotiate the clearance of their rights with the broadcasters or directly with the platform operators, whichever is the most beneficial to them. The broadcasters are also free of the onus to clear all of the rights for every platform. Note, however, that on foot of the 2019 SatCab Directive discussed in [17.3.31] and below at [32.5.01] as implemented in Ireland by SI No 357 of 2022, s 103AA was inserted into the 2000 Act in respect of transmission of programmes by direct injection (while s 103A was inserted into the 2000 Act by the Copyright and Other Intellectual Property Law Provisions Act 2019).

Must-carry and must-offer obligations for platforms

[32.4.06] Under the said s 128B of the principal Broadcasting Act 2009, a platform provider shall comply with a request by a public service provider that a particular public service audiovisual broadcasting service provided by the public service provider be retransmitted on the platform provider's platform,

---

18 s 77 (must carry and must offer obligations) of the Broadcasting Act 2009 still applies other than repeal of s 77(1)(c) and s 77(14).

19 Virgin Media is the largest digital cable television provider within the country (while Sky is a digital provider it does so by satellite and is not a cable provider).

and by a public service provider that a particular public service audiovisual on-demand media service provided by the public service provider be made available on the platform provider's platform. Conversely, a public service provider shall ensure that any public service audiovisual broadcasting service or public service audiovisual ondemand media service it provides is at all times offered to platform providers in such a way that it may be re-transmitted or made available on their platforms.

[32.4.07] The above obligations shall not preclude the conclusion of an agreement between the public service provider and the platform provider in relation to the remuneration of the public service provider by the platform provider, or fair reasonable and non-discriminatory terms of use of the public service audiovisual broadcasting service or public service audiovisual on-demand media service.

[32.4.08] If a dispute arises between a platform provider and a public service provider in relation to the remuneration of the public service provider, the dispute shall be notified to the Media Commission by the public service provider or the platform provider.

DIRECTIVE ON (RE)TRANSMISSION OF CERTAIN ONLINE TELEVISION AND RADIO PROGRAMMES

[32.5.01] In July 2022 (several months after the 2019 Copyright Directive was transposed into national law), transposition of this Directive[20] into Irish law was effected by virtue of SI No 357 of 2022.

[32.5.02] The new rules provide opportunities for broadcasters, through the country of origin principle that will facilitate the licensing of rights, to make certain programmes on their online services available across borders. Services covered are simulcasting, catch-up services and other services that complement the main broadcast, such as previews.

[32.5.03] This Directive is thus yet another crucial piece of legislation to render copyright law fit for the digital age, aimed at simplifying cross-border distribution and retransmission of television and radio programmes. The earlier Directive which it amends already facilitates[21] cross-border satellite broadcasting and retransmission by cable of television and radio programmes from other EU

---

20 Directive (EU) 2019/789 of the European Parliament and of the Council of 17 April 2019 laying down rules on the exercise of copyright and related rights applicable to certain online transmissions of broadcasting organisations and retransmissions of television and radio programmes, and amending Council Directive 93/83/EEC.

21 Broadcasters will not be obliged to make relevant programmes available online across borders. The country of origin principle is an enabling mechanism for broadcasters, who wish to offer programmes on their online services across borders, but it will not oblige them to do so.

Member States. By addressing the difficulties related to the clearance of rights, it creates the conditions allowing broadcasters and operators of retransmission services to offer wider access to television and radio programmes throughout the EU. Moreover, when combined with the AVSMD, and increase in the availability of audiovisual works via on-demand platforms, European authors will be facilitated in reaching new audiences, while making European works widely accessible to EU citizens.

[32.5.04] Heretofore, the clearance of rights for such cross-border uses was particularly burdensome: a broadcaster needed to obtain authorisations from various rightsholders, for different categories of works and other protected content, and separately for every Member State, where the programme would be available online.

[32.5.05] By establishing the country of origin principle (which will not however apply to video-on-demand services), the rights required to make certain programmes available on the broadcasters' online services (for instance their simulcasting[22] or catch-up services) are to be cleared only for the relevant broadcaster's country of principal establishment instead of for all applicable Member States. The licence fee paid by the broadcasters to rightsholders will have to reflect the audience of the programmes. The country of origin principle will help broadcasters to make certain programmes (all radio programmes, and, for television, news and current affairs programmes, as well as fully financed own productions of broadcasters) available online in other Member States. As a result, consumers will have more choice to watch and listen to online programmes transmitted by broadcasters established elsewhere in the EU.

[32.5.06] The provisions should also serve to ensure that creators, authors and rightsholders are adequately remunerated for the use of their content through 'direct injection', namely a process increasingly used by broadcasters to transmit their programmes to the public. Instead of transmitting their programmes directly to the public over the air or by wire, broadcasters send their programmes to distributors, which transmit them to the public. The Directive clarifies that when broadcasters transmit their programme-carrying signals by direct injection exclusively to distributors, and the latter transmit these to the public, there is an act of communication to the public, in which both the broadcaster and the distributors participate, and for which they need to obtain authorisation from rightsholders. This new provision will help to ensure that rightsholders are adequately paid when their works are used in programmes transmitted in this manner.

[32.5.07] The Directive applies a facilitated rights clearance mechanism – the system of compulsory collective management – to retransmission services provided through means other than cable (e.g. over internet), making it easier

[22] Simultaneous online transmission of linear broadcasts.

to obtain authorisations required to retransmit radio and television channels from other Member States. As mentioned in Chapter 17, it is unknown as yet the real and practical effects this will have on blanket music licensing in relation to broadcast of Irish television content internationally within the EU.

[32.5.08] The Directive extends the system of mandatory collective management, which is currently applicable to cable retransmissions only, to retransmission services provided through other means such as internet protocol television, satellite, digital terrestrial or online technologies. This system allows retransmission operators to clear the necessary rights in a simpler manner – they need to clear the relevant rights with broadcasters whose channels they retransmit and with collective management organisations, i.e. organisations like IMRO that represent a multitude of rightsholders and not with several individual rightsholders on a one-to-one basis (e.g. a music composer or an audiovisual performer).

Part VI

Journalism Law, Regulation and Ethics

Chapter 33

Court Reporting and Contempt of Court

INTRODUCTION

[33.1.01] Court reporting and contempt of court principles apply to traditional print and online journalism and broadcasting as they do to audiovisual and other productions by content, film and television producers. In the latter scenario, a writer's agreement in respect of a documentary or television project for instance will contain a standard warranty by the screenplay writer that the work is original, not in breach of third party copyrighted material, nor in contempt of court. In serious matters, reporters and members of the public alike can face criminal prosecution for breaching court reporting prohibitions and restrictions as occurred in the aftermath of the Ana Kriégel murder trial discussed later in this chapter.

[33.1.02] In June 2017, then Chief Justice and President of the Supreme Court, Denham CJ, called for reform of the powers afforded to the courts to deal with posting on social media of comments which may be prejudicial to pending and ongoing court cases. In October 2017, a private member's Bill was presented to Dáil Éireann by Deputy Josepha Madigan (then Minister for Culture, Heritage and the Gaeltacht) relating to contempt of court. The Bill lapsed due to dissolution of parliament in January 2020 before a general election. The courts have reiterated that contempt of court law is in need of reform. The Bill might therefore at least provide a springboard for further debate on appropriate legislation required in this area.

[33.1.03] Contempt of court is a common law doctrine. The Supreme Court has recently brought some clarity in terms of guidance[1] but there is a need for legislation to bring more.[2] Indeed, in *Irish Bank Resolution Corporation Ltd v Quinn,* the Supreme pointed out *per* Hardiman J in 2012:[3]

---

1 In *Tracey v District Judge McCarthy* [2019] IESC 14 and *Walsh v Minister for Justice* [2019] IESC 15. Both cases were heard together.

2 In *Kelly v O'Neill* [2000] 1 IR 354, Keane J commented that "our law in this area is, in many respects, uncertain and in need of clarification by legislation".

3 [2012] IESC 51 at para 7 of his dissenting judgment.

> It is 20 years now since the Law Reform Commission urged the need for statutory reform in this area, and some 31 years since such reform took place by statute in the neighbouring jurisdiction. It is most unfortunate that no positive steps have been taken here, with the result that this fraught matter has come on for resolution in an uncertain state of the law.

[33.1.04] The court was also of the view that:

> The Irish law of contempt of court is amorphous. It is extremely difficult for a lay person to understand, principally because the term "contempt of court" is used inexplicably, to mean several quite different things and it is not always clear which of them is intended. Even when the term is used by lawyers – and even judges – the distinctions are not always clear. In part, this is because, from the point of view of a party seeking to use the law of contempt to have another person fined, compelled to comply with onerous requirements, or imprisoned, it can be advantageous to cultivate a certain vagueness in the law so as to avoid the strict requirements normally and correctly imposed on a person who wishes to have his opponent stigmatised, deprived of his liberty, and confined in a convict prison.[4]

[33.1.05] More recently, in *Meath County Council v Hendy*[5] *discussed at* [33.6.13], it was noted by the High Court that "contempt procedure is notoriously complex and stubbornly resistant to judicial clarification, despite repeated efforts".

[33.1.06] In terms of court reporting, in November 2018 Clarke CJ, as he then was, speaking at a seminar organised by the Courts Service and the National Union of Journalists, stated that Irish courts were henceforth to disallow everyone[6] except bone fide members of the press and legal practitioners[7] from texting and sharing electronic communications from within courtrooms. The new practice had been agreed by the presidents of all court jurisdictions and signed on 19 November 2018. The practice direction, the provisions of which are examined later in this chapter, came into operation on 26 November 2018[8] and supplement Order 123 of the Rules of the Superior Courts, Order 67A of the Circuit Court Rules and Order 12B of the District Court Rules which restrict and regulate the recording, other than by the taking of written or shorthand notes, of court proceedings by persons other than the Courts Service.

[33.1.07] The matter of court reporting restrictions and breaches thereof came to the fore in 2019 in respect Ana Kriegel's murder trial whereat two teenage boys denied murdering the 14-year-old in a derelict farmhouse in Lucan in 2018.[9] An order banning reportage of the trial until its conclusion was lifted for all but

---

4 *Per* Hardiman J at para 1 of his judgment.

5 [2020] IEHC 142 *per* Humphreys J at para 9.

6 Including jurors.

7 Who have bona fide business in the court concerned.

8 The Courts Service, Supreme Court Practice Directions, *SC18 – Use of cameras and electronic devices in court* (2018). Available at: https://www.courts.ie/content/use-cameras-and-electronic-devices-court [Accessed 9 June 2021].

9 One of them also pleaded not guilty to violently sexually assaulting the victim.

one publisher. Earlier, McDermott J told the jurors he had decided to prohibit the publication of evidence for the duration of the trial as a "matter of law" and the order stood until any further order might be made by the court. He said it was his duty to maintain the integrity of the trial process to ensure a true verdict in accordance with the evidence. However, he decided to vary his order and the restriction henceforth only applied to one media outlet.

Coco's law and anonymity

[33.1.08] The Harassment, Harmful Communications and Related Offences Act 2020 (otherwise known as Coco's law after suicide victim Nicole 'Coco' Fox) as mentioned in Chapter 30 provides in s 5 thereof for anonymity of a victim of an offence committed under ss 2 or 3.[10] Thus, where a person is charged with an offence under ss 2 or 3, any person who publishes or broadcasts any information, a photograph of, or a photograph that includes a depiction of or any other representation of the physical likeness of the alleged victim of the offence that is likely to enable the identification of the alleged victim is, subject to any s 5(2),[11] direction, guilty of an offence. A person who is guilty of an offence under s 5(1) or (4)[12] is liable on summary conviction to a class B fine (maximum €4,000) or to imprisonment for a term not exceeding 12 months, or both, or on conviction on indictment to a fine or to imprisonment for a term not exceeding three years, or both.

THE ANA KRIÉGEL MURDER TRIAL: THE AFTERMATH

[33.2.01] In November 2019, two boys, known as Boy A and Boy B throughout their seven-week trial,[13] were unanimously found guilty by a jury of the murder[14] of schoolgirl Ana Kriegel and were sentenced at the Central Criminal Court[15] becoming the youngest offenders in Irish history to be convicted of murder. Boy B initially sought to appeal his conviction (no appeal was being sought

10 Distributing, publishing or threatening to distribute or publish an intimate image without consent with intent to cause harm or being reckless as to whether harm is caused; and recording, distributing or publishing an intimate image without consent.

11 Where judges of the court in which proceedings for an offence under ss 2 or 3 are brought consider that the interests of justice so require, they may, having taken into account the views of the alleged victim of the offence, direct that such information, photograph or representation referred to in s 5(1) as they specify may be published or broadcast in such manner and subject to such conditions (if any) as they might specify in the direction.

12 By contravening a direction given under subsection (2) including a condition in such a direction.

13 Listed in the Central Criminal Court diary under record number CCDP0099/2018A, *DPP v K L* and *DPP v A K.*

14 Boy A was also convicted of aggravated sexual assault. A term of 12 years was further imposed for that count, to be served concurrently.

15 The High Court in its criminal court capacity but here adopting procedures from the Children's Court, which for example saw lawyers and the judge wearing suits and ties rather than gowns and wigs.

against the severity of his sentence). In July 2020, Birmingham J, President of the Court of Appeal granted an application by James Dwyer SC on behalf of Boy B to exceed legal aid limits in order that he could seek the services of a UK psychologist ahead of the appeal against his conviction. The matter came before the court again in March 2022 in respect of a motion seeking to introduce fresh evidence and challenging the admissibility of matters that were not challenged at trial. However, in October 2022 Boy B withdrew his appeal altogether.

[33.2.02] In the trial court, as part of McDermott J's sentencing, he stated that the teenagers must not be named and this order will continue when they are over 18. Children's Court rules applied to their case as the boys were both 13 years old when they committed the offences in May 2018, meaning neither of the boys could be named in media coverage of the case and there were strict reporting rules mandated to prevent their being identified, even by association such that, for instance, journalists reporting on the trial could not name the school the boys attended.

[33.2.03] The judge made it clear that although the boys have been convicted and sentenced, they still cannot be publicly named. Thus, in July 2019, a journalist was fined €2,500 for inadvertently naming Boy A during a live radio broadcast. Broadcaster radio station, Cork's Red FM, was fined €10,000. In his ruling on that earlier instance in court, McDermott J said he was satisfied that the naming of the boy was done in error and was not intentional or reckless. Otherwise, if the naming had been deliberate, the action would have resulted in a prison sentence. Since the incident, the station introduced a 'dump button' whereby a seven-second delay is built into broadcasts allowing potentially problematic material to be discarded.[16]

[33.2.04] The trial judge stated the reporting ban breach must be seen in the context of the potential damage that this could visit upon wholly innocent parties who are not guilty of any offence. He said the families of the two boys had been subjected to "outrageous messaging and more, which is simply unacceptable in any decent society". It also emerged from a report in *The Journal* that a family member of Boy B had been attacked in Dublin by a group of men after he was identified as being related to the convicted murderer.[17]

[33.2.05] Even after Boys A and B turned 18, whereupon they were transferred

---

16 Eoin Reynolds, *Journalist fined €2,500 after inadvertently naming boy convicted of Ana Kriegel's murder on live radio* (2019), thejournal.ie. Available at: thejournal.ie/journalist-fined-ana-kriegel-named-4705364-Jul2019/ [Accessed 20 August 2019].

17 The victim was left with serious bruising to his face following the alleged assault. The man was on an organised night out with friends when he was approached by the group of men, one of whom was believed to have been armed with a knife (source: Garreth MacNamee, *Relative of Boy B allegedly assaulted in Dublin city centre during Ana Kriegel* trial (2019), thejournal.ie. Available at: https://www.thejournal.ie/boy-b-ana-kriegel-family-assault-4690675-Jun2019/ [Accessed 11 November 2019].

to an adult prison, it will be an offence to publicly identify them. In addition to the Red FM incident, McDermott J had already demonstrated the seriousness of these kinds of orders. In June 2019, he ordered representatives of Twitter and Facebook to appear before him after it emerged social media users had identified the 14-year-old co-accused.

[33.2.06] Solicitors for Boy B had contacted the DPP's office and alerted it to images published on Facebook alongside derogatory comments. Counsel informed the court that some of the commenters seemed to be aware that there was an order made to protect the boys' identities. The court heard that threats had been made online against the boys and against their families. A barrister for Boy A stated there was concern for the safety of their families after a tweet pointed out that there was "information on the families online if you Google their names".

[33.2.07] The judge noted that the two social media companies had acted "in good faith" and moved promptly to delete this material. Facebook at the time said it had applied photo-matching technology to prevent this content from being reshared on Facebook, Instagram or Messenger. An injunction was granted requiring the social media companies to remove any photos or other material identifying the accused of which they become aware or which is brought to their attention.

PROTECTION FOR YOUNG OFFENDERS; VICTIMS OF CRIME

[33.3.01] Under Irish law, a child over the age of ten[18] can be charged with the most serious offences such as murder, manslaughter, rape and aggravated sexual assault. According to Court Service directions,[19] the trial process in Dublin Metropolitan Children Court is subject to the following regulation:

> Young defendants accused of committing serious crimes may be vulnerable due to their age, level of maturity or disability when standing trial in the children court. The trial process should not itself expose the young defendant to avoidable intimidation, humiliation or distress. The ordinary trial process in the children courts is therefore adapted to meet those ends and ensure due regard to the welfare of the young defendant as appropriate.

---

[18] This was previously 12 years pursuant to s 52 (age of criminal responsibility) of the Children Act 2001 whereby it was conclusively presumed that no child under the age of 12 years was capable of committing an offence. Under s 129 of the Criminal Justice Act 2006, this was amended by substituting a new s 52. Section 128 also amended the title to Pt 5 of the Act of 2001 with the substitution of "Restriction on Criminal Proceedings against Certain Children" for "Criminal Responsibility".

[19] The Courts Service, District Court Practice Directions, *DC04 – Children Court* (2014). Available at: http://www.courts.ie/Courts.ie/Library3.nsf/16c93c36d3635d5180256e3f003a4580/1a800a9c20e36ce28025811b00544073?OpenDocument [Accessed 4 February 2020].

[33.3.02] Only officers of the court, relatives of the children involved, witnesses and members of the press are permitted to sit in the courtroom to hear the evidence. Under the Children Act 2001 (ss 51(1)(b) and 93) as amended ('the 2001 Act'), no report can be published or included in a broadcast which reveals the name, address or school of any child concerned in the proceedings. Neither can news reports include any particulars likely to lead to the identification of any child undergoing trial. No photographs or pictures of young defendants can be published, or images that would lead to their being identified (e.g. that of a family member). The legislation applies to matters published or included in a broadcast or other form of public communication, including social media posts.

[33.3.03] As rare exceptions to not allowing a juvenile offender to be publicly named, pursuant to s 93 of the 2001 Act,[20] the court may dispense to any specified extent with the requirements of this section in relation to a child if it is satisfied that it is appropriate to do so for reasons of public interest, for the purpose of avoiding injustice to the child, or that, in respect of a child to whom this section applies and who is unlawfully at large, it is necessary to do so for the purpose of apprehending the child, or to ensure compliance with a court order. Where the court dispenses with the requirements of this section, it shall explain in open court the reasons for its decision.

Penalties

[33.3.04] Any natural or legal person found to have identified a young offender, contrary to this legislation, could be liable *per* s 51(3) of the 2001 Act on summary conviction to a fine of (then applicable) £1,500[21] or a prison term of up to 12 months, or both. If the breach is considered more serious, on conviction on indictment an accused could face a fine of up to (then applicable) £10,000 and/or up to three years in prison. In the case of publication of the matter in a newspaper or periodical, any proprietor, editor and publisher of the newspaper or periodical can be held liable[22] as can, in the case of any broadcast, any body corporate which transmits or provides the programme in which the broadcast is made and any person having functions in relation to the programme corresponding to those of an editor of a newspaper.

[33.3.05] Leeanda Farrelly (47) was accused at Dublin District Court in May 2021 of publishing a picture of Boy A on her Facebook account on or about 19 June 2019, contrary to the 2001 Act and was sent forward by Judge John Brennan to trial at Dublin Circuit Criminal Court while in 2021 a Tallaght-based woman pleaded guilty to publishing photographs of Boy A and Boy B on Facebook.[23] These accused were two of ten defendants to appear in court over

20 As substituted by s 139 of the Criminal Justice Act 2006.

21 For euro conversion amounts, see sch 3 to the Euro Changeover (Amounts) Act 2001.

22 In the case of any other such publication, the person who publishes it.

23 On 9 March 2022 Judge Nolan for Dublin Circuit Criminal Court sentenced Louise

the identification on social media of Ana Kriégel's killers in the days following their 2019 conviction in the face of a court order preventing the then 14-year-old boys being named.

Section 252 of the 2001 Act – the murder of Brooklyn Colbert by Patrick Dillon

[33.3.06] This statutory provision was the subject of intense public controversy in October 2020 when Mr Justice Birmingham for the Court of Appeal ruled in a most surprising departure from long-standing practice with the effect that grieving parents were prevented from speaking publicly about cases where their children were the fatal victims of violence through murder or manslaughter. An application from the DPP had sought the judge to make an order confirming that s 252 of the 2001 Act made it an offence to publish anything that could identify a child who was an alleged victim of an offence, including a deceased child. The court stated:

> I appreciate the media may find the ruling surprising and that they may say that it involves a radical departure from what had been a long-established practice. They may say that the outcome is an undesirable one and may be in a position to make that argument with some force...Nonetheless, the language of the statute is clear and unequivocal and, enjoying a presumption of constitutionality as it does, must be given effect to...If change is required and if it is desired to return to previous practice where it was possible to report cases involving the deaths of children, then it is a matter requiring intervention by the Oireachtas.

[33.3.07] Given the profound effect of the judgment (which also affected child victims of sexual abuse or rape who are now adults and wish to come forward publicly, or who wish their abuser to be publicly named), it came as no surprise to media practitioners that the legislature acted with due haste to reverse the decision with enactment in April 2021 of the Children (Amendment) Act 2021 to remove the restriction on naming deceased children except in certain exceptional circumstances.

[33.3.08] Patrick Dillon of Dalgaish Park, Moyross, Limerick had his name anonymised at the Central Criminal Court in January 2021 due to an order based on the above Court of Appeal judgment. Dillon could not be named to protect the identity of his 11-year old nephew Brooklyn Colbert whom he had murdered on 3 November 2019. The sentence hearing was told that Dillon struck Brooklyn with a hammer and stabbed him 27 times in the torso, arms and neck. In early May 2021, however, on foot of the amending legislation, application was made by counsel to set aside the order made by White J to prevent the naming of the deceased child and the accused.

Heaney to 18 months' imprisonment but suspended the sentence in its entirety on strict conditions.

COURT REPORTING PRINCIPLES

[33.4.01] The importance that the judiciary attaches to the reporting of judgments by the media is perhaps best summarised by Hogan J in his 2013 High Court decision in *Allied Irish Bank Plc v Tracey (No. 2)*:[24]

> 22. The open administration of justice is, of course, a vital safeguard in any free and democratic society. It ensures that the judicial branch is subjected to scrutiny and examination and helps to promote confidence in the fair and even handed administration of justice. Any system of secret court hearings could pave the way for judicial arrogance, overbearing judicial conduct and abuse.
>
> 23. In these circumstances the public are entitled to have access to documents which were accordingly opened without restriction in open court. This is simply part and parcel of the open administration of justice which the Constitution (subject to exceptions) enjoins. Entirely different considerations would naturally arise in respect of material which was not opened in open court or which was protected by the *in camera* rules or by reporting restrictions imposed, for example, pursuant to s. 27 of the Civil Law (Miscellaneous Provisions) Act 2008.

[33.4.02] This is an extraordinarily significant ruling, placing on a constitutional footing the right and entitlement of the public to view and have access to documents which were adduced without restriction in open court. Prior to *this decision,* there was no direct authority on whether a non-party could seek access to court documents.

The role of the press

[33.4.03] *Philpott v Irish Examiner Ltd*,[25] a 2016 High Court case, concerned the *Irish Examiner* newspaper which had published certain articles on its website. The plaintiff sought to have them removed. In June 2015, the paper published an online article entitled "Former CEO loses case against hospice" and on 5 December 2015 it published an online article entitled "Ex-Marymount Hospice executive's legal case resolved".

[33.4.04] On 7 December, Mason Hayes and Curran, the then solicitors for the plaintiff issued a letter to the newspaper claiming that the article of 5 December was defamatory, skewed, not fair and accurate and that it was malicious and unprivileged. The letter, *inter alia*, required the removal of the articles from the internet. Dan Philpott was appointed as CEO of Marymount University Hospital and Hospice Limited in May 2014 but was dismissed after seven months. The reason given for the termination of his contract in the newspaper article was significant interpersonal difficulties between him and other members of staff, in particular the executive team.[26] Mr Philpott alleged, by way of whistle-blower

---

[24] [2013] IEHC 242.

[25] [2016] IEHC 62.

[26] Cited at para 12 of Barrett J's judgment.

disclosures or otherwise that charity funding was being used for needs other than palliative care to fund administration, portions of salaries, expenses of board members and other staff and that this was an improper use of funds given in good faith, and that there was alleged mismanagement of financial resources at the hospice generally.

[33.4.05] The trial judge (O'Donohoe J, Cork Circuit Court) rejected this assertion out of hand stating that it was patently clear that the Marymount Hospice was a registered charity for a considerable length of time and any further money spent from donors was for the good of the community and was fully compliant. Furthermore, the judge noted there had been no complaints made to any authority. An application was then brought to the High Court seeking removal of the two articles from the *Irish Examiner*'s website pursuant to s 33 of the Defamation Act 2009. That provision allows the court to make an order prohibiting the publication of a defamatory statement. In relation to s 33, the court stated:

> The Act of 2009 posits simply that there are three criteria which must be satisfied before an order can issue under s.33, viz:
>
> In the opinion of the court:
> (1) is the statement complained of defamatory?
> (2) does the defendant have a defence to the claim of defamation?
> (3) is that defence reasonably likely to succeed?[27]

[33.4.06] Applying this three-pronged test, Barrett J was of the view that neither of the two articles published by the *Irish Examiner*, however viewed, contained or constituted a statement that tended to injure the applicant's reputation in the eyes of reasonable members of society, and hence none of the statements complained of were defamatory. The court was of the opinion that the defence of absolute privilege was open to the newspaper in respect of both impugned articles and such defence was likely to succeed. In light of the above conclusions, the court was coerced by law into declining all of the reliefs sought by Philpott.

[33.4.07] Barrett J, when summarising the law pertaining to court reporting, noted that:

> Court reports are not just of interest to the public; they meet a great public interest. In a liberal democracy that prizes individual freedoms, all branches of government are rightly subject to the scrutiny of an ever-watchful public. Reporters perform an essential role in ensuring that members of the public learn of what is being done in their courts and why.[28]

[33.4.08] He also observed when referring to the reporters' gallery in parliaments that:

---

[27] At para 7.
[28] At para 28.

> It is by and through the media that a critical eye is so often brought to the work of all branches, offices and officers of government. This is so important a task that–except insofar as is necessary to ensure that the right of every citizen to her or his good name is protected and capable of vindication–the media must go relatively unconstrained in their efforts.[29]

Fair and accurate reporting

[33.4.09] So as not to offend against the law of defamation, reports of court proceedings must be fair and accurate. This stems from s 17(2) of the Defamation Act 2009 which provides a defence to defamation proceedings thus: it shall be a defence to a defamation action for the defendant to prove that the statement in respect of which the action was brought was a fair and accurate report of proceedings publicly heard before, or decision made public by, any court established by law in the state.

Privilege afforded to court reports

[33.4.10] When privilege (as a defence to the tort of defamation) is absolute, a defendant is entirely protected in respect of any statements made, regardless, for example, of any malice presenting. When privilege is qualified, a defendant is protected, except for statements made maliciously. In *Philpott*, therefore, were the *Irish Examiner* articles capable of attracting absolute privilege? Or to put matters otherwise, did they appear to the court to be court reports that were fair and accurate?

"Fair and accurate": the legal principles

[33.4.11] Barrett J in *Philpott* was referred to various statements of principle in the renowned English textbook, *Gatley on Libel and Slander* (12th edition), pp 310-320 and considered the principles identified below to be good law in this jurisdiction also. Accordingly, they are set out below.

[33.4.12] It is not necessary that a court report should be verbatim. An abridged or condensed court report will be privileged, provided it gives a correct and just impression of what took place in court. It is sufficient to publish a fair, summarised account of court proceedings. If the whole of a court report is a substantially accurate account of what transpired, the fact that there are slight inaccuracies or omissions is immaterial. Where an inaccuracy is of a substantial kind, a report is not privileged. Fair and reasonable latitude must be given by the courts; trifling slips do not deprive a court report of privilege. A report in a daily newspaper is not to be judged by the same strict standard of accuracy as a report coming from the hand of a trained lawyer. A more liberal view of the

[29] At para 28.

immunity of reporters is taken now than in former times. Common sense is allowed a larger share in determining any liability that may arise on their part.[30]

[33.4.13] An abridged or condensed court report must be fair and not garbled so as to produce a misrepresentation. A court report must not by deliberate suppression of some portion of the evidence give an entirely false and unjust impression to the prejudice of one of the parties involved. It is not enough to report part of the proceedings correctly, if by leaving out other parts, a false impression is thereby created. Furthermore, reports assuming a verdict are not privileged. A report which accurately sets out the summing-up or judgment of a judge is privileged, even though the summing-up or judgment may contain statements that are defamatory.

[33.4.14] Barrett J added that Gatley suggests that, in a protracted trial, a newspaper could be liable if it reported, for instance, days one to three of a trial but failed to report what happened on the conclusion. This point did not fall to be decided in *Philpott*. However, he was of the view that Irish law may well depart from what Gatley states in this regard.

Viewer complaint upheld by the BAI

[33.4.15] As discussed in Chapter 31, RTÉ *Six-One News* failed in its duty (as regards standards or codes of broadcasting) to a complainant who submitted a viewer complaint relating to a broadcast in January 2018 covering criminal proceedings in which he was the defendant at Ennis District Court. The court proceedings had concluded prior to the broadcast but the news item did not include all available facts. The exclusion of an acquittal, in particular, rendered the report misleading and unfair. The complainant therefore believed that the report was not accurate, objective or impartial.

[33.4.16] The complaint was made pursuant to the BAI's *Code of Fairness, Objectivity and Impartiality in News and Current Affairs*. The compliance committee was mindful that the information contained in the short news broadcast was factually accurate at the time of preparation. However, it noted that the report was prepared several hours before the broadcast and did not feel that sufficient steps were taken by the broadcaster to ensure that the accuracy of the report was adequate and appropriate with regard to the circumstances at the time of the broadcast. The committee was cognisant too that the update on the story was not received by the broadcaster until six minutes prior to broadcast, however, the code states that:

> Accuracy is…a fundamental principle associated with the broadcast of news

30 See para 33 of the judgment.

and current affairs content and should always take priority over the speed with which content can be delivered.[31]

The open administration of justice

[33.4.17] Public access and reporting applies only to documents which have already been freely revealed in open court and in respect of which there are no reporting or other restrictions. Different considerations might apply in the case of a document which lay hidden in discovery documents and to which no reference of any substance was made in court. In *Ewing v Ireland*,[32] the Supreme Court reiterated that a document is opened in court not only when it is read in court but also when it forms part of the court's consideration of the proceedings such as when it is read in private by a judge. As a result of Practice Direction SC15, Supreme Court legal submissions are now accessible by any member of the public requesting same.

Anonymity in relation to a medical condition

[33.4.18] Section 27 of the Civil Law (Miscellaneous Provisions) Act 2008 protects the anonymity in civil proceedings in relation to the medical condition of a party to such proceedings or to a person called or proposed to be called to give evidence in those proceedings. An application for an order under this section may be made at any stage of the proceedings and the court shall grant an order only if it is satisfied that relevant persons concerned have a medical condition, where their identification as a person with that condition would be likely to cause undue stress to them, and the order would not be prejudicial to the interests of justice. An application for an order under this section or an appeal from a refusal or grant of an application for an order under s 27 may only be made by a party to the proceedings on notice to the other party or parties to the proceedings and shall be made to the judge concerned in chambers.

[33.4.19] Each of the following who publishes or broadcasts any matter in contravention of any such order is guilty under subsection (7) of an offence and is liable on conviction on indictment to a fine not exceeding €25,000 or imprisonment for a term not exceeding three years or both: if the matter is published in a newspaper or periodical, any proprietor, editor or publisher of the newspaper or periodical; if the matter is published otherwise, the person who publishes it; if the matter is broadcast, any person transmitting or providing the programme in which the broadcast is made and any person having functions in relation to the programme corresponding to those of an editor of a newspaper.

[33.4.20] Subsection (8) provides that where a person is charged with an offence under subsection (7), it shall be a defence to prove that at the time of the alleged

---

31 At p 6 of the code.

32 [2013] IESC 44.

offence the person was not aware, and neither suspected nor had any reason to suspect, that the publication or broadcast concerned was of any such matter as is mentioned in subsection (1).[33]

[33.4.21] Subsection (11) defines a broadcast as the transmission, relaying or distribution by wireless telegraphy (radio), cable or the internet of communications, sounds, visual images or signals, intended for reception by the public generally or a section of it, whether the broadcast is so received or not; and "publish" means publish, other than by way of broadcast, to the public generally or a section of it.

Prohibition on publication or broadcast of certain matters relating to child care

[33.4.22] Section 31(1)[34] of the Child Care Act 1991 ('the 1991 Act') provides that no matter likely to lead members of the public to identify a child who is or has been the subject of proceedings under certain parts of the Act shall be published or broadcast. Note under s 31(2) that if satisfied that it is appropriate to do so in the interests of the child, the court may by order dispense with such prohibitions to such extent as may be specified in the order.

[33.4.23] Conviction for breach of this section shall result in liability on summary conviction, to a class A fine[35] or to imprisonment for a term not exceeding 12 months or both, or on conviction on indictment, to a fine not exceeding €50,000 or to imprisonment for a term not exceeding three years or both. These new penalties were introduced by s 9 of the Courts and Civil Law (Miscellaneous Provisions) Act 2013 which amended s 31 of the 1991 Act.

[33.4.24] Section 29 of the 1991 Act previously provided that proceedings under Pts III, IV or VI of the Act were to be heard otherwise than in public. However, s 8 of the 2013 Act amended s 29 so as to allow bona fide representatives of the press to be present in court during the hearing of child care proceedings under that Act, similar to the provisions relating to the presence of the press at family law proceedings. The court may nonetheless[36] on its own motion, or on application to it by a party to the proceedings or by a person on behalf of

---

33 Subsection (9) provides that where an offence under s 27(7) has been committed by a body corporate and it is proved to have been so committed with the consent or connivance of or to be attributable to any neglect on the part of persons who, when the offence was committed, were a director, manager, secretary or other officer of the body corporate, or persons purporting to act in any such capacity, those persons, as well as the body corporate, shall be guilty of an offence and shall be liable to be proceeded against and punished as if they were guilty of the first-mentioned offence.

34 As amended by s 16 of the Children Act 2001, ss 10 and 17 of the Child Care (Amendment) Act 2011 and s 9 of the Courts and Civil Law (Miscellaneous Provisions) Act 2013. See also the *in-camera* rule below.

35 A fine not exceeding €5,000 – see s 3 of the Fines Act 2010.

36 Pursuant to the inserted subsection (5A)(b)(iii) of s 29 of the 1991 Act.

a child to whom the proceedings relate, by order exclude, or otherwise restrict the attendance of, bona fide representatives of the press from the court during the hearing or particular parts of it, or prohibit or restrict the publication or broadcasting of any evidence given or referred to during the proceedings or any part of such evidence. The court under s 31 is permitted to allow the identity of the child to be revealed if it is in the interests of such child.

[33.4.25] Hence, the court might exclude the press or prohibit broadcast of evidence having taken into account such matters as the extent to which the attendance of bona fide representatives of the press might inhibit or cause undue distress to a party to the proceedings or a child to whom the proceedings relate by reason of the emotional condition or any medical condition, physical impairment or intellectual disability of the party or the child concerned; the need to protect a party to the proceedings or a child to whom the proceedings relate against coercion, intimidation or harassment; and whether information given or likely to be given in evidence might be prejudicial to a criminal investigation or criminal proceedings; and whether information would, if published or broadcast, be likely to lead members of the public to identify a party to the proceedings or a child to whom the proceedings relate.[37]

The in private (in camera) rule: rape and sexual assault

[33.4.26] Section 11 of the Criminal Law (Rape) (Amendment) Act 1990 amended s 6 of the Criminal Law (Rape) Act 1981 and now provides in s 6(1), in excluding the public from hearings, that in any proceedings in the Central Criminal Court for a rape offence or the offence of aggravated sexual assault or attempted aggravated sexual assault or of aiding, abetting, counselling or procuring the offence of aggravated sexual assault or attempted aggravated sexual assault or of incitement to the offence of aggravated sexual assault or conspiracy to commit any of the foregoing offences, the judge shall exclude from the court during the hearing all persons except officers of the court, persons directly concerned in the proceedings, bona fide representatives of the press and such other persons (if any) as judges may in their discretion permit to remain.

[33.4.27] Section 6(2) provides that the court shall exclude from the court all persons except officers of the court and persons directly concerned in the proceedings but without prejudice to the right of a parent, relative or friend of the complainant or, where the accused is not of full age, of the accused to remain in court. However, subsection (4) provides that in any proceedings to

---

37 Other considerations include the age and level of maturity of the child concerned; sensitive personal information meaning information about a person that would, in the ordinary course of events, be known only to the person or members of the family, or friends, of the person, and includes but is not limited to information relating to the medical, psychiatric or psychological history of the person, to the tax affairs of the person, and information relating to the sexual conduct or sexual orientation of the person.

which subsection (1) applies the verdict or decision and the sentence (if any) shall be announced in public.

The in camera rule: family law proceedings

[33.4.28] The purpose of the *in camera* rule is to protect the identity of the parties and any child to whom family law or child care proceedings relate. Family law cases (divorce, legal separation, maintenance, access and custody for example) are heard in the District, Circuit and High[38] Court in private to protect the privacy of the family. Only officers of the court, the parties to the case and their legal representatives, witnesses and such other people as the judge allows will be in the courtroom while the case is being heard.

[33.4.29] Section 40 of the Civil Liability and Courts Act 2004[39] ('the 2004 Act') allows solicitors, barristers and certain other categories of people approved by the Minister for Justice to attend family law cases and publish reports. Pt 2 (ss 3 to 12) of the Courts and Civil Law (Miscellaneous Provisions) Act 2013 amended s 40 of the 2004 Act by amending the *in camera* rule and thus allowing bona fide representatives of the press to attend family law cases (subject to the right of the judge to exclude any such representatives) and to publish reports. The publication of reports of family law cases is allowed under these Acts on the strict condition that no names, addresses or any other details which might identify the parties can be used. Reform of the *in camera* rule enabled the media, researchers and legal professionals to gain access to valuable information on the operation of the law in this area.

[33.4.30] However, the court may exclude representatives of the press from the court, or otherwise restrict their attendance, during the hearing or particular parts of it, or restrict or prohibit the publication or broadcasting of evidence given or referred to during the proceedings where a court is satisfied that it is necessary to do so in order to preserve the anonymity of a party to the proceedings or any child to whom the proceedings relate, by reason of the nature or circumstances of the case or as it is otherwise necessary in the interests of justice.

[33.4.31] It is an offence to contravene s 40 of the 2004 Act. Anyone breaching this prohibition will be liable on summary conviction to a class A fine or to imprisonment for a term not exceeding 12 months or both, or on conviction on indictment, to a fine not exceeding €50,000 or to imprisonment for a term not exceeding three years or both. These statutory provisions do not affect the law on contempt of court discussed below.

---

[38] Family law proceedings will only be instituted in the High Court in 'high-value' cases where there are significant assets. The High Court also deals with appeals from the Circuit Family Court.

[39] See s 40A (prohibition on publication or broadcast of certain matters) as inserted by s 6 of the Courts and Civil Law (Miscellaneous Provisions) Act 2013.

Practice direction: use of cameras and electronic devices in court

[33.4.32] The above-cited practice direction as signed by all court presidents in November 2018 provides that the taking of photographs or transmission by video or television of court proceedings, is, except where permission to do so has been given by the president of the court concerned, strictly prohibited. While any person may take notes of court proceedings in writing or in shorthand, no person other than the Courts Service or a person acting on its behalf may make a recording of proceedings before a court by means of an electronic device without seeking and receiving permission of the judge or judges presiding in the proceedings.

[33.4.33] The following persons may transmit live text-based communications during court proceedings using an electronic device[40] in silent mode: a practising member of the legal profession who has bona fide business in the court concerned; and a bona fide member of the news media profession or professional legal commentator whose professional standing is established to the court's satisfaction and who is using such device for the purpose of reporting proceedings before the court, provided such use would not, in the opinion of the judge(s), disrupt the proceedings, or prejudice the administration of justice in relation to such proceedings or any other proceedings before a court. No other person may transmit live text-based communications during court proceedings without seeking and receiving prior permission of the judge or judges presiding in the proceedings. Sanctions for breach of the practice direction include a direction that the person concerned desist from use of an electronic device, leave the courtroom, surrender the electronic device temporarily or surrender any recorded material from the electronic device as the court may direct or order.

[33.4.34] Parties, legal practitioners and other persons participating, involved in or attending court proceedings may use an electronic device in silent mode to take notes of (as distinct from recording) the proceedings provided that the use of such device does not, in the judge's opinion, disrupt the proceedings.

CONTEMPT OF COURT

Civil contempt

[33.5.01] Examples of civil contempt include wilful disobedience of a court order or judgment and wilful breach of an undertaking given to a court, which matters could involve imposition of a custodial sentence or fine.[41]

---

[40] No such electronic device may, in any event, be used in a courtroom where its use would interfere with the secure operation of the hardware, sound or other information and communications technology systems provided to support the court.

[41] A recent high-profile example involved the granting by Meenan J (High Court, November 2021) to a detective garda of permission to bring proceedings alleging civil contempt of court against the Garda Commissioner over an alleged failure to comply with an order

The Enoch Burke saga

[33.5.02] The facts of this case were well publicised relating to the suspension of the history and German teacher for refusing, based on his religious beliefs, a transgender student's wishes to be referred to as 'they". Burke was suspended on full pay pending the outcome of the disciplinary process. He continued to attend the school however notably by sitting in an empty classroom. The school obtained an interim injunction (granted by Stack J) and later an interlocutory injunction (Barrett J) requiring the suspended teacher to stay away from the campus (the validity of these orders were upheld by the Court of Appeal in March 2023).[42] Burke persisted in attending the campus in defiance of the court orders. Accordingly, the school brought an application to commit Burke to prison for civil contempt of court, which was granted by Quinn J. Burke remained in prison from September to December[43] 2022 and at all times refused to purge his contempt.

[33.5.03] Following his release from Mountjoy Prison, the contemnor began attending the school again by standing outside the school gates. In continuing breach of the High Court order not to attend his former workplace, the school brought an application seeking the attachment and committal of Burke, the sequestration of his assets or any other order which the court deemed fit. O'Moore J held that it was undesirable to jail Burke again and that the sequestration of his assets was unlikely to persuade him to comply with the court order. Accordingly, the court held in applying two earlier High Court cases[44] where coercive imprisonment was ended despite ongoing contempt) that a daily fine of €700 was the correct response to the suspended teacher's behaviour.

[33.5.04] Burke was formally dismissed from the school on 19 January 2023 but continued to present at the school gates. In lieu of imprisonment, at the date of writing at the end of April 2023, Burke remains in defiance with fines now exceeding €60,000. It is open to the court to imprison him once again for continuing contempt of court and/or in the event he commits even further contempt by not discharging accrued fines.

---

of the court made in August 2021. The order, which was made following the resolution of a civil action brought by Detective Bracken, required the commissioner to conduct a fair assessment of psychiatric injuries the garda claimed he suffered whilst performing his duties when investigating criminal gangs. The assessment had not been undertaken. If however the assessment were to be completed prior to the motion returned before the court, then that would be the end of the matter. Meanwhile, *Irish Shell Ltd v Ballylynch Motors Ltd* (unreported, Supreme Court, Lynch J, 1997 WJSC-SC 3083) confirmed that a fine may be imposed on a contemnor by a court.

42 [2023] IECA 52.

43 He was released by O'Moore J shortly before Christmas, see *The Board of Management of Wilson's Hospital School v Burke* [2022] IEHC 719.

44 *Shell v McGrath* [2006] IEHC 108 and *Wardglade Ltd v Deery* [2021] IEHC 255.

Criminal contempt

[33.5.05] Criminal contempt includes scandalising the court,[45] intentionally obstructing or disrupting court proceedings or taking an action which prejudices or interferes with the due course of any judicial proceedings or otherwise interferes with or obstructs the administration of justice, including interfering with parties, judges, juries or witnesses before and during such proceedings. As recently as 2019, the Supreme Court ruled (in the *Tracey* and *Walsh* cases) on the above issues.

[33.5.06] The original legal basis for the District Court's contempt jurisdiction is to be found in the Summary Jurisdiction (Ireland) Amendment Act 1871, s 6 of which provides:

> If any person shall wilfully insult any justice or justices sitting in any court within the police district of Dublin Metropolis, or shall commit any other contempt of such court, it shall be lawful for such justice or justices, by any verbal order, either to direct such person to be removed from such court, or to be taken into custody, and at any time before the rising of such court by warrant to commit such person to gaol for any period not exceeding seven days, or to fine such person in any sum not exceeding forty shillings.

[33.5.07] In respect of District Courts outside the Dublin Metropolitan District, a similar provision is to be found in s 9 of the Petty Sessions (Ireland) Act 1851.

CONTEMPT OF COURT CASE LAW

[33.6.01] It is fundamental to the rule of law that the courts must be able to operate effectively and that there are appropriate means to ensure this. The law of contempt of court thus developed to allow the administration of justice to operate without undue obstruction or interference. As above, there are two categories of contempt of court, criminal and civil. Criminal contempt can take the form of contempt in the face of the court, *in facie curiae* (where a person deliberately disrupts court proceedings or obstructs court proceedings in a

---

45 The Law Society's Gazette Desk reported in May 2019 that an unreserved apology had been made by Eamonn O'Neill to the President of the High Court, Kelly J for email remarks about another judge, Reynolds J about how she handled a case in which he was defendant. O'Neill is a businessman of long standing but is not a qualified lawyer. Reynolds J had previously prevented him from acting as a legal advisor. O'Neill was answering a charge of criminal contempt over emails he sent to several different people, including Gardaí, in which he said the judge was part of a "criminal conspiracy". He apologised to the court and this was accepted by Kelly P who said he wanted to offer some friendly advice not to make such allegations again and was referring to the Law Society the matter of O'Neill's seeking and receiving payment for advice given to parties involved in a High Court case. Available at: https://www.lawsociety.ie/gazette/top-stories/court-hears-apology-over-email-remarks-about-judge/ [Accessed 23 June 21].

manner prejudicial to the course of justice),[46] scandalising the court (where a person makes untrue allegations about a court or judge that might undermine public confidence in the judiciary) and *sub judice* contempt (where a person publishes prejudicial material about a pending court case that could interfere with the administration of justice).

[33.6.02] The 'scandalising the court' form of contempt was seen by Mr Justice Donal O'Donnell in the Supreme Court decision in *Walsh v Minister for Justice and Equality* as discussed below as a:

> ...controversial form of contempt of court...treated as virtually obsolescent in England and Wales in *Secretary of State for Defence v. Guardian Newspapers Ltd.* [1985] A.C. 339 at p. 347, formally abolished in that jurisdiction in 2013, and rarely invoked in this jurisdiction in recent times. At a minimum, the law of scandalizing is a dubious source of reinforcement for the law of contempt *in facie curiae*, if such is required. However, and more importantly, I do not understand the judgment which I have delivered as in any way questioning the fundamental justification for the law of contempt of court, and in particular contempt occurring in the courtroom and disrupting the proceedings.[47]

[33.6.03] It is worth noting in passing here too the comments of O'Donnell J in respect of *in facie curiae* contempt:

> I do not agree that it can be said that the law of contempt *in facie curiae* has never fallen foul of either the Constitution or the ECtHR:[48] manifestly the decision in *Kyprianou v Cyprus* (App. No.73797/01) (2007) 44 E.H.R.R. 27 amounted to a finding that the application of the traditional common law power of contempt in facie curiae, at least in some circumstances, was a breach of the ECtHR.[49]

[33.6.04] Contempt can be dealt with like any other criminal offence through a punitive sanction, such as a fine or by sentencing the person to a definite term of imprisonment. The sentence of imprisonment is intended to deal with the criminal offence that has already occurred. Civil contempt occurs when, for example, persons refuse to comply with a court order and signal that they will refuse to comply into the future. In that case, the court will commit the person to prison for contempt not for a definite term but for an indefinite period, which will end when, and only when, the person agrees to comply with the court order. The purpose of imprisonment in civil contempt is not punitive, but rather coercive: to pressurise or compel the person to comply with the order. On the other hand, the Supreme Court explained in *Keegan v de Burca*[50] that the object of criminal contempt is punitive.

---

46 This could potentially include offensive or inappropriate conduct of a barrister or a solicitor in heated exchanges or over-zealous protests to a judge.

47 At para 39 of the judgment (see fn 56).

48 Referring to the European Convention on Human Rights.

49 *supra* at para 41.

50 [1973] IR 223.

[33.6.05] In 1994, the Law Reform Commission, in its *Report on Contempt of Court,*[51] made a number of recommendations for reform of the law in this area, including that some statutory offences should be introduced to replace the existing common law of contempt. Since then, the courts have reiterated that contempt of court law is in need of reform. They have noted, for example, that the boundary between criminal and civil contempt is difficult to draw and has become blurred. The commission also published a consultation paper in 1991[52] that ran to over 400 pages on the subject.

Tracey v District Judge Aeneas McCarthy[53]

[33.6.06] The facts of this judicial review Supreme Court case initially filed against (since retired) District Court Judge McCarthy (the appeal issue being the manner in which a finding of contempt in the face of the court was made against the appellant potentially breached his rights under the Irish Constitution, under the European Convention on Human Rights or under EU law) are rather unusual and somewhat cumbersome. At any rate, they related to criminal proceedings several years prior in the District Court arising out of a road traffic prosecution rather than to matters material to the within discussion of contempt of court relating to journalists.

[33.6.07] The five-justice court unanimously allowed the appellant's appeal and granted an order of *certiorari* quashing the order of the respondent judge made on 31 May 2006 whereby Mr Tracey was committed to prison for seven days for unruly behaviour in court. The judgment clarifies issues concerning how the courts should approach contempt and disruptive behaviour. The Irish Human Rights and Equality Commission had submitted the finding of contempt against Tracey, who represented himself, breached his rights. Tracey was jailed arising from comments he made when his case, involving a charge of driving without due care and attention, was mentioned before the District Court on 31 May 2006 for the purpose of fixing a hearing date. Mr Tracey made comments including "how crooked? And you think you will get away with this? How crooked you are" which, he claimed, were directed to a Garda (rather than to Judge McCarthy) after the district judge refused to allow him read a statement to the court. As a result of the comments, the judge directed that Tracey be brought back before him and jailed him for contempt.

[33.6.08] The Supreme Court, *per* O'Donnell J was of the view that when the district judge ordered Mr Tracey be brought back before him, the situation changed since it was now possible, indeed likely, that punishment could be imposed stating:

---

51 Law Reform Commission, *Report on Contempt of Court* (LRC 47-1994).

52 Law Reform Commission, *Consultation Paper on Contempt of Court* (LRC CP4-1991).

53 [2019] IESC 14.

> In those circumstances, more elaborate procedures were called for, and a separate hearing was necessary. It may be that if such a hearing was accorded to Mr. Tracey, the outcome may have been the same, or indeed worse for him, but the issue raised here is the fundamental fairness of the procedures which were followed, and in my view he was entitled to have a separate hearing, the possibility of obtaining legal assistance, and, if appropriate, legal aid. He should also have been informed of his entitlements in this regard.[54]

Fair procedures

[33.6.09] Given the importance of fair procedures and the constitutional protection of personal liberty, the committal order (from many years prior, after time had been served and accordingly being of no real practical effect) was thus quashed. The court also noted that where a court considers it necessary to invoke the contempt jurisdiction, the person concerned should be warned, told in simple terms of the conduct considered capable of constituting contempt, and afforded the option of obtaining legal representation (including legal aid if the accused's means are insufficient). The court also made the following comments about the appropriate steps that could be taken:

> The hearing can be straightforward, but the accused person must be given a fair opportunity of defending himself or herself. Since this is in its nature a criminal offence, even if a unique one, the criminal standard of proof beyond reasonable doubt must be applied. Furthermore, there is the same right of appeal as lies from any other decision of the court.[55]

[33.6.10] When Mr Tracey then raised the issue of damages following the verdict in his favour, he was told those would have to be sought in separate proceedings.

[33.6.11] Judgment was given on the same date (25 February 2019) in the companion case of *Walsh v Minister for Justice and Equality*[56] wherein the Supreme Court (judgment by O'Donnell J, as he then was, containing a valuable and insightful account of both the history of the law of contempt and its continuing justification) dismissed a separate appeal raising similar issues brought by David Walsh arising from a hearing at Waterford Circuit Court on 31 May 2016 which, among a list of cases, dealt with possession proceedings concerning his sister. Due to Mr Walsh's behaviour and constant interruptions, an order was made to jail him for two weeks for contempt. He was freed two days later. After the Court of Appeal in March 2017 reversed the High Court ruling, the Supreme Court agreed to hear a further appeal.

[33.6.12] O'Donnell J said every court that had addressed this matter had concluded the "utterly unacceptable" conduct amounted to contempt. For reasons including when the question of imprisonment was raised, Mr Walsh was

---

54 At para 18 of the judgment.

55 At para 14, step (k) of potential steps open to a court as espoused by O'Donnell J.

56 [2019] IESC 15. O'Donnell J subsequently became Chief Justice in late 2021.

told of his entitlement to legal aid and given ample opportunity to address the issue, the court ruled that fair procedures were complied with and no injustice was inflicted on the appellant.

[33.6.13] More recently, High Court proceedings in *Meath County Council v Hendy* (March 2020), concerned Ord 44 of the Rules of the Superior Courts, orders made by Noonan J under s 57 of the Waste Management Act 1996 Act requiring the respondents to discontinue the unauthorised holding, recovery and disposal of waste on farmland in Meath (whereat up to 100,000 tonnes of waste were illegally deposited) and a battery of other reliefs including orders for remediation and payment of substantial costs exceeding €200,000 to the council. Application for coercive orders was made by counsel for the council seeking attachment and committal[57] of the first and second named respondents for neglecting to obey and comply with the terms of the previous court orders made in 2016 and 2017. The respondents submitted that they intended not to comply with the orders because it was impossible to do so. The reasons advanced for that alleged impossibility were firstly, that the second named defendant was in custody; secondly, that the first named defendant was elderly and was not involved with the running of the operation; and thirdly, that the respondents did not have the financial resources to remediate anyway.

[33.6.14] The court *per* Humphreys J took the opportunity to outline the correct process for a coercive order in respect of civil contempt as follows:

> (i) if there is some added value to a separate preliminary finding in that regard, the court can first make a finding simpliciter as to whether the respondent is in contempt or not;
> (ii) if so, the question of whether and to what extent a respondent has the capacity to comply with the order may need to be decided on, if that is an issue; and
> (iii) finally there is the question of the appropriate order, if any, on foot of any finding of contempt, which includes, but is not limited to the custodial orders referred to in Ord 44, but may include financial orders as well; and in particular if there is no capacity to comply, or limited capacity, the court may have to confine itself to noncustodial options, such as orders addressed to assets.

Earlier case law

[33.6.15] In *State (DPP) v Walsh*,[58] the two defendants had been convicted of

---

57 See also the inherent or common law jurisdiction of the court discussed by Peart J (Irvine and Hogan JJ concurring) in *McCann v AB* [2018] IECA 179 at paras 10 to 13; *Laois County Council v Scully* [2007] IEHC 212, [2009] 4 IR 488; and *Laois County Council v Hanrahan* [2014] IESC 36, [2014] 3 IR 143 wherein Fennelly J stated at p 187 that "if compliance is truly beyond the reach of one's capacity, imprisonment as a coercive means should not be resorted to. That is not to say that other measures may not be considered. Ultimately this becomes a matter for the trial judge".

58 [1981] IR 412.

contempt, in the form of scandalising the court, based on the content of a press release they had authorised which was published by *The Irish Times* newspaper. The press release attacked the legitimacy of the Special Criminal Court and alleged that the court had "so abused the rules of evidence as to make the court akin to a sentencing tribunal". The defendants did not dispute that the statement amounted to scandalising the court. They argued, however, that this meant that they were charged with a serious crime and so were entitled to a trial with a jury under Art 38.5 of the Constitution.[59]

[33.6.16] The defendants conceded that some contempt cases could be dealt with summarily, that is, without a jury, where it was necessary for the court to act with all due haste in the interests of justice, but that this was not necessary in cases of scandalising. The Supreme Court concluded that the courts can deal with contempt cases summarily where the facts are not in dispute, such as in this case, and that the defendants were therefore not entitled to a jury trial. The court, by a 3-2 majority, also decided that if the facts were in dispute, a person charged with contempt has a right to a jury trial having regard to Art 38.5.

[33.6.17] *In re O'Kelly*,[60] Kevin O'Kelly (then political correspondent for RTÉ) was called to give evidence in the trial of defendant Seán MacStiofáin, who was charged with membership of the IRA. The prosecution contended that MacStiofáin was the person who had given a taped interview to O'Kelly whereby the person on the tape claimed to be the chief of staff of the IRA. In his evidence, O'Kelly confirmed that the recording was an accurate record of the interview but he refused, on the ground that he was obliged by his professional code of conduct to refuse to reveal the source of information given in confidence, to answer a question asking him to disclose the identity of the person whose voice was recorded.

[33.6.18] The Special Criminal Court as trial court found O'Kelly guilty of contempt in the face of the court and sentenced him to three months' imprisonment. The trial against MacStiofáin then proceeded, and other prosecution evidence identified him as the voice on the tape and he was convicted of IRA membership. On appeal by O'Kelly (which was limited to an appeal against the severity of the sentence), the Court of Criminal Appeal (as it then was) held that journalists do not enjoy a constitutional immunity from disclosing information received in confidence and so the court upheld the finding of contempt. The court held, however, that although the refusal to answer the question had created "some little extra difficulty" in the case, it had not ultimately prevented the conviction for IRA membership. Therefore, the sentence of three months' imprisonment was not justified and the court imposed a fine instead.

---

[59] Which provides that, "Save in the case of the trial of offences under section 2, section 3 or section 4 of this Article no person shall be tried on any criminal charge without a jury".

[60] (1974) 108 ILTR 97.

[33.6.19] *In re Kennedy and McCann*,[61] *The Sunday World* published a story in 1976 about a custody case between a husband and wife which was at that time pending in the Supreme Court. As discussed above, custody proceedings are heard *in camera* and the names of the parties and children are anonymised. In breach of the court order, the newspaper article published the names of the parents and the children and details of the breakdown of the parents' marriage, as well as photographs. The article also alleged that in custody cases in the Irish courts, contrary to the statutory requirement that the welfare of the child be the paramount consideration, the welfare of the child was not treated as the paramount consideration, but instead money and lifestyle were regarded as the most important criteria applied by the courts. The article also implied that justice could not be obtained in the Irish courts and that, in this respect, Ireland was "a sick society" which was "hypocritical about motherhood, morality and the family".

[33.6.20] The Supreme Court accepted that free speech and the free expression of opinions are valued rights, but that Art 40.6.1° of the Constitution also provided that they are subject to limits, in particular that they "shall not be used to undermine public order or morality or the authority of the State". The court found that legitimate criticism of the courts is permissible, but in this case the article had gone beyond the acceptable limits. The court held that the article amounted to contempt of court on two counts: publication in breach of the order prohibiting publication, and publication of material intended to scandalise judges by accusing them of having corrupt and improper motives.

[33.6.21] In *Cullen v Toibín*,[62] the Supreme Court allowed *Magill* magazine to publish an article about a woman named Lyn Madden who had been a witness in the murder trial of John Cullen. At the time of the proposed publication, Mr Cullen had lodged an appeal against his conviction for murder but the appeal had not yet been heard by the Court of Criminal Appeal. The Supreme Court held that the publication of the article was unlikely to prejudice judges of that court in their determination of pure issues of law. Although the Supreme Court was critical of the decision to publish the article, it noted that freedom of the press is guaranteed by the Constitution and so should only be curtailed where such action is necessary for the administration of justice.

[33.6.22] The applicant in the 2000 case of *Kelly v O'Neill*[63] had been convicted of drugs-related offences but sentencing was postponed by the trial judge in order to examine probation reports. Prior to the sentencing hearing, *The Irish Times* published an article containing material that was not admissible in evidence before the court and that was prejudicial to the applicant. The Supreme Court held that *sub judice* contempt could be committed between the time persons are

[61] [1976] IR 382.
[62] [1984] ILRM 577.
[63] [2000] 1 IR 354.

convicted of a crime and when they are sentenced by the trial judge. In these circumstances, the trial had not yet been concluded and so the administration of justice was continuing.

[33.6.23] The trial judge had stated that he had not in fact been influenced by the article but the Supreme Court noted that the accused may nonetheless have felt that the trial was unfair and might question the impartiality of the judge in these circumstances. In addition, the Supreme Court noted that *sub judice* contempt occurs where the material is intended to interfere with the administration of justice. It does not in fact have to result in such interference. The court therefore upheld the view that this constituted contempt and that any such publication should be prohibited until sentencing had concluded.

Collapse of the Paschal Carmody trial

[33.6.24] In 2011, the *Irish Examiner* and *The Irish Times* were found to be in technical contempt of court[64] following the publication of court reports which led to the collapse of the trial of former general practitioner, Dr Paschal Carmody.

[33.6.25] The ruling on 29 April 2011 by McDonagh J at Ennis Circuit Court followed the publication by both newspapers of a court report, supplied by a freelance journalist filling in for a colleague, which contained reports of legal argument advanced in the court on a particular trial day but which had taken place in the absence of the jury and hence any reporting thereon would be prohibited. The comments should not, therefore, have been reported. Carmody was accused of defrauding the families of two terminally ill cancer patients of over €16,500 through deception by way of pretence relating to a fallacious cure. Throughout 17 days in court, the state argued that the former doctor told the families of 15-year-old Wexford teenager Conor O'Sullivan and 58-year-old Kilkenny man John Sheridan that he could cure them. The accused denied all charges.

[33.6.26] McDonagh J ruled that the publication of the reports could have affected Carmody's chance of a fair trial. Collapse of the lengthy trial inevitably and abruptly ensued prior to the final jury charge being given by the judge. Both newspapers published material on matters raised in the absence of the jury and could have been interpreted as being critical and an insult to both the judge and jury. McDonagh J said the Circuit Court must protect the integrity of its own process. The reports implied criticism of himself as well as the suggestion the jurors might not have given full attention to the proceedings, which was an insult to them.

---

64 Carol Byrne, *Newspapers found to be in technical contempt of court* (2011), irishexaminer.com. Available at: https://www.irishexaminer.com/ireland/newspapers-found-to-be-in-technical-contempt-of-court-153073.html [Accessed 20 August 2017].

[33.6.27] Senior editorial management at both papers sincerely apologised to the court for the error in publishing the reports. The trial judge accepted the apologies from both newspapers and noted that there was no malice intended. He thus found them in technical contempt of court but ruled that they had purged their contempt by their presence and apologies in court.

[33.6.28] The court, cognisant that the two newspapers had caused the trial to be aborted, questioned, however, whether it was fair to ask the people of Ireland and the accused to bear the costs. The case was transferred to Dublin Circuit Criminal Court. The newspapers had appealed the amount taxed against them which had been awarded by Clare County Registrar and, in July 2012, Dublin Circuit Criminal Court, McDonagh J continuing to deal with the matter in that circuit, upheld the amount of compensation to be awarded against the two national papers. They were fined €2,500 each and ordered to pay the costs of the DPP, the Courts Service and the former defendant, amounting to €540,000. He ordered *The Irish Times* to pay 57 percent and the *Irish Examiner* to discharge 43 percent of the costs, based on circulation figures of the newspapers published in August 2011.[65]

CODE OF PRACTICE OF THE PRESS COUNCIL OF IRELAND[66]

[33.7.01] As discussed in the Chapter 36, principle 7 (court reporting) of this code requires that the press shall strive to ensure that court reports (including the use of images) are fair and accurate, are not prejudicial to the right to a fair trial and that the presumption of innocence is respected. There is no requirement on a publication to report all of the details of evidence presented in court, so long as the details that are reported, and the overall coverage of the court case, are accurate, fair and balanced.

[33.7.02] Adherence to principle 7 is also relevant in relation to the publication of material relating to the outcome of court cases that are being or may be appealed. As many judicial proceedings in the lower courts lead to the imposition of prison sentences, such cases and their outcomes may, of course, be fully reported. However, the requirement of principle 7 for court reports to be accurate and fair means that the imposition of a jail sentence cannot, given the ever-present possibility that a defendant may be released on bail pending hearing of an appeal, be equated with imprisonment unless there is firm evidence that the defendant in the case has actually been incarcerated.

[33.7.03] The Handbook on the Code of Practice published by the Press Council of Ireland and the Office of the Press Ombudsman in January 2014

65 Clarefm News, *Court upholds costs against papers over collapse of Carmody Trial* (2012), clare.fm. Available at: http://www.clare.fm/news/court-upholds-costs-against-papers-over-collapse-of-carmody-trial/ [Accessed 21 August 2017].

66 Available at: http://www.presscouncil.ie/code-of-practice [Accessed 30 August 2017].

gives examples of complaints that have been upheld under each principle of the code. The handbook is intended as a general guide on how the Press Ombudsman applies the Code of Practice to complaints.

[33.7.04] Thus, in one complaint to the Press Ombudsman, a man complained that an article which reported on two criminal court cases in which he had been a defendant was not accurate, as it had stated that he had been sent to jail, when he had not. Although a sentence of imprisonment had been handed down, the complainant had not served time in prison and the conviction in each of the cases had been successfully appealed. The Press Ombudsman decided that reporting that the complainant had been "sent to jail" and that a judge had "jailed" him was sufficiently inaccurate to warrant a decision that the article had breached principle 7 of code. In that case, the Ombudsman also decided that the stated need for fairness in court reporting in principle 7 requires publications to complete appropriately their coverage of relevant judicial proceedings after a successful appeal against a guilty verdict which they previously reported had been brought to their attention.

[33.7.05] Another example[67] of a principle 7 breach concerned a complaint about an article which was a brief summary of a lengthy and complex decision by the Court of Justice of the EU on a number of issues referred to that court by the High Court in Ireland in connection with a long-running legal case involving the complainant. The Press Ombudsman found that the complaint was supported by persuasive evidence that the summation of the case in the article in question was a breach of principle 7 of the code.

[33.7.06] A third example of a breach given in the said explanatory handbook occurred where the editor of a newspaper group complained about the accuracy of the headline to a number of articles, each of which stated that the Circuit Court had handed down fines of €2,000 to the newspapers concerned and that they were in contempt of court. He also complained about the accuracy of statements in each of the articles that his newspapers had each been fined €1,000 for contempt of court, and that the judge had "instructed" him to attend court. The Press Ombudsman found that there was no evidence that the newspapers had been convicted of contempt of court, that they had been fined by the court, or that the complainant had been instructed by the judge to attend court. In these circumstances, he found the statements complained about were significantly inaccurate and therefore in breach of principle 7.

[33.7.07] It is important to note that this Code of Practice was not written by the Press Council or the Press Ombudsman, but by journalists themselves (including editors), and is the expression of best professional practice in journalism. The code

---

[67] Press Council of Ireland, *Code of Practice for Newspapers and Magazines* (handbook) (January 2014). Available at: http://www.presscouncil.ie/_fileupload/Handbook%20on%20Code%20of%20Practice.pdf [Accessed 10 September 2017].

has remained unchanged in all significant respects since it was first drafted under the aegis of the Press Industry Steering Committee during the 2003 to 2007 period, when the discussions that created the Office of the Press Ombudsman and the Press Council were in train.

Chapter 34

Gagging Orders and Super-Injunctions; Covert Investigative Filming and Prior Restraint Applications

GAGGING ORDERS

[34.1.01] The matter of super-injunctions (or more correctly, prior restraint or suppression orders)[1] came to the fore in May 2021 in the aftermath of the cyber attack on the Health Service Executive's information technology systems whereby the HSE secured orders from Cross J in the High Court, as then served on the dark net, against "persons unknown" to restrain any sharing, processing, selling or publishing of data stolen from HSE systems in the ransomware attack. The primary reason for seeking the injunctions was to put information service providers such as Google and Twitter on notice of the prohibition on the dissemination of such information, leading to swifter and more comprehensive removal of any such information if attempts were made to use those platforms as a conduit for publication. In his ruling on the substantive application, Cross J noted that while the HSE's application was legally unusual as the courts generally do not make orders against unidentified individuals, he was satisfied there was no legal impediment to how the proceedings were constituted. He was further satisfied the orders were necessary and the relevant criteria therefor had been met.

[34.1.02] A gagging or gag order (also termed suppression order, prior restraint order,[2] super-injunction, anonymised injunction or reporting ban, depending on the particular circumstances at bar) is an injunctive order, generally interim

---

1 Minister for Health Stephen Donnelly perhaps inadvertently referred to the High Court orders at bar as constituting 'super' injunctions. As will later be discussed, however, the orders made by the High Court in the HSE application lacked the second and hallmark leg of super-injunctions, that is, a reporting ban in the press on the existence of the order itself.

2 A term used in European Court of Human Rights jurisprudence referring to orders which restrain in advance the broadcast or publication of material but only to be granted after "careful scrutiny" whereby if it is at all possible a court should attempt to afford the defendant at least some opportunity to put before the court its case prior to the court's making any form of interim restraint order.

or interlocutory in nature pending full trial of the issues, restricting information or comment from being made public or passed onto any unauthorised third party.[3] These reliefs were originally granted to protect individuals whose lives might be at risk if their details were made public, such as child or sex offenders. However, with the passing of the Human Rights Act 1998 in England which incorporated the European Convention on Human Rights, judges began to use enactment of that statute to extend human rights law to encompass the right to privacy. The granting of a suppression order of course can bring with it the Streisand effect,[4] a phenomenon whereby an attempt to hide, remove or censor information has the unintended consequence of publicising that very information more widely, usually facilitated by the essentially impossible-to-police internet. This occurred to the detriment of footballer Ryan Giggs following the *CTB* proceedings[5] mentioned later via the surfacing of rumours on Twitter which ultimately led to Liberal Democrat MP John Hemming's use of parliamentary privilege to confirm Giggs as CTB.

[34.1.03] These injunctions may be sought, for instance, to protect the integrity of ongoing police or military operations, the privacy of victims or minors,[6] to limit the freedom of the press or, potentially, to protect commercially sensitive information.[7] Application therefor can be made in both civil and criminal

3 The phrase may sometimes also be used in the context of a private order by an employer or other institution (for example based on contractual commitments to protect trade secrets).

4 Named after actor-singer Barbara Streisand whose 2003 attempt (*Streisand v Adelman*, California Superior Court; Case SC077257) to suppress photographs of her residence in Malibu inadvertently drew further public attention to it. The superstar sued photographer Kenneth Adelman/Pictopia.com and the California Coastal Records Project for violation of privacy in a $50 million lawsuit (five actions at $10m each) endeavouring to remove an aerial photograph of her mansion from the publicly available collection of 12,000 Californian coastline photographs. Adelman photographed the beachfront property to document coastal erosion, intending to influence government policymakers. Before Streisand filed her lawsuit, the image had been downloaded from Adelman's website only a handful of times. As a result of the case, nearly half a million people visited the site over the following month. The lawsuit was ultimately dismissed and Streisand was ordered to pay the defence legal fees. Superior Court Judge Allan Goodman wrote that Streisand's complaint constituted an effort to silence Adelman's speech about a matter of public concern, protection of California's coastline, in violation of the state anti-SLAPP statute (Strategic Lawsuit Against Public Participation). Streisand was also ordered to pay Adelman's legal fees.

5 *CTB v News Group Newspapers Ltd* [2011] EWHC 1232 (QB).

6 A lifelong anonymity order was made in the case of Robert Thompson and Jon Venables in England, who were 10 years of age when they abducted and murdered two-year-old James Bulger in 1993. Venables who was given a new name on more than one occasion due to reporting breaches was released from prison in 2013. In March 2019, actress Tina Malone posted his new name and a recent photograph of him on Facebook. She was given an eight-month suspended sentence. In a legal challenge by James Bulger's father to lift the lifelong order protecting Venables' anonymity, such application was refused. The judge reasoned there was a strong possibility that if his identity were known "he would be pursued resulting in grave and possibly fatal consequences".

7 In the latter eventuality, however, redaction of information would be the preferred course of action and an order that no reference thereto could be made outside court, even if

proceedings. Restrictions on naming an accused are normally used in certain sensitive cases such as those involving sexual offences as seen in the previous chapter on court reporting. Gag orders are otherwise made by the courts by imposing reporting bans in an attempt to assure a fair trial by preventing prejudicial pre-trial publicity. All such injunctions therefore comprise a derogation from the strict principle of open justice, or in the parlance of the Constitution, that:

> Justice shall be administered in courts established by law by judges ... and, save in such special and limited cases as may be prescribed by law, shall be administered in public.[8]

Indeed, as noted in the previous chapter at [33.4.01], Hogan J in *AIB v Tracey (No. 2)* commented that:

> The open administration of justice is, of course, a vital safeguard in any free and democratic society. It ensures that the judicial branch is subjected to scrutiny and examination and helps to promote confidence in the fair and even handed administration of justice. Any system of secret court hearings could pave the way for judicial arrogance, overbearing judicial conduct and abuse.

[34.1.04] In civil law matters, with British cases in the past often involving wealthy celebrities seeking to protect their anonymity, applicants for the injunction rely both on privacy laws and on European human rights law.[9] The order's remit can extend worldwide (*contra mundum*) and in perpetuity, unless contested or revisited at a later date. The terms of suppression orders can be strict in nature such that even the fact that an injunction has been granted cannot be reported. Hence the 'super' element. In other cases, a party to proceedings may be withheld due to safety concerns. In December 2020, at preliminary application, the High Court in London ruled that the 12-year-old plaintiff in the TikTok alleged data protection breaches case mentioned in Chapter 13 could remain anonymous if the case proceeded (the case was allowed to proceed in March 2022 by further court order of Nicklin J). Warby J ruled that the girl risked being cyber-bullied by other children and TikTok users if her identity was revealed. He said she could face "hostile reactions from social media influencers who might feel their status or earnings were under threat".

---

it was mentioned in court and an order restricting public access to court documents. Lord Neuberger in *Pink Floyd* mentioned below at para [34.2.15] took the opportunity in his judgment to state, "I consider, therefore, that the present appeal provides a good opportunity for this court to make it clear that a private hearing or party anonymisation will be granted in the Court of Appeal only if, and only to the extent that, a member of the Court is satisfied that it is necessary for the proper administration of justice... in relation to appeals, the Court of Appeal should not depart from the general rule that litigation is to be conducted in public, unless a judge of that court is persuaded that there are cogent grounds for doing so.

8 Article 34.1 of the Constitution.

9 Articles 8 and 10 of the Convention.

[34.1.05] In the 2005 High Court judgment concerning Leas Cross private nursing home in Swords, north County Dublin discussed later, Clarke J (as he then was)[10] signalled that the courts were likely to favour the granting of orders restraining publication of material on people's private lives and where there is no public interest in its disclosure. However, where an order is sought to restrict the publishing of material of significant public interest, even in circumstances where that material was obtained by hidden cameras or similar "surreptitious means", Clarke J held the view that the balance would be against granting applicants "prior restraint" injunctions prohibiting publication.

[34.1.06] In figures released by Belfast High Court in early 2020 after repeated tabling of written questions to Stormont ministers by criminal law QC James Hugh Allister, leader of the Traditional Union Voice party and critic of court orders of this type, it was revealed that a record number of super-injunctions were then in force in Northern Ireland. At that juncture, over the previous seven years, eight such injunctions had been granted, of which four had been discharged. However, the subsistence of older injunctions remaining in place brought the total number to seven active orders.

SUPER-INJUNCTION AND ANONYMISED INJUNCTIONS DEFINED

[34.2.01] A so-called super-injunction is an interim injunction which firstly restrains publication of information which concerns the applicant and which is said to be confidential or private and, second, from publicising or informing others of the existence of the order and the proceedings.[11] It is this second element, namely the prohibition on the very existence of the injunction being reported in the press, which transforms this interim injunction type order into a super-injunction.

[34.2.02] An anonymised injunction is an interim injunction which prohibits publishing of information that concerns the applicant and is said to be confidential or private where the names of either or both of the parties to the proceedings are not stated. According to former President of the Supreme Court of the United Kingdom (then Master of the Rolls, Lord Neuberger), in a judicial committee report on the subject, the proper approach to anonymisation had been clarified in *JIH v News Group Newspapers Ltd*[12] in which Lord Neuberger MR delivered

---

10 Clarke J proceeded to become Chief Justice and President of the Supreme Court. He was succeeded by O'Donnell CJ in October 2021.

11 Paraphrased from page iv of a report by a UK judicial committee on super-injunctions led by Master of the Rolls, Lord Neuberger published on 19 May 2011 with a number of recommendations and observations: *Report of the Committee on Super-Injunctions: Super-Injunctions, Anonymised Injunctions and Open Justice*. Available on: https://www.judiciary.uk/wp-content/uploads/JCO/Documents/Reports/super-injunction-report-20052011.pdf [Accessed 20 June 2021].

12 [2011] EWCA Civ 42 (Lord Neuberger MR with whom Maurice Kay and Smith LJJ agreed). Here, the parties agreed the grant of an interim injunction to protect private

the Court of Appeal's unanimous judgment and therein summarised the (ten) principles (as set out in the *Appendix* to this chapter) which apply whenever a claimant seeks an anonymity order or other restraint on publication of details of a case that would normally be freely in the public domain.

[34.2.03] That case related to a story that *The Sun* newspaper intended to publish concerning an alleged affair between the claimant (a sportsman) and another. In these privacy law proceedings, JIH submitted that the general details of the story should be made reportable and that his anonymity should be retained. On the facts, the Court of Appeal held it was in order to accede to JIH's claim for anonymisation. There was obvious force in the contention that the public interest would be better served by publication of the fact that an injunction had been granted to an anonymous well-known person on the basis of certain facts than by being told that the court had granted an injunction to an identified person to restrain publication of unspecified information of an allegedly private nature.

[34.2.04] Their Lordships acknowledged the importance to the media and to wider society of being able to name JIH as the claimant. However, there was no general rule that anonymisation is more or less likely to result in greater interference with free speech and maintaining public scrutiny of the courts than precluding the publication of more extensive information about the proceedings. The crucial factor was a previous story published in the media regarding JIH's alleged liaison with YY, which bore similarities to the present allegations about JIH. If his identity was revealed without permitting the nature of the information sought to be restrained, the media and public would have easily deduced the subject matter of that information.[13]

UK gagging orders

[34.2.05] The experience by litigants is that the use and effect of suppression orders ultimately proves futile. Jeremy Clarkson who had obtained an injunction stated to the *Daily Mail* paper in the UK:[14]

> You take out an injunction against somebody or some organisation and immediately news of that injunction and the people involved and the story behind the injunction is in a legal-free world on Twitter and the internet. It's pointless.

[34.2.06] England captain John Terry (LNS) faced allegations about his private

---

information pending trial. Although also agreed between the parties, anonymity was refused by Tugendhat J. The Court of Appeal allowed an appeal from that refusal and reinstated anonymity. The court gave guidance regarding the grant of anonymity. The order in question did not contain any provision rendering it a super-injunction. Accordingly, a reasoned judgment is publicly available.

13 See para 40 of the decision.

14 *AMM v HXW* [2010] EWHC 2457.

life after unsuccessful gagging order proceedings.[15] The footballer's alleged affair with Vanessa Perroncel, the ex-girlfriend of teammate Wayne Bridge, was later reported in the press, bringing Terry the public scrutiny he sought to avoid. The judge reasoned that Terry had a robust personality and would not likely suffer distress from the revelation of these details and that:

> ...the real basis for the concern of LNS is likely to be the impact of any adverse publicity upon the business of earning sponsorship and similar income.[16]

[34.2.07] In 2011, Ryan Giggs was granted a super-injunction to prevent his affair with former Miss Wales and Big Brother star Imogen Thomas from being made public. It was reported that former Manchester United player Giggs expended some £150,000 in obtaining the order. The injunction itself was rendered worthless when, as stated, John Hemming MP availed of parliamentary privilege to name married Giggs as the mystery footballer in May 2011.

[34.2.08] Other proceedings have involved a world-famous married British actor who was granted an order from King J at London's High Court in 2011 to prevent the media reporting his relationship with a call girl. This was reported as the latest in a series of super-injunctions which made the headlines that year, as applied for by almost 30 celebrities and sports stars, in a bid to prevent lurid headlines and unflattering publicity concerning their private lives often relating to extra-marital affairs.[17]

Analysis of the UK position

[34.2.09] An analysis by *The Independent* (UK) found that more than 333 gagging orders protecting the identities of celebrities, children and private individuals were granted in the 2006 to 2011 period. At least 264 orders existed which granted anonymity to children or vulnerable adults and in a further 69 cases injunctions were granted barring the publication of the names of high-profile individuals, including 28 men accused of extra-marital affairs, and nine cases involved convicted criminals who had been granted anonymity. Orders were also granted to at least seven major companies, including the publicly-owned bank Northern Rock. The orders, some of which are permanent and some temporary, prevent publication of allegations about their commercial affairs. The 333 gagging orders in the *newspaper's study* included a company accused of pollution, a member of the public who was desirous for the press not to report his sex change, a television personality who received death threats and hundreds of anonymity orders preventing the media from taking any action that would

---

15 *Terry v Persons Unknown* [2010] EWHC 119 (QB).

16 At para 95 of Tugendhat J's judgment.

17 Irish Examiner, *'World-famous' actor wins gagging order over sex claims* (2011), irishexaminer.com. Available at: https://www.irishexaminer.com/world/world-famous-actor-wins-gagging-order-over-sex-claims-151549.html [Accessed 29 April 2018].

lead to the identification of children whose parents or carers had been accused of murder, child abuse or other crimes.

[34.2.10] Lord Neuberger MR, has said it is impossible to verify the number of rulings being handed down which make it a criminal offence to publish certain information about individuals. His report into injunctions stated:

> The absence of evidence has encouraged a view that an entirely secret process has developed in the civil courts, and that this is improper in principle, risks neutering press freedom to report matters of public interest and undermines the public's right to be informed of court proceedings.[18]

The current position

[34.2.11] Awarding of gagging orders was effectively ended in England and Wales in 2011. In saying that, in *PJS v News Group Newspapers Ltd*,[19] the UK Supreme Court by 4-1 majority reinstated an injunction (granted at first instance but discharged by the Court of Appeal) restraining publication of the fact that in 2011 the celebrity claimant in the entertainment business, PJS, had a three-way sexual encounter with AB and CD.[20]

[34.2.12] In May 2016, the Supreme Court ruled that *The Sun on Sunday* should be barred from revealing the identity of PJS on the basis that the information was private, there was no public interest in its disclosure and that, while secrecy and confidentiality may have been compromised by publicity, a court was unlikely to find that PJS's right to privacy was defeated by that fact. It held, *inter alia*, that the Court of Appeal erred in referring to a "limited public interest" in the proposed story. Criticism of a person's conduct cannot be a pretext for invasion of privacy by disclosure of alleged sexual infidelity, which is of no real public interest in a legal sense.[21] The entire matter was rather farcical however. Earlier in the year, a Scottish newspaper and others globally published full details of

---

18 Cahal Milmo, Oliver Wright and Nigel Morris, *The untold story of gagging orders* (2011), independent.co.uk. Available at: https://www.independent.co.uk/news/media/press/the-untold-story-of-gagging-orders-2288607.html [Accessed 29 April 2018].

19 [2016] UKSC 26.

20 In early April 2016, the story of PJS's sexual activities was published in a magazine in the US, and subsequently in publications in Canada, Scotland, and on the internet. The claimant's solicitors took steps to seek to remove material, but the information appeared on numerous websites and on social media. Newspapers in England and Wales reported the contents of the published judgment complaining that they could not name the persons involved. The defendant, NGN, returned to the Court of Appeal seeking discharge of the injunction on the ground that the information protected by the injunction had now entered the public domain, and therefore the injunction served no purpose and was an unjustified interference with the defendant's art 10 rights. On 18 April 2016, the Court of Appeal acceded to NGN's application and discharged the injunction subject to a stay to allow PJS to seek permission from the Supreme Court. The Supreme Court agreed to hear PJS's permission application, and, if successful, his appeal, at the same time, three days later.

21 *Per* Lord Mance at para 21 of the judgment.

the mystery couple behind the controversial injunction. The trial court order only banned newspapers in England and Wales from publishing the names of the celebrity married couple.

[34.2.13] At London's High Court in November 2016, Warby J confirmed that PJS and News Group Newspapers (NGN) had agreed a final order in the action for breach of confidence and misuse of private information. The proceedings were stayed on the basis that NGN pay a specified sum in full and final settlement of PJS's claim for damages and costs. NGN also agreed to give undertakings not to use, disclose or publish certain information and to remove and not republish certain existing articles. The undertakings extended to not publishing any information which identified or was liable to identify PJS as a party to the action, including identifying his partner or three other individuals.

Demise of the super-injunction

[34.2.14] In October 2009 when *The Guardian* newspaper reported that it had been prevented by an injunction applied for by London defamation law specialists from covering remarks made in parliament, other sources then speculated that it related to previous reports *The Guardian* had printed regarding the oil company Trafigura and its alleged waste dumping. *The Guardian* confirmed that Trafigura was the source of the gagging order, after the order of Maddison J[22] was lifted the next day. The question the paper was unable to report was from Labour MP Paul Farrelly relating to publication of internal Barclays reports documenting alleged tax avoidance schemes and the publication of the Minton report on the alleged dumping of toxic waste in the Ivory Coast, commissioned by Trafigura.

[34.2.15] The case aroused public suspicion of these types of injunction, eventually leading to a debate in the House of Commons wherein the Secretary of State for Justice revealed that the government was concerned about the over-use of super-injunctions. Former Prime Minister David Cameron and culture minister Jeremy Hunt subsequently expressed their own reservations about the manner in which the law was being enforced. Lord Neuberger's above-mentioned judicial committee report in May 2011 contained a number of recommendations and observations as set out in the *Appendix* (see also his comments relating to privacy and anonymisation at paras 62 to 69 of his judgment in *Pink Floyd Music Ltd v EMI Records Ltd*).[23] Previously, on 10 May 2011, David Cameron blamed lack of parliamentary guidance, forcing judges to rely on strict European law in their judgments. On 23 May 2011, speaking on ITV's *Daybreak*, the Prime Minister stated that the law should be reviewed as it was unsustainable.

---

22 *RJW v Guardian News and Media Ltd* [2009] EWHC 2540 (QB).

23 [2011] WLR 770; [2010] EWCA Civ 1429.

Irish proceedings

[34.2.16] In September 2017, Cloverhill District Court in Dublin lifted a gagging order that had banned the media from naming a man accused of carrying a loaded gun on a Dublin to Belfast train.[24] Mr Ciaran Ryan could then be identified as the defendant alleged to have had the semi-automatic pistol and ammunition that were seized by Gardaí on a train at Connolly Station. Judge Victor Blake lifted the reporting ban following an application by the news media. This followed a similar order by Judge Alan Mitchell who had ruled the previous month that the press could identify co-accused Nikita Murtagh alleged to have handed Mr Ryan the gun and ammunition because no legal basis for the order was advanced to him in court. Judge Gerard Jones had imposed the gagging orders (directing reporters not to reveal their names) at the request of their defence solicitors who cited safety concerns. Blake J stated that justice must be administered in public (as *per* Art 34 of the Constitution) and immediately lifted the earlier-imposed restriction order.

[34.2.17] Other than the above-cited order in respect of the HSE ransomware attack, the super-injunction type order seemingly has yet to be considered by the Irish courts. The above principle of open justice is, however, enshrined in the Constitution. As such, in the opinion of Carol Plunkett, William Fry Solicitors, if an application is made in Ireland for a super-injunction, the judiciary is likely to follow the recommendations made by the Master of the Rolls in the UK and only grant such an injunction in the most exceptional of circumstances.[25]

[34.2.18] Thus, Cross J who granted the injunctions restraining any sharing, processing, selling or publishing of data stolen from the HSE's computer systems in the 2021 cyberattack stated this was a "particularly heinous" form of blackmail where those responsible were seeking to put pressure on the HSE and the authorities to give in to the blackmailers' demands, including by hoping patients with sensitive medical data stored on the HSE system would add to those pressures. He said the consequences of the blackmailers' actions were "particularly cruel" at a time of worldwide Covid-19 pandemic and it would be "inconceivable" and "a cause of scandal" if the law was impotent or tied by excessive rules from attempting to stop this "outrage".

[34.2.19] There is nonetheless nothing to prevent an Irish celebrity from seeking a super-injunction according to Paula Mullooly, partner at media law specialists Simon McAleese solicitors. U2 guitarist The Edge obtained an injunction

---

24 Andrew Phelan, *Judge lifts gagging order in case of gun on train* (2017), independent.ie. Available at: https://www.independent.ie/irish-news/courts/judge-lifts-gagging-order-in-case-of-gun-on-train-36150094.html [Accessed 27 April 2018].

25 Carol Plunkett (with contributions by Mark O'Shaughnessy), William Fry Solicitors, *What is so Super About "Super Injunctions"*? (2011). Available at: https://www.williamfry.com/newsandinsights/news-article/2011/07/01/what_is_so_super_about_super_injunctions [Accessed 20 June 2021].

grounded on the right to privacy against *The Sunday World* to prevent disclosure of his child's leukaemia, a condition he later spoke about in public.

COVERT INVESTIGATIVE FILMING

[34.3.01] The aforementioned judgment of Clarke J (in the *Cogley*[26] and *Aherne*[27] proceedings arising out of the same intended investigative television programme and which, consequently, were heard together on the same day) is authority for the proposition that there is an entitlement to broadcast or publish material even where it has been unlawfully obtained on the basis of a legitimate public interest. This will necessarily result in the courts' exercising significant scrutiny over the public interest asserted. Clarke J was also mindful of the fact that it "is all too easy to dress up very many issues with an exaggerated or unreal public dimension". However on the facts of this case, and applying authority from New Zealand's Court of Appeal (*TV3 Network Services Ltd v Fahey*,[28] a case with very similar facts), he was more than satisfied that RTÉ had shown that there were very real, significant and weighty public interest issues involved and thus refused to grant an interlocutory injunction which would have the effect of restraining the broadcast.

The facts

[34.3.02] The programme laid very serious allegations about the manner in which the nursing home at Leas Cross was operated over a lengthy period of time. A substantial amount of the footage included in the broadcast appeared to have been filmed secretly. It was apparent that an experienced care worker was engaged by the national broadcaster to seek and take up a job at the retirement home. After a period of approximately two weeks working there, the person in question, in conjunction with the programme makers, decided that by virtue of the seriousness of the situation it was appropriate that he be equipped by RTÉ with a concealed camera. A considerable amount of footage was captured, some of which was included in the intended broadcast. A significant portion of the remainder of the broadcast involved expert commentary on the footage both shown and unshown.

[34.3.03] Both sets of proceedings were commenced in May 2005 and related to what was, at that time, the intention on the part of RTÉ to broadcast the programme on Monday 30 May. The plaintiff in the first proceedings ('the Cogley proceedings') was a director of nursing at Leas Cross. The plaintiffs in the second proceedings ('the Aherne proceedings') were the owners and occupiers of the nursing and retirement home and had carried on the business at the premises since April 1998.

26 *Cogley v Radio Telefís Éireann* [2005] IEHC 180.
27 *Aherne and Sovereign Projects Ltd v Radio Telefís Éireann* [2005] IEHC 180.
28 (1999) 2 NZLR 129.

The Cogley defamation claim

[34.3.04] In the Cogley proceedings the plaintiff based her claims squarely on defamation. She therefore contended that the court should grant an interlocutory injunction to prevent the broadcast of the programme which would injure her reputation. Two important points emerge. Firstly, an injunction can be applied for in a defamation action even if generally an injunction will not be granted where damages will instead be a more appropriate remedy. The judge based this determination on the decision of Kelly J in *Reynolds v Molocco*[29] stating as follows:

> …Kelly J. noted that damages were the ordinary and appropriate remedy for defamation and that an injunction was not. The special circumstance which seemed to have acted most strongly in favour of the exercise of the discretion to grant an injunction in that case was the conclusion reached by the learned trial judge about the financial standing of the defendant and the "virtual impossibility of ever recovering any sum awarded". It would therefore appear that even in a case where it can be clearly shown that the defendant would have no defence the court retains a discretion which can be exercised having regard to all the circumstances of the case.

[34.3.05] Here the judge was clearly not ruling out granting an injunction against RTÉ based on defamatory comment even if RTÉ would indeed be a good mark for damages and that damages would be the usual and appropriate remedy rather than granting the equitable remedy of an injunction. The second point of importance, however, is that an initial hurdle must be overcome, that is:

> …the first question that needs to be addressed in any interlocutory application in which a plaintiff seeks prior restraint on the publication or broadcast of material, on the grounds that it is defamatory is as to whether on the evidence available at the interlocutory stage, it is clear that the plaintiff will ultimately succeed at a trial. For reasons which have been fully explored in the context of interlocutory injunctions generally (from the decision of the Supreme Court in *Campus Oil v. Minister for Industry (No 2)* [1983] I.R. 88 onwards)[30] it does

---

[29] Unreported, High Court, Kelly J (11 December 1998). See also *Gilroy v O'Leary* [2019] IEHC 52 however which decision by Allen J further emphasises the reluctance of the courts, generally, to interfere with freedom of expression, as expressed by Barrett J in *Philpott v Irish Examiner* [2016] IEHC 62 because "the profound importance of free speech – a freedom inextricably linked to the freeness of our nation – is such that it is arguable that a court ought to be slow to [grant an injunction under section 33]" (Allen J referring therein to s 33 of the Defamation Act 2009).

[30] Note that on 31 July 2019 the decision of the Supreme Court in *Merck Sharp & Dohme v Clonmel Healthcare Ltd* [2019] IESC 65 brought into question the settled *Campus Oil* test for determining injunctive relief. In deciding that case, the Supreme Court set out eight factors that a court might follow in determining whether to grant an injunction. In doing so, the court emphasised the need for flexibility. One key factor applied by the court was that "robust scepticism" should be applied to arguments that damages are not adequate in commercial contract disputes. A significant question that arose from the judgment was whether this nuanced understanding of the test would apply in IP cases only, such as the patent dispute in *Merck Sharp & Dohme,* or if it would also apply to general commercial cases. In December 2019, the Court of Appeal welcomed the approach of the Supreme Court in a commercial contract dispute case particularly when it came to consider the

> not seem to me to be appropriate to ask this court at an interlocutory stage and where it will, necessarily, have available to it only a limited opportunity to consider the merits of a case, to attempt to weigh the likelihood of a plaintiff succeeding or failing. Similarly it does not seem to be appropriate to invite the court to weigh the likelihood of the defendant succeeding in maintaining any defence in defamation proceedings. Thus the plaintiff will fail to cross the first hurdle if, on the basis of the argument and materials before the court, it appears that there is any reasonable basis for contending that the defendant may succeed at the trial of the action. The defendant may succeed in defending the action for any one of a number of reasons.

[34.3.06] There could be little doubt that the programme contained accusations of the highest degree of seriousness as to the standards which operated within the nursing home concerned. It was not at all so clear however that, at least in a great many respects, a reasonable viewing of the programme would cause a viewer to conclude that Ms Cogley was culpable. Even to the extent to which a reasonable viewer might infer that the programme contended that she was blameworthy, it was by no means evident, in the light of all the evidence that was likely to be before a defamation trial jury, the jurors would necessarily conclude that any imputation of fault was not justified. Either way, the test at early application stage of likely proving successful at full trial was not readily met.

[34.3.07] In addition, much of the programme consisted of either interviews with the relatives of persons who were patients at the home, the secretly filmed footage, and the comments of experts. It seemed unlikely, therefore, that it could be denied that the events shown on the secretly filmed footage actually occurred. It may, of course, have been the case that the plaintiff would be able to persuade a jury that the way in which that film was put together and edited with expert commentary amounted to an unfair presentation of the picture to such an extent that she could succeed at full trial. However the judge did not believe a court could, at that initial stage, conclude that such an outcome, on the materials then available to it, was clear cut. On the basis therefore of established jurisprudence it did not seem to the High Court that the plaintiff in the *Cogley* proceedings had crossed the first threshold and accordingly refused her application for interlocutory relief based on defamation.

The Aherne breach of privacy and trespass claims

[34.3.08] The plaintiffs in the Aherne proceedings adopted a different approach. They relied upon the fact that in the course of the programme a significant volume of material was shown which was obtained on foot of the use of a secret camera in the circumstances referred to above and which was also otherwise unlawful, the footage having been obtained while the person concerned was a trespasser on the premises. Thus, it was contended this material was wrongfully

adequacy of damages and the balance of convenience elements of the *Campus Oil* test (see *Betty Martin Financial Services Ltd v EBS DAC* [2019] IECA 327).

obtained in breach of the plaintiffs' right to privacy and the publication should as a consequence have been restrained. It must also be noted that the plaintiffs in the Aherne proceedings did not disavow a defamation leg to their case.

[34.3.09] It was further necessary to consider the contention of the plaintiffs to the effect that there was a breach of the right to privacy of others (most especially patients). In the latter connection, the affidavit of Eddie Doyle, as executive producer of the impugned programme, noted that the content in the form in which it was intended to be broadcast sought to protect the privacy interests of patients by obscuring their identities through the technical process of pixilation, or by obtaining the consent of the patients' families to the proposed broadcast, or both. On the basis of the evidence before the court, Clarke J had no reason to believe that such measures would not effectively protect the privacy rights of the patients concerned. On that basis he was not persuaded that he should take into account any privacy rights other than those of the plaintiffs.[31]

[34.3.10] That the plaintiffs enjoyed a right to privacy was clear. Firstly, s 3 of the Broadcasting Authority (Amendment) Act 1976 amended the Broadcasting Authority Act 1960[32] by the inclusion of a provision (s 18(1B)) to the effect that "the Authority shall not, in its programmes and in the means employed to make such programmes, unreasonably encroach on the privacy of an individual". It was also clear from *Kennedy v Ireland*[33] that a right to privacy is one of the personal rights of the citizen guaranteed by, though not specifically mentioned in, the Constitution.

[34.3.11] However *Kennedy* confirmed that the right to privacy is not an unqualified right but is subject to the constitutional rights of others and to the requirements of public order, public morality and the common good. Similarly, the express recognition of an obligation to respect the privacy of others contained in the Broadcasting Acts was also not unqualified in that they placed an obligation on the Authority (at that time RTÉ) not to "unreasonably encroach" on the privacy of an individual. Accordingly, while persons such as the plaintiffs in the Aherne proceedings had a constitutional right to privacy and an arguable entitlement to ensure that the Authority did not unreasonably interfere with their privacy in the course of making and broadcasting programmes, those rights were not unqualified. It was therefore necessary to address how the right of privacy may be balanced against other competing rights and in particular

---

31 In saying that, the court emphasised that should it transpire that appropriate measures were not, in fact, taken by the programme producers for the purposes of giving reasonable and adequate protection in all the circumstances of the case to those who may have appeared on the film, nothing in this judgment should be taken as implying that such parties would be debarred from seeking a remedy in the court.

32 Both statutes were, subsequent to this 2005 judgment, largely or fully repealed respectively by the Broadcasting Act 2009 Act (which Act itself has been substantially amended – see Chapters 30 and 31).

33 [1987] IR 587.

how an assessment of the situation in respect of such competing rights should be made at an interlocutory stage such as those before Clarke J.

[34.3.12] As regards the covert filming, the court was referred to *TV3 Network Services Ltd v Fahey* in New Zealand which bore significant resemblance to this case. TV3 equipped a woman who had made accusations against a medical practitioner with a concealed video camera so that it might film an appointment which she had made to see the doctor who was the subject of misconduct accusations. The most significant difference between *TV3* and *Cogley/Aherne* was that the television station involved had, in that case, already broadcast a programme making accusations of sexual misconduct against the physician prior to the secret filming. The concealed filming therefore took place in the context of a situation whereby Fahey was already the plaintiff in defamation proceedings. However, many of the general principles identified by that judgment were equally applicable to the circumstances before Clarke J. In relation to the status of the woman who was equipped with the hidden camera, the New Zealand Court of Appeal came to the following view:

> This brings us to the third ground, trespass and invasion of privacy. Trespass is a civil wrong and entering and remaining on Dr. Fahey's premises for the purposes of confronting him with allegations of sexual and professional misconduct and surreptitiously recording the conversation could scarcely come within the terms of the normal implied licence to attend at a doctor's surgery. Clearly TV3 encouraged and facilitated X's action. As to the privacy implications discussed in Todd, The Law of Torts in New Zealand (2nd Ed. 1997) at p. 951, in terms of the Broadcasting Act 1989, TV3 was and is responsible for maintaining in its programmes and their presentation standards which are consistent with the privacy of the individual (s. 4(1)(c)) but it is not under a civil liability in respect of any failure to comply with any provisions of the section (s. 4(3)).[34]

The judgment: permitting the broadcast in the public interest

[34.3.13] On the basis of the above authority which the court found persuasive, it would seem that the plaintiff had at least made out an arguable case to the effect that the circumstances in which the surreptitious filming within Leas Cross occurred may have amounted, *prima facie*, to a trespass and breach of privacy. The implied entitlement of the individual concerned to be present as an employee would not be such as would be likely to encompass the conduct which actually occurred. Pending the establishment after a full trial of the lawfulness or otherwise of the use of such methods, Clarke J held that the balance of convenience would favour restraining RTÉ from engaging in any further trespass on the premises of the plaintiffs in the Aherne proceedings. As is always the case at an interlocutory stage, nothing in that determination he said should be taken as amounting to a final ruling as to the appropriateness or otherwise of any of the actions which had in fact been engaged in.

[34] At p 135 of the judgment, *supra* at fn 28.

[34.3.14] Nevertheless, it seemed clear from *TV3* that the mere fact that information may, arguably, have been obtained in breach of an individual's rights was not, of itself, necessarily decisive. What also needs to be weighed in the balancing exercise is the importance of any public interest issues which arise and also the extent to which damages may be an adequate remedy.

[34.3.15] The court then emphasised that at this stage anything said concerning the content of the programme should not be construed as amounting to a finding of fact by the court or that any facts alleged had been established. At an interlocutory point, a court which is asked to assess the extent of the legitimate public interest in a particular broadcast must have regard to the necessarily limited information that will be available to it at that juncture. However, subject to that caveat, the following issues of very significant public importance were potentially raised by the programme:

(a) whether the standards applied at the Leas Cross Nursing Home fall, to a very marked degree, short of the standards that could be reasonably be expected in such a home;
(b) the extent to which, in addition to its ordinary regulatory role, the above matters ought to be of concern to the authorities charged with the administration of the health service by reference to the fact that, it would appear, a significant portion of the funding of the patients who reside at the home is provided out of public funds;
(c) the extent to which the existing regulatory regime in respect of such homes has been properly administered by those charged with that task; and
(d) whether that regulatory regime is, in itself, sufficient to allow for the proper regulation of the nursing home sector.[35]

[34.3.16] The court also took into account in assessing the importance of the public interest issues involved that those who would suffer should the contentions of the programme be borne out were an extremely vulnerable section of the community with a limited (or in many cases no) voice of their own. In all those circumstances it seemed to the court that the issues raised in the programme were those of the highest public interest and that, accordingly, a very significant weight indeed needed to be attached to those matters in balancing the rights and values involved.

[34.3.17] The court was satisfied that the availability of the secret film could be said to add drama to the programme. It was equally true that having regard to the very serious accusations made in respect of the management of the nursing home it would be likely that a programme which contained those accusations, but was not supported by the surreptitious film, would be challenged. In those circumstances it appeared to the trial judge that it would be appropriate from a global perspective, using the words of his brethren in New Zealand, to also

---

[35] At para 42 of Clarke J's decision.

describe the inclusion of surreptitious film in the Leas Cross programme as "an understandable pre-emptive course of action".

[34.3.18] The judge tempered this by stating the fact that it may be understandable does not, of course, mean that it necessarily follows that it is justified or that its being understandable is decisive in relation to balancing the rights and interests involved in a prior restraint application. It was furthermore necessary to consider the legitimate public interest raised by the programme to which the court had already attributed very significant weight. Clarke J emphasised that on similar facts, but in circumstances where the material sought to be broadcast did not involve issues of significant public interest, the balancing exercise might well have resulted in the balance favouring prior restraint.

[34.3.19] Finally, as to the adequacy of damages in lieu of an injunctive order, if the accusations contained in the programme which it was intended would be broadcast by RTÉ were ultimately borne out to be correct, then any breach of privacy involved in obtaining confirmatory information which established the truth of significant accusations in the legitimate public domain would necessarily give rise to small (or even nominal) damages, which damages would clearly be an adequate remedy.

[34.3.20] Moreover, so as not to endorse unlawful filmmaking, the court was at pains to cite the Court of Appeal's conclusion in *Fahey* and to affirm that it represents the position in this jurisdiction also:

> Our decision in this case should not be seen as supporting any general proposition that the ends of news gathering justify the means. If information has been obtained in circumstances which are at least arguably unlawful that would be an important factor to weigh in the balancing exercise involved. Such unlawfulness may amount to an offence, or it may constitute a civil wrong. The more serious the breach, the stronger will be the case for restraining use of any material obtained as a result. The courts will be careful to ensure that the rights of others are properly weighed and that the media is not simply provided with an incentive to engage in and benefit from unlawful conduct whenever it claims it is acting in the exercise of freedom of expression.

[34.3.21] Hence, any claim to an entitlement to broadcast or publish material which has, arguably, been unlawfully obtained, on the basis of a legitimate public interest will necessarily result in the court's exercising significant scrutiny over the public interest asserted. Here, Clarke J was more than satisfied that RTÉ had shown that there were very real, significant and weighty public interest issues involved. For those reasons, the court refused to grant an interlocutory injunction and thus declined to restrain the subject broadcast.

Appendix

JIH v News Group Newspapers Ltd[36]

(SUMMARY BY LORD NEUBERGER MR OF THE PRINCIPLES THAT APPLY IN THE UK WHENEVER A CLAIMANT SEEKS AN ANONYMITY ORDER OR OTHER RESTRAINT ON PUBLICATION OF DETAILS OF A CASE THAT WOULD NORMALLY BE IN THE PUBLIC DOMAIN)

(1) The general rule is that the names of the parties to an action are included in orders and judgments of the court.

(2) There is no general exception for cases where private matters are in issue.

(3) An order for anonymity or any other order restraining the publication of the normally reportable details of a case is a derogation from the principle of open justice and an interference with the Article 10[37] rights of the public at large.

(4) Accordingly, where the court is asked to make any such order, it should only do so after closely scrutinising the application, and considering whether a degree of restraint on publication is necessary, and, if it is, whether there is any less restrictive or more acceptable alternative than that which is sought.

(5) Where the court is asked to restrain the publication of the names of the parties and/or the subject matter of the claim, on the ground that such restraint is necessary under Article 8, the question is whether there is sufficient general, public interest in publishing a report of the proceedings which identifies a party and/or the normally reportable details to justify any resulting curtailment of his right and his family's right to respect for their private and family life.

(6) On any such application, no special treatment should be accorded to public figures or celebrities: in principle, they are entitled to the same protection as others, no more and no less.

(7) An order for anonymity or for reporting restrictions should not be made simply because the parties consent: parties cannot waive the rights of the public.

(8) An anonymity order or any other order restraining publication made by a Judge at an interlocutory stage of an injunction application does not last for the duration of the proceedings but must be reviewed at the return date.

---

36 [2011] EWCA Civ 42.

37 Of the European Convention on Human Rights.

(9) Whether or not an anonymity order or an order restraining publication of normally reportable details is made, then, at least where a judgment is or would normally be given, a publicly available judgment should normally be given, and a copy of the consequential court order should also be publicly available, although some editing of the judgment or order may be necessary.

(10) Notice of any hearing should be given to the defendant unless there is a good reason not to do so, in which case the court should be told of the absence of notice and the reason for it, and should be satisfied that the reason is a good one.

Chapter 35

Privacy, Breach of Confidence and Parental Consent

INTRODUCTION

[35.1.01] The protection of personality rights applies to traditional and online media in the manner in which they publish images of celebrities. It also pertains to the entertainment and audiovisual sector in terms of using one's image in a commercial or for other promotional purposes, filming a public figure's private affairs, or using one's words, performance or images in a theatre play, stage show, music video, documentary, television production or feature film.

[35.1.02] In terms of privacy law, to illuminate a producer's potential exposure in the case of wrongful disclosure of private information, in legal proceedings filed in 1992 relating to *Madonna: Truth or Dare*, a docufiction chronicling the life of Madonna during her Blonde Ambition World Tour in 1990, three dancers claimed damages *inter alia* for invasion of privacy and intentional infliction of emotional distress for displaying the men's private lives (and exposing their homosexuality as regards two claimants) in the documentary. The suit against Madonna, her production company and the distributors claimed the three men had been shown in 'non-performance' scenes discussing intimate facts about their personal lives, making them the subject of contempt and ridicule. The defence countered that all participants had signed releases and the dancers willingly consented to being filmed in the knowledge that cameras would be rolling at all stages. The matter was settled in 1994 and the proceedings were dismissed.

[35.1.03] In Ireland, there is no legal right to exert control over the use of one's own image. This is also the case in the UK.[1] Other than data protection laws that also govern capturing of faces on film, which protections have been bolstered by the EU GDPR, and the criminalisation of sharing intimate images without one's consent contrary to the Harassment, Harmful Communications and Related

1 Note as regards privacy generally, the House of Lords in *Campbell* discussed below stated *per* Lord Nicholls (dissenting), "In this country, unlike the United States of America, there is no over-arching, all-embracing cause of action for 'invasion of privacy': see *Wainwright v Home Office* [2003] 3 WLR 1137. But protection of various aspects of privacy is a fast developing area of the law, here and in some other common law jurisdictions". However, some of the Law Lords did explicitly refer to the right to privacy throughout the judgment.

Offences Act 2020 ('Coco's Law', as commenced in February 2021), neither jurisdiction has a law prohibiting the unauthorised use of a person's image, name or likeness by a third party.[2] However, the European Convention on Human Rights provides[3] that all persons, subject to express exceptions,[4] have the right to respect for their private and family life, home and correspondence.[5] This was made manifest in the landmark ruling in the first of the Princess Caroline of Monaco cases (her subsequent two cases were not successful and freedom of the press prevailed). Likewise, the Constitution[6] does not specifically set out a right to privacy[7] but the courts recognise that the Arts 40 to 44 personal rights

---

2 Yet, copyright law may be invoked where a celebrity, for example, has obtained the copyright in a photograph of himself from the author. Further, where a photograph or film has been commissioned for private and domestic purposes, that person has the right to prevent copies of the work being issued or communicated to the public. Second, the tort of misuse of private information (see *PJS v News Group Newspapers Ltd* as discussed at [34.2.11]) can be used to protect individuals from unauthorised publishing of images or other information about them. The information must be private and the individual must have a reasonable expectation of privacy in relation to the information. This right flows from Art 8 of the European Convention on Human Rights. The courts have interpreted this as allowing the publishing of private information where it is in the public interest (but not simply where the public is interested in the information). See also paras 37 to 39 of the judgment of Warby J relating to the English High Court case in *HRH Duchess of Sussex v Associated Newspapers Ltd* [2020] EWHC 1058 (Ch) (discussion on whether the motives of a publisher are entirely irrelevant to a breach of privacy claim even where malice has been pleaded). Third, breach of confidence laws are similar to the tort of misuse of private information but are more likely to be appropriate where there is a commercial aspect to the information such as the principles at bar in the *Douglas v Hello!* decision – see [18.1.24]. As with misuse of private information, information may be published where it is in the public interest. In Ireland, breach of confidence was recognised by Butler J in *Carey v Independent News & Media Plc* [2021] IEHC 229 where she took into account the fact that a claim of confidentiality of "a type to which the law attaches great significance" had been made.

3 In Art 8(1) thereof.

4 As set out in Art 8(2), that is, is in accordance with the law and as is necessary in a democratic society in the interests of national security, public safety or the economic wellbeing of the country, for the prevention of disorder or crime, for the protection of health or morals, or for the protection of the rights and freedoms of others.

5 In 1981, Taoiseach Charles Haughey ordered his Justice Minister, Seán Doherty, to tap the phones of journalists Bruce Arnold, Geraldine Kennedy and Vincent Browne to ascertain who was leaking damaging government secrets to the press. In 1992, Doherty revealed that Haughey ordered the phone-taps and he was forced to resign. In October 2001, the Taoiseach, Bertie Ahern, apologised on behalf of Fianna Fáil for invading the journalists' privacy and for the unacceptable state interference.

6 The term "human rights" is not used in the Constitution. However, Arts 40 to 44 make mention of fundamental rights. The fundamental rights in the Constitution are, in effect, human rights principles by a different name.

7 Privacy and confidentiality rights (as well as journalistic privilege) fell briefly for discussion in an application for discovery by businessman Dermot Desmond pertaining to documents leaked from the Panamanian legal firm Mossack Fonseca in 2016, the much publicised 'Panama Papers', which discovery proceedings culminated in a February 2020 High Court decision of Collins J, *Desmond v The Irish Times Ltd* [2020] IEHC 95. In *Carey v Independent News & Media Plc* [2021] IEHC 229 (Butler J), the proceedings related to the fundamental right to privacy and confidentiality of a person the subject of a Garda investigation. Elsewhere, subsequent to solicitor Gerald Kean's successful

imply the right to privacy,[8] a right which is not absolute, namely, privacy rights may be limited or restricted by legislation in the interests of the common good, public order and morality.

[35.1.04] The right to privacy was first recognised in this jurisdiction in *McGee v Attorney General*[9] (concerning the then illegal importation of contraceptives). Walsh J in the Supreme Court held that "Article 41 of the Constitution guarantees the husband and wife against...invasion of their privacy by the State". In *Kennedy v Ireland*,[10] Hamilton P held in this case concerning the tapping of the plaintiff political journalists' telephone conversations by the state that the right to privacy was one of the unenumerated rights recognised by Art 40.3 of the Constitution.

Court of Appeal in Nolan

[35.1.05] More recently, the plaintiff/respondent in *Nolan v Sunday Newspapers Ltd*[11] commenced proceedings seeking an award of damages for defamation against the *Sunday World* newspaper because he considered that his good name and reputation had been seriously traduced in two separate editions of that newspaper on 15 July 2012 and again on 3 March 2013. He also claimed damages in respect of breaches of his constitutional right to privacy. Peart J for the Court of Appeal held (at para 36) that he found no basis for interfering with the trial judge's conclusion that it was the erroneous reporting of the respondent as the organiser of sex parties that caused injury to Mr Nolan's reputation and good name. The articles in question were salacious in nature and were accompanied by photographs of the respondent attending what were described as sex parties or "swingers" parties in the company of "scantily clad" females. The court awarded €200,000 for general damages for defamation as well €30,000 for punitive damages and €30,000 for exemplary damages. It made a further award of €50,000 damages for breach of the respondent's constitutional right to privacy.

[35.1.06] Peart J stated at para 87 it was not known who owned the photographs; it was implicit that the photographs would never be published in a newspaper without the consent of the other attendees who could be identified; the photographs were not taken in the public arena; and the plaintiff's consent to the photographs being taken did not amount to a waiver of his right of privacy in

---

defamation proceedings in May 2019 wherein he was awarded €160,000 by the jury (the majority finding that an article headed "Kean Caught up in CAB probe" meant Mr Kean was the subject of a probe by CAB into the criminal activities of the Hutch and Kinahan Dublin crime gangs following the Regency Hotel shootings of February 2016 and which accordingly defamed him), the matter was adjourned for when the judge was due to deal with a separate claim alleging that the article breached Kean's constitutional right to privacy. However, this claim was settled.

8 For example, one's private written communications and telephone conversations cannot be deliberately, consciously and unjustifiably interfered with.

9 [1974] IR 284.

10 [1987] IR 587.

11 [2019] IECA 141.

respect of those photographs. He concluded that they were private photographs taken for a private purpose which were never intended to be made public. He also found that the defendant was aware that the publication of the photographs was an invasion of the plaintiff's privacy as it had pixelated the faces of the other persons in the photographs and knew that Nolan did not consent to the publication of the photographs.

[35.1.07] In respect of photographs not taken in the public arena, the judgment of Kearns P in *Hickey v Sunday Newspapers Ltd*[12] noted that it was:

> …far from easy to determine where the parameters to the right of privacy may lie when placed in balance with the right of freedom of expression. One intuitively feels that a right of privacy is less easily established in public places where a person, in the words of T.S. Eliot, has had time "to prepare a face to meet the facers that you meet".

In *Hickey* the plaintiff was photographed with her son coming out of the Registry of Births, Deaths and Marriages on Lombard Street in Dublin. The photographs were taken when the photographer and plaintiffs were in a public place and performing a routine public function. There could be no expectation of privacy in that instance. That is not to say of course that photographs taken in public places are immune from suit. For audiovisual productions, clearance of photographs intended to be used should be considered as part of a thorough pre-broadcast legal review.

EUROPEAN CONVENTION ON HUMAN RIGHTS

[35.2.01] The European Convention on Human Rights ('the ECHR') is an international treaty to protect human rights and fundamental freedoms in Europe which established the European Court of Human Rights ('the ECtHR'). Any persons who feel their convention rights have been violated by a contracting party state can take a case to the ECtHR. Therefore, subjects of a documentary could initiate proceedings where the programme veers into violation of those individuals' privacy (such as revealing personal information obtained without the subjects' consent) and the country in which the persons reside, if a party to the ECHR, without justification, fails to recognise and vindicate their right to privacy in the courts, in statute or under national constitutional law. This was the position constitutionally in Germany in the first Princess Caroline case discussed below where the court found that, on the facts of that particular matter, freedom of the press was given precedence over the right to privacy. The ECtHR thus found against Germany which failed to vindicate the complainant's privacy rights under the ECHR.

12 [2010] IEHC 349 as referred to in David Kavanagh, *Photographs and Privacy – when does an expectation of privacy arise?* (2019), dilloneustace.com. Available at: https://www.dilloneustace.com/legal-updates/photographs-and-privacy-when-does-an-expectation-of-privacy-arise [Accessed 30 April 2023].

[35.2.02] Judgments of the court are legally binding on the state parties who must take measures to rectify the impugned matter. The court has the power to award damages but the amounts awarded are usually small in comparison to Irish court awards of compensation. Certain criteria apply to applications to the court, the most important of which is that a claimant must first exhaust all domestic remedies available such as those through the Irish judicial system.

UK decisions and the ECHR

[35.2.03] In *Theakston v MGN Ltd*[13] the High Court considered the scope of Art 8 ECHR when considering whether there had been a breach of confidence and breach of the right to privacy under that article in circumstances where the defendant had published photographs of the claimant, a BBC television and radio presenter, visiting a brothel in Mayfair, London. Theakston argued that the publication of the story breached his right to privacy under Art 8, that the activities had taken place in private and therefore should be treated as confidential and that there was no public interest in the publication. The *Sunday People* argued that the publication of the story was in the public interest given the concern of the BBC to ensure that presenters of programmes aimed at younger people conduct themselves appropriately in public.

[35.2.04] On 26 January 2002 Ouseley J granted an injunction to the claimant preventing the defendant from publishing photographs of the claimant inside the brothel. He refused to grant an injunction preventing the *Sunday People* from publishing an article the next day which stated that the claimant had visited a Mayfair brothel on the night of 18 to 19 December 2001 and had engaged thereat in a variety of sexual activities with three prostitutes (with one on the claimant's evidence). At the conclusion of the hearing, close to the publication deadline, the court gave a brief judgment as requested, to be followed by a fuller judgment.

[35.2.05] The court considered the material published under three headings: the fact of the claimant's attendance at the brothel; the detail of the activities; and the photographs. As to the first, he doubted whether confidence or the protection of Art 8 extended to the claimant's activities in the brothel: even if he did have rights to privacy, this was outweighed by the Art 10 (freedom of expression) rights of the newspaper. As to the second, he did not consider that the details of transient sexual relations between an unmarried man and a prostitute were confidential, and that the press's right to freedom of expression would probably defeat any injunction application at trial. However, an injunction was granted in respect of the third issue, the publication of the photographs, on the basis that freedom of expression was outweighed by the "peculiar degree of intrusion into the integrity of the claimant's personality" by their publication.[14]

---

13 [2002] EWHC 137.

14 At para 79 of the judgment.

Naomi Campbell

[35.2.06] Also in 2002, in *Campbell v MGN Ltd*,[15] supermodel claimant Naomi Campbell succeeded in her claim for damages for breach of confidence (misuse of private information) and compensation for breach of the (UK) Data Protection Act 1998 following the *Daily Mirror*'s publication of articles with accompanying photographs of her attending Narcotics Anonymous ('NA') meetings. The plaintiff claimed she suffered distress, embarrassment and anxiety which were aggravated by later publications in the *Mirror* and the defendant's conduct of the trial. The articles asserted that, contrary to her previous false assertions, she was in fact a drug addict and that she was attending meetings of NA to overcome her addiction. Some details of those meetings were published in the paper together with photographs of her leaving a meeting in Chelsea.

[35.2.07] In respect of the breach of confidence claim, the High Court court *per* Morland J considered that the details of the claimant's attendance at the meetings had the necessary quality of confidence, given that they were identifiable as private and a reasonable person of ordinary sensibilities would find their disclosure highly offensive. The court stated that the media should respect information about the private lives of celebrities or public figures which the individuals legitimately chose to keep private, as well as sensitive personal data, unless there is an overriding public interest duty to publish the information. Morland J made a modest award of £2,500 plus £1,000 aggravated damages in respect of both claims. The newspaper appealed. The Court of Appeal[16] allowed the appeal and discharged the trial judge's order. Campbell then appealed to the House of Lords.[17]

Breach of confidence / misuse of private information[18]

[35.2.08] The history of this tort (originally an action via equity proceedings rather than in the common law courts) is summarised by Lord Nicholls (dissenting with Lord Hoffman) when he stated at paras 13 and 14:

> 13. The common law or, more precisely, courts of equity have long afforded protection to the wrongful use of private information by means of the cause of

---

15 [2002] EWHC 499.

16 [2002] EWCA Civ 1373; [2003] QB 633.

17 [2004] UKHL 22.

18 Also termed unauthorised disclosure of personal information. See *Mosley v News Group Newspapers* [2008] EWHC 1777 (QB), and *McKennitt v Ash* in which Loreena McKennitt, a Canadian world music singer, sued in England to prevent publication of extracts of a book written by a former friend on the grounds of privacy (Art 8) and breach of confidence. In 2005 her former friend and employee, Niema Ash, intended to publish a book which contained intimate details of their friendship. McKennitt argued that much of the book contained confidential personal information which Ash had no right or authority to publish. The High Court found that there had been a breach of confidence and a misuse of McKennitt's private information. The Court of Appeal upheld this finding ([2006] EWCA Civ 1714).

> action which became known as breach of confidence. A breach of confidence was restrained as a form of unconscionable conduct, akin to a breach of trust. Today this nomenclature is misleading. The breach of confidence label harks back to the time when the cause of action was based on improper use of information disclosed by one person to another in confidence. To attract protection the information had to be of a confidential nature. But the gist of the cause of action was that information of this character had been disclosed by one person to another in circumstances 'importing an obligation of confidence' even though no contract of non-disclosure existed: see the classic exposition by Megarry J in *Coco v A N Clark (Engineers) Ltd* [1969] RPC 41, 47-48. The confidence referred to in the phrase 'breach of confidence' was the confidence arising out of a confidential relationship.
>
> 14. This cause of action has now firmly shaken off the limiting constraint of the need for an initial confidential relationship. In doing so it has changed its nature. In this country this development was recognised clearly in the judgment of Lord Goff of Chieveley in *Attorney-General v Guardian Newspapers Ltd (No 2)* [1990] 1 AC 109, 281. Now the law imposes a ‹duty of confidence› whenever a person receives information he knows or ought to know is fairly and reasonably to be regarded as confidential. Even this formulation is awkward. The continuing use of the phrase ‹duty of confidence› and the description of the information as ‹confidential› is not altogether comfortable. Information about an individual›s private life would not, in ordinary usage, be called ‹confidential›. The more natural description today is that such information is private. The essence of the tort is better encapsulated now as misuse of private information.

[35.2.09] Lord Nicholls went on to state that ECHR and the Strasbourg jurisprudence undoubtedly had wielded a significant influence in this area of the common law for some years and that, "The time has come to recognise that the values enshrined in articles 8 and 10 are now part of the cause of action for breach of confidence".[19]

[35.2.10] Ultimately, the majority (Lady Hale, Lord Hope and Lord Carswell) ruled in favour of Campbell, thus allowing the appeal and restoring the orders that were made by the trial judge. It was sufficiently established by the nature of the material that it was private information which attracted the duty of observing the confidence in which it was imparted to the respondents.

[35.2.11] Lady Hale ruled that the need for treatment for drug addicts was more important than the right of the public to know about it. She noted that the publication of the details of the appellant's course of treatment at NA and of the photographs taken surreptitiously in the street of her emerging from a meeting went significantly beyond the publication of the fact that she was receiving therapy or that she was engaged in a course of therapy with NA. It revealed where the treatment was taking place and the text detailed the frequency of her treatment. In this way it intruded into what had some of the characteristics of medical treatment and it tended to deter her from continuing the treatment

---

19 *supra* at fn 17 (at para 17 of the judgment).

which was in her interest and also to inhibit other persons attending the course from staying with it, when they might be concerned that their participation might become public knowledge.

[35.2.12] Likewise, Lord Carswell found it appropriate to hold that the information and the photographs went significantly beyond the revelation that the appellant was a drug addict and was engaged in drug therapy. He considered that it constituted such an intrusion into the appellant's private affairs that the factors relied upon by respondents did not suffice to justify publication. He was further unable to accept that the publication was necessary to maintain the newspaper's credibility. Meanwhile, Lord Hope ruled at para 124 of the court's judgment thus:

> 124. Any person in Miss Campbell's position, assuming her to be of ordinary sensibilities but assuming also that she had been photographed surreptitiously outside the place where she had been receiving therapy for drug addiction, would have known what they were and would have been distressed on seeing the photographs. She would have seen their publication, in conjunction with the article which revealed what she had been doing when she was photographed and other details about her engagement in the therapy, as a gross interference with her right to respect for her private life. In my opinion this additional element in the publication is more than enough to outweigh the right to freedom of expression which the defendants are asserting in this case.

[35.2.13] The above two celebrity cases demonstrate some judicial reluctance to establish a right to privacy as a separate cause of action in UK law. Instead, the courts have absorbed the right to personal privacy under Art 8 of the ECHR into the tort of breach of confidence.

[35.2.14] In July 2018, Sir Cliff Richard was awarded £210,000 in general damages after the BBC was held liable[20] for infringing his privacy rights over the filming and broadcast of a search of his property by the South Yorkshire Police in relation to allegations of historical child sexual abuse. The legendary performer had not been arrested or charged over the allegations, and the investigation was subsequently dropped by the Crown Prosecution Service due to insufficient evidence. Mr Justice Mann ruled that the singer had a reasonable expectation of privacy against both the police and the BBC. Consequently, his rights to privacy under Art 8 (as legislated for in English law by the Human Rights Act 1998) were engaged both when his home was searched and when that information was provided to the BBC by the police. Such rights were not outweighed by the BBC's Art 10 rights.

[35.2.15] After consideration of the damage to the singer's reputation, finances and health by the infringement of his right to privacy, the court arrived at the

[20] *Richard v The British Broadcasting Corporation* [2018] EWHC 1837 (Ch).

£210,000 award of damages. Mann J refused leave to appeal by the BBC on the grounds that such appeal had no real prospect of success.

IRELAND AND THE INTERNATIONAL CONTEXT

[35.3.01] The national courts in Ireland are responsible for determining allegations of human rights violations. Although Ireland has ratified a number of international human rights treaties, an individual can only invoke the protections afforded under human rights law which have been incorporated into national law, such as for example the rights protected under the Constitution, the European Convention of Human Rights Acts 2003 and 2014, and where EU law is applicable, the EU Charter of Fundamental Rights. This is because Art 29.6 of the Constitution states that no international agreement shall be part of the domestic law of the state save as may be provided by the Oireachtas. As a result, although Ireland binds itself in international law upon ratifying a human rights treaty, it only gives effect to the provisions of that treaty in domestic law through Acts of parliament, or where a treaty right is already provided for under the Irish Constitution.

[34.3.02] The lack of incorporation does not, however, mean that these standards cannot be raised in legal argument. For instance, the Irish courts can and have attached a form of persuasive authority to unincorporated international human rights instruments.[21] On exhausting all domestic remedies, it may then be open to an individual to make a complaint to a regional or international human rights body. As discussed above, at a regional level, individuals can make complaints to the ECtHR.

IRISH LEGISLATION

[35.4.01] By virtue of the European Convention on Human Rights Act 2003 ('the 2003 Act'), Irish courts are obliged to interpret Irish laws in a manner that gives effect to Ireland's obligations under the ECHR. Organs of state (such as government ministers and state bodies) are also obliged to act in compliance with the Convention. The provisions of the ECHR do not directly come into Irish law by virtue of this European legislation. Rather, its provisions have only been partially or indirectly introduced in this jurisdiction.

[35.4.02] Section 4 of the 2003 Act provides that judicial notice shall be taken of ECHR provisions and any declaration, decision, advisory opinion or judgment of the ECtHR[22] on any question in respect of which that court has jurisdiction,

---

21 In addition, certain international human rights conventions to which Ireland is a party have individual complaints mechanisms. See for example United Nations Human Rights Office of the High Commissioner at http://www.ohchr.org/EN/HRBodies/TBPetitions/Pages/HRTBPetitions.aspx.

22 And any decision or opinion of the European Commission of Human Rights and any

and a national court shall, when interpreting and applying ECHR provisions, take due account of the principles laid down by those declarations, decisions, advisory opinions, opinions and judgments.

[35.4.03] Section 5, as amended by the Court of Appeal Act 2014, provides that in any proceedings, the High Court and the Court of Appeal/Supreme Court when exercising their appellate jurisdiction, may, having regard to the provisions of s 2, on application to it in that behalf by a party, or of its own motion, and where no other legal remedy is adequate and available, make a declaration (referred to in the 2003 Act as "a declaration of incompatibility") that a statutory provision or rule of law is incompatible with the state's obligations under ECHR provisions.

PRINCESS CAROLINE OF MONACO AND THE TABLOID PRESS

[35.5.01] Three cases have come before the ECtHR in Strasbourg in respect of the private and family life of Princess Caroline Von Hannover, officially residing in Monaco but living primarily in Paris. As a member of the royal family, the applicant was president of certain humanitarian or cultural foundations but did not perform any function within or on behalf of the State of Monaco or any of its institutions. The princess' first action was successful with the court ruling in her favour in 2004. In the subsequent two actions, no violations by Germany (where the privacy breaches were alleged to have taken place) were held to have occurred.

[35.5.02] The applicant had made repeated attempts to prevent the publication in the tabloid press of photographs portraying her private life. Two series of photographs, published in 1993 and 1997, were the subject of three sets of proceedings before the German courts. The princess had on several occasions unsuccessfully applied to the German courts for an injunction preventing any further publication of the photographs that had appeared in the German magazines *Bunte*, *Freizeit Revue*, *7 Tage* and *Neue Post*. She claimed that they infringed her right to privacy and her right to control the use of her image. The photographs showed the princess and her children involved in such innocuous activities as walking, skiing, horse-riding, cycling, shopping, playing tennis and dining in a restaurant.

[35.5.03] In a landmark judgment in 1999, the German Federal Constitutional Court granted the princess an injunction regarding some of the photographs in which she appeared with her children, on the ground that the need for protection of their intimacy was greater than that of adults. However, the Constitutional Court considered that the princess, who is undeniably a contemporary public

---

decision of the Committee of Ministers established under the Statute of the Council of Europe.

figure, must countenance the publication of photographs of herself in a public place, even if they showed her in scenes from her daily life rather than engaged in her official duties. The court explained that her right to privacy was overridden by the freedom of the press and the public's legitimate interest in learning how such a person generally behaved in public.

[35.5.04] Those proceedings were the subject of the ECtHR's judgment of 24 June 2004 in *Von Hannover v Germany*,[23] in which the seven-judge court unanimously held that the German Constitutional Court decisions in question had infringed the applicant's art 8 right to respect for her private life. The publishing of paparazzi photographs taken of the princess in a public place was a violation of her right to privacy, signalling an expectation that courts throughout Europe would be encouraged to take a stronger line over the publishing of images of celebrities who do not have official functions or who do not seek public attention.

[35.5.05] When giving his concurring judgment, Judge Zupančič, concerned that the German courts had made a "fetish of the freedom of the press", expressed the time had come for the pendulum to swing to a different kind of balance between "what is private and secluded and what is public and unshielded". The publication of the photographs was found to infringe the applicant's Art 8 rights.

[35.5.06] The status quo, heralded as a victory for the protection of public figures' privacy rights, underwent a sea change with *Von Hannover (No. 2)* in 2012. The photograph in question here showed Princess Caroline and her husband on their skiing holiday in St Moritz. It accompanied an article describing the ill-health of her father, Prince Rainier III, the then reigning sovereign of Monaco. This time, the court agreed with the German courts' analysis and held that the publication, and supporting photograph, contributed to a debate of general interest. Significantly, the judgment set out five criteria (as were applied in the third case as discussed next) relevant to balancing competing Art 8 and Art 10 rights.

[35.5.07] The case of *Von Hannover v Germany (No. 3)* was the third time, since 2004, that Princess Caroline Von Hannover had complained to the ECtHR of failures by the German courts to prevent the publication of photographs which she claimed depicted her engaged in private activities. The publication at issue in *Von Hannover (No. 3)* dated from 20 March 2002. The German magazine *7 Tage* published an article relating to the trend among celebrities of renting out their holiday homes. It described in detail the Von Hannover family villa, located on an island off the Kenyan coast, setting out the furnishings, daily rental cost and activities in the area. The article featured alongside several photographs of the villa, as well as one photograph showing Princess Caroline and her husband

---

23 [2004] ECHR 294.

on holiday in an unidentifiable location. The unsuccessful challenge brought by the princess related to the latter photograph only. The court's judgment on 19 September 2013 followed a six-year appeal process in the German courts.

[35.5.08] The court unanimously held that the German Federal Court's refusal to grant an injunction prohibiting any further publication of the photograph did not constitute a breach of the applicant's privacy rights as enshrined in Art 8. The court applied the five considerations below as set out in *Von Hannover (No. 2)* and *Axel Springer AG*[24] for balancing the right to respect for private life against the right to freedom of expression.

Whether the information contributes to a debate of general interest

[35.5.09] The purpose of the article was to relay the trend among celebrities of renting their holiday homes. This could generate reactions and a dialogue among readers, thereby contributing to a debate of general interest. The court concluded that the German courts' qualification of the subject as an event of contemporary society "could therefore not be described as unreasonable". The court further remarked the text gave practically no details relating to the private life of the applicant and her husband, focusing instead on the characteristics of the Von Hannover villa.

The notoriety of the person concerned

[35.5.10] The court restated that the applicant and her husband must be regarded as public figures, unable to claim the same protection for their private life as ordinary private individuals.

The prior conduct of the person concerned

[35.5.11] The court raised the point made by the applicant that the German courts had failed to explicitly consider her efforts to keep her private life out of the press, as manifested by previous legal actions. The court, however, found that the German courts' reasoning indicated that this had been considered in substance. This, the ECtHR concluded, constituted sufficient consideration for the purpose of balancing the competing interests at stake.

Content, form and consequences of the publication

[35.5.12] The court noted that the German courts had designated the picture as being of "little format" and not of itself capable of constituting a violation of Art 8.

---

24 *Axel Springer AG v Germany* [2012] ECHR 227.

The circumstances in which the photograph was taken[25]

[35.5.13] Finally, the court observed that Princess Caroline had failed to adduce evidence before the German courts that the photograph had been taken surreptitiously or by equivalent means. The court concluded that the circumstances therefore did not require a more thorough examination as the applicant had not put forward any particular circumstances before the domestic courts so as to justify prohibiting publication of the photograph.

[35.5.14] Overall, the court considered that the German courts had given due consideration to the five criteria for the balancing exercise of freedom of the press versus the right to privacy. In these circumstances, and having regard to the margin of appreciation enjoyed by contracting states, the court unanimously concluded that the German courts had complied with their positive obligations under Art 8. Accordingly, there had been no violation of that provision in relation to Princess Caroline. This decision in *Von Hannover (No. 3)* endows publishers with substantially greater protection than its predecessor (*No. 1*) did. Publishers now need only show that the article contributes to a debate of general interest, not how or why the photograph in question supports such a contribution.

Analysis

[35.5.15] The judgment offers a clear example of the court's increasingly light-touch approach to reviewing privacy challenges since *Von Hannover (No. 2)*. Where the balancing exercise has been undertaken in conformity with the criteria laid down in ECtHR case law, the court will require strong reasons to substitute its view for that of the domestic courts.

[35.5.16] The outcome in *Von Hannover (No. 3)* follows the momentum of the pendulum swinging back towards freedom of the press in *Von Hannover (No. 2)*. Little is left of the comparatively austere legacy of the first Von Hannover ruling, in which Princess Caroline was held to be a private figure and her daily business not to contribute to an event of contemporary society. The court's deference to national courts in *Von Hannover (No. 3)* and the manner in which it glossed over the need for a link between articles of general interest and the photographs which accompany them highlight this shift.

THE *SPRINGER*[26] PRINCIPLES

[35.6.01] The applicant company in these ECtHR proceedings was the publisher of a national daily newspaper in Germany which in September 2004 published a front page article about the star of a popular television series who had been arrested at the Munich beer festival for possession of cocaine. In July 2005, the

---

25 Namely, the method of obtaining the information and its veracity.

26 *supra* at fn 24.

newspaper had published a second article, reporting that the actor had been convicted of unlawful possession of drugs following a full confession and had been fined. The actor applied for and obtained an injunction restraining publication of the second article on essentially the same grounds as for the first. That judgment was upheld on appeal. The applicant company was later ordered to pay two penal payments of €5,000 in respect of subsequent breaches of that injunction.

[35.6.02] It was held by the ECtHR however in respect of Art 10 that the domestic courts' decisions had constituted interference with the applicant company's right to freedom of expression. The court went on to determine whether the interference had been necessary in a democratic society. Applying the criteria it had established in its case law for balancing the right to freedom of expression against the right to respect for private life, the court noted, firstly, that the published articles concerned the arrest and conviction of an actor, that is, public judicial facts that could be considered to present a degree of general interest. Second, the actor was sufficiently well known to qualify as a public figure and, even though the nature of the offence was such that it would probably not have been reported on had it been committed by an ordinary individual, the fact that the actor had been arrested in public and had actively sought the limelight by revealing details about his private life in a number of interviews, meant that his legitimate expectation that his private life would be effectively protected was reduced.

[35.6.03] As regards how the information was obtained and whether it was reliable, the first article about the actor's arrest had a sufficient factual basis as it was grounded on information provided by the public prosecutor's office and the truth of the information in both articles was not in dispute between the parties. The applicant company had not acted in bad faith: not only had it received confirmation of the information from the prosecuting authorities, there was nothing to suggest that it had not undertaken a balancing exercise between its interest in publishing and the actor's right to respect for his private life before concluding, in the light of all the circumstances, that it did not have sufficiently strong grounds for believing it should preserve the actor's anonymity.

[35.6.04] As to the content, form and consequences of the publications, the articles had not revealed details about the actor's private life, but had mainly concerned the circumstances of his arrest and the outcome of the criminal proceedings. There had been no disparaging comments or unsubstantiated allegations. Nor had it been shown that the publication of the articles had resulted in serious consequences for the actor.

[35.6.05] As regards the final criterion, while the sanctions imposed on the applicant company were lenient, they had nevertheless been capable of having a chilling effect and were not justified in the light of the factors referred to above. Accordingly, the restrictions imposed on the company had not been reasonably proportionate to the legitimate aim of protecting the actor's private life. The court (12 votes to five) concluded there had been a violation of the paper's rights and ordered €17,734.28 in respect of pecuniary damage, corresponding to penalties and costs incurred in the domestic proceedings less the two penalty payments already made of €5,000.

FURTHER CASE LAW

[35.7.01] In *Einarsson v Iceland*[27] the ECtHR overturned a decision of the Iceland Supreme Court and upheld a well-known commentator's right to respect for his private life under Art 8 of the ECHR in the context of an Instagram post accusing him of rape. In terms of the third leg of the *Springer* principles, in considering whether the publication was a statement of fact or a value judgment,[28] the court found that the factual context in which the impugned statement was made and its allegation that Mr Einarsson was a "rapist" after the discontinuation of criminal proceedings against him had not been adequately taken into account by the national court.

[35.7.02] This can be contrasted with *Tamiz v UK*[29] in which the court reinforced the importance of freedom of expression in the context of online forums. In that case, vulgar comments posted on a blog operated by Google (including that a politician was a "violent racist") were held to be too trivial in character and not distributed widely enough to pose a risk to the applicant's reputation (Art 8) to warrant restricting the freedom of expression of Google and its users (Art 10). It was highlighted that comments of this nature were common on the internet and, as a politician, Tamiz was expected to tolerate them.

[35.7.03] However, a decision in July 2019 by the ECtHR found that Spanish journalists infringed upon Mexican singer Paulina Rubio's privacy rights by publishing information about her private sex life, reversing an almost decade-old decision by the Spanish Supreme Court. In 2005, Rubio sued a number of Spanish television stations and her former manager after the stations broadcast an interview with the manager discussing Rubio's sexuality, specifically whether or not she was bisexual. Her claims were dismissed in 2007. The Supreme Court upheld the decision in 2009 on the basis that Rubio's "sexual tastes" were no longer a private matter. The ECtHR ruled that this violated Art 8. The court found that journalists had a duty to "weigh the impact of the information" before publishing it. Certain elements of an individual's private life should be

---

27 App no 24703/15 [2017] ECHR (7 November 2017).

28 X had published an altered version of the front page of a magazine featuring a picture of Mr Einarsson and an interview in which he commented on the rape allegations made against him (in respect of which no prosecution was brought, the police having dismissed the matter). The altered image of Einarsson included the caption "Fuck you rapist bastard". This image was published on X's personal Instagram account.

29 App no 3877/14 [2017] ECHR (12 October 2017).

treated delicately, and journalists must use caution before spreading rumors or commenting on these aspects.

"SHARENTING"

[35.8.01] In May 2020, a Dutch court[30] ordered a woman to remove photos of her grandchildren from Facebook and Pinterest after she posted the images without permission from the children's mother and persistently declined a takedown request. While GDPR rules do not normally apply to the storage of personal data within personal circles such as family, the grandmother had made the photos public without the consent of the mother (and father in the case of one child) who had legal authority over which data of her underage children could be stored and shared.[31] Furthermore, by posting photographs on social media, they were made available to a wider audience and hence it could not be ruled out that the pictures would not come into the hands of third parties. In view of such circumstances it has not become apparent in the scope of these interlocutory proceedings that the defendant had engaged in a purely personal or household activity.

[35.8.02] When Hollywood star Gwyneth Paltrow posted an Instagram selfie while skiing with her 14-year-old daughter Apple, her daughter publicly commented to her mother in view of the actor's six millon followers that, "You may not post anything without my consent". This begs the question of whether this 'sharenting' trend is potentially a problem for children as our digital footprints ripple wider and with lasting effect. Fleeting childhood moments, sometimes of the embarrassing variety with potential adverse effects on job and career opportunities, become a permanent record. In light of the GDPR (depending on the circumstances) and wider invasion of privacy considerations, parents must thus be cognisant of their childrens' right to have a voice in how their image is disseminated online.

FILMING ISSUES: CONSENTS AND RELEASES FROM MINORS AND THEIR PARENTS

[35.9.01] The importance for producers and broadcasters of parental/guardian consent for child actors and contributors to media content (and in relation to privacy consents and waivers generally)[32] was discussed in Chapters 13, 15 and 17 and the advisability for the above reasons of having teenagers sign releases as well as their parents. The ECtHR has held[33] that domestic county and appeal

---

30 *KG ZA* 20-106, C/05/368427, X v Y [2020] (Court of First Instance of Gelderland).

31 The plaintiff and her ex-partner had joint parental authority over one child while the plaintiff had sole parental authority over her two other minor children.

32 For instance it may be prudent to involve a child psychologist when the parent of a minor features in a documentary exploring adult issues (e.g. sex, substance abuse and violence).

33 *I.V.Ţ. v Romania*, App no 35582/15 [2022] ECHR (1 March 2022).

courts in Romania had breached an 11-year-old's rights under Art 8 when dismissing her claim based on the broadcast of a television interview which had been conducted without obtaining parental consent or implementing adequate measures to protect her identity. The interview, which concerned the death of a schoolmate, had resulted in her being bullied and had caused her emotional stress.

[35.9.02] Although the child's face was blurred, she was still identifiable from the broadcast. The court emphasised that parental consent was not a mere formality, but was an important safeguard for the rights of children.

[35.9.03] Even where this news report made a contribution to a public debate, the disclosure of private information (the identity of a minor who had witnessed a dramatic event) must not be such as to exceed editorial discretion without robust justification. These considerations were more important in the present case where the court expressed doubts as to the relevance to a debate of public interest of the opinions of a child who had not witnessed the event in question first hand. The ECtHR concluded that the appellate national courts had only superficially balanced the question of the applicant's right to private life and the broadcaster's right to free expression.

Chapter 36

The Press Council of Ireland and Office of the Press Ombudsman; Protection of Journalistic Sources

INTRODUCTION

[36.1.01] In 2003, a legal advisory group on defamation established by the Minister for Justice recommended in its report that the defamation laws be updated and a statutory press council formed. While the newspaper and magazine industry welcomed news that defamation legislation would be reshaped, there was significant opposition to the concept of a statutory press council, which in fact later came to pass. The industry therefore formed the Press Industry Steering Committee comprising representatives, for instance, from Irish editions of UK titles, The National Union of Journalists and the National Newspapers of Ireland.[1]

[36.1.02] The committee's key objective was to agree a model for an independent press complaints mechanism and it thus agreed a Code of Practice. Complaints to the Press Ombudsman are based on published articles thought to involve a breach of this code. When the Press Council and Press Ombudsman offices were established, the work of the steering committee ceased.[2]

[36.1.03] The Press Council is funded by a levy applied by the Administrative Committee to member publications in accordance with their circulation numbers to meet the funding requirements of the Press Council and the Office of the Press Ombudsman.

Placement on a statutory footing

[36.1.04] Section 44 of the Defamation Act 2009, which was enacted following the establishment of the Press Council in June 2007, makes reference to a Press Council and Sch 2[3] of the Act refers to the Ombudsman. Being satisfied that

---

1 The National Newspapers of Ireland became NewsBrands Ireland in 2015.

2 Press Council of Ireland, *Press Council History*. Available on: http://www.presscouncil.ie/about-the-press-council/sub-sub-1 [Accessed 14 May 2017].

3 Schedule 2 sets out the minimum requirements in relation to the Press Council such as independence of the council, directors (13 in number) of the council (now termed

the Press Council of Ireland complied with the minimum requirements specified in the said schedule, the then Minister for Justice, Equality and Law Reform, Dermot Ahern, made an order, namely, the Defamation Act 2009 (Press Council) Order 2010[4] in which it was declared that the Press Council of Ireland shall be recognised for the purposes of the Defamation Act as the Press Council.

Press Council of Ireland

[36.1.05] In terms of legal form, the Press Council was established in June 2007 under the Companies Acts 1963 to 2006 and is responsible for the oversight of the professional principles embodied in the Code of Practice of the Press Council, and with promoting and upholding freedom of the press. It operates with the support and cooperation of member journalists and publications including online-only news publications (e.g. breakingnews.ie, Evoke.ie), magazines from *Woman's Way* to *Accountancy Ireland* and numerous national, weekly, local and student publications (such as the *Irish Examiner*, *The Sunday Business Post*, *Limerick Leader* and *Trinity Film Review*). It decides on appeals from decisions of the Press Ombudsman and on complaints referred to it directly by the Press Ombudsman. It is independent of both government and media and cannot consider complaints about publications which are not members.

OFFICE OF THE PRESS OMBUDSMAN

[36.2.01] The Office of the Press Ombudsman, established in January 2008, receives complaints from members of the public concerning articles in publications which are members of the Press Council or in respect of the behaviour of journalists if the complainant feels the Code of Practice has been breached. All information in relation to the complaint should be submitted within three months of the date of publication of the article. The Office of the Press Ombudsman will, in the first instance, attempt to resolve the matter by making direct contact with the editor of the publication concerned. It will outline the complaint to the publication and seek to resolve the matter by a process of conciliation or mediation. If conciliation is not possible, the Press Ombudsman will examine the case and make a decision based on the Code of Practice.

[36.2.02] Conciliation outcomes include personal letters of apology from the editor, publishing an apology publicly, publishing a correction or clarification (for example, if words from a funeral service eulogy were misquoted, thus causing distress to a grieving family), deletion of photographs from online publications, deletion of online articles, and amending online articles. In relation to decisions of the Press Ombudsman (where conciliation has not borne fruits), complaints will either be upheld or not upheld.

---

members of the council), publications members of the council (e.g. national newspapers), and procedures to investigate and determine complaints made to the Press Ombudsman.

4 SI No 163 of 2010.

Publication of Press Council and Ombudsman decisions

[36.2.03] Principle 10 of the Code of Practice obliges member publications to publish upheld decisions with due prominence. The guidelines as to how such decisions must be published are that decisions shall be published in full; promptly; on the same page as the original article, or further forward, subject to specified exceptions;[5] on the same day of the week as the original publication; with due prominence; unedited; and without editorial commentary by way of a headline or otherwise. In addition, it should carry the Press Ombudsman logo.

[36.2.04] Decisions of the Press Council allowing appeals by complainants against decisions of the Ombudsman, or not allowing appeals by publications against decisions of the Ombudsman, shall be published as above. In addition, each should carry the joint logo of the Press Council and the Press Ombudsman. Decisions of the Press Council upholding complaints referred to it by the Ombudsman shall also be published as above, together with the logo of the Press Council.

The ten principles of the code

[36.2.05] The preamble to the code mentions that freedom of press means the right of the press to publish what it considers to be news, without fear or favour, and the right to comment upon it – but such freedom carries responsibilities. Members of the press have a duty to maintain the highest professional and ethical standards. The code sets the benchmark for those standards. It is the duty of the Ombudsman and Press Council to ensure that it is honoured in the spirit as well as in the letter.

[36.2.06] In dealing with complaints, the Ombudsman and Press Council will give consideration to what they perceive to be the public interest. It is for them to define the public interest in each case, but the general principle is that the public interest is invoked in relation to a matter capable of affecting the public at large so that it may legitimately be interested in receiving, and the print and online news media legitimately interested in providing, information about it.

---

5 Where a complaint has been upheld in relation to an article published on the front page of a publication, the decision shall be published with due prominence on one of the first four editorial pages. Upheld decisions about online articles shall be published in full (or by use of a headlined link to the decision) on the homepage or as one of the first eight stories for a period of 24 hours, after which a link to the decision with the accompanying Press Council/Press Ombudsman logo and caption must be available on the website for a further week. If the article that gave rise to the complaint remains online, it must be permanently annotated in a prominent manner with a link to the decision. See Press Council of Ireland, *Publication Guidelines* (revised June 2018). Available at: http://www.presscouncil.ie/press-council-of-ireland-1/publication-guidelines [Accessed 31 March 2022].

Principle 1: truth and accuracy

[36.2.07] In reporting news and information, the press shall strive at all times for truth and accuracy. When a significant inaccuracy, misleading statement or distorted report or picture has been published, it shall be corrected promptly and with due prominence. When appropriate, a retraction, apology, clarification, explanation or response shall be published promptly and with due prominence.

Principle 2: distinguishing fact and comment

[36.2.08] The press is entitled to advocate strongly its own views on topics. Comment, conjecture, rumour and unconfirmed reports shall not be reported as if they were fact. Readers are entitled to expect that the content of the press reflects the best judgment of editors and writers and has not been inappropriately influenced by undisclosed interests. Wherever relevant, any significant financial interest of an organisation should be disclosed. Writers should disclose significant potential conflicts of interest to their editors.

Principle 3: fair procedures and honesty

[36.2.09] The press shall strive at all times for fair procedures and honesty in the procuring and publishing of news and information. The press shall not obtain information, photographs or other material through misrepresentation or subterfuge, unless justified by the public interest. Journalists and photographers must not obtain or seek to obtain information and photographs through harassment, unless their actions are justified in the public interest.

Principle 4: respect for rights

[36.2.10] Citizens are afforded constitutional protection for their good name. The press shall not knowingly publish material based on malicious misrepresentation or unfounded accusations and must take reasonable care in fact-checking before publication.

Principle 5: privacy

[36.2.11] Privacy is a human right, protected as a personal right in the Constitution and the European Convention on Human Rights, which is incorporated into Irish law. The private and family life, home and correspondence of everyone must be respected. Taking photographs of individuals in private places without their consent is not considered acceptable, unless justified by the public interest. Readers are entitled to have news and comment presented with respect for the privacy and sensibilities of individuals. However, the right to privacy should not prevent publication of matters of public record or in the public interest.

[36.2.12] Sympathy and discretion must be shown at all times in seeking information in situations of personal grief or shock. In publishing such information, grieving families should be taken into account and how they might be affected by such disclosure (but this should not be interpreted as restricting the right to report judicial proceedings). In the reporting of suicide, excessive detail of the means of suicide should be avoided.

[36.2.13] Public persons are also entitled to privacy. However, where persons hold public office, deal with public affairs, follow a public career, or have sought or obtained publicity for their activities, publication of relevant details of their private life and circumstances may be justifiable where the information revealed relates to the validity of the persons' conduct, the credibility of their public statements, the value of their publicly expressed views or is otherwise in the public interest.

Principle 6: protection of sources

[36.2.14] Journalists must protect confidential sources of information. This principle is detailed further in the next section. By way of comparison, the US Society for Professional Journalists' Code of Ethics, for example, includes the following requirements: verification of information before releasing it; use of original sources whenever possible; identification of (non-confidential) sources clearly – the public is entitled to as much information as possible to judge the reliability and motivations of sources; consideration of sources' motives before promising anonymity; reserving anonymity for sources who may face danger, retribution or other harm; and explanation of why anonymity was granted.[6]

Principle 7: court reporting

[36.2.15] The press shall strive to ensure that court reports (including the use of images) are fair and accurate, are not prejudicial to the right to a fair trial and that the presumption of innocence is respected. The relevant issues in this connection are discussed in Chapter 33.

Principle 8: prejudice

[36.2.16] The press shall not publish material intended or likely to cause grave offence or incite hatred against an individual or group on the basis of their race, religion, nationality, colour, ethnic origin, membership of the Traveller community, gender, sexual orientation, marital status, disability, illness or age.

Principle 9: children

[36.2.17] The press shall take particular care in seeking and presenting

6 Available at https://www.spj.org/ethicscode.asp [Accessed 21 June 2021].

information or comment about a child under the age of 16. Journalists and editors should have regard for the vulnerability of children, and in all dealings with children should bear in mind the age of the child, whether parental or other adult consent has been obtained for such dealings, the sensitivity of the subject matter, and what circumstances, if any, render the story one of public interest. Young people should be free to complete their time at school without unnecessary intrusion. The fame, notoriety or position of a parent or guardian must not be used as sole justification for publishing details of a child's private life.

[36.2.18] The Press Ombudsman in a decision of 4 December 2012 declined to uphold a complaint that the *Northern Standard* breached principle 5 (privacy) of the code. The *Northern Standard* had published a court report concerning a conviction for assault on a minor. The father of the victim wrote to the editor of the newspaper objecting to the level of detail about the assault included in the report, and the insensitive manner in which it allegedly had been reported. The newspaper defended the report and said that it had been a fair, accurate and balanced report which had not named the minor (though it accepted that the minor could be identified by other information contained in the report). The newspaper regretted the distress caused to the boy by the report but said that it had a responsibility to report on court proceedings.

[36.2.19] The father then complained to the Ombudsman that his son's privacy had not been protected or respected, and that the decision to publish the report was wholly lacking in sympathy and discretion. He referenced that his son was a minor at the time of the assault and had been greatly upset and distressed by the experience of it and the reporting of the court case. The father also claimed that the report had not been in the public interest.

[36.2.20] The editor in a submission to the Ombudsman contended that the court report had excluded overly explicit details of the assault to avoid causing distress to the victim. He said, however, that as a custodial sentence had been imposed on a first-time offender, it was necessary for a "full understanding of the Judge's ruling to present some detail as to the particular form which the assault took". He argued that the report was in the public interest "given the custodial sentence imposed and the deterrent intent of the imposition of such sentences".[7] The editor proceeded to offer his sympathy for what the boy had to endure in giving evidence and the subsequent reporting of his evidence. As the complaint could not be resolved by conciliation, it was forwarded to the Press Ombudsman for a decision.

[36.2.21] The Ombudsman considered the court report that led to the complaint

---

7 Press Council of Ireland (decided by the Press Ombudsman), *A Father and the Northern Standard* (2017), presscouncil.ie at para 4 of the report. Available at: http://www.presscouncil.ie/Decided-by-the-Press-Ombudsman/a-father-and-the-northern-standard [Accessed 1 May 2018].

as a carefully written report which endeavoured to balance sensitivity towards a minor, who was the central witness in an assault case, with the need to report on proceedings that took place in open court. Newspapers play an important part in ensuring that justice is delivered in public. Principle 5.3 of the code acknowledges that the requirement for discretion which must be shown in situations of shock is qualified by a newspaper's right to report judicial proceedings. In this instance, the Ombudsman did not believe the newspaper breached principle 5. Consequently, the complaint was not upheld.

Principle 10: publication of decisions of the Press Ombudsman/Press Council

[36.2.22] As mentioned above, when requested or required by the Ombudsman and/or the Press Council to do so, the press shall publish the decision in relation to a complaint with due prominence.

PROTECTION OF JOURNALISTIC SOURCES: JOURNALISTIC PRIVILEGE[8]

[36.3.01] The aforementioned principle 6 of the code is underpinned by international convention (Art 10 of the European Convention on Human Rights, which protects the secrecy of a source who provides confidential documents),[9] common law principles generally, domestic case law and indeed the Constitution itself.[10] Privilege might be invoked and necessary for example where the source of the information might face danger, harm or retribution (as was the case in the 1994 *Burke v Central Independent Television Plc*[11] decision of the Supreme Court) though journalists will still be compelled to answer questions or reveal sources by a court if disclosure is deemed justified by an overriding requirement in the public interest. In order words, confidentiality of journalistic sources is not an absolute or unqualified privilege.[12] Case law has also shown that non-journalists

---

8 'Journalistic privilege' was referred to by Mr Justice Gerard Hogan in *Cornec v Morrice* (see below) as "shorthand". Paragraph 42 of the judgment makes it clear that strictly speaking there is no such thing. Nevertheless, it is a useful phrase to capture the rights which journalists may enjoy in certain situations.

9 There are limitations however to the use of Art 10 as the basis for a disclosure exemption in Irish law as later discussed.

10 Article 40.6.1.i. recognises journalists' "rightful liberty of expression" on the part of the press, albeit counterbalanced by the stipulation that this rightful liberty shall not be used to undermine "public order or morality or the authority of the State". Hogan J stated in *Cornec* that this right would be meaningless if the law could not or would not protect the general right of journalists to protect their sources. In *Mahon Tribunal v Keena* discussed below at [36.3.08], the Supreme Court, while relying heavily on Art 10 of the European Convention on Human Rights, also acknowledged journalistic privilege as a constitutional principle for the first time.

11 [1994] 2 IR 61.

12 *In re O'Kelly* (discussed in Chapter 33), the Court of Criminal Appeal held that journalists do not enjoy a constitutional immunity from disclosing information received in confidence and so the court upheld the finding of contempt (this matter related to the trial of Seán MacStiofáin who was charged with membership of the IRA).

may be able to claim the protection of privilege on public interest grounds (see the facts of the 2012 High Court decision in *Cornec* [2012] IEHC 376 set out at [36.3.42]) and, accordingly, the exemption is not necessarily limited to journalists or to persons analogous to journalists.

[36.3.02] The European Court of Human Rights ('the ECtHR') frequently emphasises the value of a free press as one of the essential foundations of a democratic society, that the press generates and promotes political debate, informs the public in time of elections, scrutinises the behaviour of governments and public officials and, for these reasons, persons in public life must expect to be subjected to disclosure about their financial and other affairs, criticism and to less favourable treatment than those in private life. Generally, therefore, restrictions on freedom of expression must be justified by an overriding requirement in the public interest. The public interest in the preservation from disclosure of journalistic sources (otherwise the 'exemption from the disclosure obligation', or 'disclosure exemption') is an essential prerequisite of a free press in a democratic society.[13]

[36.3.03] Indeed in 2018, Mr Justice Charlteton, chairman of the Charleton Tribunal stated that if he were to order journalists to answer questions from the tribunal:

> ...there will be no change because the manner in which they resisted answering the question convinced me that any order I made would be absolutely futile.[14]

Case law

[36.3.04] At the time of writing, a Supreme Court appeal by the Garda Commissioner of an April 2022 Court of Appeal ruling is awaited in the case of *Corcoran* discussed below at [36.3.32] whereby the Supreme Court agreed in October 2022 to later hear the appeal. The issues raised in the case, namely the balance between the public interest and the investigation of serious crimes, and any claim of privilege, and the remedies available to courts to address these issues have not previously been ruled on by the Supreme Court.

---

13 In *Corcoran* (see para [36.3.32]), Simons J said at para 99 there was case law from the European Court of Human Rights in *Stichting* indicating that the motivation of a source (such as seeking to evade criminal accountability) was also relevant in carrying out a balancing exercise relating to a claim of journalistic privilege. He also stated there must be some doubt about the motivation of Mr Corcoran's source in seeking to have the events publicised. According to Gardaí, the events sought to reverse the effects of an eviction carried out earlier in the week following a court order. The judge noted that the motivation of the source may have been to put out a message that action would be taken against those such as security personnel (allegedly assaulted) who helped financial institutions to repossess properties. The High Court ruling was overturned and the Court of Appeal's decision will be reviewed by the Supreme Court.

14 The tribunal was established to investigate allegations by Superintendent David Taylor that he was directed, when Garda press officer in 2013 and 2014, to smear the reputation and character of whistleblower Sergeant Maurice McCabe.

Goodwin

[36.3.05] ECtHR proceedings in *Goodwin v United Kingdom*[15] concerned an order for a journalist to disclose his source. The case pertained to commercial information of a highly confidential character, being the corporate plan for the refinancing of a company. It was claimed that disclosure would threaten the business and the livelihood of its employees. The information was communicated to the journalist by a person who, though known to the journalist, wished to remain anonymous. The company managed to secure an interim injunction restraining publication. It had learned of the disclosure of the information because the journalist had contacted it to make some enquiries. The fact of this injunction was highly material to the decision of the court.

[36.3.06] The English courts, all the way to the House of Lords, made orders requiring the journalist to disclose his source. He refused. The House of Lords fined him £5,000 for contempt of court. However, in its judgment on the journalist's case, the ECtHR had this to say about journalistic sources:

> Protection of journalistic sources is one of the basic conditions for press freedom, as is reflected in the laws and the professional codes of conduct in a number of Contracting States and is affirmed in several international instruments on journalistic freedoms. Without such protection, sources may be deterred from assisting the press in informing the public on matters of public interest. As a result the vital public watchdog role of the press may be undermined and the ability of the press to provide accurate and reliable information may be adversely affected. Having regard to the importance of the protection of journalistic sources for press freedom in a democratic society and the potentially chilling effect an order of source disclosure has on the exercise of that freedom, such a measure cannot be compatible with Article 10 of the Convention unless it is justified by an overriding requirement in the public interest.[16]

The court laid emphasis on the need for any restriction on freedom of expression to be "convincingly established". It said that:

> The national margin of appreciation is circumscribed by the interest of democratic society in ensuring and maintaining a free press...In sum, limitations on the confidentiality of journalistic sources call for the most careful scrutiny by the court.[17]

[36.3.07] The court then analysed the justification put forward by the company in the national court and by the UK government in its defence to the application. It attached great weight to the fact that the injunctions granted to the company effectively prevented further dissemination of the confidential information, which had largely achieved the objective sought by the disclosure order. It accepted, nonetheless, that the injunctions could not prevent direct communication from

---

15 (1996) EHRR 123.
16 At para 39 of the judgment.
17 At para 40.

the journalist's original source to the company's customers or competitors. While accepting that these were undoubtedly relevant considerations, it considered that the additional restriction which they entailed "was not supported by sufficient reasons for the purposes of Art 10(2) of the Convention". Ultimately, the court considered that the interests protected by Art 10 "tip the balance of competing interests in favour of the interest of democratic society in securing a free press" and that:

> ...the residual threat of damage through dissemination of the confidential information otherwise than by the press, in obtaining compensation and in unmasking a disloyal employee or collaborator were, even if considered cumulatively, not sufficient to outweigh the vital public interest in the protection of the applicant journalist's source.[18]

Mahon Tribunal v Keena[19]

[36.3.08] This leading Supreme Court case on journalistic privilege which cites its own earlier case law on the issue[20] related to the Tribunal of Inquiry into Certain Planning Matters and Payments. The decision of the five-justice court in July 2009 was a landmark one that enshrined the principle of journalistic privilege and the protection of sources into Irish law for the first time.

[36.3.09] In this application, the Planning Tribunal wished to investigate a 'leak' of confidential information to *The Irish Times* and was met with a countervailing claim based on confidentiality of journalists' sources. The appeal was taken against an order made by the High Court pursuant to s 4 of the Tribunal of Inquiries (Evidence) (Amendment) Act 1997 directing a journalist and the editor of that newspaper to answer questions posed by the tribunal intended to unveil the source of documents published in the national newspaper. The first-named appellant, Colm Keena, had been a journalist for over twenty years and public affairs correspondent of *The Irish Times* and the second-named appellant, Geraldine Kennedy, was the editor of the paper.

[36.3.10] On 29 June 2006, as part of its private investigations, the tribunal wrote to wealthy businessman David McKenna, friend and supporter of Mr Bertie Ahern TD, the then Minister for Finance, seeking information in relation to certain payments said to have been made by him to Mr Ahern in late 1993.[21] The inquiries into Mr Ahern's finances were understood to have begun after allegations were made about supposed payments to him by property developer Owen O'Callaghan in relation to the Quarryvale development in west Dublin. The letter asked Mr McKenna for a detailed narrative statement setting out the

---

18 At para 45.

19 [2009] IESC 64.

20 *Mahon v Post Publications* [2007] 3 IR 338; *O'Callaghan v Mahon* [2006] 3 IR 32.

21 The tribunal had been told that the money was used to pay legal bills incurred by Mr Ahern around this time.

circumstances in which any such payment had been made. The envelope which contained this letter was marked "strictly private and confidential – to be opened by addressee only". The final paragraph of the letter was as follows:

> This inquiry is being made of you as part of the Tribunal's confidential inquiry in private. The fact of this letter or its content should not be disclosed to any third party save your legal advisor, if you should choose to seek legal advice in respect of this request.

[36.3.11] On 19 September 2006, Keena anonymously received an unsolicited copy of the letter from the tribunal to McKenna. On 21 September 2006, at which stage Mr Ahern was Taoiseach, *The Irish Times* published on its front page, under the name of the reporter appellant Mr Keena, a report with the headline "Tribunal examines payments to Taoiseach". The newspaper also destroyed the anonymous document it had received so as to protect the source.

[36.3.12] The key issue in the appeal was whether the three-justice Divisional High Court[22] was correct in deciding to make its order of 9 November 2007 which required the appellants to appear before the tribunal and to answer questions in relation to the source and present whereabouts of the documents which Mr Keena had received anonymously. The answer to that question depended on whether the High Court was correct in the manner in which it balanced the right and interest of the tribunal in seeking to uncover the source of the unauthorised disclosure and the interests of the appellants in protecting their source. The Supreme Court held that the High Court adopted an incorrect approach and thus reversed its decision.

[36.3.13] The High Court had summarised the judgments of the ECtHR concerning the balance which the courts must strike between the right to freedom of expression, on the one hand, and the interests recognised in Art 10.2 of the Convention, on the other. In the Supreme Court's view, an unanimous judgment being delivered by Fennelly J for the court, the High Court correctly said that the appellants had "cast themselves as the adjudicators of the proper balance to be struck between the rights and interests of concerned". The learned justice stated that courts cannot and should not abdicate their responsibility to decide when journalists are obliged to disclose their source. The unilateral decision of a journalist to destroy evidence with intent to deprive the courts of jurisdiction was, as the High Court had held, designed to subvert the rule of law. Accordingly, the courts cannot shirk their duty to penalise journalists who refuse to answer questions legitimately and lawfully put to them.

---

22 Proceedings were heard in the High Court by a Divisional Court composed of Johnson P, Kelly J and O'Neill J. Judgment was delivered on 23 October 2007. *Mahon v Keena* [2007] IEHC 348.

Supreme Court

[36.3.14] However, consideration was duly given to the *Goodwin* case, the result of which was that the ECtHR in Strasbourg decided that the UK was in violation of art 10. Fennelly J did not disagree with the scathing language used by the High Court in reference to the deliberate destruction by the appellants of the very documents that were at the core of the inquiry. Nonetheless, he failed to accept that the issue was whether that act was a wrongful one and deserving of the opprobrium applied to it by the High Court. Rather, it was the narrower question of whether, in circumstances where the documents no longer existed, there was a logical or causal link between that act and the order made. It did not appear to him that there was. The order now to be made had to be justified by the situation as it then existed and not by the need to mark disapproval of the unquestionably "reprehensible conduct" of the appellants. For the same reason, the Supreme Court did not consider that the High Court was correct in reaching, by reference to its summary of the great many cases decided in the ECtHR relating to the issue of freedom of expression, the conclusion that:

> ...the destruction of these documents by the defendants is a relevant consideration to which great weight must be given in striking the correct balance between the rights and interest at issue on this application.

[36.3.15] As to the import of the anonymity factor (the leaked letter was anonymously provided to *The Irish Times*), in the court's view, plainly, there was a difference between a source whose identity is known to the journalist and a completely anonymous source. Greater weight will attach to the privilege in the case of the former than the latter.

[36.3.16] If the leaked document was not headed and thus, as a matter of probability, came from a tribunal source, that might possibly assist the tribunal in its endeavour to identify the source. At the same time, a number of other hypotheses could not be excluded. One must recall that the person 'leaking' the document would, in all probability, have wished to disguise the source. Thus, by the use of a photocopying machine, the heading might be removed from an original letter. On the contrary hypothesis that it did not come from a tribunal source, but was, as the High Court expressed it "shrouded in impenetrable mystery", it clearly would not be possible to justify the making of the disclosure order.

[36.3.17] In consequence, if the apparent anonymity of the source weakened the appellants' case for resisting the order, it must correspondingly weaken the tribunal's case for obtaining it. If, as was the case in *Goodwin*, the source was a person known to the journalist, it could, at the least, be argued that there was some concrete benefit to be obtained from the making of the order. Where the source is anonymous, the benefit is speculative at best.

[36.3.18] Having fully examined the High Court judgment, the relevant ECtHR decisions and upon hearing from counsel for the tribunal and the appellants, the court at paras 68 to 70 concluded thus:

> 68. Looking at the High Court judgment as a whole, I have come to the conclusion that the great weight which it attached to the reprehensible conduct of the appellants in destroying documents led it to adopt an erroneous approach to the balancing exercise.
>
> 69. According to the reasoning of the European Court in *Goodwin,* an order compelling the appellants to answer questions for the purpose of identifying their source could only be *"justified by an overriding requirement in the public interest."* Once the High Court had devalued the journalistic privilege so severely, the balance was clearly not properly struck. On the other side, I find it very difficult to discern any sufficiently clear benefit to the Tribunal from any answers to the questions they wish to pose to justify the making of the order.
>
> 70. I would, therefore, allow the appeal and substitute an order dismissing the Tribunal's application.

Costs

[36.3.19] The matter did not end there, however, as the issue of costs was yet to be determined. Despite winning their appeal as above, the Supreme Court later in 2009 ruled[23] against the appellant editor and journalist on legal costs to the tune of €600,000[24] in what was described as "exceptional circumstances". The court held that their behaviour in destroying documents at the centre of the case did not entitle them to an order for costs in their favour. The court therefore ruled that the tribunal was fully entitled to conduct its inquiry and to seek the assistance of the High Court. The court ordered that the tribunal could recover the costs of both High Court and Supreme Court actions.

[36.3.20] Murray CJ for the Supreme Court held that this deliberate act of destruction of evidence deprived the tribunal of the possibility of conducting any meaningful inquiry into the source of the leaked letter, and such as to deprive *The Irish Times* of its normal expectation that the court would, in the exercise of its discretion, award costs which it would have been able to so do had the applicants not destroyed the documents. It followed, according to the court, that destroying the documents was not a legitimate exercise of their Art 10 right to protect their sources. The journalists' destruction of documents related to the source which justified a departure, in this exceptional scenario, from the normal rule that costs go to the winning side. As above, it directed the paper to pay all costs of the High and Supreme Court proceedings, including the costs of the tribunal.

---

23 In *Mahon Tribunal v Keena (No 2)* [2009] IESC 78.

24 RTÉ News, *Irish Times' journalists to pay €600k costs* (2009), rte.ie. Available at: https://www.rte.ie/news/2009/1126/124677-mahon/ [Accessed 20 June 2021].

[36.3.21] Eoin O'Dell[25] described this judgment as a "bizarre conclusion" that undermined the original decision that the journalists did not have to answer the tribunal's questions. If the journalists had a privilege to withhold the document and decline to answer the questions, then they had the privilege and it therefore did not matter what they did with the document. Moreover, O'Dell argued that the costs order infringed Art 10 of the European Convention on Human Rights.

[36.3.22] *The Irish Times* proceeded to argue that very point and challenged the Supreme Court's ruling in Strasbourg in proceedings lodged in May 2010 on the grounds that a number of the rights of Kennedy and Keena had been violated, in particular their rights under Art 6 of the Convention, guaranteeing a fair trial, and Art 10, guaranteeing freedom of expression. They pointed to the "chilling effect" of such an award of costs on the exercise of press freedom, pointing out that the ECtHR had already ruled[26] in the *Fressoz* decision that an order to disclose sources cannot be compatible with Art 10 unless it is justified by "an overriding requirement of public interest".

[36.3.23] The journalists argued that the proceedings taken by the tribunal were "misconceived from the outset", and they had been penalised by the Supreme Court for protecting their source; the Supreme Court's view that the document's destruction had prevented the courts from examining the case was mistaken as the Supreme Court was still able to reach a decision on the tribunal's order; and that the costs ruling would have a chilling effect on the press as journalists could now be compelled under threat of an order of costs to disclose their sources.

ECtHR ruling on costs

[36.3.24] On 30 September 2014,[27] the ECtHR by a majority rejected the argument that the costs order would have a chilling effect on free expression because as a general principle costs are a matter for the discretion of domestic courts, and secondly, the costs order would have no impact on public interest journalists who respect the rule of law, or compel disclosure of sources of information given in confidence. For the European Court, the ruling simply signified that nobody may usurp the judicial function. It said this was all the more unacceptable in light of the highly political subject matter of the case, which warranted the highest protection. It followed that the application was "manifestly ill-founded" and inadmissible. The court stated that the Convention does not confer on individuals the right to take upon themselves a role properly reserved to the courts:

> As the domestic courts underscored, this is, effectively, what the applicants did

---

25 Eoin O'Dell, *The Irish Times Goes To Strasbourg* (2010), cearta.ie. Available at: http://www.cearta.ie/2010/05/the-irish-times-goes-to-strasbourg/ [Accessed 20 June 2021].

26 *Fressoz and Roire v France* (1999) 31 EHRR 28.

27 ECtHR Application 29804/10 *Keena and Kennedy v Ireland.*

through their deliberate destruction of the very documents that were at the core of the tribunal's inquiry.[28]

[36.3.25] The ECtHR thus disagreed with the newspaper's complaint of the chilling effect of the costs order on freedom of expression. It said the costs ruling could have no impact on public interest journalists who vehemently protect their sources yet recognise and respect the rule of law.

Analysis

[36.3.26] It is clear post *Mahon Tribunal* that the privilege enjoys some degree of legal protection in Ireland. Yet, both the High and Supreme Courts there warned against any impression that journalists might enjoy an absolute entitlement to resist enquiries into the newsgathering process.[29] The Divisional Court was firmly of the view that journalists are not above the law nor are they entitled to create for themselves, where their own particular vocational interest is involved, a reserve into which the law may not go. On appeal, Fennelly J agreed that no citizen has the right to claim immunity from the processes of the law. An absolute immunity would also be out of keeping with the approach adopted by other common law[30] and international courts.[31] Indeed, Hogan J pointed out in a 2012 High Court case being the seemingly first Irish judgment to consider the position of bloggers, *Cornec v Morrice*,[32] the familiar terminology of 'journalistic privilege' is a "convenient, if slightly inaccurate, shorthand" given that "there is, in fact, in strictness, no such thing".[33]

[36.3.27] What this means is that some uncertainty remains about the precise scope of the privilege under Irish law.[34] Eoin Carolan refers to observations of Binnie J for the majority of the Canadian Supreme Court in *R. v National Post*:[35]

> To throw a constitutional immunity around the interactions of such a heterogeneous and ill-defined group of writers and speakers and whichever 'sources' they deem worthy of a promise of confidentiality and on whatever terms they may choose to offer it ... would blow a giant hole in law enforcement and other constitutionally recognised values such as privacy.

---

28 At para 48 of the judgment.

29 Simons J at paras 40 and 60 in *Corcoran* discussed below also confirmed that journalists' right to protect their sources was not absolute or inviolable using the wording of Hogan J in *Cornec*. While he was overturned, the Court of Appeal agreed that the right not to disclose journalistic sources is a constitutionally guaranteed right, albeit one which is not absolute. The matter is under appeal to the Supreme Court.

30 *Ashworth Hospital Authority v MGN Ltd* [2002] UKHL 29; *Fairfax (John) & Sons Ltd v Cojuangco* (1988) 165 CLR 346; *Branzburg v Hayes* 408 US 665 (1972).

31 *Sanoma Uitgevers BV v Netherlands* [2009] ECHR 38224/03.

32 [2012] IEHC 376.

33 [2012] 1 IR 804, at pp 821 and 818; [2012] IEHC 376 at paras 42 and 49.

34 Eoin Carolan, "Protecting public interest reporting: what is the future of journalistic privilege in Irish law?" (2017) *The Irish Jurist* 57: 187-200.

35 [2010] 5 LRC 510 at 528-529.

[36.3.28] He goes on to surmise that the disclosure exemption recognised in *Mahon Tribunal* will not apply in the face of a sufficiently clear statutory obligation to disclose. *Mahon* does not prevent the Oireachtas from enacting provisions which expressly exclude the possibility of a disclosure exemption. In addition, Carolan notes from O'Neill J's ruling in *Walsh v The News Group Newspaper Ltd*[36] that the privilege could not apply to material disclosed by a Garda in contravention of s 62 of the Garda Síochána Act 2005. Journalistic privilege which might otherwise have applied no longer applied because of the criminal nature of the conduct involved.

[36.3.29] In these High Court defamation proceedings pursued by Louis Walsh[37] against the publishers of *The Irish Sun* newspaper, the court ordered the discovery of documents relating to sexual assault allegations against Mr Walsh, subsequently admitted to be false, but not documents which might lead to the identification of unidentified sources. The court thus granted discovery of documents and rejected submissions that journalistic privilege might shield defendants where they were alleged to have given financial inducement to a false complaint of sexual assault.

[36.3.30] On the other hand, the decisions of the courts in recent years have consistently affirmed that this is a privileged constitutional position that reflects the vital role played by the press in a democratic society.[38] This is broadly consistent with the position articulated by the ECtHR in its own Art 10 case law. This raises the possibility that reliance on Art 10 as the source of a disclosure exemption – with all its associated issues – may be unnecessary. The decision of the High Court in *Cornec v Morrice* indicates the Constitution has the potential to provide a principled framework for the development of a disclosure exemption.

[36.3.31] A claim of journalistic privilege was also upheld in *Ryanair v Channel 4*[39] and in the *ex tempore*[40] judgment of Barr J in *Kean v Independent Star Ltd*.[41] In another matter, *Boyle v Governor of St Patrick's Institution*,[42] Barr J was considering an application to set aside a subpoena *duces tecum* issued to a journalist and, although the subpoena was not set aside, the learned judge ruled that the applicant did not have to reveal his confidential sources for the article.

---

36 [2012] IEHC 353.

37 This matter was settled out of court for the sum of €500,000 together with an apology from the newspaper.

38 *Irish Times v Ireland* [1998] 1 IR 359; *Mahon v Post Publications* [2007] 3 IR 338.

39 [2018] 1 IR 734.

40 A decision handed down by the judge immediately or soon after the hearing.

41 [2018] IEHC 206.

42 [2015] IEHC 410.

The Corcoran proceedings

[36.3.32] However, in *Corcoran v Commissioner of An Garda Síochána*[43] Simons J was deciding judicial review proceedings in which the applicant, a journalist, challenged the issuing and execution of a search warrant at his private residence and the seizure of his mobile phone from which the identity of his journalistic sources could be extracted (in 2018 the Garda*í* sought a limited examination of the journalist's phone as part of an investigation into an alleged violent incident at a repossessed house in County Roscommon). The court held that the public interest in the protection of journalistic sources was outweighed by the countervailing public interest in the investigation and prosecution of criminal offences.[44]

Principles enumerated by the Court of Appeal

[36.3.33] This decision was appealed to the Court of Appeal[45] which at para 97 of its judgment as delivered by Costello J set out 28 principles. As a starting point, if an issue concerning the protection of journalists' sources arises, it must first be considered under the Constitution and in particular Art 40.6.1.1° (freedom of expression). The protection afforded to journalistic sources under Art 10 of the European Convention on Human Rights is substantively the same as that under the Constitution, with the former to be attributed a high value. The court made clear once again that the right to protect journalistic sources is not absolute. The test is whether the case for the restriction on, or overriding of, journalistic privilege has been "convincingly established". A judge must therefore subject any application which will interfere with the protection of journalistic sources to "special" or "careful scrutiny". The court may only order journalists to reveal their sources if it is justified by an overriding requirement in the public interest or a pressing social need.

[36.3.34] An order authorising a search of a journalist's home and/or premises was a more drastic measure than an order to divulge the identity of a journalist's source, and an order for the compulsory surrender of journalistic material which contains information capable of identifying journalistic sources constitutes, in

---

43 [2020] IEHC 382 (principal judgment). See supplemental judgment of Simons J in [2021] IEHC 11.

44 Journalistic privilege was also discussed by the High Court in March 2021 at some length in *Carey v Independent News and Media Plc* [2021] IEHC 229 but was not decided upon. Butler J did not see the need to offer her view in the context of the proceedings before her given that the claim of privilege raised by the defendants was not one which must "inevitably succeed", adopting McKechnie J's words from the Supreme Court's ruling in *Keating v RTÉ* [2013] IESC 22. See also *Gibb v Minister for Justice* (Malley J) [2013] IEHC 238.

45 [2022] IECA 98. The High Court had ordered Gardaí to pay Mr Corcoran's legal costs, noting that the proceedings were taken in the public interest. The Commissioner of An Garda Síochana appealed this costs order, as well as the limiting of information to exclude contact details. Corcoran issued a cross-appeal, seeking a review of Simons J's findings.

itself, an interference with the journalist's/publisher's freedom to receive and impart information, even if the order is not acted upon and no source is identified.

[36.3.35] The court must be able to prevent unnecessary access to information capable of disclosing the identities of sources and the trial judge should be able to refuse to make a disclosure order, or to make a limited or qualified order, so as to protect sources from being revealed, whether or not they are specifically named in the material. Significantly, save in the case of urgency, the review and the balancing of rights must take place prior to the seizure and access of the material and an *ex post facto* review cannot retrospectively authorise a search which is invalid for breach of these requirements. In cases of urgency, it is permissible to seize but not access the material prior to the review by the court or other independent and impartial body.

[36.3.36] Costello J concluded that An Garda Síochána could apply in at least some circumstances *ex parte* to the District Court for a search warrant of a journalist's home or place of work under s 10 of the Criminal Justice (Miscellaneous Provisions) Act 1997 (as amended) provided that the minimum safeguards identified were observed. The District Court judge must be informed that the application engages or potentially engages journalistic privilege, protected by the Constitution and the European Convention, that it might be overridden and that the judge could only issue the warrant if the applicant convincingly established that there was an overriding requirement in the public interest that would justify the order. The applicant must make full disclosure in order that the District Court judge could properly balance the competing rights involved.

[36.3.37] Here the relevant safeguards had not been observed, particularly around disclosure, and the warrants had been obtained in breach of the plaintiff's constitutional rights. The issue of a warrant, even if not executed, could itself amount to a breach of constitutional rights. The defects in the warrants were not remedied by a review and *ex post facto* balancing of rights. In overturning Simons J, the court thus held the seized phone should be returned to the journalist and the information thereon should not be accessed by the Gardaí. However, it was open to the Gardaí to apply for a fresh warrant provided the appropriate safeguards were observed.

[36.3.38] As stated above, the judgment of the Court of Appeal in this important case is under appeal to the Supreme Court.

The test in RTÉ v Keating

[36.3.39] This 2013 Supreme Court case[46] established the threshold of establishing that the claim of privilege is one which must inevitably succeed. Although arising out of defamation proceedings, it concerned claims of public

[46] [2013] IESC 22.

interest privilege attaching to material comprising confidential information provided to the customs service of Revenue and used for the purposes of its enforcement functions regarding the illegal importation of drugs into the state. RTÉ had broadcast a documentary programme on this issue. The plaintiff claimed he was identifiable in the broadcast and that it was defamatory of him in circumstances where he was working as a Garda informant and, consequently, had participated in the criminal activity at the direction of An Garda Síochána.

[36.3.40] RTÉ sought third party discovery from An Garda Síochána and Revenue which was granted by the High Court without deciding on the claim of privilege which had been raised. Revenue appealed this decision. The Supreme Court denied the appeal and found that the disclosure granted was not excessive. McKechnie J stated that the court had a discretion not to order discovery in a case where a claim of privilege was bound to succeed but did not accept that this was such a case. He stated, at para 50 of the judgment:

> … in the absence of knowing how the Revenue will formulate a privilege claim in respect of what documents they might have, I am far from satisfied at this stage of the procedure that any privilege so asserted will inevitably succeed.

[36.3.41] *Keating* was followed and applied separately in two 2020 High Court decisions in *Desmond v Irish Times*[47] and *Crawley v Sunday World*.[48] These judgments are somewhat beyond the scope of this textbook, being more procedural in nature relating to applications for discovery of documents, and are briefly discussed in the *Appendix*.

New media forms

[36.3.42] In *Cornec*, orders were sought to compel two individuals – Nicola Tallant and Mike Garde – to testify for the purposes of US civil proceedings (whereby a court hearing was pending in Colorado). Both objected to the orders on various grounds, including the argument that requiring their testimony would reveal both their sources and the information provided by these sources, contrary to their journalistic privilege recognised by Irish law.

[36.3.43] In the case of Nicola Tallant, an investigative reporter with the *Sunday World*, there was no difficulty in applying the concept of journalistic privilege. The position of Mike Garde was rather more ambiguous. As the court put it, he was not a journalist in the strict sense of the term. Instead, he was a director of Dialogue Ireland, an independent charity organisation working with people who become involved in cults or fringe religions, and regularly appeared in the media and blogged about cult-related issues. Despite this, however, Hogan J had

---

47 [2020] IEHC 95.

48 [2020] IEHC 305.

no hesitation in finding that he should also benefit from a similar protection, holding that:

> While Mr. Garde is not a journalist in the strict sense of the term, it is clear that his activities involve the chronicling of the activities of religious cults. Part of the problem here is that the traditional distinction between journalists and laypeople has broken down in recent decades, not least with the rise of social media. It is probably not necessary here to discuss questions such as whether the casual participant on an internet discussion site could invoke *Goodwin*-style privileges, although the issue may not be altogether far removed from the facts of this case.
>
> Yet Mr. Garde's activities fall squarely within the "education of public opinion" envisaged by Article 40.6.1. A person who blogs on an internet site can just as readily constitute an "organ of public opinion" as those which were more familiar in 1937 and which are mentioned (but only as examples) in Article 40.6.1, namely, the radio, the press and the cinema. Since Mr. Garde's activities fall squarely within the education of public opinion, there is a high constitutional value in ensuring that his right to voice these views in relation to the actions of religious cults is protected. It does not require much imagination to accept that critical information in relation to the actions of those bodies would dry up if Mr. Garde could be compelled to reveal this information, whether in the course of litigation or otherwise. It is obvious from the very text of Article 40.6.1 that the right to educate (and influence) public opinion is at the very heart of the rightful liberty of expression. That rightful liberty would be compromised – perhaps even completely jeopardised – if disclosure of sources and discussions with sources could readily be compelled through litigation.[49]

Legislation

[36.3.44] In the absence of action by the Oireachtas it will fall to the courts yet again when faced with requests to compel disclosure to consider how a disclosure exemption should operate. Speaking against the backdrop of an alleged data breach at Independent News and Media in 2018, Taoiseach Leo Varadkar said he was open to legislating to protect journalists' sources but foresaw problems[50] and identified three complications which must be overcome.

[36.3.45] The first issue is the fact that journalism is not a regulated profession and is therefore difficult to define. To be considered a regulated professional, one must register with a professional body and uphold a certain code of conduct, and there is a mechanism by which one could be struck off the register. Journalism is not in that space. This difficulty is even more evident and pronounced now than in the past because of the emergence of the citizen journalist.

[36.3.46] Secondly, Mr Varadkar questioned whether it would be possible to limit

---

49 Paragraphs 65 and 66 of the judgment.

50 Kevin Doyle, *Legislating to protect journalists' sources difficult* (2018), independent.ie. Available at: https://www.independent.ie/business/media/legislating-to-protect-journalists-sources-difficult-taoiseach-36864823.html [Accessed 16 February 2019].

the protection and confidentiality of sources to just journalists. The Taoiseach thirdly questioned what exceptions would have to be created. For example, there is legal privilege in the case of solicitor files and doctors are protected under doctor-patient confidentiality but in no cases are those protections absolute.

[36.3.47] The Court of Appeal in *Corcoran* pointed to the desirability of more detailed legislation in and around journalistic privilege which would enable a District Court judge to tailor a warrant to ensure that it is proportionate to the particular circumstances of the case. More broadly, whether legislation will be introduced (governing journalistic privilege generally) in the aftermath of the Supreme Court's judgment when delivered remains to be seen.

Appendix

Recent cases applying *RTÉ v Keating*

[A1.1.01] In *Desmond v Irish Times* [2020] IEHC 95 (see [36.3.41]), proceedings claiming defamation, breach of privacy regarding the plaintiff's business and financial affairs and breach of a duty of confidence were brought by the plaintiff in respect of the publication by the defendant of material leaked from an international law firm. The claim was denied and a plea of fair and reasonable publication in good faith on a matter of public interest was made pursuant to s 26 of the Defamation Act 2009. Discovery was sought by the plaintiff of certain categories of material which the defendant regarded as being intended as a means to investigate the original source of the documents emanating from the law firm. Journalistic privilege was claimed and the defendant contended (as in *Carey*)[51] that the mere listing of the documents in an affidavit of discovery would run the risk of infringing the privilege.

[A1.1.02] Collins J, relying on *Keating*, took the view that journalistic privilege did not provide a shield against the making of an order for discovery in the circumstances of the case. He acknowledged the protection the law affords to journalists in respect of confidential sources but also that such protection, conveniently referred to as a privilege, was not absolute. In the particular case, the claim of privilege made did not reach the threshold required under the *Keating* test. The material before the court did not demonstrate that in the event that an order for discovery was made in relation to one or more of the categories of documents at issue, an objection to production on the basis of journalistic privilege would inevitably succeed.

[A1.1.03] The plaintiff in *Crawley* as cited above sought damages for defamation and breach of privacy arising out of the publication by the defendants of articles in which the plaintiff was described as a criminal and a range of unsavoury criminal activity allegedly attributed to him. The defendants raised a plea of truth. Discovery was sought of documents relating to the defendants' investigation into the plaintiff prior to publication of the articles and relating to the preparation of the articles. In an affidavit sworn in response to that motion, the defendants' solicitor claimed journalistic privilege in respect of the confidential sources relied on for the articles. The importance of such confidentiality was emphasised in the context of journalism dealing with serious criminal conduct. In looking at

---

51 *Carey v Independent News & Media Plc* [2021] IEHC 229.

how a similar claim of privilege had been treated in *Keating*, Hyland J observed at para 11 of her judgment:

> The Supreme Court did accept that the court has an inherent jurisdiction to refuse the application on the basis that the privilege plea must inevitably succeed. However, it noted that this was an abridgement of the normal two step process, which distinguishes between discovery and inspection obligations. If there is any possibility that the privilege plea might not succeed, then to refuse discovery would be to conflate distinct steps in a two-tier process. Therefore, where a party is refusing to swear an affidavit on the grounds of privilege, including journalistic privilege, the first inquiry must be to determine whether success on the plea is unavoidable. It is only if so that an affidavit as to documents will not be required.

[A1.1.04] On the facts of the case before her, Hyland J went on to decide that the *Keating* threshold had not been reached, stating, at paras 13 and 14 of her judgment:

> However, in this case, I am only concerned with the first step i.e. whether it is so inevitable that the defendant will be successful in its plea of journalistic privilege that I should not order discovery at all. The judgment in Keating makes it quite clear that in the majority of cases, an assertion of privilege should be determined following an identification of the document and the nature of privilege in the Schedule to the Affidavit of discovery in the normal way.

[A1.1.05] Similarly in *Carey*, Butler J (since appointed to the Court of Appeal) could not conclude that it was inevitable that the defendant would succeed in respect of a claim to privilege over each and every document that might be caught by the categories sought or a variation of same. Accordingly, the normal obligations of a party asserting privilege applied to the defendant in this case and the tests of relevance, necessity and proportionality would initially have to be met. She said that the approach of the court should be to carry out what is effectively a screening exercise. The claim should only be ruled on definitively if it is self-evidently so strong that it will inevitably succeed. The judge stated at para 64:

> …the case law makes it clear that the balance is not just between the public interest underlying the claim of privilege and that attaching to the availability of evidence for the purposes of the administration of justice but may also encompass the public importance attached to the rights a litigant is asserting through the litigation. Further, at this screening stage the court is not really looking to strike a balance between competing interests. For the claim of privilege to be allowed succeed without requiring the requested party to swear an affidavit of discovery and to formally make the claim in respect of identified documents, the scales must be overwhelmingly weighted in favour of the privilege. If a complex balancing exercise is required, it necessarily follows that the success of claim of privilege cannot be regarded as "inevitable" or "unavoidable".

[A1.1.06] The court further clarified that the screening exercise to be performed where a requested party makes a claim of privilege at the initial discovery stage, screens out only the very exceptional cases where the evidence before the court establishes that the claim of privilege is one which must succeed. In all other cases, an order for discovery should be made and the claim of privilege raised in the normal course in the affidavit of discovery. The making of an affidavit of discovery is important because it allows the requesting party to address and the court to adjudicate on the claim of privilege in respect of particular documents and in light of actual rather than abstract considerations.

Index